INTERNATIONAL ENVIRONMENTAL LAW AND WORLD ORDER

A PROBLEM-ORIENTED COURSEBOOK

Second Edition

By

Lakshman D. Guruswamy
Professor of Law
Director, National Energy-Environment
Law & Policy Institute
The University of Tulsa

Burns H. Weston
Bessie Dutton Murray Professor of Law
Associate Dean for International and Comparative Legal Studies
The University of Iowa

Sir Geoffrey W. R. Palmer, P.C., K.C.M.G., A.C.
Partner, Chen & Palmer
Barristers and Solicitors, Wellington, New Zealand
Adjunct Professor of Law
The University of Iowa

Jonathan C. Carlson
Professor of Law
The University of Iowa

with the assistance of

Jason B. Aamodt, J.D.
Sally A. Bullen, B.A., LL.B. (Hons.), LL.M.
and
Tiffany Sherman McCready, J.D.

AMERICAN CASEBOOK SERIES®

WEST GROUP

ST. PAUL, MINN., 1999

American Casebook Series, and the West Group
symbol are used herein under license.

COPYRIGHT © 1994 WEST PUBLISHING CO.
COPYRIGHT © 1999 By WEST GROUP
               610 Opperman Drive
               P.O. Box 64526
               St. Paul, MN 55164–0526
               1–800–328–9352

ISBN 0–314–22794–6

 *TEXT IS PRINTED ON 10% POST CONSUMER RECYCLED PAPER*

We are the planet, fully as much as its water, earth, fire and air are the planet, and if the planet survives, it will only be through heroism. Not occasional heroism, a remarkable instance of it here and there, but constant heroism, systematic heroism, heroism as governing principle.

— Russell Banks
Continental Drift 40 (1985)

*

*We dedicate this Book
to our Children and Grandchildren
(in chronological order)*

Anne	*Malin*
Timothy	*Dharm*
Matthew	*Martin*
Monica	*Johannes*
Holly	*Tanya*
Rebecca	*Arjun*
Bernard	*Victoria*
Rebekah	*Russell*
Dharmini	*Andrew*
Heather	*Jeremy*
Adam	*Shelby*

*and to
all other children
present and future*

*

Foreword
Maurice F. Strong

The global nature of many environmental issues—climate change, acid rain, ozone depletion, shared water and nuclear accidents, to name a few—has made national boundaries a spurious anachronism, and in some ways a dangerous fiction. In a world crying out for international solutions, educators concerned about the environment must not only pass on traditional knowledge, or train specialists who concentrate on their specific disciplines within domestic boundaries, but must also embrace an international, interdisciplinary curriculum that will equip students to become practitioners on a world stage.

One does not need to be a lawyer to appreciate that the legal academies of the world produce many of our future leaders, decision-makers and law-givers. A vitally important mission for all concerned with global environmental protection is to ensure that our potential leaders are alerted to the challenges confronting our shared planet, sensitized to their complexity, and encouraged to think creatively in finding answers to these problems. Law forms an important part of our educational curriculum, and international environmental law has a crucial role to play in helping us all to meet the global environmental challenges.

The Stockholm Conference on the Human Environment in 1972 may well have been the cocoon from which the chrysalis of international environmental law emerged as a legal subject in its own right. Whatever the occasion of its birth, there is no doubt that the subject has grown to become a crucially important facet of global environmental protection, as the multitude of treaties and other instruments found in the Documents Supplement of this book testify. The United Nations Conference on Environment and Development at Rio de Janeiro in 1992 (the Earth Summit or UNCED) demonstrated how the superstructure of global environmental protection and sustainable economic development were significantly undergirded by international legal instruments such as the Conventions on Climate Change and Biological Diversity. Having been privileged to be Secretary–General of both of these historic events, I have witnessed the growing importance and vitality of international environmental law; yet I have also noticed the dearth of comprehensive treatment of the subject. It is with great pleasure, therefore, that I welcome this book by Lakshman Guruswamy, Sir Geoffrey Palmer and Burns Weston.

To manage our common future on this planet, we will need a new global legal regime based essentially on the extension into international life of the rule of law, together with reliable mechanisms for accountability and enforcement that provide the basis for the effective functioning of national societies. We are a long way from this today. UNCED defined many of the needs for continued development of international law, including the strengthening of existing instruments and agreements on new ones. However, even this would move us only a short distance toward establishing an effective international legal regime.

The Rio Declaration and Agenda 21 are major new examples of "soft law," based on political agreement rather than on legally binding instruments. Although not binding, they nevertheless provide the basis for voluntary cooperation, which enables the action process to proceed, and paves the way for the negotiation of binding agreements. While we cannot be satisfied with these as long-term substitutes for enforceable legal measures, we should not minimize their value. After all, as long as we do not have an effective and enforceable legal regime at the international level, we must rely on political commitment as the primary basis for cooperative action in negotiating and enforcing legal instruments.

Meanwhile, the authors of this book have carefully chosen a wide range of issues that accurately mirror those challenges we currently confront. They engage the reader in soliciting answers based on a problem-solving approach which is exceptionally revealing and instructive as to the nature of the challenges as well as the solutions. I believe that both lawyers and non-lawyers will benefit from such a problem-oriented approach.

The book is exhaustively researched, analytically incisive and of enormous relevance to law and policy. It is refreshing to see a book dealing with a vitally important, yet difficult, subject living up to the highest expectations of a scholarly offering. Undoubtedly, for years to come, this book will remain an authoritative source of materials, ideas, policies and laws for that growing body of international civil servants, policy-makers, law-makers, diplomats, non-government organizations, business leaders and environmental activists concerned with the burgeoning field of international law.

Maurice F. Strong
Chairman, Ontario Hydro;
Former Secretary General, Stockholm Conference on the Human Environment (1972),
and United Nations Conference on Environment and Development (UNCED) 1992
1994

Preface

International Environmental Law (IEL), once overshadowed by its prominent parents, International Law and domestic Environmental Law, has not merely come of age. In the five years following the first edition of this book, it has continued to grow and mature demonstrating an ability to respond to global environmental challenges in a manner that its progenitors international and national laws were, and are, unable to do.

Historically, the world community assigned to International Law an essentially nightwatchman's role relative to the natural environment, leaving to domestic Environmental Law the activist's role of actually solving environmental problems. This was of course because assaults upon the natural environment either did not have or were not perceived as having much transnational impact or significance.

But clearly such is not the case today. Now, many environmental problems outstrip the capacity of an international legal order that celebrates state sovereignty and tolerates a culture or mindset that believes it only marginally important to understand and solve these problems. And much the same can be said of environmental problems that implicate domestic legal orders as well. While national environmental laws often are illuminated by, and enacted because of a conceptual understanding of environmental complexities, they possess neither the jurisdiction nor the power to deal with the extra-territorial—indeed global—implications raised by most contemporary environmental problems.

In short, contemporary problems such as global warming, ozone layer depletion, desertification, and the destruction of biodiversity essential to the entire global community demand far more. Indeed, even problems of trans-frontier pollution, long familiar to traditional International Law, require a sharp break from the juridical past.

The first edition of our problem-oriented coursebook did not purport to re-baptize International Environmental Law even in 1994. The subject had received extensive recognition and was admitted into the corpus of international law many years ago.[1] A rich volume of books, journals, and articles, as amply excerpted and otherwise noted in our text, continue to testify to the growing importance and challenge of the subject. We are conscious of exploring a subject capable of creating and developing conceptual and doctrinal frameworks sufficient to cope with both the international and environmental character of daunting transnational environmental problems.

Amidst the doctrinal and interpretative outpourings about the subject, however, ours remains the only problem-oriented coursebook on International Environmental Law. We continue to fill the gap, and therefore it behooves us to justify, albeit briefly, our pedagogical approach.

---

1. INTERNATIONAL ENVIRONMENTAL LAW (L. Teclaff & A. Utton eds., 1974) explicitly recognized the birth of the new subject, as did also J. SCHNEIDER, WORLD PUBLIC ORDER OF THE ENVI- RONMENT: TOWARDS AN INTERNATIONAL ECOLOGI- CAL LAW AND ORGANIZATION (1979), while LAW, INSTITUTIONS AND THE GLOBAL ENVIRONMENT (J. Hargrove ed. 1972) anticipated its arrival.

In choosing to write a problem-oriented coursebook rather than a treatise, we acknowledge our indebtedness to the predecessor pioneering efforts of Professors Burns H. Weston, Richard A. Falk, and Anthony D'Amato in their *International Law and World Order: A Problem-Oriented Coursebook,* also published by West Publishing Company and now in its third edition. Further, we unapologetically identify ourselves in general with those who rank issue-spotting, problem-solving, and synthesis as more important in the legal learning experience than the assimilation and comprehension of raw, disembodied knowledge. Indeed, we endorse the percipient findings of a 1942 A.A.L.S. report stating that:

> [U]nder the "problem method" deduction of legal principles becomes not the end of legal education, but the means to an end . . . , the adequate solution of problems which a dynamic society precipitates in ever new combinations. . . . The "problem method" recommends itself as a pedagogical device for re-orienting legal education to its major basic task . . . . [I]t more effectively forces the law student to reflect on the application of pertinent materials to new situations and accustoms him to thinking of case and statute law as something to be used, rather than as something merely to be assimilated for its own sake.[2]

It is our experience that the exercise of identifying and framing issues in factual context, organizing and evaluating relevant law and policy, and applying that law and policy to the facts not only hones analytical skills but kindles students' interests and fires their enthusiasm far more effectively and efficiently than doctrinal exposition. Especially when used in a simulated exercise whether it be a moot court, or a diplomatic or multilateral negotiation, the problem method provides practitioner skills of brief and memorandum writing, oral arguments, negotiating and judging in a way that mere doctrinal exposition does not.

Some who are unfamiliar with the problem method may feel that coursebooks employing the problem method lack a structured description and analysis of the substantive corpus of IEL, and do not offer the kind of expository treatment of the province of IEL presented by a treatise or even a Nutshell. We do not think such observations apply to this coursebook. While we agree that our book is primarily a teaching vehicle as opposed to a scholarly treatise on IEL, our approach to the subject does not diminish the pedagogic value of the book. Our opinion, reinforced by the fact that one of us has been involved in writing the "Nutshell" on IEL,[3] is that the preferred way of establishing, clarifying, and understanding IEL is in terms of its practice and application through problems that offer a fairly comprehensive and in depth understanding of the principal issues and doctrinal bases of IEL. This is what we have sought to do.

Because, however, IEL increasingly attracts students who have had no prior instruction either in International Law generally or in the character and scope of the global environmental challenge in particular, we begin our entire adventure, in Part I, by assuming no previous knowledge of either. Utilizing the "real

2. M. JOSEPHSON, LEARNING AND EVALUATION IN LAW SCHOOL 58 (1984). Josephson, borrowing from B. BLOOM, TAXONOMY OBJECTIVES OF EDUCATIONAL—HANDBOOK 1: COGNITIVE DOMAIN (1956), ranked learning in ascending order of difficulty and importance as: (1) knowledge, (2) comprehension or understanding, (3) issue spotting, (4) problem-solving, (5) judgment, and (6) synthesis.

3. LAKSHMAN GURUSWAMY & BRENT HENDRICKS, INTERNATIONAL ENVIRONMENTAL LAW IN A NUTSHELL (1977).

world" problem of Russian nuclear pollution of the Arctic to make our theoretical points, Part I begins with a relatively detailed doctrinal exploration of the key doctrines, principles and rules of International Law without which it is impossible to understand or apply IEL. It closes, in Chapter 4, with a hard look at "The Global Environmental *Problematique*" as viewed through diverse outlooks and approaches that may be seen to define and fashion IEL. In an essentially consensual, horizontal legal system that cannot depend on enforcement through institutionalized vertical decision-making structures typical of domestic legal orders, it is particularly important to understand the ideological, philosophical, political and psychological well-springs of international behavior. It is our hope that the perspectives delineated here will inform, fertilize, and reinforce the process of formulating answers to the issues raised in the problems in Part II.

Then, in Part II of our coursebook, pausing first in Chapter 5 to summarize the applicability of State Responsibility to environmental wrongs, we present the student, in Chapters 6-11, with a series of hypothetical problems bearing fact patterns that mirror the "real world" in which we live. We believe hypothetical problems avoid associations and biases that potentially inhibit principled analysis, while simultaneously permitting students to probe perceptively the complex webs of fact, law and policy that typically confront international law decision-making in the "real world." We have sought to achieve a compromise between the need to give students a firm grasp of the doctrines, principles, and rules of IEL and the need to stimulate in them a healthy appreciation of the difficulties involved in making these doctrines, principles and rules truly operational in everyday life.

We have chosen to categorize the problems under the environmental rubrics of atmosphere, hydrosphere, lithosphere and biosphere and a miscellaneous section, recognizing that a holistic and integrated environment may for pedagogical and analytical purposes need to be divided into its various elements. It behooves us, however, to stress that while our classification of the problems does not offer a cognitive description of the multifaceted socio-legal issues raised by them, they do in fact represent and symbolize geo-political realities as well as the bio-regions of the world.

There are at least three other ways in which the problem chapters could be organized. First, it is possible to analyze the impact of these problems according to their global, regional and transnational character. Second, it is equally reasonable to treat them as traversing international challenges posed by recognized sources of pollution or by specific pollutants, or ubiquitous social phenomena such as population growth. Finally, it is possible to classify them as problems of natural resources and biodiversity. All three approaches give rise to substantive legal regimes, principles, rules, norms and procedures that are explored and applied. They include the foundational norms of sustainable development, along with a variety of obligations dealing with pollution control, resource exhaustion and remedies.

Global issues, for example, are dealt with in chapters 12, 6, 11, 7, and 10. Global Warming, the quintessential global problem of our times is addressed by Chapter 12 on the Negotiation of a Long Range Protocol on Climate Change. This Chapter also deals with sources of specific pollutants called greenhouse gases (GHGs), and confronts the grim reality of exploding population. Population and human rights are separately addressed in Problem 11-3. In a different context, the three problems in Chapter 6 illustrate the extent to which Antarctica mirrors a wide range of other global environmental problems from biodiversity and resource conservation to pollution. The global challenges posed by diminishing biodiversity are also dealt with in a number of problems including 10-3, and 11-1, while ozone is the subject of 7-2. The impact of trade law in the form of the General Agreement on Tariffs and Trade (GATT) on the environment is dealt with in Problem 11-1.

Regional treaties are becoming an increasingly important feature of IEL, and are dealt with directly by Problems 7-1, 11-2, and 10-1. Problem 7-1 raises the issue of acid rain in the European Union, while 11-2 addresses NAFTA and the Environmental Side-Agreement. Both of these problems deal with the status and legal standing of individuals and NGOs in IEL, while Problem 10-1 concerns a regional fishing agreement dealing with conservation.

Moving on to sources and specific pollutants, sources of pollution such as land-based pollution are encountered in Problem 8-1, and vessel pollution in Problem 8-2, while those dealing with specific pollutants include Problem 7-3 on nuclear pollution, and Problem 9-2 on toxics. Other problems that deal with specific pollutants include 7-1, 7-2, 8-1, 8-2, 9-1, and 11-2. Social phenomena that have a pervasive influence on the global environment include population and human rights dealt with in 11-3, and environmental warfare in Problem 11-4.

There are a number of problems that focus directly on a variety of issues surrounding natural resources. They include Chapter 6 (Antarctica), and Problems 8-3 (groundwater), 9-3 (desertification), 10-1(fish), 10-2 (elephants), 10-3 (biodiversity) and 11-1(endangered species).

The feedback we have received about the first edition confirms our view that the problem method offers the preferred way of understanding the meaning and substantive content of the law and institutions of IEL, and remains an outstanding vehicle for teaching both analytical and practitioner skills. Placing asserted legal principles in their scientific, social, political, economic and technological context reveals their true meaning or lack of meaning, along with extent or limits of law and of lawyering with much greater clarity than didactic or Socratic methods of teaching.

Finally, in Part III, we turn to the future. In Chapter 12 we engage the student in a simulated negotiation of a fictional draft protocol to the U.N. Framework Convention on Climate Change **(Basic Document** 3.21), helping her or him to understand the complexities of the practical issues that nations encounter when regulating our environmental future, while simultaneously hammering home the significance and utility of proleptic law-making, especially in the environmental realm. And in our closing chapter, Chapter 13, we urge upon the student an impressionistic overview of the established and emerging normative, institutional and procedural responses to the theoretical and practical issues posed by the global environmental *problematique* set forth in Chapter 4, and explored in its diverse parts in each of the problems that make up Part II.

We turn now to three editorial matters. *First*, since this coursebook is organized in problem-oriented rather than doctrine-oriented fashion, we have made a special effort to provide a comprehensive substantive index. The intent is to assist instructors and students in locating subject-matter that of necessity is scattered throughout the coursebook rather than being set out in one discrete segment. *Second*, original footnotes in excerpted readings generally are omitted. However, when they are included they are denoted by numbers, with our own footnotes being indicted by letters. *Third,* we have tried to be as current as possible. Information cut-off dates for the most part being December 1998.

A concluding word about our collaboration. Despite approaching our task from different perspectives and geographic locales, and free of bonding to a particular school of jurisprudence or thought, the unique universality and commonality of our subject has been brought home to us in the astonishing confluence of our thinking on the principal issues we have traversed. It is not difficult therefore, to take common responsibility for our collective effort, including our mistakes and shortcomings. It indeed has been a collective effort, with each of us critiquing and assisting the work of the other three virtually every step of the way.

Finally, we are pleased to acknowledge with grateful appreciation, as we have done especially of Jason Aamodt, Sally Bullen, and Tiffany McCready on the title page, all who have assisted us in this endeavor. Their names and our thanks may be found in the Acknowledgments. To anyone whose name we may have inadvertently though not excusably omitted, we offer our heartfelt thanks also.

These are not times for passivity, but for active, clearheaded thinking and informed decisiveness in meeting the critical and perilous ecological conditions that face our planet. Indeed, in the spirit of novelist Russell Banks, quoted at page iii, *supra,* it is a time for "heroism as governing principle." Please join us in this exciting time, and do not hesitate to let us know your views. All are welcome.

LAKSHAM D. GURUSWAMY
Tulsa, Oklahoma

BURNS H. WESTON
Iowa City, Iowa

SIR GEOFFREY W. R. PALMER
Wellington, New Zealand

JONATHAN C. CARLSON
Iowa City, Iowa

April 1999

*

Acknowledgments

We are greatly indebted to a large number of generous people at the University of Iowa and the University of Tulsa who gave invaluably to the realization of this second edition. There of course can be no full accounting of our indebtedness, but as much as possible we seek to recognize these people and extend to them our most heartfelt thanks.

First and foremost, we wish to underscore what we have acknowledged on the title page, namely the incalculably valuable and pivotal role played by Jason Aamodt, Tiffany McCready and Sally Bullen. Others who gave generously of themselves, typically above and beyond the call of duty and always with curiosity, wisdom, and good humor, are (in alphabetical order): Yasir Aleemuddin, Brenda Carpenter, Matthew Cronin, Will Davis, Ariel Falk, Du Guangming, Craig Herkal, Scott Keefer, Michael Lissau, Ryan Maas, Lauren Redman, Jason Roberts, Edwin Rodriguez, Kendal Sheets, Vivien Uba, and Dimiter Vutov. Each is to be thanked for his or her adroit and gracious handling of various research, editorial and clerical tasks, many of them onerous.

Also deserving of very special thanks is Professor David A. Wirth of Boston College, a living example of scholarly collegiality in the finest sense. We are indebted to Professor Wirth for the initial version of the global warming negotiation in Chapter 12.

Other colleagues to whom we extend our appreciation for professional advice and assistance include: Professor Karen Kole for her help with Problem 7-1, and Byron Morris for the expert rendition of the digital maps in the Introduction, and Problems 7-1, 8-3, 9-3, 10-3, & 11-2.

The eclectic and multidisciplinary nature of many of the readings that follow require special library expertise, and this book would not have been possible without the help of the library staffs of our respective universities. We are specially indebted to Carol Arnold of the University of Tulsa Law Library for her proven professionalism, thoughtfulness and unique abilities.

For dedication and skill, in often intense situations we thank also our secretaries Mary Sleichter and Grace Newby at the University of Iowa, Rita Langford at the University of Tulsa, and Sue Lorenz, Administrative Coordinator at the National Energy-Environment Law and Policy Institute (NELPI) at the University of Tulsa.

A special thank you to the ever gracious and imperturbable Pam Siege, and the professional, understanding, skillful and accomplished staff at Westgroup who extended themselves well beyond the call of duty in dealing with a variety of challenges. They include Doug Powell, Kathy Walters and Stephanie Syata.

We are enormously grateful as well to our deans at Iowa and Tulsa for supporting our work with research assistant salaries during the past one and a half years. Their faith in us and their generosity are never taken for granted, never unappreciated, and so to them we extend our thanks as well.

Finally, as the pages following will bear ample witness, we are indebted to many authors and publishers for permission to reprint materials used in this coursebook. We acknowledge with appreciation the permission granted to reprint copyrighted material by the following authors and publishers.

We begin by expressing our gratitude to Professors Burns H. Weston, Richard A. Falk, and Hillary Charlesworth for their permission to use extensively in Chapters 1-3 materials drawn from their INTERNATIONAL LAW AND WORLD ORDER: A PROBLEM-ORIENTED COURSEBOOK (1997). We also wish to express our thanks to:

A. A. Balkemal, for permission to reprint from Dante Augusto Caponera, *The Role of Customary International Water Law, in* WATER RESOURCES POLICY FOR ASIA 365, 367-68, 372, 380-81 (1985).

A. Giuffre Editore S. P. A., for permission to reprint from *Laura Pineschi, The Antartic Treaty System and Gen. Rules of Int'l Environmental Law, in* INT'L LAW FOR ANTARTICA 187-98, 201- 07 (1987); STEPHEN BRUNNER, ART. 10 OF THE ANTARTIC TREATY REVISITED IN INTERNATIONAL LAW FOR ANTARTICA 103-109 (Francesco Franconi & Tullio Scouazzi eds.,1996).

American University Journal of International Law and Policy, for permission to reprint from C. Petsonk, *The Role of the United Nations Environment Programme in the Development of International Environmental Law,* 5 AM. U. J. INT'L L. & POL'Y 351, 367-372 (1990).

American Bar Association, for permission to reprint from Fellows of the Harvard Law School, 1992 *Trends in International Environmental Law by the editors of the Harvard Law Review* 17- 28; CEC, *International Environmental Law, SB,* 79 ALI-ABA 291 (1997); Sondra Goldschein, *Methyl Bromide: The Disparity Between the Pesticide's Phaseout Dates Under the Clean Air Act and the Montreal Protocol on Substance that Deplete the Ozone Layer,* 4 ENVTL. L. 577-607 (1998).

American Institute of Biological Sciences, for permission to reprint from G.Hardin, *Living on a Lifeboat,* 24 BIOSCIENCE 561, 561-64 (1974).

American Society of International Law, for permission to reprint from Stephen McCaffrey, *The 1997 United Nations Convention on International Watercourses,* 92 AM. J. INT'L L. 97, 99-103, 106 (1998); Sir Geoffrey Palmer, *New Ways To Make International Environmental Law,* 86 AM. J. INT'L L. 259, 262 B 63 (1992); Ruth Lapidoth, *Equity in International Law,* 81 AM. SOC. INT'L L. PROC. 138, 146-47 (1987); *Bamako Convention On The Ban Of Import Into Africa And The Control Of Transboundary Movement And Management Of Hazardous Wastes Within Africa,* Arts. 1, 4, 9, 30 I. L. M. 775 (1991); *Protocol to Amend the Vienna Convention on Civil Liability for Nuclear Damage,* 36 I.L.M. 1454 (1997); Paul Szasz, *Remarks on the Gulf War: Environment as a Weapon,* 85 AM. SOC. INT'L L. PROC. 215 (1991); Paul Szasz, *Introductory Note to the 1994 Convention on Nuclear Safety,* 33 I.L.M. 1514 (1994); Maria Stavropoulou, *The Question of a Right Not To Be Displaced,* 90 AM. SOC. INT'L L. PROC. 545 (1996); M. Glennon, *Has International Law Failed the Elephant Michael,* 84 AM. J. INT'L L. 1, 10-18, 20-23, 26-28, 30-33 (1990); Linda S. Bosniak, *State Sovereignty, Human Rights and the New UN Migrant Workers Convention,* 86 AM. SOC. INT'L L. PROC. 623 (1992); G. Palmer, *New Ways To Make International Environmental Law,* 86 AM. J. INT'L L. 259, 260, 264, 279-82 (1992); David Brown, *Widespread Migration: The Role of International Law and Institutions,* 86 AM.

Soc. INT'L L. PROC. 623 (1992); *North American Agreement on Environmental Cooperation*, 32 I. L. M. 1480, 1480 (1993); *Rio Declaration on Environment and Dev.*, Principles 1-9, 12, 13, 31 I. L. M. 874 (1992); *Stockholm Declaration of the United Nations Conference on the Human Environment*, Principles 1-3, 5, 8, 13, 21, 22, 11 I. L. M. 1416 (1972); *World Charter for Nature, Oct. 28, 1982, Principles 1-12, G. A. Res. 37/7, reprinted in,* 22 I. L. M. 455 (1983); *United Nations Security Council Resolution 687, reprinted in,* 30 I.L.M 847 (1991); Arthur C. Helton, *The Legal Dimensions of Preventing Forced Migration,* 90 AM. SOC. INT'L L. PROC. 27- 30 (1996); Anthony D'Amato, *Judge Books Concept of the Law of Nations is Seriously Mistaken,* 79 AM. J. INT'L L. 92, 99 (1985); *Helsinki Protocol on Reduction of Sulfur Emissions or Their Transboundary Fluxes by at Least Thirty Per Cent,* 27 I.L.M. 707 (1985); World Charter for Nature, *Principles 12, 21, G.A.Res. 37/7, U.N. GAOR, 37th Sess.,Supp. No. 51, at 17, U.N. Doc. A/37/51,* 22 I.L.M. (1983); *Convention on Nuclear Safety,* 33 I.L.M. 1514 (1994); *Convention on the Transboundary Effect of Industrial Accidents,* 31 I.L.M. 1330 (1992); *International Convention for the Protection of All Migrant Workers and Their Families, Arts. 1-9, 15, 22-23, 55-56, 79-83, 92, 1990, U.N. Doc. A/45/49,* 30 I.L.M. 1517 (1991); *United Nations: Convention to Combat Desertification in those Countries Experiencing Serious Drought and /or Desertification, Particularly in Africa, Arts. 1-5, 7-11, 19, 28, Annex I-Arts. 1-4, 7-8 ,* 33 I.L.M. 1328 (1994); Alan E. Boyle, *Marine Pollution Under the Law of the Sea Convention,* 79 AM. J. INT'L L. 347 347-51, 357-362, 365-67 (1985); HILLARY CHARLESWORTH, *Panel on Sources of International Law: Entrenching the Gender Bias, in* CONTEMPORARY INTERNATIONAL LAW ISSUES: OPPORTUNITIES AT A TIME OF MOMENTOUS CHANGE—PROCEEDINGS OF THE SECOND JOINT CONFERENCE OF THE AMERICAN SOCIETY OF INTERNATIONAL LAW AND THE NEDERLANDSE VERENIGING VOOR INTERNATIONAAL RECHT 615, 621-29 (1994); CHARLOTTE KU, *Panel on Sources of International Law: Entrenching the Gender Bias, in* CONTEMPORARY INTERNATIONAL LAW ISSUES: OPPORTUNITIES AT A TIME OF MOMENTOUS CHANGE—PROCEEDINGS OF THE SECOND JOINT CONFERENCE OF THE AMERICAN SOCIETY OF INTERNATIONAL LAW AND THE NEDERLANDSE VERENIGING VOOR INTERNATIONAAL RECHT 414, 416-17 (1994); United Nations Conference on Environment and Development, The Rio Declaration on Environment and Development, 31 I.L.M. 874, 874 (1992).

Aristotelian University, for permission to reprint from A. Naess, *The Deep Ecology Movement: Some Philosophical Aspects,* 8 PHIL. INQUIRY 10,12-21(1986).

Ashgate Publishing Company, for permission to reprint from D. CAPONERA, THE ROLE OF CUSTOMARY INTERNATIONAL WATER LAW 803 (1985).

Aspen Law & Business, for permission to reprint from JANIS, AN INTRODUCTION TO INTERNATIONAL LAW 1-2, 52-54 (1993).

Betsy Hartman, for permission to reprint from B. HARTMAN, REPRODUCTIVE RIGHTS AND WRONGS: THE GLOBAL POLITICS OF POPULATION CONTROL AND CONTRACEPTIVE CHOICE 20-24, 28-30, 33 (1987).

Blackwell Publishers, for permission to reprint from Antonia Layard, *Nuclear Liability Damage Reform After Chernobyl,* 5 RECIEL 218, 219, 222 (1996); Sir Gerald Fitzmaurice, *The Foundations of the Authority of International Law and the Problem of Enforcement,* 19 MOD. L. REV. 1, 8-9 (1956)..

BNA Incorporated, for permission to reprint from Roland Blassnig, *Methyl Bromide Phaseout, CFC Export Licensing Only Gains at Montreal Meeting*, 20 B.N.A. INT'L ENVT. DAILY 860 (Sept. 24, 1997); Campbell & Carpenter, *Analysis and Perspective: From Kyoto to Buenos Aires: Implementing the Kyoto Protocol on Climate Change*, 21 B.N.A. INT'L ENVT. DAILY 711- 56 (July 22, 1998); Roland Blassnig, *Nations Agree to Cuts in Productions of Methyl Bromide, Faster CGC Phase-Out*, 15 B.N.A. INT'L ENVT. DAILY 769 (Sept. 18,1997); *Marine Affairs, IMO Provisions Requiring Double Hulls on New Ships Takes Effect, Agency Announces*, 16 B.N.A. INT'L ENVT. DAILY 514 (July 26, 1993).

Boston College International and Comparative Law Review, for permission to reprint from Noemi Gal-Or, *Private Party Direct Access: A comparison of the NAFTA and the EU Disciplines*, 21 B.C. INT'L & COMP. L. REV. 1, 3-4, 13-14, 17, 21, 23, 34 (1998).

Boston University International Law Journal, for permission to reprint from John B. Heppes & Eric J. McFadden, *The Convention on International Trade in Endangered Species of Wild Fauna and Flora: Improving the Prospects for Preserving Our Biological Heritage*, 5 BOSTON U. INT'L L. J. 229, 229-32 (1987).

British Institute of International & Comparative Law, for permission to reprint from A. Boyle, *State Responsibility and International Liability for Injurious Consequences Not Prohibited by International Law: A Necessary Distinction?*, 39 I.C.L.Q. 1, 1-4, 21-24 (1990).

Brooks/Cole Publishing Company, for permission to reprint from G. MILLER, ENVIRONMENTAL SCIENCE: AN INTRODUCTION 20-24, 44-45 (1986).

Buffalo Law Review, for permission to reprint from Mark A. Montgomery, *Banning Waste Exports: Much Ado about Nothing*, 1 BUFF. J. INT'L L. 197, 203-05, 208-10, 216-18 (1994).

Butterworths Publishers, for permission to reprint from J. G. STARKE, STARKE'S INTERNATIONAL LAW 409 B 18 (11th ed.1994); J. G. STARKE, STARKE'S INTERNATIONAL LAW 36, 113, 409 - 18 (11th ed.1994).

California Western International Law Journal, for permission to reprint from Loius Renes Beres, *Towards Protection of Iraqi Crimes under International Law: Jurisprudential Foundations and Jurisdictional Choices*, 22 CAL. W. INT'L L. J. 127-134 (1991); W. Michael Reisman, *The Cult of Custom in The Late 20th Century*, 17 CAL. W. INT'L L. J. 133-35, 142-43 (1987).

Cambridge: NY Grotius Publications Ltd., for permission to reprint from ALEXANDRE KISS & DINAH SHELTON, MANUAL OF EUROPEAN ENVIRONMENTAL LAW 351-52 (1993).

Cambridge University Press, for permission to reprint from INTERNATIONAL LAW 68-74 (H. Lauterpacht ed., 1970); S. LYSTER, INTERNATIONAL WILDLIFE LAW 97-102, 105-08 (1985); THE ANTARCTIC TREATY REGIME: LAW, ENFORCEMENT & RESOURCES 128, 129-131, 229-33 (Gillian D. Triggs ed.,1987); PHILIPPE J. SANDS, CHERNOBYL: LAW AND COMMUNICATION 40-42, 44-47, 51 (1988); DAVOR VIDAS, THE EFFECTIVENESS AND THE LEGITIMACY OF THE ANTARTIC TREATY SYSTEM 61-63, 64-72, 89-90 (1996).

CATO Institute, for permission to reprint from PATRICIA ADAMS, PROPERTY RIGHTS AND BIOREGIONALISM, CATO POLICY REPORT (1995).

Chicago-Kent Law School, for permission to reprint from A. Tarlock, *The Role of Non- Governmental Organization in the Development of Int'l Envtl. Law*, 68 CHI.-KENT L. REV. 61, 69-75 (1992).

Clarendon Press/Oxford University Press, for permission to reprint from IAN BROWNLIE, PRINCIPLES OF PUBLIC INTERNATIONAL LAW 32-38, 56-57 (4th ed. 1992).

Clark Boardman Callaghan (West Group), for permission to reprint from J. JOHNSON & G. WARE, PESTICIDE LITIGATION MANUAL 1-2, 11-2 through 11-4 (1992).

Colorado Journal of International Environmental Law & Policy, for permission to reprint from Daniel Putterman, *Model Material Transfer Agreements for Equitable Biodiversity Prospecting*, 7 COLO. J. INT'L ENVTL. L. & POL'Y 149-52 (1995); Okidi, *Preservation and Protection Under the 1991 ILC Draft Articles on the Law of International Watercourses*, 3 COLO. J. INT'L ENVTL. L. & POL'Y 143, 144-145, 149, 155-172 (1992); Raymond MacCallum, *Evaluating the Citizen Submission Procedure Under the North American Agreement on Environmental Cooperation*, 8 COLO. J. INT'L ENVTL. L & POL'Y 395, 396-99, 401-02 (1997); A. Timoshenko, *Ecological Security: Global Change Paradigm*, 1 COLO. J. INT'L ENVTL. L. & POL'Y 127, 135-43 (1990).

Columbia University Press, for permission to reprint from; W. FRIEDMANN, THE CHANGING STRUCTURE OF INTERNATIONAL LAW 70 (1964); L. HENKIN, HOW NATIONS BEHAVE: LAW AND FOREIGN POLICY 13-15 (2d. ed. 1979); H. Daly, *Elements of Environmental Macroeconomics*, in ECOLOGICAL ECONOMICS THE SCIENCE AND MANAGEMENT OF SUSTAINABILITY 32, 38-40 (R. Constanza ed.1991).

Columbia University Journal of Environmental Law, for permission to reprint from J.Wylie Donald, *The Bamako Convention as a Solution to the Problem of Hazardous Waste Exports to Less Developed Countries*, 17 COLUM. J. ENVTL. L. 143, 144-45, 149, 155-72 (1992); C. O'Neil and C. Sunstein, *Economics and The Environment: Trading Debt and Techniques for Nature*, 17 COLUM. J. ENVTL. L. 93, 107-10 (1992); D. Ring, *Sustainability Dynamics: Land-Based Marine Pollution and Development Priorities in the Island States of the Commonwealth Caribbean*, 22 COLUM. J. ENVTL. L. 65, 73, 78-79, 81-98, 112-13 (1997).

Commerce Clearing House, for permission to reprint from *European Union Law Reporter* 3347-10- 23, 3347-31-32 (1995).

Community Publications Cooperative, for permission to reprint from Gernot Kohler, *The Three Meanings of Global Apartheid: Empirical, Normative, Existential*, 20 ALTERNATIVES 403, 403-04, 406-08 (1995).

Cornell University Press, for permission to reprint from Oxman, *Antarctica and the New Law of The Sea*, 19 CORNELL INT'L L. J. 211, 236 (1986); J. Barcelo, *The International Legal Regime for Antarctica*, 19 CORNELL INT'L L. J. 155, 156-61 (1986); F. Francioni, *Legal Aspects of Mineral Exploitation in Antarctica*, 19 CORNELL INT'L L. J. 163, 169-77 (1986).

Cornell University Law School, for permission to reprint from Douglas M. Zang, *Frozen in Time: The Antarctic Minerals Convention*, 76 CORNELL L. REV. 722, 735-51 (1991).

Daniel Chiras, for permission to reprint from J. Simon, *The Population Debate: The Case for More People, in* ENVIRONMENTAL SCIENCE: ACTION FOR A SUSTAINABLE FUTURE 110 (Daniel Chrias ed.,1994).

David Davies Memorial Institute of International Studies, for permission to reprint from Sylvia Maureen Williams, *The Protection of the Ozone Layer in Contemporary International Law*, 10 INT'L REL. 167, 176-77 (1990).

Denver Journal of International Law & Policy, for permission to reprint from J. Kindt, *Ocean Dumping*, 13 DEN. J. INT'L L. & POL'Y 335-38 (1984).

Duke University Press, for permission to reprint from Raven & McNeely, *Biological Extinction: Its Scope and Meaning for Us, in* PROTECTION OF GLOBAL BIODIVERSITY: CONVERGING STRATEGIES 13-30, (Lakshman Guruswamy & Jeffrey McNeely eds., 1998); FRANCIS ANTHONY BOYLE, WORLD POLITICS AND INTERNATIONAL LAW 3-14 (1985).

Dr. Jorgens Randers, for permission to reprint from JORGEN RANDERS & DONELLA MEADOWS, WESTERN MAN AND ENVIRONMENTAL ETHICS: ATTITUDES TOWARD NATURE AND TECHNOLOGY 253, 273-76 (Ian G. Barbour ed.,1973).

Dr. Ryszard W. Piotrowczi, for permission to reprint from S. BLAY, R. PIOTROWCZI & M. TSAMENYI, ANTARTICA AFTER 1991: THE LEGAL AND POLICY OPTIONS 5-19 (1989).

Earthscan Publications, for permission to reprint from MARTIN HOLDGATE, FROM CARE TO ACTION: MAKING A SUSTAINABLE WORLD 120-25 (1996); ALAN GRAINGER, THE THREATENING DESERT 1-6 (1990); Mark Gray, *The United Nations Environment Programme: An Assessment*, 20 ENVTL. L. 292, 294-96 (1990).

Environmental Politics, for permission to reprint from William M Lafferty, *The Politics of Sustainable Development: Global Norms for National Implementation*, 5 ENVT'L POLITICS 185-203 (1996); Eric Laferriere, *Environmentalism and the Global Divide*, 3 ENVT'L POLITICS 91, 94-99 (1994).

Financial Times Management, for permission to reprint from DAVID H. OTT, PUBLIC INTERNATIONAL LAW IN THE MODERN WORLD 13-16, 20-22, 23-24, 27-28, 192, 202-3 (1987).

Florida State University, College of Law, Journal Of Transnational Law & Policy, for permission to reprint from C. Fletcher, *Greening World Trade: Reconciling GATT and Multilateral Environmental Agreements within the Existing World Trade Regime*, 5 J. TRANSNAT'L L. & POL'Y 341 (1996).

Food and Agriculture Organization of the United Nations, for permission to reprint from FAO Legislative Study No. 47, 1991, Coastal State Requirements for Foreign Fishing, FAO Legislative Study, No. 21, Rev. 13-27 (1991); WILLIAM BURKE, U. N. FOOD AND AGRICULTURE ORGANIZATION (FAO) LEGILATIVE STUDY 13, 14-27, 47 (1991).

Fordham International Law Journal, for permission to reprint from Rolf Wagenbaur, *The European Community's Policy on Implementation of Environmental Directives*, 14 FORDHAM INT'L L.J. 455, 455-61, 470 (1991).

Foreign Affairs Publishers, for permission to reprint from Phillip C. Jessup, *The Reality of International Law by the Council on Foreign Relations*, 18 FOR. AFF. 244-46 (1939-40).

Foundation Press, for permission to reprint from HENRY J. STEINER ET AL., TRANSNATIONAL LEGAL PROBLEMS: MATERIALS AND TEXT 556-60 (4th ed. 1994).

Free Press Publisher, for permission to reprint from Burns H. Weston, *The Role of Law in Promoting Peace and Violence: A Matter of Definition, Social Values, and Individual Responsibility*, in TOWARD WORLD ORDER AND HUMAN DIGNITY 114, 116-17 (W. Michael Reisman & Burns H. Weston eds., 1976).

GATT BISD, for permission to reprint from, General Agreement on Tariffs and Trade, Agreement on Technical Barriers to Trade 26-28 (1979).

Georgetown Univ. Int'l Law Institute, for permission to reprint from A. Charlotte de Fontaibert et al., *Biodiversity in the Seas: Implementing the Convention on Biological Diversity in Marine and Coastal Habitats*, 10 GEO. INT'L ENVTL. L. REV. 753, 767 (1998); Howard S. Kaminsky, *Assessment of the Bamako Convention on the Ban of Import into Africa and the Control of Transboundary Movement and Management of Hazardous Wastes within Africa*, 5 GEO. INT'L ENVTL. L. REV. 77-79, 81-87 (1992); Harry Almond, *Weapons, War and the Environment*, 3 GEO. INT'L ENVTL. L. REV. 117, 118-19, 121-23, 125, 129-30, 133 (1990); Giselle Vigneron, *Compliance and International Environmental Agreements: A Case Study of the 1995 United Nations Straddling Fish Stocks Agreement*, 10 GEO. INT'L ENVTL. L. REV. 581 (1998); Jennifer R. Kitt, Note, *Waste Exports to the Developing World: A Global Response*, 7 GEO. INT'L ENVTL. L. REV. 485, 488, 491-92 (1994); Christopher N. Bolinger, *Assessing the CEC on Its Record to Date*, 28 LAW & POL'Y INT'L BUS. 1107, 1118-30 (1997).

Georgetown University Law Center, for permission to reprint from Edith Brown Weiss, *International Environmental Law: Contemporary Issues and the Emergence of a New World Order*, 81 GEO. L.J. 675, 702-07 (1993).

Green Print Ltd., for permission to reprint from J. CLARK, WHAT IS SOCIAL ECOLOGY IN RENEWING THE EARTH: THE PROMISE OF SOCIAL ECOLOGY 5-11 (1990).

Gunther Handl, for permission to reprint from Gunther Handl, *Transboudary Nuclear Accidents: The Post-Chernobyl Multilateral Legislative Agenda*, 15 ECOLOGY L. Q. 203, 222-28 (1988).

Hague Academy of International Law, for permission to reprint from Richard R. Baxter, *Treaties and Custom*, 129 RECEUIL DES COURS 25, 32-104 (1970).

Harvard Business School Press, for permission to reprint from F. CAIRNCROSS, COSTING THE EARTH- THE CHALLENGE FOR GOVERNMENTS, THE OPPORTUNITIES FOR BUSINESS 131-41 (1993).

Harvard Envt'l Law Rev., for permission to reprint from Kal Raustiala, Note, *The "Participatory Revolution" in International Environmental Law*, 21 HARV. ENVTL. L. REV. 537, 538, 542, 549, 551, 558-61, 565-67 (1997).

Harvard International Law Journal, for permission to reprint from Amy A. Fraenkel, Comment, *The Convention on Long-Range Transboundary Air Pollution: Meeting the Challenge of International Cooperation*, 30 HARV. INT'L L.J. 447, 451-52, 459, 461, 463 (1989); Avi Gesser, Comment, *Canada's Environmental Choice Program: A Model for a "Trade-Friendly" Eco-Labeling Scheme*, 39 HARV. INT'L L.J. 501, 501 (1998).

Harvard University Press, for permission to reprint from RICHARD E. BENEDICK, OZONE DIPLOMACY- NEW DIRECTIONS IN SAFEGUARDING THE PLANET 148-52 (1991).

Harvard University, Law School, Society for Law & Pub. Pol'y, for permission to reprint from Alastair Iles, *The Desertification Convention: A Deeper Focus on Social Aspects of Environmental Degradation*, 36 HARV. INT'L L.J. 207 (1995).

Hastings International & Comparative Law Review, for permission to reprint from Elizabeth B. Baldwin, Note, *Reclaiming Our Future: International Efforts to Eliminate the Threat of Persistent Organic Pollutants*, 20 HAST. INT'L & COMP. L. REV. 855, 855-62 (1997).

Heldref (Helen Dwight Reid Educational Foundation) Publications, for permission to reprint from Robert Repetto, *Earth in the Balance Sheet: Incorporating Natural Resources in National Income Accounts*, 34 ENVIRONMENT 12, 13-17, 44 (1992).

Holt Rinehart and Winston (division of Harcourt Brace), for permission to reprint from HANS KELSEN, PRINCIPLES OF INTERNATIONAL LAW 454-56 (1959).

Holmes and Meier, for permission to reprint from MOHAMMED BEDJAOUI, TOWARDS A NEW INTERNATIONAL ECONOMIC ORDER 49-50, 62-63 (1979).

Humanities Press International, for permission to reprint from K. GOURLAY, POISONERS OF THE SEAS 119-22, 140-43 (1988).

Indiana Journal of Global Legal Studies, for permission to reprint from Kyle W. Danish, *International Environmental Law and the Bottom-Up Approach: A Review of the Desertification Convention*, 3 IND. J. GLOBAL LEGAL STUD. 133 (1997).

Institute for Contemporary Studies, for permission to reprint from TODOR PANAIOTOU, GREEN MARKETS: THE ECONOMICS OF SUSTAINABLE DEVELOPMENT 57-103, 105-116 (1993).

Intergovernmental Panel on CLimate Change, for permission to reprint from THE INTERGOVERNMENTAL PANEL ON CLIMATE CHANGE, CLIMATE CHANGE 1995: THE SCIENCE OF CLIMATE CHANGE 3-7, 14-20, 23, 25-27, 31, 39-40, 312, 324 (1996).

IUCN Inter-Committee, for permission to reprint from IUCN INTER-COMMITTEE TASK FORCE ON INDIGENOUS PEOPLES, INDIGENOUS PEOPLES AND SUSTAINABILITY: CASES AND ACTION EXCERPTS (1997).

International Law Society of the Golden State School of Law, for permission to reprint from Andrea Marcus, *Transboundary Toxic Waste Disposal: Understanding the Gravity of the Problem and Addressing the Issue Through the Human Rights Commission*, 1 INT'L DIMENSIONS 11-13 (1997).

International Society of Ecological Economics, for permission to reprint from T. N. Jenkins, *Economics and The Environment: A Case of Ethical Neglect*, 26 ECOLOGICAL ECON. 151, 153, 159- 62 (1998).

IOS Press, for permission to reprint from Sam Blay & Julia Green, *The Development of a Liability Annex to the Madrid Protocol*, 25 ENVTL. POL'Y & L. 24 (1995).

Iowa State University Press, for permission to reprint from RICHARD A. FALK, REVITALIZING INTERNATIONAL LAW 3, 5-8, 91-93 (1989).

John Wiley and Sons, for permission to reprint from D. Tolbert & G. Plant, *Defining the Environment, in* ENVIRONMENTAL PROTECTION AND THE LAW OF WAR 256-60 (1991); M. KAPLAN & N. KATZENBACH, THE POLITICAL FOUNDATIONS OF INTERNATIONAL LAW 239-40 (1966); Richard A. Falk, *The Environmental Law of War: An Introduction, in* ENVIRONMENTAL PROTECTION AND THE LAW OF WAR 78, 82-88 (1991).

Journal of Maritime Law and Commerce, for permission to reprint from Mans Jacobsson & N. Trotz, *The Definition of Pollution Damage in the 1984 Protocols to the 1969 Civil Liability Convention and the 1971 Fund Convention*, 17 J. MAR. L. & COM. 467-72, 476-77, 479-81 (1986).

Kansas Journal of Int'l Law & Pub. Pol'y, for permission to reprint from I. Wani, *Poverty, Governance, the Rule of Law, and International Environmentalism: A Critique of the Basel Convention on Hazardous Wastes*, 1 KAN. J.L. & PUB. POL'Y 37, 40-45 (1991).

Kluwer Academic Publishers, for permission to reprint from Williams, *A Historical Background on the Chlorofluorocarbon Ozone Depletion Theory and Its Legal Implications, in* TRANSBOUNDARY AIR POLLUTION 267, 275-76 (1986); VIRGINIA A. LEARY, INTERNATIONAL LABOUR CONVENTIONS AND NATIONAL LAW: THE EFFECTIVENESS OF THE AUTOMATIC INCORPORATION OF TREATIES IN NATIONAL LEGAL SYSTEMS 6-9 (1982); R. Pisilo-Mazzeschi, *Forms of International Responsibility for Environmental Harm, in* INTERNATIONAL RESPONSIBILITY FOR ENVIRONMENTAL HARM 15-26 (Francesco Francioni & Tullio Scovazzi eds., 1991); QING-NAN MENG, LAND-BASED MARINE POLLUTION: INTERNATIONAL LAW DEVELOPMENT 105-06, 169-70 (1987); M. Spinedi, *Protection of the Environment Through Criminal Law*, 2 Y.B. INT'L ENVTL. L. 99-101 (1991); GERHARD BEBR, JUDICIAL CONTROL OF THE EUROPEAN COMMUNITIES 394, 396, 398 (1962); Fabian Amtenbrink, *Public Interest Litigation before European Courts*, 7 EUR. BUS. L. REV. 35-37 (1996); EBERE OSIEKE, CONSTITUTIONAL LAW AND PRACTICE IN THE INTERNATIONAL LABOUR ORGANISATION 161- 64 (1985); Tieya Wang, *The Third World and International Law, in* THE STRUCTURE AND PROCESS OF INTERNATIONAL LAW 955, 961-63, 970 (R Macdonald & D. Johnston eds., 1986); T. Gehring, *International Environmental Regimes: Dynamic Legal Systems*, 1 Y.B. INT'L ENVTL. L. 35, 47-54 (1990); OSCAR SCHACHTER, INTERNATIONAL LAW IN THEORY AND PRACTICE 55-56, 58 (1995); LOUIS HENKIN, INTERNATIONAL LAW: POLITICS,VALUES AND FUNCTIONS 22 (1998); Frederick A. Mann, *Reflections on theProsecution of Persons Abducted in Breach of International Law, in* INTERNATIONAL LAW AT A TIME OF PERPLEXITY 407, 409, 411-20 (1989); Tullio Treves, *A New Element in the Antartic System, in* INTERNATIONAL LAW FOR ANTARTICA 603-04, 609-10 (1996); EMILIO SAHURIE, THE INTERNATIONAL LAW OF ANTARTICA 352-58 (1992); JOHN W. KINDT, ANTARTIC LEGAL REGIME 194-96 (1988); SUDHIR CHOPRA, ANTARTIC LEGAL REGIME 169-76 (1988).

Law Journal-Human Rights, for permission to reprint from Jean-Marie Henckaerts, *The Current Status and Content of the Prohibition of Mass Expulsion of Aliens*, 15 HUM. RTS. L.J. 301 (1994).

Lisa B. Gregory, for permission to reprint from Lisa B. Gregory, *Your Money Or Your Life*, 6 J. CHINESE L. 45 60-78 (1992).

Macmillan Publishing Co. Simon & Schuster, for permission to reprint from JANNA THOMPSON, THE STATE AND THE ENVIRONMENT: TOWARDS INTERGRATION 275, 280-83 (1995); Burns H. Weston, *Executive Agreement, in* 2 ENCYCLOPEDIA OF THE AMERICAN CONSTITUTION 666-68 (L. Levy et al. eds., 1986); K. V. Raman, *Toward a General Theory of International Customary Law, in* TOWARD WORLD ORDER AND HUMAN DIGNITY=!27 ENVTL. L. 1209 (1997); Reed Boland, *The Environment, Population, and Women's Human Rights*, 27 ENVTL. L. 1137 (1997); Paul R. Ehrlich & Anne H. Ehrlich, *The Population Explosion: Why We Should Care and What We Should Do About It*, 27 ENVTL. L. 1187, 1188-94 (1997); Elizabeth Spahn, *Feeling Grounded: A Gendered View of Population Control*, 27 ENVTL. L. 1295 (1997); Chris Wold, *Multilateral Environmental Agreements and the GATT: Conflict and Resolution?*, 26 ENVTL. L. 841 (1996); Virginia Deane Abernethy, *Allowing Fertility Decline: 200 Years after Malthus's Essay on Population*, 27 ENVTL. L. 1097 (1997).

NY University Press, for permission to reprint from Margo Brett Baender, *Pesticides and Precaution: The Bamako Convention as a Model for an International Convention on Pesticides Regulation*, 24 N.Y.U.J. INT'L L. & POL. 557, 559-60, 562-66, 579-80, 582-83(1991).

Oceana Publications, for permission to reprint from Morin, *Canada, in* NEW DIRECTIONS IN THE LAW OF THE SEA 243, 243, 250-51 (1994); Albert E. Utton, *International Groundwater Management: The Case of the U.S.-Mexican Frontier, in* INTERNATIONAL GROUNDWATER LAW 157, 157-64 (Ludwik A. Teclaff & Albert E. Utton eds., 1981).

Organization of American States, for permission to reprint from Edith Weiss, *Environmental Disasters in International Law*, ANN. JUR. INTERAM. 141,145-50 (1986).

Oxford New York Pergamon Press, for permission to reprint from Michael Redclift, *The Meaning of Sustainable Development*, 23 GEO FORUM 395, 399 (1992); WORLD COMM. ON ENVIRONMENT & DEV., OUR COMMON FUTURE 43-54, 62-65 (1987); S. J. ANAYA, INDIGENOUS PEOPLES IN INTERNATIONAL LAW 47,51,53,98-107, 109-112 (1996); P. BIRNIE & A. BOYLE, INTERNATIONAL LAW AND THE ENVIRONMENT 150-54, 179-86 (1992); Carol Harlow, *Towards a Theory of Access for the European Court of Justice*, 12 Y.B.EUR. L. 213, 218, 229, 234, 235, 236 (1992); ROSALYN HIGGINS, PROBLEMS AND PROCESS: INTERNATIONAL LAW AND HOW WE USE IT 2-4, 19-22, 26-28 (1994).

Oxford University Press, for permission to reprint from ANTHONY CLARK AREND, INTERNATIONAL RULES: APPROACHES FROM INTERNATIONAL LAW AND INTERNATIONAL RELATIONS 289, 303-306 (1996); Alan Boyle, *Nuclear Energy and International Law: An Environmental Perspective*, 60 BRIT. Y. B. INT'L L. 257 261-65 (1989); B. SMITH, STATE RESPONSIBILITY AND THE MARINE ENVIRONMENT: THE RULES OF DECISION 34 36-43, 188-89, 198-203 (1988).

Pace University Law School, Int'l L. Rev., for permission to reprint from Muthu S. Sundram, *Basel Convention on Transboundary Movement of Harzardous Wastes: Total Ban Amendment*, 9 PACE INT'L L. REV. 1 31-4, 36-7, 42 (1997).

Pace Year Book, for permission to reprint from L. F. E. Goldie, *Environmental Catastrophes and Flags of Convenience- Does the Present Law Pose Special Liability Issues?*, 3 PACE Y. B. INT'L L. 63 63, 66-7, 81, 86-90 (1991).

Plenum Publishing Corp., for permission to reprint from F. MATSUMARA, TOXI-COLOGY OF INSECTICIDES 496 (2d ed. 1985).

Princeton University Press, for permission to reprint from Gidon Gottlieb, *Toward a Second Concept of Law, in* 4 THE FUTURE OF THE INTERNATIONAL LEGAL ORDER 331, 365-66 (C. Black & R. Falk eds., 1972).

Robert C. Balling, Arizona State University, for permission to reprint from Robert C. Balling Jr., *The Global Temperature Data*, 9 Research and Exploration 201-207 (1993).

Routledge Inc., for permission to reprint from CAROLYN MERCHANT, RADICAL ECOLOGY - THE SEARCH FOR A LIVABLE WORLD 183, 183-200 (1991); AKEHURST, AKEHURST'S MODERN INTRODUCTION TO INTERNATIONAL LAW 142 (7th ed. 1997).

Sir Geoffrey Palmer, for permission to reprint from Geoffrey Palmer, Towards a New Ocean World Order, Address to Oceans Day at the Global Forum, Rio De Janeiro June 8, 1992.

South Dakota Law Review, for permission to reprint from M. Mcdougal, *Studies in World Public Order*, 4 S. DAK. L. REV. 25, 35- 36, 50-51 (1959).

St. Martins Press, for permission to reprint from R. BOARDMAN, PESTICIDES IN WORLD AGRICULTURE: THE POLITICS OF INTERNATIONAL REGULATION 133,135-36 (1988); R. FALK, ANTARTIC TREATY SYSTEM IN WORLD POLITICS 399 (1991).

Stanford Law School, Int'l Law Journal, for permission to reprint from Jason L. Gudofsky, *Transboundary Shipments of Harzardous Waste For Recycling and Recovery Operations*, 39 STAN. J. INT'L. L. 219, 272-285 (1998).

Stanford University, Environmental Law Society, for permission to reprint from J.S. Carpenter, *Farm Chemicals, Soil Erosion, & Sustainable Agriculture*, 13 STAN. ENVTL. L. J 190, 201, 216-17, 219-20 (1994).

Stockholm International Peace Research Inst., for permission to reprint from Arthur H. Westing, *Environmental Warfare: An Overview, in* ENVIRONMENTAL WARFARE: A TECHNICAL, LEGAL AND POLICY APPRAISAL 3-10, 53-57 (Arthur H. Westing ed., 1984).

Sweet & Maxwell, for permission to reprint from L. NEVILLE BROWN & TOM KENNEDY, THE COURT OF JUSTICE OF THE EUROPEAN COMMUNITIES 17, 60-62, 107-108, 113-114, 193, 201, 207-208, 213- 214, 277-278 (1993); BING CHENG, GENERAL PRINCIPLES OF LAW - AS APPLIED BY INTERNATIONAL COURTS AND TRIBUNALS 23-25 (1953).

Taylor & Francis Inc., for permission to reprint from W. Schachte, *The Value of the 1982 UN Convention on the Law of the Sea: Preserving Our Freedoms and Protecting the Environment*, 23 OCEAN DEVELOPMENT & INT'L L. 55, 59-60 (Alastair Couper & Edgar Gold eds., 1993); S. Meese, *When Jurisdictional Interests Collide: International, Domestic and State Efforts to Prevent Vessel Source Oil Pollution*, 12 OCEAN DEV. & INT'L L. 71, 82-83 (1982).

Texas International Law Journal, for permission to reprint from Roger W. Findley, *Legal and Economic Incentives for the Sustainable Use of Rainforests*, 32 TEX. INT'L L. J. 17, 19-21, 27-30 (1997); John Warren Kindt & Samuel Pyeatt Menefee, *The Vexing Problem of Ozone Depletion in International Law and Policy*, 24 TEX. INT'L L. J. 261, 262-67, 277-282 (1989); A. Dan Tarlock, *Exclusive Sovereignty Versus Sustainable Development of a Shared*

Resource: The Dilemma of Latin American Rain Forest Man, 32 TEX. INT'L L. J. 37, 38-42, 55-57 (1997); Francesco Francioni, *The Madrid Protocol on the Protection of the Antartic Environment*, 28 TEX. INT'L L. J. 47 (1993) 48-51, 57-60.

Tulane Law Journal, for permission to reprint from Steve Charnovitz, INTER-NATIONAL ENVIRONMENTAL LAW COLLOQUIUM: GREEN ROOTS, BAD PRUNING: GATT RULES AND THEIR APPLICATION TO ENVIRONMENTAL TRADE MEASURES, 7 TUL. L. REV. 299, 310- 315, 323-324, 326- 328, 332-338 (1994).

Transnational Publishers Inc., for permission to reprint from BRUNNEE, ACID RAIN AND OZONE LAYER DEPLETION: INTERNATIONAL LAW AND REGULATION 11-14, 108-11 (1988); A. KISS & D. SHELTON, INTERNATIONAL ENVIRONMENTAL LAW 55-58, 109-13, 155-59, 350, 351, 354-56, 367-71 (1991);

U. C. L. A. School of Law, for permission to reprint from Gregory F. Maggio, *Recognizing the vital Role of Local Communities in International Legal Instruments*, 16 UCLA J. ENVTL. L. & POL. 179 (1998).

U. S. National Acid Precipitation Assessment Program, for permission to reprint from ACIDIC DEPOSITION: STATE OF SCIENCE AND TECHNOLOGY (1990).

United Nations Publishing Division, for permission to reprint from UNESCO Convention Concerning the Protection of the World Cultural and Natural Heritage, 1037 U.N.T.S. 151 (1972); Vienna Convention on the Law of Treaties, 1155 U.N.T.S. 331 (1969); Convention on Nature Protection and Wildlife Preservation in the Western Hemisphere, Arts. 1-10, 161 U.N.T.S. 229 (1940).

United Nations Environment Programme, for permission to reprint from United Nations Joint Group of Experts on the Scientific Aspects of Marine Pollution (GESAMP, 1990), GESAMP (IMO/FAO/UNESCO/WMO/IAEA/UN/UNEP Joint Group Experts on the Scientific Aspects of Marine Pollution), the State of the Marine Environment 9-25, 66-81, 90, (1990).

United Nations University Press, for permission to reprint from P. Szasz, *Restructuring the International Organizational Framework, in* ENVIRON-MENTAL CHANGE AND INTERNATIONAL LAW: NEW CHALLENGES AND DIMEN-SIONS 340, 356-76 (E. Weiss ed., 1992); E. Weiss, *Intergenerational Equity: A Legal Framework for Global Environmental Change, in* ENVT'L CHANGE AND INT'L L.: NEW CHALLENGES & DIMENSIONS 385, 410-12 (1991).

University of Arizona College of Law, Arizona J. of Int'l & Comp. Law, for permission to reprint from S. Charnovitz, *Critical Guide to the WTO's Report On Trade and Environment*, 14 ARIZ. J. INT'L & COMP. L. 341 (1997).

University of Arizona Law Review, for permission to reprint from L. Guruswamy, *Global Warming: Integrating United States and International Law*, 32 ARIZ. L. REV. 221 253-63 (1990).

University of British Columbia Press, for permission to reprint from R. M'Gonigle, *Developing Sustainability' and the Emerging Norms of International Environmental Law: The Case of Land-Based Marine Pollution Control*, CAN. Y. B. INT'L L. 169, 194-205 (1990).

University of California Press, for permission to reprint from T. Alcock, *Ecology Tankers and the Oil Pollution Act of 1990: A History of Efforts to Require Double Hulls on Oil Tankers*, 19 ECOLOGY L. Q. 97, 107-08 (1992).

University of Georgia, School of Law, Georgia Journal of Int'l & Comp. Law, for permission to reprint from Devereaux F. McClatchey, *Chernobyl and Sandoz One Decade Later: The Evolution of State Responsibility for International Disasters*, 1986-1996, 25 GEO. J. INTL & COMP. L. 659 (1996).

University of Indiana Law School Journal & William S. Hein & Co. Trustees, for permission to reprint from Faisal H. Naqvi, *Re-examining the Conceptualization of Indigenous Rights in International Law*, 71 IND. L. J. 673,714-16 (1996).

University of Michigan, for permission to reprint from William C. Burns, *The International Convention to Combat Desertification: Drawing a Line in the Sand?*, 16 MICH. J. INT'L L. 831 (1995); Steve Charnovitz, Two Centuries of Participation: NGOs and International Governance, 18 MICH. J. INT'L L. 183, 268-286 (1997).

University of Minnesota Law School, for permission to reprint from C. Feddersen, *Focusing on Substantive Law in International Economic Regulations: The Public Morals of GATT'S Article XX(A) And "Conventional" Rules of Interpretation*, 7 MINN. J. GLOBAL TRADE 75 (1998).

University of the Pacific, McGeorge School of Law, for permission to reprint from Thomas O. McGarity, *Regulating Commuters to Clear the Air: Some Difficulties in Implementing a National Program at the Local Level*, 27 PAC. L.J. 1521, 1538-53 (1996).

University of Pittsburgh Press, for permission to reprint from J. REGENS & R. RYCROFT, THE ACID RAIN CONTROVERSY 35-39, 48-51 (1988).

University of Saskatchewan Law Review, for permission to reprint from Noralee Gibson, *The Right to a Clean Environment*, 54 SASKATCHEWAN L. REV. 7 (1990).

University of Tasmania Law Review, for permission to reprint from David M. Dzidzornu & Martin Tsamenyi, *Enhancing International Control of Vessel-Source Oil Pollution Under the Law of the Sea Convention, 1982: A Reassessment*, 10 U. TASMANIA L. REV. 269, 272, 275-76, 278-79, 281-82 (1991).

University of Texas at Dallas, for permission to reprint from Rob Coppock, *Implementing the Kyoto Protocol*, 14 ISSUES IN SCIENCE AND TECH 66-74 (1998).

University of Wisconsin Press, for permission to reprint from RICHARD BILDER, MANAGING THE RISKS OF INTERNATIONAL AGREEMENT 4-11 (1981).

University Press of New England, for permission to reprint from STEPHEN DYCUS, NATIONAL DEFENSE AND THE ENVIRONMENT 140-45 (1996).

Vanderbilt Journal of Transnational Law, for permission to reprint from Asebey, *Biodiversity Prospecting: Fulfilling the Mandate of the Biodiversity Convention*, 28 VAND. J. TRANSNAT'L LAW 703, 737-46 (1995).

Vermont Law School, for permission to reprint from Stephen McCaffrey, *The Coming Fresh Water Crisis: International Legal and Institutional Responses*, 21 VT. L. REV. 803 (1997).

Virginia Journal of International Law Association, for permission to reprint from Kal Raustiala, *International Enforcement of Enforcement Under the North American Agreement on Environmental Cooperation*, 36 VA. J. INT'L L. 721, 732, 744-45 (1996); Timothy Wirth, *A Matchmaker's Challenge:*

Managing International Law and American Envt'l Law, 32 VA. J. INT'L L. 377, 392-99, 414-19 (1992).

W.W. Norton & Company, for permission to reprint from JESSICA MATHEWS, INTRODUCTION AND OVERVIEW, PRESERVING THE GLOBAL ENVIRONMENT: THE CHALLENGE OF SHARED LEADERSHIP (Jessica Mathews ed., 1991).

Wadsworth Publishing Co., for permission to reprint from J. Simon, *There is no Environmental Population or Resources Crises, in* LIVING IN THE ENVIRONMENT 29-31 (G. Tyler Miller ed.,1999).

Walter de Gruyter, Inc., for permission to reprint from G. Abi-Saab, *The Concept of International Crimes and its Place in Contemporary International Law, in* INTERNATIONAL CRIMES OF STATE: A CRITICAL ANALYSIS OF THE ILC'S DRAFT ARTICLE 19 ON STATE RESPONSIBILITY 141, 142-45 (1990).

Washington & Lee University, School of Law, for permission to reprint from John H. Jackson, *World Trade Rules and Environmental Policies: Congruence or Conflict*, 49 WASH. & LEE L. REV. 1227,1230-45 (1992); J Dunoff, *Reconciling International Trade with Preservation of the Global Commons: Can We Prosper and Protect*, 49 WASH. & LEE L. REV. 1407, 1415-21 (1992).

West Publishing Co., for permission to reprint from DAVID GETCHES, WATER LAW IN A NUTSHELL 237-41, 272 (1997); GOULD & GRANT, CASES AND MATERIALS ON WATER LAW 318-19 (5th ed. 1995); LAKSHMAN GURUSWAMY, INTERNATIONAL ENVIRONMENTAL LAW IN A NUTSHELL 20-24, 39- 56 (1997); ANTHONY D' AMATO, UNIVERSALITY VERSUS RESTRICTIVENESS IN CUSTOM, *adapted from* BURNS H. WESTON ET AL., INTERNATIONAL LAW AND WORLD ORDER 761 (1998); J. SAX ET. AL., LEGAL CONTROL OF WATER RESOURCES: CASES AND MATERIALS 448-50 (1991).

Westview Press, for permission to reprint from TERRY ANDERSON & DONALD R. LEAL, FREE MARKET ENVIROMENTALISM 9-23 (1991); G. PORTER & J. BROWN, GLOBAL ENVIRONMENTAL POLITICS 15-20, 32-33 (1991); BURNS H. WESTON, ALTERNATIVE SECURITY: LIVING WITHOUT NUCLEAR DETERRENCE 78, 79-80 (1990).

World Resources Institute, for permission to reprint from WORLD RESOURCES INST., WORLD RESOURCES 1996-97 x-xiv (1997); WORLD RESOURCES INST., GLOBAL BIODIVERSITY STRATEGY: GUIDELINES FOR ACTION TO SAVE, STUDY, AND USE EARTH'S BIOTIC WEALTH 178, 270 (1992); P. SAND, LESSONS LEARNED IN GLOBAL ENVT'L GOVERNANCE 9, 12-14 (1990).

World Watch Institute, for permission to reprint from French, *After the Earth Summit: The Future of Environmental Governance, an excerpt from* WORLD WATCH INST. MAGAZINE 38-45 (1992).

Yale Law School, for permission to reprint from Joseph H. Weiler, *The Transformation of Europe*, 100 YALE LAW L. J. 2403, 2406-07, 2419-22 (1991); P. Sands, *European Community Environment Law: The Evolution of a Regional Regime of International Environmental Protection*, 100 YALE L. J. 2511, 2518-20 (1991).

Yale University Press, for permission to reprint from MYRES S. MCDOUGAL, THE INTERPRETATION OF AGREEMENTS AND WORLD PUBLIC ORDER 3-5 (1967); CHEN, AN INTRODUCTION TO CONTEMPORARY INTERNATIONAL LAW 379-384 (1989); ECOLOGY, ECONOMICS, ETHICS 3-5, 7 (1991).

A Note on Pronouns

A word about the sometimes pesky issue of third person singular pronouns. A number of authors excerpted by us, particularly those of older vintage, have used the masculine gender ("he") when referring to that ubiquitous fictitious person to illustrate their argument. We have chosen not to challenge their choice of expression, and instead, would request the reader to construe such references in the generic sense, to include women as well as men.

*

Table of Abbreviations

The following abbreviations are used in the headnotes and footnotes to the instruments included in this documentary supplement.

A	United Nations General Assembly
Add.	Addendum
A.J.I.L.	American Journal of International Law
Alb.	Albania
AMR/SCM	Document of the Session of the Special Consultative Meeting on Antarctic Mineral Resources
App.	Appendix
ASEAN	Association of South-East Asian Nations
ATSCM	Special Consultative Meeting of Antarctic Treaty Parties
Belg.	Belgium
Can.	Canada
C/E	Council of Europe
CONF, Conf	Conference
C.M.L.R.	Common Market Law Reports
Czech.	Czechoslovakia
Den.	Denmark
Doc.	Document
E	United Nations Economic and Social Council
ECE	Economic Commission for Europe
EEC	European Economic Community
EU	European Union
FAO	Food and Agriculture Organisation of the United Nations
FCCC	Framework Convention on Climate Change
Fr.	France
G.A., GA	General Assembly
GATT	General Agreement on Tariffs and Trade
Ger.	Germany
IAEA	International Atomic Energy Agency
IAEA INFCIRC	International Atomic Energy Agency Information Circular
IAEA Leg. Ser.	International Atomic Energy Agency Legal Series
I.C.J.	Reports of Judgments, Advisory Opinions and Orders of the International Court of Justice
I.L.A.	International Law Association, Reports of Annual Conferences of the International Law Association
I.L.M.	International Legal Materials
IMCO	Inter-Governmental Maritime Consultative Organisation
IMO	International Maritime Organisation
Mtg.	Meeting
Neth.	Netherlands

N.Z.	New Zealand
No.	Number
O.A.S. Off. Rec.	Organisation of American States Official Records
O.A.S.T.S.	Organisation of American States Treaty Series
OAU	Organisation of African Unity
OEA/Ser.	Organizacion Estados Americanos Series (Organisation of American States Series)
O.E.C.D., OECD	Organisation for Economic Co-operation and Development
Off.	Official
O.J.E.C.	Official Journal of the European Communities
P.C.I.J.	Permanent Court of International Justice: Reports
Pt., pt.	Part
RES, Res.	Resolution
Rev.	Revision, Revised
S	United Nations Security Council
Ser.	Series
Sess.	Session
Stat.	U.S. Statutes at Large
Supp.	Supplement
T.I.A.S.	U.S. Treaties and Other International Acts Series
U.K.	United Kingdom
U.N., UN	United Nations
UNEP	United Nations Environment Programme
U.N. GAOR	United Nations General Assemble Official Record
U.N.J.Y.B.	United Nations Juridical Yearbook
U.N.R.I.A.A.	United Nations Reports of International Arbitral Awards
U.N.T.S.	United Nations Treaty Series
U.S.	United States
U.S.T.	U.S. Treaties
Weston	International Law and World Order: Basic Documents
W.T.O.	World Trade Organisation
Y.B.I.L.C.	Yearbook of the International Law Commission
Y.B.U.N.	Yearbook of the United Nations

Using WESTLAW
to help you understand
International Environmental Law

Introduction: As a law student, you want to master your courses as completely as possible. Obtaining that mastery is the key to higher levels of performance in law school and better preparedness for the bar exam.   Using **WESTLAW** with **West books** is an excellent way to acquire the knowledge and information necessary to understand the legal concepts that you will encounter during law school.

The following examples will show you how to use WESTLAW to quickly retrieve information that will increase your understanding of the topic areas in **Guruswamy, Palmer and Weston's International Environmental Law and World Order Problem Book**. All you need is your WESTLAW password (and WESTMATE software—if you are going to use WESTLAW from your home computer). To begin, simply type your password, enter a research session identifier and continue with one of the sections below.

I.   HOW TO RETRIEVE THE FULL TEXT OF A PRINCIPAL CASE OR NOTE CASE

The principal and note cases in this text are generally not included in full. Reading the entire case, however, may help you understand the court's reasoning and holding, and give you a better grasp of the theories involved. The authors may also provide citations to note cases for additional reading to better highlight a point of law. For example, in Chapter 5, *International Environmental Wrongs*, under note 21, the authors cite a case which provides some analysis of due diligence in terms of the "means at the disposal" of the specific state. To see the full text of that case, *Case Concerning United States Diplomatic and Consular Staff in Teheran* (U.S. v. Iran), 1980 I.C.J. 3, at 33 (page 353 this text) type

find 1980 icj 3 *(then press* **ENTER***)*

Use the format above to retrieve cases on WESTLAW, e.g., from anywhere in WESTLAW type the word **find***(or* **fi***) followed by the volume number, reporter abbreviation, and* **page number** *of the case you wish to view.*

II.   HOW TO RETRIEVE LAW REVIEW AND LAW JOURNAL ARTICLES

Often a cited law review or journal article can provide you with valuable insight into and analysis of a particular issue or topic. Your professor may even suggest or require that you read some of these articles. For example, at the middle of page 898, the authors cite Thomas Schoenbaum's article, *Free International Trade and Protection of the Environment: Irreconcilable Conflict?*, 86 A.J.I.L. 700 (1992). To view this article, first go to the WESTLAW FIND PUB-

LICATIONS INDEX (to see if the publication is on WESTLAW and to obtain the appropriate citation format) by typing

find pubs (*then press* **ENTER**)

To view publication abbreviations for law reviews and Journals, locate LAW REVIEWS (*it is the last entry*) and type its corresponding page number (and press **ENTER**). To view publications that begin with the letter **A** (for American Journal of International Law) locate the letter **A** and type its corresponding page number (and press **ENTER**). Page ahead (by using the **PAGE DOWN** key or typing **p** then pressing **ENTER**) until you locate **A**merican Journal of International Law and its WESTLAW citation format. Combine the abbreviation with the appropriate volume and page then type

find 86 Am j intl l 700 (*then press* **ENTER**)

Use the format above to retrieve law review and journal articles, e.g., from anywhere in WESTLAW type the word **find** *(or* **fi**) *followed by the* **volume number, appropriate journal or review abbreviation,** *and* **page number** *of the article you wish to view.*

III. HOW TO USE WEST'S TOPIC AND KEY NUMBER SYSTEM TO OBTAIN ADDITIONAL INFORMATION

Cases reported in West Publications are organized in its *topic* and *key number system*. The cases you read on WESTLAW contain paragraphs of information called *headnotes*. The headnotes contain concise statements of law that are designated by *topic* and *key number*. The system is designed to allow you to retrieve other cases that contain the same topic and key number, meaning that the cases will have similar "on-point" law.

Page forward in any case you are viewing until you find a topic and key number discussing a point of law relevant to your research. Then enter that topic and key number in a case law database to retrieve other cases discussing the same point of law. After finding a relevant topic and key number, see how the courts in your jurisdiction have decided the issue by searching for it in your state case law database, e.g., **il-cs** (Illinois), **ct-cs** (Connecticut), **ca-cs** (California), etc. (Look to the WESTLAW database list for appropriate database identifiers).

Follow up: Many, but not all of the law review and journal articles referenced in this book are contained in a WESTLAW database. If you have any questions about WESTLAW or the preceding sections, call West Customer and Technical Support at 1-800-WESTLAW (1-800-937-8529), or speak to your WESTLAW Academic or student representative.

Summary of Contents

*

Table of Contents

Table of Treaties and Other Instruments

References are to Pages

Table of Arbitral and Judicial Decisions

The principal cases are in bold type. Cases cited or discussed in the text are roman type. References are to pages. Cases cited in principal cases and within other quoted materials are not included.

*

INTERNATIONAL ENVIRONMENTAL LAW AND WORLD ORDER

A PROBLEM ORIENTED COURSEBOOK

Second Edition

*

Part I

THE GLOBAL ENVIRONMENT AND INTERNATIONAL LAW

INTRODUCTION

This coursebook introduces you to international environmental law primarily through the study of problems that stem from an earth-space environment increasingly threatened by humankind's disregard of the fragility of Earth's ecosystems. The problems we have fashioned are hypothetical—to avoid associations and biases that potentially inhibit principled analysis, to resist too rapid obsolescence, and to facilitate thinking about the future. At the same time, they are true to life. We are concerned that you probe as well the complex webs of fact, law, and policy that typically confront international law decision-making in the "real world." These problems will be found in Part II and reflect our belief that issue-spotting, problem-solving, and synthesis are more important in the legal learning experience than the mere assimilation of disembodied knowledge.

In this Part I, we focus upon the analytical tools you will need to work through the problems in Part II, and we have chosen to do so with an eye to the wider fundamental setting of world order in which international law and lawyering, including international environmental law and lawyering, has evolved over time, beginning with the emergence of the state system in the Seventeenth Century. Ever since that time, the guiding assumption has been that international law, including international environmental law, is primarily an instrument of, by, and for sovereign states—an assumption that has been a mixture of both ideology and fact, varying with the circumstances and interests of the strongest states. In the Twentieth Century, since the close of World War II especially, two crucial developments have compelled policy-makers, practitioners, scholars, and perhaps especially laypersons to question the adequacy, even as a matter of description, of conceiving of international law, including international environmental law, as "the Law of Nations," the law among states. The first is found in the realization of a cluster of complex integrative trends that are relocating economic and political power beyond the reach of even the most powerful states—as with the threat of environmental degradation, most pertinently, the rise of global market forces, the transnational flow of people, drugs, and popular culture, and so forth. The second has to do with the gradual but steady emergence of a global polity of individuals and groups harmed by state action and inaction, needing the protection of transnational environmental and human rights regimes, depending on citi-

1

zens' initiatives at the grassroots and among nongovernmental organizations (NGOs), to exert pressures, and increasingly capable of ensuring constructive results through direct action, including the mobilization of modern information systems and communications technologies. In this Part I, convinced that a law of humanity as the core of international legal process, is superseding by gradual—and uneven—stages the law of states, we explore the concept of international law, including international environmental law, its so-called sources, and its means of implementation by adopting a critical perspective on the statist view of international law. And we do so against the backdrop of a real and on-going problem of potentially catastrophic consequence, one involving the complexity of trying to facilitate accountability and, even more importantly, changed behavior relative to the management of ultrahazardous nuclear materials, in this instance in the Arctic and Baltic regions of Russia and neighboring Scandinavia.

Following the breakup of the Soviet Union in late 1991, newly sovereign Russia, in furtherance of arms control agreements reached between its predecessor Soviet Union, the United States and others in the late 1980s,[a] undertook to reduce drastically its nuclear and conventional armed forces. At the same time, newly independent Belarus, Kazakhstan, and Ukraine, the other inheritors of the former Soviet Union's arsenals, pursued policies aimed at complete nuclear disarmament.

The immediate impetus for the Russian arms reductions was a set of negotiations begun between the United States and the U.S.S.R. in 1982, known as the "Strategic Arms Reduction Talks" (START).[b] Aimed at reducing rather than merely limiting the superpower nuclear weapons systems, these negotiations led to the so-called START I treaty signed in 1991 and START II treaty signed in 1993.[c] In START I, both superpowers agreed to

---

a. *See especially* Treaty Between the United States of America and the Union of Soviet Socialist Republics on the Elimination of Their Intermediate–Range and Shorter–Range Missiles, Dec. 7, 1987, 27 I.L.M. 90 (1988), *reprinted in* 2 INTERNATIONAL LAW AND WORLD ORDER: BASIC DOCUMENTS II.C.30 (Burns H. Weston ed. 1994) [hereinafter Weston] and Agreement Among the United States of America and the Kingdom of Belgium, the Federal Republic of Germany, the Republic of Italy, the Kingdom of the Netherlands and the United Kingdom of Great Britain and Northern Ireland Regarding Inspection Relating to the Treaty Between the United States of America and the Union of Soviet Socialist Republics on the Elimination of Their Intermediate–Range and Shorter–Range Missiles, Dec. 11, 1987, 27 I.L.M. 60 (1988), *reprinted in* 2 Weston II.C.31.

b. START was made possible by the success of four agreements between the former Soviet Union and the United States known collectively as the Strategic Arms Limitation Treaties (SALT): Agreement on Measures to Reduce the Risk of Outbreak of Nuclear War, Sept. 30, 1971, 807 U.N.T.S. 57, *reprinted in* 2

Weston II.C.19; Agreement on Measures to Improve the USA–USSR Direct Communications Link, Sept. 30, 1971, 806 U.N.T.S. 402, *reprinted in* 2 Weston II.C.20; Treaty on the Limitation of Anti–Ballistic Missiles, May 26, 1972, 944 U.N.T.S. 13, *reprinted in* 2 Weston II.C.21; and Interim Agreement on Certain Measures with respect to the Limitation of Strategic Offensive Arms, May 26, 1972, 944 U.N.T.S. 3, *reprinted in* 2 Weston II. C.22.

c. *See* Treaty Between the United States of America and the Union of Soviet Socialist Republics on Reduction and Limitation of Strategic Offensive Arms (START I), July 31, 1991, S. Treaty Doc. No. 102–20, 102d Cong., 1st Sess., *reprinted in* 2 Weston II.C.32; and Treaty Between the United States of America and the Russian Federation on the Further Reduction and Limitation of Strategic Arms (START II), Jan. 3, 1993, S. Treaty Doc. No. 103–1, 103d Cong., 1st session. START I entered into force Dec. 5, 1994. START II has yet to enter formally into force as of this writing because, though ratified by the United States in 1996, it has yet to be ratified by the State Duma (i.e.,

reduce their strategic forces by 25 to 30 percent over a period of years, and almost immediately each began to eliminate various tactical (battlefield) nuclear weapons, including artillery shells, depth charges, land mines, bombs, and warheads carried on tactical missiles. START II called for the elimination of MIRVed ICBMs[d] and, by the year 2003 (or 2000 if the United States would be able to assist Russia in meeting that date), reductions to strategic warhead limits on each side of between 3,000 and 3,500, including a maximum of 1,700 to 1,750 submarine-launched ballistic missile (SLBM) warheads. START II also detailed the methods used to calculate these numbers, with reductions to be carried out by eliminating missile launchers and heavy bombers according to START I treaty procedures and by reducing warheads on existing ballistic missiles other than the SS–18 (according to START I counting rules).

Many of the missiles covered by START I and START II are on Russian submarines that generally are powered by two nuclear reactors (in contrast to the nuclear submarines of France, the United Kingdom, and the United States which typically are powered by one reactor).[e] Most of these Russian submarines are based in the Russian ports on the Kola Peninsula near Murmansk in the West [see Figure I–1 and Table I–1][f] and in and around Vladivostok in the East [see Figure I–2]. In and around the Murmansk Fjord, approximately 98 of an estimated 165 nuclear submarines that are part of Russia's Northern Fleet have been decommissioned as of this writing, and most have yet to have their nuclear reactors removed. The decommissioned submarines were simply cut open to remove the warheads and then patched back together and stored in the harbors. As a result, each of these submarines, while inoperative for lack of missiles, still contains the two nuclear reactors—fully fueled—that once powered them. An estimated 82 nuclear submarines are stationed in the Vladivostok area as part of Russia's Pacific Fleet, and approximately 40 of these have been similarly decommissioned.

parliament) of the Russian Federation. Notwithstanding, at a U.S.–Russian summit convened in Helsinki in March 1997, U.S. President Clinton and Russian President Yeltsin agreed on the basic elements of a START III treaty and to commence official negotiations on it just as so on as the Russian Duma finally ratifies START II. Additionally, in September 1997, U.S. Secretary of State Albright and then Russian Foreign Minister Primakov signed a Protocol to the START II treaty that aims to ease Russia's concerns over the cost of dismantling its nuclear weapons systems, that extends the time for START II's implementation to December 31, 2007, and that thereby seeks to facilitate Russia's ratification of START II. At the same time, the two foreign ministers exchanged letters codifying a commitment reached at the Helsinki Summit to deactivate by December 31, 2003, the U.S. and Russian nuclear warheads that are to be eliminated under START II, thus seeking to ensure that Russia and the United States will realize the security benefits of START II as soon as possible. *See* United States Information Agency, Fact Sheet on START II Protocol, Letters on Early Deactivation (Sept. 26, 1997) <http://www.usis.it/wireless/wf970926/97092609.htm>.

d. "MIRVed ICBMs" are intercontinental ballistic missiles with payloads comprising two or more multiple independently targeted reentry vehicles (or warheads) that engage separate targets.

e. Five countries operate nuclear-powered naval vessels at present. In addition to France, Russia, the United Kingdom, and the United States, China may be counted.

f. The nuclear-powered ships of Russia's Northern Fleet operate from at least eleven naval bases on the Kola Peninsula, including Zapadnaya Litsa, the largest and most important, located on the Litsa Fjord about 45 kilometers from the Norwegian border.

Figure I-1

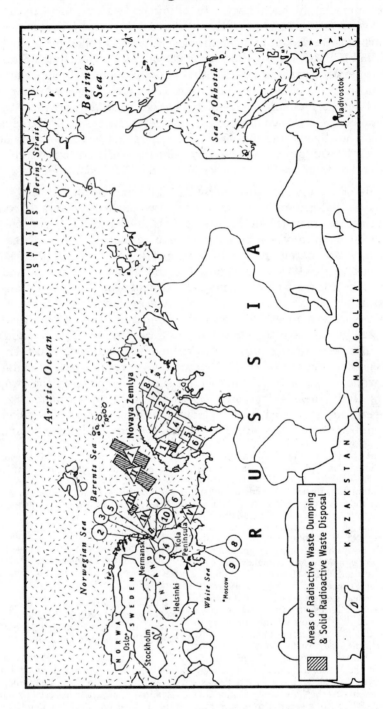

Table I-1

Sources of Radioactive Waste and Regions of Their Disposal in the Northern Seas (shown circled above)

Naval Fleet Bases	Sites of Temporary Storage of Spent Nuclear Fuel
1 Guba Nerpichia, Guba Andreeva, Bolshaya Lopatka & Malaya Lopatka bays 2 Guba Olenia & Sayda-Guba 3 Ara-Guba 4 Pala-Guba 8 Yokanga	1 Guba Andreeva 6 Yokanga 7 floating bases "Imandra", "Lepse", "Lotta" 2 floating base of the Navy for refuelling of the nuclear-powered submarine reactors
Storage and Decommissioning of Retired Naval Ships with Nuclear Power Units	**Vessel Construction and Refit Plants**
4 Polyarny 6 Yokanga 7 Murmansk (Repair Transport Facility "Atomflot") 8 Severdovinsk (water surrounding the refit wharf "Zvezdochka", Production Association "Sever")	8 Severdovinsk (Industrial Association "Sevmashpredriyatie", Product Association "Sever") 4 Polyarny (Navy refit wharf) 4 Viuzhny (refit plant "Nerpa")

Site	Activity Ci	TBq	No. of Dumps	Years	Comments
1	3320	123	22	1967-1991	3174 + ? containers 9 large objects (LO), 8 floating vessels (FV)
2	3410	126	8	1982-1984	1108 containers 104 LO
3	2027	75	8	1986-1983	472 + ? containers 4 LO, 1 FV
4	2687	99	8	1964-1978	1600 + ? containers, 6 LO, 1 FV
5	1280	47	5	1968-1975	5 LO
6	661	25	7	1966-1981	8 + ? containers, 7 LO, 4 FV
7	235	8	1	1972	1 LO
8	1845	68	3	1982-1988	146 + ? containers, 1 LO, 1 FV
Kolguev Island Chernaya Bay	40	1.5	1	1978	1 FV
(Novaya Zemlia)	300	11	1	1991	1 LO
Barents Sea	more than 100	more than 4	1	?	Barge with solid RAW in welded hull
TOTAL	**App.**	**App.**	**65**		**6508 + ? Containers, 17 FV's, 158 FV's**

All of which has created, in two concentrated areas, a huge stockpile of submarine nuclear reactors equal to about 60 percent of the nuclear power reactors presently generating civilian electric power worldwide, most of them on the Kola Peninsula, adjacent to the Barents and White seas and only one hour's drive from northern Norway and Finland [*see* Figure I–1 and Table I–1]. Indeed, combined with Russia's Atomflot fleet of nuclear-powered ice breakers in Kola Bay, the Kola nuclear power plant near Polyarny Zori, and the nuclear submarine shipbuilders in Severodvinsk, Russia's Northern Fleet of active and decommissioned submarines help to make the Kola Peninsula-White Sea region home to the largest concentration of nuclear reactors anywhere in the world.[g] Partly because most of these reactors are themselves mismanaged and partly because the waste generated by them is stored or disposed of under unsafe conditions, they present a large danger to human health and to the natural environment both on land and at sea. Also contributing to the problem are accidents on land, releasing radioactive material into the Arctic environment, and the intentional discharge of radio-

g. Adding to the toxicity of the region are more than 700,000 tons of sulphur dioxide that are each year released into the Kola Peninsula by Russian factories in Severonickel and Pe-chenganickel, where aluminum and nickel minerals are extracted practically unfiltered, endangering thousands of square miles of taiga, tundra, and mixed forests.

active pollutants on the land that later migrate into the neighboring Arctic seas. The principal facts are well documented.[h]

The Russian Shipyards

As indicated, the ships' reactors, in and around both Murmansk and Vladivostok, are not only active but derelict, having yet to be decontaminated and otherwise being managed in a manner unequal even to the (mis)management of the Chernobyl nuclear power plant near Kiev prior to its devastating explosion and "meltdown" in 1986.[i] As of this writing, indeed, the Russians appear to possess neither the knowledge nor sufficient wherewithal to remove or decontaminate the reactors; and what is more, facing continuing economic crisis, they so far have been unable to allocate even minimal funds for the undertaking (the shipyards where the removal and decontamination is supposed to take place having been funded at less than 10 percent of their requested budget). Thus the reactors constitute an enormous threat to the region in and of themselves. As stated by one highly informed source, the Norwegian-based Bellona Foundation in its 1996 report on the Russian Northern Fleet, which accounts for approximately 18 percent of the world's total nuclear reactors, "a grave situation could arise which can be pictured as a Chernobyl in slow motion."[j]

Nuclear reactors, as Chernobyl demonstrated, are made up of sophisticated equipment that require constant, high level maintenance. Maintaining Russia's existing nuclear fleet (exact numbers are difficult for both active and "moth balled" ships because they are a matter of Russian security) requires the disposal of thousands of gallons of low level radioactive waste created in coolant and cleaning water. Additionally, the fuel assemblies in each reactor need to be replaced periodically, thus generating new spent nuclear fuel waste. It is deeply troubling that the funding and personnel to maintain these reactors is thin, and may in some cases be even non-existent. The company *Kolenergo*, providing electricity to the naval bases near Murmansk, turned off the power at the Gadshievo naval base because of a long-standing unpaid energy bill amounting to about $4.5 million.[k]

---

h. For extensive detail, see T. Nilsen, I. Kudrik & A. Nikitin, The Russian Northern Fleet: Sources of Radioactive Contamination (Bellona Report No. 2:96, 1996) [hereinafter "1996 Bellona Report"], also available at <http://www.bellona.org>. *See also* Office of the President of the Russian Federation, Facts and Problems Related to Radioactive Waste Disposal in Seas Adjacent to the Territory of the Russian Federation (1993), *translated and reprinted in part* by Greenpeace Russia *in* Facts and Problems Related to the Dumping of Radioactive Waste in the Seas Surrounding the Territory of the Russian Federation (Sept. 23, 1993). For additional insights, see J. Eaton, *Kicking the Habit: Russia's Addiction to Nuclear Waste Dumping at Sea*, 23 DENVER J. INT'L L. & POL'Y 287 (1995); J. Handler, *Russia Seeks to Refloat a Decaying Fleet—The Future of the Northern Fleet's Nuclear Submarines*, INT'L DEF. REV., Jan. 1, 1997, at 43 (1997 WL 8538137); J. Handler, *The Lasting Legacy—Nuclear Submarine Disposal*, JANE'S NAVY INT'L, Jan. 1, 1998, at 11 (1998 WL 102304489); S.

Lavine, *Russian Dumping in the Sea of Japan*, 24 DENVER J. INT'L L. & POL'Y 417 (1996); K. Moody–O'Grady, *Nuclear Waste Dumping in the Oceans: Has the Cold War Taught Us Anything?*, 35 N.R.J. 695 (1995); B. Segerstahl, A. Akleyev & V. Novikov, *The Long Shadow of Soviet Plutonium Production*, 39 ENVIRONMENT 12 (Jan. 11, 1997) (1997 WL 10045034).

i. For discussion of the legal implications of nuclear accidents such as what took place at Chernobyl in 1986, see Problem 7–3 ("The Atomic Steel Mill") in Chapter 7, *infra*.

j. 1996 Bellona Report, *supra* note h, at Preface page 2.

k. According to the 1996 Bellona Report, *supra* note h at ¶ 1.3.1, "[p]ower was restored 40 minutes later when the Northern Fleet sent armed guards to the transformer station. The Northern Fleet Command ... stated that never again would *Kolenergo* dare to shut off the power." Five days later, however, "power was again shut off for 20 minutes, this time at the military shipyard *Sevmorput*." *Id*.

Much of the spent, highly radioactive waste created by the nuclear reactors is stored at the shipyards in old ships that are no longer seaworthy. These "rust buckets," now nuclear waste storage sites, afford little to no environmental security, as vividly demonstrated by the retired and rusting Atomflot supply ship *Lepse*, characterized by London's *Daily Telegraph* as "the most terrifying vessel on Earth ..., probably the world's most serious environmental threat."[l] Moored since 1982 near the center of Murmansk (population 500,000), about 100 miles from the Finnish and Norwegian borders, the *Lepse* is loaded with hundreds of damaged nuclear reactor parts and spent fuel rods, some of them more than 40 years old, holding as much radioactivity as the reactor that exploded at Chernobyl.[m] When some of this waste expanded for not having been kept cool enough, it caused the ship's waste containers, incautiously beaten shut with sledgehammers, to break. Then, in an effort to contain the radiation, part of the ship was entombed in concrete, which in turn made the *Lepse* extremely unstable and subject to capsize in a storm. No one really has any idea of how, with complete safety, to remedy this ship and other nuclear waste storage sites like it.

Dumping at Sea

Russian naval nuclear waste disposal procedures involve the dumping of thousands of barrels of radioactive waste, tons of liquid radioactive waste, damaged reactor compartments, and whole reactors removed from Russia's nuclear submarines. A number of the submarine reactors, some with their cores intact, some in stages of "meltdown," have been disposed of near the naval bases of Russia's Northern Fleet in and around Murmansk and its Pacific Fleet in and around Vladivostok. Reportedly, thirteen of these reactors are in the largest dump near Novaya Zemlya (New Land), which lies north of Murmansk near Finland and Norway.[n] Some are in 20–50 meters of water and are likely to be scoured by icebergs which routinely extend to depths of 60+ meters. Additionally, three nuclear-powered submarines have sunk in the Arctic Sea, one only 45 kilometers from Norway. On April 7, 1989, following a fire, the nuclear-powered submarine K–278, *Komsomolets*, with its two reactors and two nuclear warheads, sank to 1,685 meters depth in the Norwegian Sea, 140 kilometers off the Norwegian coast.[o] The rest of the reactors have been dumped in the Sea of Japan and in the Bering Sea off of eastern Russia.

Additionally, according to a 1993 Russian White Paper, unknown quantities of solid and liquid radioactive waste were dumped into the Barents Sea, the Sea of Japan, and the Sea of Okhotsk from 1959 to 1992 [see Figures I–1 & I–2], although it has been estimated that this dumping amounted to

---

[l.] C. Lockwood, *Russia's Time–Bomb of Nuclear Pollution*, DAILY TELEGRAPH (London) 12, Sept. 29, 1997, 1997 WL 2341783.

[m.] "The fact that the fuel roads are 'spent' only means that they are more dangerous. After being bombarded with high-energy neutrons inside a reactor for years, they are far more poisonous than when they went in." *Id.* According to the head of the Norwegian Bellona Foundation's branch office in Murmansk, Igor Kudrik, "no one is sure what happens to nuclear fuel rods that are 40 or 50 years

old.... They can fuse together. Then they are much harder to handle. You can even get a criticality, a spontaneous restarting of the nuclear reaction. No one knows what might happen when you take the lid off." *Id.*

[n.] *See* J. Handler, *The Lasting Legacy— Nuclear Submarine Disposal*, JANE'S NAVY INT'L, Jan. 1, 1998, at 11 (1998 WL 102304489).

[o.] The *Komsomolets* is a titanium-hulled submarine that once could dive to depths of up to 1,000 meters.

Figure I-2

Distribution of Radioactivity in Russia's Pacific Region

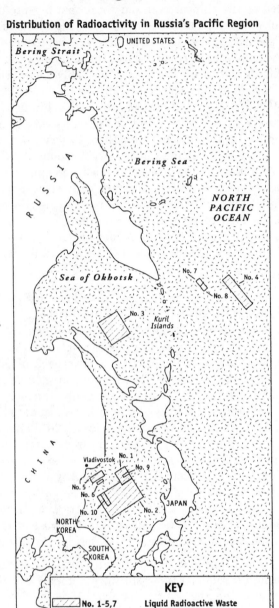

approximately 2.5 million curies of liquid low level radioactive material [see Figure I–3]. Given that one curie is equivalent to the amount of radiation released by one gram of radium, this constitutes a very large amount of radiation. The Chernobyl accident that spread radiation across Europe in

1986 released only about 100 curies of certain types of radiation. In any event, the Russian dumping of radioactive wastes has been more than twice what all other countries have dumped in the ocean. During the same era, but ending in 1984, Austria, Belgium, China, England, France, Italy, Germany, Japan, the Netherlands, New Zealand, South Korea, Sweden, and the United States also dumped low-level rad wastes, totaling 1.2 millions of curies.

Land–Based Radioactive Pollution

As one might expect, the Russian shipyards and the ocean dumping of radioactive wastes have not been the sole contributors to Russia's actual and threatened nuclear pollution of the Arctic region. Also contributing significantly to the problem is land-based pollution from radioactive sources. For example, the Mayak nuclear reprocessing plant along the north-flowing Ob and Techa rivers in Siberia (which, under growing numbers of contracts from around the world, turns nuclear fuel into weapons-grade materials), creates enormous wastes that are deposited in riverside "storage pools" containing as much as one billion curies of radioactive matter. As proven by intentional discharges of massive quantities of radioactive materials into these rivers when the Mayak plant began operations in the 1950s,[p] these pools are susceptible of breaches and therefore of releases into the Ob and Techa rivers, thence into the Kara Sea and eventually the Arctic Sea.[q] Nearby, in a related facility in Tomsk–7, a city of 500,000 that in the days of the Cold War did not even appear on the map, more than 1.2 billion curies of Russian military radioactive material are stored in caverns 200 to 400 meters below ground, a few miles from the Tom River, a tributary of the Ob River which, as noted, affects ultimately the Arctic Sea. And at Andreeva Bay not far from Norway, for yet further example, where are located the Russian Northern Fleet's largest storage facilities for radioactive waste and spent nuclear fuel, some 21,000 radioactive fuel rods stored in canisters are simply lying on the quay, exposed to the elements. The examples of land-based radioactive pollution are many.

* * *

The total amount of radioactivity resulting from Russia's mismanagement of the submarine reactors in its shipyards, from it ocean dumping of the wastes generated by them, and from its land-based pollution practices can be only estimated [see Figure I–3]. Regrettably, the Russian Federation has been less than forthcoming with the requisite information. Indeed, two people, including a former Russian naval officer working with the Bellona Foundation, currently are being held in custody by the Russian Federal Security Police (FSB), successor to the Soviet KGB, for having publicized the extent of

---

p. The problems of the Mayak plant are made even worse by nearby Lake Karachai which was used by the plant as a waste repository when the plants' storage pools were exceeded. It is so toxic that even a few minutes exposure to its radiation means certain death. The Worldwatch Institute, a leading environmental "think tank" in Washington, D.C., lists the lake as the most polluted place on Earth.

q. An equivalent plant in present-day Estonia threatens extensive radioactive contamination of the Baltic Sea near Estonia. A storage pond only 40 meters from the Baltic containing an unknown amount of radioactive waste has not been breached as of this writing. But Estonia, already financially choked by the breakup of the former Soviet Union, has been burdened with this waste problem; and, while receiving some financial and technical assistance from Sweden, it is not clear how it intends to handle the ultimate disposition of all of this radioactive material.

the derelict submarines problem. Labeled as "spies" and their records of nuclear contamination seized, they stand accused of "high treason" and under threat of the death penalty as of this writing. Not even Russian civilian authorities are allowed entry to the Northern Fleet's submarine bases to inspect for nuclear safety.

The fact remains, however, that, on the basis of information gathered from open sources in Russia and in other countries over the years, the Kola Peninsula–White Sea region may be properly described as being severely threatened by extensive radioactive pollution which, in turn, threatens to poison not just that region but, as well, the entire Arctic environment, including the northern reaches of countries such as Finland and Norway. The total amount of radioactivity in the Murmansk area alone is thought to be in the hundreds of millions of curies [see Figure I–3].

Figure I-3

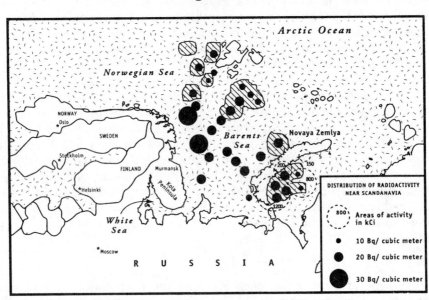

In sum, where it is not already contaminated by radioactive and other substances, the Arctic environment is grievously threatened by nuclear pollution emanating from the Russian Federation. It is a threat that the world can disregard or downplay only at its peril.

———

We now invite you to imagine yourself working as a junior lawyer in the Department of Legal Affairs of the Royal Norwegian Ministry of Foreign Affairs. Your experience is primarily in domestic environmental law gained from your first employment in Norway's Royal Ministry of the Environment. However, because of your domestic law experience, because you are analytically gifted, and because of your heritage as a member of the indigenous Saami (Lapp) people (thus your personal interest in protecting the reindeer and whale food stocks of the circumpolar Arctic region), you have been asked by your superiors to assist in the formulation of an international legal strategy that might persuade the Russian Federation to be truly aggressive in reducing the human health and environmental hazards posed by (1) its nuclear shipyard policies, (2) its disposal of the nuclear waste generated by them, and (3) its land-based pollution practices. This strategy, you are advised, includes, but is not necessarily limited to, the possibility of a memorial (i.e., brief) before the International Court of Justice in The Hague,[r] a declaration proposed for adoption by the Arctic Council,[s] and/or a negotiated agreement of some binding sort. It is January 1996, and your job, you are told, is to help prevent a gigantic international environmental disaster and to use or shape the law to deal with this frightening possibility.

You are excited by this new assignment and observe immediately that there are a number of environmental treaties and kindred instruments that appear to have, by either direct or general application, some bearing on the problem. Certain of these instruments speak directly to the practice of dumping or to the Arctic alone—e.g., the 1972 London Convention on the Prevention of Marine Pollution by Dumping of Wastes and Other Matter **[Basic Document 4.11]**, the 1991 Arctic Environmental Protection Strategy of the Arctic Council **[Basic Document 1.28]**, and the 1993 Nuuk Declaration on Environment and Development in the Arctic **[Basic Document 1.32]**. The 1972 London Dumping Convention, you note, prohibits the dumping of high-level nuclear waste. The 1991 AEP Strategy, subsumed by the Arctic Council upon its establishment in 1996, calls for adherence to the strictest relevant international standards. And the 1993 Declaration, in addition to reaffirming relevant principles of the 1992 Rio Declaration on Environment and Development **[Basic Document 1.29]**, Agenda 21 **[Basic Document 1.30]**, and the Non–Legally Binding Authoritative Statement of Principles for a Global Consensus on the Management, Conservation and Sustainable Development of All Types of Forests **[Basic Document 6.12]**, proclaims that "decisions relating to Arctic activities must be made in a transparent fashion ... to facilitate ... appropriate access to information concerning such decisions, to participation in such decisions and to judicial and administrative proceedings." Additional recommendations relating spe-

r. The International Court of Justice (ICJ), popularly known as the "World Court," has been particularly active in the international environmental law realm in recent years, so much so that, in 1993, it established a special "Chamber of the Court for Environmental Matters." For details, see *infra* Ch. 3, at 183, n.t.

s. The Arctic Council is a permanent high-level intergovernmental forum whose members consist of eight Arctic states: Canada, Denmark, Finland, Iceland, Norway, Russia, Sweden, and the United States. Established in Ottawa on September 19, 1996 when the "Ministers and Senior Representatives" of the eight states adopted the Declaration on the Establishment of the Arctic Council **[Basic Document 1.36]**, the Council—which maintains its Secretariat in Ottawa and which took as its first primary task the elaboration of rules of procedure for its meetings and those of its working groups in time for their formal adop-

tion at the Council's Ministerial Meeting in 1998—was created to promote multilateral cooperation and political action to address a wide range of Arctic issues common to its members, exclusive of matters related to military security. A key feature of the Council is the involvement of the Arctic region's indigenous peoples. In addition to the eight member nations, three organizations representing the majority of indigenous peoples in the circumpolar Arctic will be Permanent Participants: the Inuit Circumpolar Conference, the Saami Council, and the Association of Indigenous Minorities of the North, Siberia, and the Far East of the Russian Federation. Permanent participation is open to other Arctic organizations of indigenous peoples not currently represented by these three organizations provided that they meet the criteria set out in the 1996 Declaration. Participation is open also to non-Arctic states and intergovernmental organizations as observers.

cifically to land-based pollution, you observe, are to be found in Article 207 of the 1982 United Nations Convention on the Law of the Sea (UNCLOS) **[Basic Document 4.20]**, in the 1985 Montreal Guidelines for the Protection of the Marine Environment Against Pollution from Land–Based Sources (Montreal Guidelines) **[Basic Document 4.21]**, and in the 1992 Convention for the Protection of the Marine Environment of the North East Atlantic (OSPAR Convention) **[Basic Document 4.24]**. Furthermore, you note, several treaties and instruments of general applicability relate to the problem at hand, including Part 12 of UNCLOS, Principle 21 of the 1972 Stockholm Declaration on the Human Environment **[Basic Document 1.12]**, and Principle 2 of the 1992 Rio Declaration, *supra*, which direct states to ensure that activities within their jurisdiction do not cause harm to those outside their jurisdiction.

At the same time, however, you wonder if Russia, which is a party to, or signatory of, all of these instruments except for the OSPAR Convention, can be held legally accountable under them. For example, Moscow, you note, filed a declaration of non-acceptance to an extension of the 1972 London Dumping Convention to cover all radioactive materials. The 1991 AEP Strategy, though a function of the Arctic Council of which Russia is a member, calls for adherence to the strictest international standards only "as far as possible." And the 1993 Declaration as well as the 1992 instruments it reaffirms, you are advised, are widely understood to be not legally binding. You therefore ask about the possibility that these and cognate instruments, even if not binding as a matter of treaty law, may nonetheless contribute to some customary international law norms to which Russia could be beholden. To the same end, you note the existence of the 1994 Agreement between the United States of America and the Russian Federation on Cooperation in the Prevention of Pollution of the Environment in the Arctic **[Basic Document 1.34]**, requiring consultation relative to technical solutions for the elimination of radioactive and other types of pollution; the 1994 Agreement between the United States of America and the Russian Federation on Cooperation in the Field of Protection of the Environment and Natural Resources **[Basic Document 1.33]**, calling for jointly developed measures to improve the condition of the environment, including the Arctic; the 1996 Joint Communiqué and Declaration on the Establishment of the Arctic Council **[Basic Documents 1.36]**, creating an intergovernmental forum to promote effective cooperation on a wide range of Arctic issues;[t] and the 1996 Memorandum of Understanding between the Government of the United States and the Russian Federation on Cooperation in Natural and Man-made Technological Emergency Prevention and Response **[Basic Document 1.35]**, establishing that the two countries will cooperate regarding the development of emergency preparedness techniques, information sharing, and communication.

Two broad questions spring immediately to your mind. First, to what extent can the Russians be held responsible and liable for their past actions? Second, how might this impending environmental catastrophe be avoided? Numerous off-shoots of these basic questions emerge. Is the Russian government responsible for hazards to human health and the natural environment created in fulfillment of its arms control agreements? If Russia can be held

---

t. *See* note **s**, *supra*.

internationally accountable for these hazards, on the basis of what legal doctrines, principles, or rules may this be so? May Norway then lawfully threaten or impose retaliatory economic or other sanctions? May the Arctic Council? If so, according to what authority and to what extent? Is Norway bound by international law not to do so? The Arctic Council? In any event, under international law, may Norway or the Arctic Council or both demand that Russia specifically perform remedial measures designed to eliminate or reduce the health and environmental hazards it is posing? If so, what measures and according to what procedures? In addition, or in the alternative, may Norway or the Arctic Council, under international law, demand reparations from Russia for damage done? For prospective damage? If so, what damages may be assessed? Personal damages? Property damages? Punitive damages for arguable violations of international environmental law? Other damages? If any of these, in what amount and according to what valuation criteria? Criteria established by Norwegian law? Russian law? International law?

Questions, questions, questions! Overwhelmed for the moment, and knowing that you probably will have more questions later, you wisely decide to brush up on your knowledge of public international law. And to this end you turn to the Foreign Ministry's law library—which for present purposes is this coursebook and any other materials you may choose to consult in your law school's law library. We, your authors/editors, have taken it upon ourselves to provide you with some research assistance; we provide you with materials and references that may be relevant to your assignment. But like everything else in this coursebook, we do not provide you with the thinking. That is what you have to add to the materials and notes and other writings we have assembled for you.

In particular, we make no claim that the materials we have found for you are always adequate. Decisions about adequacy are for you to make—just as when you are in a library doing research, selecting some articles and books and rejecting others. Indeed, you should treat the materials we have selected much as you would a library, pulling books off the shelves and looking through them to see if there is anything you can use. Of course, our choice of materials is inevitably shaped by our own training and traditions; we are academics, the majority of us from the developed "North," and we carry a variety of baggage that belongs to this heritage. You may well disagree with the positions taken by "the authorities"—the documents, the authors—we present, and you will need to evaluate carefully the weight you choose to give to each. However, we have included ideas, comments, and questions of our own to assist you in this task. Our aim is both to help you acquire the techniques you need to identify and apply relevant international authority and to help you develop the ability to analyze and assess the existing law critically. As you will see, many traditional doctrines, principles, and rules of the international legal order respond to the interests and concerns of the powerful states, many of them former colonial powers. Today, they are not infrequently called into question by smaller nations and nations from the developing world (which now make up more than two-thirds of the membership of the United Nations) on the grounds that they often are inequitable and/or inappropriate. Increasingly, as well, women are challenging the objectivity of the international legal system, arguing that its male-dominated fora and agendas generate principles that privilege men's experiences and consequently do not take women's lives into account either seriously or at all. Other groups, such as minority indigenous peoples like the Saami, also point to the inadequacy of a system built on the artificial construct of the nation-state. So, as you work through this coursebook, always consider the politics of international environmental law. What values inform and what values are inculcated by particular doctrines, principles, and rules? Whose interests are being served? On what silences are the doctrines, principles, and rules built?

One final, related point. You will notice that the terminology of many of the authors whose work we use is sexist in that typically it refers to men as potential actors in the international legal system and beneficiaries of its doctrines, principles, and rules. This is the inevitable result of the long exclusion of women from the realm of international politics and law, former British Prime Minister Margaret Thatcher and present U.S. Secretary of State Madeleine Albright notwithstanding. It is a tangible symbol of one of the silences of international law to which we allude above and underscores the importance of imagining how different the corpus of international law might be if women from various ethnic and class backgrounds had contributed to its formation and participated equally and fully in its implementation.

Thus, with this caveat and the threat of grievous Arctic pollution in mind, you begin your exploration of international environmental law and world order, a field of growing importance in an era of increasing globalization.

Chapter One

THE CONCEPT OF INTERNATIONAL LAW

In the Introduction immediately preceding, you were asked to imagine yourself employed in January 1996 as a junior lawyer of Saami heritage working in the Department of Legal Affairs of the Royal Norwegian Ministry of Foreign Affairs. You also were asked to imagine that your superiors had invited you to assist in the formulation of an international legal strategy, potentially involving a memorial for submission to the International Court of Justice at The Hague,[a] a declaration proposed for adoption by the Arctic Council,[b] and/or a negotiated agreement of some binding sort, designed to prevent the Russian Federation from massively contaminating the circumpolar Arctic region via its derelict nuclear reactors, its disposal of the radioactive waste generated by them, and its land-based pollution practices. As your professional experience has been in domestic rather than international law, however, you find it necessary to do some background study, beginning with the definition of international law, its history, and the structure of the international legal system; and to facilitate this task, you turn to a new treatise on the subject, recently discovered by you in the Foreign Ministry's law library.[c]

A. DEFINITIONAL CONSIDERATIONS

You begin with the most basic lesson of all: clarifying the meaning of "international law" itself. The reason it is so important to address this fundamental matter of definition is because of the relative absence of courts and legislatures and police forces in the international system and therefore of the possibility of no international law at all but of something else that lawyers like to parade as international law. After all, how is it possible to have law in the relative absence of such manifestly *legal* institutions and enterprises as courts and legislatures and police forces? The question is no idle one. To the contrary, it is exceedingly important because definitions, like the words that make them up, are mental constructs—paradigms—that shape not only what

a. *See* note **q** in the Introduction at 9, *supra.*

b. *See* note **r** in the Introduction at 11, *supra.*

c. *I.e.*, this coursebook.

15

we are willing to think about, but also how we go about looking at what we are willing to think about. You know, like Lewis Carroll's Humpty Dumpty, that words use us as much as we use words. Accordingly, you commence your reading.

The task of defining "law" itself, let alone "international law," is not easy. The point is made clearly in Sir Frederick Pollock, A First Book of Jurisprudence for Students of the Common Law (1929) 3–4 (6th ed. 1994):

> We find in all human sciences that those ideas which seem to be most simple are really the most difficult to grasp with certainty and express with accuracy.... It is not surprising, then, that the student approaching the science of law should find the formal definiteness of its ideas to vary inversely with their generality. No tolerably prepared candidate in an English or American law school will hesitate to define an estate in fee simple: on the other hand, the greater have been a lawyer's opportunities of knowledge, and the more time he has given to the study of legal principles, the greater will be his hesitation in face of the apparently simple question: What is Law?

No less difficult is the task of defining "international law"—or, more precisely, of reaching agreement on what we mean by "international law." Indeed, the very reality of international law is sometimes open to challenge, on the grounds that there can be no law governing sovereign States or that it is not "real law" because States obey it only when it is in their interest to do so. As Morton Kaplan and Nicholas Katzenbach put it in The Political Foundations of International Law 5 (1961): "A number of great legal philosophers ... have ... doubted the legal character of international law, and the charges and counter-charges which pervade the international community today seem to provide empirical support for their view. Clearly some definitions of law would exclude international law."

Consider, for example, the views of John Austin, an influential English legal philosopher, considered the father of the "analytical" or "legal positivist" school of jurisprudence, who wrote in the nineteenth century. He argued that "law" is the command of a sovereign enforced by punitive sanction against persons subject to the sovereign's authority. In The Province of Jurisprudence Determined (1832) 133, 201 (1954 ed.), Austin offered this critique of the concept of "international law":

> Laws properly so called are a species of *commands*. But, being a *command*, every law properly so called flows from a *determinate* source....
> * * * [W]henever a *command* is expressed or intimated, one party signifies a wish that another shall do or forbear: and the latter is obnoxious to an evil which the former intends to inflict in case the wish be disregarded.
>
>   * * *
>
> And hence it inevitably follows, that the law obtaining between nations is not positive law: for every positive law is set by a given sovereign to a person or persons in a state of subjection to its author....
> [T]he law obtaining between nations is law (improperly so called) set by general opinion. The duties which it imposes are enforced by moral sanctions: by fear on the part of nations, or by fear on the part of

sovereigns, of provoking general hostility, and incurring its probable evils, in case they shall violate maxims generally received and respected.

In sum, to Austin the term "international law" was little more than a euphemism for international morality. International law is not "real law," not law "properly so called" because there is no apparent sovereign to command or enforce it.

Consider, too, the views of the post-World War II American "realists" (sometimes called "Neo-realists" or "Skeptics"). In World Politics and International Law 3 (1985), law professor and political scientist Francis Boyle usefully summarizes their skepticism as follows:

> From the moment of its creation as an intellectual discipline in the aftermath of the Second World War, international political science has maintained that international law and organizations are essentially irrelevant to a proper understanding of international politics and consequently are irrelevant to the progressive development of international political theory. * * * This denial of the relevance of international law and organizations to "high" international politics ... is attributable to an extreme negative reaction to the so-called legalist-moralist or utopian approach to international affairs, said to have influenced the conduct of international relations by the United States and the other Western democracies during the period between the First and Second World Wars. International political science originated from this "realist" or power-politics-oriented school of international relations. Its best exemplars [in the United States] were the writings of scholars such as Edward Hallett Carr and Hans Morgenthau, and the careers and publications of statesmen like Dean Acheson, George Kennan, and later Henry Kissinger.

> In the realist view of international relations, international law and organizations totally lack any intrinsic significance within the utilitarian calculus of international political decision making. International law, morality, ethics, ideology and even knowledge itself are mere components in the power equation, devoid of non-instrumental significance or prescriptive worth, subject to compulsory service as tools of power when deemed necessary for the vital interests of state. There are no barriers to the acquisitive nature of the nation state beyond its own inherent limitations and those constraints imposed upon it by the international political milieu. Consequently, the analysis of international relations must concentrate exclusively upon the dynamics of power politics and the machinations of that metaphysical entity known as the "balance of power." Considerations of international law do not and should not intrude into such areas. Or, if they do intrude, it should be only for the instrumental purpose of serving as a source for the manufacture of ad hoc or ex post facto justifications for decisions taken on the basis of antinomian factors such as Machiavellian power politics and nation self-interest.

Thus, once again, the term "international law" is perceived as little more than a euphemism for international morality, if that.

This "realist" response to the "legalist-moralist" or "utopian" approach to international affairs, it must be acknowledged, has not been without warrant. In a struggle that spanned three centuries, from the birth of the State system at the Peace of Westphalia in 1648 to the aftermath of World

War II, classical legal theorists, particularly those espousing the polar doctrines of naturalism and positivism, battled one another to an intellectual impasse, each purporting but failing to answer convincingly the fundamental theoretical questions of international law—its origin, its status as law, its substantive content, its reformist and transformist possibilities—and thus each failing as well to respond adequately to controversies in the "real world." While the natural law theorists (who maintained that international law binds sovereign States because law emanates from nature) ultimately were forced into retreat by the legal positivists (who maintained, as seen, that law emanates from sovereign will or consent) legal positivism also proved inadequate to the "real world" challenge; whereas natural law theory was exposed as religiously arbitrary and unverifiable, legal positivism came up short for being unable to explain either the true normative beliefs of the day or actual behavior. The result: a discipline without convincing force and effect. As observed by Nigel Purvis in *Critical Legal Studies in Public International Law*, 32 H.I.L.J. 81, 82–83 (1991): "Theoretical discourse about international law repeatedly exposed the weaknesses of the two opposing positions without finding a way either to decide between them or to overcome the division. . . . The disharmony of the discipline made all theoretic enterprises seem impossible."

Nevertheless, there developed over the years a fairly standard usage of "international law" that has had great impact upon the practice as well as the theory of international law. The Permanent Court of International Justice put it this way in an oft-quoted statement in the *Case of the S.S. "Lotus,"* 1927 P.C.I.J., ser. A, No. 10, at 18:

> International law governs relations between independent States. The rules of law binding upon States therefore emanate from their own free will as expressed in conventions or by usages generally accepted as expressing principles of law and established in order to regulate the relations between these coexisting independent communities or with a view to the achievement of common aims.

A similar formulation is found in James L. Brierly, The Law of Nations (H. Waldock 6th ed. 1963), long considered a classic in the field. "The Law of Nations, or International Law," Brierly writes, at 1, "may be defined as the body of rules and principles of action which are binding upon civilized states in their relations with one another."

These traditional rule-oriented and statist definitions have been adopted more or less formally by most—perhaps even all—of the states of our present-day world, including such distinctive powers as the United States, the independent members of The Commonwealth, the states of the European Union, the republics of the former Soviet Union, and the People's Republic of China.[d] With the passage of time, to be sure, new developments have added new elements. Thus, Section 101 of the 1986 revision of the American Law

d. For relatively recent accounts of Chinese attitudes toward international law, see, e.g., Hungdah. Chiu, *Chinese Attitudes Towards International Law in the Post–Mao Era, 1978–1987*, 21 Int'l Law. 1127 (1987); Samuel S. Kim, *The Development of International Law in Post–Mao China: Change and Continuity*, 1 J. Chinese L. 117 (1987); T. Wang, *International Law in China:Historical and Contemporary Perspectives*, 221 Recueil des Cours (Hague Acad. Int'l L.) 195 (1990).

Institute's Restatement of Foreign Relations Law takes a small step toward recognizing the relevance of non-state actors to the international legal system:

> "International law," as used in this Restatement, consists of rules and principles of general application dealing with the conduct of states and of international organizations and with their relations inter se, as well as with some of their relations with persons, whether natural or juridical.

But by and large the factual and theoretical orientation has remained the same. Statist and rule-oriented definitions of international law continue to dominate.

Despite this formal adherence to the traditional view, however, international law scholarship and decision-making has come to conceive of international law increasingly from a contextually wider, more behaviorally responsive perspective. As the following four extracts make clear, this has been due, at least in part, to a growing sophistication about law and legal process generally.

Louis Henkin, International Law: Politics, Values and Functions, 216 Recueil Des Cours (Hague Acad. Int'l L.) 22 (1989).

First, law is politics. Students of law as well as students of politics are taught to distinguish law from politics. Law is normative, and failure to abide by legal obligations invites legal remedies and brings other legal responses; politics suggests freedom of choice, diplomacy, bargaining, accommodation. In fact, however, the distinction between law and politics is only a part-truth. In a larger, deeper sense, law is politics. Law is made by political actors (not by lawyers), through political procedures, for political ends. The law that emerges is the resultant of political forces; the influences of law on State behaviour are also determined by political forces.

Second ..., law is the normative expression of a political system. To appreciate the character of international law and its relation to the international political system, it is helpful to invoke (though with caution) domestic law as an analogue. Domestic (national) law ... is an expression of a domestic political system in a domestic (national) society. A domestic society consists of people, human beings, [and] artificial juristic persons (*e.g.*, companies, associations). Domestic law is a construct of norms, standards, principles, institutions and procedures that serve the purposes of society. Law serves, notably, to establish and maintain order and enhance the reliability of expectations; to protect persons, their property and other interests; to promote the welfare of individuals (or of some of them), and to further other societal values—justice, the good life, the good society.

Similarly ..., international law is the product of its particular "society", its political system. International law, too, is a construct of norms, standards, principles, institutions and procedures. The purposes of international law, like those of domestic law, are to establish and maintain order and hence reliable expectations, to protect "persons", their property and other interests, to further other values. But the constituency of the international society is different. The "persons" constituting international society are not [primarily] individual human beings but political entities, "States", and the society is [primarily] an inter-State system, a system [primarily] of States.

Myres S. McDougal, *The Impact of International Law Upon National Law: A Policy–Oriented Perspective*, 4 S. DAK. L. REV. 25, 35–36 (1959), *reprinted in* MYRES S. McDOUGAL & ASSOCIATES, STUDIES IN WORLD PUBLIC ORDER 157, 169–70 (1960).

[T]he most appropriate [*i.e.*, usable] conception [of international law] requires emphasis not upon rules alone or operations alone, but upon rules and operations, and, further, not upon authority alone or control alone, but upon authority and control. Rules taken alone cannot be made to serve adequately to describe decisions or to account for decisions or to predict decisions or to appraise the consequences of decision, much less to perform all these tasks at once. Focus upon operations only—when among the most important variables affecting decisions are the perspectives of participants, including their demands for values, their identifications, and their expectations about past and future events—is equally sterile. In comparable token, authority alone, when effective power is not at its disposal and expectations of decision in accordance with community prescription lack realism, is not law but sheer illusion. Effective control, on the other hand, when it asserts decision, in the sense of imposition or threat of severe deprivation, without regard for community expectations about how and what decision should be taken, is not law but naked power or unilateral coercion. The recommendation we make, from perspectives of human dignity and for efficiency of inquiry into varying patterns of authority and control, is, accordingly, that international law be regarded not as mere rules but as a whole process of authoritative decision in the world arena, a process in which authority and control are appropriately conjoined and which includes, along with an inherited body of flexible prescriptions explicitly related to community policies, both a structure of established decision-makers and a whole arsenal of methods and techniques by which policy is projected and implemented.

ROSALYN HIGGINS, PROBLEMS AND PROCESS: INTERNATIONAL LAW AND HOW WE USE IT 2–4 (1994).

There is a widely held perception of international law as "rules"—rules that are meant to be impartially applied but are frequently ignored. It is further suggested that these rules are ignored because of the absence of effective centralized sanctions—and, in turn, that all of this evidences that international law is not "real law" at all.

The view that international law is a body of rules that fails to restrain states falls short on several counts. In the first place, it assumes that law is indeed "rules". But the specialized social processes to which the word "law" refers include many things beside rules. Rules play a part in law, but not the only part. I remain committed to the analysis of international law as process rather than rules and to the view I expressed many years ago, when I said:

> When ... decisions are made by authorized persons or organs, in appropriate forums, within the framework of certain established practices and norms, then what occurs is *legal* decision-making. In other words, inter-

national law is [like all law] a continuing process of authoritative decisions. This view rejects the notion of law merely as the impartial application of rules. International law is the entire decision-making process, and not just the reference to the trend of past decisions which are termed "rules." There inevitably flows from this definition a concern, especially where the trend of past decision is not overwhelmingly clear, with policy alternatives for the future.[1]

Thus "rules" are just accumulated past decisions. And, if international law was just "rules", then international law would indeed be unable to contribute to, and cope with, a changing political world. To rely merely on accumulated past decisions (rules) when the context in which they are articulated has changed—and indeed when their content is often unclear—is to ensure that international law will not be able to contribute to today's problems and, further, that it will be disobeyed for that reason.

The rejection of the perception of law as "rules" entails a necessary consequence. It means that those who have to make decisions on the basis of international law—judges, but also legal advisers and others—are not really simply "finding the rule" and then applying it. That is because the determination of what *is* the relevant rule is part of the decision-makers' function; and because the accumulated trend of past decisions should never be applied oblivious of context. Although this reality has been regarded as anathema by many traditionalists, it was well understood by Sir Hersch Lauterpacht. He rejected the notion that the judicial function meant finding the appropriate "rule" in an impartial manner. The judge, he argued, does not "find rules" but he "makes choices"—and choices "not between claims which are fully justified and claims which have no foundation at all but between claims which have varying degrees of legal merit."[2]

The reasons why some insist that international law is "rules," and that all international lawyers have to do is to identify them and apply them, are not hard to find. They are an unconscious reflection of two beliefs, deeply held by many international lawyers. The first reason is that, if international law is regarded as more than rules, and the role of the authorized decision-maker as other than the automatic applier of such rules, international law becomes confused with other phenomena, such as power or social or humanitarian factors. The second reason is that it is felt by many that only by insisting on international law as rules to impartially applied will it be possible to avoid the manifestation of international legal argument for political ends.

I . . . deal with each of these reasons in turn, and [state] why I do not agree with them. To seek to contrast law with power (in which task the perception of law as "rules" plays an essential [role]) is fundamentally flawed. It assumes that law is concerned only with the concept of authority and not with power, or control. International law *is* indeed concerned with authority—and "authority" not just in the sense of binding decisions, but in the broader sense of jurisdictional competence, and more. Myres McDougal has explained:

---

1. Rosalyn Higgins, *Policy Considerations and the International Judicial Process*, 17 INT'L & COMP.L.Q. 58, 58–59 (1968).

2. HERSCH LAUTERPACHT, THE DEVELOPMENT OF INTERNATIONAL LAW BY THE INTERNATIONAL COURT 399 (1958).

By authority is meant expectations of appropriateness in regard to the phases of effective decision processes. These expectations specifically relate to personnel appropriately endowed with decision-making power; the objectives they should pursue; the physical, temporal and institutional features of the situations in which lawful decisions are made; the values which may be used to sustain decision, and so forth . . .[3]

So far, so good. But it is *not* the case, as is frequently supposed, that international law is concerned with authority *alone*, and that "power" stands somehow counterpoised to authority, and [has] nothing to do with law, and is indeed inimical to it. This view—which banishes power to the outer darkness (that is to say, to the province of international relations)—assumes that authority can exit in the total absence of supporting control, or power. But this is a fantasy. The authority which characterizes law exists not in a vacuum, but exactly where it intersects with power. Law, far from being authority battling against power, is the interlocking of authority with power. Authority cannot exist in the total absence of control. Of course, there will be particular circumstances when power overrides authority. On such occasions we will not have decision-making that we can term lawful. But that is *not* to say that law is about authority *only*, and not about power too; or that power is definitionally to be regarded as hostile to law. It is an integral element of it.

What then of the other argument—that a perception of international law as other than neutral rules inevitably leads to bias and partiality? A classical statement of this view was made by Judges Fitzmaurice and Spender in the *South West Africa Cases* in 1962, when they wrote:

We are not unmindful of, nor are we insensible to, the various considerations of a non-judicial character, social, humanitarian, or other . . . but these are matters for the political rather than for the legal arena. They cannot be allowed to deflect us from our duty of reaching a conclusion strictly on the basis of what we believe to be the correct legal view.[4]

This formulation reflects certain assumptions: that "the correct legal view" is to be discerned by applying "rules"—the accumulated trend of past decisions, regardless of context or circumstance—and that "the correct legal view" has nothing to do with applying past decisions to current contexts by reference to objectives (values) that the law is designed to promote.

The classical view, so brilliantly articulated by Fitzmaurice but shared by very many others, is that international law can best perform its service to the community exactly by distancing itself from social policy. As the International Court of Justice put it in 1966: "Law exists, it is said, to serve a social need; but precisely for that reason it can do so only through and within the limits of its own discipline. Otherwise, it is not a legal service that would be rendered."[5] Of course, the International Court of Justice thought it self-evident as to where the law *does* draw "the limits of its own discipline". But what is self-evident to one is merely question-begging to another.

3. Myres McDougal, et al., *The World Constitutive Process of Authoritative Decision,* 19 J. LEGAL EDUC. 253, 256 (1966).

4. South West Africa Cases, 1962 I.C.J. 319, 466 (joint diss. op.).

5. South West Africa Cases, 1966 I.C.J. 6, at para. 49.

Reference to "the correct legal view" or "rules" can never avoid the element of choice (though it can seek to disguise it), nor can it provide guidance to the preferable decision. In making this choice one must inevitably have consideration for the humanitarian, moral, and social purposes of the law. As I have written elsewhere:

> Policy considerations, although they differ from "rules", are an integral part of that decision making process which we call international law; the assessment of so-called extralegal considerations is *part of the legal process*, just as is reference to the accumulation of past decisions and current norms. A refusal to acknowledge political and social factors cannot keep law "neutral", for even such a refusal is not without political and social consequence. There is no avoiding the essential relationship between law and politics.[6]

Because I believe there is no avoiding the essential relationship between law and policy, I also believe that it is desirable that the policy factors are dealt with systematically and openly. Dealing with them systematically means that all factors are properly considered and weighed, instead of the decision-maker unconsciously narrowing or selecting what he will take into account in order to reach a decision that he has instinctively predetermined is desirable. Dealing with policy factors openly means that the decision-maker himself is subjected to the discipline of facing them squarely (instead of achieving unconsciously desired policy objectives by making a particular choice, which is then given the label of "the correct legal rule"). It also means that the choices made are open to public scrutiny and discussion.

Burns H. Weston, *The Role of Law in Promoting Peace and Violence: A Matter of Definition, Social Values, and Individual Responsibility, in* Toward World Order and Human Dignity 114, 116–17 (W. Reisman & B. Weston eds., 1976).

The word "law" has . . . several diverse applications. Yet despite this fact we use the term with relative everyday ease. With little conspicuous difficulty, we use it to refer to matters essentially outside human intervention, as when we speak of "the law of gravity" or "the law of supply and demand"; and we use it to refer to matters which are, conversely, the product of human intervention, as when we speak of "the law of contracts," "criminal law," "the law of torts," "property law," and all the other breadwinners of the legal profession. Similarly, within the context of human intervention, we use it to refer to those social patterns which evolve essentially without benefit of centralized decisionmaking mechanisms, as when we speak of "customary law" or "international law"; and we use it to refer to those social patterns which evolve from highly articulated command and enforcement structures, as when we speak of all those executive orders, legislative enactments, and judicial decisions we call "the law of Iowa" or "the law of the United States of America." The point is, of course, that none of these uses is incorrect. Fundamentally, each is proper. However applied, the concept "law" repre-

6. Rosalyn Higgins, *Integrations of Authority and Control: Trends in the Literature of International Law and Relations, in* Towards World Order and Human Dignity 79, 85 (B. Weston & W. Reisman eds., 1976).

sents, in the end, a set of events whose common property is sanctioned regularity.

To most people, however, including many lawyers, this sanctioned regularity called "law," insofar as it pertains to social arrangements, is conceived largely as a body of rules affirmatively prescribed and enforced by the sovereign State, to the general exclusion of those regularities which, somehow mysteriously divorced from "the law," we are wont to call "customary morality." Except for the international lawyers and "jurisprudes" who take the challenge of defining "law" seriously, little attention is paid to those normative principles and practices which result from self-determinative interactions in the private sphere. Consider, thus, why Amy Vanderbilt's New Complete Book of Etiquette, manifestly descriptive of ordered social behavior in the absence of positive sovereign command, is not ordinarily considered relevant to law school study. Tenaciously wedded to the Legal Positivist tradition of nineteenth century English jurist John Austin and his followers, we cling to the belief that law is entirely or almost entirely a function of government—that it bespeaks only what governments say and do—and that it has little or no relation to what evolves in the absence of governmental intervention. So narrow a conception, I submit, is empirically unwarranted and socially detrimental, at least in the long run. It feeds the insidious notion that law is, or that it must be, as if some natural law of physics, only the expression of the will of the strongest.

But how, then, do we define "law" so as to avoid transforming the mere *characteristics* of the popular model into the *prerequisites* of a comprehensive theory about law; so as to avoid the allegation that law is not, or that it cannot be, the expression of the will of all or most of the people? The answer: to think upon law in functional rather than institutional terms, and from this perspective to acknowledge its invention, its application, and its appraisal both within and beyond the formal corridors of power. Law does not live by executives and legislators and judges alone. It lives also by individual human beings such as ourselves, pushing and pulling through reciprocal claim and mutual tolerance in our daily competition for power, wealth, respect, and other cherished values. To turn a phrase, law is legitimized politics—a Hydra-headed process of social decision, involving persons at all levels and from all walks of public and private life who, with authority derived both explicitly and implicitly from community consensus or expectation, and supported by formal and informal sanction, effect those codes or standards of everyday conduct by which we plan and go about our lives.

Discussion Notes/Questions

1. The traditional definition of international law emerged at a time when the principal actors on the world stage consisted of a small number of relatively homogeneous nation-states, mostly in Europe. Today, the international system has expanded greatly to include not only a large number of States of widely different ideological persuasion and levels of economic development from all regions of the globe, but also worldwide and regional international organizations, multinational business enterprises, transnational interest groups, and other non-state actors. When the U.N. was founded in 1945, it had fifty-one members, mainly European nations. Fifty years later, its membership stands at 185 states, of whom the majority are from the developing world. What implications does this

have for the international legal system? To what extent is a definition of international law created for a simpler state-centric era still valid today? Should the new developments provoke a different definitional response? Does the following excerpt from T. Kuhn, The Structure of Scientific Revolutions 111–13 (2d ed. 1970) suggest some answers?

Examining the record of past research from the vantage of contemporary historiography, the historian of science may be tempted to exclaim that when paradigms change, the world itself changes with them. Led by a new paradigm, scientists adopt new instruments and look in new places. Even more important, during revolutions scientists see new and different things when looking with familiar instruments in places they have looked before. It is as if the professional community had been suddenly transported to another planet where familiar objects are seen in a different light and are joined by unfamiliar ones as well. Of course, nothing of quite that sort does occur: there is no geographical transplantation; outside the laboratory everyday affairs usually continue as before. Nevertheless, paradigm changes do cause scientists to see the world of their research-engagement differently. * * * [Indeed,] [s]urveying the rich experimental literature from which ... examples [of perceptual transformation] are drawn makes one suspect that something like a paradigm is prerequisite to perception itself. What a man sees depends both upon what he looks at and also upon what his visual-conceptual experience has taught him to see. In the absence of such training there can only be, in William James's phrase, "a bloomin' buzzin' confusion."

2.   Henkin, *supra*, asserts that international law is an expression of international society. Given the well-known ethnic, ideological, socioeconomic, and political cleavages that have characterized world affairs from East to West and North to South, to what extent is it possible to speak of a present-day international society or world community? Philip Allott writes, in Eunomia: New Order for a New World 418 (1990):

International law has been the primitive law of an unsocial international society. Itself a by-product of that unsocialization, it has contributed to holding back the development of international society as society. Failing to recognize itself as a society, international society has not known that it has a constitution. Not knowing its own constitution, it has ignored the generic principles of a constitution.

What do "society" and/or "community" mean? And to what extent can international law lay claim to universality? Is such a claim essential for international law to be called "law"? For domestic law to be called law?

3.   In the extracts, *supra*, by Myres McDougal and Rosalyn Higgins (now a judge on the International Court of Justice), law generally and international law in particular are defined as a "process of authoritative and controlling decision." What is the meaning of "process"? Of "authoritative decision"? Of "controlling decision"? What do they mean by "authority"? By "control"? In *Myres S. McDougal and Twentieth–Century Jurisprudence: A Comparative Essay*, in Toward World Order and Human Dignity: Essays in Honor of Myres S. McDougal 3, 14 (W. Reisman & B. Weston eds., 1976), Australian legal scholar William L. Morrison summarizes McDougal's conception of law as follows:

Law is conceived as a social process of authoritative and controlling decision.... [S]ocial process refers to interactions among participants in a context which maintain relatively stable, but not necessarily formally organized, patterns of value shaping and sharing. *Decisions* are taken to be commitments attended by threats of severe deprivation or extremely high indulgence. They are said to be *authoritative* when they are, in a stipulated degree, in accordance with community expectation about who is to make them, about the criteria in accordance with which they should be made, and about the situations in which, and the procedures by which, they are to be made. They are said to be *controlling* [emphasis added] when the outcome sought is in fact realized to a significant degree.

To what "stipulated degree" of accord with "community expectation" about decision-making must decisions be to qualify as *legal* decisions? Do you agree that, by implication, law does not exist when decisions are attended by threats of only mild rather than "severe" deprivation or merely high rather than "extremely high" indulgence? Or when the outcome sought is realized to only a modest rather than a "significant" degree? Why? Why not? Elsewhere McDougal writes (together with Harold D. Lasswell and W. Michael Reisman):

> By "law" or "authoritative decision" we refer to a process of decision characterized both by expectations of authority and by effective control. It may be observed, however, that no decision process, whatever the size of the community, is wholly effective. The aggregate degree of effectiveness of an authority system must be sufficient to sustain expectations of future decision largely in conformity with demanded authority. The precise degree of effectiveness or "control" required for "law"—whether in national or international arenas—cannot, thus, be stated absolutely; it is a function of context and will vary. An authoritative and controlling decision can be contrasted with decisions involving only effective power ("naked power") or mere barren authority ("pretended power"). We see "naked power" in action when a strong empire coerces a weak neighboring polity, and nothing happens. We identify "pretended power" when a superseded monarch vainly claims acceptance as the legitimate head of the body-politic from which [he/she] has been expelled.

M. McDougal, H. Lasswell, & W. M. Reisman, *The World Constitutive Process of Authoritative Decision, in* International Law Essays 192, 193 (M. McDougal & W. M. Reisman eds., 1981).

4. Burns Weston, *supra*, suggests that rules and patterns of social etiquette may be designated as "law." Is this appropriate? Consider the following quotation from Amy Vanderbilt's New Complete Book of Etiquette: The Guide to Gracious Living ix-xii (1971):

> The word "etiquette" . . . covers much more than "manners," the way in which we *do* things. [This guide] is considerably more than a treatise on a code of social behavior. . . . For we must all learn the socially acceptable ways of living with others in no matter what society we move. Even in primitive societies there are such rules, some of them as complex and inexplicable as many of our own. * * * I believe that knowledge of the rules of living in our society makes us more comfortable even though our particular circumstances may permit us to elide them somewhat. Some of the rudest and most objectionable people I have ever known have been technically the most "correct." Some of the warmest, most lovable, have had little more than an innate feeling of what is right toward others. But, at the same time, they have had the intelligence to inform themselves . . . on the rules of social intercourse as related to their own experiences. Only a great fool or a great genius is likely to flout all social grace with impunity, and neither one, doing so, makes the most comfortable companion.

If this quotation does not lead to the conclusion that rules and patterns of social etiquette are "law," is international law properly called "law"? If so (or if not), what do we mean by "law"? Does it require the participation, direct or indirect, of the state, as is implied by the standard curricula of most law faculties? If so, does that mean that it is not possible to have private legal systems? Does "law" include custom? If so, when is custom not law? In this connection, see *infra* ch. 2.

5. What are the principal indicia of "law" in national communities? In the world community? Do they differ? If not, how not? If so, is it valid to define "law" to include both domestic or municipal (i.e., national) and international law?

6. As for international legal system, does the absence of a central legislature matter? The absence of an international court with general, compulsory jurisdiction? The absence of an executive agency with enforcement powers? If so, how? If not, why not?

7. In *International Law and the Controversy Concerning the Word "Law"*, 22 B.Y.B.I.L 146, 159–62 (1945), Glanville Williams contended that the jurisprudential debate over the reality of international law is merely a debate about words. Do you agree?

B. INTERNATIONAL LAW IN HISTORICAL AND CONTEMPORARY PERSPECTIVE

As you prepare to assist your superiors in the Norwegian Foreign Ministry in the formulation of a legal strategy to prevent a radioactive disaster in the circumpolar Arctic region, you now feel more refreshed about what international law purports to be. But you are hazy about its origins, about the factors that have shaped its growth and development, and about the extent to which, over the years, it has been successful or unsuccessful in preventing and mitigating conflicts and disputes of one sort or another. So, you sensibly elect to read further.

1. HISTORICAL PERSPECTIVES

According to Arthur Nussbaum, A Concise History of the Law of Nations (1953 rev. ed.), "the law of nations"—or international law—can be traced to approximately 3100 B.C. when a treaty was concluded between two Mesopotamian city-states. The next three selections make no attempt to report this entire history. They do, however, take stock of the principal events and perspectives that, both before and since the beginnings of the State system (around the Peace of Westphalia in 1648), have shaped the evolution and scope of contemporary international law theory and practice.[e]

e. According to George Finch, THE SOURCES OF MODERN INTERNATIONAL LAW 313 (1937), the following factors "appear to have exerted an influence on growth and development of the principles of modern international law": (1) the spread of Roman law through Western Europe; (2) the revival of trade and commerce during the Middle Ages; (3) the formation of leagues of trading towns for the protection of their trade and citizens engaged in trade; (4) the development of maritime law made necessary by the spread of international trade on the sea; (5) the growing custom on the part of states to send and receive permanent legations; (6) the establishment of permanent standing armies; (7) the Renaissance and the Reformation; (8) plans for maintaining international peace; (9) the discovery of America; and (10) the American Revolution.

MARK W. JANIS, AN INTRODUCTION TO INTERNATIONAL LAW 1 (1988).

The roots of international law go deep into history. In early religious and secular writings, there are many evidences of what we now know as international law; there are, for example, the detailed peace treaties and alliances concluded between the Jews and the Romans, Syrians, and Spartans. The Romans knew of a *jus gentium*, a law of nations, which Gaius, in the second century, saw as a law "common to all men," a universal law that could be applied by Roman courts to foreigners when the specific law of their own nation was unknown and when Roman law was inapposite. Later, in the seventeenth century, the Dutch jurist [Hugo] Grotius [1583–1645] argued that the law of nations also established legal rules that bound the sovereign states of Europe, then just emerging from medieval society, in their relations with one another. Grotius' classic of 1625, *The Law of War and Peace*, is widely acknowledged, more than any other work, as founding the modern discipline of the law of nations, a subject that, in 1789, the English philosopher Jeremy Bentham renamed "international law."[f] Nowadays, the terms the law of nations and international law are used interchangeably.[g]

STARKE'S INTERNATIONAL LAW 11–14 (I. Shearer 11th ed., 1994).

The history of the law of nations during the two centuries after Grotius was marked by the final evolution of the modern nation-state system in Europe, a process greatly influenced by the Treaty of Westphalia of 1648 marking the end of the Thirty Years' War, and ... was further enriched by the writings and studies of a number of great jurists. Side by side there proceeded naturally a kind of action and reaction between the customary rules and the works of these great writers; not only did their systematic treatment of the subject produce the best evidence of the rules, but they suggested new rules or principles where none had yet emerged from the practice of states. . . .

The most outstanding writers of the seventeenth and eighteenth centuries following [Grotius] were Zouche (1590–1660), Professor of Civil Law at Oxford ... and an Admiralty Judge, Pufendorf (1632–1694), Professor at the University of Heidelberg, Bynkershoek (1673–1743), a Dutch jurist, Wolff (1679–1754), a German jurist and philosopher, who constructed an original, systematic methodology of international law and the law of nature, Moser (1701–1795), a German Professor of Law, von Martens (1756–1821), also a German Professor of Law, and Vattel (1714–1767), a Swiss jurist and diplomat, who was greatly influenced by the writings of Wolff, and who perhaps of

f. For a famous discussion of Grotius' contribution to international law, see Hersch Lauterpacht, *The Grotian Tradition in International Law*, 23 BRIT. Y.B.I.L. 1 (1946).

g. The author goes on to write, at 2:

At least since the end of the Thirty Years War in 1648, world politics has principally involved the relations of more or less independent sovereign states. An important part of international law has consequently had to do with the establishment of a set of mutual-

ly agreed-upon rules respecting the nature of these states and their fundamental rights and obligations inter se. If there is a single international legal principle underlying the modern state system it probably is the one neatly framed by Montesquieu in 1748 and offered to Napoleon in 1806 by Talleyrand "that nations ought to do to one another in peace, the most good, and in war, the least evil possible."

these seven men proved to have the greatest influence, and found the widest acceptance, wider even than that extended to Grotius. In the eighteenth century, there was a growing tendency among jurists to seek the rules of international law mainly in custom and treaties, and to relegate to a minor position the "law of nature", or reason, as a source of principles. This tendency was extremely marked, for instance, in the case of Bynkershoek's writings and found expression particularly also in the works of Moser, and von Martens. There were, however, jurists who at the same time clung to the traditions of the law of nature, either almost wholly, or coupled with a lesser degree of emphasis upon custom and treaties as components of international law. As contrasted with these adherents to the law of nature, writers such as Bynkershoek who attached primary or major weight to customary and treaty rules were known as "positivists".

In the nineteenth century international law further expanded. This was due to a number of factors which fall more properly within the scope of historical studies, for instance, the further rise of powerful new States both within and outside Europe, the expansion of European civilization overseas, the modernization of world transport, the greater destructiveness of modern warfare, and the influence of new inventions. All these made it urgent for the international society of States to acquire a system of rules which would regulate in an ordered manner the conduct of international affairs. There was a remarkable development during the century in the law of war and neutrality, and the great increase in adjudications by international arbitral tribunals following the *Alabama Claims Award* of 1872 provided an important new source of rules and principles. Besides, States commenced to acquire the habit of negotiating general treaties in order to regulate affairs of mutual concern. Nor was the nineteenth century without its great writers on international law. The works of jurists belonging to a number of different nations contributed significantly to the scientific treatment of the subject; among them were Kent (American), Wheaton (American), De Martens (Russian), Kluber (German), Phillimore (British), Calvo (Argentinean), Fiore (Italian), Pradier–Fodere (French), Bluntschli (German), and Hall (British). The general tendency of these writers was to concentrate on existing practice, and to discard the concept of the "law of nature", although not abandoning recourse to reason and justice where, in the absence of custom or treaty rules, they were called upon to speculate as to what should be the law.

Other important developments have taken place in the twentieth century. The Permanent Court of Arbitration was established by the Hague Conferences of 1899 and 1907. The Permanent Court of International Justice was set up in 1921 as an authoritative international judicial tribunal, and was succeeded in 1946 by the present International Court of Justice. Then there has been the creation of permanent international organizations whose functions are in effect those of world government in the interests of peace and human welfare, such as the League of Nations and its present successor, the United Nations, the International Labour Organization, the International Civil Aviation Organization, and others. . . . And perhaps most remarkable of all has been the widening scope of international law to cover not only every kind of economic or social interest affecting States, but also the fundamental rights and freedoms of individual human beings.

It is characteristic of the latter-day evolution of international law that the influence of writers has tended to decline, and that modern international lawyers have come to pay far more regard to practice and to decisions of tribunals.... "[N]atural law" writers have ceased to command the same degree of influence as formerly, perhaps because of the emergence of a number of States outside Europe which did not inherit doctrines of Christian civilization such as that of "natural law", or which possessed traditional cultures impelling them towards differing perceptions with respect to law and legal procedure. These new states (in particular the Afro–Asian group) have challenged certain of the basic principles of international law, stemming from its early European evolution in the seventeenth and eighteenth centuries, albeit they have to some extent recognized natural law in regard to certain concepts, e.g., self-determination. Moreover, many long-standing rules and concepts of international law have been subjected to severe strains and stresses under the impact of modern developments in technology, of modern economic exigencies, and—not least—the more enlightened sociological views and attitudes which prevail today.

Above all, there is the rapidly changing world situation to which the traditional system of international law must adapt itself. The era of East–West rivalry between blocs led by the two superpowers has given way to a more natural—in a sense—order of things in which states are asserting their individual self-interest. This development has its ugly side when it is impelled by ethnic or religious intolerance or by authoritarian ideologies. The notion of the Third World—a term coined at the Bandung Conference [of] 1955 to indicate states not aligned with either the Western or the Communist blocs— has given way to a category of "developing states", within which exists a subcategory of desperately poor "least developed states". Trade has become the major concern of the developed states as they vie for markets and self advancement, not only in traditional goods and commodities but also in technology, in which intellectual and industrial property rights play an important role. Of particular concern to developing states is the increasing degree to which trade, development assistance, respect for human rights, and the protection of the natural environment have become linked, not always to their immediate advantage. New hope is emerging for the effective end of the threat of nuclear arms. Another positive sign is the more co-operative spirit demonstrated in the United Nations Security Council since the end of the Cold War which may enable the Charter provisions for collective world security to be realized more effectively. But structural and political problems remain to be solved within the United Nations system. Apart from this, international law is now called upon to find new rules or guidelines to govern the fields of nuclear and thermonuclear energy (indeed of all forms of energy, having regard to events since 1973, and the depletion of oil reserves), and scientific research generally, to provide special régimes for various areas of international trade (e.g., the international sale and international sea-carriage of goods), to regulate state activities in the upper atmosphere and in the cosmos, to protect and control the natural environment, to control the growth of world population ... , to deal with the trans-border flow of computer data ... , and to establish a new legal regime for the exploration and exploitation of the resources of the seabed beyond the limits of national sovereignty.

RICHARD A. FALK, REVITALIZING INTERNATIONAL LAW 91–93 (1989).

Efforts in this century to deal with problems of international society have concentrated on four sorts of areas that exhibit both the capacities and the severe limits of international law and international institutions. The area of greatest success has been what I would call the *management of complexity*. There has been a surprisingly resilient capacity on the part of sovereign states ... to contrive mutually beneficial ways of dealing with the ... implications of interdependence.

The second area of effort, but one where until recently there has been less success despite strong efforts, has been the *containment of conflict within tolerable limits*. A major aspect of that containment has been the effort to build procedures and a consensus prohibiting aggressive uses of force. To abandon this search for agreed limits on conflict ... [would represent] a serious deterioration in the quality of international order.

The third area of considerable significance has been of relatively recent origin and is what I would call broadly the *promotion of decency in the world*; this has taken two principal forms. Perhaps the most important form is the notion that poverty and mass misery are matters not only of domestic concern, but also ... matters that affect the quality of international life as a whole including the possibilities of the space age, a psychological reality to our identity as a single species. Emerging alongside and underneath national and civilizational interests is a human interest that is not just sentimental; it is real. We are risking at this time, to the extent that we neglect this human interest, moral as well as physical extinction....

* * *

Those problems involving the promotion of decency in relation to equity and development also have as their other side the whole question of human rights and the degree to which we tolerate torture, mass killing, extreme repression, and, to some extent, not only tolerate it but reinforce it by the kinds of foreign policies that are pursued. Again, to the extent we do that, we deny our own dignity and esteem and are caught up in a process that is exceedingly destructive in its consequences....

The fourth general task and challenge has to do with the *avoidance of catastrophe*. It is here we encounter a colossal failure on the part of international law and the organized international community. The degree to which nuclear weapons have been accepted without being subjected to any serious scrutiny ... suggests an astounding degree of complacency.... These weapons of mass destruction overwhelm the traditional law of war and yet how many law journal articles or serious treatment of these issues can one find?[h]

h. For notable exceptions, see Richard A. Falk et al., *Nuclear Weapons and International Law*, 20 INDIAN J. INT'L L. 541 (1980); Burns H. Weston, *Nuclear Weapons Versus International Law: A Contextual Reassessment*, 28 MCGILL L. J. 542 (1983); Peter Weiss et al., *Draft Memorial in Support of the Application by the World Health Organization for an Advisory Opinion by the International Court of Justice on the Legality of the Use of Nuclear Weapons under International Law, Including the WHO Constitution*, 4 TRANSNAT'L L. & CONTEMP. PROBS. 709 (1994); and Symposium, *Nuclear Weapons, The World Court, and Global Security*, 7 TRANSNAT'L L. & CONTEMP. PROBS. No. 2 (1997). *See also, e.g.*, E. MAORIS, PROHIBITION OF NUCLEAR WEAPONS:

The fundamental question, of course, is one of political will to achieve restraint. Such restraint is absent in the centers of power, thereby accenting the impotence of moral and legal reasoning. But this distance between the normative and the practical is something we need to acknowledge and interpret in an honest way; it is far better to take account of this distance than to pretend it does not exist.

2. CONTEMPORARY PERSPECTIVES

The historical evolution of international law and relations has stimulated considerable critical thinking in recent years. The next five extracts illustrate the most notable of the intellectual currents presently influencing international law's continuing development. The first is a voice from the "Third World," challenging many of international law's basic principles because of their early European derivation. The second elaborates on the themes of the first from the perspective of race and racism in global society. The third decries the pervasive patriarchy that dominates the organizational and normative structures of international law. The fourth reports on an intellectual enterprise that perceives international law as mainly an incoherent and self-validating ideological construct said to be incapable of responding to the fundamental questions of international life. And the fifth voices a cautiously optimistic world order view that international law is already in transition to a law of humanity through the agency of civil society.

MOHAMMED BEDJAOUI, TOWARDS A NEW INTERNATIONAL
ECONOMIC ORDER 49–50, 62–63 (1979).

Traditional international law is derived from the laws of the capitalist economy and the liberal political system. From these two sources it derives the elements and factors of a certain consistency to be found in its theoretical construction and in the terms of its actual rules.

The [juridical] order set up by the former international society gave the impression of neutrality or indifference. But the laissez-faire and easy-going attitude which it thus sanctioned led in reality to ... the seizure of the wealth and possessions of weaker peoples. Classic international law in its apparent indifference was *ipso facto* permissive. It recognized and enforced a "right of dominion" for the benefit of the "civilized nations". This was a colonial and imperial right, institutionalized at the 1885 Berlin Conference on the Congo.

In addition to ratifying the European countries' right to conquer and occupy the territories concerned, international law recognized the validity of "unequal treaties", essentially leonine, whereby the weaker people for a long time delivered up their natural wealth on terms imposed on them by the stronger States. Neutral or indifferent, international law was thus also a formalistic law, attached to the semblance of equality which barely hid the flagrant inequalities of the relationships expressed in these leonine treaties.

It was also a law eminently suited to the protection of the "civilized countries" privileges, through the interests of their nationals. By virtue of

THE RELEVANCE OF INTERNATIONAL LAW (1990); N. SINGH, NUCLEAR WEAPONS AND INTERNATIONAL LAW (1959); CHRISTOPHER G. WEERAMANTRY, NUCLEAR WEAPONS AND SCIENTIFIC RESPONSIBILITY (1987).

diplomatic protection and intervention, the law enabled the nationals of the countries concerned to obtain, in certain States, advantages which were not even awarded to the citizens of those States.

International law made use of a series of justifications and excuses to create legitimacy for the subjugation and pillaging of the Third World, which was pronounced uncivilized. * * * However, the consistency of the system required that the freedom of action allotted by international law to a "civilized" State should be matched by the same freedom for any other civilized State. This accepted international law was thus obliged to assume the essential function of reconciling the freedom of every State belonging to the family of "civilized nations" with the freedom of all other States in the same family.

To keep in line with the predatory economic order, this international law was thus obliged simultaneously to assume the guise of: (a) an *oligarchic law* governing the relations between civilized States members of an exclusive club; (b) a *plutocratic law* allowing these States to exploit weaker peoples; (c) a *non-interventionist law* (to the greatest possible extent), carefully drafted to allow a wide margin of laissez-faire and indulgence to the leading States in the club, while at the same time making [it] possible to reconcile the total freedom allowed to each of them. However, this matter of controlling rival appetites was not taken very far.

Until the League of Nations came into being, this international law was simply a European law, arising from the combination of regional fact with material power, and transposed as a law dominating all international relations. The European States thus projected their power and their law on to the world as a whole. Here we come to the real nature of the so-called "international" law, to its substance and even to the reality of its existence. As it had been formed historically on the basis of regional acts of force, it could not be an international law established by common accord, but an international law given to the whole world by one or two dominant groups. This is how it was able to serve as a legal basis for the various political and economic aspects of imperialism.

This classic international law thus consisted of a set of rules with a geographical basis (it was a European law), a religious-ethical inspiration (it was a Christian law), an economic motivation (it was a mercantilist law) and political aims (it was an imperialist law).

Until the recent period of successive decolonizations, there was no perceptible change in this law as a backing for imperialism, apart from the fact that the emergence of the two super-great powers eclipsed the European influence and provoked a large-scale revision of the boundaries of spheres of influence in the world. * * * Traditional international law has always lagged behind emerging trends, set fast in its function of conserving a *status quo* which takes little account of the changes in the international community and the needs it expresses. * * * Like a mastodon crushing the interests of the Third World countries, while the latter attempt with great difficulty to shift it, traditional international law "is, as a whole, the embodiment of situations of predominance of the strong over the weak".[8]

---

8. C. Chaumont, *Cours Général de Droit*   350, 343 (1970–I).
International Public, 130 Recueil des Cours

But it is mainly in the economic sphere that the dichotomy between law and reality appears most clearly. This may be seen, for example, in connection with the activities of the multinational firms. Although they dominate the world economy and cause incalculable prejudice to the underdeveloped countries, these enterprises, which snap their fingers at all legal or moral standards, have so far not once been called to order or taken to task by international law. They are to economic domination what the colonial companies of the nineteenth century were to political domination. Although they are the ones who determine international relationships, these giant enterprises are left untouched by international law.

This historical retrospect revealing the origins of the disastrous economic situation from which the world now suffers, enables the true nature of international law to be perceived. Under cover of neutrality and the refusal of any political affiliation, it has permitted colonization, the exploitation of man by man, and racial discrimination. Through formal, abstract regulations, it has facilitated and legalized the enrichment of the affluent countries through the impoverishment of the poor countries.

But this law, which has done nothing to help poor countries, may nevertheless be improved thanks to them. This is the task which the developing countries have undertaken, being resolved to free international law from its paralyzing formalism and its heavy armour of hypocrisy, and to steer it towards a nobler, more humane and more essential goal—the promise of development.

Gernot Köhler, *The Three Meanings of Global Apartheid: Empirical, Normative, Existential*, 20 ALTERNATIVES 403, 403–04, 406–08 (1995).

Political concepts can have alternative meanings, depending on the type of discourse in which they are employed. * * * As an empirical concept, global apartheid describes the structure of global society [and] is similar to several others, such as *industrialized—developing countries, First World—Third World, North-South, imperialism, center-periphery, world system, global stratification*, and others. * * * [It] has been defined as "a structure of world society [reflecting] extreme inequality in cultural, racial, political, economic, and legal terms, as . . . South African apartheid."[9]

In this structure, "the affluent white minority possesses a disproportionately large share of world society's political, economic, and military power."[10] A similar description of the "system of global apartheid" is as follows: The "most economically developed and affluent countries are banding together to protect their privileged position in much the same way that South Afrikaners and others of European descent sought to maintain their dominance in South Africa."[11] One author speaks of a "diplomacy of apartheid on a global scale" that is "a dangerous exercise in the maintenance of inequality."[12]

* * *

9. Gernot Köhler, *Global Apartheid*, 4 ALTERNATIVES—A JOURNAL OF WORLD POLICY 263, 267 (1978).

10. *Id.*

11. ANTHONY H. RICHMOND, GLOBAL APARTHEID: REFUGEES, RACISM, AND THE NEW WORLD ORDER 216 (1994).

12. J.-C. RUFIN, L'EMPIRE ET LES NOUVEAUX BARBARES (1991), here quoted from the German

Global Apartheid as a Negative Norm

The concept of global apartheid can be used [also] as a normative concept, in which case it implies a value judgment. The value judgment is: "That which we call global apartheid is as wrong, unjust, and objectionable as South African apartheid before Mandela." This statement requires further clarification, especially (1) to specify what is meant by global apartheid; (2) to explain in what sense it is wrong, unjust, and objectionable; and (3) to explain the basis on which this negative judgment is justified.

The target of the accusation implicit in the term global apartheid varies somewhat between writers, who may direct their negative judgment toward either (1) the entire world ("global society," "world order," "world structure"), or (2) one part of the world—namely, the North of the world or the dominant states of the North, or (3) certain policies by the North or certain states of the North, which may include international and domestic policies.

The content of the accusation implied in *global apartheid* is that the accused (that is, the world, the North, or a policy) exhibits global apartheid, practices global apartheid, or promotes global apartheid. Typically, the details of this accusation are as follows:

1. The *world order* is accused of

   · Exhibiting *"extreme inequality"* or *"gross inequities."* These inequities are between rich and poor countries and/or between the North and the South of the world and/or between the whites and nonwhites of the world, and/or between men and women, as in gendered global apartheid.[13] These inequities are manifest in multiple dimensions: economic, social, health, power, violence, security from violence, and others.

   · Exhibiting *"domination"* by the North over the South of the world by military, economic, or other means, and *"subjugation"* and oppression of the South.[14]

   · Exhibiting more *violence* and instability in the South than in the North.

   · Exhibiting economic *"exploitation"* of the South by the North.

   · Exhibiting *"structural racism"*[15] between the white North and the nonwhite South.

2. The *North* of the world is accused of

   · Being affluent while oppressing the poor South; being affluent while exploiting the poor South; or being affluent while neglecting the poor South.

   · Controlling, dominating, or oppressing the South by various means and "recolonizing" the South.

translation: Das Reich und die Neuen Barbaren 247 (1991).

13. D. Williams, *Gendered Global Apartheid: Women, Imperialism and the Struggle for Civil Society*, article from Internet, gopher, University of Colorado, Virtual Seminar, Reading List, 1994.

14. Arijit Mukherji, *Economic Apartheid in the New World Order, in* Altered States: A Reader in the New World Order 108 (P. Bennis & M. Moushabeck eds., 1993).

15. Ali Mazrui, *Global Apartheid: Structural and Overt*, 19 Alternatives—A Journal of World Policy 186 (1994).

· Pursuing policies of racial segregation on a world scale, and thus of "institutionalized racial segregation."

· Preventing poor nonwhites of the South from entering and working in rich white countries.

· Being "overtly racist" and preaching the racial inferiority of nonwhites.

· Practicing domestic racism within the North.

3.   Various *policies* of the North are similarly accused, including foreign and domestic policies, toxic waste disposal policies, and so on.

The Normative Basis of the Accusations

The above accusations against the existing "world order" and the North and its policies are based on several fundamental values and norms. It is claimed, explicitly or implicitly, that global apartheid violates the norms of

· *Justice and fairness*. The situation, structure, or behaviors are judged to be unjust and unfair.

· *Basic needs*. Irrespective of justice and fairness considerations, the basic needs for the necessities of life, including food, shelter, security, and dignity, are not met for vast numbers of people in the present world order.

· *Human rights*. The human rights of vast numbers of people are violated, including the rights to life, liberty, and employment.

· *Equality*. The norm of universal equality is grossly violated.

· *Democracy*. The domination and/or oppression of a majority by a minority violates principles of political democracy. In South Africa, Mandela and the ANC used the "one man, one vote" principle and slogan as their goal.

· *Racial nondiscrimination*. Global apartheid grossly violates the norm of racial nondiscrimination.

Furthermore, it is alleged that global apartheid replicates, on a world scale, the negative norm of apartheid.

This institutionalized practice of separate and unequal development of racial groups (segregation), combined with white minority rule over nonwhite majorities, has been condemned by the world community in the case of South Africa prior to Mandela, revealing a worldwide opinion, if not consensus, that a combination of gross inequality, minority rule, and racism is unacceptable to the modern mind.

HILARY CHARLESWORTH, ET AL., FEMINIST APPROACHES TO INTERNATIONAL LAW, 85 AM. J.INT'L L. 613, 615, 621–29 (1991).

[A] feminist account of international law suggests that we inhabit a world in which men of all nations have used the statist system to establish economic and nationalist priorities to serve male elites, while basic human, social and economic needs are not met. International institutions echo these same priorities. * * * [W]e argue that the international legal order is virtually impervious to the voices of women and propose two related explanations for this: the organizational and normative structures of international law.

The Organizational Structure of International Law

The structure of the international legal order reflects a male perspective and ensures its continued dominance. The primary subjects of international law are states and, increasingly, international organizations. In both states and international organizations the invisibility of women is striking. Power structures within governments are overwhelmingly masculine: women have significant positions of power in very few states, and in those where they do, their numbers are minuscule. Women are either unrepresented or underrepresented in the national and global decision-making processes.

States are patriarchal structures not only because they exclude women from elite positions and decision-making roles, but also because they are based on the concentration of power in, and control by, an elite and the domestic legitimation of a monopoly over the use of force to maintain that control. This foundation is reinforced by international legal principles of sovereign equality, political independence and territorial integrity and the legitimation of force to defend these attributes.

International organizations are functional extensions of states that allow them to act collectively to achieve their objectives. Not surprisingly, their structures replicate those of states, restricting women to insignificant and subordinate roles. Thus, in the United Nations itself, where the achievement of nearly universal membership is regarded as a major success of the international community, this universality does not apply to women.

* * *

Women are excluded from all major decision making by international institutions on global policies and guidelines, despite the often disparate impact of those decisions on women. Since 1985, there has been some improvement in the representation of women in the United Nations and its specialized agencies. It has been estimated, however, that "at the present rate of change it will take almost 4 decades (until 2021) to reach equality (*i.e.*: 50% of professional jobs held by women)."[16] This situation was recently described as "grotesque."[17]

The silence and invisibility of women also characterizes those bodies with special functions regarding the creation and progressive development of international law. Only [two women have] sat as a judge on the International Court of Justice[i] and no woman has ever been a member of the International Law Commission.[j] Critics have frequently pointed out that the distribution of

16. Equal Time, July 1985, at 5.

17. Brian Urquhart & Erskine Childers, A World in Need of Leadership: Tomorrow's United Nations 29 (1990).

i. Currently, only one woman, Professor Rosalyn Higgins from the United Kingdom, serves as a judge on the International Court of Justice. Previously, in a case decided by the World Court in 1985, Mme. Suzanne Bastid of France sat only as a judge *ad hoc*.

j. The International Law Commission is a subsidiary body of the U.N. General Assembly established in 1947 and consisting of thirty-four members (originally fifteen, until 1956) chosen by the General Assembly for five-year terms on the basis of their recognized expertise in international law and charged, per Article 13 of the U.N. Charter [**Basic Document 1.3**], to "initiate studies and make recommendations for the purpose of encouraging the progressive development of international law and its codification." The Commission holds one session per year, lasting from eight to eleven weeks in Geneva, Switzerland. Since it began its work in 1948, the Commission has explored a wide variety of topics deemed suitable for codification, including, *inter alia*, the law of consular intercourse and immunities, of nationality, of the sea, of State responsibility,

judges on the Court does not reflect the makeup of the international community, a concern that peaked after the decision in the *South West Africa* cases in 1966.[18] Steps have since been taken to improve "the representation of the main forms of civilization and of the principal legal systems of the world" on the Court, but not in the direction of representing women, [over] half of the world's population. * * * [And despite] the common acceptance of human rights in an area in which attention can be directed toward women, they are still vastly underrepresented on UN human rights bodies. . . .

* * *

Why is it significant that all the major institutions of the international legal order are peopled by men? Long-term domination of all bodies wielding political power nationally and internationally means that issues traditionally of concern to men become seen as human concerns, while "women's concerns" are relegated to a special, limited category. * * * The orthodox face of international law and politics would change dramatically if their institutions were truly human in composition; their horizons would widen to include issues previously regarded as domestic—in the two sense of the word. . . .

The Normative Structure of International Law

[I]nternational jurisprudence assumes that international law norms directed at individuals within states are universally applicable and neutral. It is not recognized, however, that such principles may impinge differently on men and women; consequently, women's experiences of the operation of these laws tend to be silenced or discounted.

The normative structure of international law has allowed issues of particular concern to women to be either ignored or undermined. For example, modern international law rests on and reproduces various dichotomies between the public and private spheres, and the "public" sphere is regarded as the province of international law. One such distinction is between public international law, the rules about conflicts between nation-states, and private international law, the rules about conflicts between national legal systems.[19] Another is the distinction between matters of international "public" concern and matters "private" to states that are considered within their domestic jurisdiction, in which the international community has no recognized legal interest. Yet another is the line drawn between law and other forms of "private" knowledge such as morality.

At a deeper level one finds a public/private dichotomy based on gender. One explanation feminist scholars offer for the dominance of men and the male voice in all areas of power and authority in the western liberal tradition

and of treaties. In addition, it has dealt with a number of matters delegated to it by the General Assembly, among them: Draft Articles on State Responsibility [**Basic Document 1.10**]; a Draft Code of Crimes Against the Peace and Security of Mankind [**Basic Document 7.28**]; a definition of "aggression"; an opinion regarding the establishment of an international judicial organ for the trial of persons charged with genocide and related other crimes; and a formulation of the Principles of International [Penal] Law Recognized in the Charter and Final Judgment of the Nuremberg Tribunal [**Basic Document 7.27**].

18. South West Africa (Eth. v. S. Afr.; Liber. v. S. Afr.) (Second Phase), 1966 I.C.J. 6.

19. Among common law countries, the expression "conflicts of law" is typically substituted for the expression "private international law," the preferred expression among civil law countries.

is that a dichotomy is drawn between the public sphere and the private or domestic one. The public realm of the work place, the law, economics, politics and intellectual and cultural life, where power and authority are exercised, is regarded as the natural province of men; while the private world of the home, the hearth and children is seen as the appropriate domain of women. The public/private distinction has a normative, as well as a descriptive, dimension. Traditionally, the two spheres are accorded asymmetrical value: greater significance is attached to the public, male world than to the private, female one. The distinction drawn between the public and the private thus vindicates and makes natural the division of labor and allocation of rewards between the sexes. Its reproduction and acceptance in all areas of knowledge have conferred primacy on the male world and supported the dominance of men.

* * *

Although the scientific basis of the public/private distinction has been thoroughly attacked and exposed as a culturally constructed ideology, it continues to have a strong grip on legal thinking. The language of the public/private distinction is built into the language of the law itself: law lays claim to rationality, culture, power, objectivity—all terms associated with the public or male realm. It is defined in opposition to the attributes associated with the domestic, private, female sphere: feeling, emotion, passivity, subjectivity. . . .

In one sense, the public/private distinction is the fundamental basis of the modern state's function of separating and concentrating juridical forms or power that emanate from the state. The distinction implies that the private world is uncontrolled. In fact, the regulation of taxation, social security, education, health and welfare has immediate effects on the private sphere. The myth that state power is not exercised in the "private" realm allocated to women masks its control.

What force does the feminist critique of the public/private dichotomy in the foundation of domestic legal systems have for the international legal order? Traditionally, of course, international law was regarded as operating only in the most public of public spheres: the relations between nation-states. We argue, however, that the definition of certain principles of international law rests on and reproduces the public/private distinction. It thus privileges the male world view and supports male dominance in the international legal order.

[The authors next illustrate their thesis by reference to the "generally accepted" international right to freedom from torture as defined in Article 1(1) of the 1984 United Nations Convention against Torture and Other Cruel, Inhuman or Degrading Treatment or Punishment, 1465 U.N.T.S. 85, *reprinted in* 3 Weston III K.2. They point out, *inter alia*, that the Convention's definition of torture, in addition to using the male pronoun which "immediately gives the definition a male, rather than a truly human, context", deliberately "relies on a distinction between public and private actions that obscures injuries . . . typically sustained by women"; that it insists upon a primary and secondary intention to inflict suffering that necessarily excludes, for example, the victimization of women and children via "widespread and apparently random terror campaigns by both governments and guerilla groups in times of civil unrest or armed conflict"; and that it requires that "a public official or a person acting in official capacity ... be implicated in the pain and suffering" involved, thus relegating the prohibited conduct exclusively to the "public realm". The authors also point out that "States are not considered responsible if they have maintained a legal and social system in which violations or physical and mental integrity are endemic", noting that the International Law Commission, which drafted the 1984 convention, "did not widen the concept of imputability to incorporate such acts." They then conclude:]

The assumption that underlies all law, including international human rights law, is that the public/private distinction is real: human society, human lives can be separated into two distinct spheres. The division, however, is an ideological construct rationalizing the exclusion of women from the sources of power. It also makes it possible to maintain repressive systems of control over women without interference from human rights guarantees, which operate in the public sphere. By extending our vision beyond the public/private ideologies that rationalize limiting our analysis of power, human rights language as it currently exists can be used to describe serious forms of repression that go far beyond the juridically narrow view of international law....

Editors' Note

Starting in the early 1980s, a provocative attempt to rethink the basis of traditional legal theory began to make itself felt in the field of international law, challenging the view of law as rational, objective, and principled by deconstructing traditional legal argument and thereby exposing the contradictions and indeterminacies of legal doctrines, principles, and rules. An extension of the "post-modern" legal scholarship called "critical legal studies" (CLS) or "critical jurisprudence" (with its intellectual origins in Legal Realism, New Left anarchism, Sartrean existentialism, neo-progressive historiography, liberal sociology, radical social theory, and empirical social science), this "New Stream"[k] of internationally-oriented inquiry has had as a unifying theme, as noted by Nigel Purvis, *Critical Legal Studies in Public International Law*, 32 Harv.Int'l L.J. 81 (1991), large antipathy for what New Stream scholars David Kennedy (of the United States) and Martii Koskenniemi (of Finland) have called "conceptual pragmatism."[l] The term refers to the liberal international law scholarship that, in the wake of World War II, sought to transform the discipline by removing it from "the theoretical and doctrinal disharmony that had characterized much of its history."[m] Purvis summarizes, at 88–92:

k. Professor David Kennedy coined this term in *A New Stream of International Legal Scholarship*, 7 Wis. Int'l L. J. 1, 6 (1988).

l. David. Kennedy, *supra* note **l**, at 1–7; Martti Koskenniemi, From Apology to Utopia: The Structure of International Legal Argument 131–91 (1989).

m. Purvis explains, at 84–86:

Conceptual pragmatists sought to use doctrinal analysis to mediate between positivism and naturalism. Recognizing the need for abstraction, they sought to turn abstraction into functionalism ... , producing a fantastic

diversity of idiosyncratic theories about international law. Numerous schools of conceptual pragmatism developed. Most important among them were [the] "Rule-approach" [i.e., the work of such theorists as Georg Schwarzenberger, James Brierly, and Lassa Oppenheim, "who emphasized abstracted doctrinal definitions and rules"], [the] "Policy-approach" [i.e., the work of Harold Lasswell and Myres McDougal and their associates], Skepticism [i.e., the "realists" whose ranks included scholars and statesmen such as Hans Kelsen, Leo Gross, Louis Henkin,

[Incorporating] insights from normative philosophy, critical theory, structuralism, anthropology, prepositional logic, literature, sociology, politics, and psychiatry * * *, New Stream scholarship [has] been directed against "the tragic voice of post-war public law liberalism"[19] ... [and] has advanced on four principal fronts. Contemporary [critical] international law scholars have maintained (1) that the logic of liberalism in international law is internally incoherent; (2) that international legal discourse operates within a constrained structure; (3) that international legal analysis is indeterminate; and, (4) that whatever authority international law may have is self-validated.

While paralleling claims made by CLS scholars outside the international law field, these criticisms have been presented by New Stream scholars, Purvis notes, "as a unified theory of international legal analysis...." *Id.* at 92.

Illustrative is the following passage from Martii Koskenniemi, *From Apology to Utopia: The Structure of International Legal Argument* 40–42, 44–48 (1989):

There are two ways of arguing about order and obligation in international affairs. One argument traces them down to justice, common interests, progress, nature of the world community or other similar ideas to which it is common that they are anterior, or superior, to State behaviour, will or interest. They are taken as a given normative code which precedes the State and effectively dictates how a State is allowed to behave, what it may will and what its legitimate interests can be. Another argument bases order and obligation on State behaviour, will or interest. It takes as given the existence of States and attempts to construct a normative order on the basis of the "factual" State behaviour, will and interest. Following Walter Ullmann, I shall call these the *"descending"* and *"ascending" patterns of justification.*[20]

The two patterns—or sets of arguments—are both exhaustive and mutually exclusive.... The former is premised on the assumption that a normative code *overrides* individual State behaviour, will or interest.... The latter is premised on the assumption that State behaviour, will and interest are determining of the law.... Either the normative code is superior to the State or the State is superior to the code. A middle position seems excluded.

It should not be difficult to recognize the normative/concrete opposition in these two argumentative patterns. The descending pattern privi-

Hans Morgenthau, George Kennan, and Dean Acheson and who considered international law to be no more than what nations did in fact, preferring description and resisting abstraction], and idealism [e.g., scholars and jurists such as Alejandro Alvarez and Mohammed Bedjaoui who "were prone to speculate about the existing normative character of international life"].... Each [of these schools] hoped to construct a view of international law that did not depend on the two rival theories about the fundamental nature of the international order. * * * [In the end, however,] all forms of modern conceptual pragmatism ... failed to escape the naturalism/positivism debate.... Within their pragmatic concepts the naturalism/positivism indeterminism reemerged in other dichotomies: idealism/realism, normativity/concreteness, rules/processes, law/policy, and utopias/apologies. Each of these dichotomies paralleled the irreconcilable sides of the classical debate.

19. *Id.* at 2.

20. Walter Ullmann, Law and Politics in the Middle Ages: An Introduction to the Sources of Medieval Political Ideas 30–31 (1975)....

leges normativity over concreteness while the ascending pattern does the reverse.... The patterns oppose each other as they regard each other too subjectively. From the ascending perspective, the descending model falls into subjectivism as it cannot demonstrate the content of its aprioristic norms in a reliable manner (*i.e.*, it is vulnerable to the objection of utopianism). From the descending perspective, the ascending model seems subjective as it privileges State will or interest over objectively binding norms (*i.e.*, it is vulnerable to the charge of apologism).

Consequently, international legal discourse cannot fully accept either of the justificatory patterns. It works so as to make them seem compatible. The result, however, is an incoherent argument ... as it incorporates *contradictory assumptions* about what it is to argue objectively about norms. This gives rise to conflicting legal arguments and the inability to prefer any of them.

* * *

Thus, *we cannot consistently prefer either set of arguments*. Adopting a descending pattern will seem political and subjective either because it assumes the existence of a natural morality or because it creates an arbitrary distinction between States. An ascending pattern will seem political and subjective because it cannot constrain at all. It simply accepts as law whatever the State will choose to regard as such at any moment. Both must be included in order to make law seem objective, that is, normative and concrete and, as such, something other than politics.

The standard strategy of reconciliation is recourse to *tacit consent*. That is, we assume that though the law can be justified only by subjective acceptance, no *present* acceptance is needed for its application. The norm is binding because the State had agreed by means of conduct, an anterior statement, during the *travaux préparatoires*, or the like. This seems to preserve the law's concreteness while maintaining its normative force. But this reconciliation is a failure.... [A]cceptance *cannot* be invoked against a State denying it without assuming either 1) that the law-applier "can know better" what the State has agreed to[,] or 2) that there is some non-acceptance-related criterion whereby we can judge whether acceptance is present or not. Both points involve assuming an objective theory of justice; the former under the guise of "objective interests", the latter by reference to a naturalistic theory of good faith, reasonableness, or the like. Both are vulnerable to the objection about utopianism.

Reconciliation is impossible. This results from the way both sets of arguments are based on the assumption that they overrule each other. Moreover, this is their *only* distinct sense. The point of making a descending argument is that it can override subjective acceptance. To make an ascending argument is to assume that subjective acceptance can overrule any alternative justification. The arguments are meaningful only in mutual exclusion.

The dynamic of international legal argument is provided by the contradiction between the ascending and descending patterns of argument and the inability to prefer either.... Consequently, doctrine is forced to maintain itself *in constant movement from emphasizing concrete-*

ness to emphasizing normativity and vice-versa without being able to establish itself permanently in either position.

Different doctrinal and practical disputes turn out as transformations of this contradiction. Any doctrine, argument or position can be criticized [as] either utopian or apologist. The more it tries to escape from one, the deeper it sinks into the other. This will explain why familiar disputes keep recurring without there seeming to exist any way of disposing of them permanently. Law is contrasted to discretion, "positivism" to "naturalism", consent to justice, sovereignty to community, autonomy to organization[,] and so on.

The result is a curiously incoherent doctrine which is *ad hoc* and survives only because it is such. It retreats into general statements about the need to "combine" concreteness and normativity, realism and idealism which bear no consequence to its normative conclusions. It then advances in an *ad hoc* manner, emphasizing the contextuality of each solution—undermining its own emphasis on the general and impartial character of its system. . . . The doctrine's own contradictions force it into an impoverished and unreflective pragmatism. On the one hand, the "idealist" illusion is preserved that law can and does play a role in the organization of social life among States. On the other, the "realist" criticisms have been accepted and the law is seen as distinctly secondary to power and politics. . . .

The contradictions outlined in an abstract way give theoretical expression to the common feeling that international law is somehow "weak" or manipulable. One rule or argument seems to justify mutually opposing solutions. The same solutions are regularly justified by reference to contradictory arguments or rules. This feeling is ultimately explained by the *contradictory nature of the liberal doctrine of politics.* . . .[21] The weakness of international legal argument appears as its incapability to provide a coherent, convincing justification for solving a normative problem. The choice of solution is dependent on an ultimately arbitrary choice to stop the criticisms at one point instead of another.

Koskenniemi then concludes, at 48: "In other words, my argument is that international law is singularly useless as a means for justifying or criticizing international behaviour. Because it is based on contradictory premises it remains both over- and underlegitimizing: it is overlegitimizing as it can ultimately be invoked to justify any behaviour (apologism); it is underlegitimizing because [it is] incapable of providing a convincing argument on the legitimacy of any practices (utopianism)."

Thus, voicing New Stream thinking, Koskenniemi's project is to show, as summarized by Hilary Charlesworth in *Subversive Trends in the Jurisprudence of International Law*, 1992 Proceed. A.S.I.L. 125, 126, that "the very notion of an objective legal order seems to conflict with the liberal rejection of all but subjective, individual values" and that, therefore, "[liberal] interna-

---

21. Liberalism's internal contradictions have frequently been the subject of analysis. [T]he most useful . . . [argue] that liberal political theory contains two separate strands: 1) the postulate of individual freedom and 2) a programme for collective decision. The strands are contradictory. Any political decision infringes individual freedom as liberalism cannot consistently define "freedom" otherwise than as absence of (collective) constraint.

tional legal argument cannot achieve the objective resolution of disputes, claimed as its principal virtue, with the aim of 'open[ing] up a possibility for alternative descriptive—and simultaneously normative—characteristics of the world in which states live.' "[22] But as Koskenniemi asks later, *supra*, at 497, "[d]oes this imply losing a commitment to the whole, to peace and world order?" Koskenniemi answers, at *id.*:

> No, but it does force one into seeing the commitment in a new light. It is not a commitment which seeks to realize given principles or ready-made social arrangements. It aims to construct the whole as a structure of open political conflict and constant institutional revision. The whole will be seen as a system which enables, as far as possible, particularized solutions, aimed at realizing authentic commitment. But it gives no intrinsic weight to solutions, once adopted, and it is ready to make constant adjustments once this seems called for. It positively *excludes imperialism and totalitarianism*. Beyond that, however, it makes no pretention to offer principles of the good life which would be valid in a global way.

In other words, "the lawyer [must] recognize that solving normative problems in a justifiable way requires ... wide knowledge of social causality and of political value and, above all, capacity to imagine alternative forms of social organization to cope with conflict." *Id.* at 498. Koskenniemi concludes: "As international lawyers ..., we [are] not relieved from the painful task of living and choosing in the midst of political conflict. Instead of impartial umpires or spectators, we [are] cast as players in a game, members in somebody's team. It is not that we need to play the game better, or more self-consciously. We need to reimagine the game, reconstruct its rules, redistribute the prizes." *Id.* at 501.

Richard A. Falk, *The World Order Between Interstate Law and the Law of Humanity: The Role of Civil Society Institutions*, Notes for a Lecture at the Foundation Opera Campana Dei Caduiti, International University of Peoples' Institutions for Peace, Roverto, Italy (July 29, 1993).

The [contemporary] notion of world order is situated between interstate [*i.e.*, international] law and the law of humanity, although not necessarily at all in the middle. The interstate is presumably the past, a time when clearly the interstate dimension dominated our understanding of international law, but not the more distant past when states in the modern sense didn't exist.

The law of humanity is associated with the future, it is more a matter of potentiality than of history or experience. It is prefigured, and to some extent embodied, in the substance and theory of the international law of human rights. Its formal reality has been established through the primary agency of states, and qualifies as a domain of interstate law. But the historical potency of the international law of human rights is predominantly a consequence of its implementation through the agency of civil society.

This agency of civil society needs to be understood in two senses. Firstly, in the transnational nongovernmental sense, typified by Amnesty Internation-

22. *Id.* at xxiii.

al and the various regional "watch groups," that is, voluntary associations of citizens using information about abusive behavior on the part of states, exerting influence to obtain compliance, and failing this, to disclose information about abuses that challenges the legitimacy of the accused state. Here, the preoccupation is with the well-being of the individual human being, and as such, satisfies one aspect of the law of humanity (in contrast, interstate law is preoccupied with the interests of the state as promoted by its official representatives).

There is a second dimension of the agency of civil society in relation to the law of humanity: it is the activation of peoples to pursue their emancipation from oppressive structures of governance, social movements legitimated by their aspirations being embodied in interstate law. The movements of emancipation in Eastern Europe, as for instance, Solidarity in Poland and Charter 77 in Czechoslovakia, that were sustained, in part, by the realization that their most fundamental grievances had already been validated by the state that was offering such blatant resistance. In this kind of setting, the law of humanity is buried in the forms of interstate law, but must be exhumed, and made operative, by the militancy of civil society.

World order, then, is a composite reality, reflecting the persisting influence of states on its normative order, yet also exhibiting the effects of voluntary associations and social movements that are motivated by the law of humanity, and situated in civil society. The global spread of political democracy, with its roots in constitutionalism, makes those persons within the territorial space controlled by the sovereign state increasingly aware of their political, moral, and legal option to appeal to broader communities in the event of encroachment on their basic human rights.

The character of the law of humanity is not self-evident. It could mean law that is enacted by and for the peoples of the world, as distinct from the elites that act in lawmaking settings on behalf of states. Such a usage would correspond with "the rights of peoples," the innovation associated with the efforts of the radical Italian parliamentarian, Lelio Basso, leading to the establishment in the mid–1970s of the Permanent Peoples Tribunal with its site in Rome. Such an innovation is itself explicitly conceived to be a counter-institution intended to expose the abuses of states and the deficiencies of international institutions, and to provide civil society with its own autonomous voice. The formalization of this voice by way of legal instruments (for instance, The Algiers Universal Declaration on the Rights of Peoples (1976) *reprinted in* 3 Weston III V.2) and acts (for instance, the various decisions of the Permanent Peoples Tribunal) constitutes the substance of the law of humanity so conceived. In this regard, then, states are not regarded as appropriate agents for the development of the law of humanity, and it depends on civil society to establish new forms for law-creation and law-application.

It is also necessary to distinguish the law of humanity from the phenomenon of globalization, although there are some connections that will be noted as well. Interstate law presupposed the autonomy of the territorial state, although such a presupposition was always a legal fiction given the hierarchical reality of geopolitics. During most of the period of the ascendancy of the state, the largest part of humanity was excluded from its protective structures associated for convenience sake with the Peace of Westphalia (1648), being subordinated within the frame of one or another variety of imperial geopolitics. That is, the interstate system was primarily a regional system centered in Europe, and only because the region projected its power globally did the illusion arise of a world system. Ironically, it is only in recent decades, with the collapse of colonialism, that interstate law was an encompassing global reality. The irony arises because at this historical point of climax for interstate law as a framework of formal membership, the realities of interdependence and integration undermine the presupposition of autonomy, rendering partially obsolete the claims of interstate law.

There is a certain confusion that follows from distinguishing the law of humanity as "the other" in relation to interstate law. During the modern period the ideology of the state included the claim that such a system of distinct sovereignties upheld the wellbeing of humanity, that interstate law was the best vehicle by which to achieve the objectives of the law of humanity. In this regard, interstate law, with its positivist disposition was seen as an improvement upon the naturalist approach that rested on a vague foundation of universalism that didn't correspond with the specific interests, cultural diversities, and concrete values of separate peoples organized on the basis of distinct national identities. That is, the state reconciled the particular with the general in a satisfactory manner so long as territoriality approximated economic, social, political, and cultural reality. Of course, here too, adequacy depended on fiction as illustrated by the terminology of nation-state, a juristic conception of nationality that often obscured the presence within state boundaries of several ethnic groups with separate, often antagonistic, psychopolitical conceptions of national identity. The state-fracturing impact of the right of self-determination when extended to "peoples" (as in Article 1 of the human rights covenants [**Basic Documents 7.13 & 7.14**] and in the post–1989 practice relating to the former Yugoslavia and Soviet Union) has exploded once and for all the misleading pretension of designating states as "nation-states."

But, arguably, the erosion of territoriality has undermined the major premise of interstate law and its derivative claim to operate as the guardian of human wellbeing. This erosion can be understood from different angles: matters of vulnerability-the state has lost the capacity to uphold security in light of nuclear weaponry and long-range delivery systems; matters of environmental protection-the state cannot safeguard its territory from the adverse effects of extra-territorial behavior nor can it by its own efforts maintain the global commons (oceans, atmosphere); matters of economic viability-the state, even those that are well-endowed and large, can no longer provide an adequate framework for economic activity, and is gradually being superseded by an array of international regimes and by the regionalization and globalization of capital markets and corporate and banking organization. In these three types of erosion, the wellbeing of humanity requires law to be operative on a regional, or global, scale that corresponds to the scope of operations. It is here, however, that interstate realities persist, and the law of humanity is mainly in the dreaming (or pure aspirational phase). Interstate law provides what control there is in relation to war/peace and environmental issues, and except for the European Community, with respect to transnational economic activity. Thus, the inability of interstate law to rise to these challenges and the failure of the law of humanity to take effective shape is one way to express a critical view of world order; the deep structural quality of these criticisms also helps understand why even such a momentous historical occasion as the ending of the Cold War and the reuniting of Europe can have only a superficial relevance to an inquiry into prospects for the emergence of the law of humanity in an effective form.

Discussion Notes/Questions

1.   To understand the origins and development of international law is to understand world history. How, generally, would you describe the development of international law over the course of history?

2.   Through Starke–Shearer, *supra*, we can trace the emergence of the modern state system and the coordinate development of international law on the basis, at least initially, of "natural law" theorizing. Starke, however, suggests a trend away from such theorizing in the direction of positivist thinking in recent times. Do you agree? What about the experience of World War Il, the Nuremberg and Tokyo trials, and, recently, the rapid development of international human rights law? Do not these events attest to the re-emergence of once discredited natural law theory? In fact, there may be a newly emerging consensus on enduring values. Not so long ago it was fashionable to defer to anthropologists who, when investigating remote societies, claimed that all values were relative to time, place, and culture. But in a deep sense the Second World War and the development of weapons of global destruction may have changed our earlier attitudes. It is increasingly hard to maintain that any value is as good as another, that any morality is only a matter of social pressure and culturally determined, that any action by a government is all right as long as it has the support of its own people. What do you think?

3.   Which of the forces shaping the organization and interrelation of human societies from early to modern times do you consider to have been most important in shaping the development of international law? Why? How? Is there a Western bias? A class bias? A racial bias? A male bias? Do they persist? Is it a matter merely of perception or is it one of real substance?

4.   The first Falk extract, *supra*, observes that international law and the organized international community have amounted to "a colossal failure" in the avoidance of catastrophe. Do you agree? Assuming Falk to be correct, do you believe there are grounds for optimism that the practitioners of international law and policy can and will reverse this pattern? Why? Why not?

5.   In the continuation of his essay, Professor Köhler, *supra*, asks, at 408: "If the world had a court of justice where global apartheid was a punishable crime on a level with such crimes as waging [a] war of aggression or genocide, would the North be guilty or not guilty of such a crime?" How do you answer this question? What are your reasons?

6.   The Charlesworth–Chinkin–Wright extract, *supra*, asserts that the dichotomy drawn by international law (as well as national law) between public and private spheres of action prevent international legal processes from being gender neutral and consequently prejudice the position and role of women relative to men in international (and national) society. What do Charlesworth–Chinkin-Wright mean? How does the public-private dichotomy to which they refer prejudice women?

7. Bedjaoui, Köhler, and Charlesworth–Chinkin–Wright, *supra*, all point to deep structural dislocations and malignancies in the international system. If it is true that law is an essentially conservative profession, how, if at all, might international law serve a reformist or transformist role in relation to these dislocations and malignancies?

8. Purvis, in the Editors' Note, *supra*, observes, at 116, that "the most disappointing aspect of the New Stream literature has been its failure to commit to an affirmative image of international law's role in the world order"—in contrast to, for example, the "conceptual pragmatism" of the policy science approach of Harold Lasswell and Myres McDougal toward which New Stream scholars display some hostility. Rosalyn Higgins, a policy science scholar, now I.C.J. judge, writes as follows of critical jurisprudence in Problems and Process: International Law and How We Use It 8–9 (1994):

> [Critical legal studies] has more in common with policy science than either the policy scientists or the critical realists might wish to acknowledge. For both schools, the legal theory is applicable to law in general and not just to international law.... Both take as the starting-point that law is deeply rooted in social theory. Both locate legal process in social context and make the place of values quite explicit. Both reject law as rules and exceptions. But the critical-studies scholar will see law as contradictions or as essentially indeter-minate at its core rather than as complementary or competing norms between which choices have to be made in particular circumstances. The critical-studies scholar believes that these contradictions are either historically con-tingent or inherent in the human experience. This view leads to the pessimis-tic conclusion that what international law can do is to point out the problems but not assist in the achievement of goals.

Do you agree with Judge Higgins' conclusion? Disagree? Why? What would Koskenniemi say? Note that his vision of world order "positively *excludes imperi-alism and totalitarianism.*"

9. The second Falk extract, *supra*, describes the present world order as somewhere between "interstate law" and "the law of humanity," but moving in the direction of "the law of humanity." What does Falk mean?

10. In their introduction to Rethinking Human Rights: Challenges for Theo-ry and Action (1989), Indian scholars Smitu Kothari and Harsh Sethi write, at 9:

> [W]hile recourse to law, or appealing to the state to enforce the law or legislate new ones, will and possibly must remain an important, maybe even the primary strategy to transform the human condition, equally important is to evolve and popularise a social praxis, rooted in the need of the most oppressed communities, that seeks to create shared norms of civilized exis-tence. In any final instance, it is only this—a shared vision of how we want to live as a collectivity—that can provide us the moral basis of evolving our own conduct.

Would Falk, on the basis of the second Falk extract, *supra*, agree with this statement, which, on final analysis, is skeptical of the law as a progressive social change agent? Do you agree with it? Why? Why not? How might Bedjaoui, Köhler, and Charlesworth–Chinkin–Wright respond?

11. For an insightful critique by a contemporary Indian scholar of "the most persuasive Western theories of international law"—"realist" (Morgenthau); "poli-cy science" (McDougal–Lasswell); "world order" (Falk)—and of the Soviet ap-

proach to international law as well (Tunkin), see B. Chimni, International Law and World Order: A Critique of Contemporary Approaches (1993).

C. IS INTERNATIONAL LAW REALLY LAW?

In reviewing the definition of "international law" (*supra* Section A) as you prepare for the formulation, with your Norwegian Foreign Ministry superiors, of a legal strategy to offset environmental catastrophe in the circumpolar Arctic region, you read some general observations supporting the proposition that international law deserves the title "law," a proposition that you found also to be assumed in the brief historical and contemporaneous views you just considered (*supra* Section B). But you are aware that much of the general public is skeptical about the "legal" status of international law. Are there really any means, many would ask, for legally impugning the Russian Federation for its policies and activities? Is it not paradoxical to talk about law operating among "sovereign" states? Does not international law exist in name only, as merely a language for brokering international relations and politics? You again turn to your treatise.

A modern-day example of skepticism about international law is to be found, as we saw in Section B, *supra*, in the "New Stream" scholarship of "Critical Legal Studies" (CLS) or "critical jurisprudence." As observed, New Stream scholars attack conclusory statements about law, which they perceive as commonly concealing the socioeconomic and political agendas of those with effective power. To the CLS theorist, objectivity does not exist except within the minds and prejudices of the naive. In *International Law, World Order and Critical Legal Studies*, 42 Stan. L. Rev. 811, 833–34 (1990), Philip Trimble summarizes an important aspect of the CLS argument in the context of international law:

> A quick look at the rules of international law shows why governments love international law. Contrary to the ... view of law as a restraint on unruly governments, international law confirms much more authority and power than it denies. For example, the basic rule of international law is that a state generally has the exclusive authority to regulate conduct within its territory. International law thus confers authority to control entry and exit, to establish police control, to determine economic structure, to tax, to regulate, and to reinforce in many other ways the power and legitimacy of government. Public international law also grants governments sovereignty over air space and control over the continental shelf and economic resources 200 miles into the sea.

> Of course, each rule conferring authority on a government denies it to all others. The United States government may be restrained in attempts to enforce its law in Canada, and Japanese fishermen may be barred from fishing near California's coast. Nevertheless, governments have little interest in extending their authority to that extent, at least when compared with their interest in controlling matters at home. For the most part governments do not want to invade other countries or apply their law or send their fishermen to other territories. To be sure,

there are exceptions, and these exceptions can be of vital importance to the actors involved. In the aggregate, however, they are less important than the effect of the general rules.

Even the rules of public international law that expressly restrain government authority may at the same time give a government an excuse to impose its authority throughout its own society so that it can effectively discharge its obligations under international law. International human rights law, for example, promotes national judicial review, general criminal law procedures, and a host of objectives that can best be met by assertions of national government power, especially against village or other traditional structures. For example, a government's international responsibility for injuries to aliens gives that government a mandate to control local officials and practices.

Even when the rules do prevent a government from doing something that it otherwise wants to do . . ., it may decide to forego the short-term advantages derived from violating those rules because it has an overriding interest in maintaining the overall system. The rules comprising the system as a whole enable each government to achieve welfare goals for important parts of its population, and hence solidify its standing and legitimacy. . . . The rules of international law accordingly are very congenial to governments. They mostly justify or legitimate the practical exercise of state power.

For the CLS theorist, then, the claims of rational or objective rules only cloak the real forces behind all legal language and structure: politics and the struggle for power.

Skepticism about international law is also found among those who are attracted to the command theory of law, which considers that the only "law" worth talking about is the "law" that is enforced. Citizen A sues Citizen B; A wins in court; B is very unhappy and refuses to pay the judgment; the sheriff seizes B's assets and pays them over to A. It is the last action—that of the sheriff or, in some cases, the military—that the command theorists emphasize as giving the entire process the name "law." Nineteenth Century legal philosopher John Austin, the quintessential command theorist, denied absolutely the propriety of treating "international law" as part of legal science: "[T]he greatest logical error of all that is committed by many continental jurists, who include in public law, not only the law of political conditions, of crimes, and of civil and criminal procedure, but also international law; which is not positive law at all, but a branch of positive morality." 2 J. Austin, Lectures on Jurisprudence 176–77 (R. Campbell ed., 1875).

When people look at international law, they have difficulty finding the international equivalent of a sheriff. Especially when a nation is the "defendant," they ask how any alleged "law" can be enforced against it. Nation A sues Nation B; A wins in an international court; B is very unhappy and refuses to pay the judgment. Then what? Suppose Nation A launches a war of retaliation against Nation B. Is such a war the equivalent of "enforcement action"? Theoretically one might so allege, but there is no guarantee that Nation A will win. Indeed, what if Nation B wins?

It is considerations such as these that have led many to conclude, akin to John Austin, that there is no such thing as international law because there is no third-party "command" that is routinely enforceable .. As Gidon Gottlieb explains, "[d]ominant legal theories all relate to the legal order of vertical systems ... in which, to borrow Professor Falk's phrase, there is a vertical or hierarchical relationship between unequal centers of power. This is in contrast to systems in which there is a horizontal or nonhierarchical order between equal centers of power."[23] Thus leading modern-day legal positivist H. L. A. Hart has written, in The Concept of Law 209 (1961):

> [T]hough it is consistent with the usage of the last 150 years to use the expression "law" here, the absence of an international legislature, courts with compulsory jurisdiction, and centrally organized sanctions have inspired misgivings, at any rate in the breasts of legal theorists. The absence of these institutions means that the rules for states resemble the simple form of social structure, consisting only of primary rules of obligation, which, when we find it among societies of individuals, we are accustomed to contrast with a developed legal system. It is indeed arguable, as we shall show, that international law not only lacks the secondary rules of change and adjudication which provide for legislatures and courts, but also a unifying rule of recognition specifying "sources" of law and providing general criteria for the identification of its rules. These differences are indeed striking and the question "Is international law really law?" can hardly be put aside.

Hart argues, in effect, that international law is not a system or process but a set of rules, and that, lacking any basic rules of recognition, it is not law.

But the command-oriented conception of law upon which this skepticism rests is almost universally rejected by modern legal theorists, even as a description of domestic legal systems. Thus Roger Fisher has written, in a now classic essay based primarily on United States experience, *Bringing Law to Bear on Governments*, 74 Harv. L. Rev. 1130, 1132–34 (1961):

> [I] suggest that we lawyers, in uncritically accepting the command theory and applying it to international law have ourselves been guilty of woolly thinking. I suggest that in denying the status of international law because there is no apparent sovereign issuing the commands, we show a limited understanding of how [for example] a court system operates in its relations with a government. In blandly assuming that all law rests on superior force, we have ignored the cases in which the government loses a judgment and honors it.
>
> Is organized force essential to such compliance? Clearly it is not. When a judgment is entered against the United States in the Court of Claims, no superior sovereign compels Congress to vote an appropriation. The judgment is paid because that is the law; but the law is not the articulate voice of a superior sovereign. When, in the *Youngstown* case, the Supreme Court ordered the Secretary of Commerce to return the steel mills which the President had ordered him to seize, the Court had no regiments at its command. But despite the fact that the Supreme Court sitting in Washington had no greater force at its command vis-à-vis the Government than does the International Court of Justice sitting at The Hague, the steel mills were returned.

23. Gidon Gottlieb, *The Nature of International Law: Toward a Second Concept of Law,* in THE FUTURE OF THE INTERNATIONAL LEGAL ORDER 331, 332 (C. Black & R. Falk eds., 1972).

The more closely one examines law within this country and within others, the less significant seems the element of force. Even such hard, positive laws as the criminal and tax laws depend ultimately on compliance with them by the Government, and the general pattern is one of compliance. To be sure, Congress, on perhaps a dozen occasions, has failed to honor a judgment of the Court of Claims. But the Government, which is never without funds or absent from the jurisdiction, has a far better record than the private judgment debtor. This record, even if less than perfect, demonstrates that a pattern of governmental compliance can be secured without a supragovernmental police force.

Moreover, even where the organized force of a superior sovereign is available it may be difficult to make a government comply. If a government is not persuaded to obey by other reasons, superior force alone may not be enough. In *Virginia v. West Virginia* the Supreme Court had before it the continuing failure of the West Virginia legislature to raise and appropriate the funds needed to pay Virginia that share of its public debt which West Virginia had undertaken upon becoming a separate state. Assuming that the United States Army was at the Court's disposal, what should the Army do to enforce the judgment? Should it seize the state capitol and sell it at auction? Should it raise funds at the point of a gun? If so, from whom? However effective force or the threat of force may be when applied to an individual, it is difficult to bring force to bear on a political enterprise which offers no obvious point of application. So long as a rule runs only to a political entity rather than to individuals, a superior power must face the problem of trying to apply force to an abstraction.

And to Professor Fisher's dissent may be added the curious fact that international law, despite very few centralized or hierarchical command and enforcement structures, is widely obeyed on the whole. Writes Louis Henkin in How Nations Behave—Law and Foreign Policy 47 (2d ed. 1979): "It is probably the case that *almost all nations observe almost all principles of international law and almost all of their obligations almost all of the time.* Every day nations respect the borders of other nations, treat foreign diplomats and citizens and property as required by law, observe thousands of treaties with more than a hundred countries."

Actually, not even legal positivists such as H.L.A. Hart, who rests his concept of law primarily upon the model provided by municipal legal systems, agree with the positivist view as originally or traditionally conceived. While not accepting international law as "law" in the same way or to the same degree they do domestic or municipal (i.e., national) law, neither do they insist on "law" as solely a matter of orders (the command of the sovereign) backed by threats (sanctions). Thus Hart, for example, likens international law to the law of "primitive communities" which, he says, are lacking in so-called secondary *rules of recognition* (for conclusive identification of the authoritativeness of primary or substantive community norms), *rules of change* (for empowering individuals or groups to introduce or eliminate old primary or substantive norms), and *rules of adjudication* (for enabling individuals or groups to make authoritative determinations of the question whether a primary or substantive norm has been broken), though *not* in so-called primary *rules of obligation* ("that general attitude of the group towards its own standard modes of behaviour" that imposes "restrictions on the free use of violence, theft, and deception"). These latter "primary rules of obligation," he maintains, provided they are supported by majority consensus, may be understood to reflect at least a minimal legal system because, along with the "secondary rules" of "recognition," "change," and "adjudication," they help to make up "the heart of a legal system." *See* H. Hart The Concept of Law 89–95, 212–15 (1961). Hart writes, at 212–13:

> To argue that international law is not binding because of its lack of organized sanctions is tacitly to accept the analysis of obligation contained in the theory that law is essentially a matter of orders backed by threats. This theory ... identifies "having an obligation" or "being bound" with "likely to suffer the sanction or punishment threatened for disobedience". Yet ..., this identification distorts the role played in all legal thought and discourse of the ideas of obligation and duty. Even in municipal law, where there are effective organized sanctions, we must distinguish ... the meaning of the external predictive statement "I (you) are likely to suffer for disobedience", from the internal normative statement "I (you) have an obligation to act thus" which assesses a particular person's situation from the point of view of rules accepted as guiding standards of behaviour. It is true that not all rules give rise to obligations or duties; and it is also true that the rules which do so generally call for some sacrifice of private interests, and are generally supported by serious demands for conformity and insistent criticism of deviations. Yet once we free ourselves from the predictive analysis and its parent conception of law as essentially an order backed by threats, there seems no good reason for limiting the normative idea of obligation to rules supported by organized sanctions.

Hart continues (and concludes), at 214–15:

> [T]here is general pressure for conformity to the [primary rules of international obligation]; claims and admissions are based on them and their breach is held to justify not only insistent demands for compensation, but reprisals and countermeasures. When the rules are disregarded, it is not on the footing that they are not binding; instead efforts are made to conceal the facts. It may of course be said that such rules are efficacious only so far as they concern issues over which states are unwilling to fight. This may be so, and may reflect adversely on the importance of the system and its value to humanity. Yet that even so much may be secured shows that no simple deduction can be made from the necessity of organized sanctions to municipal law, in its setting of physical and psychological facts, to the conclusion that without them international law, in its very different setting, imposes no obligations, is not "binding", and so not worthy the title of "law".

In short, says Hart, international law deserves to be called "law" even if its analogy to domestic or municipal law is more in its content than its form.

Thus it is possible to say that the command theory of law and legal process is no longer in ascendancy, having given way to other, more complex theories about national and international law. But if it is not necessarily the threat of force that induces governmental compliance with law in general, and international law in particular, on what basis is it possible to say that international law really is law and that it has force and effect most, if not all, of the time? This question has been asked by even a former judge of the International Court of Justice, Philip C. Jessup, in a now classic statement, *The Reality of International Law,* 18 Foreign Aff. 244 (1939–40), at 244–46:

> Why do Foreign Ministers and Secretaries of State consult legal advisers about international law? * * * In most cases the layman is impressed by the reality of breaches of international law and is not sufficiently aware of the reality of reliance upon it. He does not pause to wonder why foreign offices bother to maintain legal staffs, which are an expense and sometimes a hindrance to the execution of policy. A distinguished student has remarked that in the seventeenth century "state papers are full of allusions and appeals not merely to reasons of policy but to principles of right, of justice and of equity–to the authority of public law and to those principles and rules by which the rights of the weak are protected against the invasion of superior force by the union of all who are interested in the common danger."
>
> Why has this been true for three centuries? Why have the nations been willing ... to subscribe to a budget ... for the maintenance of the [World Court]? ... Why have the governments of the United States and Mexico filled reams of paper with legal arguments concerning the property rights of American citizens in the latter country? Why does the Constitution of the United States, which, according to Chief Justice Marshall, cannot be presumed to contain any clause which "is intended to be without effect," give Congress the power "to define and punish ... offenses against the law of nations"? Why has the United States Supreme Court, like the courts of most other countries, asserted that "international law is part of our law"? Why do people commonly emphasize the "lawlessness" of certain nations which have come to be known as "aggressors"?
>
> There must be some reason for this habitual invocation of international law—an invocation which is even more frequent than the assertion of its nonexistence. Perhaps a subconscious human urge, a variety of wishful thinking, seeks to give reality to the ancient maxim: *ubi societas, ibi ius.* Perhaps "international law" is merely a slogan of diplomacy, like "manifest destiny," "the white man's burden," or "*Lebensraum.*" Surely it is often a convenient weapon for a ministry of propaganda anxious to win the support of world opinion. Yet if international law has no reality, what is the use of convincing peoples in other lands that one's opponent is a violator of that law? Shall we chorus with the Pirate King: "A paradox, a paradox, a most ingenious paradox"? One would scarcely deny that international law is a comparatively weak sister of private law. Yet a great lawyer–John Bassett Moore—bears testimony as the result of wide experience and study that "international law is on the whole as well observed as municipal law."

How might Jessup have answered the questions he asks? How does one convincingly argue that international law really is law and that it has force and effect most if not all of the time? We here consider two principal responses: (1) the existential/obligation argument, and (2) the reciprocity/sanctions argument.[n]

1. THE OBLIGATION/EXISTENTIAL ARGUMENT

Sir Gerald Fitzmaurice, *The Foundations of the Authority of International Law and the Problem of Enforcement*, 19 MOD. L. REV. 1, 8–9 (1956).

The real foundation of the authority of international law resides ... in the fact that the States making up ... international society recognize it as binding upon them, and, moreover, as a system that *ipso facto* binds them as members of that society, irrespective of their individual wills. * * * [I]t is not consent, as such, that creates the obligation, though it may be the occasion of it. It is a *method* of creating rules, but it is not, in the last resort, the element that makes the rules binding, when created. In short, consent could not in itself create obligations unless there were already in existence a rule of law according to which consent had just that effect.... Others have put it in the following way: "There is a customary rule of international law that the consent of the States to a rule makes that rule binding upon them." Be it so; but then, of course, the difficulty is merely removed a stage further back, and the inquirer will have to ask what is the juridical foundation for this customary rule itself, and what is it that makes *that* rule binding. To this question it is very difficult to give an answer. It can be said, with [Hans] Kelsen, that the reason why a customary rule is binding is that there is an antecedent and still more fundamental legal principle to the effect that "States have a duty to go on behaving as they have customarily behaved"— but then what is the source of *that* duty? Or can it be held, with [Sir Hersch] Lauterpacht, that the antecedent principle that confers binding force on customary rules is one according to which the general will of the community must prevail, and there is a duty to conform to that will as expressed in customary rules of law—but here again a duty is postulated that has itself ... to be accounted for. The point is that, however the matter is put, finality can, in the nature of the case, never be attained. The discussion merely enters what is known to the mathematicians as an infinite regress—a series in which each proposition is explicable in terms of the previous one, and derives its validity from it; but this antecedent proposition itself requires to be accounted for by a similar process.

JAMES L. BRIERLY, THE OUTLOOK FOR INTERNATIONAL LAW 5 (1944).

The best evidence for the existence of international law is that every actual state recognizes that it does exist and that it is itself under obligation to observe it. States may often violate international law, just as individuals often violate municipal law; but no more than individuals do states defend their violations by claiming that they are above the law. It is only the philosopher in his study who sometimes makes that claim on their behalf. States may defend their conduct in all sorts of other ways, by denying that the

---

n. The authors are indebted to Professor Anthony D'Amato for this analytical approach, which he initiated in International Law and World Order: A Problem–Oriented Coursebook (B. Weston, R. Falk & A. D'Amato eds., 2d ed, 1990).

rule they are alleged to have broken is a rule of law, by appealing to a supposed right of self-preservation superior to the ordinary law, and by other excuses more or less sincerely believed in as the case may be; but they do not use the explanation which would obviously be the natural one if there were any doubt that international law has a real existence and that they are bound by it.

ANTHONY D'AMATO, INTERNATIONAL LAW: PROCESS AND PROSPECT 10–11 (1987).

Suppose we were to read all the communications that governments officially make to one another: letters, speeches, proclamations, treaties, agreements, diplomatic initiatives, and so on. Suppose we read these with an eye toward whether the language contained in these communications refers to "law" and is "legal" language. In brief, we would be engaging in a "content analysis" of these communications to see whether what is being asserted and claimed therein can properly be called "legal." We will find, indeed, that much of the content of international communications is self-consciously grounded in legal terminology. There should be nothing surprising about this, considering the fact that lawyers typically help draft these documents and speeches. We will find, indeed, that the more important the communication the more likely it is cast in legal terms, and the more likely it is that lawyers have played a role in drafting it.

We might then want to argue that, given the reality of this legal language, it would be rather absurd to maintain that "law" is not involved in these intergovernmental communications. If the relevant actors call it "law," who are we to say that they are all wrong? ... [T]he very utilization of legal language in intergovernmental communications is an argument for the proposition at least that governments resort to "law" in their attempts to influence each other; or refer to "law" in an attempt to be legal and thus ward off disapproval of other states.

Burns H. Weston, *Law and Alternative Security: Toward a Just World Peace, in* Alternative Security: Living Without Nuclear Deterrence 78, 79–80 (B. Weston ed. 1990).

[B]arring some truly radical change in the present State-centric structure of international relations, improbable in the near-term (at least outside Western Europe), it seems futile to imagine any legal initiative or set of legal initiatives that *alone* could ... [safeguard] core national interests, real or imagined. Embarked though the world surely is upon an historical transformation of major proportion (at least as great as what took place at the end of the Thirty Years' War and the onset of the Westphalian system in 1648), we still live in the *global* Middle Ages, characterized by more than [185] separate fiefdoms, each with a monopoly control over the military instrument and each only barely accountable in any formal sense to each other or to the larger arenas in which each operates....

[But this] is not to say that international law is without any utility at the present time. As the late Professor William W. Bishop, Jr., counseled pithily over [three] decades ago, "under present conditions all [States] need international law in order to continue to exist together on this planet."[24] And what is more, it performs, all things considered, remarkably well. Every hour of every day ships ply the sea, planes pierce the clouds, and artificial satellites roam outer space. Every hour of every day communications are transmitted, goods and services traded, and people and things transported from one country to another. Every hour of every day, transactions are made, resources exploited, and institutions created across national and equivalent frontiers. And in all these respects, international law (by which I mean the many processes of authoritative and controlling transboundary decision at all levels or social organization that help to regulate such endeavors) is rather well observed on the whole; it is an important and relevant force in the ordering of human relationships worldwide. True, the international legal system is by no means adequate in its force and effect, and this is particularly true in the realm of war and peace.... But no legal system, not even the most advanced, can boast absolute effectiveness; and all legal systems, again including the most advanced, typically display a certain impotence when it comes to politically volatile or otherwise intractable issues of public policy.

Gidon Gottlieb, *The Nature of International Law: Toward a Second Concept of Law, in* 4 THE FUTURE OF THE INTERNATIONAL LEGAL ORDER 331, 365–66 (C. Black & R. Falk eds., 1972).

It is correct to assert that a legal order exists when:

1. international actors (for example, states) accept sets of fairly specific rules, principles, and policies as binding—in the sense that they recognize they are not at liberty to disregard them—and as proper standards for assessing the legality of their own actions;

2. international actors make demands, claims, complaints, and proposals to each other on the basis of such binding rules, principles, and policies and seek to settle their differences by reference to them;

3. international actors attempt to secure compliance with such rules, principles, and policies and there is a measure of congruence between state action and accepted law;

4. there are organizations established under such rules, principles, and policies and acting pursuant to them;

5. there is a measure of consensus between international actors about the content of the rules, principles, and policies accepted as binding, and about criteria for identifying them;

6. these rules, principles, and policies regulate significant aspects of the relationships between international actors and are designed to limit their unfettered discretion in decision-making;

7. international actors are committed to accept the guidance of these binding rules, principles, and policies in good faith and to apply them evenhandedly in all situations.

24. W. Bishop, Jr., *General Course of Public International Law*, 115 RECUEIL DES COURS 147, 467 (1965–II).

Such a legal order involves then *a process of authoritative decision-making* leading to unavoidable principled choices between competing goals and policies. It requires a measure of congruence between state action and accepted law. This congruence is a central feature of *the existence of any legal system*. Accordingly, the earnestness with which major powers act upon international law considerations in good faith, and the intensity of their commitment to its principles and objectives, are good measures of the existence of such a system. Deviant practices, invoking one set of standards for oneself and another for adversaries, stretching concepts to legitimize national policies of questionable legality, all these tend to undermine the existence of the international legal order. The health of a legal system is thus subject to fluctuations, declining at times of crisis and tension when legal scruples may be ignored to accommodate pressing political interests.

2. THE RECIPROCITY/SANCTIONS ARGUMENT

James L. Brierly, *Sanctions*, 17 TRANSACT. GROT. SOC'Y 68 (1932).

... [T]he habitual observance of International Law suggests, what every international lawyer knows to be the case, that there do exist sanctions behind the law. The real difference in this respect between municipal and International Law is not that the one is sanctioned and the other is not, but that in the one the sanctions are organized in a systematic procedure and that in the other they are left indeterminate. The true problem for consideration is therefore not whether we should try to create sanctions for International Law, but whether we should try to organize them in a system. In both kinds of law obedience is the rule and disobedience the exception, and in both the real inducing cause of the general obedience is the same....

LOUIS HENKIN, HOW NATIONS BEHAVE—LAW AND FOREIGN POLICY 29–30 (2d ed. 1979).

Every nation derives some benefits from international law and international agreements. Law keeps international society running, contributes to order and stability, provides for common enterprise and mutual intercourse. Because it limits the actions of other governments, law enhances each nation's independence and security; in other ways, too, by general law or particular agreement, one nation gets others to behave as it desires. General law establishes common standards where they seem desirable. Both general law and particular agreement avoid the need for negotiating anew in every new instance; both create justified expectation and warrant confidence as to how others will behave.

All these advantages of law and agreement have their price. Law limits freedom of action: nations are "bound" to do (or not to do) other than they might like when the time to act comes. Political arrangements legitimized by law are more difficult to undo or modify. Stability and order mean that a particular nation is not free to be disorderly or readily to promote external change. To promote its own independence and security and the inviolability of its territory, to control the behavior of other governments, a nation may have to accept corresponding limitations on its own behavior. For the confidence bred by law, one pays the price of not being free to frustrate the expectations of others.

Myres S. McDougal, *The Impact of International Law Upon National Law: A Policy–Oriented Perspective*, 4 S. Dak. L. Rev. 25, 50–51 (1959), *reprinted in* Myres S. McDougal & Associates, Studies in World Public Order 157, 186–87 (1960).

It may perhaps require emphasis that, despite the absence from the world arena of a centralized executive organ, there are ample sanctions—if sanctions be defined as implementing techniques or available base values—at the disposal of the general community of states, assuming a willingness by states to employ sanctions, for securing that inclusive prescriptions are honored in actual conduct by a reasonable conformity. Exactly the same base values (power, wealth, respect, enlightenment, and so on) and exactly the same instruments of policy (diplomatic, ideological, economic, and military) may be used in support as in attack upon inclusive policy. The history of state interactions reveals a constant flow of examples in which all these base values and all these instruments of policy have been employed, in many differing combinations and in organized and unorganized modalities, for the enforcement of community prescription. The difficulty is that, on occasion, what has been missing is not efficient procedures but rather the appropriate predispositions of decision-makers, the general community consensus, necessary to sustain the application of sanctions. Decision-makers act ... like other men, to maximize their values as individuals and as members of all the groups and associations, including the state, with which they identify. The important decision-makers of the world arena have ... been able to clarify a long-term common interest in the enforcement of many inclusive prescriptions—such as with respect to the allocation of resources, the protection of diplomats, the making of agreements, the distribution of jurisdiction over particular events, and so on—and for sanctioning such prescriptions have established an elaborate network of expectations about reciprocal claim and mutual tolerance, promise of reciprocity and threat of retaliation, which in the main secures a high degree of effective application. For other prescriptions, such as the community prohibition of unauthorized violence, common interest has not yet been clarified in comparable degree, effective elites are not yet fully convinced that in destroying others they will destroy themselves, and expectations of enforcement are accordingly low. The task of enhancing the effectiveness of inclusive prescriptions in the world arena remains, in measure, a task of enlightenment.

Anthony Clark Arend, *Toward an Understanding of International Legal Rules, in* International Rules: Approaches From International Law and International Relations 289, 303–306 (R. Beck, A. Arend & R. Vander Lugt eds., 1996).

[A]s [already] noted ..., one of the reasons for the estrangement that developed between international relations theorists and international legal scholars was a growing perception by adherents of the Realist School that international law did not matter, that legal rules did not play a significant, independent role in international relations. With the more recent [i]nternational relations literature on international regimes, it has become more acceptable to discuss the relevance of international rules to international rules to international relations. For the regime theorists, the question was normally posed in the new idiom—Do regimes matter? Given our specific interest in international legal rules, we would simply ask—Do international legal rules matter? Does international law matter?

[W]e answer this question affirmatively. International legal rules do matter in international relations. They are not merely epiphenomenal. To elaborate on this hypothesis, [we] explore three potential roles of international legal rules: (1) giving structure to the international system, (2) influencing state behavior, and (3) regulating the activity of certain nonstate actors.

International Law and the Structure of the International System

When scholars explore the question of the relationship of international legal rules to international relations, they frequently focus on the role these rules play (or do not play) in the foreign policy decision-making processes in particular cases. . . . They do often, however, examine the role that legal rules play in constituting the structure of the international system. As Andrew Hurrell observes, "Rationalist models of co-operation miss the crucial link between costs and benefits of specific rules and the role of international law as constitutive of the structure of the state system itself."[25] But how does international law constitute the international system?

As many of the Sociological (Reflectivist) Institutionalists have noted, there are a number of ways in which international law constitutes the structure of the state system. We will note several. First, international law enshrines the doctrine of sovereignty. The concept of sovereignty—the notion that states are independent, that they can be bound by no higher law without their consent, that they are juridically equal—is one of the assumptions underlying international relations. While we agree with the standard caveats about the notion of sovereignty—it may not be absolute, it may undergo change, it can be distinguished from empirical autonomy,[26] and so on—the concept forms a most basic operating principle of international affairs. It is ingrained in the minds of all international actors and can be considered one of the primary building blocks of the modern international system.

Second, an inextricably related to the first point, international law establishes the criteria for membership in the international system. It determines when a particular international actor will enjoy certain rights and duties at the global level. International law, for example, establishes criteria for statehood. It determines when an entity can be regarded as a state. In so doing, international law confers legitimacy on states. International legal rules also determine when nonstate actors will be endowed with rights and duties. It determines, for example, when an international organization can enter into international agreements and when the decisions of such an organization can be binding on members.

---

25. Andrew Hurrell, *International Society and the Study of Regimes, in* REGIME THEORY AND INTERNATIONAL RELATIONS 49, 59 (V. Rittberger ed., 1993).

26. As Robert O. Keohane explains: "As a legal concept, the principle of sovereignty should not be confused with the empirical claim that a given state in fact makes its decisions autonomously." *International Institutions: Two Approaches*, 32 INT'L STUD. Q. 379, 385 (1988).

Third, international law provides a language for diplomacy. Even Nigel Purvis, commenting on the New Stream of international legal scholarship, observes that "[o]n the most basic level, sovereigns seem to take for granted the propriety of engaging in international legal discourse (instead of some other type of discourse) when they seek to resolve international issues."[27] When international actors speak, they use the idiom of international law. Decision-making elites in states assert their positions in terms of legal rights. They make *legal* claims. When, for instance, a state decides to use armed force, it will invariably present its claim in terms of international law. It is rare indeed for a state to justify its actions solely on the basis of political, practical, or even moral factors. Some reference to legal principles is made in virtually every case. When the United States invaded Grenada in 1983, or Argentina seized the Falkland (Malvinas) Islands in 1982, or Iraq moved into Kuwait in 1990, these states justified their actions in legal terms.

Likewise, if a state is critical of the behavior of another state, it will frequently castigate that state for failure to abide by its *legal* obligations. Many states criticized the [former] South African system of apartheid as a violation of international human rights law; the United States accused the [former] Soviet Union of violating the Anti–Ballistic Missile Treaty by establishing a phased-array of radar at Krasnoyarsk.

Fourth, international law gives normative value to actions and claims made by international actors. As Frederich Kratchowil has noted, the international legal order "specifies the steps necessary to insure the validity of their official acts and assigns weight and priority to different claims."[28] In other words, when states or other international actors contemplate a particular action, legal rules provide guidance about what procedure to follow for the act to be perceived as legitimate. During the [Persian] Gulf War, for example, international law provided a procedure that the United States and its allies could use to ensure that the action against Iraq would receive the maximum degree of legitimacy.[o] ... In addition, once a state or other international actor has acted, international legal rules reflect certain normative judgments about the legitimacy of the action. Thus, when Iran denied immunity to diplomats from the United States, the act was perceived to be "wrong." Similarly, when the United Nations sent peacekeeping troops into Cambodia to supervise a transition to power, other international actors believed that action to be "right."

International Law and the Behavior of States

In playing a constitutive role in the international system, we believe that international law is extremely relevant to international relations. The Sociological (Reflectivist) Institutionalists make this useful contribution to the understanding of the role of legal rules. Other scholars from a more "rationalistic" approach might explore the question of rules a bit differently. They

27. Nigel Purvis, *Critical Legal Studies in Public International Law*, 32 HARV. INT'L L.J. 81, 110 (1991).

28. FRIEDRICH KRATCHOWIL, RULES, NORMS AND DECISIONS: ON THE CONDITIONS OF PRACTICAL AND LEGAL REASONING IN INTERNATIONAL RELATIONS AND DOMESTIC AFFAIRS 251 (1989).

o. *But see* Burns H. Weston, *Security Council Resolution 678 and Persian Gulf Decision–Making: Precarious Legitimacy*, 85 AM. J. INT'L L. 516 (1991).

would ask whether any theory can be developed that will explain and predict the role that legal principles play in specific foreign policy decision[s]. In other words, can any theoretical insights be gleaned as to what role *specific* legal rules play in *specific* cases that are decided by *specific* decision-makers?

This is an area where much research needs to be done. It presents one of the most tricky theoretical questions.... [In the tradition of Legal Positivism, we] believe that international legal rules are created by the consent of states. Accordingly, we believe that the rules were created to reflect the interests of states. If this is the case, can these legal rules have an independent influence on state behavior? As Andrew Hurrell note[s], "[t]he central problem ... for regime theorists and international lawyers is to establish that laws and norms exercise a compliance pull of their own, at least partially independent of the power and interests which underpinned them and which were often responsible for their creation."[29] He explains that "[t]o avoid empty tautology it is necessary to show not only that the rules exist and that they are created and obeyed primarily out of self-interest or expediency, but that they are followed even in cases when a state's self-interest seems to suggest otherwise." It is easy to demonstrate that, in cases where international law is consistent with immediate policy goals, states will follow the law. But what about cases where there is a conflict between international legal rules and other specific policy goals? What will decision-makers do in those cases?

In an effort to stimulate further empirical research on this question, we would suggest several tentative hypotheses about the role of international legal rules in the actual decision-making process.

First, foreign policy decision-makers will almost always attempt to find out what international law says about a contemplated course of action. They may choose not to comply with the law, but they will wish to know its content. We believe that it would be rare indeed for a state to be unconcerned about what the law provided. Accordingly, the foreign ministries of virtually all states have certain individuals charged with informing decision-makers about what they believe international law is on a particular issue.

Second, the higher the degree of authority and control of a particular rule, the more likely it is to be followed, even though it may be in the immediate short-term interest of the state not to follow the rule. A state does not particularly want to be perceived as a "law breaker." The stronger the rule, the more likely the state will be seen as violating the rule.[30]

Third, the more easily the rule could be violated reciprocally to the detriment of the state in question, the more likely the state is to comply with the rule. [Norway], for example, is probably not inclined to shoot [Russian] diplomats, deny [Russian] flagships innocent passage through the territorial sea, or kill [Russian] prisoners of war, if [the Russian Federation] could reciprocate in kind.

It is our hope that these and other hypotheses can be tested by empirical research.... Clearly, for any comprehensive theory to be developed, scholars

---

29. *Supra* note 25, at 53.

30. This hypothesis draws on the arguments of Professor Franck. *See* THOMAS M.

FRANCK, THE POWER OF LEGITIMACY AMONG NATIONS (1990).

must examine the behavior of a wide range of states and a variety of issues areas.

International Law and the Behavior of Nonstate Actors

Finally, another way in which legal rules matter in international relations relates to the behavior of nonstate actors. As noted previously, international law determines who the legitimate actors in the international system are and establishes that nonstate actors can lay a role in international relations. The function of international law, however, goes beyond this simple acknowledgment. International law regulates the behavior of nonstate actors in the international system much as domestic law regulates the behavior of actors in the domestic legal system. Whenever a person takes an international flight or sails on the high seas, that individual's behavior is controlled by accepted [international] legal rules. When someone mails a letter, it arrives at its destination without violation or much controversy. Accordingly, they tend to be neglected in discussions of the role of international law. They are, nonetheless, extremely important in providing order to innumerable international transactions that take place. Indeed, if the amount of private or other nonstate interaction increases, these types of legal rules will play an even more critical role in international relations.

Discussion Notes/Questions

1. As noted above, even modern-day legal positivists concede the existence of international law. If the extracts from H.L.A. Hart, *supra*, are representative, however, they make this concession in a somewhat limited sense; they ascribe to international law an elementary character analogous to the law found, ostensibly, in "primitive communities." According to Hart at least, international law manifests "primary rules of obligation," which are at "the heart a legal system," but not "secondary rules" of "recognition," "change," and "adjudication," which likewise are at "the heart of a legal system." Do you agree with Professor Hart's assessment of the primitiveness of international law? Why? Why not? Is he correct in saying that the world community lacks rules of recognition, change, and adjudication? That so-called primitive communities lack such rules? Is it possible that Professor Hart may be exalting form over function?

2. Brierly, Fitzmaurice, Henkin, Weston, Gottlieb, and Arend, *supra*, agree that international law exists. How do their assessments differ from that of Hart? To what do they point to substantiate their existential claim? Can you point to any other evidence? Does the way you think about the question depend on how you define "international law"?

3. Professor Gottlieb refers to the existence of a "process of authoritative decision-making." What is a "process of authoritative decision"? What makes it authoritative? What makes the decisions resulting from it authoritative? How do we know when a decision is "authoritative and controlling" and when it constitutes the exercise of merely "naked power"? How can we tell when a particular exercise of power is unauthoritative or lawless?

4. Is Professor D'Amato persuasive in arguing that scholars may not dispute the proper usage of the term "law" if the relevant actors in the international arena use that term? If he says that scholars have no right to tell the actors that their use of the term "law" is incorrect, what about the opposite? Do the international actors have the right to prescribe the meaning of "law" to scholars?

5. Out of concern for the fundamental status of international law, many scholars variously dwell upon the concepts of reciprocal "obligation" and "sanction" to validate the "binding" force of international law. What do they mean by these terms? Does Brierly shed any light on this question? Henkin? McDougal? Arend? Do the meanings attached to the terms depend on how writers define "international law"?

6. Do nation-states regard themselves as bound to comply with international law rules? Do private individuals and groups (corporate and otherwise) regard themselves as bound to comply with municipal law rules? Is any legal system entirely successful in preventing deviant behavior? If so, when? If not, when? Does Trimble shed any light on these questions?

7. In everyday parlance, we often talk about "the law of the jungle." Can there be a "law" of the jungle? Or is the jungle characterized by an absence of law? Is there "order" in the jungle? Is "law" synonymous with "order"? Is there international order? Is there international law? If so, is the law and/or order of the international system no more and no less than "the law of the jungle"? Why? Why not?

8. What are the preconditions for effective law in the world community? In national society? Do you perceive any differences between the two? In kind? In degree? Is some system of external or third-party enforcement required? Is voluntary compliance (i.e., self-enforcement) sufficient?

9. Generally speaking, are national legal systems more effective or less effective than the international legal system? How? Why? Compare, in this connection, the following two comments:

> . . . I think it is very important to stress that it is true that 90 percent of the present system of international law is working [reasonably well]. Of course, we are worried about the remaining 10 percent in which we say the law is not working well enough just as we are worried domestically about teenage delinquency or about violations of human rights. Yes, we have the same problem internationally. We have the problem of proper international behaviour in the crucial area on which the peace of the world depends; and here, of course, I cannot say we have an adequate system. We are still far away from a system of world law which would really maintain peace and security, and of course this is what we are worried most about. L. Sohn, *The Effectiveness of International Law*, in Essays on International Law 58, 63 (M. Nawaz ed., 1967).

> [O]n empirical grounds, given the number of civil wars, wars of secession and *coups d'état* since—let us say—1945, a good case can he made out for saying that *public* international law is more efficacious than public law within States. At any rate, whether or not such a judgment is sustainable, those who would judge international law would do well, on grounds of logical consistency, to start out by taking a hard look at the performance of *national* legal systems. Ian Brownlie, *The Reality of International Law*, 52 Brit. Y.B.I.L. 1, 2–3 (1981).

With whom do you agree? Sohn? Brownlie? Both? Taking "effectiveness" to refer to the extent to which compliance with community norms is achieved, what conclusions do you reach when you act upon Professor Brownlie's suggestion?

10. Is there any legal system more effective than a national legal system in securing compliance with authorized norms? If so, which one(s) and why? If not, why not? Is there any legal system less effective than the international legal

system? If so, which one(s) and why? If not, why not? Do your answers depend at least in part on how you define "legal system"? On the degree to which any given legal system can boast "legitimacy," as discussed by Arend, *supra*? On whether or not one is considering "micro" and/or "private" legal systems (e.g., the NCAA, the high church) as well as "macro" and/or "public" legal systems? All of the above? None of the above?

11. Deprivation of entitlements, as Arend, *supra,* implies, may be international law's way of promoting enforcement of its norms, but entitlements clearly are only one kind of value that states hold dear. There are many more tangible kinds of values that states safeguard and that are vulnerable to attack by other states. Indeed, when one considers the enormous range of ways to "harm" a state, one begins to get a picture of the diversity and subtlety of the notion of "enforcement" in international law.

Consider in this connection Herman Kahn's "escalation ladder" of reactions by one or more States to the actual or alleged illegalities of another, excerpted from Herman Kahn, *Escalation and its Strategic Context, in* National Security 475 (D. Abshire & R. Allen, eds. 1963). Which of the following responses, all taken from id. at 482–87, do you consider legal, appropriate, rational?

a. *Retortions.* Acts by one government to seek redress for, or prevent recurrence of, an undesired act by another government are called retortions. For example one can: (1) recall an ambassador for lengthy consultation; (2) refuse to facilitate negotiations on other issues; (3) make overtures to the other side's enemies; (4) denounce a treaty; (5) make same kind of legal or economic reprisal; (6) push resolutions in the U.N. against the other side; (7) replace an official in a key spot by one who is known to be "hard" or "tough"; (8) start a violent publicity campaign, indulge in mass meetings, spontaneous public demonstrations, and so on.

b. *Show of force.* There are various ways of showing force: direct or indirect, silent or noisy. A direct show of force might consist of massing troops in a certain area, placing naval units in a certain sea, evicting diplomatic representatives, etc. An indirect show of force might be an increase in the draft call, the test firing of missiles, or the conduct of maneuvers. All these shows of force may be silent; or they may be accompanied by a press campaign and official speeches in which it is specifically stressed that the "enemy's" behavior or the need to rectify injustice has "forced us to do what we are doing."

c. *"Legal" harassment.* In addition to perpetrating "internal" acts whose major purpose is to show committal, anger or preparation, one can harass the opponent's prestige, property, or nationals "legally." For example, one can embargo the shipment of goods to a certain country, or one could even actuate a "peaceful" blockade. This could be done outright or under the guise of being something else. For example, the Soviets [were able to] deny access by rail transportation to West Berlin under the pretext that the railroads [were] out of order. One could also interfere with shipping, claiming that public health or safety measures require it. One could put vessels in port and force them to stay there, perhaps, by enforcing arbitrary health or safety regulations. One might confiscate bank deposits or other property of the opposing government or its nationals. One can arrest or expel on trumped-up charges some of the other side's nationals who are within one's own borders.

d. *Violent harassment.* If the crisis is still not resolved, acts of violence or other incidents designed to harass, confuse, exhaust, violate, discredit, frighten, and otherwise harm, weaken, or demoralize the opponent or his allies and friends may be manufactured. Bombs may be dropped by unauthorized or anonymous planes; enemy nationals within one's border can be arrested and charged with real or fancied crimes; embassies may be stoned or raided; soldiers guarding the border may be shot. There may be kidnapping or assassination of important, or (more likely) unimportant personalities, or the limited use of paramilitary actions such as guerrilla warfare, piracy, sabotage, terror, ambushes, border raids, and other terror tactics. Reconnaissance probing operations or other intelligence activities may be increased. There may even be overflights or other invasions of sovereignty. Harassing acts can also be verbal—either abusive or threatening in nature.

12.   Is there any good reason not to consider international law as law?

Chapter Two

INTERNATIONAL LEGAL PRESCRIP-
TION: THE "SOURCES" OF IN-
TERNATIONAL LAW

Having cultivated your understanding of the concept of international law, you now turn (in your capacity as a junior lawyer recruited by the Department of Legal Affairs of the Royal Norwegian Foreign Ministry to help prevent a radioactive disaster in the Arctic) to the matter of international legal prescription. You turn, that is, to the matter of how international law is made, where we look to find the doctrines, principles, and rules that help to make up its content, and how we tell that a particular doctrine, principle, or rule actually has the force and effect of law. No other aspect of your review of international law is likely to be more important than this one, and none or few could be more difficult. You are aware of the dearth of centralized legislative, judicial, and executive institutions in the international legal system. You know there is no world legislature that can create binding laws. You know there is no elaborate global system of courts with compulsory jurisdiction to interpret the law. And you know there are no centralized executive agencies (*e.g.*, police forces) authorized to apply it. Furthermore, you know that, in international law, one must deal with competing sovereignties that, for the most part, are not subject to the dictates of centralized command and enforcement structures, or at least not yet on a globally significant basis. Still, there are prescriptive (*i.e.*, law-making) processes by which expectations of authority and control become accepted as doctrines, principles, and rules of international law—that is, there are "sources" of international law from which the norms (doctrines, principles, and rules) of international law may be extrapolated, including the doctrines, principles, and rules applicable to environmental protection.

Your understanding of these so-called sources of international law is fuzzy, however, so you decide to resume your study, knowing that this is the best way to respond, at least initially, to the request for your assistance in the formulation of an international legal strategy designed to prevent the Russian Federation from massively contaminating the circumpolar Arctic region via its derelict nuclear reactors, its disposal of the radioactive waste generated by them, and its land-based pollution practices. Thus, you reopen your treatise, turn to the chapter entitled "International Legal Prescription: The 'Sources' of International Law," and begin reading.

———

You begin by observing that the term "sources" is set off by quotation marks, as often it is, and you ask why. Another textbook addresses this question by another question, using the hydrographical analogy or metaphor of a spring: "Is [the source of a spring] the place where water from the spring first appears on the surface of the ground," it asks, "or is it some subterranean area?"[a] You sense that the answer could be either or both of these alternatives, at least as applied to law or legal process. The water from the spring on the surface of the ground can be analogized, you think, to the statutes, administrative regulations, treaties, judicial decisions, customs, and other informational or material sources that communicate the doctrines, principles, and rules that are the corpus of the law in any given community; and the water that is found in some subterranean area can be equated, you believe, with the underlying community expectations that project the legal doctrines, principles, and rules and help to give them binding force and effect. You are aware, however, that, as Professor M. H. Mendelson warned in a working paper to the International Law Commission[b] in 1988, *Appendix to First Report of the Rapporteur (1986): Formation of International Law and the Observational Standpoint*, 63 International Law Association: Report of the Conference 941, 954 (1988), "in all discussions of theory metaphors should be treated with caution." Also, you are aware that, metaphorical considerations aside, the meaning of the term "sources" has been the subject of controversy. Professor Mendelson explains, at *id.* 954–55:

> In international law, a certain amount of confusion has been caused by the fact that the term ["source"] is used by different people in different senses. In particular, whilst some use the word to denote the formal processes by which law is made, others extend it to factors which merely contribute to the evolution, or ascertainment of the existence, of a legal rule. This led Schwarzenberger, for instance, to abandon the term "source" altogether and to distinguish between "law-creating processes" and "law-determining agencies."[1] Others, more impressed with the fact that, in a decentralized society, both the creation and the application of the law are often carried out by the same entities (States in particular), and that it is not always easy to distinguish between the two processes in practice, have preferred to speak of "the world constitutive process of authoritative decision"[2] or "the international legal process".[3] Yet again, Fitzmaurice has persuaded a number of authors to distinguish between "sources of law" (e.g. custom) and "sources of obligation" (e.g. treaties).[4] Also, the exposition of sources is sometimes interwoven with discussion of

a. The International Legal System—Cases and Materials 51 (W. Holder & G. Brennan eds. 1972).

b. *See supra* note j in Chapter 1, at 37.

1. George Schwarzenberger, The Inductive Approach to International Law 19, 21 (1965).

2. Myres McDougal et al., *The World Constitutive Process of Authoritative Decision,* *in* International Law Essays 191 (Myres McDougal & W. M. Reisman, eds. 1981).

3. *E.g.*, Antonia Chayes et al., International Legal Process (2 vols. 1968).

4. *Some Problems Regarding the Formal Sources of International Law, in* Symbolae Verzijl 153 (1958).

the basis of obligation in international law. And finally, there is controversy about some possible candidates for inclusion in the category of formal sources of international law.

Nevertheless, as Professor Mendelson concludes, at *id.* 956, "the expression 'source of international law' is too well entrenched and, if the appropriate discriminations are made, perhaps too convenient, to be wholly abandoned. . . ."

And so you turn to a widely accepted statement that indicates at least the "material sources" of international law, namely, Article 38 of the Statute of the International Court of Justice [**Basic Document 1.4**],[c] which is the principal judicial organ of the United Nations and which, together with its unfortunately-named predecessor, the Permanent Court of International Justice, is popularly known as "the World Court." Article 38 of the I.C.J. Statute (the World Court's constitution) reads as follows:

Article 38

1.   The Court, whose function is to decide in accordance with international law such disputes as are submitted to it, shall apply:

> **(a) international conventions, whether general or particular, establishing rules expressly recognized by the contesting states;**
>
> **(b) international custom, as evidence of a general practice accepted as law;**
>
> **(c) the general principles of law recognized by civilized nations;**
>
> **(d) subject to the provisions of Article 59,[d] judicial decisions and the teachings of the most highly qualified publicists of the various nations, as subsidiary means for the determination of rules of law.**

2.   This provision shall not prejudice the power of the Court to decide a case *ex aequo et bono*, if the parties agree thereto.

Technically speaking, you are aware, Article 38 is meant to apply to the I.C.J.; it is, after all, a provision of the legal instrument that governs the World Court. But you know too that Article 38 has come to have a life beyond the World Court, helping to define the legal authority upon which decision-makers and theorists of all kinds decide cases, solve problems, and advocate policies in the international realm. Additionally, its enumeration of "sources" or law-making processes is not complete. Drawn word-for-word from the statute that governed the Permanent Court of International Justice between World Wars I and II, its text does not account explicitly for the innovations in international prescription that have emerged since that earlier time—for conspicuous example: the resolutions and declarations of the United Nations and other international governmental institutions, many of which are of great

---

c. Hereinafter sometimes referred to as "the I.C.J. Statute."

d. Article 59 of the I.C.J. Statute reads: "The decision of the Court has no binding

force except between the parties and in respect of that particular case."

importance to the laws of war, to human rights, and to other matters pertinent to the prosecution of war crimes and associated atrocities. Nevertheless, Article 38 does address the historically primary "sources" of international legal authority, and it is therefore fitting, you conclude, to revisit their meaning and significance.

A. TREATIES

The first "source" of international law listed in Article 38 is "international conventions," which is another name for "treaties." Generally speaking, putting treaties first makes sense. A nation should be held to its own formal promises, which typically are the result of extensive deliberation and negotiation; and because a treaty—defined in Article 2(1)(a) of the 1969 Vienna Convention on the Law of Treaties **[Basic Document 1.7]** to mean "an international agreement concluded between States in written form and governed by international law"—is an instrument containing the *mutual* promises of signatory States, it should be an especially strong "source" of law against such a nation. Thomas Hobbes, in constructing his "Leviathan" model of the State, began with the social contract—a mythical pact among the founders of society based purely upon mutual consent. He knew that the reader, even if living in a state of anarchy (Hobbes wrote during the civil war in England), would be persuaded by an appeal to the promises made by the reader's own forbears. The idea of consent to a rule is very powerful evidence that the rule is "binding" upon the consenting parties; and it therefore should come as no surprise that one of the most basic principles of international law is the principle of *pacta sunt servanda*, to wit, that nations are bound to keep the promises they make.

Thus, while the enumeration of "sources" in Article 38 may be misleading if that enumeration is seen as giving absolute priority to treaties over custom (or other law-making processes),[e] treaties are a powerful "source" of international legal authority.[f] Of course, as you contemplate, in your Norwegian Foreign Ministry capacity, the seeming disregard of treaties pertinent to Russia's Arctic pollution practices—for example, the the 1972 London Convention on the Prevention of Marine Pollution by Dumping of Wastes and Other Matter **[Basic Document 4.11]** and the 1982 United Nations Convention on the Law of the Sea ("UNCLOS") **[Basic Document 4.20]**, treaties to which both Norway and the Russian Federation are party—you wonder whether this fact is fully appreciated by those who determine policy in

---

e. For comment, see Discussion Note/Question 3 in "Concluding Notes/Questions" at the end of this chapter.

f. Sometimes, indeed, treaties of very long-standing, as evidenced in the 1957 *Lake Lanoux Arbitration* between France and Spain, for example, which arguably established the principle that a State has the duty to give notice when its actions may impair the environmental interests of another State but which turned on the interpretation of a treaty negotiated 100 years earlier! *See Lake Lanoux Arbitration*, 12 U.N.R.I.A.A. 281 (1957) (citing the Treaty of Bayonne of Dec. 1, 1856). *See also* the 1929 *Case Relating to the Territorial Juris-*

diction of the International Commission of the River Oder, P.C.I.J. (ser. A) No. 23, at 5 (Sept. 10) (interpreting the 1919 Versailles Peace Treaty to require equality for all riparian States in the whole course of a navigable internationalized river) and the 1937 *Diversions of Water from the Meuse Case*, P.C.I.J. (ser. A/B) No. 70, at 4 (June 28) (interpreting an 1863 treaty as authorizing States freedom of action in their own territory provided they do not endanger the physical well-being of their neighbors). Each of these cases is excerpted or summarized as **[Basic Documents 8.1, 8.2 and 8.3]**.

Moscow, and, if so, how they have been able to rationalize their behavior in light of them. Taking no chances, you decide to explore the nature, meaning, and significance of treaties further, and, in particular, the extent to which they give international law shape and substance.

1. THE IMPORTANCE OF TREATIES

PETER MALANCSUK, AKEHURST'S MODERN INTRODUCTION TO
INTERNATIONAL LAW 36–37 (7th Rev. ed. 1997).

Treaties are of growing importance in international law.... Modern technology, communications and trade have made states more interdependent than ever before, and more willing to accept rules on a vast range of problems of common concern—extradition of criminals, safety regulations for ships and aircraft, economic aid, copyright, standardization of road signs, protection of foreign investment, environmental issues, and so on. * * * Treaties are the major instrument of co-operation in international relations, and co-operation often involves a change in the relative positions of the states involved (for example, rich countries give money to poor countries). Treaties, therefore, are often an instrument of change—a point which is forgotten by those who regard international law as essentially a conservative force.

MYRES S. McDOUGAL ET AL., THE INTERPRETATION OF AGREEMENTS
AND WORLD PUBLIC ORDER 3–5 (1967).

Even in a community which aspires only to minimum public order, in the sense of the prevention and repression of unauthorized violence, agreements are of central importance: agreements, explicit and implicit, are indispensable for establishing a stability in peoples' expectations which lessens predispositions for arbitrary resort to violence. In a community which projects, beyond minimum order, the goals of an optimum public order, in the sense of the greatest production and widest sharing of all human values, agreements assume an even greater significance. In such a community agreements serve both to secure that values are shaped and shared more by persuasion than coercion and to organize initiatives for the effective employment of resources in the maximum production and distribution of valued social outcomes.

The important role of agreements in the most comprehensive contemporary community of [humankind] relates, thus, to both minimum order and optimum order. It is by agreement most broadly conceived—that is, when agreement is conceived to include the whole flow of peoples' collaborative behavior—that the effective participants in earth-space power processes establish an overall "constitutive process"—identifying authoritative decision-makers, projecting fundamental community objectives, affording structure of authority, providing bases of power in authority and other values, legitimizing or condemning different strategies in persuasion and coercion, and allocating competence among effective participants over different authority functions and value interactions for the maintenance of a modest minimum order. It is by agreement, further, when agreement is no less broadly conceived, that the established decision-makers perform the important authority function of prescribing, of "legislating," general community policies about the detailed activities which comprise world social process in pursuit of all values. It is by agreement also, when the basic constitutive process of the general community is appropriately maintained, that the many different participants in the world social process—territorially organized communities, international governmental organizations, political parties, pressure groups, private associations, and individuals express their creative initiatives and organize their base values to get on with the world's work in producing and distributing new values.

Given this important role of agreements in contemporary earthspace public order, the urgent need for appropriate general community procedures and principles to facilitate the making and application of agreements can scarcely require elaboration. The urgency of this need can, further, be expected to accelerate in proportion as the interdependencies of peoples accelerate in the emerging new ... era, with both its threats of potentially comprehensive destruction and its promises of a productivity in all values hitherto beyond fantasy.

Geoffrey Palmer, *New Ways to Make International Environmental Law* 86 AM. J. INT'L L. 259, 262– 63 (1992).

[T]he proliferation of international [environmental] agreements has been enormous. There are more than a hundred multilateral [environmental] instruments in force, many of which were negotiated since the [1972] Stockholm Declaration [of the United Nations Conference on the Human Environment] [**Basic Document 1.12**]. The UNEP[g] register listed 152 as of May 1991.[h] In the years since the Stockholm Declaration, there have been some prodigious achievements in the negotiation of conventions dealing with global environmental problems. The United Nations Convention on the Law of the Sea [**Basic Document 4.20**] is an obvious example.... The many famous victories include instruments on long-range transboundary pollution, notification and assistance regarding nuclear accidents, endangered species, and the movement and disposal of hazardous waste. The [1985] Vienna Convention for the Protection of the Ozone Layer [**Basic Document 3.14**] and its progeny amount to perhaps the most substantial achievement of all.

Many of these instruments were stimulated by the activities of UNEP, which has launched various initiatives to develop new policies: action plans, a multitude of soft law instruments and framework conventions. UNEP's Montevideo plan set out a comprehensive program for the progressive development of international environmental law that, in 1991, is in the course of being revised for the next ten years.

While the number of instruments is impressive, and some of them will have slowed down [environmental] degradation, it cannot be assumed that they have led to an improvement in the overall situation. A strong argument can be made that, during the time these instruments were being developed, the environmental situation in the world became worse and is deteriorating further.... Furthermore, many international agreements do not necessarily mean many ratifications. Frequently, there appears to be a long lag in securing widespread ratification because of insufficient incentives for nations

---

g. I.e., the United Nations Environment Programme, headquartered in Nairobi, Kenya.

h. More than 135 of these instruments are reprinted in 5 Weston.

to sign up.... Nor is there any institutional mechanism to provide nations with incentives to comply when they have ratified. Moreover, ratification itself says nothing about whether the agreed standards are being observed. In many instances monitoring is difficult; in some instances it is simply not being done....

2. DEFINITION, NATURE, AND SIGNIFICANCE OF TREATIES

STARKE'S INTERNATIONAL LAW 397–98, 401 (I. Shearer 11th ed. 1994).

A treaty may be defined, in accordance with the definition adopted in article 2 of the [1969 Vienna Convention on the Law of Treaties] **[Basic Document 1.7]**, as an agreement whereby two or more states establish or seek to establish a relationship between themselves governed by international law. So long as an agreement between states is attested, provided that it is not one governed by domestic national law, and provided that it is intended to create a legal relationship, any kind of instrument or document, or any oral exchange between states involving undertakings[,] may constitute a treaty, irrespective of the form or circumstances of its conclusion....

* * *

The form in which treaties are concluded does not in any way affect their binding character. To take an extreme illustration of this principle it is not even necessary that a treaty be in writing.[i] An oral declaration in the nature of a promise made by the Minister of Foreign Affairs of one country to the Minister of Foreign Affairs of another and in a matter within his or her competence and authority may be as binding as a formal written treaty. International law does not as yet require established forms for treaties, and here content and substance are of more importance.

Treaties go under a variety of names, some of which indicate a difference in procedure or a greater or a lesser degree of formality. Thus , besides the term "treaty" itself, the following titles have been given: (1) *Convention*. (2) *Protocol*. (3) *Agreement*. (4) *Arrangement*. (5) *Procès-Verbal*. (6) *Statute*. (7) *Covenant*. (8) *Declaration*. (9) *Modus Vivendi*. (10) *Exchange of Notes (or of Letters)*. (11) *Final Act*. (12) *General Act*.... As to the term "treaty" itself, this tends to be given to formal agreements relative to peace, alliance, or the cession of territory, or some other fundamental matter.

DAVID H. OTT, PUBLIC INTERNATIONAL LAW IN THE MODERN WORLD 23–24 (1987).

Types of treaties. Treaties may be either *bilateral* (between only two parties) or *multilateral* (between more than two parties).

Nature of treaties. A treaty may serve in effect as an international contract between two states, or it may be what will be called here a "law-making" treaty, or it may very rarely have a legislative effect.

i. *But see* article 2(1)(a) of the 1969 Vienna Convention on the Law of Treaties [Basic **Document 1.7**].

Contractual treaties. Some writers (*e.g.* Sir Gerald Fitzmaurice) have suggested that treaties are strictly speaking sources of obligation rather than sources of law. That is, treaties of the kind intended do not establish a regime of legal principles and rules against which the conduct of the parties can be measured, but rather simply state the mutual obligations which the parties have undertaken to perform. Treaties which have this character may properly be called "contractual" by analogy to contracts in private law.

"Law-making" treaties. "Law-making" treaties are concerned with establishing general norms or overall legal regimes in accordance with which the parties to such a treaty agree to order their conduct and relations with each other.

Whereas the operative effect of a contractual agreement may come to an end when the parties have done (or failed to do) certain specified things, a law-making treaty may involve an open-ended commitment to a certain legal regime without regard to the parties' performance of reciprocal obligations. * * * The U.N. Charter [**Basic Document 1.3**], as regards the members of the organization, ... functions as a constitutional and law-making treaty whereby, for example, the members have general obligations to the international community not to disrupt international peace and security as well as bilateral obligations to each other in that regard.

"Legislative" treaties. Although there is no reason in principle why states should not establish law-making treaties for themselves, there is an objection in principle to what we are calling here "legislative" treaties, *i.e.*, treaties concluded by some states which purport to determine law and obligations incumbent upon other states that are not parties.

Customary international law[j] and Article 34 of the Vienna Convention [**Basic Document 1.7**] adopt the position that in general a treaty does not create obligations or rights for a third state without its consent. The effect of this would be that there are no legislative treaties in the sense described, but occasionally suggestions are nevertheless made that certain treaties are in fact legislative.

Lord McNair, for example, argued that there could be "dispositive" treaties creating or affecting territorial rights and effectively imposing legal consequences on third parties, and "constitutive or semi-legislative" treaties establishing international legal regimes of one kind or another.

In 1920 a commission of jurists appointed by the League of Nations to consider the legal position regarding the Aaland Islands, lying at the mouth of the Gulf of Bothnia between Sweden and Finland, concluded that a treaty of 1856 created a special international status for the islands such that every interested state (whether party to the 1856 treaty or not) had the right to insist upon compliance with the treaty provisions.

In the *Reparation for Injuries Suffered in the Service of the United Nations Case* (1949),[k] the World Court held that the U.N. Charter created the U.N. as an entity possessing "objective international personality" such that Israel, though not a member of the U.N. at the relevant time, was obliged to

---

j. *See infra* Section B of this chapter, at 98.   **k.**   1949 I.C.J. 174 (Advisory Opinion).

acknowledge the U.N.'s existence and pay it damages for the assassination of the U.N.'s representative in Jerusalem by Jewish terrorists.

Professor Hans Kelsen has gone further and suggested that the Charter imposes general obligations on non-members by virtue of Article 2(6), which requires the U.N. to "ensure" that states which are not members of the United Nations act in accordance with the organisation's principles. Professor Kelsen himself call this a "revolutionary" application of the Charter, and precisely for that reason it has been strongly contested by many writers.

HANS KELSEN, PRINCIPLES OF INTERNATIONAL LAW 454–56 (R. Tucker 2d Rev. ed. 1966).

[B]y concluding a treaty the contracting states apply a norm of customary international law—the rule *pacta sunt servanda* (treaties must be, or ought to be, observed, that is, have binding force)—and at the same time create a norm of international law, the norm which presents itself as the treaty obligation of one or all of the contracting parties, and as the treaty right of the other or the others. Legal obligations and legal rights are always the function of a legal norm determining the behavior of an individual. The term "norm" designates the objective phenomenon whose subjective reflections are obligation and right. The statement that the treaty has "binding force" means nothing but that the treaty is or creates a norm establishing obligations and rights of the contracting parties. Thus the treaty has a law-applying and at the same time a law-creating character. It has a law-applying character because every conclusion of a treaty is the application of the rule of general international law *pacta sunt servanda*; it has a law-creating function because every treaty constitutes obligations and rights that, prior to the conclusion of the treaty, had not yet existed, obligations and rights which come into existence by the treaty.

MORTON A. KAPLAN & NICHOLAS DEB. KATZENBACH, THE POLITICAL FOUNDATIONS OF INTERNATIONAL LAW 239–40 (1961).

In the view of legal scholars, the "law of treaties" is largely derived from general principles of contract common to the various domestic legal systems. The consensual approach to international law promotes this analytical method. So, too, does the fact that most treaties are formally bilateral arrangements between two states, rather than general "legislation" for the international community. Many such arrangements are cast in the form, and perhaps even have the substance, of mutual advantage and reciprocal rights, thus promoting a "bargain" concept characteristic of a contractual prototype. But it is sobering to remember, too, that the parties to these "contracts" are political entities, represented by governments subject to the vicissitudes of politics, and that they double as international legislators. The contract analysis can be overdone, for there may be overriding considerations which demonstrate that it is no longer in the interest of the community as a whole to insist on literal compliance with a particular agreement, or situations where it is not possible politically for a government to honor its international commitments. It is certainly unrealistic now, and even yesterday, to think of the international community as little more than a series of bilateral arrangements among various participants. * * * [T]reaties are almost always something more than, or different from a contractual arrangement. And the legislative analogy helps us to see why this is true.

RICHARD B. BILDER, MANAGING THE RISKS OF INTERNATIONAL AGREEMENT 4–11 (1981).

International agreements are typically used to establish exchange or cooperative relationships between or among nations, based on reciprocity. They will occasionally, however, be used to serve other purposes as well, such as to communicate foreign policy positions, convey threats, encourage the growth of international institutions, achieve propaganda objectives, lay a basis for future bargaining, or accomplish primarily internal purposes.... Collectively, these agreements establish an extensive and intricate network of cooperation on a wide variety of subjects, ranging from the broad concerns embraced in the United Nations Charter **[Basic Document 1.3]**, Charter of the Organization of American States,[1] or International Covenants on Human Rights **[Basic Documents 7.13 & 7.14]**, to the narrower and more specialized problems dealt with in agreements on radio frequencies, oil pollution, control of narcotics, fisheries, or uniform weights and measures.

In the last analysis, of course, international agreements are only pieces of paper and nations can and on occasion do violate their agreements. But agreements are very special pieces of paper, which serve to reinforce the expectations of their parties by drawing upon deeply and widely held human norms, developed over millennia of social experience, supporting the sanctity of solemnly made promises. There is ample evidence that nations generally take their agreements very seriously, treat them as real commitments, and do not enter into them lightly. Indeed, if nations did not believe international agreements were useful and effective, they would not bother to enter into so many of them and would enter into them with less care and deliberation than they usually do....

The various factors which influence nations to observe their treaty obligations have often been noted. First, since cooperative agreements are consensual, a nation will not usually enter into such an agreement unless it believes that the agreement is in its interest and intends to comply with it; thus, if for no other reason, a nation will normally perform its part of the bargain because it wants reciprocal performance by its treaty partner. Second, nations share a common interest in maintaining the usefulness of the treaty device as a way of ensuring stable expectations and will not lightly impair the integrity of this device. Third, most nations and government officials feel a normative sense of obligation to prove trustworthy and keep their word and will not want to be thought of as untrustworthy or "cheaters." [Louis] Henkin points out that "[e]very nation's foreign policy depends substantially on its 'credit'—on maintaining the expectation that it will live up to international mores and obligations. Considerations of 'honor,' 'prestige,' 'leadership,' 'influence,' 'reputation,' which figure prominently in government decisions, often weigh in favor of observing law. Nations generally desire a

1.   119 U.N.T.S. 3, 1 Weston I.B. 14).

reputation for principled behavior, for propriety and respectability."[5] Fourth, nations and their officials have a very practical stake in maintaining a reputation for credibility and living up to their commitments; if they break their treaties, other nations will be less willing to enter into further agreements with them. As [Thomas] Schelling comments, "[w]hat makes many agreements enforceable is only the recognition of future opportunities for agreement that will be eliminated if mutual trust is not created and maintained and whose value outweighs the monetary gain from cheating in the present instance."[6] Fifth, nations will ... be concerned with possible retaliation of the imposition of sanctions by its treaty partner or other nations or international organizations in the event it fails to comply with its obligations. Finally, there is much to suggest that once a nation concludes an agreement, political and bureaucratic inertia alone tend to induce compliance. Bureaucrats are creatures of law and will generally find it more comfortable simply to keep a treaty than to go to the effort of breaking it. Moreover, as [Abram] Chayes points out in a thoughtful article on arms control agreements, "verification and enforcement mechanisms do not provide the only forces operating to insure [sic] compliance, and probably not the most important ones. An agreement that is adopted by a modern bureaucratic government will be backed by a broad official consensus generated by the negotiating process, and will carry personal and political endorsement across the spectrum of bureaucratic and political leadership. These are exceedingly hard to undo and reverse, the more so since, once the treaty goes into effect, they are reinforced by the ponderous inertia of the bureaucracy."[7] [Fred] Iklé similarly notes that "[w]here breach of an agreement necessitates a clear-cut action requiring complicated decisions, democratic governments may encounter institutional obstacles to a violation."[8] In short, a fear that nations enter into international agreements with the idea of cheating or tricking the other side assumes a Machiavellian rationality and flexibility of which most governments are not capable in the real world.

Nonetheless, to say that international agreements usually work does not mean that nations regard them as establishing completely rigid commitments or deal with treaty problems solely in legalistic terms.... [G]overnment officials probably look at questions of treaty obligation and breach more flexibly and in a broader context than traditional legal analysis assumes. For them, an agreement will often be not simply an instrument for creating legal rights and obligations but a multipurpose foreign policy tool, constituting one element in the more complex pattern of their nation's overall foreign policy. In this broader context, other foreign policy objectives will sometimes be more important than ensuring performance of the agreement. Indeed, decisions respecting international agreements will sometimes turn on solely domestic rather than foreign policy considerations; internal political pressures may dictate participation in agreements which otherwise make little sense, or prevent participation in agreements of great potential benefit. Moreover, government officials will recognize that agreements are made with varying

---

5. LOUIS HENKIN, HOW NATIONS BEHAVE—LAW AND FOREIGN POLICY 48 (1968).

6. THOMAS SCHELLING, THE STRATEGY OF CONFLICT 45 (1960).

7. Antonia Chayes, *An Inquiry Into the Working of Arms Control Agreements*, 85 HARV. L. REV. 905, 968 (1972).

8. Fred IKLÉ, HOW NATIONS NEGOTIATE 8 (1964).

degrees of commitment—that some are meant to be taken less seriously than others; that changing expectations and external or domestic circumstances can create pressures for one or more parties which must be pragmatically dealt with if the agreement is not to break; and that treaty disputes are more likely to signal real problems in the balance and fairness of the agreement than to result from attempts to "cheat." Consequently, they will tend to see the obligation to perform agreements in good faith in terms of these realities, to be interpreted and judged not only by the past balance of forces in which the treaty was formed but also by the present and future balance of forces in which it must be implemented. Finally, while legal rights and obligations will affect the perceived legitimacy of the different parties' positions in the event of a dispute, and thus their respective strategies in trying to resolve the dispute, law alone will not necessarily determine either the parties' responses or the eventual outcome. Government officials will be aware that a particular treaty dispute is only one incident in what must inevitably be a continuing relationship with the other nation; in an interdependent world, most countries will have little choice but, sooner or later, to do business with each other. As is often the case in business contract disputes, pressing one's treaty partner unduly, "taking him [sic] to court," or winning the dispute may be poor long-run policy, and accommodation and compromise through negotiation and express or tacit amendment will often appear much more sensible. The net result of these perceptions and tendencies towards accommodation is that in the real world, international agreements, far from creating once-and-for-all expectations and commitments, constantly change and evolve as the circumstances and the parties' expectations change.

CHARLOTTE KU, *Panel on Sources of International Law: Entrenching the Gender Bias, in* CONTEMPORARY INTERNATIONAL LAW ISSUES: OPPORTUNITIES AT A TIME OF MOMENTOUS CHANGE—PROCEEDINGS OF THE SECOND JOINT CONFERENCE OF THE AMERICAN SOCIETY OF INTERNATIONAL LAW AND THE NEDERLANDSE VERENIGING VOOR INTERNATIONAAL RECHT 414, 416–17 (1994).

Most of interstate behaviour regulated by the approximately 40,000 treaties in force as of 1993 has not been examined from a gender perspective. The vast majority of treaties were negotiated by men; decisions about signing those instruments were made by men; and domestic constitutional processes for ratification or accession usually excluded women, *de facto* if not *de jure*. Treaties are not gender neutral. Indeed, gender bias in treaties may originate in the very nature of the obligation treaties represent. Feminist writer Nancy Hirschmann points out that the concept of a voluntary obligation promotes a structural gender bias "[b]y declaring that all obligations, to be such, must be taken voluntarily, consent theory ignores or denies what women's experience reveals [. . .] that obligations do in fact exist that are not chosen but stem from the history and character of human relationships" ["Freedom, Recognition, and Obligation: A Feminist Approach to Political Theory", 83 *American Political Science Review* 1229 (1989)].

* * *

The scarcity of women taking part in the stages of treaty-making, viz. 1) negotiation, 2) signature, 3) ratification or accession, 4) reservation, 5) entry into force[,] and 6) registration, underscores the likelihood of gender bias in the structure or framework that will emerge from such treaties.

There are no legal requirements about the form of negotiation. The complexity of the treaty dictates whether negotiation will consist of a telephone call from [e.g.] Washington to The Hague between deputy assistant secretaries or a decade-long conference involving 150 governments. The germane issue is whether a gender perspective is accommodated by he people doing the negotiating. With women still a small fraction of those on the front lines of treaty creation and with the participation of women regarded as more appropriate in some subject areas than in others, there is every reason to believe that lack of input from women in this formative stage affects every aspect of treaties.

Those doing the negotiation may have a voice about whether or not a state signs the instrument after the final text has been adopted. Thus the same lack of participation by women is present at this stage. An interesting question is whether women who have leadership roles in negotiations are taken seriously when they make recommendations about signature. In this instance, the voice may be strong or weak depending on the practices of a particular state or who the negotiator is without specific considerations of gender, but the absence of women in these leading roles increases the potential for gender bias.

Each state is free to establish its own processes of ratification. The important question ... is whether these processes are gender biased. We hypothesize that this might occur in two principal ways. First, foreign ministry officials make recommendations to their executives about whether ratification or accession is in the national interest. If the foreign ministry bureaucracy does not reflect gender diversity, this may be reflected in those recommendations. Second, ratification requires the consent of a legislative body which is generally dominated, numerically and organizationally, by males, so the likelihood that women's perspectives will be considered at this stage of the process is also minimal.

There are several significant ways in which reservations may reflect gender bias. On the most obvious level are reservations that explicitly exclude provisions designed to assure equal treatment of men and women. For example, Article III of the 1953 Convention on the Political Rights of Women[n] provides that "women shall be entitled to hold public office and to exercise all public functions, established by national law, on equal terms with men, without any discrimination".... The Kingdom of the Netherlands offered a reservation excluding "succession to the Crown in conformity with relevant constitutional provisions."[o] While some would argue that such reservations have no practical value, they surely have symbolic importance. Reservations and other statements may provide the best way to get an overview of gender bias in treaties.... [They] are likely to reflect deeper convictions within governments and the society as a whole after forces beyond the diplomatic corps have begun to operate. They provide a vehicle whereby domestic political realities emerge that might otherwise be masked by diplomatic rhetoric.

n. 193 U.N.T.S. 135, *reprinted in* 3 Weston   **o.** 790 U.N.T.S. 130.
III.C.9.

We hypothesize that certain treaties that seek to extend rights to women will have trouble garnering the requisite number of parties to enter into force. Political forces within states that have neither signed more ratified such conventions may work behind the scenes to try to prevent entry into force because of the pressures that such treaties might bring to bear on domestic policy. For example, if a treaty assuring women's rights and access to abortion were signed, one can be certain that "pro-life" forces in the US would do all they could to see that the US did not accede to such a treaty. Conversely, there may be domestic or international political pressures encouraging a state to sign a treaty, although a sufficient consensus to ensure its ratification does not exist. A government may nevertheless choose to reap the benefits of favourable press and public reaction to signature in the full knowledge that decision-makers have no intention of proceeding with ratification.

One of the principal reasons for the [UN Charter] provision to register treaties with the UN (Article 102) **[Basic Document 1.3]** was to discourage secret diplomacy. But it is entirely possible that states may wish that certain of their treaties, probably including those that exacerbate gender inequality, are not widely available. We know that UN members are not very reliable when it comes to registering their treaties; treaties that were never registered with the League of Nations of the UN may make up more than one third of all treaties signed since 1920. The possibility of public scrutiny of treaty obligations may do little at the outset to eliminate unacceptable practices, but the full disclosure of all treaties may ultimately work to change undesirable behaviour, including that which discriminates against women.

3. CONCLUSION AND ACCEPTANCE OF TREATIES

Starke's International Law 409–18 (I. Shearer 11th ed. 1994).

(2) Negotiation and adoption

Negotiations concerning a treaty are conducted either through discussions in the case of bilateral treaties or by a diplomatic Conference, the more usual procedure when a multilateral treaty is to be adopted. In both cases the delegates remain in touch with their governments, they have with them preliminary instructions which are not communicated to the other parties, and at any stage they may consult their governments and, if necessary, obtain fresh instructions. As a matter of general practice, before appending their signature to the final text of the treaty, delegates do obtain fresh instructions to sign the instrument whether with or without reservations.

The procedure at diplomatic Conferences runs to a standard pattern. Apart from Steering Committees, Legal and Drafting Committees are appointed at an early stage to receive and review the draft provisions proposed by the various delegations. Usually, too, the Conference appoints a prominent delegate to act as rapporteur in order to assist the Conference in its deliberations. Besides the formal public sessions of the Conference, many parleys are conducted in the "corridors", in hotel rooms, and at special dinners and functions. The results of these appear in due course in the decisions reached by the Conference.

Article 9, paragraph 2 of the Vienna Convention [on the Law of Treaties] **[Basic Document 1.7]** provides that the adoption of a treaty text at an international conference is to take place by the vote of two-thirds of the states present and voting, unless by the same majority these states decide to apply a different rule.

It should be mentioned that in respect of certain subjects at least, the procedure of adoption of multilateral instruments by diplomatic Conferences has been replaced by the method of their adoption by the organs of international institutions; for example, by—among others—the United Nations General Assembly, the World Health Assembly, and the Assembly of the International Civil Aviation Organization [ICAO]. The Conventions adopted by such Assembly are opened for signature or acceptance by member or non-member states.

* * *

(3) Authentication, signature and exchange of instruments

When the final draft of the treaty has been agreed upon, the instrument is ready for signature. The text may be made public for a certain period before signature.... The act of signature is usually a most formal matter, even in the case of bilateral treaties. As to multilateral conventions, signature is generally effected at a formal closing session (*séance de clôture*) in the course of which each delegate steps up to a table and signs on behalf of the head of state or government by whom they were appointed.[p]

Unless there is an agreement to dispense with signature, this is essential for a treaty, principally because it serves to authenticate the text. The rule, as stated in article 10 of the Vienna Convention, is that the text may be authenticated by such procedure as is laid down in the treaty itself, or as is agreed to by the negotiating states, or in the absence of such agreed procedure, by signature, signature ad referendum, initialling, or by incorporation in the Final Act of the conference. In practice, also, the text of an instrument may be authenticated by the resolution of an international organisation. If a treaty is signed, it is important that the signature should be made by each of the delegates at the same time and place, and in the presence of each other. Furthermore, the date of the treaty is usually taken to be the date on which it was signed.

* * *

It is a common practice to open a convention [or treaty] for signature by certain states until a certain date after the date of the formal session of signature. Generally, this period does not exceed nine months. The object is to obtain as many parties to the convention as possible, but inasmuch as new signatories can only be allowed with the consent of the original signatories, a special clause to this effect must be inserted in the convention. A current practice is to open a convention for signature to all members of the United Nations and the specialised agencies, to all parties to the Statute of the International Court of Justice [**Basic Document 1.4**], and to any other state invited by the [U.N.] General Assembly. During the period mentioned, each state may sign at any time, but after the expiration of the period no further

p. Sometimes not merely a delegate but a   *Starke's International Law, infra.*
Head of State will sign a treaty. *See, e.g.,*

signatures are allowed and a non-signatory state desiring to become a party must accede or adhere to the convention but cannot ratify, inasmuch as it has not signed the instrument. . . .

A further expedient has been, by the so-called *acceptance formula clause*, to open an instrument for an indefinite time for: (a) signature, without reservation as to acceptance; (b) signature subject to, and followed by later acceptance; and (c) acceptance simpliciter, leaving states free to become bound by any one of these three methods. The term "acceptance", used in this clause, has crept into recent treaty terminology to denote the act of becoming a party to a treaty by adherence of any kind, in accordance with a state's municipal constitutional law. The principal object of this clause was indeed to meet difficulties which might confront a potential state party under its municipal constitutional rules relative to treaty approval.

* * *

Effect of signature

The effect of signature of a treaty depends on whether or not the treaty is subject to ratification, acceptance, or approval.

If the treaty is subject to ratification, acceptance, or approval, signature means no more than that the delegates have agreed upon a text and are willing to accept it and refer it to their governments for such action as those governments may choose to take in regard to the acceptance or rejection of the treaty. It may also indicate an intention on the part of a government to make a fresh examination of the question dealt with by the treaty with a view to putting the treaty into force. In the absence of an express term to that effect, there is no binding obligation on a signatory state to submit the treaty to the national legislature for action or otherwise. On the other hand, it is laid down in [Article 18 of] the Vienna Convention that, where a treaty is subject to ratification, acceptance, or approval, signatory states are under an obligation of good faith to refrain from acts calculated to defeat the object of the treaty until they have made their intention clear of not becoming parties. . . .

Where a treaty is subject to ratification, acceptance or approval, it is sometimes expressly stipulated in the treaty or in some related exchange of notes that, pending ratification, acceptance, or approval, the instrument is to operate on a provisional basis as from the date of signature. . . .

If the treaty is not subject to ratification, acceptance, or approval, or is silent on this point, the better opinion is that, in the absence of contrary provision, the instrument is binding as from signature. . . . Also many treaties relating to minor or technical matters, generally bearing the titles "Agreement", "Arrangement" or "Procès-Verbal", are simply signed but not ratified, and operate as from the date signature is appended.

* * *

(4) Ratification

The next stage is that the delegates who signed the treaty or convention refer it back to their governments for approval, if such further act of confirmation be expressly or impliedly necessary.

In theory, ratification is the approval by the head of state or the government of the signature appended to the treaty by the duly appointed plenipotentiaries. In modern practice, however, it has come to possess more significance than a simple act of confirmation, being deemed to represent the formal declaration by a state of its consent to be bound by a treaty. So in article 2 of the Vienna Convention, ratification was defined to mean "the international act ... whereby a state establishes on the international plane its consent to be bound by a treaty". Consistently with this, ratification is not held to have retroactive effect, so as to make the treaty obligatory from the date of signature.

* * *

Ratification and municipal constitutional law

The development of constitutional systems of government under which various organs other than the head of state are given a share in the treaty-making power has increased the importance of ratification. At the same time in each country the procedure followed in this regard differs. For instance, often states will insist on parliamentary approval or confirmation of a treaty although the treaty expressly provides that it operates as from signature, whereas other states follow the provisions of the treaty and regard it as binding them without further steps being taken.

* * *

Some treaties make signature subject to "acceptance" or "approval"; these terms may then denote a simplified form of ratification. In fact, in article 2 of the Vienna Convention, "acceptance" and "approval" have received the same definition as ratification, while the provisions of article 14 as to when ratification imports consent to be bound by a treaty apply mutatis mutandis to acceptance and approval.

Absence of duty to ratify

The power of refusing ratification is deemed to be inherent in state sovereignty, and accordingly at international law there is ... [no] duty to ratify a treaty. Furthermore, there is no obligation other than one of ordinary courtesy to convey to other states concerned a statement of the reasons for refusing to ratify.

* * *

Obligation not to defeat the object and purpose of a treaty prior to its entry into force

The rule stated by article 18 of the Vienna Convention [not to defeat the object and purpose of a treaty following signature or expression of consent to be bound but prior to the treaty's entry into force] is regarded as one of customary international law.... The effect of this rule is not to make an unratified treaty, or one not yet in force, in all respects binding, for that would be to deprive those steps of meaning. Rather, a state is bound by good faith not to take up or persist in an action or posture fundamentally at variance with the treaty until it has definitively disavowed its intention to proceed to the ratification of the treaty that it has signed.

Exchange or deposit of ratifications

Unless the treaty itself otherwise provides, an instrument of ratification has no effect in finally establishing consent to be bound by the treaty until the exchange or deposit, as the case may be, of ratifications, or at least until some notice of ratification is given to the other state or states concerned, or to the depositary of the treaty, is so agreed[q].... The same rule applies to an instrument of acceptance or approval.

In the case of bilateral treaties, ratifications are exchanged by the states parties concerned and each instrument is filed in the archives of the Treaty Department of each state's Foreign Office. Usually a Procès-Verbal is drawn up to record and certify the exchange.

[This] method of exchange is not appropriate for the ratification of multilateral treaties. Such a treaty usually provides for the deposit of all ratifications in a central headquarters such as the Foreign Office of the state where the treaty was signed....

(5) Accessions and adhesions

In practice, when a state has not signed a treaty it can only accede or adhere to it. According to present practice, a non-signatory state may accede or adhere even before the treaty enters into force. * * * No precise form is prescribed by international law for an instrument of accession, although generally it is in the same form as an instrument of ratification. A simple notification of intention to participate in a treaty may be sufficient.

* * *

(6) Entry into force

The entry into force of a treaty depends upon its provisions, or upon what the contracting states have otherwise agreed[r] .... As already mentioned, many treaties become operative on the date of their signature, but where ratification, acceptance, or approval is necessary, the general rule of international law is that the treaty concerned comes into force only after the exchange or deposit of ratifications, acceptances, or approvals by all the states signatories. Multilateral treaties now usually make entry into force dependent on the deposit of a prescribed number of ratifications and like consents to be bound—usually from six to about thirty-five. Sometimes, however, a precise date for entry into force is fixed without regard to the number of ratifications received. Sometimes, also, the treaty is to come into operation only on the happening of a certain event....

Editors' Note

When states signal their consent to be bound by a treaty, they sometimes also signal a wish to qualify that consent; they indicate that they accept the treaty in general but that, for constitutional or other reasons, they have reservations regarding certain of its provisions. The question then arises: what is the effect of a unilateral attempt to modify a treaty? In Public International Law in the Modern World 192 (1987), David H. Ott addresses the issue as follows:

q. *See* the Vienna Convention on the Law of Treaties [**Basic Document 1.7**], art. 16.

r. *Id.*, art. 24(1).

With a bilateral treaty an attempt to do this by a reservation would destroy the parties' original understanding of the agreement and would amount to a counter-offer and a reopening of negotiations. The other party would then accept or reject the reservation as, in effect, part of a new agreement. If the reservation were not acceptable, the treaty would fail.

In the case of a multilateral treaty the situation is more complicated. If one state makes a reservation, some of the existing parties may accept it and consider that the reserving state is a party to the treaty, while other existing parties may reject the reservation and consider that the reserving state is not a party.

The result would be that the applicability of the treaty's provisions would be in doubt and there would be disagreement about which states were parties and which were not. This could present a particular problem with regard to the treaty's coming into force. Most treaties require the adherence of a specified number of states before that can happen. If the adherence of some reserving states were in doubt, it might prove impossible to determine whether or when the treaty has entered into force, with serious consequences for the parties and the international community in general.

The traditional response to this problem was to assume that a multilateral treaty was, in effect, a contract between all the existing parties on one side and the reserving state on the other. The choice for the reserving state would then be to accept without reservation what they had already agreed or alternatively to persuade them *all* to change their agreement in line with the reservation. This response was said to emphasize the *integrity of the convention*, that is, the integrated wholeness of the text, which was not to be undermined by reservations. In this view, unless all the existing parties to a multilateral treaty agreed to a reservation, the attempted adherence of the reserving state would be null and void.

The problem usually came to a head at the time when the reserving state communicated its qualified adherence to the *depositary*, the state of organisation designated in the treaty as responsible for keeping records of the treaty and maintaining the official list of the parties to it. Should the depositary enter the reserving state's name on that list or not?

This question found its way to the World Court by way of a U.N. General Assembly request for an advisory opinion on whether reservations were permitted to avoid the compulsory jurisdiction of the Court under the 1948 Convention on the Prevention and Punishment of the Crime of Genocide [**Basic Document 7.10**]. The Court, minimizing the contractual (as opposed to legislative) character of the Genocide Convention, rejected the contention that the parties to the Convention could stipulate reservations to any provision they disliked. Otherwise, the Court concluded, state parties could act in "complete disregard of the object and purpose of the Convention." *Reservations to the Convention on the Prevention and Punishment of the Crime of Genocide*, 1951 I.C.J. 15, 24 (Advisory Opinion). In this conclusion, the Court ruled consistently with Articles 2(d) and 19–21 of the 1969 Vienna Convention on the Law of Treaties [**Basic Document 1.7**] which indicate the generally accepted view that reservations are permissible except when (a) they are prohibited by the treaty, (b) they are not included among expressly authorized reservations, and (c) they are otherwise incompatible with the object and purpose of the treaty.

A "reservation," however, is not the only device used to signal a qualification to treaty consent. In addition, State parties resort to "understandings" and "declarations." In *Reservations to Multilateral Treaties: The Goal of Universality,* 71 Iowa L. Rev. 295, 298–300 (1985), Catherine L. Piper distinguishes these "treaty-qualifying" communications:

> The three major classifications of treaty-qualifying unilateral statements are reservations, understandings, and declarations. A reservation is a formal declaration that acts to limit or modify the effect of the treaty in application to the reserving state. A reservation is external to the text of the treaty and is an attempt to alter the negotiated package. Because reservations are made outside of the treaty negotiations, their amendment to the multilateral treaty may conflict with the original text of the treaty. The ultimate effect of the reservation will depend on the practice or rule of reservations applied and the existence or nonexistence of special provisions within the treaty governing inclusion and effect of reservations.

> The term "understanding" is used to designate a statement not intended to alter or limit the effect of the treaty, but rather to set forth a state's interpretation or explanation of a treaty provision. In practice, understandings are sometimes used to provide a memorandum of the nation's interpretation at the time of signing in case of future judicial or arbitral proceedings.

> A "declaration" is a unilateral statement of policy or opinion that, like an understanding, is not intended to alter or limit any provision of the treaty. It is considered to have the least effect on the original treaty text and is used primarily to articulate a signatory's purpose, position, or expectation, concerning the treaty in question.

> The use of the labels "reservation," "understanding," and "declaration" have created much confusion on both the international level and the domestic level. The problem arises because the label attached is not conclusive as to the substantive effect the statement has on the treaty. This is especially evident when dealing with understandings. A state may condition acceptance of a treaty on a specific interpretation, which may later be found contrary to the plain language of the treaty of intended meaning of other parties. As such, the understanding in effect alters or modifies the original treaty and amounts to a reservation. If a state were allowed to determine conclusively the treatment of a unilateral statement by attaching a label, the statement could alter the multilateral treaty and negate the application of reservation law. It is necessary, therefore, to distinguish qualifying statements by comparing the substance or contents of the statement with the original text of the treaty. If the qualifying statement in application alters the legal effect of the treaty, the statement should be considered a reservation and be governed by the applicable reservation law.

The Vienna Convention **[Basic Document 1.7]** has attempted to clarify the labeling confusion by formulating a broad definition of reservations that tends to focus on the substance of the statement rather than the label attached: " 'reservation' means a unilateral statement, however phrased or named, made by a State ... whereby it purports to exclude or modify the legal effect of certain provisions of the treaty in their application to that State.' "

The Vienna Convention rule includes all unilateral statements, regardless of their labels, under the term "reservation" if the substantive content of the statement alters the effect of the treaty. The determination of whether a statement is a reservation is generally left to the other treaty signatories. The law of reservations, therefore, must be viewed as one governing all unilateral qualifying statements because the interpretative effect of any one statement may vary with the evaluating party.

4. AMENDMENT OF TREATIES

As time passes and circumstances change, reasons for altering agreements mount. Treaties are no less vulnerable in this respect than other agreements. Accordingly, many treaties, both bilateral and multilateral, contain provisions that establish a procedure for their amendment. In the case of bilateral treaties, typically either party may propose an amendment, but unanimity of agreement between both parties must be obtained for the proposed amendment to be adopted. In the case of multilateral treaties, typically any one or more of the parties may initiate the procedure established for amendment and usually only majority approval of the proposed amendment (commonly two-thirds or three-fourths majority) is required for it to be adopted. In each case, however, the amendments usually enter into force only after they have been accepted or ratified by *all* the contracting parties. Articles 39 and 40 of the 1969 Vienna Convention on the Law of Treaties **[Basic Document 1.7]**, requiring amendments to be concluded and entered into force in the same way as treaties themselves, set out the generally accepted rules regarding these matters.

This traditional process of modifying treaties by negotiating and concluding new agreements has been found to respond not quickly enough to more or less fast changing circumstances—as in the discovery, for recent example, of a more rapidly depleting ozone layer than had been anticipated in the emission-curbing schedules set forth in the 1987 Montreal Protocol on Substances that Deplete the Ozone Layer **[Basic Document 3.18]**. Though adding much-needed rigor to the 1985 Vienna Convention for the Protection of the Ozone Layer **[Basic Document 3.14]**, the Montreal Protocol has itself modified by numerous agreements. In his famous treatise on the law of treaties, Lord McNair, noting the complexity of highly technical multilateral treaties, anticipated this problem when he observed that we are here addressing "one of the weakest spots in the now existing system of States." A. McNair, The Law of Treaties 534 (1961). "[I]t must be admitted," he continued, "that no national society which is not equipped with legislative and administrative machinery for effecting changes could hope to hold together for long. International society is clearly groping its way towards the creation of some escape from the present effect of the rule requiring consent of all the parties affected by a change...." *Id.* Earlier, in *International Legislation*, 19 Iowa L. Rev. 177 (1934), Lord McNair noted that some technical multilateral treaties contained provisions by which, within certain narrowly defined limits, the parties had agreed to permit treaty modifications by majority vote.

Today, echoing this history, an increasing number of treaties, especially environmental treaties, establish a bifurcated norm-modifying procedure, pursuant to which the fundamental obligations enunciated in the treaties are made subject to the traditional, rather difficult amendment process, while administrative and technical details are permitted to be altered informally and therefore quickly; a general framework is set forth in the treaty proper which is supported by administrative and technical annexes that can be modified easily without amending the "framework treaty." Professor Frederic Kirgis, Jr., has noted this "nontraditional" rule-altering technique in the context of the "constituent instruments" of the International Labour Organization (ILO), the Universal Postal Union (UPU), the World Health Organization (WHO), the International Civil Aviation Organization (ICAO), and the International Maritime Organization (IMO): "The constituent instruments of most specialized agencies contain amendment procedures that bind all members if some fraction—often two-thirds—of the total membership adopts and ratifies the amendment." Frederic L. Kirgis, Jr., *Specialized Law–Making Processes*, in 1 United Nations Legal Order 109, 121 (C. Joyner & O. Schachter eds. 1995). Noting that this norm-modifying "process of prolepsis" (*i.e.*, of providing an answer to an issue in anticipation of a circumstance that makes the answer applicable) has "clear applicability to global environmental problems," Sir Geoffrey Palmer observes favorably that "[t]he proleptic method of avoiding the rule of unanimous consent has already been employed in the environmental sphere in the Montreal Protocol on Substances that Deplete the Ozone Layer of 1987 **[Basic Document 3.18]**. Some little-noticed innovations," he adds, "were made that certainly go beyond the technical and change the rule of unanimous consent in dramatic ways." Sir Geoffrey Palmer, *New Ways to Make International Environmental Law*, 86 Am. J. Int'l L. 259, 274 (1992).

5. TERMINATION OF TREATIES

Most treaties have a limited life span; many are concluded for a limited duration only and state parties always are free to suspend or terminate a treaty at any time by agreement. *See, e.g.*, Articles 54–59 of the 1969 Vienna Convention on the Law of Treaties **[Basic Document 1.7]**. A treaty may cease to operate, however, for reasons other than the agreement of the parties—for example, by virtue of breach, impossibility of performance, change of circumstances, or denunciation and withdrawal, as detailed in Section 3 of the Vienna Convention and as summarized in the readings that follow.

PETER MALANCZUK, AKEHURST'S MODERN INTRODUCTION TO
INTERNATIONAL LAW 142–43 (7th Rev. ed. 1997).

Article 60(1) of the Vienna Convention [on the Law of Treaties] **[Basic Document 1.7]** provides: "A material breach of a bilateral treaty by one of the parties entitles the other to invoke the breach as a ground for terminating the treaty or suspending its operation in whole or in part." The injured state's power to terminate or suspend a treaty is one of the main sanctions for breach of a treaty, but it is not the only one; there is nothing to prevent the injured state claiming compensation instead of, or in addition to, exercising its rights under Article 60(1).

The problem is more complicated if the treaty is multilateral. Obviously, breach by state A cannot entitle state B to denounce the treaty, because that would not be fair to states C, D, E, and so on. Accordingly, Article 60(2) provides:

A material breach of a multilateral treaty by one of the parties entitles:

(a) the other parties by unanimous agreement to suspend the operation of the treaty in whole or in part to terminate it either:

 (i) in the relations between themselves and the defaulting state, or

 (ii) as between all parties;

(b) a party specially affected by the breach to invoke it as a ground for suspending the operation of the treaty in whole or in part in the relations between itself and the defaulting state;

(c) any party other than the defaulting state is to invoke the breach as a ground for suspending the operation of the treaty in whole or in part with respect to itself if the treaty is of such a character that a material breach of its provisions by one party radically changes the position of every party with respect to the further performance of its obligations under the treaty.

An example of the type of treaty contemplated by paragraph 2(c) is a disarmament treaty. Clearly, breach of a disarmament treaty by one party constitutes a very serious threat to each of the other parties. But should this entitle one of the injured parties to create a similar threat to the other injured parties? Would it not be more appropriate to deal with the problem under paragraph 2(a)? It is in any case doubtful whether paragraph 2(c) really reflects customary law.

It is generally agreed that a right to terminate does not arise unless the breach is a material (that is, serious) one. Article 60(3) defines a material breach as "(a) a repudiation of the treaty not sanctioned by the present convention; or (b) the violation of a provision essential to the accomplishment of the object of purpose of the treaty". This definition is defective, because it does not make clear that violation of an essential provision does not constitute a material breach unless it is a serious violation. If a state makes a treaty to deliver 5,000 tons of tin and delivers only 4,999 tons, a literal interpretation of Article 60(3) would imply that the other party would denounce the treaty because of this minor violation of an essential provision—which is repugnant to common sense.

Breach does not automatically terminate a treaty; it merely gives the injured party or parties an option to terminate or suspend the treaty, and, according to Article 45, an injured party loses the right to exercise this option if, after becoming aware of the facts:

(a) it shall have expressly agreed that the treaty ... remains in force or continues in operation, as the case may be; or

(b) it must by reason of its conduct be considered as having acquiesced ... in its [that is, the treaty's] maintenance in force or in operation, as the case may be.

The power of the injured party or parties to terminate or suspend a treaty may also be modified or excluded by the treaty itself.

DAVID H. OTT, PUBLIC INTERNATIONAL LAW IN
THE MODERN WORLD 202–03 (1987).

Termination or suspension because of supervening impossibility of performance. Under Article 60(1) of the Vienna Convention [on the Law of Treaties] **[Basic Document 1.7]** a state may terminate a treaty or withdraw from it if it becomes impossible to perform because of "the permanent disappearance or destruction of an object indispensable for the execution of a treaty". A temporary impossibility is a ground only for suspension of the treaty's operation. But a party may not invoke impossibility of performance for these purposes if the impossibility results from that party's own breach of the treaty or of some other international obligation towards the other parties to the treaty.

Termination or withdrawal because of fundamental change of circumstances. The Vienna Convention in Article 62 gives a limited right to a state to terminate or withdraw from a treaty because the circumstances under which it became a party no longer exist. The fundamental change of circumstances must, however, be one "not foreseen by the parties" and:

(a) the existence of those circumstances must have been an essential basis of the parties' consent to be bound by the treaty; and

(b) the effect of the change must be radically to transform the extent of obligations still to be performed under the treaty.

But termination or withdrawal is not permitted in this situation if the treaty establishes a boundary or if the fundamental change is the result of a breach by the party invoking it as reason for termination or withdrawal.

Suspension of the treaty's operation is also permitted on the same terms as termination or withdrawal.

Behind Article 62 lies a long history in customary international law of what is called the doctrine of *rebus sic stantibus* ("things staying as they are"). The doctrine supposed that it was an implicit provision in many treaties (a *clausula rebus sic stantibus*) that the parties would consider themselves bound by the treaty only so long as the fundamental circumstances that prompted it remained in existence.[s]

---

s. Professor Ott cites the Fisheries Jurisdiction Case (Merits), 1974 I.C.J. 3, noting that the World Court indicated that Article 62 is "in many respects" a codification of customary law.

PETER MALANCZUK, AKEHURST'S MODERN INTRODUCTION
TO INTERNATIONAL LAW 142 (7th Rev. ed. 1997).

Article 56 of the Vienna Convention [**Basic Document 1.7**] provides:

1. A treaty which contains no provision regarding its termination and
    which does not provide for denunciation or withdrawal is not subject
    to denunciation or withdrawal unless:

    (a) it is established that the parties intended to admit the possibility
        of denunciation or withdrawal; or

    (b) a right of denunciation or withdrawal may be implied by the
        nature of the treaty.

2. A party shall give not less than twelve months' notice of its intention
    to denounce or withdraw from a treaty under paragraph 1.

It follows from the wording of Article 56 that a right of denunciation or
withdrawal can never be *implied* if the treaty contains an *express* provision
concerning denunciation, withdrawal, or termination.

It is uncertain to what extent Article 56 reflects customary law; this is
particularly true of paragraph 1(b), which was added to the text of Article 56
at the Vienna conference by 26 votes to 25 with 37 abstentions. The provisions of Article 56 (especially paragraph 1(b)) reflect the views of most British
writers, but many continental writers thought there could never be an implied
right of denunciation or withdrawal under customary international law.
However, in *Nicaragua v. U.S.A.*, the International Court of Justice seems to
have accepted that Article 56 was an accurate statement of customary law.[t]

Treaties of alliance and certain types of commercial treaties are often
cited as the main examples of the kind of treaty in which a right of
denunciation or withdrawal can be inferred from the nature of the treaty,
within the meaning of Article 56(1)(b). A similar inference can also probably
be made in the case of treaties conferring jurisdiction on international courts.[u]

Customary international law requires reasonable notice to be given
whenever an implied right of denunciation or withdrawal is exercised. Article
56(2) adds greater precision by requiring notice of at least twelve months.

6. INTERPRETATION OF TREATIES

LAKSHMAN GURUSWAMY & BRENT HENDRICKS, INTERNATIONAL
ENVIRONMENTAL LAW IN A NUTSHELL 20–24 (1997).

Not unlike other areas of international law, many principles of [interna-
tional environmental law (IEL)] embodied in treaties are vague and nebulous
for a number of reasons. Among the more important of these reasons is that
treaties are drafted, not by gods, but by humans who are unable to anticipate
and provide for every factual or legal contingency that might arise in the
future. To meet unforeseen contingencies, resort is made to abstractions and
concepts of wide scope which almost by definition lack specificity and exacti-
tude, and require interpretation before they can be applied to the facts of a
case. When an unpredicted case arises, the extent to which it might be
covered by existing provisions through interpretation gives rise to contention.

In addition, there is a tendency for drafting conferences to resort to
aspirational and hortatory expression when they cannot agree upon specific

---

t. 1984 I.C.J. 392, at 420.   **u.** *Id.*

obligations. Furthermore, and conversely, when parties to a treaty want to move beyond the aspirational to the obligatory, but are unable to agree on the formulation of such an obligation, they sometimes leave it to be resolved by interpretation on a later occasion.

Treaties are replete with a variety of formulations that do not amount to obligations of effect. These include: aspirational norms; general norms containing inchoate and open-textured obligations; and formulations of rules or principles that codify contentious or competing rules. Illustrations of aspirational and inchoate obligations abound in recent treaties. For example, according to the Climate Change Convention **[Basic Document 3.21]**, parties, according to their "common but differentiated responsibilities" (not defined), shall take climate change considerations into account "to the extent feasible" [art. 4(1)(f)]. The Biodiversity Convention **[Basic Document 6.11]** is choked by obligations of aspiration, such as "as far as possible and as appropriate," [arts. 5,6,7] and in accordance with a party's "particular conditions and capabilities" [art. 6]. The Basel Convention on the Control of Transboundary Movements of Hazardous Wastes and their Disposal (Basel Convention) **[Basic Document 5.6]** . . . requires each party to take "appropriate measures" to minimize the generation of hazardous wastes [art. 4(2)(a)] and also requires that parties manage wastes in an "environmentally sound" manner [art. 4(2)(d)]. The Protocol to the 1979 Convention on Long-Range Transboundary Air Pollution Concerning the Emissions of Nitrogen Oxides or their Transboundary Fluxes **[Basic Document 3.19]** . . . requires parties to "act as soon as possible" in article 2(1) and "without undue delay" in article 7.

While the previous citations serve as examples of aspirational norms and inchoate and open-textured obligations, other provisions embody general duties and competing norms that remain undefined, thus creating difficulties of interpretation. A possible conflict in the way general duties and competing norms are resolved may be found in the Biodiversity Convention and [the United Nations Convention on the Law of the Sea (UNCLOS0) **[Basic Document 4.20]**. The Biodiversity Convention . . . strikes a balance between sovereign rights over natural resources and the duty not to cause transboundary damage in art. 3, but does so somewhat differently to the way the same balance is expressed in article 192 of UNCLOS. . . . Such a divergence obviously creates interpretive problems in arriving at the general obligation and in reconciling the conflicting norm between respective treaties.

Two interconnected questions concerning treaty interpretation require further attention: (1) Who is empowered to interpret a treaty and (2) how or according to what rules is the law interpreted? Interpretation in IEL operates in a manner similar to national legal systems in which the interpretive task is undertaken by courts and judicial tribunals, as well as administrative agencies charged with implementing the statute in question.

International courts include the International Court of Justice, but the ICJ depends on the acquiescence of the parties for its jurisdiction. . . . Judicial or arbitral tribunals created by treaties such as UNCLOS or the Climate Change Convention are also empowered to interpret the law. Interpretation may further be rendered by the declarations of Diplomatic Conferences such as the 1972 Stockholm Conference on the Human Environment, the 1992

United Nations Conference on Environment and Development (UNCED), and the General Assembly of the United Nations. Increasingly, interpretation is made by the institutions created by environmental treaties such as the permanent annual conferences of international regimes or even expert organizations. . . .

The Vienna Convention [on the Law of Treaties] **[Basic Document 1.7]** outlines basic rules of treaty interpretation. Article 31 stipulates that a treaty shall be interpreted in good faith in accordance with the ordinary meaning to be given to the terms of a treaty in their context and in the light of its object and purpose [which is principally to give effect to the intentions of the parties]. Article 32 allows for supplementary means of interpretation where interpretation according to article 31 leaves the meaning ambiguous or obscure, or leads to a result that is manifestly absurd or unreasonable. While these appear to be reasonably objective rules, they are not self-executing and need to be applied by an interpreter. The process of applying the rules creates an unavoidably subjective human element and can result in demonstrable differences of opinion. * * * For example . . . , the Meeting of the Parties under the Montreal Protocol interpreted some of its provisions in an expansive and even non-textual fashion.

Editors' Note

Articles 31 and 32 of the 1969 Vienna Convention on the Law of Treaties **[Basic Document 1.7]**, drafted by the International Law Commission, represent a sharp departure from a once popular view of treaty interpretation previously espoused by, among others, the Institute of International Law[v]— that is, the viewpoint that only the language of a treaty counts, not the "supposed intentions" of the parties, and that therefore a treaty is to be interpreted only according to its words, according to their "plain and natural meaning."[w] Another departure, more radical than that of the International Law Commission and the Vienna Convention that it drafted, is the "policy-oriented and configurative" approach advocated in Myres S. McDougal, Harold A. Lasswell, & James C. Miller, *The Interpretation of Agreements and World Public Order* (1967). Eschewing the views of both the Institute of International Law and the International Law Commission, this controversial but critically acclaimed treatise holds that (a) it is the intentions of the parties—their "genuine shared expectations"—that should, together with overriding community policies, preeminently concern the interpretative enterprise; and (b) that everything that throws light on those expectations (including, obviously, the text of the treaty) should be included in the interpreter's investigations. Thus, because "[t]he communications which constitute an international agreement . . . are functions of a larger [than textual] context" (*id.* at 58), and as such "may be affected by any and all the variables in the process of agreement and its context" (*id.* at 11), the authors refuse to make

v. The Institute of International Law (or Institut de Droit International) is a transnational non-governmental organization founded in Belgium in 1873 for the purpose of developing and codifying international law. Its membership comprises persons chosen as a result of their contributions to the field of international law. It currently is headquartered in Geneva, Switzerland.

w. *See, e.g., Comments of Sir Eric Beckett on the Report of M. H. Lauterpacht (of the Second Commission of the Institute of International Law) on the Interpretation of Treaties,* 43–I ANN. INST. DR. INT'L 437–39 (1950).

the text the exclusive or even near-exclusive indicator of party expectation and community preference. Consequently, they urge the investigation of *all* relevant "pre-outcome" (*i.e.*, negotiation), "outcome" (i.e., text), and "post-outcome" (*i.e.*, subsequent conduct) indices of such intention and preference. The Yale professors do not stop here, however. Proposing a host of "principles of content and procedure" designed to facilitate the fullest possible marshalling of all evidence relevant to party intention and community preference, *and refusing to accept any preordained hierarchy of factual inquiry* (because "[t]he significance of any particular factor may in different contexts vary greatly in relation to other factors"—*id.* at 116), they recommend a series of "goals of interpretation" (including the goal of according the highest possible deference, compatible with other constitutional policies, to the genuine shared expectations of the particular parties) for the purpose of guiding decision-makers through the labyrinths of interpretation and from which they deduce particular policies to fit exact issues so as "to give effect to the goals of a public order of human dignity"[x] (*id.* at 40):

> [O]ur recommended goals of interpretation are based on the fundamental expectation that future events cannot fail to be affected in some degree by any decision outcome. The decision-maker who engages in acts of interpretation is in search of the past and present; but the past and present are pursued as a way of accomplishing a future result. Obviously, decision of the particular case calls for action affecting the future relations of the parties, and particular consequences are expected to follow the decision. Results are not, however, restricted to the fate of the immediate parties, even when precautions are taken to circumscribe the significance of the decision as precedent. The chain of effect may prove to be visible for a very short time or it may be discerned for long periods and in many jurisdictions. In any event, effects are not to be eliminated by wishing or pretending that they will not occur.

> The goals of interpretation that we propose take into consideration the obligation of any decision-maker to act rationally in harmony with the fundamental objectives of the community whose authoritative spokesman he is. Decision outcomes have consequences that can and ought to be affected by deliberate efforts to further the realization of the basic pattern of value distribution and the fundamental institutions that are compatible with the preferred system of public order.

Id. at 39–40. For explanatory critiques of the McDougal–Lasswell–Miller study, see Richard A. Falk, *On Treaty Interpretation and the New Haven Approach: Achievements and Prospects*, 8 V.J.I.L. 323 (1968); Gidon Gottlieb, *The Conceptual World of the Yale School of International Law*, 21 World Politics 108 (1968); and Burns H. Weston, *Book Review*, 117 U. Pa. L. Rev. 647 (1969).

Discussion Notes/Questions

1. We noted in our discussion of treaties that Article 2(1) of the 1969 Vienna Convention on the Law of Treaties [**Basic Document 1.7**] defines "treaty" to

---

x. A "public order of human dignity" is elsewhere defined by McDougal to mean a "public order in which values are shaped and shared more by persuasion than coercion, and which seeks to promote the greatest production and widest possible sharing, without discriminations irrelevant to merit, of all values among all human beings." MYRES MCDOUGAL & ASSOCIATES, STUDIES IN WORLD PUBLIC ORDER 987 (1960).

mean "an international agreement concluded between states in written form and governed by international law...." Article 2(1) goes on to add the following words: "whether embodied in a single instrument or in two or more related instruments and whatever its particular designation...." Thus, if an agreement is called a "convention," "protocol," "arrangement," "statute," "procès-verbal," "statute," "declaration," "modus vivendi," "exchange of notes," "final act," or "general act," it still is a "treaty" if it fits the above definition. Does an "Executive Agreement" amount to a "treaty"? When, in 1972, governments adopted the Stockholm Declaration of the United Nations Conference on the Human Environment [**Basic Document 1.12**] or when, at the "Earth Summit" in 1992, they adopted the Rio Declaration on Environment and Development [**Basic Document 1.29**], a program of action called "Agenda 21" [**Basic Document 1.30**], and a declaration on the protection of forests [**Basic Document 6.12**] did they, in so doing, adopt "treaties"?

2. Who may conclude (i.e., legally enter into) treaties? Article 6 of the Vienna Convention [**Basic Document 1.7**] reads, in its entirety, as follows: "Every State possesses capacity to conclude treaties." Does this provision answer the question posed? What is a "state"? Would it be possible for a treaty to define the meaning of "state"? Or, since states, according to article 6, are the entities that enter into treaties, would it be possible to have a treaty define the parties to it? Under the terms of article 6, can the United Nations Organization enter into a treaty? The World Health Organization? The Vatican? Liechtenstein? Iowa? Oklahoma? Are the terms of article 6 exclusive?

3. Charlotte Ku, *supra*, contends that the negotiation, signature, ratification or accession, reservation, entry into force, and registration of treaties are subject to gender bias in favor of men. Do you agree? If so, does it make any difference? What would be the effect of the absence of a gender bias in the negotiation, signature, ratification or accession, reservation, entry into force, and registration of treaties?

4. The negotiation, adoption, and ratification of treaties is commonly referred to by international lawyers as "the international legislative process." Are treaties, like domestic law statutes, the embodiment of "legislation" for the international community? As we have seen, some theorists look upon treaties as essentially "contractual" rather than "law-making" in character. Is this a valid viewpoint? Is the distinction important? Might it affect our judgment about the legal effects of different environmental treaties? How? How not?

5. When does a treaty become "binding" (i.e., enforceable)? Article 84(1) of the Vienna Convention [**Basic Document 1.7**] provides that it "shall enter into force on the thirtieth day following the date of deposit of the thirty-fifth instrument of ratification or accession." As of this writing, however, the Vienna Convention has not entered into force for a majority of the world's major powers (the United States being among the non-ratifiers, in contradistinction to the former Soviet Union which became a party to the Convention on May 29, 1986). Arguably, therefore, the Vienna Convention is not yet "binding" law generally. On the other hand, it already has become widely cited in state papers, in international treaty negotiations, and in the writings of international law specialists, as well as having been ratified by such countries as Australia, Canada, Denmark, Finland, Japan, the Netherlands, New Zealand, Sweden, and the former West Germany as well as the former U.S.S.R. This development is due in part to the care with which the Convention was drafted and to the fact that most nations participated in its drafting. Also, it is due to the fact that many of its provisions

are restatements of what, by 1969, was considered to be the customary international law of treaties and treaty interpretation. Accordingly, was the Vienna Convention necessary in the first place?

6. Many environmental treaties cannot really be successful if not joined by all or many states. A good example is the 1985 Vienna Convention on the Protection of the Ozone Layer [**Basic Document 3.14**] and its progeny. Without a system that can bind all or most nations, all efforts to protect the ozone layer would be, arguably, in vain. Or is it possible for treaties to be binding on non-ratifying states? Consider article 11 of the Vienna Convention:

> The consent of a State to be bound by a treaty may be expressed by signature, exchange of instruments constituting a treaty, ratification, acceptance, approval or accession, or by any other means if so agreed.

Observe that article 11 does not prescribe an absolute means of consenting to a treaty. Indeed, it says, if anything, that the means are unimportant; that we have not to worry about some technical legal difference between "signature," "ratification," "acceptance," or "approval". Who then, has to worry? When? What if a treaty provides that it will enter into force when it is "signed"? Could the United States, with its constitutional requirements, ever "sign" such a treaty? Would a diplomat have the power to sign? How could he/she get the power?

7. As we have seen, states often wish to make a reservation or some other qualifying statement when ratifying a treaty. Should environmental treaties permit or disallow reservations and other qualifying expressions? Would not reservations often be contrary to the purpose of environmental agreements? On one hand there is the need to have as many states join such treaties, on the other hand reservations could render the whole treaty ineffective. What do you think?

8. We see, in general, that the Vienna Convention [**Basic Document 1.7**] modernizes notions of consent to treaties. What counts is that a state clearly consents. The form of consent is unimportant so long as there is agreement among the states party to a particular treaty as to what the proper form will be. Thus, drafters of any new treaty surely will (or should) specify the way the treaty will enter into force. It may provide, and typically does provide, that the treaty will become operative when it is ratified by the parties. If it is a multilateral treaty, it may provide, like the Vienna Convention itself, that the treaty will enter into force only after a specified number of nations have ratified or acceded to it. Alternatively, it may provide that the treaty will enter into force *as between the ratifying parties* so that the states that sign *and* ratify will bind each other even if other states hold out.

9. Can or should a right to denounce or unilaterally withdraw from a treaty be implied in environmental treaties when they contain no explicit denunciation and/or withdrawal provision? Considering that generally it is important to have maximum participation in an environmental treaties to facilitate their effectiveness, would not such a right render an environmental treaty ineffective? If so, might it not be persuasively argued that a right to denounce or unilaterally withdraw does not exist in the absence of an provision expressly guaranteeing such a right?

10. What would constitute a material breach of an environmental treaty, justifying denunciation and/or withdrawal? What would constitute a fundamental change of circumstances? Is a broad or narrow interpretation of "material breach" and "change of circumstances" to be preferred? Why? Who should have the burden of proof? Why?

11. The 1969 Vienna Convention [**Basic Document 1.7**] may be described as an attempt at the codification of one aspect of international law. In domestic (i.e., national) law systems, codification has been an important historical process, beginning in modern times with the Napoleonic Code and finding many analogues throughout the world since then. In the United States, first with Chancellor Kent's codification of the laws of New York, the various states have from time to time enacted comprehensive "codes" (which constitute compilations of statutes and their amendments) so as to tighten up gaps among pre-existing statutes. Also, proponents of codification have urged the enactment of statutes to replace the prior common law generated by the courts but not yet embodied in legislation, the most ardent of the codifiers hoping that there would be no further need for common law development in the courts. But this "ideal" never has been realized in fact; the infinite variety of human experience has outdistanced the most visionary of codifiers, serving up new questions never contemplated by them. Also, when the codes themselves use vague and all-embracing words (e.g., "the decision in a tort action should be awarded against the negligent party") their words do not serve adequately as guides for future litigation, and therefore court decisions relating to the codes evolve a vast detailing and specification of the ambiguous provisions. On the basis of Vienna Convention articles 2 and 6 noted in Discussion Notes/Questions 1 and 2, *supra*, is it possible to say that the same fate may befall the Vienna Convention? Can it be said that the Convention offers little by way of precise guidance for future treaty interpretation? Consider these questions when examining other provisions from the Convention.

12. How can the Vienna Convention [**Basic Document 1.7**] purport to "codify" the international law on treaties? Is not its success as a codification instrument dependent upon international acceptance of its provisions? Is not its success dependent also upon the extent to which its provisions merely restate existing customary law? These questions present difficult logical problems; but, for better or worse, similar questions may be asked of any attempt to codify or restate the law, domestic or international.

13. Does the codification of the international law of treaties facilitate or inhibit the development of world order? Would you conclude the same thing in respect of the codification of laws within nations, such as the Uniform Commercial Code in the United States? Why? Why not? In looking at the international situation, is there a fundamental difference owing, say, to the nature of the parties subject to the codification—i.e., states in greatly different stages of development with greatly varying needs and capabilities relative to resources and power? Are these differences so great as to preclude the possibility of uniform rules that can advance the cause of peace, social justice, economic well-being, and environmental sustainability worldwide? This last question is among the more important that can be asked of the international legal process as a whole, and therefore should be kept in mind throughout.

14. Why do treaty negotiations often take years? Why do states hesitate to conclude international environmental treaties? To what extent do domestic factors (e.g., a full-employment economy) play a role? Should they play a role? Why? Why not?

15. As noted, many environmental treaties provide for simplified amendment procedures when it comes to administrative and technical details? Does this approach meet environmental needs? The amendments still have to be negotiated and often will take a long time. Can you think of faster or more efficient amendment procedures? Better procedures, from the standpoint of responsiveness

to particular environmental needs? Not infrequently, a so-called technical change will constitute in reality a major modification of a treaty, but according to the treaty provisions the state parties are not obliged to ask for the approval of their respective parliaments. Accordingly, national politicians often are skeptical about such procedures because they fear that the procedures facilitate circumvention of national approval prerogatives. What do you think?

16. As we have seen, it is possible to identify at least three approaches to treaty interpretation. Which one do you prefer? Which makes the most sense (a) from a theoretical point of view, (b) from a practical (or operational) point of view, and (c) from both points of view. If you were in a position to render an authoritative interpretation of a written legal instrument other than a treaty (e.g., a constitution, code, statute, resolution, administrative ruling, contract, etc.), which of the three approaches would you adopt, if any? Would it depend on the nature of the instrument? Whether you were situated in a domestic or international arena? Other considerations? Do any of the identified three approaches to treaty interpretation serve as an unambiguous means for resolving disputes relative to provisions in treaties (and other legal instruments)? Is an unambiguous means for resolving such disputes possible? More or less possible? Which of the three approaches, if any, is likely to approximate this unambiguous ideal? Why?

B. CUSTOM

Next among the "sources" of international law listed in Article 38 of the I.C.J. Statute **[Basic Document 1.4]** is "international custom, as evidence of a general practice accepted as law." Prior to World War II when the development of international law via treaties was less popular than it is today, international law consisted for the most part of doctrines, principles, and rules developed through the customary practice of states. Indeed, prior to World War II, custom often was viewed, if not as the principal "source" of international law, as at least equal to treaties in this regard.

But you are uncertain about the details. Eager to impress your superiors at the Norwegian Foreign Ministry, you ask yourself: What exactly is customary international law? What does it mean to talk about "a general practice accepted as law"? Is it binding on all states or only on some states? What constitutes evidence of it? Can treaties give rise to it? Does it include rules prohibiting radioactive pollution? If so, by what process do these rules arise? How do we know when a given state practice has matured into a rule of customary international law?

To these and related questions you now turn. They are important questions because customary law still plays an important role in contemporary international legal process, not least in international environmental law (despite the emergence of treaties as a major "source" of international law in this and other realms). As noted by Alexandre Kiss and Dinah Shelton, in International Environmental Law (1991), at 105–07:

> To speak of rules of customary international law in a field as new as that of international environmental law may appear surprising. However, it is possible to discern among current norms "evidence of a general practice, accepted as law", even though only a short period of time has elapsed.

The Conference on the Law of the Sea which met between 1973 and 1982 adopted one of the most important modern international treaties. During the long process of its elaboration, in which all states of the world participated, a certain number of existing rules were codified, but there also arose a consensus on several new norms. On the basis of this consensus an international practice formed, even before adoption of the new treaty. This was particularly the case with the exclusive economic zone, now codified in part V of the [United Nations Convention on the Law of the Sea **[Basic Document 4.20]**], where it was recognized from the beginning that coastal states have sovereign rights for the purpose of conserving and managing living and non-living natural resources and have jurisdiction to preserve the marine environment.[y] It was also accepted that coastal state jurisdiction to legislate regarding ships in innocent passage through the territorial sea includes measures to conserve marine biological resources and preserve the marine environment and to prevent, reduce and control marine pollution.[z]

On other points one may observe emerging rules of customary international law, at different stages of their evolution. The formulation of nonbinding principles undoubtedly plays an important role in this process.[aa] Another factor is the repetition of specific rules in numerous international texts.[bb] Third, it is possible that the process of formulating a rule which may or may not have been applied by different states creates a rather rapid consensus which leads to general acceptance of the rule in state practice.[cc] * * * [For example,] [o]ne of the rules which had emerged from state practice [at the time of the nuclear reactor accident at Chernobyl in 1986],[dd] largely based on repeated conventional requirements, was the obligation to urgently notify states at risk of having their environment adversely affected by any situation or any event. The non-application of this principle by the U.S.S.R. after Chernobyl made it necessary to formulate the norm explicitly based on the parallel conventional provisions. Thus, 58 states signed an agreement in Vienna on early notification of a nuclear accident **[Basic Document 3.16]**. As its title indicates, it provides that states should give notification without delay of any nuclear accident which will or might lead to radioactive consequences for another state [and it] entered into force with unusual speed one month later. The speed of codification of this rule can only be explained by the circumstances and by the recognition of a prior customary international duty to notify.

It can be argued that several other customary rules of international environmental law have emerged or are emerging in state practice. In particular, it clearly seems required that no state cause or allow its

y. *See, e.g.,* Problems 8–1 ("Land–Based Pollution in the Indian Ocean") and 8–2 ("An Oil Tanker Spill in Angloboer's Coastal Waters") in Chapter 8, *infra,* and Problem 10–1 ("Driftnet fishing in the South Pacific") in Chapter 10, *infra.*

z. *See, e.g.* , Problems 8–1 ("Land–Based Pollution of the Indian Ocean") and 8–2 ("An Oil Tanker Spill in Angloboer's Coastal Waters") in Chapter 8, *infra.*

aa. *See* Section F(1) of this chapter, at **149,** *infra.*

bb. *See* Editors' Note and text immediately following at **100-106** in this section, *infra. See also,* Section F(1) of this chapter at **149,** *infra.*

cc. *See* Section F(2) of this chapter at **164** *infra.*

dd. *Se, e.g.,* Problem 7–3 ("The Atomic Steel Mill") in Chapter 7, *infra.*

territory to be used to cause damage to the environment of other states. This norm first arose in international jurisprudence[ee] and was formulated in principle 21 of the [1972] Stockholm Declaration (of the United Nations Conference on the Human Environment) **[Basic Document 1.12]** before being adopted and reaffirmed in numerous other binding and nonbinding international instruments. The duty to cooperate, announced by principle 24 of the Stockholm Declaration, also appears to have acquired this status, as well as reflecting a fundamental norm of the entire United Nations system. Other principles may be cited which form the core of the international common law of the environment. In sum, it is possible to speak of a body of customary international environmental law composed of fundamental principles underlying the entire [international] system and applicable to all environmental subjects.

Thus, customary international law, in relation to the global environment as well as to other worldly fields, facilitates the interpretation of treaties and otherwise contributes to the development of international law by addressing issues unregulated by treaties and other "sources" of international law. And, as a result of each of these functions, it paves the way for the codification of doctrines, principles, and rules through treaties (multilateral and bilateral), domestic legislation, and other international and national means of standard-setting. Not to be overlooked either, it oftentimes defies the second-level priority textually assigned to it by Article 38 of the Statute of the International Court of Justice **[Basic Document 1.4]**, not infrequently demonstrating greater precision than treaties in reflecting community expectations of authority and control. The need to understand the meaning of customary international law, you conclude, is thus manifest. And so, once again, you return to your review.

Editors' Note

In his essay *Toward a General Theory of International Customary Law, in* Toward World Order and Human Dignity 365 (W. Reisman & B. Weston, eds. 1976), Venkata Raman writes, at 365–66:

> Even within highly organized communities, where legislative and adjudicative functions are formally the prerogative of centralized institutions, it generally is recognized that legislation and adjudication do not exhaust the process by which "law" is prescribed. It is familiar knowledge that in applying [legal] prescriptions to any complex interaction there is a continuing interplay between the formulated and the unformulated components [of legal prescription]—evident whether a decisionmaker is concerned with interpreting a business contract or the constitution of the community itself—and custom generally is seen as a dependable guide for ascertaining what is truly regarded as "authoritative" at any given time. Even in societies structured to look to formal institutions for guidance, the lawmaking process cannot be described adequately without acknowledging the part played by customary practice. This is not just because of the reverence with which societies regard tradition in their social interac-

---

ee. *See, e.g.*, the cases excerpted and summarized in Section 8 of the documentary supplement to this Coursebook.

tion. What is often treated functionally as [legal] prescription may not be readily traceable to any formal official source, just as a significant part of what is popularly termed "legislation" may have little or no relevance to community expectations of authority and control. Mistaking the structure for the function, many assume that custom is a technique of "primitive" societies and legislation a technique of "civilized" societies.

Thus Professor Raman concludes, perceptively, that "legal prescription" (or law-making) may be seen, in "primitive" *and* "advanced" societies alike, as "a comprehensive and continuing *process of communication* comprising primarily an agreement process, a process of formal enunciation through parliamentary organs, and the customary process." *Id.* at 365. In the first two of these process categories, he observes, "legal prescription is communicated in some stylized linguistic form" (i.e., contracts, legislation, treaties, etc.); in the last or customary process, it is communicated "through uniformities of behavior." *Id.* Customary international law, in other words, "refers generally to the *unformulated* component of [legal] prescription [or law-making]." *Id.* (Emphasis added.)

DAVID H. OTT, PUBLIC INTERNATIONAL LAW IN THE MODERN WORLD 13–16 (1987).

The process of forming customary law. The essence of the formation of customary international law is the gradually combining effect of the practice of a number of states with regard to a particular type of legal problem or situation.... The question then is: at what point ... [does] the rule come into existence?

To help in this determination international law has developed tests to be applied in evaluating instances of observed state action. One must examine the evidence for the nature, extent and significance of state practice and determine whether that practice establishes that the required elements of custom are present and have in fact combined to generate a rule of law.

It is usual to distinguish customary law that is found in this way from mere *usage*, that is, a habitual state activity that is not required by international law but is observed as a matter of goodwill at the discretion of the particular state.[ff]

The problem of evaluating the evidence for state practice. In general, the examination of state activities is concerned with what states actually do when faced with a particular problem. The difficulty is that states may act out of some momentary interest which leads them away from what a more considered judgment might suggest international law requires. * * * In examining state actions, then, the international lawyer must be very careful not to attach undue weight to any particular act of state self-interest.[gg]

ff. "Although occasionally the terms are used interchangeably," writes Ian Brownlie in Principles of Public International Law 4–5 (4th ed. 1990), " 'custom' and 'usage' are terms of art and have different meanings. A usage is a general practice which does not reflect a legal obligation, and examples are ceremonial salutes at sea and, apart from a recent convention, the giving of customs exemption to the personal baggage of diplomatic agents."

gg. Anthony D'Amato writes, in The Concept of Custom in International Law (1971), at 88–89:

What is an "act" of a state? In most cases, a state's action is easily recognized. A state sends up an artificial satellite, tests nuclear

The evidence of state practice. With that caveat in mind, however, the lawyer may consider as evidence of state practice a wide variety of things, some of more value than others.

There are first the documents generated by states in their conduct of foreign relations. Diplomatic correspondence, policy statements, press releases, and opinions of official legal advisers may all come within this category.

Then one may find more general expressions of a state's views on international law in such things as official manuals on legal questions. Both the United States and the United Kingdom publish manuals on the law of war which may be taken as expressions of each state's views on the conduct of military activities.

The actual decisions of governments on questions with some international legal relevance are often good indications of state practice. Similarly, legislation and judicial decisions of the state's higher courts[hh] may reflect that state's practice on the international legal issues raised.

On the international level, the comments by a state on draft treaties produced by the U.N. International Law Commission,[ii] or the voting of that state in international bodies (particularly the U.N. General Assembly),[jj] may offer good indications of a state's practice—may indeed even in some sense be state practice.

More generally, the language used in the treaties a state signs may reflect its practice, as may also a pattern of treaties in which a state has fairly consistently agreed to a certain view of the relevant international law in agreements with its treaty partners.

It is within the framework of such evidences of state practice that the international lawyer must decide whether the elements of customary law are present.

The elements of custom. Once it has been determined what is the real practice of states with regard to some legal point, that practice must next be examined to see whether it reflects what are generally recognized to be the indispensable elements whose presence transforms practice into customary law. . . .

Element 1: opinio juris. This is the belief that a certain practice is obligatory as a matter of law. Thus Article 38(1)b of the I.C.J. Statute **[Basic Document 1.4]** speaks of a "general practice *accepted as law*". If a practice is

weapons, receives ambassadors, levies customs duties, expels an alien, captures a pirate vessel, sets up a drilling rig in the continental shelf, visits and searches a neutral ship, and similarly engages in thousands of acts though its citizens and agents. On the other hand, a claim is not an act. As a matter of daily practice, international law is largely concerned with conflicting international claims. But the claims themselves, although they may *articulate* a legal norm, cannot constitute the material component of custom. For a state has not done anything when it makes a claim; until it takes enforcement action, the claim has little value as a prediction of what the state will actually do.

Harder to recognize as an "act" is a state's decision not to act in a situation where it could have acted. When the first Sputnik circled the globe, the non-actions of the states over whose territory the satellite passed were just as significant to the formation of custom as the action of the [former] Soviet Union in sending it up.

hh. *See infra* Section D of this chapter, at **137**.

ii. *See supra* note **j** in Chapter 1, at 37.

jj. *See infra* Section F(1) of this chapter, at **149**.

not so accepted, but is regarded as simply a discretionary act performed out of a political or other non-legal motives, then it is an example of usage which may merely reflect international friendliness or diplomatic tact—what international law calls comity.

In the *Asylum Case* (1950)[kk] the World Court emphasised the importance of a practice being the expression of a right belonging to one party and a duty lying on the other party. Without that nexus of legal obligation, and the *opinio juris* which recognises it, there is no custom.

Unfortunately, although this requirement of *opinio juris* makes practical sense as a means of distinguishing custom from comity, it is illogical insofar as it requires new rules of customary law to be generated by a process which must assume a belief that those rules are *already* legally binding.

Nevertheless, the World Court has insisted on this and the main question in several cases has been how to decide whether a practice is motivated by *opinio juris* or not. In the *Lotus Case* (P.C.I.J. 1927),[ll] the court indicated that one could not infer *opinio juris* from a particular practice unless the state involved was "conscious of having a duty" in that regard. This has been criticised as requiring the judges and others to determine the psychological viewpoint of a state as if it were a real person. Several respected writers have suggested that the better position is to infer *opinio juris* from practice which reasonably bears that inference unless there are clear indications from the state to the contrary. But in the *North Sea Continental Shelf Cases* (1969)[mm] the court reiterated the *Lotus* view although a slight shift occurred in *Nicaragua v. US* (1986).[nn]

Element 2: duration. This has to do with the length of time a practice has been followed. Long duration may be helpful in establishing a custom, but the I.C.J. indicated in the North Sea Continental Self Cases that even a short duration might suffice when state practice has been extensive and virtually uniform. In other words, a short duration may be offset to some extent by a strong showing with regard to the remaining elements of custom. . . .

Element 3: uniformity and consistency. Uniformity means that the practice of states should not vary greatly from state to state. Consistency implies that there should not be contradictions or discrepancies in the practice of states between one relevant instance and another.

Element 4: generality. This relates to whether a practice is fairly widespread among a majority of states: a practice common in only one area of the world or observed by only a minority of states would not generate international customary law for all. However, all states may be bound by custom arising from generally followed practice without the need for universality.

It may be possible, nevertheless, for a state which objects to a particular general practice to avoid in certain circumstances being obligated as a matter

kk. Asylum (Colom./Peru), 1950 I.C.J. 266.

ll. (Fr. v. Turk.), 1927 P.C.I.J. (ser. A) No. 10, at 4.

mm. (F.R.G./Den.) (F.R.G./Neth.), 1969 I.C.J. 3. For a brief extract from this case, see text at **107**, *infra*.

nn. Military and Paramilitary Activities in and against Nicaragua (Nicar. v. U.S.) (Merits), 1986 I.C.J. 14.

of customary law. The *Anglo-Norwegian Fisheries Case* (1951)[oo] is generally understood to recognize the possibility of a state's being a *persistent objector* and thus not bound by a particular custom on account of having objected to the relevant practice right from the beginning of its transformation into a rule of customary international law. On the other hand, a *subsequent objector*, which remained silent while the custom was in the process of formation and spoke out only after it had become law, would not be able to escape being obligated unless other affected states acquiesced in the subsequent objector's attempt to avoid being bound.

These observations about the position of states that object to a rule of customary law are important for a corollary that is implicit in them, namely, that if a state makes neither a persistent objection nor a subsequent objection to a particular rule, then that state is bound by the rule, even without an explicit acceptance.

RUDOLF BERNHARDT, *Customary International Law New and Old Problems* 19 THESAURUS ACROASIUM 199, 215 (1992).

[C]an "customary law" come into existence without custom, as "instant" customary law in the words of Bin Cheng?[9] The contradiction in the formula should not conceal the problem, *i.e.* whether in exceptional circumstances law—aside from treaty law—can come into existence spontaneously. I would not exclude this possibility if two conditions are met. There must be quasi-unanimity in the community of States that a certain rule is necessary, and this unanimity must not be counterbalanced by adverse practices. If, for instance, the representatives of States in a universal organization or conference express the unanimous opinion that tests of nuclear weapons or the stationing of weapons of mass destruction in space and on celestial bodies should be totally excluded, why should this not create new law? Can the *opinio juris sive necessitatis* suffice in certain circumstances, if no adverse practices exist? I would answer this question affirmatively despite the undeniable dogmatic difficulties.

ROSALYN HIGGINS, PROBLEMS AND PROCESS: INTERNATIONAL LAW AND HOW WE USE IT 19–22 (1994).

One of the special circumstances of international law is that violations of law can lead to the formation of new law. Of course, this characteristic is more troublesome for those who regard law as rules, and less troublesome for those who regard law as process. But whether one believes that international law consists of rules ... derived from consent or natural law; or whether one believes international law is a process of decision-making, with appropriate reliance on past trends of decision-making in the light of current context ... , there still remains the question of how the "rules" or the "trends of decision" change through time. And, in so far as these rules or trends of decisions are based on custom, then there is the related question of what legal significance is to be given to practice that is inconsistent with the perceived rules or trends of decision.

oo. Fisheries (U.K. v. Nor.), 1951 I.C.J. 116.

9. Bin Cheng, *United Nations Resolutions on Outer Space: "Instant" International Customary Law?*, 5 INDIAN J. INT'L L. 23 (1965).

Some rule-based international lawyers are apt to see rules as immutable. Repeated violations of these rules are to them a reflection of the reality that at the end of the day international law is dependent upon power[;] and, if there is a divergence between the two, it is power politics that will prevail. This was the view of Georg Schwarzenberger and, of course, is a view widely held by non-lawyers, and by students of international relations.... For those who regard international law as a process, however, the situation presents itself rather differently. That which we describe *as law* is the confluence of authority and control. Where there is substantial non-compliance, over a period of time, the norms concerned begin to lose their normative [*i.e.,* juridical] character. What has been lost is the community expectation that claimed requirements of behaviour reflect legal obligation.

But even for those who view international law as process, there are some difficult questions. What exactly causes a norm to lose its quality as law? Conceptually, this question is, of course, the same as that put regarding the formation of custom. To ask what is evidence of practice required for the loss of obligatory quality of a norm is the mirror of the evidence of practice required from the formation of the norm in the first place. As we have seen, for the formation of custom, practice and *opinio juris* are required.

If a customary rule loses its normative quality when it is widely ignored, over a significant period of time, does this not lead to a relativist view of the substantive content of international law, with disturbing implications? Let us take a spectrum of possibilities. In the *South West Africa Cases* South Africa argued that there was not in reality any norm of [racial] non-discrimination, as—regardless of the way states voted on resolutions on the issue—the great majority of states routinely discriminated against persons of colour. This argument arose in the context of whether a norm of non-discrimination had ever developed and come into existence.[10] A second example: all states agree that international law prohibits genocide (and that this total prohibition is today rooted in customary international law and not just in treaty obligations). So what if some states from time to time engage in genocide? Here we may safely answer that genocide, while it sometimes occurs ... , is certainly not the majority practice. The customary law that prohibits genocide remains intact, notwithstanding appalling examples of non-compliance. Let us look at a third, more difficult example. No one doubts that there exists a norm prohibiting torture. No state denies the existence of such a norm; and, indeed, it is widely recognized as a customary rule of international law by national courts.[11] But it is equally clear from, for example, the reports of Amnesty International, that *the great majority* of states systematically engage in torture. If one takes the view that non-compliance is relevant to the retention of normative quality, are we to conclude that there is not really any prohibition of torture under customary international law? The International Court of Justice touched on this issue in a rather general way in *Nicaragua v. United States,* when determining the law on intervention and permitted use of force. It said:

10. South West Africa Cases (Eth. v. S. Afr.) (Liber. v. S. Afr.) (Second Phase), 1966 I.C.J. 6.

11. *See, e.g.,* Filártiga v. Peña-Irala, 630 F.2d 878 (2d Cir. 1980).

If a State acts in a way prima facie incompatible with a recognized rule, but defends its conduct by appealing to exceptions or justifications contained within the rule itself, then whether or not the State's conduct is in fact justifiable on that basis, the significance of that attribute is to confirm rather than to weaken the rule.[12]

For lawyers who do not approach matters from the perspective of the battle between "legal rules" and "power politics", this last type of example presents very real difficulties. The answer seems to have been found by some embracing, if not a hierarchical normativity, then a weighted normativity.... Essentially, the argument seems to be that, if [certain rules such as rules against aggression and on self-defence] are not treated as "rules of higher normativity" than ordinary rules, then they cannot be treated differently from ordinary rules so far as the evidence of practice is concerned; and, if they cannot be treated differently, then disaster will ensue. To assert an immutable core [of] norms which remain constant regardless of the attitudes of states is at once to insist upon one's own personal values (rather than internationally shared values) and to rely essentially on natural law in doing so. This is a perfectly possible position, but it is not one I take.

* * *

The answer, in my view, lies elsewhere. First, we must not lose sight of the fact that it is the practice of the vast majority of states that is critical, both in the formation of new norms and in their development and change and possible death. Thus, even if genocide and the killing of prisoners of war regrettably sometimes occur, if this is not the usual practice of most states, the status of the normative prohibitions is not changed. No special attribution of "high normative status" is needed. More difficult is the question of torture, because we are told, by reputable bodies in a position to know, that the majority of states in the world do engage in this repugnant practice. It is at this point that a further factor comes into play.

New norms require both practice and *opinio juris* before they can be said to represent customary international law. And so it is with the gradual death of existing norms and their replacement by others. The reason that the prohibition on torture continues to be a requirement of customary international law, even though widely abused, is not because it has a higher normative status that allows us to ignore the abuse, but because *opinio juris* as to its normative status continues to exist. No state, not even a state that tortures, believes that the international law prohibition is undesirable and that it is not bound by the prohibition. A new norm cannot emerge without both practice and *opinio juris*; and an existing norm does not die without the great majority of states engaging in both contrary practice and withdrawing their *opinio juris*.

Editors' Note

Can a treaty give rise to customary law that is binding on all nations? At the turn of the Twentieth Century, a number of British scholars took the view that treaties prescribe only the contractual obligations of States, that they

12. *Supra* note **mm**, at 103.

have no legal force and effect beyond them, and that their provisions could be declaratory or in derogation of customary law but that they could not alter it. The late Professor Richard Baxter, a former judge of the I.C.J., took a different view. In a carefully reasoned Hague lecture, he argued that a treaty provision can "pass" into customary international law subject to the proviso that there be some acquiescence to the provision (or rule) by the non-party States affected (though he did not indicate how this acquiescence might be substantiated). We reproduce an excerpt from this lecture below. But first let us consider how the World Court has dealt with this question, as it did in the 1969 *North Sea Continental Shelf* cases and the 1986 case concerning *Military and Paramilitary Activities in and Against Nicaragua.*

NORTH SEA CONTINENTAL SHELF CASES (JUDGMENT) (F.R.G./DEN.) (F.R.G./NETH.), 1969 I.C.J. 3, 41–45.

[These cases involved three States (the Federal Republic of Germany, Denmark, and The Netherlands) bordering on the North Sea and asserting conflicting claims to its undersea land masses known as the "continental shelf." Denmark and The Netherlands claimed that the dispute should be decided according to the "principle of equidistance" per Article 6 of the 1958 Geneva Convention on the Continental Shelf [**Basic Document 4.3**]. The Court rejected the application of the Convention inasmuch as West Germany was not a party to it. It also rejected another claim advanced by Denmark and The Netherlands, to wit, that the equidistance principle in Article 6 of the same Convention had become part of the *corpus* of general international law and, in particular, customary international law. It addressed the question of whether a treaty give rise to customary law as follows:]

70. ... [Denmark and The Netherlands contend] that even if there was at the date of the Geneva Convention [on the Continental Shelf] no rule of customary international law in favour of the equidistance principle, and no such rule was crystallized in Article 6 of the Convention, nevertheless such a rule has come into being since the Convention, partly because of its own impact, partly on the basis of subsequent State practice—and that this rule, being now a rule of customary international law binding on all States, including therefore the Federal Republic, should be declared applicable to the delimitation of the boundaries between the Parties' respective continental shelf areas in the North Sea.

71. In so far as this contention is based on the view that Article 6 of the Convention has had the influence, and has produced the effect, described, it clearly involves treating that Article as a norm-creating provision which has constituted the foundation of, or has generated a rule which, while only conventional or contractual in its origin, has since passed into the general *corpus* of international law, and is now accepted as such by the *opinio juris*, so as to have become binding even for countries which have never, and do not, become parties to the Convention. There is no doubt that this process is a perfectly possible one and does from time to time occur: it constitutes indeed one of the recognized methods by which new rules of customary international law may be formed. At the same time this result is not lightly to be regarded as having been attained.

72.   It would in the first place be necessary that the provision concerned should, at all events potentially, be of a fundamentally norm-creating character such as could be regarded as forming the basis of a general rule law. Considered *in abstracto* the equidistance principle might be said to fulfil this requirement. Yet in the particular form in which it is embodied in Article 6 of the Geneva Convention, and having regard to the relationship of that Article to other provisions of the Convention, this must be open to some doubt. In the first place, Article 6 is so framed as to put second the obligation to make use of the equidistance method, causing it to come after a primary obligation to effect delimitation by agreement. Such a primary obligation constitutes an unusual preface to what is claimed to be a potential general rule of law. . . . Secondly the part played by the notion of special circumstances relative to the principle of equidistance as embodied in Article 6, and the very considerable, still unresolved controversies as to the exact meaning and scope of this notion, must raise further doubts as to the potentially norm-creating character of the rule. Finally, the faculty of making reservations to Article 6, while it might not of itself prevent the equidistance principle being eventually received as general law, does add considerably to the difficulty of regarding this result as having been brought about (or being potentially possible) on the basis of the Convention: for so long as this faculty continues to exist . . . , it is the Convention itself which would, for the reasons already indicated, seem to deny to the provisions of Article 6 the same norm-creating character as, for instance, Articles 1 and 2 possess.

73.   With respect to the other elements usually regarded as necessary before a conventional rule can be considered to have become a general rule of international law, it might be that, even without the passage of any considerable period of time, a very widespread and representative participation in the convention might suffice of itself, provided it included that of States whose interests were specially affected. In the present case however, the Court notes that, even if allowance is made for the existence of a number of States to whom participation in the Geneva Convention is not open, or which, by reason for instance of being land-locked States, would have no interest in becoming parties to it, the number of ratifications and accessions so far secured is, though respectable, hardly sufficient. That non-ratification may sometimes be due to factors other than active disapproval of the convention concerned can hardly constitute a basis on which positive acceptance of its principles can be implied. The reasons are speculative, but the facts remain.

74.   As regards the time element, the Court notes that is over ten years since the Convention was signed, but that it is even now less than five since it came into force in June 1964. . . . Although the passage of only a short period of time is not necessarily, or of itself, a bar to the formation of a new rule of customary international law on the basis of what was originally a purely conventional rule, an indispensable requirement would be that within the period in question, short though it might be, State practice, including that of States whose interests are specially affected, should have been both extensive and virtually uniform in the sense of the provision invoked; and should moreover have occurred in such a way as to show a general recognition that a rule of law or legal obligation is involved.

75.   The Court must now consider whether State practice in the matter of continental shelf delimitation has, subsequent to the Geneva Convention,

been of such a kind as to satisfy this requirement.... [S]ome fifteen cases have been cited in the course of the present proceedings, occurring mostly since the signature of the 1958 Geneva Convention, in which continental shelf boundaries have been delimited according to the equidistance principle—in the majority of the cases by agreement, in a few others unilaterally—or else the delimitation was foreshadowed but has not yet been carried out.... [However, there are] several grounds which deprive them of weight as precedents in the present context.

76. To begin with, over half the States concerned, whether acting unilaterally or conjointly, were or shortly became parties to the Geneva Convention, and were therefore presumably ... acting actually or potentially in the application of the Convention. From their action no inference could legitimately be drawn as to the existence of a rule of customary international law in favour of the equidistance principle. As regards those States, on the other hand, which were not, and have not become parties to the Convention, the basis of their action can only be problematical and must remain entirely speculative. Clearly they were not applying the Convention. But from that no inference could justifiably be drawn that they believed themselves to be applying a mandatory rule of customary international law. There is not a shred of evidence that they did and ... there is no lack of other reasons for using the equidistance method, so that acting, or agreeing to act in a certain way, does not of itself demonstrate anything of a juridical nature.

77. The essential point in this connection—and it seems necessary to stress it—is that even if these instances of action by non-parties to the Convention were much more numerous than they in fact are, they would not, even in the aggregate, suffice in themselves to constitute the *opinio juris*;—for, in order to achieve this result, two conditions must be fulfilled. Not only must the acts concerned amount to a settled practice, but they must also be such, or be carried out in such a way, as to be evidence of a belief that this practice is rendered obligatory by the existence or a rule of law requiring it. The need for such a belief, *i.e.*, the existence of a subjective element, is implicit in the very notion of the *opinio juris sive necessitatis*. The States concerned must therefore feel that they are conforming to what amounts to a legal obligation. The frequency, or even habitual character of the acts is not in itself enough. There are many international acts, *e.g.*, in the field of ceremonial and protocol, which are performed almost invariably, but which are motivated only by considerations of courtesy, convenience or tradition, and not by any sense of legal duty.

78. In this respect the Court follows the view adopted by the Permanent Court of International Justice in the *Lotus* case ... (*P.C.I.J., Series A, No. 10,* 1927, at p.28).[pp] ... [T]he position is simply that in certain cases—not a great number—the States concerned agreed to draw or did draw the boundaries concerned according to the principle of equidistance. There is no evidence that they so acted because they felt legally compelled to draw them in this way by reason of a rule of customary law obliging them to do so—especially considering that they might have been motivated by other obvious factors.

* * *

pp. *See supra* text at note ll.

81.   The Court accordingly concludes that if the Geneva Convention was not in its origins or inception declaratory of a mandatory rule of customary international law enjoining the use of the equidistance principle for the delimitation of continental shelf areas between adjacent States, neither has its subsequent effect been constitutive of such a rule; and that State practice up-to-date has equally been insufficient for the purpose.

MILITARY AND PARAMILITARY ACTIVITIES IN AND AGAINST NICARAGUA (NICAR. v. U.S.) (MERITS) 1986 I.C.J. 14.

[*Eds.*—In 1984, Nicaragua instituted proceedings against the United States in the World Court alleging military and paramilitary acts by the United States in Nicaragua in violation of international law. The United States contested the jurisdiction of the Court on several grounds, including a reservation it had made in accepting the Court's jurisdiction to the effect that its acceptance would not apply to disputes concerning the application of a treaty—in this case, the United Nations Charter **[Basic Document 1.3]** and the Charter of the Organization of American States [119 U.N.T.S. 3], Nicaragua responded by arguing that its claim was based on not only the Charter but also on rules of customary international law that were similar in content to the Charter and applicable to the facts in the case. The Court accepted the Nicaraguan argument for the reasons given in the ensuing extract from the Court's lengthy opinion.]

182.   The Court concludes that it should exercise the jurisdiction conferred upon it by the United States declaration of acceptance under Article 36, paragraph 2, of the Statute **[Basic Document 1.4]**, to determine the claims of Nicaragua based upon customary international law notwithstanding the exclusion from its jurisdiction of disputes "arising under" the United Nations and Organization of American States Charters.

183.   In view of this conclusion, the Court has next to consider what are the rules of customary international law applicable to the present dispute. For this purpose, it has to direct its attention to the practice and *opinio juris* of States; as the Court recently observed,

> "It is of course axiomatic that the material of customary international law is to be looked for primarily in the actual practice and *opinio juris* of States, even though multilateral conventions may have an important role to play in recording and defining rules deriving from custom, or indeed in developing them." (*Continental Shelf (Libyan Arab Jamahiriya/Malta), I.C.J. Reports 1985, pp. 29–30, para. 27.*)

In this respect the Court must not lose sight of the Charter of the United Nations and that of the Organization of American States, notwithstanding the operation of the multilateral treaty reservation. Although the Court has no jurisdiction to determine whether the conduct of the United States constitutes a breach of those conventions, it can and must take them into account in ascertaining the content of the customary international law which the United States is also alleged to have infringed.

184.   The Court notes that there is in fact evidence, to be examined below, of a considerable degree of agreement between the Parties as to the content of the customary international law relating to the non-use of force

and non-intervention. This concurrence of their views does not however dispense the Court from having itself to ascertain what rules of customary international law are applicable. The mere fact that States declare their recognition of certain rules is not sufficient for the Court to consider these as being part of customary international law, and as applicable as such to those States. Bound as it is by Article 38 of its Statute to apply, *inter alia*, international custom "as evidence of a general practice accepted as law", the Court may not disregard the essential role played by general practice. Where two States agree to incorporate a particular rule in a treaty, their agreement suffices to make that rule a legal one, binding upon them; but in the field of customary international law, the shared view of the Parties as to the content of what they regard as the rule is not enough. The Court must satisfy itself that the existence of the rule in the *opinio juris* of States is confirmed by practice.

185.   In the present dispute, the Court, while exercising its jurisdiction only in respect of the application of the customary rules of non-use of force and non-intervention, cannot disregard the fact that the Parties are bound by these rules as a matter of treaty law and of customary international law. Furthermore, in the present case, apart from the treaty commitments binding the Parties to the rules in question, there are various instances of their having expressed recognition of the validity thereof as customary international law in other ways. It is therefore in the light of this "subjective element"—the expression used by the Court in its 1969 Judgment in the *North Sea Continental Shelf* cases (*I.C.J. Reports 1969, p. 44*)—that the Court has to appraise the relevant practice.

186.   It is not to be expected that in the practice of States the application of the rules in question should have been perfect, in the sense that States should have refrained, with complete consistency, from the use of force or from intervention in each other's internal affairs. The Court does not consider that, for a rule to be established as customary, the corresponding practice must be in absolutely rigorous conformity with the rule. In order to deduce the existence of customary rules, the Court deems it sufficient that the conduct of States should, in general, be consistent with such rules, and that instances of State conduct inconsistent with a given rule should generally have been treated as breaches of that rule, not as indications of the recognition of a new rule. If a State acts in a way prima facie incompatible with a recognized rule, but defends its conduct by appealing to exceptions or justifications contained within the rule itself, then whether or not the State's conduct is in fact justifiable on that basis, the significance of that attitude is to confirm rather than to weaken the rule.

187.   The Court must therefore determine, first, the substance of the customary rules relating to the use of force in international relations, applicable to the dispute submitted to it. The United States has argued that, on this crucial question of the lawfulness of the use of force in inter-State relations, the rules of general and customary international law, and those of the United Nations Charter, are in fact identical. In its view this identity is so complete that, as explained above ... , it constitutes an argument to prevent the Court from applying this customary law, because it is indistinguishable from the multilateral treaty law which it may not apply. In its Counter–Memorial on jurisdiction and admissibility the United States asserts that "Article 2(4) of

the Charter is customary and general international law". It quotes with approval an observation by the International Law Commission to the effect that

> "the great majority of international lawyers today unhesitatingly hold that Article 2, paragraph 4, together with other provisions of the Charter, authoritatively declares the modern customary law regarding the threat or use of force" (*ILC Yearbook*, 1966, Vol. II, p. 247).

The United States points out that Nicaragua has endorsed this view, since one of its counsel asserted that "indeed it is generally considered by publicists that Article 2, paragraph 4, of the United Nations Charter is in this respect an embodiment of existing general principles of international law". And the United States concludes:

> "In sum, the provisions of Article 2(4) with respect to the lawfulness of the use of force are 'modern customary law' (International Law Commission, *loc. cit.*) and the 'embodiment of general principles of international law' (counsel for Nicaragua, Hearing of 25 April 1984, morning, *loc. cit.*). There is no other 'customary and general international law' on which Nicaragua can rest its claims."

> "It is, in short, inconceivable that this Court could consider the lawfulness of an alleged use of armed force without referring to the principal source of the relevant international law—Article 2(4) of the United Nations Charter."

As for Nicaragua, the only noteworthy shade of difference in its view lies in Nicaragua's belief that

> "in certain cases the rule of customary law will not necessarily be identical in content and mode of application to the conventional rule".

188.   The Court thus finds that both Parties take the view that the principles as to the use of force incorporated in the United Nations Charter correspond, in essentials, to those found in customary international law. The Parties thus both take the view that the fundamental principle in this area is expressed in the terms employed in Article 2, paragraph 4, of the United Nations Charter. They therefore accept a treaty-law obligation to refrain in their international relations from the threat or use of force against the territorial integrity or political independence of any State, or in any other manner inconsistent with the purposes of the United Nations. The Court has however to be satisfied that there exists in customary international law an *opinio juris* as to the binding character of such abstention. This *opinio juris* may, though with all due caution, be deduced from, *inter alia*, the attitude of the Parties and the attitude of States towards certain General Assembly resolutions, and particularly resolution 2625 (XXV) entitled "Declaration on Principles of International Law concerning Friendly Relations and Co-operation among States in accordance with the Charter of the United Nations" **[Basic Document 1.8]**. The effect of consent to the text of such resolutions cannot be understood as merely that of a "reiteration or elucidation" of the treaty commitment undertaken in the Charter. On the contrary, it may be understood as an acceptance of the validity of the rule or set of rules declared by the resolution by themselves. The principle of non-use of force, for example, may thus be regarded as a principle of customary international law,

not as such conditioned by provisions relating to collective security, or to the facilities or armed contingents to be provided under Article 43 of the Charter. It would therefore seem apparent that the attitude referred to expresses an *opinio juris* respecting such rule (or set of rules), to be thenceforth treated separately from the provisions, especially those of an institutional kind, to which it is subject on the treaty-law plane of the Charter.

189. As regards the United States in particular, the weight of an expression of *opinio juris* can similarly be attached to its support of the resolution of the Sixth International Conference of American States condemning aggression (18 February 1928) and ratification of the Montevideo Convention on Rights and Duties of States (26 December 1933) [165 U.N.T.S. 19], Article 11 of which imposes the obligation not to recognize territorial acquisitions or special advantages which have been obtained by force. Also significant is United States acceptance of the principle of the prohibition of the use of force which is contained in the declaration on principles governing the mutual relations of States participating in the Conference on Security and Co-operation in Europe (Helsinki, 1 August 1975) [73 Dep't State Bull. (1975)], whereby the participating States undertake to "refrain in their mutual relations, *as well as in their international relations in general*," (emphasis added) from the threat or use of force. Acceptance of a text in these terms confirms the existence of an *opinio juris* of the participating States prohibiting the use of force in international relations.

190. A further confirmation of the validity as customary international law of the principle of the prohibition of the use of force expressed in Article 2, paragraph 4, of the Charter of the United Nations may be found in the fact that it is frequently referred to in statements by State representatives as being not only a principle of customary international law but also a fundamental or cardinal principle of such law. The International Law Commission, in the course of its work on the codification of the law of treaties, expressed the view that "the law of the Charter concerning the prohibition of the use of force in itself constitutes a conspicuous example of a rule in international law having the character of *jus cogens*"[qq] (paragraph (1) of the commentary of the Commission to Article 50 of its draft Articles on the Law of Treaties, *ILC Yearbook*, 1966–II, p. 247). Nicaragua in its Memorial on the Merits submitted in the present case states that the principle prohibiting the use of force embodied in Article 2, paragraph 4, of the Charter of the United Nations "has come to be recognized as *jus cogens*". The United States, in its Counter-Memorial on the questions of jurisdiction and admissibility, found it material to quote the views of scholars that this principle is a "universal norm", a "universal international law", a "universally recognized principle of international law", and a "principle of *jus cogens*".

RICHARD R. BAXTER, *Treaties and Custom*, 129 RECUEIL
DES COURS 25, 32–104 *passim* (1970–I).

[Article 38 of the Vienna Convention on the Law of Treaties [**Basic Document 1.7**]] did no more than recognize that treaty law can pass

qq. *I.e.*, a peremptory principle or norm from which, it is claimed, no derogation is permitted. For discussion of the doctrine of *jus cogens*, see the Editors' Note, *infra* at **132**.

into customary international law.[rr] [It] did not address [itself] to how this transformation takes place * * *; [but] there are three ways in which the [customary] law-declaring quality of a treaty might be established:

The first is that the treaty, through appropriate language in the preamble or elsewhere would state that it incorporates nothing but customary international law.

The second is through the *travaux préparatoires* of the treaty ... [which] could make it clear that the treaty was intended to be declaratory of existing customary international law.

The third would be through comparison of provisions of the treaty with customary international law, whereby it might be established that certain articles of the treaty or all of its contents are, as it were, an accurate photograph of the law. This third process hardly facilitates the proof of customary international law, because the declaratory quality of the treaty must be established through the proof of customary international law, and that is the very law to be established through recourse to the treaty.... [This] merely interjects an unnecessary further step in the proof of the law. * * * [Thus,] instances of attempts to conclude international agreements purportedly declaratory of existing customary international are rare and can, in extreme cases, have an adverse effect on the bringing into force of the agreement amongst a substantial number of States.

* * *

Treaties that do *not* purport to be declaratory of customary international law at the time they enter into force may nevertheless with the passage of time pass into customary international law.[ss] * * * [But a] word of warning is needed at this point. In certain instances it may be difficult to determine whether a tribunal which held a treaty to reflect the state of customary international law at a certain moment in time meant that the treaty had from the outset been declaratory of customary international law or that the treaty had in the course of time and with general acceptance by non-parties passed into general international law. * * * [Nevertheless,] [t]he International Court conceded in the *North Sea Cases* that a treaty provision can develop into a rule of customary international law.[tt] ...

* * *

Any summing-up of the phenomenon whereby norms come to be transmuted into norms of customary international law must recognize that the process is simply a special application of the normal rules for the creation of customary international law. The norm of the treaty is taken up by non-parties in such a way that State practice is "extensive and virtually uniform." The really difficult questions are the perennial ones about the proof of "a general practice accepted as law": how extensive and how uniform must acquiescence in the rule be? Are the views of all States to be given equal weight or does one pay particular regard to the views of States that have a

rr. Article 38 reads: "Nothing in articles 34 and 37 precludes a rule set forth in a treaty from becoming binding upon a third State as a customary rule of international law, recognized as such."

ss. Emphasis added.

tt. *See* para. 71 in the immediately preceding reading.

particular interest in the subject-matter of the treaty? How large a role does *opinio juris* play? * * * The multilateral treaty is no short-cut in the proof of customary international law, since it must always be proven that the treaty does reflect customary international law. But the existence of the treaty does mean that there is an agreed starting point—and attractive force to which non-party practice will be drawn like iron filings to a magnet. Once it is established through judicial decision or other authoritative pronouncement that the treaty provision has passed into customary international law, reliance on precedent can simplify proof of the state of the law in subsequent instances. At that point the international community will know that it is bound by one agreed text rather than by a norm which must be derived by legal reasoning from a variety of ambiguous and possibly inconsistent State practice. Of course, if the conduct of non-parties can cause a treaty norm to pass into general international law, it can likewise force the treaty norm out of customary law. But this is simply a manifestation of the way in which customary international law always changes and grows.

* * *

Treaties will continue to exercise a most important impact on the content of general international law. Even if all States should expressly assume the obligations of codification treaties, regard will still have to be paid to customary international law in the interpretation of those instruments, and the treaties will in turn generate new customary international law growing out of the application of the agreements.

Anthony D'Amato, *Universality vs. Restrictiveness in Custom*, adapted from Burns H. Weston et al., INTERNATIONAL LAW AND WORLD ORDER: A PROBLEM-ORIENTED COURSEBOOK 76 (2d ed. 1990).

If customary international law is "universal," then it is binding on *all* States. However, if it is not universal, then the question is left open as to whether, indeed, it is binding on any given State. Even a cursory look at the vast literature on the subject will show what the competing considerations are.

(a) Favoring the Universality of Custom: The "Objectivist" or "Sociological" View

Assume that it is, say, the Seventeenth Century and that Great Britain and The Netherlands are locked in a debate over the far-reaching question of the freedom of the high seas. "At that time," recount Anthony A. D'Amato & John L. Hargrove, *An Overview of the Problem*, in Who Protects the Ocean? 20–21 (J. Hargrove ed. 1975), "the Netherlands was the dominant maritime country, and its leading international lawyer, Hugo Grotius, spelled out the arguments in favor of freedom of navigation on all the oceans. John Selden for England countered in favor of a closed sea."[13]

What really was at issue in this debate was the paying of tariffs to another nation for navigational use of the high seas off its coast. Grotius,

---

13. Later, when England became the dominant naval power, England espoused freedom   of the seas.

representing an aspiring naval power, did not want Dutch ships to have to pay for a license to navigate and trade with a distant power; he feared the proliferation of fees from all countries along the route. Selden, on the other hand, believed that England stood to gain more than it would lose by the imposition of such fees in the waters around England, affecting not only trade with England but also trade through the Straits of Gibraltar.

But England was unable to enforce this collection of fees, and so the Dutch view of freedom of the high seas prevailed as between the two countries, and a customary practice respecting this view developed between them. Did this mean that the new custom between Great Britain and The Netherlands—freedom of navigation on the high seas—applied to all other countries? Does it today apply automatically between Australia and the United States?

If the establishment of a legal custom between two or more States is automatically universalized, a proposition about which there is disagreement, the answer is of course "yes." But how does a principle of law become "automatically" universalized?

We need look no further than ordinary case law. Smith sues Jones and wins. A rule of law in *Smith v. Jones* is thus established and, through the force of precedent, deemed to apply to all future litigants similarly situated. In this way, the common law is certainly a rather undemocratic process. But it is quite normal and acceptable. If the same issue litigated in *Smith v. Jones* came up later in *Brown v. Green*, we would think it strange that the court in the latter case would refuse to follow the rule of *Smith v. Jones*. Such a refusal, we would say, would make the law unpredictable and uncertain. Thus, even though neither Brown nor Green were around when *Smith v. Jones* was decided, the rule of *Smith v. Jones* affects both Brown and Green in their dealings with one another.

If we take this "common law" analogy and apply it to customary international law, then the custom of freedom of navigation on the high seas—even if provable only between Great Britain and The Netherlands at a given point in time in the Seventeenth Century—becomes automatically extended to all nations wishing to navigate on the high seas. Historically, of course, it was the Grotian position that prevailed, and today it is even hard to find a copy of Selden's *Mare Clausum* in a law library.

(b) Favoring the Restrictiveness of Custom: The "Participatory" or "Voluntarist" View

Many writers have objected to this universalization thesis. For example, in past decades the former Soviet Union strenuously objected; and, today, many Third World countries say that the universalization of custom is "undemocratic" because it signals the extension to them of principles of law that had their origin in customs established primarily among the industrialized, liberal economy nations of the Western world over which they had little or no control. They do not want to be "told" what to do by customary practices in which they did not participate. Hence, various "voluntarist" theories have evolved, holding that rules of customary international law apply only to those nations that have participated in the custom.

Consider, thus, the late Russian (formerly "Soviet") legal scholar Grigorii Tunkin, in G. Tunkin, Theory of International Law 127–31 (W. Butler trans. 1974):

> The thesis that a customary norm of international law recognized by a significant number of states is binding on all other countries enjoys wide support in contemporary bourgeois international legal literature. * * * The concept ... is actually based upon the presupposition that a majority of states may dictate norms of international law binding upon all other states in international relations.
>
> * * *
>
> This concept is in blatant contradiction to the fundamental principles of international law, especially the principle of equality of states.
>
> * * *
>
> As regards newly emergent states, legally they have the right not to recognize a particular customary norm of general international law. If, however, a new state enters without reservations into official relations with other countries, this signifies that it accepts the specific complex of principles and norms of prevailing international law as being the basic principles of relations among states.
>
> * * *
>
> The doctrine that customary norms of international law recognized as such by a significant number of states are binding upon all states not only has no basis in contemporary international law but also conceals a very great danger. This doctrine in essence justifies the attempts of a specific group of states to impose upon new states, socialist or newly emergent states of Asia and Africa, for example, certain customary norms which never have been accepted by the new states and which may be partially or wholly unacceptable to them.... [S]uch attempts undoubtedly may lead to serious international complications.

To become a norm of international law of universal application, in other words, a customary norm must be recognized by all the States affected by it.[14]

14. A more recent prominent view emanating from the former Soviet Union, less confining than that of Professor Tunkin but still sympathetic to the "participatory" or "voluntarist" view, may be found in Rein Müllerson, *Sources of International Law: New Tendencies in Soviet Thinking*, 83 AM. J. INT'L L. 494 (1989). An Estonian now teaching international law at King's College London, Müllerson wrote, at 504:

I do not entirely agree with Professor Tunkin. I find it too abstract to say that a newly born state is not bound by customary norms of general international law.... On entering the international system ... , a new state requires (and has a right to require) that other states respect its sovereignty; it wants other states not to use force against it, not to interfere in its internal affairs, and so on.

And this state automatically has to be deemed to have accepted these elementary or basic norms of contemporary international law. That is why I am convinced that at least norms of *jus cogens* [i.e., peremptory norms] are obligatory for all states, including new states.

As for other norms of general customary international law, I think that, theoretically, a new state does not have to accept all of them automatically. It may propose new rules; it may try to conclude treaties derogating from existing customary norms that do not have the character of peremptory norms (*jus cogens*). But practically, of course, a state that is just entering the existing international system has to recognize most norms of customary international law.

Thus if under this "participatory" or "voluntarist" theory we want to apply the customary law of, say, transfrontier atmospheric pollution to a particular State, we would have to do historical research into the question of whether that State "participated" in the formation of the law of transfrontier atmospheric pollution or whether it rejected such norms. Surely we can expect the historical evidence to be mixed at best, and probably nonexistent in most instances.

More generally, when we look to "participation" (in some form or another) in the custom-formation process, we probably will find that, when actual cases come up, the nations party to them probably will *not* have participated in the relevant custom! For if they had, then the cases probably would not have come up; the practices between the States would have been in accordance with the custom. Cases only arise when we have divergent practices, and divergent practices usually indicate that both sides have not participated in the relevant custom-formation process.

So we see that any theory short of universality is likely to leave us with very little relevant international law to apply to disputes between States. Our view is that the "universality" principle of customary international law probably has prevailed, but this is only a guess. One should look to the leading cases on custom to obtain a more informed answer.

Editors' Note

In light of the foregoing discussion by Professor D'Amato, consider the *Asylum Case* (Colom. v. Peru), 1950 I.C.J. 266, and the *Anglo-Norwegian Fisheries Case* (U.K. v. Nor.), 1951 I.C.J. 116. In the former, the I.C.J. stated, at 277–78, that "[e]ven if it could be supposed that ... a custom [of diplomatic asylum] existed between certain Latin American States only, it could not be invoked against Peru" which, far from having by its attitude adhered to it, has on the contrary repudiated it.... Similarly, in the latter, after rejecting as a rule of customary international law a claimed ten-mile baseline rule for bays,[uu] the Court stated, at 131, that, "[i]n any event, the ten-mile rule would appear to be inapplicable as against Norway, inasmuch as she has always opposed any attempt to apply it to the Norwegian coast." These pronouncements invoke what in the past has been a seldom claimed exception to the universality principle known as the persistent objector rule, to wit, that a customary rule, though it may come into being over the opposition of one state or a few states (assuming a sufficient degree of general acceptance), will not bind those who object persistently to it—which is to say that in international law there is no majority rule with respect to the formation of customary law.

Though seldom relied upon in the past, this persistent objector rule is likely to be increasingly invoked in the future as new principles of customary law emerge from majority positions in intergovernmental conferences and in the organs of the United Nations and other international institutions. *See, e.g.*, Ted L. Stein, *The Approach of the Different Drummer: The Principle of*

uu. The "baseline" is the line from which the breadth of the territorial sea and other maritime zones of coastal States is measured.

the Persistent Objector in International Law, 26 H.J.I.L. 457, 463–69 (1985). Accordingly, the rule is today attracting ever more attention. *See, e.g.*, Jonathan I. Charney, *The Persistent Objector Rule and the Development of Customary International Law*, 56 B.Y.B.I.L. 1 (1985). It also is attracting controversy. *See, e.g.*, Olufemi Elias, *Some Remarks on the Persistent Objector Rule in Customary International Law*, 1991 Denning L. J. 37, who observes, *inter alia*, that "[a] striking feature of the discussions about the existence and vitality of the persistent objector rule is the lack of a common statement of the rule itself." *Id.* at 38. Rudolf Bernhardt upon the rule and its dilemmas in *Customary International Law New and Old Problems*, 19 Thesaurus Acroasium 199, 219–20 (1992):

> Since, on the one hand, a strict majority rule is hardly compatible with the structure of [the international] community and the sovereignty of its member States, and, on the other hand, the emergence of new rules should not be made totally dependent on unanimity, a solution seems to be that all States which accept a new rule or at least acquiesce in regard to its application are bound, and only those which persistently reject the new rule are not bound. This proposal would seem to satisfy the interests at stake, but it leaves a good number of very difficult questions open. Is one persistent objector enough to exclude its being bound by a new norm? The answer seems to be yes, but can it not be relevant how strong the objection is and which interests are at stake? And what is the legal position if a persistent objector rejects a norm which is widely considered to be a norm of *jus cogens*? This has been discussed for the [former] practice of apartheid [in South Africa], but other examples [can] also be found. If a State which is not a member of the United Nations would persistently deny the validity of the prohibition of the use of force at least in certain circumstances, would this mean that the objector is not bound? What is the situation in regard to the persistent rejection of the right of self-determination by one State or a small group of States, or the permanent violation of basic human rights?

There are no easy answers to these questions. Surely the constancy and intensity with which an objector dissents should bear some influence. But how much influence and under what circumstances? And surely, too, certain basic values or fundamental principles of the world community as expressed through customary international law should be binding upon a persistent objector even though these values or principles may have been rejected from the start. But which ones and who is to decide according to what criteria? As Bernhardt observes in conclusion, at 220, "[t]he formation and the content of customary law are not governed by strict logical rules; instead they follow the development of the international community." Again, thus, we are left to follow the leading cases and incidents on custom as they evolve.

Tieya Wang, *The Third World and International Law*, in THE STRUCTURE AND PROCESS OF INTERNATIONAL LAW: ESSAYS IN LEGAL PHILOSOPHY DOCTRINE AND THEORY 955, 961–63, 970 (R. Mac-Donald & D. Johnston eds., 1983).

Although Third World countries are adamantly opposed to the imperialistic, colonialistic, oppressive and exploitative principles and rules of traditional [*i.e.*, customary] international law, they do not reject international law itself. Some western international lawyers, such as Brierly, believe that the new nations are inclined to look on international law as an alien system imposed on them by western nations.[15] Others, such as Jennings, doubt that the newly-independent states consider themselves bound in all respects by laws whose formation they had no part in.[16] In fact, the Third World objects only to parts of traditional international law; it has never and does not object to all of the rules of international law. To be sure, much of international law predates the gaining of independence by the Third World nations and was therefore created without their participation and by a process dominated by a minority of powerful states. Be this as it may, the march of history cannot be halted. International relations and international law are constantly developing and advancing. The newly-independent nations do not exist in a vacuum. There must be intercourse between nations and no nation has any choice but to subscribe to those principles and rules of international law which are necessary for its regulation. For this reason, the newly-independent nations do respect international law. Many, in fact, have explicitly acknowledged the effectiveness of international law in their constitutions. This point has been stressed by Third World writers. Anand, for example, makes the observation that none of the new nations has ever denied the binding effect of international law and, in fact, have unquestionably accepted the validity of the bulk of international law.[17]

The attitude taken by the Third World towards international law is very clear: it neither accepts nor rejects international law in its entirety. As Hazard puts it, "No one is asking that the books be burned and that we start afresh in rejection of the lessons history has given us as to the rules which minimize friction."[18] The Third World, however, will not suffer the continued existence of the principles and rules established to protect the interests of imperialism and colonialism.... [T]he Third World requires that international law be gradually re-written to reflect the revolutionary changes which have taken place since the Second World War. To this end, Third World nations have been eagerly participating in "legislative" activities.

As subjects of international law, Third World nations are fully qualified to participate in the making of international law. Moreover, as a group, the Third World is not without clout; it has been playing and will continue to play a very significant role in the development of international law. As Henkin pointed out, "The ways of the law have been importantly affected also by the fact that there are now more than [185] states, [185] makers of international law, [185] judges of each other's behavior"[19] a fact of no small import. Nations belonging to the Third World account for more than one half of these [185] states. Their collective importance to the formation and development of international law should not be underestimated.

15.   JOSEPH BRIERLY, THE LAW OF NATIONS 43 (H. Waldock 6th ed. 1963).

16.   R. Jennings, *The Progress of International Law*, 34 BRIT.Y.B.I.L. 350 (1958).

17.   Ram P. Anand, New States and International Law 62 (1972).

18.   J. Hazard, in 57 PROCEED. AM. SOC. INT'L L. 79 (1963).

19.   LOUIS HENKIN, HOW NATIONS BEHAVE—LAW AND FOREIGN POLICY 122 (2d ed. 1979).

Editors' Note

"Without denigrating the considerable utility of customary international law," writes Mark Janis in *An Introduction to International Law* 52–53 (2d ed. 1993), "it must be admitted that this form of international law is subject to a number of sometime crippling faults." He then outlines three:

First and foremost is the fact that oftentimes state practice is so diverse that it may be difficult or even impossible to find enough consistency [or uniformity] of practice to warrant drawing a customary international legal rule from it. . . . If no treaty can be found to authoritatively regulate a matter, it is by no means certain that customary international law will provide a definite rule to fill the gap.

Second, even if one state, judge, or other observer decides that the available evidences establish a norm of customary international law, there is no assurance that another decisionmaker will reach the same conclusion. Customary international law is found by a more or less subjective weighing of the evidence and subjective scales tilt differently in different hands. . . .

Third, the very process of making customary international law often stimulates conflict. When states have differing views of what international law ought to be and when they cannot agree to make common rules by treaty, then they may well act and react in international relations in a fashion consciously designed to make customary international law or, at least, to block another state's preferred version of the right rule from becoming customary international law or to establish an exception to the rule. . . .

Janis might usefully have recorded another deficiency of customary international law: its gender bias to the detriment of women and women's concerns. After noting customary law's quantitative and qualitative requirements (state practice and *opinio juris*), Professor Christine Chinkin has remarked insightfully as follows:

The focus on official government action in the requirements of customary law makes the question [of customary law formation] one of simple exclusion. It leaves out the possibly many and varied practices of its citizens. There is an assumption of monolithic behaviour by the state, a single line of practice that can be viewed as state practice, without regard to the diversity of views and actions that may in fact exist. The low level of representation of women in high-ranking government positions has . . . been noted. The effect in this context is that women's voices are not heard in the decision-making processes that lead to identifiable state practice.

However, there are other ways beyond simple lack of participation in which the determination of rules of customary law works to exclude the interests of women. . . . First, in some instances where the facts of state practice do not conform with assertions of customary law, there has been a tendency to disregard the reality in preference for the statements of governments that such acts are prohibited. . . . However, this approach does not allow a determination of a rule of customary law condemning violence against women that is likely to win widespread acceptance. [Second,] unlike other human rights abuses, violence against women is not even verbally condemned as illegal in many societies, but instead is regarded as acceptable on social, traditional or religious grounds.... It is impossible to assert that there is strong evidence of *opinio juris* to allow contrary state practice to be discounted. * * * The task for women has therefore been to struggle to have gender-specific violence placed on the international agenda and to take steps within the public arena whereby a rule of customary law may be generated.

Panel on Sources of International Law: Entrenching the Gender Bias, in Contemporary International Law Issues: Opportunities at a Time of Momentous Change—Proceedings of the Second Joint Conference of the American Society of International Law and the Nederlandse Vereniging voor Internationaal Recht (at The Hague, July 22–24, 1993) 418, 418–19 (1994).

W. Michael Reisman, *The Cult of Custom in the Late 20th Century*, 17 CAL. W. INT'L L. J. 133, 133–35, 142–43 (1987).

Legislation involves the deliberate and explicit establishment of community policy through prescribed procedures, usually in specialized institutions.... Custom, in contrast, concerns the *implicit* creation of norms through the behavior of a few politically relevant actors who are frequently unaware that law is being, or has been, made. Custom is supposedly indistinguishable from the aggregate flow of community behavior and thus has traditionally been associated with primitive societies lacking institutional articulation. While those who wish to use law as a means of affirmatively shaping future social arrangements have viewed custom as an anachronism and an atavism ... , those conservatives who just like old things and some scholars who appreciate so-called "free-market arrangements," have extolled custom for what they believe are its inherent efficiency and democracy.

Custom rapidly regained currency in the international context after the United States [in 1982] repudiated the [1982] Law of the Sea Treaty **[Basic Document 4.20]**, the most ambitious international legislative project since the drafting of the United Nations Charter. Although the action was traumatic for the international legislative process, the President [Ronald Reagan] of the United States ... announced that the renouncement [would] have little effect on lawmaking for the uses of the oceans: Most of the substance of the treaty, in fact, *mirabile dictum*, that is everything except the parts we dislike, is customary law anyway, meaning that it is a part of international law irrespective of the President's action.

* * *

However, we must ask ourselves whether custom can really address the needs of global civilization in the late 20th [and early 21st centuries]. If purposive legislation is so important an instrument for clarifying and implementing policy in an industrial and science-based civilization such as ours, how can we dispense with it in the much more complicated and varied global civilization? Mr. Reagan and his spokesmen told us [that] everything in the draft [Law of the Sea] Convention—except for the seabed resources regime— was custom anyway. That is rather puzzling in that our delegates were arguing over much of it in international legislative chambers only weeks earlier. Moreover, few American leaders would agree [then or now] that what majorities do in international conferences, much less what particular governments say there, is *ipso facto* custom or *eo ipso* evidence of it.

There are, in short, more than a few intellectual problems with this revivalist jurisprudence. It is hard to escape the suspicion that this great leap backward to custom [was] a device to conceal an entirely different political and legal maneuver. Obviously, custom will always survive in large measure for there will always be a great deal of macro- and micro-law secreted in the interstices of social life, like the hidden bulk of the proverbial iceberg. The question is about the tip of the iceberg: Can we really dispense with the international equivalent of legislation?

I think the answer is obvious. No one, I submit, seriously believes that custom is replacing deliberate international legislation.... What is being signalled is opposition to the *quantity* and the *style* of formal international legislation as it has developed in the last twenty [now thirty plus] years. The setting of necessary legislation is being shifted from the most inclusive and open international arenas, such as the General Assembly and universal conferences, to more limited alliance, regional and, within them, value sectoral conferences from which most of the new majority in the United Nations will be excluded. The "all states" trend of the last forty [now fifty plus] years, seeking to bring *everyone* into an inclusive conference arena, is being reversed in favor of a network of restrictive-access legislative arenas. Because this shift from the floors of the world legislatures to back rooms elsewhere is inconsistent with venerated international legal myth, it is more convenient, if less accurate, to describe it as the resurgence of custom.

* * *

[T]he new slogan of custom assumes that in the broader arena of real world power, numbers will not count at all. This, however, is a myopic view.... The fact is that, though the voting rules of the General Assembly magnify the power of the Third World, its members are part of the world power process and must be taken account of in future deliberations.... In or out of the General Assembly or an *ad hoc* international conference, the Third World must be contended with. It is autistic fantasy to assume that the Third World can be conjured away merely by substituting the word "custom" for "legislation". Realistically, even without the United States [or other major powers], the numerical majority does have power. No [major power] can afford to believe that, just because it stands aloof, legal arrangements cannot be made....

In addition to procedural fantasies in the custom slogan, there are also related substantive fantasies. It should be clear to anyone with the faintest understanding of international life that customary processes of lawmaking cannot deal with the enormous problems facing the world such as the debt crisis, the complex arrangements involved in a space station, the staggering detailed problems involved in meshing economically interdependent but functionally different national economies, the arranging of transnational defense against and suppression of terrorism and so on. However much one extols custom, deliberate multilateral legislation must continue. But, concealed under the rubric of custom, there will be important changes.

Discussion Notes/Questions

1. In his book *Global Order—Values and Power in International Politics* (2d ed. 1990), political scientist Lynn H. Miller writes as follows, at 88:

> [W]hat happens when, because of a malfunction of some kind, the traffic lights at a busy intersection suddenly fail? The symbol of government ceases to operate; yet we would not expect every semblance of social order there to break down as a result. The drivers of the cars approaching that intersection still have a mutual interest in their own safety. As a result, they almost certainly will begin to create an ordering, or quasi-governmental, system of their own, perhaps even without any verbal communication. We should expect such drivers at least to slow down when they see the traffic lights not functioning, and then proceed only when they deem it safe. Logically, each will defer to the driver who arrives at the intersection next before him [sic], for if all drivers do that, none will be more minimally inconvenienced, and a depend able stop-and-go system, clear to all, will be in place.

Does this passage help to explain how rules of customary international law come about? Can you relate it to the theoretical discussion of the elements of custom as explained in the foregoing readings? Does it help to clarify the "quantitative" element? The "qualitative" element? Neither? Both?

2. What is the distinction between "custom" and "usage"? "Custom" and "habit"?

3. As we have seen, one of the elements of customary international law is state practice. But, specifically, what state practice? Must it be some kind of action? Is a vote in the U.N. General Assembly (where resolutions are presumptively not binding) as opposed to the U.N. Security Council (where resolutions are presumptively binding) state practice? Do domestic executive, legislative, or judicial statements constitute state practice? If so, is it relevant by what internal organ state action is taken? Can acts of omission be a form of practice? If so, under what circumstances? Must the absence of action have been deliberate? Further:

   a. How general must state practice be to establish customary law? How many states are needed? Does one consider only the practice of affected states? Is the practice of some states more important than that of others? Can there be a customary rule if the United States or some other major power has a different state practice from the majority of states? Can there be regional customary international law? Bilateral customary international law?

   b. How much consistency is required to have state practice? How does one determine whether the state practice is consistent or not since the circumstances will be different in every case? How far back in time must we go to determine whether there is consistency? Or inconsistency? Is one inconsistency or are several minor inconsistencies sufficient to negate a customary rule?

   c. How much time must pass to create state practice? May a single act constitute state practice sufficient to establish customary law? Is it possible to have instant customary law? If so, is this desirable? Undesirable?

   d. How can there be "a general practice accepted as law," to quote Article 38(1)(b) of the Statute of the International Court of Justice [**Basic Document 1.4**] in the case of an omission or absence of action?

4. Another key element of customary international law is captured in the expression *opinio juris* or *opinio juris sive necessitatis*. What does this mean?

a. How does one determine the existence of this subjective element, *opinio juris*? Is it not determined by the consistency of state practice? Is it anything more than a tacit agreement among states? If not, then why is it necessary that there be this separate subjective element to establish customary international law? Does it not all add up to the fact that customary law consists only of one element? Or is something else involved? If so, what?

b. Can we assume an *opinio juris* because a state practice is socially necessary or suited to international needs? Can there be a customary international rule if all states agree on the norm in theory but none act in accordance with it in practice?

c. Whose *opinio juris* is relevant for the purpose of establishing customary international law? Can a state have an opinion, legal or otherwise? If we respond by saying that states, or governments, have opinions in the form of policies, who, then, speaks for the state or government? What if the government is not representative of the people?

d. Article 38(1)(b) of the I.C.J. Statute speaks of "a general practice accepted as law." How can there be an acceptance of law in the case of an omission or absence of action?

5. Upon whom is customary international law binding? Are dissenting and non-participating states bound by customary rules? Is the burden upon the dissenting state to resist the binding effect of a customary international law rule? If so, when and how must a state express its opposition? Does only a persistent objection deny the binding effect of the customary rule? If so, what qualifies as a persistent objection? Does a qualified persistent objection prevent the creation of the rule or is the rule not binding only on the particular state? Is customary law binding on states that were not in existence at its creation?

6. It is said that treaties can create customary international law. But *how* does a treaty create customary? And where do we draw the line between a treaty obligation and a customary rule? Can customary international law come into being via a treaty that has not been ratified or entered into force? Can resolutions and declarations of the General Assembly and other quasi-parliamentary institutions establish customary international law?

7. Can state practice negate a treaty commitment or obligation? What happens to a customary law rule when the supporting state practice changes? Is there law during the period of transition? What rules do we apply then, if any?

8. In an actual case, how does the international lawyer determine whether or not there exists a rule of customary law to be applied in that case? Can he or she look at judicial decisions and the teachings of qualified international law publicists to prove that a certain conduct constitutes a rule of customary international law? How do courts and arbitral tribunals do it? Do they engage in or refer to a detailed study of state practice? Is it not true that most of the time courts and arbitral tribunals simply announce that a particular customary law rule exists and that they rarely examine the actual state practice or consider whether it is accompanied by the subjective element of *opinio juris*?

9. What is the value, if any, of customary international law today, particularly in relation to major world order problems? Does the process of customary law-making meet the needs of a Twenty-first Century global civilization? Can customary law change quickly enough to keep pace with scientific and technological

technology breakthroughs? Is it adequately democratic to be representative of different legal expectations in a multicultured world?

C.   GENERAL PRINCIPLES OF LAW

As a third "source" of international law, what, you ask, in your capacity as a junior lawyer in the Norwegian Foreign Ministry, are "general principles of law recognized by civilized nations"? And how do they supplement treaties and customary law? The answers to these questions, you discover, depend in part on who you ask.

The phrase, you recall, was inserted in the Statute of the Permanent Court of International Justice—predecessor to the International Court of Justice, as already noted—to assist in the resolution of cases where neither treaty law nor customary law provides an answer. However, the concept means different things to different people. As Professor Mark Janis writes in An Introduction to International Law 55 (2d ed. 1993), "some [scholars] liberally suggest that the availability of general principles as a source of international law permits international lawyers to apply natural law, while others restrictively contend that general principles of law may be international law only when drawn from customary international practice"—for example, Legal Positivists who insist upon State consent as a precondition to the establishment of any international law rule (hence their stress upon the qualitative element, or *opinio juris*, in the making of customary law) and who therefore are loathe to admit to international legal rules that are based on *nonconsensual* foundations (such as natural law). But "the most usual approach to general principles of law as a source of international law," Professor Janis continues, "relies upon techniques of comparative law. The basic notion is that a general principle of law is some proposition of law so fundamental that it will be found in virtually every legal system." Id. On the other hand, you query, is there really any reason why "general principles of law" cannot have all three meanings. After all, international tribunals had for many years relied upon all three meanings even before the phrase was inserted into the P.C.I.J.'s Statute in 1920.

And what, by the way, is meant by the expression "civilized nations"? Does it include Germany, the homeland not only of Bach, Beethoven, and Brahms (and Kant, Goethe, and Schiller) but also of Adolf Hitler, the killer of over six million Jews? In the light of Hiroshima and Nagasaki—so far, mercifully, the only instance of innocent men, women, and children being incinerated and radiated by nuclear warfare—does it include the United States? For that matter, does it include the Russian Federation, given its deliberate dumping of radioactive waste and its persecution of persons who seek to expose and reverse the practice? Also, may "general principles" be invoked to supplement or modify what treaty law and customary international law have to say on a given subject—say, Russia's dumping of spent reactors from its Northern and Pacific nuclear submarine fleets—or may they be referred to only to fill gaps that treaty law and customary law fail to fill?

All of these and related questions compel you to resume your review of public international law. You turn to your treatise yet again.

HERSCH LAUTERPACHT, INTERNATIONAL LAW 68–
74 (Elihu Lauterpacht ed., 1970)

The fact that, on the face of it, there are no provisions of a treaty or of customary international law directly applicable to a given situation does not necessarily mean that there exists a gap in the law and that there is, therefore, no room for the application of international law.... [W]hen there might ... appear to exist a clear gap in the law as laid down by custom or treaty, international practice [custom?] recognizes, and the very existence of the international community necessitates, a residuary source of law on which States are entitled to act and by reference to which international courts are bound to render decisions. That residuary source is, in the language of Article 38 of the Statute of the Court **[Basic Document 1.4]**, the body of "general principles of law recognized by civilized nations."

What is the meaning of that expression? These "general principles" are not, as such, principles of moral justice as distinguished from law; they are not rules of "equity" in the ethical sense; nor are they a speculative law conceived by way of deductive reasoning from legal and moral principles. They are, in the first instance, those principles of law, private and public, which contemplation of the legal experience of civilized nations leads one to regard as obvious maxims of jurisprudence of a general and fundamental character— such as the principle that no one can be judge in his own cause, that a breach of a legal duty entails the obligation of restitution, that a person cannot invoke his own wrong as a reason for release from a legal obligation, that the law will not countenance the abuse of a right, that legal obligations must be fulfilled and rights must be exercised in good faith, and the like. The International Court of Justice and its predecessor have occasionally acted on these and other general principles of law. So have international tribunals generally.

However, the recourse to and the utility of general principles of law are not confined to fundamental, or abstract, maxims of jurisprudence of a general character. "General principles of law" are, and have been, a legitimate source of judicial decision and State action in regard to specific rules and situations. * * * Whenever a question arises which is not governed by an existing rule of international law imposing an obligation upon a State or, in the absence of such a rule, acknowledging by implication its freedom from obligation, or in which the existing rule required elucidation or development, the rich repository of "general principles" may be legitimately resorted to by a tribunal, a Government, or the scholar grappling with a novel or difficult situation. Such instruction is available not automatically but only as the result of a search which may be exacting....

On occasions, the search for a general principle of law may fail to offer direct assistance for the reason that national systems of law differ with regard to the particular subject. Even in such cases the negative result may not be altogether without usefulness inasmuch as it may throw light on the intricacies of the problem involved. However, experience shows that in the vast majority of cases such differences are limited to questions of form and procedure and that behind national differences of technique and approach there asserts itself an essential uniformity of the law—a reminder that the increasingly frequent description of general principles of law as the modern law of nature is no mere form of words.

Finally, in the rapidly expanding field of relations between Governments which are substantially indistinguishable from that of ordinary commercial relations between private persons, circumstances call, on that account, for the application of general principles of law approximating to general principles of private law in the restricted sense. Thus, there has been a growing number of treaties between Governments providing for the sale or exchange of goods, the grant or opening of a credit, the loan of money or guarantee of a debt, the lease of property of an ordinary private law character, and the like.... [S]ome of these treaties ... may be governed by ... the rules of private law of one of the contracting parties. However, the circumstances of these transactions do not as a rule point to an intention of the parties to submit to the law of the other party. In view of this the relations in question ... are more properly governed by what has been described as the commercial law of nations, namely, general principles of private law applicable to the transaction in question."[vv]

The same may apply to agreements, especially in the sphere of private law, between one [intergovernmental] organisation and another, between [intergovernmental] organisations and States, and, probably, between [inter-governmental] organisations and private individuals. The relations between public international organizations and their officials—an expanding field of international administrative law—[also] call for the application of "general principles of law" in that particular sphere.

Bin Cheng, General Principles of Law—As Applied by International Courts and Tribunals 23–25 (1953).

[T]he line of demarcation between custom and general principles of law recognized by civilized nations is often not very clear, since international custom or customary international law, understood in a broad sense, may include all that is unwritten in international law, *i.e.*, both custom and general principles of law. In Article 38 [of the I.C.J. Statute] **[Basic Document 1.4]**, however, custom is used in a strict sense, being confined to what is a general practice among States accepted by them as law....

In the definition of [general principles of law], there is also the element of recognition on the part of civilized peoples but the requirement of a general

---

vv. *See, e.g.,* Award of Lord Asquith of Bishopstone in the Matter of an Arbitration Between Petroleum Development (Trucial Coast) Ltd. and the Sheikh of Abu Dhabi, 1 I.C.L.Q. 247, 250 (1952):

What is the "Proper Law" applicable in construing this [oil concession] contract? This is a contract made in Abu Dhabi and wholly to be performed in that country. If any municipal system of law were applicable, it would prima facie be that of Abu Dhabi. But no such law can reasonably be said to exist. The Sheikh administers a purely discretionary justice with the assistance of the Koran; and it would be fanciful to suggest that in this very primitive region there is any settled body of legal principles applicable to the construction of modern commercial instruments. Nor can I see any basis on which the municipal law of England could apply. On the contrary, Clause 17 of the agreement, cited above, repels the notion that the municipal law of any country, as such, could be appropriate. The terms of that clause invite, indeed prescribe, the application of principles rooted in the good sense and common practice of the generality of civilised nations—a sort of "modern law of nature." I do not think that on this point there is any conflict between the parties.

practice is absent. The object of recognition is, therefore, no longer the legal character of the rule implied in an international usage, but the existence of certain principles intrinsically legal in nature.... Principles are to be distinguished from rules.... This part of international law does not consist ... in specific rules formulated for practical purposes, but in general propositions underlying the various rules of law which express the essential qualities of juridical truth itself, in short of Law. Thus Lord Phillmore, who proposed the formula [of Article 38], explained that by general principles of law he meant "maxims of law."[20] But how is it possible to ascertain whether a given principle is a principle of law and not of another cognate social discipline, such as religion or morality? The recognition of its legal character by civilized peoples supplies the necessary element of determination. Lord Phillmore also explained that the principles referred to in Article 38 I (c) were those which were "accepted by all nations *in foro domestico*."[21] M. de La Pradelle took them to mean that general principles of law were the basis of the municipal law of all or nearly all States.[22] The recognition of these principles in the municipal law of civilized peoples, where the conception of law is already highly developed, gives the necessary confirmation and evidence of the juridical character of the principle concerned. The qualification "recognized by civilized nations" was intended to safeguard against subjectivity and possible arbitrariness on the part of the judge. It should be noticed, however, that the word *nation* was originally used in the sense of "people" rather than "State." The qualifying epithet "civilized" was, therefore, necessary in order to exclude from consideration systems of law of primitive communities which were not yet civilized....

Hanna Bokor–Szegö, *General Principles of Law, in*
INTERNATIONAL LAW: ACHIEVEMENTS AND PROSPECTS
213, 214–15 (M. Bedjaoui ed. 1991).

[T]he origin of the expression "civilized nations" goes back to the colonial era, when the international community was mainly composed of European States. For a long time, this "traditional" international law meant, basically, European international law. This law was gradually expanded with the founding of the United States of America and subsequently the accession to independence of the Central American and South American States. Yet despite the expansion of international law, the gulf which existed at that time between the juridical status of States subject to international law and that of dependent territories persisted and indeed widened. The expression "civilized nations" clearly reflected the wish to see international legal conflicts settled in terms of Anglo–Saxon [law] (common law) and the law of the European continental States based on Roman law, or according to legal systems derived from one or [the] other of these. After the First World War, and even more so after the Second, the composition of the international community changed radically with the accession to independence of a large number of States in Asia and Africa. The participation by the socialist States in international relations helped to bring pressure to bear on the "traditional" reference frames of international law. In 1973, some governments strongly criticized the

---

20. LORD PHILLIMORE, PROCÈS-VERBAUX 335.   **22.** *Id.*
21. *Id.* at 335.

expression "civilized nations" in their reply to the United Nations Secretary–General's questionnaire on a revision of the role of the International Court of Justice, considering it to be a relic of out-dated colonialism, and proposing that it be defeated. * * * The prevailing view *is that today the expression "civilized nations"—as contained in [Article 38 of] the Statute of the International Court of Justice—should be understood as meaning sovereign States irrespective of their political system and the degree of development of their economy.*

Oscar Schachter, International Law in Theory and Practice 50–53 (1991).

[The] category, general principles of municipal law, has given rise to a considerable body of writing and much controversy. Article 38(1)(c) of the Statute of the Court **[Basic Document 1.4]** does not expressly refer to principles of national law but rather [to] general principles "recognized by civilized nations". The travaux préparatoires reveal an interesting variety of views about this subparagraph during the drafting stage. Some of the participants had in mind equity and principles recognized "by the legal conscience of civilized nations". (The notion of "legal conscience" was a familiar concept to European international lawyers in the nineteenth and early part of the twentieth century.) Elihu Root, the American member of the drafting committee, prepared the text finally adopted and it seemed clear that his amendment was intended to refer to principles "actually recognized and applied in national legal systems."[23] The fact that the subparagraph was distinct from those on treaty and custom indicated an intent to treat general principles as an independent source of law, and not as a subsidiary source. As an independent source, it did not appear to require any separate proof that such principles of national law had been "received" into international law.

However, a significant minority of jurists holds that national law principles, even if generally found in most legal systems, cannot *ipso facto* be international law. One view is that they must receive the *imprimatur* of State consent through custom or treaty in order to become international law. The strict positivist school adheres to that view. A somewhat modified version is adopted by others to the effect that rules of municipal law cannot be considered as recognized by civilized nations unless there is evidence of the concurrence of States on their status as international law. Such concurrence may occur through treaty, custom or other evidence of recognition. This would allow for some principles, such as *res judicata*, which are not customary law but are generally accepted in international law....

Several influential international legal scholars have considered municipal law an important means for developing international law and extending it into new areas of international concern.... The growth of transnational commercial and financial transactions has also been perceived as a fruitful area for the application of national law rules to create a "commercial law of nations", referred to as a "vast *terra incognita*".

---

23. Humphrey. Waldock, *General Course*   Cours 237 (1965).
on Public International Law, 115 Recueil des

Despite the eloquent arguments made for using national law principles as an independent source of international law, it cannot be said that either courts or the political organs of States have significantly drawn on municipal law principles as an autonomous and distinct ground for binding rules of conduct. It is true that the International Court and its predecessor the Permanent Court of International Justice have made reference on a number of occasions to "generally accepted practice" or "all systems of law" as a basis for its approval of a legal rule. (But curiously the Court has done so without explicit reference to its own statutory authority in Article 38(I)(c).) Those references to national law have most often been to highly general ideas of legal liability or precepts of judicial administration. In the former category, we find the much-quoted principles of the *Chorzów Factory* case[24] that "every violation of an engagement involves an obligation to make reparation" and that "a party cannot take advantage of his own wrong". These maxims and certain maxims of legal interpretation, as for example, *lex specialis derogat generalis*, and "no one may transfer more than he has", are also regarded as notions intrinsic to the idea of law and legal reasoning. As such they can be (and have been) accepted not as municipal law, but as general postulates of international law, even if not customary law in the specific sense of that concept.

The use of municipal law rules for international judicial and arbitral procedure has been more common and more specific than any other type of application. For example, the International Court has accepted *res judicata* as applicable to international litigation;[25] it has allowed recourse to indirect evidence (*i.e.*, inferences of fact and circumstantial evidence)[26] and it has approved the principle that legal remedies against a judgment are equally open to either party.[27] Arbitral tribunals have applied the principle of prescription (or laches) to international litigation relying on analogies from municipal law. Lauterpacht's *Private Law Sources and Analogies of International Law*, written in 1926, still remains a valuable repository of examples, as does Bin Cheng's later work on *General Principles as Applied by International Courts and Tribunals*.

But considerable caution is still required in inferring international law from municipal law, even where the principles of national law are found in many "representative" legal systems. The international cases show such use in a limited degree, nearly always as a supplement to fill in gaps left by the primary sources of treaty and custom.... The most important limitation on the use of municipal law principles arises from the requirement that the principle be appropriate for application on the international level. Thus, the universally accepted common crimes—murder, theft, assault, incest—that apply to individuals are not crimes under international law by virtue of their ubiquity. In the *Right of Passage Over Indian Territory* case (Port. v. India),[28] the Court rejected arguments that the municipal law of easements found in

24. Factory at Chorzów (Ger. v. Pol.) (Merits), 1928 P.C.I.J. (ser. A) No. 21, at 93, 17, 19.

25. Effect of Awards Made by the United Nations Administrative Tribunal, 1956 I.C.J. 53 (Advisory Opinion).

26. Corfu Channel (U.K. v. Alb.) (Merits), 1949 I.C.J. 4.

27. Judgments of the Administrative Tribunal of the ILO Upon Complaints Made Against UNESCO, 1956 I.C.J. 77, at 85–86. (Advisory Opinion).

28. Right of Passage Over Indian Territory (Port. v. India) (Merits), 1960 I.C.J. 6.

most legal systems were appropriate principles for determining rights of transit over State territory. Similarly, a contention that the law of trusts could be used to interpret the mandate of South Africa over South West Africa (Namibia) did not win approval as international law but it may possibly have had an indirect influence on the Court's reasoning in its advisory opinions. Lord McNair, in an individual opinion, in the 1950 Advisory Opinion on the *International Status of South West Africa*, expressed a balanced conclusion on the subject of analogies from private law that merits quotation here.

> "International law has recruited and continues to recruit many of its rules and institutions from private systems of law ... The way in which international law borrows from the source is not by means of importing private law institutions 'lock, stock and barrel', ready-made and fully equipped with a set of rules ... In my opinion the true view of the duty of international tribunals in this matter is to regard any features or terminology which are reminiscent of the rules and institutions of private law as an indication of policy and principles rather than as directly importing these rules and institutions."[29]

I would subscribe to this general formulation and stress the requirement that the use of municipal law must be appropriate for international relations.

At the same time, I would suggest a somewhat more positive approach for the emergent international law concerned with the individual, business companies, environmental dangers and shared resources. Inasmuch as these areas have become the concern of international law, national law principles will often be suitable for international application. This does not mean importing municipal rules "lock, stock and barrel", but it suggests that domestic law rules applicable to such matters as individual rights, contractual remedies, liability for extra-hazardous activities, or restraints on use of common property, have now become pertinent for recruitment into international law. In these areas, we may look to representative legal systems not only for the highly abstract principles of the kind referred to earlier but to more specific rules that are sufficiently widespread as to be considered "recognized by civilized nations"....

Editors' Note

There have been frequent assertions by states and others that certain principles of international law, whether nationally or internationally derived, are so fundamental as to be considered *jus cogens*—for example, the basic principles of territorial sovereignty and *pacta sunt servanda*, found among the "general principles of law recognized by civilized nations" as well as in customary international law. But what is this notion of *jus cogens*? Writes Malcolm Shaw, in International Law (3rd ed. 1991), at 99: "The concept of *jus cogens* is based upon an acceptance of fundamental and superior values within the system and in some respects is akin to the notion of public order or public policy in domestic legal orders." To this may be added Professor Janis' observation that "*[j]us cogens* is a norm thought to be so fundamental that it

29. International Status of South–West Africa, 1950 I.C.J. 128, at 148 (Advisory Opinion).

invalidates rules consented to by states in treaties and custom.... *Jus cogens* postulates an international public order potent enough to invalidate some norms that particular states might otherwise establish for themselves." Mark W. Janis, An Introduction to International Law 62 (2d ed. 1993). *See,* in this connection, articles 53 and 64 of the Vienna Convention on the Law of Treaties **[Basic Document 1.7]** entitled, respectively, "Treaties Conflicting with a Peremptory Norm of General International Law (Jus Cogens)" and "Emergence of a New Peremptory Norm of General International Law (Jus Cogens)." Consider also the following excerpt from *Starke's International Law* 48–49 (I. Shearer 11th ed. 1994):

> [M]ention should be made of the concept of *jus cogens* ... which may ... operate to invalidate a treaty or agreement between States to the extent of the inconsistency with any of such principles or norms.... There is undoubtedly some analogy between *jus cogens* and the principles of public policy which at common law render a contract void if it offends against these, such as the principle that parties cannot by agreement between themselves oust the ordinary courts from their jurisdiction. For example, in the international field, a treaty for the purpose of carrying out operations of piracy *jure gentium* would be void and would not be enforced by an international tribunal. Assuming that this analogy holds good, one must correspondingly bear in mind some of the metaphors used by harassed common law judges to describe the doctrine of public policy, such as "a very unruly horse," "treacherous ground," and "slippery ground." Critics of the concept of *jus cogens* in international law have also urged that it may be resorted to as a means of avoiding onerous treaty obligations, or even to justify interference in matters otherwise falling within the domestic jurisdiction of States.

> One major difficulty is related to the identification of norms of *jus cogens*. First, should this function of identification be performed solely by multilateral law-making Conventions, or may a norm of *jus cogens* evolve through the same process as in the case of customary rules of international law? Article 64 of the Vienna Convention on the Law of Treaties provides that "if a new peremptory norm of general international law emerges, any existing treaty which is in conflict with that norm becomes void and terminates". The word "emerges" shows that is was contemplated that a norm of *jus cogens* could be one of customary international law. Second, there is a lack of consensus as to what, at the present time, are norms of *jus cogens....*

But see Roberto Ago, *The Law of Treaties in Light of the Vienna Convention,* 134 Hague Recueil (Hague Acad. Int'l L.) 297, 324 n. 37 (1971–III) (editors' transl.), who views the doctrine of *jus cogens* applicable to

> ... the fundamental rules concern the safeguarding of peace and notably those which prohibit recourse to force or the threat of force; fundamental rules of a humanitarian nature (prohibitions of genocide, slavery, racial discrimination, protection of rights essential to the human person in times of peace and in times of war); rules which forbid infringement of the independence and the sovereign equality of States; rules which ensure to all members of the international community the enjoyment of certain common resources (high seas, outer space, etc.).

Arguably, *jus cogens* doctrines, principles, and rules forbidding infringement of the independence and sovereign equality of states (applicable to the Russian Federation's management of its nuclear arsenal) can work against the goals of international environmental protection (applicable to the Russian Federation's disposal of its radioactive waste). But others cited by Ago in 1971—rules which ensure to all members of the international community the enjoyment of certain common resources—clearly do not.

Hilary Charlesworth, *Sources of International Law: Entrenching the Gender Bias, in* CONTEMPORARY INTERNATIONAL LAW ISSUES: OPPORTUNITIES AT A TIME OF MOMENTOUS CHANGE—PROCEEDINGS OF THE SECOND JOINT CONFERENCE OF THE AMERICAN SOCIETY OF INTERNATIONAL LAW AND THE NEDERLANDSE VERENIGING VOOR INTERNATIONAAL RECHT 421, 421–24 (July 22–24, 1993).

The "general principles of law recognized by civilized nations" are perhaps the most controversial source of international law. What I want to argue is that while general principles can be an essentially conservative force in entrenching the gender bias in international law, this source of law may also offer the possibility of transformation.... Professor Cherif Bassiouni has argued that, in the face of increasing global interdependence, customary and conventional law are not always adequate to respond to major contemporary issues, such as human rights, the environment, economic development and international criminality.[ww] He contends that general principles may take up the slack, indeed that they may become "the most important and influential source of international law in this decade."[xx]

What might be a feminist approach to this? * * * If one looks at the traditional way in which general principles are defined, it suggests they may well be a vehicle by which the androcentric assumptions of national legal systems are reproduced and reinforced in the international legal sphere. The subordination of women to men through both the structure and substance of law is one truly universal feature of national legal systems; implicitly, and sometime explicitly, a core legal concept. All national legal systems have been fashioned by men ... and reflect the interests of their designers.... A real danger of bringing general principles of domestic law into the international law system is that they will simply transpose the gender bias of national legal systems to the international plane. * * * [Additionally, a] core feature of many national legal systems is their concern to distinguish legal activity from politics and morality.... This leads to a very narrow form of dispute-resolution in which parties are viewed detached from their actual social context. Imbalances in social and economic power between individuals are regarded as irrelevant in legal terms.... Incorporation of general principles of this sort into the international sphere will not advance women's equality.

A second feminist criticism of Article 38(1)(c) is that it makes quite explicit the consensual assumptions of the international legal order; that the general principles can be translated to the international plane because all or some states have recognized them as such. Any feminist analysis of the

ww. M. Cherif Bassiouni, *A Functional Approach to General Principles of International Law*, 77 MICH. J. INT'L L. 768 (1990).

xx. *Id.* at 769.

international legal order must tackle this institutionalization of state perspectives in law-making. For a long time feminists accepted the state as a neutral institution which could be persuaded to accommodate women's interests, but this project has failed and has led to new understandings of the state.... [W]omen ... form the largest group whose interests remain unacknowledged in the state structure.

[T]he few general principles which are generally accepted as international law tend to be procedural or otherwise without immediate implications for gender. * * * One category of general principles, *jus cogens*, involves ... substantive commitments. [However, it] is not a properly universal one ... ; [it] reflect[s] a male perspective of what is fundamental to international society that may not be shared by women or backed up by women's experience[s] of life ... , [with] [w]omen ... relegated to the periphery of communal values. My aim is not to challenge the powerful symbolic significance of *jus cogens*, but to argue that the symbolism is itself skewed and gendered. The content of *jus cogens* would be much richer if women's lives contributed to the designation of international fundamental values. The violations of human rights typically included in the catalogue of *jus cogens* norms are of undoubted seriousness: genocide, slavery, murder, systematic racial discrimination, etc. The silences of the list, however, indicate that women's experiences have not directly contributed to it. For example, although race discrimination consistently appears in *jus cogens* inventories, discrimination on the basis of sex does not. And yet, sex discrimination is an even more widespread injustice, affecting the lives of more than half the world's population.

How can a feminist analysis contribute to the development of general principles as a source of international law? One of the ways is to identify all the silences of the category and to ask, for example, why violence against women is not prohibited as a general principle of both national and international law? ... NGOs can have a particularly important role in this respect....

Another way that could improve general principles from a feminist perspective is to de-emphasize the state as their source. Accepting statehood and sovereignty as givens in the international legal order narrows our imaginative universe and the possibilities of reconstruction. Developing general principles of international law from the activities of international organizations is one way of reducing the androcentric influence of statehood. Another approach is a feminist reconstruction of the category of general principles. For example, notions of equity are often acknowledged as general principles and these could be developed to include the advancement of sexual equality. Feminist rethinking of *jus cogens* would give prominence to a range of human rights, including the right to sexual equality, to food, to reproductive freedom, to be free from fear of violence and oppression, and to peace. * * * [I]t should be possible for even traditional international legal theory to accommodate rights that are fundamental to the existence and dignity of [over] half the world's population.

Discussion Notes/Questions

1. The preceding extract by Hilary Charlesworth, citing M. Cherif Bassiouni, argues for the proposition that "general principles" provide a rich opportunity for developing new norms of conventional and customary international law and for

developing a supplemental source to conventional and customary international law. In this regard, consider the following quotation from Morton A. Kaplan & Nicholas deB. Katzenbach, *The Political Foundations of International Law* 263 (1961):

> As vague and discretionary as the injunction to use "general principles of law" may be, it is a limitation upon, rather than an extension of, the capacity of courts and other decision makers applying international law. We can see that this is true if we review the long and inconclusive debate about whether or not international arbitrators are free to decide *ex aequo et bono*—according to concepts of "justice and fairness."[yy] Prevailing doctrine is that they are not free to do so unless specifically authorized by the parties, which rarely occurs. The phrasing suggests an absence of objective standards required by the judicial function. Although we suspect that it makes little difference to the decision arrived at, preference for "general principles of law" is a preference for principles that are as definite as possible. It reflects consensus that agreement would be impossible if nations had to agree on new rules or if judges were free to create new norms unrestrained by recorded common experience.

Does this quotation cause you to alter any conclusions you may have reached about "general principles" as a "source" of international law? Does it cause you to wonder about the capacity of international law, as circumscribed by article 38 of the I.C.J. Statute **[Basic Document 1.4]** to me et the unprecedented challenges to world order brought about by growing transnational economic and technological interdependence? How might Schachter, *supra*, react to this quotation?

2.   Note that international tribunals often refer to general or well-recognized principles of international law when referring to rules of international customary law as opposed to "general principles of law recognized by civilized nations," *e.g.*, the principles of state sovereignty, territorial integrity, equality, non-intervention, self-defense, etc. So do international law publicists. Professor Schachter, *supra*, appears to consider them as "general principles" within the meaning of Article 38(1)(c) of the I.C.J. Statute **[Basic Document 1.4]**. Do you agree with this conclusion? If so, what happens to the distinction between general principles of customary international law and general principles of law recognized by civilized nations?

3.   "General principles of law recognized by civilized nations" is the third listed "source" of international law in article 38 of the I.C.J. Statute **[Basic Document 1.4]**, after treaties and custom. Can you imagine a situation in which a general principle might take precedence over a treaty or a custom accepted as law, and thus challenge the hierarchy or sequence set forth in article 38?

4.   It is widely recognized among leading comparative law authorities that the major legal systems of the world include (a) the Romanist–Germanic–Civilist legal systems, (b) the Common Law legal systems, (c) the Marxist–Socialist legal systems, (d) the Islamic legal systems, and (e) the Asian legal systems. *See, e.g.*, René David, Les Grands Systèmes de Droit Contemporaires 22–32 (5th ed. 1973). Is it reasonable to suppose that a "general principle of law recognized by civilized nations" cannot become part of international law unless it is recognized by all of these legal systems? A majority? One or two? When it comes to resolving international legal disputes, is it possible that some legal systems may be more

yy.   *See* Section E of this chapter, *infra* at
143.

helpful than others in supplying the necessary legal principles? If so, is it reasonable to suppose that a "general principle" can become part of international law *without* being recognized by all the major legal systems?

5. Notice that Article 38(1)(c) of the I.C.J. Statute [**Basic Document 1.4**] refers to "general principles of law *recognized* by civilized nations" (emphasis added). Does this mean that there must be some sort of consent to, or acknowledgment of, a general principle before it can become part of international law? If so, how is that consent or acknowledgment manifested? Is a tacit agreement sufficient? Must the general principle have matured into a rule of customary international law? Or is a general principle something that does not require "State practice" and therefore, to become part of international law, is not dependent on achieving customary law status?

6. Recall that, in theory, treaties are binding only on states that have consented to be bound by them and that customary international law is binding on a state only if it has not objected persistently. Is a "general principle of law recognized by civilized nations" binding on a state that has explicitly rejected—or refused to *recognize*—that principle? Does your answer depend on how you define "law" or on the school of jurisprudence that commands your intellectual loyalty?

7. Oscar Schachter, *supra*, argues that a municipal law principle must be not only "general" and "recognized" but also "appropriate" for international application to become part of international law. What conclusions may we draw from this viewpoint relative to the expansion and strengthening of international law? How would an international lawyer transform a national norm into an international one? What would be required?

8. Roberto Ago contends, *supra*, that the prohibition of genocide is a prohibition having *jus cogens* status. One may add that it has had this status for quite some time. It surely is beyond doubt, for example, that the United States, which did not become a full party to the 1948 Convention on the Prevention and Punishment of the Crime of Genocide [**Basic Document 7.10**] until 25 November 1988, could not have entered into any treaty or other arrangement sometime before that date that would have had as its intent the killing or other infliction of serious mental or bodily harm of a national, ethnical, racial, or religious group as such (contrary to Articles I and II of the Convention). Might it, then, be fairly maintained that a government that deliberately kills or harms, say, an indigenous people as part of an effort to exploit the resources of a rainforest is violating not only, possibly, a treaty prohibition but a "general principle of law" with *jus cogens* status as well? Consider, in this connection, Problem 10–3 ("A Rain Forest and the Guahibo are Threatened in Amazonia and Caribia") in Chapter 10, *infra*.

D. JUDICIAL DECISIONS AND THE TEACHINGS OF HIGHLY QUALIFIED PUBLICISTS

You now have renewed understanding that international legal authority may be derived from treaties, custom, and general principles of law—traditionally viewed as the primary means through which international law is made. You note from article 38(1)(d) of the I.C.J. Statute [**Basic Document 1.4**], however, that there are yet other acknowledged "sources" of international law, to wit, "judicial decisions and the teachings of the most highly qualified publicists of the various nations, as subsidiary means for the determination of rules of law." But what judicial decisions? International ones only? National ones also? If so, which? The highest tribunals only? Adjudicative ones only? Other third-party decision-making processes? And who are "the most highly qualified publicists"? Is there a list of them available somewhere? Is there some special standard to be applied? And why are they and "judicial decisions" designated as only "subsidiary means" for ascertaining rules of international law? Would a judicial decision by a Norwegian court with jurisdiction over, say, a stray Russian nuclear submarine be binding upon Russian courts? Should the work of, say, a scholar who has spent a lifetime at understanding and explaining a particular aspect of international law be thus seconded?

1. JUDICIAL DECISIONS

It is clear that a judicial decision in a case involving international law can and will be cited for its persuasiveness by parties to an international legal dispute, the decisions of courts and other tribunals being seen often to affirm or announce a treaty-based rule or interpretation, a rule of customary international law, or a general principle of international law. Explicitly mentioned in Article 38(1)(d) of the Statute of the International Court of Justice **[Basic Document 1.4]**, judicial decisions are seen as trustworthy evidence of what the law really is on a given subject; and this point is verified, in any event, by most of the leading international adjudicative and arbitral decisions that have helped to lay the foundations and otherwise articulate the substance of the emerging, modern-day customary international law of global environmental protection.[zz]

Each of these "judicial decisions" and others like them, however, are subject to the qualification, clearly stated in Article 38(1)(d) of the I.C.J. Statute, that they have no more than "subsidiary" value when it comes to their serving as reliable "sources" for international law doctrines, principles, and rules—a qualification that indicates, at least in theory, the reluctance of states, and perhaps most particularly states with a Civil Law tradition, to give to courts and other third-party decision-makers too much of a role in law-making. In addition, although a function of the same reluctance, there is Article 59 of the I.C.J. Statute which states that decisions of the World Court in contentious cases have no binding force except as between the parties and in respect of the case under consideration. The fact is, however, that the World Court itself and other tribunals as well have striven to follow their own and other previous rulings to ensure a measure of certainty and predictability in the development of international law, in a manner akin to the doctrine of precedent (*stare decisis*) well-known to the Common Law but theoretically foreign to the Civil Law upon which so much of international law has been erected. Indeed, in the course of interpreting and carefully distinguishing their prior judgments, the World Court and other tribunals will sometimes actually *make* law and not merely *determine* it,[aaa] not least in its advisory opinions.[bbb]

---

zz. These cases are excerpted or summarized in Section 8 of the documentary supplement to this coursebook.

aaa. *See, e.g.,* Fisheries (U. K. v. Nor.), 1951 I.C.J. 116; Nottebohm (Liech. v. Guat.), 1955 I.C.J. 4.

bbb. *See, e.g.,* Reparations for Injuries Suffered in the Service of the United Nations,

But as may be noted from the leading cases that have helped to lay the foundations of modern-day international law, "judicial decisions" as a "source" of international law need not be rendered solely by international adjudicative tribunals, such as the International Court of Justice. Frequently—perhaps the majority of times—the "judicial decisions" cited by parties to an international legal dispute will consist of arbitral awards (as opposed to *adjudicated* decisions *stricto sensu*) and, indeed, cases in *national* courts where issues of international law often are adjudicated (particularly in the absence of known pertinent precedent on the international plane). While technically not directly "binding," judges, arbitrators, and other third-party decision-makers—as a matter of training and habit—traditionally look to the disposition of other courts and tribunals in factually similar cases when attempting to reach decisions of their own. In this sense, strictly "binding precedent" is perhaps less important than the acknowledged fact that judges and analogous decision-makers typically attempt to adhere to prior third-party decisions whenever possible.

One other key point merits responsible attention, namely, the gendered way in which judicial and quasi-judicial bodies interpret and apply international (and national) law. The point was explicitly addressed in relation to international judicial bodies at the Second Joint Conference of the American Society of International Law and the Nederlandse Vereniging voor Internationaal Recht in July 1993. Comparing the way the principles of equal treatment and non-discrimination as between men and women have been interpreted and applied by the European Court on Human Rights, the Court of Justice of the European Communities, and the U.N. Human Rights Commission, Dutch law professor Titia Loenen noted, in general, "a male bias [that] reflect[s] masculine norms and values under the guise of objectivity and neutrality," i.e., "[a] legal focus ... on formal equality" that "start[s] from the presumption that men and women should always be treated the same [despite] the social and/or economic differences between men and women." Titia Loenen, *Sources of International Law: Entrenching the Gender Bias, in* Contemporary International Law Issues: Opportunities at a Time of Momentous Change—Proceedings of the Second Joint Conference of the American Society of International Law and the Nederlandse Vereniging voor Internationaal Recht 424, 424–27 (July 22–24, 1993). A "[s]tarting point for any court," Professor Loenen argued, "should be a contextual instead of an abstract approach to the concepts of equality and [non-discrimination]" that acknowledges "gender disadvantage." *Id.* at 428–29.

2. THE TEACHINGS OF PUBLICISTS

Under Article 38(1)(d) of the I.C.J. Statute **[Basic Document 1.4]**, the teachings of scholars (in French: *la doctrine*)—to which this coursebook gives obvious deference—are given a high, albeit "subsidiary," priority as an independent "source" of international law. Certainly this fact is gratifying to those who take up the study of international law as a life's work, the more so because it represents a significant break from the positivist doctrine of "sources" that became dominant in the Nineteenth Century and that contin-

1949 I.C.J. 174 (Advisory Opinion); Reservations to the Convention on Prevention and Punishment of the Crime of Genocide, 1951 I.C.J. 15 (Advisory Opinion).

ues to have substantial influence today, namely, an insistence upon empirically verifiable prescriptions that reveal themselves primarily, if not exclusively,
in the "will" of states through treaties and customary practice accepted as
law. But to what extent, precisely, do scholarly writings actually contribute to
the formation of international law? The following quotations from two celebrated domestic court decisions and from three "highly qualified publicists"
are instructive. In reading them, bear in mind the fact, already several times
noted, that the vast majority of international law publicists are men.

The Paquete Habana, The Lola, 175 U.S. 677, 700 (1900).

International law is part of our law, and must be ascertained and
administered by the courts of justice of appropriate jurisdiction, as often as
questions of right depending upon it are duly presented for their determination. For this purpose, where there is no treaty, and no controlling executive
or legislative act or judicial decision, resort must be had to the customs and
usages of civilized nations; and as evidence of these, to the works of jurists
and commentators, who by years of labor, research and experience, have made
themselves peculiarly well acquainted with the subjects of which they treat.
Such works are resorted to by judicial tribunals, not for the speculations of
their authors concerning what the law ought to be, but for trustworthy
evidence of what the law really is.

West Rand Central Gold Mining Co. v. The King,
2 King's Bench 391, 402 (K.B. 1905).

[T]he views expressed by learned writers on international law have done
in the past, and will do in the future, valuable service in helping to create the
opinion by which the range of the consensus of civilized nations is enlarged.
But in many instances their pronouncements must be regarded rather as the
embodiments of their views as to what ought to be, from an ethical standpoint, the conduct of nations inter se, than the enunciation of a rule or
practice so universally approved or assented to as to be fairly termed, even in
the qualified sense in which that word can be understood in reference to the
relations between independent political communities, "law."

D. W. GREIG, INTERNATIONAL LAW 47–8 (2D ED. 1976).

[H]ow influential are juristic writings in the development of international
law? Historically, before there existed any great wealth of state practice or
judicial precedent, writers on international law held a pre-eminent position
and it was impossible not to rely heavily on the writings of Suarez and
Gentilis in the sixteenth century, of Grotius (volume II of whose *De Jure Belli
ac Pacis* earned him the title of "Father of the Law of Nations"), Zouche and
later Pufendorf in the seventeenth century, and the so-called "positivists",
Bynkershoek, Moser and Van Martens, and the "Grotian" Vattel, of the
eighteenth century. Even today, particularly where the law is uncertain, the
advocate before an international tribunal, or the legal adviser to the foreign
affairs department of a state, will make occasional reference to the works of
these writers, the so-called "classics of international law", though more
frequent citation is made to contemporary writings, particularly to Oppen-

heim's treatise,[ccc] and to various monographs and articles on specialised fields of international law. [However,] [e]ven if it is possible to demonstrate the significance of international juristic writings to the advocate or legal adviser from the frequency with which use is made of such writings in written and oral pleadings submitted by states parties to cases before the International Court [of Justice], it is less apparent what impact these citations have either on the practice of states, or on actual decisions.

OSCAR SCHACHTER, INTERNATIONAL LAW IN THEORY AND PRACTICE 38–39 (1991).

[A]n examination of legal positions and argumentation of governments reveals that generally heavy reliance [has been] placed on principles and rules formulated in the [major] treatises [on international law]. In theory, most of the treatises written in the latter part of the nineteenth century and in the twentieth adhered to the doctrine of sources and the requirement of objective validation of claims on the basis of such sources. But the doctrinal adherence was significantly modified in the treatises themselves. Many of the treatises relied predominantly on quotations and paraphrases of statements by earlier writers of principles and rules. These were supported in many cases by references to State practice or judicial decision. But such references were frequently selected to confirm the norm that had been formulated by earlier writers or by the writer of the treatise. When we examine these treatises, we can readily see that pronouncements of impressive generality (and aphoristic form) were transmitted from treatise to treatise, quoted in judicial decisions and governmental statements.... [T]he selective tendency of the writers, especially their propensity to quote the generalities of other writers, meant that their statements of existing law were steps removed from the ideal of an inductive approach.

Furthermore, the scientific character of these scholarly works are ... suspect because of the tendency in many of them to reflect positions and outlooks of their national States.... We are not really surprised by this though it is incompatible with the premise of scientific positivism.... These observations are not meant to suggest that deliberate bias of a national or political kind is characteristic of treatises and scientific articles. It is rather to point out that relatively few juristic studies, no matter how positivist in theory, fail to betray their national or ideological origins and indeed that more than a few clearly support partisan positions. That a degree of bias is inescapable is recognized by the common assumption that more credible judgments on controversial issues of international law were more likely if made by a broadly representative body than by persons (however expert) from a single country or a particular political outlook.... If the question [before the International Court of Justice and other international bodies] concerns international law, it has become more usual to include citations of writers from a broad range of States, including the new States and those with different social systems. This reflects the expanded composition of the international community and a greater awareness that a heterogeneous society

---

ccc. *I.e.*, LASSA OPPENHEIM, INTERNATIONAL   [vol. 1]; 7th ed., 1952 [vol. 2]).
LAW: A TREATISE (H. Lauterpacht 8th ed., 1955

cannot have its law authoritatively determined by scholars from a small group of States.... But it does not follow that reliance on a plurality of writers brings one closer to the primary sources. Whether one or many, the jurists still engage in generalizing and abstraction that adds to the distance between their pronouncements of *lex lata* and the raw data of the sources.

Discussion Notes/Questions

1. As observed, Article 59 of the I.C.J. Statute [**Basic Document 1.4**] forbids the decision of the Court from having binding force except as between the parties and in respect of the case under consideration. Many respected publicists claim that this prohibition applies to cases decided by *all* international tribunals. *See, e.g.*, Hersch Lauterpacht, The Development of International Law by the International Court 20–22 (rev. ed. 1958). They also note the traditional view that *national* tribunals express only the legal opinions of states of which they are organs. In part these viewpoints are the result of the Civil Law tradition which, in addition to an historical resistance to "judge-made" law in favor of legislation or codification, has greatly influenced the development of international law over the centuries. Historical explanations aside, are these viewpoints useful from the standpoint of the progressive development of international law? Would adherence to judicial or arbitral precedent via the doctrine of *stare decisis* help or hinder that development? If there are no unambiguous answers to a particular issue on the basis of international legal authority, does it make sense to disregard nationally-based judicial or arbitral decisions?

2. The reputation of a court, whether national or international, depends in part on its ability to arrive at decisions free of political influence or pressure. Most observers give the I.C.J. high points in this regard. A relatively recent exception may be found in the United States response to the case brought by Nicaragua against the United States for its support of military and paramilitary activities against Nicaragua in the early 1980s. *See Case Concerning Military and Paramilitary Activities in and Against Nicaragua* (Nicar. v. U.S.), 1986 I.C.J. 14. The United States boycotted the Court and rescinded its acceptance of the compulsory jurisdiction of the Court in this instance because it believed the Court to be politically biased in the case brought by Nicaragua to seek vindication for its contention that it was being victimized by United States support of the *Contra* insurgents. *See* Abraham D. Sofaer, *The United States and the World Court*, U.S. Dep't State Bureau Pub. Aff., Current Policy No. 769 (Dec. 1985). Professor Thomas Franck argued that the Nicaragua decision has to be interpreted objectively in light of the U.S. role as a superpower entrusted "with responsibility for the defense of the free world." *See* Thomas M. Franck, Judging the World Court 23–71 (1986). How can international law provide a framework for restraint and cooperation in the face of such a mandate? Should a major power be willing to risk defeat in the World Court or any other international tribunal on such questions as a contested use of force? On other questions?

3. The International Court of Justice at The Hague is not the only permanently constituted international tribunal. While there are not many, the Court of Justice of the European Union in Luxembourg, the Benelux Court of Justice in Brussels, the European Court of Human Rights in Strasbourg, France, and the Inter–American Court of Human Rights in San José, Costa Rica are not to be overlooked. Except for the I.C.J., however, all have limited subject-matter jurisdiction. Would the world benefit from an array of courts of general jurisdiction? How might this be accomplished? What would be the utility, given the "subsidiary"

status accorded judicial decisions under article 38 of the I.C.J. statute and widely accepted, at least in theory, to apply to all international tribunals?

4. Write Alexandre Kiss and Dinah Shelton, *International Environmental Law* 108 (1991):

> While major books entirely devoted to international environmental law remained exceptional until the end of the 1980s, a mass of articles has appeared since 1972. Other significant sources are the works of scientific and professional associations which formulate applicable principles in this field, such as the 1979 Athens resolution of the International Law Institute on pollution of rivers and lakes in international law [58 Ann. l'Institut Dr. Int'l 193 (1979)], and the numerous texts of the International Law Association, including the Helsinki rules on the uses of the waters of international rivers (1966) **[Basic Document 4.6]** [and] principles concerning land-based marine pollution (1972) **[Basic Document 4.10]**, demonstrating a consensus in doctrine on a certain number of applicable norms. Also important are the activities of the European Council on Environmental Law, a scientific body which seeks legal solutions for European countries based on comparative law.

In addition, one should mention an increasing number of law journals specialized to international environmental law. *See, e.g.,* 1 Y. B. Int'l Envtl. L. (1990).

5. Note that most of the international jurists excerpted thus far have been men. Is this significant for the development of international law?

E. EQUITY

So far in your preparation for the formulation of an international legal strategy to offset the possibility of disastrous radioactive pollution at the hands of the Russian Federation in the Arctic region, you have reconsidered only those "sources" of international legal authority that are acknowledged in article 38(1) of the I.C.J. Statute **[Basic Document 1.4]**. You now turn to article 38(2), which states that article 38 "shall not prejudice the power of the Court to decide a case *ex aequo et bono,* if the parties agree thereto." You sense that, to ensure just results, it is important to explore the meaning of this provision and the place of equity in international law generally.

DAVID H. OTT, PUBLIC INTERNATIONAL LAW IN
THE MODERN WORLD 20–22 (1987).

Equity in international law: in the reservoir of principles or autonomous? In international law the position of equity is less restricted [than in national law], though there are theoretical problems regarding where it fits into the scheme of Article 38. When the *Diversion of Water from the Meuse Case* (1937) **[Basic Document 8.2]** was before the Permanent Court of International Justice, Judge Hudson, concurring, supported the view that equity was a part of international law and meant essentially "general principles of justice" derivable from the principles observable in national legal systems. Thus, equity would appear in this view to be a part of [the] reservoir of [general principles of law recognized by civilized nations].[ddd]

ddd. A close reading of Judge Hudson's opinion permits the conclusion, however, that the applicability of equity does not depend on its introduction via general principles of law:

In more recent years, however, the I.C.J. has appeared to conceive of equity's being implicit in the rules of international law in a more general way than Judge Hudson did. In the *North Sea Continental Shelf Cases*,[eee] the Court indicated that just and equitable decisions find their "objective justification in considerations lying not outside but within the rules".[fff] In the *Fisheries Jurisdiction (Merits) Case* (1974)[ggg] it saw the main problem as "not a matter of finding simply an equitable solution, but an equitable solution derived from the applicable law".In the *Continental Shelf (Tunisia v. Libya) Case* (1982)[hhh] the World Court continued the process of making equity an autonomous feature of international law. It said in part:

> Equity as a legal concept is a direct emanation of the idea of justice. The court whose task is by definition to administer justice is bound to apply it. In the course of the history of legal systems the term "equity" has been used to define various legal concepts. It was often contrasted with the rigid rules of positive law, the severity of which had to be mitigated in order to do justice. In general, this contrast has no parallel in the development of international law; the legal concept of equity is a general principle directly applicable as law. Moreover, when applying positive international law, a court may choose among several interpretations of the law the one which appears, in the light of the circumstances of the case, to be closest to the requirements of justice ... [The court] is bound to apply equitable principles as part of international law, and to balance up the various considerations which it regards as relevant in order to produce an equitable result. While it is clear that no rigid rules exist as to the exact weight to be attached to each element in the case, this is very far from being an exercise of discretion or conciliation; nor is it an operation of distributive justice.

This view of equity implies a conception that has moved some distance from the reservoir of principles idea insofar as it sees equity arising from the nature of international law as a system seeking to achieve justice rather than from the specific principles of national legal systems.

What are widely known as principles of equity have long been considered to constitute a part of international law, and as such they have often been applied by international tribunals.... The Court has not been expressly authorized by its Statute to apply equity as distinguished from law.... Article 38 of the Statute expressly directs the application of "general principles of law recognized by civilized nations", and in more than one nation principles of equity have an established place in the legal system. The Court's recognition of equity as a part of international law is in no way restricted by the special power conferred upon it "to decide a case ex aequo et bono, if the parties agree thereto".... It must be concluded, therefore, that under Article 38 of the Statute, *if not independently of that Article*, the Court has some freedom to consider principles of equity as part of the international law it must apply.... [Emphasis added.]

In this case, the Court refused to grant a remedy to the Netherlands against Belgium because "one party which is engaged in a continuing non-performance of [its] obligations should not be permitted to take advantage of a similar non-performance of that obligation by the other party" (diversion of water from the Meuse in violation of a treaty of 1863).

eee. *Supra* note **mm**. *See also* text in Section B of this chapter, at **98**.

fff. The case dealt with the delimitation of the shelf, it will be recalled, in a circumstance involving a concave coast. After the Court found that the relevant provisions of the 1958 Convention on the Continental Shelf [**Basic Document 4.3**] did not apply to the case, it found that in this matter customary international law required such delimitation to be established by reference to equitable principles.

ggg. Fisheries Jurisdiction (U.K. v. Ice.) (Merits), 1974 I.C.J. 3.

hhh. 1982 I.C.J. 18.

Ex aequo et bono. Article 38(2) of the I.C.J. Statute [**Basic Document 1.4**] gives the court power to decide a case *ex aequo et bono, i.e.,* according to what is fair and appropriate, if the parties to the case agree. This is not the same as applying equity within the established system of law. *Ex aequo et bono* implies deciding according to what suits the facts of the case, regardless of the law. This is often said to be in effect a licence for the court to legislate in the sense of creating new law for the parties, and is rarely resorted to because hardly ever authorised by the parties in cases before the court.

OSCAR SCHACHTER, INTERNATIONAL LAW IN THEORY AND PRACTICE 55–56, 58 (1991).

No concept of international law resists precise definition more than the notion of equity. It is often defined by listing approximate synonyms that seem equally elusive: fairness, justice, reasonableness, good faith. Apart from the imprecision of these terms, they are not adequate to convey the full use of equity in legal reasoning. Its almost protean character tempts one to speak of "equity in its infinite variety". But ... it is [nonetheless] convenient to distinguish the following five uses of equity and equitable principles:

(1) Equity as a basis for "individualized" justice tempering the rigours of strict law.

(2) Equity as consideration of fairness, reasonableness and good faith.

(3) Equity as a basis for certain specific principles of legal reasoning associated with fairness and reasonableness: to wit, estoppel, unjust enrichment, and abuse of rights.

(4) Equitable standards for the allocation and sharing of resources and benefits.

(5) Equity as a broad synonym for distributive justice used to justify demands for economic and social arrangements and redistribution of wealth.

* * *

Equitable principles of a ... specific substantive character have come to have an especially significant role in regard to shared resources and delimitation problems. It is interesting that these equitable principles of a "legislative" character have been developed in large measure by judicial or arbitral bodies, influenced by the work of nongovernmental international law bodies. One notable example has been the emergence of principles for the equitable sharing of rivers, lakes and ground waters that are a common resource of two or more States. The arbitral award of 1957 in the *Lac Lanoux* case between France and Spain [**Basic Document 8.3**] was a significant step in recognizing the claims of equitable sharing in limiting unilateral acts of riparian States. The Helsinki Rules on the Uses of the Waters of International Rivers adopted by the International Law Association in 1966 [**Basic Document 4.6**] and the resolution of the Institut de droit international on Pollution of Rivers and Lakes, adopted in 1979,[iii] have advanced specific criteria for weighing the many factors that bear on the equities of sharing common resources.

iii. 58 ANN. L'INSTITUT DR. INT'L 193 (1979).

Ruth Lapidoth, *Equity in International Law*, 81
PROCEED. AM. SOC. INT'L L. 138, 146–47 (1987).

The advantages of the application of equity are obvious: in adjudication, it enhances the chances of bringing the law nearer to justice, which is one of the main objects of every legal system. It makes it possible to adapt the rule to individual cases and to prevent injustice resulting from the generality of law and from the impossibility of the legislature to predict in advance all possible situations that might arise. * * * In difficult negotiations, reference to an abstract although perhaps ambiguous equity or equitable principles may help the parties to reach an agreement that otherwise might be impossible.

The disadvantages should not be overlooked, however.... The subjectivity of the contents of equity is particularly dangerous in the international legal order due to the heterogeneity of the international community. Moreover, the notions that one may have of justice depend on his or her links to a certain ethical environment and to the municipal legal system in which he or she has grown up.

The great qualities of law are its generality, clarity, certainty and predictability. None of these virtues would exist in an individualized system of equity.

Moreover, if equity is part of international law, it is not only a source of inspiration for the judge and arbitrators, but also may be relied upon by the parties to justify their behavior. The possibility to invoke equity in a legal system with no compulsory jurisdiction may provide states with many loopholes and subterfuges that will help them to evade the application of the law.

* * *

Nevertheless, despite these shortcomings, equity is part of the law and has to be applied appropriately, in order to prevent grave injustice and to fill gaps. The need for equity in the administration of international law even has grown recently because more and more rules of law are of a rather general or abstract character, and because of the need to share and distribute the newly discovered natural and technological resources.

Editors' Note

The utility of equity as a means of sharing and distributing scarce resources, as noted in the extract by Ruth Lapidoth, *supra*, is a focus of concern of the article *The International Role of Equity-as-Fairness*, 81 Georgetown L. Rev. 563 (1993) by Thomas M. Franck & Dennis M. Sughrue. The authors write, at 572, 580 and 590–91:

Since World War II, equity-as-fairness has become relevant to one of the most vexing problems facing international courts: the allocation of scarce resources among states. This problem arises primarily from the failure of the earth's system of territorial boundaries to resolve satisfactorily the attribution of certain resources, such as the riches of the continental shelf. Equity brings important advantages to this task, affording judges a measure of discretion, within a flexible structure, commensurate with the uniqueness of each dispute and the rapid evolution of new resource recovery and management technology.

International lawyers are engaged in a debate as to the proper role of equity in this context. This debate shows that at least three approaches to equitable allocation have emerged. In the first model, which may be labelled "corrective equity," equity occupies the important, but fringe, role of tempering the gross unfairness that sometimes results from the application of strict law. In the second model, "broadly conceived equity," equity displaces law but is still rule-based, evolving into a set of principles for the accomplishment of an equitable allocation. In the third model, "common heritage equity," equity serves a dual creative function: determining the conditions for exploitation and ensuring the conservation of humankind's patrimony.

A relatively recent invocation of the "common heritage equity" model described by Franck and Sughrue is the theory of "intergenerational equity" advanced by Professor Edith Brown Weiss in Fairness to Future Generations: International Law, Common Patrimony, and Intergenerational Equity (1989).

Discussion Notes/Questions

1.   What is the difference between law and equity? The relationship? Can equity serve to create law? Consider this last question in light of the following proposal of Professor Edith Brown Weiss in *Intergenerational Equity in International Law*, 81 Proceed. Am. Soc'y Int'l L. 126, 126–30 (1987):

We live on a small, relatively new, and fragile planet—Earth. We have inhabited this planet for only 3–4 million years, a brief interlude compared to the 160 million years of the dinosaurs. Today we have the power to alter planet Earth, irreversibly, on a global scale, in many different ways. While we may develop new technologies to prevent some environmental disasters, it is by no means certain that technology can provide a sufficient response. For the first time we must be concerned as members of the human species with the condition of the natural and cultural heritage of our planet that we pass to future generations and with our own ability to enjoy the legacy from past generations.

This [essay] sets forth a theory of intergenerational equity in international law and applies it to the natural and cultural patrimony of our planet. The theory assumes that each generation receives a natural and cultural legacy in trust from previous generations and holds it in trust for future generations. This imposes certain planetary obligations upon each generation to conserve the quality and diversity of the natural and cultural resource base for future generations and gives it certain planetary rights to use the legacy. These planetary obligations and planetary rights form the basis of a proposed doctrine of intergenerational equity, or justice among generations. For these obligations and rights to be enforceable, they must be incorporated into international law or into national and subnational legal systems.

* * *

...   There are four criteria that should guide the development of principles of intergenerational equity. First, the principles should encourage equality among generations, neither authorizing the present generation to exploit resources to the exclusion of future generations nor imposing unreasonable burdens on the present generation to meet indeterminate future needs. Second, they should not require one generation to predict the values of future generations. Third, they should be reasonably clear when applied to foreseeable situations. Fourth, they must be shared generally by different cultural traditions and be acceptable generally to different economic and political systems.

We should adopt three basic principles of intergenerational equity obligations. First, each generation should be required to conserve the diversity of the natural and cultural resource base, so that it does not restrict unduly the options available to future generations in addressing their problems and satisfying their own values. This principle is called "conservation of options." Second, each generation should be required to maintain the quality of the planet so that it is passed on in no worse condition than the present generation received it. This is the principle of "conservation of quality." Third, each generation should provide its members with equitable rights of access to the legacy from past generations. This is the principle of "conservation of access."

These three principles of intergenerational equity serve as constraints on the two extreme cases that define the boundaries of intergenerational equity: the preservation and the consumption models. Rights of access and use serve as a brake on the preservationist model; obligations to conserve quality and diversity act as constraints on the consumption/opulent model. They are designed to ensure that each generation received it and will have an opportunity to use the resources of the planet to improve economic and social conditions.

These proposed principles constrain the actions of the present generation in developing and using the planet. They do not dictate the details of how members of the present generation should manage their resources, however. They do not require that we predict preferences for future generations, which would be difficult, if not impossible, to do. Rather, they try to ensure at a minimum a reasonably secure and flexible natural resource base for future generations and a reasonably decent and healthy human environment for present and future generations.

Professor Weiss thus gives us an example of how equity might play a role in international environmental law. Is it implicit in her recommendation that conventional and customary rules are not flexible enough to meet the needs of the global environment? For a fuller explication of Professor Weiss' thesis, see E. Weiss, In Fairness to Future Generations: International Law, Common Patrimony, and Intergenerational Equity (1989).

2. Why has the World Court never explicitly stated that it applies equity or equitable principles? Might a reference to a specific equitable rule have raised too much criticism? What problems attend the application of equitable principles? Do they give third-party decision-makers too much discretion? Do they risk too much subjectivity in legal decision?

3. Ruth Lapidoth, *supra*, says that the "great qualities" of law include its clarity, certainty, and predictability. Do you agree? Professor Lapidoth also expresses concern that equity, which she says does not have these "virtues," would be relied upon, if as part of international law, to justify potentially unwanted subjectivities; one person's "justice" would be another's "injustice." Do you agree? How might such negative consequences be avoided?

4. Franck–Sughrue and Weiss give us examples of how equity can and might play a role in international environmental law. Is it implicit in their commentaries that conventional and customary rules are not flexible enough to meet the needs

of the global environment? Or at least some of those needs? Can you think of other areas of international life that might benefit from the "common heritage equity" model or a version thereof? Would it or any other equity model assist in a case against the Russian Federation for its radioactive pollution of the Arctic region? For example, "intergenerational equity" relative to the sustainability of indigenous populations such as the Saami?

5. Is it possible to argue that all cases are decided according to "equity" in some sense of that word? If so, is the notion of "equity" a vacuous concept? Or does it have some substantive significance as a "source" of international law rules?

F. OTHER "SOURCES" OF INTERNATIONAL LAW

Up to this point in your preparations to assist the Royal Norwegain Ministry of Foreign Affairs, you have reconsidered only those "sources of international law" that are expressly chronicled in Article 38 of the Statute of the International Court of Justice [**Basic Document 1.4**]. But there are possible others, and it is to these that you now turn: the resolutions of international governmental organizations (IGOs) such as the United Nations and its allied agencies, expressions of consensus, declarations of intent, and so forth. The resolutions of the U.N. General Assembly and Security Council having been given the most serious attention in recent years, however, you consider them primarily.

But you approach these "other 'sources' " with caution; although international law may be derived from them, you recall from your formal studies that what counts in the end, at least in the world order presently constituted, is the attitude of states toward these law-creating processes and their practices among one another. However much any potentially law-making process may stress that a given norm is a rule of international law, the acid test, especially in an essentially "horizontal" and voluntarist legal system such as the current international legal system, is whether nations accept that norm as one governing their international relations. The caveat applies, of course, to every "source" of international law without exception.

1. UNITED NATIONS AND OTHER INTERGOVERN-MENTAL ORGANIZATIONAL RESOLUTIONS

Though nowhere mentioned in Article 38 of the I.C.J. Statute [**Basic Document 1.4**], declarations and resolutions of the United Nations, its allied agencies, and other intergovernmental organizations have been increasingly cited since 1945 as "evidence" for rules of international law, not least in the international environmental realm. For this reason they merit our attention. It should be understood, however, that, while the readings that follow focus primarily on U.N. General Assembly declarations and resolutions, their essential teachings apply also to the declarations and resolutions of other intergovernmental organizations. In addition to the U.N. and its specialized agencies, there exists a vast array of intergovernmental organizations, both global and regional, that contribute to the codification and development of international law. By interpreting their respective charters, by adopting and implementing declarations and resolutions, and by sponsoring treaties in their spheres of influence and competence, these diverse organizations contribute substantially to the creation and development of international law. In contrast to the United Nations and its allied agencies, however, all of which have global jurisdiction, these other IGOs tend to have less universal importance or significance. The same may be said, as a consequence, of their legal utterances.

DAVID H. OTT, PUBLIC INTERNATIONAL LAW IN THE MODERN WORLD 20–22 (1987).

[Consider] the problem of the effect of [United Nations] General Assembly resolutions in the creation of new law. There are basically four possibilities:

(*a*) that such resolutions have no legal effect;

(*b*) that they are authoritative interpretations of the pre-existing law in the U.N. Charter;

(*c*) that they help create customary law;

(*d*) that they have an almost legislative effect.

Possibility (a): no legal effect. This argument depends on the statement in the U.N. Charter, Article 10 **[Basic Document 1.3]**, that the General Assembly may only "discuss" matters within the scope of the Charter and "make recommendations". By definition these are not orders and cannot have the binding effect necessary to create legal obligations and duties. It is sometimes also suggested that the act of voting for a mere recommendation cannot be state practice contributing to the growth of customary law since, it is said, the knowledge that the recommendation is not binding prevents the requisite *opinio juris*. Even if a state indicated that it felt obliged to vote for a certain recommendation, the obligation (and hence the rule of customary law) would exist independently and not in the resolution itself.

* * *

Possibility (b): authoritative interpretations. This view is less troubled by the limitations imposed by restriction of the Assembly to discussion and recommendation. International law recognises ... that the interpretation of a treaty may be affected by the subsequent practice of the parties to it. It is not too far from this to say that voting in the Assembly in favour of certain interpretations of the Charter ... amounts to practice that may clarify and develop the relevant Charter provisions.

This understanding is particularly apt when applied to resolutions that take the form of declarations of principle on legal questions, most notably the Universal Declaration of Human Rights of 1948 **[Basic Document 7.11]**. Thus, in the *Filártiga v. Peña-Irala* case[iii] a United States federal court in 1980 said, on the question of whether torture was prohibited under international law, that "U.N. declarations are significant because they specify with great precision the obligations of member nations under the Charter".

A somewhat similar view of the role of General Assembly resolutions was put forward by Judge Jessup in his dissenting opinion in the *South West*

iii.   630 F.2d 876 (2d Cir.1980).

Africa Cases (1966).[kkk] The judicial task of the court was, he said, to interpret constitutional documents like those in that case (and like the U.N. Charter) by applying contemporary international community standards for which statements in General Assembly resolutions provided proof.

Possibility (c): creation of customary law. This could arguably happen in one of three ways:

(*a*) A state's vote in favour of a resolution might be state practice with *opinio juris* because the state regards the resolution as in itself legally binding. But this notion is open to the objection that under the U.N. Charter most General Assembly resolutions are only recommendatory and therefore cannot be binding.

(*b*) A state's vote for a resolution could be state practice with *opinio juris* because the vote is an acknowledgement by the state that the content of the resolution accords with the requirements of international law and cannot legitimately be rejected. From this possibility some writers have gone a step further to speak of a process of "parliamentary diplomacy" whereby the will of the international community can be quickly and accurately reflected in resolutions, with the accumulation of such authoritative pronouncements producing new international law. Judge Tanaka, dissenting in the *South West Africa Cases* (1966), described the process as "the middle way between legislation by convention and the traditional process of custom making". The court in the *Filártiga* case ... implicitly endorsed this view with regard to resolutions on human rights. . . .

(*c*) The resolution may enunciate principles or rules which later state practice (with *opinio juris*) adopts as customary law. This role for General Assembly resolutions is widely accepted, but one should remember that in this situation the subsequent practice, and not the resolution *per se*, is what is generating the new law.

Possibility (d): quasi-legislative effect. After the General Assembly in December 1963 adopted unanimously the "Declaration of Legal Principles Governing the Activities of States in the Exploration and Use of Outer Space",[lll] the United States representative said that a resolution of that kind, approved unanimously, "represented the law as generally accepted in the international community". This was understood to mean that one resolution of that kind could create law where none had existed previously, in effect could legislate new international law. The view was contested at the time and remains debatable.

The key to the American claim was the unanimity with which the resolution was adopted. If a resolution purporting to set out new "law" were adopted only by a majority, the situation would be different. In the *Texaco v Libya* arbitration of 1977,[mmm] the arbitrator held that such a resolution, if not simply reaffirming previously existing law (*lex lata*), would be merely *de lege ferenda*, that is, a suggestion of what the law ought to be rather than a statement of what it presently is. Although many international lawyers would

---

kkk. *Supra* note 10.

lll. G.A. Res. 1962, U.N. GAOR, 18th Sess., Supp. No. 15, at 15, U.N. Doc. A/5515 (1963).

mmm. *Reprinted in* 17 I.L.M. 1 (1978).

accept this opinion in principle, considerable room for disagreement remains in trying to determine which resolutions it applies to.

ROSALYN HIGGINS, PROBLEMS AND PROCESS: INTERNATIONAL LAW AND HOW WE USE IT 26–28 (1994).

[P]rominent among [the] activities [of international organizations] is the passing of resolutions that purport to be declaratory of contemporary international law. Can we reject their legal relevance *simply* on the ground that they are recommendatory, or incapable of directly binding the membership at large?[nnn] What status is therefore to be accorded them?

There are a great range of opinions. Looking along a spectrum, we can perhaps see at one end those who are deeply sceptical, in the generalized fashion, about the relevance of General Assembly resolutions—such writers as Judge Sir Gerald Fitzmaurice, Judge Stephen Schwebel, and Sir Francis Vallat, Professors David Johnson and Gaetano Arangio–Ruiz. The Englishmen in this group all arrive at their position primarily by an emphasis in their writings, or judicial decisions, on the recommendatory nature of Assembly resolutions and their inability to bind.... Judge Schwebel and Professor Arangio–Ruiz arrive at their position through a different route. They fully accept that resolutions can contribute to the formation of customary international law, but express deep scepticism as to whether this really happens.

Professor Arangio–Ruiz says that General Assembly resolutions do not in fact contribute to the evolution of custom because states "don't mean it".... "That is to say, states often don't meaningfully support what a resolution says and they almost always do not mean that the resolution is law."[30] Judge Schwebel then adds a piercingly important point. Agreeing that states "don't mean it", he says: "This may be truer still of resolutions adopted by 'consensus'."[31] Thus the size of the majority has nothing to do with the intentions of the states voting for it.

Somewhere towards the middle of the spectrum there are other international lawyers who downplay the significance of Assembly resolutions as non-binding, but accept that it would be wholly exceptional for any single resolution to have normative results. They argue ... [that] the decentralized method of international law-making can cause the metamorphosis of "General Assembly recommendations from non-binding resolutions to inchoate normative principles".[32] Certain resolutions may be a first step in the process of law creation; and looked at as a whole, they may in certain circumstances (depending on subject-matter, size and margin of majorities, *opinio juris*) be evidence of developing trends of customary law.

nnn. Earlier, Professor (now Judge) Higgins writes, at 24: "It is, of course, beyond all doubt that the drafters of the [U.N.] Charter" **[Basic Document 1.3]** deliberately declined to give the General Assembly legislative authority. In other than budgetary matters, the resolutions of the General Assembly are recommendatory and not directly binding: see the wording of Articles 10, 11, 12, 13, and 14.

30. Gaetano Arangio–Ruiz, *The Normative Role of the General Assembly of the United Nations and the Development of Principles of Friendly Relations*, 137 RECUEIL DES COURS 419 (1972–III).

31. Stephen M. Schwebel, *The Effect of Resolutions of the UN General Assembly on Customary International Law*, 1979 PROCEED. AM. SOC. INT'L L. 301 (1979).

32. C. Joyner, *UN General Assembly Resolutions: Rethinking the Contemporary Dynamics of Norm–Creation*, 11 Calif. W. Int'l L. J. 445, 464 (1981).

At what could be termed the radical end of the spectrum are those who invest Assembly resolutions with considerably greater legal significance. In this context can be mentioned Richard Falk, who has written of the "quasi-legislative" competence of the General Assembly,[33] and Jorge Castañeda, who has argued that, through its repeated efforts to declare principles of international law, the General Assembly has secured powers beyond the recommendatory powers listed in the UN Charter **[Basic Document 1.3]**.[34]

Underlying these positions are many complicated and interesting issues, one or two of which may be mentioned briefly. When we look at resolutions as a first step in the formation of custom, or as part of the evidence of the existence of general practice, is it enough that we look at the resolutions alone?

Judge Schwebel has insisted that, because *opinio juris* remains a critical element, one must look to see if states "mean" what they voted for—and looking at their practice outside the United Nations is one way we can ascertain this. The [1977] arbitral award of Professor Dupuy in the *Texaco Case*[35] is interesting in this context, as well as in many others. It will be recalled that (unlike Judge Lagergren, when faced with similar issues in the *BP v. Libya Case*[36]) Dupuy closely examined the series of resolutions that are collectively regarded as the New International Economic Order resolutions, to see whether the traditional requirements for compensation had changed. He found that General Assembly Resolution 1803 [G.A.Res. 1803, U.N. GAOR, 17th Sess., Supp. No. 17, at 15, U.N.Doc. A/5217] represented current international law, for it had passed with the support of the industrialized capital exporting states as well as the capital importing states; however, the same consensus was never really apparent in the voting on the Charter for Economic Rights and Duties **[Basic Document 7.2]** and the Declaration on the [Establishment of A] New International Economic Order [G.A.Res. 3201, U.N. GAOR, 6th Spec. Sess., Supp. No. 1, at 3, U.N.Doc. A/9559 (1974)]. In other words, Dupuy was engaged in trying to ascertain whether a resolution expressed a consensus on what was the existing customary rule. But one must take care not to use General Assembly resolutions as a short cut to ascertaining international practice in its entirety on a matter—practice in the larger world arena is still the relevant canvas, although UN resolutions are a part of the picture. Resolutions cannot be a *substitute* for ascertaining custom; this task will continue to require that other evidence of state practice be examined alongside those collective acts evidenced in General Assembly resolutions.

So far we have spoken of [General] Assembly resolutions. Yet we must not lose sight of Security Council resolutions in our examination of the process of creating norms in the international system. Professor Tunkin, in his 1956 study on the fundamental principles of contemporary international law,[37] indicated that decisions of the UN Security Council are not strictly speaking sources of international law. They have an *ad hoc* effect and may create binding obligations, but they are not sources of general applicabili-

33. Richard Falk, *On the Quasi–Legislative Competence of the General Assembly*, 60 AM. J. INT'L L. 782 (1966).

34. JORGE Castañeda, Legal Effects of United Nations Resolutions (1970).

35. Texaco Overseas Petroleum Co. v. Libyan Arab Republic, [1977] 53 I.L.R. 389 (1979) [*see also supra* note **mmm**].

36. [1977] 53 I.L.R. 297 (1979).

37. GRIGORII I. TUNKIN, OSNOVY SOVREMENNOGO MEZHDUNARODNOGO PRAVA (1956).

ty. . . . I think that this view is largely right—though sometimes the substance of the Security Council work, and the fact that it is legal work repeated year in and year out, makes it engage in the processes of customary [law] development as well as the mere imposing of obligation.

* * *

As with much of international law, there is no easy answer to the question: What is the role of resolutions of international organizations in the process of creating norms in the international system? To answer the question we need to look at the subject-matter of the resolutions in question, at whether they are binding or recommendatory, at the majorities supporting their adoption, at repeated practice in relation to them, at evidence of *opinio juris*. When we shake the kaleidoscope and the pattern falls in certain ways, they undoubtedly play a significant role in creating norms.

Editors' Note

Another response to the question of the legal nature of General Assembly resolutions is what van Hoof has called the "other source" or "new source" approach. G. van Hoof, Rethinking the Sources of International Law 184 (1983). Rather than link General Assembly resolutions to one or more of the traditional "sources" set forth in Article 38 of the I.C.J. Statute **[Basic Document 1.4]**, this approach argues that those resolutions constitute a separate, independent "source" of international law. The late Nigerian jurist T. Olawale Elias, a former member and President of the World Court, may be the most conspicuous advocate of this view. He once wrote:

> Those states that vote for a particular resolution by the requisite majority are bound on the grounds of consent and of estoppel. Those that abstain are also bound on the ground of acquiescence and tacit consent, since an abstention is not a negative vote; while those that vote against the resolution should be regarded as bound by the democratic principle that the majority view should prevail when the vote has been free and fair and the requisite majority as been secured.

Modern Sources of International Law, in Transnational Law in a Changing Society: Essays in Honor of Philip C. Jessup 34, 54 (W. Friedmann, L. Henkin & O. Lissitzyn eds., 1972).

A more cautious assessment, but still close enough to be identified with the "other source" or "new source" approach, may be seen in the writings of Louis B. Sohn, a long-time student of the United Nations. According to Professor Sohn, unanimously approved General Assembly declarations, such as the Declaration on Principles of International Law Concerning Friendly Relations and Cooperation among States **[Basic Document 1.8]**, may be seen as "leading to the creation of new international law applicable to all States" and as representing "a new method of creating customary international law." L. Sohn, *The Development of the Charter of the United Nations: the Present State*, in The Present State of International Law and Other Essays 39, 52 (M. Bos ed. 1973). Van Hoof observes: "Despite his reference to customary international law, Sohn's treatment of the unanimous declarations leaves no doubt that he in fact drops the requirement of *usus* [*i.e.*, practice]" and that therefore one is faced here with "not just a new method of creating customary international law, but rather a new method of creating international law *tout court* [*i.e.*, altogether]." J. van Hoof, *supra*, at 185.

Finally, there is a school of thought, dubbed the "soft law" approach, that views General Assembly resolutions and other such prescriptive communications as not creating full-fledged rules of international law capable of fitting into the traditional "sources" categories but nonetheless fulfilling, in van Hoof's words, "at least some, if not a great number of the criteria required for rules to be considered rules of international law and [which therefore] cannot be put aside as non-law." J. van Hoof, *supra*, at 187–88. This "soft law," Pierre–Marie Dupuy avers, must be understood as "not merely a new term for an old (customary) process" but as "both a sign and product of the permanent state of multilateral cooperation and competition among the heterogeneous members of the contemporary world community," the existence of which "compels us to re-evaluate the general international law-making process and, in so doing, illuminates the difficulty of explaining this phenomenon by referring solely to the classical theory of formal sources of public international law." P.-M. Dupuy, *Soft Law and the International Law of the Environment*, 12 Mich. J. Int'l L. 420, 435 (1991). It is, he says, "a trouble maker because it is either not yet or not only law" and includes theoretically non-binding instruments "such as recommendations and resolutions of international organizations, declarations and 'final acts' published at the conclusion of international conferences and even draft proposals elaborated by groups of experts" create and delineate "goals to be achieved in the future rather than actual duties, programs rather than prescriptions, guidelines rather than strict obligations." *Id.* at 420 and 428. Illustrative, he observes, is the 1972 Stockholm Declaration on the Human Environment [**Basic Document 1.12**]. "Although, from a formal point of view, the Declaration is only a non-binding resolution," he writes, "many of its 'principles,' particularly Principle 21, have been relied upon by governments to justify their legal rights and duties . . . , [and] subsequent State practice has been, no doubt, influenced by such provisions." *Id.* at 422.

But why, one may ask, do governments generate and accept "soft" in contrast to "hard" law? Because, Sir Geoffrey Palmer, former Prime Minister of New Zealand, says, "it is so politically convenient." Geoffrey Palmer, *New Ways to Make International Environmental Law*, 86 Am. J. Int'l L. 259, 269 (1992). Hard law in the form of international custom, he writes, "takes time and often a lot of state practice before it hardens into a legally enforceable rule, [and] [t]reaties take a long time to negotiate and nations tend to shy away from the specificity they often involve." *Id.* Palmer elaborates at 269–70, noting the effect of "soft" law along the way:

> Resort to soft law leaves large amounts of discretion to states. The standards are often so vague that third-party adjudication would be impossible even if it were provided for. Often the standards themselves are discretionary. What is important about these instruments is not so much the form in which they appear but the manner in which the obligations, if any, created by them are expressed. Frequently, what is expressed is a series of political statements or values. The Stockholm Declaration [**Basic Document 1.12**] is a good example.

* * *

All politicians know the value of ambiguity. It can serve to secure agreement where agreement may otherwise not be achieved. International instruments are frequently drafted with studied ambiguity. Such an approach may have deceptive elements to it and may create wrong impressions, but it promotes feelings of international comity and cooperation that are very valuable. Since political leaders and countries must continue dealing with one another, it is better that those dealings be based on agreement than on disagreement—and soft law solutions produce agreement.

More importantly, soft law solutions change the political thinking on an issue. They alter the circumstances in which an issue is considered; they cause opinion to coalesce. These changes can be a very important catalyst in securing an agreement with a harder edge later. Soft law solutions can thus be useful steps on a longer journey. Soft law is where international law and international politics combine to build new norms....

Political decision makers are influenced by soft law solutions. No political leader wants to endorse an empty declaration. They usually take a lot of care with the language since they have to defend it in the media and other public forums. The political impact of the statement is their prime concern, usually its impact on domestic political opinion. They want to have achieved something that is politically significant. Press statements are taken seriously by the politicians who make them. International instruments involving political leaders from other countries are taken even more seriously. Such soft law documents are often produced by lengthy negotiations simply because the statement is perceived to have political consequences of a serious sort....

Considering that the system is somewhat short of means for establishing norms, it would be a great mistake to get too excited from an analytical point of view about the dangers of soft law.... [It] is a concept of both range and flexibility. It ranges from material that is not law at all, through a long spectrum to material so close to being hard law as to be indistinguishable from it.... It is a vital part of the continuous process of building norms.

ALEXANDRE KISS AND DINAH SHELTON, INTERNATIONAL
ENVIRONMENTAL LAW 109–13 (1991).

[R]esolutions constitute a new source of international law not foreseen by the Statute of the International Court of Justice [Basic Document 1.4], or at least establish a new technique for creating international juridical norms. This technique is particularly effective in establishing law for new fields like human rights, exploration and exploitation of outer space and the deep seabed, and environmental law.

1.   Binding Resolutions

One of the principal characteristics of international organizations is that very few have the power to adopt legally binding texts. Only three among all the organizations which are concerned with matters of environmental protection have such power.

In an extremely limited way, the Security Council of the United Nations can play a role in this regard, by virtue of the Convention on the Prohibition of Military or Any Other Hostile Use of Environmental Modification Techniques [**Basic Document 7.30**].[ooo] According to article 5 of the Convention, each state party which has reason to believe that another state party is violating its obligations can file a complaint with the Security Council [which, in turn,] may undertake an inquiry with the power to decide that the state bringing the complaint has been or might be harmed due to a violation of the Convention . . . [and] recommend dispute-settlement procedures.

The Organization for Economic Cooperation and Development (OECD) has wider competence in the field of environmental protection. In order to achieve its objectives, this organization of market-economy industrial states can take decisions which, unless otherwise stated, bind all its members [although] the nature of this organization as an agency of study and consultation is such that in practice binding environmental decisions are infrequent . . . [and relate to] matters where the exercise of state power is not significantly affected.

The reverse is true of the European Communities, which are invested with the right to take binding action for the members through two means: "regulations" binding in all their elements and directly applicable in all member states, and "directives" binding each state to achieve a given result but leaving the means and methods to individual state control. . . .

2.　Nonbinding Resolutions

Resolutions issuing from conferences or international organizations can be classified, according to their contents, in three categories: directive recommendations, programs of action, and declarations of principles.

a.　*Directive recommendations.* Directive recommendations form the bulk of acts in which intergovernmental organizations address themselves to states members. In order to understand the significance of such recommendations, one should recall that in joining an international institution, member states freely accept certain obligations which are often drafted in general or abstract terms; it remains for the organization's component organs to explicate and detail these obligations in the concrete cases which arise. Interpretation and application of such obligations generally take place through resolutions adopted by the organs competent to speak on behalf of the organization. However, because state members usually guard their sovereignty . . ., they reserve the right to decide if they will apply these resolutions. Thus, the latter cannot be formally obligatory; they are instead recommendations or guidelines addressed to states members in order to indicate how they would accomplish the obligations of membership.

Directive recommendations concerning the environment play a fundamental role in the activities of most intergovernmental organizations, both regional and universal. In particular, there exist OECD recommendations regarding such subjects as the relationship between the environment and economy, the management of natural resources and wastes, chemical, transfrontier pollution, the management of coastal zones, and tourism.

ooo. *See* Problem 11–4 ("Environmental Warfare in Khalifan") in Chapter 11, *infra,* where this convention is considered in some detail.

b.   *Programs of action.* While directive recommendations are addressed to state members of an international organization, programs of action are primarily aimed at the organizations which draft them, setting forth the activities to be undertaken within a given period of time. . . .

The best-known action plan is no doubt the "Action Plan for the Human Environment", adopted by the 1972 Stockholm Conference on the Human Environment.[ppp] The text is composed of 109 recommendations, sometimes addressed to governments, sometimes to international organizations, sometimes to both. It contains not only an indication of actions to be taken, but also directive recommendations. It has served, in fact, as the basis for a large number of environmental measures taken since its adoption, including the global environmental assessment plan (Earthwatch) to survey the state of the planetary environment. It has also been the foundation of global conventions, studies sponsored by various intergovernmental organizations, and UNEP's regional seas program in 1974.[qqq]

c.   *Declarations of principles.* Among nonbinding resolutions and similar texts, especially those issuing from international conferences, a special place must be given to declarations of principles. These differ from directive recommendations in that they do not envisage precise action to be undertaken; they limit themselves to fixing general guidelines which states should follow. Thus, they may exercise a considerable influence on the development of subsequent legal rules.

A fundamental objective of any legal system is to protect by direct or indirect means values recognized as essential within society. . . . In the evolution of every cause the formulation of new social values and their recognition are particularly important. They can be achieved through declarations adopted and proclaimed in the name of society at an international level by organizations or international conferences.

All environmental law is founded on the recognition of new or [the] reemergence of former values. Thus, when the 1972 Stockholm Declaration **[Basic Document 1.12]** proclaims [in its Principle 2] that "[t]he natural resources of the earth, including the air, water, land, flora and fauna, and especially representative samples of natural ecosystems must be safeguarded for the benefit of present and future generations", it recognizes the value of protecting these resources. This recognition is especially important because it includes elements which formerly lacked economic value because of their easy availability, such as air, water, and soil, or because extreme anthropocentric views denied their worth, such as wildlife and natural ecosystems. Thus, new values can be formulated in nonbinding texts, prior to being definitively established in more formal, obligatory instruments.

Most principles proclaimed in declarations have reappeared in one form or another in conventional [i.e., treaty] texts, in the mandate given to international institutions, and in the practice of states. While international environmental law has not utilized its declarations of principles with the same

---

ppp. Also now well known is the more recent Agenda 21, an action plan that emerged from the United Nations Conference on Environment and Development (UNCED) in Rio de Janeiro in June 1992. [*See* **Basic Document 1.29**].

qqq. As earlier noted, UNEP is an acronym for the United Nations Environment Programme, established by the U.N. General Assembly with headquarters in Nairobi, Kenya.

vigor as international human rights law ..., the influence of the Stockholm Declaration and the World Charter for Nature **[Basic Document 1.21]** is undeniable, if more diffuse. Other declarations of principles of more limited aims have directly led to the creation of obligatory norms. These include the European Water Charter,[rrr] the 1974 OECD recommendation containing principles relative to transfrontier pollution **[Basic Document 3.6]**, and the 1978 UNEP statement of principles of conduct in the field of environment for the guidance of states in the conservation and harmonious utilization of natural resources shared by two or more states.

Finally, even where declarations of principles are not directly transformed into binding rules, they may serve to guide states in adopting legislation. It seems certain that without the Stockholm Declaration numerous national laws would not have been adopted or would have been significantly different.

Editors' Note

Reflecting on the kind of discussion that is represented by the foregoing readings, David Kennedy writes, in *International Legal Structures* 39–40 (1987):

> Commentators often discuss new sources of international law in ways which characterize them as either hard or soft. When these two rhetorical strands are used in this way, it is difficult to terminate the discussion in any definitive way—not so much because new sources each entertain both hard and soft rhetorics as because each can be characterized as either hard or soft and neither characterization alone seems a persuasive basis for the new source's authority. Resolutions of the United Nations General Assembly have been treated in precisely this fashion. Since the General Assembly formally has no general legislative function in public international law, Article 38 makes no mention of its various textual outputs. Commentators have nonetheless struggled to think about U.N. resolutions within the rhetoric of sources. General Assembly resolutions are thought to be binding to the extent that they express state consensus or systemic justice. Those who argue that they express consent are opposed to the argument that General Assembly delegates lack the requisite capacity or intent. Those who argue that resolutions embody principles of systemic justice are opposed by argument that resolutions express a mere passing consensus—rule or tyranny of the majority.

Consider Professor Kennedy's observations in the light of Professor Myres McDougal's reported remarks in a panel discussion on *The Effect of U.N. Resolutions on Emerging Legal Norms*, 1979 Proceed. Am. Soc'y Int'l L. 300, responding to the panel chairman's (Anthony D'Amato's) opening instruction that "[t]he purpose of the panel was to examine the controversy concerning the legal implications surrounding U.N. resolutions and to assess the status of purported legal norms that were created through a process of mutual accommodations and consensus":

---

rrr. Council of Europe, European Water Charter, adopted May 26, 1967, *reprinted in* Legal Problems Relating to the Non–Navigational Uses of International Watercourses: Supplementary Report by the Secretary–General, [1974] II Y.B. INT'L L. COMM'N 342, 342–43, U.N. Doc. A/CN.4/274, *also reprinted in* DANTE A. CAPONERA, THE LAW OF INTERNATIONAL WATER RESOURCES 210 (1980).

Professor McDougal remarked that "sources of international law" presented not merely a theoretical problem, but in actuality, a very practical problem. The first question any operating lawyer would want to know was, "Who is going to decide my case?"; the second question which would naturally follow would be, "Who is making the law?" These were not just theoretical inquiries. Legal norms did not simply exist; they were manifested in a continuous process of evolution and hence emanate from several different sources.

For instance, in Article 38 of the Statute of International Court of Justice **[Basic Document 1.4]**, the traditional sources of international law were enumerated.... These were not homogenous sources; they represented not only the most deliberate form of expression—formal agreement—but also the least deliberate form—the vast flow of expectations derived from uniformities in decision and behavior.

Regarding custom, it was supposed to arise when uniformities of behavior gave rise to expectations about authority and control in persons engaged over a long period of time in that behavior. Accordingly, the primary function of the longevity requirement was to clarify and substantiate what expectations were in fact held by members of the community.

In a real sense, then, the U.N. machinery entailed a facile means for finding out what the international community's expectations were concerning lawful and unlawful activities. In this regard, the concept of "binding obligation" became little more than meaningless noise if it omitted expectations of the community concerning authority (i.e., who is competent to make decisions) and control (i.e., what sanctions are in fact available to carry out decisions). As Hans Kelsen had noted, every norm possessed factual contingency, a policy content, and a sanctioning component. Hence, a norm must carry expectations of authority and control. In short, when looking for legal norms, we were actually searching for indices which express these expectations of authority and control.

Professor McDougal then posited that the notion of consensus was much too limited. The key to law was not consent, but expectation. It was not the intent of the communicator that held principal importance; rather, it was whether a certain policy expectation was shared by both the communicator and the communicatees. The key question was what did the community expect? For instance, at one time the laying of mines at sea had been considered wholly illegal. However, after parties had repeatedly engaged in this practice during two world wars, it had become accepted by the international community as being lawful. The intent of the communicator—be it a U.N. organ or any other party—was not of paramount consideration; rather, primacy should go to the expectations about authority and control which the communicator created for the larger community.

Consequently, it had to be realized that these expectations were being created all the time, in many different ways. There was in constant process an explicit, continuous flow of international agreements, as well as an outpouring of official decisions by courts and legislative bodies. Not to be overlooked either in this respect was the behavior of private parties engaged in multifaceted transnational activities. No one of these sources of law carried ultimate or exclusive importance; in each case, particular inferences might be drawn about expectations, but in the greatest likelihood, they would come from several diverse sources.

To be sure, the United Nations provided a forum for evaluating what the international community thought the law was. Yet, in order to decide whether a U.N. statement reflected an accurate description of what peoples' expectations were concerning the law, one needed to know several facts: Who voted for that statement? Who voted against it? What was the relative and effective power of these voters? How compatible is the asserted policy with past expectations? What followed from the resolution? What were the expectations coming from other sources? And so on.

The Chairman then interjected a hypothetical case for Professor McDougal's consideration. Suppose a U.S. oil company wanted to drill for oil on the deep seabed. Would this profit-seeking behavior be illegal in light of recent U.N. pronouncements [such as] the Declaration of the Principles Governing the Sea-Bed and Ocean Floor, and the Subsoil Thereof, Beyond the Limits of National Jurisdiction [**Basic Document 4.8**], or would the very conduct of drilling, with its concomitant profit expectations, be creating a new norm of legality?

Professor McDougal replied that the answer depended upon who voted for the moratorium resolution and other factors. If the United States and Western Europe—the principal nations having the technological capability to perform these exploitation activities—had voted against the resolution, then the expectations needed to change existing legality would probably be insufficient. The requirements for putting an end to an existing prescription were the same as for creating a new prescription.

* * *

In reply to Professor McDougal's comments, Professor Garibaldi argued that it was incongruous to maintain that the binding nature of a General Assembly resolution depends on its acceptance by the major powers and, at the same time, that the major powers' opinions are irrelevant to the larger issue of whether some General Assembly resolutions are binding at all. The differences between his and Professor McDougal's views lay in the criterion of validity taken as reference. Community expectations constituted an *a priori* criterion; the speaker preferred an empirical criterion, more closely tied to the realities of international life.

Mr. Schwebel [now Judge Schwebel, President of the International Court of Justice] stated that if a major power or powers voted against a General Assembly resolution, that resolution could not *ipso facto* be considered declaratory of international law, or constitutive of what international law was.

Professor McDougal then responded that no nation state could effectively prevent the process of law creation. This related back to an ancient anthropological observation regarding what law was all about. Law served as a process of clarifying and implementing common interests of people, through explicit communications and by inferences from their behavior.

This represented the most fundamental law in any society, namely, customary law. The argument was neither theoretical nor *a priori* ; it was just an observation of historical fact. Furthermore, what was important in the legislative process was not the secret intent of the legislator, but rather the expectations which that legislation created for the community. Hence, the whole flow of behavior and inferences would guide expectations about content, authority, and control.

* * *

As a concluding remark, Mr. Schwebel stated that he hoped and believed that Professor McDougal was not correct about the increasing legal significance attributed to the General Assembly's actions. The United States shared the perception with those governments who instructed their delegates on the assumption that how they voted in the United Nations was not law creative, and should not give rise to the kind of expectations about which Professor McDougal had spoken. One could not just argue that particular reality away. The widespread attitude of many states in the United Nations, especially those in the West, was: "So what? It is only a recommendatory resolution of the United Nations, so what does it matter? Why should we offend our friends in the Third World by voting against it?" In the light of this fact, to arrive at a conclusion that would hold these resolutions as binding or law creating would be at best questionable.

Discussion Notes/Questions

1. Is a resolution of the U.N. General Assembly a "source" of international law because it states a "general principle of law" that nations have accepted by virtue of their membership in the United Nations? Customary international law? Which? Is it an independent "source" in its own right?

2. Echoing the views of Professor Dupuy reported in the Editors' Note, *supra*, and agreeing with him that "international organizations and conferences . . . contribute to the evolution and adoption of legal norms," Rudolf Bernhardt, in *Customary International Law New and Old Problems*, 19 Thesaurus Acroasium 199, 212–13 (1992), nevertheless cautions that "one should avoid the misleading notion of soft law and instead recognize that international practices and pronouncements of international organizations and conferences can contribute to the creation of *real customary law*" (emphasis added). States Bernhardt, at 212, "rules are either part of the law or legally not binding; they cannot be binding and non-binding at the same time." Do you agree with Bernhardt? Why? Why not?

3. Are resolutions of the U.N. General Assembly binding on the member States? Are some of them binding? What do U.N. Charter articles 10, 11, 12, 13, and 14 say? Are resolutions of the Security Council binding? What does Charter Article 25 say? What is the difference between "resolutions," "declarations," and "recommendations"?

4. Note that many legal scholars from northern industrialized countries deny the binding effect of U.N. General Assembly resolutions. Is this because developing countries are in the majority in that forum and that the industrialized world does not want to be bound by what they might call "the tyranny of the Third World majority"? Is it possible that the question of the legal effect of General Assembly resolutions is more political than legal?

5.   Judge Rosalyn Higgins, *supra*, states that "decisions of the UN Security Council ... may create binding obligations, but they are not sources of general applicability." Does this mean that Security Council resolutions do not "count as law"? If not, what does it mean?

6.   In The Development of International Law through the Political Organs of the United Nations (1963), Professor [now Judge] Higgins observes that the law-creating role of political organs such as those of the United Nations "enables a quantitative problem of some magnitude." In this particular connection, she asks, at 6: "How many resolutions incorporating the same legal doctrine must be passed before that doctrine is deemed an international custom? How many states must vote in favour of those resolutions?—a simple majority?—a two-thirds majority? Must all the major powers be in favour of the implied legal prescription?" How would you answer these questions?

7.   In *China, The United Nations, and World Order* 466–67 (1979), Samuel S. Kim assesses the contribution of the People's Republic of China to the development of international law:

China's legal practice of invoking certain General Assembly resolutions, in particular, the NIEO [new international economic order] resolutions which fall neatly into the category of the evolving international law of development, as the authoritative reference for her U.N. multilateral diplomacy can only contribute to the process of redefining and relegitimizing the sources of international law.... If a new international legal order is ever to be established, it is not likely to come from the advisory opinions of contentious judgments of the I.C.J. or from a definitive or formalistic codification of a new multilateral convention. It is most likely to evolve and crystallize from the political process of collective legitimization in the domain of justice.

In short, repeated references to certain resolutions in state practice may well have the effect of transforming consensus into consent in the Assembly's norm-formulating, value-realizing, and law-declaring activities. If this analysis is correct, the well-established Chinese legal practice of invoking General Assembly resolutions would have the two legal consequences. First, it will make it increasingly difficult for China to defy Assembly resolutions without suffering a serious credibility problem in her multilateral diplomacy. Second, it will contribute to the process of broadening the scope of the Assembly's law-developing and law-legitimizing functions. In other words, the most significant "contribution" of China toward the establishment of a new international legal order may lie in its participation in the General Assembly's long-term amending process of international law.

8.   Suppose all the nations of the world were to agree to give full legislative power to the United Nations. Would that be desirable? What would be gained? Lost? What restrictions might there be, if any, on that legislative power? Who would define the restrictions? Who would interpret them? Would there have to be an international "Supreme Court"? If so, who would appoint the judges? Would the judges be capable of being impartial if a matter affected their own nations' vital interests? What other particularistic questions would be appropriate—indeed necessary—to ask? In this connection consider the following questions: is the world "ready" for centralized decision-making? would centralized decision-making be more "rational" than what we have now? Assuming centralized decision-making would be more "rational," should each nation get a vote? should "mini-states" have the vote on a equal basis with, say, Australia, Brazil, China, India, Nigeria, Russia, or the United States?

9. What does McDougal, *supra*, mean when he says that the issue of the legal effect of U.N. resolutions and other prescriptive communications is one of community expectation, not consent? How does one substantiate community expectation? Is it easier or harder to substantiate than consent?

2. CONSENSUS AND GENERALLY ACCEPTED STANDARDS

As seen in the preceding discussion concerning the declarations and resolutions of international organizations, it often is loosely claimed that the consensus of states can be a "source" of international law. One should ask anyone making such a statement what is meant by "consensus." Is the claim a mere truism? If all the states in the world believe that proposition X is a rule of general customary law binding on all states, then who can say otherwise? Certainly not Professor McDougal, who argues that the key to law is not consent, but expectation. *See* the remarks of Myres McDougal, *supra*, in *The Effect of U.N. Resolutions on Emerging Legal Norms*, 1979 Proceed. Am. Soc. Int'l L. 300. After all, no one other than "all the states" can define what international law is! Thus, to restate the truism: "international law consists of the international consensus about international law."

There is another key question: most practically, how can we establish what all the states believe? Many commentators have suggested that when the United Nations passes a resolution by unanimous vote, the content of that resolution *is* "international consensus" and hence becomes part of general customary law. What do you think of this position? Does the concept of "consensus" *add* anything to the discussion in the preceding section about the force and effect of U.N. resolutions?

The following summary paragraph from Ulrich Fastenrath, Lücken im Völkerrecht 291 (1991) provides a convenient overview that can help answer some of these questions. The insertion of the word "consensus" in brackets throughout is the result of an editorial judgment that the author, in translating from the German, mistakenly adopted the word "consent" instead of the word "consensus."

> Among the controversial sources of international law is [consensus]....
> According to the theory of [consensus] developed by *D'Amato* and *Cheng*
> on the basis of psychological legal positivism, a norm is a legal one if
> states agree to see it as such. No express consent is necessary; acquies-
> cence is sufficient. Ethiopia and Liberia pursued such a line of reasoning
> in the *South West Africa* cases.[sss] Presumably, according to this view,
> consent could be withdrawn at any time. This result is avoided by *Onuf's*
> theory of recognition. Like the theory just mentioned, it is based on the
> view that law is what states recognize as such. However, *Onuf* does not
> construe common consent as a psychological fact but, in a more sociologi-
> cal way, as a society's convention on the existence of a certain norm.
> Once such a convention has been established it cannot simply be invali-
> dated by changing one's mind. On the other hand, no formal cancellation
> is necessary. Rather, according to the speech-act theory, a point must be
> reached where the convention on the existence of the norm is not

sss. *Supra* note 10.

generally accepted anymore. A much more stringent effect is attributed to [consensus] by *Verdross, Simma,* and *van Hoof.* According to them, a norm established by [consensus] is valid until it is abrogated or modified by a new norm. Conversely, these authors are much more reluctant in accepting the legal character of a rule established by [consensus]. However, they provide no evidence why such a norm can be nullified or modified only by a new norm. It is well conceivable and, in international law, even common practice that legal rules stemming from different sources are changed or invalidated in different ways.

Closely related, if not identical, is the conception of "generally accepted international standards," a phrase that has surfaced in recent years mainly in relation to law of the sea and other environmental domains. *See, e.g.,* Restatement (Third) of the Foreign Relations Law of the United States §§ 502, Comment *c* of which states that "once a [marine safety] standard has been generally accepted, a state is obligated in particular to apply it to all ships flying its flag and to adopt any necessary laws or regulations." *See also,* Comment *b* to § 601 which declares that a similar principle requires all States to conform to international rules and standards derived from international conventions or adopted by international organizations pursuant to such conventions. Commenting, Professor Oxman writes, in *The Duty to Respect Generally Accepted Standards*, 24 N.Y.U. J. Int'l L & Pol. 109, 143–44 (1991):

> The duty [to respect generally accepted standards] entails a legally binding obligation to observe generally accepted standards. This obligation, however, is created by general acceptance of a standard in fact, rather than by the procedure by which the standard was articulated. Thus, it creates a useful bridge between so-called "soft law" and "hard law." This, indeed, was part of its original function. Where appropriate, standards (or guidelines) can be developed in a somewhat more relaxed procedural environment which is not specifically designed to generate legally binding obligations as such; yet those same standards can become legally binding if they become generally accepted. * * * The effect ... is to impose a legal obligation on a state to respect a standard which it would not otherwise be legally bound to respect. The consensual requirements of international law for the imposition of legal obligations are not offended by this proposition; those requirements have previously been satisfied through acceptance of the general duty either by treaty or by customary international law. It is unnecessary to restrict the scope of the duty itself to conform to such requirements.

Discussion Notes/Questions

1. In *On Consensus*, 8 Can. Y. B. Int'l L. 104, 117 (1970), Anthony D'Amato took up the question of the weight to be given a dissenting vote by a major power in respect of a U.N. resolution:

> [W]e need not assume that the dissenting state be a powerful or major state or the leader of a bloc of states; such considerations of "weight" which often creep into the discussions of publicists confuse might with right in a manner which may these days be as anachronistic as gunboat diplomacy, let alone unjustifiable. The advent of the nuclear era has paradoxically created impotency in the highest places. Interbloc nuclear balance, the counterproductively excessive power of nuclear weapons, and the ability owing to

modern mass communication of small nations to rally to the side of any one of them threatened by a larger power, make it necessary in any discussion of international law—which itself is designed to persuade the reader and not to force him to accept a position—to assume equality of states before the law and genuine reciprocity.

But could it not be argued that "major powers" should have a larger voice in determining the content of international law because (a) they usually have large populations, and "people count, not states"; (b) they command significant resources, including military resources that can be a force for world stability and order; (c) they are often more articulate about international law? How would a small power, or a Third World nation, respond?

2.   Is "consensus" as a possible "source" of international law anything more than the qualitative element of customary law (*opinio juris*) without the quantitative element of customary law (*usus*, or state practice)? Or is it both? And if it is both, how does it differ from customary law?

3.   NON–CONVENTIONAL CONCERTED ACTS AND DECLARATIONS

It is common practice for governments to engage in collaborative acts that evince common understandings and outlooks but which are not viewed, at least not initially, as part of conventional or customary international law. Typically they are expressed in intergovernmental communications and *communiqués*. Sometimes, indeed, they are chronicled in more formal instruments, *e.g.*, the 1972 Stockholm Declaration on the Human Environment **[Basic Document 1.12]** and the 1992 Rio Declaration on Environment and Development **[Basic Document 1.29]**. Deemed technically non-binding, they are nonetheless substantially observed. The same is true of so-called gentlemen's agreements, characteristic of the practice of the International Monetary Fund.

In addition, presumptively non-legal intergovernmental declarations outside the framework of an international organization have been used to settle disputes and chart the course for future relations. Noteworthy examples include the declarations at the Yalta, Potsdam, and Cairo conferences at the end of World War II relating to postwar territorial disposition and political organization. Professor Schachter, in International Law in Theory and Practice 129 (1991), describes these declaratory communications as official state acts from which "it is appropriate to draw inferences that the States concerned have recognized the principles, rules, status and rights acknowledged." He continues: "This does not mean that 'new law' or a new obligation is created. However, where the points of law are not entirely clear and are disputed the evidence of official positions drawn from these instruments can be significant." *Id*. Schachter then adds, at 130:

> States entering into a non-legal commitment generally view it as a political (or moral) obligation to carry it out in good faith. Other parties and other States concerned have reason to expect such compliance and to rely on it. What we must deduce from this, I submit, is that the political texts which express commitments and positions of one kind or another are governed by the general principle of good faith. Moreover, since good

faith is an accepted general principle of international law, it is appropriate and even necessary to apply it in the legal sense.

Discussion Notes/Questions

1. According to J. Garner, *The International Binding Force of Unilateral Oral Declarations,* 27 Am. J. Int'l L. 493 (1933), unilateral declarations of states may give rise to international legal obligations by way of estoppel. However, the intention of a state making such a declaration must necessarily be a critical factor, as must also an element of publicity. But what constitutes a sufficient indication of intent and sufficient publicity for a unilateral declaration to be deemed binding? Indeed, given that states and governments do not have minds, how is it possible to determine the requisite intent in the first place? Does the customary law theory of *opinio juris* bear any relevance here? Consider in these connections that, in the *Nuclear Tests Cases,* wherein Australia and New Zealand challenged the atmospheric nuclear testing of France at its Muroroa atoll in the South Pacific, the World Court determined a unilateral declaration by France to halt further atmospheric testing to be a legally binding commitment sufficient to render the case moot. *See* 1973 I.C.J. 99, 135.

2. If, as Schachter, *supra*, contends, voluntary governmental declarations are to be governed by the general principles of good faith (and its corollary estoppel), why is it necessary to posit a "source" of law distinct from "general principles of law recognized by civilized nations"? *See* section E, *supra*.

Concluding Discussion Notes/Questions

1. The expression "sources of international law" is at best ambiguous. Worse, because it understates both the derivation and scope of law-creating processes, it is misconceived and therefore misleading. The case is persuasively made by professors McDougal, Lasswell, and Reisman who, in a seminal essay, observe that the law-creating processes which by tradition we call "sources" of law are best seen in terms of the seven component functions which comprise the various types of legal decision: intelligence, promotion, prescription, invocation, application, termination, and appraisal. *See* Myres S. McDougal et al., *The World Constitutive Process of Authoritative Decision, in* 1 The Future of the International Legal Order 73 (R. Falk & C. Black eds. 1969).

Especially relevant is what these authors call the "prescriptive [or law-making] function." In *The Prescribing Function in World Constitutive Process: How International Law is Made,* 6 Yale Studies in World Public Order 249 (1980), McDougal and Reisman write, at 250: "The making of law is a decision function which may be conveniently described as prescription. By prescription, we refer to a process of communication which creates, in a target audience, a complex set of expectations comprising three distinctive components: expectations about a policy content; expectations about authority; and expectations about control." And "to speak meaningfully of law," they emphasize, "all three components must be copresent." *Id.* at 251.

Professor Reisman elaborates elsewhere, in *International Lawmaking: A Process of Communication,* 1981 Proceed. Am. Soc. Int'l L. 101, 108, as follows:

[P]rescriptive or law-making communications ... carry simultaneously three coordinate communication flows in a fashion akin to the coaxial cables of modern telephonic communications. The three flows may be briefly referred to as the policy content, the authority signal and the control intention. Unless each of these flows is present and *effectively mediated* to the relevant audience, a [legal] prescription does not result. [Emphasis added.]

Equally important, Reisman adds, the three components *"must continue to be communicated* for the prescription, as such, to endure; if one or more of the components should cease to be communicated, the prescription undergoes a type of desuetude and is terminated." *Id.*

McDougal and Reisman are concerned to avoid, among other things, certain of the confusions and disabilities that accompany the traditional approaches to the question of whether an international rule of law has in fact been made or does in fact endure. The mainstream *opinio juris* test which bids inquiry into what states "believe" a rule to be, they point out for example, does not lend itself easily, if at all, to empirical verification. Nor, one might add, does it rest altogether comfortably in a world increasingly beset by fundamental challenges to the primacy of the nation-state as a global claimant and decision-maker.

Do McDougal and Reisman make it easier for you to understand—i.e., do they help to demystify—how law, particularly international law, is made? Might their behavioralist approach affect the manner in which you, as a member of Judge Goldstone's legal staff, prepare for the prosecution of persons responsible for war crimes and other atrocities in the former Yugoslavia and Rwanda? How? Would it help to ask why we and other authors set off the term "sources" with quotation marks?

3.   Does there exist a hierarchy among the various "sources" of international law? Would you say that international law decision-makers are expected to treat the "sources" of international law embraced by Article 38 of the I.C.J. Statute **[Basic Document 1.4]**, or at least the first three major "sources" (treaties, custom, and general principles) noted therein, in hierarchical or sequential manner? Why? Why not? Consider the following extract from W. Michael Reisman, Nullity and Revision—The Review and Enforcement of International Judgments and Awards 555–58 (1971):

> The root problem of enumerated sources such as are found in article 38 is that of priorities. In point of fact, the problem of priorities is artificial, since authoritative international policy does not present itself for application with a convenient label affixed, specifying its source. International prescription is an ongoing process. The purport of a convention cannot be grasped without consideration of prior and subsequent customary developments, their consonance with general principles, and the responses of quasi-authoritative doctrine. Initial focus on any one source will encounter a parallel necessity to be considered in the context of all other sources.

> A construction of article 38 or a comparable compromissory source enumeration that gives priority to one source over all others will clearly effect decision. In many cases, it may obstruct conformity to current public order requirements. It is thus urgent that the order of enumeration in "applicable law" clauses be treated only as an order of investigation and not as an order of substantive priority.

> The point can be demonstrated by a hypothetical case in which a bilateral treaty applies to a particular dispute. Will a tribunal seised of the dispute properly acquit itself of its function by resorting exclusively to the convention? It is submitted that it will not. In the first place, it is impossible to decide a case by exclusive resort to conventional law. The very act of construing a treaty involves application of customary principles of interpreta-

tion, general principles, and presumptions; performance of both of the latter tasks is rarely accomplished without resort to doctrinal writings.

In the second place, exclusive resort to one expression of policy will rarely give an accurate indication of the actual expectations and demands of the parties. Policy clarification is continuous; a written document represents only one element at one point in time. The document cannot, for example, reflect customary development subsequent to redaction.

* * *

Finally, exclusive resort to a document may well result in an accurate "legal decision" that is, nonetheless, inconsistent with minimum and maximum community goals. This will result in an extremely poor or ineffective decision. But this danger is avoided if there is mandatory resort to general principles, including consideration and recognition of community goals.

These general policy recommendations are consonant with the legislative history of article 38. The Committee of Jurists had formulated that provision with the preliminary statement, "in the order following." The French text emphasizes the notion of priorities even more, stating, *en ordre successif* The committee's formulation was not unanimous. Although a number of members were firmly in favor of a weighted priority, Ricci–Busatti sought a formulation that would constrain the proposed [Permanent Court of International Justice] to examine all the sources simultaneously, taking cognizance of their interrelations. His concern was with their effect on decision and not on the preliminary examination. "If the expression '*en ordre successif*' only meant that a convention should be considered before, for instance, customary law, it is unnecessary." [Lord] Phillimore appeared to agree with this point of view. Though a member of the majority, he thought the phrase was secondary in importance, since he felt that this was the logical order in which any jurist would approach the problem. But Phillimore did not appear to have considered the enumeration as weighted in favor of any particular source.

In the discussion in the committee of the [League of Nation's] first Assembly, the word "in the order following" were struck. At the United Nations Conference on International Organization in 1945, the question of stating a weighted priority was reconsidered but rejected. The observers from the P.C.I.J., Judges Guerrero and Hudson, stated that the enumeration itself did not have a normative character and was not intended "to stipulate the order in which they are to be resorted to." Thus the order of source enumeration in a *compromis* should not be deemed to set up priorities in favor of one source over another unless the *compromis* specifically demands it. Even in the latter case, the necessities for decision will require consultation of all sources.

Do you agree with Reisman? What happens if a provision in a treaty clearly conflicts with a rule of customary international law? Is there a way to resolve the conflict according to the strategy suggested by Professor Reisman? Suppose a treaty between States *A* and *B* clearly conflicts with customary law rights that *A* and *B* had in the absence of the treaty. Which prevails, the treaty or the custom? In considering your answer to this question, ask yourself why *A* and *B* signed the treaty when there were underlying customary rights in its absence. Would it matter which came first or last in time?

4. Consider the following remarks by Liesbeth Lijnzaad of the Faculty of Law of the University of Limburg, in Maastricht, The Netherlands:

Traditional international law is concerned with states.... What I find striking in the present international system is the lack of interest in the interests of people that states can get away with. That is related to the methods of creation of international law and the international legal system in which there is no central authority. In a domestic legal system there is a central authority which can steer if things go wrong. So if we try to change the indifference to the interests of people in the international legal system, that would have to include the methods of creation of law.

Sources of International Law: Entrenching the Gender Bias, in Contemporary International Law Issues: Opportunities at a Time of Momentous Change: Proceedings of the Second Joint Conference of the American Society of International Law and the Nederlandse Vereniging voor Internationaal Recht 432 (July 22–24, 1993). Can you suggest how Professor Lijnzaad's concerns might be met? She suggests that feminist legal analysis might be helpful, commenting at 432–33:

> [F]eminist legal analysis is comparable to socialist legal theory of which the basic idea is that the law belonging to the superstructure is governed by production relationships in the base. There is a similarity between the way in which feminist legal analysis sees law as being created by what we all experience in everyday life. If you agree with this impression that might mean that we could look to socialist legal analysis and find ways of dealing with everyday problems.

Do you agree? In any event, on the basis of Professor Lijnzaad's comments and the chapter in general, would you say that the law-creating processes of the international law system are any different from the law-creating processes of municipal law systems? If so, what differences do you perceive? If not, why not? Consider Morton H. Kaplan & Nicholas deB. Katzenbach, *The Political Foundations of International Law* 235 (1961):

> The techniques employed and the sources invoked are strikingly parallel in the domestic and international systems. The difference lies largely, as we have noted, in the difficulty of developing a system of legislation comparable to that developed by domestic governments, and of segregating, as a result, governmental functions structurally in the manner characteristic of domestic societies. The international process remains relatively undeveloped as a governmental system.

Chapter Three

THE APPLICATION OF INTERNATIONAL LAW

A. THE APPLICATION OF INTERNATIONAL LAW IN THE CASE OF THE KINGDOM OF NORWAY AND THE RUSSIAN FEDERATION

It is Spring 1998, a little over two years since you completed your review of the fundamentals of public international law so as to assist your colleagues in the Royal Norwegian Ministry of Foreign Affairs in the formulation of an international legal strategy that might persuade the Russian Federation to be truly aggressive in reducing the human health and environmental hazards posed by (1) its nuclear shipyard policies, (2) its disposal of the nuclear waste generated by them, and (3) its land-based pollution practices. This strategy, you had been advised, was to include, but not necessarily be limited to, the possibility of a memorial (i.e., brief) before the International Court of Justice in The Hague,[a] a declaration proposed for adoption by the Arctic Council,[b] and/or a negotiated agreement of some binding sort. Your job, you knew, was to help prevent a gigantic international environmental disaster and to use or shape the law to deal with this frightening possibility.

Naturally, many questions arose in your mind at the time. Not least because of the urgency of the situation facing your government and others vis-à-vis the long-term sustainability of the circumpolar Arctic region, you were particularly concerned to understand how international law is enforced or applied. The application of international law doctrines, principles, and rules, you knew very well, is indispensable to their counting as law. Unless they are applied to some degree, signaling an intention if not always a capacity to make them fully effective or controlling, they remain essentially aspirational or hortatory exercises—*moral* prescriptions perhaps, but not *legal* ones.

Thus, you asked yourself, through precisely what mechanisms of international legal decision-making might the many issues arising out of Russia's nuclear waste disposal practices be most quickly and effectively resolved? The

---

a. *See supra* note **r** in the Introduction at 11.

b. *See supra* note **s** in the Introduction at 11.

International Court of Justice, you determined, was not likely to be within easy or quick reach because the Russian Federation had submitted to the World Court's compulsory jurisdiction only on a selective case by case basis, and thus far not at all in respect of any environmental issues so far as you could tell. Moreover, you concluded, the wisdom of an adversarial or contentious proceeding before the World Court was at least debatable if not altogether infelicitous under the circumstances. Nor did the Arctic Council seem a likely forum considering that, at the time, it still had to establish its rules of procedure and that, in any event, it was precluded from dealing with matters related to military security,[c] manifestly implicated in the instant case. So, you asked yourself, what else might be available? The United Nations General Assembly? The Security Council? The Organization for Security and Cooperation in Europe? Some other decision-making institution? Would Russia be obliged, as a matter of international law, to submit to at least some third-party arbiter? If so, according to what sources of legal authority? If not, what would be left for Norway to do? If a third-party decision is rendered, requiring the Russian Federation to make good to Norway in one way or another, you know that it does not matter whether the decision is rendered by an ad hoc or permanently constituted panel or tribunal. But, you ask yourself, can it be enforced against Russia? If so, how and to what extent? If not, why not? And what, then, is the precedential significance of the decision, if any?

Your review of international law, in particular its application or enforcement, quickly provided you with answers to these and related questions.[d] As you already had inferred from the possibility of a suit before the International Court of Justice and from newspaper accounts of decisions of the Dispute Settlement Body of the World Trade Organization (WTO)[e] and the International Tribunal for the Law of the Sea, the application of international law does sometimes go forward, despite well-known limitations upon jurisdiction and access, through recourse to third-party decision-makers such as courts and arbitral tribunals, both permanent and temporary, on the international as well as the national plane. Particularly striking, you noted, is the increase in permanently constituted and highly specialized regional tribunals such as the European Court of Justice (of the European Communities and European Union) in Luxembourg; the Benelux Court of Justice in Brussels; the European Court of Human Rights in Strasbourg; and the Inter–American Court of Human Rights in San José (Costa Rica). However, you soon discovered, in an essentially voluntarist legal system such as the international legal system where there is primarily horizontal or nonhierarchical order among formally equal centers of legal authority, where few centralized command and enforcement structures are capable of compelling parties to comply with the rules, and where autointerpretation prevails, legal prescriptions are relatively *infrequently* applied by courts, arbitral panels, and other such third-party decision-makers. Instead, they are applied mainly by national officials—functioning as claimant, judge, and police officer, often simultaneously[f]—in an ongoing

c. *Id.*

d. *See infra* Section B of this chapter at 181, which bears closely upon the materials that immediately follow.

e. *See* 1994 WTO Understanding on Rules and Procedures Governing the Settlement of Disputes [Basic Document 7.8]. *See also in-*

fra Problem 11–1 ("The Environment and GATT Collide in Albion").

f. The French jurist Georges Scelle has used the term *dédoublement fonctionelle* to refer to the fact that a law officer (a lawyer for a government who also is an official of that government) typically has a double function: to

transnational process of unilateral determination *and reciprocal* claim and response.[g]

Thus, more or less familiar with much of what we associate with the application of international law (including the "table skills" of negotiation, good offices, mediation, conciliation, arbitration, and adjudication),[h] you were not surprised when, a little over two years ago, you learned from your superiors at the Royal Norwegian Foreign Ministry that a decision had been made to pursue a negotiated settlement with the Russian Federation regarding its nuclear waste disposal practices. A binding treaty between Norway and the Russian Federation, it had been concluded, would be the most efficient and effective way to achieve Norway's environmental and human health goals. And you agreed with this conclusion. Aware of the kindred agreements reached by the United States with the Russian Federation relative to the latter's Arctic pollution practices,[i] it appeared to you that Moscow was receptive to such arms-length dealing.

Whereupon, for the next approximately two years, and encouraged along the way by a September 1996 "Declaration on Arctic Military Environmental Cooperation" (AMEC) that you helped draft for signature by the defense ministers of Norway, Russia, and the United States [**Basic Document 1.37**],[j] you and your colleagues engaged in intense and ultimately successful negotiations with your Russian counterparts. On May 26, 1998, on the occasion of a state visit of Norway's King Harald V to Russia, Norwegian Foreign Minister Knut Vollebaek and Russian Minister for Nuclear Energy Yevgeny Adamov signed an "Agreement on Environmental Cooperation with the Dismantling of Russian Nuclear Powered Submarines Withdrawn from the [Russian] Navy's Service in the Northern Region, and the Enhancement of Nuclear and Radiation Safety" [**Basic Document 1.39**], reproduced in full following the next paragraph.

By all known accounts, the May 26, 1998 Agreement, which entered into force upon signature, marked a major milestone in enhancing nuclear safety in the Arctic region, at least as between Norway and Russia. In particular, as

make claims (as advocate) on behalf of her or his country, and to pass upon claims (as judge) made against her or his country by foreign countries or their citizens.

g. For sophisticated explication, see Myres McDougal et al., *The World Constitutive Process of Authoritative Decision, in* 1 THE FUTURE OF THE INTERNATIONAL LEGAL ORDER 73 (R. Falk & C. Black eds. 1969). *See also* LUNG-CHU CHEN, AN INTRODUCTION TO CONTEMPORARY INTERNATIONAL LAW ch. 24 (1989).

h. "Viewed comprehensively," writes Professor Lung-chu Chen, "[the] application [of law] may embrace the following sequential features: exploration of potentially relevant facts, including the precipitating events and their larger context; exploration of potentially relevant policies; identification of significant facts; determination of the authoritative policies applicable; making of the decision, including the projection of future relations between the parties; enforcement; and review." LUNG-CHU CHEN, *supra* note **g**, at 376.

i. *See* the 1994 Agreement between the United States of America and the Russian Federation on Cooperation in the Field of Protection of the Environment and Natural Resources [**Basic Document 1.33**]; the 1994 Agreement between the United States of America and the Russian Federation on Cooperation in the Prevention of Pollution of the Environment in the Arctic [**Basic Document 1.34**]; requiring consultation relative to technical solutions for the elimination of radioactive and other types of pollution; and the 1996 Memorandum of Understanding between the Government of the United States and the Russian Federation on Cooperation in Natural and Man-made Technological Emergency Prevention and Response [**Basic Document 1.35**].

j. The Declaration is sometimes referred to, at least by Norwegian officials, as "the AMEC agreement." *See infra* notes **o** and **p** and accompanying text at 180.

provided in Article 1, Norway agreed to render "free technical assistance" to the Russian Federation "in the form of delivery of equipment, technology transfer, provision of financial means[,] and services" for "an early, environmentally safe and cost-effective dismantling" of Russia's nuclear powered submarines, "including the management of spent nuclear fuel and radioactive waste ... formed thereby ..."; and Russia, for its part, agreed to use the free technical assistance provided by Norway "exclusively for [these] purposes." More particularly still, the Agreement expressly enumerated an inexhaustive list of projects that it would cover (Article 2) and provided that both Norway and Russia "will facilitate the involvement of third parties in [the] financing and/or practical implementation of [such] projects...." (Article 8).[k] In addition, the agreement removed two major stumbling blocks that had threatened to stall cooperation between the two countries: (1) exemption from Russian taxes, duties, and fees on technical assistance grants, provided for in Article 5; and (2) indemnification relative to lawsuits that might arise following a nuclear incident or damage to property owned by the Russian Federation, provided for in Article 9. Finally, the Agreement provided for the establishment of a joint Norwegian–Russian commission to coordinate and control its implementation (Article 3) and for arbitration in accordance with internationally recognized arbitration rules in the event of disagreement between the two parties (Article 9).

AGREEMENT
between the Government of the Kingdom of Norway and the Government of the Russian Federation on environmental cooperation in connection with the dismantling of Russian nuclear powered submarines withdrawn from the Navy's service in the northern region, and the enhancement of nuclear and radiation safety[l]

The Government of the Kingdom of Norway and the Government of the Russian Federation, hereinafter referred to as the "Parties";

Considering the Declaration of 26 March 1996 on the foundations of relations between the Kingdom of Norway and the Russian Federation, the Agreement of 3 September 1992 between the Government of the Kingdom of Norway and the Government of the Russian Federation on environmental cooperation, the Agreement of 10 January 1993 between the Government of the Kingdom of Norway and the Government of the Russian Federation on early notification in case of a nuclear accident and exchange of information on nuclear facilities,[m] the Agreement of 15 December 1995 between the Ministry of Defence of the Kingdom of Norway and the Ministry of Defence of the Russian Federation on defense-related environmental cooperation, the Memorandum of 4 October 1995 on Norwegian–Russian cooperation in the area of nuclear safety, the Vienna Convention of 21 May 1963 on Civil Liability for Nuclear Damage;

k. *See infra* note l.

l. Reproduced at the courtesy and with the permission of the Royal Norwegian Embassy, Washington, D.C. Text reproduced also as **Basic Document 1.39.**

m. *See also* the 1986 IAEA Convention on Early Notification of a Nuclear Accident [**Basic Document 3.16**] and the 1986 IAEA Convention on Assistance in the Case of a Nuclear Accident or Radiological Emergency [**Basic Document 3.17**].

Emphasizing that each state has the obligation to ensure that activities within its jurisdiction or control do not cause environmental damage in other states or in areas outside of national jurisdiction;

Reaffirming their commitment to the protection and preservation of the environment in areas adjacent to the Norwegian–Russian border, on the basis of the principles and priorities of the Declaration of 14 June 1991 on the protection of the Arctic environment, the Declaration of 11 January 1993 on Cooperation in the Barents Euro–Arctic region, the Action Programme for the environment adopted by the Barents Euro–Arctic Council on 15 June 1994, and the Declaration of 19 September 1996 on the establishment of the Arctic Council [**Basic Document 1.36**],

Have agreed as follows:

Article 1

1. The Norwegian Party shall render free technical assistance to the Russian Party in the form of delivery of equipment, technology transfer, provision of financial means and services in order to contribute to an early, environmentally safe and cost-effective dismantling of Russian nuclear powered submarines withdrawn from the Navy's service in the northern region, including the management of spent nuclear fuel and radioactive waste which is formed thereby, and to enhance nuclear and radiation safety at nuclear power plants ant other nuclear facilities.

2. The free technical assistance from the Norwegian Party in accordance with this Agreement is provided on agreement between the Parties within the framework of the Storting's budget appropriations."

3. The Russian Party shall use the free technical assistance provided by the Norwegian Party exclusively for the purposes listed in paragraph 1 of this article.

Article 2

1. The Parties shall cooperate in order to promote the realization of the following projects:

   — Emptying and decommissioning of the storage facility for spent nuclear fuel from Russian nuclear powered submarines in Andreyev Bay (Murmansk oblast), and the development of methods for the management of this fuel;

   — Establishment of an interim storage facility for spent nuclear fuel from ships' reactors at the production association "Mayak" (Chelyabinsk oblast);

   — Design, construction and commissioning of a temporary storage facility for solid waste at Andreyev Bay (Murmansk oblast);

   — Design, construction and commissioning of a specialized self-propelled vessel for the transport of containers with spent nuclear fuel;

   — Construction and commissioning of four specialized railway cars for the transport of containers with spent nuclear fuel;

n. The "Storting" is the Norwegian parliament.

— Modernization and commissioning of an interim storage facility for liquid radioactive waste at the "Zvezdochka" shipyard (Severodvinsk, Arkhangelsk oblast);

— Delivery of a mobile facility for treatment of liquid radioactive waste (Murmansk);

— Dismantling of the floating technical base "Lepse" (Murmansk);

— Modernization of the facility for treatment of liquid radioactive waste at the repair and technical enterprise "Atomflot" (Murmansk);

— Enhancement of operational safety at the Kola nuclear power plant (Polyarnye, Zori).

2.   If the Parties so agree, other projects may also be added to those listed in paragraph 1 of this article.

Article 3

1.   A joint Norwegian–Russian commission, hereinafter referred to as the "Commission," shall be established to coordinate and control the implementation of this Agreement.

2.   The Commission shall take and recommend any measures it deems necessary for an effective implementation of the cooperation within the framework of this Agreement, including approval of projects and cooperation programmes proposed by involved organizations of the Parties.

3.   The meetings of the Commission shall be held at regular intervals, but at least once a year, alternately in Norway and the Russian Federation, unless otherwise agreed.

4.   The competent authorities for the purpose of this Agreement are: for the Norwegian Party—the Royal Norwegian, Ministry of Foreign Affairs; for the Russian Party—the Ministry of the Russian Federation for Atomic Energy.

5.   The implementation of projects as foreseen in article 2 shall be based on individual agreements for each project, hereinafter referred to as "project agreements" or "contracts," to be concluded between Norwegian and Russian organizations.

6.   The cooperation shall be carried out on the basis of the national legislation of the Parties, as well as conventions to which both Parties have acceded and internationally recognized principles and recommendations for nuclear and radiation safety and environmental protection.

7.   The project agreements or contracts shall be endorsed by the competent authorities of the Parties.

Article 4

1.   The Norwegian Party shall, according to established procedures deliver equipment, materials and other goods, transfer technology and provide financial means and services to Russian recipients or customers within the framework of this Agreement in accordance with the provisions of each project agreement or contract.

2.   The Russian recipients or customers shall receive the equipment, materials and other goods which are provided by the Norwegian Party according to

the procedures established in the Russian Federation, and undertakes to use the equipment, materials and goods solely for the purposes specified in article 1, Paragraph 1.

3.   The Russian Party shall ensure that the free technical assistance provided by the Norwegian Party is used for the implementation of projects listed in article 2 of this Agreement.

4.   The design, construction, delivery and commissioning of technical means and objects financed by funds provided by the Norwegian Party shall be conducted in accordance with the legislation, norms and regulations of the Russian Federation. The procedure for execution of the work shall be prescribed by the project agreements or contracts.

5.   Training of Russian personnel for the qualified operation of equipment which is delivered shall be foreseen by the respective project agreements or contracts.

6.   The Parties shall mutually provide effective protection of intellectual and industrial property rights in accordance with the national legislation of the Parties, and in accordance with international agreements to which they are a party. The recipient or customer and the contractor may agree on additional terms in each project agreement or contract.

Article 5

1.   Equipment and materials which are imported into the territory of the Russian Federation as free technical assistance for the implementation of this Agreement, and which are financed by funds provided by the Norwegian Party, shall be exempt from taxes, customs duties and other fees in accordance with the legislation of the Russian Federation.

2.   Exemption in accordance with paragraph 1 of this article shall be granted on terms not less favourable than those accorded to technical assistance provided free of charge by any third party.

Article 6

1.   Any disagreement concerning the interpretation of individual provisions of this Agreement or its implementation shall be resolved through consultations between the Parties. Consultations shall take place not later than three months after one of the Parties has so requested.

2.   In case of any divergence between this Agreement and the provisions of project agreements or contracts which are concluded within the framework of this Agreement, the provisions of this Agreement shall prevail.

3.   The Parties may conclude additional agreements on any question that might arise in the course of the implementation of this Agreement.

4.   The provisions of this Agreement may be amended on written agreement between the Parties.

Article 7

1.   At the request of one of the Parties, the Parties shall hold meetings and consultations in order to examine the implementation of the project agreements or contracts.

2. The Norwegian Party is accorded the right to verify and control that equipment, technology and financial means provided free of charge to the Russian Party as technical assistance is used in accordance with the terms of this Agreement. The procedure for verification and control shall be established in the project agreements, contracts or in separate agreements.

3. Each Party shall declare which data and information are to be considered confidential in connection with the implementation of the projects listed in article 2 of this Agreement. Confidential data and information relating to concrete projects within the framework of this Agreement shall not be made public, or disclosed to any individual or legal person who does not participate directly in the implementation of this Agreement without the written permission of the Party that has provided such information.

Article 8

1. The provisions of this Agreement shall not affect the rights and obligations of the Parties under international agreements they have previously concluded, or their membership in international organizations.

2. The Parties will facilitate the involvement of third parties in financing and /or practical implementation of projects listed in article 2 of this Agreement.

Article 9

1. With the exception of claims for damage or injury against individuals arising from their premeditated actions, the Russian Party shall bring no claims or legal proceedings against the Norwegian Party and its personnel or contractors, subcontractors, consultants, suppliers of equipment or services at any tier and their personnel, for indirect, direct or consequential damage to property owned by the Russian Federation. This paragraph shall not apply to legal actions brought by the Russian Party to enforce the provisions of contracts to which it or a Russian national is a party.

2. With the exception of claims for damage or injury against individuals arising from their premeditated actions, the Russian Party shall provide for the adequate legal defence of, indemnify, and shall bring no claims or legal proceedings against the Norwegian Party and its personnel, contractors, subcontractors, consultants, suppliers of equipment or services at any tier and their personnel in connection with third party claims in any court or forum arising from activities undertaken pursuant to this Agreement for injury or loss or damage occurring within or outside the territory of the Russian Federation that results from a nuclear incident occurring within the territory of the Russian Federation.

3. Without prejudice to paragraphs 1 and 2 of this article nothing in this article shall be interpreted to prevent legal proceedings or claims against nationals of the Russian Federation or permanent residents on the territory of the Russian Federation.

4. The provisions of this article shall not prevent indemnification by the Parties for damage in accordance with their national laws.

5. Nothing in this article shall be construed as acknowledging the jurisdiction of any court or forum outside of the Russian Federation over third party

claims for which paragraph 2 of this article applies, except as provided for in paragraph 9 of this article and in any other case where the Russian Federation has pledged itself to acknowledge and execute a legal decision on the basis of provisions of international agreements.

6.   Nothing in this article shall be construed as waiving the immunity of the Kingdom of Norway or the Russian Federation with respect to potential third-party claims that may be brought against either of the Parties.

7.   The provisions of this article shall—if so requested by the contractor—be incorporated into the project agreements or contracts by the issue, by or on behalf of the Russian Party, of an indemnity confirmation letter to the contractor.

8.   In case a nuclear incident has occurred which may lead to the fulfilment of the obligation to compensate damage, the Parties shall hold consultations upon request by one of the Parties.

9.   As regards its obligations in this article to the contractors, subcontractors, consultants, suppliers of equipment or services at any tier and their personnel, the Russian Party undertakes to have any conflict, controversy or claim arising out of or in relation to this article, if not settled amicably within three months, referred to and finally resolved by arbitration in accordance with the UNCITRAL Arbitration Rules. The national legislation of the Parties shall not be applied for the resolution of any conflict, controversy or claim.

10.   Any payments related to the indemnification in paragraph 2 of this article shall be made promptly and in a convertible currency.

11.   The obligations concerning liability for nuclear damage undertaken by the Russian Party in accordance with the present article shall be valid for objects which are the subject of cooperation under this Agreement, and shall remain in effect regardless of any subsequent transfer of ownership of these objects, termination of this Agreement or the expiry of its validity.

Article 10

1.   This Agreement shall enter into force on signature and shall remain in force for a period of five years. The Agreement shall be extended for additional five-year periods on written agreement between the Parties at the expiry of each five-year period.

2.   Each Party may inform in writing the other Party of its intention to denounce this Agreement at any time. The Agreement shall cease to have effect six months after written notice of denunciation has been received from either of the Parties through diplomatic channels.

3.   At the expiry of the validity of this Agreement, the Parties shall consult each other concerning the conclusion of projects started during this period when the Agreement was in effect.

Done in the city of Moscow, this 26th day of May 1998 in duplicate, in the Norwegian, Russian and English languages, all three texts being equally authentic. In case of any divergences of interpretation of the texts in Norwegian and Russian, the text in English shall prevail.

For the Government of the Kingdom of Norway s/Knut Vollbaek	For the Government of the Russian Federation s/Yevgeny Adamov

Thus, in the late 1990s, did Norway pursue the safe handling and ultimate disposal of large amounts of radioactive waste and spent nuclear fuel resulting from Russia's dismantling of its retired nuclear submarines in the Arctic region. It remains a formidable challenge that, from Norway's perspective at least, requires the maximum possible third-party involvement and support. Hence, according to Norwegian officials, the inclusion of "the AMEC agreement'"[o] of September 1996 **[Basic Document 1.37]** among the May 1998 Agreement's Article 2 projects "is a precondition for Norway's moving ahead with these [Article 2] projects beyond the feasibility study stage."[p] Norway's ultimate aim "is to help establish a *multilateral* umbrella mechanism, through which third parties will enjoy the same terms of cooperation with the Russian federation as are now in force on a [Norwegian–Russian] bilateral basis—providing *inter alia* for tax and nuclear liability exemption for third parties that may wish to cooperate on any relevant nuclear safety project in Northwest Russia. Norwegian authorities hope that the bilateral agreement now in force will form an important building block in establishing such a mechanism."[q]

———

Much can be learned from the May 1998 Norwegian–Russian Agreement about international law and politics, including the manner in which international law is applied as well as prescribed. To the application of international law in general, on both the international and national planes, we now turn.

Discussion Notes/Questions

1. Was the May 1998 Norwegian–Russian Agreement a victory for international law or did it constitute merely a political settlement? If the former, why? If the latter, why?

2. Was the May 1998 Norwegian–Russian Agreement a victory for Norway? The Russian Federation? Both? Neither? How might Norway's environmental concerns vis-à-vis Russia's Arctic nuclear pollution practices have been better handled, resolved? How might environmental problems of the sort posed in this case be avoided in the future? Should nuclear disarmament agreements be required to address them expressly?

3. What significance attaches to the fact that the May 1998 Norwegian–Russian Agreement was determined, per Article 10, to remain in force for only five years and to be subject to denunciation by either Norway or Russia at any time?

o. *See supra* note **j** and accompany text, at 173.

p. Letter from Bjorn Brede Hansen, Embassy Secretary, the Royal Norwegian Embassy (Washington, D.C.), to Professor Burns Weston 1 (Sept. 8, 1998) (original on file with Professor Weston, copy on file with Professor Guruswamy). Information concerning all of Norway's ongoing nuclear clean-up projects in northwest Russia as of this writing may be found in the Norwegian Plan of Action on Nuclear Safety (1997–98) (original on file with Professor Weston, copy on file with Professor Guruswamy).

q. Memorandum from Bjorn Brede Hansen, Embassy Secretary, the Royal Norwegian Embassy (Washington, D.C.) to Professor Burns Weston 2 (Sept. 8, 1998) (original on file with Professor Weston, copy on file with Professor Guruswamy).

4.   Norwegian authorities refer to the May 1998 Norwegian–Russian Agreement as a "framework agreement"? Why? How does it differ, if at all, from other agreements not so designated?

B.   THE APPLICATION OF INTERNATIONAL LAW IN GENERAL

1.   THE APPLICATION OF INTERNATIONAL LAW ON THE INTERNATIONAL PLANE

Among the vast majority of international law decisions that are rendered on the international plane around the world every hour of every day, those that are rendered via the *adjudicative arena* of third-party decision-making with which we are so familiar in our national legal systems, are today, as noted earlier, in a distinct minority. Not that such decision-making is unimportant or unusual. To the contrary, it is prized for its impartiality and deliberateness. But the fact remains: the application of international law on the international plane goes forward most commonly *not* in arenas characterized by third-party decision-making (e.g., arbitration and adjudication),[r] but in arenas characterized by processes of unilateral determination and reciprocal response, to wit:

> the *diplomatic arena*, typically on a foreign office to foreign office basis, utilizing both persuasive (e.g., fact-finding, negotiation, reporting) techniques[s] and coercive (e.g., economic, military) instruments of policy, in routine and exceptional circumstances alike;

> the *parliamentary-diplomatic arena*, through recourse to formal conferences, both official and unofficial;

> the *parliamentary arena*, in legislative and quasi-legislative assemblies on the global, regional, and national levels (as in such institutions as the United Nations Security Council or General Assembly, the General Assembly of the Organization of American States, and the Congress of the United States); and

> the *executive arena* via the secretariats of such international governmental organizations as the United Nations, the European Council, and NATO.

Never to be overlooked, of course, though it is highly susceptible of major abuse, is, in addition, resort to unilateral and collective *measures of self-help*, relying upon all the instruments of governmental policy—diplomatic, ideological, economic, and military. The next reading addresses these matters with helpful efficiency.

---

r. To the extent that an ultimate settlement *is not* contingent on the consent of the disputing parties, good offices, mediation, and conciliation may be included among the techniques that are located within the adjudicative arena of third-party decision-making.

s. To the extent that an ultimate settlement *is* contingent on the consent of the disputing parties, then good offices, mediation, and conciliation may be included among the persuasive techniques that are located within the diplomatic arena of unilateral determination and reciprocal response.

LAKSHMAN GURUSWAMY & BRENT HENDRICKS, INTERNATIONAL
ENVIRONMENTAL LAW IN A NUTSHELL 39–56 (1997).

[T]he vertical command and power structure governing domestic politics within nations is conspicuously absent within the international legal order. In international society, power or authority rests on a horizontal base made up of co-equal sovereign states, and can be built into a pyramidal structure only if these nations consent to and join in such an endeavor. While piecemeal building upon the base has resulted in the substantial corpus of [International Environmental Law (IEL)], there is no overarching pyramid of authority consisting of law-making, law-interpreting, law-implementing, or law-enforcing institutions. The absence of institutions cloning those within nation states does not signify a complete void in international implementing institutions. On the contrary, what we have are international implementing agencies and mechanisms correlated to the international society in which we live. They merit examination, and we begin with the many international organizations that facilitate the implementation of IEL, and follow this by examining compliance mechanisms, diplomatic avenues and judicial remedies as methods of implementation.

A. INSTITUTIONS AND ORGANIZATIONS

Despite the impressive growth of IEL and its expanding domain, there is still no single institution or organization that serves environmental protection in the way that the World Trade Organization (WTO) advances, interprets, implements, and enforces the concept of free trade.... The institutions and organizations enlisted to advance IEL are fractured, fragmented, and divided along functional, regional, bureaucratic, and geo-political lines. It is useful to take note of the more important of these entities.... They are classified as Global Organizations, Regional Organizations, and Treaty Specific Organizations.

1. GLOBAL ORGANIZATIONS

The United Nations was founded in 1947 before the dawning of environmental awareness, and its Charter [**Basic Document 1.3**] creates seven principal organs including the General Assembly, the Security Council, the Economic and Social Council (ECOSOC), and the International Court of Justice (ICJ).... The UN Charter neither creates an environmental organ nor specifically mandates the protection of the environment.

A number of international organizations created by treaty or agreement have been brought into a familial relationship with the UN pursuant to charter provisions, and are known as Specialized Agencies of the UN. They enjoy juridical personality and may exercise rights and duties as subjects of international law. A number of them have broadly interpreted their constituent treaties to adopt an environmental competence. Those presently assuming environmental responsibilities include the Food and Agricultural Organization (FAO), the International Labor Organization (ILO), the World Health Organization (WHO), the World Meteorological Organization (WMO), the International Maritime Organization (IMO), the UN Educational, Scientific, and Cultural Organization (UNESCO), and the International Atomic Energy Agency (IAEA).

While the IAEA does not possess Specialized Agency status as such, it plays a role in advancing environmental protection along with other semi-autonomous UN bodies such as the UN Development Program (UNDP), the United Nations Institute for Training and Research (UNITAR), and the United Nations Conference on Trade and Development (UNCTAD). After the 1972 United Nations Conference on Environment and Development (UNCED), the General Assembly of the UN created the Commission on Sustainable Development (CSD) as a functional commission of ECOSOC. Perhaps the most important of the UN Organizations, the UN Environmental Program (UNEP) was created by a General Assembly resolution, not by treaty or agreement.

UNEP was established to act as a focal point for environmental action and coordination, but possesses no executive power. All UNEP programs are financed directly by member states. Consequently, its mission is to persuade and convince states of the need for environmental action, provide information, expertise and advice, and sponsor treaties. It has accomplished these limited objectives credibly.

Increasingly, incentives, financial mechanisms, and technology transfers have become part of the architecture of IEL, and it is necessary to take note of the more important of the institutions involved. The World Bank group consists of the International Bank for Reconstruction and Development (IBRD), the International Development Bank (IDA), and the International Finance Corporation (IFC). The World Bank has developed a bad record by encouraging environmentally damaging developments, but appears to be mending its ways. The Global Environment Facility (GEF) was established in 1990 on an experimental basis to provide financial and technical assistance to developing countries to promote environmental protection. It was restructured along permanent lines in 1994 and is a potential source of green funds for *Agenda 21* [**Basic Document 1.30**], the United Nations Framework Convention on Climate Change (Climate Change Convention) [**Basic Document 3.21**], and the Convention on Biological Diversity (Biodiversity Convention) [**Basic Document 6.11**].

A review of global environmental institutions would not be complete without a reference to two legal institutions: 1) the International Court of Justice (ICJ), and 2) the International Law Commission (ILC). The ICJ is the principal judicial organ of the UN system, and exercises jurisdiction by consent. It has now set up an environmental chamber[t] and recently demon-

---

t. I.C.J. Communiqué 93/20, issued by the World Court on July 19, 1993, reported the formation of a "Chamber of the Court for Environmental Matters":

The following information is communicated to the Press by the Registry of the International Court of Justice.

The Statute of the Court [**Basic Document 1.4**] provides, in Article 36, paragraph 1, as follows:

"The jurisdiction of the Court comprises all cases which the parties refer to it and all matters specially provided for in the Charter of the United Nations [**Basic Document 1.3**] treaties and conventions in force."

At present, out of eleven cases on its docket, the full Court is seised of two cases, namely those concerning Certain Phosphate Lands in Nauru (Nauru v. Australia) and the Gabcikovo–Nagymaros Project (Hungary/Slovakia) with important implications for international environmental law on matters relating to the environment.

The Statute of the Court also provides, in Article 26, paragraph 1, as follows:

"The Court may from time to time form one or more chambers, composed of three or more judges as the Court may determine, for dealing with particular categories of cases;

strated in the Advisory Opinion on the Threat or Use of Nuclear Weapons that it is capable of addressing vexing environmental issues and applying the law to changing situations [Legality of the use by a State of Nuclear Weapons in Armed Conflict, 1996 I.C.J. 93 (July 8)].[u] The ILC was created by the UN General Assembly to work toward the codification and development of international law, and it has reported on subjects of great importance to IEL such as state responsibility and international watercourses.

2. REGIONAL ORGANIZATIONS

A number of regional organizations are playing an important role in developing IEL. The most important of these is the European Union (EU), formerly known as the European Community (EC) and the European Economic Community (EEC). The EU is the most advanced form of international organization in the world and is evolving into a confederation. It possesses three key attributes lacking in other international organizations: 1) law-making agencies; 2) law-interpreting and enforcing agencies; and 3) a court with compulsory jurisdiction. Clothed with explicit environmental jurisdiction, the EU has enacted a large number of environmental laws over a wide range of subject areas. The extent of its corpus of environmental law, and the changing jurisprudential character of EU, deters us from dealing with EU law [here]. Other regional bodies of note are the Council of Europe, the Organization for Economic Cooperation and Development (OECD), the Organization of American States (OAS), and the South Pacific Regional Organization.

3. SPECIFIC TREATY ORGANIZATIONS

Many treaties set up rudimentary international organizations in the form of institutional arrangements for their implementation. They range from *ad hoc* conferences to more permanent institutional structures. A number of

for example, labour cases and cases relating to transit and communications."

In the past the Court has considered the question of the possible formation of a chamber to deal with environmental matters. On those occasions it took the view that it was not necessary to set up a standing special chamber, emphasising that it was able to respond rapidly to requests for the constitution of a so-called "ad hoc" Chamber (pursuant to Article 26, paragraph 2 of the Statute) which could deal also with any environmental case.

In view of the developments in the field of environmental law and protection which have taken place in the last few years, and considering that it should be prepared to the fullest possible extent to deal with any environmental case falling within its jurisdiction, the Court has now deemed it appropriate to establish a seven-member Chamber for Environmental Matters composed as follows: Judges Schwebel, Bedjaoui, Evensen, Shahabuddeen, Weeramantry, Ranjeva and Herczegh.

The Members of the Chamber, who have been elected by secret ballot, will serve for an initial period of six months and will enter upon their duties on 6 August 1993.

The case concerning Certain Phosphate Lands in Nauru (Nauru v. Australia) was settled between the parties out of court not long after Communiqué 93/20 was issued, in an amount that closely approximated the damages sought by Nauru from Australia—indicating, arguably, that the Court's influence extends beyond its usual adjudicative functions in achieving the peaceful settlement of international disputes (at least in respect of environmental matters). Merely announcing that it would hear the case appears to have pressured the parties (particularly Australia) to resolve their differences.

u. For pertinent commentary, see Burns H. Weston, *Nuclear Weapons and the World Court: Ambiguity's Consensus*, 7 Transnat'l L. & Contemp. Probs. 371 (1997).

them are called conferences of the parties, which include a permanent secretariat and a budget, and in some cases, special science advisory bodies. A representative sample of these include the sporadic conference of the parties under the [1985] Vienna Convention for the Protection of the Ozone Layer (Vienna Convention on Ozone) **[Basic Document 3.14]** ... , and regular meetings of the parties under the Montreal Protocol on Substances that Deplete the Ozone Layer **[Basic Document 3.18]**.... Additionally, the Climate Change Convention **[Basic Document 3.21]** ... institutes an annual conference of the parties, and the Biodiversity Convention **[Basic Document 6.11]** ... provides for a conference of the parties on regular intervals. Finally, the Paris Convention for the Prevention of Marine Pollution from Land–Based Sources (1974 Paris Convention) **[Basic Document 4.14]** ... requires regular meetings of the Paris Commission, while the Convention on International Trade in Endangered Species of Wild Fauna and Flora (CITES) **[Basic Document 6.5]** ... sets up a conference of the parties that meets at least every two years.

4. NON–GOVERNMENTAL ORGANIZATIONS (NGOs)

Global NGOs are playing an increasingly important role in IEL. We mention three out of hundreds to illustrate their diversity and spread. The World Conservation Union (IUCN) is a unique hybrid comprised of non-governmental conservation groups, states, and public law entities such as universities and research institutes. The World Wildlife Fund (WWF) is a non-governmental conservation group whose goals parallel those of IUCN. WWF finances conservation strategies throughout the world. A third is the Earth Council endorsed by the Earth Summit which assists grassroots organizations to press for the implementation of sustainable development....

NGOs have become established actors in the implementation of environmental law for a number of reasons. To begin, they are closer to the people affected by environmental degradation, and represent them more faithfully and diligently than their governments. Second, having played a major role in organizing the once invisible colleges of scientists to study the effects and impacts of various environmental problems, and having participated in the making of treaties, they have a legitimate and well-founded interest in the implementation of IEL. Third, the international character of these organizations embraces the concept of global as distinct from national environmental protection, and their large numbers have given them an undeniable international political standing.

As such, NGOs exert pressure on nations and international organizations to comply with IEL, but they have not yet attained the status of States as subjects of international law. There are fundamental conceptual problems in their achieving theoretical parity with States within a legal system comprised of sovereign states alone. However, on a functional level there ought not to be objections to states or international organizations allowing NGOs to perform the role of private attorneys general empowered to protect the international environment. Some treaties point the way in this direction.

For example, the IAEA has granted consultative status to NGOs having special competence in the field [Rules on Consultative Status of NGOs with the Agency, IAEA Doc. INFCIRC/14, (1959)]. The Convention on the Protection of the Environment Between Denmark, Finland, Norway and Sweden (Nordic Treaty) **[Basic Document 1.16]**, art. 2, ... goes further and grants all legal persons, including individuals, and non-governmental organizations the right to protest and vindicate environmental rights and duties in the legal systems of the parties. So, too, does the European Union [see Treaty Establishing the European Community [298 U.N.T.S. 3] ... ; *see also* Case t–585/93, Stichting Greenpeace, et al. v. Commission, 695 B.O. 219 (Ct. First Instance 1995)]. The Convention for the Protection of the Marine Environment of the North–East Atlantic (OSPAR Convention) **[Basic Document 4.24]** ... , like most recent environmental treaties, goes even further by granting NGOs observer status—a role which entitles them to participate in the meetings of the parties, and to submit reports, but not to vote [arts. 11(1) & (2)].

Formal treaty provisions are not the only means of obtaining NGO input. For example, the Commission on Sustainable Development is mandated to receive input from NGOs relating to the implementation of Agenda 21 **[Basic Document 1.30]** ... , ¶ 3 (h) (1992). Even more striking, the Inspection Panel of the World Bank was created to provide an independent forum for private citizens who believe that they or their interests have been or could be directly harmed by a project financed by the World Bank. In a number of cases the World Bank has taken action pursuant to the claims and reports of the Inspection Panel .....

B.   COMPLIANCE MECHANISMS

The international organizations we have noted are not possessed of the power and authority of legislative, executive, and judicial bodies that supervise and enforce the implementation of national laws. It is important, therefore, that the substantive rules of international law should first possess an internal force or dynamic that makes sense to the parties and invokes an attitude of compliance rather than non-compliance. Treaty negotiators try to formulate and endow substantive rules with some compliance generating character that induces implementation without the need for supervision. Second, conventions or treaties also create institutions and techniques that induce compliance and confer power on appropriate authorities to deal with non-compliance. In order to secure compliance, treaties have instituted various processes, procedures and techniques. As we have seen, some set up their own institutions, while others delegate power to existing international organizations such as those mentioned above. Individual treaties contain varying baskets of measures addressing such tasks, and provide *inter alia* for the following: interpretation, research, information and data collection and/or dissemination, monitoring, reporting, reviews of performance, rule-making by experts subject to differing types of confirmation, and management by international organizations. These compliance mechanisms call for further description.

To begin, [there is] the importance of interpretation ... as a method of implementing a treaty.[v] The interpretation and implementation of the Montreal Protocol **[Basic Document 3.18]** provides illustrations—more adventur-

---

v.   Regarding treaty interpretation, see *supra* Section A(6) in Chapter 2, at 91.

ous than others—of how interpretation and other processes are used as compliance techniques.... The First Meeting of the Parties under the Montreal Protocol clarified and interpreted various treaty obligations, including those in Annex A which expressly stated that the Ozone Depletion Potential (ODP) figure for one of the halons was "to be determined." Inserting an ODP figure technically required amending the Annex of the Protocol, and involved a circuitous procedure, plus ratification by two thirds of the parties. Instead, the parties inserted an ODP figure into the Annex of the Protocol by way of interpretation, thereby circumventing the more cumbersome and demanding amendment procedures.

The Second Meeting continued further along these lines, and states adopted a comprehensive "Amendment" to the Montreal Protocol that came into force upon ratification by one third of the parties, even though the explicit language of the Protocol itself required amendments to be ratified by two thirds of the parties. They also established an Interim Multilateral Fund to support ozone friendly technology in developing countries even though there was no provision either in the framework convention or the Protocol that authorized such a step. The Second Meeting of the Parties also adopted a "non-compliance procedure" not provided for in the Protocol, that allowed for the amicable resolution of disputes to be finally determined not by a judicial body but by a decision of the Meeting of the Parties. Finally, the "noncompliance procedure" adopted by the Second Meeting of the Parties sets up an "Implementation Committee" which deals with non-compliance and reports to the Meeting of the Parties.

In addition to implementation, research to ascertain the true environmental impacts and effects of any activities identified in a treaty is of crucial importance. This is particularly the case when dealing with a framework treaty that requires later protocols to deal with unfolding facts. Treaties are replete with references to research. For example, the parties to the Vienna Convention on Ozone [**Basic Document 3.14**] ... undertake to carry out research and scientific assessments on a variety of activities that may affect the ozone layer. These assessments include research into the physics and chemistry of the atmosphere, health and biological effects, and effects on climate of a variety of chemicals that might have a potentially deleterious effect on the ozone layer [arts. 2 & 3 & annex 1]. The Climate Change Convention [**Basic Document 3.21**] ... calls for research on the causes, effects, magnitude, and timing of climate change, and the economic and social consequences of various response strategies [arts. 4(g) & 5], and sets up a subsidiary body for scientific and technological advice [art. 9]. The Biodiversity Convention [**Basic Document 6.11**] ... seeks to promote research that, *inter alia*, contributes to the conservation and sustainable use of biological diversity [art. 12] and sets up a subsidiary body on Scientific, Technical, and Technological Advice [art. 25].

The three treaties mentioned above also call for data collection and the dissemination of research and data. The purpose of the dissemination of research and data is to facilitate compliance. Reporting requirements may include the information obtained from research and data collection, and can take the form of reports by a particular international treaty organization to the parties, or more often, reports by the parties to the international organization or the other parties. The objective of reporting is to bring compliance into the sunlight of scrutiny by other parties and the treaty machinery. The importance of reporting as a technique to secure compliance is illustrated in the Climate Change Convention. All parties are obliged to communicate to the Conference of the Parties a general description of steps taken to implement the Convention, including a detailed description of anthropogenic emissions by sources and removal by sinks [arts. 4(1)(a) & (j); 12(1)(a) & (b)]. The reporting responsibilities of developed countries is even more onerous [art. 12(2)].

Assessments and reviews of performance are tied to reporting. On the basis of the reports and research made available, the parties or a specific treaty organization may assess the extent of implementation and the progress made towards objectives. The Climate Change Convention entrusts this responsibility to the Conference of the Parties [art. 7(e)], while the Montreal Protocol requires assessment and review of control measures based on the reports submitted by a panel of experts at least every four years [art. 6].

Where a framework treaty institutes an objective, or final goal, the task of approaching it is usually undertaken in steps and requires interim measures. The task of making these rules and drawing up other measures, or recommending what they should be, is sometimes delegated to a group of scientific experts. We have seen that panels of experts have been set up under the Montreal Protocol, while the Climate Change Convention and the Biodiversity Convention have each created special scientific bodies. In our discussion on the amendment of treaties[w], we noticed how the use of protocols and scientific annexes is directed at avoiding the tortuous process of treaty amendment. We have also noted above how annexes under the Montreal Protocol are amended. In addition, Chapter Eight on Antarctica offers examples of how the Commission under the Convention on the Conservation of Antarctic Marine Living Resources (CCAMLR) **[Basic Document 2.4]** is possessed of management powers that will help nations comply with that treaty regime.

International treaty rules inhabit a consensual legal order and the implications of non-compliance with such rules stand in sharp relief to the comparable non-implementation of statutory rules within national legal systems. In the absence of bodies empowered to enforce compliance, the pressing goal of the parties to a treaty is to persuade the defaulter to comply. A medley of diplomatic and administrative measures are employed to secure such compliance. Judicial supervision leading to court-type decisions are available but are resorted to only in rare instances, and many environmental treaties provide for negotiation, conciliation, and arbitration as alternatives or preconditions to court litigation.

C. DIPLOMATIC AVENUES

Many environmental treaties require that parties resort to diplomatic and other means of settling their differences before resorting to judicial or quasi-judicial settlement of disputes. They include: CITES [art. XVIII] **[Basic Document 6.5]**; the Convention for the Prevention of Pollution from Ships (MARPOL) . . ., art 10 **[Basic Document 4.12]**; the Convention on Interna-

w. *See supra* Section A(4) of Chapter 2, at 87.

tional Liability for Damage Caused by Space Objects (Space Liability Convention) ... art. IX **[Basic Document 3.5]**; the Vienna Convention on Ozone [art. 11(1)] **[Basic Document 3.14]**, the Climate Change Convention [art. 14] **[Basic Document 3.21]**; and the Biodiversity Convention [art. 27(1)] **[Basic Document 6.11]**. These provisions signal the importance of diplomatic means for securing treaty compliance, and a number of treaties in fact institutionalize consultation between parties: the 1974 Paris Convention [art. 9(1)] **[Basic Document 4.14]**; the Nordic Convention [art. 11] **[Basic Document 1.16]**; and the Convention on Long–Range Transboundary Air Pollution (LRTAP) ..., art. 5, **[Basic Document 3.8]**. Thus, diplomatic pressures and consultations are part of the implementing architecture of IEL.

D. JUDICIAL REMEDIES

Apart from regulatory regimes supervised by or through agencies established by treaty, judicial enforcement provides another avenue for securing compliance with the law. Judicial remedies could be used to obtain specific acts of compliance and can act as deterrents by bringing embarrassment, perhaps ignominy, to bear on wrongdoing states. In a community of nations where good standing and reputation are important, judicial remedies may have some use even though they lack mechanisms for enforcement.

It is necessary, at the outset, to point out that the arrangements in a number of environmental treaties allow private individuals to prosecute claims for breaches of a treaty within national courts—even though this practice is highly unusual in most areas of international law. *See*, for example, the Nordic Convention, art. 3 **[Basic Document 1.16]** ... , the Convention on Third Party Liability in the Field of Nuclear Energy (Paris Nuclear Liability Convention) ... , art. 3 **[Basic Document 3.1]** ... , the Vienna Convention on Civil Liability for Nuclear Damage (Vienna Nuclear Liability Convention) ... , art. II **[Basic Document 3.23]** ... , and the International Convention on Civil Liability for Oil Pollution Damage, art. III **[Basic Document 4.25]**.... [Elsewhere,] we refer to the potential for developing national remedies for implementing international treaties.

Much more commonly, judicial or quasi-judicial remedies within IEL are invoked through inter-state litigation, and are based on the grievance remedial principles of "state responsibility" or international tort law that enables one state to demand *ex-post* compensation and other relief for harm caused to it by another state. Typically, adjudication arising under international laws governing such questions is handled by international courts, tribunals, and arbiters, and not national courts or institutions. Despite ongoing efforts to enlarge the domain of public international law by giving standing to injured persons other than states, such as NGOs and even private citizens, the actors in public IEL remain confined almost exclusively to state parties.

———

In sum, to effectuate the policies and priorities defined by international environmental law, one is well advised to cast a skeptical eye upon traditional approaches to implementation in favor of more sophisticated functional or programmatic techniques for making collective choices and taking positive action. Traditional *ex post* adjudicative approaches tend to emphasize primarily exclusive interests in the protection and preservation of the natural environment, although not always. As is noted by one astute observer, "both appellants in the [Australian and New Zealand] *Nuclear Tests* cases before the International Court of Justice[x] claimed to be representing not only their own exclusive interests but also the compatible inclusive common interests of the entire international community." J. Schneider, World Public Order of the Environment: Towards an International Ecological Law and Organization 91 (1979). "Australia asserted," Schneider continues,

> not only that the deposit of radioactive fall-out on its territory [was] in violation of Australia's own sovereignty and territorial integrity but also that

> [t]he right of Australia and its people, in common with other States and their peoples, to be free from atmospheric nuclear weapons tests by any country is and will be violated . . . [and that] the interference with ships and aircraft on the high seas and in the superjacent airspace, and the pollution of the high seas by radioactive fall-out, constitute infringements of the freedom of the high seas.[1]

> New Zealand made analogous assertions, including that continuation of the testing "violates the rights of all members of the international community, including New Zealand."[2] The Court neither passed judgment nor commented on this point. It has, of course, been held in the *Reparations* case that international organizations may bring claims against governments on behalf of their collective membership (or of individual victims)[3] . . . .

Id. at 91–92. Still, as Schneider goes on to point out, "the problem remains of under what conditions one state may appoint itself champion for the inclusive interests of the world community on a particular issue." Id. at 92. Thus, *ex ante* regulatory approaches brought about by multilateral agreement and implemented through collective measures may be seen to speak more for the common inclusive interest than the alternative *ex post* adversarial-adjudicative approach. The next two readings confirm this view.

ALEXANDRE KISS & DINAH SHELTON, INTERNATIONAL ENVIRONMENTAL LAW 55–58, 155–59 (1991).

INTERNATIONAL INSTITUTIONAL COOPERATION

Protecting the environment poses problems of enormous qualitative and quantitative variety. By the end of the 1960s, international organizations were forced to become involved, and most global and regional, intergovernmental as well as nongovernmental organizations were represented at the 1972 Stockholm Conference. In turn, Principle 25 of the Stockholm Declaration **[Basic Document 1.12]** provides:

---

x. (Austl. v. Fr.), 1974 I.C.J. 253; (N.Z. v. Fr.), 1974 I.C.J. 457. *See also* **Basic Document 8.6**.

1. Application Instituting Proceedings on Behalf of Australia, quoted in I.C.J. Interim protection, Order of 22 June 1973, 1973 I.C.J. 135, 139.

2. *Id.*

3. Reparations for Injuries Suffered in the Service of the United Nations, 1949 I.C.J. 174 (Advisory Opinion). . . .

States shall ensure that international organizations play a coordinated, efficient and dynamic role for the protection and improvement of the environment.

This role is important for several reasons. First ..., mankind is far from having complete knowledge about the environment, its current and potential deterioration, and the remedies which should be adopted. During the two decades since Stockholm, the role of long-range atmospheric pollution in the destruction of forests, reduction in the stratospheric ozone layer, deforestation and desertification, and concern about global climate change have arisen as issues requiring study and action. Rapid evolution in knowledge makes necessary permanent assessment of the environment, in most cases on an international level or in cooperation with researchers from other countries. In this regard international organizations are indispensable, because effective assessment requires coordination of environmental monitoring to fully obtain and evaluate information on global environmental trends. Moreover, what is known about the environment suggests that the solution to environmental problems lies in the management of natural resources. To be truly efficient, such management must be international and continuously supervised. For this as well, international organizations are crucial. Finally, international organizations representing the common interests of mankind can serve to demonstrate the interdependence of environmental quality, development, product control and energy resource management.

These various tasks necessitate a continuity of cooperative structure which can be assured only by permanent institutions. Institutional permanence is necessary also for the development of international environmental law. Clearly, elaboration and adherence to international standards are indispensable to prevent deterioration of the environment. In addition, there must be mechanisms to supervise application of the rules. By itself, entry into force of standards usually does not and cannot ensure resolution of the problems addressed. Evolution of the state of the environment and knowledge of it requires virtually constant revisions of the rules, adapting existing instruments and their application. These tasks also demand sustained cooperation and an institutional framework.

A. *Functions*

There are many structural and functional parallels among international organizations, with their activities regarding the environment similar and often overlapping.

1) *Research* plays a particularly important role in the activities of international organizations. While they rarely carry out their own scientific research, organizations often undertake studies of comparative or international law prior to drafting international treaties, recommendations, directives, and model laws. In this regard the detailed work of the FAO [Food and Agriculture Organization] and the OECD [Organization for Economic Cooperation and Development] can be cited. Where research programs require major scientific contributions, in general the member states undertake them. In this situation the role of international organizations is to ensure coordination of the tasks delegated to one or more states and to disseminate the results of the research. In certain cases, financial assistance is given to carefully selected

projects, as is done by the EEC [European Economic Communities] Commission, or research contracts are concluded with experts or research groups, as done by UNESCO [United Nations Educational, Scientific, and Cultural Organization] and the OECD.

2) *Exchange of information* concerning national and international studies and projects and, in certain cases, the results of research is another important aspect of cooperation within international organizations. All international organizations which are to some degree concerned with environmental protection are at the same time places for the collection and exchange of information. Some international organizations also prepare a synthesis of information received. The synthesis may concern a given problem, such as reports prepared by the United Nations Economic Commission for Europe, or may address the whole state of the environment, as for example, the annual report of the United Nations Environment Program.

3) *Regulatory functions* are often exercised by international organizations. They consist of drafting new norms proposed to members states, either recommendations or, more rarely, obligatory decisions, draft treaties or international rules. Some drafts follow the normal path of adoption of international instruments, i.e., elaboration by a group of experts followed by submission to a diplomatic conference, without this necessarily leading to adherence by every member state. Another means of standard-setting may occur when a treaty devoted to a specific aspect of environmental protection creates its own organ of implementation. In such cases, the organ is often given responsibility for elaborating rules for application of the treaty or for modifying existing norms, sometimes contained in detailed appendices. When such power is conferred, states generally maintain their right to withhold acceptance of any changes through formulating explicit objections.

4) *Supervising implementation* of the norms generally does not extend to coercive action, such as policing the high seas to catch polluters. Of course, in rare cases such power may be granted, as in Article 24 of the Canberra Convention on the Conservation of Antarctic Marine Living Resources **[Basic Document 2.4]** which establishes an international system of "observation and inspection." However, much more frequently states parties submit reports to designated international organs on the implementation of international norms by national authorities.

5) *Management of natural resources* by an international organization is no doubt the most progressive measure of international cooperation in the field of environmental protection. There are few examples. However, Article V(2) of the 1957 Interim Convention on the Conservation of North–Pacific Fur Seals confers on its Commission power to recommend to states parties appropriate measures concerning the size, sex, and age composition of the seals taken each year. There is also a system for mineral resource management of the deep seabed provided in Chapter XI of the 1982 Law of the Sea Convention **[Basic Document 4.20]**, in which protection of the marine environment holds a high place.

B.   Division of Labor

Both nationally and internationally, concerns about the environment touch most areas of activity of public agencies and institutions. As a result, a large number of organizations are engaged in studies or actions aimed at protecting the biosphere, raising questions of how to divide the necessary work.

The first and obvious criterion applicable on the international level is the scope of competence granted each organization; thus, the World Health Organization is concerned with problems which can affect human health, the International Maritime Organization with ocean pollution, and the Food and Agriculture Organization with problems of water and soil.

Another criterion is geographic. Certain environmental questions can be dealt with either on a global level, essentially by institutions within the United Nations system, or on a regional basis by regional organizations, or, finally, on a subregional level, where a few states are concerned with the solution to a concrete problem of limited geographic scope. The latter include the pollution of a water course or a lake; protected areas in a border zone; and the protection of endemic species of wild fauna.

Of course, this division of labor poses the formidable problem of coordinating the activities of different institutions. However, this is no different from the problem governments face within their frontiers of determining whether an agency or organ should have primary responsibility and large power to control all those who may have to intervene to protect the various environmental sectors or whether a specific agency should be invested only with the task of coordinating the activities of other organs. In the environmental field only the last solution is possible. Within the United Nations, an Administrative Coordinating Committee (ACC), an inter-institutional organ, ensures cooperation and coordination among all bodies concerned in implementation of environmental programs. One of its activities is to submit to the Governing Council of the United Nations Environment Program an annual report on international cooperation in the field of the environment. The preparatory process for ACC discussions on the environment is undertaken by the Executive Director of UNEP. Thus, UNEP plays the role of coordinator and advocate, its primary means of action being persuasion and, in certain cases, financial assistance.

REGULATION OF ENVIRONMENTAL SECTORS

International environmental law is generally organized to regulate the broad sectors of the environmental—oceans, inland waters, air, soil, and wildlife—even though many problems such as toxic wastes and global warming independently affect several or even all sectors.... [I]t is useful to look at regulatory techniques which are common to the various sectors and which characterize both domestic and international environmental law.

A.   Legal Techniques Common to Different Sectors

There are several regulatory techniques of proven value in environmental protection. Three which appear frequently in environmental treaties are licensing, lists, and standard-setting.

Licensing regimes act to prohibit certain activities unless a permit has been accorded by the proper authorities. Permits can be general, concerning an entire type of activity, or specific, required in precise cases. A typical example of a licensing scheme is found in article 4 of the London Convention on the Prevention of Marine Pollution by Dumping of Wastes and other Matter [**Basic Document 4.11**]:

> 1.   In accordance with the provisions of the Convention, Contracting Parties shall prohibit the dumping of any wastes or other matter in whatever form or condition except as otherwise specified below:
>
>> a) the dumping of wastes or other matter listed in Annex I is forbidden;
>>
>> b) the dumping of wastes or other materials listed in Annex II requires a prior special permit;
>>
>> c) the dumping of all other wastes or matter requires a prior general permit.

The following paragraph of the same article provides that a permit may be issued only after careful consideration of certain factors, which are set forth in Annex III of the Convention and include the characteristics and composition of the product to be dumped, the dumping site and the method to be used.

Annexes I and II list the different categories of waste. The use of such lists is another characteristic of international environmental law. It permits individualizing situations and gives the regulations some flexibility. In the London Convention, a different treatment is afforded to each list of wastes based on their toxicity or the dangers they pose to the marine environment and on their persistence. Any waste or other substance that does not appear on one of the lists is controlled by the general permit requirement of article 4(c).

Annex I is the "black list", those substances which are the most dangerous: organohalogen compounds, mercury and its compounds, cadmium and cadmium compounds, high-level radioactive wastes, and any materials produced for biological and chemical warfare. Persistent materials which are not biodegradable are added: plastics and other synthetic materials such as netting and ropes which may remain suspended in the sea. These are products which, apart from polluting the water and beaches, can seriously ravage marine animal life, especially marine mammals. The final items on the black list are crude oil, fuel oil, heavy diesel oil, and hydraulic fluids whose effects are known on the ocean, marine life, beaches and coastlines in general. The only exception to the ban on dumping these products is for "substances which are rapidly rendered harmless by physical, chemical or biological processes in the sea".

If the norm seems clear, its application has been less so. The identification of wastes containing mercury, cadmium or organohalogen compounds often necessitates extended research to obtain information which is not readily available. The problem is even more apparent with another convention which uses the blacklist technique: the Convention for the Protection of the Rhine against Chemical Pollution [**Basic Document 4.16**]. It lists 83 substances for which limits are established, based on a catalogue of 1,500 potential blacklist substances, compiled through an EEC Commission study. Obviously, there are practical difficulties in enforcing a ban on dumping such a lengthy list of substances.

The same is true for the somewhat less dangerous wastes listed in Annex II of the London Convention [on the Prevention of Marine Pollution by

Dumping of Wastes and Other Matter]. This "grey" list comprises those materials and substances whose dumping requires special precautions and for which specific prior authorization is necessary. The substances include waste not covered by Annex I which contains significant amounts of arsenic, lead, copper, zinc, and their compounds, organosilicon compounds, cyanides, fluorides, pesticides and their by-products. In addition, the presence of all the prior substances, plus beryllium, chromium, nickel, vanadium, and their compounds must be considered before a permit is issued for dumping large quantities of acids or alkalis. Finally, the grey list also includes objects which could present a serious obstacle to fishing or navigation: containers, scrap metal and other bulky wastes liable to sink to the sea bottom.

The dumping of all other wastes requires a general permit. Further, states parties are required to take all practicable steps to prevent marine pollution by dumping and to constantly monitor the dumping of wastes. However, the Convention only concerns deliberate dumping outside the normal operations of ships and other uses of the sea, being concerned with the use of the sea as a general waste disposal site.

The technique of lists is extremely widespread in laws to protect ocean waters as well as inland waters from dumping of wastes, discharge of substances by ships during normal operations, land-based pollution, and dumping in rivers or groundwaters. Such lists are found not only in international treaties, but in EEC directives, such as the May 4, 1976, directive on Pollution caused by Certain Dangerous Substances Discharged into the Aquatic Environment of the Community [L129 O.J.E.C. 23 (1976)], and the December 17, 1979, directive on the Protection of Groundwater against Pollution caused by Certain Dangerous Substances [L20 O.J.E.C. 43 (1980)].

In each case, the use of lists avoids too much technical detail being included in the basic norms and also permits modification of the listed substances without going through the often cumbersome amendment process.

The same technique has been applied in numerous instruments for the protection of wildlife. For example, the Washington Convention on International Trade in Endangered Species of Wild Fauna and Flora (CITES) [Basic Document 6.5] is supplemented by three appendices listing: (1) species threatened with extinction, (2) all species which are vulnerable to such threat, and (3) those which need regulation to prevent or restrict exploitation. Trade in Appendix I species is strictly limited in order to avoid threatening their survival. Permits for such trade may be granted only in exceptional circumstances and, significantly, are required both by the exporting and the importing state.

For those species included in the second Appendix, permits to trade are required under somewhat less strict conditions. Finally, trade in species listed in Appendix III, for which a state party obtained regulation in order to prevent or restrict exploitation, is subject to more general controls. This method of protection has been utilized in nearly all treaties aimed at protecting wildlife, in EEC directives, and in national law. Although the situation is different from water pollution, the same advantages and disadvantages are present. The rules are clear and the lists are relatively easy to alter. However, customs officials may be unfamiliar with all the listed items or with the appearance of many of the regulated species, especially the numerous protected plants.

The third technique of protection is environmental standard-setting, the fundamental task of legal regulation. A distinction may be made between four categories of norms:

1. *Quality standards* for the environment fix the maximum permissible level of pollution in the different sectors. Such a standard may set the level of mercury permissible in rivers, or the level of sulfur dioxide in air, or the noise level impacting houses near a freeway. Quality standards can vary according to the particular utilization of the environmental sector. For example, for inland waters a distinction is made between drinking water, agricultural waters, bathing waters, and fishing waters. EEC directives concerning each "type" of water show the impact of the diverse uses on quality norms. Quality norms can also vary in geographic scope, covering national or regional zones, or a particular environmental source, such as a specific river or lake.

2. *Emission standards.* The objective of these norms is to specify the quantity of pollutants, or their concentration in discharges, which can be emitted by a given source. Often the discharge sector is determined: groundwaters, ocean waters, air. The emission of polluting substances can be measured by a unit of time, a fixed period, or by a given activity or operation. As a general rule, emission standards apply to fixed installations, such as factories or homes, while mobile sources of pollution are regulated by product standards, discussed below. Emission standards establish obligations of result, leaving to the polluter the free choice of means to conform to the norm. Thus, a regulated paper mill could either obtain a water purification system or choose to change its production processes. Emission standards may vary depending on the environmental sector, the number of polluters and the capacity of the sector to absorb pollutants. Variations also appear due to particular climatic or other conditions, for example, higher smoke emission standards will apply during smog alerts caused by air inversion layers or persistent fog.

3. *Process standards* establish certain specifications applicable to fixed installations. For example, they may impose a particular production procedure on a factory in order to protect the environment. In contrast to emission standards, process standards establish the means of production and do not leave the polluter with a choice of methods to reduce emissions. Often, these norms require the installation of purification or filtration systems.

4. *Product standards* fix the physical or chemical composition of items such as pharmaceuticals or detergents, or the handling, presentation and packaging of products, particularly those which are toxic, or the levels of pollutants which the product can emit during its use, such as automobile emission standards. For economic reasons, these standards are usually industry wide, utilized to adopt uniform rules with the aim of preserving human health. Product standards can take numerous forms. One norm may specify the composition of products such as chemical substances or motor vehicle or factory engine emissions; another may list substances whose use is forbidden in certain products; for example, the use of mercury in pesticides. Product standards also can serve to standardize products for purposes other than

environmental; e.g. professional organizations or industries may adopt them for quality control.

For several reasons the implementation of such norms on the international level requires standardization of the methods and measures imposed. First, issues of competitive disadvantage act as a disincentive to unilateral environmental regulation. Second, unilateral measures which are taken by one country due to a high priority given environmental protection could be imposed extraterritorially if there is considerable political pressure to take action. Third, adequate enforcement of standards regarding products and substances in international trade or having transboundary effects requires common standards, documents, and certification clearly understood by national officials charged with their application.

PATRICIA W. BIRNIE & ALAN E. BOYLE, INTERNATIONAL
LAW AND THE ENVIRONMENT 179–86 (1992).

OTHER METHODS OF DISPUTE SETTLEMENT
(1) International Adjudication

Resort to the International Court of Justice or to binding arbitration has been of limited significance in the development of international environmental law, although the seminal contribution of the small number of arbitral awards and ICJ judgments [may be] observed....[y] Adjudication may be relevant, however, as a means of supervising treaty compliance, and in determining applicable rules and principles of general international law.

(a) Adjudication and Treaty Compliance

Adjudication as a means of ensuring treaty compliance is rarely used in instruments concerned with environmental matters. Three European treaties dealing with wildlife conservation, pollution of the Rhine, and land-based sources of marine pollution allow any party to refer disputes concerning their "interpretation or application" to arbitration,[4] while the 1972 London Dumping Convention [Basic Document 4.11] provides for such disputes to be referred unilaterally to arbitration or by agreement to the ICJ. The 1958 Geneva Convention on Fishing and Conservation of Living Resources [Basic Document 6.3] requires certain conservation disputes to be submitted to a special commission, whose decisions are binding, but subject to review after two years. The treaty is not widely ratified, and the special commission procedure has never been invoked. A few more treaties allow optional acceptance of the compulsory jurisdiction of the ICJ or arbitration in the event of dispute, or include these among the methods parties may agree to use. Many environmental treaties have no dispute settlement clause at all; others require only the use of negotiation, or in a few cases, conciliation.

This pattern is consistent with the view that international adjudication, based on rules of international law, has too many disadvantages in an

---

y. *See, e.g.,* the cases noted in Section 8 of the documentary supplement to this coursebook.

4. 1979 Berne Convention on the Conservation of European Wildlife and Natural Habitats, Article 18, E.T.S. 104; 1976 Convention on the Protection of the Rhine Against Chemicals, Article 15 [Basic Document 4.16]; 1974 Paris Convention for Prevention of Marine Pollution from Land-based Sources, Article 21 [Basic Document 4.14].

environmental context to be widely attractive to states as a primary means of dispute settlement. The inclusion of a formal compliance procedure in the 1987 Montreal Protocol **[Basic Document 3.18]** to the Ozone Convention **[Basic Document 3.14]** emphasizes the importance of collective supervision by the parties in this context, while the protocol's relatively weak dispute settlement clause indicates its secondary role and the continuing opposition of many states to compulsory adjudication.

But it does not follow that resort to judicial machinery is necessarily inconsistent with primary reliance on political and institutional methods of treaty supervision. This can be observed in the *ICAO Council* case,[5] where Article 84 of the Convention on International Civil Aviation gave the ICJ jurisdiction over disputes concerning the "interpretation or application" of the convention. In rejecting the argument that it was deprived of jurisdiction in a dispute concerning the competence of the ICAO Council, the court observed:

> the appeal to the court contemplated by the Chicago Convention and the Transit Agreement must be regarded as an element of the general regime established in respect of ICAO. In thus providing for judicial recourse by way of appeal to the court against decisions of the Council concerning interpretation and application ... the Chicago treaties gave member states, and through them the Council, the possibility of ensuring a certain measure of supervision by the Court over those decisions. To this extent, these treaties enlist the support of the Court for the good functioning of the organization and therefore the first reassurance for the Council lies in the knowledge that means exist for determining whether a decision as to its own competence is in conformity or not with the provisions of the treaties governing its action.

This judicial review function in respect of matters of treaty interpretation and application is particularly important where international institutions are endowed with significant powers or where such powers are conferred on states. This is why the 1982 UNCLOS **[Basic Document 4.20]** makes extensive provision for compulsory judicial settlement of disputes by the proposed Law of the Sea Tribunal, by arbitration, or by the Sea–Bed Disputes Chamber. If a stronger model of multilateral decision-making is to be developed in the environmental field, as the Montreal Protocol to the Ozone Convention suggests, then the argument for judicial review becomes stronger and more important, and the 1982 UNCLOS can be seen as a possible precedent in this respect.

(b) Dispute Settlement Under the 1982 UNCLOS

Article 286 of the 1982 UNCLOS **[Basic Document 4.20]** is a general provision for unilateral reference of disputes concerning interpretation or application of the Convention to the Law of the Sea Tribunal, the ICJ, or an arbitral tribunal constituted under the provisions of the Convention. The court or tribunal chosen will also have jurisdiction to interpret or apply international agreements "related to the purposes of the Convention" if they so provide. Article 286 is broad [in] scope. It includes allegation that "a coastal state has acted in contravention of specified international rules and

---

5.   1972 I.C.J. 46.

standards for the protection and preservation of the marine environment which are applicable to the coastal state . . ." or, in more general terms, that a flag state has failed to perform its obligations. But, although fisheries disputes are also in general subject to compulsory jurisdiction, there are far-reaching exceptions in this case, which exclude disputes relating to the exercise of sovereign rights over living resources in the EEZ [Exclusive Economic Zone], including the determination of a total allowable catch, harvesting capacity, and the allocation of surpluses. Allegations of a failure by coastal states to ensure proper conservation and management of stocks must, however, be submitted to conciliation, though its outcome is without mandatory effect. Disputes concerning activities in the deep sea-bed area, including the acts of the ISBA or violation of the convention's sea-bed articles or of other regulations by states parties fall within the separate jurisdiction of the sea-bed disputes chamber.

These provisions [which took effect when the convention came into force on November 16, 1994] raise certain problems of overlapping authority and fragmentation in the judicial elaboration of the [L]aw of the Sea. But they are indicative of the importance of judicial supervision in controlling the exercise of jurisdiction and authority conferred by the [c]onvention on states, particularly coastal states, and on international institutions. It is one of the very few treaties under which environmental disputes will be within the compulsory jurisdiction of international tribunals.

The 1982 UNCLOS is concerned with [a] much wider range of issues, however; it was intended to be a "package deal" whose provisions would represent a global consensus, from which only limited derogation would be permitted. Compulsory third-party dispute settlement is thus an integral element in a [c]onvention whose integrity and consistent application were among the primary interests of many states involved in its negotiation. Judicial supervision can be seen in this context as an essential means of stabilizing a complex balance of rights and duties, while accommodating inevitable pressure for continued development of the law to fit new circumstances. Few of these considerations apply with the same force to other environmental treaties, which in most cases are less concerned with the allocation and control of power than with facilitating co-operative solutions to common problems. In this context institutional supervision remains in general the more appropriate means of control and development.

(c) The European Court of Justice

The European Community has competence both to adopt environmental regulations and directives, and to conclude treaties on conservation matters and environmental protection. It is party to a number of European pollution treaties, including the 1974 Paris Convention for the Prevention of Pollution from Land-based Sources **[Basic Document 4.14]**, the 1979 Geneva Convention on Long–Range Transboundary Air Pollution **[Basic Document 3.8]**, and 1976 Rhine Chemicals and Chlorides Conventions **[Basic Documents 4.16 & 4.17]**. It has also ratified or signed a number of important global instruments, including the 1973 CITES Convention **[Basic Document 6.5]**, the 1985 Vienna Convention for the Protection of the Ozone Layer **[Basic Document 3.14]** and subsequent protocols, and the 1989 Basel Convention for the Control of Transboundary Movement of Hazardous Wastes **[Basic**

Document 5.6]. The Community also concludes fisheries agreements on behalf of all member states. Most of these are "mixed agreements" to which both the Community and member states are parties, in so far as they deal with matters not exclusively within the competence of member states alone or of the [C]ommunity alone.

The European Court of Justice is a regional international tribunal with powers of judicial supervision over the enforcement and implementation of such treaties by member states and the Community. Under Articles 169 and 170 of the EC Treaty[z] cases may be brought to the [C]ourt by the European Commission, or by other member states alleging non-compliance by a member state with its obligations under the EC treaties. This extends to treaties ... which are concluded by the Community with non-members under the procedure laid down in Article 228(1) and which are therefore also binding on member states. In the case of "mixed agreements", however, enforcement powers can only be invoked in respect of those provisions which relate to obligations within the Community's sphere of competence. There is also a procedure under Article 175 of the EC Treaty whereby a failure of the Community to act may be reviewed by the Court.

It must be observed that neither Articles 169 nor 170 permit enforcement actions against member states by private individuals or organizations. Nor, it seems, can such persons rely on the Community's failure to act against a member state as the basis for proceedings before the Court under Article 175. At most, individuals or environmental organizations may petition the Commission to take action, but [C]ommunity law makes no wider provision for public interest litigation before the court as such. Nevertheless, the procedures available have allowed the Commission to bring successful actions in a number of environmental cases involving non-compliance with treaties to which the Community is a party. Although member states cannot be compelled to implement the Court's judgments, and have not done so in all cases, both the tradition of adherence to the rule of law in most member states and the political pressure which other members can exert in cases of non-compliance serve to ensure that in most cases the Court's findings are observed.

The EEC system represents the most highly developed form of regional supervision applicable to environmental matters. While it constitutes an important model because of the prominence given to judicial supervision, it should not be assumed that this has universal significance given the rather special relationship on which the Community's extensive system of political and legal integration rests.

(d) Adjudication and Customary Law

States are of course free to resort to adjudication as a means of settling questions of customary international law, or general principles of law, in environmental disputes ..., [but] they have been reluctant to do so. Two points may be developed. The first problem is that the jurisdiction of the ICJ is based on consent; it has no general jurisdiction to hear applications

z. Treaty Establishing the European Economic Community, Mar. 25, 1957, 298   U.N.T.S. 11, *reprinted in* 1 Weston I.B. 7.

submitted unilaterally save to the extent provided by Article 36(2) of the Statute of the Court [**Basic Document 1.4**], or in other treaties. Secondly, the Court decides cases in accordance with international law. There are limitations on its ability to reform or develop established rules of law, even where states are agreed that change is necessary. Thus in the 1974 *Icelandic Fisheries* case,[6] the Court was able to depart only to some extent from established customary rules, but failed to reach a solution acceptable either to the parties or to the international community as a whole. In these circumstances, negotiation is likely to be a more successful method of law-making. Where the law is less clear, states face substantial uncertainty in submitting the outcome to the Court's jurisdiction, and the Court itself may be unwilling to adjudicate if, as in the *Nuclear Tests*[7] cases, there is no consensus on the rules applicable to the dispute. In a subject where legal rules are still developing, and underlying consensus not yet fully established, the role of adjudication is likely to be limited.

These factors help explain the reluctance of states to resort to judicial machinery, even in situations such as the Chernobyl disaster, or acid rain in Europe and North America. The possibility that a judicial award might establish precedents with unwelcome implications for the plaintiff state is also a significant factor in many environmental disputes, and favours negotiated solutions and resort to multilateral treaties as the most predictable means of balancing the conflicting interests of those concerned. This may change as consensus on some basic rules of environmental protection begin to emerge, however. Moreover, the sporadic acceptance of the ICJ's compulsory jurisdiction does mean that from time to time important issues of environmental significance will continue to come before it, as in the *Nauru* case.[8]

(2) Diplomatic Methods of Settlement

(a) Mediation and Good Offices

These methods of dispute settlement involve the assistance of a third party in facilitating negotiations. The process is voluntary and works only if the parties want to reach agreement. The use of international institutions for these purposes [is manifest], and a number of environmental treaties allow for the possibility of mediation or good offices. The main virtue of both types of settlement process is that the parties are able to avoid taking adversarial roles, while the third party is not involved in a formal adjudication.

(b) Conciliation and Inquiry

Conciliation and inquiry involve more than facilitating negotiations. In the former a third party may be empowered to indicate possible solutions, which may include finding on matters of law and of fact. Commissions of inquiry will normally deal only with fact-finding. The parties are not obliged to accept the findings or proposed solutions, however.

Conciliation is provided for in the case of fisheries disputes under the 1982 UNCLOS [**Basic Document 4.20**]; it is also one of the roles of the US–Canadian International Joint Commission. The compliance procedure adopted

---

6. 1974 I.C.J. 3.

7. 1974 I.C.J. 457; *See also* [**Basic Document 8.6**].

8. 1 Y.B. Int'l Envtl. L. 271 (1990).

under the Montreal Protocol [**Basic Document 3.18**] to the Ozone Convention [**Basic Document 3.14**] may also correspond to conciliation.

Provision for inquiry is unusual in environmental treaties despite the issues of fact which frequently arise. But there are many instances of states resorting to scientific inquiry to establish the causes or consequences of environmental pollution. The 1991 ECE Convention on Environmental Impact Assessment [**Basic Document 1.27**] also provides for an inquiry procedure to determine whether a proposed activity is likely to have a significant adverse transboundary impact. A number of European states have proposed the establishment of a similar procedure to be operated by UNEP [United Nations Environment Programme].

Discussion Notes/Questions

1. As Guruswamy & Hendricks observe, and as Kiss & Shelton and especially Birnie & Boyle confirm, adjudication, including adjudication by the International Court of Justice, has so far not had a very extensive role in the settlement of international disputes, environmental and otherwise. An explanation for this lackluster state of affairs is not hard to find, at least as regards the I.C.J. Regardless of the Court's substantive competence to hear virtually any dispute brought before it, per Article 36(2) of its Statute [**Basic Document 1.4**], its procedural competence rests, per Article 36(1), on the willingness or consent of the contending parties, and for the most part, as Birnie & Boyle make clear, states are reluctant to submit their legal disputes to the Court. As Oscar Schachter has written of international adjudication generally:

> Litigation is uncertain, time consuming, troublesome. Political officials do not want to lose control of a case that they might resolve by negotiation or political pressures. Diplomats naturally prefer diplomacy; political leaders value persuasion, manoeuvre and flexibility. They often prefer to "play it by ear," making their rules to fit the circumstances rather than submit to pre-existing rules. Political forums, such as the United Nations, are often more attractive, especially to those likely to get wide support for political reasons. We need only compare the large number of disputes brought to the United Nations with the few submitted to adjudication. One could go on with other reasons. States do not want to risk losing a case when the stakes are high or be troubled with litigation in minor matters. An international tribunal may not inspire confidence, especially when some judges are seen as "political" or hostile. There is apprehension that the law is too malleable or fragmentary to sustain "true" judicial decisions. In some situations, the legal issues are viewed as but one element in a complex political situation and consequently it is considered unwise or futile to deal with them separately. Finally we note the underlying perception of many governments that law essentially supports the *status quo* and that courts are [not] responsive to demands for justice or change.

Oscar Schachter, *International Law in Theory and Practice—General Course in Public International Law*, 178 Recueil des Cours (Hague Acad. Int'l L.) 9, 208 (1982–V).

2. Should states be more willing to submit their international disputes to judicial settlement? Would increased resort to international adjudication help to develop and strengthen international law? Would it advance the cause of world peace? Of global ecological balance? Consider in these respects the preceding extract from Birnie & Boyle; also the following extract from Daniel Partan,

Increasing the Effectiveness of the International Court, 18 Harv. Int'l L. J. 559, 561 (1977), identifying three functions of the World Court specifically that can be said to characterize international adjudication generally:

> The effectiveness of the International Court, like that of any international institution, must be examined in terms of the purpose and functions of the Court. At the risk of over-simplification, three functions of the International Court might be distinguished. First, the Court functions as a vehicle for the peaceful settlement of international disputes. Second, in articulating international law and applying that law to disputes before it, the Court exerts a major influence on the progressive development of international law. Third, in carrying out its dispute settlement and law development roles, the Court must balance claims for legal change against claims for the enforcement of established rights under traditional international law.... [S]ubject to many intense differences of views as to their proper exercise, the three functions just stated would probably enjoy wide acceptance as a framework within which to define the Court's role and measure its effectiveness.

For extensive and insightful elaboration on these and related themes, see R. Bilder, *International Dispute Settlement and the Role of International Adjudication*, 1 Emory J. Int'l Disp. Resol. 131 (1987). *See also* R. Bilder, *An Overview of International Dispute Settlement*, 1 Emory J. Int'l Disp. Resol. 1 (1986); Richard Builder, *The Settlement of Disputes in the Field of the International Law of the Environment*, 144 Recueil des Cours 139 (Hague Acad. Int'l L. 1975–I); J. Merrills, *International Dispute Settlement* (1984).

3.   When states do give their consent to adjudication, including adjudication by the International Court of Justice, often they do so on a case by case basis, pursuant to a special agreement known as a *"compromis."* In many other instances, as in the present problem, it is given by general declaration, recognizing the Court's jurisdiction, per Article 36(2) of the Court's Statute **[Basic Document 1.4]**, "as compulsory *ipso facto* and without special agreement, in relation to any other state accepting the same obligation."

These general declarations, however, lending support to Oscar Schachter's observations in Discussion Note/Question 1, supra, can and do serve to limit the I.C.J.'s jurisdiction. As authorized by Article 36(3) of the Court's Statute, general declarations concerning the Court's jurisdiction "may be made unconditionally or on condition of reciprocity on the part of several or certain states, or for a certain time"; and accordingly declarations have in fact varied from unconditional acceptances of the Court's compulsory jurisdiction to those that are highly qualified. The 1946 United States Declaration, since repealed (as hereinafter explained), is illustrative of the qualified sort and reads in pertinent part as follows:

> [T]he United States of America recognizes as compulsory ipso facto and without special agreement, in relation to any other state accepting the same obligation, the jurisdiction of the International Court of Justice in all legal disputes hereafter arising concerning:
>
> a.   the interpretation of a treaty;
>
> b.   any question of international law;
>
> c.   the existence of any fact which, if established, would constitute a breach of an international obligation;
>
> d.   the nature or extent of the reparation to be made for the breach of an international obligation;

Provided, that this declaration shall not apply to

a. disputes the solution of which the parties shall entrust to other tribunals by virtue of agreements already in existence or which may be concluded in the future; or

b. disputes with regard to matters which are essentially within the domestic jurisdiction of the United States of America as determined by the United States of America; or

c. disputes arising under a multilateral treaty, unless (1) all parties to the treaty affected by the decision are also parties to the case before the Court, or (2) the United States of America specially agrees to jurisdiction. . . .

Declaration by the President of the United States of America, Aug. 14, 1946, respecting recognition by the United States of America of the compulsory jurisdiction of the International Court of Justice, 61 Stat. 1218, T.I.A.S. No. 1598, 4 Bevans 140, 1 U.N.T.S. 9.

Note especially the last eight words of reservation b: "as determined by the United States of America." Popularly known as the "Connally Amendment," after Senator Tom Connally of Texas (Chairman of the Senate Foreign Relations Committee when the Declaration was adopted), this language was for many years severely criticized by proponents of a stronger World Court, since, pursuant to the reciprocity doctrine embodied in Article 36(3) of the I.C.J. Statute, a state may use another state's reservation to defeat the jurisdiction of the Court. In addition, it was censured for its self-judging and self-serving character. In the words of former Vice President Hubert Humphrey, the amendment "hampered the effectiveness of the Court [while rendering] little advantage and much embarrassment to this country." Hubert Humphrey, *The United States, the World Court and the Connally Amendment*, 11 Va. J. Int'l L. 310, 311 (1971).

Proponents of a stronger World Court were to be yet further disappointed by the United States, however, following the Court's decision, on November 26, 1984, in *Military and Paramilitary Activities in and Against Nicaragua* (Nicar. v. U.S.) (Jurisdiction and Admissibility of the Application), 1984 I.C.J. 392, *reprinted in* 24 I.L.M. 59 (1985), that it had jurisdiction to adjudicate Nicaraguan claims alleging violations of international law by the United States in and against Nicaragua in the aftermath of the Sandinista Revolution. In an earlier letter to the U.N. Secretary-General dated April 6, 1984, the United States had declared its "inherent right" to modify its August 1946 Declaration by excluding from the Court's jurisdiction "disputes with any Central American state or arising out of or related to events in Central America. . . . " Letter to U.N. Secretary–General Concerning Non–Applicability of Compulsory Jurisdiction of the International Court of Justice with Regard to Disputes with Central American States, *reprinted in* 23 I.L.M. 670 (1984). After the Court, in its November 26 judgment, denied that the United States had the right to thus modify its 1946 Declaration (ergo the Court's jurisdiction), the U.S. Department of State issued a formal statement flatly denying the Court's jurisdiction and declaring a withdrawal by the United States from further proceedings in the case. Statement on the Withdrawal from the Proceedings Initiated by Nicaragua in the International Court of Justice (Jan. 18, 1985), 85 Dep't State. Bull. 64 (March 1985), *reprinted in* 24 I.L.M. 246 (1985). Thereafter, on October 7, 1985, ignoring the World Court's November 26, 1984 ruling, the United States terminated its 1946 Declaration and withdrew from the Court's compulsory jurisdiction altogether. *See* Letter to U.N. Secretary–General Concerning Termination of Acceptance of Compulsory Jurisdiction of the International Court of Justice (Oct. 7, 1985), 86 Dep't State Bull. 67 (Jan. 1986). This withdrawal of the United States from the World Court's compulsory jurisdiction and the Court's November 26, 1984 jurisdictional ruling prompted a heated debate among international lawyers. *See, e.g.,* Herbert Briggs, *Nicaragua v. United States: Jurisdiction and Admissibility,* 79 Am. J. Int'l L. 373 (1985); Anthony A. D'Amato, *Comment: Modifying U.S. Acceptance of the Compulsory Jurisdiction of the World Court,* 79 Am.J.Int'l L. 385 (1985); Monroe Leigh, *Comment: Military and Paramilitary Activities In and Against Nicaragua (Nicaragua v. United States of America),* 79 Am.J.Int'l L. 442 (1985); Patrick Norton, *The Nicaragua Case: Political Questions Before the International Court of Justice,* 27 Va. J. Int'l L. 459 (1987); W. Michael Reisman, *Has the International Court Exceeded Its Jurisdiction?,* 80 Am. J. Int'l L. 128 (1986). *See also* U.S. Decision to Withdraw from the International Court of Justice: Hearing Before the Subcomm. on Human Rights and International Organizations of the House Comm. on Foreign Affairs, 99th Cong., 1st Sess. (1985) (especially statements by Abraham D. Sofaer, Legal Adviser, Department of State; Professor Richard N. Gardner, Columbia University School of Law; and Professor Burns H. Weston, Independent Commission on Respect for International Law and University of Iowa College of Law). However, it should be noted that withdrawal from adherence to the compulsory jurisdiction of the Court does not signify withdrawal from the Court's jurisdiction in all cases and for all purposes; the United States is subject to the Court's jurisdiction under the compromissory provisions of over 70 treaties, under which disputes arising under the said treaties may be referred to the Court on the application of any party. See, in this connection, Frederick Morrison, *Treaties as a Source of Jurisdiction, Especially in U.S. Practice,* in The International Court of Justice at a Crossroads 58 (L. Damrosch ed. 1987).

Do you agree with the position taken by the United States Government? How might the U.S. action affect the work of the World Court in the future?

As of this writing, there are no indications that the United States will soon reaccept the Court's compulsory jurisdiction except on a case by case basis and in respect of specific types of disputes. Imagine yourself as a lawyer in the Office of the Legal Adviser of the U.S. Department of State. Would you, in this capacity, recommend such a selective step or would you argue against it? If you would not so recommend, why not? If you would so recommend, would you simultaneously recommend some qualifying language? For example, would you recommend that a United States declaration of acceptance of the general compulsory jurisdiction of the Court not extend to such disputes as were mentioned in the 1946 United States declaration, *supra*? To disputes in respect of which any party to the dispute has accepted the compulsory jurisdiction of the Court less than, say, a year prior to the filing of the application bringing the dispute before the Court? To disputes that relate to ongoing armed hostilities between the parties? Why? Why not? Bear in mind that, first in the *Nuclear Tests Cases* [(Aust. v. Fr.) 1974 I.C.J. 253 and (N.Z. v. Fr.) 1974 I.C.J. 457 **[Basic Document 8.6]**] and later in the Iranian *Hostage Case* [Case Concerning United States Diplomatic and Consular Staff in Tehran (United States v. Iran) 1979 I.C.J. 23], as well as most recently in the case of *Nicaragua v. United States, supra,* respondent States have chosen to boycott the Court in the face of ongoing litigation, ergo to leave it in a position of rendering essentially *ex parte* decisions whose force and effect, in our decentralized international legal system, is thus necessarily compromised. For this and related considerations, see The United States and the Compulsory Jurisdiction of the International Court of Justice (A. Arend ed. 1986); Anthony D'Amato, *Modifying U.S. Acceptance of the Compulsory Jurisdiction of the World Court,* 79 Am. J.

Int'l L. 385 (1985); Louis B. Sohn, *Suggestions for the Limited Acceptance of Compulsory Jurisdiction of the International Court of Justice by the United States*, 18 Ga. J. Int'l & Comp. L. 1 (1988).

See generally Thomas M. Franck, Judging the World Court (Twentieth Century Fund Paper, 1986); The International Court of Justice at a Crossroads (L. Damrosch ed. 1987). For extensive discussion on how and in what ways to revive the World Court, see Richard A. Falk, Reviving the World Court (1986).

4. As pointed out by Birnie & Boyle, *supra*, the usefulness of such non-adjudicative means of international dispute settlement as mediation and conciliation is limited because they cannot be successful without the cooperation of the disputants. The techniques of mediation and good offices work , they write, "only if the parties want to reach agreement" and that, in respect of the techniques of conciliation and inquiry, "the parties are not obliged to accept the findings or proposed solutions." Does this mean that decisions reached via these non-adjudicative modalities of international dispute settlement do not have the force and effect of law? What if the parties choose to treat these decisions as binding? What then?

5. For discussion of non-adjudicative means of dispute settlement, see J. G. Merrills, International Dispute Settlement (1984); J. Simpson & H. Fox, International Arbitration: Law and Practice (1959). For discussion of non-adjudicative as well as adjudicative means of dispute settlement in the environmental realm, see Richard Bilder, *The Settlement of Disputes in the Field of the International Law of the Environment*, 144 Recueil des Cours 139 (Hague Acad. Int'l L. 1975–I); Richard Builder, *An Overview of International Dispute Settlement*, 1 Emory J. Int'l Disp. Resol. (1986).

2. THE APPLICATION OF INTERNATIONAL LAW ON THE NATIONAL PLANE

If international law were relevant only in foreign offices, intergovernmental organizations, tribunals such as the International Court of Justice, and other decision-makers on the international plane, then, though still deserving of serious study, it would be confined to limited amounts of conflict resolution across national boundaries. In fact, however, international law comes up often in national (domestic or municipal) decision-making arenas. International law, Hans Kelsen once argued, is thoroughly pervasive, serving as the ultimate legitimization of national law (although this is, of course, a theoretical argument). More evidently, it is resorted to, in varying degree, for the actual *rules of decision* in domestic litigation and settlement; and increasingly this is so in the environmental realm. As one international environmental law scholar observed already a decade and a half ago:

> As far as national tribunals are concerned . . . , there is some indication of an emerging trend towards a widening of their portals in transnational environmental matters. When an incident has caused oil pollution damage in the territory (including territorial sea) of a particular state or states (wherever the escape or discharge responsible may have occurred), the International Convention on Civil Liability for Oil Pollution Damage **[Basic Document 4.25]** stipulates that actions for compensation may only be brought in the courts of the damaged state(s); it does additionally, however, commit each contracting state to "ensure that its Courts

possess the necessary jurisdiction to entertain such actions for compensation." With regard to any kind of transnational environmental nuisance or damage, Denmark, Finland, Norway, and Sweden have provided for access of each other's nationals to their courts. More specifically, they have agreed that any person who is or may be affected by a nuisance caused by environmentally harmful activities or is seeking compensation for damage caused by such activities in another contracting state

> shall have the right to bring before the appropriate Court or Administrative Authority of that State the question of the permissibility of such activities, including the question of measures to prevent damage, and to appeal against the decision of the Court or the Administrative Authority to the same extent and on the same terms as, legal entity of the State in which the activities are being carried out.

Without an explicit international agreement, a Canadian citizen and a Canadian environmental organization were early permitted to intervene in litigation in US courts under the National Environmental Policy Act of 1969 to ensure representation of their own separate interests.[9]

Jan Schneider, *World Public Order of the Environment: Towards an International Ecological Law and Organization* 91 (1979).

In any event, to the extent that national courts do decide cases of international consequence, it may be said that they act as agents of the international legal order. If international law were relevant only in foreign offices, intergovernmental organizations, and third-party decision-making arenas such as the International Court of Justice, then, though the subject still would be deserving of serious study, it would be confined to limited amounts of conflict resolution across national boundaries.

Thus, in this sense of the resort to international law in domestic law systems we find a vast extension of the influence of international law. Therefore, before we plunge into the problems in Part II of this coursebook, we here present material concerning the incorporation of international law as a basis for decision in national courts. In so doing, we focus primarily on the incorporation of international law as a rule of decision in *American* courts. We do this in part because this coursebook is designed mainly for American law students but largely because space does not permit a survey of all national legal systems in this regard. It should be understood, however, that the issues raised in the United States relative to the interrelation of national and international law have their analogues in the legal systems of most other countries and therefore have broad relevance.

Starke's International Law 71–72 (I. Shearer ed., 11th ed. 1994).

Nothing is more essential to a proper grasp of the subject of international law than a clear understanding of its relation to State law. A thorough acquaintance with this topic is of the utmost practical importance. Particularly is it of value in clarifying the law of treaties—perhaps the most important branch of international law, and one which impinges so frequently on the domain of State law. * * * The two principal theories are known as *monism*

---

9. Wilderness Society v. Morton, 463 F.2d 1261 (D.C.Cir. 1972).

and *dualism*. According to monism, international law and State law are concomitant aspects of the one system—law in general; according to dualism, they represent two entirely distinct legal systems, international law having an *intrinsically* different character from that of State law. Because a large number of domestic legal systems are involved, the dualist theory is sometimes known as the "pluralistic" theory, but it is believed that the term "dualism" is more exact and less confusing.

IAN BROWNLIE, PRINCIPLES OF PUBLIC INTERNATIONAL LAW 31–33 (5th ed. 1998).

The theoretical issue [of the relation of municipal and international law] is normally presented as a clash between dualism (or pluralism) and monism. Both these schools of thought assume that there is a common field in which the international and municipal legal orders can operate simultaneously in regard to the same subject-matter, and the problem then is, which is the master? It is at once obvious that when the issue is taken up in this form a limit has already been set to the controversy and certain solutions ruled out. Dualist doctrine points to the essential difference of international law and municipal law, consisting primarily in the fact that the two systems regulate different subject-matter. International law is a law between sovereign states: municipal law applies within a state and regulates the relations of its citizens with each other and with the executive. On this view neither legal order has the power to create or alter rules of the other. When municipal law provides that international law applies in whole or in part within the jurisdiction, this is merely an exercise of the authority of municipal law, an adoption or transformation of the rules of international law. In case of a conflict between international law and municipal law the dualist would assume that a municipal court would apply municipal law.

Monism is represented by a number of jurists whose theories diverge in significant respects. In the United Kingdom Hersch Lauterpacht has been a forceful exponent of the doctrine. In his hands the theory has been no mere intellectual construction, and in his work monism takes the form of an assertion of the supremacy of international law even within the municipal sphere, coupled with well-developed views on the individual as a subject of international law. Such a doctrine is antipathetic to the legal corollaries of the existence of sovereign states, and reduces municipal law to the status of pensioner of international law. The state is disliked as an abstraction and distrusted as a vehicle for maintaining human rights: international law, like municipal law, is ultimately concerned with the conduct and welfare of individuals. International law is seen as the best available moderator of human affairs, and also as a logical condition of the *legal* existence of states and therefore of the municipal systems of law within the sphere of the legal competence of states.

Kelsen has developed monist principles on the basis of formal methods of analysis dependent on a theory of knowledge. According to the bases of Kelsen's thought, monism is scientifically established if international and municipal law are part of the same system of norms receiving their validity and contents by an intellectual operation from a basic norm. This basic norm he formulates as follows: "The States ought to behave as they have customarily behaved." When the basic norm came to support a system of international law, the principle of effectiveness contained therein, which allows revolution to be a law-creating fact, and accepts the first legislators of a state, provided the basic norm of national legal orders, i.e. the effectiveness of the new internal legal orders established on the basis of acts which may be contrary to the previous constitution. Then, it follows: "Since the basic norms of the national legal orders are determined by a norm of international law, they are basic norms only in a relative sense. It is the basic norm of the international legal order which is the ultimate reason of validity of the national legal orders, too." Whilst Kelsen establishes monism on the formal bases of his own theory, he does not support the "primacy" of international law over municipal law: in his view the question of "primacy" can only be decided on the basis of considerations which are not strictly legal. One may speculate whether Kelsen has avoided an element of assumption when he establishes that the basic norm of international law in some sense determines the validity of the national basic norm: the validity of each could rest on a relation of interdependence rather than a "hierarchical" relation.

There is also a monist-naturalist theory, which, superficially at least, resembles Kelsen's provision of a universal basic norm. According to this theory the international and municipal legal orders are subordinate to a third legal order, usually postulated in terms of natural law or "general principles of law," superior to both and capable of determining their respective spheres.

Editors' Note

The fact is, as international law scholar Edwin A. Borchard once wrote, that both the dualist and monist schools regarding the interrelation of national and international law are "partly right and partly wrong." Edwin Borchard, *The Relation Between International Law and Municipal Law*, 27 Va. L. Rev. 137, 140 (1940). Borchard continued:

> The error of each school appears to lie in the unwillingness to admit a principle of coordination between the two systems. They do have a relation and an easily established one. Although it is true that international law is addressed to States as entities, it exerts a command upon law-abiding States not to depart from its precepts, subject to international responsibility. The domestic instruments that the State employs to perform its international obligations are a matter of indifference to international law. It may employ statute or administrative official or judicial control. It may directly incorporate international law into the local system, or it may incorporate only treaties and not customary law. Its failure to enact the necessary implementing legislation or law may impose upon it international responsibility, as in the case of the *Alabama* claims. On the other hand, should its local legislation arrogate to itself privileges not permitted by international law, it will be bound either to make restitution or to pay damages through arbitration or diplomacy.

> In the United States the courts are by the Constitution bound to give effect to treaties which even an aggrieved individual may invoke. In England, the rule is different, for there treaties must be adopted or converted into legislation before they become invocable in the courts. But in both cases the treaty is binding on the nation and will be enforced, notwithstanding a conflicting municipal statute, by such instrumentalities as international law

possesses. The American courts, like the English, are said to consider international law a part of the law of the land. And this is true, for international law will in principle be enforced directly in the municipal courts provided there is not statute *contra*. Where a reconciliation between international law and municipal law is possible, the courts will make it. Where there is a statute which conflicts with international law, instances of which will presently be noted, the courts must perforce give effect to the statute even as against the treaty, provided the treaty is earlier in time. But this merely indicates that the municipal economy or administration is so arranged that the enforcement of the international obligation is vested not in the courts but in a different department. This phenomenon has led to the inference that the municipal law enforceable in the courts prevails over a contrary rule of international law, which is enforceable by the Executive at the initiative of the aggrieved foreigner or his government. But this merely means that the courts have no local authority to give effect to international law *when it conflicts with municipal statute*, but that such function is vested in this country in the Secretary of State, who is the agent of the American people for the enforcement of international law. The rule that finally prevails on the American people is the rule of international law as evidenced in the taxes they may have to pay to make good the aberrations of the municipal statute.

Id. at 143–45.

The late Myres S. McDougal, arguably the preeminent international law theorist of the last half century, gave theoretical expression to Borchard's observations as follows:

From the perspective of our recommended conception of law, both international and national, as a process of authoritative decision, the problem of the impact of international law upon national law may now be given a much sharper focus. The problem is not, as the Austinians think, one of determining a relationship between mere rules of international morality and exclusive sovereign command; or, as the dualists think, of achieving some kind of logical explanation of how absolutely sovereign states can be subordinated to, or coordinated by, "binding" international rules; or, as the monists think, of demonstrating the common "validity" of a hierarchy of rules by syntactical derivations from the top of a rule pyramid downward or from the bottom upward. The problem is rather one of the reciprocal impact or interaction, in the world of operations as well as of words, of interpenetrating processes of international and national authority and control. The relevant hierarchies, if hierarchies are relevant, are not of rules but of entire social and power processes. The world power process as a whole may indeed perhaps be insightfully viewed as a complex hierarchy of power processes of varying degrees of comprehension (global, hemispheric, regional, national, local), with the more comprehensive affecting "inward" or "downward" the less comprehensive, and the latter in turn affecting "outward" or "upward" the former. The metaphor of "nesting" tables or cups might be apt if such tables and cups could be conceived as being in process of constant interaction and change. On the level of formal authority, there is in the power processes a thorough, continuing interpenetration of decision-makers, structures of interaction, and demanded policies, with the officials of international authority, for example, often acting in the arenas of national authority, and vice versa. On the level of effective power, of the factors which actually shape authoritative decision, it is a common-place that individuals, private associations, parties, and pressure groups bring their base values to bear upon all levels of authority, and with little respect for state boundaries. The important questions are: how, and with what access to decision by interested participants, are inclusive policies, purporting to express a common interest, actually prescribed in the world arena for regulating the practices of states; what balance between the inclusive competence of the general community of states and the exclusive competence of particular states, in terms of control over interactions assigned to each, is in fact established by such prescription; in what degree, and by what practices, are inclusively prescribed policies effectively applied in action, in external and internal arenas, to regulate states both in their external strategies and in their internal policies; and, finally, how compatible are the aggregate effects achieved, by the impact of international upon national processes of authority, with shared values of human dignity?

Myres McDougal, *The Impact of International Law Upon National Law: A Policy-Oriented Perspective*, 4 S.D. L. Rev. 25, 37–38 (1959), *reprinted in* Myres McDougal et al. *Studies in World Public Order* 157, 171–72 (1960).

Accurate though Borchard and McDougal were in describing the "real world" in which we live, the monist and dualist approaches to the interrelation of national and international law nevertheless find formal expression in the constitutive orders of modern legal systems. Three examples follow.

A. The *monist approach* to the relationship between national and international law, prevalent in civil law countries that borrow heavily from the German legal experience, is illustrated by Articles 24–26 of the Basic Law for the Federal Republic of Germany (especially Article 25), as quoted in 6 Constitutions of the Countries of the World 50 (A. Blaustein & G. Flanz eds., 1985):

Art. 24

(1) The Federation may, by legislation, transfer sovereign powers to inter-governmental institutions.

(2) For the maintenance of peace, the Federation may enter a system of mutual collective security; in doing so it will consent to such limitations upon its rights of sovereignty as will bring about and secure a peaceful and lasting order in Europe and among the nations of the world.

(3) For the settlement of disputes between states, the Federation will accede to agreements concerning a general, comprehensive and obligatory system of international arbitration.

Art. 25

The general rules of public international law are an integral part of federal law. They shall take precedence over the laws and shall directly create rights and duties for the inhabitants of the federal territory.

Art. 26

(1) Acts tending and undertaken with the intent to disturb the peaceful relation between nations, especially to prepare for aggressive war, are unconstitutional. They shall be made a punishable offence.

(2) Weapons designed for warfare may not be manufactured, transported or issued except with the permission of the Federal Government. Details shall be regulated by a federal law.

B. The *dualist approach* to the relationship between national and international law, manifest in the United Kingdom and elsewhere in The Commonwealth where the Common Law prevails, is more or less illustrated by New Zealand law. We quote from Paragraph 44, Appendix E of Legislative Change: Guidelines On Process and Content (rev. ed. 1991), a report of New Zealand's Legislation Advisory Committee adopted as an official government policy by the New Zealand cabinet:

> International law and practice make it clear that various representatives of the state ... have authority to negotiate and adopt or authenticate the text of [a] treaty. Other officials may also be given specific authority to undertake a negotiation or to agree to a treaty text.

These functions are executive functions. The Privy Council made that clear in 1937 in a Canadian case from which it is convenient to quote ...:

> It will be essential to keep in mind the distinction between (1) the formation, and (2) the performance of the obligations constituted by a treaty, using that word as comprising any agreement between two or more sovereign States. Within the British Empire there is a well-established rule that the making of a treaty is an executive act, while the performance of its obligations, if they entail alteration of the existing domestic law, requires legislative action. If the national executive, the government of the day, decide to incur the obligations of a treaty which involve alteration of law they have to run the risk of obtaining the assent of Parliament to the necessary statute or statutes. To make themselves as secure as possible they will often in such cases before final ratification seek to obtain from Parliament an expression of approval. But it has never been suggested, and it is not the law, that such an expression of approval operates as law, or that in law it precludes the assenting Parliament, or any subsequent Parliament, from refusing to give its sanction to any legislative proposals that may subsequently be brought before it.... Once [obligations undertaken in treaties] are created, while they bind the State as against the other contracting parties, Parliament may refuse to perform them and so leave the State in default. In a unitary State[aa] whose Legislation possesses unlimited powers the problem is simple. Parliament will either fulfil or not treaty obligations imposed upon the State by its executive. The nature of the obligations does not affect the complete authority of the Legislature to make them law if it so chooses. (*Attorney-General for Canada v Attorney-General for Ontario* [1937] AC 326, 347–48)

* * *

This question [of how treaties are given effect in New Zealand] arises at two levels, the international and the national.... So far as national implementation is concerned, the passage ... quoted from the Privy Council in the Canadian case provides the starting point. While the government can enter into treaties it cannot, by that action alone, change the rights and duties of individuals or of the state under the law of New Zealand. If such changes are called for then legislation will be necessary.

Many treaties do not have a direct impact on the rights and duties of individuals. They can operate without legislative support. The obligations arising under alliances or the Charter of the United Nations provide an example. For the most part those obligations are met through the powers

---

aa. *E.g.*, New Zealand, in contrast to a   United States.
federated state such as Brazil, Germany, or the

which the government has under the prerogative and the common law to administer its foreign relations and to deploy its armed forces....

In a second category of cases, New Zealand law will already conform, or largely so, with the treaty to which the government is proposing to become a party. That view was taken for instance of the International Covenants on Civil and Political Rights and on Economic, Social and Cultural Rights....

In the third case, New Zealand law is not in compliance with the proposed treaty obligations. Legislative action will have to be taken. It might be taken by the executive under delegated authority if Parliament has conferred that authority (as with UN sanctions or in the case of extradition and double taxation agreements for instance), or the action might have to be taken by Parliament.

* * *

Legislative provisions giving effect to treaty obligations can take one of two broad forms. They might be more or less conspicuously woven into the texture of existing legislation. That is so for instance of that part of international criminal law which can be found in the Crimes Act 1961....

The second method is more direct. The particular treaty provisions are set out and are given the force of law in New Zealand. Legislation relating to extradition, double taxation, and diplomatic and consular privileges and immunities uses that method for instance....

Even if a treaty is not given direct force by legislation, it might nevertheless have significance in the operation of our legal system. For instance[bb]

(a) The treaty might be declaratory of customary international law on a particular topic ... and customary international law *is* part of the law of New Zealand.

(b) Courts will if possible interpret statutes consistently with international obligations. But if the statute plainly contradicts the treaty, that interpretative course is not available.

C. A *mixed dualist-monist approach* to the interrelation of national and international law is illustrated by Article VI(2) of the United States Constitution, which reads as follows:

This Constitution, and the Laws of the United States which shall be made in Pursuance thereof; and all Treaties made, or which shall be made, under the Authority of the United States, shall be the supreme Law of the Land; and the Judges in every State shall be bound thereby, any Thing in the Constitution or Laws of any State to the Contrary notwithstanding.

This mixed approach in the constitutive order of the United States, however, making treaties automatically part of "the supreme Law of the Land" but giving them no greater status than the Constitution or acts of Congress, tilts operationally in a dualist direction. The readings in subsections (a) and (b), immediately following, illustrate this point.

bb. In the two instances that follow, New Zealand (and other Commonwealth countries) may be seen to borrow from the monist tradition, allowing the incorporation of customary international law directly into the local common law without requiring an enabling act of Parliament.

(a) The Interrelation of International Agreements and National (United States) Law

Burns H. Weston, *Treaty Power*, 4 ENCYCLOPEDIA OF THE AMERICAN CONSTITUTION 1910–11 (L. Levy, et al. eds., 1986).

To enhance the pledged word of the United States in foreign relations, the Framers of the Constitution granted to the President, in cooperation with the Senate, the power to make and enter into treaties. They also provided that this power should vest exclusively in the federal government. The Framers neglected to define the term "treaty," however, leaving its meaning to subsequent clarification. Today, under ... United States law, the term "treaty" usually denotes only those international agreements that are concluded by the federal government and ratified by the President upon receiving the advice and consent of the Senate. All other international agreements— executive agreements, for example—are brought into force for the United States upon a constitutional basis other than senatorial advice and consent.

The process of treaty making involves negotiation, signature, ratification, exchange of instruments of ratification, publication, and proclamation; but, other than prescribing that two-thirds of the senators present must give their advice and consent to the ratification of a treaty, the Constitution is silent on the subject. In the early days of the Republic, it was thought that the Senate would participate with the President by giving its advice and consent at every negotiating juncture. Today, it is the accepted practice for the President to solicit the advice and consent of the Senate only after a treaty has been negotiated and signed, although in many—especially important—instances, Senate and even House committees play active roles in advance of the conclusion of a treaty, sometimes on their own initiative, sometimes at the behest of the executive branch.

Once the negotiation of a treaty is complete, the President decides whether to sign the treaty and, if so, whether to submit it to the Senate for advice and consent to ratification. If the Senate is perceived as hostile, the President may choose to let the treaty die rather than suffer defeat. If the Senate receives the treaty, it refers the treaty to the Committee on Foreign Relations, which may or may not report the treaty to the full Senate for its advice and consent. Committee inaction is the usual method for withholding consent to controversial treaties. Sometimes the executive branch will request that the committee withhold or suspend action. Few treaties are defeated by direct vote of the full Senate.

After the Senate gives its advice and consent to ratification, often subject to "reservations," "understandings," and "declarations" initiated by the Senate or the executive branch itself (to clarify, alter, or amend the treaty), the treaty is returned to the President for ratification. The President may choose to ratify the treaty or to return it to the Senate for further consideration. The President also may choose not to ratify the treaty at that time.

After a treaty is ratified, which is a national act, some international act— typically the exchange or deposit of instruments of ratification—usually is required to bring the treaty into force. Also upon ratification, the President issues a proclamation making the treaty officially public. There is disagreement over whether proclamation of a treaty is constitutionally required before the treaty takes effect domestically, but it is the norm to issue such a proclamation which, in any event, is useful in determining the date on which the treaty enters into force.

The Constitution does not limit the treaty power explicitly. Moreover, no treaty or treaty provision has ever been held unconstitutional. Nevertheless, it is generally agreed that such limitations exist. For example, the Supreme Court held, in *Reid v. Covert* (1957),[cc] that treaties may not contravene any constitutional prohibition, such as those of the Bill of Rights or in the Thirteenth, Fourteenth, and Fifteenth Amendments. Further, although *Missouri v. Holland* (1920)[dd] largely disposed of the argument that the subject

cc. 354 U.S. 1 (1957).

dd. 252 U.S. 416 (1920). *Missouri v. Holland* is especially worth noting because it concerned the constitutionality of an *environmental* treaty, between the United States and Great Britain (for Canada) for the protection of migratory birds. The treaty provided that the United States and Canada would enact legislation prohibiting the "killing, capturing or selling" of birds except in accordance with regulations promulgated by the federal government. The State of Missouri brought suit to enjoin enforcement of a federal regulation enacted pursuant to the treaty on the grounds that the powers reserved to it under the Tenth Amendment had been invaded. Prior to this case, Congress had attempted to regulate the hunting of migratory birds through the interstate commerce clause, but the effort was voided on the ground that this was a subject matter left to the separate states under the Tenth Amendment. Thus, as the State of Missouri saw it, the treaty approach—giving to Congress what Congress did not have without a treaty—represented a usurpation of the power of the separate states and consequently a subversion of federal-state relations as envisioned by the Founding Fathers. In a 7–2 decision, with Mr. Justice Holmes delivering the majority opinion, the Supreme Court upheld the treaty and regulation, contending that the dispute required reference to more than the Tenth Amendment. Mr. Justice Holmes wrote:

To answer this question it is not enough to refer to the Tenth Amendment, reserving the powers not delegated to the United States, because by Article 2, Section 2, the power to make treaties is delegated expressly, and by Article 6 treaties made under the authority of the United States, along with the Constitution and laws of the United States made in pursuance thereof, are declared the supreme law of the land. If the treaty is valid there can be no dispute about the validity of the statute under Article 1, Section 8, as a necessary and proper means to execute the powers of the Government. . . .

* * *

. . . The treaty in question does not contravene any prohibitory words to be found in the Constitution. The only question is whether it is forbidden by some invisible radiation from the general terms of the Tenth Amendment. We must consider what this country has become in deciding what that amendment has reserved.

The State [of Missouri] . . . founds its claim of exclusive authority upon an assertion of title to migratory birds, an assertion that is embodied in statute. No doubt it is true that as between a State and its inhabitants the State may regulate the killing and sale of such birds, but it does not follow that its authority is exclusive of paramount powers. To put the claim of the State upon title is to lean upon a slender reed. Wild birds are not in the possession of anyone; and possession is the beginning of ownership. The whole foundation of the State's rights is the presence within their jurisdiction of birds that yesterday had not arrived, tomorrow may be in another State and in a week a thousand miles away. If we are to be accurate we cannot put the case of the State upon higher ground than that the treaty deals with creatures that for the moment are within the State borders, that it must be carried out by officers of the United States within the same territory, and that but for the treaty the State would be free to regulate this subject itself.

As most of the laws of the United States are carried out within the States and as many of them deal with matters which in the silence of such laws the State might regulate, such general grounds are not enough to support Missouri's claim. Valid treaties of course "are as binding within the territorial limits of the States as they are elsewhere throughout the dominion of the United States." Baldwin v. Franks, 120 U.S. 678, 683 (1887). No doubt the great body of private relations usually fall within the control of the State, but a treaty may override its power. . . .

Here a national interest of very nearly the first magnitude is involved. It can be protect-

matter of treaties is limited by the Tenth Amendment, it remains possible, as the Court hinted in *DeGeofroy v. Riggs* (1890),[ee] that the treaty power may be limited by "restraints . . . arising from the nature . . . of the states."

Beyond these limitations, however, the treaty power is perceived as a broad power, extending to all matters of "international concern," a phrase that some claim limits the treaty power, but that the courts have used to illustrate the power's broad scope. Ordinarily it is difficult to show that a treaty matter is not of international concern even in the presence of domestic effects.

In addition to granting the power to make and enter into treaties, the Framers of the Constitution provided that resulting treaties, together with the duly enacted laws of the United States, should constitute part of the "supreme law of the land." Thus, as well as giving rise to international legal obligations, treaties have force as domestic law, to be applied as federal statutes and consequently to prevail at all times over inconsistent state laws (assuming no conflict with the Constitution).

Still, not all treaties are automatically binding on American courts. Aside from the general constitutionality requirement, two additional conditions must obtain for treaties to have domestic effect. First, a treaty must not conflict with a subsequent act of Congress. This is in keeping with the judiciary's interpretation of the supremacy clause, ranking treaties and acts of Congress equally and therefore ruling that the law later in time prevails. With the sole exception of *Cook v. United States* (1933),[ff] cases in this area have involved conflicts between an earlier treaty and a later statute, with the latter prevailing. The courts presume, however, that Congress does not intend to supersede treaties, and consequently the courts are disposed toward interpretations that will achieve compatibility between treaties and federal statutes on the same subject.[gg]

Second, for a treaty to bind courts it must be "self-executing" or, alternatively, "non-self-executing" but supported by enabling legislation. Such was the holding in *Foster v. Neilson* (1829).[hh] Judicial decisions vary widely in their application of this requirement, however. The distinction between "self-executing" and "non-self-executing" treaties is more easily

---

ed only by national action in concert with that of another power. The subject matter is only transitorily within the State and has no permanent habitat therein. But for the treaty and the statute there soon might be no birds for any powers to deal with. We see nothing in the Constitution that compels the Government to sit by while a food supply is cut off and the protectors of our forests and our crops are destroyed. It is not sufficient to rely upon the States. The reliance is vain, and were it otherwise, the question is whether the United States is forbidden to act. We are of opinion that the treaty and statute must be upheld.

ee.   133 U.S. 258 (1890).

ff.   288 U.S. 102 (1933).

gg.   There are at least two exceptions to the "last in time" rule, one limiting and the other reinforcing the impact of international agreements within the United States. First, it has been held not to validate an *executive* agreement which, though last in time, was found to conflict with a substantive Federal statute. Seery v. United States, 127 F.Supp. 601 (Ct. Claims 1955). And second, pursuant to Article VI(2) of the Constitution [**Basic Document 1.1**], it has been shown not to operate in the case of state or local legislation, thereby giving effect to constitutionally valid treaties even when they pre-date the conflicting state or local laws, and even, indeed, when they are found to be "non-self-executing." Asakura v. City of Seattle, 265 U.S. 332 (1924).

hh.   27 U.S. 253 (1829).

stated than applied. A determination that a treaty fits one category or the other may be shown to depend on subjective, at times political, considerations.

Although the Constitution is silent on the question of who has the power to suspend or terminate treaties and under what circumstances, it is generally accepted that the President has such power, *without* the advice and consent of the Senate, based on the President's established constitutional authority to conduct the foreign affairs of the United States. A challenge to the President's authority in this connection has thus far arisen only in the one case of *Goldwater v. Carter* (1979),[ii] and that case was decided, on purely jurisdictional grounds, against the challenge. . . .

Burns H. Weston, *Executive Agreements*, 2 Encyclopedia of the American Constitution 666–68 (L. Levy, et al. eds., 1986).

Executive agreements—that is, international agreements concluded between heads of state or their representatives, commonly without the necessity of parliamentary approval—are nowhere explicitly authorized in the Constitution. The Constitution is silent about international agreement-making except as it vests in the President, in cooperation with the Senate, the power to make and enter into treaties. Nevertheless the principle has long been established that the capacity of the United States to negotiate and enter into international agreements is not exhausted by the treaty power. . . .

The expression "executive agreement," which is not widely used outside the United States but which has its equivalents abroad, is understood by the Department of State to refer, in general, to any international agreement brought into force relative to the United States without the advice and consent of the Senate that is constitutionally required for treaties. In particular, it is understood to refer to three kinds of agreements: those made pursuant to, or in accordance with, an existing treaty; those made subject to congressional approval or implementation ("congressional-executive agreements"); and those made under, and in accordance with, the President's constitutional powers ("sole executive agreements"). None of these executive agreements is subject to the formal treaty-making process specified in Article II, section 2, clause 2, of the Constitution.

A treaty-based executive agreement, provided that it is within the intent, scope, and subject matter of the parent treaty, has the same validity and effect as the treaty itself and is subject to the same constitutional limitations. Deriving from one of the elements of "the supreme law of the land," it takes precedence over all inconsistent state laws and follows the customary rule favoring the instrument later in time in case of inconsistency with a federal statute. A conspicuous example of a treaty-based executive agreement is the traditional *compromis* defining the terms of submission to adjudication or arbitration under a basic convention. Another is found in the hundreds of status of forces agreements and other agreements required to carry out the North Atlantic Treaty, the linchpin of United States policy in Europe since World War II.

A congressional-executive agreement is based on either a prior or a subsequent act of Congress authorizing the making of the agreement or

ii.   481 F. Supp. 949 (D.D.C.1979).

providing general authority for the executive action needed internationally to implement the legislation in question. The scope or subject matter of the agreement is the same whether the congressional act comes before or after the negotiation of the agreement: the act of Congress often takes the form of an authorization to enter into or effectuate an agreement already negotiated. In principle, however, the agreement must reside within the joint powers of Congress or the President in order to have constitutional validity. An agreement outside the legal competence of Congress or the President, authorities generally agree, would be unconstitutional. On the other hand, as the American Law Institute has commented, "the source of authority to make a congressional-executive agreement may be broader even than the sum of the respective powers of Congress and the President," and "in international matters the President and Congress together have all the powers of the United States inherent in its sovereignty and nationhood and can therefore make any international agreement on any subject."[jj] In any event, partly out of a concern to check and balance the President in the conduct of foreign affairs, the vast majority of executive agreements entered into by the United States ... are of this type. Like its treaty-based counterpart, deriving from one of the elements of "the supreme law of the land," the congressional-executive agreement supersedes all inconsistent state law and follows the customary rule favoring the instrument later in time in case of inconsistency with a federal statute.

Sole executive agreements are international agreements entered into by the President without reference to a treaty or statutory authority, that is, exclusively on the basis of the President's constitutional powers as chief executive and commander-in-chief, responsible for United States foreign relations and military affairs. Department of State records indicate that only a small percentage of executive agreements are of this type and that the great majority have dealt with essentially routine diplomatic and military matters. Accordingly, with relatively minor exception ..., they have had little direct impact upon private interests and therefore have given rise to little domestic litigation. However, in part out of fear that the President might undertake by international agreement what would be unconstitutional by statute, as in fact occurred in *Missouri v. Holland* (1920),[kk] such agreements have not been free of controversy. Two issues in particular stand out.

First there is the question, not yet conclusively settled, of whether Congress may legislate to prohibit or otherwise limit sole executive agreements. Although comprehensive limitations on such agreements ... have so far failed to be adopted, Congress has nonetheless occasionally restricted presidential authority in ways that appear to preclude some executive agreements.... The validity of such restrictions upon presidential authority has been challenged by Presidents and has yet to be determined by the Supreme Court.

Second, while it is widely accepted that the President, under the "executive power" clause, has the authority to conclude sole executive agreements that are not inconsistent with legislation in areas where Congress has primary

---

jj.   1 Restatement (Third) of the Foreign Relations Law of the United States § 303 Reporters' Note 7 (1987).

kk.   *Supra* note **cc.**

responsibility, there is a question as to whether the President alone may make an agreement inconsistent with an act of Congress or, alternatively, whether a sole executive agreement may supersede earlier inconsistent congressional legislation. The prevailing view, rooted in the belief that it would be unconscionable for an act of a single person—the President—to repeal an act of Congress, is that sole executive agreements are inoperative as law in the United States to the extent that they conflict with a prior act of Congress in an area of congressional competence. This is the position taken by a federal appeals court in *United States v. Guy W. Capps, Inc.* (4th Circuit, 1953)[ll] and by the American Law Institute. The Supreme Court has not yet rendered a definitive decision in these respects, however.

The foregoing two issues aside, there is broad agreement about the scope and effect of sole executive agreements as a matter of constitutional law. Like the other two kinds of executive agreements, they are subject to the same limitations applicable to treaties, they are not limited by the Tenth Amendment, and they supersede all inconsistent state law.[mm]

(b) The Interrelation of Customary International Law and National (United States) Law

The following two cases outline in broad fashion the role of customary international law before American courts.

The Paquete Habana, The Lola 175 U.S. 677, 20 S.Ct. 290, 44 L.Ed. 320 (1900).

MR. JUSTICE GRAY delivered the opinion of the Court.

These are two appeals from decrees of the District Court of the United States for the Southern District of Florida, condemning two fishing vessels and their cargoes as prize of war.

Each vessel was a fishing smack, running in and out of Havana, and regularly engaged in fishing on the coast of Cuba; sailed under the Spanish flag; was owned by a Spanish subject of Cuban birth, living in the city of Havana; was commanded by a subject of Spain, also residing in Havana; and her master and crew had no interest in the vessel, but were entitled to shares, amounting in all to two thirds of her catch, the other third belonging to her owner. Her cargo consisted of fresh fish, caught by her crew from the sea, put on board as they were caught, and kept and sold alive. Until stopped by the blockading squadron, she had no knowledge of the existence of the war, or of any blockade. She had no arms or ammunition on board, and made no attempt to run the blockade after she knew of its existence, nor any resistance at the time of the capture.

* * *

Both the fishing vessels were brought by their captors into Key West. A libel for the condemnation of each vessel and her cargo as prize of war was there filed on April 27, 1898; ... and on May 30, 1898, a final decree of

---

ll. 204 F.2d 655 (4th Cir.1953), *aff'd on other grounds*, 348 U.S. 296 (1955).

mm. *See, e.g.,* United States v. Belmont, 301 U.S. 324 (1937); United States v. Pink, 315 U.S. 203 (1942).

condemnation and sale was entered, "the court not being satisfied that as a matter of law, without any ordinance, treaty or proclamation, fishing vessels of this class are exempt from seizure."

* * *

We are then brought to the consideration of the question whether, upon the facts appearing in these records, the fishing smacks were subject to capture by the armed vessels of the United States during the recent war with Spain.

By an ancient usage among civilized nations, beginning centuries ago, and gradually ripening into a rule of international law, coast fishing vessels, pursuing their vocation of catching and bringing in fresh fish, have been recognized as exempt, with their cargoes and crews, from capture as prize of war.

This doctrine, however, has been earnestly contested at the bar; and no complete collection of the instances illustrating it is to be found, so far as we are aware, in a single published work, although many are referred to and discussed by the writers on international law, notably in 2 Ortolan, *Regles Internationales et Diplomatie de la Mer*, (4th ed.) lib. 3, c. 2, pp. 51–56; in 4 Calvo, *Droit International*, (5th ed.) §§ 2367–2373; in De Boeck, *Propriété Privée Ennemie sous Pavillon Ennemi*, §§ 191–196; and in Hall, *International Law*, (4th ed.) § 148. It is therefore worth the while to trace the history of the rule, from the earliest accessible sources, through the increasing recognition of it, with occasional setbacks, to what we may now justly consider as its final establishment in our own country and generally throughout the civilized world.

[The Court then proceeds to review the history of the rule through a lengthy examination of State practice, beginning with the issuance of orders by Henry IV to his admirals in 1403 and 1406. It recites that France, Spain, Holland, England, Prussia, the United States, Japan, and other States had long followed the custom of exempting enemy fishing vessels from capture, even in the absence of treaties, although there sometimes had been exceptions to this custom. Referring to Lord Stowell's decision in *The Young Jacob and Johanna* (1798), 1 C. Rob 20, the Court went on:]

But some expressions in his opinion have been given so much weight by English writers, that it may be well to examine them particularly. The opinion begins by admitting the known custom in former wars not to capture such vessels—however, "but this was a rule of comity only, and not of legal decision." Assuming the phrase "legal decision" to have been there used, in the sense in which courts are accustomed to use it, as equivalent to "judicial decision," it is true that, so far as appears, there had been no such decision on the point in England. The word "comity" was apparently used by Lord Stowell as synonymous with courtesy or good will. But the period of a hundred years which has since elapsed is amply sufficient to have enabled what originally may have rested in custom or comity, courtesy or concession, to grow, by the general assent of civilized nations, into a settled rule of international law....

International law is part of our law, and must be ascertained and administered by the courts of justice of appropriate jurisdiction, as often as questions of right depending upon it are duly presented for their determination. For this purpose, *where there is no treaty, and no controlling executive or legislative act or judicial decision,*[nn] resort must be had to the customs and usages of civilized nations; and, as evidence of these, to the works of jurists and commentators, who by years of labor, research and experience, have made themselves peculiarly well acquainted with the subjects of which they treat. Such works are resorted to by judicial tribunals, not for the speculations of their authors concerning what the law ought to be, but for trustworthy evidence of what the law really is. *Hilton v. Guyot*, 159 U.S. 113, 163, 164, 214, 215.

Wheaton places among the principal sources of international law, "Text-writers of authority, showing what is the approved usage of nations, or the general opinion respecting their mutual conduct, with the definitions and modifications introduced by general consent."

As to these he forcibly observes: "Without wishing to exaggerate the importance of these writers, or to substitute, in any case, their authority for the principles of reason, it may be affirmed that they are generally impartial in their judgment. They are witnesses of the sentiments and usages of civilized nations, and the weight of their testimony increases every time that their authority is invoked by statesmen, and every year that passes without the rules laid down in their works being impugned by the avowal of contrary principles." *Wheaton's International Law*, (8th ed.) § 15.

Chancellor Kent says: "In the absence of higher and more authoritative sanctions, the ordinances of foreign States, the opinions of eminent statesmen, and the writings of distinguished jurists, are regarded as of great consideration on questions not settled by conventional law. In cases where the principal jurists agree, the presumption will be very great in favor of the solidity of their maxims; and no civilized nation, that does not arrogantly set all ordinary law and justice at defiance, will venture to disregard the uniform sense of the established writers on international law." 1 Kent Com. 18.

[The Court then reviews the opinions of French, Argentine, English, German, Swiss, Dutch, Austrian, Spanish, Portuguese, and Italian writers on international law, and thereafter continues.]

This review of the precedents and authorities on the subject appears to us abundantly to demonstrate that at the present day, by the general consent of the civilized nations of the world, and independently of any express treaty or other public act, it is an established rule of international law, founded on considerations of humanity to a poor and industrious order of men, and of the mutual convenience of belligerent States, that coast fishing vessels, with their implements and supplies, cargoes and crews, unarmed, and honestly pursuing their peaceful calling of catching and bringing in fresh fish, are exempt from capture as prize of war.

The exemption, of course, does not apply to coast fishermen or their vessels, if employed for a warlike purpose, or in such a way as to give aid or information to the enemy; nor when military or naval operations create a necessity to which all private interests must give way.

* * *

---

nn. Emphasis added.

This rule of international law is one which prize courts, administering the law of nations, are bound to take judicial notice of, and to give effect to, in the absence of any treaty or other public act of their own government in relation to the matter.

* * *

Upon the facts proved in either case, it is the duty of this court, sitting as the highest prize court of the United States, and administering the law of nations, to declare and adjudge that the capture was unlawful, and without probable cause; and it is therefore, in each case,

Ordered, that the decree of the District Court be reversed, and the proceeds of the sale of the vessel, together with the proceeds of any sale of her cargo, be restored to the claimant, with damages and costs.

[MR. CHIEF JUSTICE FULLER with whom concurred MR. JUSTICE HARLAN and MR. JUSTICE MCKENNA, dissented on the ground that the practice of exempting enemy fishing vessels from capture had not become a customary rule of international law, but was only a rule of comity or courtesy and had not been authorized by the President.]

Garcia–Mir, et al. v. Meese, Fernandez–Roque, et al. v. Meese 788 F.2d 1446 (11th Cir.1986).

JOHNSON, CIRCUIT JUDGE:

* * *

This is an appeal and cross-appeal from the final decision of the trial court ordering the government to prepare and implement a plan to provide individual parole revocation hearings for unadmitted aliens. The appellees-cross appellants ["appellees" or "aliens" or "Mariels"] are a certified class of Mariel Cuban refugees who were accorded a special immigration parole status by the Refugee Education Assistance Act of 1980. The district court has broken the class into two sub-classes. The "First Group" includes those who are guilty of crimes committed in Cuba before the boat-lift or who are mentally incompetent. They have never been paroled into this country. The "Second Group" consists of all other Mariels—those who, because there was no evidence of criminal or mental defect, were paroled under the provisions of the general alien parole statute, 8 U.S.C.A. 1182(d)(5) (1985) [i.e., authorized to remain free in the United States pending resolution of their status], but whose parole was subsequently revoked. All are currently detained in the Atlanta Penitentiary.

* * *

B. *International Law:*

The public law of nations was long ago incorporated into the common law of the United States. *The Paquete Habana*, 175 U.S. 677, 700 (1900); *The Nereide*, 13 U.S. (9 Cranch) 388, 423, 3 L.Ed. 769 (1815); *Restatement of the Law of Foreign Relations Law of the United States (Revised)* § 131 comment d (Tent. Draft No. 6, 1985) [hereinafter cited as *"Restatement 6"*]. To the extent possible, courts must construe American law so as to avoid violating principles of public international law. *Murray v. The Schooner Charming Betsy*, 6 U.S. (2 Cranch), 64, 102, 118 (1804); *Lauritzen v. Larsen*, 345 U.S. 571, 578 (1953). But public international law is controlling only "where there is no treaty and no controlling executive or legislative act or judicial decision...." 175 U.S. at 700. Appellees argue that, because general principles of international law forbid prolonged arbitrary detention, we should hold that their current detention is unlawful.

We have previously determined that the general deportation statute, 8 U.S.C.A. 1227(a) (1985), does not restrict the power of the Attorney General to detain aliens indefinitely. *Fernandez–Roque II*, 734 F.2d at 580 n.6. But this does not resolve the question whether there has been an affirmative legislative grant of authority to detain. As to the First Group there is sufficiently express evidence of congressional intent as to interdict the application of international law. Pub. L. No. 96–533, Title VII, § 716. 94 Stat. 3162 (1980), *reprinted at* 8 U.S.C.A. § 1522 note.

The trial court found, correctly, that there has been no affirmative legislative grant to the Justice Department to detain the Second Group without hearings because 8 U.S.C.A. § 1227(c) does not expressly authorize indefinite detention.... Thus we must look for a controlling executive act. The trial court found that there was such a controlling act in the Attorney General's termination of the status review plan and in his decision to incarcerate indefinitely pending efforts to deport.... The appellees and the *amicus*[10] challenge this by arguing that a controlling executive act can only come from an act by or expressly sanctioned by the President himself, not one of his subordinates.... They rely for that proposition upon *The Paquete Habana* and upon the *Restatement of the Law of Foreign Relations Law of the United States (Revised)* § 131 comment c (Tent. Draft No. 1, 1980) [hereinafter cited as "Restatement 1"].

As to *The Paquete Habana*, that case involved the capture and sale as war prize of several fishing boats during the Spanish–American War. The Supreme Court found this contrary to the dictates of international law. The *amicus* characterizes the facts of the case such that the Secretary of the Navy authorized the capture and that the Supreme Court held that this did not constitute a controlling executive act because it was not ordered by the President himself. This is a mischaracterization. After the capture of the two vessels at issue, an admiral telegraphed the Secretary for permission to seize fishing ships, to which the Secretary responded that only those vessels " 'likely to aid the enemy may be detained.' "175 U.S. at 713, 20 S.Ct. at 304. Seizing fishing boats aiding the enemy would be in obvious accord with international law. But the facts of *The Paquete Habana* showed the boats in question to be innocent of aiding the Spanish. The Court held that the ships were seized in violation of international law because they were used solely for fishing. It was the *admiral* who acted in excess of the clearly delimited authority granted by the Secretary, who instructed him to act only consistent with international law. Thus *The Paquete Habana* does not support the proposition that the acts of cabinet officers cannot constitute controlling

10. The Lawyers Committee for Human Rights filed a brief as *amicus curiae* in support of the appellees.

executive acts. At best it suggests that lower level officials cannot by their acts render international law inapplicable. That is not an issue in this case, where the challenge is to the acts of the Attorney General.

As to the *Restatement* 1, the provision upon which *amicus* relies has been removed in subsequent drafts. The most recent version of that provision notes that the President, "acting within his constitutional authority, may have the power under the Constitution to act in ways that constitute violations of international law by the United States." The Constitution provides for the creation of executive departments, *U.S. Const.* art. 2, § 2, and the power of the President to delegate his authority to those departments to act on his behalf is unquestioned.... Likewise, in *Restatement* 6, § 135 Reporter's Note 3, the power of the President to disregard international law in service of domestic needs is reaffirmed. Thus we hold that the executive acts here evident constitute a sufficient basis for affirming the trial court's finding that international law does not control.

Even if we were to accept, *arguendo*, the appellees' interpretation of "controlling executive act," *The Paquete Habana* also provides that the reach of international law will be interdicted by a controlling judicial decision....

Discussion Notes/Questions

1. "Nothing is more essential to a proper grasp of the subject of international law," writes Starke, *supra*, "than a clear understanding of its relation to State law." Do you agree? Why?

2. Which of the three theories set forth in the above readings, describing the relationship between international and municipal law, do you most agree? Monism? Dualism? McDougal's "nesting cup" or "nesting table" theory? Which best reflects the "real world" as you perceive it?

3. The foregoing readings bear witness to the fact that nation-states variously commit themselves to the domestic application of international law. For example, note the bold, wholesale incorporation of international law by the Basic Law (or Constitution) of the German Federal Republic, *supra*, and compare this with the provisions of the United States Constitution, *supra*, together with the language of the U.S. Supreme Court in *The Paquete Habana, supra*. In general, by what means, through what decision-making institutions, and to what degree do nation-states give "binding force and effect" to international law domestically? Is their commitment satisfactory in this respect? Unsatisfactory? Why?

4. Sometimes even a *treaty* ratified by a state will not be given "binding force and effect" within that state itself. In the United States, the refusal by a court to give domestic legal effect to a treaty can theoretically come about because the treaty itself is found by the court to be unconstitutional. But apart from the unconstitutionality question, there has developed in American courts a distinction between treaties that are "self-executing" versus those that are "non-self-executing" the latter being not automatically binding on the courts.

When is a treaty "self-executing" or, alternatively, "non-self-executing"? In the words of Chief Justice Marshall, "when the terms of the [treaty] stipulation import a contract—when either of the parties [have] engaged to perform a particular act—the treaty addresses itself to the political, not the judicial department; and the legislature must execute the contract before it can become a rule for the Court." *Foster v. Neilson*, 27 U.S. (2 Pet.) 253, 314, 7 L.Ed. 415 (1829). Thus, a treaty which requires no legislation to make it operative within the national legal order is said to be "self-executing." This seemingly clear-cut distinction, however, turns out to be more easily stated than applied. For example, in *Sei Fujii v. State*, 217 P.2d 481(Cal.App.1950), the California District Court of Appeals, citing Articles 1, 55, and 56 of the United Nations Charter [**Basic Document 1.3**] and Articles 1, 2, and 7 of the Universal Declaration of Human Rights [**Basic Document 7.11**], invalidated certain California land laws discriminating against aliens. On appeal, however, although reaching the same results on constitutional grounds, the California Supreme Court found that the U.N. Charter provisions (and by implication, those of the Universal Declaration) were *not* "self-executing." *Sei Fujii v. California*, 38 Cal.2d 718, 242 P.2d 617 (1952). Stated Chief Justice Gibson, id. at 724, 242 P.2d at 621 "they [the U.N. Charter provisions] are framed as a promise of future action by the member nations." Significantly, the U.S. Supreme Court never has addressed the question of whether the U.N. Charter's human rights provisions are "self-executing" or not. See also Problem 11–2, supra.

5.   Anthony D'Amato has argued that the distinction between self-executing and non-self-executing treaties is largely irrelevant because in any imaginable case an individual simply would not be able to show a violation of a treaty right if that treaty could be labeled "non-self-executing." Professor D'Amato reasons as follows in *Judge Bork's Concept of the Law of Nations Is Seriously Mistaken*, 79 Am. J. Int'l L. 92, 99 (1985):

> A non-self-executing treaty ... binds the states parties to it to enact legislation that will implement the treaty principles in their own domestic spheres. Hence, a non-self-executing treaty can only be *violated* if a party to it fails to pass the requisite implementing legislation. In the event of such a failure, that party will be in breach of the treaty vis-à-vis other parties, but the breach will consist solely in that party's failure to enact the requisite legislation. Suppose, for example, that the United States enters into a treaty with Poland containing the provision that Polish ham should be allowed to be sold in American supermarkets without interference by state or local government, and that the United States undertakes to implement this principle by passing the appropriate legislation. If, after the treaty enters into force, the United States fails to enact the legislation, Poland will have a legitimate complaint that the United States has committed a breach of the treaty. Now suppose that an importer asks for a restraining order in court against local officials seeking to bar the sale of Polish ham.... The court ... [should hold that] there has been no violation of the treaty that is relevant to the importer's lawsuit. The "violation" of the treaty that has occurred has nothing to do with Polish ham, or the right to import and sell Polish ham. Rather, the "violation" is at an entirely different level, consisting of the failure of Congress to pass implementing legislation.

> Technically speaking, the importer of Polish ham would only have a claim, akin to a shareholder's derivative lawsuit, against the United States Congress, charging that as a member of the public he has been deprived of a property interest (profits in the sale of Polish ham) owing to the failure of Congress to live up to its treaty commitments to Poland. Under present U.S. law, such a lawsuit would have practically no chance of success; it would be barred by lack of standing, the "political question" doctrine and the general constitutional right of Congress to enact or not to enact legislation. But I spell it out here to [underscore] ... that an individual is not directly "hurt" (except in this attenuated sense of a citizen's derivative lawsuit against Congress) by a "violation" of a non-self-executing treaty.

Do you agree? Could the importer of Polish ham argue that the treaty is in fact self-executing and that hence there is no need for implementing legislation by Congress? Consider the Charter of the United Nations [Basic Document 1.3], especially Articles 55 (dealing with human rights). Can this clause be argued to be self-executing? What does Article 56 add? If a nation *fails* to implement Article 56, are the rights contained in Article 55 illusory for the people in that nation?

6.   The United States has become party to the International Covenant on Civil and Political Rights [Basic Document 7.14]. Will it pass muster with the U.S. Supreme Court? Consider Article 5. Additionally, can you speculate as to what attitude the Supreme Court might take were it to have the "self-executing"/"non-self-executing" issue of the U.N. Charter's [Basic Document 1.3] human rights provisions presented to it? What factors would have to be taken into account? Purely "legal" factors? Finally, suppose a human rights treaty were to be signed by the President on January 1, given advice and consent to ratification by the Senate, after national elections, on June 1 of the following year, but was contravened by a clearly intended conflicting act of Congress on September 1 of the year of signature. What result? Would the treaty be binding on the American courts? Consider in this connection Articles 11–18 of the Vienna Convention on the Law of Treaties [Basic Document 1.7].

7.   In the words of Mr. Justice Gray in *The Paquete Habana*, supra, "[i]nternational law is part of our [United States] law, and ... where there is no treaty, and no controlling executive or legislative act or judicial decision, resort must be had [by American courts] to the customs and usages of civilized nations...." Thus, just as international tribunals, *stricto sensu*, look to "international custom, as evidence of a general practice accepted as law" (in the words of Article 38 of the Statute of the International Court of Justice [Basic Document 1.4], so also do American courts look to custom as a "source" of law for resolving transnational conflicts. Did the Supreme Court apply a rule of customary international law as the rule of decision in *The Paquete Habana*? Or did it apply, as dissenters Fuller, Harlan, and McKenna contended, only as a rule of "comity" or "courtesy"? If the latter, what is the difference between a rule of customary international law, on the one hand, and a rule of comity or courtesy, on the other? If the former, on what data did Mr. Justice Gray rely to substantiate the rule of customary international law upon which, arguably, his majority opinion was premised? And further, if in fact he did ground his decision on customary international law, where did he get his authority to do so? Finally, what was the holding in this case? What would the Court have held if there had been no reference to "the law of nations" in the President's proclamation? Alternatively, what would the Court have held if Congress had provided in its declaration of war that all Spanish vessels would be subject to arrest and capture?

8.   How might the qualifying language of *The Paquete Habana* ("and no controlling executive or legislative act or judicial decision") as discussed in *Garcia-Mir* impact upon the application by U.S. courts of a customary international environmental rule?

9.   What would happen if the U.S. Supreme Court were to hold, in a particular case, that the United States Government had violated international law *per se*? Would such a ruling be decisive as to whether in fact the United States had violated international law? Within the United States? Externally? Why?

10.   Does the President of the United States have authority to violate the rules of international law? Consider the off-putting answer to this question by Professor Abram Chayes, former Legal Adviser to the Department of State:

When I first heard about this panel on whether the U.S. Government can violate international law I was reminded of the story of a Georgia deacon who was asked if he believed in baptism by total immersion. He said: "Believe in it? Hell, I've seen it done!"

One of the problems we have to face most carefully is that the President never says he will violate international law. The Congress never explicitly authorizes the President to violate international law. Congress may authorize a specific action under a conclusive presumption that the action does not violate international law. Of course, there may be debate in the Senate or House as to whether there is a violation of international law.

11. One thing at least is clear! A state cannot get out of its international legal obligations merely because one of its municipal courts says so. For example, if a municipal court of State A holds, erroneously, that a treaty between States A and B does not give certain rights to State B citizens temporarily visiting in State A, and as a result a State B tourist is thrown into a State A jail without a hearing and explanation of the charge as required (let us assume) by the treaty, that holding of the municipal court of State A cannot be decisive upon State B. But then what happens? Does the tourist remain in jail? What might State B do about it? Might it complain on a diplomatic level to State A? Would such a complaint avoid friction? Retaliation? Would State A's government bring "pressure" upon the State A municipal judge who ignores the treaty? Could it? Might State B? Should it? Might there be other consequences?

12. As we end Part I of this coursebook, have we left you with more *questions* about international law or more *answers* ? What is more important for an international lawyer—to know the answers to questions that are asked, or to know what questions to ask? Make a note of your present response. Then, after you have completed Part II of this coursebook, come back to this question and see if your response has changed.

Chapter Four

THE GLOBAL ENVIRONMENTAL PROBLÉMATIQUE: OUTLOOKS AND APPROACHES

The purpose of this chapter is to introduce you to the problems of the global environment in a manner that allows their nature and quality to be readily discerned, and, to this end, to introduce you also to a range of outlooks and approaches that are essential for their proper understanding. It is not anticipated that any solutions will become apparent. Indeed, there is disagreement about what the problems are and how they rank in importance. It will be enough if the multifaceted nature of the problems emerges, with some appreciation, as well, for the breadth and depth of the intellectual perspectives that are available for thinking about them.

The point is, of course, that the international lawyer who wishes to deal with environmental problems must have at least some grasp of these problems through the disparate insights of the other disciplines: economics, geography, history, mathematics, philosophy, politics, the social sciences, and, of course, the physical sciences. In one way or another, therefore, all of these disciplines are represented in the readings that follow. But note: except for the 1992 Rio Declaration on Environment and Development [**Basic Document 1.29**] at the end of the chapter, no legal material will be found among them—which actually should come as no surprise. Law often is the last of the general disciplines, a societal gatekeeper, commonly selecting, adapting, and finally incorporating the ideas of others into governing law and policy; and in the case of international environmental law this truism is no mere cliché. The international environmental lawyer who actually practices in the field, particularly in its law-making processes, must deal with scientists, government officials (especially those worried about the economic consequences of policy change), diplomats, non-governmental environmental organizations, and countless others (not to mention participating in interminable international conferences held in faraway places) because it usually falls to the lawyer to co-ordinate the proceedings, assimilate the findings, and draft the outcomes of others in a form that becomes an international convention or other legally commanding instrument. And the skill required to do these and related things is remarkably wide-ranging, requiring understanding of all the disciplines that bear upon the international environmental law-making and law enforcement process—to make sense of them, to bring all their insights together, to cumulate them, order them, and otherwise marshal them in support of strategies of progressive management and reform. So, while the readings in this chapter may seem remote from lawyers' concerns, in fact, in the real world of international environmental law, they are representative of the basic literacy that is absolutely required to practice in the field in a responsible and conscientious way.

We begin with definitions. It always is useful to start with definitions, and in this instance it is essential since even the term "environment" is not free of conceptual difficulty. It is a term that has become stretched and distended with time, so that what it encompasses now is a question for debate. Added to which, there is some elementary terminology that is necessary to understand. The second segment of this chapter focuses upon what some people think the problems are. The problems make up what we have chosen to call "the global environmental *problématique*." There is no uniform approach to the problematique; the readings afford different shades of emphasis and proceed often from different analytical constructs. However, beginning in the early 1970s and broadening through the late 1980s and early 1990s, there does appear to have emerged widespread agreement that serious ecological problems do exist, and on a major scale. This is a conviction shared by your authors, or we hardly would have bothered to prepare this coursebook. But it is a conclusion that is capable of being contested nonetheless. All of the readings on all sides of the debate must be approached with a critical and skeptical mind, another quality that conscientious lawyers bring to the task of analyzing and solving problems.

There are a number of key phenomena that pervade and therefore help to define the global environmental *problématique*: energy and the seemingly limitless demand of human beings for it is one; the world's population—its size and projected levels of growth—is another. Both of these phenomena relate to the availability of natural resources, their depletion, and the consequences of their depletion upon economic well-being. Thus it is fitting that the global environmental *problématique* be considered first in terms of these pervasive phenomena and thereafter in terms of the more particularistic environmental realms upon or within which they have made themselves felt: the atmosphere, the hydrosphere, the lithosphere, and the biosphere (physical environments around which, it may be noted, the problems in Part II are principally organized). Along the way, we consider several "overviews," including the early and well known "limits to growth" and "tragedy of the commons" perspectives.

The third and final segment of this chapter is the most difficult and the one that is likely to frustrate you, the reader, the most. It is an attempt to bring together a variety of perspectives through which to view the global environmental *problématique*, a variety of perspectives that turns out to be astonishingly wide and that consequently poses significant difficulties for policy-making and law-making. Consensus is hard to come by in this field because what the viewer sees depends very much upon the lens through which he or she is gazing. And, yet, it is consensus that is essential to arrive at international agreements.

Some of the perspectives presented here can be viewed as analytical frameworks of a systematic type through which transnational environmental problems might be handled. Others are of a looser, less analytical sort, shading into ideological positions. The ecologists look at the world differently than the economists. Indigenous peoples see the problems differently from feminists. Those who believe that the "deep ecology" approach is right will not be convinced by the "sustainability" analysis. The latter can now be regarded—rightly or wrongly—as the officially sanctioned approach of the international community, having been accepted by the United Nations Conference on Environment and Development (UNCED) when, in June 1992, it adopted the Rio Declaration on Environment and Development [**Basic Document 1.29**]. Of course, international political reality and the nature of international organization places yet a different set of constraints over the entire scene.

It is to be understood, however, that, in putting forward a variety of perspectives on the global environmental *problématique*, it is not our intention to approve one approach or concept over another. All have something to offer; none enjoys a monopoly on the truth. This is a menu approach, not a definitive set of recommended analytical paradigms. While many of the perspectives have some analytical power, none is alone capable of explaining everything. Indeed, you will feel a measure of frustration when you finish this chapter because no one insight will emerge as *the* beacon by which to navigate through the rest of your global environmental study. You will, however, know the range of approaches available and be able to place issues in context; you will know the range of factors against which international environmental problems must be considered.

Final conclusions cannot be arrived at in this chapter. If any are even available—and about this there is dispute—their consideration must await concluding Chapter 13, infra, entitled "The Future of International Environmental Law." In this concluding chapter, we return to the themes raised here. In the meanwhile, particularly when you engage in the "Recommended Reflective Exercise" found in each problem of Part II, beware that, after reviewing the perspectives set forth in this chapter, you are likely to have some of your fundamental assumptions about life in the world significantly challenged.

A.   SOME DEFINITIONAL CONSIDERATIONS

1.   ENVIRONMENT

Gordon Young, *Environment: Term and Concept in the Social Sciences*, 25 Soc. Sci. Info. 83–84 (1986).

Environment has ... become an easy but individualistic code word, utilized in all sorts of contexts, resulting in imperfect, unclear, even misleading dialogues and in the oversimplified reduction of complex matters to a single word. Because of such confusion, because ecology and "the environment" remain conspicuous in the media and in popular awareness, because they have become so prominent in the social science literature, and because ecology—including human ecology—is about the relationships between organisms and *environment*, whatever the meaning, it seems not only appropriate but urgent to explore the various definitions of, and alternatives to, this difficult word....

* * *

Environment is derived from the French words *environ* or *environner*, meaning "around", "round about", "to surround", "to encompass"; these in turn originated from the Old French *virer* and *viron* (together with the prefix *en*), which mean "a circle", "around", "the country around", or "circuit". Etymologists frequently continue to the conclusion that, in English usage, *environment* is the total of the things or circumstances around an organism (including humans) though *environs* is limited to the "surrounding neighborhood of a specific place—the neighborhood or vicinity".

Even an abbreviated etymological encounter with the word environment provokes two persuasive suggestions for possible restructuring of contemporary definitions: first, that the word environment is identified, to some extent at least, with a totality, the *everything* that encompasses each and all of us, and that this association is well enough established not to be lightly dismissed; second, that the word's origin in the phrase "to environ" indicates a process derivative, one that alludes to some sort of action or interaction, at the very least implying that the encompassing is active, in some sense reciprocal; that the environment, whatever its nature, is not simply an inert phenomenon to be impacted without response or without affecting the organism in return.

THE DICTIONARY OF ECOLOGY AND ENVIRONMENTAL
SCIENCE **(Henry W. Art et al. eds., 1993).**

environment The whole sum of the surrounding external conditions within which an organism, a community, or an object exists. Environment is not an exclusive term; organisms can be and usually [are] part of another organism's environment.

2. ENVIRONMENTALISM

THE DICTIONARY OF HUMAN GEOGRAPHY 136
(Ronald J. Johnston ed., 1986).

Environmentalism The philosophies and practices which inform and flow from a concern with the environment.... One of the more recent approaches is a celebration and exploration of "the close and enriching affective bond between people and the environments that they create, inhabit, manipulate and conserve, visit, or even, imagine".[1] ... [O]ne of the most trenchant criticisms of a rather different approach, which has clearly been preoccupied with the formulation of environmental policy and which consists of those versions of systems analysis which have been directed towards the control of the ecosystem, is that its interests are essentially technocratic rather than ecocentric, concerned with means rather than ends.... Certainly, early investigations of the interface between human and physical systems were mainly technical, involved with strategies of environmental management, but

---

1. VALUED ENVIRONMENTS (John R. Gold &
Jacquelin Burgess eds., 1981).

later investigations of "control systems" have at least recognized the central importance of ethical issues as well. According to Bennett and Chorley,[2] for example, "the environmental imperative requires changes in social values" towards "a more conservation-oriented system". To this extent, they come much closer to the mainstream of environmentalism, which "is about conviction—conviction that a better mode of existence is possible, conviction that *Homo Sapiens* is capable of recognizing his dilemmas and taking responsive action" and which often flows into movements "opening up our minds and our organizations to new ideas about fairness, sharing, permanence and humility".[3] And many of those movements are profoundly political. . . .

3. ANTHROPOCENTRISM

DICTIONARY OF PHILOSOPHY (Dagobert Runes ed., 1983).

Anthropocentric: Literally, centering in man. A term which may be used in connection with extreme humanism, viewing the world in terms only of human experience.

J. Seed, *Anthropocentrism, in* DEEP ECOLOGY-LIVING AS IF NATURE MATTERED 243 (Bill Devall & George Sessions eds., 1985).

"Anthropocentrism" or "homocentrism" means human chauvinism. Similar to sexism, but substitute "human race" for "man" and "all other species" for "woman."

Human chauvinism, the idea that humans are the crown of creation, the source of all value, the measure of all things. . . .

4. ECOLOGY

ANDY CRUMP, DICTIONARY OF ENVIRONMENT AND DEVELOPMENT: PEOPLE, PLACES, IDEAS AND ORGANIZATIONS (1991).

Ecology The study of the relationships between all living organisms, plants, animals and humans, and the environment, including the ways in which human activities affect other wildlife populations and alter natural surroundings. Modern ecology dates from the work of Charles Elton in the 1930s and is concerned with the relationship of different species both with each other and with biological, physical and chemical components of the environment, or habitat, in which they live. A community of organisms, of either the same or differing species, and the habitat in which they live is called an ecosystem. The effect of human intervention on such ecosystems can be predicted to some extent, enabling effective conservation of wildlife and management of wildlife resources. An understanding of ecology has enabled scientists to develop methods for the biological control of pests and means to improve crop production.

---

2. ROBERT J. BENNETT & RICHARD J. CHORLEY, ENVIRONMENTAL SYSTEMS: PHILOSOPHY, ANALYSIS AND CONTROL (1978).

3. TIMOTHY O'RIORDAN, ENVIRONMENTALISM 300 (1981).

THE CONCISE OXFORD DICTIONARY OF ECOLOGY
(Michael Allaby ed., 1994)

ecology The scientific study of the interrelationships among organisms and between organisms, and between them and all aspects, living and non-living, of their environment.

Discussion Notes/Questions

1. Why are the definitions of "environment," "environmentalism," and "anthropocentrism" important to the study of international environmental law? What are definitions? Might it be said that they are paradigms? What are paradigms and how do they affect us?

2. How do the seemingly superior capabilities of humanity mesh with ecological analysis? Human beings have the ability to make major impacts on the biosphere. At what point do these impacts become "unnatural"?

3. Do you agree that "nature" and "environment" are separate concepts?

4. Ecology is a well-established branch of science. Cognizant of its lessons, how is it that humanity continues and even increases activities that work against the interests of diversity and stability, e.g. pesticide use—regarding which see Problem 9–2 ("Toxic Pollution in Yoribo and Bamileko") in Chapter 9, *infra*?

5. To accept criticisms about development projects (such as dams) as valid, there must be some acceptance of the inherent value of ecosystem stability. Many human beings value the benefits of hydroelectric power over the lives of fish, which dams affect. If human beings can survive despite ecosystem degradation, is the latter a real concern? Should it be factored into policy decisions? If so, how? If not, why not?

6. Monoculture production such as forest plantations often are suggested as a way of preserving the natural environments. Does it matter that they are "the least stable systems" if they slow the rate of destruction in other, more diverse ecosystems?

7. For any definitional problems, refer to A. Crump, Dictionary of Environment and Development: People, Places, Ideas and Organizations (1991); A. Gilpin, Dictionary of Environmental Terms (1976); B. Goodal, Dictionary of Human Geography (1987); The Dictionary of Human Geography (R. Johnson ed., 1986); D. Lukhaup, Dictionary of Environmental Protection (1992); and other similar texts.

B. WHAT IS THE PROBLEM?

Ever since the first Earth Day in 1970, our natural environment has been noisily rediscovered. Genuine efforts at population control, resource conservation, and pollution abatement have been made. But humans continue to be born at exponential rates, leading to exponential population growth, and the squandering of nonrenewable resources, the wanton killing of precious life species, and the overall contamination of delicate ecosystems persist with only marginal relief. To date, albeit with increasing exception, there is only small evidence that humankind is seriously prepared, psychologically or politically, to assume the courageous planetary stewardship—heroism—that is needed to avoid major disasters. Eloquent new rhetoric to the contrary notwithstanding, governments remain committed to elusive self-sufficiencies and to economic expansion as the *sine qua non* of social progress and well-being. Pollution is widely perceived as *the* central theme of environmental concern, except when there is talk or movement in the direction of competitive resource grabs. Few evince wholesale regard for "the closing circle"[4] and the consequent need to see our world as a total living organism, with appropriate coherent policies to match.

On the other hand, as Jessica Tuchman Mathews writes in her *Introduction and Overview*, to Preserving the Global Environment: The Challenge of Shared Leadership 15, 20 (Jessica Tuchman Mathews ed. 1991), there appears to have developed, beginning in the late 1980s, "an explosion of interest" in these and related environmental issues that have been around since the early 1970s. And Mathews asks: Why? "The lessening nuclear threat undoubtedly played a role," she observes. But as she goes on to conclude, cautioning that "our perspective today is too short to allow an accurate historical assessment," it is clear that "this was not the only, or even the major, force at work." Id. Whereupon Mathews proceeds to explain the new "explosion of interest" and, in so doing, to clarify generally the nature of the global environmental *problématique*. She writes, at 20–26:

> Public attitudes were clearly influenced by a steady drum-beat of internationally reported events: the oil price rise and widespread shortages that opened the decade; the chemical accident at Bhopal; the decimation of European and high-altitude U.S. forests from acid rain and other air pollutants; Chernobyl; ozone depletion and the discovery of a "hole" in the ozone layer over Antarctica; drought and famine in Africa; the Rhine River chemical spill; the homeless freighter that sailed the world for two years without finding a place to unload its cargo of toxic ash; steadily rising rates of tropical deforestation and of species extinction; closed beaches from Western Europe to the Baltic to New Jersey; the Exxon Valdez oil spill; and as the decade closed, an outbreak of freakish weather—drought and record-breaking heat in the U.S., devastating floods in Bangladesh, the most powerful hurricane ever measured, and the warmest winter in Moscow in more than a century—bringing intense new concern to the possibilities of global greenhouse warming.

> Governments were influenced also by insights flowing from a new field of research known as earth systems science, or more simply, global change. Composed of studies that criss-cross the traditional boundaries of geology, ecology, oceanography, chemistry, paleobiology, and meteorology, earth systems science emerged for several reasons. Research over the previous thirty years had erased the old notion of a stable and fully formed planet, replacing it with a picture of a planet that is naturally in constant flux. The signs of this activity—earthquakes, volcanoes, mountain building, and continental drift—could now be consistently explained. The increased attention to change was buttressed by advancing understanding of the high degree of interaction among the planet's nonliving realms—water, the atmosphere, rocks, and soils—and its living realm, the always evolving biosphere, which overlaps each of these. Together these two trends virtually demanded a new approach to research.

---

4. *See* BARRY COMMONER, THE CLOSING CIRCLE: NATURE, MAN AND TECHNOLOGY (1972).

Technological advance was also crucial, because for the first time it became physically possible to measure global phenomena on a vast scale and to handle and analyze the resulting mass of data. Remote sensing devices on satellites and airplanes and improvements in computer capabilities are the best known of these, but highly sophisticated new sensing devices on land and at sea also began to provide extraordinary insights into huge swaths of the planet that were largely unexplored. A new British long-range sonar, for example, discovered twenty-eight new volcanoes on the ocean floor on its first voyage.

Earth systems scientists studied the four chemical elements essential to life—carbon, nitrogen, phosphorous, and sulfur—and quickly found that their natural cycles through earth, air, water, and living things were being affected on a global scale by human activities. Humankind is altering the natural carbon cycle largely through the combustion of fossil fuels, having increased the natural carbon dioxide (CO_2) concentration in the atmosphere by 25 percent in the last 130 years, mostly in the last three decades. We are also *doubling* the amount of nitrogen that nature makes available to living things through the production of commercial fertilizer. One minor class of chemical compounds, the chlorofluorocarbons, is depleting the life-giving stratospheric ozone layer.

Nonchemical changes are equally massive. On land, soil erosion and deforestation are accelerating the flow of sediments and nutrients to the ocean in some places, while dams built for irrigation and electricity interrupt the natural flow in others. Deforestation in the Amazon, for example, could multiply the river's discharge manyfold in the near future, while the Colorado and the Nile, which each once discharged more than a million tons of suspended matter annually, now discharge essentially none. The loss of species—now estimated to stand at four per hour—utterly disrupts the natural balance between speciation [i.e., the evolutionary formation of a new biological species] and extinction.

The more closely scientists looked at the planet's structure and metabolism, from the top of the stratosphere to the ocean canyons, the more the evidence of rapid change accumulated. A sense of urgency gradually filtered through to governments that humans are now the principal agent of environmental change on the planet, and that if humanity is to live successfully with its ability to alter natural systems, it must first understand those systems and the ways in which human society depends on their normal functioning. Unless policies change, some scientists warned, human impacts on the planet are so profound and so rapid that irreversible damage could occur before—to put it bluntly—we have any idea of what we are doing.

Beyond the headline-grabbing events and the scientific discoveries, public and official views were also influenced by social and economic trends clearly linked to environmental conditions that seemed to augur ill for the future. The 1980s opened with a famine in Africa. By mid-decade, per capita gross national product (GNP) in sub-Saharan Africa was falling at the appalling rate of 4.2 percent per year. The region was also the only place in the world where per capita food production and consumption were declining. It had—has—the world's highest rate of population growth, by far the highest fertility rate; the highest infant, child, and maternal mortality rates; and the lowest life expectancy. It has the heaviest reliance on imported food, the greatest proportion of land area losing its fertility, and the largest percentage of the population suffering from severe malnourishment. It has the world's greatest dependence on fuelwood for energy, and accounts for a bare 1 percent of commercial energy consumption. Looking ahead, the Economic Commission for Africa predicted in 1983 that if these current trends continued, the prospects for the region in 2008 were "almost a nightmare ... characterized by a degradation of the very essence of human dignity."

As the 1980s progressed, a surprising international consensus grew that "the first answer" to Africa's crisis, in the words of Food and Agriculture Organization (FAO) Director–General Edouard Saouma, lies in the management and protection of its natural resources. The stress on Africa's cropland, rangeland, and forests will, if not soon relieved, "impose savage limits" on future production. This widely shared, though by no means universal, view that Africa's uniquely fragile and unforgiving environment lies at the heart of its development challenge represented a striking break with the past.

Global trends also promised future stress. Throughout the decade, academic and official studies used UN population projections, prepared in 1980, that saw global population ultimately stabilizing at about 10 billion people. In the spring of 1989 the UN Fund for Population Activities revealed that growth had been considerably more rapid than projected, and, if the current trend continued, the earth's population would stabilize not at 10 billion but at a hard-to-imagine crowd of 14 billion—almost triple the present figure. And while concern mounted over greenhouse warming and how it might be controlled, global energy use marched rapidly upward, rising by almost 3 percent in 1987 and 3.5 percent in 1988.

Probably the most influential trend of the decade was the gradually spreading realization that environmental mismanagement—not just environmental cleanup—imposes large economic costs. As countries in Central America and Southeast Asia, endowed a few decades ago with vast hardwood forests, faced the prospect of soon becoming timber importers, precepts of forest management that preserve the forests while producing a steady annual income acquired new salience. As agricultural projects failed on land converted from tropical forests, governments began to count the fiscal costs of subsidizing the conversion. As a species of perennial corn—potentially worth billions—was saved on the point of extinction, scientists could point with new credibility to the costs of an extinction rate conservatively estimated at one hundred species per day. A widely publicized 1985 study, *Natural Disasters: Acts of God or Acts of Man?*, pointed out the degree to which droughts, floods, and famines, once assumed to be wholly uncontrollable, were in fact caused or exacerbated by human-caused environmental degradation. Around the world, for example, soil erosion on newly populated upland watersheds was contributing to flooding hundreds of miles downstream.

The costs of environmental decline were also being measured in human suffering as "environmental refugees" proliferated. In 1985 two-thirds of all refugees in the world were African. A large proportion of these were fleeing not war, but the consequences of devegetation and soil loss that made it impossible to grow food where they lived. In Haiti, where one-sixth of the population left, deforestation that stripped much of the country of topsoil was as powerful an impetus to leave as were the brutal Duvalier regimes. Even now, as borders open in Eastern Europe, the newspapers are full of accounts of families moving in search of breathable air.

All of these environmental troubles and warning signs must be set against the remarkable achievements of the postwar era. In the forty years since 1950, global economic output has grown fourfold, outstripping population, which doubled, by a healthy margin. Life expectancy has grown by one-third—the average person can now expect to live to be sixty years old (seventy-four in the developed countries). Infant mortality dropped by half in the developing countries, from 180 deaths per thousand births, to eighty-two, and by three-quarters in the industrialized countries, from fifty-six to fifteen. Most of these improvements, it should be noted, slowed dramatically or came to a complete halt for most of the developing world in the 1980s. Per capita income actually declined in Latin America and Africa, and rates of improvement in infant mortality decelerated sharply.

Global agricultural performance presents a similarly mixed picture. From 1965–85, food production grew by 59 percent—a 10 percent per capita improvement. Yet in 1988 the World Bank estimated that outside China almost a billion people—one-fifth of the world's population—suffered from hunger. Thus in spite of decades of rapid growth in agricultural productivity, including the Green Revolution and steady expansion of agricultural land at the expense of forest and wilderness, there were more hungry people on the planet as the postwar era drew to a close than there had ever been before.

Institutionally, the record of environmental achievement is also hard to assess. International attention to the environment began on a large scale in 1972 with the Stockholm Conference on the Human Environment and the founding of the United Nations Environment Programme (UNEP). At that time only twenty-five countries possessed national environmental ministries, eleven of them in the developing world. Environmental action was understood to be principally a matter of preventing or cleaning up pollution, and in the developing countries was seen as a luxury to be afforded only after industrialization. At worst, the developed countries' environmental concerns were attacked as "environmental imperialism" or even seen as a conspiracy designed to squelch economic growth in the developing countries and preserve the global division between rich and poor.

By the mid–1980s, more than 140 countries—110 of them in the developing world—had national environmental agencies, though many of them remain chronically underfunded, poorly staffed, and near the bottom of the ministerial power hierarchy. The emphasis had shifted from pollution to the management of such resources as forests, fisheries, rangeland, soils, genetic diversity, and wetlands. Environmental degradation was now seen to be as much a consequence of poverty, the result of billions of individuals striving for a living, as of successful industrialization. More and more leaders of developing countries viewed environmental and resource conservation as integral elements of economic development. In words that could not have been uttered a decade earlier, World Bank President Barber Connable concluded that "economic growth based on any other premise is a costly illusion." The focus of activity shifted steadily from local to regional to global.

The realization that environmental issues will be a major concern of international relations in the 1990s has caught both diplomats and environmentalists unprepared. There is little in the way of scholarly or human resources to support the policy choices that must be made. Only a few political scientists, international lawyers, or individuals with broad experience in multilateral diplomacy are well versed in the environmental issues. On the other side, only a few environmental experts have experience in international relations. Economists are still employing tools that distort or ignore the contributions of natural resource consumption and send badly misleading signals to policy makers. All sides recognize the absence of a common language and body of knowledge. Moreover, time is short: many key negotiations are in their formative stages.

The readings in Subsection 1, immediately following, elaborate in some detail upon the themes struck by Jessica Mathews.

1. THE PROBLEM IN GENERAL

We begin with an excerpt from a book entitled *Limits to Growth*, commissioned by an international group of business people known as "the Club of Rome," that made a deep and lasting impact on the consciousness of the world when it was first published in 1972. Thereafter we highlight another seminal writing—*The Tragedy of the Commons*—that likewise has endured since its first publication in *Science* in 1968. Each of these writings, consistent with the viewpoint of Jessica Mathews, perceives the existence of a global environmental *problématique*. This perspective is not universally shared, however, and thus it is fitting to present also a contrary view, which we do in the form of an excerpted essay by Julian L. Simon, a well known scholarly skeptic. We close, by way of rejoinder, because we do not share the Simon view, with three readings that not only presuppose the existence of a global environmental *problématique* but outline in more technical terms its underlying scientific nature.

DONELLA H. MEADOWS ET AL., THE LIMITS
TO GROWTH 25–31, 34–38 (1972).

All five elements basic to the study reported here—population, food production, industrialization, pollution, and consumption of nonrenewable natural resources—are increasing. The amount of their increase each year follows a pattern that mathematicians call exponential growth. Nearly all of mankind's current activities, from use of fertilizer to expansion of cities, can be represented by exponential growth curves.... Since much of this book deals with the causes and implications of exponential growth curves, it is important to begin with an understanding of their general characteristics.

THE MATHEMATICS OF EXPONENTIAL GROWTH

Most people are accustomed to thinking of growth as a *linear* process. A quantity is growing linearly when it increases by a constant amount in a constant time period. For example, a child who becomes one inch taller each year is growing linearly. If a miser hides $10 each year under his mattress, his horde of money is also increasing in a linear way. The amount of increase each year is obviously not affected by the size of the child nor the amount of money already under the mattress.

A quantity exhibits *exponential* growth when it increases by a constant percentage of the whole in a constant time period. A colony of yeast cells in which each cell divides into two cells every 10 minutes is growing exponentially. For each single cell, after 10 minutes there will be two cells, an increase of 100 percent. After the next 10 minutes there will be four cells, then eight, then sixteen. If a miser takes $100 from his mattress and invests it at 7 percent (so that the total amount accumulated increases by 7 percent each year), the invested money will grow much faster than the linearly increasing stock under the mattress. The amount added each year to a bank account or each 10 minutes to a yeast colony is not constant. It continually increases, as the total accumulated amount increases. Such exponential growth is a common process in biological, financial, and many other systems of the world.

Common as it is, exponential growth can yield surprising results—results that have fascinated mankind for centuries. There is an old Persian legend about a clever courtier who presented a beautiful chessboard to his king and requested that the king give him in return 1 grain of rice for the first square on the board, 2 grains for the second square, 4 grains for the third, and so forth. The king readily agreed and ordered rice to be brought from his stores. The fourth square of the chessboard required 8 grains, the tenth square took 512 grains, the fifteenth required 16,384, and the twenty-first square gave the courtier more than a million grains of rice. By the fortieth square a million rice grains had to be brought from the storerooms. The king's entire rice supply was exhausted long before he reached the sixty-fourth square. Exponential increase is deceptive because it generates immense numbers very quickly.

A French riddle for children illustrates another aspect of exponential growth—the apparent suddenness with which it approaches a fixed limit. Suppose you own a pond on which a water lily is growing. The lily plant doubles in size each day. If the lily were allowed to grow unchecked, it would completely cover the pond in 30 days, choking off the other forms of life in the water. For a long time the lily plant seems small, and so you decide not to worry about cutting it back until it covers half the pond. On what day will that be? On the twenty-ninth day, of course. You have only one day to save your pond.

It is useful to think of exponential growth in terms of *doubling time*, or the time it takes a growing quantity to double in size. In the case of the lily plant described above, the doubling time is 1 day. A sum of money left in a bank at 7 percent interest will double in 10 years. There is a simple mathematical relationship between the interest rate, or rate of growth, and the time it will take a quantity to double in size. The doubling time is approximately equal to 70 divided by the growth rate....

MODELS AND EXPONENTIAL GROWTH

Exponential growth is a dynamic phenomenon, which means that it involves elements that change over time. In simple systems, like the bank account or the lily pond, the cause of exponential growth and its future course are relatively easy to understand. When many different quantities are growing simultaneously in a system, however, and when all the quantities are interrelated in a complicated way, analysis of the causes of growth and of the future behavior of the system becomes very difficult indeed. Does population growth cause industrialization or does industrialization cause population growth? Is either one singly responsible for increasing pollution, or are they both responsible? Will more food production result in more population? If any one of these elements grows slower or faster, what will happen to the growth rates of all the others? These very questions are being debated in many parts of the world today. The answers can be found through a better understanding of the entire complex system that unites all of these important elements.

Over the course of the last 30 years there has evolved at the Massachusetts Institute of Technology a new method for understanding the dynamic behavior of complex systems. The method is called System Dynamics.[5] The basis of the method is the recognition that the *structure* of any system—the many circular, interlocking, sometimes time-delayed relationships among its components—is often just as important in determining its behavior as the individual components themselves. The world model described in this book is a System Dynamics model.

Dynamic modeling theory indicates that any exponentially growing quantity is somehow involved with a *positive feedback loop*. A positive feedback loop is sometimes called a "vicious circle." An example is the familiar wage-price spiral—wages increase, which causes prices to increase, which leads to demands for higher wages, and so forth. In a positive feedback loop a chain of cause-and-effect relationships closes on itself, so that increasing any one element in the loop will start a sequence of changes that will result in the originally changed element being increased even more.

Editors' Note

When *Limits to Growth* was first published in 1972, many viewed it as a prediction of doom, although its authors intended it as a challenge for the future. The three summary conclusions the authors made in 1972 were as follows:[d]

1. If the present growth trends in world population, industrialization, pollution, food production, and resource depletion continue unchanged, the limits to growth on this planet will be reached sometime within the next 100 years.

---

5. A detailed description of the method of System Dynamics analysis is presented in JAY W. FORRESTER'S INDUSTRIAL DYNAMICS (1961) and PRINCIPLES OF SYSTEMS (1968).

d. DONELLA H. MEADOWS, ET AL., THE LIMITS TO GROWTH xiii (1972).

The most probable result will be a sudden and uncontrollable decline in both population and industrial capacity.

2.   It is possible to alter these growth trends and to establish a condition of ecological and economic stability that is sustainable far into the future. The state of global equilibrium could be designed so that the basic material needs of each person on earth are satisfied and each person has an equal opportunity to realize his or her individual human potential.

3.   If the world's people decide to strive for this second outcome rather than the first, the sooner they begin working to attain it, the greater will be their chances of success.

Twenty years later, the same authors, using the same analytical techniques, wrote a sequel: Donella H. Meadows, et al., Beyond the Limits (1992). The intervening years did not alter their conclusions very much. They concluded in 1992 that "the three conclusions we drew [in 1972] are still valid, but they need to be strengthened."[e] "Now," they said, "we would write them this way:"

1.   Human use of many essential resources and generation of many kinds of pollutants have already surpassed rates that are physically sustainable. Without significant reductions in material and energy flows, there will be in the coming decades an uncontrolled decline in per capita food output, energy use, and industrial production.

2.   This decline is not inevitable. To avoid it two changes are necessary. The first is a comprehensive revision of policies and practices that perpetuate growth in material consumption and in population. The second is a rapid, drastic increase in the efficiency with which materials and energy are used.

3.   A sustainable society is still technically and economically possible. It could be much more desirable than a society that tries to solve its problems by constant expansion. The transition to a sustainable society requires a careful balance between long-term and short-term goals and an emphasis on sufficiency, equity, and quality of life rather than on quantity of output. It requires more than productivity and more than technology; it also requires maturity, compassion, and wisdom.

These conditions constitute a conditional warning, not a dire prediction. They offer a living choice, not a death sentence. The choice isn't necessarily a gloomy one. It does not mean that the poor must be frozen in their poverty or that the rich must become poor. It could actually mean achieving at last the goals that humanity has been pursuing in continuous attempts to maintain physical growth.[f]

Garrett Hardin, *The Tragedy of the Commons*, 162 SCIENCE 1243, 1244–45 (1968).

The tragedy of the commons develops in this way. Picture a pasture open to all. It is to be expected that each herdsman will try to keep as many cattle as possible on the commons. Such an arrangement may work reasonably satisfactorily for centuries because tribal wars, poaching, and disease keep the numbers of both man and beast well below the carrying capacity of the land. Finally, however, comes the day of reckoning, that is, the day when the long-desired goal of social stability becomes a reality. At this point, the inherent logic of the commons remorselessly generates tragedy.

e. DONELLA H. MEADOWS, ET AL., BEYOND THE   **f.** *Id.* at xv-xvi.
LIMITS xv (1993).

As a rational being, each herdsman seeks to maximize his gain. Explicitly or implicitly, more or less consciously, he asks, "What is the utility to *me* of adding one more animal to my herd?" This utility has one negative and one positive component.

1) The positive component is a function of the increment of one animal. Since the herdsman receives all the proceeds from the sale of the additional animal, the positive utility is nearly $+1$.

2) The negative component is a function of the additional overgrazing created by one more animal. Since, however, the effects of overgrazing are shared by all the herdsmen, the negative utility for any particular decision-making herdsman is only a fraction of -1.

Adding together the component partial utilities, the rational herdsman concludes that the only sensible course for him to pursue is to add another animal to his herd. And another; and another.... But this is the conclusion reached by each and every rational herdsman sharing a commons. Therein is the tragedy. Each man is locked into a system that compels him to increase his herd without limit—in a world that is limited. Ruin is the destination toward which all men rush, each pursuing his own best interest in a society that believes in the freedom of the commons. Freedom in a commons brings ruin to all.

Some would say that this is a platitude. Would that it were! In a sense, it was learned thousands of years ago, but natural selection favors the forces of psychological denial. The individual benefits as an individual from his ability to deny the truth even though society as a whole, of which he is a part, suffers. Education can counteract the natural tendency to do the wrong thing, but the inexorable succession of generations requires that the basis for knowledge be constantly refreshed.

* * *

In an approximate way, the logic of the commons has been understood for a long time, perhaps since the discovery of agriculture or the invention of private property in real estate. But it is understood mostly only in special cases which are not sufficiently generalized. Even at this late date, cattlemen leasing national land on the western ranges demonstrate no more than an ambivalent understanding, in constantly pressuring federal authorities to increase the head count to the point where overgrazing produces erosion and weed dominance. Likewise, the oceans of the world continue to suffer from the survival of the philosophy of the commons. Maritime nations still respond automatically to the shibboleth of the "freedom of the seas." Professing to believe in the "inexhaustible resources of the oceans," they bring species after species of fish and whales closer to extinction.[5]

The National Parks present another instance of the working out of the tragedy of the commons. At present, they are open to all, without limit. The parks themselves are limited in extent—there is only one Yosemite Valley—whereas population seems to grow without limit. The values that visitors seek in the parks are steadily eroded. Plainly, we must soon cease to treat the parks as commons or they will be of no value to anyone.

5. S. McVay, 216 SCIENTIFIC AMERICAN 13 (1966).

What shall we do? We have several options. We might sell them off as private property. We might keep them as public property, but allocate the right to enter them. The allocation might be on the basis of wealth, by the use of an auction system. It might be on the basis of merit, as defined by some agreed-upon standards. It might be by lottery. Or it might be on a first-come, first-served basis, administered to long queues. These, I think, are all the reasonable possibilities. They are all objectionable. But we must choose—or acquiesce in the destruction of the commons that we call our National Parks.

Pollution

In a reverse way, the tragedy of the commons reappears in problems of pollution. Here it is not a question of taking something out of the commons, but of putting something in—sewage, or chemical, radioactive, and heat wastes into water; noxious and dangerous fumes into the air; and distracting and unpleasant advertising signs into the light of sight. The calculations of utility are much the same as before. The rational man finds that his share of the cost of the wastes he discharges into the commons is less than the cost of purifying his wastes before releasing them. Since this is true for everyone, we are locked into a system of "fouling our own nest," so long as we behave only as independent, rational, free-enterprisers.

The tragedy of the commons as a food basket is averted by private property, or something formally like it. But the air and waters surrounding us cannot readily be fenced, and so the tragedy of the commons as a cesspool must be prevented by different means, by coercive laws or taxing devices that make it cheaper for the polluter to treat his pollutants than to discharge them untreated. We have not progressed as far with the solution of this problem as we have with the first. Indeed, our particular concept of private property, which deters us from exhausting the positive resources of the earth, favors pollution. The owner of a factory on the bank of a stream—often has difficulty seeing why it is not his natural right to muddy the waters flowing past his door. The law, always behind the times, requires elaborate stitching and fitting to adapt it to this newly perceived aspect of the commons.

The pollution problem is a consequence of population. It did not much matter how a lonely American frontiersman disposed of his waste. "Flowing water purifies itself every ten miles," my grandfather used to say, and the myth was near enough to the truth when he was a boy, for there were not too many people. But as population became denser, the natural chemical and biological recycling processes became overloaded, calling for a redefinition of property rights.

Editors' Note

As influential as the Hardin analysis has been, it has not been without its detractors. A somewhat recent example is found in *Whose Common Future?: Reclaiming the Commons*, THE ECOLOGIST 12–13 (1993):

> According to Hardin, any commons ... "remorselessly generates tragedy" since the individual gain to each user from overusing the commons will always outweigh the individual losses he or she has to bear due to its resulting degradation. As many critics have pointed out, however, and as Hardin himself later acknowledged, what he is describing is not a commons

regime, in which authority over the use of forests, water and land rests with a community, but rather an open access regime, in which authority rests nowhere; in which there is no property at all; in which production for an external market takes social precedence over subsistence; in which production is not limited by considerations of long-term local abundance; in which people "do not seem to talk to one another"; and in which profit for harvesters is the only operating social value.

The Ecologist authors continue: "The difference is crucial. Far from being a 'free-for-all', use of the commons is closely regulated through communal rules and practices." *Id*. at 13.

Julian Simon, *There Is No Environmental, Population or Resource Crisis, in* Living in the Environment: An Introduction to Environmental Science 29, 29–31 (George Tyler Miller, Jr. ed., 7th ed. 1992).

[Most people who address] environmental and resource problems [begin] with the proposition that there is an environmental and resource crisis. If this means that the situation of humanity is worse now than in the past, then the idea of a crisis—and all that follows from it—is dead wrong. In almost every respect important to humanity, the trends have been improving, not deteriorating.

Our world now supports 5.4 billion people. In the nineteenth century, the earth could sustain only 1 billion. And 10,000 years ago, only 1 million people could keep themselves alive. People are living more healthily than ever before, too.

One would expect lovers of humanity—people who hate war and worry about famine in Africa—to jump with joy at this extraordinary triumph of the human mind and human organization over the raw forces of nature. Instead, they lament that there are so many human beings and wring their hands about the problems that more people inevitably bring.

The recent extraordinary decrease in the death rate—to my mind, the greatest miracle in history—accounts for the bumper crop of humanity. Recall that it took thousands of years to increase life expectancy at birth from the 20s to the 30s. Then, in just the last 200 years, life expectancy in the advanced countries jumped from the mid–30s to the 70s. And, starting well after World War II, life expectancy at birth in the poor countries, even the very poorest, has leaped upward (averaging 64 on 1990) because of progress in agriculture, sanitation, and medicine. Average life expectancy at birth in China, the world's most populous country, was 68 in 1990, an increase of 24 years since the 1950s. Is this not an astounding triumph?

In the short run, another baby reduces income per person by causing output to be divided among more people. And as the British economist Thomas Malthus argued in 1798, more workers laboring with existing capital results in less output per worker. However, if resources are not fixed, then the Malthusian doctrine of diminishing resources, resurrected by today's doom-and-gloom analysts, does not apply. Given some time to adjust to shortages with known methods and new inventions, free people create additional resources.

It is amazing but true that a resource shortage resulting from population or income growth usually leaves us better off than if the shortage had never arisen. If firewood had not become scarce in seventeenth-century England, coal would not have been developed. If coal and whale oil shortages hadn't loomed, oil wells would not have been dug.

The prices of food, metals, and other raw materials have been declining by every measure since the beginning of the nineteenth century, and as far back as we know. That is, raw materials have been getting less scarce instead of more scarce throughout history, defying the commonsense notion that if one begins with an inventory of a resource and uses some up, there will be less left. This is despite, and indirectly because of, increasing population.

All statistical studies show that population growth doesn't lead to slower economic growth, though this defies common sense. Nor is high population density a drag on economic development. Statistical comparison across nations reveals that higher population density is associated with faster instead of slower growth. Drive around on Hong Kong's smooth-flowing highways for an hour or two. You will then realize that a large concentration of human beings in a small area does not make comfortable existence impossible. It also allows for exciting economic expansion, if the system gives individuals the freedom to exercise their talents and pursue economic opportunities. The experience of densely populated Singapore makes it clear that Hong Kong is not unique, either.

In 1984, a blue-ribbon panel of scientists summarized their wisdom in *The Resourceful Earth*. Among the findings, besides those I have noted above, were these:

- Many people are still hungry, but the food supply has been improving since at least World War II, as measured by grain prices, production per consumer, and the death rate from famine.

- Land availability won't increasingly constrain world agriculture in coming decades.

- In the U.S., the trend is toward higher-quality cropland, suffering less from erosion than in the past.

- The widely published report of increasingly rapid urbanization of U.S. farmland was based on faulty data.

- Trends in world forests are not worrying, though in some places deforestation is troubling.

- There is no statistical evidence for rapid loss of plant and animal wildlife species in the next two decades. An increased rate of extinction cannot be ruled out if tropical deforestation is severe, but no evidence about linkage has yet been demonstrated.

- Water does not pose a problem of physical scarcity or disappearance, although the world and U.S. situations do call for better institutional management through more rational systems of property rights.

- There is no persuasive reason to believe that the world oil price will rise in coming decades. The price may fall well below what it has been.

● Compared with coal, nuclear power is no more expensive and is probably much cheaper under most circumstances. It is also much cheaper than oil.

● Nuclear power gives every evidence of costing fewer lives per unit of energy produced than does coal or oil.

● Solar energy sources (including wind and wave power) are too dilute to compete economically for much of humankind's energy needs, though for specialized uses and certain climates they can make a valuable contribution.

● Threats of air and water pollution have been vastly overblown. The air and water in the United States have been getting cleaner, rather than dirtier.

We don't say that all is well everywhere, and we don't predict that all will be rosy in the future. Children are hungry and sick; people live out lives of physical or intellectual poverty and lack of opportunity; war or some other pollution may do us in. *The Resourceful Earth* does show that for most relevant matters we've examined, total global and U.S. trends are improving instead of deteriorating.

Also, we do not say that a better future happens automatically or without effect. It will happen because men and women—sometimes as individuals, sometimes as enterprises working for profit, sometimes as voluntary nonprofit-making groups, and sometimes as governmental agencies—will address problems with muscle and mind, and will probably overcome, as has been usual through history.

We are confident that the nature of the physical world permits continued improvement in humankind's economic lot in the long run, indefinitely. Of course, there are always newly arising local problems, shortages, and pollutions, resulting from climate or increased population and income and new technologies. Sometimes temporary large-scale problems arise. But the world's physical conditions and the resilience in a well-functioning economic and social system enable us to overcome such problems, and the solutions usually leave us better off than if the problem had never arisen. That is the great lesson to be learned from human history.

Discussion Notes/Questions

1. What are the differences in the conclusions reached by the authors in the above extracts? Can they all be right? Can the views be reconciled?

2. What can be said for and/or against the views put forward?

3. Are there weaknesses in the *Limits to Growth* analysis? If so, what are they? How, if at all, can the analysis be faulted?

4. Does the *Tragedy of the Commons* analysis alter the conclusions put forward by Mathews? By the other authors in this subsection? Is it compatible with them?

5. Does Hardin's gender-specific language reflect more than the time of writing? What are the assumptions that Hardin makes about human nature? Do they reflect only the competitive, rational, individualist (and perhaps male) attributes that capitalism, particularly free-market capitalism, presupposes? If they do, does that detract from the validity of his thesis?

6. Was it merely the "tribal wars, poaching, and disease" that allowed the commons to be cared for in the past? Is Hardin's description of society a Western or First World description only? Does the issue of unequal distribution of resources have a place in Hardin's analysis?

7. Which of Hardin's "several options" are most realistic? If rights of entry were allocated on the basis of some agreed-upon standards, what sort of standards should they be?

8. Are property rights the answer? If factory owners had ownership rights over parts of the river, would that mean they would be less likely to pollute it?

9. If pollution only becomes a problem when population increases, is there any moral dimension to environmental degradation?

10. What arguments are available to refute Julian Simon's analysis? Is there a global environmental crisis or isn't there?

11. How should international policymakers respond to such analyses?

12. How certain should a policymaker be before deciding to act?

13. For additional pertinent reading, see Common Property Resources: Ecology and Community-based Sustainable Development (F. Berkes ed., 1989); A Theory of Resource Allocation Under Communal Property Rights (G. Glomm & R. Lagunoff eds., 1990); G. Hardin, Managing the Commons (1977); J. Kohn, *Thinking in terms of System Hierarchies and Velocities: What makes Development Sustainable?* 26 Ecological Economics 173 (1998); The Question of the Commons: The Culture and Ecology of Communal Resources (B. McCay & J. Acheson eds., 1987); T. G. Moore, Climate of Fear: Why We Shouldn't Worry About Global Warming (1998); E. Ostrom, Governing the Commons: The Evolution of Institutions for Collective Action (1990); K. Turekian, Global Environmental Change: Past, Present, and Future (1996).

Editors' Note

We turn now to the three laws of thermodynamics, all three of which are critical to a proper understanding of the relationship of energy and resources. The first law states that heat can be converted into work and *vice versa*, that the amount of work is equal always to the quantity of heat, and that heat can be expressed in terms of energy. The second states that when a free exchange of heat takes place between two bodies as a self-sustaining and continuous process the heat must always be transferred from the hotter to the colder body. And the third law states that every substance has a definite entropy (i.e., the availability of energy to do work) that approaches zero as its temperature approaches absolute zero (273.1°C). As the energy becomes unavailable the entropy is said to increase. Reflecting upon these scientific laws, Nobel Prize chemist Frederick Soddy has observed, tantalizingly, that "[t]he laws of thermodynamics control the rise and fall of political systems, the freedom or bondage of nations, the movements of commerce and industry, the origins of wealth and poverty, and the general physical welfare of the human race."[h] The following two extracts help to explain why.

GEORGE TYLER MILLER, JR., ENVIRONMENTAL SCIENCE:
AN INTRODUCTION 20–24, 44–45 (1986).

We talk about consuming or using up material resources, but actually we don't consume any matter. We only borrow some of the earth's resources for

h. As quoted in GEORGE TYLER MILLER, JR., ENVIRONMENTAL SCIENCE: AN INTRODUCTION 20 (1986).

awhile—taking materials from the earth, carrying them to another part of the globe, processing them, using them, and then discarding, reusing, or recycling them. In the process of using matter we may change it to another form, but in every case we neither create nor destroy any measurable amount of matter. This circumstance is expressed in the **law of conservation of matter**: In any physical or chemical change, matter is neither created nor destroyed but merely changed from one form to another.

This law tells us that there is no "away." *Everything we think we have thrown away is still here with us, in one form or another.* We can collect dust and soot from the smokestacks of industrial plants, but these solid wastes must then go somewhere. We can collect garbage and remove solid sludge from sewage, but these substances must either be burned (perhaps causing air pollution), dumped into rivers, lakes, and oceans (perhaps causing water pollution), or deposited on the land (perhaps causing soil pollution and water pollution).

Although we can certainly make the environment cleaner, the law of conservation of matter says that we will always be faced with pollution of some sort. This means that we must *trade off* one form of pollution for another. This tradeoff process involves making controversial scientific, political, economic, and ethical judgments about what is a dangerous pollution level, to what degree a pollutant must be controlled, and how much we are willing to pay to reduce the amount of a pollutant to a harmless level. Now let's look at energy and the two energy laws to learn more about what we can and cannot do on this planet.

* * *

First Energy Law What energy changes occur when you drop a rock? Because of its position, the rock in your hand has a higher potential energy than the same rock at rest on the ground. Has energy been lost or used up in this process? At first glance it seems so. But according to the law of conservation of energy, also known as the first law of thermodynamics, in any ordinary physical or chemical process energy is neither created nor destroyed but merely changed from one form to another. The energy lost by a *system* or collection of matter under study (in this instance, the rock) must equal the energy gained by the *surroundings* or *environment* (in this instance, air molecules and soil particles moved by the impact of the rock). This energy law holds for all systems, living and nonliving.

Let's consider what really happens. As the rock drops, its potential energy is changed into kinetic energy—both its own and that of the air through which it passes. The friction created when the rock drops through the air causes the gaseous molecules in the air to move faster, so their average temperature rises. This means that some of the rock's original potential energy has been transferred to the air as heat. When the rock hits the ground, more of its mechanical energy is transferred to particles of soil. The energy lost by the rock (system) is exactly equal to the energy gained by its surroundings. In studying hundreds of thousands of mechanical processes (such as the rock falling) and chemical processes (such as the burning of a fuel), scientists have found that no detectable amount of energy is either created or destroyed. *Energy input always equals energy output.*

Although most of us know this first energy law, we sometimes forget that regarding energy quantity, it means that we can't get something for nothing. In the words of environmentalist Barry Commoner, "There is no free lunch." For example, we often hear that we have huge amounts of energy available from the world's deposits of oil, coal, natural gas, and nuclear fuels (such as uranium). The first law of thermodynamics tells us that we really have much less useful energy available than these estimates indicate because *it takes energy to get this energy.* We must use large amounts of energy to find, remove, and process these fuels. The only energy that really counts is the *net useful energy* or *useful energy yield* available for use after subtracting the energy needed to make this energy available from the total energy in the resource.

* * *

Second Energy Law and Energy Quality Because according to the first law energy can neither be created nor destroyed, you might think that there will always be enough energy. Yet when you fill a car's tank with gasoline and drive around, something is lost. If it isn't energy, what is it? The *second law of energy,* also known as the *second law of thermodynamics,* provides the answer to this question.

Energy varies in its *quality* or ability to do useful work. For useful work to occur, energy must move or flow from a level of high-quality (more concentrated) energy to a level of lower quality (less concentrated) energy. The chemical potential energy concentrated in a lump of coal or a tank of gasoline and the concentrated heat energy at a high temperature are forms of high-quality energy. Because they are concentrated, they have the ability to perform useful work in moving or changing matter. In contrast, dispersed or less concentrated heat energy at a low temperature has little remaining ability to perform useful work.

In investigating hundreds of thousands of conversions of heat energy to useful work, scientists have found that some of the energy is always degraded to a more dispersed and less useful form, usually as heat given off at a low temperature to the surroundings. This is a statement of the second energy law, another name for the second law of thermodynamics: No transfer of heat energy to useful work is 100 percent efficient. Thus, the supply of concentrated, high-quality energy available to the earth is being continually depleted and the supply of low-quality energy is being continually increased so that the total energy remains the same.

* * *

According to the first energy law we will never run out of energy, but according to the second law we can run out of high-quality, or useful, energy. *Not only can we not get something for nothing (the first law), we can't even break even in terms of energy quality (the second law).*

The second energy law also tells us that high-grade energy can never be reused. *We can recycle matter but we can never recycle high-quality energy.* Fuels and foods can be used only once to perform useful work. Once a piece of coal or a tank of gasoline has burned, its high-quality potential energy is lost forever. This means that the net useful, or high-quality, energy available from fossil fuels, uranium, or any concentrated energy source is often less than that predicted by the first energy law. . . .

The Second Energy Law and Increasing Disorder The second energy law can be stated in a number of ways. For example, since energy tends to flow or change spontaneously from a concentrated and ordered form to a more dispersed and disordered form, the *second energy law* also can be stated as follows: Heat always flows spontaneously from hot (high-quality energy) to cold (lower quality energy). You learned this the first time you touched a hot stove. A cold sample of matter such as air has no heat energy dispersed in the random motion of its molecules. This is why heat energy at a low temperature can do little if any useful work.

* * *

These observations all suggest that a *system* of matter spontaneously tends toward increasing randomness or disorder, often called *entropy*. But you may have already thought of some cases that contradict this hypothesis. What about living organisms, with their highly ordered systems of molecules and cells? You are a walking, talking contradiction of the idea that systems tend spontaneously toward increasing disorder or entropy. We must look further.

* * *

Thus, *all forms of life are tiny pockets of order maintained by creating a sea of disorder around themselves.* The primary characteristic of modern industrial society is an ever-increasing use or flow of high-quality energy to maintain the order in our bodies and the pockets of order we call civilization. As a result, today's industrialized nations are adding more entropy or disorder to the environment than any society in human history.

* * *

To survive, you and every other form of life must have an almost continuous *input* of both energy and matter. Merely receiving energy and matter, however, will not keep you alive. An *output* of degraded energy (heat) and waste matter must also flow from an organism. For the organism to remain alive, the input and output of energy and matter must be in balance. Thus, life depends on the *one-way flow of both matter and energy*.

To be self-sustaining, the ecosphere and any ecosystem *depend on matter cycling*—not matter flow—and *energy flow*. At the ecosystem and ecosphere levels, life depends on energy flow because, according to the second law of thermodynamics, *energy quality can never be recycled*. In any ecosystem, high-quality energy enters (usually as sunlight), moves through organisms, and eventually escapes to space as low-quality heat energy.

Life at the ecosystem and ecosphere levels, however, depends on matter cycling, not on one-way matter flow, because according to the law of conservation of matter, matter can neither be created nor destroyed, only changed from one form to another. While the chemicals essential for life must eventually be cycled completely in the ecosphere, chemical cycling in an ecosystem need not be as complete. Some of this matter flows from one ecosystem to another because the various ecosystems on earth are interconnected.

Thus, *we can generally answer the question "What happens in an ecosystem?" by saying that energy flows and matter cycles.* These two major ecosystem functions connect the various structural parts of an ecosystem so that life is maintained. . . .

GARETH HARDIN, LIVING WITHIN LIMITS 140–43 (1993).

The ease with which useful energy can be captured has a great deal to do with the physical quality of life. Cheap energy means abundant supplies of energy-requiring goods; when energy becomes expensive, people start complaining of shortages. In the last three centuries an increasing fraction of our daily energy supply has come from petroleum, gas, and coal. What can we say about human history in the light of the supplies of fossil energy?

Graphing the rate of use of each fossil energy source yields a bell-shaped curve. [Figure 4–1] gives Hubbert's projection of the world's use of petroleum over time. Until the year 1900 the level of world production was too low to show on the scale of this figure. Then it rose exponentially almost until the present. After 1973 the path departed more and more from an exponential curve due to increasingly tighter supplies. At some point (here estimated to be about 1995, but the date is not precise) the curve of petroleum use will bend over and start heading downward. As indicated in the figure, 80 percent of the oil will be used up in a mere fifty-six years, scarcely more than a moment in the history of mankind. All but a small percentage of the extractable oil will be taken from the ground in less than two centuries.

Figure 4-1

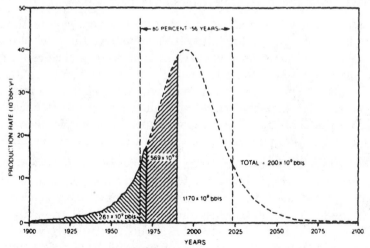

Figure 4-1. Complete lifetime curve for world petroleum "production." (After Hubbert, 1974.)

A similar graph for coal extraction would look much the same, but it would begin earlier and peak later than the oil curve. Comparable curves must hold for natural gas, tar sands, oil shales, and peat, but the numerical data are less reliable. Lumping all the energy data together produces the graph shown in [Figure 4–2]. This curve has come to be known as "Hubbert's pimple."

Figure 4-2

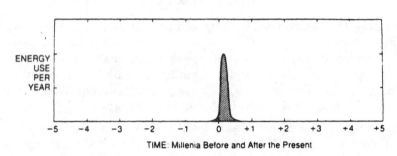

Figure 4-2. "Hubbert's pimple" on the face of history, showing past and future course of fossil energy use by human beings.

The part of the curve that lies in the future is conjectural, of course, but there can be little doubt of its essential correctness. To feel the full impact of reality, one should, in imagination, extend the curve far beyond the bounds of the printed page.... *Homo sapiens*—our species—has been in existence for about one hundred thousand years. The progenitor species go back at least a million years. Were we to extend the curve backward a million years it would reach to the left of this printed page for about forty feet.

For all but a few hundred years of that time the curve of fossil fuel usage is nearly flat on the horizontal axis, not visibly above the level of usage = 0. The curve started rising only yesterday, as it were—specifically, about six hundred years ago, when we started using coal in significant quantities. From all the signs, the human species is only a few score years away from the peak of the curve. After that the curve will fall rapidly until it once more lies prostrate on the zero line. The prosperous period of our fossil-energy-fueled civilization can be no more than a pimple on the lifeline of human existence.

[T]he ability to extract meaning from graphs is an essential part of "numeracy." Hubbert's pimple is a test of that ability. As one traces this curve from the evanescent present into the unavoidably near future the numerate viewer experiences something of a cold chill traveling down his spine. If words will help, the restrained summary Hubbert wrote in [1949] should be of aid [Box 4–1]. Those who understand Hubbert's pimple find its implications as incompatible with easy optimism as Gibbons' *Decline and Fall of the Roman Empire*.

Box 4-1

Box 4.1 - History through Hubert's Eyes

Human history can be divided into three distinct successive phases. The first, comprising all history prior to about 1800, was characterized by a small human populations, a low level of energy consumption per capita, and very slow rates of change. The second, based upon the exploitation of the fossil fuels and the industrial metals, has been a period of continuous and spectacular exponential growth. However, because of the finite resource of the Earth's fossil fuels and metallic ores, the second phase can only be transitory. Most of the ores of the industrial metals will have been mined within the next century. The third phase, therefore, must again become one of slow rates of growth, but initially at least with a large population and a high rate of energy consumption. Perhaps the foremost problem facing mankind at present is that of how to make the transition from the present exponential growth phase to the near steady state of the future by as noncatastrophic a progression as possible.

"Energy from Fuels," 1949

To date, from the beginning of time until we become entangled in the veil of the future, the curve of human population growth is essentially identical with the curve of fossil energy usage. The near identity of the two curves must be more than coincidence. Human life and civilization requires steady inputs of energy. The number of human lives, and the scale of energy use per capita to which we have become accustomed, produce so high a rate of energy demand that the thought of exhausting fossil energy resources is scary. To see what lies ahead of us—*and not very far ahead of us, at that*—we need to look at a magnification of the yet-to-be-developed part of the curve where the turning takes place [Figure 4–3] below.

Too many of our people unfortunately expect the curve of available energy (the dashed line) to continue to increase exponentially forever. As energy inputs start to fall short of our exponential expectations there will be a period that is characterized by widespread fear and denial of the facts. This will be followed by what we can only designate by the pitifully inadequate word "shock." Beyond that lies the pain of "social chaos"—also inadequate words.

All this is within the veil of the future, so it cannot be dignified by the name "fact." The exhaustion of fossil fuel resources is certain enough to be called a fact. The human reactions of fear, denial, shock, and pain are also facts; but, being information-mutable facts, they are facts of a different order. Such facts are subject to some control (modification) by human decisions, by human effort and by human will. (But what sort of fact is *human will*?)

Figure 4-3

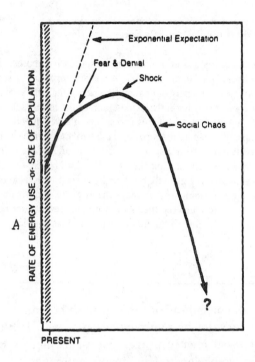

Figure 4-3. A plausible future f o r
the coupled variables of energy
use and population size, unless
the human species mends its
ways.

Can we develop a new and significant supply of energy? Is nuclear energy such a one? Theoretically, the *per capita supply* of energy can be increased by reducing the number of people making demands on the environment. Or a "shortage" can be done away with by lowering per capita energy demands. Both possibilities are denigrated as "utopian" by most people, but the mythical man-from-Mars (who is, by hypothesis, a perfectly intelligent and all-knowing being) might well, after examining the human situation on earth, ask: "What's the trouble? There's no reason on earth you earthlings cannot accept, in plenty of time, the necessity of *stopping* exponential growth. When you understand what has to be done, *stop*."

No reason on earth why exponential expectations cannot be eliminated? Quite so: no reason on *earth*. The trouble is not exactly "on earth": the problem is *in our heads*. Not in one human head, but in a collectivity of many human heads. Solving problems that are "in our heads" is much more difficult than solving problems "on earth." We need to take a closer look at some of the curious processes that take place in the minds of human beings as they become aware of problems created by human successes in gaining a partial mastery of nature.

Discussion Notes/Questions

1. Thermodynamic realities suggest that the continued drive for development is nonsensical. Can thermodynamics and development be reconciled? Is "sustainable development" an oxymoron?

2. Should we just accept as inevitable the gradual reduction in high quality energy? What would it mean ethically to do so? Should there be any limits on the rate at which we "spend" it? On what basis should limits be imposed, if any?

3. Heavily industrialized societies are by far the biggest users of high quality energy. Is this a major issue of equity relative to the Third World?

4. Is energy efficiency the answer to thermodynamic limitations? Should we stop looking for oil and put our faith in technological solutions?

5. How do we bring about changes to peoples' thinking, as Hardin suggests?

6. Is greater use of nuclear energy an answer to the problems raised in this segment?

7. For additional pertinent reading, see B. Commoner, The Closing Circle: Nature, Man and Technology (1972); M. Faber, H. Niemes, G. Stephen & L. Freytag, Entropy, Environment and Resources: An Essay in Physio–Economics (1987); J. Kohn, *Thinking in Terms of System Hierarchies and Velocities: What Makes Development Sustainable?* 26 Ecological Economics 173 (1998); J. Peet, Energy and the Ecological Economics of Sustainability (1992); I. Prigogine & I. Stengers, Order Out of Chaos: Man's New Dialogue with Nature (1984).

2. THE PROBLEM IN GEOPHYSICAL CONTEXT

In this subsection, we provide an overview of the global environmental *problématique* in particular geophysical contexts, that is, with reference to the atmosphere, the hydrosphere, the lithosphere, and the biosphere. The World Resources Institute regularly surveys the state of the geophysical environment. We provide you with the Executive Summary from the WRI's 1996–97 publication. It is strongly recommended that the reader give these materials special notice because, in addition to meriting attention in their own right, they serve as introductions to most of the problems that make up Part II. Without them, the problems in Part II are not adequately comprehended.

WORLD RESOURCES INSTITUTE, WORLD RESOURCES
1996–97, at x-xiv (1997).

Population Growth

Current population trends are cause for both optimism and concern. Some developing countries are moving rapidly toward population stability. But other countries are experiencing rapid population growth, usually accompanied by high levels of poverty, limited progress for women, and high levels of internal and international migration. Overall, the world population is increasing by more than 86 million people every year. Such rapid growth places enormous pressure on natural resources, urban infrastructure and services, and governments at all levels, especially in the poorest countries where growth is most rapid.

Global population will continue to grow for many decades to come, reflecting the demographic inertia of countries in which a large fraction of the population has not yet reached child-bearing age. In the U.N. medium population projection, working population reaches about 10 billion by the middle of the next century before gradually leveling off. Much of that growth occurs in the next few decades and is concentrated in a few regions, such as Africa and Asia. In these projections, fertility is assumed to decline from current levels in developing regions of the world. Projected fertility rates cannot be taken for granted, however; policies that influence fertility rates— provision of family planning services, alleviation of poverty, and improvements in education, health care, and economic opportunities, especially for women—can have a marked effect on future population levels.

Freshwater Supplies

One environmental consequence of growing nations is increasing pressure on natural resources. Demand for water is growing rapidly as populations and industrial activity expand and irrigated agriculture (the largest use) continues to increase. From 1940 to 1990, for example, withdrawals of freshwater from rivers, lakes, and underground aquifers increased by a factor of four. Many current patterns of water withdrawals are clearly unsustainable, such as pumping from subsoil aquifers at rates far greater than they are recharged. Water shortages are already critical in some regions, posing obstacles to continued development and threats to freshwater habitats.

The future availability of water for human use depends on how water resources are managed; water can, in principle, be reused many times. Future pressures on water resources can thus be seen as a measure of the management challenge that water-short regions will face. According to one estimate, between 1 billion and 2.4 billion people (13 to 20 percent of the projected world population) will live in water-scarce countries by 2050. Africa and parts of western Asia appear particularly vulnerable. Policies that improve the efficiency of water use, avoid waste, and preserve supplies (by controlling water pollution and maintaining watersheds) can markedly extend the availability of scarce supplies. Particularly important are more efficient irrigation systems, appropriate water pricing and removal of harmful subsidies, upgrading and improved maintenance of urban water distribution systems, control or treatment of industrial wastewater and urban sewage effluents, and cooperative management of shared watersheds and river basins.

Food Security

Water scarcity has a direct impact on food security. Indeed, many countries facing water scarcity may not be able to support irrigated agriculture at levels necessary to feed future populations from domestic agricultural activities. Soil erosion and degradation, especially in fragile tropical and subtropical environments, also threaten the continued productivity of agricultural lands. Overfishing threatens to damage fisheries and lower future harvests, denying many developing regions an important source of protein.

These trends may put severe strains on the world's ability to increase global food production in parallel with population growth. Nonetheless, most recent assessments suggest that global food production—the supply end of the equation—has the capability to keep pace with rising global demand.

There is less optimism about the prospects for reducing undernutrition and improving food security. Even if global food supplies are adequate, the inability of poor nations to pay for food imports, along with an inadequate distribution infrastructure and the inability of poor families to buy food, means that many people will continue to go hungry. For 1990 to 1992, the U.N. Food and Agriculture Organization (FAO) identified 27 countries as having low or critical food security indexes. In sub-Saharan Africa, for example, FAO projects that the number of undernourished people could rise from 175 million to some 300 million by 2010.

Food trade is projected to nearly double between 1990 and 2010, but trade and food aid may not fill the food security gap. Policies that strengthen agricultural research and extension systems, promote sustainable intensification and more sophisticated management of agricultural resources, and develop more effective agricultural markets in developing countries could play a major role in helping these countries to meet their own food needs. Policies that increase rural employment and access to land and credit and that strengthen the capacity of developing country governments can also have an important indirect impact on food security.

Energy and Climate

Energy use is already high in the developed countries and is increasing rapidly in many developing countries as they industrialize. Three different studies of future energy demand conclude that global energy use is virtually certain to rise considerably in coming decades. These studies find plausible increases in the range of 34 to 44 percent by 2010 and 54 to 98 percent by 2020. The projected growth is concentrated in Asia (a 100 percent increase from 1990 to 2010) and Latin America (a 50 to 77 percent increase over the same period). Moreover, most of the expanded production will come from fossil energy sources—coal, oil, and natural gas—in the absence of specific policies to alter market incentives. The so-called "new renewables" such as solar, wind, and farm-grown energy crops are expected to provide only 2 to 4 percent of global energy supplies from 1990 to 2020 if current practices and strategies continue.

These projections imply that local and regional air pollution is likely to increase significantly in rapidly developing regions and that global emissions of greenhouse gases will increase as well, greatly increasing the risk and potential impact of global climate change. Emissions of carbon dioxide from industrial activity climbed 38 percent during the 20 years prior to 1990 and are expected to rise another 30 to 40 percent by 2010.

These projected trends make clear that significant changes will be required in energy strategies and practices in all major regions of the world to stabilize global emissions of greenhouse gases. Even greater efforts and, almost certainly, a transition to nonfossil energy sources will be required to eventually reduce emissions and hence stabilize atmospheric concentrations, the ultimate goal of the Global Climate Convention. Policies that encourage more efficient use of energy, that tax energy-based pollution or provide market incentives for the introduction of renewable energy sources, and that facilitate use of the best available technologies for energy consumption and production are well known, if not always easy to implement. Given the growing scientific consensus on global climate change—reflected in the finding by the Intergovernmental Panel on Climate Change that there is "a discernible human influence on global climate"—these policies deserve far greater attention.

Critical Ecosystems at Risk

Coastal habitats, some of the richest storehouses of marine biodiversity, provide one example of how critical ecosystems are increasingly threatened. About 60 percent of the global population lives within 100 kilometers of the coastline, drawing heavily on coastal and marine habitats for food, building sites, transportation, recreational areas, and waste disposal. According to a new study by the World Resources Institute, 51 percent of the world's coastal ecosystems appear to be at significant risk of degradation from development-related activity. Europe, with 86 percent of its coastline at high or medium risk, and Asia, with 69 percent in these categories, are the regions most threatened by degradation. Worldwide, nearly three fourths of marine protected areas within 100 kilometers of continents or major islands appear to be at risk.

Forest losses are continuing at a rapid rate. A new FAO study shows that fully 20 percent of all tropical natural forest cover was lost from 1960 to 1990. Temperate forest cover, too, has declined, primarily in developing countries. Natural forest cover declined 8 percent in developing countries during the 1980s, although this loss was partially offset by new forest plantations and growth in wooded areas outside forests.

Forest losses in developing countries echo earlier deforestation in developed countries. North America has lost an estimated 20 percent of its original forest cover; the countries of the former Soviet Union, 35 percent; and Europe, 60 percent. Many remaining undisturbed forests are at risk from logging, and fragmentation of forest cover is widespread. Air pollution and fire suppression practices have also contributed to declining forest health.

There is still no international consensus on how to protect forests, nor is it clear that the world community is ready to move forcefully toward managing forests on a sustainable basis. Many efforts are under way to explore policy instruments in areas such as forest management and trade in forest products; others are focusing on improving information about forests and developing greater consensus about appropriate practices.

Discussion Notes/Questions

1. What relationship exists between the forms of environmental degradation outlined here and the level of the world's population?

2. What do the problems of the atmosphere, hydrosphere, lithosphere, and biosphere have in common? To what extent are they completely separate from each other?

3. The issue of population comes up later in the book in Problem 11–3 ("Population Control Meets Human Rights in Hanguo") in Chapter 11, *infra*, but at this stage what, if anything, do you think the world should be doing about it?

4. How does biodiversity fit in? Why is it valuable? What do we lose when species become extinct?

5. What ways can you suggest to deal with each of the problems outlined above?

6. What grounds for optimism exist in the current situation? What grounds for pessimism?

7. Can the world's population reasonably be expected to understand the material you have read? What would they do if they did understand it? Is greater public education called for?

8. Has anything you have read so far caused you to change the way you think about the global environment?

C. PERSPECTIVES AND APPROACHES

As was noted at the beginning of this chapter, this segment focuses on different ways of thinking about the predicament of the global environment. Much of the material is controversial, even ideological; some of it is scientific. Politics and economics offer important insights not only on how to think about environmental problems but on how to put them right. It would be satisfying to present analytical material that, upon mastery, would offer up solutions. But, alas, this cannot be done at this historical time. The fact is that there simply are many eclectic and vastly differing ways of looking at the problem; and what is important is to ask what the strengths and weaknesses of each perspective or approach are. How can it be criticized? What facts support the views expressed? What factors does it fail to take into account? Is the approach practical in the sense that it will facilitate policies that are capable of implementation?

An interesting question is whether the various perspectives and approaches should be thought of as compatible with one another or as mutually exclusive? Would it be possible to develop further perspectives or approaches by combining various of their elements? Important ethical issues arise. Does nature have rights? If so, what rights? Are deep ecology and ecofeminism compatible? Can economics provide a holistic approach to environmental problems or only a set of incentives in some instances? What are the differences between sustainable development and steady-state economics? These are the kinds of questions to be considered when making your way through these materials.

You should use these materials also to develop your personal approach to the problems of the global environment. Which of the perspectives most accords with your views? Do some of the perspectives force you to reconsider your own views? Is it all too vague and theoretical to make any difference in how policy will be developed in the real world, or do some of these views constitute the inarticulate major premise on which much of international environmental law rests?

An important caveat: While international environmental thought and action has its parallels in national environmental policy and practice, and while many domestic environmental issues are also issues internationally, and *vice versa*, those environmental problems that are truly international cannot be solved by local decisions, unless the same decisions are taken by each country at roughly the same time (which, of course, is improbable). The sovereignty of nation-states, the dynamics of international relations, the relative absence of centralized command and enforcement structures on the international plane—these and other complexities mean that international solutions are fraught with difficulties that are not ordinarily encountered in the domestic sphere. For example, economists will say that making polluters pay the cost of the their pollution is a good principle that will prevent the development of "externalities" and assist in securing the efficient allocation of resources. But if the only way to achieve these goals is to impose a tax, then a capacity to impose the tax must exist. At present, however, the international system has no authority or ability to tax. So, then, how can the "polluter pays" principle be enforced? Is the principle merely hortatory in character? Or does it somehow have some real "bite"? Questions such as these of course raise difficult issues surrounding the interaction of international and domestic law, something we considered in Section B(2) of Chapter 3, *supra*, and a subject to which we shall return in concluding Chapter 13.

Finally, we emphasize that it is impossible to do complete justice to the outlooks and approaches presented here. Many of the authors have written extensively in the field, and in excerpting from their voluminous writings distortions or misrepresentations are possible. However, we have done our best to keep faith with their views and to present them accurately. The idea is to offer at least a snapshot of the most important conceptual thinking that has gone into consideration of the global environmental *problématique*.

1. SOCIO–POLITICAL ANALYSIS

GARETH PORTER & JANET WELSH BROWN, GLOBAL ENVIRONMENTAL
POLITICS 15–20, 32–33 (1991).

Introducing Global Environmental Politics

Global environmental politics is not a single issue but a complex set of issues, each of which has its own structure and dynamics. But the scope of the issue area is defined by two dimensions of any international environmental problem: the scope of environmental consequences of the economic activity in question and the geographical scope of the states and nonstate actors involved in the issue. If the consequences are global, or if the actors in the issue transcend a single region, we consider it a global environmental issue.

Issues involving threats to the integrity of the biosphere on which all human life depends—the planet's climate, atmosphere, land, oceans, and seas—are clearly global environmental issues. The destruction of the world's tropical forests also falls within its scope, because of the reach of both biological and political consequences. Forest loss affects climate change (fluctuations in climate due to accumulations of greenhouse gases) and forests are storehouses of biological wealth that is important to the world economy and society. Moreover, states and nongovernmental organizations (NGOs) from both industrialized and developing countries as well as international organizations have become involved in policies that address the degradation of the biosphere.

Threats to the survival of whale species and to the African elephant and threats to the wilderness of the Antarctic are also global environmental issues because they have involved states from developed as well as developing countries. The issue of the international hazardous-waste trade involves both developed and developing countries, with environmental consequences for both, depending on how the issue is addressed by the international community. Long-range transboundary air pollution, including acid rain, does not affect all regions of the world, but it has been the subject of multilateral negotiations involving Europe and North America.

Most global environmental politics involve multilateral negotiations to reach global agreements aimed at reducing transnational environmental hazards. The development assistance agencies of large donor countries like Japan and the United States, the multilateral financial institutions such as the World Bank and International Monetary Fund and even the General Agreement on Tariffs and Trade (GATT) **[Basic Document 7.1]** make decisions that have direct or indirect impacts on global environmental issues. As global environmental activism has grown and the environmental arena has widened, all major institutions (including private businesses) that make authoritative decisions affecting the world economy and environment have come under scrutiny and become targets of lobbying and pressure by environmental groups.

Global environmental negotiations seek to achieve effective international cooperation under circumstances in which the environmental interests of states diverge. States have different combinations of internal economic and political forces that influence their policies toward environmental issues. The actual costs and risks of environmental degradation, moreover, are never distributed equally among all states, so some are less motivated than others to participate in international efforts to reduce environmental threats. Nor do states have the same perceptions of equitable solutions to environmental issues. Yet despite these disparate interests, states must strive for unanimity, at least among those states that significantly contribute to and are significantly affected by a given environmental problem. In every global environmental issue there is at least one and sometimes more than one group of states whose cooperation is so essential to a successful agreement for coping with the environmental problem in question that they have an effective veto power over the agreement. When these states indicate their doubts or outright opposition to the agreement, they become veto states and form veto coalitions.

* * *

Because of the importance of veto power, an economically powerful state may not be able to impose a regime on a much smaller state if the latter is strongly opposed to it. Thus, some key developing countries may credibly threaten to reject a global climate-change agreement, even though almost every industrialized state is now committed to a regime for regulating carbon emissions and even though these states are dependent on highly industrialized states for markets, capital flows, and technology. And if bargaining turns to the distribution of costs and benefits, it is precisely the inability to bear the costs of the policies required to contribute to the global environmental action that gives developing countries a strong basis for demanding compensation and other forms of favorable treatment in global negotiations.

A second characteristic of global environmental politics is that they tend to reflect the structure of the global economy. First, a number of global environmental issues involve, either directly or indirectly, trade relations between states that are producers and exporters of a particular good and states that are importers of the good, and those roles tend to define the political dynamics of that issue. The issue of international hazardous waste trading, for instance, is defined by the relationship between industrialized countries that are exporting the waste and developing countries that are potential importers. The issues of international trade in endangered species and tropical deforestation are defined by the roles of the developing countries that export the illegal wildlife products and the major economies that import them. On tropical deforestation, trade relations between tropical timber exporters and consuming nations are critical to the dynamics of the issue.

In each of these issues, the roles and relative bargaining influences tend to be defined by a country's position in the economic relationship in question. In some cases, it is the producing-exporting countries that have the veto power; in others, it is the importing countries. In one case—tropical deforestation—both producers and importers have roughly equal veto power, making for much greater difficulty in forging a global regime. But industrialized states and developing states do not have equal veto power over the outcomes. Although a relatively few developing states may have the ability to either prevent an agreement from being reached or to bargain for special treatment on some environmental issues, the major economic powers have the ability to do that on every environmental issue.

There are other ways in which economic power may affect the outcomes. The ability of an economic power to give or withhold economic benefits such as market access for textiles, fish products, or financial resources can persuade states dependent on such benefits to avoid open opposition to the power's own policy. If the economically strong states can reach agreement on a given international environmental problem, they can use the threat of trade sanctions against smaller states who refuse to cooperate as leverage to get them to go along with the agreement. Such sanctions, for example, are built into the Montreal Protocol on Substances that Deplete the Ozone Layer to discourage nonparticipants from exporting CFCs. Even more importantly, however, the ability and willingness of the major donor states to commit resources to global environmental issues determines whether or not an international agreement is possible on several issues recently negotiated or now under negotiation.

The third characteristic of politics in this issue area is that traditional power relations based on military power have no direct impact on the outcomes of specific international environmental conflicts. Global environmental politics, by its very nature, does not give rise to a hegemonic power in the traditional sense of the ability to coerce other states into accepting the hegemon's position on a particular environmental issue. The conceptual and value basis of security politics is so far removed from that of environmental politics that it is difficult to conceive of military force being used to influence the outcomes of global environmental issues. When the United States has played a lead role in working for international cooperation, it has been despite, rather than because of, its military power. Of course, military power may have an indirect effect on outcomes by diverting the resources and attention of policy-makers and thus reducing the ability or willingness of a state to play a lead role on an environmental issue.

Although the actors found in the issue areas of security and economic politics—international organizations, states, and business firms—all play distinct roles in the political process in the environmental arena, a distinctive characteristic of environmental politics is the importance of public opinion and nonprofit NGOs, especially environmental NGOs, that are both national and international in scope. Environmental issues, like human rights issues before them, have mobilized the active political interest of large numbers of citizens in key countries, inducing shifts in policy that helped turn the tide in a number of environmental issues. Public opinion, channeled through electoral politics and NGOs, has had a substantial, if not decisive influence on the outcomes of global bargaining on whaling, Antarctic minerals, and ozone depletion, and could be a key factor in negotiations on global climate change. Public opinion has not played comparable roles in the security and economic issue areas, which have been much more heavily dominated by bureaucratic elites and special interests. This is not to say that public opinion has never had a substantial impact on national security policies or on the outcomes of security issues (the Vietnam War being an obvious example), but such instances are relatively rare.

Discussion Notes/Questions

1. Is it possible that there be a separate discipline of international environmental law or is it so political such that it is inextricable from international environmental politics?

2. What is the relevance of short term political office to environmental issues? Is there any realistic chance that the interests of future generations will be seriously considered?

3. If scientific evidence is what motivates environmental action on a global scale, does that spell doom for issues where there is scientific uncertainty (e.g., climate change)?

4. Could the problem of veto power be addressed or are the realities of economics and power too conclusive? What does the experience at the 1992 "Earth Summit" (UNCED) in Rio de Janeiro add to this analysis?

5. What are the limitations of public opinion? How important is the voting public? Are some environmental issues more charismatic than others?

The following readings highlight the interrelationship between North South politics and international environmental issues. Eric Laferriere discusses the existing and likely impact of global environmental degradation on North–South relations. The excerpt from Edgar Asebey and Jill Kempenaar comes from an article about biodiversity prospecting under the terms of the Biodiversity Convention. The authors describe recent experiences in biodiversity prospecting and analyze the traditional roles of the North and South. The excerpt reproduced here discusses the possibility of cartelization of genetic resources by developing countries.

Eric Laferriere, *Environmentalism and the Global Divide,* 3 Envtl. Pol. 91, 94–99 (1994).

Environmental Problems and the Global Divide

A focus on environmental politics, however, leads naturally to a discussion of the relationship between rich and poor: income inequalities are indeed part and parcel of the dynamic of environmental degradation. The rich-poor gap, as environmental *problematique*, would ideally be approached in its entirety—that is, both within countries and between countries. In other words, a thorough study of the impact of environmental problems and environmentalism on political relations would seek to identify commonalities or differences between national and non-national experiences. In this study, the less ambitious objective is to focus on the global rich-poor gap, and on the North–South patterns of relations which are associated with it. "The association of 'North–South' with 'the global', however, does not void the utility of the latter concept. In fact, it seeks to emphasise that, in this integrated global polity, the North–South divide represents probably the single most important political problem, a 'critical issue' around which elites and challengers gravitate in the pursuit of their respective utopias. The significance of the environmental crisis for North–South relations thus clearly unfolds. The mutual dependence inherent in globality is displayed most clearly, of course, in the 'commons' problems mentioned above. But it extends beyond them. Southern dependence on the North is quite real in local matters related to health care and sustainable production. These are typical Southern problems, intricately linked to pollution and ecologically destructive practices, whose alleviation 'requires' (at least according to elites) Northern capital and 'technology/knowledge.' On the other hand, Northern dependence, and the consequent 'power of denial' 'claimed by the South', is rooted in the political demands of the North's globalist environmentalism: Northern environmental groups are keenly interested in curtailing environmental problems in the South, and the latter is fully aware of the bargaining chip which it can extract from such 'emotional attachment'."

Recognising environmental degradation as a global issue of concern, what is its existing and likely impact on North–South relations? A global problem such as environmental degradation can just as much create or increase conflict (if parties cannot agree on a solution) as it can prompt affected actors to initiate a dialogue on broader issues. Indeed, existing evidence suggests that although Northern governments have used coercive mechanisms of environmental problem-solving (such as lending conditionality), they also have accepted the principle of compensatory funding for Third World expenses linked to environmental protection and sustainable development (of course, the sheer level of compensation can, and has, become a serious issue of contention).

There are several reasons why the environmental question can worsen North–South relations. For instance, as hinted above, the types of environmental preoccupations differ from North to South. The North carries a globalist discourse, laced with scientific interests and aesthetic considerations: for instance, Northern countries want the South to protect its tropical forests so as to reduce global warming, preserve access to untapped reservoirs of organic materials necessary for biotechnological and medical research, and maintain nature's grandeur. Northern actors want to minimise the South's existing and potential contribution to environmental problems affecting Northern interests. As for the South, it perceives environmental problems through the lenses of public health and sustainable local production, and insists that these problems be addressed internationally before yielding on commons issues and conservationist policies.

Charges of "neo-imperialism" under environmental garb are thus often levied, especially with existing and opportunity costs involved. Not only does the environmental agenda differ between the two hemispheres, a definite Northern reluctance to bear the full costs of global environmental policies is viewed with much suspicion in the South. The latter correctly claims that Western development policies are most responsible for global pollution and resource depletion while the world economic order has institutionalised Southern impoverishment, which itself fuels local environmental abuse. In other words, Southern elites perceive environmentalism as a Northern phenomenon designed either to legitimise protectionism or aid restraint or to forestall the growth of an autonomous industrial power base for the South. Burdened by debt and the socio-economic problems that it fuels, the South is hardly willing to delay growth projects and "waste" money on pollution control.

In sum, assuming that environmental concerns are solidly implanted on the global agenda and actively pursued by at least some sectors of the Northern political elite, there are many reasons to believe that the urgency of environmental crises induces sustained pressure on the South for domestic sacrifices; at the same time, Southern states are well aware of their power of denial in environmental affairs and have used it in the hope of extracting Northern commitments. The potential for increased North–South conflict is especially evident in current recessionary times.

On the other hand, some market-based factors could be invoked to link environmental issues to North–South cooperation. Many opponents of the proposed North American Free Trade Agreement have argued that disparities in the implementation of environmental legislation would act as a magnet for polluting industries wishing to avoid American and Canadian standards in favour of looser restrictions in Mexico. If this assumption is valid, and if liberal forces do have the upper hand in coalition politics, then environmental problems, far from being the object of international dispute for their resolution, become an impetus for increased levels of trade depending precisely on the *status quo*. However, the argument can just as easily be turned around: protectionist and environmentalist forces may well exaggerate the extent to which environmental control costs are indeed uppermost on industry's priority list, and effectively discourage instances of North–South cooperation (which, if pursued, may in fact generate the necessary wealth for environmental policies—though this benign view of the market can be debated). In other words, the environment, as it relates to trade, either raises barriers between North and South or, perversely, brings inter-hemispheric *rapprochement*.

Another market-based example will illustrate the point. The North–South trade in toxic wastes has been the object of virulent denunciations from African governments, prompting a sharply worded resolution at the OAU and setting the stage for the drafting of a global convention, in 1989. However, this weak display of international law has yet to be ratified by the necessary minimum of parties for its implementation. Most probably, this reflects the tremendous economic benefits, for both North and South, of using the Third World as a dumping ground for hazardous wastes: waste disposal in the South is ten times cheaper than in the North, while the South gets access to a source of revenue which would vanish under a strong North–South environmental regime.

This said, the market does not necessarily violate the interests of nature, at least in principle. Americans have long advocated market mechanisms to control pollution. Having introduced the concept of tradeable pollution permits, which sets a 'tolerable' aggregate ceiling of emissions but allows efficient plants to sell their share of pollution rights to less efficient ones, and having implemented the idea domestically the US has urged the adoption of a similar mechanism at the global level. Applied to the problem of global warming, the scheme would use the country rather than the plant as an emitting unit and authorise 'excessive' individual greenhouse gas emissions, providing that a global maximum be respected. This problem-solving mechanism might hence elicit the cooperation of key, reticent Third World countries (such as China and India) into a global regime. However, the numerous obstacles (political, definitional, practical) facing the adoption of such a revolutionary plan are overwhelming. Moreover, market-based environmental problem-solving may say relatively little about the impact of environmental problems on global relations. It may demonstrate that the *market* is an appealing approach, enticing co-operation for the resolution of *any* common problem; but it does not suggest that common environmental problems are, in their essence, conducive to co-operation.

To summarise, the global problem posed by environmental degradation may well modify North–South relations. An optimist would argue that the urgency of the situation has ensured the presence of environmental issues on the global agenda, that the North cannot extract environmental compliance from the South through traditional means of coercion, and that the intensity of the South's economic crisis and own environmental crisis must stimulate its participation in co-operative schemes destined to reduce pollution and implement sustainable development patterns. The pessimist, on the other hand, would assume that the same urgency is pushing Northern countries to harden their economic policies towards the South so as to elicit rapid compliance to Northern environmental dictates, while the South cares relatively little about environmental questions and seeks to extract huge commitments from the North by the use of the environmental bargaining chip. Optimism and pessimism could also drive arguments assuming little or no efforts at North–South problem-solving: trade could benefit from the *status quo* in the regulatory gaps, but could suffer from attempts at using environmental arguments as disguised non-tariff barriers; left untouched, pollution and resource depletion would also, in the long run, cause serious conflict (directly or indirectly) as rich and poor societies become embroiled in finger-pointing exercises.

Janna Thompson, *Sustainability, Justice and Market Relations,* *in* Markets, The State and the Environment: Towards Integration, 275, 280–283 (Robyn Eckersley ed., 1995).

Global Environmental Justice

The least well off people of the world are not generally found in Australia or the developed countries of the Western world. They are living in the *favelas* of Rio de Janeiro or the deserts of North Africa and increasingly in the blighted industrial slums of the former Soviet Union. The World Bank estimates that one billion people in the world live below a poverty line of $370 per year. The worst forms of environmental degradation and the worst effects of industrial development are also found in these developing or under-developed parts of the world. The problems of poverty and environmental degradation are closely associated. Impoverished people are more likely to exploit marginal lands, to tolerate unsafe and polluting industries, or to allow their land to be stripped of natural resources.

Moreover, poor countries can often not afford environmental reforms. Susan George argues that poor countries are not in the position to phase out the use of pesticides, since people depend too much on the extra productivity that they make possible. Even a temporary setback would be a disaster for many people. Nor can many Third World governments afford to meet the terms of agreements to cut down on the emission of greenhouse gases. Forcing them to do so by threatening to withhold aid or trade is likely to result in making the poorest part of the population even worse off.

Not all environmental programs are bad news for the poorest people of the world. Aid given to villagers to improve their farming methods, conservation projects that employ local people, education programs aimed at women and the development of environmentally sound local industries and coopera-tives can have the effect of restoring degraded environments, slowing down population growth and at the same time improving the lot of the least well off. Nevertheless, it is unlikely that such projects by themselves are an answer to Third World poverty and environmental degradation.

To most people it seems obvious that the development of industry and the economies of Third World countries is the only feasible solution to the problem of poverty. The United Nations declares that the people of the world have a 'right to development', which it defines as 'a comprehensive economic, social, cultural and political process, which aims at the constant improvement of the well-being of the entire population and of all its individuals on the basis of their active, free and meaningful participation in the development and in the fair distribution of benefits resulting therefrom'. Environmentalists will add that this development must lead to environmental sustainability, both nationally and internationally. The two goals, it seems, should go together. People who are better off are also in the position to protect their environment better.

Some environmentalists are sceptical about the very possibility of achiev-ing development, equity and sustainability for everybody. Rudolf Bahro, for example, does not regard the dream of development as feasible: 'On a world scale industrialisation cannot be achieved any longer, for the earth will not yield the material consumption of the North American middle class for the 10 to 15 billion people of the next century'. The right of development does not require that everyone in the world achieve the standard of living of the North American middle class. But it is hard to imagine that sustainable development can be achieved in an equitable way unless the countries of the developed world are prepared to transfer some of their wealth to the poor of the world. Do we, the relatively rich, have a duty of justice to the impoverished people of the world, and if so, what is required of us?

The wealthy people of the world bear a large part of the responsibility for poverty and environmental destruction in the Third World. Apart from the colonial legacy, which still adversely affects some areas of the world, the world market operates in a way that disadvantages the poor. Industrialised countries, as Jacobs remarks, 'export unsustainability'. Simply because they are wealthy, they can often avoid the externalities of their economic activity and thrust them onto people in the Third World. They can afford to buy up scarce resources, determine where and how goods should be produced, and export their waste products elsewhere. Their demands for food and fibre result in lands being deforested to grow commercial crops and local people being denied basic goods.

Since the activities of the wealthy substantially contribute to the plight of the poor and the destruction of Third World environments, it seems that justice demands that the wealthy take responsibility for undoing the harm. Jacobs suggests that we have a moral duty to compensate Third World people for the damage we have done. We could, for example, discharge the debts owed by many Third World governments to international banks. However, there are a number of problems with compensation, whatever form it takes. One of them is that Third World governments would not necessarily use the benefits received either to improve the lot of the least well off or to make environmental reforms. Some governments and aid organisations insist that recipient governments use money for particular projects, but as Jacobs notes, attaching strings to the use of compensation payments does not accord very well with the idea that these payments are not aid, but what we owe to those we have harmed. In any case, it might be difficult to ensure that governments do use benefits in an environmentally sound way once they have received them.

There are more serious problems with the idea that justice demands that the wealthy compensate the poor. Who, exactly, owes benefits to whom? Much of the damage to people and environments has been done not by individuals or even states but by multinational companies. Governments and citizens have only limited control over what these organisations do. In fact, it is difficult to determine whom to hold responsible for what is simply the normal operation of the international market. Governments have a limited control over their domestic economy and can thus be held responsible for regulating economic affairs so that the least well off are not disadvantaged, but individual states or companies have virtually no control over the operation of the international market. Even the power of the USA over world economic affairs has diminished significantly in the past two decades, and though some multinationals have a powerful position in Third World countries, they must still do what is necessary to survive in an increasingly competitive international market. But if agents, whether individuals, companies or states, are simply doing what is necessary for their own viability in a world economic system, then it is more difficult to regard anyone in particular as being morally responsible for the export of unsustainability, and there is not much point in singling out particular agents for punishment. This does not mean that appeals to justice are meaningless or pointless in world society, or that we have no duties to the least well off. Rather, the problem of assigning responsibility to particular agents suggests that what is needed is a collective global strategy for solving the related problems of poverty and environmental degradation. Our primary duty of justice is to do what we can to implement this strategy.

Edgar J. Asebey & Jill D. Kempenaar, *Biodiversity Prospecting:*
Fulfilling the Mandate of the Biodiversity Convention, 28
VAND. J. TRANSNAT'L L. 703, 737–746 (1995).

POTENTIAL ALTERNATIVE: RESTRICTION OF SUPPLY

When the United States initially refused to sign the Biodiversity Convention in 1992, Venezuela retaliated by refusing to sign any new scientific collaboration agreements with United States corporations for the study of genetic resources. Such retaliation was hardly a surprise to the global community as international environmental organizations at the Rio de Janeiro summit had predicted such action. Venezuela's move was by no means the sole act of an international renegade. Since the Convention was opened for signature, many source countries established or made more stringent, "regulations on the collection and export of biological resources in an effort to both control and capture some of the [attendant] economic benefits."[i] In essence, Venezuela chose to treat the Biodiversity Convention as an international benchmark for the conduct of corporations wishing to undertake genetic exploration within its borders, denying access to countries that refused to accede to the voluntary code of conduct. Ultimately, the United States did sign the Biodiversity Convention, and the incident received only passing attention.

This seemingly small confrontation is extremely important, however, because it sets crucial precedent for similar actions in the future. The significance of the action is underscored by the actor that chose to boycott United States investors: Venezuela, a member of the Organization of Petroleum Exporting Countries (OPEC).

Developing countries may seek to increase their revenue from biodiversity prospecting by increasing the market value of their genetic resources through supply restrictions and coercive imposition of favorable conditions. In its least threatening form, this could be accomplished with the voluntary cooperation of multinational pharmaceutical corporations through creation of codes of conduct. In the alternative, developing countries may seek to create higher market value for their genetic materials by developing one or more genetic resource cartels. Cartelization and the rise of codes of conduct are not mutually exclusive mechanisms. They may overlap, follow one another in progression, or act as two extreme points on a continuum. In either case, they are a response to the enduring features of prior approaches: the absence of an inherent market value in genetic material, developing countries' lack of individual bargaining power, and the absence of value-adding processes within source countries.'

The historical discussion above illustrated the reality that multinational corporations of the North do not value biodiversity and genetic materials *per se*; the countries of the South are compensated, if at all, based upon the value added to their resources by refinement. This is an unsurprising result given the North's historically easy access to the South's genetic materials. As with

---

i. Julie M. Feinsilver, *Biodiversity Prospect-*   PROSPECTING 21, 22 (A.H. Zakri ed., 1995).
ing and Realities, in PROSPECTS IN BIODIVERSITY

all natural resources, the laws of supply and demand are applicable to the cost of biological resources. When demand remains constant but supply is restricted, the price of a good will increase. This basic law of supply and demand can be harnessed by the South to achieve its goals of increased revenue, technology transfer, economic development, and improved environmental protection. Several authors refer in passing to the possibility of collective action to reduce supply in several contexts related to biodiversity, but none seriously examine the possibility of concerted action by the South as a mechanism through which the South can attain its goals.

Collective action by the South will fall along a continuum from a series of isolated unilateral standards to a broad-scale cartel that drastically restricts Northern corporations' access to genetic resources. One scenario, voluntary multilateral regional coordination, analogous to the U.N. Codes of Conduct, falls in the middle of the spectrum, and probably represents the most likely possibility. A number of countries with gene-rich resources might confer and formulate an agreement among themselves. Such an agreement would require genetic prospectors to satisfy a series of specific conditions in exchange for the right to collect or examine genetic samples. In the absence of significant technology transfer, one of the conditions would almost certainly be a royalty rate much higher than the customary one to three percent and an up-front payment for access to the resource. Such a condition would meet developing countries' needs for increased revenue. Other likely conditions include requiring the multinational corporation to locate permanent research and development facilities within the source country, conduct extensive scientific training of local personnel, and transfer significant quantities of technology to the source country. These conditions would meet the developing countries' needs for economic development and acquisition of scientific know-how and hardware.

Myriad contractual issues ranging from access to and use of ethnobotanical knowledge to technology to conservation could be addressed in such a code. The result might be boilerplate contractual language for use in bilateral agreements, or perhaps a document to which multinational pharmaceutical corporations would have to formally agree in order to gain access to any of the signatory nations' resources. The agreement could be as broad or as detailed as political realities would allow; it would be dictated by what the source countries thought they could realistically extract from potential prospectors and by the number of signatories and strength of the coalition. If a sufficient number of nations signed a multilateral genetic prospecting code, multinational corporations' access could be so restricted as to force them to comply with the conditions of the accord. In a worst-case scenario, all gene-rich developing countries might flatly deny multinational corporations access to genetic resources unless multinational corporations complied with source countries' terms. Given that the worst-case scenario would require unprecedented cohesive multilateral action, however, such an extreme result seems unlikely.

Industries, such as pharmaceutical manufacturers, that were opposed to the Biodiversity Convention maintain that compensation to developing countries should be negotiated contractually between the parties rather than by international agreement or national legislation, which the Convention requires on some issues. A code of conduct instigated by developing countries can be seen as falling within the purview of contractual negotiations, albeit collective negotiations confined only by the South's economic realities. Market factors will limit the compensation that developing countries can realistically demand. At the same time, however, collective action will prevent nations of the South from being individually disadvantaged when they enter bilateral negotiations with multinational corporations.

Taken to the extreme, restricting supply to create valuation of plant resources *per se* could result in a genetic resource cartel—a new OPEC. Aggressive multilateral cooperation among the biodiversity rich nations of the developing world could potentially starve the North of biological resources. Such cartelization would likely start among countries who find they have little to lose by cutting off the North's access. Countries that were promised only a three percent royalty of sales, which may not materialize for decades, might be willing to sign a multilateral accord that offers the hope of realistic compensation.

There is already international precedent for multilateral agreements that impose limitations on multinational corporations' behavior. Although never completed, the U.N. Model Code of Conduct for Transnational Corporations gives an illuminating glimpse at the demands the South has made on Northern multinational corporations for almost two decades. Moreover, Northern multinational corporations outside the pharmaceutical industry regularly develop their own codes of conduct. The codes are usually specific to a given industry and are association-based, applying both within the United States and, to some extent, internationally. Such codes are often environmental, but address more visibly pressing concerns, such as hazardous materials. Private codes are proliferating throughout the developed world, creating a universe of voluntary commitments to better environmental practices by multinational corporations. Significantly, however, even the most conscientious corporations almost never adhere to their codes of conduct in relations with developing countries.

Domestic regulatory policy within the United States is also moving toward voluntary compliance. The system is being redesigned to stimulate voluntary corporate initiatives and to reward or punish companies on the basis of the policies and management practices they adopt. Taken in the aggregate, there appears to be a pervasive movement toward constructing mechanisms that induce multinational corporations to comply voluntarily with environmental requirements.

The most well-known precedent relevant to this discussion is, of course, the creation of the OPEC oil cartel and its control on global oil supplies in the early 1970s. In the OPEC context, access to a natural resource took on the political cast of a battle between countries of the North and South, as oil exporting nations sought to demonstrate and solidify a fundamental political recognition of their national sovereignty.

Individual nations are already beginning to coordinate restricted access to their genetic resources. The Venezuelan and Indian position discussed previously are not the only examples of movements which threaten to tighten the supply of genetic resources. The presidents of Belize, Costa Rica, El Salvador, Guatemala, Honduras, Nicaragua, and Panama signed a nonbinding resolution that encouraged the passage of internal laws to regulate the extraction of medicinal plants and other biogenetic substances. The next logical step is for them to create an enforcement mechanism which will make such pro-restriction resolutions binding.

A cartel effort would be built upon the platform of shared perceptions that underpins the label "South," which when properly used, refers to an observable process in international politics. The "bloc diplomatic behavior" exhibited by nations of the South, especially when they are represented by the Group of 77 (the Nonaligned Movement), is underpinned by several fundamental shared perceptions: (1) Status quo institutional structures (particularly GATT and the International Monetary Fund) and attendant political and economic processes are deeply biased against developing countries; (2) the North has constructed a system of international impediments to the South's economic growth; and (3) Southern nations share the goal of achieving higher levels of political influence and economic welfare in international relations.

If the ties which bind the South into a cohesive political entity are not strong enough to support a unitary cartel effort, then cartelization may occur along regional lines drawn for other purposes. In South America, for example, the nations of the Andean Common Market have cooperated with each other in creating a draft framework for access to genetic resources. Similarly, the nations that participated in the Contadora process of the mid–1980s could be expected to become an early focal point for collective efforts to reduce the North's access to biological resources. However, multinational pharmaceutical corporations will prefer to keep their options open and acquire genetic samples from numerous geographic locations, institutions, and collection agencies. If too many regional cartels develop, their effectiveness will be compromised. Thus, various cartels can be expected to coordinate with one another for maximum effectiveness.

The potential financial benefits of cartelization are not without some risk. One risk of cartelization is that the Northern multinational corporations might play a long waiting-game, gambling that the South's immediate financial needs are so pressing that individual nations will break the united front in order to fulfill their needs for revenue. This is especially likely with the growing prominence of a combinatorial chemistry, which is capable of producing millions of compounds in a short time for testing in high-throughput screening systems. This, undoubtedly, will reduce the demand for natural products as the starting materials for drug discovery screening. Such a strategy would cut off a large portion of the cartel members' revenue from biodiversity prospecting for several years.

A second risk is that the governments of the North might play political hardball on economic issues of greater importance to the South, such as loan rescheduling and various other forms of trade treatment. These risks seem unlikely, however, because the United States cherishes its position as the global biotechnology leader, and United States companies desire the South's resources at least as much as source countries wish to allow the access.

The history of OPEC amply demonstrates a third risk: factionalization within the cartel itself. Bilateral disagreements within a large cartel may be a never-ending threat to the harmony of the group and its ability to remain cohesive for the greater benefit of all involved. This fact suggests that a series of smaller regional cartels would be more likely to achieve the South's objectives than one large cartel. Multinational corporations could certainly attempt to manipulate internal tensions in an effort to weaken the cartel's control of accessible genetic resources by playing one member off another.

A fourth risk is that the North might attempt to sanction Southern cartel members for restricting access to their resources in violation of the Biodiversity Convention. However, if the North fails to honor its Convention duty to provide technology transfer, technical and scientific cooperation, and financial resources, the South will be able to justifiably evade its Convention obligation to provide access. The Convention recognizes that developing countries' duty to provide access is conditioned upon ample support from developed countries.

It is not clear from the Convention to what degree the South could restrict access and still be in compliance. The interpretation of "access" may ultimately be quite loose. The majority of signatories are nations of the South and, as they ratify the Convention, their enabling domestic legislation will almost certainly adopt a broad interpretation of their powers to provide and restrict access. The Convention frequently uses the phrases "mutually agreeable terms" and "subject to mutual agreement" when discussing access, and this could provide an escape clause for cartel members. Presently, Northern corporations can argue that their bilateral contracts with developing countries constitute "mutually agreed terms" despite the multinational corporations' strong bargaining power. Conversely, the phrase "mutually agreed terms" could be construed to allow the nations of the South to drive an extremely hard bargain with the North by threatening restricted access to genetic resources. A final risk is that attempts to control the flow of biological materials could result in black market smuggling of raw genetic materials; a market and infrastructure already exists.

Discussion Notes/Questions

1. Laferriere considers the impact of environmental problems on North–South relations. Is the analysis much different when considering the impact of North–South relations on environmental problems?

2. How valid are claims of neo-imperialism? Should the South be forced to share the North's environmental concerns? To what extent should the North provide financial assistance for environmentally beneficial action by the South?

3. Is the North–South issue a matter of justice? If so, what are the obligations of wealthy countries in relation to environmental problems in the South?

4. Does cartelization of genetic resources pose a real threat? Would it be a legitimate use of political power? Do powerful economies use analogous strategies?

5. Are voluntary agreements and undertakings by business entities a tool of environmental law?

6. Is international (environmental) law capable of regulating multinational pharmaceutical companies?

7. Is cartelization uniquely relevant to bio-prospecting due to the lack of inherent market value in genetic material? Would cartelization result in a beneficial environmental outcome?

8. For additional pertinent reading on international environmental politics, see N. Adams, Worlds Apart: The North/South Divide and the International System (1993); J. Kauffman, *Global Environmental Politics: Lessons from Montreal*, 14 Env'tl Impact Assessment Review 3 (1994); P. Nelson, *Deliberation, Lever-*

age or Coercion? The World, NGOs, and Global Environmental Politics: Comment on Payne, 34 J. Peace Res. 467 (1997); OECD, Strengthening Environmental Co-operation with Developing Countries (1989); The International Politics of the Environment: Actors, Interests, and Institutions (A. Hurrell & B. Kingsbury eds. 1992); J. O'Neill, Ecology, Policy and Politics: Human Well-Being and the Natural World (1993); *Developments in Law: International Environmental Law*, 104 Harv. L. Rev. 1484 (1991); G. Palmer, *The Earth Summit: What Went Wrong at Rio?*, 70 Wash. U. L. Q. 1005 (1992); R. Payne, *Deliberating Global Environmental Politics*, 33 J. Peace Res. 129 (1996); E. Von Wizacker, Earth Politics (1993); P. Wapner, *On the Global Dimensions of Environmental Challenges*, 13 J. Pol. & Life Sciences 173 (1994).

Porter and Brown allude to the interrelationship between environment and security. There is a body of academic writing specifically concerned with that interrelationship (refer Discussion Note 6 below). The thesis has been advanced that environmental problems will increasingly cause security threats. The following reading by Marc Levy is a critique of that thesis. We have provided you with the introduction and conclusion of Levy's article, which provide a summary of his analysis. Levy concludes that although there is a link between environment and security, it is of very little importance.

Marc A. Levy, *Is the Environment a National Security Issue?*, 20 INT'L SEC. 35, 35–37, 60–62 (1995).

In the spring of 1994, when the U.S. government was trying to put its less-than-successful intervention in Somalia behind it while contemplating future troubles in Haiti, an *Atlantic Monthly* article painted a picture of the world in which such conflicts could be expected to magnify and spread. Robert Kaplan's "The Coming Anarchy" captured Washington's attention with its dire vision of a world beset with collapsing state authority. President Clinton was reported to have scribbled marginal notes on his personal copy, and citation of it became practically *de rigueur* for Cabinet members appearing before Congress. Much of Kaplan's analysis centered on the role of environmental degradation in sparking "the coming anarchy," and his article therefore marks a decided elevation of the environment and security debate.

However, to call it a debate is to stretch things. Since the late 1980s, when public discussion of environment and security links began in earnest, a ground swell of support for the core proposition that environmental degradation constitutes a security risk has encountered hardly any voices of dissent. Critics of the core idea have voiced their opinion by way of silence rather than debate, perhaps hoping the discussion would fade away. But because the ideas are getting more, rather than less, attention, it is time to subject them to a serious review.

This essay examines the proposition that global environmental degradation is a security threat to the United States. I focus on three distinct forms of connection between the environment and security, which I term the existential, the physical, and the political. This article reviews each link and evaluates each on its own terms. All of these views pertain to links *from* processes of environmental degradation *to* deterioration in security positions. Connections that run in the opposite direction (from use of force to deterioration in environmental quality) are not examined here.

Adherents to the existential view, such as Jessica Tuchman Mathews and Norman Myers, argue that certain aspects of the global environment are so intimately connected to our deepest national values that they are constitutive of our security interests. When these environmental values are threatened, our security is threatened, *ipso facto*. I argue that this position has no basis except as a rhetorical device aimed at drumming up greater support for measures to protect the environment. These advocates probably hope for more than is realistic in this regard, because the rhetorical act of pointing out that environmental degradation endangers important national values begs the question of how such values ought to be traded off against one another. In addition, the political task of gaining support for the environment may in many cases fare better on the level of low politics than high politics, as I explain.

I find that proponents of the direct physical link between environment and U.S. security have serious arguments worth considering, but that these arguments require difficult assessments of competing alternative responses. A combination of prevention, adaptation, and "letting nature take its course" is likely to emerge as optimal. This conclusion is unsettling to many advocates of the environment and security link, but unsurprising to students of security studies: it amounts to an argument that to "roll back" global environmental change is forbiddingly costly, and that a better policy consists of a combination of "containment" and "co-existence."

Finally, this paper finds that the indirect, political threat from environmental degradation (involving environmental refugees, resource wars, and so on) is at once both the weakest substantive threat to U.S. security and the strongest intellectual challenge to the field of security studies. That is, the United States has the least to fear from political conflicts caused by environmental harm (because such conflicts are likely to be limited to regions removed from direct U.S. interests); but nonetheless this is where the academic community has the most catching up to do, because the question of how regional conflicts emerge and evolve is one of the most neglected areas of security studies, and analysts have made a strong case that environmental degradation is an important causal factor. I argue, however, that to conclude that we need more research on environmental causes of conflict *per se* is wrong. The reason we do not know much about the role of the environment in sparking regional conflict is not that we have neglected the environment. On the contrary, few good studies of regional conflict neglect natural resources as central factors. Rather, we do not know much about the role of the environment in causing conflict because we do not know much about what causes regional conflict overall. What we need, if we wish to come to grips with any "coming anarchy," is research on conflict, not on the environment.

* * *

The assertion that many environmental problems constitute security risks is correct, and is of very little importance.

The purely rhetorical line of argumentation that urges us to consider environmental problems and security problems as by their very nature inseparable is probably destined to disappear. Whatever needs for attention-getting may have been present in the late 1980s, they are past now. If the problems these writers point to are really as serious as they say, then the more pressing need is not for more "new thinking" but for effective solutions.

The existential strand of the environment and security literature may have been unique to the historical moment in which it emerged. At a time when environmental awareness was rapidly rising among publics, politicians were competing for "green" votes, a global convention was succeeding at eliminating a whole class of dangerous compounds, and the Cold War was ending, for many in the environmental community the world seemed poised on the threshold of a new age. It was possible to pose the question (with all seriousness) in a mainstream journal: "Could the time be coming when as much lasting security can be purchased through trees as through tanks?"[j]

Those heady days of optimism are past. The world of 1995 looks nowhere near as primed for a nudge toward ecotopia as the world of 1989 did. Proposals for new thinking are giving way to more appropriate attention to work on developing creative solutions to specific problems. Those writers who continue to brandish the environment-qua-security rhetorical sword are likely to find themselves unable to communicate with those who view security in conventional terms.

I argue that ozone depletion and climate change are the only significant environmental problems that currently pose a direct physical harm to U.S. interests. While both problems can thus properly be considered as security problems, and both warrant serious responses, it is not clear whether engaging in the first task facilitates the second. Although many analysts accept in principle the connection between these environmental risks and security, there is no evidence that this affects in any way the kind of research they undertake or the kind of recommendations they make. The equation does not appear to do any great good, and the ozone example suggests that in some cases better results can be obtained without it.

Other important environmental problems that have security implications do so through indirect routes, through processes of violent conflict in domestic and regional settings in the developing world. But to respond effectively to these problems one needs to deepen understanding of regional and civil conflict; the environment occupies only one of many causal roles. By the time one moves from understanding conflicts to recommending responses, the environment is likely to fade far into the background.

So in the end, the pleas to consider the environment as a security issue lead us further and further from the environment and security nexus. Examination of direct threats to American values settles within the traditional domain of environmental policy studies and stays there. Examination of indirect threats stemming from phenomena such as violent conflict in the Third World settles in another traditional domain—studies of war and unrest—and stays there. Neither path delivers on the promise of what Mathews calls a "new way of thinking," but perhaps what we need is better old

j. Norman Myers, *Environment and Securi-*   *ty* 74 FOREIGN POL'Y 23, 41 (1989).

thinking. In fact, now that the environmental advocates have got everyone's attention, this is precisely the time to turn away from slogans and toward the more mundane work of integrating environmental considerations into research and analysis.

Discussion Notes/Questions

1. Is Levy unduly sceptical, or do current environmental problems spell a redefinition of security? What if the worst case scenario of climate change comes to pass?

2. Can environmental concerns ever be considered more important than traditional military threats?

3. Is the environment and security thesis valuable as a political tool?

4. If effective environmental management is to be achieved on a global scale, will State sovereignty in its present sense need to be discarded? Would the relaxation of State sovereignty necessarily mean a more limited role for the military?

5. Is it relevant that political conflicts caused by environmental harm are geographically remote from the United States?

6. For additional pertinent reading, see S. Dalby, *Ecological Discourse: 'Environmental Security' and Political Geography* 16 Progress in Human Geography 503 (1992); J. Galtung, Environment, Development, and Military Security: Towards Alternative Security Doctrines (1982); T. Homer–Dixon, *Environmental Scarcities and Violet Conflict: Evidence from Cases* 19 Int'l. Security 8 (1994); R. Pethig, Conflicts and Co-operation in Managing Environmental Resources (1992); L. Brock, *Security Through Defending the Environment: An Illusion? in* New Agendas for Peace Research: Conflict and Security Reexamined (E. Boulding ed. 1992); N. Eberstedt, *Population Change and National Security*, 70 For. Aff. 115 (1991); T. Homer–Dixon, *On The Threshold: Environmental Changes as Causes of Acute Conflict*, 16 Int'l Security 76 (1991); P. Mische, *Ecological Security and the Need to Reconceptualize Sovereignty*, 14 Alternatives 389 (1989).

2. ECONOMIC ANALYSIS

Editors' Note

The economic analysis of environmental issues and policy provides a conceptual framework for analysing questions related to international environmental law. The primary focus of environmental economics is the identification of effective and efficient mechanisms of environmental protection. Mainstream economics is in agreement on a number of fundamental points of analysis:

● Where natural resources, including air, water and land are unowned, unregulated and can be exploited by any person, a 'tragedy of the commons' results which leads inevitably to their over-exploitation and ruin. In contrast, where property rights to natural resources are defined and enforced, individual or communal owners have strong incentives to husband them.

● Prices for goods and services should reflect the full cost of production, including the cost of the environmental and natural resources that are used. Paying the full cost of inputs ensures that users make appropriate decisions about resources. However, at present environmental costs are very imperfectly accounted for, so that producers often do not pay the full cost of the harms they generate. Making polluters pay for the damage they cause ensures that they are accountable for their actions, and gives them incentives to seek less damaging (and therefore less costly) ways of doing things.

● Protecting the environment implies a willingness to sacrifice. Cleaning up a polluted river, for example, means that other things have to be given up, because cleaning up is costly and the money and effort involved could have been spent elsewhere. The sacrifices made to clean up the environment tend to increase exponentially as the environment gets cleaner, while the benefits of additional units of environmental purity tend to fall. The benefits of a cleaner environment must be balanced against the cost of achieving it. Beyond some point, the costs of additional purity exceeds the benefits, so it is not economically sensible to pursue a policy of complete environmental purity. Trade-offs are inevitable; zero environmental risk is not a feasible goal.

● Evaluating environmental policies and projects involves specifying the objective and assessing all the costs and benefits of achieving it. It leads to policy recommendations that balance competing demands on resources in order to improve community well-being. However, assembling and correctly weighing the requisite information is a dauntingly formidable task. There is often uncertainty about the nature, extent, causation and timing of environmental problems and the risks they pose. Information on the effectiveness and costs of alternative instruments to clean up the environment is also scarce. Policy decisions must therefore inevitably be made with highly imperfect information. Environmental policy is most effective when it encourages new knowledge and is responsive to new information.

● Incentives matter. Policy mechanisms that utilise market instruments and harness incentives are generally, but not always, more likely to achieve effective environmental protection than regulatory or 'command and control' policies. Well designed market instruments with enforceable property rights and prices that reflect the true costs of resource use provide an institutional framework that relies on the incentives of individuals acting in their own self-interest to protect the environment. The role of government is to establish the property rights (such as the right to discharge waste water in terms of the maximum permitted level of pollution) and to enforce them. In contrast, command and control policies are typically ineffective in protecting the environment, and can often have perverse consequences, exacerbating rather than ameliorating environmental problems. These problems arise because the political process in which regulation is made is subject to manipulation by interest groups seeking policies that favour them at the expense of others. These difficulties are inherent in the political process and apply not only to domestic but also to international environmental policies. Furthermore, command and control policies offer inadequate incentives to search for more cost-effective approaches to environmental problems and suffer from a scarcity of information that hampers their effective implementation.

The economic view that incentive-based instruments are more typically effective in protecting the environment than command and control regulation is in sharp contrast to the views of many environmentalists. The economic view is that incentives are important and that given the opportunity, interest groups including firms, lobbyists, and government organizations themselves will use the political process to press their advantage. In contrast, the environmentalist view is often based on a presumption that environmental regulation is intended to and does protect the public interest in the environment.

The challenge of resource management is to devise and select legal and political institutions that protect and preserve natural and environmental resources. Many of the world's critical environmental resources such as the oceans, the air, groundwater and fisheries are managed as open-access resources that anyone can use. Such open access has international implications. Excessive extraction from an aquifer can reduce the amount of groundwater in a neighboring country; damming a river can reduce downstream flows that affect agriculture and fisheries in another country. These external effects are not limited to neighboring countries. Factory pollution can produce acid rain a continent away.

Improved institutional arrangements that define even partial property rights that allow exchange can mitigate these problems. Yet it can be difficult to define property rights to the air, groundwater or the oceans. Nevertheless, technologies are now available that make it possible to measure and track cross-boundary air pollution and make it easier to develop and use internationally tradeable property right systems.

Defining and enforcing property rights can be costly. Also, the costs of negotiating and exchanging property rights, which are fundamental to the way that markets function, may be high. These high costs imply that the use of property rights will only be worthwhile when the costs of defining, enforcing and exchanging them (the transactions costs) are low. In these situations the ability to exchange property rights means that the best use is made of the resource. In economic terms, it is used efficiently. It does not matter who holds the property right and who pays whom for its use. An efficient allocation of resources would always be reached. This is the conclusion of a celebrated article by Nobel Laureate Ronald Coase, The Problem of Social Cost, 3 J. Law & Econ. 1 (1960). In such a world pollution would not be a problem for the collective good, since polluters could pay for the pollution they create or those affected could bribe the polluters not to pollute.

However, when transactions costs are high, then the allocation of rights does matter. Who has the legal right to pollute determines who will pay. Defining property rights may not be worthwhile if the environmental costs are low. But without defined property rights externalities may remain, imposing environmental costs internationally and resulting in environmental degradation. Countries that burn large quantities of fossil fuels can continue to impose costs on others. Yet these other countries do not have an effective means of paying polluting countries not to pollute or of being compensated for the environmental harms that they endure. The International Law of State Responsibility (outlined in Chapter 5) places great restrictions on the imposition of any sort of liability in the international plain, in contrast to practice at the domestic level which allows those affected to sue polluters.

Any international effort to deal with cross-border environmental issues faces enormous difficulties. Typically policy decisions are made within a milieu of great uncertainty. There is generally scientific uncertainty about the causation, nature, timing and extent and probability of environmental problems. There is also considerable technical uncertainty about the mechanisms required for abatement. Also, there is typically economic uncertainty about the costs and benefits of the environmental problem and the possible solution. Not only is the magnitude of these costs and benefits unknown, but there is also uncertainty about who (regions, countries or industries) can expect to bear the costs and enjoy the benefits.

Such uncertainty has important consequences. It can lead to severe disagreements among those with different expectations of the probable effects. Differences in the incidence of the likely costs and benefits also lead those who expect to be affected to oppose or support international measures to deal with environmental issues according to the net benefits they expect to receive. Disagreements between countries on international environmental control measures are generally ground-ed in these differences.

It is therefore by no means clear how effectively economic instruments for the control of cross-boundary environment problems can be applied at the internation-al level. International environmental decisions must be taken by governments acting under enormous scientific, technical and economic uncertainty as well as domestic political pressures driven by a range of interest groups. It is not altogether surprising that the environmental policies advocated by economic theory are not as yet reflected in international measures dealing with cross-boundary environmental problems.

Lawrence Summers, *Summers on Sustainable Growth*, THE ECONOMIST, May 30, 1992, at 65.

In this letter, a reply to our Economics Focus of May 9th, the World Bank's chief economist defends the application of economics to the environment.

SIR—You accept too credulously the arguments of those who criticize econom-ic approaches to the environment. Certainly, the idea of sustainable develop-ment has drawn attention to environmental problems that were ignored for too long. But there is no intellectually legitimate case for abandoning accepted techniques of cost-benefit analysis in evaluating environmental investments, either by using abnormally low discount rates or, worse yet, by invoking special criteria regarding sustainability.

The argument that a moral obligation to future generations demands special treatment of environmental investments is fatuous. We can help our descendants as much by improving infrastructure as by preserving rain forests, as much by educating children as by leaving oil in the ground, as much by enlarging our scientific knowledge as by reducing carbon dioxide in the air. However much, or little, current generations wish to weigh the interests of future generations, there is every reason to undertake invest-ments that yield the highest returns.

That means holding each investment, environmental and non-environ-mental, to a test of opportunity cost. Each project must have a higher return (taking account of both pecuniary and non-pecuniary benefits) than alterna-tive uses of the funds. Standard public non-environmental investments like sewage-treatment facilities, education programmes, or World Bank transport projects have returns of more than 10%. Most private investors apply even higher "hurdle rates" in evaluating investments, generally 15% or more, because higher-return alternatives are available.

Once costs and benefits are properly measured, it cannot be in posterity's interest for us to undertake investments that yield less than the best return. At the long-term horizons that figure in the environmental debate, this really matters. A dollar invested at 10% will be worth six times as much a century from now as a dollar invested at 8% [*see* Table 4–1].

Miraculous Interest

Table 4–1.

The value over time of $1

for:	invested at 8%	10%
10 Years	2.2	2.6
20	4.7	6.7
30	10	17
40	22	45
50	47	117
75	321	1,272

The premise that our first priority should be to do more for our descendants is, anyway, debatable. Surely it is ethically relevant that our grandchildren will in all likelihood be much better off than we are. While nobody can accurately predict long-term growth rates, remember that standards of living are three times higher than 60 years ago in the United States, seven times higher in Germany and almost ten times higher in Japan. Should my American grandparents have reduced their standard of living, when life was considerably more nasty, brutish and short than now, to leave raw materials in the ground for my benefit?

To think so implies an odd morality. What is the better course for rich countries: to put more aside for a posterity that will be far richer than we are, or to do more to help the world's poor now? I, for one, feel the tug of the billion people who subsist on less than $1 a day in 1992 more acutely than the tug of future generations.

Some environmentalists talk about stewardship. They say we have an obligation to pass on to our children what has been passed on to us. Of course, we all wish our children to be better off than we are. But any investment that would make the difference between rising and falling living standards would pass a cost-benefit test at standard discount rates.

The reason why some investments favoured by environmentalists fail such a test is that their likely effect on living standards is not so great. Take the most serious global problem—climate changes from greenhouse gases. In the worst-case scenario of the most pessimistic estimates yet prepared (those of William Cline of the Institute for International Economics), global warming reduces growth over the next two centuries by less than 0.1% a year. More should be done: dealing with global warming would not halt economic growth either. But raising the spectre of our impoverished grandchildren if we fail to address global environmental problems is demagoguery.

Some suggest that whatever happens to an economy's productive potential, it is always wrong to damage any part of its natural patrimony irreversibly. But what is irreversible damage? Clearly, cutting down some trees and burning some scarce natural gas is all right, because sufficiently close substitutes are available. At the other extreme, no sane person would favour causing the extinction of hundreds of species to build a dam, if other poverty-reducing strategies were available. In every case, the question returns to trade-offs between costs and benefits. Chanting the mantra of sustainability is not enough.

In applying the standard cost-benefit paradigm to the environment, however, two issues do come up.

First, some advocate treating environmental investments differently, on the grounds that they are alternatives to consumption, not to other investments. This partly depends on how additional environmental spending is financed. But that is essentially a political judgment. Honest analysts should not endorse projects if proposals yielding higher returns are available. And given the extremely high interest rates at which most of the world's consumers are willing to borrow, consumption should not in any case be lightly sacrificed.

Second, it is argued that environmental damage is both uncertain and possibly irreversible. The right way to allow for the unusual riskiness of environmental decisions is to estimate the benefits of environmental investment generously, making special allowance for the value of options that they preserve. However plausible it may seem to reduce the discount rate to allow for risk, this reflects an elementary fallacy. To apply a specially low discount rate merely increases the weight attached to risks in the distant future as compared with risks in the near future—which makes no sense.

Environmentalists who point to the damage done by dams, power plants and roads evaluated according to standard economic criteria have a point. The answer does not lie in blanket sustainability criteria, or in applying special discount rates, but in properly incorporating environmental costs into the appraisal of projects. The grim fact is that no careful analysis was done of many of the projects which environmentalists condemn. The world's problem is not too much cost-benefit analysis, but too little that is done well. Plenty of environmental improvements can pass rigorous cost-benefit tests. There is no need to cook the books.

Discussion Notes/Questions

1.   What is the economic basis for Summers' faith in ever-increasing living standards? Is it borne out by the evidence to date?

2.   Would it be legitimate for today's poor to resent government policies that saved resources for future generations?

3.   Does making polluters pay for the environmental damage they cause simply give them a "license to pollute"?

4.   How can trade-offs be made between standards of living for people and the preservation of the natural environment?

5.   Should society bear some of the pollution "costs" on the grounds that they are a necessary part of industrial society? If polluters were made to pay fully for their costs, might society as a whole suffer from the reduced range, and increased cost of products?

6.   Could the problem of measuring pollution costs obstruct any meaningful attempt to include pollution on the balance sheet? What is the cost of an increased risk of cancer?

7.   For additional pertinent reading, see E. Barbier et al., Paradise Lost? The Ecological Economics of Biodiversity (1994); P. Bartelmus, *Whither Economics? From Optimality to Sustainability?* 2 Env't & Dev. Econ. 321 (1997); P. G. Brown, *Towards an Economics of Stewardship: The Case of Climate* 26 Ecological Econ. 11 (1998); N. Dorfman & R. Dorfman, Economics of the Environment: Selected Readings (1993); R.C. Dower & M.B. Zimmerman, The Right Climate for Carbon Taxes: Creating Economic Incentives to Protect the Atmosphere (1992); Markets, The State and the Environment: Towards Integration (R. Eckersley ed., 1995); E. Kula, Economics of Natural Resources and the Environment (1992); M. Max–Neef, From the Outside Looking In: Experiences in "Barefoot Economics" (1992); M.

Redclift, *Economic Models and Environmental Values: A Discourse on Theory, in* Sustainable Environmental Management: Principles and Practice (R. Turner ed., 1988); R. Repetto & D. Austin, The Costs of Climate Protection: A Guide for the Perplexed (1997); The Group of Green Economists, Ecological Economics: A Practical Programme for Global Reform (1992).

TERRY L. ANDERSON & DONALD R. LEAL, FREE
MARKET ENVIRONMENTALISM 9-23 (1991).

RETHINKING THE WAY WE THINK

Most natural resource and environmental policy has been premised on the assumption that markets are responsible for resource misallocation and environmental degradation and that centralized, political processes can correct these problems. In general, the failure of markets is attributed to private decision makers who do not take into account all costs and benefits, to the unequal availability of information to all buyers and sellers, or to monopolies distorting prices and output. In essence, market failure is blamed on the lack of information, inappropriate incentives, or both. To counter market failures, centralised planning is seen as a way of aggregating information about social costs and social benefits in order to maximise the value of natural resources. Decisions based on this aggregated information are to be made by disinterested resource managers whose goal is to maximise social welfare.

Economic analysis in general and natural resource economics in particular have approached resource policy as if there is a "socially efficient" allocation of resources that will be reached when scientific managers understand the relevant trade-offs and act to achieve the efficient solution. For example, forest resources are supposed to be managed to achieve the "greatest good for the greater number" through "multiple use management" undertaken by an "elite corps of professionals". When problems with management are recognised, they are attributed to "bad people in government" and the solution is to replace them with better trained, better financed managers.

But there is a more realistic way of thinking about natural resource and environmental policy. This alternative recognises and emphasises the costs of coordinating human actions. There is no assumption that costs of engaging in a transaction are zero or that there is perfect competition. To the contrary, understanding alternative policies requires that we specify coordinating costs and discover why and where competitive forces may not be working.

This analytical framework applies equally to markets and politics. If all people lived alone on remote islands, there would be no costs of coordination; but in a complex society where people gain from trade, interacting individuals must measure and monitor the actions of one another. In the marketplace, consumers must signal to suppliers what quantity and quality of products they demand at what prices; suppliers must determine which products to produce and which input combinations to use. Both demanders and suppliers must monitor one another to ensure that products are delivered and paid for. To the extent that actions can be effectively measured and monitored, demanders and suppliers will internalise costs and benefits, profit will be made, and efficient resource allocation will be a by-product.

Similarly, citizens who demand goods and services from government must monitor the politicians and bureaucrats who supply them. Like a consumer displeased with food purchased from the supermarket, a citizen who is unhappy with the actions of his political representative has experienced the cost of measuring and monitoring supplier performance. Outcomes do not always reflect citizens' desires; the political process may supply too many of goods like nuclear arms or too little goods like quality education. As with market analysis, policy analysis must focus on how well the political process internalises costs and benefits to citizens and their political agents so that resources will not be squandered.

In rethinking natural resource and environmental policy, two facts must be recognised. First, *incentives matter to all human behaviour*. No matter how well intended professional resource managers are, incentives affect their behaviour. Like it or not, individuals will undertake more of an activity if the costs of that activity are reduced; this holds as much for bureaucrats as it does for profit-maximising owners of firms. Everyone accepts that managers in the private sector would dump production wastes into a nearby stream if they did not have to pay for the cost of their action. Too often, however, we fail to recognise the same element at work in the political arena. If a politician is not personally accountable for allowing oil development on federal lands or for permitting an agency to dump hazardous wastes into the environment, then we can expect too much development or too much dumping. Moreover, when the beneficiaries of these policies do not have to pay the full cost, they will demand more of each from political representatives.

Second, *information costs are positive in both the private and political sectors*. In a world of scarcity, both private and political resource managers must obtain information about the relative values of alternative uses. When one resource use rivals another, trade-offs must be made. Resource managers can only make these trade-offs based on the information coming to them or on their own values. If they believe lumber is more valuable than wildlife habitat, trees will be cut. Timer managers may know how fast trees grow under certain conditions, but they cannot know what the value of the growth is without incurring some cost in obtaining that information. The lumber market provides information on timber value as a commodity, but information about the value of wildlife habitat and environmental amenities is more costly because those markets are less developed. Private timber managers for International Paper, for example, are being forced to consider wildlife habitat in their timber production decisions because prices tell them that consumers are willing to pay increasingly more for hunting, camping, and recreation. Political managers who "give away" recreational services from political lands lack this price information and have less incentive to react to changing values.

When incentives matter and information is costly, resource management is complicated so that it is not sufficient to rely on good intentions. Even if the superintendent of national parks believes that grizzly bear habitat is more valuable than more campsites, his good intentions will not necessarily yield more grizzly bear habitat. In a political setting where camping interests have more influence over a bureaucrat's budget, his peace and quiet, or his future promotion, intentions will have to override incentives if grizzly bear habitat is to prevail. But if a private resource owner believes that grizzly bear habitat is more valuable and can capitalize on that value, then politics will not matter.

Moreover, if those who demand grizzly habitat are willing to pay more than those who demand campsites, then incentives and information reinforce one another. Management simply cannot be adequately analysed without careful attention to the information and incentives that actors face under alternative institutional arrangements.

Scientific Management or Economics Without Prices

For years economists have tried to use computer modeling techniques to stimulate the market allocation of natural resources. The U.S. Forest Services, for example, developed FORPLAN, a forest stimulation model to specify the necessary conditions for efficient national forest use. The rationale of such models is simply that if the additional or marginal value of one resource use is greater than another, then allocation will be improved if the resource is reallocated from the latter to the former. This form of analysis teaches us that there are many margins for adjustment and that few decisions have all-or-nothing consequences. When water is allocated for fish or irrigation, trade-offs must be made; it is not an either-or decision. Put simply, neither demand nor supply is unresponsive to price changes. If prices rise, then demanders will make marginal adjustments by shifting consumption to the nearest substitutes; suppliers will adjust by substituting among resources and technologies.

The logic of this analysis combined with models and computers that can stimulate resource use can lure policy analysts into believing that the maximisation of resource value is a simple matter. Unfortunately, in this case logic and simplicity are not good guides because they mask the information costs and incentives. Consider the case of multiple use management of the national forests, where the scientific manager is supposed to trade off timber production, wildlife habitat, aesthetic values, water quality, recreation, and other uses to maximise the value of the forest. Because the managers are not supposed to be motivated by profit or self-interest, it is assumed that they will impartially apply economic theory and quantitative methods to accomplish efficient resource allocation. The scientific manager, armed with the economic concepts of marginal analysis, is supposed to be "always analytical.... Always, the economist's reasoning, his analytical framework ... , and his conclusions are exposed forthrightly to the examination and criticism of others. In these ways, *scientific objectivity* is actively sought."[k]

To apply marginal analysis to multiple use, decision makers must attach values to the relevant margins. Scientific management assumes that these values are known and, therefore, that there is an efficient solution. The decision maker must only acquire the "correct" information about resource values in alternative uses and reallocate those resources until marginal equalities hold. Management is simply the process of finding the socially optimal allocation. Thomas Sowell has captured the traditional resource economics perspective on information:

> Given that explicitly articulated knowledge is special and concentrated ... the best conduct of social activities depend upon the special knowledge of the few being used to guide the actions of the many ... Along

k.   ALAN RANDALL, RESOURCE ECONOMICS 36   (1981).

with this has often gone a vision of intellectuals as disinterested advisors . . .[l]

If knowledge of values that must be traded off against one another were "special and concentrated," then scientific management might be possible. But as F.A. Hayek has pointed out,

> the economic problem of society is . . . not merely a problem of how to allocate "given resources"—if "given" is taken to mean given to a single mind which deliberately solves the problem set by these "data." It is rather a problem of how to secure the best use of resources known to any of the members of society, for ends whose relative importance only these individuals know. Or, to put it briefly, it is a problem of utilisation of knowledge not given to anyone in its totality.[m]

The very information and knowledge necessary for trade-offs made using scientific management are subjective and are only revealed through human action.

As analytical tools, economic models focus on the importance of marginal adjustments, but they cannot instruct managers in which trade-offs to make or which values to place on a resource. In the absence of subjective individual evaluations, the marginal solutions derived by sophisticated efficiency maximisation models are unachievable ideals. Unfortunately, these models have been used as guides to tell resource managers how to achieve efficient allocation; in fact, they can only provide a way of thinking about trade-offs. Managers argue that these models have added sophistication and authority to political management efforts, allowing shadow prices (that is, prices that are not real but images of what would exist if there was a market) to be derived and used in lieu of actual market processes. The Forest Services and the Bureau of Land Management, enamored with these models, assume that with sufficient data and large enough computers it is possible to produce wise and efficient management plans. Forest economist Richard Behan stated that the planning acts that guide the Forest Service mandate "with the force of law that forest plans can be rational, comprehensive, and essentially perfect."[n] But no matter how rational or comprehensive they may be, models built on marginal analysis will always be constrained by information requirements.

The market process generates information on the subjective values that humans place on alternative resource use as individuals engage in voluntary trades. The decentralised decisions made in markets are crucial, because "practically every individual has some advantage over all others in that he possesses unique information of which beneficial use might be made, but of which use can be made only if the decisions depending on it are left to him or made only if the decisions depending on it are left to him or are made with his active cooperation." Once we understand that most knowledge is fragmented and dispersed, then "systemic coordination among the many supersedes the special wisdom of the few." Traditional economic analysis has failed to recognise this fundamental point. The information necessary for "efficient"

l. THOMAS SOWELL, A CONFLICT OF VISIONS 46 (1987).

m. Frederich A. Hayek, *The Use of Knowledge in Society*, 35 THE AMERICAN ECONOMIC REVIEW 519–520.

n. Richard W. Behan, *RPA/NFMA—Time to Punt* 79 J. FORESTRY 802 (1981).

resource allocation depends on the knowledge of the special circumstance of time and place.

The idea of scientific management has also misguided public policy because it ignores the incentives of decision makers in the political sector. The economic analysis of markets focuses on incentives in the form of prices that determine the benefits and costs that decision makers face. Market failure is said to result when any benefits are not captured or costs are not borne by decision makers. The existence of these externalities or third-party effects means that either too little of a good is produced in the case of uncaptured benefits or too much in the case of unborne costs. A system of private water allocation, for example, may not provide a sufficient supply of instream flows for wildlife habitat and environmental quality because owners of water cannot easily charge recreationalists and environmentalists who benefit from free-flowing water. And too much pollution exists because firms do not have to pay the full cost of waste disposal, so they "overuse" the air or water as a garbage dump. Such under-or over-protection is often taken as a sufficient condition for taking political control of resource allocation.

There is, however, an asymmetry in the analysis of market and political processes because of a failure to recognise that the *political sector operates by externalising costs*. Consider the reasoning that political agents apply to scientific management. When land is diverted from timber production to wilderness, there is an opportunity cost associated with the reallocation. Private landowners interested in maximising the value of the resource must take this cost into account in the "price" of wilderness. The bureaucratic manager or politician who does not own the land, however, does not face all the opportunity costs of his decisions. He will take the values forgone into account only if the political process make him do so. If we assume that the political process worked perfectly (which is the equivalent of *assuming* that markets work perfectly), then the countervailing powers of the opposing sides would internalise the benefits and costs for the decision maker.

But there is little reason to believe that the political process works perfectly or even tolerably well. Because politicians and bureaucrats are rewarded for responding to political pressure groups, there is no guarantee that the values of unorganised interests will be taken into account *even if* they constitute a majority of the population. For example, most Americans will pay marginally higher prices for petroleum products if oil production is not allowed in the Arctic National Wildlife Refuge. Because this cost to each individual is low and the costs of information and action are high relative to the benefits, each person will remain rationally ignorant; that is, he will not become informed on the issue. But organised groups that favour preserving wildlife habitat in the pristine tundra can gain by stopping drilling in the refuge. To the extent that those who benefit from wildlife preservation do not have to pay the opportunity costs of forgone energy production, they will demand "too much" wildlife habitat. In the absence of a perfect political process, we must depend on good intentions to overpower the special interest incentives built into the imperfect system. This takes a giant leapof faith.

Traditional thinking about natural resource and environmental policy ignores the most basic economic tenet: *incentives matter*. Markets with positive costs of eliminating third-party effects have been compared with a political process where those costs are ignored or assumed to be zero. Consider the approach taken in a leading natural resource economic textbook:

> ... "the government" is a separate agent acting in the social interest when activity by individuals fails to bring about the social optimum ... we discuss some limits of this approach, but it permits us to abstract from the details of the political process.[o]

When we abstract from the details of the political process, we ignore incentives inherent in that process. Daniel Bromley claimed that government agencies are

> politically responsible to the citizenry through the system of ... elections and ministerial direction. However imperfect this may work, the *presumption* must be that the wishes of the full citizenry are more properly catered to than would be the case if all environmental protection were left to the ability to pay by a few members of society given to philanthropy.[p]

But why must we "presume" that the "wishes of the full citizenry are more properly catered to"? And what does "full citizenry" mean? Is there unanimous consent? Does a majority constitute the "full citizenry" when voting turnout is traditionally low? Bromley also charged that "claims for volitional exchange are supported by appeal to a body of economic theory that is not made explicit," but there is little made explicit when we "abstract from the details of the political process" by presuming "that the wishes of the full citizenry are more properly catered to" in the political process.[q]

Because traditional thinking about resource and environmental policy pays little attention to the institutions that structure and provide information and incentives in the political sector, practitioners often seem surprised and puzzled that efficiency implications from their models are ignored in the policy arena. In the private sector, efficiency matters because it influences profits; in the political sector, prices and incentives are often very different. Political resource managers make trade-offs in terms of political currencies measured in terms of special interest support; at best, this unit of account provides imprecise measures of the subjective values of citizens.

The incentive structure in the political sector is complicated because the bottom line depends on the electoral process where votes matter not efficiency. Because voters are rationally ignorant, because benefits can be concentrated and costs diffused, and because individual voters seldom (and probably never) influence the outcome of elections, there is little reason to expect that elections will link political decisions to efficiency in the same way that private ownership does in the market process.

Under private ownership, profits and losses are the measure of how well decision makers are managing. Even where shareholders in a large company have little effect on actual decisions, they can observe stock prices and annual reports as a measure of management's performance. In other words, private ownership gives owners both the information and the incentive to measure performance. In the political sector, however, both information and incentives

o. John M. Hartwick & Nancy D. Olewiler, The Economics of Natural Resource Use 18 (1986).

p. Daniel W. Bromley, Property Rights and the Environment: Natural Resource Policy in Transition 55 (1988).

q. *Id.* at 54.

are lacking. Annual budget figures offer information about overall expenditures and outlays, but it is not clear who is responsible and whether larger budgets are good or bad. Even when responsibility can be determined, there is no easy way for a citizen to "buy and sell shares" in the government. Therefore, citizens remain rationally ignorant about most aspects of political resource allocation and rationally informed about issues that directly affect them. The rewards for political resource managers depend not on maximising net resource values but on providing politically active constituents with what they want with little regard for cost. Although it may not be possible to state precisely what is maximised by politicians and bureaucrats, it is clear that efficiency is not the main goal. If political resource managers were to follow the tenets of traditional natural resource economics, it would have to be because there were honest, sincere people (professional managers) pursuing the public interest.

Anthony Fisher has provided perhaps the best summary of the problem:

We have already abandoned the assumption of a complete set of competitive markets ... But if we now similarly abandon the notion of a perfect planner, it is not clear, in my judgment, that the government will do any better. Apart from the question of the planner's motivation to behave in the way assumed in our models, to allocate resources efficiently, there is the question of his ability to do so.[r]

Without information and incentives, scientific management becomes economics without prices.

Getting the Incentives Right

The constraint on the gains from trade in market processes is that each party to a transaction must measure and monitor the activities of the other. If individuals were self-sufficient, these costs disappear, but they would also forgo the gains from specialisation and trade. Hence, the problem we all face is to trade off the gains from specialisation against the costs of measuring and monitoring the performance of those with whom we interact.

This framework is useful for examining relationships in the political sector where citizens "hire" politicians or bureaucrats to produce certain goods and services. At a minimum, this relationship grants to the government a monopoly on the use of coercion, which enables it to enforce voluntary contracts between individuals. In addition, citizens may assign to the state the role of producing goods for which coercion is necessary because the costs of measuring and monitoring voluntary transactions are prohibitive. For example, if the costs of excluding fishermen from a free-flowing stream are high, then there will be little incentive for the private sector to provide this amenity; market failure is said to result in the under production of these "public goods." By using the coercive power of government to charge all citizens (or at least all fishermen), this problem can be overcome. Unfortunately, this solution raises another problem: How can the citizens be certain that the state is producing the desired bundle of public goods? Indeed, the fundamental dilemma of political economy is: Once the state has the coercive power to do what voluntary (market) action cannot do, how can that power be constrained from being usurped by special interests?

r. Anthony C. Fisher, Resource and Environ-   mental Economics 54 (1981).

At least two variables are important in determining the resolution of this dilemma. First, the complexity of the good in question will have a direct bearing on the ability of a consumer or citizen to measure the performance of suppliers. If lands managed by the political sector produce timber, measuring the board feet of production may be simple; but if those same lands are for "multiple use," then it is much more costly to determine how closely actual results approximate the results desired. Goods such as environmental quality, risk management, soil conservation, national heritage, and wilderness values are all costly to measure.

The second determinant will be the costs of monitoring political agents who provide public goods, and these costs will be directly related to the proximity, both in time and space, of the agent to the citizen. Monitoring the behaviour of a local zoning board is less costly than monitoring the behaviour of the director of the National Park Service. Furthermore, before we had telephones and computers, monitoring agent behaviour was more costly because of the time required for communication. A free press and free access to governmental information reduced these costs. At the same time, however, the multitude of decisions made at various levels of government and the large number of constituents represented by each political agent raised the cost of monitoring.

Because the same kinds of costs exist with market transactions, we must complete the analysis by comparing the measurement and monitoring costs of the political sector with those of the private sector. For all market transactions, both buyers and sellers must incur measurement and monitoring costs. The buyer must consider a product's value in quantity and quality terms and weigh that value against alternative goods. The seller must monitor production and discover mechanisms for making sure buyers cannot enjoy the benefits of the good without paying. For example, a hunter purchasing hunting rights must consider the value of the hunting experience relative to other opportunities. The seller must determine whether it is worth enhancing hunting opportunities and whether nonpaying hunters can avoid paying the fee (that is, trespassing) while still reaping the benefits. If the costs for either buyer or seller are sufficiently high, the potential net gains from trade will be reduced and trades may not take place.

There are three important characteristics of private sector transactions, however, that tend to mitigate these costs. First, measurement costs are greatly reduced in market transactions by prices. Prices convey valuable, condensed information that allows consumers to compare and aggregate inputs and outputs. In the absence of price information that transforms subjective values into an objective measure, comparing values of alternative resource uses is difficult. Because many governmental goods and services are not priced, transaction costs are higher in the political sector.

Prices also allow a measure of efficiency through profits and losses. If a shareholder wants to know how well the management of his farm is performing, he can at least consult the profit-and-loss statement. This is not a perfect measure of performance, but continual losses suggest that actual results differ from those that are desired. This can tell the shareholder that he should consider alternative managers who can produce the product. Compared to the political sector where the output of government is not priced and where agency performance is not measured by the bottom line, profits and losses in the private sector provide concise information with which owners can measure the performance of their agents.

Second, the political and private sectors differ in the degree to which measurement and monitoring costs are borne by those who demand the goods. In the political process, votes ultimately decide who the suppliers will be. In order to make good decisions, voters must gather information about alternative candidates or referenda issues and vote on the basis of that information. If an individual invests a great deal of effort into becoming informed and votes on what is best for society, he does a service for his fellow citizens. If the voter is not well informed and votes for things that will harm the society, then this cost is spread among all voters. In other words, well-informed voters produce a classic public good, and, as with any public good, we can expect voters to under-invest in becoming informed, thus remaining "rationally ignorant." In contrast, consumers in the private sector bear the costs of being informed, but they also reap the benefits of good choices and bear the costs of bad ones. When a landowner hires a forest manager, he will seek information on the manager's ability and he will monitor his performance. If the landowner assumes none of these costs and gets a bad manager, then the owner will bear the costs directly; if he pays the costs and management quality is improved, then the benefits are internalised to the landowner in the form of higher profits. It is the clear assignment of these profits and losses that distinguishes the private from the political sector.

Third, private sector relationships differ from those in the political sector in terms of the cost of choosing alternative suppliers. In the political sector, if a citizen does not believe he is getting from government the goods and services he desires, then he can attempt to sway a majority of the voters and elect new suppliers or he can physically move from one location to another. In either case, the costs of changing suppliers is much higher than in the private sector, where there is greater competition among potential agents. For example, if a local supermarket does not sell what a customer desires, then he has many alternative producers from whom to choose. Even in the more complex case of corporate managers, a stockholder can easily change agents by selling shares in one company and purchasing shares in another. In short, because changing suppliers in the private sector does not require agreement from a majority of the other consumers, change is less costly. This condition imposes a strong competitive discipline. In general information through prices, internalization of costs and benefits from monitoring by individuals, and agent discipline imposed by competition reduce measurement and monitoring costs.

Where market transactions fail to occur for natural resources and environmental amenities, it is usually because the costs of measuring and monitoring resource use are high. For example, suppose a landowner is deciding whether to forgo one type of production to enhance an aesthetic quality. If the aesthetic quality is a beautiful flower garden, a high fence may be sufficient to exclude free riders and capture the full benefits from the product. If the trade-off is between cutting trees and preserving a beautiful mountainside, however, excluding casual sightseers may be far too costly.

The key, therefore, to effective markets in general and free market environmentalism in particular is the establishment of well-specified and transferable property rights. When a conservation group purchases a conservation easement on a parcel of land, the exchange requires that property rights be well defined, enforced, and transferable. The physical attributes of the resources must be specified in a clear and concise manner; they must be measureable. For example, the rectangular survey system allows us to define ownership rights over land and clarifies disputes over ownership. The system may also help us define ownership to the airspace over land, but more questions arise here because of the fluidity of air and the infinite vertical third dimension above the ground. If property rights to resources cannot be defined, then they obviously cannot be exchanged for other property rights.

Property rights also must be defendable. A rectangular survey may define surface rights to land, but conflicts are inevitable if there is no way to defend the boundaries and prevent other incompatible uses. Barbed wire provided an inexpensive way to defend property rights on the western frontier; locks and chains do the same for parked bicycles. But enforcing one's rights to peace and quiet by "fencing out" sound waves may be much more difficult, as will keeping other people's hazardous wastes out of a groundwater supply. Whenever the use of property cannot be monitored or enforced, conflicts are inevitable and trades are impossible.

Finally, property rights must be transferable. In contrast to the costs of measuring and monitoring resource uses, which are mainly determined by the physical nature of the property and technology, the ability to exchange is determined largely by the legal environment. Although well defined and enforced rights allow the owner to enjoy the benefits of using his property, legal restrictions on the sale of that property preclude the potential for gains from trade. Suppose that a group of fishermen values water for fish habitat more highly than farmers value the same water for irrigation. If the fishermen are prohibited from renting or purchasing the water from the farmers, then gains from trade will not be realised and potential wealth will not be created. Moreover, the farmer will have less incentive to leave the water in the stream.

In sum, free market environmentalism presupposes well-specified rights to take actions with respect to specific resources. If those rights cannot be measured, monitored, and marketed, then there is little possibility for exchange. Garbage disposal through the air, for example, is more of a problem than solid waste disposal in the ground because property rights to the Earth's surface are better defined than property rights to the atmosphere. Private ownership of land works quite well for producing timber, but measuring, monitoring, and marketing the land for endangered species habitat requires entrepreneurial imagination.

Imagination is crucial to free market environmentalism, because it is in the areas where property rights are evolving that resource allocation problems occur. Where environmental entrepreneurs can devise ways of marketing environmental values, market incentives can have dramatic results. It is important to recognise that any case of external benefits or costs provides fertile ground for an entrepreneur who can define and enforce property rights. A stream owner who can devise ways of charging fishermen can internalise the benefits and costs and gain an incentive to maintain or improve the quality of his resource. The subdivider who puts covenants on deeds that preserve open space, improve views, and generally harmonize development with the environment establishes property rights to these values and captures the value in higher asset prices.

The property rights approach to natural resources recognises that property rights evolve depending on the benefits and costs associated with defining and enforcing rights. This calculus will depend on such variables as the expected value of the resource in question, the technology for measuring and monitoring property rights, and the legal and moral rules that condition the behaviour of the interacting parties. At any given time, property rights will reflect the perceived benefits and costs of definition and enforcement. To observe actions that are not accounted for in market transactions—that is, for which property rights have not been specified—and call them externalities or market failure ignores the evolutionary nature of property rights. As the perceived costs and benefits of defining and enforcing property rights change, property rights will evolve.

This does not mean that there is no role for government in the definition and enforcement process or that property rights will always take all costs and benefits into account. The costs of establishing property rights are positive and *potentially* can be reduced through governmental institutions, such as courts. Furthermore, because transaction costs are positive, contracts that take costs into account will not always be forthcoming. In the case of water pollution from sources that cannot be identified (with current technology) at low costs, for example, the definition and enforcement of property rights governing water use may be impossible. And excluding non-payers from enjoying a scenic view may be costly enough that a market cannot evolve under current technologies and institutions. In these cases, there is a utilitarian argument for considering government intervention. But there is still no guarantee that the results from political allocation will work very well. If markets produce "too little" clean water because dischargers do not have to pay for its use, then political solutions are equally likely to produce "too much" clean water because those who enjoy the benefits do not pay the cost.

Conclusion

Traditional economic analysis stresses the potential for market failure in the natural resource and environmental arena on the grounds that externalities are pervasive. Free market environmentalism explicitly recognises that this problem arises because it is costly to define and enforce rights in both the private and political sectors. In fact, the symmetry of the externality argument requires that specific attention be paid to politics as the art of diffusing costs and concentrating benefits. Assuming that externality problems in the environment can be solved by turning to the political sector ignores the likelihood that government will externalise costs. Just as pollution externalities can generate too much dirty air, political externalities can generate too much water storage, clear-cutting, wilderness, or water quality.

Free market environmentalism emphasises the importance of market processes in determining optimal amounts of resource use. Only when rights are well-defined, enforced, and transferable will self-interested individuals confront the trade-offs inherent to a world of scarcity. As entrepreneurs move to fill profit niches, prices will reflect the values we place on resources and the environment. Mistakes will be made, but in the process a niche will be opened and profit opportunities will attract resource managers with a better idea. Remember that even externalities offer profit niches to the environmental entrepreneur who can define and enforce property rights to the unowned resource and charge the free-riding users. In cases where definition and enforcement costs are insurmountable, political solutions may be called for. Unfortunately, however, those kinds of solutions often become entrenched and stand in the way of innovative market processes that promote fiscal responsibility, efficient resource use, and individual freedom.

Discussion Notes/Questions

1. Is preserving the environment an ethical or an economic issue?

2. Does the economic approach to environmental issues imply that economists are anti-environment?

3. If international property rights solutions are impractical today, does this mean that they are impossible forever?

4. Does the market approach to environmental issues imply that there is no role for government?

5. For additional pertinent reading, see Eco–Sanity: A Common–Sense Guide to Environmentalism (J.L. Bast et. al., eds., 1994); W. Beckerman, Pricing for Pollution: An Analysis of Market Pricing and Government Regulation in Environmental Consumption and Policy (1990); D. Bromley, Environment and Economy: Property Rights and Public Policy (1991); P. Hoeller AD & J. Nicolaisen, A Survey of Studies of the Cost of Reducing Greenhouse Gas Emissions (Working Paper No. 89 OECD, 1990); M.S. Greve & F.E. Smith Jr, Environmental Politics: Public Costs Private Rewards (1992); S.E. Landsburg, The Armchair Economist, Economics and Everyday Life (1993); L. Lave, *Greenhouse Scenarios to Inform Decision Makers, in* The State of Humanity (J. Simon ed., 1995); D. Pearce & R. Turner, Packaging Waste and the Polluter Pays Principle: A Taxation Solution (1992); R. Turner, Environmental Policy: An Economic Approach to the Polluter Pays Principle (1992).

Herman Daly, *Elements of Environmental Macroeconomics,* *in* Ecological Economics: The Science and Management of Sustainability 32, 38–40 (R. Costanza ed., 1991).

Cowboy, Spaceman, or Bull in the China Shop?

If one starts from the vision of the economic process as an open subsystem of a closed finite total system, then the question of how big the subsystem should be relative to the total system is hard to avoid. How then have we managed to avoid it? In two ways: first, by viewing the economic subsystem as infinitesimally small relative to the total system, so that scale becomes irrelevant because it is negligible; second, by viewing the economy as coextensive with the total system. If the economy includes everything, then the issue of scale relative to a total system simply does not arise. These polar extremes correspond to Boulding's colorful distinction between the "cowboy economy" and the "spaceman economy." The cowboy of the infinite plains lives off of a linear throughput from source to sink, with no need to recycle anything. The spaceman in a small capsule lives off of tight material cycles and immediate feedbacks, all under total control subservient to his needs. For the cowboy, scale is negligible; for the spaceman, scale is total. There is no material environment relative to which scale must be determined; there is no ecosystem, only economy. In each of these polar cases, the only problem is allocation. Scale is irrelevant.

It is only in the middle ground between cowboy and the spaceman that the issue of scale does not get conflated with allocation. But, as Boulding realized, the middle ground happens to be where we are. Between the cowboy and the spaceman economies is a whole range of larger and smaller "bull-in-the-china-shop economies" where scale is a major concern. We are not cowboys because the existing scale of the economy is far from negligible compared to the environment. But neither are we spacemen, because most of the matter-energy transformations of the ecosystem are not subject to human control either by prices or by central planning. In a finite system subject to the conservation of mass, the more that is brought under our economic control, the less remains under the spontaneous control of nature. As our exactions from and insertions back into the ecosystem increase in scale, the qualitative change induced in the ecosystem must also increase, for two reasons. The first is the law of thermodynamics (conservation of matter-energy). The taking of matter and energy out of the ecosystem must disrupt the functioning of that system even if nothing is done to the matter and energy so removed. Its mere absence must have an effect. Likewise, the mere insertion of matter and energy into an ecosystem must disrupt the system into which it is newly added. This must be the case even without appealing to any qualitative degradation of the matter and energy thus relocated. The second reason is the second law of thermodynamics which guarantees that the matter-energy exacted is qualitatively different from the matter-energy inserted. Low-entropy raw materials are taken out, high-entropy wastes are returned. This qualitative degradation of the matter-energy throughout, along with the purely quantitative dislocation of the same, induces changes in the ecosystem which to us are surprising and novel because our information and control system (prices) assumes nonscarcity (nondisruptability) of environmental source and sink functions. Economic calculation is about to be overwhelmed by novel, uncertain and surprising feedbacks from an ecosystem that is excessively stressed by having to support too large an economic subsystem.

How big should the subsystem be relative to the total ecosystem? Certainly this, the question of optimal scale, is the big question for environmental macroeconomics. But since it is such a difficult question, and since we cannot go back to the cowboy economy, we have acquired a tendency to want to jump all the way to the spaceman economy and take total control of the spaceship earth. The September 1989 special issue of *Scientific American* entitled "Managing Planet Earth" is representative of this thrust. But, as environmentalist David Orr points out, God, Gaia or Evolution was doing a nice job of managing the earth until the scale of the human population, economy and technology got out of control. Planetary management implies that it is the planet that is at fault, not human numbers, greed, arrogance, ignorance, stupidity, and evil. We need to manage ourselves more than the planet and our self-management should be, in Orr's words, "more akin to child-proofing a day-care centre than to piloting spaceship earth." The way to child-proof a room is to build the optimal scale playpen within which the child is both free and protected from the excesses of its own freedom. It can enjoy the light and warmth provided by electrical circuits beyond its ken, without running the risk of shorting out those circuits, or itself, by experimenting with the "planetary management technique" of teething on a lamp cord.

Our manifest inability to centrally plan economies should inspire more humility among the planetary managers who would centrally plan the ecosystem. Humility should argue for the strategy of minimizing the need for planetary management by keeping the human scale sufficiently low so as not to disrupt the automatic functioning of our life support systems, thereby forcing them into the domain of human management. Those who want to take advantage of the "invisible hand" of self-managing ecosystems have to recognize that the invisible hand of the market, while wonderful for allocation, is unable to set limits to the scale of the macroeconomy. Our limited managerial capacities should be devoted to institutionalizing an economic Plimsoll line that limits the macroeconomy to a scale such that the invisible hand can function in both domains to the maximum extent. It is ironic that many free marketeers, by opposing any limit to the scale of the market economy (and therefore to the increase in externalities), are making more and more inevitable the very central planning that they oppose. Even worse is their celebration of the increase in GNP that results as formerly free goods become scarce and receive a price. For allocation it is necessary that newly scarce goods not continue to have a zero price—no one disputes that. The issue is that, for all we know, we might have been better off to remain at the smaller scale at which the newly scarce goods were free and their proper allocative price was still zero. The increase in measured national income and wealth resulting as formerly free goods are turned into scarce goods is more an index of cost than of benefit, as was recognized by the classical economist Lauderdale back in 1819.[20]

Discussion Notes/Questions

1. Given that human society is essentially organized by economics, need we consider how it fits within a wider framework which is less directly relevant?

2. Should the dividing line between human activities and the environment be consciously set? Are economists best placed to do that?

3. Is the setting of limits irreconcilable with free market policies?

4. How do we know where the boundaries of the economy are?

5. For additional pertinent reading, see: H. Daly, Steady–State Economics: The Economics of Biophysical Equilibrium (1977); H. Daly & J. Cobb, For the Common Good: Redirecting the Economy Toward Community, The Environment, and a Sustainable Future (1989).

3. ETHICS

Martin Holdgate, From Care to Action: Making a Sustainable World 120–125 (1996).

The ethic of care for the environment

People do what they believe is right, advantageous, necessary or unavoidable.... [W]e are all guided by a vision, and one problem of today's world is

20. James M. Lauderdale, An Inquiry into the Nature and Origin of Public Wealth and into the Means and Causes of its Increase (1819).

that the visions are often blurred, while expediency has become stronger than principle in many societies. As we seek practical action, we have to look again at the principles that should guide it.

The heart of the message of *Caring for the Earth* is that development has to be people-centered and conservation-based. Conservation is a social policy with care for nature, and the sustainable use of natural resources as its objective. We need development that provides a real improvement in the quality of human life and at the same time conserves the vitality and diversity of the Earth. We shall only get it—we shall only get the kind of community action we need, and the kind of strategies we need—if individuals are convinced and move forward together.

For this very reason *Caring for the Earth* begins with the ethical principles for a sustainable society. To quote some key sentences:

> Living sustainably depends on accepting a duty to seek harmony with other people and with nature. The guiding rules are that people must share with each other and care for the Earth. Humanity must take no more from nature than nature can replenish. This in turn means adopting life-styles and development paths that respect and work within nature's limits.

One founding principle provides the base for all the others. It is:

Respect and Care for the Community of Life

> This principle reflects the duty of care for other people and other forms of life, now and in the future. It means that development should not be at the expense of other groups or later generations. We should aim to share fairly the benefits and costs of resource use and environmental conservation among different communities and interest groups, among people who are poor and those who are affluent, and between our generation and those who will come after us.

> All life on earth is part of one great interdependent system, which influences and depends on the non-living components of the planet— rocks, soils, waters and air. Disturbing one part of this biosphere can affect the whole. Just as human societies are interdependent and future generations are affected by our present actions, so the world of nature is increasingly dominated by our behaviour. It is a matter of ethics as well as practicality to manage development so that it does not threaten the survival of other species or eliminate their habitats. While our survival depends on the use of other species, we need not, and should not, use them cruelly or wastefully.

The question is how we can change attitudes so that this principle is accepted at all levels of society, and is translated into personal, social and national policy.

The environmental ethic is founded on a belief in people as a creative force, and in the value of every human individual and each human society.

> An ethic is important because what people do depends on what they believe. Widely shared beliefs are often more powerful than government edicts. The transition to sustainable societies will demand changes in how

people perceive each other, other life and the Earth; how they evaluate their needs and priorities; and how they behave.

We need to re-state and win support for the ethic of living sustainably because:

- it is morally right;

- without it the human future is in jeopardy; poverty, strife and tragedy will increase;

- individual actions are, perhaps for the first time, combining to have global effects;

- no major society yet lives according to a value system that cares properly for the future of human communities and other life on earth.

Developing this theme, *Caring for the Earth* emphasizes the need for support from the religious community, because they have spoken for centuries about the individual's duty of care for fellow humans, and of reverence for divine creation. It equally emphasizes the need for support from secular groups concerned with the principles that should govern relationships among people, and with nature. It points out that an ethic defines both rights and responsibilities. And it calls for a series of actions, first to develop the world ethic for living sustainably, second to promote it at national level, third to implement it through action in all sectors of society and finally to establish a world organization to monitor implementation of the world ethic and to prevent and combat serious breaches in its observation. ...The needs were debated at the IUCN General Assembly in Buenos Aires.

Developing the ethic

Environmental ethics is a relatively new subject despite having its origins in classical Greek thought, and no doubt thinking of similar antiquity in other cultures. In recent attempts to address the fundamental basis for social action, the ethical approach has begun with an analysis of the factors that produce attitudes—and ethics has been treated, according to Professor RJ (Sam) Berry, 'not as a branch of academic philosophy but in the fundamental sense of expression of moral understanding, usually in the form of guidelines or rules of conduct, involving evaluations of value or worth.'

Professor Ron Engel, Chair of the IUCN Working Group on Ethics, leading the discussion in Buenos Aires, stressed the need to find a middle way between a universalism which is culturally imperialistic and a relativism which denies any universally shared values and principles. He commented that:

> Over the course of the past several decades there have been many calls for a world ethic that will bring into one common discourse and practice our duties to one another and to the earth, Some call it a 'global ethic', others an 'earth ethic', others an 'ethic for survival', others an 'ethic of living together worldwide', and others an 'ethic of global solidarity'.

Ethics is not something imposed by one group, class or profession on others.

> In fact, it is precisely the opposite. It is the one activity that most self-evidently makes us equals. Most simply put, ethics is the ability to

distinguish good and evil, right and wrong, in our relationships to one another, and in our relationships to all of life. Thus we are all ethicists.

But ethics is not only our inherent birthright: it is also embedded in culture; indeed it is primarily by means of culture that moral values are transmitted, criticized and transformed. Ethics are taught, thought about, practised, reformed by means of religions, by means of national and local traditions, by means of family life and educational institutions, by means of art, ritual and sacred places, by means of law, philosophy, politics and also, as many would hold, by the sciences.

Chatsumarn Kabilsingh of Thammasat University, Thailand, discussed the elements of a sustainable world ethic from a Buddhist perspective. Recognizing the deterioration in the world environment, he had a simple and clear diagnosis:

> Governments at national and international levels are trying very hard to cope with all these impossible crises. More often, they try to make some sincere amendment at the bottom line, and not at the root cause of it. Surprisingly enough, the cause of all these troubles are here within our hearts, and not to be sought outside.

> Let us try to understand the basic and simple truth of man (and woman). We consist mainly of two parts—mind (or spirit) and body. It is an utter necessity that mind must be the master to control and order the physical body. The crucial point is—one must have a trained and righteous mind so that the person can direct the body in the right direction. This is the basis for global ethics.

> People with righteous minds must be peaceful within themselves as individuals and they must be peaceful with the world outside. But how can they remain peaceful when the world is exploited to the point of threatening humanity's own survival?

Buddhists (like followers of many other faiths) emphasize that humanity is part of nature, and when nature is exploited or harmed, so are people. We do not stand apart or above, and attempts to conquer nature are vain. Buddhists do not believe that the world is a creation from the mind of God, but the consequence of certain fundamental laws, in whose unfolding human beings originated as divine, spiritual entities that came down to the world, were attracted by it, and became a part of it. As such, their conduct can significantly affect the courses of nature. When people are righteous, nature itself runs aright: when people are greedy and destructive, whether through ignorance or deliberate choice, things go wrong.

This contrasts, of course, with the Christian, Judaic and Islamic view that the world of nature and all living things, including humanity, are created beings: the works of God. Clever Tabaziba of Zambia set out this perspective in Buenos Aires when he said:

> The divine presence of the spirit in creation binds us as human beings together with all created life. We are accountable before God in and to the community of life, an accountability which has been imaged in various ways (as servants, stewards and trustees, as tillers and keepers, as carers for creation, as nurturers, as co-workers). This calls for attitudes of compassion and humility, respect and reverence. Creation protests its

treatment by human beings. It groans and travails in all its parts. Ecological equilibrium has been severely broken through misinterpretation of our faith.

The need for a spiritual rebirth has been emphasized by writers and thinkers outside orthodox religion, including Dag Hammarskjold and Andre Malraux. Looking through the statements of essential belief in 14 different religions, summarized by their adherents in the *Source Book for the Community of Religions* published in 1993, what stands out is that in all there is an awareness of a spiritual being who stands above and beyond the world (and is usually seen as its creator), an affirmation of the spiritual nature of people and of their importance to the creative being, and a strong emphasis on our responsibility to care for one another and for the world. In contrast to modern secular statements which emphasize human 'rights', religions emphasize duties—to worship, to help others, to be of service to all living beings, to pursue peace. Most recognize the need for change in a world where self-seeking has become dominant, but many also emphasize that change is easy—if it is led by the spirit....

All concur in the belief that there is integrity, unity, in the creation and that the establishment of justice, peace, and harmony between humanity and the rest of creation is an essential goal for the world. As Pope John Paul II has put it 'there is only one community, and it consists of all peoples ...Men turn to various religions to solve mysteries of the human condition which today as in earlier times burden people's hearts.' This leads to the practical conclusion that any environmental ethic must tackle the linked themes of unity and diversity. We are global citizens. We inhabit a shared Earth, and an increasingly interdependent world civilization, and if it is to survive that civilization must be guided by shared values. Moreover, there are no global values that are not local values: the foundation for global agreements and the basis for their implementation lie alike in attitudes and ethical approaches in many places and cultures. Each person's ethic will be guided by each person's deeper beliefs.

The environmental ethic we need is universal but diverse. It should draw on various faiths, principles and forms of expression in a mutually creative way. It isn't that 'anything goes'—but that the diverse inputs should come together to build a whole that is greater and richer than the sum of the parts. Translated to the secular world, it should lead to equity in law. This was emphasised by Lothar Gundling of the IUCN Environmental Law Centre in Bonn, who commented that: 'equity is a basic principle of any normative order. As such, equity is not a new subject in law. It is often linked to the common law legal system where it exists to supplement established common law rights and duties ...In essence the idea of equity is universal.'

Summing up the discussions in Buenos Aires, Nigel Dower and Richard Tarasofsky concluded that:

a world ethic may mean one or more of the following three things:

a)an ethic whose **content** is global: that is, one that incorporates specific principles, values and rules that are to be accepted by and applicable to people generally throughout the world;

b)an ethic that specifies the **scope or domain** of obligation and responsibility as worldwide: that is, a person accepting it accepts some responsibility to promote or protect what is of value anywhere in the world, or takes the state of the world as a whole as an object of practical concern;

c)an ethic which is fairly generally, if not universally, accepted by people throughout the world.

Dower and Tarasofsky emphasized that:

it is important to link global obligation with global responsibility. Whatever may have been the case in the past, the idea of responsibility needs now to be closely linked to patterns of causality flowing from our acts, and must therefore take into account the effects of our actions, individually and collectively, outside our country, outside human domain, and beyond the present time.

Other key conclusions were:

● the search for a world ethic will fail if the test is universal acceptance: even general acceptance is unlikely at present—'What one can do is try to build a world ethic on the basis of consensus', recognizing that there is a long way to go;

● the acceptance of a world ethic will not eliminate conflicts in many particular situations. Even where people accept the same guiding principles, there will be debate over the reliability and meaning of stated facts, and over the probability of different outcomes;

● ethical obligation depends on a sense of contract: a sense of obligation by the human individual to others and to the natural world;

● it is important to develop and publicize a clear statement of principles or premises upon which global and national action is to be based;

● these principles must represent a convergence of ideas involving the whole nature, properties and management of the Earth;

● the principles must describe responsibilities rather than define rights.

Policy based on, and expressing, the ethic needs to express a global sense of obligation and responsibility, a commitment to care for the Earth, and a strong linked commitment to social justice both between groups of people alive today and between generations.

Timothy N. Jenkins, *Economics and the Environment:*
***A Case of Ethical Neglect,* 26 Ecological Econ. 151,**
153, 159–62 (1998).

The ethical dimension

The conventional picture of development treats science, values and resources as exogenous inputs into a system of technological and social organisation. Since the organisation and efficiency of resource use improve over time, development is linear and progressive. An ecologically more realistic view, however, would treat nothing as exogenous: values and knowledge, as well as social organisation and technology, would be seen as subsystems co-evolving with, and influencing, each other. Development could then be defined as a qualitative as well as quantitative process which raises living standards in a manner which does not sacrifice the social and ecological balance achieved over centuries.

This suggests that it is inadequate to address ecological and social problems by relying entirely on pragmatic utilitarian moral attitudes in combination with scientific understanding of natural systems. Some form of 'environmental reverence' is also required which requires a metaphysical grounding.

* * *

Ethical escape from the developmental dilemma

One solution might be the development of a new international ecologist ethic for modern life which draws upon traditions in which an ecological conscience exists. An important element of such an ethic would be to recognise the drawbacks of the Western heritage. Traces of it are to be found in the emerging concept of 'ecodevelopment' (promoted by the UN) which involves the formal incorporation of environmental awareness and protection into economic decision-making (Williams, 1994). Initiatives such as the Rio Summit are also in this vein. Ironically, the main input would be modern science: the Newtonian/Cartesian/Comtist view that humans are divinely appointed to run an objective, inert and external natural world is now replaced in scientific theory by an appreciation of evolution, organicism, and interactive ecological conditions. Much of the current environmental crisis is attributable to the inconsistency between the atomistic/mechanistic image of nature derived from Greek traditions and the holistic/organic reality disclosed by modern ecology and physical science.

* * *

[I]n this vein, there is a clear postmodern re-emergence of a Leopoldian 'land ethic' in the West, which is slowly (and in some areas not so slowly) changing public policy and popular culture. Such an ethic is premised on the idea that an individual is a member of an interdependent community, with all that this implies with regard to social and antisocial conduct, and that the community's boundaries are extendible to include 'land' in its broadest sense (i.e. the natural world). Although there are dangers that such a 'bottom up' movement could become aberrant, these trends are encouraging even if their main impact so far has been confined to superficial forms of resource conservation and improvement.

The growth of this postmodern land ethic has been aided by an appreciation of non-Western traditional cultures by Westerners for which the predominant culture of materialism is unsatisfactory, and by inputs from non-Westerners concerned at the indiscriminate Westernisation of their own societies. The argument here is not that the arising ethic should necessarily be grounded in, or derived from, any non-Western ethic, Chinese or otherwise. This would be unrealistic for the same reason as the resurrection of lost traditions is infeasible. Ethical traditions are embedded in particular spatial and temporal circumstances and are unlikely to flourish where circumstances change (the lack of resistance to Westernisation noted in the case of China and elsewhere is a case in point) or when dis-embedded from the circumstances within which they arose. Rather, the new ethic stands a good chance of taking root in widely differing environmental, cultural and economic circumstances. It is based on scientific and philosophical developments and on an appreciation of the concordance of such developments with ideas already extant in a variety of cultural traditions. It also has the advantage that scientific thinking has already penetrated widely into non-Western belief systems. This optimism need not be dented by Tuan's concern about discrepancy between ideals and past behaviour: if a new ethic passes the twin tests of philosophical acceptability and practical effectiveness in the West, then its efficacy elsewhere is likely.

In time, unsustainable Western lifestyles may be modified by this post-modern land ethic, as evolutionary processes ensure selection and survival of cognitive cultures which best map ecological exigencies. A new benign postmodernism may then follow the malign modernist model into the policy-making of both 'developed' and 'developing' countries, and we should not underestimate how quickly moral attitudes can change. However, in the modern technological era where environmentally destructive power is easily acquired, this is dependent on poor countries first reaching an acceptable threshold level of material prosperity. It is ironic that the recognition of agrosystemic and environmental problems in the West has coincided in China with the embrace of unsustainable farming practices such as declining use of organic recycling, disappearance of complex crop rotations, increasing use of synthetic fertilisers and pesticides, and the use of ever deeper aquifers for irrigation water.

* * *

In arguing for a postmodern land ethic, we assume, that environmental problems are a moral, rather than an institutional issue and that their solution lies in changing personal moral values rather than in institutional action. This view contrasts importantly with reliance on institutional change in that it requires personal confrontation with the specific results of our daily activities on the environment, but it conforms with the current political vogue for individual responsibility. It is therefore necessary to set out in general terms the philosophical and practical directions which a postmodern land ethic will have to take to be effective.

On the philosophical level, its main objective should be to combat the current promotion of irresponsible technological civilisation inspired by an obsolete worldview by seeking to increase ecological literacy and to remove obstacles to human affinity with nature through a thorough programme of education and information. Such a programme should seek to dispel misrepresentations of the world which lead to harmful human interventions, particularly those misrepresentations apparent in mainstream science and economics which represent the world as inert, mechanical and purposeless. It would also recognise the persistent fallacy (originally derived from Locke) of attempting to defy the entropy law through the ontological substitution of money for low-entropy resources in order to portray the material accumulation process as potentially limitless. While, in principle, economic actions can be ethically evaluated under existing individualistic, utilitarian and anthropocentric worldviews, a postmodern land ethic can provide a more suitable evaluation framework which goes beyond effects on people and even covers effects on natural phenomena such as pests which may conventionally be given zero or negative values.

On the practical level, such an ethic should set up a moral challenge to the legitimacy of current economic arrangements and undermine the currently dominant paradigm of "development", with its structures of increasing material possession and consumption, dependence, technology transfer, and "catching up". It is important to recognise that "well-being" does not keep pace with material accumulation, and that improvements in living standards are not simply a unidimensional quantitative growth process. An alternative multidimensional qualitative view of progress would emphasise the inalienable internal goods of self-cultivation and respect diversity, self-reliance, continuity and sustainability. The shift from quantitative to qualitative thinking itself dramatically reduces the "development gap" and introduces doubt about progress defined in materialistic terms. For example, the GDP per capita of industrial countries is more than six times higher than that of "developing" countries, yet their "human development index" is only 1.6 times higher Vol. 336 No. 7929 THE ECONOMIST (1995); and US GDP per capita has more than doubled since 1950, yet its "genuine progress indicator" has fallen by one quarter Vol. 336 No. 7933 THE ECONOMIST (1995).

* * *

Conclusion

Without an appropriate ethical base, attempts to regulate environmental interventions using the law and using markets are insufficient and ineffective tools for achieving sustainability since they are based on egotistical self-interest and fear of punishment. The real task of those concerned to promote human progress is to cultivate a spirit of affirmation for the natural world from which an ethical obligation for safeguarding the natural environment will inevitably flow. A relational view of the self 'transforms egoism to environmentalism', and spiritual perspective is necessary if nature is to become value-laden rather than simply fact.

Discussion Notes/Questions

1. What is meant by the term "ethics" in the context in which it is being discussed?

2. How can an ethical approach be reconciled with an economic approach?

3. What are our fundamental beliefs as a society? Do we have any? Is there a postmodern land ethic?

4. Is it valid to assume that environmental problems are a moral rather than institutional issue, as Jenkins does?

5. Does religious history assist the analysis?

6. For additional reading, see R. Attfield, *Environmental Ethics and Intergenerational Equity*, 41 Inquiry 207 (1998); D. Botkin, Discordant Harmonies (1990); A. De–Shalit, Why Posterity Matters: Environmental Policies and Future Generations (1995); J.R. des Jardins, Environmental Ethics (1993); R. Goldstein, *Green Wood in the Bundle of Sticks: Fitting Environmental Ethics and Ecology into Real Property Law*, 25 B.C. Envtl. Aff. L. Rev. 347 (1998); O. Johansson–Stenman, *The Importance of Ethics in Environmental Economics with a Focus on*

Existence Values, 11 Envtl. & Res. Econ. 429 (1998); B. Norton & B. Hannon, *Environmental Values: A Place–Based Approach* 19 Envtl. Ethics 227 (1997); J.Rachels, The Elements of Moral Philosophy (1990); C. D. Stone, The Gnat Is Older Than Man—Global Environment and Human Agenda (1993); G. W. Trompf, *Ethics and Environmental Conservation*, 24 Envtl. Conservation 301 (1997); D. Van De Veer & C. Pierce, People, Penguins and Plastic Trees (1986).

4. SOCIAL ECOLOGY

John Clark, *What Is Social Ecology?*, in RENEWING THE EARTH: THE PROMISE OF SOCIAL ECOLOGY 5, 5–11 (John Clark ed., 1990).

Social Ecology is a comprehensive holistic conception of the self, society, and nature. It is, indeed, the first ecological philosophy to present a developed approach to all the central issues of theory and practice. It sets out from the basic ecological principle of organic *unity in diversity*, affirming that the good of the whole can be realized only through the rich individuality and complex interrelationship of the parts. And it applies this fundamental insight to all realms of experience.

In affirming such a holistic approach, Social Ecology rejects the dualism that has plagued Western civilization since its beginnings. A dualism that sets spirit against matter, soul against body, humanity against nature, subjectivity against objectivity, and reason against feelings. A dualism that is intimately related to the social divisions that are so central to the history of civilization: ruler versus ruled, rich versus poor, urban versus rural, "civilized" versus "savage", male versus female, in short, the dominant versus the dominated.

In opposition to this dualism, Social Ecology proposes a principle of *ecological wholeness*, which Bookchin defines as "a dynamic unity of diversity" in which "balance and harmony are achieved by ever-changing differentiation." As a result, "stability is a function not of simplicity and homogeneity but of complexity and variety."[21] The entire course of evolution is seen as a process aiming at increasing this diversification. Thus, there is an ever increasing richness of diversity, not only in the sense of biological variety and interrelatedness, but also in the sense of richness of *value*.

Accordingly, evolution should be looked upon as a process of planetary development having *directiveness*, and involving the progressive *unfolding of potentiality*.

* * *

[T]he entire process of development of life and mind is a movement toward the attainment of value. For Bookchin, "the universe bears witness to an ever striving, developing—not merely moving—substance, whose most dynamic and creative attribute is its increasing capacity for self-organization into increasingly complex forms."[22] Life and mind are not random, chance occurrences in a dead and unconscious universe. Rather, there is a tendency within substance to produce life, consciousness, and self-consciousness. A

---

21. MURRAY BOOKCHIN, THE ECOLOGY OF FREE-DOM: THE EMERGENCE AND DISSOLUTION OF HIERARCHY 24 (1981).

22. Murray Bookchin, *Toward a Philosophy of Nature, in* DEEP ECOLOGY 229 (Michael Tobias ed., 1984).

tendency to differentiate itself, to issue in diversity and complexity in all realms of being.

* * *

According to Social Ecology, this holistic, developmental understanding of organic systems and their evolution has enormous importance for ethics and politics. Indeed, only if the place of humanity in nature and natural processes is understood can we adequately judge questions of value. We then see our own experience of valuing and seeking the good as part of the vast process of the emergence and development of value in nature. Value is achieved in the course of each being, according to its particular nature, attaining its good to the greatest degree possible.

Yet, from an ecological point of view, the realization of the planetary good is not merely the sum of all the particular good attained by all beings. For the biosphere is a *whole* of which these beings are parts, and a *community* of which they are members. The common planetary good can therefore be conceptualized only in a non-reductionist, *holistic* manner. The essential place of humanity in the attainment of this good cannot be underestimated. This is true in large part because of the technical capacity of humanity either to aid evolutionary development through judicious and restrained cooperation with nature or to put an end to the process through nuclear annihilation or degradation of the biosphere. But, in a more fundamental sense, humanity's role in nature results from the fact that our species constitutes the most richly developed realm of being to emerge thus far in the earth's evolutionary self-realization.

To say this is not to adopt an *anthropocentrism* that makes humanity the final or even the only end of nature. Neither is it a *biocentrism* that would ignore evolutionary developments for the sake of biological egalitarianism. Rather, it is *ecocentric* in the sense that it requires humanity to situate its good within the larger context of the *planetary good*, and to transform reason into *planetary reason*. As Bookchin states, "the greatest single role" of an ecological ethic is "to help us distinguish which of our actions serve the thrust of natural evolution and which of them impede it."[23]

Human society must therefore transform itself, and renew itself, using ecological wisdom, so that it becomes a social ecological system within a natural ecological system. It must be seen as "an ecosystem based on unity-in-diversity, spontaneity, and non-hierarchical relationships."[24] This demands that a new *ecological sensibility* pervade all aspects of our social existence. Such a sensibility perceives "the balance and integrity of the biosphere as an end in itself."[25] It also recognizes the intrinsic goodness of the self-realization process (the Tao or "way") of all the diverse beings that share our planetary ecocommunity.

As the mentality of non-domination replaces the prevailing hierarchical outlook, there emerges "a new animism that respects the other for its own sake and responds *actively* in the form of a creative, loving, and supportive

---

23. *Supra* note 21, at 342.   **25.** *Id.* at 59.

24. Murray Bookchin, Toward an Ecological Society 69 (1980).

symbiosis.''[26] The mutualism found throughout nature thereby attains its highest development in a mutualistic system of values and perceptions. This new sensibility will give direction to the process of regeneration that must take place at all levels, from nature, to the community, to the individual person.

The renewal of nature is perhaps the most self-evident task today for an ecological movement. According to Social Ecology, it is necessary to create ecocommunities and eco-technologies that can restore the balance between humanity and nature, and reverse the process of degradation of the biosphere. An ecological community will not attempt to dominate the surrounding environment, but rather will be a carefully integrated part of its ecosystem. Rather than continuing the system of obsessive, uncontrolled production and consumption, the community will practice true *economy*, the careful attending to and application of "the rules of the household". The extent to which humans can have a desirable impact on the ecosystem can be decided only through careful analysis of our abilities to act on behalf of nature, and of the detrimental effects of our disturbances of natural balances.

A pre-condition for the achievement of harmony with nature is the attainment of harmony and balance within society itself. Mechanistic organization based on political and economic power must be replaced by an organic community regulated through common ecological values and a commitment to a common life. The post-scarcity society advocated by Bookchin does not transcend the "realm of necessity" through vastly increased production and consumption of commodities. Nor by a more "equitable" distribution of existing material goods to "the masses". A society does not fight addiction to harmful substances by even-handedly administering increased doses to each citizen.

Rather, the ecocommunity will achieve abundance through a critical analysis and reshaping of its system of needs. The development of an ecological sensibility will create an awareness of the importance of cultural and spiritual richness: that which comes from close human relationships, from aesthetic enjoyment, from the unfolding of diverse human potentialities, from spontaneity, play, and all activities liberated from the deadening hand of productive and consumptive rationality. The ecocommunity will seek greater simplicity, and reject the mystifying and dehumanizing economic, technical, and political systems that prevail in mass society. It will highly value the complexity of developed personality, of subtle skills, of disciplined intelligence, of liberated imagination. In short, the greatest wealth of an ecocommunity will consist in the flowering of a richly elaborated libertarian and community culture.

The social forms that will emerge from such a culture will themselves embody the ecological ideal of unity-in-diversity. A fundamental unit will be the commune, a closely knit, small community based on love, friendship, shared values, and commitment to a common life. It is founded on the most intimate "kinship", whether or not this kinship is also biological. In addition, cooperative institutions in all areas of social life will be formed: mutualistic associations for child care and education, for production and distribution, for cultural creation, for play and enjoyment, for reflection and spiritual renewal.

---

26. *Supra* note 21, at 268.

Organizations will be based not on the demands of *power*, but rather on the *self-realization of persons* as free social beings.

Such a transformation requires vast changes in our conception of "the political". As Bookchin states it, "society, conceived of as a diversified and self-developing ecosystem based on complementarity, poses a very distinct notion of politics" that stresses "human scale, decentralization, non-hierarchy, communitarianism, and face-to-face interaction between citizens."[27] The ideal method of decision-making is consensus, which requires an outcome based on a full recognition of the worth and competence of all involved in the process. But to the extent that this is impossible, the most participatory forms of democracy are necessary, if the values of freedom and community are to be synthesized in practice. Ultimate authority must be retained at the level of the local community—the level of lived experience.

Discussion Notes/Questions

1. Social ecology applies ecological understandings to human society. Does it make sense to use a framework from the natural world to analyze the artificiality of human civilization?

2. Social ecology claims to be attuned to history yet advocates a return to an organic society. Does this represent a naive appreciation of historical developments? Are we being asked to take giant steps back in time? Does social ecology belong in another (earlier) era?

3. Clark talks of the deadening hand of productive and consumptive rationality. Is social ecology more or less value-imbued than the economic approach? How can competing values be evaluated and/or reconciled?

4. Social ecologists talk of the ecosystem evolving as a whole. What about the role of human beings in determining that evolution? If human beings are having a disproportionate impact, can they be considered as merely part of an evolving ecosystem?

5. For additional pertinent reading, see: J. M. Boles, *James Rorty's Social Ecology: Technology, Culture, and the Economic Base of an Environmentally Sustainable Society* 11 Org. & Envt. 155 (1998); M. Bookchin, The Modern Crisis (1986); ___, Remaking Society (1989); J. Clark, *Marx's Inorganic Body*, 11 Envtl. Ethics 243 (1989); R. Eckersley, *Divining Evolution: The Ecological Ethics of Murray Bookchin*, 11 Envtl. Ethics 99 (1989); R. Hood, *Rorty and Postmodern Environmental Ethics* 183 Envtl. Ethics 183 (1998); V. Routley, *On Karl Marx as an Environmental Hero*, 3 Envtl. Ethics 237 (1981).

5. DEEP ECOLOGY

Arne Naess, *The Deep Ecological Movement: Some Philosophical Aspects*, 8 PHIL. INQUIRY 10, 12–21 (1986).

What I advocate and argue for is this: even those who completely subsume ecological policies under the narrow ends of human health and well-being cannot attain their more modest aims, at least not fully and easily, without being joined by supporters of deep ecology. They need what these

---

27. Murray Bookchin, *The Radicalization of Nature*, in COMMENT, July 1, 1984, at 7.

people have to contribute, as this will work for them more often than it works against them. Those in charge of environmental policies, even if they are resource-oriented (and growth tolerating?) decision makers, will increasingly welcome if only for tactical and not fundamental reasons, what deep ecologists have to say. Even though the more radical ethic may seem nonsensical or untenable to them, they know that its advocates are doing in practice conservation work that sooner or later must be done. They concur with the practice, although they operate from diverging theories. If I am right, the time is ripe for professional deep ecologists to breach their silence and freely express their deepest concerns. A bolder advocacy of deep ecology by those who are working within the shallow, resource-oriented "environmental" sphere is the best strategy for regaining some of the strength of this movement among the general public, and thereby to contribute, however modestly, toward a turning of the tide.

What do I mean by saying that even the more modest aims of shallow environmentalism have a need for deep ecology? We can see this by considering the World Conservation Strategy prepared by the International Union for Conservation of Nature and Natural Resources (IUCN) with the advice, cooperation and financial assistance of the United Nations Environmental Programme (UNEP) and the World Wildlife Fund (WWF). The argument in this important publication is through and through homocentric in the sense that all its recommendations are justified in terms of their effects upon human health and well-being. Even the recommended environmental ethic, with its attendant environmental education campaign, has humans in harmony with nature for human good. "A new ethic, embracing plants and animals as well as people, is required for human societies to live in harmony with the natural world on which they depend for survival and well-being."[28] Such an ethic would surely be more effective if it were acted upon by people who believed in its validity, rather than by those who merely believe in its usefulness. This, I think, will come to be understood more and more by those in charge of educational policies. Quite simply, it is indecent for a teacher to proclaim an ethic only for tactical reasons. Further, this point applies to all aspects of world conservation strategy. Conservation strategy will be more eagerly implemented by persons who love what they are conserving, and who are convinced that what they love is intrinsically lovable. Such lovers will not want to hide their attitudes and values, but rather will increasingly give voice to them in public. They have a genuine ethic of conservation, not merely a tactically useful instrument for social and political ends.

In short, environmental education campaigns can fortunately combine anthropocentric arguments with a practical land and sea ethic based either on a deeper and more fundamental naturalistic philosophical or religious perspective, and on a set of norms resting on intrinsic values. But the inherent strength of this overall position will be lost if those who work professionally on environmental problems do not give public testimony to these fundamental norms.

This article is hortatory in the positive etymological sense of that word. I seek "to urge, incite, instigate, encourage, cheer" (Latin: hortari). This may

28. INTERNATIONAL UNION FOR CONSERVATION OF NATURE AND NATURAL RESOURCES, WORLD CONSER-   VATION STRATEGY: LIVING RESOURCE CONSERVATION FOR SUSTAINABLE DEVELOPMENT § 13 (1980).

seem unacademic in a philosophical journal, but I consider it justifiable because of an intimate relationship between hortatory sentences and basic philosophical views. . . .

What Is Deep Ecology?

The term "deep ecological movement" has so far been used without trying to define it. One should not expect much from definitions of movements. Think of terms like "conservatism," "liberalism," or "feminist movement." And there is no need that supporters should adhere to exactly the same definition. In what follows, a set of principles, or key terms and phrases, agreed upon by George Sessions and myself, are tentatively proposed as basic to deep ecology.

(1) The well-being and flourishing of human and non-human Life on Earth have value in themselves (synonyms: intrinsic value, inherent value). These values are independent of the usefulness of the non-human world for human purposes.

(2) Richness and diversity of life forms contribute to the realization of these values and are also values in themselves.

(3) Humans have no right to reduce this richness and diversity except to satisfy vital needs.

(4) The flourishing of human life and cultures is compatible with a substantial decrease of the human population. The flourishing of non-human life requires such a decrease.

(5) Present human interference with the non-human world is excessive, and the situation is rapidly worsening.

(6) Policies must therefore by changed. These policies affect basic economic, technological, and ideological structures. The resulting state of affairs will be deeply different from the present.

(7) The ideological change is mainly that of appreciating life quality (dwelling in situations of inherent value) rather than adhering to an increasingly higher standard of living. There will be a profound awareness of the difference between big and great.

(8) Those who subscribe to the foregoing points have an obligation directly or indirectly to try to implement the necessary changes.

* * *

Deep Versus Shallow Ecology

A number of key terms and slogans from the environmental debate will clarify the contrast between the shallow and deep ecology movements.

A. *Pollution*

Shallow approach: Technology seeks to purify the air and water and to spread pollution more evenly. Laws limit permissible pollution. Polluting industries are preferably exported to developing countries.

Deep approach: Pollution is evaluated from a biosphere point of view not centering on its effects on human health, but on life as a whole including life conditions of every species and system. The shallow reaction to acid rain is to avoid action by demands of more research, demands to find species of trees tolerating high acidity etc., whereas the deep approach concentrates on what is going on in the total ecosystem and asks for a high priority fight against the economy and technology responsible for acid rain.

The priority is to fight deep causes of pollution, not merely the superficial, short range effects. The third and fourth worlds cannot afford to pay the total cost of the war against pollution in their regions, and consequently they require the assistance of the first and second worlds. Exporting pollution is not only a crime against humanity, but also against life.

B. Resources

Shallow approach: The emphasis is upon resources for humans, especially for the present generation in affluent societies. On this view, the resources of the earth belong to those who have the technology to exploit them. There is a confidence that resources will not be depleted because, as they get rarer, a high market price will conserve them, and substitutes will be found through technological progress. Further, animals, plants, and natural objects are valuable only as resources for humans. If no human use is known, they can be destroyed with indifference.

Deep approach: The concern here is with resources and habitat for all life forms for their own sake. No natural object is conceived of solely as a resource. This then leads to a critical evaluation of human modes of production and consumption. It is asked: to what extent does an increase here favor ultimate values in human life? To what extent does it satisfy vital needs, locally and globally? How can economic, legal, and educational institutions be changed to counteract destructive increases? How can resource use serve the quality of life rather than the economic standard of living as generally promoted in consumerism? There is an emphasis here on an ecosystem approach rather than just the consideration of isolated life forms or local situations. There is a long-range maximal perspective of time and place.

C. Population

Shallow approach: The threat of (human) overpopulation is seen mainly as a problem for developing countries. One condones or even cheers population increases in one's own country for shortsighted economic, military, or other reasons; an increase in the number of humans is considered a value in itself or as economically profitable. The issue of "optimum population for humans" is discussed without reference to the question of the "optimum population" of other life forms. The destruction of wild habitats caused by an increasing human population is accepted as an inevitable evil. Drastic decreases of wild life forms tend to be accepted as long as species are not driven to extinction. Animal social relations are ignored. The long term substantial reduction of the global human population is not seen as a desired goal. One has a right to defend one's own borders against "illegal aliens," no matter what the population pressures elsewhere.

Deep approach: It is recognized that excessive pressures on planetary life conditions stem from the human population explosion. The pressure stemming from industrial societies is a major factor, and population reduction must have a high priority in those societies, as well as in developing countries. Estimates of an optimal human population vary. Some quantitative estimates are 100 million, 500 million, and 1000 million, but it is recognized that there must be a long range, humane reduction through mild but tenacious political and economic measures. This will make possible, as a result of increased habitat, population growth for thousands of species which are now constrained by human pressures.

Discussion Notes/Questions

1. Is Naess suggesting that human beings are of no more value than any other part of nature (e.g. fleas and rocks)? Can such a proposition be taken seriously?

2. Does the deep ecology philosophy accord most closely with the scientific limitations of ecology and thermodynamics? Does it have any more virtue in this respect than the social ecology analysis?

3. Deep ecology endorses the notion that there is intrinsic value in the natural environment. Does this idea have sufficient acceptance to render deep ecology the basis for a new society?

4. If environmental problems continue to get worse, could we be forced to adopt principles of deep ecology?

5. For additional pertinent reading, see: F. Capra, The Turning Point: Science, Society and the Rising Culture (1982); C. Chamberlin, *Citizenship as the Practice of Deep Ecology*, 31 Spring 142 (1997); B. Devall & G. Sessions, Deep Ecology: Living as if Nature Mattered (1985); S. Flader, Thinking Like a Mountain: Aldo Leopold and the Evolution of an Ecological Attitude Toward Deer, Wolves, and Forests (1974); S. Harding, *What is Deep Ecology?* 185 Resurgence 14 (1997); A. Leopold, A Sand Country Almanac (1968); W. Fox, *Deep Ecology: A New Philosophy of Our Time?*, 14 The Ecologist 194 (1984); E. Goldsmith, *Gaia: Some Implications for Theoretical Ecology* 18 The Ecologist 64 (1988); A. Naess, *Intuition, Intrinsic Value and Deep Ecology*, 14 The Ecologist 201 (1984); Z. Naveh, *From Biodiversity to Ecodiversity: New Tools for Holistic Landscape Conservation* 21 Int'l. J. Ecology & Env't 1 (1995); M. Peterson & T. Peterson, *Ecology: Scientific, Deep and Feminist* 5 Envtl. Values 123 (1996); Deep Ecology: An Anthology (M. Tobias ed., 1985).

6. INDIGENOUS PEOPLES' PERSPECTIVE

INDIGENOUS VIEWS OF LAND AND THE ENVIRONMENT 1 (Shelton H. Davis ed., World Bank Discussion Paper No. 188, 1993).

For thousands of years prior to the rise of industrial society, human beings practiced modes of livelihood, used the land, and managed natural resources in ways different to our own. Today, large areas of the planet are still inhabited by the descendants of these ancient or traditional peoples. It is estimated that there are over 250 million indigenous peoples, comprising more than 4 percent of the world's population, and living in over 70 countries. What distinguishes indigenous peoples from other populations is their strong, collective attachment to their ancestral lands and the habitats where they live.

For most indigenous peoples, land is not viewed as a "commodity" which can be bought or sold in impersonal markets, but rather a substance endowed with sacred meanings which defines their existence and identity. Similarly, the trees, plants, animals, and fish, which inhabit the land are not "natural resources," but highly personal beings which form part of their social and spiritual universe. This close attachment to the land and environment (what some observers have described as a "stewardship of the earth") is the defining characteristic of indigenous peoples. Cosmologically and philosophically, it links together many geographically and culturally diverse peoples throughout the world.

IUCN INTER-COMMISSION TASK FORCE ON INDIGENOUS PEOPLES, INDIGENOUS PEOPLES AND SUSTAINABILITY: CASES AND ACTIONS 36-38 (1997).

The concept of sustainability is embodied in indigenous agricultural systems, and historical evidence exists which demonstrates the sustained productivity of indigenous systems in some cases for thousands of years on the same land. The first aspect of linking indigenous systems and sustainability is therefore to investigate and learn about ways in which Indigenous Peoples' knowledge systems already embody sustainability principles.

Indigenous communities possess an 'environmental ethic' developed from living in particular ecosystems. This ethic cannot be regarded as universal, but indigenous systems do tend to emphasize the following specific values and features:

– cooperation;

– family bonding and cross-generational communication, including links with ancestors;

– concern for the well-being of future generations;

– local scale, self-sufficiency, and reliance on locally available natural resources;

– restraint in resource exploitation and respect for nature, especially for sacred sites.

The spiritual nature of indigenous systems

Although Indigenous Knowledge is highly pragmatic and practical, Indigenous Peoples generally view this knowledge as emanating from a spiritual base: all Creation is sacred, the sacred and secular are inseparable, spirituality is the highest form of consciousness, and spiritual consciousness is the highest form of awareness. In this sense, a dimension of Indigenous Knowledge is not local knowledge, but knowledge of the universal as expressed in the local.

In indigenous cultures, experts exist who are peculiarly aware of Nature's organizing principles, sometimes described as entities, spirits, or natural law. Knowledge of the environment depends not only on the relationship between humans and Nature, but also between the visible world and the invisible spirit world. According to Opoku, the distinctive feature of traditional African religion is that it is:

A way of life, [with] the purpose of ... order[ing] our relationship with our fellow men and with our environment, both spiritual and physical. At the root of it is a quest for harmony between man, the spirit world, nature, and society . . .

In indigenous experience, states Opoku, the unseen is as much a part of reality as that which is seen. The spiritual is as much a part of reality as the material, and there is a complementary relationship between the two, with the spiritual being more powerful than the materials. The community is of the dead as well as the living. And in nature, behind visible objects lie essences, or powers, which constitute the true nature of those objects.

The holistic nature of indigenous systems

Indigenous Peoples frequently view themselves as guardians and stewards of nature. Harmony and equilibrium among components of the Cosmos are central concepts in most indigenous cosmologies. Agriculture, for example, can provide 'balance for well-being' through relationships not only among people, but also nature and deities. In this concept, the blessing of a new field represents not mere spectacle, but an inseparable part of life where the highest value is harmony with the Earth. Most Indigenous Knowledge traditions recognize linkages between health, diet, properties of different foods and medicinal plants, and horticultural/natural resource management practices—all within a highly articulated cosmological/social context.

Indigenous Knowledge embraces information about location, movements, and other factors explaining spatial patterns and timing in the ecosystem, including sequences of events, cycles, and trends. For Indigenous Peoples the main significance of their knowledge systems is that their connection to land and the relationships and obligations that arise from that connection are the core of their identity. Indigenous agrocentric culture in the Peruvian Andes illustrates the special relationships between culture and the land.

Discussion Notes/Questions

1. Who are indigenous peoples? Should they be treated as a unified group?

2. How should the views of indigenous peoples be reconciled with the views of non-indigenous peoples?

3. What impact should the views of indigenous peoples have on international environmental law decision-making? How should past injustices be addressed?

4. For additional pertinent reading, see: S. J. Anaya & S. T. Crider, *Indigenous Peoples, the Environment, and Commercial Forestry in Developing Countries: The Case of Awas Tingni, Nicaragua* 18 Hum. Rts. Q. 345 (1996); K. Bosselmann, *The Right to Self-determination and International Environmental Law: An Integrative Approach*, 1 N.Z.J. Envtl. L. 1 (1997); J. Callicott, *Traditional American Indian and Western European Attitudes Toward Nature: An Overview*, 4 Envtl. Ethics 293 (1982); *Focus: Beware Green Imperialists* 154 New Scientist 14 (1997); A. Gray, Between the Spice of Life and the Melting Pot: Biodiversity Conservation and Its Impact on Indigenous Peoples (1991); J. Hughes, American Indian Ecology (1983); M. Stavropoulou, *Indigenous Peoples Displaced from their Environment: Is There Adequate Protection?* 5 Col. J. Int'l. Envtl. L. 105 (1994); IUCN, Indigenous Peoples and Sustainability: Cases and Actions (1997); A. Tunks, *Tangata Whenua Ethics and Climate Change*, 1 N.Z.J. Envtl. L. 67 (1997); A. Wiggins, *Indian Rights and the Environment*, 18 Yale J. Int'l L. 345 (1993).

7. ECOFEMINISM

CAROLYN MERCHANT, RADICAL ECOLOGY—THE SEARCH
FOR A LIVABLE WORLD 183, 183–200 (1991).

In Kenya, women of the Green Belt movement band together to plant millions of trees in arid degraded lands. In India, they join the chipko (tree-hugging) movement to preserve precious fuel resources for their communities. In Sweden, feminists prepare jam from berries sprayed with herbicides and offer a taste to members of parliament: they refuse. In Canada, they take to the streets to obtain signatures opposing uranium processing near their towns. In the United States, housewives organize local support to clean up hazardous waste sites. All these actions are examples of a worldwide movement, increasingly known as "ecofeminism," dedicated to the continuation of life on earth.

Ecofeminism emerged in the 1970s with an increasing consciousness of the connections between women and nature. The term, "ecofeminism," was coined by French writer Françoise d'Eaubonne in 1974 who called upon women to lead an ecological revolution to save the planet.[38] Such an ecological revolution would entail new gender relations between women and men and between humans and nature.

Developed by Ynestra King at the Institute for Social Ecology in Vermont about 1976, the concept became a movement in 1980 with a major conference on "Women and Life on Earth: Ecofeminism in the 80s," and the ensuing Women's Pentagon Action to protest anti-life nuclear war and weapons development.[39] During the 1980s cultural feminists in the United States injected new life into ecofeminism by arguing that both women and nature could be liberated together.

Liberal, cultural, social, and socialist feminism have all been concerned with improving the human/nature relationship and each has contributed to an ecofeminist perspective in different ways (see Table 4–3).[40] Liberal feminism is consistent with the objectives of reform environmentalism to alter human relations with nature from within existing structures of governance through the passage of new laws and regulations. Cultural ecofeminism analyzes environmental problems from within its critique of patriarchy and offers alternatives that could liberate both women and nature.

38. Francoise d'Eaubonne, *Feminism or Death, in* NEW FRENCH FEMINISMS: AN ANTHOLOGY (Elaine Marks & Isabelle de Courtivron eds., 1980).

39. Ynestra King, *Toward an Ecological Feminism and a Feminist Ecology, in* MACHINA EX DEA (Joan Rothschild ed., 1983).

40. ALISON M. JAGGAR, FEMINIST POLITICS AND HUMAN NATURE (1983); Karen J. Warren, *Feminism and Ecology: Making Connections*, 9 ENVTL. ETHICS 3 (1987).

Feminism and the Environment

Table 4-3

	Nature	Human Nature	Feminist Critique of Environmentalism	Image of a Feminist
Liberal Feminism	Atoms Mind/Body dualism Domination of nature	Rational Agents Individualism Maximization of self-interest	"Man and his environment" leaves out women	Women in natural Resources and environmental sciences
Marxist Feminism	Transformation of nature by science and technology for human use Domination of nature as a means to human freedom Nature is material basis of life: food, clothing, shelter, energy	Creation of human nature through mode of production, praxis Historically specific —not fixed Species nature of humans	Critique of capitalist control of resources and accumulation of goods and profits	Socialist society will use resources for good of all men and women Resources will be controlled by workers Environmental pollution could be minimal since no surpluses would be produced
Cultural Feminism	Nature is spiritual and personal Conventional science and technology problematic because of their emphasis on domination	Biology is basic Humans are sexual reproducing bodies Sexed by biology/ gendered by society	Unaware of interconnectedness of male domination of nature Male environmentalism retains hierarchy Insufficient attention to environmental threats to women's reproduction (chemicals, nuclear war)	Woman/Nature both valorized and celebrated Reproductive freedom Against pornographic depiction of both women and nature Cultural ecofeminism
Socialist Feminism	Nature is material basis of life: food, clothing, shelter, energy Nature is socially and historically constructed Transformation of nature by production and reproduction	Human nature created through biology and praxis (sex, race, class, age) Historically specific and socially constructed	Leaves out nature as active and responsive Leaves out women's role in reproduction and reproduction as a category Systems approach is mechanistic and dialectic	Both nature and human production are active Centrality of biological and social reproduction Dialectic between production and reproduction Multileveled structural analysis Dialectical (not mechanical) systems

Social and socialist ecofeminism ground their analyses in capitalist patriarchy. They ask how patriarchal relations of reproduction reveal the domination of women by men, and how capitalist relations of production reveal the domination of nature by men. The domination of women and nature inherent in the market economy's use of both as resources would be totally restructured. Although cultural ecofeminism has delved more deeply into the woman-nature connection, social and socialist ecofeminism have the potential for a more thorough critique of domination and for a liberating social justice.

Ecofeminist actions address the contradiction between production and reproduction. Women attempt to reverse the assaults of production on both biological and social reproduction by making problems visible and proposing solutions (see Table 4–3). When radioactivity from nuclear power-plant accidents, toxic chemicals, and hazardous wastes threatens the biological reproduction of the human species, women experience this contradiction as assaults on their bodies and on those of their children and act to halt them. Household products, industrial pollutants, plastics, and packaging wastes invade the homes of First World women threatening the reproduction of daily life, while direct access to food, fuel, and clean water for many Third World women is imperiled by cash cropping on traditional homelands and by pesticides used in agribusiness. First World women combat these assaults by altering consumption habits, recycling wastes, and protesting production and disposal methods, while Third World women act to protect traditional ways of life and reverse ecological damage from multinational corporations and the extractive industries. Women challenge the ways in which mainstream society reproduces itself through socialization and politics by envisioning and enacting alternative gender roles, employment options, and political practices.

Many ecofeminists advocate some form of an environmental ethic that deals with the twin oppressions of the domination of women and nature through an ethic of care and nurture that arises out of women's culturally constructed experiences. As philosopher Karen Warren conceptualizes it:

An ecofeminist ethic is both a critique of male domination of both women and nature and an attempt to frame an ethic free of male-gender bias about women and nature. It not only recognizes the multiple voices of women, located differently by race, class, age, [and] ethnic considerations, it centralizes those voices. Ecofeminism builds on the multiple perspectives of those whose perspectives are typically omitted or undervalued in dominant discourses, for example Chipko women, in developing a global perspective on the role of male domination in the exploitation of women and nature. An ecofeminist perspective is thereby ... structurally pluralistic, inclusivist, and contextualist, emphasizing through concrete example the crucial role context plays in understanding sexist and naturist practice.[41]

An ecofeminist ethic, she argues, would constrain traditional ethics based on rights, rules, and utilities, with considerations based on care, love, and trust. Yet an ethic of care, as elaborated by some feminists, falls prey to an essentialist critique that women's nature is to nurture.[42]

An alternative is a partnership ethic that treats humans (including male partners and female partners) as equals in personal, household, and political relations and humans as equal partners with (rather than controlled-by or dominant-over) nonhuman nature. Just as human partners, regardless of sex, race, or class must give each other space, time, and care, allowing each other to grow and develop individually within supportive nondominating relationships, so humans must give nonhuman nature space, time, and care, allowing it to reproduce, evolve, and respond to human actions. In practice, this would mean not cutting forests and damming rivers that make people and wildlife in flood plains more vulnerable to "natural disasters"; curtailing development in areas subject to volcanos, earthquakes, hurricanes, and tornados to allow room for unpredictable, chaotic, natural surprises; and exercising ethical restraint in introducing new technologies such as pesticides, genetically-engineered organisms, and biological weapons into ecosystems. Constructing nature as a partner allows for the possibility of a personal or intimate (but not necessarily spiritual) relationship with nature and for feelings of compassion for nonhumans as well as for people who are sexually, racially, or culturally different. It avoids gendering nature as a nurturing mother or a goddess and avoids the ecocentric dilemma that humans are only one of many equal parts of an ecological web and therefore morally equal to a bacterium or a mosquito.

41. KAREN J. WARREN, TOWARD AN ECOFEMINIST ETHIC, STUDIES IN THE HUMANITIES 140, 151 (Dec. 1988).

42. Karen J. Warren, *The Power and the Promise of Ecological Feminism*, 12 ENVTL. ETHICS 125 (1990).

Janet Biehl, *Viewpoint: Perspectives on Ecofeminism,*
18 ENVTL. ACTION 19 (1992).

It might surprise many female ecological activists to learn that they have a mystical connection with nature that men do not possess. It may further surprise them to learn that when they fight development in their communities, a mysterious "goddess" is inspiring them. Still further, having researched ecological destruction and presented testimony before planning commissions and other government bodies, it may surprise them to learn that rationality is not after all their strong suit.

Having relied upon scientific studies of the effects of toxic wastes on a river or lake, they may be surprised to learn that science is their enemy, rather than corporations and that magic ... and myths are the means of choice for altering the present state of affairs. Having worked with diverse members of their community in the name of building an ecological society, radical female ecological activists around the world, in short, may be surprised to learn that, thanks to a reworking of traditional male stereotypes of women into a more "positive" form, they are now part of a movement called ecofeminism.

* * *

Somehow, women ecologists are expected to accept a hoary sexist identification with nature as part of a program not only to save the biosphere but to liberate women. In particular, women of color are accorded the dubious honor of being the "closest" to nature, over the strong objections of many women of color.

* * *

Fortunately, it is possible to be a feminist and an ecological activist without accepting ecofeminist baggage.... Women who seek to build a non-hierarchial ecological society can reclaim their genuinely human heritage—as rational (as well as emotional) beings, as people capable of public, grassroots democratic practice (as well as private, intimate concerns) of a broad human solidarity—a struggle that includes fighting the specific oppression of women.

Discussion Notes/Questions

1. Studies by psychologist Carol Gilligan show that women are far more likely to endorse an ethic of care. *See* Carol Gilligan, In a Different Voice: Psychological Theory and Women's Development (1982). In recognition that the environment could do with some care, ought not women to be given an essential role in managing it?

2. If we are to avoid biologically-based assumptions about women, does feminism add anything much to the discussion? If values such as caring and nurturing are only learned by women, are they merely one facet of the human value system? Would the philosophy of humanism therefore be equally instructive?

3. Is it useful to try and link various critiques of mainstream society? Would the combined forces of feminists, Marxists, and environmentalists provide a

formidable political lobby? Alternatively, would their somewhat diffuse interests undermine their potency?

4. Does Merchant's notion of a partnership with the environment deny humanity's dependence on it?

5. For additional pertinent reading, see H. Afshart, Women, Development and Survival in the Third World (1991); J. Biehl, Rethinking Ecofeminist Politics (1991); C. Bretherton, *Global Environmental Politics: Putting Gender on the Agenda?* 24 Rev. of Int'l. Studies 85 (1998); S. Griffin, Women and Nature (1978); Healing the Wounds: The Promise of Ecofeminism (J. Plant ed., 1989); J. Cheney, *Eco–Feminism and Deep Ecology*, 9 Envtl. Ethics 115 (1987); M. Peterson & T. Peterson, *Ecology: Scientific, Deep and Feminist* 5 Envtl. Values 123 (1996); V. Plumwood, *Women, Humanity and Nature*, 48 Radical Philosophy 6 (1988); S. Tanner, *Women and the Sustainable Development Commission*, 13 Women and Environments 51 (1993); K. Warren, *Feminism and Ecology: Making Connections*, 9 Envtl. Ethics 3 (1987).

8. SUSTAINABLE DEVELOPMENT

WORLD COMMISSION ON ENVIRONMENT AND DEVELOPMENT, OUR COMMON FUTURE[nn] 43–54, 62–65 (1987).

Sustainable development is development that meets the needs of the present without compromising the ability of future generations to meet their own needs. It contains within it two key concepts:

- the concept of "needs", in particular the essential needs of the world's poor, to which overriding priority should be given; and

- the idea of limitations imposed by the state of technology and social organization on the environment's ability to meet present and future needs.

Thus the goals of economic and social development must be defined in terms of sustainability in all countries—developed or developing, market-oriented or centrally planned. Interpretations will vary, but must share certain general features and must flow from a consensus on the basic concept of sustainable development and on a broad strategic framework for achieving it.

Development involves a progressive transformation of economy and society. A development path that is sustainable in a physical sense could theoretically be pursued even in a rigid social and political setting. But physical sustainability cannot be secured unless development policies pay attention to such considerations as changes in access to resources and in the distribution of costs and benefits. Even the narrow notion of physical sustainability implies a concern for social equity between generations, a concern that must logically be extended to equity within each generation.

I. The Concept of Sustainable Development

The satisfaction of human needs and aspirations is the major objective of development. The essential needs of vast numbers of people in developing

---

nn. Also known as the Brundtland Commission Report, after Norwegian Prime Minister Gro Brundtland, who chaired the Commission.

countries—for food, clothing, shelter, jobs—are not being met, and beyond their basic needs these people have legitimate aspirations for an improved quality of life. A world in which poverty and inequity are endemic will always be prone to ecological and other crises. Sustainable development requires meeting the basic needs of all and extending to all the opportunity to satisfy their aspirations for a better life.

Living standards that go beyond the basic minimum are sustainable only if consumption standards everywhere have regard for long-term sustainability. Yet many of us live beyond the world's ecological means, for instance in our patterns of energy use. Perceived needs are socially and culturally determined, and sustainable development requires the promotion of values that encourage consumption standards that are within the bounds of the ecologically possible and to which all can reasonably aspire.

Meeting essential needs depends in part on achieving full growth potential, and sustainable development clearly requires economic growth in places where such needs are not being met. Elsewhere, it can be consistent with economic growth, provided the content of growth reflects the broad principles of sustainability and non-exploitation of others. But growth by itself is not enough. High levels of productive activity and widespread poverty can coexist, and can endanger the environment. Hence sustainable development requires that societies meet human needs both by increasing productive potential and by ensuring equitable opportunities for all.

An expansion in numbers can increase the pressure on resources and slow the rise in living standards in areas where deprivation is widespread. Though the issue is not merely one of population size but of the distribution of resources, sustainable development can only be pursued if demographic developments are in harmony with the changing productive potential of the ecosystem.

A society may in many ways compromise its ability to meet the essential needs of its people in the future—by overexploiting resources, for example. The direction of technological developments may solve some immediate problems but lead to even greater ones. Large sections of the population may be marginalized by ill-considered development.

Settled agriculture, the diversion of watercourses, the extraction of minerals, the emission of heat and noxious gases into the atmosphere, commercial forests, and genetic manipulation are all examples of human intervention in natural systems during the course of development. Until recently, such interventions were small in scale and their impact limited. Today's interventions are more drastic in scale and impact, and more threatening to life-support systems both locally and globally. This need not happen. At a minimum, sustainable development must not endanger the natural systems that support life on Earth: the atmosphere, the waters, the soils, and the living beings.

Growth has no set limits in terms of population or resource use beyond which lies ecological disaster. Different limits hold for the use of energy, materials, water, and land. Many of these will manifest themselves in the form of rising costs and diminishing returns, rather than in the form of any sudden loss of a resource base. The accumulation of knowledge and the development of technology can enhance the carrying capacity of the resource base. But ultimate limits there are, and sustainability requires that long before these are reached, the world must ensure equitable access to the constrained resource and reorient technological efforts to relieve the pressure.

Economic growth and development obviously involve changes in the physical ecosystem. Every ecosystem everywhere cannot be preserved intact. A forest may be depleted in one part of a watershed and extended elsewhere, which is not a bad thing if the exploitation has been planned and the effects on soil erosion rates, water regimes, and genetic losses have been taken into account. In general, renewable resources like forests and fish stocks need not be depleted provided the rate of use is within the limits of regeneration and natural growth. But most renewable resources are part of a complex and interlinked ecosystem, and maximum sustainable yield must be defined after taking into account system-wide effects of exploitation.

As for non-renewable resources, like fossil fuels and minerals, their use reduces the stock available for future generations. But this does not mean that such resources should not be used. In general the rate of depletion should take into account the criticality of that resource, the availability of technologies for minimizing depletion, and the likelihood of substitutes being available. Thus land should not be degraded beyond reasonable recovery. With minerals and fossil fuels, the rate of depletion and the emphasis on recycling and economy of use should be calibrated to ensure that the resource does not run out before acceptable substitutes are available. Sustainable development requires that the rate of depletion of non-renewable resources should foreclose as few future options as possible.

Development tends to simplify ecosystems and to reduce their diversity of species. And species, once extinct, are not renewable. The loss of plant and animal species can greatly limit the options of future generations; so sustainable development requires the conservation of plant and animal species.

So-called free goods like air and water are also resources. The raw materials and energy of production processes are only partly converted to useful products. The rest comes out as wastes. Sustainable development requires that the adverse impacts on the quality of air, water, and other natural elements are minimized so as to sustain the ecosystem's overall integrity.

In essence, sustainable development is a process of change in which the exploitation of resources, the direction of investments, the orientation of technological development, and institutional change are all in harmony and enhance both current and future potential to meet human needs and aspirations.

II.   Equity and the Common Interest

Sustainable development has been described here in general terms. How are individuals in the real world to be persuaded or made to act in the common interest? The answer lies partly in education, institutional development, and law enforcement. But many problems of resource depletion and environmental stress arise from disparities in economic and political power. An industry may get away with unacceptable levels of air and water pollution because the people who bear the brunt of it are poor and unable to complain effectively. A forest may be destroyed by excessive felling because the people living there have no alternatives or because timber contractors generally have more influence than forest dwellers.

* * *

The search for common interest would be less difficult if all development and environment problems had solutions that would leave everyone better off. This is seldom the case, and there are usually winners and losers. Many problems arise from inequalities in access to resources. An inequitable land-ownership structure can lead to overexploitation of resources in the smallest holdings, with harmful effects on both environment and development. Internationally, monopolistic control over resources can drive those who do not share in them to excessive exploitation of marginal resources. The differing capacities of exploiters to commandeer "free" goods—locally, nationally, and internationally—is another manifestation of unequal access to resources. "Losers" in environment/development conflicts include those who suffer more than their fair share of the health, property, and ecosystem damage costs of pollution.

As a system approaches ecological limits, inequalities sharpen. Thus when a watershed deteriorates, poor farmers suffer more because they cannot afford the same anti-erosion measures as richer farmers. When urban air quality deteriorates, the poor, in their more vulnerable areas, suffer more health damage than the rich, who usually live in more pristine neighbourhoods. When mineral resources become depleted, late-comers to the industrialization process lose the benefits of low-cost supplies. Globally, wealthier nations are better placed financially and technologically to cope with the effects of possible climatic change.

Hence, our inability to promote the common interest in sustainable development is often a product of the relative neglect of economic and social justice within and amongst nations.

III. Strategic Imperatives

The world must quickly design strategies that will allow nations to move from their present, often destructive, processes of growth and development onto sustainable development paths. This will require policy changes in all countries, with respect both to their own development and to their impacts on other nations' development possibilities....

Critical objectives for environment and development policies that follow from the concept of sustainable development include:

- reviving growth;
- changing the quality of growth;
- meeting essential needs for jobs, food, energy, water, and sanitation;
- ensuring a sustainable level of population;
- conserving and enhancing the resource base;
- reorienting technology and managing risk; and
- merging environment and economics in decision making.

* * *

IV. Conclusion

In its broadest sense, the strategy for sustainable development aims to promote harmony among human beings and between humanity and nature. In the specific context of the development and environment crises of the 1980s, which current national and international political and economic institutions have not and perhaps cannot overcome, the pursuit of sustainable development requires:

- a political system that secures effective citizen participation in decision making,

- an economic system that is able to generate surpluses and technical knowledge on a self-reliant and sustained basis,

- a social system that provides for solutions for the tensions arising from disharmonious development,

- a production system that respects the obligation to preserve the ecological base for development,

- an international system that fosters sustainable patterns of trade and finance, and

- an administrative system that is flexible and has the capacity for self-correction.

These requirements are more in the nature of goals that should underlie national and international action on development. What matters is the sincerity with which these goals are pursued and the effectiveness with which departures from them are corrected.

Michael Redclift, *The Meaning of Sustainable Development*, 23 GEOFORUM 395, 399 (1992).

Sustainable development is a term which is subject to considerable interpretation, depending on the context of the discussion, and the audience for the debate. The discussion of sustainability has revealed some major differences between protagonists, during the 5 years since the Brundtland Commission published its report *Our Common Future*.

* * *

In Our Common Future the Brundtland Commission placed the emphasis in sustainable development on meeting human needs, rather than the protection of nature of the biosphere.

* * *

From within a radical Green perspective what needs to be sustained, in the course of pursuing sustainable development, is the natural resource base. This is cogently expressed by Rees.[43] ... In his opinion the term "sustainable development" has been stripped of its original concern with ensuring future

43. William E. Rees, *The Ecology of Sustainable Development*, 20 THE ECOLOGIST 18   (1990).

ecological stability as it has come to be embraced by the political mainstream. In Rees' view it is no longer a challenge to the conventional economic paradigm, but rather a laboured excuse for not departing from continued economic growth.

This view of the primacy of ecological considerations, although given most emphasis in radical Green thinking, is an important component of a broader current of opinion. This tradition concentrates attention on the resource base, and particularly renewable resources, as the "object" of sustainability. The major threat to the long-term sustainability of the Earth's resources is identified in the key indices of resource degradation, in the loss of soil and water quality, and the inability of the atmosphere to absorb air pollution.

* * *

Not all advocates of sustainable development regard ecological objectives as having primacy over human commitments. Barbier[44] argues, for example, that "sustainable economic development is ... directly concerned with increasing the material standard of living of the poor at the 'grassroots' level, which can be quantitatively measured in terms of increased food, real income, educational services, health-care, sanitation and water supply, emergency stocks of food and cash.... In general terms, the primary objective is reducing the absolute poverty of the world's poor through providing lasting and secure livelihoods". The emphasis here is very clearly on meeting social and economic objectives, rather than ecological ones.

* * *

The emphasis on the human purposes to which sustainability should be dedicated is illustrated even more clearly by Bartelmus[45] who argues that "sustainable development maintains a particular level of income by conserving the sources of that income, the stock of produced and natural capital". Conservation, on this reading, means more than the conservation of the planet's life-support systems. It also includes the physical infrastructure and services, the "man-made" capital, that makes up much of the built environment. We have come a long way from radical Green views of sustainability.

* * *

[T]here are at least two sets of contradictions which soon become evident when sustainable development is discussed.

First, embedded in much of the "sustainability" thinking is an important difference of emphasis. Some writers view sustainability as a serious issue because nature is a major constraint on further human progress. They are concerned, basically, with the price paid by the conventional growth model if the warnings we receive from the environment, the "biospheric imperatives", are ignored. The solution, then, is either to develop technologies which avoid the most dire environmental consequences of development, or to take measures to assess environmental losses in a more realistic way, thus reducing the danger that they will be overlooked by policymakers.

44. Edward Barbier, Economics, Natural-Resource Scarcity and Development 103 (1989).

45. Peter Bartelmus, Environment and Development 12 (1987).

Other writers take a rather different view. For them the principal problem is that "human progress" carries implications for nature itself, and should cause us to re-examine the "ends" of development, as well as the means. This view is shared by a variety of people; radical ecologists, eco-feminists and Deep Ecologists. For writers of these different ideological persuasions finding technical solutions to environmental problems, including ways of costing environmental losses . . . is ultimately self-defeating.

Second, considering "sustainable development" within a North–South framework requires attention to the contradictions imposed by the structural inequalities of the global system. Green concerns in the North, such as alternatives to work and ways of making work more rewarding, can often be inverted in the South, where the environment is contested not because it is valued in itself, but because its destruction creates value. In the South struggles over the environment are usually about basic needs, strategies to survive, rather than "lifestyles", and the cost to the individual of pursuing individual self-interest is often carried by the group or collectivity (the basis of the "tragedy of the commons" argument). There is no point in appealing, under these circumstances, to idealism or altruism to protect the environment, when the individual and household are forced to behave "selfishly" in their struggle to survive.

Discussion Notes/Questions

1. Does sustainable development attempt to keep too many factions happy?

2. Sustainable development accepts that human beings are, for the most part, anthropocentric. It accepts that we live in an industrial society and that we are intent on continued development. Can it be argued that the greatest virtue of sustainable development is its courageous recognition of realities?

3. Does the term have political currency in that it creates a dialogue between environmentalists and developers? Alternatively, has it lost its value because of its constant "hijacking" by developers?

4. Is the Brundtland Report becoming more or less relevant as time goes by? Are the outcomes of the 1992 Earth Summit at Rio consistent with the spirit of the Report?

5. For additional pertinent reading, see F. Archibugi, Economy and Ecology: Towards Sustainable Development (1989); R. Braidotti, et al., Women, the Environment and Sustainable Development (1993); M. Carley, Managing Sustainable Development (1993); M. Holdgate, From Care to Action: Making a Sustainable World (1996); IUCN, A Sustainable World: Defining and Measuring Sustainable Development (T.C. Trzyna ed., 1995); R. Jolly, Adjustment with a Human Face: Protecting the Vulnerable and Promoting Growth (1987); S. Latouche, The End of Affluent Society: An Exploration of Post–Development (1993); M. Meister & P.M. Japp, *Sustainable Development and the Global Economy: Rhetorical Implications for Improving the Quality of Life* 25 Communication Res. 399 (1998); S. Pandey, *Women, Environment and Sustainable Development* 41 Int'l. Social Work 339 (1998); D. Pearce, Sustainable Development: Economics and Environment in the Third World (1990); G. Piel, Only One World: Our Own to Make and Keep (1992); M. Redclift, Sustainable Development: Exploring the Contradictions (1987); W. Sacks, The Development Dictionary: A Guide to Knowledge as Power (1992); F. Schuurman, Beyond the Impasse: New Directions in Development Theory (1993); J. Seabrook, Pioneers of Change: Experiments in Creating a Humane Society

(1993); R. Verburg & V. Wiegel, *On the Compatibility of Sustainability and Economic Growth*, 19 Envtl. Ethics 247 (1997); H.H. Webster, *Some Comparisons of Canadian and U.S. Attitudes/Behaviour Concerning Sustainable Development* Canadian Rev. of American Studies 1 (1998).

9. THE WORLD'S RESPONSE AT RIO

The perspective on the global environmental *problématique* that has been the most influential and that now has the official imprimatur of virtually every government in the world is the sustainable development approach outlined in the report of the World Commission on Environment and Development and extracted in Subsection 9, *supra*. The report and the ideas it contains stimulated the holding of the largest diplomatic gathering the world has ever seen, at Rio de Janeiro in June 1992.

The conference, officially known as the United Nations Conference on Environment and Development (UNCED) and popularly dubbed the "Earth Summit," was preceded by a number of U.N. General Assembly resolutions defining its agenda.[o] UNCED was preceded, twenty years before, in 1972, by the United Nations Conference on the Human Environment in Stockholm, Sweden. The Stockholm Conference made an important contribution to the debate on the global environment and the 1972 Stockholm Declaration of the United Nations Conference on the Human Environment [**Basic Document 1.12**] made a significant series of statements about what needed to be done, with some of its principles making their way into customary international law since then.

At Rio in 1992, a number of significant instruments in international environmental law were concluded. The main outputs were:

● the Rio Declaration on Environment and Development [**Basic Document 1.29**], a short statement of principles revolving around sustainability;

● Agenda 21, an enormous action plan of forty chapters comprising recommendations to governments;[p]

● a Convention on Biological Diversity [**Basic Document 1.30**];

● a Framework Convention on Climate Change [**Basic Document 3.21**];

● a Statement of Principles for a Global Consensus on the Management, Conservation and Sustainable Development of Forests [**Basic Document 6.12**], which had been intended as a "hard law" convention but which failed in this form for lack of agreement; and

● an agreement within the context of Agenda 21 to establish a "Sustainable Development Commission," since established, to monitor progress in implementing the Rio Declaration [*see* **Basic Document 1.29**].

The leading instrument was the Rio Declaration, the full text of which is set out following this introductory note (as well as in the documentary supplement to this coursebook). Like many declarations concluded at massive

---

o. See, e.g., United Nations Conference on Environment and Development, G.A. Res. 44/228, U.N. GAOR, 44th Sess., Supp. No. 49, at 151; G.A. Res. 43/196, U.N. GAOR, 43d Sess., Supp. No. 49, at 147, U.N. Doc. A./43/49 (1989).

p. For excerpts, see [**Basic Document 1.30**].

international meetings, the Rio Declaration was not intended to contain enforceable obligations in the manner that treaties do. Nation-states usually prefer "soft law" documents; they like to agree on high-sounding resolutions of principle that do not actually require them to do anything very specific. The Rio Declaration is such an instrument. Nevertheless, it contains a set of mission statements that would be of substantial benefit if adopted around the world.

The Declaration is based on the principle of sustainable development. Almost everything within it points to the need to adopt sustainable development policies. It does not, however, explain the legal and policy content of sustainable development, nor does it indicate how to achieve it. One may ask, for example, how the economic interests of future generations are to be weighed against the economic interests of present generations? How might one balance the question of ecological "bottom lines" against the question of community and individual interests: jobs and short-term economic advancement? These issues are difficult to resolve. Nations need more guidance on how to confront these issues than the high sounding principles that are contained in the Rio Declaration and the additional guidance that is intended to come from the detailed action plan called Agenda 21.

Principle 1 of the Rio Declaration states that "[h]uman beings are at the center of concerns for sustainable development. They are entitled to a healthy and productive life in harmony with nature." Principle 3 provides that "[t]he right to develop must be fulfilled so as to equitably meet development and environmental needs of present and future generations." To achieve sustainable development, Principle 4 directs that "environmental protection shall constitute an integral part of the developmental process and cannot be considered in isolation from it." Principle 5 continues: "All states and all people shall cooperate in the essential task of eradicating poverty as an indispensable requirement for sustainable development . . .". And the Declaration adds, in Principle 6, that "[t]he special situation and needs of developing countries, particularly the least developed and those most environmentally vulnerable, shall be given special priority." Principle 8 goes further: "To achieve sustainable development and a higher quality of life for all people, States should reduce and eliminate unsustainable patterns of production and promote appropriate demographic policies."

Thus the Rio Declaration embodies a tension between protecting the environment and promoting economic development. It is a contradiction that does not appear to be resolved by the Rio Declaration. But one thing is clear: the Rio Declaration makes sustainable development the driving force in international efforts to address the global environmental *problématique*. For this reason, it is the most important of the perspectives or approaches contained in this chapter, and therefore vitally important to comprehend. We set it out in its entirety here so that it can be easily and fully discussed.

THE RIO DECLARATION ON ENVIRONMENT AND DEVELOP-MENT OF THE UNITED NATIONS CONFERENCE ON ENVIRONMENT AND DEVELOPMENT[qq] June 14, 1992, UNCED Doc. A/CONF. 151/5.Rev. 1, 31 I.L.M. 874 (1992).

Preamble

The United Nations Conference on Environment and Development,

Having met at Rio de Janeiro from 3 to 14 June 1992,

Reaffirming the Declaration of the United Nations Conference on the Human Environment, adopted at Stockholm on 16 June 1972, and seeking to build upon it,

With the goal of establishing a new and equitable global partnership through the creation of new levels of cooperation among States, key sectors of societies and people,

Working towards international agreements which respect the interests of all and protect the integrity of the global environmental and developmental system,

Recognizing the integral and interdependent nature of the Earth, our home,

Proclaims that:

Principle 1

Human beings are at the centre of concerns for sustainable development. They are entitled to a healthy and productive life in harmony with nature.

Principle 2

States have, in accordance with the Charter of the United Nations and the principles of international law, the sovereign right to exploit their own resources pursuant to their own environmental and developmental policies, and the responsibility to ensure that activities within their jurisdiction or control do not cause damage to the environment of other States or of areas beyond the limits of national jurisdiction.

Principle 3

The right to development must be fulfilled so as to equitably meet developmental and environmental needs of present and future generations.

Principle 4

In order to achieve sustainable development, environmental protection shall constitute an integral part of the development process and cannot be considered in isolation from it.

Principle 5

All States and all people shall cooperate in the essential task of eradicating poverty as an indispensable requirement for sustainable development, in order to decrease the disparities in standards of living and better meet the needs of the majority of the people of the world.

Principle 6

The special situation and needs of developing countries, particularly the least developed and those most environmentally vulnerable, shall be given

qq. See also [Basic Document 1.29].

special priority. International actions in the field of environment and development should also address the interests and needs of all countries.

Principle 7

States shall cooperate in a spirit of global partnership to conserve, protect and restore the health and integrity of the Earth's ecosystem. In view of the different contributions to global environmental degradation, States have common but differentiated responsibilities. The developed countries acknowledge the responsibility that they bear in the international pursuit of sustainable development in view of the pressures their societies place on the global environment and of the technologies and financial resources they command.

Principle 8

To achieve sustainable development and a higher quality of life for all people, States should reduce and eliminate unsustainable patterns of production and consumption and promote appropriate demographic policies.

Principle 9

States should cooperate to strengthen endogenous capacity-building for sustainable development by improving scientific understanding through exchanges of scientific and technological knowledge, and by enhancing the development, adaptation, diffusion and transfer of technologies, including new and innovative technologies.

Principle 10

Environmental issues are best handled with the participation of all concerned citizens, at the relevant level. At the national level, each individual shall have appropriate access to information concerning the environment that is held by public authorities, including information on hazardous materials and activities in their communities, and the opportunity to participate in decision-making processes. States shall facilitate and encourage public awareness and participation by making information widely available. Effective access to judicial and administrative proceedings, including redress and remedy, shall be provided.

Principle 11

States shall enact effective environmental legislation. Environmental standards, management objectives and priorities should reflect the environmental and developmental context to which they apply. Standards applied by some countries may be inappropriate and of unwarranted economic and social cost to other countries, in particular developing countries.

Principle 12

States should cooperate to promote a supportive and open international economic system that would lead to economic growth and sustainable development in all countries, to better address the problems of environmental degradation. Trade policy measures for environmental purposes should not constitute a means of arbitrary or unjustifiable discrimination or a disguised restriction on international trade. Unilateral actions to deal with environmental challenges outside the jurisdiction of the importing country should be avoided. Environmental measures addressing transboundary or global environmental problems should, as far as possible, be based on an international consensus.

Principle 13

States shall develop national law regarding liability and compensation for the victims of pollution and other environmental damage. States shall also cooperate in an expeditious and more determined manner to develop further international law regarding liability and compensation for adverse effects of environmental damage caused by activities within their jurisdiction or control to areas beyond their jurisdiction.

Principle 14

States should effectively cooperate to discourage or prevent the relocation and transfer to other States of any activities and substances that cause severe environmental degradation or are found to be harmful to human health.

Principle 15

In order to protect the environment, the precautionary approach shall be widely applied by States according to their capabilities. Where there are threats of serious or irreversible damage, lack of full scientific certainty shall not be used as a reason for postponing cost-effective measures to prevent environmental degradation.

Principle 16

National authorities should endeavour to promote the internalization of environmental costs and the use of economic instruments, taking into account the approach that the polluter should, in principle, bear the cost of pollution, with due regard to the public interest and without distorting international trade and investment.

Principle 17

Environmental impact assessment, as a national instrument, shall be undertaken for proposed activities that are likely to have a significant adverse impact on the environment and are subject to a decision of a competent national authority.

Principle 18

States shall immediately notify other States of any natural disasters or other emergencies that are likely to produce sudden harmful effects on the environment of those States. Every effort shall be made by the international community to help States so afflicted.

Principle 19

States shall provide prior and timely notification and relevant information to potentially affected States on activities that may have a significant adverse transboundary environmental effect and shall consult with those States at an early stage and in good faith.

Principle 20

Women have a vital role in environmental management and development. Their full participation is therefore essential to achieve sustainable development.

Principle 21

The creativity, ideals and courage of the youth of the world should be mobilized to forge a global partnership in order to achieve sustainable development and ensure a better future for all.

Principle 22

Indigenous people and their communities, and other local communities, have a vital role in environmental management and development because of their knowledge and traditional practices. States should recognize and duly support their identity, culture and interests and enable their effective participation in the achievement of sustainable development.

Principle 23

The environment and natural resources of people under oppression, domination and occupation shall be protected.

Principle 24

Warfare is inherently destructive of sustainable development. States shall therefore respect international law providing protection for the environment in times of armed conflict and cooperate in its further development, as necessary.

Principle 25

Peace, development and environmental protection are interdependent and indivisible.

Principle 26

States shall resolve all their environmental disputes peacefully and by appropriate means in accordance with the Charter of the United Nations.

Principle 27

States and people shall cooperate in good faith and in a spirit of partnership in the fulfillment of the principles embodied in this Declaration and in the further development of international law in the field of sustainable development.

*

Part II

PROBLEMS IN INTERNATIONAL ENVIRONMENTAL LAW AND WORLD ORDER

INTRODUCTION

We began our study of international environmental law by exploring the sources and application of environmental law, guided and instructed by a frightening real life challenge posed by the manner in which the Russians are dealing with their nuclear fleet. These true, as distinct from hypothetical facts, initiated us into the study of international law: the progenitor of international environmental law (IEL).

In this section of our book we move on to examine other sets of facts. These facts, unlike the facts in the Introduction, are hypothetical not real. As indicated in the Preface, a basic feature of this coursebook (deliberately so called because it is not a "casebook" that relies heavily upon judicial opinions drawn from "cases") is its use of hypothetical problems to bring you face to face both with the multiple crises that now substantially define the global environment and with the norms, institutions, and procedures through which the international legal system purports to do something about them.

Hypothetical problems are pedagogically useful, we believe, because, among other virtues, they help to avoid the unwanted associations and biases of the "real world" that potentially inhibit principled analysis. Moreover, IEL is a new and developing subject that, because of its youth, is unable to rely on an established corpus of precedents, cases or "real" experience like its prominent parents International Law and Domestic Environmental Law. It is important that we define and refine the legal norms, in hypothetical scenarios, that can be invoked to deal with similar situations when encountered in the real world. We are persuaded that the "problem method" is the best way to tackle the range of policy choices that actually and potentially are available to decision-makers when confronting, from a legal perspective, this or that aspect of the global environmental *problématique*.

We begin, in Chapter 5, with a look at the Law of State Responsibility and International Liability as it has developed so far in relation to transboundary environmental harms. It is critical that this chapter be *thoroughly* comprehended; all the hypothetical problems that follow, in Chapters 6 through 11, will in one way or another depend upon it, and you therefore will be asked to return to it time and time again.

Next, in Chapter 6, we present you with the first of the hypothetical problems that are the core of this coursebook. It deals with the multi-issue complexity of legally safeguarding "the global commons"—in this case, Antarctica. This is followed by a series of hypothetical problems, in Chapters 7 through 10, in which you are asked to consider how law can help to protect the earth-space environment in which we live: the atmosphere, the hydrosphere (oceans and water resources), the lithosphere (land and soils), and the biosphere (biodiversity).

Finally, in Chapter 11, we address the problem of protecting the global environment against four particular conditioning factors: trade, population growth, and warfare. These are not the only factors that condition our ability to protect the global environment, to be sure. They are, however, among the most pervasive and for this reason merit our concentrated attention.

We turn now to Chapter 5—which, we remind you, you will be asked to revisit with much frequency. Study it carefully *before* you proceed to the problems that lie in store. Like Part I (and especially Chapter 2 therein), its teachings will touch upon each of the problems you will encounter.

Chapter Five

INTERNATIONAL ENVIRONMENTAL WRONGS

Chapter Four, which concluded Part I, presented a range of outlooks and approaches, gathered from various disciplines, canvassing the essential social, political, and scientific context of international environmental law (IEL). In this chapter, which commences Part II, you are introduced to concepts and doctrines deemed essential for understanding and evaluating the nature of the actual legal remedies available when confronting transnational environmental problems.

Legal remedies arise from the fundamental principle of justice that loss be shifted from the victim to the perpetrator, and that the victim be entitled to some form of reparation. This principle straddles the legal systems of nation states as well as the international community of nations, and constitutes the common jurisprudential foundations of tort law and remedies in domestic legal systems, and the law of state responsibility and liability in public international law.

None of the hypothetical problems that comprise this Part II—indeed, few transnational environmental problems generally—can be legally handled without invoking and applying the concepts, principles, and viewpoints presented here, to wit, the three interlocking doctrines, principles, and rules of "State Responsibility," (SR) "International Liability,"(IL) and "Civil Liability" (CL). These three approaches to compensation and reparation, admittedly replete with differing theoretical perspectives, deal with what we call the "Law of International Environmental Wrongs." Despite their common foundations in tort law, they have tended to be treated in a fragmented rather than an integrated manner. We begin with an overview or road-map that describes, clarifies, and attempts to integrate these different approaches to compensatory and remedial justice in IEL.

The readings immediately following our introduction key into, and etch in further detail, some of the complex elements of this area of law. You are urged to scrutinize them closely not only because they are essential for understanding and evaluating transnational environmental problems generally, but because, as already indicated, you will frequently be called upon to consult all or part of them in the problems and exercises that make up the next five chapters. They constitute a prelude, as it were, to Chapters 6 through 11.

A. EDITOR'S INTRODUCTION

1. STATE RESPONSIBILITY

As signified by its name, SR deals with a body of law which holds a state responsible for environmental harm or damage caused to another state. Derived initially from the traditional norms of state responsibility for the treatment of aliens and their property, this jurisprudence is rooted in the long-accepted proposition that states, the so-called subjects of international law, are responsible for such violations of that law as are attributable to them and that, consequently, they are legally obligated to other aggrieved states to make reparations whenever such attributable violations occur.[a] The central point about SR is that the parties to the action are states, not the polluter or the victim. Because the state acts as a proxy for the actual parties, SR can only arise if the plaintiff or petitioner state decides to espouse or undertake an action on behalf of the victim. Conversely, as we shall see, states are not responsible for all actions arising from within their jurisdiction, unless the actions of the polluter are attributable to the defendant or respondent state. SR is a species of tort law. It is based on grievance remedial principles that enable one state to demand *ex-post* compensation and other relief for harm suffered by it. Litigation in cases involving state responsibility is adjudicated by international courts and tribunals.

2. THE LIMITED IMPORTANCE OF STATE RESPONSIBILITY

The majority of the materials that follow are directed toward understanding the meaning and application of SR, and the cognate principle of IL. Some aspects of SR and IL are riddled with difficulties, and it is necessary that we try to untangle the confusing and contradictory strands of thinking that enmesh the subject. At the same time, it behooves us to take note of the limited and restricted applicability of SR and IL. These two remedies have been modeled on the assumption that sovereign independent states are the only significant and critical actors in IEL,[b] and that the involvement of states provides the necessary legal machinery for access to environmental justice and reparation.

This is a dubious assumption. While there is no question that states are important and will remain key legal players in IEL, we live in an interconnected world inhabited by other powerful legal actors. Among them, national and transnational corporations, private individuals, and non-governmental organizations (NGOs) have assumed importance on the global legal stage. They are subjects of legal regimes other than SR and IL, and this note, *inter alia,* will sketch the role and growth of CL as it emerges as an alternative or concurrent legal method of obtaining relief and compensation.

Moreover, the considerable theoretical attention given to SR and IL stands in stark contrast to their conspicuous absence in environmental

---

a. *See, e.g.,* Factory at Chorzów (Merits) (Germany v. Poland), 1928 P.C.I.J. (ser. A) No. 17, at 4.

b. Edith Brown Weiss, *International Environmental Law in Transition, in* TRILATERAL PERSPECTIVES ON INTERNATIONAL LEGAL ISSUES: RELEVANCE OF DOMESTIC LAW & POLICY 95, 96 (Michael K. Young & Yuji Iwasawa eds., 1996).

treaties. The stubborn fact is that questions of how to claim compensation for the breach of international environmental obligations, either in national or international forums, have for the large part been deliberately neglected or omitted. While states accept the principle or "primary rule" that a wrong gives rise to SR, they have balked at setting up the procedural or "secondary rules" that enable and facilitate the recovery of damages or compensation.[c]

This disjunction between theory and practice is crystallized by article 235 of the United Nations Convention on the Law of the Sea (UNCLOS) dealing with "Responsibility and liability." After asserting that "[s]tates are responsible for the fulfilment of their international obligations concerning the protection and preservation of the marine environment" it affirms that "[t]hey shall be liable in accordance with international law" [235(1)]. Recognizing the absence of mechanisms for establishing liability and assessing compensation, it quickly goes on to require that states should cooperate in the " ... further development of international law relating to responsibility and liability for the assessment of and compensation for damage ..." [235(3)]. In doing so, UNCLOS highlights the lack of international laws and procedures addressing the compensatory or remedial aspects of SR.

State prosecution of claims based on SR have conspicuously been wanting. Apart from the omission of states to invoke SR for the substantial damage following the blaze at a Sandoz chemical warehouse, [344 *infra*] the nuclear accident at Chernobyl [Editors Note, Problem 7–3, 542] offers striking evidence of the reluctance of states to base claims on SR.

Citizens of many countries of Europe, Scandinavia, and even the Americas felt the fall out from the serious accident at one of the four reactors at the state run nuclear power plant in Chernobyl near Kiev in the former Soviet Union. This resulted in widespread radioactive contamination of air, water, and soil; and caused direct damage to milk producing cattle, vegetables, and other food supplies. Huge quantities of milk, vegetables, and food had to be destroyed, and the costs of remediation amounted to hundreds of thousands of dollars.

Despite this, none of the injured countries made any claims based on SR. The reason for their abstinence is open to conjecture. It may have been in the self interest of other nuclear power generating states not to create a precedent based on SR that could be cited against them at some future date. It is possible that they did not wish to expend good money after bad by pursuing the Soviets who were in no position to pay any damages because of their weak economic plight. Perhaps, despite the strong facts, states were not sure that this case gave rise to SR. For whatever reason, the lack of response by injured states after the Chernobyl accident is strong evidence of their reluctance to use or even assert SR.

3. INTERNATIONAL OBLIGATIONS

The foundational principle of SR, as of tort law, is the concept of a "wrongful act." A state commits an internationally "wrongful act" if it

---

c. The analytical distinction between "primary" and "secondary" rules of SR, first suggested in the commentary to the ILC Draft Articles, is explicated by J. Combacau & D. Alland, *"Primary" and "Secondary" Rules in the Law of State Responsibility Categorizing International Obligations*, 16 N.Y.U. J. INT'L L. & POL. 8 (1985).

violates or breaches an international obligation, found in treaty or customary law. In theory all obligations, whether general or specific, contained in treaties as well as in customary law have the potential to give rise to SR.

An obligation could be very general. For example, the obligation could be that of good neighborliness that places responsibility on states to ensure that activities within their jurisdiction or control do not cause damage to the environment of other states or to areas beyond their jurisdiction. *See* **Basic Document 1.12**, and section C of this chapter, "Attempts at Codification," *infra*. Another general obligation, because it does not specify exactly what a state should do, is that placed on states to supply security or to implement civil liability mechanisms as required by the nuclear treaties discussed below in section A. 9. On the other hand, there are very specific obligations such as those relating to time tables for reduction of ozone damaging chemicals, and monitoring or reporting of ozone levels which could also give rise to state responsibility.[d]

4a. APPLICATION OF SR

According to the International Law Commission's (ILC) codification of the law of SR in its Draft Articles on State Responsibility **[Basic Document 1.10]**: "Every internationally wrongful act of a State entails the international responsibility of that State" [article 1], and "there is an internationally wrongful act of a State when the conduct is attributable to the State under international law; and . . . that conduct constitutes a breach of an international obligation of the State." [article 3(a) & (b)].

Despite the acceptance of the principle that the breach of an obligation is a wrong that gives rise to SR, conceptual problems abound. There is an ongoing dispute as to the elements of an *international wrong*. For exploration of these difficulties, see Professor Riccardo Pisillo–Mazzeschi's article, *Forms of International Responsibility for Environmental Harm,* in section D. 1 *infra*.

4b. "FAULT" AND SR

Controversy surrounds the question as to whether "fault" (wrongful intention or negligence) is a necessary ingredient of a wrongful act that is prohibited by international law. It can be argued that a requirement of fault must be implied in all primary obligations because there could be no wrong (state responsibility *stricto sensu*) without fault. Impelled by the theoretical cogency of this doctrinal thesis, the ILC accepted the need for fault in cases of state responsibility *stricto sensu* in its draft articles on state responsibility. At the same time, it appreciated the practical need to deal with the reality of environmental harm caused *without fault* and attempted to establish a parallel basis for reparation in circumstances where there was no wrongful intention or negligence. In effect, the ILC attempted to create a form of strict liability for harmful acts under a less detractive name, which we have called *International Liability. See, International Law Commission Draft Articles on*

---

d. *International Law Comm'n Draft Articles on State Responsibility*, Adopted by the International Law Comm'n at its 1642nd Meeting, arts. 20 & 21, U.N. Doc. A/35/10 (1981) [hereinafter ILC Draft on State Responsibility].

International Liability for Injurious Consequences Arising Out of Acts Not Prohibited by International Law [**Basic Document 1.9**].

5. INTERNATIONAL LIABILITY

The ILC's attempt to articulate an alternative jurisprudential basis for accommodating strict or absolute liability for lawful activities which cause environmental harm without fault or negligence, has been criticized, inter alia, by Professor Alan E. Boyle in, *State Responsibility and International Liability for Injurious Consequences Not Prohibited by International Law: A Necessary Distinction?*, which we have excerpted in section D. 1, *infra*. Without getting into the details of this rather tortuous debate, an approach based on general principles of law suggests that we should examine the primary obligation in question to determine if fault is an ingredient or element of the breach giving rise to a wrong. If fault is an element of breach of the primary obligation, then it is a requirement of SR. If not, we should imply fault only if there are other reasons for so doing. If, for example, the obligation we are examining is the one restated in article 21 of the Stockholm Declaration [**Basic Document 1.12**], the fact that it does not require the transboundary harm to be caused intentionally or negligently suggests that fault is not a requirement. But does this mean that article 21 imposes strict or even absolute liability? Some commentators and environmental treaties have declined to answer this question in the affirmative, arguing that fault is a ubiquitous requirement of all wrongs. They argue that an affirmative answer will create a regime of no fault *liability* that supercedes fault-based *responsibility* for all practical purposes.

The idea of replacing SR with IL, which would make states liable without the need to establish even a duty of care based on a due diligence standard, has been criticized. See the writings of Brian D. Smith and A. Boyle, in section D. 1, *infra*. Such critics would rather stay with a graduated concept of SR based on differentiated standards ranging from due diligence to strict and absolute responsibility, than move to IL.

6. STRICT AND ABSOLUTE LIABILITY

The concepts of strict and absolute liability have not been authoritatively defined, but standards of strict liability are less rigorous than absolute liability, and may constitute no more than a reversal of the burden of proof, allowing a defending state to establish circumstances precluding wrongfulness or liability. Absolute or objective liability on the other hand is more conclusive and prohibits, or very severely limits, evidence of circumstances precluding liability. The examples cited below, while illustrative of these distinctions, do not remove all of the doubts still surrounding them.

The Space Liability Convention illustrates absolute liability under a SR regime. Where damage is caused to the surface of the earth or to aircraft in flight, it asserts that, "[a] launching State shall be absolutely liable to pay compensation for damage caused by its space object. . . ." [article II]. The Space Liability Convention draws a distinction between absolute liability [article II] and fault liability [article III]. While absolute liability is imposed for damage to the surface of the earth [article II], damage resulting elsewhere can result in liability only where fault is established [article III].

Other examples are taken from regimes dealing with CL, discussed below, but are illustrative of the common distinction between absolute and strict liability. The 1992 International Convention on Civil Liability for Oil Pollution Damage (CLC) **[Basic Document 4.25]** illustrates strict liability. It places liability on the owner of the ship subject to exceptions such as war, hostilities, certain kinds of natural phenomena, and acts of a third party [article III(2) of CLC]. Three conventions on nuclear liability: 1) the 1960 Paris Convention on Third Party Liability in the Field of Nuclear Energy **[Basic Document 3.1]** 2) the 1997 Vienna Convention on Civil Liability for Nuclear Damage **[Basic Document 3.23]**, and 3) the Convention Relating to Civil Liability in the Field of Maritime Carriage of Nuclear Materials **[Basic Document 4.9]** each implement a system of absolute liability, even though that term is not expressly mentioned; and they admit of certain very limited exceptions based on armed conflict and civil war.

7.   ATTRIBUTION, CAUSATION AND EXHAUSTION OF LOCAL REMEDIES

Apart from proving the breach of an obligation, with or without fault, a wrongful act must be attributed to a state for SR to arise. In the case of environmental wrongs, the acts resulting in the wrong must be laid at the feet of the state or an agency of the state. Because transboundary environmental wrongs are often committed by private parties, it is necessary to attribute the wrong to the agency or government department that authorized, mandated or failed to prevent the wrongful action. *See*, ILC Draft on State Responsibility, articles 5–10.

In addition, a claimant for judicial remedies, whether based on SR, IL, or CL must prove damage and causation. This can be difficult, particularly where there is more than one source of the impugned pollutant as illustrated by the case of acid rain. Sweden, for instance, had to resort to very elaborate monitoring and measuring devices to trace the source of acid rain to a particular suspect country whether it were the United Kingdom or Germany, or both.

Procedurally, there is also a rule, subject to exceptions, regarding the exhaustion of local (national) remedies before preferring an international action. This rule is discussed in section D. 3 of the readings, *infra*.

The remedies sought attempt to restore the injured party to its position prior to the wrong. The judicial tribunal can regulate future actions and order compensation as happened in the Trail Smelter Case, and it can declare the rights of parties and order interim measures as was done in the Nuclear Test Cases I.

8.   TRAIL SMELTER ARBITRATION

The *Trail Smelter Arbitration* **[Basic Document 8.4]**, a well known public international law case dealing with transboundary pollution, is invariably cited in any discussion of state responsibility. The facts of that case also serve the double purpose of illustrating how a civil liability system under national law could have dealt with the transnational wrongs suffered in that case. In the Trail Smelter Arbitration sulphur dioxide fumes from a Canadian smelter were causing damage in the state of Washington in the United States. Farmers in the U.S. who suffered damage were prevented from bringing an action in U.S. courts because of jurisdictional difficulties. The first of these jurisdictional problems arose from the fact that the company owning the smelters had its place of business and was a company registered in Canada. A second jurisdictional problem arose from the *locus delicti* or the fact that the act which initiated the damage, and therefore the tort, occurred in Canada. Even if the plaintiffs were able to overcome this difficulty and persuade a U.S. court to assume jurisdiction on the basis that the harm inflicted or damage suffered was in the U.S., the plaintiffs still faced a number of other difficulties.

One of these other problems is the "proper law" to be applied by the court. Should it be Canadian or U.S. law? And if the applicable law was Canadian, to what extent did Canadian law permit recovery of damages in cases where the harm suffered was in a jurisdiction different to that from which it originated? The doctrine of *forum non conveniens* dealing with the appropriate forum for an action, raises another question. Are the U.S. courts an appropriate forum for deciding a case such as this?

These were among the reasons why it was necessary for the U.S. to espouse and advocate the claims of the Washington farmers and negotiate a treaty in which Canada accepted responsibility for provable damage. An arbitral tribunal was created under that treaty to find a solution that was just to all parties. The principles articulated by that arbitral tribunal in deciding this case have become one of the pillars of state responsibility. The arbitrators determined that "under the principles of international law, ... no state has the right to use or permit the use of its territory in such a manner as to cause injury by fumes in or to the territory of another, or properties or persons therein when the case is of serious consequence and the injury is established by clear and convincing evidence." It went on to conclude that the "Dominion of Canada is responsible in international law for the conduct of the Trail Smelter. Apart from the undertakings in the Convention, it is, therefore, the duty of the Government of the Dominion of Canada to see to it that this conduct should be in conformity with the obligation of the Dominion under international law as herein determined."

9. CIVIL LIABILITY

While states painfully and slowly struggle to create rules of compensation under international law, whether based on SR or IL, they have set up a third set of rules and regimes based on civil liability that channel responsibility for an environmental wrong on the polluter rather than the state. CL regimes are usually established by treaty and place only residual duties, that could give rise to SR, upon states. These regimes of CL have the potential to be expanded into vehicles for environmental protection.

It is worth considering the extent and manner in which the farmers in the *Trail Smelter* case could have been compensated through other legal avenues. For example, the U.S. and Canada could have entered into a treaty in which their respective courts were granted jurisdiction to hear cases where damage occurred outside their ordinary jurisdiction. This approach might follow the recommendations of the Organization for Economic Co-operation and Development (OECD),[e] that provides for access to domestic courts and remedies by national and foreign entities on a non-discriminatory basis. It could also have ensured that an order by a court vested with jurisdiction under the treaty could be enforced in either country.

This principle of non-discrimination has now been incorporated into the Convention on the Law of the Non–navigational Uses of International Watercourses [**Basic Document 4.30**]. Article 32 provides that watercourse states shall not discriminate against injured parties on the basis of nationality or residence or place where the injury occurred in granting persons access to judicial or other areas of remedial justice.

Claims based on CL enjoy substantial advantages over those originating in SR or IL. To begin, a victim has direct access to justice (whether courts or administrative agencies) and does not have to await espousal or adoption by his/her country. As we have seen, decisions to prosecute claims based on SR are taken only in rare circumstances and victims are often held hostage to the politics of their own country. Second, even where states premise their case on SR the time taken in doing so often is inordinately long because the machinery of states is notoriously slow. Third, the victim is forced to rely upon the state and not an advocate or attorney of his/her choosing, to present and argue the case. Fourth, the absence of a liability regime makes recovery of damages very difficult.

Admittedly, a victim who files an action in a foreign state faces some obstacles arising from the differences of legal systems, language, procedure and execution. But the constitutive treaty establishing a CL regime can address these difficulties. The constitutive treaty could place duties on the contracting parties relating to non-discrimination, access to justice, security for payment of damages, and thereby remove or ameliorate these difficulties.

a. Treaty Overlay

Where CL regimes are created, the primary responsibility for environmental harm is usually placed on the polluter and not the state. It is important to note that modalities for doing justice to the aggrieved parties, by placing the burden of compensation on private corporations and individuals have in fact been created by a number of treaties. The United Nations Convention on the Law of the Sea (UNCLOS) [**Basic Document 4.20**], which is emerging as a constitution for the oceans, requires states to "ensure that recourse is available in accordance with their legal systems for prompt and adequate compensation or other relief in respect of damage caused by pollution of the marine environment by natural or juridical persons under their jurisdiction."[f] Civil liability remedies against private and corporate entities are also underscored by a number of other treaties.

e. *Recommendation of the Council for the Implementation of a Regime of Equal Right of Access and Non-discrimination in Relation to* *Transfrontier Pollution*, OECD, May 17, 1977, 16 I.L.M. 977 (1977) [**Basic Document 3.7**].

f.   UNCLOS, art. 235(2).

The recent Convention on the Non–navigational Uses of International Watercourses **[Basic Document 4.30],** following the OECD recommendation, expressed the principle that domestic or national courts can and should grant environmental relief and compensation, as one of "Non-discrimination." According to article 32 where a person suffers or is under a serious threat of suffering significant transboundary harm, the state in which the harm originated should grant the injured person "in accordance with its legal system, access to judicial or other procedures, or a right to claim compensation or other relief. . . ."

The same principle is embodied in a cluster of other treaties dealing with a range of activities including the peaceful use of nuclear energy; the operation of nuclear ships; maritime carriage of nuclear materials; oil pollution; the carriage of dangerous goods by road, rail and inland navigation vessels;[g] North American free trade;[h] and protection of the Antarctic.[i] The legal regimes addressing the peaceful use of nuclear energy and oil pollution are illustrative of this seam of law.

The treaties dealing with the peaceful use of nuclear energy include the 1960 Paris Convention on Third Party Liability in the Field of Nuclear Energy **[Basic Document 3.1]**, the 1997 Vienna Convention on Civil Liability for Nuclear Damage (1997 Vienna Convention) **[Basic Document 3.23]**, and the 1997 Convention on Supplementary Compensation for Nuclear Damage **[Basic Document 3.24]**. What is important about these treaties is that they place primary liability not on the state, qua state, but on the operator of the nuclear installation. In the event of the state being the operator, CL will of course, attach to the state but not on the basis of SR. These treaties only place residual or ancillary duties on the state which could give rise to SR.

For example, the 1997 Vienna Convention places liability on the operator of a nuclear installation alone,[j] and restricts jurisdiction solely to the courts of the party where the accident occurred.[k] What is noticeable is that the state is not held responsible for the actions of the operator according to the principles of state responsibility. Instead, the state is under a more limited duty to ensure that any claims against the operator are satisfied through the availability of funds, and the necessary security.[l] This duty could give rise to SR.

The field of oil pollution is governed by treaties, including for example, the 1992 International Convention on Civil Liability for Oil Pollution Damage (1992 CLC) **[Basic Document 4.25]**, and the 1992 International Convention on the Establishment of an International Fund for Compensation for Oil Pollution Damage (1992 Fund Convention) **[Basic Document 4.26]**. Like the treaties dealing with civil nuclear power, these oil pollution treaties place liability for oil pollution damage on the owner, or other individuals or corporations involved in the enterprise of the carriage of oil from one location

---

g. Bjorn Sandvik & Satu Suikkari, *Harm and Reparation in International Treaty Regimes: An Overview, in* HARM TO THE ENVIRONMENT: THE RIGHT TO COMPENSATION AND THE ASSESSMENT OF DAMAGES 57, 57–58 (Peter Wetterstein ed., 1997).

h. *See,* North American Agreement on Environmental Cooperation, arts. 5–6, 32 I.L.M. 1480 (1993) [hereinafter NAAEC], a side-agreement to NAFTA **[Basic Document 7.4]**.

i. Convention on the Regulation of Antarctic Mineral Resource Activities, art. 8 **[Basic Document 2.7]**.

j. Vienna Convention on Civil Liability for Nuclear Damage, art. II (5) **[Basic Document 3.23]**.

k. *Id.* art. 11.

l. *Id.* art. VIII.

to another.[m] They do not establish a regime of state responsibility under public international law.

The North American Agreement on Environmental Cooperation (NAAEC) **[Basic Document 7.4]** also provides national remedies of a more limited nature. This environmental side-agreement obligates each Party to ensure that judicial, quasi-judicial and administrative proceedings are available under its laws to sanction or remedy violations of its environmental laws.[n] It grants access to and empowers interested private persons to seek relief by way of damages or injunctions in the courts of that state Party, where the laws of that Party have been broken.[o] While the environmental side-agreement opens the door to persons other than those within the jurisdiction of the state Party concerned, the cause of action is limited to the breach of the laws of that Party. Unlike the regimes dealing with civil nuclear power or oil pollution, the side-agreement does not create a new regime of environmental laws that can be vindicated in the national courts of any of the state Parties.

b. Civil Liability Litigation

A civil liability case from Europe, in which the plaintiffs claimed environmental damages based on tort, illuminates the extent to which national courts can deal with cases of transnational environmental injury provided they are vested with appropriate jurisdiction by international agreement. The international agreement that enabled this case to proceed was the Convention on the Jurisdiction and the Enforcement of Judgments in Civil and Commercial Matters[p] (Enforcement of Judgments Convention). This convention had established uniform jurisdictional rules for national courts in the Member States of the then European Economic Community (EEC), now the European Union (EU), regarding disputes between parties domiciled in different Member States.

In *Bier v. Mines de Potasse d'Alsace SA* [1976] ECR 1735, a French company in Alsace discharged massive amounts of chlorides into the Rhine. The chloride allegedly damaged nursery gardens in Holland and the Dutch Supreme Court upheld the assertion of jurisdiction by a Dutch court despite the argument that releases of the chlorides into the Rhine were lawful at the points of discharge in Alsace, France. The European Court of Justice (ECJ) affirmed, basing itself on the Enforcement of Judgements Convention.[q] Subsequently, a Dutch court applied Dutch law concerning environmental damage, and rejected the defense that the conduct was lawful.[r]

By contrast in the case of the Sandoz fire,[s] and as we have seen, in the Chernobyl disaster, no actions based on SR were prosecuted. In October 1986,

---

m. GOTTHARD GAUCI, OIL POLLUTION AT SEA: CIVIL LIABILITY AND COMPENSATION FOR DAMAGE 89–119 (1997).

n. NAAEC, art. 5(2).

o. NAAEC, art. 6(2) & (3).

p. Sept. 27, 1968, 15 1972 J.O. (299) 32.

q. The ECJ held that the article 5(3) containing the expression "place where the harmful event occurred," must be understood as being intended to cover both the place where the damage occurred and the place of the event

giving rise to it. In the result the defendant may be sued, at the option of the plaintiff, either in the courts of the place where the damage was suffered or in the courts of the place where the event took place.

r. ANDREAS F. LOWENFELD, INTERNATIONAL LITIGATION AND THE QUEST FOR REASONABLENESS 30 (1996).

s. The account of this case relies on Hans Ulrich Jessurun d'Oliveira, *The Sandoz Blaze: The Damage and the Public and Private Liabil-*

a fire broke out in a chemical warehouse belonging to Sandoz S.A., a major chemical manufacturer in Switzerland. The warehouse, located on the banks of the river Rhine, contained large quantities of pesticides and other harmful chemicals; and the firefighters employed unsophisticated fire fighting methods, using huge quantities of water to extinguish the fire. Ten to fifteen thousand cubic meters of water, containing over 30 tons of toxic chemicals–including insecticides, herbicides, and fungicides–flowed directly into the Rhine due to the absence of a catchment area (customarily built as a precautionary measure to prevent this kind of direct discharge from chemical plants). The chemicals resulted in serious damage to fisheries, killed off all eels, and severely damaged the fauna and flora of the Rhine. It also posed grave threats to human health in France, Germany and Holland and even shut off the Dutch from their principal source of drinking water: the Rhine.

There are a number of treaties protecting the Rhine against pollution, to which Switzerland is a party [**Basic Documents 4.16 & 4.17**]. There is no doubt that numerous provisions of these treaties relating to the care, storage, auditing, and emergency measures pertaining to the chemicals in the warehouse had been violated. Despite this, there were no claims based on SR, and none of the injured states made any direct claims against the Swiss Confederation for damages suffered by them.

Professor Jessurun d'Oliviera has commented that the German, French and Dutch governments privatized their claims by seeking reparations against Sandoz rather than the Swiss government. His observations reinforce the political reality that states will not litigate issues based on SR for good reason. The majority of claims were settled out of court, with the help of the Swiss government within three years. This contrasts to the fourteen years taken over the *Mines de Potasse d'Alsace* case, and ten years for the Amoco–Cadiz litigation.[t] While the riparian states did not pursue actions based on SR, it is open to conjecture that the possibility of an action based on SR induced the Swiss government to exert pressure on Sandoz to settle the cases.

10. CONCLUSION

What we see is the emergence of new international laws based on civil liability (CL) that break away from the inherited system of state-controlled law that gave rise to state responsibility (SR), and international liability (IL). We live in a world in which national and international laws and regulations governing corporations and individuals, in matters of trade, commerce, health, communications, and the environment have become more important than those controlling states. This must of necessity mean that SR and IL will lose their primacy as the principal legal instruments for governing environmental protection. CL opens the door to NGOs and other private parties to use the legal system to protect the environment in a way not permitted by SR or IL.

Such a development does not mean that remedies based on SR and IL completely lose their utility or their importance. Instead SR and IL assume new significance and vitality when used as interlocking remedies in conjunc-

ities, in INTERNATIONAL RESPONSIBILITY FOR ENVIRONMENTAL HARM 429, 434–43(Francesco Francioni & Tullio Scovazzi eds., 1991).

t. *Id.* at 440–41.

tion with civil liability (CL). Many CL regimes are established by treaties that place subsidiary but nonetheless important duties on states. For example, the 1997 Vienna Convention on Civil Liability [**Basic Document 3.23**] makes the operator and not the state liable for injuries and damage caused by any accident. It also requires the state to provide adequate security to ensure that the operators will pay up. A state that does not provide such security will be violating an obligation that may be actionable under SR. Again, in the Sandoz blaze the fact that SR could have given rise to actions against Switzerland may have prompted the Swiss government to pressure Sandoz into paying up. There can be little doubt that SR and IL will continue to play an important role in IEL.

B. ARBITRAL AND JUDICIAL DECISIONS

Noted below are most of the leading international adjudicative and arbitral decisions, several of them pre-dating World War II, that have helped to lay the foundations of the emerging, modern-day customary international law of global environmental protection. The first three involve disputes arising out of the use of shared water resources and are therefore grouped together, but all should be carefully studied before proceeding to Section C.

Summary of Case Relating to the Territorial Jurisdiction of the International Commission of the River Oder (Czech., Den., Fr., Ger., Swed., U.K./Pol.), 1929 P.C.I.J. (ser. A.) No. 23, at 5 [Basic Document 8.1].

Summary of Diversion of Water from the Meuse Case (Neth. v. Belg.), 1937 P.C.I.J. (ser. A/B) No. 70, at 4 [Basic Document 8.2].

Summary of Lac Lanoux Arbitration (Spain v. Fr.), 12 U.N.R.I.A.A. 281 (1957) [Basic Document 8.3].

Trail Smelter Arbitration (U.S. v. Can.), 3 [1941] U.N.R.I.A.A. 1938, 1963–81 (1949) [Basic Document 8.4].

Corfu Channel Case (U.K. v. Alb.), 1949 I.C.J. 4 [Basic Document 8.5].

Nuclear Tests Cases (Austl. v. Fr.; N.Z. v. Fr.), 1974 I.C.J. 253, 457 [Basic Document 8.6].

C. ATTEMPTS AT CODIFICATION

Stockholm Declaration of the United Nations Conference on the Human Environment, Adopted by the UN Conference on the Human Environment at Stockholm, June 16, 1972, Report of the UN Conference on the Human Environment, June 15–16, 1972, Principles 21 and 22, U.N. Doc. A/CONF.48/14/Rev.1 at 3 (1973), UN Doc. A/CONF.48/14 at 2–65, and Corr. 1 (1972), 11 I.L.M. 1416 (1972) [Basic Document 1.12].

Rio Declaration on Environment and Development, June 14, 1992, Principles 2 and 7, UNCED Doc. A/CONF.151/5/Rev. 1, 31 I.L.M. 874 (1992) [Basic Document 1.29].

United Nations Convention on the Law of the Sea, Dec. 10, 1982, Article 235, U.N. Doc. A/CONF.62/122, 21 I.L.M. 1261 (1982) [Basic Document 4.20].

Legal Principles for Environmental Protection and Sustainable Development, Adopted by the Experts Group on Environmental Law of the World Commission on Environment and Development, June 1986, Articles 11 and 21, in Environmental Protection and Sustainable Development (1987) [Basic Document 1.22].

Restatement (Third) of the Foreign Relations Law of the United States, §§ 601–604 (1987) [Basic Document 1.23].

United Nations International Law Commission Draft Articles on State Responsibility, Pt. 1, Arts. 1–19; Pt. 2, Arts. 1–5, 44 U.N. GAOR Supp. (No. 10), at 190–93, 218–19 U.N. Doc. A/44/10 (1989) [Basic Document 1.10].

International Law Commission Draft Articles on State Responsibility, pt. 1, arts. 1–19; pt. 2, arts. 1–5, Adopted by the International Law Commission 12 July 1996. Report of the International Law Commission on the Work of its Forty-eighth Session. U.N. Doc. A/51/10 and Corr. 1, *reprinted in* 37 I.L.M. 440 (1998) [Basic Document 1.10].

United Nations International Law Commission, Draft Articles on International Liability for Injurious Consequences Arising out of Acts Not Prohibited by International Law, arts. 1–17, U.N. Doc. A/CN.4/423 [Basic Document 1.9].

D. THE TEACHINGS OF PUBLICISTS

1. HARMFUL ACTS: FORMS AND IMPLICATIONS

EDITORS OF THE HARVARD LAW REVIEW, TRENDS IN INTERNATIONAL
ENVIRONMENTAL LAW 19–28 (1992).

[T]he imposition of state responsibility requires the breach of an international obligation. For transboundary pollution [and other transnational environmental harms], responsibility attaches to conduct attributable to the state that violates the principle of *sic utere tuo ut alienum non laedas*.[1]

Under the principle *sic utere*, a state has a duty to refrain from acts that would cause injury to persons or property located in the territory of another state. The 1938 *Trail Smelter* arbitration introduced the principle into international environmental jurisprudence. **[Basic Document 8.4]** A few subsequent decisions by international courts and tribunals have ratified the *sic utere* principle in international law.[2] International legal scholars have similarly asserted that transfrontier pollution [and transnational environmental harms] [violate] principles of customary international law. Indeed, the 1987 *Restatement (Third) of the Foreign Relations Law [of the United States]* **[Basic Document 1.23]**, whose "principles" for environmental law "are rooted in customary international law,"[3] specifies that a state must take all necessary measures, to the extent possible, to prevent activities within its jurisdiction or control from causing significant injury to the environment outside its jurisdiction. The *Restatement* also codifies the state's responsibility "for any significant injury resulting from such violation, to the environment of areas beyond the limits of national jurisdiction."[4] Moreover, states have ratified international treaties and declarations reaffirming the obligation to prevent significant transboundary injury[,] [f]or example, Principle 21 of the [1972] Stockholm Declaration on the Human Environment **[Basic Document 1.12]**. . . .

* * *

The last two decades have witnessed the proliferation of scholarly literature on international liability for transnational pollution . . . , [treating] the subject as if any actual regime exists for adjudicating disputes and imposing liability upon a state for activities within its jurisdiction or control that injure the environment of another state. Meanwhile, the International Law Commission (ILC) of the United Nations has set its thirty-four experts to the task of

---

1. The Principle dictates that "one should use his own property in such a manner as not to injure that of another." BLACK'S LAW DICTIONARY 1380 (6th ed. 1990).

2. *See, e.g.*, Corfu Channel (U.K. v. Alb.) **[Basic Document 8.5]** (affirming "every State's obligation not to allow knowingly its territory to be used for acts contrary to the rights of other states"). Many commentators

interpret *Corfu Channel* as establishing a principle of state responsibility for transfrontier pollution.

3. RESTATEMENT (THIRD) OF THE FOREIGN RELATIONS LAW OF THE UNITED STATES §§ 601-604 introductory note (1987).

4. *Id.* § 601(2)(b).

codifying doctrines of state responsibility and international liability from customary international law. Other international organizations, such as the Organization for Economic Cooperation and Development (OECD), the United Nations Environment Programme (UNEP), and the World Commission on Environment and Development (WCED), have similarly extrapolated rules of liability for states from customary practices, general principles of law, treaties, charters, and international judicial decisions.

Notwithstanding the close attention ... , no operational system for adjudicating liability has emerged. The International Court of Justice (ICJ) has heard only one dispute of note, the *Nuclear Tests* case **[Basic Document 8.6]**, and international arbitration has entered only a few notable cases.... No state even brought suit against the Soviet Union following the 1985 Chernobyl accident, although more than twenty states registered significant increases in radioactivity levels. Moreover, no downstream states sought any remedy under international law against Switzerland for the damages caused by the 1986 Sandoz spill of toxic chemicals into the Rhine River, despite possible Swiss violations of a treaty that provided for arbitration of all disputes. Publicists' efforts at codifying standards of conduct notwithstanding, international liability remains an empty abstraction.

Moreover, the scant international environmental case law that does exist possesses little precedential value because the cases are decided not on environmental liability grounds but rather on narrow mootness or treaty grounds. Thus, neither scholars nor international judges can legitimately rely upon these cases to generate more specific liability rules.... Even the Trail Smelter arbitration, heralded as "the *locus classicus* of international legal principles on transnational pollution,"[5] has limited precedential value, because the tribunal determined Canadian responsibility from the terms of a *compromis* reach between the [United States and the United Kingdom (for Canada)] and never considered whether Canada's conduct violated rules of customary international law.

The scarcity of noteworthy decisions and their limited precedential value have stifled doctrinal development and rendered an embryonic liability system unable to communicate expectations about the consequences of action or inaction to prospective [environmentally injurious] states. The dearth of case law deprives the principle of *sic utere* of the specificity that application to particular instances ... would arguably furnish. Instead, *sic utere* remains an abstraction, an empty concept that commentators hope to fill with substantive content, preferably content bearing the imprimatur of the United Nations or some other international organization.

Yet the illusory nature of liability for transboundary environmental harm hardly stems from a simple failure to develop specific content for the principle of *sic utere*. Rather, the lack of case law reflects the refusal of states to countenance even the partial relinquishment of sovereignty that submission to binding third-party adjudication would entail.... The challenge for the publicists, then, lies in the promulgation of an international liability regime that so advances the interests of states that nations will surrender some of

---

5. Gunther Handl, *Territorial Sovereignty*   Am. J. Int'l L. 50, 60 (1975).
and the Problem of International Pollution, 69

their sovereign rights to participate in the system. By deriving duties from immanent [i.e., existing or intrinsic] principles and customs of international law, however, publicists have presupposed that vague *customs* coincide sufficiently with the shared *interests* of states to secure eventual acceptance of the liability regime. [It is not unreasonable to suggest] that the publicists may have assumed what they first should have set out to prove.

Riccardo Pisillo–Mazzeschi, *Forms of International Responsibility for Environmental Harm, in* International Responsibility for Environmental Harm 15, 15–17, 18–26 (Francesco Francioni & Tullio Scovazzi eds., 1991).

[I]nternational practice shows that the States have now accepted a general principle of responsibility for environmental harm: that is, the principle that they must answer for environmental harm caused by activities they have carried out or allowed within their own territory or by activities that are under their control. Yet there still remain many uncertainties as to the exact content and the limits of such a principle. In particular, one of the most important problems, and the one which is the subject of the present chapter, concerns the legal basis and the form of international responsibility for environmental harm.[u]

In addressing this problem, we must first clarify what forms, theoretically and generally, the international responsibility of States may take. In this regard, we can basically identify three different regimes of responsibility for a wrongful act and one regime of liability without a wrongful act.

The first regime of responsibility for a wrongful act is the one of fault responsibility. According to the traditional view, ... it is up to the victim State to prove, in addition to the breach of the international obligation, the psychological fault (wilful or negligent conduct) of the organs of the State accused of the wrongful act. According ... to a different thesis, and one which I prefer, emphasis must be placed on the content of a particular category of primary obligations of the State and therefore one must speak of a regime of responsibility for breach of due diligence obligations (considering due diligence as an objective and international standard of behavior).

Fault responsibility is in contrast to objective responsibility (or responsibility without fault). In the traditional view, ... responsibility does not require fault, but arises from the mere breach of an international obligation. We can identify two different regimes of objective responsibility: objective and relative responsibility (or strict responsibility), when the State accused of the wrongful act may invoke ... circumstances precluding wrongfulness allowed by international law; and objective and absolute responsibility, when no circumstance precluding wrongfulness is allowed....

Lastly ..., alongside these three different forms of responsibility for a wrongful act, there must ... be allowed the possibility of ... liability without

u. In another paragraph, the author notes: "In contemporary international law the term 'responsibility' usually means the consequences arising from the breach of an international obligation; while the term 'liability' means the duty to compensate damage in the absence of a violation of international law.... [Here] the term 'responsibility' will be used as a generic term when dealing with the problems common to both 'responsibility' and 'liability.'"

a wrongful act. Such [a] regime is characterized by the fact that the obligation to pay compensation, or, more generally, liability, arises from lawful activities, on the basis of the mere causal link between these activities and the damage done. For this reason, such form of liability is, by its own nature, objective and absolute.

Liability without a wrongful act must be clearly contrasted to responsibility for a wrongful act.... [I]n the doctrine there is often conceptual and terminological confusion. Indeed, many authors, in referring to liability without a wrongful act, speak of objective responsibility or of strict responsibility. In this way, they erroneously assume that the distinction between responsibility for a wrongful act and liability without a wrongful act corresponds to the distinction between fault responsibility and responsibility without fault.

Having theoretically and generally defined the possible forms of international responsibility of States, we must now deal with the specific problem concerning the form of international responsibility for environmental harm. This problem will be dealt with first in the perspective of conventional law and then in the perspective of customary law.

I. Responsibility for Environmental Harm in Conventional International Law

In conventional international law on the protection of the environment, there are sometimes agreements that contain fairly precise rules on responsibility, which indicate the form of responsibility applicable in case of breach of treaty obligations or in case of damage. For example, the 1972 Convention on International Liability for Damage Caused by Space Objects [**Basic Document 3.5**] expressly provides two different forms of responsibility: absolute liability without a wrongful act for damage caused on the surface of the earth or to aircraft in flight (Art. II) and fault responsibility for other kinds of damage (Art. III).

* * *

In reality, however, the existence of precise treaty rules on responsibility is very rare. Indeed, in most agreements on environmental protection, either there are no rules at all on responsibility or there are only very general and vague rules. In such a situation, in order to establish whether responsibility for breach of treaty rules exists, and what the form of such responsibility is, in each case the exact nature of the primary obligations laid down by the treaty must be identified.

In this context, several categories of primary obligations, to which correspond various forms of responsibility, can be found in environmental treaty law.

First of all, the treaty may contemplate very general commitments concerning cooperation among the States Parties. The vagueness and the uncertainty of such commitments raises doubts as to their binding nature and therefore also doubts as to the possibility of enforcing international responsibility for their breach. Commitments of this kind are, for example, laid down in the 1979 Geneva Convention on Long Range Transboundary Air Pollution [**Basic Document 3.8**] (see, especially, Arts. 2, 3, 4, 5). Confirmation that they are non-binding commitments is given by the fact that the Convention excludes that international responsibility is applicable in the event of their breach. Indeed, the Convention expressly states in a footnote that it does not contain rules on State responsibility.

There are, then, other conventions which, after establishing commitments among the States Parties to cooperate, only lay down an abstract principle of responsibility and provide that the States Parties pledge themselves to adopt in the future precise rules regarding responsibility. See, for example, [Article 12 of] the 1976 Barcelona Convention for the Protection of the Mediterranean Sea Against Pollution **[Basic Document 4.15]**. . . .

Secondly, the treaty may establish true obligations to prevent pollution. Actually, the great majority of existing treaties, in laying down general obligations binding on the States, provide obligations mainly of this kind. Indeed, many agreements contain a special clause, in which the States pledge themselves to take "all appropriate measures" or to make "appropriate efforts" to control and reduce sources of pollution in the area or in the space concerned. This is to be done both by establishing technical and administrative procedures in their own territory or regarding activities under their control and sometimes by organizing procedures for informing other States in the event of pollution. It is clear that such agreements do not establish the strict obligation not to pollute (obligation of result), but only the obligation to "endeavor" under the due diligence rule to prevent, control, and reduce pollution. For this reason the breach of such obligation involves responsibility for fault (*rectius*: for lack of due diligence).

* * *

Thirdly, it may happen that a treaty, in order further to specify and substantiate the States' obligations concerning the environment, contains rules which expressly prohibit certain polluting activities, and therefore places on the States real and strict obligations not to pollute (obligations of result). Evidently, to the breach of such obligations there corresponds objective responsibility (usually relative). For example, [Article 1(1) of] the UN Convention on the Prohibition of Military and any other Hostile Use of Environmental Modification Techniques **[Basic Document 7.30]** lays down an obligation of result. . . .

Lastly, it is possible that a treaty on environmental protection establishes forms of liability without a wrongful act. In this respect, the most well-known multilateral treaty is the already-cited one on international liability for damage caused by space objects. However, there are also several bilateral agreements which establish international liability for extra-territorial damage suffered by a Contracting Party and resulting from whatever type of activity carried out in the territory of the other Contracting Party. . . .

In conclusion, an overall evaluation of conventional international law on the protection of the environment shows that various categories of obligations can be found to whose breach there correspond all the possible forms of international responsibility. In reality, the weight of the practice adopts due diligence obligations regarding prevention, to whose breach there corresponds responsibility for fault (or for lack of due diligence). Nevertheless, one should not exclude the possibility that the States might establish by treaty obligations of result, to which there correspond forms of objective responsibility (relative or absolute), or might even establish forms of liability without a wrongful act.

II. Responsibility for Environmental Harm in Customary International Law

The problem of the form of responsibility for environmental harm is much more complex and controversial in customary international law....

1. *The Doctrine*

Legal doctrine is very divided as to the basis and the form of international responsibility for environmental harm in customary international law. One can roughly identify three main views, which we should examine separately.

The first view tends to resolve the problem in the framework of liability without a wrongful act. Indeed, some authors hold that the application of modern technology to industrial activities and to hazardous activities has created a special situation; this is, that on the one hand scientific progress requires that certain activities cannot be prohibited while, on the other, reparation must be provided for the damage that they cause. According to these authors, this situation has made the traditional criteria of State responsibility inadequate and has brought about effects in international law on responsibility, similar to those that have been seen in national law, through the creation of new principles on responsibility and especially concerning forms of liability without a wrongful act.

At first these authors attempted to place the new problems in the framework of responsibility for abuse of rights; subsequently, they developed the theory of risk liability for ultra-hazardous activities, and, lastly, they extended the application of this latter theory to the protection of the environment. In particular, with regard to environmental protection, they hold that the State in whose territory the source of pollution is located is *in any case* liable and obligated to pay compensation simply as a result of the occurrence of significant transnational environmental harm. According to some authors, this rule derives from general principles of law recognized by civilized nations. According to others . . . , the trend towards liability without a wrongful act for transnational damage is by now well-established in international practice at the conventional, diplomatic, and judicial level.

In sharp contrast to the above view, a good part of the literature opposes the trends favoring the affirmation of liability without a wrongful act in certain areas of general international law; such authors hold firmly to traditional positions on responsibility, and maintain that, in *general international law*, reparation for damages and, more generally, responsibility, can arise only from the breach of a specific international obligation and therefore from a wrongful act.

On the basis of this, the solution to problems created by the protection of the environment is no longer seen in the perspective of responsibility but in that of primary rules. One must evaluate whether there have been developments, not in the area of responsibility but in the area of primary rules, through the birth of new rules which set limits on State sovereignty. One must, in particular, find out what are the substantive rules of general international law in force in the environmental sector, in order to determine whether there are general obligations of the States, what is possibly the content of such obligations (that is, whether they are due diligence obligations or obligations of result), and whether, therefore, their breach results in forms of responsibility for fault (or for lack of due diligence) or in forms of objective responsibility (relative or absolute). In other words, the discussion must move from the field of responsibility to the field of primary obligations of a general character binding on the States.

Nevertheless, it is precisely with regard to the discovery of such obligations that, in the above view, three different theses can be identified.

Under the first thesis, general international law up to now has not set any limits on the States as to the use of their territory and therefore it has not as yet laid down any customary obligations of the States with regard to protection of the environment. The supporters of this thesis point out that the existing international practice is for now too scanty to justify such an important limit on State territorial sovereignty.

The second thesis, supported by the majority, holds, instead, that today there do exist limits to territorial sovereignty which arise from real general obligations of the States with regard to environmental protection. In particular, there exists a general rule concerning the environment, which, according to different views, can be traced back to a specific custom, or to relations between neighboring States, or to principles such as *nerninem laedere* or the non-injurious use of the territory.

However, according to this second thesis, such general rule does not entail the prohibition of any pollution, that is, an obligation of result, but only an obligation of prevention limited by the due diligence standard; that is, only the obligation of the States to undertake appropriate measures, which are normally required by a "civilized State", to prevent substantial pollution. Therefore, the breach of such obligation involves responsibility for a wrongful act based on fault (or owing to lack of due diligence). We note that the wrongfulness is not to be attributed to the polluting activity, but to the conduct of the State with regard to such activity. Therefore, the State's conduct will be wrongful if such State has not used all possible measures to prevent the damage that are laid down by the due diligence standard; on the contrary, the conduct of the State that has used such measures will be lawful.

Lastly, still within the general position contrary to liability without a wrongful act ... , [s]ome authors ... hold that the customary norms on pollution contain not only due diligence obligations but also obligations of result, whose breach creates objective responsibility. Yet these authors do not specify which customary obligations on protection of the environment are due diligence obligations and which are obligations of result.

As we can see, there is a sharp contrast between the general position favoring liability without a wrongful act and the one favoring responsibility for a wrongful act. Moreover, as we said at the outset, we can find in the more recent doctrine a third general view, one which attempts to overcome this contrast between the two above radical positions, by trying to reconcile them. This view includes a series of theories, whose common denominator is the attempt to allow the coexistence, with regard to environmental protection, of a general regime of responsibility for a wrongful act based on fault along with special regimes of a residual nature which, in special cases, provide for liability without a wrongful act.

The special rules which, in some cases, link liability to the simple fact of pollution instead of to wrongful conduct are variously interpreted by different authors. For example, according to some authors, liability without a wrongful act applies to environmental harm caused by hazardous or ultra-hazardous activities, such as nuclear activities, outer space activities, and activities involving exploration and transportation of hydrocarbons; and this stems from a general principle of law recognized by civilized nations. According to others, liability without a wrongful act applies when harmful activities occur whose wrongfulness is excluded by certain circumstances precluding wrongfulness (such as, for example, force majeure or a fortuitous event) and when it is a question of activities that "certainly" cause substantial environmental harm but there is a great disparity between the costs necessary to avoid the damage and the importance of the damage itself. Lastly, according to still other authors, liability without a wrongful act applies when a "recognizably relevant" transnational risk exists that cannot be eliminated with reasonable caution and when the damage represents "a typical effect of such risk".

As we can note, the theses we have just examined—even if they partly differ—assign a role both to responsibility for a wrongful act and to liability without a wrongful act with regard to protection of the environment.

This basic idea seems to be, on the whole, accepted also by the ILC [International Law Commission]. In fact, the ILC, on the one hand, in its works on State responsibility, has clarified that the breach of rules concerning the environment may constitute a wrongful act and even, in some cases, an international crime. On the other hand, in its works on international liability for acts not prohibited by international law, the ILC has considerably developed, with regard to the environment, the concept of liability, as a primary obligation to provide reparation. However, the concept of liability is not intended to bypass and to substitute the concept of responsibility for a wrongful act. First of all, the Special Rapporteurs Quentin–Baxter and Barboza expressly made clear that the regime of liability for transnational damage to the environment does not exclude at all a parallel regime of responsibility for a wrongful act. Secondly, we must note that, within the regime of international liability, the initial approach of Rapporteur Quentin–Baxter, entirely aimed at placing international liability in the framework of primary rules, was to a great extent modified by Rapporteur Barboza who more and more tends to bring obligations of prevention within a regime of responsibility for a wrongful act based on fault and obligations to provide reparation within a regime of risk liability.

* * *

Alan E. Boyle, *State Responsibility and International Liability for Injurious Consequences Not Prohibited by International Law: a Necessary Distinction?* 39 INT'L & COMP. L.Q. 1, 1–4, 21–24 (1990).

The topic "International Liability for the Injurious Consequences of Acts Not Prohibited by International Law" has been on the agenda of the International Law Commission since 1978. Despite adopting an ever narrower focus, it remains a difficult and controversial one. There are two major reasons for this.

First, at a theoretical level, it is not clear that the conceptual basis on which it is distinguished from State responsibility is either sound or necessary. Second, at a more practical level, it is questionable whether it represents a useful basis for codification and development of existing law and practice relating to environmental harm, the field in which the Commission has mainly located the topic.

From either perspective, it is liable to seem at best a questionable exercise in reconceptualising an existing body of law, or at worst, a dangerously retrograde step which may seriously weaken international efforts to secure agreement on effective principles of international environmental law. The purpose of this article is to explore the arguments for the new topic and to examine briefly the Commission's main proposals.

Status, Origins and Scope of the Topic

Present Status

The first special rapporteur presented his preliminary report to the Commission in 1980. Four more reports, a schematic outline and five draft articles followed. A new special rapporteur was appointed in 1985. He has delivered five reports and proposed revised draft articles, which make some significant changes in the original outline. It is clear that the Commission is still some distance from agreement on the content and form of its final conclusions, and some members of the United Nations Sixth Committee[v] remain unconvinced of the topic's value or critical of certain aspects. Much work thus remains to be done.

* * *

The Scope of the Topic

Responsibility for acts not in themselves wrongful was equated by some members of the Commission with "responsibility for risk", or "liability without fault". Activities in outer space, or involving nuclear energy or connected with the environment were given as examples which might support this form of responsibility. Professor Quentin Baxter noted in his preliminary report that "the specific context in which the topic is discussed has always been that of environmental hazard",[6] and there is no doubt that this is what Commission members had in mind initially.

When the matter reached its agenda as a separate item, however, the Commission avoided exclusive identification with environmental protection, and sought rules of a more general nature, which could also include forms of harm arising out of economic or monetary activities. This was reflected in the first draft of the rapporteur's schematic outline.

---

v. The Sixth Committee of the U.N. General Assembly is responsible for all legal matters of concern to the General Assembly, including the activities of the International Law Commission which reports to it.

6. 1 Y.B.I.L.C. 24, para. 4 (II–1980).

It quickly became apparent, however, that the precedents on which the Commission would have to rely came exclusively from the environmental field or dealt only with physical transboundary harm. They included the *Trail Smelter* and *Lac Lanoux Arbitrations* [**Basic Documents 8.4 & 8.3**], the *Corfu Channel Case* [**Basic Document 8.5**], pollution liability treaties, and the Law of the Sea Convention 1982 [**Basic Document 4.20**]. There was no comparable basis for establishing or codifying principles in the sphere of economic relations, and the rapporteur concluded that "there is no possibility of proceeding inductively from the evidence of State practice in the field of the physical uses of territory to the formulation of rules or guidelines in the economic field".[7] With the agreement of the Commission and the Sixth Committee of the General Assembly, he therefore decided to confine future work to environmental matters, by concentrating on activities with physical transboundary consequences affecting the use or enjoyment of territory, or other areas within the control of States. The present rapporteur has made this environmental perspective explicit in his revised draft articles, presented to the Commission in 1988.

Thus, in practice, the Commission's work on injurious consequences of acts not prohibited by international law has become an attempt to codify and develop aspects of international environmental law, overlapping in part with the law of State responsibility for breach of environmental obligations and in part with the Commission's simultaneous effort to codify the law relating to the non-navigational uses and environmental protection of international watercourses.

* * *

Viability and Necessity: Conclusions

The apparent distinctions which the Commission has drawn between State responsibility and international liability are in many cases implausible. It is difficult to resist the conclusion that much of what the Commission is now proposing could be conceptually contained within a regime of obligations whose breach entailed State responsibility. "Liability", like "responsibility", is now used by the Commission to refer to obligations and the consequences of their breach; the primary obligations of notification, consultation and harm prevention are acknowledged to exist in customary law and to carry responsibility for breach; the notion that activities incurring responsibility for harm are unlawful and prohibited can be seen as misconceived and oversimplified; and the elements of harm, knowledge and control are all drawn directly from comparable use in a State responsibility context. The only elements of the topic which merit the Commission's efforts to construct a separate regime are the concept of strict liability for environmental harm and the balance of interests sought by the rapporteurs. But even these could be dealt with within the concept of State responsibility, provided it is clear what the substantive environmental obligations of States are.

The rapporteurs have always accepted the coexistence of their proposed regime with that of State responsibility; the more one examines the elements which are supposed to differentiate them, however, the weaker these become.

---

7.   1 Y.B.I.L.C. 205, para. 15 (II–1983).

If this is the case, it would have been wiser to concentrate not on the topic as originally conceived, but to approach it from the altogether more practical and less theoretically questionable standpoint of codifying and developing a set of basic environmental obligations for States. This is a task in which other organisations, such as the United Nations Environment Programme or the International Maritime Organisation, or States themselves, have been engaged with much greater success. Treaties already define in many specific situations what the environmental obligations of States are. In some cases the measures to be taken are precisely stated, as for example in the 1973 International Maritime Organisation's Marine Pollution Convention **[Basic Document 4.12]** which sets detailed standards for the control of pollution from ships. In other cases, a looser standard is employed, requiring States only to "endeavour" to control a particular problem or to take "all reasonable measures" or "all necessary measures" to do so. Both formulations can be used to give content to a duty of due diligence in the control of harmful activities; and to set international or regional standards of conduct aimed at the prevention of environmental harm.

Thus in practical terms due diligence can now offer a workable standard by which to judge the responsibility of States for environmental harm. It has the added advantage that its definition in treaty practice can be related to the needs of each case, and offer clear evidence of the support of States. What is now needed is the elevation of this standard into general customary law: in effect a globalisation of environmental obligations comparable to what has been achieved for the marine environment by the Law of the Sea Convention and related treaties. This would provide both an adequate basis for responsibility and for the obligation of harm prevention sought by Rapporteurs Quentin–Baxter and Barboza. After some hesitation, the Commission's 1989 articles do appear to be heading in this direction. The rapporteur has noted the need to give "an equally important role to the concepts of harm and risk",[8] and his draft articles on prevention, assessment, notification and negotiation reflect contemporary developments in international environmental law and practice. The only serious objection to this course is that it may still be premature for the Commission to undertake such an ambitious task of codification and development, and it may be the wrong forum for a matter of such political sensitivity. Nevertheless the Legal Principles and Recommendations of the World Commission on Environment and Development **[Basic Document 1.22]** already exist as one possible model and it has its own work on international watercourses on which to draw.

There is still a case, however, for looking at the adoption of a stricter standard of responsibility for damage in some situations. A few treaties, such as the 1972 Convention on International Liability for Damage Caused by Space Objects **[Basic Document 3.5]**, have already done this. But it is not yet a widely accepted standard. There remains doubt over whether it applies to all cases of a high risk of serious damage, to unforeseeable accidents or harm, or only to those cases provided for by treaty. The Chernobyl accident has exposed the lack of agreement on these issues,[w] and it is now necessary to address generally the question when it is appropriate and acceptable to expect States to make good losses inflicted without lack of due diligence. This is not a

8. U.N. Doc. A/CN.4/L.438, para. 44, at 22 (1989).   **w.** *See infra*, Problem 7–3 ("The Atomic Steel Mill").

task which necessitates extended theoretical analysis; it is more a matter of deciding whether a general principle is possible, how it should be defined, and if generality is too ambitious, to what specific activities it should be applied.

Finally, while a balancing of interests in environmental disputes is probably a necessary and inevitable condition of progress in the regulation of the global environment, this is also not an issue which needs a new conceptual framework for the subject. It is better tackled in the context of developing appropriate remedies for the breach of environmental obligations, including those breaches which pose only a risk of possible harm. The role of injunctions and declarations in international law needs careful reconsideration for this purpose, for while there is no difficulty postulating an obligation of harm prevention based on standards of diligent conduct such as the MARPOL Convention **[Basic Document 4.12]**, there remains great uncertainty, following the *Nuclear Tests Cases* **[Basic Document 8.6]**, over the existence of adequate preventive or preemptive remedies to enforce such standards.

Thus, the Commission's present approach to the topic of international liability can best be summarised as a combination of two elements. On the one hand, it is busy elaborating a set of substantive and procedural primary obligations aimed at protecting the environment and other States from serious harm. These obligations draw largely on existing legal developments and precedents. On the other hand, the Commission's principle of causal liability provides a largely novel basis for reparation complementing State responsibility or operating in cases where responsibility does not arise. As such, it is only questionably supported by State practice and existing law.

The assumption that such a principle is desirable is not itself in question here. Rather, the main problems concerning the Commission are to identify its proper scope and its conceptual basis. There is some reason to believe that it has begun to answer the first of these questions satisfactorily, and to move away from earlier concentration on conceptual distinctions between the present topic and the principle of State responsibility. As we have seen here, that issue has largely been unproductive and frequently misconceived. The voluminous and often turgid character of much of the early work on this topic belies the essential modesty of what is now emerging: much less a counterpart to the principle of State responsibility than was originally conceived, it has become simply an attempt to codify and develop aspects of international environmental law.

Editors' Note

In most cases, state responsibility is invoked when individual states have actually suffered harm. We now explain a cognate cluster of three concepts and obligations, particularly as they are pertinent to international environmental law—obligations *erga omnes*, rules *jus cogens*, and international crimes—which are said to engage state responsibility even where injury in fact cannot be proved. These obligations constitute a relatively new and important phenomena in international law, embracing "community" as distinct from "individual" grievances relevant to state responsibility. They are especially relevant to international environmental law because many environmental harms affect either directly or indirectly the entire international community. The global environment constitutes a huge, intricate, delicate, and interconnected web in which a touch here or palpitation there sends tremors throughout the whole system. Obligations *erga omnes*, rules *jus cogens*, and international crimes respond to this state of affairs by permitting environmental wrongs to be guarded against by all nations. Central to their legal character is the distinction between international obligations that can be vindicated only when a state demonstrates actual injury to itself and those that are of such importance to the international community that individual states are authorized to vindicate the obligations even if they have not suffered direct harm themselves. These latter community obligations, it may be said, give rise to community rights. A corollary is that the rules governing standing to vindicate such rights are changed also.

The first case seeking to vindicate community rights without having to show individual harm (or standing) ended in failure. In *South West Africa* (Eth. v. S. Afr.) (Liber. v. S. Afr.) (Second Phase), 1966 I.C.J. 6, Liberia and Ethiopia (the Applicants) instituted proceedings against South Africa for practicing apartheid and committing various other breaches of international law in South West Africa (now Namibia) in violation of its mandate under the League of Nations mandate system. The Applicants had not suffered injury themselves, but pressed their claims as members of the League of Nations who had an interest in South Africa performing its obligations under international law. The International Court of Justice asserted, however, the need to show actual injury before a breach of international law could be prosecuted, holding that Liberia and Ethiopia could not exercise rights they did not individually possess. At 1966 I.C.J. 47, it characterized the rights claimed by the Applicants as amounting to

> a plea that the Court should allow the equivalent of an "actio popularis" or right resident in any member of a community to take legal action in vindication of a public interest. But although a right of this kind may be known to certain municipal systems of law, it is unknown to international law as it stands at present. . . .

It seems clear that the unarticulated major premise of the World Court was that the appropriate domestic law analogy for dealing with this vexed international problem was tort law governed by applicable rules of civil procedure.

It may be reasonably argued, however, that this inclination to apply private law remedies sounding in tort to public international law has persisted far too long. As Elihu Root, addressing himself to the absence of a "general recognition of the right of nations to object," long ago observed:

> Up to this time breaches of international law have been treated as we treat wrongs under civil procedure, as if they concerned nobody except the particular nation upon which the injury was inflicted and the nation inflicting it. There has been no general recognition of the right of other nations to object. . . . If the law of nations is to be binding . . . , there must be a change in theory, and violations of the law of such character as to threaten peace and order of the community be deemed to be a violation of the right of every civilized nation to have law maintained and a legal injury to every nation. . . . Wherever in the world the laws which should protect the independence of nations, the inviolability of their territory, the lives and property of their citizens, are violated, all other nations have a right to protest against the breaking down of the law.[x]

x. Elihu Root, *The Outlook for International-al Law*, 9 AM. SOC'Y INT'L L. PROC. 2, 7–9 (1915).

But it was not until *Barcelona Traction, Light and Power Company, Limited* that the World Court articulated a different vision and theory from that adopted in the case of *South West Africa*. It stated that:

> an essential distinction should be drawn between the obligations of a state toward the international community as a whole, and those arising vis-à-vis another state.... By their very nature the former are the concern of all states. In view of the importance of the rights involved, all states can be held to have a legal interest in their protection: they are obligations erga omnes.[y]

These obligations derive, the Court went on to observe, "from the outlawing of acts of aggression, and of genocide, as also from the principles and rules concerning the basic rights of the human person, including the protection from slavery and racial discrimination."[z] "Others," it noted further, "are conferred by international instruments of universal or quasi-universal character." Id.

The examples given by the I.C.J. could well be expanded to embrace significant environmental harms. Indeed, this was precisely the view of Australia and New Zealand in the *Nuclear Tests* cases [**Basic Document 8.6**]. They asserted an obligation *erga omnes* prohibiting nuclear testing, and claimed the right of every state, including themselves, to vindicate this community right. Unfortunately, the Court chose not to decide this issue.

Rules *jus cogens* are a species of the genus of obligations *erga omnes*. Their distinguishing feature is their indelibility that arises from their hierarchical superiority to all other international rules except subsequent *jus cogens* rules addressing the same issue. They are exceptional rules of international law, peremptory norms, that cannot be set aside by acquiescence or treaty, only by the formation of a subsequent rule to contrary effect. Thus article 53 of the Vienna Convention on the Law of Treaties [**Basic Document 1.7**], which voids treaties conflicting with peremptory norms of international law (jus cogens), states that:

> a peremptory norm of general international law is a norm accepted and recognized by the international community of states as a whole as a norm from which no derogation is permitted and which can be modified only by a subsequent norm of general international law having the same character.

The Vienna Convention thus makes clear that the *ratios legis* of *jus cogens* are located in obligations *erga omnes*. However, not all obligations *erga omnes* have *jus cogens* status. Only those rules that are seen by the international community as having constitutional import rise to this status.

Finally, international crimes constitute a species of obligations *erga omnes* that are even more difficult to establish than *jus cogens*. In article 19(2) of its Draft Articles on State Responsibility [**Basic Document 1.10**], the International Law Commission distinguished intentional crimes from intentional delicts (torts):

> An internationally wrongful act which results from the breach by a State of an intentional obligation so essential for the protection of fundamental interests of the international community that its breach is recognized as a crime by that community as a whole constitutes an international crime.

Article 19 then goes on to explicate, in subparagraph 3, that a "serious breach of an international obligation of essential importance for the safeguarding and

---

y. Barcelona Traction, Light and Power Company, Limited (Belg. v. Spain) (Second Phase), 1970 I.C.J. 3, at 32.

z. *Id.*

preservation of the human environment, such as those prohibiting massive pollution of the atmosphere or of the seas" may result in an international crime. It is worth noting that only "serious breaches" of obligations *erga omnes* qualify as international crimes. In its commentary, the I.L.C. explains that while some breaches of a rule of *jus cogens* might amount to a crime, rules *jus cogens* are much broader than crimes. See 2 Y. B. Int'l L. Comm'n pt. 2, at 120 (1976).

To sum up, there exist three types of community obligations: *erga omnes, jus cogens*, and international crimes, found in descending order of frequency. This emerging public law dimension of state responsibility merits scrutiny in any analysis of international environmental wrongdoing.

Marina Spinedi, *Protection of the Environment Through Criminal Law* 2 Y. B. Int'l Envtl. L. 99, 99–101 (1991).

In 1991, the most important development concerning the protection of the environment through criminal law was the adoption on first reading by the International Law Commission (lLC), at its forty-third session, of the Draft Code of Crimes against the Peace and Security of Mankind **[Basic Document 7.28]**. One of the crimes listed in the Code is the causing of "widespread, long-term and severe damage to the natural environment."

The draft Code deals exclusively with the responsibility of individuals, be they private persons or State organs. It does not deal with the responsibility that could be incurred by the State for an act or an omission attributable to it.

* * *

The existence of international criminal responsibility of the State for a willful destruction of the environment such as that committed by Iraq during the Gulf war has not been expressly advanced.

In its resolution 687 of 3 April 1991 **[Basic Document 7.32]**, the UN Security Council affirmed that Iraq "is liable under international law for any direct loss, damage, including environmental damage and the depletion of natural resources [...] as a result of Iraq's unlawful invasion and occupation of Kuwait" (paragraph 16) and it created a Fund to pay compensation for such damage (paragraph 18). During the discussions at the [General Assembly's] Sixth Committee on the item of exploitation of environment as a weapon ... , speakers invoked financial responsibility of the State in addition to personal criminal responsibility of State organs.

According to Art. 19, para. 3(d) of the Draft Articles on State Responsibility **[Basic Document 1.10]** adopted on first reading by the ILC in 1976, an international crime of the State may result from "a serious breach of an international obligation of essential importance for the safeguarding and preservation of the human environment, such as those prohibiting massive pollution of the atmosphere or the seas." However, the characterization of a wrongful act of the State as a "crime" in the ILC's Draft did not have as its aim indicating that such a wrongful act entailed the punishment of the State or other forms of responsibility close to that provided for in the criminal law of modern domestic legal systems. It had only as its aim indicating that such a wrongful act was particularly serious and that: a) it entailed a regime of responsibility more severe than that attached to "ordinary" wrongful acts (including subjection to the sanctions provided for by the UN Charter); and b) it injured all the States. The positions taken by States in relation to the willful massive pollution caused by Iraq in the Gulf region seem to confirm that only in this sense can one speak of international "crimes" of States.

Georges Abi–Saab, *The Concept of "International Crimes" and Its Place in Contemporary International Law, in* INTERNATIONAL CRIMES OF STATE: A CRITICAL ANALYSIS OF THE ILC'S DRAFT ARTICLE 19 ON STATE RESPONSIBILITY 141, 142–45 (J. Weiler et al. eds., 1989).

My first question ... is ... whether, as a matter of positive law, the concept or category of "international crimes" constitutes a part of the corpus of contemporary international law....

* * *

A. *Historically,* I would say that whatever was the status of the question before 1945, the UN Charter **[Basic Document 1.3]** created a clear situation according to which, at least as far as peace and security are concerned, we have a consecration in legal and institutional terms of one supreme value, a value that social scientists would now call a "public good": the necessity and indivisibility of peace.... The legal system is no longer unhinged; it does not just float; it has a center and an orbit revolving around that center: that value. All the rest has to be situated in relation to that pivot, which determines the degrees of freedom that can be accommodated within the system.

Around the same time, in the immediate aftermath of World War II, we have, also based on the Charter the upsurge of the movement for the international protection of human rights both within and outside the UN,[aa] followed closely by the revision of the Red Cross Conventions, leading to the adoption of the four Geneva Conventions [on the laws of war] of 1949[bb] which, while reaffirming certain preexisting principles, introduced new legal techniques for their better safeguard and protection. In other words, a new trend reveals itself: certain values are singled out and protected by legal norms in a way which is a-typical of what existed before, i.e. the protective norms have particular characteristics and their violation graver legal effects.

This is a purely empirical observation, a description of historical development. But the awareness or perception of it, i.e. its being taken cognizance of is another matter. Kelsen, in his *Principles of International Law* (1952) distinguishes between a legal norm, which is the pattern of behaviour prescribed by law and the legal consequences attached to its violation, and a legal rule which he defines as a scientific description of the norm, its formulation or articulation in terms of law. In other words, norms are the legal raw materials while rules are the way we perceive and present them. The perception usually lags behind the phenomena, behind the emergence of the norms in the legal

---

aa. *See, e.g.,* the 1948 Universal Declaration of Human Rights **[Basic Document 7.11]**, the 1966 International Covenant on Economic, Social and Cultural Rights **[Basic Document 7.13]**, and the 1966 International Covenant on Civil and Political Rights **[Basic Document 7.14]**; *reprinted in* 3 Weston III. A.3.

bb. *Reprinted in* 2 Weston II.B.11, II.B.12, II.B.13 & II.B.14.

system. Perception needs time, and lawyers are usually cautious; they don't hurry to draw conclusions, even from things that are before their very eyes.

Perhaps it took us too long a time to discover that here we have new normative stuff that has to be conceived and presented in a different way. But we came to it all the same. Thus . . . , I have no hesitation to say that with the Charter, with some characteristics of the Geneva Conventions and of the Human Rights instruments, we are facing new legal phenomena, new types of norms of international law, from which flow different legal effects and which require a different treatment. I would add that . . . their violation constitutes what has come to be called "international crimes". The fact that we have not instantaneously perceived all the consequences of this new phenomenon and drawn all the conclusions, does not mean that it [does] not exist. After all, law, like all social phenomena, is a continuous unfolding, a continuous process of elaboration.

* * *

B. Sociologically, this legal development is not difficult to explain. . . . [O]nce the international community considers certain interests or values to be primordial or essential, it is logical that it clothes them with greater legal protection, and that graver consequences [are] attached to the violation of their protective norms.

The wider significance of this development . . . is that the international community is remoulding its legal order from a purely atomistic one (i.e. undifferentiated and unicellular) into one with an incipient hierarchical normative structure.

C. Technically speaking, the question remains whether the concept of "international crimes" . . . can be or is already integrated in the international legal order. The . . . question . . . [can be answered by] inductively examining the status of the examples given in article 19 of the International Law Commission's Draft Articles on State Responsibility **[Basic Document 1.10]**.

Paragraph 2 of that article provides a general definition of international crimes which tallies perfectly with the preceding analysis, while paragraph 3 provides, on a non exhaustive basis, four examples of such crimes:

Subject to paragraph 2, and on the basis of the rules of international law in force, an international crime may result, *inter alia*, from:

(a) a serious breach of an international obligation of essential importance for the maintenance of international peace and security, such as that prohibiting aggression;

(b) a serious breach of an international obligation of essential importance for safeguarding the right of self-determination of peoples, such as that prohibiting the establishment or maintenance by force of colonial domination;

(c) a serious breach on a widespread scale of an international obligation of essential importance for safeguarding the human being, such as those prohibiting slavery, genocide and *apartheid*;

(d) a serious breach of an international obligation of essential importance for the safeguarding and preservation of the human environment, such as those prohibiting massive pollution of the atmosphere or of the seas.

The first thing that strikes in this text is the affirmation, in its opening phrase, that these examples of international crimes are provided "on the basis of the rules of international law in force"; an affirmation which has to be given all the weight it deserves, emanating, as it does, from the International Law Commission.

As far as (a) is concerned, I need not repeat here what I have already said about the central place in the UN Charter of the principle of prohibition of the threat or use of force and the grave consequences that attach to its violation. The same can also be said about (b), though the special legal regime evolving around the principle of self-determination, and reflecting the high rank and particular importance attributed to it by the international community, owes as much to subsequent practice as to the initial prescriptions of the Charter.

Large scale gross violations of human rights envisaged in (c) may be considered by some as a less evident example. But I have no hesitation in considering it a good, i.e. a correct, one. ... This is reflected in the particular regime of the Geneva Conventions and of the different human rights instruments, in article 60, paragraph 5, of the Vienna Convention on the Law of Treaties [**Basic Document 1.7**], etc. They all bear witness to an emerging special regime which, while drawing its strands from these diverse instruments, is being forged through the intensifying practice of international organs, to provide special protection to what the international community considers as basic human rights.

* * *

The fourth example (d), of article 19, the case of large scale pollution, is the one that has been criticized most. Perhaps its *ratio legis* was not made sufficiently clear. But if we consider that major tampering with the ecological balance can put human existence into jeopardy then preserving and protecting this balance becomes even more vital as a supreme value needing special protection than peace and security; at the very least, threats to it can be considered as extreme cases of threat to peace and security, being, as they are, directed against the very existence of the human race or minimally against human communities in their entirety. All we hear and read now about the nuclear winter, etc., is very frightening indeed, and clearly illustrates the incalculable and unforeseeable consequences of such serious threats, or tampering with the ecological balance.

All I am saying is that if the international community posits certain values and considers them supreme (and I think that at least verbally, this has taken place in relation to the categories mentioned above, particularly the first three; and in any case for the maintenance of international peace and security ...), then we have to accept the consequence which is a special regime of responsibility attaching to the violation or norms protecting these supreme values.

2. ATTRIBUTION OF RESPONSIBILITY

EDITORS OF HARVARD LAW REVIEW, TRENDS IN INTERNATIONAL
ENVIRONMENTAL LAW 17–19 (1992).

To invoke state responsibility for extraterritorial pollution [and other transnational environmental harms], the complaining state must ... establish that the offending conduct is attributable to the defendant state. . . .

* * *

[I]nternational jurisprudence has established that acts committed by a state's organs or agents in violation of an international obligation may be attributed to the state. The position of the state organ within the governmental structure does not alter the extent to which the conduct of the organ may be imputed to the state. For example, states may be held responsible for the conduct or omissions of their legislative bodies or their courts. Even *ultra vires* acts may be attributed to the state, as long as the state organ has acted with the state's apparent authority.

Although international law attributes the conduct of police, legislatures, and administrative officials to the state, these state organs and representatives rarely have a hand in producing transboundary pollution. State-owned commercial entities, however, can harm the environment beyond national jurisdiction. But scholars have given scant attention to the question whether such conduct is attributable to the state, and the law remains inchoate on this point. One scholar suggests that "[w]hen the state elects to act in a central role in a commercial enterprise, through organization, ownership, capitalization, receipt of profits, administration and similar involvements, that action dictates that the entity be treated, at least for purposes of international attribution, as a 'public' representative of the state."[9]

If the conduct of private parties is in question, principles of international jurisprudence require states to exercise "due diligence" to prevent conduct that, if performed by the state, would breach its primary international duties. Thus, a state has an obligation to take all reasonable measures to prevent substantial transboundary pollution. For example, when a state fails to enact adequate environmental regulations, the polluting conduct can be attributed to that state, and the state breaches its international duties. If a state exercises due care but private parties within its jurisdiction or control nonetheless inflict substantial harm upon the environment of another state, the source state must take all necessary steps to punish the offenders. Otherwise, the polluting conduct may be attributed to the state.

BRIAN D. SMITH, STATE RESPONSIBILITY AND THE MARINE ENVIRONMENT: THE RULES OF DECISION 34, 36–43 (1988).

[T]o what extent does state responsibility arise with respect to conduct of individuals who, as to such specific conduct, may not be deemed state organs or representatives? As most individual actors, in environmental and other contexts, fall within the "private" category, the answer is critical.

* * *

What, then, are the obligations of the state which arise with respect to private conduct? The state must first exercise "due diligence" to *prevent*

---

9. BRIAN D. SMITH, STATE RESPONSIBILITY AND THE MARINE ENVIRONMENT: THE RULES OF DECISION 30 (1988).

conduct which, if the state were the actor, would breach its international obligations. If such conduct nevertheless occurs, the apprehension and punishment of the offenders must be "diligently" pursued.... As the *Janes* Tribunal concluded: "If the nonprosecution and nonpunishment of crimes (or of specific crimes) in a certain period and place occurs with regularity, such nonrepression may even assume the character of nonprevention and be treated as such."[10] The obligation to apprehend and punish wrongdoers, then, is but an expression of the general obligation to prevent private individuals from engaging in conduct in which the state is prohibited to engage.

One distinction between the obligations of prevention and punishment should be underscored. When responsibility and a consequential duty to compensate follow a breach of the duty to exercise due diligence to prevent, a causal relationship generally exists between the state's omission and the private conduct, i.e. but for the failure of the state, the conduct might have been prevented. An *ex post facto* failure to punish, on the other hand, cannot logically have any direct causal connection with the private conduct. Even if punishment is, appropriately, conceived as a means of contributing to prevention through enhancing respect for legal processes, a causal relationship between a specific failure to punish and the prior conduct of the offender is difficult to draw. The issue of the appropriate measure of compensation, given the absence of a causal connection to the consequences of the violative conduct, therefore remains in dispute.

* * *

[A]s to the content of the duty, [ILC Rapporteur] Garcia–Amador was quite correct in reporting to the ILC that "the rule of 'due diligence' cannot be reduced to a clear and accurate definition which might serve as an objective and automatic standard for deciding, regardless of the circumstances, whether a state was 'diligent' in discharging its duty of vigilance and protection."[11] It is, however, possible to identify certain relevant factors. Analysis of the feasibility of effective state action is, for example, evident in cases concerning responsibility for insufficient diligence in the prevention of injury. Findings that no reasonable degree of diligence could have prevented the event have thus contributed to denials of responsibility. Conversely, states have been deemed responsible following a conclusion that effective action could have been taken. Foreseeability of private conduct is a related factor frequently playing a principal and explicit role in the decisions of arbitral tribunals as to whether states have acted with diligence.

The factor perhaps most disputed is whether such questions of diligence should be assessed in light of the capabilities and practices of the particular state or subjected to an international standard. The positions taken in the leading case of the *Alabama Claims* illustrate the conflict.[12] The United States asserted a claim against Great Britain for violation of a neutral's obligation of due diligence to prevent conduct supportive of a belligerent, based on the

---

10. The Janes Case (U.S. v. Mex.), [1925] 4 U.N.R.I.A.A. 82, at 118 (1951).

11. F. V. Garcia–Amador, *Draft Articles on the Responsibility of the State for Injuries Caused in its Territory to the Person or Property of Aliens, reprinted in* Recent Codification of the Law of State Responsibility for Injuries to Aliens 27 (F. V. Garcia–Amador et al eds., 1974).

12. The Alabama Claims (U.S. v. U.K.), [1872] I J.B. Moore, History and Digest of the International Arbitrations to Which the United States Has Been a Party 495 (1898).

construction and equipping of a Confederate vessel within British jurisdiction. Britain responded that it had indeed exercised the required level of diligence, i.e. *diligentia quam in suis* or that which "a nation is in the habit of employing in the conduct of its own affairs."[13] The Tribunal, finding Britain responsible, implicitly accepted the American perspective of an objective test of due diligence. Support for such an international definition may be found in a number of arbitral awards: the *Neer* case specifically subjected a state's conduct in punishing the killer of an alien to "the test of international standards";[14] a failure of due diligence to prevent injury to aliens was found in the *Montijo* Case regardless of the incapacity of the particular state to perform adequately.[15] Eagleton's position is representative of that of a number of publicists: "the regular or even the utmost activity of the state may here, as elsewhere, be regarded as insufficient because of the failure of the State to measure up to the international standard."[16]

The contrary position remains that the circumstances of the particular state define the standard of "due diligence". In its extreme form, arising in the jurisprudence of the treatment of aliens, this view has been expressed in terms of the obligation to afford aliens only the same measure of protection from private conduct provided citizens, without any reference to international minima. This purely subjective approach has encountered substantial contemporary opposition. Even recent literature, however, is replete with evidence of the relevance of the specific circumstances of the state. Garcia–Amador, for example, speaks of diligence in light of the "resources available to the state".[17] Friedmann argues that the degree of control over private activity exercised in totalitarian regimes implies a higher standard of due diligence.[18] Numerous authorities, including, most notably, the ICJ in the [1980] *Iran Hostages* Decision, have analysed due diligence in terms of the "means at the disposal" of the specific state.[19] Yet, one need not conclude that such views are inconsistent with an objective standard. Rather, the contemporary view would seem to be a hybrid of the two approaches: the diligence of the state will be considered in light of its particular capacities and practices; if, however, its conduct falls below an international minimum standard, responsibility will nevertheless lie.

The interests at stake in the particular case constitute another recognized factor central to decisions regarding state due diligence. A number of significant cases have spoken in terms of a response proportional to the nature of the threatened or actual injury. In fact, there appear to be certain specific categories of interests, or conduct affecting interests, which demand a stricter level of diligence by the state. The most traditional of these relates to the

13. *Id.* at 600.

14. The Neer Case (U.S. v. Mex.), [1926] 4 U.N.R.I.A.A. 60, at 61 (1951).

15. The Montijo Case (U.S. v. Colombia), [1874] II J.B. Moore, History and Digest of the International Arbitrations to Which the United States Has Been a Party 1421, at 1444 (1898).

16. C. Eagleton, The Responsibility of States in International Law 89–90 (1928).

17. *Supra* note 11, at 130.

18. "The range of injurious acts is infinitely great, and the most totalitarian state cannot fully control the movements of many millions of individuals. On the other hand, the 'due diligence' required of every state in the supervision of its citizens may, on the circumstances of the case, make the proof of guilt easier against totalitarian states than against others." W. Friedmann, *The Growth of State Control over the Individual and Its Effect upon the Rules of International State Responsibility*, 139 B.Y.B.I.L. 118, 143 (1938).

19. Case Concerning United States Diplomatic and Consular Staff in Tehran (U.S. v. Iran), 1980 I.C.J. 3, at 33.

protection of the person and property of diplomats. Following the dispute between Italy and Greece regarding the assassination of members of the *Tellini* diplomatic mission resident in Greece, the League of Nations Committee of Jurists defined state obligations with respect to such matters as follows:

> The responsibility of the State is only involved by the commission in its territory of a political crime against the persons of foreigners if the State has neglected to take all reasonable measures for the prevention of the crime and the pursuit, arrest and bringing to justice of the criminal.
>
> The recognized public character of a foreigner and the circumstances in which he is present in its territory entail upon the State a corresponding duty of special vigilance on his behalf.[20]

The other principal category for which an elevated due diligence requirement is imposed consists of matters for which the State is held to a strict standard of responsibility.... [T]he presence of strict responsibility as a regime of customary law is rather controversial.... It is important to note at this point, however, during the discussion of general principles, that an assertion of strict responsibility for private conduct does not demand deviation from the rules of attribution. Rather, as to such conduct, due diligence merges into a strict regime. The diligence required of the state is simply that necessary to prevent the private conduct. A failure to prevent is a failure of due diligence. If one were to assume, for example, a regime of strict responsibility for the consequences of "ultrahazardous" activity within the state, the integrity of the general principles of attribution need not be disturbed in order to find the state strictly responsible when private ultrahazardous conduct causes injury to a neighbour. The responsibility of the state arises not out of the conduct itself but the state's failure to achieve the required standard of diligence, i.e. that necessary to prevent injury.

The final point to be made concerning due diligence is simply that the emphasis on the territorial character of the obligation evident throughout the literature ought not to suggest that the state may not, depending on the character of the primary obligation, be required to exercise due diligence with respect to conduct outside the state. A brief look at the issue dictates a significant and contrary conclusion: in certain circumstances, the state must exercise territorial or extraterritorial legal authority, or both, to satisfy the demands of due diligence.... Eagleton summarizes the logic of the linkage:

> Since international law must prevail within each state, all states in consequence thereof are burdened with the obligation of respecting the rights, within their own territories, of other states or their members. The responsibility of the state for the acts of individuals is therefore based upon, the territorial control which it enjoys, and which enables it, and it alone, to restrain and punish individuals, whether nationals or not, within its limits.[21]

Such comments, however, reflect the particular character of the subject which dominated and shaped the traditional jurisprudence of state responsibility: treatment of aliens. The conduct with which this specific subject is concerned is, by definition, territorial; to assert the territorial limits to due

---

20. 5 League of Nations 1924 O.J. (524).   **21.** *See supra* note 16.

diligence with respect to the treatment of aliens is to state a truism. Not all of the state's primary obligations, however, are so limited. In many areas (e.g. neutrality and aggression), international law operates to prohibit conduct which may occur beyond the borders of the state. It must be submitted that the obligation of due diligence attaches even to distinctly extraterritorial conduct. Logically, the state must exercise all available means to prevent and punish conduct anywhere which, if committed by the state, would violate international obligations.

The state's legal authority, of course, constitutes the means available to it for action either within or outside its territory. Due diligence in the context of certain primary obligations, then, is, properly viewed as an obligation to act to the extent of such legal authority. The language of Judge Ammoun in the 1971 *Namibia* Case is instructive:

> [States]   must show due diligence in preventing any individual or collective act contrary to neutrality. This obligation relates to nationals and subjects, and to foreign residents ... for a State which undertakes an obligation commits its own subjects and those who live under its law, and must employ every kind of means, legislative, administrative and judicial, by which it governs.[22]

... The legal authority of the state does not, however, end at its borders; each state possesses a measure of extraterritorial prescriptive legal authority, most clearly, for example, over its own nationals. A state performing with due diligence should logically be required to exercise such jurisdiction to proscribe for its nationals extraterritorial conduct which, if the state were the actor, would violate international law. Two points support this conclusion. First, the prescription itself may prevent such conduct. Thus, if a causal connection can be established, state responsibility and a consequential obligation to compensate should arise for a failure to exercise such authority. Moreover, it is only through the enforcement of such extraterritorial prescriptions that the state may fulfill the complementary due diligence obligation of punishment.

3. EXHAUSTION OF LOCAL REMEDIES

C. F. Amerasinghe, Local Remedies in International Law 359–361, 366 (1990).

The Rule [of local remedies] sprang up primarily as an instrument designed to ensure respect for the sovereignty of hosts states in a particular area of international dispute settlement. * * * [T]he *raison d'etre* of the rule is the recognition given by members of the international community to the interest of the host state, flowing from its sovereignty, in settling international disputes of a certain kind by its own means before international mechanisms are invoked.

* * *

Although the value attached to respect for the sovereignty of the host or respondent state is at the heart of the implementation of the rule, there is

22. The Legal Consequences for States of the Continued Presence of South Africa in Namibia (South West Africa) Notwithstanding Security Council Resolution 276 (1970) (Advisory Opinion), 1971 I.C.J. 16, at 95 (Sep. Opin. of J. Ammoun).

evidence ... that ... in the rule's application [the] values ... of the national State of the alien and of the international community have to be taken into consideration.

* * *

[I]t is reasonable to expect that the rule should operate essentially as a means of securing economically and efficiently the settlement of international disputes.... Thus, while on the one hand, a sovereign State is given every opportunity of settling such disputes equitably through its organs, ... on the other, it is logical that some recognition should also be given to the counter-vailing interests of all parties concerned in efficient justice without financial waste

* * *

To use the words of Judge Schwebel, ... the tendency has been to apply a "rule of reason" in the "interpretation of the reach of the requirement of the exhaustion of local remedies."[23]

IAN BROWNLIE, PRINCIPLES OF PUBLIC INTERNATIONAL LAW 496, 497–500 (5th ed. 1998).

The role of the local remedies rule is seen more readily if three situations are distinguished.

(1) When the act complained of is a breach of an international agreement or customary law, and is not a breach of local law then the rule is inapplicable.

(2) When the act complained of is a breach of local law only, then it is only the subsequent conduct of the state of the forum which can create responsibility. If the authorities interfere with the course of justice or certain standards are not observed, then a denial of justice has occurred and responsibility results from it.

(3) When the act complained of is a breach both of local law and of an international agreement or customary law, the rule of exhaustion of local remedies applies.

* * *

(b) The local remedies rule applies when effective remedies are available in the national system. In certain circumstances recourse to local remedies is excused. The remedies to be exhausted comprise all forms of recourse as of right, including administrative remedies of a legal nature "but not extra-legal remedies or remedies as of a grace."[24] The best test appears to be that an effective remedy must be available "as a matter of reasonable possibility."[25] No effective remedy is available if a point of law which could have been taken on appeal has previously been decided by the highest court, or if the only issue on appeal would be one of fact and the higher courts lack the power to review

---

23. The Elettronica Sicula S.p.A. (ELSI) Case, 1989 I.C.J. 94.

24. Finnish Ships Arbitration (1934), RIAA iii. 1479.

25. *See*, Lauterpacht, Sep. op., Norwegian Loans case, ICJ Reports 157-39; Fitzmaurice,

37 BY (1961) 59-64; Tanaka, Sep. op., Barcelona Traction case (second phase), 1970 I.C.J. 144-5.

findings of fact. However, the local law may be uncertain on such issues as the principles of sovereign immunity, the Act of State doctrine, or the interpretation of gold clauses, and the consequence is that an international tribunal should show caution in drawing conclusions on the availability of a local remedy. It must be noted, however, that a fair number of writers and arbitral awards have been willing to presume ineffectiveness of remedies from the circumstances, for example on the basis of evidence that the courts were subservient to the executive. A final and major point remains. A remedy is effective if it does justice to the claim in the local courts: "a remedy cannot be ineffective merely because, if the claimant is in the wrong, if will not be obtainable."[26]

4. REMEDIES

PATRICIA W. BIRNIE & ALAN E. BOYLE, INTERNATIONAL LAW AND THE ENVIRONMENT 150–54 (1992).

Where the responsibility of a state is established, an obligation to make appropriate reparation arises. This can entail extensive consequences. The injured state may require the other to:

(i) discontinue the act;

(ii) apply national legal remedies;

(iii) re-establish the situation existing before the act in question, or to the extent that this is impossible, pay corresponding compensation;

(iv) provide guarantees against repetition.

The effect of these requirements was indicated in the *Chorzów Factory* case: "reparation must, as far as possible, wipe out the consequences of the illegal act and re-establish the situation which would, in all probability, have existed if that act had not been committed."[27] Additionally, the injured state may enjoy rights of reprisal and suspension of its legal obligations towards the offending state. If it is accepted that a wrongful act is also an international crime, other states will also incur a duty of non-recognition of its legality.

Reparation in the law of state responsibility is not an inflexible concept, however. As Brownlie observes: "the interaction of substantive law and issues of reparation should be stressed."[28] The appropriateness of particular forms of reparation, or of other remedies, thus depends on the circumstances of individual cases. In environmental disputes, states will primarily be concerned with preventing anticipated injury in breach of obligation, securing adequate guarantees against repetition, or obtaining compensation for environmental injury. It must also be remembered that restitution of the environment may often be impossible, impracticable, or not economically justifiable.

(a) Preventive Remedies

Although the ICJ has power to make interim orders of protection which are comparable to interlocutory injunctions, the *Nuclear Tests* cases [**Basic Document 8.6**] suggest that an international tribunal cannot grant injunc-

---

26. Fitzmaurice, 37 B.Y. 60 (1961).

27. *Supra* note a, at 336.

28. IAN BROWNLIE, SYSTEM OF THE LAW OF NATIONS: STATE RESPONSIBILITY 234 (1983).

tions or prohibitory orders restraining violations of international law. This is an obvious weakness in the potential use of international judicial tribunals to deal with cases involving environmental risks to other states. It casts serious doubts on the capacity of the system of state responsibility to secure compliance with environmental obligations, rather than simply to compensate states for the consequences of their breach. Declaratory judgments have, however, been employed by international tribunals in interpreting treaties and affording satisfaction in cases of breach of customary obligations, and some writers have also argued that a declaration may be equivalent to an injunction where it is used as a means of passing judgment on the legality of proposed conduct. A strong dissent by four judges favoured this form of remedy in the *Nuclear Tests* cases, but the majority took a more restrictive view of the Court's power. Their decision suggests that: "problems which do not involve any direct injury to a particular state but rather affect the international community as a whole cannot be dealt with by means of a bilateral claim for a declaratory judgment." States seeking to complain of injury to the environment of common areas may thus be confined to diplomatic protest and measures of retorsion, or resort to international supervisory institutions.

(b) Repetition and Future Conduct

The *Trail Smelter* case **[Basic Document 8.4]** does indicate that states may be enjoined to take measures to prevent repetition of environmental injury for which they have been held responsible. In that case Canada was ordered to adopt a regime for regulating the future operation of the smelter, including the payment of compensation for any damage which recurred notwithstanding compliance. Although Canada had [no] right to cause serious injury to the United States, its right to continue to operate the smelter was maintained. Thus, despite admission by Canada of a breach of obligation, a balance of interests between the two parties was achieved through the tribunal's order, and indeed this formed the main object of the arbitration. There is no reason in principle why in other situations an international tribunal should not approach the question of responsibility for continuance of environmentally harmful activities in this way, using the remedies at its disposal to achieve a balance of interests. It does not inevitably follow that state responsibility is a system in which "the winner would take all", and lead to the prohibition of harmful activities. Negotiated settlements of environmental disputes have normally been equally sensitive to the need to achieve an equitable solution, without thereby weakening the underlying rules of international law which structure their negotiations.

(c) Restitution and Compensation

Where environmental harm or injury is suffered by the claimant state, compensation for damage is likely to be the normal remedy sought by way of an international claim. Controversy surrounding restitution in international law makes it "difficult to state the conditions of its application with any certainty,"[29] and there are no examples of its use in an environmental context. Legal restitution, that is an order for the repeal or alteration of some legislative, judicial, or administrative act, may be appropriate where a treaty provision or international standard is not complied with. The *Trail Smelter*

---

29. *Id.* at 222.

award comes close to restitution in this sense in so far as it compels the more diligent regulation of the smelter.

What is mainly in issue, however, is whether harm not quantifiable in terms of damage to property or economic loss is recoverable by way of monetary compensation. This question is significantly dependent on the content of [a] state's primary obligations of environmental protection. To the extent that these do cover the protection of common areas, ecosystems, wildlife, or wilderness areas, reparation should include clean-up costs, damage limitation, and possible re-instatement of the environment. State practice and judicial precedent are too limited in this field to draw confident conclusions, but reparation for such damage occurring to a state's territory is covered by a number of modern liability treaties or provisions, and may possibly be inferred in the Cosmos 954 claim.[30] It is also included in the ILC's proposed regime of international liability **[Basic Document 1.9]**.

In principle, compensation should fully restore the injured party's position. There is some evidence, however, that the application of a strict or absolute liability principle may entail a limitation of damages. In the Cosmos 954 claim Canada did not recover its full costs of $14 million, but claimed $6 million, and settled for $3 million. In its proposed regime of international liability, the ILC has adopted the position that harm must "in principle, be fully compensated", but may be reduced if it appears equitable to share certain costs among the states concerned. However, the 1972 Space Objects Liability Convention **[Basic Document 3.5]** provides that compensation shall be determined in accordance with "international law and the principles of justice and equity", but must be sufficient to restore the party on whose behalf the claim is presented "to the condition which would have existed if the damage had not occurred". Moreover, the international precedents do not go so far as the civil liability treaties, where specific monetary limits on compensation are an essential part of a complex scheme of loss distribution. Thus it is uncertain how far the measure of reparation in international law is limited and whether this depends on the choice of liability standard.

(d) Breach

Apart from an obligation to offer reparation, a breach of treaty may additionally entitle the injured state to retaliate by taking proportionate countermeasures aimed at restoring equality between the parties, or to terminate or suspend the treaty in relation to a party in material breach, as provided for by Article 60 of the Vienna Convention on the Law of Treaties **[Basic Document 1.7]**. The application of these responses depends in part on the object and purpose of the treaty concerned, and for that reason may be inappropriate in the case of multilateral co-operation treaties, including those concerned with environmental protection. In such cases resort to international supervisory institutions is a preferable method of ensuring the continued integrity of the treaty regime.

Discussion Notes/Questions

1. What are the legal bases and legal consequences of state responsibility? How has the structural function of international responsibility within the international legal system evolved during the last decade or two?

30. Claim for Damage Caused by Cosmos 954, 18 I.L.M. 902 (1979).

2. Philip Allott strongly criticizes the International Law Commission's work on state responsibility. Objecting to the very idea that "every intentionally wrongful act of a State entails the international responsibility of that State," he argues:

> Two especially vicious consequences result from using responsibility as a general and independent category in international law. First, it consecrates the idea that wrong-doing is the behavior of morally responsible human beings. It therefore obscures the fact that breaches of international law are attributable formally to the legal persons known as states but morally to the human beings who determine the behavior of states.

> Second, if responsibility exists as a legal category, it must be given legal substance. In particular, general conditions of responsibility have to be created which are then applicable to all rights and duties. The net result is that the deterrent effect of the imposition of responsibility is seriously compromised, not only by rationalizing it (the first vicious consequence) but also by leaving room for argument in every conceivable case of potential responsibility (the second vicious consequence). When lawyers leave room for argument there is much room for injustice.[cc]

Do you agree with Allott? Is his criticism valid? Are the dangers he sees a necessary consequence of the idea of state responsibility?

3. As seen, the International Law Commission has been studying the question of transnational environmental harm as it relates to "international liability for injurious consequences arising out of acts *not* prohibited by international law" (emphasis added) in particular whether, in this context, a state's obligations relative to transboundary harm include a duty to prevent, inform, negotiate, and/or repair. As of this writing, it has provisionally concluded that only the failure to repair would result in international liability. Additionally, a majority of the Commission is of the view that, regarding prevention, its proposals should be merely recommendatory, that the prior consent of a potentially harmed state is not required for an activity to be authorized, and that, in the matter of repair (or compensation), the liability should be shared between the private operator (with primary liability) and the state (with secondary or residual liability). Critics of the ILC's approach, such as Alan E. Boyle, *supra*, have argued against liability for lawful activities. Liability should arise, they contend, only for noncompliance with "primary rules" of conduct specifying the behavior or inaction that would be internationally required, including possibly a duty to compensate for all transboundary harm arising out of designated extrahazardous activities. With whom do you agree? Why?

4. For additional pertinent reading, see Ian Brownlie, System of the Law of Nations: State Responsibility (1983); Gadkowski, International Liability of States for Nuclear Damage (1989); ___, International Crimes of State: A Critical Analysis of the ILC's Draft Article 19 on State Responsibility (J. Weiler, A. Cassese, & M. Spinedi eds. 1989); International Responsibility for Environmental Harm (F. Francioni & T. Schovazzi eds. 1991); F. Malekian, International Criminal Responsibility of States: A Study on the Evolution of State Responsibility with Particular Emphasis on the Concept of Crime and Criminal Responsibility (1985); B. Smith, State Responsibility and the Marine Environment: The Rules of Decision (1988); U.N. Codification of State Responsibility (S. Spinedi & B. Simma eds. 1987); P.

---

cc. Philip Allott, *State Responsibility and the Unmaking of International Law*, 29 HARV. INT'L L.J. 1, 13–14 (1988).

Allott, *State Responsibility and the Unmaking of International Law*, 29 H.I.L.J. 1 (1988); D. Bederman, *Contributory Fault and State Responsibility*, 30 V.J.I.L. 335 (1990); P.–M. Dupuy, *The International Law of State Responsibility: Revolution or Evolution*, 11 Mich. J. Int'l L. 105 (1989); G. Kasoulides, *State Responsibility and Assessment of Liability for Damage Resulting From Dumping Operations*, 26 San Diego L. Rev. 497 (1989); S. Scott, *Codification of State Responsibility in International Law: A Review and Assessment*, 9 A.S.I.L.S. Int'l L. J. 1 (1985); M. Straus, *Causation As An Element of State Responsibility*, 16 L. & Pol'y Int'l Bus. 893 (1984).

Chapter Six

MANAGING THE GLOBAL COMMONS
IN ANTARCTICA

Antarctica. A remote continent, unique in so many respects. It is, therefore, necessary to introduce you to its special characteristics. The wise application of law and policy to this area depends upon such knowledge. It is, in fact, a heightened awareness of this vast continent's unique qualities that is largely responsible for the increased attention that recently has been given to the legal safeguards needed to protect it. Today, there is a considerable amount of international law that relates to Antarctica, including a complex treaty system.

In fact, it is with this international law in mind that, following our description, we invite you to wrestle with a multi-issue problem that we hope will engage and inform you relative to some of the more difficult environmental law issues that arise in relation to this vast realm. Our intent, through fictional scenarios that we believe are realistically capable of taking place in Antarctica, is to sensitize you, as student and potential advocate and policymaker, to the ecological-legal challenge that Antarctica presents. A challenge which is, in a word, daunting, so fragile is the Antarctic environment. Oil spills, for example, of which there have been several in recent times, can affect the Antarctic ecosystem much more seriously than spills do other parts of the world. Preservation of biodiversity in Antarctica also is key. While there is more aquatic life than might be expected—whales, seals, penguins, and birds—the history of human exploitation of some of these species has been at various times catastrophic. And now tourism poses fresh threats, with a potential for damage far beyond what so far has been experienced. Thus, the Antarctic environment requires the utmost professional as well as ecological sensitivity and acumen. However remote, Antarctica does not exist by itself, unconnected to the rest of the world. To the contrary, it exerts great influence upon the ecology of the entire world, and for this reason alone, requires to be taken seriously into legal account.

Finally, throughout this chapter, but in sections B(3) and C especially, we ask you to consider and recommend, against this backdrop, alternative norms, institutions, and/or procedures that you believe might do better than existing arrangements to contend with the situations posed by the multi-issue problem presented. We ask you to think about the policy options available and imaginable for Antarctica's long-term governance. This "reflective assignment" is as inevitable as it is useful and desirable. Questions about Antarctica's international legal regime are necessarily of the most fundamental sort: whether states claiming sovereignty over certain parts of Antarctica can and should have exclusive jurisdiction or legal control over the areas claimed; whether states not party to, or members of the Antarctic Treaty System (ATS) can and should be bound by the norms that flow from it; whether the governance of Antarctica should be internationalized through the United Nations or some other multilateral agency or method; and so forth. In short, in addition to presenting an extraordinarily rich intersection of environmental and international law issues, Antarctica is a paradigmatic case of a global commons. It requires for its enlightened regulation and management the most fertile of imaginations–well trained in the art of the possible, but not insistent upon immediate feasibility.

And so, we wish you a pleasant legal journey around the coldest continent on Earth. Along the way, keep in mind that many of the issues of law and policy raised here apply also to other global and international environmental problems.

A. ANTARCTICA: A BRIEF PORTRAIT

Editors' Note

A vast mountain continent, Antarctica has an awe-inspiring fascination no words can capture. It is a place of great grandeur and natural beauty. Also, it is a place where some of the most heroic deeds of modern-day exploration have taken place—which means that serious exploration on land has been possible only in the Twentieth Century, and even then in circumstances of great privation.

Two hundred million years ago, Antarctica was joined to Africa, Australia, India, New Zealand, and South America, forming the Gondawanaland supercontinent. Over millions of years, these continents drifted apart. As of thirty million years ago, they were almost in the same positions they are today (see Figure 6–1, infra). Antarctica drifted to a polar position and began to experience a winter of more than five months without sunlight.

Today, Antarctica is covered almost completely by ice. Without its ice cap, it covers an area of approximately 2.7 million square miles (or 699,297.3 million hectares). With its ice cap it covers an area larger than the United States (some 5.4 million square miles, or 1,398,594.6 million hectares), and boasts a diameter of about 2,800 miles (or 4,509 kilometers), making it the fifth largest continent. It also is the highest, driest, and coldest continent in the world. About ninety-eight percent of this expanse is buried beneath a thick ice sheet. Falling snow and ice crystals maintain the depth of the ice sheet at an average of more than 7,000 feet (or 2,133.6 meters) and up to 13,450 feet (or 4,099.6 meters) thick in some places.

The Antarctic ice sheet represents about 90 percent of the world's ice and 68 percent of the world's freshwater. Thus, it not only dominates the climate of the area but also has an influence that extends to the equator and beyond in the form of cold air, cold water currents, and migratory bird and sea life. If all the ice were to melt, it would raise the levels of the world's oceans between 160 and 200 feet (or 48.8 and 60.9 meters). About one-third of the land which supports the ice sheet lies below the surface of the sea. The 2,400 mile (or 3,864.7 kilometers) long mountain ranges which subdivide the continent are some of the longest on Earth with many high peaks. As a consequence, the Antarctic has a mean height more than three times that of any other continent.

Figure 6–1

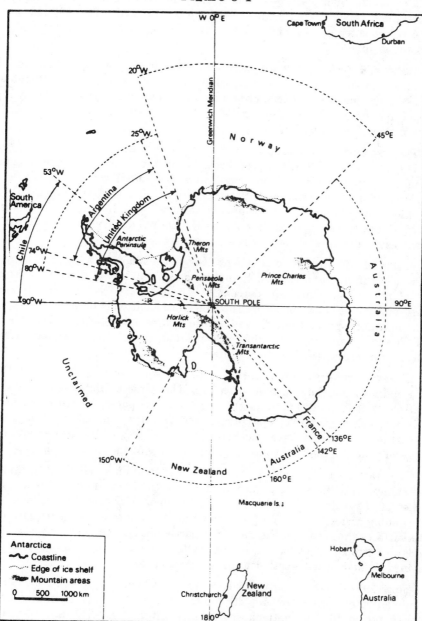

Figure 6.1. Map of national claims in Antarctica

The main characteristic of the Antarctic climate is severe low temperatures. While the continent receives a surprising amount of sunlight in spite of its five to six months "winter night" (more solar radiation reaches the South Pole during the Antarctic summer than is received at the equator in an equivalent period), the sunlight does not result in much surface heat because most of the sunlight is reflected back into space by the snow and sea ice. Thus, temperatures range in summer from slightly below freezing at the coast to an average of −36°F (or −37.7°C) on the high plateau. In the winter, the coasts and plateaus experience temperatures between −40°F and −90°F (or −40°C and −67.7°C). The world's lowest recorded temperature of −129.3°F (or −89.61°C) was measured at the base of Vostok in July 1983.

Also, Antarctica is a very dry continent, receiving just enough precipitation to allow snow to accumulate. The high winds in some parts of the continent whip this snow up and the powdery blizzards can reduce visibility to zero. It is not unusual for these conditions to occur for up to two out of three days in August, which is the stormiest month.

Thus isolated, almost totally covered by ice, and having an exceedingly cold, dry climate, Antarctica has never been hospitable to colonization by plants, animals, or human beings. Ferns, freshwater fish, amphibians, and reptiles are found today only as fossils; and it is the only continent where humans are not indigenous and where civilizations have never developed. Indeed, Antarctica is the last continent to be explored. It remains the continent about which the least is known, especially its effect on global environmental processes.

Forms of life on the frozen continent have adapted in unusual ways for survival in the cold and the low humidity, and for living on the ice or the salty soils of the region. Only two percent of Antarctica is ice-free—mainly coastal areas—and this is where most life is found. Birds and seals breed and raise their young on the ice or land but depend on the rich resources of the ocean for their food. The sea–abounding with whales, fish, squid, and krill as important elements of the marine ecosystem–is rich with life.

However, terrestrial life is very limited and slow-growing in the cold, windy, dry conditions and long winter darkness. The largest land-based animal is a flightless midge 3 mm. long and the vegetation is sparse, consisting of lichens, algae, mosses, fungi, microscopic plants, and two flowering species that grow at the northern tip of the Antarctic Peninsula. A variety of freshwater and saline lakes and ponds on the land contain a limited range of aquatic animals.

The coastal areas free of ice are where most human activities are concentrated—mainly scientific stations and field activities. Ground-level climate in the largest of these areas is warmer in the summer and considerably drier than surrounding areas. Once free of ice, they tend to stay free, partly because of the bare surfaces that soak up the heat and partly because snowfall is minimal and winds are strong. Many of the largest valleys, such as the "dry valleys" near McMurdo Sound, contain both salt and freshwater lakes.

Since 1957–58, the International Geophysical Year, Antarctica has been used by human beings primarily as a site for scientific research. A multilateral treaty entered into in 1959 by nations interested in Antarctica—The Antarctic Treaty **[Basic Document 2.1]**—established methods for international cooperation in scientific exploration and for preservation of Antarctica for peaceful purposes. In addition, state practice under the treaty has developed in ways designed to protect the fragile environment. Along with the oceans, the atmosphere, the moon and other celestial bodies, Antarctica is now increasingly accepted as part of what has come to be known as "the global commons." Concern about preserving the Antarctic environment has grown because the continent exerts great influence on the world's climate and weather systems.

LEE KIMBALL, SOUTHERN EXPOSURE: DECIDING
ANTARCTICA'S FUTURE 4–5 (1990).

Antarctica's southern seas are highly productive for two reasons, and both are geographical. The Southern Ocean is unique in that it circles the earth unbroken by land masses. Its northern boundary is referred to as the Antarctic convergence, a boundary some 20 to 30 miles wide between 50 and 60 degrees south latitude where cold Antarctic surface waters meet warmer sub-Antarctic waters to the north. The convergence also marks a change in ocean currents and the northern limit of most Antarctic marine species.

Southern Ocean waters are the densest on Earth. When the sea freezes over around Antarctica, salt is ejected back into the water. When the sea ice melts again in the Antarctic spring, it mixes relatively fresh water back into the ocean. This process influences oceanic circulation in ways not yet fully understood.

The cold Antarctic surface waters are rich in nutrients and support abundant marine life. In general, growth of oceanic phytoplankton is influenced by light, nutrient supply, and temperature in the surrounding environment. In the Antarctic, it is now believed, light is the driving force in the productivity of the marine ecosystem. During winter, photosynthesis and thus phytoplankton growth is limited by the lack of light as days shorten and the frozen sea ice blocks exposure to sunlight. As spring and summer arrive, the breakup and melting of the sea ice release "ice" algae living where ice meets water. These algae thrive on sunlight and nutrients, creating phytoplankton "blooms" that in turn nurture the annual cycle of the Antarctic food web. As more and more sea ice melts, moving northward and nearer the continent, the bloom follows the path exposed to the sun.

Antarctic winds also play a role in these phytoplankton blooms because they affect water turbulence and mixing. During the harsh Antarctic winter, the winds stir up nutrients, raising them nearer the surface, poised for the coming of sunlight in the spring. This winter "store" is uncovered for the waiting algae as the sea pack ice peels back in spring. The ejection of salt when the sea ice freezes during the winter also mixes the waters vertically.

Geography plays a part in the food chain itself too. In most ocean ecosystems, the chain has four or five links [see Figure 6–2]: simple plants or phytoplankton grow by processing the ocean's microscopic raw material nutrients. The phytoplankton are consumed by zooplankton, which in turn feed fish, birds, and sea mammals at the top of the chain. And each organism in the sequence uses part of the food it eats to reproduce and to fuel its own body. By the time it reaches the top of the food chain, only 10 to 15 percent of the original energy is left.

In some cases, life is simpler in Antarctica. Much of the intervening plant and animal life that lengthens food chains in temperate and tropical waters does not occur in Antarctica's harsh waters. Instead, much more efficiently, a two- to three-step process—a sort of fast-food chain—recycles ocean wastes into higher life forms.

The key difference in Antarctica is that so many species depend on krill, two inch shrimp that drift in kilometer-wide masses across the sea surface catching simple plant plankton in basket-shaped filters around their mouths. Many of the larger species in residence—fish, birds, squid, penguins, and some seals—eat the krill. Even many species of whales, the largest of Earth's animals, strain the Antarctic waters through sieve-like baleen plates and survive almost entirely on krill. Three-step chains (phytoplankton-krill-whales) co-exist with more complex chains (phytoplankton-krill-fish-penguin-leopard seal-whale) to make up the Antarctic food web.

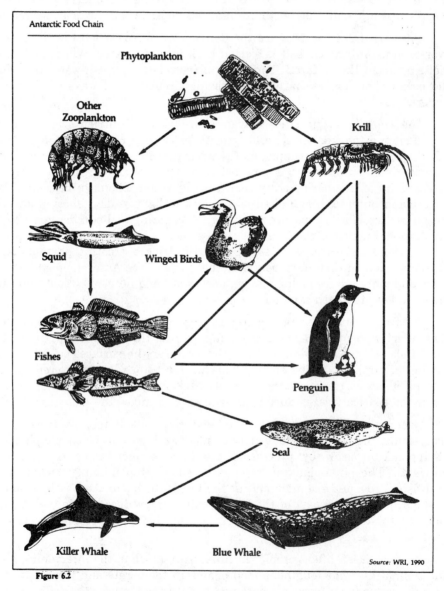

Antarctic Food Chain

Phytoplankton

Other Zooplankton

Krill

Squid

Winged Birds

Fishes

Penguin

Seal

Killer Whale

Blue Whale

Source: WRI, 1990

Figure 6.2

Obviously, krill is plentiful. No reliable count has yet been taken, but estimates of the standing stock range up to a total of 600 million tons. Without sufficient data, scientists also differ over figures for annual krill production, with estimates ranging from 40 to 150 million metric tons—the high end equalling about twice the world's fish catch.

Krill are rich in protein and at their best taste much like shrimp. Over the years krill have been touted as a major potential food source, but even mixing them with cheese into a sandwich spread has failed to win them a following, and the crustaceans have proven expensive to catch and preserve. The Soviet Union and Japan have created krill industries, but most of the catch is still used for animal feed. New techniques to quick-freeze krill and serve them as shrimp have been developed, but market demand has been slack.

Martin Holdgate, *Regulated Development and Conservation of Antarctic Resources, in* THE ANTARCTIC TREATY REGIME 128, 129–31 (Gillian Triggs ed., 1987).

The history of Antarctica provides some glaring examples of the consequences of unregulated development. One of the best-known followed Cook's discovery of South Georgia, with its teeming population of fur seal (*Arctocephalus gazella*), in 1774. Some 1.2 million animals were taken from the island before 1822, and a further million from the South Shetland region in the same period.[1] Sealers similarly devastated the stocks on other sub-Antarctic islands including Kerguelen, and on the temperate islands south of New Zealand. Elephant seals were slaughtered in large numbers for oil during the same period. After a minor recovery in the late nineteenth century, followed by a resumption of sealing, the southern fur seal stocks were so depleted that hardly any individuals at all were seen until the late 1920s, when a small population was found in the Willis Islands near South Georgia. The subsequent recovery of the population on that island (at a rate of increase of 16.8% per annum so that some 90 thousand pups were being born a year in the mid-1970s), is one of the more remarkable wildlife recovery stories of this century. It is paralleled by less spectacular recoveries of other southern stocks, and also by a considerable increase in the numbers of elephant seal which had not been so severely depleted.

The catastrophic impact of sealing occurred because the resources were "open access"; that is, they were unregulated by governments and each sealing captain found himself in competition with all the others. Although some of the more enlightened ones, like James Weddell, recognized that they were destroying a resource which with more prudence might have yielded a steady return indefinitely, it was in nobody's interests to exercise restraint.

A similar but more interesting and complicated pattern followed in the exploitation of the Southern Ocean whale stocks. This industry began in the early years of the twentieth century, and was initially shore-based with factories on South Georgia, the South Orkney Islands, the South Shetland Islands, and in the New Zealand region. Although the first station was only built in 1904, within 3 years Antarctic whaling produced more oil than the rest of the world's whaling areas put together. The British government attempted to prevent over-fishing by issuing licenses for the factories in the

---

1. William N. Bonner, *The Fur Seal of South Georgia*, 56 BRITISH ANTARCTIC SURVEY SCIENTIFIC REPORTS 1 (1968); M. Payne, *Growth of a Fur Seal Population*, 279 PHILOSOPHICAL TRANSACTIONS OF THE ROYAL SOCIETY OF LONDON 69 (1977).

South Atlantic region, which were all within British-administered territory. Revenues from the whaling industry were used to fund the *Discovery* Investigations which had two ships almost continuously at sea in the southern summers between 1925 and 1939. These voyages laid the foundations of our understanding of the oceanography and marine ecology of the Southern Ocean, and provided a commendable example of an attempt to lay a foundation of scientific knowledge as the basis for the regulation of an industry. Unfortunately, the development of more profitable pelagic factory ships and catcher fleets which were not tied to a limited range from a shore station allowed the focus of whaling to shift to the high seas, beyond any national controls, and this in turn led to the competitive depletion of stocks, first of Blue whales (*Balaenoptera musculus*) and then of Fin and Sei whales, in a pattern that is now well known. Recent estimates suggest that the present stocks of Blue whales are now no more than 5% of the original, with Humpback whales at 3%, Fin at 21% and Sei at 54%.[2]

As Gulland ... has pointed out, the declines or collapses of seals, whales and, in the last decade, certain fin-fish stocks, in the circum-Antarctic regions are not peculiar to this part of the world. As Gulland puts it:

[V]irtually every commercially attractive exploited fish stock has been allowed to decline below its most productive level. These declines have not often turned into catastrophic collapses largely because of two factors—the high reproductive capacity of most fish makes them less vulnerable to sustained over exploitation than the mammals, and most fishing fleets can move to alternative resources when stocks and catch rates in one area begin to decline. The events in the Southern Ocean should therefore not be ascribed to some unusual degree of greed or shortsightedness on the part of the harvesters, but are the predictable results of unmanaged exploitation of a common-property, open-access resource.[3]

Nonetheless, the situation was more acute in the Antarctic regions than in the Arctic, and most of the other fishery zones of the world, because in the far south there was not the framework of unquestioned national sovereignty over the land areas, nor a regional fisheries convention. Until recently, the only regulatory body was the International Whaling Commission (IWC) which, from 1946 onwards, fought a protracted rearguard action to bring the whaling industry into balance with the resource on which its future depended.[a]

The IWC's experience with whaling did point to certain lessons.... The first was the necessity for good quantitative scientific information on the stocks of the exploited resource, so that the consequences of alternative policies could be evaluated. The IWC did not reach the stage of reasonably thorough statistical analysis until 1960. By this stage, the Blue whales had

2. Richard Maitland Laws, *Seals and Whales in the Southern Ocean*, 279 PHILOSOPHICAL TRANSACTIONS OF THE ROYAL SOCIETY OF LONDON 81–96 (1977).

3. John A. Gulland, *The Antarctic Treaty System as a Resource Management Mechanism*, in THE ANTARCTIC TREATY REGIME 116, 117 (Gillian Triggs ed., 1987).

a. The International Whaling Commission was established pursuant to, and receives all its statutory authority from, the 1946 International Convention for the Regulation of Whaling [**Basic Document 6.2**]. For details, see, *e.g.*, Patricia Birnie, *International Protection of Whales*, 37 Y. B. WORLD AFF. 240, 243–61 (1983); Gare Smith, *The International Whaling Commission: An Analysis of the Past and Reflections on the Future*, 16 NAT. RESOURCES L. 543 (1984). *See also* Problem 10–1 ("Driftnet Fishing in the South Pacific") in Chapter 10, *infra*.

virtually ceased to be exploitable, and the Fin whales were on the point of catastrophic decline. The industry was now faced with a choice between immediate and drastic catch reductions, which would have meant the writing off of much investment, or the continuance of whaling for a limited number of years in order to recoup on those investments, with the virtual certainty of termination thereafter. The IWC was powerless to dictate a solution, and the industry opted for the latter course, bringing down its quotas, but not sufficiently rapidly to create optimum conditions for the recovery of the whale stocks and the perpetuation of its own future.

> **John W. Kindt,** *A Regime for Ice–covered Areas: The Antarctic and Issues Involving Resource Exploitation and the Environment, in* THE ANTARCTIC LEGAL REGIME 187, 194–96 **(Christopher Joyner & Sudhir Chopra eds. 1988).**

The first significant exploration of the Southern Ocean and Antarctica occurred from 1772 to 1775 when Captain Cook circumnavigated practically the entire continental area of Antarctica. Thereafter, occasional landings were made in the Antarctic areas, but the systematic exploration of Antarctica did not begin until Roald Amundsen's scientific expedition in 1897. In 1912, Amundsen reached the South Pole, and the ill-fated British expedition of Captain Robert Scott reached the South Pole shortly after Amundsen.

From the 1880s to the beginning of World War II, several countries engaged in a "race for the continent" of Antarctica. During this period, seven countries made territorial claims allegedly justified by; (1) discovery and occupation; (2) performance of administrative acts; and (3) the concomitant principles of contiguity, continuity, and the sector theory. Those seven countries making territorial claims and the years of their initial claims were:

    a.   the United Kingdom, 1908;

    b.   New Zealand, 1923;

    c.   Australia, 1933;

    d.   France, 1938;

    e.   Norway, 1939;

    f.   Chile, 1940; and

    g.   Argentina, 1942.

These countries have become known as the "claimant States" [*see* Figure 6–1, *supra*].

A rationale involving "discovery" or "exploration" to support territorial claims in Antarctica was utilized by Argentina, Australia, Chile, France, Norway, and the United Kingdom. The theory supporting these claims asserts that sovereign rights arise from the exploration of territory that was allegedly first seen or crossed by explorers from the country asserting the claim. The "occupation" or "effective occupation" basis for sovereign claims rationalizes that discovery confers inchoate title upon the discovering country. Although discovery alone cannot support a claim, the inchoate title bars territorial claims by other countries for an undefined period after the discovery. During this undefined period, the claimant state must perfect title through occupation of the territory, otherwise the title fails. Argentina and Chile have also claimed jurisdiction based on the "performance of administrative acts" in Antarctic areas; for example, the occurrence of births and marriages (which may have been carefully orchestrated by these claimant States).

The "contiguity" theory of sovereign rights over Antarctic areas was asserted by Argentina, Australia, Chile, New Zealand, and South Africa. Under the contiguity theory, these countries claimed special entitlements and tried to justify their actions based on their relative proximity to Antarctica. The "continuity" theory alleges claims similar to those under the "occupation" theory, and both theories are invalid for similar reasons. Finally, the "sector" theory defines Antarctic territorial boundaries according to longitudinal lines which converge on the South Pole from one of two types of baselines: (1) the mainland boundaries of a claimant State, or (2) the length of the Antarctic coast claimed by the State.

Contrary to the claimant States, five other countries did not assert territorial claims although they had also established a nexus with Antarctica by conducting research and exploratory efforts. After World War II, these five States asserted that they would neither assert nor recognize any territorial claims to Antarctica. Known as the "nonclaimant States", they included Belgium, Japan, South Africa, the USSR, and the United States. While the nonclaimant States did not recognize any territorial claims to Antarctica, these governments admonished that they were only holding their claims in abeyance and still reserved the right to assert their claims in the future. To fortify their policy of "nonrecognition", the nonclaimant States argued that the claimant States had not occupied any substantial part of their claimed territories and that Antarctica *per se* could not be subjected to territorial claims because of its unique environment and status.

During the 1950s, disputes between claimant and nonclaimant States highlighted the need for resolving the conflicting nature of these theories, and as a carryover project from the International Geophysical Year during 1957–1958, the United States invited both claimant and nonclaimant States to send representatives to Washington, D.C., for the purpose of negotiating a treaty to govern the Antarctic. The conference was convened on Oct. 15, 1959 and all 12 claimant and nonclaimant States were participants. The product of the conference was the Antarctic Treaty **[Basic Document 2.1]**, which entered into force in June 1961. Reflecting the U.S. position after 1959, the *Second Restatement of Foreign Relations Law* stated that:

> The largest remaining area of unacquired territory, Antarctica, is subjected by the Antarctic Treaty ... to a special regime dedicating Antarctica to peaceful purposes and scientific investigation and holding in abeyance conflicting claims of sovereignty in the area. In becoming a party to the agreement, a state does not renounce or prejudice any such claim. See Article IV. The United States, which is a party to the Treaty, has made no territorial claim in the area and does not recognize the claims of others.[4]

Similar to the United States, the actual and potential claims of all parties to the Antarctic Treaty were, of course, placed in abeyance under Article IV.

4. RESTATEMENT (SECOND) OF FOREIGN RELA-   TIONS LAW § 11, Reporter's Note (1962).

This provision of the Antarctic Treaty represents a remarkable achievement as it permits peaceful activities to continue in Antarctica despite the conflicting claims to Antarctic territory. In practical terms, for over 25 years peaceful activities have been pursued and disputes settled under the Antarctic Treaty.

In addition to Article IV, the Antarctic Treaty contains several other provisions which implement unique policies. The most laudable policy which the Antarctic Treaty has spawned consists of the demilitarization and denuclearization of an entire continent. Ocean dumping of nuclear wastes is also prohibited. While provisions for on-site inspections have traditionally been almost impossible to negotiate, the Antarctic Treaty authorizes on-site inspections of all installations, stations, equipment, vessels, and aircraft.

The flexibility of the Antarctic Treaty system has permitted resolution or abeyance of disputes, and this flexibility has also allowed the system to accommodate changing circumstances. The Antarctic Treaty is neatly supplemented by two other conventions and a set of Agreed Measures:

a.   the Convention for the Conservation of Antarctic Seals **[Basic Document 2.3]**,

b.   the Agreed Measures for the Conservation of Antarctic Fauna and Flora (Fauna and Flora Conservation Measures) **[Basic Document 2.2]**, and

c.   the Convention on the Conservation of Antarctic Marine Living Resources (Antarctic Living Resources Convention or CCAMLR) **[Basic Document 2.4]**.

During the early 1980s, the Consultative Parties began negotiating a regime to govern Antarctic nonliving (i.e., mineral) resources; at the same time, States outside of the Antarctic Treaty system began to question several aspects of the Antarctic Treaty system, including the Antarctic Treaty itself. Consequently, new approaches were developed for considering Antarctic issues.

B.   THE COMPLEXITY OF THE ANTARCTIC ENVIRONMENT: A MULTI–ISSUE PROBLEM

SECTION 1. FACTS

As evidenced by several recent and widely publicized events, Antarctica's resources have proven increasingly vulnerable to economic and political exploitation. Of particular interest have been the following:

A.   *Polar Petroleum Corporation Explores for Oil and Gas*

In the late Nineteenth Century, sealers and whalers from New Britain, a southern hemispheric nation, visited Antarctica and established huts along Antarctica's coast from which to conduct their harvesting operations during the summer season. In 1910, when interest in Antarctic exploration was at its zenith, the government of New Britain asserted sovereignty over the area and has done so consistently ever since. In 1958, the International Geophysical

Year, it established a scientific research station in the area, which it has since occupied the year round, although with reduced numbers during the winter months.

Polar Petroleum Corporation (PPC), a company incorporated in Liechtenstein,[b] is actively engaged in oil and gas exploration in the world's polar regions. About three years ago, PPC undertook oil and natural gas exploration on the coastal margin of one of Antarctica's "dry valleys" (areas that are among the driest places on earth, with no rainfall for the last two million years). This exploration, which turns out to have taken place on the territory claimed by New Britain, went undetected for the first year. Shortly thereafter, however, scientists and students from New Britain's Antarctic Scientific Programme discovered PPC's operation and immediately reported evidence of it (including photographs) to the New Britain government. The government of New Britain protested to PPC on the grounds that the latter's exploration violated the 1959 Antarctic Treaty, to which New Britain is a party; and, additionally, that it violated New Britain's claim of territorial sovereignty over the region in question. Under New Britain law, a license from the government of New Britain is required to explore for oil and gas anywhere within New Britain's claimed territorial jurisdiction, and failure to secure one is an offense punishable by a fine of U.S. $100,000 for every day the activity continues. The legislation explicitly states that it extends to New Britain's Antarctic territory.

After consulting its legal counsel, PPC served notice upon the government of New Britain that it considered its operations to be lawful under the 1959 Treaty and, further, that it considered New Britain's assertion of jurisdiction against PPC to be invalid because, it contended, "New Britain's territorial claim is not recognized by other nations." Whereupon New Britain, having no ice breakers necessary to remove the drilling equipment, called upon the United States for logistical support. The United States, after initial hesitation, agreed that the equipment should be removed, proceeded to remove it, and finally took the equipment into custody at its Antarctica base at McMurdo Sound.

Soon after, PPC filed suit in the United States District Court for the District of Columbia praying for return of the oil rig, compensation for its financial losses, and a declaratory judgment stating that its exploration activities in Antarctica were lawful. After bilateral negotiations between New Britain and the United States, it was agreed that New Britain would appear before the court to assert for itself its claim to sovereignty over the Antarctic territory in dispute. All procedural issues having been resolved and all issues of fact having been stipulated as above, the case now awaits legal argument. Liechtenstein is not a party to the 1959 Antarctic Treaty or its associated agreements.

b. The usual though not absolute convention with problems in this coursebook is to use fictional jurisdictions to avoid unwanted associations. In this problem, some of the jurisdictions are real—Liechtenstein and the United States. It is important, therefore, to stress that any relationship between these countries and the facts of this problem is purely coincidental and that, in any event, no reflection on the policies of these countries is intended. The same disclaimer is made in respect of all other problems in this coursebook.

B. *Andea Promotes Tourism*

Andea is an economically nascent South American country with a small scientific research base in Antarctica located on Edward VII Peninsula close by the Ross Sea in an area not claimed by any nation but adjoining land claimed by New Zealand (*see* Figure 6–1, *supra*). A non-consultive party to the 1959 Antarctic Treaty, Andea signed the 1991 Protocol on Environmental Protection to the Antarctic Treaty just after it was negotiated in 1991. The nations present at the negotiations—both consultive and non-consultive parties—agreed in the Final Act that they all would ratify the Protocol quickly and that, until they did so, they all would act in accordance with the Protocol in so far as that was possible. But Andea was under pressure from a strong domestic environmental lobby. Thus, to secure favorable publicity that would help his government in an up-coming national election, Andea's Foreign Minister, His Excellency Enrique Carrasco, made the following press statement:

On behalf of the Government of Andea, I welcome the Environmental Protection Protocol to the Antarctic Treaty.

It is the general understanding of the parties to the Treaty contained in the Final Act that the Protocol will be ratified quickly and that, until ratification is complete, all nations will act in accordance with the Protocol as far as possible. Andea believes this most strongly.

The [Andean] Cabinet has discussed the matter, and we give the following firm guarantee to our Antarctic Treaty partners: Andea will follow the provisions of the Protocol in every respect possible, and we will treat the Protocol as presently binding international law.

Sr. Carrasco went on to say, in conclusion: "I am sure that all of the nongovernmental organizations in Andea, which made such an impact on the fashioning of our Government's Antarctic policy, will be pleased with the position we have taken."

Copies of the foregoing statement were sent to all foreign embassies in Andea, and Andea's ambassadors were instructed to distribute copies to the foreign offices of all countries to which they were accredited.

Shortly thereafter, the incumbent government of Andea won the national election, but so far has done nothing to ratify the Protocol. Indeed, Andea's interest in Antarctica has taken a new turn. To increase its foreign exchange earnings, Andea began bringing quantities of tourists to its Antarctic base. At the peak of the season, as many as 300 people from all over the world were brought by ships and ski planes to visit the scientific station, to take guided tours of the nearby penguin rookeries, and to watch the whales, penguins, and icebergs at the ice edge.

Last year, with the scientific research base full of tourists, more electrical power was needed for the base, so Andea decided to bring in a small but efficient nuclear generator to provide the additional power required. Andea did not notify the other parties to the Antarctic Treaty of its intentions. Nor did it carry out any environmental impact assessment. On the advice of Andean scientists (who thought it would be safer to activate the nuclear generator in Andea where all technical backup could be assured rather than wait to assemble the device in the hostile environment of Antarctica), Andea arranged for a nuclear generator to be activated in Andea, loaded it on a military plane scheduled to fly to Andea's Antarctic base to remove seventeen barrels of hazardous chemicals, and dispatched it to Antarctica by air as planned.

The weather, however, deteriorated, and the plane crashed into a mountain adjacent to Andea's base, killing the flight crew and, in addition, spreading the "hot" radioactive materials aboard the plane over a wide area. The resulting increases in levels of radiation forced an emergency evacuation of all people at the base. With the assistance of the *HMNZS Nelson*, a New Zealand naval vessel, the people were evacuated.

About three months ago, after a series of severe winter storms of great force, scientists and technicians appointed by the United Nations Environment Programme (UNEP) and specially protected against radiation, returned to the area to assess the damage. All penguins within ten miles were found to have perished and high levels of radiation were discovered to be present in the sea, with the result that krill, fish, seals, and whales in the area had died. In addition, the scientists and technicians discovered that winter storms had ruptured the seventeen barrels of hazardous substances that had been awaiting removal by the plane. The substances comprised chemicals used in scientific drilling operations as well as detergents, varnishes, paints, and sealants used in the construction and operation of tourist facilities. A trail of greenish-black ooze had made its way along the ice shelf into the Ross Sea, causing serious pollution. Trash also littered the area.

As a result of this environmental disaster, and because it became doubtful as to whether Andea would have the resources necessary to provide adequate cleanup, New Zealand (also a party to the 1959 Antarctic Treaty) took action to sequester all of Andea's assets within New Zealand's jurisdiction, condemning Andea's action as "in violation of international law" and requesting Andea to "cease and desist" from all operations in Antarctica "until such time as efforts are successful to restore the area to its former condition." Other states party to the 1959 Antarctic Treaty soon followed New Zealand's lead, citing, in addition, the 1989 Basel Convention on the Control of Transboundary Movements of Hazardous Wastes and Their Disposal [**Basic Document 5.6**], another treaty to which Andea is a party.

Objecting to these actions by New Zealand and the other members of the Antarctic Treaty regime, Andea, invoking article XI(1) of the 1959 Treaty, proposed a resolution of the dispute "by negotiation, inquiry, mediation conciliation, arbitration, judicial settlement, or other peaceful means." Concerned to establish firm legal precedent in its favor, however, New Zealand and its 1959 Treaty partners refused. After consulting with one another, and invoking article XI(2) of the 1959 Treaty, they proposed, instead, to refer the dispute to the International Court of Justice. After much deliberation, Andea consented to this proposal and the case is now awaiting argument at The Hague.

C. *Malacca Hunts Seals*

For several years, Malacca, a newly industrialized country in Southeast Asia that is not a party to the 1959 Antarctic Treaty and the subsequent, associated instruments (including the 1972 Convention for the Conservation of Antarctic Seals), has advanced the argument at the United Nations, on its own behalf and on behalf of a number of like-minded countries, that the Antarctic Treaty regime is nothing more than an exclusive "rich men's" club whose member states ought not to be allowed by themselves to make the rules governing Antarctica because the subcontinent is part of the Common Heritage of Mankind (CHM). Thus, Malacca argues, an Antarctic regime is required "that is truly universal in character and committed to serving the interest of the entire international community."

In the last Antarctic summer season, the Government of Malacca dispatched a sealing expedition to Antarctic waters to test the validity of its jurisdictional claims. Notwithstanding the provisions of the 1972 Seals Convention, its official expedition hunted and killed 300 seals of a species totally protected by the 1972 Convention and exceeded by 200 the number allowed to be taken of species permitted to be exploited under the Convention. Some of the seals were taken from Antarctic territories claimed by certain of the Antarctic Treaty partners and some from the fifteen percent claimed by no nation.

Having learned of Malacca's intentions, Greenpeace sent its ship *MV Gondawana* to the area. The ship, which had a helicopter, was able to capture on film scenes of bloody carnage in which seals were clubbed to death. Subsequently widely distributed to television networks, these scenes caused widespread public outrage. Resolutions condemning the action were adopted by the United Nations General Assembly and by other international organizations, and many governments registered stern diplomatic protests. Most importantly, all of the parties of the Antarctic Treaty regime, invoking article X of the Treaty, protested to the Government of Malacca about the killing of the seals and the consequent imperiling of the fragile Antarctic ecosystem.

Malacca, believing it had adequately made its jurisdictional point, quickly stopped its sealing operation and offered to submit its dispute with the Antarctic Treaty parties to international arbitration. It recommended that three arbitrators expert in international law be appointed—one by the Treaty partners, one by Malacca, and a third presiding arbitrator chosen by the other two. This proposal was accepted and a *compromis* was agreed to, requiring the arbitral panel to decide the dispute in accordance with international law.

SECTION 2. QUESTIONS PRESENTED

In contrast to the later problem-oriented chapters in this coursebook, the many primary and secondary issues in this problem are *not* identified explicitly. Instead, trusting in your analytical talents, we leave these for you to determine—just as you would do, in fact, in the "real world" of every day legal practice. However, to facilitate clear analysis, we give you an assist; we arrange your reading assignments topic by topic and indicate the factual scenario or scenarios in the problem for which they are most relevant. Each topic bears a direct relation to the primary and secondary issues involved and can be analyzed and discussed separately.

SECTION 3. ASSIGNMENTS

A. Reading Assignment

Study the Readings presented in Section 4, *infra*, and the Discussion Notes/Questions that follow. Also, to the extent possible, consult the accompanying bibliographical references.

B. Recommended Writing Assignment

Prepare a comprehensive, logically sequenced, and *argumentative* brief in the form of an outline of the primary and subsidiary *legal* issues you see requiring resolution by the United States District Court, the International Court of Justice, and the ad hoc international arbitral panel convened in the above three scenarios. Also, from the perspective of an independent objective judge, indicate which side ought to prevail on each issue in each scenario and why. Retain a copy of your issue-outline/brief for class discussion.

C. Recommended Oral Assignment

Assume you are legal counsel for the parties involved in each of the above three scenarios of this problem (as designated by your instructor); then, relying upon the Readings (and your issue-outline if prepared), present a 10–15 minute oral argument of your government's likely positions before the decision-makers identified.

D. Suggested Reflective Assignment

Consider (and recommend) alternative norms, institutions, and/or procedures that you believe might do better than existing world order arrangements to contend with situations of the kind posed by this problem. In so doing, but without insisting upon *immediate* feasibility, identify the particular transition steps that would be needed to make your alternatives a reality.

SECTION 4. READINGS

The readings in this section are grouped according to the following subheadings: (A) The Antarctic Treaty and Related Issues, (B) Resource Management and Exploitation, and (C) Environmental Degradation and Pollution. They presuppose your knowledge of the Law of International Environmental Wrongs as elaborated in Chapter 5, *supra*. They cannot be adequately understood nor can the factual scenarios to which they relate be accurately analyzed and discussed without Chapter 5 firmly in mind. In short, Chapter 5 should be considered part of your reading assignment.

A. The Antarctic Treaty and Related Issues

The following readings relate primarily but not exclusively to the first scenario in this problem ("Polar Petroleum Corporation Explores for Oil and Gas"), *supra*. It should be possible to deal with the issues in that scenario after reviewing the readings here and in subsection B, *infra*.

1. **Charter of the United Nations June 26, 1945, arts. 1, 2, 74, 59 Stat. 1031, T.S. No. 993, 3 Bevans 1153, 1976 Y.B.U.N. 1043 [Basic Document 1.3].**

2. **The Antarctic Treaty Dec. 1, 1959, 12 U.S.T. 794, T.I.A.S. No. 4780, 402 U.N.T.S. 71 [Basic Document 2.1].**

3. **Resolution on the Question of Antarctica Dec. 17, 1984, G.A. Res. 39/152, U.N. GAOR, 39th Sess., Supp. No. 51, at 94, U.N. Doc. A/39/51 (1984) [Basic Document 2.6].**

4. **Resolution on the Question of Antarctica Dec. 15, 1989, G.A. Res. 44/124, U.N. GAOR, 44th Sess., Supp. No. 49, at 91, U.N. Doc. A/44/49 (1989) [Basic Document 2.8].**

5. **Juan Barcelo,** *The International Legal Regime for Antarctica*, 19 CORNELL INT'L L. J. 155, 156–61 (1986).

A. The Antarctic Treaty System

From 1908 to the early 1940s the following seven countries, in the order listed, claimed sovereignty over different sectors of Antarctica (totaling approximately 85% of the land area): the United Kingdom, New Zealand, France, Australia, Norway, Chile, and Argentina [*see* Figure 6–2, *supra*]. The claims were based not on effective occupation, but on early exploratory and scientific expeditions, and to some extent on marine resources exploitation. The claims of the United Kingdom, Chile, and Argentina overlap, thus these countries refuse to recognize one another's claims. Moreover, the United States and the Soviet Union (and all other countries of the world not making territorial claims to Antarctica themselves) have refused to recognize any territorial claims. Both the United States and the Soviet Union engaged in early activities on the subcontinent and thus have a basis for a territorial claim, but each has refused to reduce that claim to specific territory—in effect reserving the right to claim all of Antarctica, or at least an interest in all of Antarctica. About 15% of Antarctica is not expressly claimed by any country.

In the two decades prior to adoption of the Antarctic Treaty of December 1, 1959 **[Basic Document 2.1]**, the countries in the region seemed at times on the verge of open conflict. There were various flare-ups among the states with overlapping claims. The seven claimant states sought at every turn to reaffirm their claims vis-à-vis nonclaimants. There was also a growing fear, especially during the 1950s, that the cold-war military rivalry between the United States and the Soviet Union would spread to Antarctica.

B. Three Goals: Demilitarization, Scientific Cooperation, and Environmental Preservation

To avoid these pitfalls, the seven claimant states and five others (U.S., U.S.S.R., Japan, Belgium, and South Africa)—twelve states in all—entered the 1959 Antarctic Treaty. The Treaty has two primary goals: 1) to preserve Antarctica as an area for peaceful uses only; and 2) to promote freedom of scientific investigation throughout the continent. To achieve these ends, the Treaty prohibits all military activities, weapons testing, nuclear explosions, and disposal of nuclear wastes in Antarctica. It also guarantees freedom of scientific enquiry in Antarctica and obligates the parties to exchange scientific personnel and experimental results. The treaty parties have taken decisions within the treaty system that articulate a third goal: protecting the unique environment and ecosystem of Antarctica. Although no treaty language announces this purpose with complete clarity, the Treaty does prohibit nuclear explosions and radioactive waste disposal in Antarctica and calls for the treaty parties to consult on the "preservation and conservation of living resources in Antarctica."[3]

C. Article IV: Standstill on Territorial Claims

Article IV, concerning the rights of the claimant and nonclaimant states, is the cornerstone of the Treaty. It uniquely sidesteps the intractable issue of territorial claims by providing that none of the agreed upon cooperative activities under the Treaty is to prejudice or affect in any way the legal rights and claims of either the claimant or nonclaimant states. No new claims are to arise; no enlargement of existing claims is to occur; and no renunciation, diminution, or denial of claims is to be grounded upon the parties' cooperative activities under the Treaty. Because of Article IV's pivotal role, its operative language is worth repeating here:

> No acts or activities taking place while the present Treaty is in force shall constitute a basis for asserting, supporting or denying a claim to territorial sovereignty in Antarctica or create any rights of sovereignty in Antarctica. No new claim, or enlargement of an existing claim, to territorial sovereignty in Antarctica shall be asserted while the present Treaty is in force.

Two other treaty provisions buttress this central feature of the Antarctic legal regime: 1) all decisions are to be taken by unanimity; and 2) all decision-making parties are entitled to free and unhindered on-site inspection of all installations and all vessels and aircraft (at points of loading and unloading) in Antarctica. The unanimity provision assures both claimants and nonclaimants that nothing will be permitted in Antarctica that would prejudice their respective claims or legal positions. On-site inspection ensures full compliance with the treaty provisions and subsequent implementing agreements.

The treaty parties have also bound themselves to prevent even non-party states from acting in any way inconsistent with the goals and principles of the Antarctic Treaty. Article X provides that each treaty party "undertakes to exert appropriate efforts, consistent with the Charter of the United Nations, to the end that no one engages in any activity in Antarctica contrary to the principles or purposes of the present Treaty." Thus, under Article X the treaty parties would be obligated to resist any efforts of non-party states to assert new claims to sovereignty over any area of Antarctica, to infringe the freedom of scientific inquiry, to use any part of Antarctica for military purposes, or to act in a way that imperils the fragile Antarctic ecosystem.

During or after the year 1991, if any decision-making party so requests, the treaty parties are obligated to hold a conference to review the operation of the Antarctic Treaty system.

3. Antarctic Treaty, art. IX(f) [Basic Document 2.1].

D. Two–Tiered Treaty Party Structure

For decision-making purposes the parties to the Antarctic Treaty fall into two groups; 1) the so-called "consultative parties" (who have the power to make decisions); and 2) the "non-consultative parties" (who technically have no vote).

1. Consultative Parties

The consultative, or decision-making, parties meet biennially to consider pending issues concerning the governance of Antarctica and implementation of the Treaty. The consultative parties are the original twelve parties to the 1959 Treaty and six additional countries who were later adherents: Poland (1977), West Germany (1981), Brazil (1983), India (1983), the People's Republic of China (1985), and Uruguay (1985). Any party to the Treaty can become a consultative party through demonstrating "interest in Antarctica by conducting substantial scientific research activity there, such as the establishment of a scientific station or the despatch of a scientific expedition." The six non-original consultative parties achieved consultative party status in this manner, and five of these did so in the last five years.

2. Non-consultative Parties

There are also fourteen non-consultative parties to the 1959 Treaty. These countries have acceded to the Treaty but have not established a scientific presence in Antarctica sufficient to give them the rights of a consultative party. Since 1983, the consultative parties have invited the non-consultative countries to attend the decision-making meetings with observer status. The fourteen non-consultative countries are: Bulgaria, Cuba, Czechoslovakia, Denmark, Finland, East Germany, Hungary, Italy, the Netherlands, Papua New Guinea, Peru, Romania, Spain, and Sweden. Two of this group— Italy and Sweden—have recently planned and conducted scientific investigations in Antarctica and are thus poised to become full consultative parties.

At their biennial meetings the consultative parties have adopted a number of recommendations, covering such matters as environmental protection and preservation of species, exchange of scientific information, tourism, communications, and the procedural aspects of decision making. They have also completed two additional treaties: (1) the 1972 Convention for the Conservation of Antarctic Seals [**Basic Document 2.3**]; and (2) the 1980 Convention on the Conservation of Antarctic Marine Living Resources [**Basic Document 2.4**].

6.   Stefan Brunner, *Article 10 of the Antarctic Treaty Revisited,* *in* INTERNATIONAL LAW FOR ANTARCTICA 103, 103–09 (Francesco Francioni & Tullio Scovazzi eds., 1996).

1.   Introduction

Art. 10 of the Antarctic Treaty [**Basic Document 2.1**] reads:

Each of the Contracting Parties undertakes to exert appropriate efforts, consistent with the Charter of the United Nations, to the end that no one engages in any activity in Antarctica contrary to the principles or purposes of the present Treaty.

It has been said that "article 10 of the Treaty is clear."[4] There remain, however, several problems of interpretation which are worth mentioning:

—Who are the "no ones"? Individuals or States or both? Should or could a distinction be made between governmental and non-governmental expeditions? Are jurisdictional aspects covered, or does the provision concern only State obligations? Does "no ones" refer only to third States and their respective nationals or to Contracting Parties as well, even to those with consultative status?

—What exactly are the "principles and purposes of the Treaty"? Do they have anything to do with the principles and objectives furthered by recommendations?

—Has subsequent practice distinguished between obligations to be observed by Contracting Parties without consultative status on the one hand and by Consultative Parties on the other hand?

—What is the significance of the specific reference to the Charter of the United Nations?

2.   Article 10 and third States: Which principles and purposes?

Quite an extensive debate has focused on the problem of whether art. 10 reflects the lack of a third party effect and its implicit admission, or, on the contrary, whether it constitutes an "assertion of competencies" vis-a-vis third States.[5]

Sometimes art. 10 is in fact used as a counter argument against any third party effects of the treaty. . . . It could, however, be argued that art. 10 would not be superfluous in case of a third party effect, because it is one thing when an obligation, which is owed to you and others, is breached, and quite another thing when you are obliged to actively prevent or to react to such a breach.

On the other hand, it has been suggested that art. 10 itself is the vehicle to bring about third party obligations.[6] The theories to this effect have to circumvent several legal obstacles, among others, art. 38(1)(a) of the Statute of the International Court of Justice **[Basic Document 1.4]**, which refers to "international conventions, whether general or particular, *establishing rules expressly recognized* by the contesting states"[7] and the existing "customary law of treaties" which has been codified and progressively developed in the Vienna Convention on the Law of Treaties **[Basic Document 1.7]**. As far as the relationship of third States to treaties is concerned international law is essentially based on the notion of sovereignty.

On a first level, the *principle of territorial sovereignty* is the basis of the distinction between treaties providing for obligations and treaties providing for rights. If it could be maintained that the signatory powers had already

4.   Roberto Guyer, Antarctica's Role in International Relations, in ANTARCTIC RESOURCES POLICY 267, 278 (F. Orrego Vicuña ed., 1983).

5.   *See* Bruno Simma, *Le Traite antarctique: Crée-t-il un "regime objectif" ou non?*, *in* INTERNATIONAL LAW FOR ANTARCTICA 137 (Francesco Francioni & Tullio Scovazzi eds., 1987); IAN BROWNLIE, PRINCIPLES OF PUBLIC INTERNATIONAL LAW 266 n.2 (3d ed. 1979).

6.   *See* Guyer, *supra* note 4, at 278–79; ECKART KLEIN, STAATSVERTRAGE IM VÖLKERRECHT. RECHTSFRAGEN TERRITORIALER SONDERREGIME 62–63 (1980); ULRICH NUSSBAUM, ROHSTOFFGEWINNUNG IN DER ANTARKTIS 122–27 (1985).

7.   . . . Emphasis added.

established a sovereign title, before they entered into the Antarctic Treaty, third parties would clearly be obliged to observe the "conditions for use," i.e. the conditions for exercising a right, the only important legal question being, whether they have acquired any right at all. The vast majority of writers do not follow this avenue, including those who rely on art. 10 as a device for producing *erga omnes* effects. They argue that an "obligation to respect" has subsequently been created for third parties by the "Treaty as such" (as opposed to the Treaty proceeding from and being based on the prior "obligation to respect sovereignty"). This approach includes, therefore, the—legally well founded—admission that the preexisting claims were not sufficiently founded in international law, and consequently that a title had not then been perfected.

According to this view the Treaty as such, and art. 10 in particular, are intended to create obligations for third parties; *the principle of sovereign equality* works, however, with regard to obligations on a second level and requires express consent to the provision concerned which has unfortunately never taken place. Sophisticated devices have been designed to overcome this dilemma. One theory perceives art. 10 as a Janus-faced provision serving both as an *obligation inter partes* and as a *claim erga tertios*. Accordingly, the silence of third parties is not to be interpreted as disagreement because express consent to a treaty provision providing for obligations is lacking, but it must, on the contrary, be understood as acquiescence in the assertion of competences which lies behind art. 10.

At this stage a closer examination of art. 10 seems necessary to solve the puzzle about its function and legal significance. The primary function of every treaty provision is still to create duties for the parties to the treaty and not for outsiders. Which duties does art. 10 create? Art. 10 obliges the parties to prevent anyone from doing nasty things in Antarctica. Which activities are to be regarded as nasty things depends on the meaning of "principles and purposes". What the parties are allowed to do against third States and their nationals under general international law and, correspondingly, which efforts they are obliged to exert according to art. 10 depends on whether the Treaty has any third party effects at all and, if so, which. The proviso of "consistency with the Charter of the United Nations" is another point where possible third party effects come into the picture. If there are no legal obligations for third States, nothing more than moral persuasion or retorsion could lawfully be exerted, and hence be called for in art. 10. If, however, such obligations existed, at least reprisals would be permissible against third States. Equally only the lawful exercise of enforcement jurisdiction is required by art. 10.

It should be examined whether the legality of the use of force against third parties depends on the validity of claims or possible *erga omnes* effects of the Treaty. If a third State launches an attack against an Antarctic station, it goes without saying that self-defence according to art. 51 of the U.N. Charter **[Basic Document 1.3]** is permissible irrespective of the claims to sovereignty and their validity under international law. The establishment of a military base in Antarctica by a third party would constitute an armed attack, i.e. a violation of territorial integrity comparable to troops crossing a frontier, only if there were a sovereign in Antarctica, be it that the claimant States had a valid title to their sectors (which would leave the problem of the unclaimed sector), be it that Antarctica were a *de jure* condominium with distinct legal personality, falling as such within the scope of art. 51 of the U.N. Charter. If, however, a legal evaluation were to come to the conclusion that there is no sovereign in Antarctica, whose territorial integrity could be violated, the mere establishment of a military base would not amount to an armed attack, and such an installation could not lawfully be destroyed in self defence once it has been established. It is debatable whether the picture would change and the destruction of the base would have to be considered legal, if the third State were bound by the provisions concerning non-militarization of Antarctica as norms of general international law. The answer depends on the permissibility of "reprisals involving the use of force," a celebrated subject of academic controversy.[8] The *opinio juris* expressed in the Friendly Relations Declaration **[Basic Document 1.8]** and elsewhere indicates that reprisals must not amount to the use of force. Therefore the legality of the use of force according to art. 51 of the U.N. Charter depends entirely and exclusively on the validity of the territorial claims except for the above-mentioned cases of immediate attacks; in other words: in the absence of a valid title to territory, military force could not lawfully be employed by the parties to the Treaty alone, even if the rules to be enforced had become legally binding for third States.

This result is not as disastrous as it may appear at first sight, because the parties could at any rate bring this situation, which might lead to international friction or give rise to a dispute, to the attention of the Security Council, either individually in their capacity as members of the United Nations according to art. 35(1) of the U.N. Charter or collectively as members of a regional arrangement in conformity with art. 53(1) of the U.N. Charter, which requires prior authorization of the Security Council for all enforcement actions.

These enforcement actions are measures under the authority of the Security Council and may therefore be directed against non-members of the regional arrangement; the Charter does, on the other hand, not grant any semi-legislative competencies to treaties under chapter VII. Thus, the parties to the Treaty may use force against third States with the authorization of the Security Council irrespective of the validity of the claims and of possible *erga omnes* effects of the Treaty.

This intricate legal situation explains an important aspect of the reference to the Charter of the United Nations in art. 10 of the Antarctic Treaty.

7. Douglas M. Zang, *Frozen in Time: The Antarctic Minerals Convention*, 76 CORNELL L. REV. 722, 735–51 (1991).

A precondition to the existence of any legal order is recognized authority. Whether the authority comes from a formalized "rule of recognition," or from a fluid set of shared community values, the existence of some basic norm from which all valid legal principles originate distinguishes a legal order from a system based upon the arbitrary exercise of power. In international law the fundamental source of authority is consensus in the recognition of the legitimacy of a legal norm. To be consistent with international law, then, any exercise of state action in the international realm must be recognized as legitimate. This requirement of recognized legitimacy applies to the exercise

8. *See, e.g.,* Derek Bowett, *Reprisals Involving Recourse to Armed Force*, 66 AM. J. INT'L L. 1 (1972); W. Hester, Gewaltverbot und Repressalien (1973).

of jurisdiction. In order to claim the authority to prescribe or enforce a rule of law, an actor must be able to point to a principle of international law which grants that authority.

A.   The Exercise of Jurisdiction in Antarctica

There is a continuing debate over whether the Treaty System purports to exercise jurisdiction over nonparty states in Antarctica. If the [Antarctica] Treaty **[Basic Document 2.1]** applies only to Treaty member states and their nationals, then nonparty states presumably have no strong grounds for objecting to the current regime. The Treaty would not compromise rights of nonparties, and nonparties would not be constrained by externally imposed obligations. As to the Convention [for the Regulation of Antarctic Mineral Resource Activities (CRAMRA) **[Basic Document 2.7]**], however, the outcome of this debate is not conclusive.

In contrast to the [Antarctic] Treaty, the Convention clearly contemplates the exercise of jurisdiction over Antarctica, and over the activities of nonparty states in Antarctica. Article 3 of the Convention states that "[n]o Antarctic mineral resource activities shall be conducted except in accordance with this Convention." The parties to the Convention thereby assert that they will grant the right to undertake mineral resource activities only to those who comply with their terms and conditions. Article 3, of course, assumes that the right to develop mineral resources is theirs to grant. Furthermore, it assumes that they may deny that right to any entity unwilling to abide by the terms of the Convention.

The Convention's claim to jurisdiction over all mineral resource activities, including those of nonparty states, together with an administrative structure which limits participation in the decision making process necessitates the assertion of some legitimate basis of authority. Absent such recognized authority, the Convention is fundamentally inconsistent with international law.

B.   Possible Sources of Authority

There is no clearly defined set of legal principles that supports the exercise of territorial jurisdiction. The international lawmaking process is continuous and fluid, dependent upon consensus to establish its legitimacy. Although the fluidity of international law makes its content difficult to define, three generally recognized legal principles would be most likely to support the exercise of jurisdiction in Antarctica: territorial sovereignty, the objective treaty doctrine, and customary international law. For various reasons, however, none of the three justifies the current legal regime established by the Treaty System.

1.   *Territorial Sovereignty*

Territorial sovereignty describes a sovereign's competence to exercise legislative, executive, and judicial functions within its dominion. The authority of a territorial sovereign generally is absolute and exclusive, and thus is analogous to the authority that an owner exercises over his property under private law. Under this principle, the establishment of a legal order such as the Treaty System, with its imposition of rights and obligations, is within the competence of the territorial sovereign of Antarctica.

Either the claimant states severally, or the Treaty consultative parties collectively, may assert territorial sovereignty in Antarctica. If each of the individual claimants holds valid title to its claimed sector, then their participation in the Treaty System provides a legitimate basis for the sovereignty of the consultative parties. The Treaty System could thus be viewed as a regional arrangement, competent to determine regional matters of "peace and security" as provided for in the United Nations Charter.

Alternatively, if the individual claims are amalgamated, a de facto condominium may exist.[9] According to this view, the consultative parties are entitled to exercise a form of collective sovereignty over Antarctica by virtue of either their collective activity or the pooling of their independent claims. Declaration of a de facto condominium has two significant advantages for the consultative parties. First, it would not require the resolution of conflicting territorial claims. Second, even if an individual territorial claim is not legally strong enough to stand on its own, the consultative parties together would have a consolidated claim to traditional territorial sovereignty stronger than any other state or group of states. Assertion of territorial sovereignty, either individually or as a condominium, must be supported by a principle of territorial acquisition. To claim territory as part of a sovereign's dominion, international law must recognize the means of acquisition as legitimate. The category of principles of territorial acquisition is ill-defined, but the following survey considers principles that are at least colorable as applied to Antarctica.

a. Discovery

According to the discovery principle, valid legal title to territory and the right to exercise territorial sovereignty accrues from the act of discovery itself. While none of the states that currently asserts a claim in Antarctica relies solely on the principle of discovery, seven states utilize discovery as partial support for their claim: France, Australia, New Zealand, Norway, the United Kingdom, the United States, and the Soviet Union.

Discovery, however, is no longer widely recognized as a sufficient basis for sovereignty. The *Island of Palmas* case[10] supports this view. *Island of Palmas* involved a dispute between the United States and the Netherlands, both of which claimed sovereignty over the Island of Palmas, or Miangas, in the Philippines. The Netherlands based its claim upon actual occupation of the island, whereas the United States claim derived from an earlier Spanish claim based on discovery. The Permanent Court of Arbitration held in favor of the Netherlands, stating that acts of discovery alone, without any attempt to exercise control, cannot confer title to territory.

Furthermore, there are a number of practical difficulties with the discovery principle. For example, its does not set forth which specific acts constitute discovery. Nor does it provide for the verification of claims, or the resolution

---

9. A condominium in international law is defined as territory "under the *joint tenancy* of two or more States, these several States exercising sovereignty conjointly over it, and over the individuals living thereon." LASSA OPPENHEIM, INTERNATIONAL LAW: A TREATISE 453 (1962).

See also Daniel O'Connell, *The Condominium of the New Hebrides*, 43 BRIT. Y. B. INT'L L. 71 (1968–69).

10. Island of Palmas (U.S. v. Neth.) 2 U.N.R.I.A.A. 829 (1982).

of disputes between conflicting claims. Finally, discovery alone does not determine the geographical extent of a claim.

b. Occupation

Historically, an individual could obtain title to previously unclaimed territory by occupying it.[11] The more stringent doctrine of effective occupation, developed during the nineteenth century, requires state-sanctioned, permanent occupation and settlement in order to perfect title. Under the effective occupation doctrine, possession must be actual, continuous, and useful. An effective occupation may follow the establishment of an "inchoate title" through initial acts of possession or discovery. Settlement or a consistent pattern of activity must follow such acts in order to maintain a territorial claim. Inchoate title allows the claimant to relate its claim back to the initial act of possession, thereby granting it priority over subsequent competing claims.

The exact quantum of activity required to establish an effective occupation is unclear. Given the size of Antarctica, however, the largely scientific activities of the Treaty parties are insufficient to constitute effective occupation or to perfect inchoate title. The presence of the Treaty parties in Antarctica consists mainly of isolated scientific stations that occupy only small areas; this presence does not reach the level of permanent settlement and administration required under the theory of effective occupation.

Commentators have argued that inhospitable environments call for a reduced standard in applying the doctrine of effective occupation. In support of such a view, some commentators have cited the *Eastern Greenland* case,[12] which involved a dispute over the competing claims of Denmark and Norway to the eastern coast of Greenland. Denmark had established permanent settlements on the southern and western coasts, but proclaimed its intention to exercise sovereignty over the entire island, including the eastern coast where it had no significant presence. Norwegian fishermen had maintained bases on the eastern coast for centuries, but Norway had not formally asserted a claim until this litigation arose. The Permanent Court of International Justice held in favor of Denmark. The commentators suggest that the court based its decision upon a finding that, given the harsh conditions prevailing in that region, Denmark's minimal presence in eastern Greenland was sufficient to establish an effective occupation. However, the outcome in *Eastern Greenland* was not determined by effective occupation. Instead, the decision rested upon the fact that Denmark's claim went essentially unchallenged for centuries, and that Norway made statements which could be interpreted as recognizing the validity of Denmark's claim[13]. In other words, the decision in *Eastern Greenland* did not rest upon the validity of Denmark's means of acquisition, but rather upon Norway's implicit recognition of Denmark's claim. *Eastern Greenland* does not, therefore, provide support for claimant states who assert that isolated scientific activities are sufficient to

11. Before the rise in European exploration and colonialization in the middle of the 15th century, the only unclaimed lands were newly formed islands. The individual who first occupied these islands acquired title. Donald Grieg, *Sovereignty, Territory and the International* *Lawyer's Dilemma*, 26 Osgoode Hall L. J. 127, 140 (1988).

12. Legal Status of Eastern Greenland (Den. v. Nor.), 1933 P.C.I.J. (ser. A/B) No. 53, at 22 (Apr. 5).

13. *Id.* at 50–53.

constitute an effective occupation under a reduced standard applicable to inhospitable regions.

c.   Propinquity

The theory of propinquity provides that when a state acquires sovereignty over part of a geographical unit, it acquires sovereignty over the entire unit. As applied to Antarctica, sovereignty over a section of the Antarctic coast translates into a claim to sovereignty over the adjacent inland region. Thus claimant states may contend that the establishment of a small research station supports a claim to the entire geographical unit within which the station is situated. This theory has the advantage of not requiring effective occupation of an entire area. Propinquity is, however, ambiguous and uncertain in its application. Given the inherent difficulty of determining what constitutes a distinct geographical unit in Antarctica, the territorial extent of such a claim would be unclear. Furthermore, although scholars developed the theory of propinquity to support European colonial claims during the nineteenth century, the theory was explicitly rejected at the Berlin Congo Conference of 1885 by those for whose benefit it was developed.

d.   Sector Theory

Sector theory, developed with respect to the Arctic polar region, provides that states whose territory extends above the Arctic Circle[14] acquire sovereignty over the triangular sector with a baseline which extends between the extreme eastern and western limits of that state's northern coastline, and with the apex at the north pole. States asserting claims in Antarctica, with the exception of Norway, have relied to some extent upon the sector theory. The method of delineating claims under this theory superficially accords with the actual territorial claims in Antarctica, which happen to be triangular. By its own definition, however, the sector theory should not apply to Antarctica since no state's territory extends below the Antarctic Circle. In fact, no state's territory extends below sixty degrees south latitude, the baseline of the seven extant claims.

Sector theory has never gained wide recognition in the international community. The United States, Denmark, and Norway, which are all Treaty parties, and one of which (Norway) is a claimant state, have explicitly rejected the sector theory. Objections have been based in part upon the conflict with the requirement of effective occupation, the arbitrary placement of baselines, and the conflict with freedom of the high seas.

e.   Uti Posseditis

The *uti posseditis* principle suggests that the Antarctic claims of Chile and Argentina are legitimate as a matter of historic right. In the Bull Inter Caetera Divinae of 1493, Pope Alexander VII divided the unclaimed regions of the world between Spain and Portugal. Antarctica falls within the half of the world ostensibly granted to Spain. When Argentina and Chile seceded from Spain in 1810, they retained the Spanish claims. While the grant was intended to be binding upon third parties, only Spain and Portugal, the two

14. The countries involved were Canada,   and Norway.
the United States, the Soviet Union, Denmark,

states who had requested papal intervention, recognized the pope's authority to make such a disposition. This arcane theory has never gained wide acceptance. Given the lack of international consent to the papal disposition, it is not a convincing basis for jurisdiction over Antarctic mineral resources.

* * *

3. Customary International Law

Article 38 of the Statute of the International Court of Justice [**Basic Document 1.4**] lists as one of the four sources of international law "international custom, as evidence of a general practice accepted as law." A customary rule of law has two components: the general practice of states, and the recognition by states that this general practice has become law (*opinio juris*). The general practice element requires a demonstrable pattern of unambiguous and consistent state practice. There is disagreement, however, over the amount of time which must elapse before a general practice or asserted principle becomes binding as customary law. The recognition of the practice must be widespread, but need not be universal. A multilateral agreement such as the Treaty or the Convention may provide the source for rules of customary international law. On occasion, standards of conduct which were binding initially only by virtue of their explicit stipulation in an international agreement became enforceable rules of customary law through widespread acceptance among the international community. Products of such an evolution include the principle of freedom of the seas, and the minimum standards of protection owed to foreigners. Furthermore, an international agreement may create customary law that binds not only the parties to the agreement, but also third parties. Article 38 of the Vienna Treaty on Treaties [**Basic Document 1.7**] supports this view, providing that the principle of *pacta tertiis* does not "preclude a rule set forth in a treaty from becoming binding upon a third State as a customary rule of international law, recognized as such."

B. Resource Management and Exploitation

The following readings relate to the first scenario in this problem ("Polar Petroleum Corporation Explores for Oil and Gas"), *supra*. It should be possible to deal with the issues in that scenario after reviewing the readings here and in subsection A, *supra*.

1. **Convention on the Regulation of Antarctic Mineral Resources Activities (CRAMRA), June 2, 1988, 27 I.L.M. 868 (1988) [Basic Document 2.7].**

2. **Protocol on Environmental Protection to the Antarctica Treaty Oct. 4, 1991, arts. 2–4, 6–8, 30 I.L.M. 1461 (1991). [Basic Document 2.9].**

3. **United Nations Convention on the Law of the Sea Dec. 10, 1982, arts. 192–196, 207, U.N. Doc. A/CONF.62/122, 21 I.L.M. 1261 (1982) [Basic Document 4.20].**

·4. **Emilio Sahurie, The International Law of Antarctica 352–58 (1992).**

Minerals on Land

The physical characteristics of Antarctica make it difficult to obtain a complete and substantial knowledge of its geology. A major obstacle is the ice sheet that covers 98% of the continent. Thus, despite the fact that Antarctic geoscience has grown in the last years and that oil companies and state agencies have conducted several surveys, the information on minerals that geologists have provided in the last two decades, with some notable exceptions in a few areas, is scant and basically redundant.

The existence of minerals in Antarctica, however, seems undeniable: The mere fact that it is a continental landmass is strong evidence in and of itself. All the other continents—especially Africa, Australia, and South America, which together with Antarctica formed the great landmass called Gondwanaland—are rich in all sorts of minerals. Most scholars now accept the existence of the supercontinent of Gondwanaland in the early Mesozoic era, 200 million years ago.[15] The history of its break-up and the evolution of its fragments into South America, Africa, Australia, and Antarctica can best provide information in evaluating the potential resources in Antarctica. In addition, direct evidence of ore minerals has resulted both from geological analysis of rocks, and from the limited prospecting that has been done.

There is no reason to speculate that Antarctica has no mineral resources. The little prospecting done shows impressive results. But more is needed. A comprehensive search, delineation and economic assessment of the ore-bodies buried under Antarctic ice are tasks that have been neglected as a result of the lack of political certainty about the status of resources in Antarctica.... It is important to bear in mind, however, that because of current costs of operation in Antarctica, and prevalent market conditions, only those deposits of high concentration and value might be worth exploiting in the future.

[The author next observes that Antarctica is known or speculated to have deposits, often in large quantities, of iron (in East Antarctic and the Antarctic Peninsula); copper (on the Antarctic Peninsula, on islands west of the Antarctica Peninsula, and in the Transantarctic Mountains); molybdenum (on the Antarctic Peninsula and in Eastern Antarctica); coal (in the Transantarctic Mountains and in Eastern Antarctica); uranium (in ice-free areas of Antarctica); chromium, nickel, and cobalt (in the Pensacola Mountains and on the Antarctic Peninsula); and such other minerals as gold, silver, titanium, lead, zinc, niobium, and tantalum (on the Antarctic Peninsula, in Adelie Land, and in East Antarctica). He notes also the existence, albeit "not in amounts of economic significance," of such industrial minerals as graphite, micas, kyanite, fluorite, rock crystal, and phosphate (especially in East Antarctica). He then continues:]

Offshore Resources

Oil

Despite the opinion of some experts, the existence of oil deposits in Antarctica can no longer be in doubt. Several reports produced in the last

---

15. Campbell Craddock, *Antarctica and Gondwanaland, in* ANTARCTIC GEOSCIENCE 3 (C. Craddock ed., 1982); Gilbert Guillaume, *Oil as a Special Resource: Problems and Experiences, in* ANTARCTIC RESOURCES POLICY 185, 186 (Francisco Orrego Vicuña ed., 1983).

years, and a growing interest of states and business associations in the oil potential of Antarctica, are strong evidence.

Soviet officials have suggested that Antarctica has larger oil resources than Alaska, and that exploration and exploitation would follow in the near future. Indeed, the Soviets have carried out aeromagnetic surveys in diverse parts of the continental shelf of Antarctica. Aeromagnetic surveys permit a first appraisal of the structure of sedimentary rocks; these are of interest as a possible source of petroleum. A more direct indication is given by multi-channel seismic surveys, which measure the return of shock waves sent through materials below the sea floor. This method, introduced in Antarctica by Norway in 1976, has been regularly used by oil companies searching for oil. Several other studies have been conducted by West German, American, French, Australian, Japanese, and Chilean geologists. This increase in research has resulted from steady international pressure for figures to ascertain the value of oil resources. A great deal of the research has been concentrated in the Ross Sea and Weddell Sea basins [*see* Figure 6-2, *supra*], which appear promising not only because of their hydrocarbon potential, but also because they are free of permanent ice. This would avoid logistical problems and permit the use of technology based on experience in the Arctic. The Ross Sea is in the area claimed by New Zealand, and the Weddell is in Western Antarctica, where the Argentine, British, and Chilean claims overlap. Also, the Amundsen Sea continental margin, which is in the unclaimed sector, and the Bellingshausen Sea continental margin in Western Antarctica are considered promising areas for oil exploitation.

Estimates on recoverable oil vary. In 1973, an internal report of the U.S. Geological Survey put the figures at 15 billion barrels in the Ross, Weddell, and Bellingshausen seas.[16] But in 1974, the *Wall Street Journal* citing U.S. Geological Survey sources, raised the figures to 45 billion barrels.[17] This is far higher than the proven reserves of Alaska and the British sector of the North Sea put together. Another U.S. government report mentioned tens of billions of barrels in the most promising areas; in 1979, a Gulf Oil representative stated that the potential of the most promising areas in the Ross and Weddell seas was in the range of 50 billion barrels, "but could be much more."[18] Several oil companies have indicated interest in the area, including Texaco, Gulf, Arco, and Exxon. Some have applied for licenses; others would consider immediate prospecting if the political condition permitted it....

Minerals on the Ocean Floor

The sea bottom of the Southern Ocean has significant concentrations of manganese nodules, especially beneath the Antarctic convergency at about 60° south latitude. Other areas in the Pacific Ocean, however, are richer and have conditions more favorable than the hostile environment of the Southern Ocean.

---

16. Nancy Wright & Paul Williams, *Mineral Resources of Antarctica*, U.S. GEOLOGICAL SURVEY CIRC. 705 (1974); Barbara Mitchell, *Resources in Antarctica*, 1 MARINE POL'Y 91 (1977).

17. J. Spival, *The Energy Crisis Spurs Idea of Seeking Oil at the South Pole*, WALL ST. J., Feb. 21, 1974, at 1.

18. *Id.*

Icebergs

Water soon will be the most valuable mineral resource we can mine from the earth. Water, perhaps the most necessary of the natural resources, is becoming one of the scarcest. Glaciers hold the world's greatest reserve of fresh water. More than 70% of the usable fresh water is in the Antarctic icecap, and 1.4 trillion tons of ice break off every year in the form of huge icebergs that eventually melt into the Southern Ocean. This is the equivalent of one thousand billion tons of water.

The concept of transporting water great distances may be better grasped by thinking of comparable achievements. In Roman times water was brought by aqueducts to Rome from the Alps hundreds of miles away. Pipelines transport oil and gas cross-continent. Water is routed long distances to inhabited areas by shifting it from one river system to another, by using canals, by pumping it or sending it through mountain tunnels.

The desperate need in some areas for more water has changed views about bringing icebergs to warmer latitudes. In 1966 President Johnson of the United States submitted to Congress a program to meet future water needs, urging the study of the possibility of towing Arctic icebergs to southern California. There have been several iceberg-towing discussions over the years. Experts have suggested that Antarctic icebergs could be pulled by tugs to northwestern Australia and the Atacama Desert in northern Chile. They would be beached there and the melted water pumped inland. The problem of ice melting could be overcome by using the cold currents offshore which come from a polar direction, by towing only very large icebergs, and by giving icebergs an insulated cover.

According to studies, towing icebergs to Saudi Arabia, a project to be undertaken by Saudi Arabia in association with a French enterprise, would be technically feasible, and the cost much less than the current price to Saudi cities of $0.79 per cubic meter of desalinated sea water. Costs of water delivered to dry areas in the Southern Hemisphere such as Australia, Africa, Chile, and Peru, and perhaps California, would be even cheaper.

In fact, the water that a large iceberg contains is substantial; a medium size iceberg which rises 50 feet above the water, which is 450 feet thick and half a mile on a side, weighs about 90 million tons. At $0.50 per ton, the value of the water would be $45 million.

5. Editors' Note. Something of a crisis developed within the Antarctic Treaty System (ATS) in the last few years relative to environmental threats posed by the exploitation of mineral and other resources. There was some interest in mineral exploration following the OPEC oil shocks of the 1970s, and the parties to the Antarctic Treaty **[Basic Document 2.1]** made a serious effort to negotiate an additional convention to deal with the matter. Despite years of diplomatic effort, however, they were forced to back off under the increasing pressure of environmental opinion.

In truth, environmental considerations were not perceived as important when the Antarctic Treaty was negotiated. The Treaty's only provisions dealing with environmental issues are those that prohibit nuclear explosions and the disposal of radioactive waste in Antarctica,[e] and one in which consultative meetings are given the task of recommending measures directed at, *inter alia*, the preservation and conservation of living resources in Antarctica.[f]

The first serious attempt to introduce some protective environmental measures occurred in 1964, with the adoption of the Agreed Measures for the Conservation of Antarctic Fauna and Flora **[Basic Document 2.2]**. Pursuant thereto, the Antarctic Consultative Parties (ATCPs) declared that the Antarctic is a "Special Conservation Area" and they imposed restrictions on certain activities having the potential to harm the Antarctic environment. The Agreed Measures did not take effect until the early 1980s, however, because they were not ratified by all the states that negotiated them.

Subsequently, in 1972, the ATCPs negotiated the Convention for the Conservation of Antarctic Seals **[Basic Document 2.3]**. The Convention establishes permissible annual catches for three species found in the Southern Ocean, and forbids the killing or capturing of three other species. It also divides the year into a "Closed Season" and a "Sealing Season," provides that each "zone" is to be totally closed to all sealing operations for one year in six, and establishes "Seal Reserves" to protect the main breeding areas of Antarctic seals.

In 1982, in the face of mounting pressures by distant-water fishing states (e.g., Japan) to exploit Antarctica's living resources, particularly krill, the Treaty parties adopted the Convention for the Conservation of Antarctic Marine Living Resources (CCAMLR) **[Basic Document 2.4]**. CCAMLR is significant for the fact that it introduces the "ecosystem concept" to the management of the marine resources of the Southern Ocean, with article II laying down conservation principles for any harvesting activities. The Convention is therefore a model for other treaty regimes aimed at protecting marine and other resources.

Other measures bearing on the protection of the Antarctic environment include the 1975 Code of Conduct for Antarctic Expeditions and Station Activities (unpublished) and the 1979 rules for the guidance of visitors to the Antarctic (unpublished). These measures were agreed to under the structure of the Treaty itself.

Outside the structure of the Antarctic Treaty itself has been the matter of controlling mineral exploitation and mining activities generally. The Antarctic Treaty says nothing about minerals exploitation and its control because mining in Antarctica was not an issue when the ATS was adopted. When, however, in 1982 it became a hotly debated issue, the negotiation of a minerals regime for Antarctica—including environmental protections—was begun. The end result, after extended negotiations involving many complex issues, was the 1988 Convention for the Regulation of Antarctic Mineral Resource Activities (CRAMRA) **[Basic Document 2.7]**.

Large efforts to oppose CRAMRA, however, were mounted by international environmental groups, with Jacques Cousteau of the Cousteau Society playing an important oppositional role. The governments of France and

---

e. *See* art. V(1) & (2).   **f.** *See* art. IX(1)(f).

Australia opposed ratification of the Convention despite their participation in the negotiations and their apparent agreement with the result; and the government of New Zealand, whose Deputy Secretary of Foreign Affairs Chris Beeby had chaired the CRAMRA meetings, also changed its mind. So did other ATCPs. The result is that CRAMRA has yet to enter into force. Moreover, it is unlikely to do so; and when this probability became apparent, shortly after the negotiation of CRAMRA, there occurred a diplomatic scramble to negotiate something else. Unless another agreement were reached, it was understood, the very future of the ATS as a whole would be in jeopardy. Thus, in 1991, the Protocol on Environmental Protection to the Antarctic Treaty **[Basic Document 2.9]** was completed.

For all the environmental protection diplomacy that took place during the 1980s, however, a word of caution: in practice, the reality of environmental protection has not always corresponded with the claim of the Antarctic Treaty parties that the protection of the environment is their foremost concern. In some cases, there have been deliberate and knowing breaches of the letter and spirit of the Treaty. The state parties have been reluctant to criticize each other, probably because they perceived that such criticism would threaten the unity of the ATS itself.

The 1991 Protocol

The 1991 Protocol **[Basic Document 2.9]** was negotiated in rapid time and applies to the same geographic area as the Antarctic Treaty itself: the land and fast ice areas south of 60° south latitude. It is composed of twenty-seven articles plus four technical annexes, four of which–dealing with environmental impact assessment, conservation of fauna and flora, waste disposal, and marine pollution–have been agreed to by the parties. Further annexes can be appended. Signatories are committed to comprehensive protection of Antarctica and its ecosystems, and Antarctica is designated a natural reserve, devoted to peace and science.

Under the Protocol, all activities in Antarctica are subject to prior environmental evaluation. It establishes institutions—most notably a Committee for Environmental Protection—to ensure the safeguarding of environmental values, and it covers compliance, emergency response action, and dispute settlement. In addition, it includes an affirmative undertaking to "elaborate rules and procedures relating to liability for damage" for activities in the Antarctic Treaty area and, in article 7, prohibits mineral activities other than those for scientific research. Indeed, to take the minerals issue off the agenda, the Protocol cannot be reviewed for fifty years unless there is unanimous consent. After fifty years, any nation may call for a review; but a modification to allow mining requires agreement by a majority of the parties, including three-quarters of the consultative parties. Early drafts of the Protocol gave each of the ATCPs an effective mining veto. However, as this was unacceptable to the United States, the final version does not.

Finally, the Protocol provides that it will not enter into force until after it has been ratified by all states which are ATCPs as of the date on which the Protocol was adopted. All twenty-six Consultative Parties have now ratified the Protocol; thus, it came into force on January 14, 1998. Amendments, dealt with in article 25, involve a number of complexities, there being a relationship between the amendment processes of the original Treaty and the Protocol amendment provisions.

Thus the new Protocol responds to mounting public concern over environmental issues in Antarctica. Will it significantly influence the environmental practice of States? Will its prohibition on mining have the force of customary law after fifty years? As the same Antarctica Treaty parties still are given special status, it is difficult to say. The future of Antarctica is not easy to predict.

The World Park Proposal

To really understand the pressures over minerals that mounted within the Antarctic Treaty System, it is useful to note the historical development of the Antarctic "World Park" proposal, which originated at the Second World Conference on National Parks held in 1972. In 1975, at the eighth Antarctic Treaty Consultative Meeting, New Zealand proposed informally that Antarctica be declared a "World Park." This proposal was made against the background of meetings in 1970 and 1972 that included discussions of the possibility of exploration of minerals in Antarctica. In 1969, Texaco had asked the United States Department of State about prospecting for minerals in Antarctica but had been discouraged. Other governments had been approached about mining also.

The World Park proposal was put forward as a bold package deal. It involved banning mineral activity, the United Nations taking on the administration of Antarctica, and the renunciation of all state territorial claims. Though bold, however, the proposal failed for lack of support within the ATS.

Environmental groups, on the other hand, have consistently urged the ATS consultative parties to set Antarctica aside as a world park. Greenpeace International, the Environmental Defense Fund, the Cousteau Society, and the Antarctic and Southern Ocean Coalition groups command a substantial following in the public opinion of the countries comprising the ATS, and all have been active in advocating a world park regime.

In 1989, in a joint initiative, Australia and France announced that they would support protecting Antarctica as a world park. Their announcement meant that CRAMRA, the negotiation of which had been completed only the previous year, was in serious trouble, as its ratification required Australian and French agreement. Furthermore, in October 1990, the U.S. House of Representatives approved a ban on mining in Antarctica. CRAMRA died, at least for the foreseeable future, and the 1991 Protocol on Environmental Protection to the Antarctic Treaty **[Basic Document 2.9]** thus was negotiated in its place.

6. Francesco Francioni, *The Madrid Protocol on the Protection of the Antarctic Environment*, **28** Tex. Int'l. L.J. 47, 48–51, 57–60 (1993).

I. INTRODUCTION

During 1988, at Wellington, New Zealand, when the Consultative Parties to the Antarctic Treaty adopted the Convention on Antarctic Mineral Resources (CRAMRA) **[Basic Document 2.7]**, commentators welcomed the event as a significant step forward for expanding and consolidating the system of international co-operation regarding Antarctica, a process instituted in 1959 by the Antarctic Treaty **[Basic Document 2.1]**. The new convention ended six years of difficult negotiations.

* * *

The success that seemed to surround the new agreement, however, was destined to prove somewhat ephemeral. Some of the Consultative Parties who had actively participated in the mineral negotiations–Australia, France, Belgium, and Italy—very soon found themselves faced with intransigent domestic opposition incited by non-governmental environmental organisations, which expertly co-operated with political forces and which had a strong grip on public opinion. Unconvinced by the system of strong environmental guarantees that CRAMRA introduced, these organisations and the movement they encouraged sought to completely prohibit any mineral exploitation on the continent, no matter how controlled. Playing to the feelings aroused worldwide by environmental disasters occurring in the period following the adoption of the Wellington Convention–the wreck in Antarctic waters of the Argentine ship *Bahia Paraiso* and the Alaskan disaster of the *Exxon Valdez*–the environmentalist movement pleaded to set aside the mineral-development option and for a new approach based on the preservation of the continent as a natural park and a zone dedicated to science.

The effects of this environmental campaign were soon felt. The parliamentary debate in some countries holding Antarctic Consultative status, such as Belgium and Italy, led to the adoption of resolutions or even actual legislation that restricted their governments from undertaking or permitting mineral development in the Antarctic. In the United States, a country strongly interested in the Antarctic mineral regime and already a signatory to the Wellington agreement, the opposition to CRAMRA found expression in an Act of Congress that called upon the administration to start negotiations to ban mineral development.

This process of critical review of CRAMRA climaxed when Australia and France decided to postpone signing the mineral convention. This decision prevented the consensus necessary to enact the convention because the participation of all countries claiming sovereign rights in the Antarctic, including France and Australia, was an essential condition for the formation of the organs of the mineral regime. With hopes of CRAMRA's rapid entry into force thus extinguished, diplomatic efforts to resolve the impasse focused on the environmental issues.

At the Paris meeting of October 1989, the Consultative Parties decided to begin special negotiations to adopt a general instrument dedicated exclusively to the protection of the Antarctic environment. . . .

The Protocol was adopted and opening for signature during [a] session held in Madrid in October 1991 on the eve of the regular consultative meeting held at Bonn.

Against the background of this difficult train of negotiations and the displacement of CRAMRA, the Madrid Protocol on the Protection of the Antarctic Environment (Madrid Protocol) **[Basic Document 2.9]** stands as the first instrument of international agreement to provide a comprehensive system of rules and procedures binding upon and applicable to all human activity in an area beyond the limits of national jurisdiction.

* * *

THE SYSTEM OF THE ANNEXES

Following a technique now widely employed in the conventions of international environmental law, the Madrid Protocol was conceived as a framework agreement, adaptable to the varying needs of environmental protection through a system of technical annexes that are adopted in consultative meetings and derive their obligatory force directly from the norms of the Madrid Protocol. The advantages of such systems are well recognised. This system avoids the slow and complex process of revising the original instrument and negotiating for a new agreement, as well as bypassing the cumbersome internal procedure normally required for ratification, approval, or acceptance of the revisions or amendments. In contemporary practice, the system of annexes has developed into two basic models. One model provides for the adoption of an annex by a majority of the contracting parties to the treaty and within a certain period of time allows its automatic entry into force for all the contracting parties, reserving the possibility of withdrawal (opt-out clause) for parties who do not want to, or cannot, accept the relative obligations. The other model involves adopting the annex by unanimity or by consensus and requires an acceptance procedure on the part of the contracting states.

In the field of environmental law, it is the first of these models which offers the guarantees of speed and adaptability required by the changing needs of environmental protection. Unfortunately, the Antarctic environmental negotiations did not permit adoption of this model. Although it was the subject of a specific proposal within the ambit of the draft conventions presented by the group of four, it would have altered the Antarctic decision making process–primarily the rule of consensus–which conflicted with the need of continuing that process unchanged. Article 9 of the Madrid Protocol provides that the annexes should be adopted and become effective in conformity with article IX of the Antarctic Treaty, which sets forth the procedures for adopting measures in furtherance of the Antarctic treaty system. This means that (1) only the Consultative Parties can participate in decisions concerning the adoption of further annexes or amendments to existing annexes; (2) such decision making must occur by consensus; and (3) the new measure of environmental protection, or amendments to those actually in force, must be accepted by the Contracting States, whether Consultative or non-Consultative Parties.

This solution presents the disadvantage of an insufficient capacity to respond to new environmental problems or new risks posed by human activity or technology because, in response to fears that a different system would be destined to fail, it continues the consensus system of administrating Antarctica. It allows one state or a small minority of states, perhaps motivated by special interests opposed to the general interest in protecting the Antarctic environment, to block the adoption of measures supported by a large majority. No interpretative device can overcome this obstacle since it derives from one of the constitutional elements of the Antarctic system itself.

Concerning the problem of when new annexes or their amendments enter into force, even though the Madrid Protocol expressly provides for effectiveness in accordance with article IX of the Antarctic Treaty, part of the original proposal remains and allows automatic entry into force with the right of dissenting states to opt out within a given time limit. The Madrid Protocol provides that the regular procedure for entry into force may be derogated when the annex itself provides "for amendments and modifications to become effective on an accelerated basis".[g] Therefore, regarding measures of particular urgency, an amendment to the annex in force can still be adopted by consensus. Such amendment may become effective automatically within a prescribed period of time, with the exception that it not apply to Contracting Parties who raise objections. Apart from this rule, the result of automatic applicability of the annexes to the environmental protocol would be generally achieved if the theory of the direct applicability of resolutions adopted by the Consultative Parties were accepted. Hopefully, this theory, supported by recent authoritative doctrine, may find application in the procedures of the Antarctic Treaty, which remain marked by the desire of the states to maintain a system of express acceptance of the resolutions adopted by the consultative meetings by notification to the depositary of the Treaty.

THE MATERIAL PRINCIPLES OF ENVIRONMENTAL PROTECTION

The Madrid Protocol **[Basic Document 2.9]** establishes a regime of Antarctic environmental protection based in large measure on the expansion and enhancement of principles already in effect in the Antarctic system or in international environmental law. At the same time it introduces several new principles, whose mandatory character assigns a new role and new objectives for the Antarctic system. Article 3 of the Madrid Protocol states these six new principles.

First, every activity in the Antarctic must be planned and conducted in such a way as to *limit its negative impact on the Antarctic environment*. This rule is not new; it occurs as a corollary of Principle 21 of the 1972 Stockholm Declaration **[Basic Document 1.12]** and is confirmed in the Declaration in the *World Charter of Nature* **[Basic Document 1.21]** adopted by the General Assembly of the United Nations in 1982.

Second, *minimising environmental impact must also apply to the ecosystems* dependent upon and associated with the Antarctic. This principle permits extension of the sphere of enforcement for the Madrid Protocol beyond the area of enforcement of the Antarctic Treaty.

Third, *the concept of damage to the Antarctic environment is an essentially ecological concept and is not dependent on an economic-proprietary assessment*. This is evident from article 3(2)(b) which deals with

> i) adverse effects on climate or weather patterns; ii) significant adverse effects on air or water quality; iii) significant changes in the atmospheric, terrestrial . . ., glacial or marine environments; iv) detrimental changes in the distribution, abundance or productivity of species . . . of fauna and flora; v) further jeopardy to endangered or threatened species . . . ; or vi) degradation of, or substantial risk to, areas of biological, scientific, historic, aesthetic or wilderness significance.

g. Madrid Protocol, article 9, para. 3 [Basic Document 2.9].

Fourth, *all activities in the Antarctic must be planned and conducted on the basis of sufficient information* in order to evaluate in advance their impact on the Antarctic environment, to determine in timely fashion negative environmental effects, and to cope speedily and effectively with any accidents that might occur.

Fifth, Antarctic activities must be planned and conducted in a manner which *gives priority to scientific research* and to the designation of the Antarctic as a vast scientific laboratory beneficial to an understanding of the global environment. Finally, all activity in the Antarctic must be subject to *regular monitoring*.

While these six principles were introduced into the Madrid Protocol without particular difficulty, other more innovative principles engendered considerable differences of opinion and made the whole course of negotiations difficult. These more innovative principles include designating the entire Antarctic as a natural reserve, the general obligation to assess the environmental impact of all human activity in the Antarctic, and prohibiting mineral development activity.

7. Christopher C. Joyner, *The Effectiveness of CRAMRA*, in Governing the Antarctic: The effectiveness and legitimacy of the Antarctic Treaty System 152, 171 (Olav Schram Stokke & Davor Vidas eds., 1996).

The Legal Status of CRAMRA Today

It is important to recognise that CRAMRA is not dead legally. The Convention may be politically bankrupt at the present time, but its status as a legal instrument technically remains that of an active Convention caught up in the process of ratification. Granted, its purpose has been overtaken by the ban on mining and environmental provisions in the Madrid Protocol. Granted, too, that it is unlikely that any state will now seek to accede to or ratify CRAMRA in the foreseeable future. The fact is, however, that while politically inert, CRAMRA is not legally defunct. It remains open for accession by any statute that is a Contracting Party to the Antarctic Treaty. There is no expiration date for ATCP accession to or ratification of that instrument. Hence, the status of CRAMRA remains stuck in a static condition of legal limbo. Should the time ever come when a minerals regime might be desirable or necessary, the procedural process for CRAMRA's entry into force would be legally available. Even so, if the Madrid Protocol should fail in national ratification efforts or collapse some time in the future, the greater likelihood appears that governments will opt to borrow the best features of CRAMRA and incorporate them into a new regulatory regime. The perceived ineffectiveness of CRAMRA may well have tarnished even its future acceptability among some Consultative Parties.

8. Davor Vidas, *The Antarctic Treaty System and the Law of the Sea*: *A New Dimension Introduced By the Protocol*, in Governing the Antarctic: The Effectiveness and Legitimacy of the Antarctic Treaty System 61, 61–63, 64–72, 89, 90 (Olav Schram Stokke & Davor Vidas eds., 1996).

INTRODUCTION

Discussions on the relationship between the 1982 United Nations Convention on the Law of the Sea (hereinafter LOS Convention) **[Basic Document 4.20]** and the Antarctic Treaty System (ATS) are becoming more urgent due to recent developments within both regimes. The LOS Convention entered into force on 16 November 1994, supplemented by the 1994 Agreement relating to the implementation of Part XI of the United Nations Convention on the Law of the Sea of 10 December 1982 (hereinafter Implementation Agreement). The 1991 Protocol on Environmental Protection to the Antarctic Treaty **[Basic Document 2.9]**, which–as we shall see in this chapter–introduced a change in the *normative* relationship between the ATS and the law of the sea, also has good prospects of entry into force in the near future. [Editor's Note: the 1991 Protocol entered into force on 14 January 1998.]

* * *

THE ANTARCTIC MARITIME AREA AND THE LAW OF THE SEA

Views seem to have diverged not only in connection with the question *how* to apply the law of the sea in general, and the LOS Convention in particular, to the Antarctic maritime area, but–prior to this–*whether* the LOS Convention is indeed applicable to that area at all. Several authors have pointed out that the Third United Nations Conference on the Law of the Sea (1973–82; hereinafter UNCLOS III) has intentionally failed to deal with this area: i.e., that the wording of the LOS Convention was no product of chance, but that the Antarctic was excluded deliberately from UNCLOS III negotiations. In contrast to this, the 1986 Report of the UN Secretary–General stressed:

> It is a global convention applicable to all ocean space. No area of ocean space is excluded. It follows that the Convention must be of significance to the Southern Ocean in the sense that its provisions also apply to that ocean.[h]

Similarly, Orrego has argued:

> the exclusion of Antarctica from the ambit of the 1982 Convention's application would have required an express provision to that effect, which certainly is not the case.[i]

Moreover, the same author has pointed out that the basic concepts of the law of the sea–such as the territorial sea, the continental shelf, the exclusive economic zone and the regime of the high seas–have all become part of customary international law and can thus be applied to Antarctica independently of any conventional regime. The view that the general law of the sea is of significance for the Antarctic maritime area has prevailed in the doctrine.

If the law of the sea in general, and the LOS Convention in particular, is made applicable to the Antarctic maritime area, the question remains: *how* to apply it? In connection with this, Vukas has stressed that:

h. UN doc. A/41/722, Nov. 17, 1986, at 29.

i. Francisco Orrego Vicuña, *The Law of the Sea and the Antarctic Treaty System: New Approaches to Offshore Jurisdiction, in* THE ANT- ARCTIC LEGAL REGIME 101 (Christopher C. Joyner & Sudhir K. Chopra eds., 1988) [hereinafter Vicuña].

the regimes of the seas adjacent to the coast have been developed on different physical and legal realities than those existing in Antarctica.[j]

First, the existing rules of the law of the sea have been conceived for waters adjacent to coasts not possessing such specific properties as those caused by the Antarctic ice structures. Second, the law of the sea, as embodied both in customary and in conventional rules, relies on two basic concepts: the concept of the *coastal state* and the concept of the *baselines of the territorial sea*, derived from the first concept. It was due to the different approaches of the states concerned with respect to the issue of sovereignty claims to Antarctica that the law of the sea was initially approached from divergent "positions of principle". These positions of principle were based on the view of either the existence or the non-existence of state sovereignty in Antarctica. They led to a purely legal logical exposition of the two essentially different lines of reasoning.

Both of them have taken a common point of departure–the notion of the coastal state. This notion is among the key concepts of the law of the sea, as it provides the basis for delimitation of different legal regimes for the marine and submarine areas, with their respective disparate statuses. While the coastal state possesses a certain degree of legal power over the marine and submarine areas situated relatively close to its coast (the internal waters, the territorial sea, the contiguous zone, the exclusive economic zone and the continental shelf), such legal power is not recognised by the law of the sea rules for the marine and submarine areas situated relatively distant from its coast (the high seas, the seabed outside the limits of national jurisdiction). This legal order is based on the general customary law of the sea, which is embodied partly in the provisions of the four conventions adopted at the First UN Conference on the Law of the Sea (Geneva 1958) and entirely in the provisions of the 1982 LOS Convention.

Furthermore, states which are not coastal do not possess legal power over the marine and submarine areas (sovereignty, sovereign rights and territorial jurisdiction). Moreover, an area that is "coastal" in a geographical sense but without the recognised legal elements of statehood accordingly may not possess the power of the coastal state over the adjacent marine and submarine areas.

Thus, the fact of the existence of the coastal state is the backbone of all legal regimes in the law of the sea where the state exercises some degree of legal power based on its territory as well as the relevant fact for determining the limits of the law of the sea regimes characterised by the absence of a state's territorial jurisdiction. Indeed, the starting question has been formulated: does a coastal state exist in Antarctica? For the claimant states, the answer is in the affirmative, with all the consequences resulting from the rules of the law of the sea, as already summarised above. For the non-claimant states, the answer is in the negative, again with all the consequences resulting from the rules of the law of the sea.

Regarding the latter view, the law of the sea determines that all parts of the sea not included in the exclusive economic zone, in the territorial sea or in

j. Budislav Vukas, *Commentary, in* THE LAW OF THE SEA: WHAT LIES AHEAD? PROCEEDINGS OF THE 20TH ANNUAL CONFERENCE OF THE LAW OF THE SEA INSTITUTE 405 (Thomas M. Clingan, Jr. ed., 1988)[hereinafter Vukas].

the internal waters of a state, or in the archipelagic state, are the high seas. Applying this rule to the status of the Antarctic marine area along with the hypothesis of the non-existence of the coastal state, the conclusion is, clearly, that *all* the sea south of 60°S latitude is high seas. And if the entire sea surrounding the Antarctic is high seas, then there is no sovereignty or sovereign rights of individual states over the seabed and its subsoil as well. In lacking the continental shelf regime, the entire submarine area under the Antarctic high seas, together with its natural resources, is outside the limits of national jurisdiction. However, there have been two lines of reasoning available when it comes to the legal interpretation of the regime of the submarine areas situated beneath the high seas, but beyond the outer limits of the continental shelf. According to one, advocated by the technologically most developed states, the regime of the high seas shall be applied analogously to such submarine areas, indeed including all the analogous high seas freedoms with regard to the natural resources of such submarine areas. According to another view, advocated by a large group of developing states, the seabed outside the limits of national jurisdiction and its natural resources are considered in international law a common heritage of mankind. In summing up, when cumulatively applied to the Antarctic maritime area, the above views based on the "positions of principle" may lead only to deadlock. If theory were consequently put into practice, this would lead to irreconcilable legal solutions.

The Law of the Sea and the Antarctic Treaty System

The above interpretation of the law of the sea rules—and their application to the Antarctic maritime area based on the positions of principle—fails to take into consideration the *substance* of the regimes at the sea adjacent to the coast, whose *raison d'être* does not lie solely in the existence of the coastal state. As emphasised by Vukas:

> there are some interests, activities, and relations, non-existent in the high seas, that have to be regulated in the coastal waters independently of the existence of coastal sovereignty: for example, the prevention of land-based pollution, the prevention of infringement of sanitary regulations applied on land, the protection of coastal species, the regulation of discharging or embarking, etc.[k]

Moreover, the logical constructions based on the positions of principle may be maintained as long as one claims that the proper way to determine the legal status of the Antarctic maritime area is solely by applying the rules of the general law of the sea to that area. Such a line of reasoning, however, fails to take into consideration the *complexity of the normative situation*: the problem lies not in the application of one legal system (the law of the sea) to the factual situation (the Antarctic maritime area) but in the combined application of the two legal systems (the law of the sea *and* the ATS) to the same factual situation. The 1958 Geneva Conference on the Law of the Sea codified the then-existing customary law of the sea, pre-dating the adoption of the Antarctic Treaty by only one year. Since then, these two legal systems have had a parallel development, the former resulting in the 1982 LOS Convention and the latter in today's ATS. The system which has grown up on

---

k. Vukas, *supra* note j, at 406.

the basis of the Antarctic Treaty has clearly established a special body of rules tailored to the special circumstances of the Antarctic. Hence, the present legal status of the Antarctic maritime area may be properly determined by *two* international systems of rules in conjunction: the ATS and the general international law of the sea.

One important factor is the unique geophysical circumstances in the Antarctic, especially various ice structures. However, other factors have led the ATS into the regulation of the specific issues otherwise regulated by the law of the sea: according to what is known today, significant natural resources in the Antarctic Treaty area may be found predominantly in its maritime area, which is characterised by its unique ecosystem. Thus, the initially restricted scope of the Antarctic Treaty has been widened through the ATS' developing rules relevant to the management of the Antarctic marine resources. As observed by Orrego, it is for this reason that solutions to the pertinent legal problems have begun to emerge within the context of various resource regimes.[l] Hence, the vital need for an Antarctic resources policy has led to a gradual revision of the initial "positions of principle".[m] This, in turn, has had implications for the applicability of the general law of the sea to the Antarctic maritime area. At this point, Orrego links resource regimes with Article VI of the Antarctic Treaty (with implications for the extent of applicability of the law of the sea in general), by concluding that:

> questions of jurisdiction and economic utilisation related to offshore maritime areas and the high seas have been dealt with through practice within the system and the development of its special regimes.[n]

While analysing the relationship between the ATS and the law of the sea from another perspective, Vukas arrives at a similar conclusion:

> Although Article 6 of the Antarctic Treaty is drafted in a somewhat ambiguous manner, it is obvious that south of 60° South latitude the high seas regime, subject to the principles of the Antarctic Treaty, applies. In respect of the living resources, the 1980 Conservation Convention is an important addition to the applicable general rules.[o]

To sum it up, this line of reasoning leads us to the conclusion that the proper approach lies not in the direct application of the general law of the sea to the Antarctic maritime area but in the concurrence of the two existing systems of legal norms, that is, the law of the sea (mainly as codified in the 1982 LOS Convention) and the ATS. At that stage, it might be asserted, these two normative systems, when combined in a complex legal mosaic, offer the most acceptable basis for building the legal regime for the Antarctic maritime area.

Although this approach delves considerably deeper into the essence of the specific situation of the Antarctic maritime area, it still leaves several fundamental questions open. As it obviously takes its point of departure in the general area of the law of the sea, this approach seeks primarily to determine which aspects of the law of the sea are relevant and applicable to the Antarctic maritime area. In doing so from the perspective of general law, it

---

l. Vicuña, *supra* note i, at 97–98.

m. *Id.* at 98.

n. *Id.* at 101.

o. Vukas, *supra* note j, at 405.

still has to cope with the core problem: territorial claims in Antarctica. Thus, even in the conjunctive treatment of the two legal systems applicable to the Antarctic maritime area, the law of the sea perspective nevertheless relies upon the coastal state concept. Perhaps the best solution one may invent in such a situation is the ambivalent phrase "bifocal approach".

THE ANTARCTIC TREATY SYSTEM PERSPECTIVE ON THE LAW OF THE SEA QUESTIONS

The ATS has introduced and gradually developed its own perspective to the law of the sea questions, which made it possible to bridge the difficulties connected with the traditional concepts of the general law of the sea. Under the ATS, the concept of the coastal state has in fact acquired its "functional equivalent", conceptualised by van der Essen as the joint jurisdiction of the Consultative Parties over the Antarctic area.[p] Joyner has observed that the legal basis for the ATS' self-designed resource management and jurisdictional functions in waters offshore Antarctica is derived in large part from its political authority, which might attain persuasiveness owing to the acknowledged success of the ATS over the past thirty years.[q]

The common policy adopted by the Consultative Parties in establishing the resource regimes has led to the reconciliation of otherwise irreconcilable positions of principle. Significantly, the resource regimes do not differentiate between claimed and unclaimed sectors in the Antarctic. Here, one could argue that the ATS breaks with the fixity of legal concepts, in going beyond the freedom-sovereignty-commons trichotomy of ordering systems, which had proven itself unsuited for allocating authority in Antarctica.

Although largely innovative and suited for the special circumstances of the Antarctic, the ATS resource regimes have still implied the necessity of compromising between the Antarctic regional peculiarities and the requirements stemming from the already established general legal rules as well as policy considerations. However, it is maintained in the remaining part of this chapter that the Protocol has introduced a qualitatively new dimension in the ATS in this respect. The shift from the mineral resource regime to the environmental protection regime has had significant consequences with regard to the regulation of the status of the Antarctic submarine areas....

A NEW DIMENSION INTRODUCED BY THE PROTOCOL

Recent developments within the ATS have added to the controversy of the relationship between the ATS and the law of the sea, in particular with respect to the status of the Antarctic submarine areas. The law of the sea order has created two separate regimes for the submarine areas beyond the outer limits of the territorial sea: the continental shelf, and the regime for the seabed beyond the limits of national jurisdiction (the latter being, according to the LOS Convention, together with its resources the common heritage of mankind). Both regimes are largely concerned with the exploration and exploitation of minerals. While the coastal state exercises sovereign rights over the continental shelf for the purpose of exploring it and exploiting its

---

p. *See* Alfred van der Essen, *The Application of the Law of the Sea to the Antarctic Continent, in* ANTARCTIC RESEARCH POLICY: SCIENTIFIC LEGAL AND POLITICAL ISSUES 233, 235 & 242 (Francisco Orrego Vicuña ed., 1983).

q. CHRISTOPHER C. JOYNER, ANTARCTICA AND THE LAW OF THE SEA 89, 98–99 (1992).

natural resources, the minerals recovered from the Area may only be alienated in accordance with Part XI of the LOS Convention and the rules, regulations and procedures of the International Seabed authority. True, Part XI of the LOS convention has been substantially reformed by the 1994 Implementation Agreement; however, the *redistributive element* of the common heritage of mankind concept persisted in this thorough revision of Part XI. Thus, if applicable, both the continental shelf and the Area regimes of the LOS Convention would allow for mineral resources activities in the seabed offshore Antarctica. In contrast, the Protocol has introduced the prohibition of any activity relating to mineral resources, other than scientific research, in the Antarctic Treaty area. This may indicate that compatibility between the ATS and the general law of the sea is reduced.

* * *

[T]he Protocol has introduced prohibition on any activity relating to mineral resources, other than scientific research. This excludes the aspect of utilisation found in the regimes of the continental shelf and the Area, and characteristic for CRAMRA as well. In this context, it is not only that the Protocol has superseded CRAMRA: it also implies that the *ratio* of both the continental shelf and the Area concepts no longer exists for the Antarctic submarine area. The most important continental shelf rights involve the exploration and exploitation of its mineral resources: and they are now banned by the Protocol. Regarding the concept of the Area, as embodied in Part XI of the LOS Convention, it is obvious that, if mining is prohibited, there is nothing left for economic distribution pursuant to the common heritage of mankind principle. The prohibition of mineral resource activities in the Antarctic, apart from being embodied in the Protocol, has since 1989 been consistently demanded by the states which are not parties to the Antarctic Treaty, as well as recurring in the texts of UN General Assembly resolutions.

It is in this sense, then, that this chapter claims that the Protocol has introduced a new dimension into the relationship between the ATS and the law of the sea. We may now arrive at two theses as to the ATS' law of the sea dimension: first the concept of the coastal state has lost considerable weight in the Antarctic maritime area; when needed, its functions are performed by the ATS rather than by individual states. And second, the specific legal concept introduced in the ATS through the adoption of the Protocol offers a prism through which to view the law of the sea for the Antarctic maritime area as well as the need for rethinking some general law of the sea concepts from the perspective of the Antarctic Treaty System.

C. *Environmental Degradation and Pollution*

The following readings relate to the second and third scenarios in this problem ("Andea Promotes Tourism" and "Malacca Hunts Seals"), *supra*. It should be possible to deal with the issues in those scenarios after reading and considering the readings here and in subsection A ("The Antarctic Treaty and Related Issues"), at 378, *supra*.

1.   Arbitral and Judicial Decisions [Basic Documents 8.1 through 8.11].

2. Stockholm Declaration of the United Nations Conference on the Human Environment, Adopted by the UN Conference on the Human Environment at Stockholm, June 16, 1972, Part I and Principles 1, 2, 4–7, Report of the UN Conference on the Human Environment, June 15–16, 1972, UN Doc. A/CONF.48/14/Rev.1 at 3 (1973), UN Doc. A/CONF.48/14 at 2–65, and Corr. 1 (1972), 11 I.L.M. 1416 (1972) [Basic Document 1.12].

3. World Charter for Nature, Oct. 28, 1982, Principles 1–3, 6, G.A. Res. 37/7, U.N. GAOR, 37th Sess., Supp. No. 51, at 21, U.N. Doc. A/37/L.4 and Add. 1 (1982) [Basic Document 1.21].

4. Rio Declaration on Environment and Development, June 14, 1992, Principles 1, 2, 7, UNCED Doc. A/CONF.151/5/Rev. 1, 31 I.L.M. 874 (1992) [Basic Document 1.29].

5. The Antarctic Treaty, Dec. 1, 1959, arts. I, III, V, X, 12 U.S.T. 794, T.I.A.S. No. 4780, 402 U.N.T.S. 71 [Basic Document 2.1].

6. Protocol on Environmental Protection to the Antarctic Treaty, Oct. 4, 1991, arts. 2–4,6–8, Annexes I & III, 30 I.L.M. 1461 (1991) [Basic Document 2.9].

7. Convention on the Control of Transboundary Movements of Hazardous Wastes and Their Disposal, Mar. 22, 1989, arts. 1–4, 9, 10, 28 I.L.M. 657 (1989) [Basic Document 5.6].

8. Convention for the Conservation of Antarctic Seals, Feb. 11, 1972, arts: 1–3, 11 I.L.M. 251 (1972) [Basic Document 2.3].

9. Convention on the Conservation of Antarctic Marine Living Resources (CCAMLR), May 20, 1980, arts. I, II, VII, IX, X, 19 I.L.M. 841 (1980) [Basic Document 2.4].

10. Tullio Treves, *Compulsory Settlement of Disputes: A New Element in the Antarctic System,* **in** INTERNATIONAL LAW FOR ANTARCTICA **603, 603–04, 609–10 (Francesco Francioni & Tullio Scovazzi eds., 1996).**

COMPULSORY SETTLEMENT OF DISPUTES IN THE 1991 MADRID PROTOCOL

When the Madrid Protocol on Environmental Protection to the Antarctic Treaty of 4 October 1991 (PEPAT) **[Basic Document 2.9]** enters into force [Editor's Note: entered into force on 14 January 1998], compulsory jurisdiction, that is, the possibility of bringing a dispute before an international judicial or arbitral body at the request of one Party, will become, for the first time, an element of the Antarctic system. Indeed, the Antarctic Treaty of 1959 **[Basic Document 2.1]** and the Convention on the Conservation of Antarctic Marine Living Resources of 20 May 1980 **[Basic Document 2.4]** only foresaw the possibility that the International Court of Justice alone, in the case of the Treaty, or, in the case of the Convention, the International Court of Justice together with a court of arbitration, be seized "with the consent, in each case, of all Parties to the dispute". In addition neither the Convention for the Conservation of Antarctic Seals of 1 June 1972 **[Basic Document**

2.3], nor the amendment thereto of 16 September 1988 contained provisions on the settlement of disputes.

The Wellington Convention on the Regulation of Antarctic Mineral Resource Activities of 2 June 1988 (CRAMRA) **[Basic Document 2.7]**, to the contrary, contains elaborate provisions on the settlement of disputes. These provisions certainly are a point of departure for those contained in PEPAT. The political circumstances leading to the adoption of PEPAT, as well as the prohibition of any activity relating to mineral resources contained in its Art. 7, indicate however, that while the Antarctic Treaty Parties appear willing to ratify the Madrid Protocol and let it enter in force, the contrary seems true as regards the Wellington Convention. Thus, in all likelihood, compulsory settlement of disputes will become a component of the Antarctic System through the Madrid Protocol and not through the earlier Wellington Convention.

The PEPAT provisions on the settlement of disputes, similarly to those of CRAMRA, do not rule out diplomatic means of settlement, namely procedures leading to an agreement for the settlement of the dispute, nor judicial or arbitral means of settlement if agreed by the Parties after the dispute has arisen.[r] They introduce, however, the possibility of unilaterally instituting proceedings before the International Court of Justice or an Arbitral Tribunal (Art. 20, para. 1) as well as a mechanism for a choice of dispute settlement procedures inspired by that of Art. 287 of the 1982 Law of the Sea Convention (Art. 19) **[Basic Document 4.20]**. Compulsory jurisdiction is, however, limited *ratione materiae* (Art. 19, para. 1; Art. 20 para. 2), even though no optional exceptions are permitted.

* * *

THE CHOICE BETWEEN THE INTERNATIONAL COURT OF JUSTICE AND AN ARBITRAL TRIBUNAL

The courts or tribunals to which a State Party may unilaterally refer a dispute as permitted by the Protocol, are the International Court of Justice and an Arbitral Tribunal, whose functions and structure are set out in a thirteen-article Schedule to the Protocol. The mechanism chosen for determining which of these two procedures applies in a specific case is similar to that contained in the 1982 UN Law of the Sea Convention (the "Montreux" formula of Art. 287 of that Convention).

According to para. 1 of Art. 19, each Party, at signature, ratification or accession, may choose in a written declaration one of the two above mentioned procedures. If all the Parties to a dispute have chosen the same means of settlement, the dispute shall be submitted to that means (Art. 19, para. 4). If this is not the case, the Arbitral Tribunal is given the privileged position of being the "residual" body competent to settle the dispute. This has two distinct implications. First, a Party that has not made the written declaration mentioned above, or whose declaration is no longer in force, shall be deemed to have accepted the competence of the Arbitral Tribunal (para. 3. Of Art. 19). Second, where the Parties to a dispute have not made the same choice, the dispute may be submitted to the Arbitral Tribunal (para. 5 of Art. 19).

---

r. PEPAT, art. 18 [Basic Document 2.9].

Questions arise when one or more of the Parties have accepted the compulsory jurisdiction of the International Court of Justice under Art. 36, para. 2, of the Court's Statute. First, let us consider the case in which both Parties to the dispute have accepted the "optional clause". When neither such Party has made the choice according to Art. 19 of PEPAT, the Parties may be deemed to have agreed on submitting their dispute to the ICJ according to Art. 18 of PEPAT. The operation of Art. 18 shall not be affected by the declarations made under para. 1 of Art. 19 (so states para. 2, and this statement would seem to extend to presumed declarations under para. 3). Thus, the competence of the ICJ would include also aspects of PEPAT for which compulsory jurisdiction is excluded under the rules of the Protocol. This would not apply, it would seem, to matters "within the scope" of Art. IV of the Antarctic Treaty. On matters excluded by reservations to the acceptance of the "optional clause" but not excluded from compulsory jurisdiction under PEPAT the Arbitral Tribunal would remain competent as these would be matters not covered by the agreement between the Parties and on which no concurrent choice would have been made.

As regards the case in which, while both Parties have accepted the "optional clause", one has also chosen the ICJ according to Art. 19 of PEPAT, such choice is without effect according to PEPAT. Consequently, the observations made above apply to this case also.

As regards the case in which one Party to the dispute has accepted the "optional clause" and the other has made a choice for the ICJ under Art. 19 of PEPAT it would seem that this is a situation in which both Parties have accepted the ICJ under Art. 18. It seems correct to consider the will to confer jurisdiction to the ICJ as prevailing on the consideration that one of the two expressions of such will was not made having Art. 18 of PEPAT in mind. The jurisdiction of the Court will be limited, nevertheless, to the matters falling neither under reservations to the acceptance of the optional clause by one Party nor under the limitation of Art. 20, para 2. On matters covered by the compulsory disputes settlement clauses of PEPAT, and remaining outside the jurisdiction of the Court, it will be possible to resort to arbitration.

11. Laura Pineschi, *The Antarctic Treaty System and General Rules of International Environmental Law*, in INTERNATIONAL LAW FOR ANTARCTICA 187, 187–98, 201–07 (Francesco Francioni & Tullio Scovazzi eds., 1987).

Two general duties emerge from the set of rules which make up the international law of the environment. The first prohibits transboundary environmental interference, impeding the States from causing harmful consequences for the environment of other States or of areas outside national jurisdiction because of activities conducted under their own control. The second, which supports the first, calls on the States to cooperate in the duty of preventing and abating transboundary environmental interference. Exchange of information, consultations, and the equitable use of shared resources are the principal ways by which this duty is accomplished in State practice.

As general rules, these obligations will apply both to States party to the Antarctic Treaty System and to third States. As regards the former, general rules will be applicable independently from the space and time limits of the

Antarctic Treaty [**Basic Document 2.1**], while third States, by means of general rules, will be bound to preserve the Antarctic environment from detrimental changes. The preservation of Antarctica from substantial contamination, which is a problem of worldwide interest, given the strict interrelation between the fragile Antarctic ecosystem and the entire environmental balance of the planet, shall therefore be assured, aside from whatever discussion about the objective character of the rules of the Antarctic Treaty System may arise.

On the other hand, the rules enacted by the parties to the Antarctic Treaty System in the field of environmental protection are numerous and detailed. Only one rule of the Antarctic Treaty, Art. IX, makes an explicit reference to problems of an environmental character and empowers the Consultative Parties to adopt recommendations for the protection and conservation of living resources. However, since the first consultative meetings, the parties have shown that they consider the task in wider terms and that they consider the environmental system to which they belong, and its living resources, to be worthy of protection.

At present the particular rules of the Antarctic Treaty System embrace the Agreed Measures for the Conservation of Antarctic Fauna and Flora of 1964 [**Basic Document 2.2**], the London Convention for the Conservation of Antarctic Seals of 1972 [**Basic Document 2.3**], the Canberra Convention on the Conservation of Antarctic Marine Living Resources [**Basic Document 2.4**] (hereinafter: CCAMLR) of 1980 and the many recommendations, adopted by the Consultative Parties with regard to man's impact on the environment and the regulation of scientific and touristic activities. Under these rules, some areas now benefit from such special protection as specially protected areas or sites of special scientific interest. Proper guarantees against detrimental changes to the environment are also provided for in the draft regime for the exploration and exploitation of Antarctic mineral resources which has been under discussion among the Consultative Parties for several years.

* * *

The obligation to prevent or abate transboundary environmental interference, which causes, or risks causing, substantial harm to the environment of other States or of areas outside national jurisdiction, may be considered a well established rule of general international law.

The prohibition against causing transboundary environmental interference has been applied in international jurisprudence mainly with reference to cases of atmosphere or water pollution. The following well-known statement was made by the arbitral tribunal deciding over the dispute between the United States and Canada in the *Trail Smelter* arbitration [**Basic Document 8.4**] on 11 March 1941. The tribunal held the Canadian government responsible for the emission of toxic fumes into American territory:

> under the principles of international law, as well as of the law of the United States, no State has the right to use or permit the use of its territory in such a manner as to cause injury by fumes in or to the territory of another or the properties or persons therein, when the case is

of serious consequence and the injury is established by clear and convincing evidence.[24]

In the *Lake Lanoux* case (*Spain v. France*) [**Basic Document 8.3**], which was decided by arbitral award on 16 November 1957, the sameprinciple of international law was invoked in relation to the utilization of international watercourses. In that case the tribunal considered that the general rule was not to be applied because the French project did not cause an alteration of the shared waters, but the actual existence of such a rule in current international law was not discussed:

> ... Thus, if it is admitted that there is a principle which prohibits the upstream State from altering the waters of a river in such a fashion as seriously to prejudice the downstream State, such a principle would have no application to the present case, because it has been admitted by the Tribunal ... that the French scheme will not alter the waters of the Carol....[25]

In United Nations General Assembly resolutions the duty of prevention and abatement of transboundary environmental interferences assumes a general significance. The rule set forth by Principle 21 of the Declaration on the Human Environment adopted in Stockholm in 1972 (hereinafter: Stockholm Declaration) [**Basic Document 1.12**], for example, includes every kind of activity which can cause harm without any reference to a particular source of pollution (as in the *Trail Smelter* award: "injury by fumes") or to the habitat violated (as in the *Lake Lanoux* case: alteration of the waters of a watercourse). Even the space dimension, considered as the expression of territorial sovereignty, and the human interests connected to it, is considerably attenuated. Thus, if in the *Trail Smelter* arbitration the general rule was set forth to prohibit States from using their *territory* in such a manner as to cause detrimental changes to the *territory* of another State ("territory of another State or the properties or persons therein") according to Principle 21 of the Stockholm Declaration, every State is responsible for activities which cause detriment to the *environment* of other States or of *areas outside any national jurisdiction* and which can be ascribed to it by means of any connecting element, territorial or personal:

> States have, in accordance with the Charter of the United Nations and the principles of international law, the sovereign right to exploit their own resources pursuant to their own environmental policies, and the responsibility to ensure that activities within their jurisdiction or control do not cause damage to the environment of other States or of areas beyond the limits of national jurisdiction.[26]

Finally, the obligation to prevent severe pollution becomes, in the codification work of the International Law Commission, absolute. The obligation to preserve the human environment from massive pollution of the atmosphere and of the seas has been inserted by Art. 19 of the Draft Articles on State Responsibility [**Basic Document 1.10**] among the rules considered so essen-

---

24. Trail Smelter Arbitration, at 1965 [**Basic Document 8.4**].

25. Lake Lanoux Arbitration, at 281 [**Basic Document 8.3**].

26. Stockholm Declaration of the United Nations Conference on the Human Environment, Principle 21 [**Basic Document 1.12**].

tial for the protection of fundamental interests of the international community that their breach must be considered an international crime:

> 2. An internationally wrongful act which results from the breach by a State of an international obligation so essential for the protection of fundamental interests of the international community that its breach is recognized as a crime by that community as a whole constitutes an international crime.

> 3. Subject to paragraph 2, and on the basis of the rules of international law in force, an international crime may result, *inter alia*, from:

> ... d) a serious breach of an international obligation of essential importance for the safeguarding and preservation of the human environment, such as those prohibiting massive pollution of the atmosphere or of the seas.

Whether international law already provides, after the violation of the obligations listed in Art. 19, for more serious consequences than those generally connected to the violation of an international obligation is a problem which is impossible to go into here in any depth. What we are anxious to underline, instead, is the character of the positive obligation of existing international law that the International Law Commission has attributed to the cited categories, as though giving into the temptation, which the Commission had stated several times it was trying to resist, to codify even the content of the obligations breached (the "primary rules") with the rules regulating State responsibility. As the chairman of the drafting committee, Sahovic stated when explaining the text of the draft article:

> ... it was plain from the words "on the basis of the rules of international law in force" that the examples of the categories or fields enumerated were based strictly on the rules of international law as they existed today.[27]

Such a statement becomes even more important if we consider the explicit reference made in Art. 19 to examples of environmental pollution. The original draft (Art. 18.3(c)) which made general reference to "the conservation and the free enjoyment for everyone of a resource common to all mankind" would have raised not a few problems of interpretation:

> ... if a ship polluted the sea with oil, it would breach the obligation to conserve a resource common to all mankind, but would not be committing an international crime. On the other hand, if a State conducted large-scale nuclear tests near the territory of another State, that could be called an international crime.

The definitive version of the rule, however, is not without weaknesses. The reference in paragraph 3(d) to forms of massive pollution of the atmosphere and the seas as examples of breaches of the general rule prohibiting serious environmentally detrimental changes does not appear satisfactory, and during the discussions within the International Law Commission, it was not without its critics. It was pointed out that:

27.   1 Y. B. Int'l L. Comm'n 240 (1976).

Paragraph 3(d) concerned the biosphere, and its examples should not be limited to the atmosphere and the seas. Massive pollution could occur in rivers, lakes, canals or even whole areas of the territory of States.

Castañeda proposed to include deliberate action to bring about environmental change among the examples listed in paragraph 3(d) while Ushakov proposed *tout-court* to delete the reference to massive pollution of the atmosphere and the seas, affirming that:

> the reference to "preservation of the human environment" suggested the biosphere in general not merely the atmosphere or the seas.

However, if we consider that the reference to massive pollution of the atmosphere and the seas as only an illustrative, and not an exhaustive, character, these failings are not to be overstated to the detriment of the important contribution of Art. 19 to the further development of international environmental law. As special rapporteur Ago defined it vis-a-vis other crimes such as slavery, genocide, or apartheid which are destined (or so it is hoped) to disappear, the violation of environmental balance is a crime of the future. The only rule among those listed in paragraph 3 of Art. 19 to be not directly contemplated by the United Nations Charter **[Basic Document 1.3]** or the Universal Declaration of Human Rights **[Basic Document 7.11]**, it is for the first time set forth in absolute terms. On the one hand, in order to consider a State responsible for a crime of massive pollution, it is not necessary that pollution materially crosses the borders of States. On the other, the environmentally unlawful act becomes an event which is relevant for the international community as a whole. Unlike international delicts which imply a bilateral relationship between the guilty State and the victim State, international crimes entail responsibility towards all other States. Consequently, in the case of massive pollution, every State, not only those who have directly suffered from the harmful event, will be entitled to consider its rights affected.

The general prohibition of transboundary environmental interferences may be extended to the protection of the Antarctic environment under a twofold interpretation.

Principle 21 of the Stockholm Declaration in fact can be interpreted both as a preventive measure against environmental interference detrimental for the Antarctic environment that may arise in the territory of any State, as well as the prohibition of activities undertaken in Antarctica detrimental for the environment of other States, of areas outside national jurisdiction, such as the high seas, or of other Antarctic areas. Consequently, every State will be obligated to prevent and abate environmental interference, developing from activities under their control, in their territory or directly in the Antarctic area. However, for the States which claim sovereign rights over the Antarctic territory, if pollution strictly confined to the claimed area can be considered contrary to international law, it will be by virtue of the rules of environmental protection of the Antarctic Treaty System.

When we consider the Antarctic Treaty System, the space limits which are to be referred to are the geographical coordinates to which the Antarctic Treaty applies, the Agreed Measures for Conserving Fauna and Flora, and the Convention for the Conservation of Antarctic Seals (south of 60° south latitude) or the CCAMLR (the Antarctic Convergence as defined in Art. 1.4 of the Convention), and not the boundaries, often disputed, inside which some

States intend to exercise their sovereign claims. Therefore, the State polluting its own area, prosecutable under general international law only upon demonstration of the groundlessness of its territorial claims, might be considered responsible for the violation of rules of the Antarctic Treaty System also inside the sector claimed.

As to specific activities, the Antarctic Treaty System provides for some prohibitions and substantial restrictions. Activities prohibited in Antarctica, because they are explicitly banned by Arts. I and V of the [Antarctic] Treaty, are measures of a military nature, nuclear explosions, and the disposal of radioactive waste. However, the nuclear hazard, and the risks intrinsically connected to it, have not been barred from the fragile Antarctic environment. Art. V does not prohibit the use of radioactive material and the precautionary measures adopted up to now by the Consultative Parties for experiments involving the use of radio-isotopes (prior notification must be given) have essentially been suggested after considering the possible impact of experiments of that nature on subsequent scientific research in the same area:

> ... The Representatives, *Recognizing* that experiments involving the use of radio-isotopes may jeopardize subsequent scientific investigations in the same locality ... *Recommend* to their Governments that, when experiments involving the use of radio-isotopes in the Antarctic Treaty Area are planned, they should provide appropriate information on such experiments to other Consultative Parties as early as possible, preferably six months in advance, but in any event, annually.[28]

* * *

The obligation to prevent or abate transboundary environmental interferences is a duty of due diligence: every State is required to watch over interferences which actually cause substantial harm or potentially risk causing such harm abroad. As a duty of due care, a lack of control and vigilance is sufficient to entail State responsibility without speaking of fault in its true sense:

> ... la "surveillance" à laquelle l'État est tenu, loin d'apparâitre comme un élément subjectif de sa responsabilité, elle constitue l'objet même de l'obligation qui s'impose à lui et dont la violation le rend responsable sans qu'il ait à faire intervenir la notion de faute au sens propre du mot.[29]

In order to evaluate State conduct, however, we must know the *measure* of the "due diligence", which is a particularly delicate operation if we consider that the rule prohibiting transboundary pollution includes the prevention of the environmental risk. When we say risk, we mean a potential negative event whose consequences are neither known nor foreseeable with certainty. The probability that the negative event will happen may be foreseen statistically only in some cases; in others, in relation to events which are not well-known, it will be only considered as a possibility. Intrinsically ambiguous ..., the duty of due diligence cannot be measured in the abstract nor defined *a priori*....

28. Handbook of the Antarctic Treaty System, Rec. VI–6, 3201–3202 (1970).

29. CHARLES ROUSSEAU, 5 DROIT INTERNATIONAL PUBLIC 21 (1983).

International jurisprudence and State practice developed outside environmental law have tried, however, to give some general criteria for the evaluation of "in due diligence."

On the one hand, one parameter, which in many cases is reasonable, consists in demanding from the States a positive action proportional to the means which they have at their disposal. The standard of the *diligentia quam in suis*, suggested by arbiter Huber in deciding the dispute concerning the Spanish Zone of Morocco Claims (Great Britain v. Spain—1925), sums up the content of due diligence for that case:

> The vigilance which a State is required to guarantee in accordance with international law, can, applying by analogy a term of Roman law, be characterized as diligentia quam in suis. This rule, which is in conformity with the basic principle of the independence of States in their internal affairs, in fact, offers States the degree of severity which they can reasonably expect for their nationals.[30]

To impose foreign legislative patterns would be in contrast with the principle of sovereign independence of States, and to require that the means which the States have at their disposal be up to the circumstances would imply imposing an unbearable strain on the States. As suggested by Principle 23 of the Stockholm Declaration **[Basic Document 1.12]**, what has been said can be applied for the evaluation of the behaviour of less developed States in the field of prevention and abatement of transboundary pollution:

> Without prejudice to such criteria as may be agreed upon by the international community, or to standards which will have to be determined nationally, it will be essential in all cases to consider the systems of values prevailing in each country and the extent of the applicability of standards which are valid for the most advanced countries but which may be inappropriate and of unwarranted social cost for the developing countries.

On the other hand, under certain circumstances, the standard of *diligentia quam in suis* might be inadequate for considering the international obligation fulfilled. For particularly hazardous activities, in fact, one would obviously assume that more rigorous behaviour is expected from a State, just as with regard to the treatment of aliens. In this case a State is required to adopt a minimum standard demanded by international law regardless of the treatment reserved to nationals.

Consequently, the duty of "due diligence" will be proportional not only to the objective possibilities of every State, but also to the extent of damage to be prevented. The more serious the consequences which may develop, the more serious the measures which the State is requested to adopt.

In the field of environmental protection, an area in which the notion of risk is implicit, the evaluation of State behaviour presumes a prior comparison between the economic or environmental value which must be defended and the negative variation that the potentially foreseen harm may have with regard to the same value. Knowledge and prior evaluation of the sources and the causes of risk, on one hand, and the potential target which must be protected, on the other, are the foundations of environmental protection

30. Spanish Zone of Morocco Claims (Gr. Brit. v. Spain), 2 U.N.R.I.A.A. 120 (1925).

policy. However, it is not always possible to assess *a priori* the incidence of certain activities on the environmental balance of some areas. Under certain circumstances, activities normally practiced because they are considered to be of low risk may lead to irreversible environmental changes if undertaken in particularly fragile ecosystems. Therefore, the assessment of the risk will have to be made case by case, according to specific circumstances.

A particular and effective method for the assessment and prevention of environmental harm consists in environmental impact assessments. By means of these procedures it is possible to predetermine the effects which planned activities may have. Provisions for the assessment of environmental impact before undertaking certain activities and the adoption of alternative practices when serious risk of environmental change is evident may be found in various national laws. Similar provisions are frequently inserted in treaties or adopted in the resolutions of international organizations.

The adoption of environmental impact assessment at present cannot be considered to be more than a progressive trend of international law; we can hardly say that States consider such a practice legally binding under general international law. However, it is undeniable that environmental impact assessments appear to be the most effective method of supplying a scientific foundation to legal evaluations and consequently facilitate the determination of the standards according to which the behaviour of one State vis-à-vis a probable harm can also be considered satisfactory from the legal point of view.

12.   Editors' Note. Antarctica's polar location, the vast bulk of its ice mass, and the huge extent of the surrounding seas mean that the continent has a fundamental influence on the atmosphere, the oceans, and the biological conditions of the entire global system. In turn, the impact of human activities elsewhere on Earth is felt in Antarctica.

For these reasons, among others, the International Geosphere–Biosphere Programme uses Antarctica as part of its worldwide network of regional research centers and sites to gather data and analyze global change problems. A pristine laboratory within which, by examining the ice, changes in global pollution rates and world climates can be monitored, Antarctica is a natural resource in itself. And, being the repository of much of the world's freshwater in the form of continental and sea ice, it is, in turn, especially sensitive to global climate change. Global warming can cause Antarctica's ice to melt and thereby contribute to global sea level change.

Antarctica's vulnerability to events elsewhere was revealed by the discovery, in 1985, of an ozone hole above it. This ozone hole—which first appears each year in September (when ozone levels plunge by over a third) and lasts until November—results in an increase in ultraviolet (UV) radiation exposure for Antarctic ecosystems. UV radiation has mutagenic and lethal effects on plant and animal cells, and preliminary experiments in Antarctica indicate that the marine phytoplankton are already UV stressed.

Some possible effects of this development may include far-reaching effects on the Southern Ocean ecosystem and a decrease in species diversity in the terrestrial ecosystem as a whole. Thus, the Antarctic food web could be affected, and this, in turn, would have a major effect throughout the food chain. For example, UV-induced food scarcity could have a significant effect on fish, seals, penguins, and whales. Indeed, stocks of certain whale species in the Southern Ocean are already depleted to the point where they may never recover. If food is limited because of increased competition, prey population reductions, or overharvesting, increased UV impacts would further complicate recovery.

In sum, the Antarctic environment is fragile. All human activity in the region (and to some extent even beyond) has some sort of adverse impact on it. Scientific operations have left a legacy of environmental problems (and, as noted below, tourism has the potential to do likewise). But not necessarily at the hands of Antarctic Treaty System (ATS) members alone. Pakistan, which opposed the ATS in the United Nations, established a summer station in the area claimed by Norway in 1991. This is not the first time a country outside the Antarctic Treaty has established a base and done scientific research in Antarctica. India was the first and South Korea the second. Neither are consultative parties.

The actual and potential impact of human activity upon Antarctica is the subject of the remainder of this note.

Science

Science has a major impact on the Antarctic environment. During the 1980s, often to satisfy more political than scientific motivations, the number of nations with scientific programmes on the continent nearly doubled. Some stations are townships rather than small scientific bases (in the Antarctic summer season there are about 1,000 people at the United States stations), and typically involve the construction of bases and logistic support facilities, like airstrips, by different nations in close proximity to each other. All of which means greater environmental degradation.

For example, in May 1990, several thousand king penguins on a Macquarie Island breeding colony died, apparently in a stampede. The proximity of a large-supply aircraft flying at low altitude was consistent with the disturbance.

Also, Antarctic stations tend to disregard environmental protection agreements, like the Code of Conduct for Waste Disposal (unpublished) and the Agreed Measures **[Basic Document 2.2]**. The legacy is one of pollution, with high levels of PCBs found in marine sediments, pesticide residues and other organochlorines in biological samples, and heavy metal contamination in soil. Few stations have containment facilities to prevent damage from fuel spills. What is more, Antarctic stations are turning to incineration to reduce volumes of waste. But this only transfers the impact of waste from soil and water to the air. Burning can result in new toxic products forming, the impact of which on the ecosystem is unknown.

Consider the following extract from Lorne Kriwoken, *Antarctic Environmental Planning and Management: Conclusions from Casey, Australian Antarctic Territory*, 27 Polar Record 1, 4–6 (1990), which evaluates the impacts of just one Antarctic station:

> [I]mpact upon the environment caused by the rebuilding of Australian Antarctic stations is not confined to "existing station areas". The new Casey [settlement] occupies a new site 0.7 km from the old. Appropriate recognition of the sensitivity of the ice-free land, and particularly the nearby protected area, was not given prior to station expansion. The arrival of engineers and construction crews brought many more people

into the area, infrastructure and facilities expanded, and impact on the whole of the surrounding ice-free area increased significantly.

The extended Casey area has become a high-density settlement with large energy consumption and waste disposal requirements. The impact of the rebuilding programme is well documented: associated air pollution is having short-term and long-term environmental impact on the adjacent terrestrial ecology.[31] SSSI [Site of Special Scientific Interest] No 16, containing rich lichen and moss communities and supporting long-term taxonomic, ecological, and physiological research, has been seriously degraded. At the 1985 Senate Standing Committee on National Resources evidence was received that:

> ... a lake beside Casey dramatically altered as a result of ground in the catchment being disturbed, resulting in glacier flour entering the lake; cement dust broadcast extensively; plastic cement bags disposed of by throwing them in the sea, only to re-appear on the shores; morainic rock at Mawson being used to feed rock-crushers for concrete production; various engineering manipulations to provide adequate water supply, particularly to meet the heavy demands of the water-flush toilet system being introduced....[32]

The three periods of expansion have cumulatively degraded the environment of Bailey and Clark peninsulas. Neither of the old stations has been cleared, so impacts have therefore spread over an unnecessarily large area; in just over 30 years 9.5 hectares (ha) of the ice-free land surrounding Newcombe Bay have been irreversibly changed (Table 6–1). In addition, there are three field huts within 22 km of Casey.

The length and complexity of roads, an excellent index of clustering of station facilities, has increased ten-fold (Table 6–1). Approximately 2 km of road now service a widely dispersed station area, with associated increases in fuel consumption, dust, and congestion. Fuel consumption for station operation has increased over four-fold (Table 6–1). The new road on the causeway linking old and new Casey has been subject to an increased level of maintenance activity. Until the old station is closed and removed, fuel use will remain high. The AAD [Australian Antarctic Division (an Australian government agency)] "notice of intention" made no mention of the problems of a widely dispersed station and increased fuel consumption.

Table 6–1—Environmental impacts of Wilkes, "Old" Casey, and "New" Casey stations.

Operating period	Winter population	Summer population	area* (ha)	length of roads**	fuel usage (1x1000)***	construction
Wilkes	18–25	45	1.5	200	200	0.5 '56–69
"Old Casey"	22–28	45	2	200	-410	4 '69–88
"New Casey"	25–35	80	2	2000	-700	8+ '88–

* Includes remote radio communications facilities. ** Index of clustering of station facilities. *** Includes only power station fuel consumption; fuels used for vehicles and field work would be extra. *Editor's Postscript:* In a ten-week operation over the 1990–91 season, pressurized gas, chemicals, fuels and explosives remaining at the derelict station Wilkes, were identified and rendered safe.

31. R. Lewis Smith, Environmental Impact and Related Matters in the Casey Station Area (1986) (unpublished manuscript on file with Cambridge, British Antarctic Survey).

32. 1985 Senate Standing Committee on National Resources, The Natural Resources of the Australian Antarctic Territory, Parliamentary Paper No. 495/1985, at 75 (1985).

Increased station population has not brought about a proportional increase in scientific personnel. The winter population has not changed greatly in 30 years, but summer population has almost doubled (Table 6–1); most visits are occurring when the ice-free terrestrial ecosystem is most vulnerable to impact. The AAD "notice of intention" did not cite any increase in numbers of associated impact on the terrestrial ecosystem.

Scientific commitment to Casey seems to be eroding. The glaciology programme has stopped, with only a summer drilling programme planned. In 1988–89 one biologist over-wintered. If stations are justified for their scientific role, Casey is almost solely justified by its terrestrial biology programme. Critical to this research is the adjacent SSSI, the very area that the rebuilding programme placed in jeopardy. Ecosystems close to new Casey are fragile, with small capacity to absorb change, including fellfield communities of lichen and mosses.[33] Vulnerability of the moss beds was recognized in the "notice of intention", and one site alternative was rejected because of its potential impact.[34] However, new Casey stands on the northern edge of the most sensitive area. The question of minimizing its impact by locating it on the site of old Casey does not seem to have warranted serious consideration.

Though moss beds immediately southeast of new Casey received their SSSI status in 1985, both old and new Casey operations had already adversely affected the area. Concrete mixing sent a plume of alkaline cement dust from the batching plant, often covering the adjacent moss beds and contaminating the soil,[35] . . . and a two ha moss bed adjacent to new Casey and outside the SSSI was almost killed by pollution. SSI status has not ensured adequate protection from station activity; close proximity, though ideal for research, maximizes chances of disturbance. Cables servicing the radio transmitter at the south end of the protected area have been laid directly on the moss beds . . . and, with the cycle of freeze and thaw, have become embedded. These are the very moss critical to the terrestrial biology programme which largely justified Casey's existence.

Wilkes, on a 1.5 ha site, consists of dilapidated wood and canvas buildings, abandoned heavy equipment, fuel drums, wood, wire, cable, and plastic. . . . The site cannot readily be cleaned up by Casey personnel; rehabilitation will require a massive collaborative effort, presumably between Australia and the United States, with removal of dangerous and environmentally deleterious substances given high priority. As a former

33. W.S. BENNINGHOFF & WILLIAM BONNER, MAN'S IMPACT ON THE ANTARCTIC ENVIRONMENT: A PROCEDURE FOR EVALUATING IMPACTS FROM SCIENTIFIC AND LOGISTIC ACTIVITIES 44 (1985).

34. PARLIAMENTARY STANDING COMMITTEE ON PUBLIC WORKS, MINUTES OF EVIDENCE RELATING TO

REDEVELOPMENT OF AUSTRALIAN ANTARCTIC BASES, PART I AND II, at 580 (1981).

35. See Lewis Smith, supra note 31.

IGY [International Geophysical Year] station Wilkes may have some historic value; there could be a case for restoring one or more buildings of historic importance and developing interpretative and educational material for future visitors.

Waste materials have been generated from the rebuilding programme and the old Casey site, and a formal comprehensive waste management programme is needed to deal with it. Old Casey, like Wilkes, may include representative buildings of historic importance that should be preserved. Berms surrounding bulk fuel storage tanks are needed to contain fuel in the event of a leakage or spillage, and careful monitoring is needed during fuel transfer operations.

This illustration of the problems of constructing settlements in Antarctica is typical of the operations of countries exploring the continent.

One of the difficulties is that Antarctic operators are often both the developer, supporting supply and building activities; and the environmental watchdog, enforcing environmental policy. Not surprisingly, development and operational priorities take precedence over environmental planning and management. Station areas do not have management plans to deal with all human activities associated with the station. Management plans, if complied with, could help ensure the protection of terrestrial and marine environments.

What is the justification for scientific research in Antarctica? The discovery of the glycoprotein antifreeze in Antarctic has a spin-off for stabilizing ice cream. Is this an adequate justification? What is an adequate justification? What should be the limits of scientific investigation? Is it not enough to know that the ecosystem exists? Given their impact on the environment, do scientists have any more right to intrude than tourists? Should there be greater regulation of scientific programs and operations? Who should exercise that regulation and on what authoritative basis?

Tourism

What if a tourist killed penguins? What if a vessel taking tourists to the site capsized, polluting the area and wiping out the penguins? What if a helicopter flight caused a stampede in a penguin colony during the breeding season, causing the deaths of a large number of chicks and breeding pairs, and thereby endangered the population? Who would be liable?

Tourism began in the Antarctic in 1966, but is not well-established. Businesses operate tours on a competitive basis. Most tourists come by sea, either on nature tours, mostly in small vessels, or on the more traditional kind of cruise in larger passenger ships. A small number of tourists come by air.

The impacts of tourism vary. Nature tours generally have inflatable launches which allow landings to be made almost anywhere. This means that there is an impact on wildlife in the field. The traditional type of cruise lands at research stations, and has an impact there. Private or semi-commercial adventure tourism is growing.

Tourism involves about four to five thousand people, active mainly in a period of three months of the year. Tourist visitors now equal the number of science and science support staff on the continent. Antarctic tourism is likely to increase. Land-based tourism is likely to grow, probably using ski-equipped aircraft or wheeled aircraft operating on ice-strips.

There have been a number of serious tourist accidents in Antarctic—tour ship groundings, sinkings of tourist ships (*Southern Quest* and *Bahia Paraiso*—*see infra*), and serious air disasters (one on Mount Erebus). These accidents highlight difficulties with the Antarctic Treaty regime. Who is liable for air safety, marine pollution and oil spill prevention, and contingency and emergency response planning? Who should be responsible for tourist operations that go wrong and consequently pollute the environment or destroy local ecosystems?

A major problem is how to educate people who go to Antarctica about the fragility of the Antarctic environment. So fragile is it, indeed, that it is legitimate to ask whether tourism should be permitted at all. A dilemma is, of course, that tourists go home with a commitment to protecting Antarctica, thereby influencing the political climate on the future of Antarctica. Should tourism be regulated? For example, should tourists be limited to defined tourist areas? Should there be a restriction on numbers? How should that decision be made—on a country by country basis, or by some other method such as a ballot or an auction? Should there be a minimum standard that tourist operations must meet? Should there be comparable standards between government and non-government activities on the ice? Should there be regulation of aspects like safety, self-sufficiency, environmental impact, and emergency preparedness? Under what authority could any of this be done? Should *individuals* have a duty under international law to protect the Antarctic environment?

The 1991 Environmental Protection Protocol

Antarctica needs a complex set of regulations based squarely on sound conservation principles to protect the Antarctic region. It requires an integrated and binding environmental protection regime. Does the 1991 Environmental Protection Protocol [**Basic Document 2.9**] provide this?

The 1991 Protocol is designed to address the problems of human activity in Antarctica—waste disposal, marine pollution, the protection of wildlife, plants, habitats, and natural and historic features, uses of Antarctic ice, commercial fishing, tourist and recreational activities, and scientific research activities such as drilling. Does it have the capacity to deal with these matters? Can it deal with the cumulative impacts of activities by individual States? For example, the approach to setting up stations and bases in the Antarctic is ad hoc. Can the Protocol achieve the grouping of bases around shared facilities and infrastructures? Can it deal with cross-media pollution? What are its strengths and weaknesses? Does it provide a model for other global environmental issues?

Additionally, how does the environmental protection regime put in place by the new Protocol differ from the World Park concept? Can an Antarctic World Park be implemented within the framework of the Antarctic Treaty System? Should one all-embracing convention (as proposed by some) have been negotiated from the start instead? Might the Antarctic Park concept be implemented within the framework of the United Nations? If so, how?

Marine Pollution

In 1989, Argentina's supply ship, the *Bahia Paraiso*, grounded after a visit to Palmer Station.[s] The accident released approximately 170,000 gallons of diesel fuel, jet fuel, and lubricating oil into the marine environment, some of which was carried out to sea while much of the rest found its way onto the shores of nearby islands. Three hundred sixteen people were on board the ship at the time of the accident (most of them tourists), and they were taken to the nearby Palmer Station. The area is of interest, to scientists especially, because of its abundant wildlife.

Measures to prevent oil spilling from the damaged vessel were taken quickly. A Chilean navy oceanographic ship surrounded the vessel with a light boom. Staff from Palmer Station used their fleet of "zodiacs" (small inflatable boats) and the ship's lifeboats to recover drums, CNG cylinders, and other floating debris. In the United States, the National Science Foundation (which had invested a considerable sum in the research work at Palmer Station) assembled a team of experts and equipment to fly to Buenos Aires to join their research vessel RV *Polar Duke*. They arrived within about eight days, installed a heavier boom around the *Bahia Paraiso*, collected surface oil, and used chemical dispersants to break up patches of oil. Two Argentine vessels and a Chilean vessel assisted with the operations, including the sealing of the *Bahia Paraiso* to stop further leaking. The ship was eventually salvaged.

Soon after the grounding of the *Bahia Paraiso*, scientists found dead and dying krill washed up in tidal pools. Limpets, the main food source for kelp gulls, also were affected. Subsequently, skuas, penguins, and cormorants in a nearby colony were affected. Studies show that the animals most affected by the oil spill are those which regularly move in and out of the water.

The case of the *Bahia Paraiso* illustrates the possible effects and the difficulties that are associated with shipping accidents and marine pollution incidents in Antarctica. The *Bahia Paraiso* involved a relatively minor oil spill. What would be the likely consequences of an *Exxon Valdez*-type oil spill in Antarctica? The more human activity in Antarctica and the more ships that go there, the greater is the risk of accident leading to major marine pollution.

Mining

The future exploration and exploitation of mineral resources in Antarctica is likely to impact negatively on the Antarctic environment in two ways. First, there is the potential for damage to the marine ecosystem (as well as on shore from the operation of support facilities). The release of large amounts of crude oil into the Southern Ocean from tanker accidents and well blowouts, for example, could destroy the local ecosystem. Because oil takes much longer to degrade in the cold Antarctic temperatures than it does in the warmer climates, such mishaps would likely contaminate the krill (which form the bottom of the marine food chain) and thereby affect the well-being of both marine and land ecosystems. Second, a rise in particulate matter associated with oil and mineral development could alter the ability of Antarctica's ice cap to reflect the sun's heat, which in turn could cause the atmosphere to warm.

---

s. Named after American explorer Nathaniel Palmer who, in 1820, discovered Palmer Peninsula, 60° West, without realizing that it was part of a continent.

Also, an increase in pollution could ruin Antarctica as a global laboratory for monitoring worldwide pollution levels.[t]

Icebergs

Antarctica has incredible fresh water reserves. What if someone decided to export icebergs to supply freshwater to water-short countries? Who has sovereignty over icebergs? Does the law of the sea apply to them? What international law would apply to the activity? What international law *should* apply?

Role of Non-governmental Organizations

In recent times, nongovernmental organizations have had major influence in the shaping of policy about Antarctica. In particular, they have been instrumental in arousing public concern about the future of the continent, thereby shaping political attitudes and action. Greenpeace had an environmental and scientific programme in Antarctica, dating from 1985 until 1992. Two facilities were used for this, the expedition ship *MV Gondawana* and World Park Base at Cape Evans, Ross Island. Its role in the Antarctic was largely as an environmental watchdog. Greenpeace conducted environmental inspections of Antarctic bases and field sites and published a report at the end of each season. The scientific programme included collaborative research with a number of scientists from several nations. World Park Base was closed in 1992.

D. Issues for the Future

Antarctica, as the three foregoing problems demonstrate, provides a laboratory for international environmental law. However, since no nation can claim sovereignty over it, must its problems be solved in the same way as other environmental problems? Are there approaches that might work for other global or regional environmental issues that will not work for Antarctica? Are there approaches that might work for Antarctica that might not work for other global or regional environmental issues?

1. Sam Blay & Julia Green, *The Development of a Liability Annex to the Madrid Protocol*, 25 ENVTL. POL'Y & L. 24 (1995).

Introduction

After the rejection of the 1988 Minerals Convention [**Basic Document 2.7**], the Antarctic Treaty Consultative Parties (ATCPs) adopted the Madrid Protocol on Environmental Protection to the Antarctic Treaty (hereinafter referred to as the Protocol) [**Basic Document 2.9**] aimed at creating a comprehensive regime for the protection of the Antarctic environment. As an operational instrument, the Protocol has two unique aspects: the first is that it is an umbrella instrument that deals with international relations concerning Antarctica in very broad terms. The specific details of each activity likely to impact on the environment, and thus requiring regulation, are left to be dealt with in a series of annexes attached to the Protocol. Provision is made in

t. *See* U.S. DEPARTMENT OF STATE, FINAL ENVIRONMENTAL IMPACT STATEMENT ON THE NEGOTIATION OF AN INTERNATIONAL REGIME FOR ANTARCTIC MINERAL RESOURCES (1982).

Article 9 for further annexes, should they be necessary over time. The second aspect is that, even though the Protocol deals with the protection of the Antarctic environment, the central issue of liability for damage to the environment is not addressed in it. In this regard, the ATCPs "undertake to elaborate rules and procedures relating to liability for damage arising from activities taking place in the Antarctic Treaty area and covered by [the] protocol". Like other more specific issues, the question of liability is left to be dealt with in a separate annex.

So far, only a handful of states have ratified the Protocol. However, there is little doubt that at some time in the future the Protocol will receive the requisite ratifications to bring it into force. [*Editors' Note*: The Protocol came into force on 14 January 1998]. With this in mind, at the XVIIth Antarctic Treaty Consultative Meeting (ATCM) in Venice in November 1993, it was recommended that a meeting of legal experts be convened to deal with the issue of a liability annex to the Protocol, in fulfilment of the obligation in Article 16.

Among the ATCPs, the issue of liability for environmental damage is not new. The issue arose under the Convention for the Regulation of Antarctic Mineral Resource Activities (hereinafter referred to as CRAMRA) **[Basic Document 2.7]** where it was considered central, but was not resolved. While the parties agreed that there was need for specific liability provisions to underpin the stringent requirements of CRAMRA, they came to no agreement on the actual details of liability. Given the centrality of the issue to the operation of CRAMRA, Article 8(9) provided that neither permits for exploration nor development could be issued before the entry into force of the liability protocol.

Since the Protocol does not permit mineral resource activities in Antarctica, the adoption of a liability annex is not made a condition precedent to the operation of the Protocol. In this regard the resolution of the issue of liability lacks the urgency it once commanded under CRAMRA. This notwithstanding, the ATCPs are committed to adopting an instrument on the liability if they are to live up to their obligations under Article 16. Whatever their undertakings under the Protocol may be, the negotiation of a liability annex is certain to test their commitment to the protection of the Antarctic environment. This is because given the unique legal regime concerning the region, the question of liability for environment damage to it involves complex issues of law and policy. This paper examines some of these issues, and canvasses some solutions and approaches that may be adopted by the ATCPs.

The Necessity of a Liability Annex to the Protocol

The attempts to conclude a liability annex to the Protocol presupposes that such a regime is necessary. But is a liability annex to the Protocol or indeed any regime on liability for environmental damage necessary to support the implementation of the Protocol? It may be suggested that the liability annex to the Protocol is necessary because the Protocol specifically requires it under Article 16. Such an answer begs the question, because the question still remains; is the annex necessary for the efficient implementation of the Protocol? The Antarctic Treaty System (ATS) incorporates several instruments aimed at protecting the region's environment. However none of these includes specific liability provisions concerning the activities of states in Antarctica. Thus apart from the rules of international law that cover general issues of environmental protection as may be applicable to Antarctica, the liability of states for environmental damage in the region is far from clear or indeed hardly established. Even though the Antarctic Treaty Parties generally deal with questions of liability in punitive terms under their respective domestic legislation, this usually covers the activities of their own nationals or their sectors of jurisdiction exclusively, and the pieces of legislation tend to vary in their standards of care and their bases of liability. This situation is a reflection of the mosaic of instruments in the ATS all purporting to deal with the protection of the Antarctic environment. In the absence of any substantive rules concerning liability for damage to the region, it is logical to develop a uniform system of determining liability as part of the general regime under the Protocol.

But would the adoption of a liability annex make any significant difference to the effective implementation of the Protocol? The ATS has been in operation for well over three decades now and for all this period, it has been without an instrument on liability as such. Even though substantive efforts to protect the Antarctic environment are recent phenomena, there is no evidence to suggest that the absence of a formal liability instrument has been detrimental to the protection of the Antarctic environment or encouraged the wanton pollution in the area. As noted earlier, unlike CRAMRA, the operation of the Protocol is not made conditional on the adoption of a liability instrument. This is an important distinction between the two agreements. It gives the impression that the Treaty parties themselves admit that in the absence of resource exploitation on the continent that may have potential adverse implications for the region's environment, and minimal instances of deliberate or negligent degradation of the environment, a liability regime, while desirable, is not exactly vital for the operation of Protocol. If this is the case then the lack of urgency is likely to slow down the negotiation process for the liability annex.

Even though a formal regime on liability does not appear vital for the implementation of the Protocol, we must caution against undue delays in adopting one. Given the concern over the protection of the region's vulnerable environment and the many efforts to protect it, a clear statement clarifying the principles and the bases for determining liability is well overdue. The history of Antarctic so far indicates that the most potent threat to the region's environment, in the absence of mineral resources activities there, and for which a liability annex would be most appropriate, are oil spills. As the case of the *Exxon Valdez* clearly indicates, the costs associated with clean-up can be quite considerable. In the context of Antarctica, the responsibility for the clean-up campaign, and associated attempts to "repair" the environment and protect affected species, in the absence of a formal liability regime could well be a matter for controversy. If the treaty states are committed to the protection of the Antarctic environment as evidenced by their adoption of the Protocol, then they need not wait for an *Exxon Valdez* type incident before debating the details of liability.

The Policy Basis for A Liability Regime

In law, liability connotes the ascription of responsibility to an identifiable party for a particular event. It is thus an essential feature of law enforcement.

Its central purpose may be to help penalise and deter, as in criminal cases, or to help allocate the cost of compensation and/or restitution as in civil cases. In environmental law, liability tends to serve all these purposes. However, the utility of any concept of liability depends on the object in respect of which the liability may arise, and the subject to whom liability may attach. In the specific case of Antarctica, while the object of liability is easily identifiable, the legal status of the object in terms of its ownership and sovereignty is far from settled. This in turn has the potential to complicate the legal standing of states which may claim to be potential plaintiffs, the compensation they may be entitled to or the penalties they may be capable of imposing, not to mention the corresponding implication for any defendants. These issues will be addressed in detail later in this paper. For the moment, we will note that if the liability annex is to be of value, then it must be premised on a sound policy basis and with specific objectives in mind.

We propose that any liability regime for Antarctica should have at the very least four principal objectives: First, definition of what constitutes damage to the Antarctic environment. Second, in so doing, it should afford minimal defences to ensure that there are no loopholes that could be exploited by parties which may otherwise be liable. Third, it should seek to provide the maximum protection possible, preferably through a system of strict liability while taking account of particular Antarctic idiosyncrasies. Such an approach will necessarily call for the drawing of a desirable balance between the need to protect the region's environment on the one hand and the need to open up the region for scientific research, commercial activities such as off-shore fishing, and recreational issues such as tourism. Fourth, it should provide for both compensation for losses suffered as a result of conduct that causes damage and for responsibility for cleaning up and restoration of the damaged environment and the associated or dependent ecosystems. Any liability regime must be practical and functional. It must draw a good balance between the dichotomy of environmental protection and permitted uses. A very stringent regime may well be impractical. On the other hand; a regime that is too liberal may lose its essence.

Given the peculiar nature of Antarctica, what should one expect the law or policy maker to aim at in a liability regime for environmental damage to the region? A liability instrument could be aimed at penalising actual polluters and deterring potential ones. But the modern history of Antarctica does not warrant such a focus. While there is ample evidence of some localised environmental damage arising from station and research activities, there is nothing to suggest that Antarctica and the Southern oceans are used as waste disposal grounds as such. Indeed, in the case of oil spills, in the few instances on record, environmental damage occurred as a result of accidents rather than deliberate conduct. Where mishap is the principal cause of the damage, a principle or instrument of deterrence will be of little value. While a policy instrument or a law can minimise the possibilities of accidents by requiring specific safety measures, by their nature, accidents can hardly be stopped by legislative means. Admittedly, environmental damage arising from waste mismanagement at Antarctic stations is caused either intentionally or negligently. However, in modern times, most, if not all ATS with stations on the continent, are known to employ elaborate and sometimes sophisticated techniques of waste management ranging from recycling to transportation of the waste out of the region, in an effort to keep its environment clean. Such stations are thus hardly the appropriate subjects for a deterrence-oriented liability regime.

Alternatively, the policy or law maker can choose to focus liability on compensation and restitution. In this regard more attention will be given to the determination of who bears the cost of rectifying or cleaning up any damage to the environment and a clarification of the basis for liability generally. In the opinion of the authors, this would be a more desirable focus for the liability annex. The modern history of Antarctica clearly indicates a lack of any concise regime for the determination of liability. Thus when the Argentinean ship *Bahia Paraiso* spilt its cargo of oil off the coast near Anvers Island in 1989, while the fact of an accident was not in dispute, what remained unclear and unresolved were the extent of liability of the flag state and the vessel operators. The real difficulty with the protection of the Antarctic environment is not a phenomenon of persistent degradation of the region's near-pristine environment, but the absence of a clear strategy incorporating the cost of cleaning up and related measures once the damage occurs. The liability annex presents the ATCPs with an important opportunity to establish the principles of liability for all activity in Antarctica and to deal with such cases.

In drawing up the liability annex, it is important that the ATCPs are clear as to the theoretical or policy basis of the instrument. The policy basis they settle on will determine the general direction of the instrument and its approach to many fundamental questions. It is of course possible for the liability instrument to incorporate the two-policy basis of penalty and deterrence on the one hand, and compensation and restitution on the other hand. However, such a combination will require caution, because they can lead to complex results. For instance, if one adopted penalty and deterrence as the principal basis for the liability, then in the formulation of the instrument, one would necessarily have to make provision for excuses and defences against liability. This is because in general terms, once can hardly justify punishing an offender for a conduct that is neither negligent nor deliberate. On the other hand if one makes compensation and restitution the primary focus of liability, then fault need not be the basis of liability. In this case, the instrument can opt for strict or absolute liability. Thus a party may be held liable for the damage if the event causing the damage is attributable to the party irrespective of whether it was intentional or negligent. Where the focus of liability incorporates both deterrence and compensation, the provisions of the instrument will need to reflect such a basis adequately.

Editors' Note

A Group of Legal Experts has been working on a Liability Annex. The Group met during the Antarctic Treaty Consultative Meeting XXII held in Norway, 25 May—5 June 1998, and discussed the following outstanding issues in relation to the draft Liability Annex: the definition of "operator" and how liability might be imposed on operators; joint and several liability; insurance; and dispute settlement. The Group reported to the ATCM during Meeting XXII, and it was decided to dissolve the Group now that the report is complete. The Meeting decided to move further discussions on the Liability Annex to Working Group I of the ATCM.

2.   Richard Falk, *The Antarctic Treaty System: Are There Viable Alternatives?,* **in** THE ANTARCTIC TREATY SYSTEM IN WORLD POLITICS 399 **(Arnfinn Jorgensen–Dahl & Willy Ostreng eds., 1991).**

The governance of Antarctica, ingeniously combining the virtues of international cooperation with the reality of state sovereignty, is the closest thing to "a world order miracle" that the world has known. For more than three decades, despite antagonisms between the United States and the Soviet Union and the strongest geopolitical ambitions of several states with territorial claims in Antarctica, a loose administrative framework evolving out of the 1959 foundational treaty has succeeded in keeping Antarctica demilitarized and free from wider currents of international conflict. These results have been achieved by a group of states, the original twelve treaty partners plus a gradually increasing number of adhering states, resulting in a current arrangement comprised of 39 Consultative States.

The limited number of participating states reflected both the dynamics of self-selection, and a degree of acquiescence by a world community then essentially disinterested. For critics it is questionable whether such a limited number of states can continue to represent the global interest in Antarctica under the differing circumstances that exist in the 1990s when many non-treaty states are sensitive to their absence from such a regime and when environmental public opinion is raising doubts as to whether any sort of statist arrangement can provide satisfactory environmental protection. Indeed, it explains why alternatives to the Antarctic Treaty System (ATS) are being discussed, given the ATS record of remarkable achievement, including responsiveness to criticism. At first glance, even exploring alternatives may seem like a dubious undertaking. Why erode confidence in the most successful experiment in international cooperation in the whole history of international relations?

3.   Gillian Triggs, *The United Nations in Antarctica? A Watching Brief,* **in** THE ANTARCTIC TREATY REGIME 229–33 **(Gillian Triggs ed., 1987).**

Diplomats, scientists and government officials are now more ready to concede that some form of external accommodation must be made [relative to Antarctica's governance]. Assertions of common heritage over Antarctic resources cannot be ignored, if only because of the power of the United Nations (UN) to develop a rival regime creating international discord and rendering unworkable any regime adopted by the Consultative Parties.

The notion that the United Nations should have some role in Antarctica is of long standing. Proposals for United Nations involvement were made after the Second World War and again by India in 1956. It was not, however, until September 1982 that the Malaysian Prime Minister, Dr. Mahathir, raised the issue in a speech at the United Nations General Assembly in which he called for a meeting to "define the problem of these uninhabited lands". He alleged that the Antarctic Treaty **[Basic Document 2.1]** was a neocolonial document which "does not reflect the true feelings of the members of the United Nations". He suggested further that all claimants to Antarctic territorial sovereignty "must give up their claims so that either the United Nations can administer these lands or the present occupants act as trustees for the nations of the world".

In the following year, Malaysia successfully argued for Antarctica to be included on the agenda for the General Assembly. After debate, a resolution was adopted calling upon the Secretary–General to conduct a comprehensive, factual and objective study on Antarctica and to report back in 1984. The Secretary–General submitted his report to the 39th Session in November 1984; however, as delegations had no time to examine the report it was decided to retain the question of Antarctica on the agenda for the 40th Session in 1985. Nonetheless, Malaysia's attempt to seek the establishment of an *ad hoc* United Nation's Committee on Antarctica was unsuccessful.

The Secretary–General reported that states have various views on the question of a common heritage as it applies in Antarctica. Some argue that, because they accept that territorial sovereignty in Antarctica is valid, common heritage has no relevance in Antarctica; others argue that the concept is a logical extension of an international trend established in outer space and the deep seabed; and others take the position that flaws in the Antarctic Treaty system can be adjusted in an evolutionary way to meet the interests of the international community. It is significant that whilst some states consider that the notion of a common heritage applies in Antarctica they also take the position that it can be given effect within an expanded and reformed treaty. Thus there is no cohesive "Third World" view which is necessarily juxtaposed to that of the Treaty Parties, and there is no cohesive or clearly defined block view taken in General Assembly debates.

The Question of Antarctica was debated at the 40th session of the General Assembly and three resolutions were passed.

—One, submitted on behalf of the Group of African States, urges Antarctic Treaty Consultative Parties to exclude the racist apartheid regime of South Africa from participation in meetings of Consultative Parties.

—The second resolution requests the Secretary–General to update and expand the present study on the Question of Antarctica, by specifically addressing the question of availability of information from Consultative Party meetings, the involvement of specialized agencies of the United Nations and intergovernmental organizations in the Antarctic Treaty system and the significance of the United Nations Convention on the Law of the Sea in the Southern Ocean.

—The third resolution invites the Consultative Parties to inform the Secretary General of their negotiations to establish a minerals regime and to confirm that any exploitation of Antarctic resources will ensure international peace and security, protection of the Antarctic environment, non-appropriation and conservation of Antarctic resources and "the international management and equitable sharing of the benefits of such exploitation".

As to the first resolution, the Consultative Parties are unlikely to expel South Africa from meetings. South Africa's role as a Consultative Party remains, for this reason, a focus for conflict both within the United Nations and the Antarctic Treaty system.

As to the second resolution, the Parties noted at the Thirteenth Consultative meeting, the need to ensure freer availability of information about the Antarctic Treaty system. They recommended to their governments that, among other things, an Antarctic Treaty handbook should be maintained as a current compilation of all Recommendations and other actions and that final reports should provide full and accurate records of meetings. Consultative Parties have, nonetheless, maintained confidentiality with regard to negotiations for a minerals regime. Such documents as are available have been leaked and are dated. While the reason for confidentiality can be understood as agreement is more likely in the absence of a public debate upon a draft which merely represents negotiating options, a more politically sensitive approach might have been to demonstrate international responsibility for Antarctica within the Treaty system by consulting openly with interested groups and making working documents available.

The second resolution also considers the role of other organizations in the Antarctic system. It reflects the criticism that the Treaty Parties have operated in virtual isolation from other relevant international bodies. The closest links have been between the Consultative Parties and the Scientific Committee on Antarctic Research (SCAR) of the International Council of Scientific Unions (ICSU)—links which grew from the role the ICSU played in developing cooperation between the Consultative Parties during the International Geophysical Year. The ICSU itself has consultative status with the United Nations Economic and Social Council (ECOSOC) ..., [the] Food and Agricultural Organisation (FAO), and working relations with the International Trade Organisation (ITO), World Health Organisation (WHO), and World Meteorological Organisation (WMO). It is these links which demonstrate that, a wide range of interaction exists between the Antarctic Treaty system and the United Nations and other relevant scientific bodies. The Consultative Parties did not consider this issue at the Thirteenth Consultative meeting. However, the General Assembly resolution on this question some days after this meeting should stimulate some response at the next meeting in 1987.

The second resolution concerns the impact of the 1982 Convention on the Law of the Sea in the Southern Oceans (UNCLOS) [Basic Document 4.20]. As described in Part II, the International Seabed Authority has jurisdiction beyond the limits of national jurisdiction which, on one view, includes the deep seabed surrounding Antarctica. While there may have been a silent agreement at UNCLOS negotiations to exclude the Southern Oceans, the Convention itself makes no exclusion of polar regions nor, indeed, does it make any special provision for the regulation of the Arctic or Antarctic.

The third resolution is simply a request for information. Nonetheless, the preambular clauses demonstrate the central purposes of the resolution. They recall declarations adopted by non-aligned countries in New Delhi in 1983, and again in Luanda in 1985, and by the Organisation of African Unity in Addis Ababa in 1985. The resolution records the fact that no states other than Antarctic Treaty Parties are privy to the minerals negotiations, and recognises that the exploration and use of Antarctica should be in the interests inter alia of promoting international cooperation for the benefit of mankind as a whole. It remains to be seen how much detailed information the Secretary–General will be given, but the General Assembly has made clear the premises upon which any acceptable minerals regime must be based.

As the General Assembly continues its information-gathering on Antarctica the Consultative Parties are attempting to meet criticism of the Treaty system. At the Thirteenth Meeting, the Parties considered the need for environmental impact assessment of scientific activities and for a revised code of conduct for expeditions. They also considered possible additional measures to protect the Antarctic environment particularly where activities are concentrated in certain areas. It was recommended that governments should invite SCAR to undertake a review of waste-disposal aspects of scientific research and logistical activities. It was also recommended that governments should invite SCAR to offer scientific advice on the system of protected areas in Antarctica and on steps that could be taken to improve the availability of scientific data. It was recommended that governments should cooperate where their stations are established in the same areas to avoid adverse environmental effects arising from their activities.

Finally, the Parties decided that the decision to invite Non–Consultative Parties to the Thirteenth Meeting should now be placed on a permanent basis. There was further discussion on the question of inviting other international organizations to appoint observers to Consultative Party meetings, but this matter was left unresolved. It may be doubted whether these discussions and recommendations quite meet the criticism that decision-making under the Antarctic Treaty System is exclusive, undemocratic and discriminating against small states. There is substance to the argument however, that those who are directly engaged in Antarctic activities are, through their experience in Antarctica, well placed to take decisions which affect matters such as scientific programmes and environmental protection. It is also true of the present Consultative Parties that there is no ideological or economic division on North/South or East/West lines within the Treaty framework.

While the negotiations and recommendations of the Thirteenth Consultative meeting demonstrate the "art of the possible", they may be a long way from satisfying the concerns of environmentalists or of political opponents within the General Assembly. It is difficult to speculate upon the future role of the United Nations in Antarctica. When doing so, however, it should be remembered that each of the permanent members of the Security Council is a Consultative Party under the Antarctic Treaty. It has also been noted that the parties represent a high percentage of the world's population and most geographical, economic and ideological interests, with the exception of the states of Africa. Any state may accede to the Antarctic Treaty and its related conventions. These facts suggest that it might be possible to demonstrate responsible management of Antarctica within the Antarctic Treaty system and to defuse demand for universal regulation. For the present, the Secretary General is merely to report, and moves to establish a special UN Committee on Antarctica have thus far been defeated. The UN can be expected to maintain a watching brief on Antarctic activities and to play a closer role in the negotiations upon a minerals regime.

4. Sudhir Chopra, *Antarctica as a Commons Regime: A Conceptual Framework for Cooperation and Coexistence*, in THE ANTARCTIC LEGAL REGIME 163, 169–76 (Christopher Joyner & Sudhir Chopra eds., 1988).

It is much like putting old wine in new bottles when one considers the "commons regime" in terms of modern economic values. Modern concepts are basically derived from Roman law concepts, sometimes with little variation.

Modern concepts include: (1) free access to the commons regime (i.e., *res communis*, which is also described as "inclusive use"), and (2) the common heritage of mankind regime. These two regimes carry different economic connotations and implications. Analysis of the Antarctic Treaty **[Basic Document 2.1]** regime in light of these concepts will facilitate determining the nature of the Antarctic commons regime.

The Commons Regime Under Free Access

According to Russett and Starr, in the modern world, increasingly "more objectives of States *require* group action because of interdependence ... desire for alliances or other aspects of security."[36] They describe the commons regime with free access as a "tragedy of the commons," and prescribe that in contemporary times it is necessary to pool resources and efforts in order to develop an effective management system which will ensure orderly activity and an optimum level of resource consumption from the commons pool. Failure to do so, they argue, will result in chaotic situations where overuse of a finite resource will soon leave the commons pool in a depleted condition, leaving both those who overused the resource, and those who never used it, with nothing at all. In sum, Russett and Starr envision the circumstance where one State voluntarily observes the optimum level of resource exploitation, but others do not, thus leading to a situation in which no State will be encouraged to observe any rules. The result will be complete chaos.

There is no doubt that a regime based on free access to commons resources can prove disastrous. A striking example is the circumpolar seas in the Southern Ocean which suffered species extinctions in the past due to excessive whaling and seal fishing. It is therefore not surprising that a special convention committed to conservation and management of Antarctic marine living resources was concluded in 1980.

The Antarctic Treaty parties established a new resource regime through the Marine Living Resource Convention **[Basic Document 2.4]** to regulate and conserve the resources of the Southern Ocean. Through this instrument, the Treaty regime added a new element to the existing free access commons regime—joint regulation of the commons by a select group of concerned States; consequently, the earlier free access oceans regime was transformed into a controlled and regulated Antarctic marine living resources regime. The new living resource regime can now be defined as a free access commons regime, which allows free access to the marine living resources of the area with regulatory powers to control harvesting in the region, including the high seas south of 60° South Latitude.

It is difficult to assess the position of claimant States regarding the living resources regime. Clearly, it is of interest to both claimants and non-claimants alike that the area covered under this "commons regime" be regulated to ensure that harvesting in the region should not exceed maximum sustainable yield, and that these levels should be monitored on a regular basis. There is no doubt that exclusion of this area from the free access, unregulated commons regime of the high seas in the long term is in the interest of all. Apparent concessions given by claimant States by way of permitting Treaty

36. BRUCE RUSSETT & HARVEY STARR, WORLD
POLITICS: THE MENU FOR CHOICE 514 (1981).

Parties to harvest living resources in areas adjacent to their claims sectors, amount to gradual liquidation of their sovereignty claims.

The minerals regime is quite different from the living resources regime. An early start is assured for technologically advanced States in the Antarctic minerals regime. The high level of technology required to carry out economically viable activity is confined to a few major States. Also, these States are interested in a safe and secured regime to gain access to oil resources. Such an activity is possible only through cooperation and development of a regime which guarantees assured access under a free access regime. The common pool regime thus needs to be regulated in an organized manner with strict control over environmental protection measures. That is exactly the thrust of the ... [1988] Minerals Agreement **[Basic Document 2.7]**. Since the objectives and interests of States are different in this regime, it is natural that rules concerning access to the commons area are also different.

The main difference is in the operative area. All three conventions dealing with the Antarctic define the area covered under their respective regimes as south of 60° South Latitude. But at the same time these conventions have different operative effects, with the result being that the nature of each commons regime presented is changed. The operative disparities are: (1) The Antarctic Treaty regime is a free access regime without recourse to resource activity; (2) The Marine Living Resource regime, as implied by the term marine resources, is mainly operative in the Southern Ocean area; its operative effect lies not on the continent or continental shelf area, although its jurisdiction may; (3) The minerals regime, in contrast to two earlier regimes, will have an operative effect on Antarctica and its continental shelf, although its jurisdiction shall extend far beyond continental shelves into the high seas.

The nature of the minerals regime for Antarctica depends on its operative elements. The commons regime of mineral resources in Antarctica is likely to be extensively regulated to serve two purposes: (1) to protect the fragile environment; and (2) to restrict "free access" to regime members. While the first condition may be a legitimate concern, the second is merely a by-product of the first. In effect, this "commons regime" will have quite restricted access due to the high standards required to operate in the area, thus giving access to only a few States who are technologically-advanced and can afford to engage Antarctic minerals activity. Theoretically, this is a commons regime which prima facie offers free access. But the stringent operative standards required under the regulated regime virtually eliminate the free access to the area.

There is another difference between this minerals regime and the marine living resources regime. While resource exploitation in the latter regime is open to any State irrespective of whether or not the State is a party to the Living Resource Convention, the former regime's "free access" in its widest application is limited to States who become parties to the new convention. It is far easier to satisfy the scientific activity qualification set for the Living Resource Convention than it will be to qualify for the minerals activity.

For claimant States, establishment of a free access commons regime for mineral activity runs contrary to their objectives. This regime would further dilute their claims of sovereignty and undercut protection of those claims while they remained frozen under Article IV of the [Antarctic] Treaty. For non-claimant States, this regime is more palatable since in theory it gives "free access" to the commons for all nonclaimant Treaty parties. Their position is further secured because it is a regulated regime developed through cooperation in an atmosphere of political interdependence.

The Antarctic "commons regime" denies free access to non-parties of the regime. By increasing the number of member States in the Treaty system, Treaty powers have strengthened their resource regimes. What we have now is a regime effectively insulated from the rest of the world—one which will enjoy an exclusive pool of commons resources by excluding the rest of the world. And within this regime only a privileged few with means and technology will have real access to the pool of commons. Losers in this regime are the less developed countries, irrespective of whether they are within or outside the Treaty system.

A free access "commons regime" in Antarctica under the present system is therefore not a commons regime in effect, but a structure to avoid outside pressures with the support of other Treaty parties. In this complicated setup, the Treaty regime at once protects the interests of technologically advanced States while the development of a regulated resource further assures them of security and cooperation. What we see here is genuine interdependence between claimant States and other Treaty parties. This is not an ideal regime from the perspective of the vast majority of States, for it does not fulfill the dream of a true "commons regime." At best, this is a regional regime serving the interests of a select few.

The commons regime, as envisioned under the common heritage of mankind (CHM) principle, is very different from the free access regime. Objectives of the CHM regime as elaborated by Arvid Pardo are: (1) the areas designated as common heritage shall not be appropriated; (2) the use of the area and resources which fall under the common heritage shall be carried out by a common management system; (3) there shall be active and equitable sharing of benefits derived from the exploitation of the common heritage area and resources; (4) the area shall be reserved for future generations (environmental protection); and (5) the area shall be used for peaceful purposes.[37]

As discussed by Pardo and Borgese, these elements are based on economic objectives. Through them, a functional approach is envisioned to achieve the equitable sharing of the common heritage of mankind. This approach assures that the area and its resources, which belong to no one, shall be used only in the interest of all peoples by designating them to be the common heritage of mankind.

The first element of CHM requires that neither the area nor its resources shall be appropriated. The theory of non-appropriation holds that the area and its resources shall not be annexed, by way of sovereignty, or sovereign rights, or through the free access regime of the commons. This raises an obligation on the part of those States active in the area not to appropriate

37. Arvid Pardo & Elisabeth Borgese, New International Economic Order and the Law of the Sea 10 (1976); Christopher Joyner, *Antarctica and the Common Heritage of Mankind*, 79 Am. Soc. Int'l L. Proc. 62 (1985); ___, *Legal Implications of the Concept of Common Heritage of Mankind*, 35 I.C.L.Q. 190 (1986).

what is common to all. Resource exploitation or use of the area should take place under a common management system.

Under the CHM doctrine, the Antarctica regime would be expected to completely forgo sovereignty claims and any basis for those claims. Since sovereignty claims are nonoperative under the Antarctic Treaty the condition that the ownership rights be negated is satisfied in part. Under the Treaty system, Antarctica is not owned by anyone and is managed jointly by the Treaty parties. While active sovereignty or ownership rights are absent from the Antarctic Treaty system, rights for use and resource exploitation have been separately provided for under the appendage resource regimes. The requirement that resources not be appropriated is not protected any more. The Antarctic Treaty system has been developing more along the lines of a free access commons regime than a regime based on ownership rights—a fact which makes it easier to appropriate the resources without appropriating the area.

The second element of the CHM regime requires that there should be a common management system. This element is the basis of the CHM doctrine, as it provides the framework through which the goal of common sharing can be achieved. It is through a common management system that a truly international regime can be developed. An international structure with universal participation to assure that interests of all mankind shall be protected is essential. Through this element a global democratic decision-making process is envisioned; common management is essential, for without it exploitation of resources would be chaotic.

Both the Antarctic Treaty and the resource regimes developed under the Treaty system provide for common management. However, this conception of common management is far from the universal participation required under a CHM regime. Although the Antarctic Treaty and its attendant regimes can be joined by acceding to the appropriate treaty, mere accession does not guarantee States Consultative Party status. For a State to acquire such a status, it must demonstrate through substantial activity its interest in Antarctica. It is this qualification clause which runs contrary to the spirit of the CHM doctrine. A CHM regime is designed for universal participation; restrictions or qualifications based on selective economic criteria deny economically weaker States an equal opportunity to participate. Therefore, though a common management system has been developed to regulate the Antarctic regimes, the presence of a qualification clause implies that the common management system is available to only a few States.

There is no room for equitable sharing, except for minimal contribution to exploitation.... Equitable sharing of economic benefits is in sharp contrast to the "free access" regimes. A commons regime based on equitable sharing does not permit appropriation of benefits by the exploiter. Antarctic resource regimes are in sharp conflict with this objective of the CHM regime. The Antarctic regime is based on free access and free enjoyment under a regulated system. There is no room for equitable sharing, except for minimal contribution to effectuate the regulatory machinery.

The fourth element requires that the area and its resources should be reserved for future generations. This objective envisions a rational system of resource exploration which will save the area and its resources from depletion and contamination. Environmental protection by way of pollution control and conservation is expected. Unless environmental protection is assured, the area and its resources are unlikely to be available to future generations. Antarctic resource regimes are quite aware of these concerns. Both regimes dealing with resources have elaborate provisions for pollution control as well as conservation.

Lastly, the objective of peaceful use of the area is common in both the CHM regime and the Antarctica regime. Perhaps the Antarctica regime is the only regime in the world which has effectively upheld this objective.

There is a sharp difference between a CHM regime and the present Antarctic Treaty regime. The latter is based on participation of a select group of States, and resource exploitation on the basis of free access[;] the CHM regime is structured on non-appropriation of resources and equitable sharing of proceeds.

Antarctica as an International Regime: a Framework for Cooperation and Coexistence

Development of an International Space Regime Under the Antarctic Treaty System

The main characteristics of the Antarctic Treaty regime are: freedom of scientific research and investigation; international cooperation; the banning of nuclear explosions and disposal of radioactive waste material; inspection of all bases by any Treaty party; denial of exclusive rights and interests to resources; common interest in conservation and environmental protection; and common interest to use the area under the Treaty regime for peaceful purposes only. These principles are clearly not applicable to any sovereign regime; rather they are more akin to international space regimes.

These principles, which were primarily designed to resolve the stalemate between claimant States and the conflict between claimant and non-claimant States, have over the years established themselves as sound, workable notions of international law. Acceptance by claimant States of principles clearly alien to national sovereignty or jurisdictional control establishes a de facto international regime. Despite efforts of contracting parties to avoid giving the clout of an international space regime to Antarctica, in practice, acceptance of these principles by the Treaty parties has reinforced the effectiveness of these norms.

Yet the restriction on attaining Consultative Party status in the Antarctic Treaty continues to be an unresolved issue. And, because of restricted membership, it is perhaps difficult to classify the Antarctica regime as simply another international space regime. Nevertheless, the recent change in the attitude of Antarctic Treaty Consultative parties to accept new members, though cautiously, is welcomed. It is definitely a step towards gradual internationalization. However, such a change in policy does not seem to be a willing one; rather it has been developed in order to protect the Antarctica regime from external pressures. The fact that liberalization of attitudes by the ATCPS will accommodate only a few cautiously selected new States as full members, to secure political gains, needs to be examined carefully. Does this situation mean that only a few States, those States who have shown interest in Antarctica by conducting scientific activity, will be selected on the basis of their political weight in international political blocs? Or will any State which qualifies under scientific criteria be welcomed? These are questions which can only be answered in the future. The present trend seems to favor only those States which can benefit and help in the survival of the Antarctic regime by not pursuing this issue seriously in other international forums. Perhaps it might not be wrong to suggest that if the international community wants global or near global participation in Antarctic affairs, it will have to continue to raise the Antarctic issue in every possible international forum.

A Framework for Cooperation and Coexistence

It is evident that the Antarctica regime differs from the CHM regime of the seabed and the free access regime of the high seas. It is unique in the sense that it does not even resemble traditional regimes of *res communis* or *res nullis*. A drastic change in its basic nature seems unlikely. However, some adjustment to accommodate the growing pressure of the world community is expected. How much, and what exactly will be conceded by the Treaty system, depends on the unity among those States seeking changes. An approach of confrontation is less likely to work in the case of Antarctica—it is not the Law of the Sea Conference. This distinction becomes clear when one realizes that the Law of the Sea Conference negotiated every conceivable aspect of ocean law from scratch. In the case of Antarctica, there is no conference to structure a new regime, and it appears highly unlikely that a regime which has functioned relatively well will be dismantled to facilitate placing the scrambled situation on the United Nations agenda. A more pragmatic approach would be to concede those issues which are impossible to renegotiate. Endorsement of certain basic principles of the Treaty by the countries seeking change also will help in confidence building. Since much of the current tension between Antarctic treaty powers and several outside states has been caused by resource regimes, it would seem most appropriate to seek moderate change pertaining to resource activity and its consequences. A framework for a compromise regime should include both what ought to be preserved and what ought to be changed.

Discussion Notes/Questions

1. As is evident from the foregoing readings, Antarctica's delicate ecosystem is much in need of enlightened and effective planning, management, and policing. Reports such as Kriwoken's (in Reading 12, *supra*), for example, documenting the impact of existing Antarctic stations, highlight this need especially vividly. Even states that are party to instruments that specifically address environmental protection (Australia in Kriwoken's report) cannot be relied upon to safeguard the Antarctic environment in relatively unobtrusive involvements let alone in circumstances where resource exploitation *per se* may be directly undertaken.

One solution is the environmental impact assessments (EIAs) endorsed by article 4 of the 1988 Convention for the Regulation of Antarctic Mineral Resource Activities (CRAMRA) [**Basic Document 2.7**] and article 8 and Annex I of the 1991 Protocol on Environmental Protection to the Antarctic Treaty [**Basic Document 2.9**]. The EIAs provided for in the 1991 Protocol, for example, relate to all stages of an activity (including decommissioning of a project) and must address alternatives and potential cumulative impacts if they are more than "minor or transitory." There is some provision for comment by the public, the

Committee for Environmental Protection (CEP), and the Antarctic Treaty Consultative Meetings (ATCM).

The issue of whether and, if so, how the CEP should consider Comprehensive Environmental Evaluations (CEEs) was raised at the CEP during the Antarctic Treaty Consultative Meeting (ATCM XXII) held in Norway, May 25—June 5, 1998. It arose during a discussion on the process for handling a United States CEE on a project to rebuild South Pole Station. This was the first CEE to come before the Committee following the ratification of the 1991 Protocol. There were major differences of opinion between the United States and almost all other Parties about the role of the CEP. The US maintained that the CEP's role was to advise on procedure only and not on issues of substance. The US argued that the CEP was not obliged to review every draft CEE submitted to the parties. Other delegations argued that the Protocol clearly instructed the CEP, as the committee of experts, to provide comprehensive advice to the ATCM and that this necessarily involved reviewing every CEE. As a result of this debate there was no substantive discussion on the CEE for the South Pole Rebuild and the Committee did not provide advice to the ATCM on the CEE.

Other weaknesses of the scheme include the discretion left to countries promoting the activity. While requirements for publicity and exchange of documents may induce enlightened practices to some extent (such publicity is the ultimate sanction where an activity breaches objectives and principles), vested interests are likely to influence decisions as to what constitutes a "minor or transitory impact."

Another weakness is represented by the overlap of interests where a governmental agency is responsible for both the EIA and for promoting the proposed activity. There also is the problem of private operations whose management is left largely to individual countries.

In addition, the 1991 Protocol makes exceptions for emergencies involving human safety or life, ships, aircraft, high value equipment, or protection of the environment. How might some of these gaps be closed by modifications to the EIA provisions? In early 1993, in *Environmental Defense Fund v. National Science Foundation*, 986 F.2d 528 (D.C.Cir.1993), reversing *Environmental Defense Fund v. Massey*, 772 F.Supp. 1296 (D.D.C. 1991), a suit brought by the United States government during the administration of President George Bush, the United States Circuit Court of Appeals for the District of Columbia, ruled that the National Environmental Policy Act, which requires EIAs for all U.S. government projects, applied to two incinerators the U.S. National Science Foundation want to build in Antarctica. Recently elected President Bill Clinton declined to appeal the ruling. What is the significance of this precedent? How might former President Bush's administration have responded?

2. The problem of ensuring the enlightened and effective planning, management, and policing of Antarctica's delicate ecosystem is further complicated by the encouragement given to scientific research under the existing legal regime for Antarctica. The 1991 Protocol on Environmental Protection to the Antarctic Treaty [**Basic Document 2.9**], for example, which prohibits mineral activities generally, authorizes them for scientific research purposes.

A similar deference may be found in Article VII of the International Convention for the Regulation of Whaling [**Basic Document 6.2**], which provides that state parties may grant permits to catch whales for the purpose of scientific research notwithstanding anything contained within the Convention to the contrary. Following the adoption of a whaling moratorium in 1982, this exception appears to have become an avenue for abuse, as suggested by the increase in permit applications corresponding directly to the time when the moratorium took effect. International pressure has limited the abuse, but there are no legally binding restraints.

This whaling example raises the issue of possible abuse of scientific exceptions to mining in Antarctica; mineral prospecting could conceivably occur under the veil of scientific research. Would such abuse breach other obligations agreed to? How could such conflicts be resolved? What sorts of regulatory safeguards might be instituted to deal with the problem? To what extent would abuse of the research exception affect the suggestion that the mining prohibition might gain customary law status after fifty years? *See, e.g.,* S. Andresen, *Science and Politics in the International Management of Whales,* 13 Marine Pol'y 99 (1989); P. Birnie, *International Legal Issues in the Management and Protection of the Whale: A Review of Four Decades,* 29 N.R.J. 903 (1989).

3.   Yet another example of the problem of enlightened and effective planning, management, and policing of Antarctica's delicate ecosystem is found in the fact that none of the legal instruments pertaining to Antarctica prohibit the use of nuclear power.

In the 1960s, the United States was the first to install nuclear equipment in Antarctica, a 1.8 megawatt pressurized water reactor located at the McMurdo base as an experiment with cheaper forms of power production. Production began in 1962 and continued for ten years. According to the United States, the only serious problem that arose during this ten-year period was a fire caused by the hydrogen by-product of the reactor. Greenpeace International contested these claims, contending instead that the ten-year period was characterized by shutdowns, fire damage, and radiation leakages.

In 1972 a U.S. Navy cost-effectiveness study concluded that it was economically unjustified to overhaul and upgrade the power plant. Subsequently, the plant was closed down and demolished. Greenpeace claims that the demolition cost $1 million and that the reactor and large quantities of radioactive earth and rocks had to be shipped back to the United States. It was not until May 1979 that the site was released for unrestricted use and declared to be "decontaminated to levels as low as reasonably achievable."

See John May, *The Greenpeace Book of Antarctica: A New View of the Seventh Continent* (1989).

4.   There are a number of connections between the management of Antarctica and the problem of ozone depletion.

First, Antarctica was the scientific laboratory in which discoveries were made about dramatic decreases in the ozone layer, which in turn led to rapid progress in the international legal regime now governing ozone depletion. As an example, the Montreal Protocol [**Basic Document 3.18**] which resulted from these findings adjust the chlorofluorocarbon (CFC) control measures from a 20% reduction from 1986 levels by the year 1994 and 50% by 1999, to a 50% reduction by 1995 for developed nations, 85% by 1997, and a total phase-out by the year 2000. *See* J. Mintz, *Progress Toward a Healthy Sky,* 16 Yale J. Int'l L. 571 (1991).

Second, the ozone hole that appears over Antarctica poses great danger to the delicate Antarctic ecosystem. The increase in ultraviolet radiation could mean a decrease in species diversity such that the whole Antarctic food chain could be affected. *See* M. Voyteck, *Addressing the Biological Effects of Decreased Ozone on the Antarctic Environment,* 19 Ambio 52 (1990). In working to decrease the emission of ozone-depleting substances, the legal regime governing such emissions works indirectly to protect the Antarctica environment.

A more tenuous link is made, however, between the relative success of the legal regime governing ozone depletion and a future solution for Antarctica management. The success of the ozone regime is attributable largely to an understanding of the need to account for the concerns of the developing countries (which, to date, are not primarily responsible for CFC emissions). The London Amendments, for example, establish a multilateral fund and system of technological transfer for the developing countries. Disagreement over an Antarctic management regime, on the other hand, stems at least in part from a concern that only some countries will benefit. Like the ozone problem, Antarctica involves potential profit-making by individual nations with impacts on the environment, but unlike the ozone problem it is further complicated by competing sovereignty claims.

There is good reason to suggest that representatives from the developed world should heed their own (ozone) example in dealing with Antarctica. The assumption is that if the benefits of exploitation are widely shared, there is greater chance that crucial environmental protection concerns will be widely shared as well. Are there inherent differences between ozone and Antarctica which are significant relative to legal regulation? Inherent commonalities?

For further discussion concerning ozone depletion, *see* Problem 7–2 ("Nueva Granada Versus the Ozone Layer") in Chapter 7, *infra*.

5. The matter of policing Antarctica is addressed explicitly by the Antarctic Treaty in its provisions for on-site inspections by the Treaty parties. It is commonly recognized, however, that such monitoring does not take place on any great scale. There appears to be an unspoken policy that recognizes the mutual benefits of non-exercise of inspection provisions. There also is the problem of non-Treaty parties. While non-Treaty parties cannot claim invasion of sovereign territory (a claim even Treaty parties cannot sustain), neither do they grant consent for inspection in the way that the Treaty parties do.

As indicated in the above readings, Greenpeace International acted unofficially to fill the Antarctic inspection gap from 1985 until it relinquished this role in 1992. Accordingly, it is now pertinent to consider who can best fulfil this important policing function. While the Antarctic Treaty System has been congratulated for its relatively conflict-free management, if this is to the detriment of environmental integrity a more internationalized intrusion in the form of monitoring and enforcement is arguably necessary. What body should serve this function? Is this an ideal situation for United Nations involvement? Could U.N. participation in Antarctica form part of a wider "environmental police force"? How much reliance can be placed on a body such as the Committee for Environmental Protection, provided for in the 1991 Protocol to The Antarctic Treaty on Environmental Protection [**Basic Document 2.9**]? Bear in mind that, during negotiations for the Minerals Convention [**Basic Document 2.7**], the Consultative Parties consistently rejected proposals for an independent Antarctic protection agency to play a monitoring role. Perhaps the relative independence of NGOs such as Greenpeace International renders them the only effective candidates. But, if so, who should fund them, and under what authority?

6. Like Antarctica, the Arctic region has its share of sovereignty problems, albeit of a different sort. At least seven Arctic Ocean boundary disputes remain unresolved. Canada, for example, has formally claimed complete sovereignty over its waters while the United States, primarily for strategic military reasons,

maintains that the Northwest Passage is an international strait subject to the right of transit passage.

Despite the strategic military importance of the Arctic region, however, commentators have begun to record an increase in regional cooperation born of a growing awareness of Arctic ecosystem realities. The Arctic region, like Antarctica, plays a critical role in controlling global climate. Also, it offers in substantial proportions the hydrocarbon and mineral resources thought to exist in Antarctica. Additionally, circumpolar nations share environmental concerns in the form of wind, weather patterns, and wildlife, and the potential melting of the polar ice pack caused by the greenhouse effect is yet a further uniting concern. Accordingly, Arctic-rim scientists have begun recently to explore the need for a formal scientific cooperation arrangement similar to Antarctica's Scientific Committee on Antarctic Research (SCAR). *See* J. Vanderzwaag, et al., *Towards Regional Ocean Management in the Arctic: From Co-existence to Cooperation*, 37 U.N.B.L.J. 1 (1988).

Thus, while Antarctic history has been lauded for its relative harmony, increased Arctic cooperation perhaps provides lessons for Antarctica. The above example suggests that increased awareness of the systemic nature of environmental problems creates a more holistic perception of the area and therefore how it should be managed. Historical examples (e.g., driftnet fishing) show that public awareness of environmental issues can translate well into political awareness and legal action. How might such awareness be cultivated and exploited with respect to effective Antarctic management?

7. The principle of the "common heritage of mankind" (CHM), which is central to a proper understanding of Antarctica and its relation to the rest of the planet, raises interesting conceptual issues for international environmental law. The undivided rights suggested by the notion of "common," for example, could refer to ownership rights or, alternatively, to user rights. "Heritage" could imply transmission to future generations, in which case some regulation would be required to prevent resource destruction, or it could be understood merely to imply that the resource has been handed down from past generations. Further still, it could be taken to suggest a more intrinsic value, akin to the idea of treasure.

There is some move to replace the CHM principle with, the perhaps more appropriately named, "common concern of mankind". But the inclusion of "mankind" in both formulations carries the obvious problem of "man-made" gender-exclusive language. Also, there is the issue of whether "mankind" can in fact be the subject of international law, a domain traditionally reserved for States. Does it mean the collectivity of all people and, if so, who can legitimately speak for it?

As noted in the above readings, there is some general consensus as to the meaning of CHM. However, it should not be forgotten that, during negotiations for the 1982 Law of the Sea (LOS) Convention **[Basic Document 4.20]** relative to the deep sea-bed, there was much dispute between developed and developing countries as to how it should be interpreted.

In Antarctica, where, as noted, the CHM principle has been said to be applicable, there is the additional problem of sovereignty claims. Does the historical example of the LOS Convention and Antarctica's additional complexities mean that the CHM principle is best left out of proposed management regimes such as those suggested for the deep sea-bed or Antarctica?

8. *Bibliographical Note.* For further discussion concerning the principal themes addressed in this problem, consult the following additional specialized materials:

a. The Antarctic Environment in General

I. Anderson, *Oil and Geological Chaos Found off Antarctica,* 106 New Scientist 9 (1985); F. Auburn, *The Antarctic Environment,* 1981 Y. B. World Aff. 248 (1981); D. Drewry, *The Antarctic Physical Environment, in* The Antarctic Treaty Regime: Law, Environment and Resources 6 (G. Triggs ed., 1987); A. Hemmings, *Antarctica in Transition* 284 Forest and Bird 38 (1997); C. Joyner, Antarctica and the Law of the Sea (1992); Antarctic Ecology (R. Laws ed., 1984); ___, *Scientific Opportunities in the Antarctic, in* The Antarctic Treaty Regime: Law, Environment and Resources 28 (G. Triggs ed., 1987); ___, *Science as an Antarctic Resource, in* The Future of Antarctica: Exploitation Versus Preservation 8 (G. Cooke ed., 1990); J. May, The Greenpeace Book of Antarctica: A New View of the Seventh Continent (1989); J. Stewart, Antarctica: An Encyclopedia (1990); R. Willan & D. Drewry, *The Mineral Resource Potential of Antarctica: Geological Realities, in* The Future of Antarctica: Exploitation Versus Preservation 25 (G. Cooke ed., 1990).

b. Antarctica Treaty System in General

Antarctic Challenge: Proceedings of an Interdisciplinary Symposium, June 22–24, 1983 (R. Wolfrum ed., 1984); Antarctic Challenge II: Proceedings of an Interdisciplinary Symposium, Sept. 17–21, 1985 (R. Wolfrum ed., 1986); Antarctic Politics and Marine Resources: Critical Choices for the 1980s (L. Alexander & L. Carter eds., 1985); Antarctic Resources Policy (F. Orrego Vicuña ed., 1983); *Antarctic Treaty: XX Consultative Meeting* 26 Env't Pol'y & L. 160 (1996); F. Auburn, Antarctic Law and Politics (1982); ___, *Consultative Status under the Antarctic Treaty,* 28 I.C.L.Q. 514 (1979); J. Barcelo, *The International Legal Regime for Antarctica,* 19 Cornell Int'l L. J. 163 (1986); P. Beck, The International Politics of Antarctica 1986); P. Bergin, *Antarctica, the Antarctic Treaty Regime, and Legal and Geopolitical Implications of Natural Resource Exploration and Exploitation,* 4 Fl. Int'l L. J. 1 (1988); P. Birnie, *The Antarctic Regime and Third States, in* Antarctic Challenge II, at 239 (R. Wolfrum ed., 1986); B. Boczek, *The Soviet Union and the Antarctic Regime,* 78 A.J.I.L. 834 (1984); B. Boleslaw, *Specially Protected Areas as an Instrument for the Conservation of the Antarctic Nature, in* Antarctic Challenge II, at 65 (R. Wolfrum ed., 1986); W. Bonner & D. Walton, Key Environments: Antarctica (1985); K. Brennan, *Criteria for Access to the Resources of Antarctica: Alternatives, Procedures and Experience Applicable, in* Antarctic Resources Policy 217 (F. Orrego Vicuña ed., 1983); P. Bruckner, *The Antarctic Treaty System from the Perspective of a Non–Consultative Party to the Antarctic Treaty, in* U.S. Polar Research Board, Antarctic Treaty System: An Assessment 315 (1986); *Consultative Parties Focus on Environment, Tourism, and the Treaty System at 18th Meeting,* 29 Antarctic J. of U.S. 4 (1994); S. Eilers, *Antarctica Adjourned? The U.N. Deliberations on Antarctica,* 19 Int'l Lawyer 1309 (1985); L. Elliott, Continuity and Change in Cooperative International Regimes: the Politics of the Recent EnvironmentDebate in Antarctica (1991); V. Fuchs, *Antarctica: its History and Development, in* Antarctic Resources Policy 13 (F. Orrego Vicuña ed., 1983); V. Golitsyn, Antarctica: The International Law Regime (1983); M. Holdgate, *Environmental Factors in the Development of Antarctica, in* Antarctic Resources Policy 77 (F. Orrego Vicuña ed., 1983); International Law for Antarctica (F. Francioni & T. Scovazzi eds., 1996); C. Joyner, *Legal Implications of the*

Concept of the Common Heritage of Mankind, 35 I.C.L.Q. 190 (1986); ___, *Japan and the Antarctic Treaty System,* 16 Ecology L. Q. 155 (1989); L. Kimball, *The Role of Non–Governmental Organizations in Antarctic Affairs, in* The Antarctic Legal Regime 33 (C. Joyner & S. Chopra eds., 1988); R. McColloch, *Recent Developments: Protocol on Environmental Protection To the Antarctic Treaty,* 22 Ga. J.Int'l & Comp. L. 211 (1992); J. Myhre, The Antarctic Treaty System: Politics, Law, and Diplomacy (1986); F. Orrego Vicuña, Antarctic Mineral Exploitation—The Emerging Legal Framework (1988); M. Peterson, Managing the Frozen South: The Creation and Evolution of the Antarctic Treaty System (1988); P. Quigg, A Pole Apart: The Emerging Issue of Antarctica (1983); C. Redgwell, *Antarctica,* 39 I.C.L.Q. 474 (1990); ___, *Antarctica,* 40 I.C.L.Q. 976 (1991); D. Rothwell, *The Antarctic Treaty: 1961–1991 and Beyond,* 14 Sydney L. Rev. 62 (1992); J. Rowland, *The Treaty Regime and the Politics of the Consultative Parties, in* The Antarctic Legal Regime 11 (C. Joyner & S. Chopra eds., 1988); Y. Rybakov, *Juridical Nature of the 1959 Treaty System, in* U.S. Polar Research Board, Antarctic Treaty System: An Assessment 33 (1986); E. Sahurie, The International Law of Antarctica (1992); Governing the Antarctic: The Effectiveness and Legitimacy of the Antarctic Treaty System (O. Schram Stokke & D. Vidas, eds., 1996); R. Scully, *The Antarctic System: Overview and Analysis, in* Antarctic Politics and Marine Resources: Critical Choices for the 1980s 3 (L. Alexander & C. Hanson Lynne eds. 1985); ___, *The Evolution of the Antarctic Treaty System—The Institutional Perspective, in* U.S. Polar Research Board, Antarctic Treaty System: An Assessment 391 (1986); ___, *Institutionalisation of the Antarctic Treaty Regime, in* Antarctic Challenge 283 (R. Wolfrum ed., 1986); D. Shapley, The Seventh Continent: Antarctica in a Resource Age (1985); K. Shusterich, *The Antarctic Treaty System: History, Substance, and Speculation,* 39 Int'l J. 800 (1984); S. Slevich, Antarctica in the Modern World (1985); R. Thakur & H. Gold, *The Antarctic Treaty Regime: Exclusive Preserve or Common Heritage?,* 32 Foreign Aff. Rep. 169 (1983); The Antarctic Legal Regime (C. Joyner & S. Chopra eds., 1988); The Antarctic Treaty Regime: Law, Environment and Resources (G. Triggs ed., 1987); The Antarctic Treaty System in World Politics (A. Jorgensen–Dahl & W. Ostreng eds., 1991); The Future of Antarctica: Exploitation versus Preservation (G. Cook ed., 1990); *The International Legal Regime for Antarctica: A Symposium,* 19 Cornell Int'l L. J. 155 (1986); *The New Nationalism and the Use of Common Spaces* (J. Charney ed., 1982); G. Triggs, *The Antarctic Treaty Regime: A Workable Compromise or a "Purgatory of Ambiguity"?,* 17 Case W. Res. J. of Int'l L. 165 (1985); A. Watts, *The Antarctic Treaty as a Conflict Resolution Mechanism, in* U.S. Polar Research Board, Antarctic Treaty System: An Assessment 65 (1986); ___, *Liability for Activities in Antarctica—Who Pays the Bill to Whom, in* Antarctic Challenge II, at 147 (R. Wolfrum ed., 1986); U.S. Polar Research Board, Antarctic Treaty System: An Assessment (1986); R. Woolcott, *The Interaction between the Antarctic Treaty System and the United Nations System, in* U.S. Polar Research Board, Antarctica Treaty System: An Assessment 375 (1986).

c.   The Antarctic Treaty Regime: Jurisdiction

Auckland District Law Society, *How Strong Is New Zealand's Claim to the Ross Dependency,* N.Z.L.J. 76 (1980); D. Bederman, *Exploring the Foreign Country Exception: Federal Tort Claims in Antarctica,* 21 Vand. J. Trans. L. 731 (1988); R. Bilder, *The Present Legal and Political Situation in Antarctica, in* The New Nationalism and the Use of Common Spaces 167 (J. Charney ed., 1982); B. Carl, *The Need for a Private International Law Regime in Antarctica, in* The Antarctic Legal Regime 65 (C. Joyner & S. Chopra eds., 1988); B. Conforti, *Territorial Claims in Antarctica: a Modern Way to Deal with an Old Problem,* 19 Cornell Int'l

L. J. 249 (1986); H. Fox, *The Relevance of Antarctica to the Lawyer, in* The Antarctic Treaty Regime: Law, Environment and Resources 77 (G. Triggs ed., 1987); D. Hinkley, *Protecting American Interests in Antarctica: the Territorial Claims Dilemma,* 39 Naval L. Rev. 43 (1990); J. W. Huber, *NEPA's extraterritorial application in Antarctica* 14 J. Energy Nat. Resources & Envtl. L. 193 (1994); E. Johnson, *Quick, Before it Melts: Towards a Resolution of the Jurisdictional Morass in Antarctica,* 10 Cornell Int'l L. J. 173 (1976); C. Joyner, *The United States and Antarctica: Rethinking the Interplay of Law and Interests,* 20 Cornell Int'l L. J. 65 (1987); E. Luard, *Who Owns the Antarctic?,* Foreign Aff. 1174 (Summer 1984); T. Parriott, *Territorial Claims in Antarctica: Will the United States be Left Out in the Cold?,* 22 Stanford J. Int'l L. 67 (1986); R. Scott, *Protecting United States' Interests in Antarctica,* 26 San Diego L. Rev. 575 (1989); S. Scott, *The Geopolitical Organization of Antarctica, 1900–1961: The Case for a Revisionist Analysis* 11 Austl. J. L. & Soc'y 113 (1995); B. Simma, *The Antarctic Treaty as a Treaty Providing for an "Objective Regime,"* 19 Cornell Int'l L. J. 189 (1986); G. Triggs, International Law and Australian Sovereignty in Antarctica (1986); ———, *The Antarctic Treaty System: Some Jurisdictional Problems, in* The Antarctic Treaty Regime: Law, Environment and Resources 88 (G. Triggs ed., 1987); R. Trolle—Anderson, *The Antarctic Scene: Legal and Political Facts, in* The Antarctic Treaty Regime: Law, Environment and Resources 57 (G. Triggs ed., 1987).

d.   Antarctica and the Law of the Sea

D.   Cheever, Antarctica and the Exclusive Economic Zone (Int'l Stud. Ass'n, 1983); R. Harris, *The Antarctic Regime and the Law of the Sea Convention: an Australian View,* 21 V.J.I.L. 727 (1981); C. Joyner, *Exclusive Economic Zone and Antarctica,* 21 V.J.I.L. 691 (1981); ———, *Antarctica and the Law of the Sea: Rethinking the Current Legal Dilemmas,* 18 San Diego L. Rev. 415 (1981); ———, *Antarctica and the Law of the Sea: An Introductory Overview,* 13 Ocean Dev. & Int'l L. 277 (1983); ———, Antarctica and the Law of the Sea (1992); M. C. Kennicutt et al, *Human Contamination of the Marine Environment—Arthur Harbor and McMurdo Sound Antarctica* 29 Envtl. Sci. & Tech. 1279 (1995); J. Kindt, *Ice Covered Areas and the Law of the Sea: Issues Involving Resource Exploitation and the Antarctic Environment,* 14 Brooklyn J. Int'l L. 27 (1988); F. Orrego Vicuña, *The Application of the Law of the Sea and the Exclusive Economic Zone to the Antarctic Continent, in* Antarctic Resources Policy 243 (F. Orrego Vicuña ed., 1983); ———, *The Law of the Sea and the Antarctic Treaty System: New Approaches to Offshore Jurisdiction, in* The Antarctic Legal Regime 97 (C. Joyner & S. Chopra eds., 1988); B. Oxman, *Antarctica and the New Law of the Sea,* 19 Cornell Int'l L. J. 211 (1986); M. Peterson, *Antarctic Implications of the New Law of the Sea,* 16 Ocean Dev. & Int'l L. 137 (1986); D. R. Rothwell, *A Maritime Analysis of Conflicting International Law Regimes in Antarctica and the Southern Ocean* 15 Austl. Y.B. Int'l. L. 155 (1994); A. van der Essen, *The Application of the Law of the Sea to the Antarctic Continent, in* Antarctic Resources Policy 231 (F. Orrego Vicuña ed., 1983); A. Young, *Antarctic Resource Jurisdiction and the Law of the Sea: a Question of Compromise,* 11 Brooklyn J. Int'l L. 45 (1985).

e.   Management and Exploitation of Mineral Resources

F.   Auburn, *Legal Implications of Petroleum Resources of the Antarctic Continental Shelf,* 1 Ocean Y.B. 500 (1978); ———, *Antarctic Minerals and the Third World,* Fram: J. of Polar Stud. 201 (Winter 1984); R. Bentham, *Antarctica: A Minerals Regime,* 8 J. Energy & Natural Resources L. 120 (1990); H. Burmester,

Liability for Damage From Antarctic Mineral Resource Activities, 29 V.J.I.L. 621 (1989); J. Burgess, *Comprehensive Environmental Protection of the Antarctic: New Approaches for New Times, in* The Future of Antarctica: Exploitation versus Preservation 53 (G. Cook ed., 1990); S. Burton, *New Stresses on the Antarctic Treaty: Toward International Legal Institutions Governing Antarctic Resources,* 65 Va. L. Rev. 421 (1979); J. Carroll, *Of Icebergs, Oil Wells, and Treaties: Hydrocarbon Exploitation Offshore Antarctica,* 19 Stanford J. Int'l L. 201 (1983); J. Charney, *The Future Strategies for an Antarctic Mineral Resource Regime—Can the Environment Be Protected, in* The New Nationalism and the Use of Common Spaces 206 (J. Charney ed., 1982); S. Chopra, R. Scully, C. Beeby, R. Hayton, & C. Joyner, *The Antarctic Minerals Agreement: Remarks,* 83 Proceed. Am Soc'y Int'l L. 204 (1989); D. Cook Waller, *Death of a Treaty: the Decline and Fall of the Antarctic Minerals Convention,* 22 Vand. J. Transnat'l L. 631 (1989); A. Davis, *Protecting Antarctica: Will a Minerals Agreement Guard the Door or Open the Door to Commercial Exploitation?,* 23 George Wash. J. Int'l L. Econ. 733 (1990); C. Davis, *Hiding our Heads in the Snow: the Dilemma of Non-living Resources in Antarctica,* 15 Syracuse J. Int'l L. & Commerce 431 (1989); F. Francioni, *Legal Aspects of Mineral Exploitation in Antarctica,* 19 Cornell Int'l L. J. 163 (1986); R. Friedheim & T. Akaha, *Antarctic Resources and International Law: Japan, the United States, and the Future of Antarctica,* 16 Ecology L. Q. 119 (1989); J. Heap, *The Political Case for the Minerals Convention, in* The Future of Antarctica: Exploitation versus Preservation 44 (G. Cook ed., 1990); B. Heim, *Exploring the Last Frontiers for Mineral Resources: A Comparison of International Law Regarding the Deep Seabed, Outer Space, and Antarctica,* 23 Vand. J.Transnat'l L. 819 (1990); I. Hendry, *The Antarctic Minerals Act 1989,* 39 I.C.L.Q. 183 (1990); M. Infante, *The Continental Shelf of Antarctica: Legal Implications for a Regime on Mineral Resources, in* Antarctic Resources Policy 253 (F. Orrego Vicuña ed., 1983); C. Joyner, *The Antarctic Minerals Negotiating Process,* 81 A.J.I.L. 888 (1987); C. Joyner & P. Lipperman, *Conflicting Jurisdictions in the Southern Ocean: The Case of an Antarctic Minerals Regime,* 27 Va J. Intl L. 1 (1986); G. Lohmeier, *Keeping Cool Amidst the Ice: Addressing the Challenge of Antarctic Mineral Resources,* 2 Emory J. Int'l Dispute Resolution 141 (1987); B. Murphy, *Antarctic Treaty System: Does the Minerals Regime Signal the Beginning of the End?,* 14 Suffolk Transnat'l L. J. 523 (1991); E. Newman, *The Antarctic Mineral Resources Convention: Developments from the October 1986 Tokyo Meeting of the Antarctic Treaty Consultative Parties,* 15 Den. J. Int'l L. & Pol'y 421 (1987); B. Oxman, *Evaluating the Antarctic Minerals Convention: The Decision–Making System,* 21 U. Miami Inter–Am. L. Rev. 17 (1989); J. Pedehl & D. Roghwell, *New Zealand and the Convention on the Regulation of Antarctic Mineral Resource Activities (CRAMRA): An Unhappy Divorce?,* 22 Victoria U. Wellington L. Rev. 23 (1992); R. Rich, *A Minerals Regime for Antarctica,* 31 I.C.L.Q. 709 (1982); H. Tetzeli, *Allocation of Marine Resources in Antarctica: Problems and a Possible Solution,* 10 Hastings Int'l & Comp. L. Rev. 525 (1987); G. Triggs, *Negotiation of a Minerals Regime, in* The Antarctic Treaty Regime: Law, Environment and Resources 182 (G. Triggs ed., 1987); A. Watts, *Antarctic Mineral Resources: Negotiations for a Mineral Resources Regime, in* The Antarctic Treaty Regime: Law, Environment and Resources 164 (G. Triggs ed., 1987); ___, *The Convention on the Regulation of Antarctic Mineral Resource Activities 1988,* 39 I.C.L.Q. 169 (1990); ___, *The Convention on the Regulation of Antarctic Mineral Resource Activities,* 39 I.C.L.Q. 169 (1990); J. D. Weiss, *The Balance of Nature and Human Needs in Antarctica: The Legality of Mining* 9 Temp. Int'l. & Comp. L.J. 387 (1995); W. Westermeyer, The Politics of Mineral Resource Development in Antarctica: Alternative Regimes for the Future (1984); *Who Has the Right of Exploitation, and the*

Right to Prevent Exploitation, of the Minerals in Antarctica, 79 Proc. Am. Soc. Int'l L. 58 (1985); M. de Wit, Minerals and Mining in Antarctica; Science and Technology, Economics and Politics (1985); R. Wolfrum, *The Use of Antarctic Non–Living Resources: The Search for a Trustee?, in* Antarctic Challenge 153 (R. Wolfrum ed., 1984); D. Zang, *Frozen in Time: The Antarctic Mineral Resource Convention,* 76 Cornell L. Rev. 722 (1991).

f. Protection of the Marine Environment

R. Andersen, *On Solid International Ground in Antarctica: A U.S. Strategy for Regulating Environmental Impact on the Continent,* 26 Stanford J. Int'l L. 93 (1989); N. Bankes, Environmental Protection in Antarctica: A Comment on the Convention on the Conservation of Antarctic Marine Living Resources, 19 Can. Y. B. Int'l L. 303 (1981); J. Barnes, *The Emerging Convention on the Conservation of Antarctic Marine Living Resources: An Attempt to Meet the New Realities of Resource Exploitation in the Southern Ocean, in* The New Nationalism and the Use of Common Spaces 239 (J. Charney ed., 1982); S. Blay, *New Trends in the Protection of the Antarctic Environment: The 1991 Madrid Protocol,* 86 A.J.I.L. 377 (1992); B. Boczek, *The Protection of the Antarctic Ecosystem: A Study in International Environmental Law,* 13 Ocean Dev. & Int'l L. 347 (1983); J. Bondareff, *The Congress Acts to Protect Antarctica,* 1 Territorial Sea J. 223 (1991); W. Bonner, *Recent Developments in Antarctic Conservation, in* The Antarctic Treaty Regime: Law, Environment and Resources 143 (G. Triggs ed., 1987); D. Butterworth, *Antarctic Marine Ecosystem Management,* 23 Polar Record 37 (1986); L. Corodonnery, *Area Protection and Management in Antarctica: A Proposed Strategy for the Implementation of Annex V of the Madrid Protocol Based on Information Management* 14 Envt'l. & Plan. L. J. 38 (1997); C. Deihl, *Antarctica: An International Laboratory,* 18 B. C. Env. Aff. L. Rev. 423 (1991); J. Couratier, *The Regime for the Conservation of Antarctica's Living Resources, in* Antarctic Resources Policy 139 (F. Orrego Vicuña ed., 1983); D. Edwards & J. Heap, *Convention on the Conservation of Antarctic Marine Living Resources: a Commentary,* 20 Polar Record 353 (1981); F. Francioni, *Liability for Damage to the Common Environment: The Case of Antarctica* 3 Rev. European Community & Intl. Envt'l. L. 223 (1994); R. Frank, *The Convention on the Conservation of Antarctic Marine Living Resources,* 13 Ocean Dev. & Int'l L. 291 (1983); ___, *The Convention on the Conservation of Antarctic Marine Living Resources,* 13 Ocean Dev. & Int'l L. 291 (1983–84); J. Gardam, *Management Regimes for Antarctic Marine Living Resources—An Australian Perspective,* 15 Melbourne U. L. Rev. 279 (1985); J. Gulland, *The Antarctic Treaty System as a Resource Management Mechanism—Living Resources, in* U.S. Polar Research Board, Antarctic Treaty System: An Assessment 221 (1986); ___, *The Antarctic Treaty System as a Resource Management Mechanism, in* The Antarctic Treaty Regime: Law, Environment and Resources 116 (G. Triggs ed., 1987); ___, *The Management Regime for Living Resources, in* The Antarctic Legal Regime 219 (C. Joyner & S. Chopra eds., 1988); R. Hofman, *The Convention on the Conservation of Antarctic Marine Living Resources, in* Antarctic Politics and Marine Resources: Critical Choices for the 1980s, at 113 (L. Alexander & L. Carter Hanson eds., 1985); M. Holdgate, *Regulated Development and Conservation of Antarctic Resources, in* The Antarctic Treaty Regime: Law, Environment and Resources 128 (G. Triggs ed., 1987); M. Howard, *The Convention on the Conservation of Antarctic Marine Living Resources: A Five-Year Review,* 38 I.C.L.Q. 104 (1989); C. Joyner, *Oceanic Pollution and the Southern Ocean: Rethinking the International Legal Implications for Antarctica,* 24 N.R.J. 1 (1984); K. Kock, *Present Knowledge of Antarctic Marine Living Resources and Means of Ensuring the Compliance with Protection Mea-*

sures, in Antarctic Challenge II, at 47 (R. Wolfrum ed., 1986); R. Lagoni, *Convention on the Conservation of Marine Living Resources: A Model for the Use of a Common Good, in* Antarctic Challenge 93 (R. Wolfrum ed., 1984); W. MacKenzie et al., *Implementing the Convention on Conservation of Antarctic Marine Living Resources: the Legislative Process, in* Antarctic Politics and Marine Resources: Critical Choices for the 1980s, at 129 (L. Alexander & L.Carter Hanson eds., 1985); T. Nagata, *The Implementation of the Convention on the Conservation of Antarctic Marine Living Resources: Needs and Problems, in* Antarctic Resources Policy 119 (F. Orrego Vicuña ed., 1983); D. Overholt, *Environmental Protection in the Antarctic: Past, Present, and Future,* 28 Can. Y. B. Int'l L. 227 (1990); M. Poole, *Liability for Environmental Damage in Antarctica,* 10 J. Energy & Natural Resources L. 246 (1992); S. Seach, *Conflicting Interests in Antarctica: People or Nature?,* 5 Temple Int'l & Comp. L. J. 109 (1991).

g. *Exploitation of Icebergs*

G. Graham, *Ice in International Law, in* 7 Thesaurus Acroasium 489 (1977); T. Lundquist, *The Iceberg Cometh?: International Law Relating to Antarctic Iceberg Exploitation,* 17 N.R.J. 1 (1977); P. Schwerdtfeger, *Antarctic Icebergs as Potential Sources of Water and Energy, in* Antarctic Challenge II, at 377 (R. Wolfrum ed., 1986); P. Wadhams, *The Resource Potential of Antarctic Icebergs, in* Iceberg Research 9 (No. 10, April 1985); E. Zuccaro, *Iceberg Appropriation and the Antarctic's Gordian Knot,* 9 Cal. W. Int'l L. J. 405 (1979).

h. *Antarctica and Tourism*

I. Nicholson, *Antarctic Tourism—The Need for a Legal Regime?, in* Antarctic Challenge II, at 191 (R. Wolfrum ed., 1986); R. Reich, *Tourism in the Antarctic: Its Present Impact and Future Development, Dissertation, Diploma in* Polar Studies (Scott Polar Research Institute, 1979); R. Thomson, *Transport and Tourism in Antarctic Development, in* El Desarrollo de la Antártica 290 (F. Orrego Vicuña ed., 1977).

i. *Antarctica and Demilitarization*

H. Almond, *Demilitarization and Arms Control: Antarctica,* 17 Case W. Res. J. Int'l L. 229 (1985); J. Goldblat, *The Arms Control Experiment in the Antarctic,* SIPRI Y. B. 477 (1973); T. Hanevold, *Inspections in Antarctica,* 2 Cooperation & Conflict 103 (1971); R. Purver, *Security and Arms Control at the Poles,* 39 Int'l J. 88 (1984); D. Shapley, *Antarctica: Why Success?, in* US–Soviet Security Cooperation: Achievements, Failures, Lessons 307 (A. George et al. eds., 1988).

j. *Whither Antarctica? Future Policies*

J. Barnes, *The Future of Antarctica–Environmental Issues and the Role of NGOs, in* Antarctic Challenge II 413 (R. Wolfrum ed., 1985-86); P. Beck, *Another Sterile Annual Ritual? The United Nations and Antarctica 1987,* 24 Polar Rec. 207 (1988); ___, *The UN Goes Green on Antarctica: The 1989 Session,* 26 Polar Rec. 323 (1990); ___, *Antarctica, Vina de Mar and the 1990 UN Debate,* 27 Polar Rec. 211 (1991); S. Blay, Antarctica After 1991: The Legal and Policy Options (1989); S. Chopra, Antarctica as a Commons Regime: A Conceptual Framework for Cooperation and Coexistence, in The Antarctic Legal Regime 163 (C. Joyner & S. Chopra eds., 1988); G. Cook, *Possible Future Developments, in* The Future of Antarctica, Exploitation versus Preservation 95 (G. Cook ed., 1990); *The Future of the Antarctic Regime: New Directions,* 85 Proc. Am. Soc. Int'l L. 461 (1991); M. Haron, *Antarctica and the United Nations—The Next Step?, in* Antarctic Challenge II, at 321 (R. Wolfrum ed., 1986); M. Hayashi, *The Antarctica Question in the United Nations*, 19 Cornell Int'l L. J. 275 (1986); B. Herber, *Mining or World Park? A Politico-economic Analysis of Alternative Land Use Regimes in Antarctica*, 31 N.R.J. 839 (1991); L. Kimball, *The Future of the Antarctic Treaty System: Environmental Community Suggestions, in* Antarctic Politics and Marine Resources: Critical Choices for the 1980s, at 237 (L. Alexander & L. Carter Hanson eds., 1985); M. Koch, *The Antarctic Challenge: Conflicting Interests, Co-operation, Environmental Protection and Economic Development*, 15 J. Mar. L. & Com. 112 (1984); C. Moneta, *Antarctica, Latin America, and the International System in the 1980s: Toward a New Antarctic Order?*, 23 J. Interamer. Stud. & World Aff. 29 (1981); G. Mosley, *The Natural Option: The Case for Antarctic World Park, in* Australia's Antarctic Policy Options 307 (S. Harris ed. 1984); Report on Antarctica (L. Kimball ed., 1991); D. Rothwell, A World Park for Antarctica: Foundations, Developments and the Future (Antarctic and Southern Ocean L. & Pol'y Occasional Papers 3, 1990); J. Rowland, *Whither Antarctica? Alternative Strategies, in* The Antarctic Treaty Regime: Law, Environment and Resources 218 (G. Triggs ed., 1987); Southern Exposure: Deciding Antarctica's Future (L. Kimball ed., 1990); R. Scully, *Alternatives for Cooperation and Institutionalization in Antarctica: Outlook for the 1990s, in* Antarctic Resources Policy 281 (F. Orrego Vicuña ed., 1983); E. Tenenbaum, A World Park for Antarctica: The Common Heritage of Mankind, 10 Va. Envtl. L. J. 109 (1990); The UN and the Antarctic Treaty System: A Panel, 80 Proceed. Am Soc'y Int'l L. Proc. 269 (1986); G. Triggs, *The United Nations in Antarctica? A Watching Brief, in* The Antarctic Treaty Regime: Law, Environment and Resources 229 (G. Triggs ed., 1987); M. White, *Common Heritage of Mankind: An Assessment*, 14 Case W. Res. J. Int'l L. 509 (1982).

Chapter Seven

PROBLEMS IN PROTECTING
THE ATMOSPHERE

The Earth's atmosphere, a mixture of gases and water vapor essential to earthly life and good health, is today being threatened. Industrial and other human activities are altering its chemical balance and consequently endangering the life forms it supports, causing long-term contamination of the food chain, sickness, and related assaults upon the biosphere. Acid rain, ozone depletion, and radioactive fallout, while less tangible than many other forms of pollution, are among the principal culprits.[a]

Broadly speaking, "acid rain" refers to the deposition from the atmosphere—in the form of fog, dew, frost, rain, sleet, hail, snow, and dry deposits—of acidic "inputs" into the Earth's ecosystems, derived from sulphur and nitrogen oxide emissions brought about by automotive, industrial, and other human activity. The ozone layer, a thin upper-atmospheric shield that protects earthly life from the ultraviolet rays of the sun, is being destroyed by chlorofluorocarbons, halons, and other human-made substances that interfere with the way ozone is created and broken down, consequently reducing its concentration in the upper atmosphere. And radioactive fallout refers to the introduction of toxic nuclear material into the environment by a variety of means, among them nuclear power plant mishaps of one sort or another.

Ironically, each of these threats to the atmosphere is largely a result of human "progress." Sulphur and nitrogen oxides derive from industrial innovations such as combustion. Ozone-depleting substances are used in refrigerators, air-conditioners, spray propellants, and other luxuries of modern— mainly "First World"—life. The use of nuclear power for energy and economic production evidences ever more increasing and intense demands for higher standards of living.

Despite their similar human-based origins, however, these threats raise different issues of law and policy. While the sources of acid rain lie ostensibly in the midst of industrial society, the causal links are complex and there is debate about precisely how dangerous acid rain really is. Ozone is a somewhat

a. So also, of course, is the build-up of "greenhouse gases" in the atmosphere (or "global warming") which threatens, among other things, to alter the earth's climate. This issue, however, has been reserved for a negotiation exercise in Chapter 12, *infra*. Accordingly, see Chapter 12 for helpful readings on this subject.

simpler proposition. Not only are a few countries and companies responsible for much of the offending production, but alternatives to ozone-depleting substances exist. And the control of radioactive contamination must account for a range of opinions regarding the safety of nuclear power and, consequently, for disparities in its use.

On the other hand, all three atmosphere-threatening problems share in common the need to account in law and policy for disparate production and consumption patterns as between different countries and regions of the world. Disparate—particularly disproportionate—production and consumption patterns, one can argue, should create different degrees of legal accountability and responsibility. And in this connection legal protection of the atmosphere additionally must take into account disparate commitments to prevention and redress. In so doing, however, recognition of the differing capabilities of developed and developing countries to modernize technology and practices is mandatory. Such recognition is essential for the success of any environmental regulatory regime.

Finally, legal protection of the atmosphere is today restricted, as is true of so many environmental concerns, by the time-honored notion of state sovereignty. Innovative arguments based on state responsibility, preemptory norms of environmental protection (*jus cogens*), rights and duties, and civil liability must remain cognizant of that stumbling block yet work actively to surmount it when and where protection of the environment requires it.

In the ensuing three problems, these and related issues are addressed.

Problem 7–1

Acid Rain in Savoy

SECTION 1. FACTS

Throughout most of the Twentieth Century, the European Republic of Swabia, like its neighbors elsewhere in Europe, has developed a variety of industries, including hydro-electric and coal-fired steam generation facilities, along and near the Schöner Fluss, a river that originates in the north and flows south through Swabia and neighboring Savoy en route to the Mediterranean Sea (*see* Figure 7–1). As a result of this extensive growth in the Schöner Fluss valley and the adjoining areas, Swabia, which relies heavily on its abundance of high sulfur coal, has experienced numerous air pollution problems. The soiling of buildings, deteriorating freshwater fisheries and forest productivity, together with a variety of public health concerns, have forced the government to take a number of measures to reduce pollution. It generally is recognized, however, that much remains to be done.

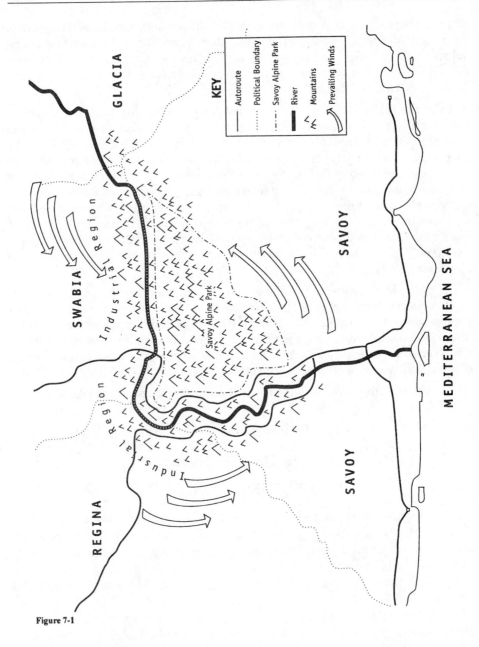

Figure 7-1

After descending through Swabia, the Schöner Fluss flows west alongside an extensive alpine range that separates Swabia from the Republic of Savoy. After several hundred miles, it then veers south into Savoy in a series of deep and scenic gorges before reaching Savoy's lowlands and ultimately the Mediterranean Sea. For many years, the narrow, winding road along the river valley was a favorite route of many Europeans driving south on holiday to the Mediterranean and its warmer climes. In the mid–1970s, the Government of Savoy expanded the road to a four-lane *autoroute* which traversed each side of the Schöner Fluss; and the drive from the sub-alpine forests of southern Swabia through the forested mountain valleys of Savoy, which enjoys four months of summer sunshine, quickly became a mecca for European travelers. Today, nearly a million cars make the trip through the region on most summer weekends.

In 1985, responding to a proposal of the Global Alliance for Nature (GAN) (a nongovernmental environmental organization with branch offices in every member state of the EU), Savoy created a national park called the Savoy Alpine Park (SAP). This park encompasses the northeastern bank of the Schöner Fluss and much of the eastern mountain range within Savoy. Pursuant to a submission made to the World Heritage Committee by Savoy, the SAP was included in the World Heritage List as a natural area "of outstanding universal value from the point of view of science, conservation or natural beauty."[b] The GAN applauded this recognition of the SAP and, in cooperation with Savoy, showcased the SAP as one of its centers for environmental education and eco-tourism initiatives. This resulted in a significant growth of tourists into the SAP and, pursuant to further discussions, Savoy agreed to give the GAN thirty percent of the fees levied for entrance into the SAP.

In the late 1980s and early 1990s, the Savoyard government began to notice that a summer haze or "smog" periodically descended upon the Schöner Fluss Valley, irritating the eyes, throats, and lungs of Schöner Fluss Valley motorists. It also noticed that the forests along its mountainous border with Swabia were suffering from some kind of blight, with large numbers of conifer and hardwood trees beginning to die. The trees affected were those most exposed to the atmosphere, i.e., the tallest or those on edges or openings in the forests. The branches showed a general discoloration and loss of needles from inside outward and midcrown upward followed by a general reduction of tree vigor, the loss of fine roots, leading ultimately to the death of the trees. Additionally, buildings were affected. Metal gutters became corroded, discoloration or spalling of stone on building facades set in, and the paint on many structures cracked and peeled.

The haze or "smog" and the loss of scenic trees adversely affected its booming tourist industry, and Savoy feared that these problems would be compounded by the stripping of other vegetation from Savoy's mountainsides (which, besides adding to the scenery, helps prevent winter avalanches). In response, the government of Savoy undertook a series of studies to determine the cause of the problem. These studies determined that sulfur dioxide (SO_2) and nitrogen oxide (NO_x) emanating from Swabia's industrial plains and river valleys were being carried by prevailing winds into Savoy, and returning to Earth as acid deposition and urban haze at such a rate as to seriously threaten the sustainability of Savoy's forests and other vegetation, its freshwater lakes, and its streams. The studies also concluded that, notwithstanding, both Swabia and Savoy were in compliance with the "limit values" set under the two EEC directives dealing with sulfur dioxide and nitrogen oxide (i.e. Council Directive 80/779 of August 30, 1980, and Council Directive 85/203 of March 27, 1985, respectively).

Alarmed at the results of these studies and their ominous implications for the future, Savoy notified Swabia of its intention to adopt, under article 4(2)

---

b. UNESCO Convention for the Protection of The World Cultural and Natural Heritage,   November 16, 1972, article 2 [**Basic Document 7.18**].

of EEC Directive 80/779, more stringent "guide values" for sulfur dioxide in the Schöner Fluss region; and, as required by article 11(1) of Directive 80/779, Savoy invited Swabia to engage in "prior consultations" on the matter. Swabia declined, however, presenting to Savoy its own study which revealed, first, that no "significant" emissions had crossed its frontier into Savoy; and, second, that the smog in Savoy was caused primarily by volatile organic compounds (VOCs) emitted by the constant and growing stream of motor vehicles that traveled Savoy's highways. Thirdly, Swabia's study noted the close proximity of other industrial countries and the consequent great difficulty in ascribing any acid deposition solely to sources located in Swabia.

Outraged by this response, Savoy quickly adopted strict "guide values," and soon thereafter their monitoring of the region revealed rain with a pH value of 3.9, together with high concentrations of sulfur dioxide, in violation of the new standards. Whereupon Savoy again complained to Swabia and, in so doing, requested that the two countries "hold consultations with a view to remedying the situation" under article 11(2) of Directive 80/779. Also, it alleged that Swabia was in breach of international environmental law prohibiting transboundary pollution and demanded compensation for the resulting damage. But once again Swabia declined, citing its previous position and again offering its own study to Savoy as evidence of compliance.

Frustrated by Swabia's apparent intransigence, Savoy officially complained to the Commission of the European Union (Commission) with a view toward bringing the matter before the European Court of Justice (ECJ) under article 170. In complaining to the Commission, Savoy chronicled events including its implementation of more stringent measures and offered its study as clear evidence of Swabia's violation of article 11(2) of Directive 80/779, and of the rule of international law prohibiting transboundary pollution. The Commission requested that both Savoy and Swabia present their arguments before the Commission. However, three months passed and the Commission had not ruled upon the issue. Pursuant to article 170, Savoy has brought the matter before the ECJ.

In a concurrent development, Swabia's GAN office initiated an action in the Swabian courts alleging Swabia's violation of Directive 80/779, and claiming damages for the loss of revenue stemming from the pollution of the SAP. The GAN relied on the direct, vertical applicability of Directive 80/779. The GAN appealed the issue through the Swabian court system and the Supreme Court of Swabia agreed to request the ECJ for a Preliminary Ruling under article 177.

The ECJ has consolidated both causes of action and requests Swabia, Savoy, the Commission, the GAN, and the Advocates General to submit oral and written observations to the Court. The ECJ has decided to consider whether Swabia is guilty of an infringement of the relevant European Union (EU) directives and, if so, whether Swabia bears any "state responsibility" for damage caused to Savoy. Furthermore, the ECJ will consider whether Swabia has violated international law in general. Both Swabia and Savoy were members of the European Community and now belong to the European Union (EU).[c] Also, both are parties to the 1979 Geneva Convention on Long–Range

---

c. For the purposes of this problem, assume that European Community (EC) Directives dealing with stationary sources (e.g., combustion plants, incinerators, vehicles, and

Transboundary Air Pollution, the 1982 World Charter for Nature and the 1972 World Heritage Convention. Only Savoy is a party to the 1985 Helsinki Protocol on Reduction of Sulfur Emissions or Their Transboundary Fluxes by at Least Thirty Per Cent.

SECTION 2. QUESTIONS PRESENTED

1. Has Swabia violated EU law or more general international law by refusing to consult with Savoy?

2. Is Swabia responsible or liable to Savoy and/or the GAN under EU law or more general international law for any acid deposition Savoy may be experiencing; and in this connection, upon whom should the ECJ place the burden of proof?

SECTION 3. ASSIGNMENTS

A. Reading Assignment

Study the Readings presented in Section 4, *infra*, and the Discussion Notes/Questions that follow. Also, to the extent possible, consult the accompanying bibliographical references.

B. Recommended Writing Assignment

Prepare a comprehensive, logically sequenced, and *argumentative* brief in the form of an outline of the primary and subsidiary *legal* issues you see requiring resolution by the ECJ. Also, from the perspective of the independent Advocate General or an ECJ judge (as designated by your instructor), indicate which side ought to prevail on each issue and why. Retain a copy of your issue-outline/brief for class discussion.

C. Recommended Oral Assignment

Assume you are legal counsel for Swabia, Savoy, the Commission, or the GAN (as designated by your instructor); then, relying upon the Readings (and your issue-outline if prepared), present a 15–20 minute oral argument of your party's likely positions before the ECJ.

D. Recommended Reflective Assignment

Consider (and recommend) alternative norms, institutions, and/or procedures that you believe might be more effective than existing world order arrangements in resolving situations of the kind posed by this problem. In so doing, but without insisting upon *immediate* feasibility, identify the particular transition steps that would be needed to make your alternatives a reality.

their fuels) are irrelevant and have no application. Assume also that the European Economic Community (EEC) and European Community (EC) laws referred to in the readings that follow are laws of the European Union established by the 1992 Maastricht Treaty on European Union [see **Basic Document 1.6**].

SECTION 4. READINGS

1.   JAMES L. REGENS & ROBERT W. RYCROFT, THE ACID RAIN CONTROVERSY 35–9, 48–51 (1989).

What is acid rain and why should we be concerned about it? Acid rain commonly refers to what is identified more precisely as the wet and dry processes for the deposition from the atmosphere of acidic inputs into ecosystems. Thus, all forms of precipitation—not just rain—can be acidic. Indeed, the definition includes acidifying compounds that are deposited in dry form. As a result, *acid deposition* is the scientifically accurate and all-encompassing term for acid rain. For simplicity as well as by conventional usage, however, the term *acid rain* is commonly used to include both precipitation and dry deposition.

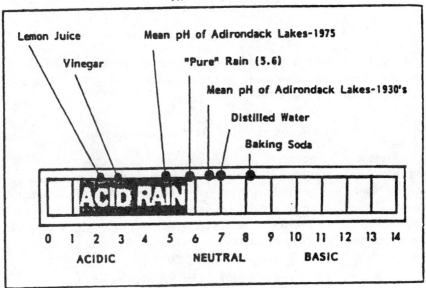

Source: U.S. Environmental Agency (1980)

Since acids release hydrogen ions in a water solution, the relative acidity or alkalinity of any solution is typically described by the percentage of hydrogen ions that a water solution contains measured on the logarithmic potential hydrogen (pH) scale.... The further a reading is from 7.0, below or above, the more acid or base the substance is. Because pH expresses the negative logarithm of acid concentration, interpreting changes in chemical composition can be confusing for many laypersons. The lower the pH value, the higher the acidity. Each full pH unit drop represents a tenfold increase in acidity. For example, a solution whose pH value equals 4.0 contains ten times as much acid, not just 20 percent more, than one measuring 5.0 on the pH scale. And, it is one hundred times more acidic than a substance with a pH of 6.0.

Figure 7–1.3

Schematic View of the Acid Deposition Problem

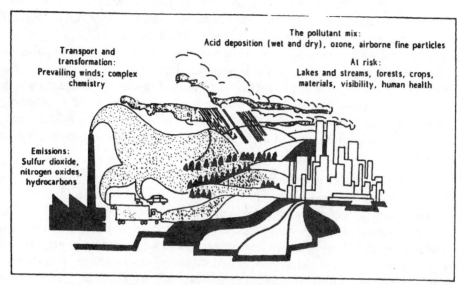

Source: U.S. Office of Technology Assessment (1984)

All forms of precipitation—rain, snow, sleet, hail, fog, and mist—are naturally somewhat acidic, and human activities have made them more so. For example, in industrial regions, the pH of rainfall is often around or below 4.0, and it has been measured as low as 2.6. In pure water, the "natural" acidity value often is assumed to be pH 5.6, calculated for distilled water in equilibrium with atmospheric carbon dioxide concentrations.... The ratio of anthropogenic to natural sulfur emissions is on the order of at least 3:1 and it is over 7:1 for nitrogen oxide emissions. Thus, because manmade rather than natural sources for the sulfur and nitrogen oxides released into the atmosphere for conversion to acids predominate in North America and Europe, the atmospheric chemistry suggests that reducing anthropogenic emissions of acid rain's major causes should reduce the aggregate level of acidic deposition, although it may have less impact on some sensitive receptor areas than popular impressions imply.

Environmental Effects

Acid deposition and/or sulfur and nitrogen oxide emissions are said to affect ecosystems and human health both directly and indirectly. [S]uch emissions can have direct effects, such as the acidification of lakes and streams, plant damage, or reduced forest growth, as well as indirect effects on human health or reduced visibility.... Critics of additional controls, however, maintain that the "high acid rain research effort provides ample data showing that the link between SO_2 emissions and the acidity of rain is far weaker than generally supposed, and, further, that the link between acid rain and ecological damage is even weaker, or nearly nonexistent."[1] What, then, do we know about the environmental impact of acid rain?

1. A. Katzenstein, *Acid Rain: A Further Look at the Evidence,* 24 POWER ENGINEERING 32 (1986).

Conclusive evidence points to chemical and biological changes, including fish kills, in lakes and streams that have limited capacities to neutralize acidic inputs. This can affect sport fishing, tourism, and other values associated with aquatic resources.... Evidence of damage to nonaquatic ecosystems, especially forest, is largely circumstantial. In part, this reflects limited research. It also reflects the often synergistic nature of effects attributable to air pollution in the ambient environment, which is more analogous to a chemical soup than individual, discrete pollutants exerting effects in a noninteractive fashion. As a result, impacts are plausible, and evidence of nonaquatic effects, especially on forest productivity, is growing. For example, adverse effects on forests may result from the leaching out of soil nutrients or through the mobilization of toxic metals....

As a result, many are concerned about the harmful, long-term effects of acid deposition on trees—particularly spruce, pine, aspen, and birch.... Because causal linkages are complex, conclusions about forest effects remain somewhat equivocal. However, acid deposition does appear to be one of various stresses affecting forest ecosystems, although obviously acid rain is not the only potential culprit. A combination of atmospheric pollutants— acidic deposition, sulfur dioxide, ozone—as well as drought, temperature shifts, pathogens, and heavy metals like lead have been implicated.

Unlike the effects on aquatic ecosystems and the possible effects on forests, no clear evidence of a direct link between ambient levels of acid deposition and injury to agricultural crops has been demonstrated.... The emerging consensus that acid deposition fails to damage crops is not surprising, since farmers use agricultural practices to manage acidic and alkaline inputs to their soils.

Concern has also been expressed about the impact of acid deposition on outdoor sculpture, historic monuments, buildings, and other structures. Environmentalists refer frequently, because of their emotional appeal, to the damage to priceless artifacts like the Parthenon or the Statue of Liberty. Damage to the Acropolis has been traced primarily to emissions from nearby traffic and from an oil refinery only a few kilometers away. The Statue of Liberty sits in New York Harbor, where the sea water typically measures around pH 8.2 and 8.4, which is highly alkaline. Its damage appears to have resulted from failed insulation that allowed electrolytic corrosion to take place between the statue's copper sheathing and iron framework, as well as from a century's exposure to corrosive sea salts.... As a consequence, while field studies have linked materials damage to air pollution, such damage is most prevalent in urban areas with high concentrations of ambient sulfur dioxide. This suggests the impact of primarily local rather than distant sources.

Finally, unlike respirable sulfates or fine particulate matter, acid deposition does not appear to represent a direct threat to human health. Limited health risks may be associated with acid fog episodes or the leaching of metals such as lead into drinking water supplies, although most drinking water supply systems already have treatment facilities for liming to neutralize acid inputs, thereby preventing metals leaching.

2. Jutta Brunnée, Acid Rain and Ozone Layer Depletion: International Law and Regulation 11–14 (1988).

Anthropogenic Emissions

Acid rain is primarily the result of anthropogenic emissions of sulphur oxides and nitrogen oxides which are common byproducts of our modern industrial society.

i) Sulphur

Sulphur is presently considered the most important factor in the acidification process. Some 100 million years ago fossil fuels—such as oil, coal and some ores—began to be built up from decomposing animals and plants. Those organisms contributed certain amounts of sulphur they had absorbed from their environment to the mixture. Therefore the oil, coal, and ore we use today contain, according to the geographical area they originate from, varying amounts of sulphur.

The predominant sources of sulphur oxides are the burning of fossil fuels in thermal power plants and smelting processes which refine nonferrous metal ores (nickel, copper, lead, zinc, etc.). Further emission sources are fuel combustion by industrial, commercial, and residential users, other industrial processes (such as petroleum refining and sulphate pulping), and combustion of gasoline in motor vehicles. . . . In most OECD countries the energy sector is the major emission factor, with industrial uses in second position.

ii) Nitrogen Oxides

It is interesting to note that nitrogen is not only found in fuels, but also makes up 80% of the atmosphere. Therefore, the decisive factors for the actual formation of nitrogen are the combustion process and the temperatures at which it is carried out. Since nitrogen oxides occur through oxidation of nitrogen in the fuels and in the combustion of air, the presence of nitrogen oxides will increase with increasing combustion temperature.

Anthropogenic emissions of NO_x originate mainly from the transportation sector, the energy sector and industrial processes. The dominating factors appear to be motor vehicles (about 40%), closely followed by fossil fueled power plants (about 30%).

Transport, Transformation, and Deposition of Acid Pollutants

[M]ost of the primary pollutants emitted into the air undergo changes during their residence time. This is of particular importance to the phenomenon of acid rain, since the substances discussed above are only precursors to the secondary pollutants which eventually harm the environment.

In the 1960s and 1970s tall smoke stacks were built in response to the occurrence of severe local pollution problems. They blow pollutants high up into the air where prevailing winds transport the pollutants far beyond the local area. Therefore, tall stacks are a major factor in the generation of acid rain.

* * *

Tall stacks are linked to an increased occurrence of acid rain because the atmospheric residence time of pollutants introduced into higher moving air masses is usually longer than that of substances originating from low level sources. Consequently sulphur dioxides and nitrogen oxides are much more exposed to the processes which transform them into acidifying secondary pollutants.

The transformation itself can be described as a two-step process. The first step is the oxidation of some of the gaseous SO_2 or NO_x emissions into sulphate or nitrate particles. The second step is the transformation of the particles into sulfuric or nitric acid in the presence of water vapor—either in the air or on the ground.

* * *

While sulphur oxides are thought to be responsible for about two-thirds of the acidity in precipitation, nitric contributions appear to be gaining importance.

3.   Amy A. Fraenkel, Comment, *The Convention on Long–Range Transboundary Air Pollution*: *Meeting the Challenge of International Cooperation*, 30 HARV. INT'L L.J. 447, 451–52, 459, 461, 463 (1989).

In Europe, monitoring studies have shown that acid deposition involves not merely two or three countries, but the entire region: every European country both exports and imports acidifying compounds across its boundaries. Further, the impact of acid deposition is distributed unevenly: some countries are "net importers" and others "net exporters" of the precursor emissions of SO_2 and NO_x. In one half of the European countries monitored through the currently employed Cooperative Program for Monitoring and Evaluation of Long–Range Transboundary Air Pollution (EMEP), the majority of pollution is attributable to foreign sources. For example, more than 60% of the sulphur deposition in Norway, Sweden, Switzerland, Austria, the Netherlands and Eastern Canada originates in other countries. In Switzerland, less than 15% of sulphur deposited in 1980 came from Swiss sources, with the rest coming from Italy, France, West Germany, Austria, the United Kingdom (UK), East Germany, Spain, Czechoslovakia, Belgium, Poland, Hungary, the Netherlands and others. Thus, in the European context, neither unilateral efforts by an affected country nor bilateral agreements can be effective in addressing the problem....

* * *

UNCERTAINTIES IN LINKING EMISSIONS TO ENVIRONMENTAL DAMAGE

Unlike "traditional" transboundary air pollution, where the source of environmental damage was generally thought to be identifiable, acid deposition involves a relationship between emissions and damage that is far from simple. While there is general agreement that SO_2 and NO_x may be carried miles away from their source of emission to damage other areas, there remains the difficulty of linking a specific country's emissions to damage in another country. In the European context, where so many countries are involved, the question is especially complex. Weather patterns, chemical transformation in the atmosphere and interaction with other pollutants further complicate the uncertainty. With respect to pollution control schemes, it is therefore unclear which emissions should be reduced to produce the greatest environmental benefit to a given area. This issue is most sensitive for countries found to be net exporters of acidifying compounds, as the international onus to reduce pollution lies heavily on them.

* * *

A [further] complicating factor is that even if countries agree that pollution from a given source or country does harm a specific area, other agents or variables may have a profound effect on the ultimate harm. For example, certain areas are naturally more sensitive than others to acid deposition due to their soil composition.[2] Other natural or anthropogenic (man-made) stresses will also be a factor in the effect of air pollutants.[3] Additionally, other pollutants, such as ozone, may act in conjunction with acid deposition to cause damage.[4] Such compounding factors may complicate sorting out the contribution of acid deposition to the effects noted, e.g., forest decline.

National Responses to the Call for Emission Reductions

Countries have responded to the above uncertainties and obstacles in different ways. . . .

A key factor in a country's willingness to agree to concrete pollution reductions at the international level is its national self-interest. Factors affecting national self-interest include the environmental damage suffered by a given country, political pressure to address environmental issues, domestic economic interests, and the costs of reducing pollution. The most fundamental consideration is whether a country is a net importer or a net exporter of acidifying compounds. Net exporters, especially those which are less impacted by acid deposition themselves, may have little incentive to control their emissions. Other factors include the availability of control options as well as the costs of control, which may vary significantly between countries due to differences in their fuel use patterns. For countries such as Bulgaria and East Germany, which have a large supply of high-sulphur coal, emissions limits might mean importing cleaner fuel, changing fuel use, or paying exorbitant control costs for facilities using high-sulphur coal. Some countries, such as France, have been able to achieve reductions in air pollution through increased reliance on nuclear energy. However, this option may be limited for other countries, such as West Germany and Switzerland, due to domestic political opposition to nuclear power. Another consideration is that less industrialized countries are understandably of the view that their economic development should not be retarded merely because of the current concern with air pollution, caused by the prior industrial growth of their neighbors.

4. Editors' Note. In *Acid Rain: The Problem*, 17 EPA J. 18, 18–20 (1991), Ned Helme and Chris Neme write: "The acid rain program, part of the Clean Air Act Amendments of 1990, embodies the major policy principles supported by the Alliance for Acid Rain Control: reducing national sulfur dioxide emissions by 10 million tons below 1984 levels." The authors contin-

---

2. For example, in Scandinavia, the soil is naturally poor and has a low buffering capacity, i.e., its ability to neutralize acid deposition is limited.

3. *Final Draft Report of the UN ECE Critical Levels Workshop* 3–8, Bad Harzburg, Federal Republic of Germany, March 14–18, 1988.

4. *Id.* at 9–10.

ue: "Nevertheless, [the] NAPAP[d] report concludes that acid rain is not a catastrophic environmental problem. The NAPAP study concluded that the number of acidic lakes has grown only slightly over the last 10 years and that forest damage from acid rain has been limited to high-elevation stands."

On the other hand, while recent scientific studies such as the NAPAP report indicate that acid rain is not as devastating as originally thought, many Europeans—especially the Germans and Scandinavians—remain convinced that acid rain is a terrible problem. It is widely believed in Europe that acid rain is responsible for the destruction of approximately 50 percent of Germany's Black Forest (Schwarzwald); and as one drives along the roads of the former East Germany, yellow treetops are clearly visible and bear witness to a phenomenon known as "crown die-back," which is said to have killed many trees. In Scandinavia, freshwater lakes are deemed to have suffered acidification on a scale large enough to have caused a significant decline in fish populations. In the introduction to their important 1983 study of acid rain in Europe, Gregory Wetstone and Armin Rosencranz comment as follows:

> Irreversible changes may be occurring in the soils and forests of widespread areas of Europe and, perhaps, North America as well. Recent studies have found that acid rains can leach important plant nutrients from forest soils, and free toxic metals normally bound in soil materials that may be harmful to vegetation and animal life. Buildings, statuary, and other man-made materials, including precisely monuments such as the Parthenon and the Colosseum, are reportedly also suffering acid rain damage. Effects on crops, drinking water, and even human health are under investigation.

Gregory Wetstone & Armin Rosencranz, *Acid Rain in Europe and North America: National Responses to an International Problem—A Study for the German Marshall Fund of the United States* 3 (1983).

The controversy among scientists as to the seriousness of acid rain makes determination of liability for environmental harm across national boundaries that much more difficult. For further discussion of acid rain in Europe, see S. Rissberger, *On the Brink of an Ecological Calamity: Acid Rain, Transboundary Air Pollution and Environmental Law in West Germany*, 12 Syracuse J. Int'l L. 325 (1985). See also Economic Commission for Europe, Transboundary Air Pollution: Effects and Control, U.N. Doc. ECE/EB.AIR/B (1986); W. Bown, *Europe's Forests Fall to Acid Rain*, 127 New Scientist 17 (Aug. 11, 1990); Note, *Acid Rain in the European Community: A Hard Rain's A–Gonna Fall*, 16 Brook. J. Int'l L. 621 (1990).

5.   Joseph E. Barnard & Alan A. Lucier, *Report 16: Changes in Forest Health and Productivity in the United States and Canada*, in Acidic Deposition: State of Science and Technology, Summary Report of the U.S. National Acid Precipitation Assessment Program 135, 137–38 **(Patricia M. Irving ed., 1991).**

---

d. *I.e.*, the National Acid Precipitation Assessment Program, a 10–year scientific study   sponsored by the U.S. Congress.

16.1 Introduction and Scope

Forests, like all plant communities, are constantly changing. Change occurs on many spatial and temporal time scales through natural and human-caused disturbance and through the processes of evolution, succession, and biomass accumulation....

Forest health problems associated with insects, pathogens, climatic stresses, and normal maturation and senescence of trees and stands are natural features of forest ecosystems ... Such problems may develop gradually or suddenly depending on environmental conditions and the characteristics of the species involved.

[F]orest health problems are classified as "declines" [in ecosystem quality] if they are (1) not the result of normal maturation and senescence, (2) not clearly attributable to a single predominant natural factor, and (3) sufficiently severe and extensive to be detected by routine forest monitoring or special field investigation. Symptoms of decline may include abnormal growth reduction, loss and discoloration of foliage, and increased rates of branch and whole tree mortality. Some or all of these symptoms may be present and they can be caused by a variety of natural and human-made factors....

* * *

16.2 Major Conclusions

[M]ajor conclusions about forest health and air quality in the United States and Canada are drawn from the available scientific information....

16.2.1 Regional Forest Health

Conclusion 1: The vast majority of forests in the United States and Canada are *not* affected by decline.

There is no evidence of an overall or pervasive decline in which acidic deposition is known to be a predominant cause. Only in cases where forests are frequently exposed to highly acidic fog or cloudwater is there evidence that acidic deposition is a significant contributing factor to observed forest health problems.

* * *

16.2.5 Ozone Impacts

Conclusion 5: Ozone is the pollutant of greatest current concern with respect to possible regional scale impacts on North American forests. Ozone is the key factor in a decline of pines in ... California. It is also imposing varying degrees of stress on trees over broad areas in other parts of the United States and Canada....

* * *

The extent to which ozone is affecting forest productivity and ecosystem diversity remains to be determined. Experiments with seedlings have shown that many species across the United States and Canada have genotypes that are adversely affected by ambient levels of ozone. It is difficult to confidently extrapolate the experimental results because mature trees in forest stands may respond to ozone differently than seedlings grown under experimental conditions. In areas outside the Los Angeles Basin, effects of ambient ozone on tree species have not been shown to cause forest health problems other than visible injury and growth loss in sensitive individuals. The long-term effects of chronic ozone exposure warrant further investigation.

16.2.6 Long-term Effects

Conclusion 6: Compared to ozone and many nonpollutant stress factors, acidic deposition appears to be a relatively minor factor affecting the current health and productivity of most forests in the United States and Canada. Most forests in the United States and Canada are receiving acid rain at doses that have not had a serious impact on health and productivity. The possibility of long-term (several decades) adverse effects on some soils appears realistic. Sulfate deposition increases leaching losses of nutrient cations [or kations] from many different forest soils and over the long term may reduce the fertility of soils with low buffering capacity or low mineral weathering rate.

* * *

16.3 Synthesis

[A]n intensive short-term effort has not supported initial concerns that North American forests are suffering widespread damage caused by acidic deposition. Most forests are apparently healthy. Known forest health problems are in most cases attributable to natural stresses and/or past land management practices. . . .

6. Thomas O. McGarity, *Regulating Commuters to Clear Air: Some Difficulties in Implementing a National Program at the Local Level*, 27 Pac. L. J. 1521, 1524–27 (1996).

The health and environmental effects of exposure to ozone in the ambient air, like the health and environmental effects of many pollutants, are a subject of much debate. Studies convincingly demonstrate that ozone causes "immediate, short term changes in lung function and increased respiratory (problems) among healthy adults and children who exercise moderately or heavily during periods of elevated ozone concentrations."[5] Exposure to ozone for one or two hours at levels encountered in cities like Los Angeles, New York, and Houston can cause decreases in lung function and pronounced symptoms like coughing and pain when breathing deeply, but these effects appear to be reversible.[6] It is becoming increasingly clear that the acute adverse effects of exposure to a particular concentration of ozone in the atmosphere depend upon both the duration of exposure and the intensity of the individual's physical activities during the time of exposure.[7]

* * *

The Contribution of Automobile Emissions

---

5. United States Congress, Office of Technology Assessment, Catching Our Breath: Steps for Reducing Urban Ozone 39 (1989) [hereinafter OTA Ozone Report].

6. *Id.* at 39–40, 54.

7. *Id.* at 40–41.

Photochemical oxidants are formed when certain hydrocarbon compounds, sometimes called volatile organic compounds (VOCs), combine with oxides of nitrogen (NO_x).[8] As a measure of the concentration of photochemical oxidants in the atmosphere, regulatory agencies rely upon the more easily measured concentration of ozone. In hot summer months, there is probably a natural background concentration of ozone of about 0.04 ppm (one-third of the 0.12 ppm national primary ambient air quality standard) attributable largely to vegetative emissions of hydrocarbons. Automobiles are major contributors to both VOC emissions and NO_x emissions in urban areas. The relative contributions of automobiles and other mobile sources to VOC emissions vis-a-vis stationary sources present a question to which there is no clear answer, because existing VOC emissions inventories are quite poor and emissions models are highly uncertain.[9] Since the formation of photochemical oxidants depends upon sunlight and temperature and because stagnant air tends to limit pollutant dispersal, ozone concentrations tend to be highest on hot sunny days when the wind is not blowing.[10]

One of the most perplexing aspects of arriving at regulatory solutions to the problem of photochemical oxidants is the phenomenon of "ozone transport." Because photochemical oxidants remain in the air for a considerable period of time, prevailing winds can transport ozone that is initially formed over a city to surrounding rural areas.[11] Ozone plumes can spread over large distances that include both urban and rural areas. For example, photochemical oxidants that originate in New York sometimes pollute the air over Boston.[12] This phenomenon can greatly complicate efforts to reduce ozone in particular areas. It may often be the case, especially on the East Coast, that a 100% reduction of VOC emissions in one area will not be sufficient to meet air quality standards in that area because of ozone transported from other areas.[13]

7. Philippe Sands, *European Community Environmental Law: The Evolution of a Regional Regime of International Environmental Protection*, 100 YALE L.J. 2511, 2518–20 (1991).

Characterizing the Community legal order correctly is an important task for at least two reasons. First, Community environmental law is the only reasonably comprehensive and effective international (albeit regional) model available to the rest of the international community as it attempts to legislate international environmental law on a global and regional basis. Second, the Community has itself become an important actor in international environ-

8. OTA OZONE REPORT, *supra* note 5, at 97. Oxides of nitrogen are pollutants in their own right, and EPA promulgated primary and secondary NAAQS for one of the oxides of nitrogen—nitrogen dioxide. 40 C.F.R. § 50.11 (1995). Currently only one area, Los Angeles, has not attained the NO_x standards, and it may soon be redesigned. U.S. EPA, NATIONAL AIR QUALITY AND EMISSIONS TRENDS REPORT 1991 1–8 (1992). Exposure to nitrogen dioxide in high enough levels can irritate the lungs and lower resistance to respiratory illness, especially in children and in persons already suffering from respiratory diseases. EPA has recently

decided not to revise either of the standards for nitrogen dioxide. *See Standard for Nitrogen Dioxide Adequate to Protect Health, Environment, EPA Says*, 26 ENV'T REP. (BNA) No. 13, Oct. 13, 1995, at 1033.

9. OTA OZONE REPORT, *supra* note 5, at 26.

10. *Id.* at 97.

11. *Id.* at 23.

12. *Id.*

13. *Id.* at 23–24.

mental lawmaking, forcing important procedural mutations that may enable other regional groupings to participate more effectively in international fora.

The need to develop international environmental law is now a major preoccupation of the international community. A twenty-year review of the 1972 Stockholm Conference [took] place in Brazil at the June 1992 United Nations Conference on Environment and Development. Significantly, Community environmental law, one of the most tangible consequences of the 1972 Stockholm Conference [**Basic Document 1.12**], [became] a "role model" for participants at [the 1992] Brazil Conference. The question is how "international," and how appropriate, is the Community model?

The Community legal order, including its environmental law, remains a part of the old order of public international law from which it grew. Its approach is rooted in an international agreement, the Treaty of Rome [*see* **Basic Document 1.6**], whose validity and effect continue to be governed by traditional rules of international law. In the case of *Van Gend en Loos*, the European Court called the Community "a new legal order of international law."[14] As such, the Community joins other specialized legal orders of international law, such as the European Convention of Human Rights[5] regional human rights law and the international administrative law that international administrative tribunals apply.

The Community legal order is innovative, however, and it has significantly moved the "goalpost" of traditional international law. It extends the scope of possibilities available under international law. One important achievement is the wholesale change in our perceptions of how international law can work as a dynamic and effective force. The Community legal order has done so most notably by granting to nonstate actors rights that they can enforce before national courts and the European Court of Justice, by applying the doctrines of direct effect, supremacy, and implied powers, and by instituting a decision-making process based on qualified majority, rather than unanimous, voting. While, as Professor Weiler[6] recognizes, each of these doctrines existed under traditional international law, the Community legal system and the European Court have given them flesh.

* * *

Professor Weiler describes the Community legal order as "a truly self-contained legal regime with no recourse to the mechanism of state responsibility, at least as traditionally understood, and therefore no reciprocity and countermeasures, even in the face of actual or potential failure." Whether one believes that state responsibility is a substantive rule of international law or simply "a general term for all the consequences of wrongdoing," it exists in the Community legal order as in any other discrete international legal order. Neither application of Community law in the national courts nor recourse to Article 177 can force a member state to remedy a breach of the Treaty of

14. Case 26/62, Van Gend en Loos v. Netherlands Inland Revenue Admin., 1963 E.C.R. 1, 2.

5. European Convention for the Protection of Human Rights and Fundamental Freedoms, Nov. 4, 1950, Europ. T.S. No. 5, 213 U.N.T.S. 221, *reprinted in* 3 Weston.

6. Professor Weiler is author of *The Transformation of Europe*, an analysis of the legal developments in the European Community. 100 YALE L.J. 2403 (1991).

Rome. Rather, recourse to Articles 169 and 170, which give the European Court of Justice jurisdiction over alleged wrongdoing and breaches of the Treaty of Rome by member states, will provide, at a minimum, attempts at remedies. The European Court has compulsory jurisdiction, and its powers under Articles 169 to 172 in contentious proceedings involving issues of state responsibility are similar to those of the International Court of Justice.

The Community legal order differs from general international law in that the Community allows nonstate actors to trigger action by an independent international actor (the Commission) which then alleges the breach of an international legal obligation (a Community law) before the compulsory jurisdiction of an international court (the European Court). Despite this procedure's weaknesses, which Professor Weiler highlights, it is unique both in its scope and in bringing into the enforcement process members of the international community other than states.

The Community legal order is an important step in the progressive development of international law. It builds upon the historic foundations of traditional international law. As such, the Community's rules on environmental protection constitute a part of international environmental law and can contribute to its progressive development, whether in the Caribbean, the South Pacific, the Americas, or globally.

8. Rolf Wagenbauer, *The European Community's Policy on Implementation of Environmental Directives*, 14 FORDHAM INT'L L.J. 455, 455–61, 470 (1991).

Under the Treaty Establishing the European Economic Community (the "EEC Treaty") [**Basic Document 1.6**], the "directive" is one of the most widely used legal instruments. As far as environmental protection policy is concerned, the directive has been the most important instrument from the early 1970s when the European Economic Community (the "EEC" or the "Community") first took an interest in this field of activity.

* * *

I.   The Directive and the Necessity of Implementation

Article 189 of the EEC Treaty sets out the legal nature of the directive:

A directive shall be binding, as to the result to be achieved, upon each Member State to which it is addressed but shall leave to the national authorities the choice of form and methods.[15]

Accordingly, the nature of a directive, a binding legal act as to results which leaves the method to achieve those results open to national authorities, implies that legislation takes place in two steps. First, the competent Community institution adopts a directive following the procedure indicated in the relevant EEC Treaty provision.[16] The Council of Ministers of the European Communities (the "Council"), which acts on proposals from the Commission, is usually the institution competent to adopt environmental protection di-

---

15. EEC Treaty [**Basic Document 1.6**], art. 189.

16. These procedures are usually based on EEC Treaty articles 100a or 130a. Prior to the Single European Act, procedures were based on articles 100 and 235. *See* Single European Act, 1987 O.J. (L 169) 1, Common Mkt. Rep. (CCH) ¶ 21,000, *reprinted in* 1 Weston. *See also* **Basic Document 1.6**.

rectives. After adoption by the Council, the directive is notified to the Member States. One of the directive's final articles will generally state the date or time within which Member States must implement the directive in national law.

After adopting the directive, the Member State must implement it. Article 189 obliges Member States to implement the directive, to guarantee the enforcement of the directive, and to modify existing national law accordingly. The "form and methods" by which Member States achieve this result are left to the individual Member States' discretion.

* * *

A. Case Law Concerning the Forms and Methods of Implementation

Court of Justice case law provides interesting clarifications of Member State obligations to implement directives. The Court has addressed repeatedly the question of which Member State regional entity is competent to implement directives. In general, the Court has done so when the Member State objected to implementing a directive because national constitutional law required implementation by regional or local entities. The Court of Justice responded unambiguously to this objection: "each Member State is free to delegate powers to its domestic authorities as it considers fit and to implement the directive by means of measures adopted by regional or local authorities."[17] This ruling is of particular relevance for Member States with a federal structure (such as Germany) or with decentralized legislative competencies (such as Belgium). According to the ruling, the Commission's contact should be solely with the Member States' central authority, notwithstanding the national-law question of which authority is competent to implement the directive.

The Court of Justice has clarified the means by which a Member State must implement a directive. For instance, to implement directives, Member States must use national provisions with the same legal status as previous regulations. The Court has further held that "each Member State should implement the directives in question in a way which fully meets the requirements of clarity and certainty in legal situations." The Court has also noted that "[m]ere administrative practices, which by their nature can be changed as and when the authorities please and which are not publicized widely enough cannot in the circumstances be regarded as a proper fulfillment of the obligation imposed by Article 189 on Member States to which the directives are addressed."[18] In addition, the Court noted that "according to the consistent case law ... each Member State must implement directives in a manner which fully meets the requirement of legal certainty and must consequently transpose their terms into national law as binding provisions."[19]

B. The "Binding Nature" of the Directive

The Court of Justice has, quite rightly, underlined repeatedly that prompt implementation of directives is particularly important since imple-

---

17. Case 97/81, Commission v. Netherlands, 1982 E.C.R. 1791, 1804, Common Mkt. Rep. (CCH) ¶ 8842.

18. Case 102/79, Commission v. Netherlands, 1980 E.C.R. at 1486, Common Mkt. Rep. (CCH) ¶ 8673.

19. Case 239/85, Commission v. Belgium, 1986 E.C.R. 3645, 3659, Common Mkt. Rep. (CCH) ¶ 14,383 (with conclusions by Advocate General da Cruz Vilaça).

menting measures are left to Member State discretion. If implementation is delayed, the directive would be ineffective to remedy discrimination resulting from differences in Member State rules after implementation deadlines expire. Accordingly, the Court has rejected a variety of excuses which Member States have made when charged with failure to implement a directive. Among those rejected are the following:

— The Member State concerned attributes direct effect to the provisions of the directive and alleges that giving direct effect is equivalent to normal implementation;

— The time allowed for implementation is insufficient;

— Other Member States failed to implement the directive in due time;

— A governmental crisis prevented implementation;

— Non-implementation was due to the premature dissolution of the Member State national legislature;

— Internal difficulties or provisions of the national constitution caused non-implementation;

— Constitutionally independent institutions caused internal difficulties preventing timely implementation;

— Current practice within the Member State conforms with the directive; all that remains is to conform national law to the established practice and the directive.

In other words, Member States must adopt measures giving full effect (*effet utile*) to the directive, notwithstanding the circumstances preventing timely implementation. A Member State may not, therefore, refer to "provisions, practices or circumstances" existing in that Member State's legal system to justify failure to meet the obligations and time limits of Community directives.[20] "General principles of constitutional or administrative law" may, however, render superfluous implementation by specific legislation.[21]

II. The Enforcement of Directives

As compared with the powerful regulation—which plays a minor role in environmental protection law—the "directive" has decisive weaknesses. A "regulation" is true Community-wide law with direct effect. A regulation grants direct rights to and imposes charges on private parties without interference of national law. The feature that the directive has in common with the regulation is that it is binding law. The directive must, however, be implemented and the national law changed accordingly. Upon Member State failure to implement a directive, the Commission may take enforcement action.

* * *

20. Case 52/75, Commission v. Italy, 1976 E.C.R. 497, 516, Common Mkt. Rep. (CCH) ¶ 14,092 (preliminary ruling requested by Tribunal de Premiere Instance Liège).

21. Case 29/84, Commission v. Germany, 1985 E.C.R. 1661, Common Mkt. Rep. (CCH) ¶ 14203.

3. Early Commission—Member State Consultation

[U]ntil now, with a few exceptions, implementation was solely in the hands of Member States. The Commission intervened only when it appeared that implementation did not take place in due time or was incorrect. In the future, the Commission could be involved more closely in the implementation process. First, Member States and the Commission should start early discussions concerning implementation problems and possible solutions. To arrive at this, there should be a general obligation for Member States to consult the Commission on all legislative measures having an environmental impact. Such an obligation is already in force in the field of transport policy. It would be a positive step to introduce similar rules in environment policy, thereby averting erroneous developments which could later on lead to infringement procedures. Additionally, early dialogue would help to avoid later confrontation.

9.   European Union: Consolidated Version of the Treaty Establishing the European Community, Mar. 25, 1957, arts. 2, 3(L), 10, 211, 220, 221, 226, 227, 232, 234, 269, reprinted in 37 I.L.M. 56 (1998) [Basic Document 1.6].

10.   Vienna Convention on the Law of Treaties, May 23, 1969, arts. 2, 31, 32, 34, 35, 53, 1155 U.N.T.S. 331 (1969) [Basic Document 1.7].

11.   UNESCO Convention for the Protection of The World Cultural and Natural Heritage, November 16, 1972, 1037 U.N.T.S. 151. [Basic Document 7.18].

12.   Helsinki Protocol on Reduction of Sulfur Emissions or Their Transboundary Fluxes by at Least Thirty Per Cent, July 8, 1985, 27 I.L.M. 707 (entered into force Sept. 2, 1987) [Basic Document 3.15].

13.   EEC Council Directive 80/779, arts. 1–5, 11, 1980 O.J. (229) 30 [Basic Document 3.10].

14.   EEC Council Directive 85/203, arts. 1–5, 11, 1983 O.J. (87) 2 [Basic Document 3.13].

15.   *Sources and Nature of EU Environmental Law and Policy*, 3 Eur.Union L.Rep. (CCH) 3347–1, 3347–10 to 3347–23, 3347–31 to 3347–32 (1995).

Direct effect

While recommendations and opinions have no binding force, much of the secondary legislation (regulations, directives and decisions) creates rights and obligations which can, in certain circumstances, be relied upon by individuals before the courts of the member states. This is known as *direct effect* (see *NV Algemene Transport-en Expeditie Onderneming van Gend & Loos v Nederlandse Administratie der Belastingen* (Case 26/62) (1963) ECR 1).

The direct effect doctrine means that where a provision of Community law:

—is clear and unambiguous;

—is unconditional; and

—does not depend for its operation upon further action being taken by the Community or local authorities,

authorities in member states, including courts and tribunals must apply the provision to the benefit of individuals in the member states, even if the provision has not been incorporated into national law.

* * *

The precautionary principle

The precautionary principle is not defined in the treaty, however, in international law, the precautionary principle:

"... ensures that a substance or activity posing a threat to the environment is prevented from adversely affecting the environment, even if there is no conclusive scientific proof linking that particular substance or activity to environmental damage" (J. Cameron and J. Abouchar, "The precautionary principle: a fundamental principle of law and policy for the protection of the global environment" 1991, 14 *Boston College Int'l & Comp L R* 1).

The precautionary principle requires a non-scientifically based evaluation of the relative costs of regulatory inactivity, and involves a balancing of social, political, cultural and economic considerations. Article 130r(2) requires that Community environmental policy must be based on the precautionary principle.

[P]recautionary action generally applies where irreversible damage is threatened and can be applied to, inter alia, global warming, loss of species, electromagnetic fields, and emission of toxic substances.

* * *

The polluter-pays principle

The polluter-pays principle means that the costs of clean-up or prevention of environmental damage should be borne by the polluter. This principle has a comparatively long history in EC environmental policy. The EC adopted the principle in its first programme of action on the environment in 1973 (OJ 1973 C112/1). In 1975, the Council recommended that the EC, at the Community level, and the member states, in their national environmental legislation, apply the polluter-pays principle, according to which:

"... natural or legal persons governed by public or private law who are responsible for pollution must pay the costs of such measures as are necessary to eliminate that pollution or to reduce it so as to comply with the standards or equivalent measures ... laid down by the public authorities" (Council Recommendation 75/436, OJ 1975 L194/1).

EU citizens and environmental groups

EU citizens have standing in national courts to enforce member states' obligations through the direct effect doctrine where a Community directive, regulation or decision is first of all clear and unambiguous, secondly unconditional, and thirdly its operation does not depend on further action being taken by Community or national authorities. Accordingly, provisions of EC environmental law that lay down maximum values for permissible discharges, that prohibit certain activities or the use of certain substances, or that specify that individuals are to be informed or consulted can be seen as having direct effect (L Kramer, *The Implementation of Community Environmental Directives within Member States: Some Implications of the Direct Effect Doctrine* (1991) 3 *JEL* 1 39). Kramer has defined the following as capable of having direct effect:

... Directive 80/779 (standards for sulphur dioxide and suspended particulates, OJ 1980 L229.30);

... Directive 85/203 (nitrogen oxide, OJ 1985 L87/1);

[F]urthermore, where a directive states that its primary purpose is to protect human health, the ECJ has held that citizens are thereby granted rights where a specific limit value is established to breath air of that quality.

* * *

Damages

Where member states have violated rights provided for in environmental directives, liability for damages may result by application of art. 5 of the EC Treaty which requires member states to take all appropriate measures to ensure fulfilment of their obligations under Community law. In *Francovich v Italy* (Joined Cases C–6/90 and C–9/90) the ECJ held that it is a principle of Community law that member states are obliged to pay compensation for harm caused to individuals by breaches of Community law for which the member states can be held responsible. The court ruled that state liability for failure to fulfill its obligation to take all the measures necessary to achieve the result prescribed by a directive gives rise to a right to compensation where the following three conditions are met:

(1) the result required by the directive includes conferring rights for the benefit of individuals;

(2) it is possible to identify the content of these rights by reference to the provisions of the directive; and

(3) there is a causal link between the breach of the state's obligation and the harm suffered by the injured parties.

16. ALEXANDRE KISS & DINAH SHELTON, MANUAL OF EUROPEAN ENVIRONMENTAL LAW 351–52, *excerpt from* LUDWIG KRAMER, THE EUROPEAN COMMUNITY AND ATMOSPHERIC POLLUTION (1993).

Environmental directives aimed at air pollution establish quality objectives for the entire Community. Such objectives are fixed for sulphur dioxide and particulates,[22] lead,[23] and nitrogen dioxide.[24] Other directives fixing limits have been announced but not formally proposed.

These three directives require the establishment of measuring stations in areas where the concentration of pollutants is considered to be the most heavy. However, they leave to the Member States the choice of the precise location where these stations are to be installed. Given that they indicate only in a vague way the criteria determining the number of these stations, there is a great variation in the number installed from one state to another. To this

22. Directive 80/779, 1980 O.J. (L 229).   **24.** Directive 85/203, 1985 O.J. (L 87).
23. Directive 82/884, 1982 O.J. (L 378).

must be added the fact that the measuring instruments and the methodology are such that small changes lead to very different results.

Member States have the possibility, in sensitive zones, not to adhere to the limit values set by the directives. Such zones should be designated and communicated to the Commission within a certain period following adoption of the directive in question. At the same time, Member States should submit clean-up programmes with a time-table which assures that air pollution is reduced as rapidly as possible and in any case before 1989 (lead), 1993 (sulphur dioxide and particulates) or 1994 (nitrogen dioxide).

Subsequently, its seems apparent that Member States have designated the appropriate zones, but have not established the corresponding programmes designed to assure a progressive improvement in air quality within these zones. As the regular reports on the implementation of the directives and asserted violations are not always transmitted in the time required, supervision of the effective application of the directives remains very difficult. In other words, it is not clear whether the limits set by the directives are exceeded nor, in such cases, where the violations occur.

17. Ludwig Kramer, E.C. Treaty and Environmental Law 99, 101–02, 105–06 (2d ed. 1995).

Article 130t

Article 130t was introduced into the Treaty by the Single European Act. The Maastricht Treaty slightly changed the wording and added that national measures, which were maintained or introduced, had to be notified to the Commission. The Article balances the Member States' right to adopt measures to protect the environment against Community provisions.

* * *

Article 130t applies only if the Community has adopted rules on the basis of Article 130s. Article 130t says nothing about the form which the Community rules must take. It is therefore immaterial whether they are set out in a directive, a regulation or a decision to accede to an international convention.

[T]he measures must be adopted "pursuant to Article 130s". Article 130t does not, therefore, apply if the Community adopts environmental legislation based on, say, Articles 43 or 100a.

[O]nly "more stringent" protective measures are permitted under Article 130t. Consequently, the Member States may not adopt different measures from the Community. On the contrary, the tougher protective measures must aim in the same direction and come closer than the Community rules to attaining the objectives of Article 130s(1).

* * *

Measures adopted under Article 130t must be notified to the Commission. There is no time-limit for such notification and the measures must not be notified to the Commission in draft form.... It follows from general principles of the Treaty and in particular from Article 5, that Member States are under obligation to inform the Commission as early as reasonably possible of their national measures—and of their intention to maintain them.

18.   L. NEVILLE BROWN & TOM KENNEDY, THE COURT OF JUSTICE OF THE EUROPEAN COMMUNITIES 17, 60–62, 107–08, 113–14, 193, 201, 207–08, 213–14, 277–78 (4th ed. 1994).

Introduction

There is ... at Luxembourg the dichotomy made in several continental legal systems between, on the one hand, those who sit in judgment—the Bench, as we would say in England, or *la magistrature assise* as the French jargon puts it, and, on the other, "the standing judiciary" (*la magistrature debout*), by which are meant the six advocates general. The latter do not themselves sit in judgment but rather stand to proffer advice to the Bench of how it should decide the cases before the Court. . . .

* * *

Advocates General

While the functions of a judge are generally understood, the role of the advocate general in the Court is less easily grasped, especially in countries where the legal system has no precise equivalent. His title, too, is something of a misnomer, since he is really no more an advocate than he is a general.[25] On the contrary, he is a member of the Court.

* * *

It is the main task of the advocate general, again according to Article 166, "acting with complete impartiality and independence, to make, in open court, reasoned submissions on cases brought before the Court of Justice, in order to assist the Court in the performance of the task assigned to it in Article 164." This he does by delivering what is termed an "opinion," (in French, *"conclusions"*), after the case has been heard and normally at a later hearing, in which he gives the judges his view of the case and seeks to help them reach their judgment. Usually in his opinion he will review the facts of the case, deal with the submissions of the parties and of any others who have taken part in the proceedings, review the law, and finally express his own opinion on how the judges should decide the case. He takes no further part in the case and does not attend the private meetings at which the judges deliberate.

* * *

Procedure Under Article 169

An action by the Commission under Article 169 involves three phases. The formal procedure is invariably preceded in practice by the commission writing a letter to the member State warning of its breach and inviting its comments. If this does not settle the matter, and in two cases out of three it does, then the first formal step is for the Commission to invite the State formally to submit its observations on the alleged breach, after which, if it is not satisfied by the explanations or undertakings given by the State, the Commission will deliver a reasoned opinion.

[I]f the State is recalcitrant, the second phase in the procedure is for the Commission to bring the matter before the Court. Settlements are sometimes

---

25. A quip first made by the first advocate general from the United Kingdom, J.-P. War- ner in *Some Aspects of the European Court of Justice* 14 S.P.T.L. 16 (1976).

made at this stage. The third and final phase is for the Court to give judgment.

Procedure Under Article 170

The alternative procedure to Article 169 is that under Article 170 which permits any Member State to bring another Member State before the Court if it considers the latter has failed to fulfill an obligation under the Treaty. This form of action has rarely been used. Like the procedure under Article 169, Article 170 is in successive phases. The first phase requires the complaining State to bring the alleged infringement before the Commission. The Commission must then deliver a reasoned opinion, as under Article 169, after allowing the States concerned to submit their observations. Only then ... may the complaining State bring the defaulting State before the Court.

* * *

Preliminary Rulings

In many ways the most important aspect of the work of the Court is its jurisdiction to give "preliminary rulings" under Article 177 EC....

As we have seen, disputes involving Community law, whether between individuals or companies, or between private parties and the national authorities of the Member States, never come directly before the Court of Justice, but before the courts and tribunals of the Member States. The treaty provisions enable the Court of Justice, at the request of the national court, to rule on questions of Community law which arise in such litigation. This jurisdiction is exclusive to the Court of Justice....

* * *

The procedure on a reference is in all cases the same.... First it should be noted that a decision to refer can be taken only by a national court. In practice such a decision will usually be taken at the instance of the parties or of one of them; but the court may also take the step of its own motion, even contrary to the express wishes of the parties. When a reference is made, the proceedings before the national court are generally stayed for the period, currently about 18 months in most cases, until the ruling is given. The procedure before the Court of Justice is, as we have seen, an interlocutory step in the action before the national court; but the Community institutions concerned (that is, the Commission in all cases ...) and all Member States, as well as the parties to the action before the national court, have the opportunity of submitting observations, both in writing and at an oral hearing, before the Court of Justice. When the ruling has been given, it is sent to the national court, and the proceedings there are resumed.

* * *

In the historic *Van Gend en Loos* case, ... the Court for the first time held that a provision of Community law "produces direct effects and creates individual rights which national courts must protect" (Case 26/62 (1963) ECR 1 at p. 16)....

* * *

[T]he notion of direct effect of Community law, coupled with the jurisdiction of the Court to give a preliminary ruling and so to determine the scope of the individual's rights and obligations, is a more powerful weapon (than the discretionary remedy of the Commission or Member State acting on the individual's behalf) (explanatory added). The individual has no direct remedy, before the Court, against the default of a State. The remedy lies in the national court with the use of Article 177 where appropriate, and with a possible action in damages for such default.[26]

* * *

Courts and Tribunals Obliged to Refer

Under the last paragraph of Article 177 ... a court or tribunal against whose decision there is no judicial remedy under national law is not merely entitled, but obliged, to refer a question, if it considers that a decision on that question is necessary to enable it to give judgment. A reference in such a case is not discretionary but mandatory.

* * *

Legal Representation

A Member State or a Community institution is represented by an agent appointed for the case, assisted, as necessary, by an advisor or lawyer. Member States appear quite frequently; apart from their role as parties in direct actions, usually as defendants in proceedings by the commission under Article 169 EC, Member States frequently make use of their right to submit observations in references from national courts.

* * *

The Council and the Commission are usually represented by a member of their respective Legal Services, although they occasionally instruct private practitioners. The role of the legal Service of the Commission is particularly important. The Commission, apart from appearing as applicant or defendant in most contentious cases, always submits observations in references from national courts, and can assist the Court be explaining the background to the particular Community instrument in question, which it will usually be responsible for drafting. It can also supply information on the economic context of the provision, or on the way in which it has been implemented in the Member States.

19. Noemi Gal–Or, *Private Party Direct Access: A Comparison of the NAFTA and the EU Disciplines* 21 B.C. Int'l & Comp. L. Rev. 1, 13–14, 17, 23, 34 (1998).

A private party may have several identities and forms. It may consist of an individual person, a small business, a multinational corporation, an interest group, or a class registered as an association. The financial and legal

26. See the momentous decision in Cases C–6, 9/90, Francovich v. Italian State, 1991 ECR I–5357. For commentary on *Francovich* and its impact: see James E. Hanft, *Francovich and Bonifaci v. Italy: EEC Member State Liability for Failure to Implement Community Di-rectives* 15 Fordham Int'l 1237 L.J.(1991–92); K. Parker, *State Liability in Damages for Breach of Community Law* L.Q.R. 181 (1992); and Josephine Steiner, *From Direct Effect to Francovich: Shifting Means of Enforcement of Community Law,* 18 Eur. L.Rev. 3 (1993).

resources at the disposal of the private party may determine its nature. Accordingly, the legally unincorporated person may litigate as (1) an individual, (2) a "litigation coalition" representing a group of individuals coalescing for a particular ad hoc case and purpose, (3) a group that registered separate applications, but is heard as a joint case, (4) a "membership association" protecting a common mutual interest (e.g., staff associations, trade unions, consumer, and environmental associations) either as intervenors or as plaintiffs, and (5) as "representative groups" acting only as intervenors in litigation for non-parties and claiming to represent the public interest. The "legal" person, however, must have "the necessary independence to act as a responsible body in legal matters." This classification reflects the road EU law has traveled since its inception, gradually expanding to include social conflicts, in addition to economic issues, as important causes of action.

* * *

The Treaties lack an EU notion of a legal person. When examining the capacity of a legal person to bring an action, the Court resorts to the relevant national law. "Thus, the legal personality under national law is required to exercise the right of action, as provided for by the Treaties."[27]

* * *

The doctrine of "direct effect" was devised to allow the individual the option of proceeding against the Member State in the national court.

* * *

[T]he EU's goals encompass social, cultural, environmental, and even political issues as part of the integration process. Embedded in a customs union, achievement of these goals is enhanced in the harmonization of trade law; enforceability is secured through the device of "direct effect," whereby individuals enjoy direct access to EU law via their national courts. The EU has thus been evolving into a quasi-federal legal system where "constitutional" judicial review and an appellate court system are available at the highest level, namely the ECJ. Due to a persisting lack of clarity separating the jurisdiction of the EU courts from the national courts, gaps in private party access to remedies still exist. These gaps can be bridged only by the private party's invocation of national litigation in order to gain indirectly access to the EU courts. There remains, however, a large body of non-direct effect law which gives rise to disputes between individuals and EU institutions (and between Member States and institutions as well) that cannot be addressed in the national courts. In this area, there is only limited room available for direct access by private parties to EU legal recourse through EU institutions, including litigation for final judgment.

* * *

The judicial procedures provided by the EC Treaty are concentrated in Articles 169, 177, and 173. Article 169 gives the Commission the sole right to file proceedings regarding the non-, or deficient, implementation of Communi-

27. GERHARD BEBR, DEVELOPMENT OF JUDICIAL   (1981).
CONTROL OF THE EUROPEAN COMMUNITIES 32

ty law by Member States. Under Article 170, Member States also have the right to file such proceedings. These articles exclude the private party for both purposes of direct litigation and intervention. Under Article 177, the private party may be represented by the Member State which files a preliminary reference with the ECJ. The national court makes the reference. Both the parties to the action before that court and the Member State in which it is situated have the right to submit written and oral observations to the ECJ independently. This procedural device may be used to review the validity of Community legislation, as well as to protect private party rights arising from the Community's legal order against any obstructing national legislation. As this procedure requires representation by the state, the question of standing is subject to disparities among the various national legal orders.

20.   GERHARD BEBR, DEVELOPMENT OF JUDICIAL CONTROL OF THE EUROPEAN COMMUNITIES 394, 396, 398 (1981).

So far the Court has been very liberal in admitting a referral of a national court. Thus, for example, in one instance the Court maintained that " . . . when a national court . . . refers a provision of Community law for interpretation, it is to be *supposed* that the said court . . . considers this interpretation necessary to enable it to give judgment in the action."[28] And it significantly added that it " . . . cannot require the national court . . . to state expressly that the provision which appears to that court . . . to call for an interpretation is applicable."[29] This ruling follows the well established jurisprudence according to which the Court may not review or appreciate the relevance of questions for the pending litigation which a national court raised.

* * *

The jurisdiction of the Court is established by a request of a national court for a preliminary ruling—provided, of course, the referral is duly made and admissible.

* * *

In *Rheinmühlen*[30] the Court forcefully confirmed this view. "In the interests of clarity and legal certainty, this Court must abide by the decision to refer, which must have its full effect so long as it has not been revoked."

The national court is thus, so to speak, the master of the preliminary proceeding—at any time it may withdraw its request and deprive the Court of its jurisdiction. But is this strict respect of the request of a national court also justified when its decision to refer is appealed to a higher court? As may be inferred from its case law, the Court assumes so on several grounds. Firstly, it follows logically from the strict separation of the Community and national jurisdiction. Thus—and this is the second point—the pursuit of the litigation is a matter for national courts, governed by the national rules of procedure. The Court may not interpret these rules but this would be so if it would consider the effect such an appeal may have on the pending preliminary proceeding. Thirdly, and this follows from the preceding considerations, the

---

28. Preliminary ruling 5/77 (Tedeschi v. Denkavit [1977] ECR 1555,1574

29. *Id.*

30. Preliminary ruling 146/73, Rheinmühlen-Düsseldorf v. Einfuhr-und Vorratsstelle fur Getreide . . . , 1974 E.C.R. 139.

referral of a national court is the only relevant and decisive factor in establishing the Court's jurisdiction. These considerations carry ultimately, in the Court's view, a greater weight than the consequences likely to result from a preliminary ruling which meanwhile became devoid of object because the superior court quashed the decision of reference.

21.   Fabian Amtenbrink, *Public Interest Litigation before European Courts*, 7 EUR. BUS. L. REV. 35, 35-37 (1996).

[P]ublic interest may to some extent be involved in preliminary reference procedures under Article 177 EC. On the one hand, that provision can be used as a tool to review the validity of Community legislation in favour of *public interest*. On the other hand, preliminary rulings by the ECJ can also help to protect the rights of citizens arising from the Community's legal order against any national legislation that stands in the way. The Court fixes the premises according to which a national court then declares a Member State's legal act compatible/incompatible with Community or national law. Indeed, as *Caranta* observes: "National courts have only to pull the trigger, the aim has already been taken."[31] Nevertheless, the value of Article 177 EC with respect to public interest litigation is diminished by the fact that the pursuit of *public interest* before national courts by private individuals and interest groups is subject to the different national procedural rules on *locus standi*. National standing requirements, aimed at preventing *actio popularis*, may often result in the indirect participation of *public interest* via the support of individual interest litigation, *ie* individual plaintiffs, by public interest groups.

22.   Carol Harlow, *Towards a Theory of Access for the European Court of Justice*, 12 Y.B. EUR. L. 213, 218, 229, 234, 235-36 (1992).

[T]he argument of this article is first, that more space is needed for public interest representation in the Court of Justice; secondly, that standing and intervention are facets of the same problem of access and need to be considered in tandem; and, finally, that the procedures of the Court of Justice in fact contain mechanisms which can supply these needs without introducing undue complexity or adding unduly to the Court's backlog.

* * *

It might be argued that pluralist representation of the public interest is ensured through the doctrine of privileged access to the Court by Member States and Community institutions.

* * *

Article 20 of the Statute permits the "Member States, Commission and Council" to submit "observations" in any preliminary reference under Article 177. Nowhere are the international law origins of the Court of Justice more clearly reflected.

A.   INTERVENTIONS

How in practice do the privileged applicants use their rights? The pattern of litigation is necessarily sporadic but something about the behaviour of the

---

31. Roberto Caranta, The Judicial Protection Against Member States: The Indirect Effects of Art. 173, 175 and 177, Conference paper (1995).

member States can be learned from statistics regularly compiled by the Court of observations in Article 177 cases. These show that the right to make observations or intervene has been freely used by the Member States.

* * *

In the Court of Justice, ... an individual may challenge only an *individuated* administrative act by which he is directly affected. Thus the jurisdiction of the Court of Justice is effectively narrower than that of a typical administrative court in that challenge to Community normative acts can be mounted only by the privileged applicants. This limitation has been described by Maurice Lagrange as *"une amputation serieuse de la competence normale d'une juridiction administrative"*. It has also been contrasted unfavourably with the jurisdiction of a "mature federation" such as the United States or Germany, which do offer judicial review to their citizens on a wide basis.

* * *

The Article 177 procedure may also allow the restrictions on direct entry to be bypassed by putting the validity of a general Community act or regulation indirectly in issue.

* * *

Article 177 References

[T]he doctrine of "direct effect" (which created rights enforceable against the Member States in national courts and allows the validity of national acts and policies to be tested against Community law) has been described as the strongest plank in the Court's strategy for the protection of *individual* rights by the Community legal order. Again, preliminary references under Article 177 have been called "the principal avenue whereby *individuals* may make use of the rights and (duties) bestowed on them by the EC legal order. The range of subject-matter is theoretically wide, mirroring the case-load of national civil and administrative courts. To pick at random from the case-law, individuals have sought to establish freedom of movement, queried income tax assessments, claimed social security benefits, equal pay and damages for invalid administrative action, protested against discrimination, and challenged nationalization, immigration policies, and disputed elections."

* * *

[T]he system of legal protection established by the Treaty, as set out in Article 177 in particular, implies that it must be possible for every type of action provided for by national law to be available for the purpose of ensuring observance of Community provisions having direct effect, on the same conditions concerning admissibility and procedure as would apply were it a question of ensuring observance of national law.

* * *

[I]t has been suggested that standards set by the Community environmental directives might give rise to rights enforceable "where appropriate, before the national courts."[32] To put this differently, environmental directives

32. Cases 361/88, 59/89, Commission v. Germany 1991 E.C.R. 2567, 2602.

could either give rise to a civil law right of damages for statutory nuisance or oblige national courts to permit challenges to the validity of national environmental law. In this way, a path would be opened via Article 177 into the [European] Court of Justice for private applicants who at present have to rely on the Commission to bring infringement proceedings under Article 169. The two systems would thus act as a rachet to open up standing provisions across the Community.

23. *International Environmental Wrongs*, Chapter 5, *supra* at **335.**

24. World Charter for Nature, Oct. 28, 1982, Principle 12, 21, G.A. Res. 37/7, U.N. GAOR, 37th Sess., Supp. No. 51, at 17, U.N. Doc. A/37/51, 22 I.L.M. 455 (1983). [Basic Document 1.21].

25. Convention on Long–Range Transboundary Air Pollution (LRTAP), Nov. 13, 1979, arts. 1–5, 18 I.L.M. 1442 (1979). [Basic Document 3.8].

26. JUTTA BRUNNÉE, ACID RAIN AND OZONE DEPLETION: INTERNATIONAL LAW AND REGULATION 108–11 (1988).

THE DUTY TO CONSULT AND NEGOTIATE

It is less clear whether, beyond the duty of notification or information, states are also obliged to consult with potentially harmed neighboring states. Some authors contend that there is a general duty of consultation in transfrontier pollution cases. Others claim that the existing evidence of confirming *opinio juris* and state practice is, especially regarding air pollution, not sufficient.

With respect to water resources, the principle of consultation is widely accepted as a rule of customary international law. The 1909 Boundary Waters Treaty between the United States and the United Kingdom/Canada provides an early example. With the International Joint Commission (IJC) the parties set up a body which, as one of its major tasks, offered a forum for consultations. Further support for the existence of the principle can be derived from the *Lac Lanoux* case **[Basic Document 8.3]**....

* * *

The principle of consultation has as well been recognized by the International Court of Justice in the *North Sea Continental Shelf* cases[33] and the *Fisheries Jurisdiction Case.*[34]

In support of a broader applicability of the principle it can be argued that it emanates from the obligation of peaceful settlement of disputes underlying the United Nations Charter **[Basic Document 1.3]**.... Although duty to engage in consultations or negotiations on transboundary air pollution can certainly not be derived directly from the peaceful settlement principle, the latter does provide a guideline for the conduct of states in the case of a

33. North Sea Continental Shelf Cases (Judgment) (Federal Republic of Germany/Denmark) (Federal Republic of Germany/Netherlands), 1969 I.C.J. 3. *See* excerpt from these cases in Chapter 2, *supra* at 107.

34. Fisheries Jurisdiction Case (U.K. v. Iceland), 1974 I.C.J. 3, 31, 32.

dispute arising because of unlawful transfrontier pollution. A duty to consult or to negotiate would arise under the Charter mainly, perhaps only, if the continuation of the dispute threatened international peace and security (Article 33 United Nations Charter). Thus far disputes about transfrontier air pollution have not represented such a threat.

In the context of dispute settlement a recommendation with regard to negotiation is formulated in Article XXX of the Helsinki Rules [on the Uses of the Waters of International Rivers **(Basic Document 4.6)**]: "In case of a dispute between States as to their legal rights or other interests ... they should seek a solution by negotiation." Further references can be found, for example, in Article 13 of the 1979 ECE Convention [on Long–Range Transboundary Air Pollution (LRTAP) **(Basic Document 3.8)**], Article 11 of the Vienna Ozone Layer Convention **[Basic Document 3.14]**, and Article 30 of the ASEAN Agreement. However, one has to be careful to distinguish negotiations or consultations held in order to settle an already existing dispute from consultations held prior to potentially harmful activities. In the latter context the OECD recommendations of 1974 and 1977 **[Basic Documents 3.6 & 3.7]** provide indications of a duty to engage in consultations. In Principle 7 the 1974 Recommendation says that: "Countries should enter into consultation on an existing or foreseeable transfrontier pollution problem at the request of a country which is or may be directly affected and should diligently pursue such consultations on this particular problem over a reasonable period of time." The other documents mentioned with regard to a duty to inform equally lend support to the existence of an obligation to consult. General Assembly Resolution 3129 **[Basic Document 1.14]**, Article 3 of the Charter of Economic Rights and Duties of States **[Basic Document 7.2]**, and the UNEP Draft Principles of Conduct **[Basic Document 1.18]** all make reference to consultations to be engaged in by states sharing a natural resource.

Further evidence of the acceptance of a duty to consult on existing or potential transfrontier air pollution problems are the Council of Europe's 1971 Resolution on Air Pollution in Frontier Areas, Articles 8, 10, 11 of the Mexican–United States Agreement on cooperation in the border area, Article 3 of the Canada–United States MOI, Articles 3 and 5 of the ECE Convention on Long–Range Transboundary Air Pollution, Articles 18–21 of the ASEAN Convention, and Article 6 of the Vienna Convention on the Protection of the Ozone Layer. The Mexican–United States agreement, the ASEAN Convention and the Vienna Convention on the Protection of the Ozone Layer do not refer to consultations prior to specific activities. There the duty to consult is directed towards the development and administration of the respective agreements. An example at the regional level is to be found in the "Nordic Convention" between Denmark, Finland, Norway, and Sweden. Article 11 stipulates that:

> Where the permissibility of environmentally harmful activities which entail or may entail considerable nuisance in another contracting State is being examined by the Government or by the appropriate Minister or Ministry of the State in which the activities are being carried out, consultations shall take place between the States concerned if the Government of the former State so requests.[35]

35. *Reprinted in* 13 I.L.M. 591 (1974).

It could be asked whether States actually consider themselves obligated to consult with concerned countries or whether they only do so at their convenience. One would expect that the large number of countries that support the consultation principle feel an obligation to consult in relevant cases. States may, of course, argue that a significant danger of transfrontier air pollution does not exist, but this in itself indicates that in principle they recognize the duty to consult. The above-mentioned examples of European state practice, particularly those involving border area commissions, support this view. The International Boundary and Water Commission (IBWC) established between Mexico and the United States, and the United States–Canada IJC point in the same direction. However, it should be remembered that the IBWC is primarily concerned with technical issues; consultations on other matters appear to take place on a rather ad hoc basis. Although not displaying a regular pattern, the transfrontier pollution cases between the United States and Canada indicate that both countries are willing to engage in consultations.

In summary, I am concluding that state practice is too scattered to lend support to the existence of a general rule of prior consultation or even negotiations. In many cases the existing practice has evolved around particularly significant risks of harm.

For cases of air pollution causing or threatening to cause *significant* transboundary harm it can therefore be concluded that a rule of customary international law obliges states to consult with concerned neighboring states. But it must be stressed once again that the obligation is only one to consult or to negotiate in good faith and not one to actually reach an agreement. States have thus far not been ready to agree on such a caveat to their sovereignty.

Discussion Notes/Questions

1. Regarding causation and proof in respect of state responsibility for transfrontier environmental harm, consider the following from Jutta Brunnée, *Acid Rain and Ozone Depletion: International Law and Regulation* 119 (1988):

> In transfrontier air pollution cases one of the most difficult aspects is to actually establish a chain of causation between the alleged polluter and the damage suffered. For a state attempting to hold another state responsible, an additional difficulty arises from the burden of proof. Generally, each side has to prove facts on which it banks its rights and claims. The victim country might thus have to prove the existence of the rule broken by the polluting state *and* the causation of the damage. Considering that most evidence with respect to the latter may well be beyond the reach of the victim country, such distribution of the burden of proof does not seem equitable. If we placed more emphasis on territorial integrity, we could more readily establish an assumption that transfrontier pollution is illegal. This would result in a shift of the burden of proof, at least with regard to the existence of rules prohibiting pollution. However, at this point it does not seem likely that major source countries would favor such a shift. Also, in some cases victim countries may at another occasion assume the role of the polluter. Thus they too may not be willing to press too hard for a general shift of the burden of proof in order to "protect" themselves from future claims.

2. A state is responsible only for activities that can be "attributed" to it. Attribution may easily be proved where the polluting activity is carried out by the state itself or by its agencies. But what if transboundary pollution is caused by

private entities and enterprises? Can their actions be attributed to the state? As Problem 10–3 ("A Rainforest and the Guahibo Are Threatened in Amazonia and Caribia") demonstrates, this is a more difficult question and still is surrounded by controversy. In the instant problem, it has been assumed that any pollution arising from within its boundaries is attributable to Swabia. This cannot always be assumed in other cases. Consider, in this regard, subsection D(2) of Chapter 5, *International Environmental Wrongs, supra,* p. 366, discussing "Attribution of Responsibility."

3. The NAPAP study (Reading 5, *supra*) raises an important question: Have we spent billions of dollars on killing a phantom dragon of acid rain? The debate is by no means over, but we must again face up to an issue endemic to environmental decision making: How certain must we be before action is taken? On the one hand, delay may aggravate pollution and make remedial action more expensive. On the other hand, in a world that compels us to take from Peter to pay Paul, the money spent on acid rain may well be the money denied to action on global warming. Could it be argued that the demand for greater certainty may be justified in the case of acid rain, where the consequences are remediable, but not in the case of global warming where the results of inaction may be irremediable?

4. *Bibliographical Note.* For further discussion concerning the principle themes addressed in this problem, consult the following specialized materials:

(a) *Specialized Books/Monographs.* Acid Rain: The Relationship Between Sources and Receptors (J. White ed. 1988); R. Boyle & R. Boyle, Acid Rain (1983); J. Brunnée, Acid Rain and Ozone Layer Depletion: International Law and Regulation (1988); J. Carroll, Acid Rain: An Issue in Canadian–American Relations (1982); T. Crocker, Economic Perspectives on Acid Deposition Control (1984); S. Elsworth, Acid Rain (1984); R. Gould, Going Sour (1985); A. Kahan, Acid Rain: Reign of Controversy (1986); J. McCormick, Acid Earth: The Global Threat of Acid Pollution (1985); J. Merrills, International Dispute Settlement (1991); Organization of Economic Cooperation and Development, Environmental Effects of Electricity Generation (1985); R. Ostmann, Acid Rain (1982); F. Record, D. Bubenick, D. & R. Kindya, Acid Rain Information Book (1982); J. Regens & R. Ryecroft, The Acid Rain Controversy (1989); J. Schmandt, J. Clarkson, & H. Roderick, Acid Rain and Friendly Neighbors: The Policy Dispute Between Canada and the United States (1988); The Acid Rain Debate: Scientific, Economic, and Political Dimensions (E. Yanarella & R. Ihara eds. 1985); Transboundary Air Pollution: International Legal Aspects of the Co-operation of States (1986); World Commission on Environment and Development, Our Common Future (1987).

(b) *Specialized Hearings/Reports.* J. Barnard & A. Lucier, *Report 16: Changes in Forest Health and Productivity in the United States and Canada, in* Acidic Deposition: States of Science and Technology, Summary Report of NAPAP (P. Irving ed., Sept. 1991); Federal/Provincial Research and Monitoring Committee (RMCC), Assessment of the State of Knowledge on the Long–Range Transport of Air Pollutants and Acid Deposition (August 1986); J. Lammers, First (Preliminary) Report of the ILA Committee on Legal Aspects of Long–Distance Air Pollution in ILA, Report of the Sixty-first Conference 377 (1984); Swedish Royal Ministry for Foreign Affairs and Swedish Royal Ministry of Agriculture, Air Pollution Across National Boundaries: The Impact on the Environment of Sulphur in Air and Precipitation (1972); Transboundary Air Pollution–Effects and Control: Report Prepared Within the Framework of the Convention on Long–Range Transboundary Air Pollution (1986); U.S. Congress, Office of Technology Assessment, Acid Rain and Transported Air Pollutants: Implications for Public Policy

(1984); U.S. House of Representatives, Acid Rain: Hearings Before the Subcommittee on Oversight and Investigation of the Committee on Interstate and Foreign Commerce (1980); ___, Effects of Air Pollution and Acid Rain on Forest Decline: Oversight Hearing Before the Subcommittee on Mining, Forest Management and Bonneville Power Administration of the Committee on Interior and Insular Affairs (1984).

(c) *Specialized Articles/Book Chapters.* W. Bown, *Europe's Forests Fall to Acid Rain,* 127 New Scientist 17 (Aug. 11, 1990); A. Fraenkel, *The Convention on Long–Range Transboundary Air Pollution: Meeting the Challenge of International Cooperation,* 30 H.I.L.J. 447 (1989); J. Galloway & E. Cowling, The Effects of Precipitation On Aquatic and Terrestrial Ecosystems—A Proposed Precipitation Chemistry Network, 28 J. Air Pollution Control Associations 229 (1978); A. Gottlieb, *Acid Rain: A Common Problem, A Joint Solution,* 4 J. Mineral L. & Pol'y 1 (1988); G. Handl, *Territorial Sovereignty and the Problem of Transnational Pollution,* 69 A.J.I.L. 50 (1975); ___, *National Uses of Transboundary Air Resources: The International Entitlement Issue Reconsidered,* 26 N.R.J. 405 (1986); N. Helme & C. Neme, *Acid Rain: The Problem,* 17 EPA J. 18, 18–20 (1991); N. Higton & M. Chadwick, *The Effects of Changing Patterns of Energy Use on Sulfur Emissions and Depositions in Europe,* 11 Ambio 324 (1982); A. Katzenstein, *Acid Rain: A Further Look at the Evidence,* 24 Power Engineering 32 (1986); A. Marsh, *Environmental Issues in Contemporary European Politics, in* The European Transition from Oil 121 (G. Goodman, L. Kristoferson, J. Hollander eds. 1981); B. Molski & W. Dmuchowski, *Effects of Acidification on Forests and Natural Vegetation, Wild Animals and Insects, in* Acidification and Its Policy Implications 29 (T. Shneider ed. 1986); Note, *Acid Rain in the European Community: A Hard Rain's A–Gonna Fall,* 16 Brook. J. Int'l L. 621 (1990); M. Pallemaerts, *Judicial Recourse Against Foreign Air Polluters: A Case Study of Acid Rain In Europe,* 9 Harv. Envtl. L. Rev. 143 (1985); J. Paul, *Urban Air Quality: The Problem,* 17 EPA Journal 23 (Jan.-Feb. 1991); S. Rissberger, *On the Brink of an Ecological Calamity: Acid Rain, Transboundary Air Pollution and Environmental Law in West Germany,* 12 Syracuse J. Int'l L. 325 (1985); P. Sands, *European Community Environmental Law: The Evolution of a Regional Regime of International Environmental Protection,* 100 Yale L. J. 2511 (1991); R. Wagenbauer, *The European Community's Policy on Implementation of Environmental Directives,* 14 Fordham Int'l L. J. 455 (1990–91); G. Wetstone, *Air Pollution Control Laws in North America and the Problem of Acid Rain and Snow,* 10 Envtl. L. Rep. 50001 (February 1980); G. Wetstone & A. Rosencranz, *Transboundary Air Pollution: The Search for an International Response,* 8 Harv. Envtl. L. Rev. 89 (1984).

Problem 7–2

Nueva Granada Versus the Ozone Layer

SECTION 1. FACTS

Nueva Granada is a developing nation of nearly thirty-five million people in southern South America. In recent years, Nueva Granada's economic situation has gradually improved, in part because of an increasingly prosperous agricultural sector. Part of the reason for this success has been the growing use by local farmers of modern farming techniques, including the heavy use of fertilizer and pesticides. In addition, trade agreements calling for the liberalization of agricultural trade have opened up foreign markets to Nueva Granadan exports. Nueva Granadan farmers have found that the United States is a particularly lucrative export market for local fruits and vegetables, especially during January–March, the U.S. winter season.

One of the pesticides which has entered into widespread use in Nueva Granada is methyl bromide. Methyl bromide, a colorless, odorless gas, is a powerful and effective tool for controlling pests at several stages in the production and transportation of food crops. Although methyl bromide is extremely toxic to humans (exposure at high levels can cause permanent disability or death), its usefulness is such that the food industry values it highly and uses it widely, despite the health risks it poses for workers. Methyl bromide is used to fumigate soil before crops are planted, to treat crops directly during storage or shipment, and to eradicate a variety of pests, including insects and rodents, from warehouses, food-processing plants and common carriers.

According to the U.S. Environmental Protection Agency, about 76,000 tons of methyl bromide is used globally each year. The bulk of the use is in soil fumigation, and the heaviest use (about 43%) occurs in North America, mostly in the United States. Nueva Granada's use is relatively low, about 1000 tons annually, less than 2% of total global use.

In addition to posing health hazards to workers who use it, methyl bromide are an ozone-depleting substance, with a relatively high ozone-depleting potential (ODP). A particular problem with methyl bromide is that its various uses all involve high rates of release of the gas into the atmosphere. When methyl bromide is injected into the soil for soil fumigation, 50–95% of the gas eventually reaches the atmosphere. The rate is 80–95% for methyl bromide used in commodity treatment and over 90% when the gas is used for structural pest control. Those who are concerned with the continuing problem of ozone depletion view the elimination of methyl bromide as a major objective.

Nueva Granada was an early signatory of the two main international instruments that relate to the earth's ozone layer, the 1985 Vienna Convention for the Protection of the Ozone Layer and the 1987 Montreal Protocol on Substances that Deplete the Ozone Layer; however, despite its early adherence to these instruments, Nueva Granada has joined other developing nations in refusing to sign or ratify any of the subsequent amendments to the Montreal Protocol. In particular, it has refused to adhere to the 1990 London Amendments, the 1992 Copenhagen Amendments, and the 1997 Montreal Amendments. Methyl bromide was not added to the group of substances controlled by the ozone treaty system until its inclusion was mandated by the 1992 Copenhagen Amendments, and Nueva Granada has taken no steps to discourage methyl bromide use by its agriculture industry. Indeed, underground brine deposits containing high concentrations of bromide salts (used in the production of methyl bromide) have recently been discovered in Nueva Granada, and the government is considering inviting a major producer of methyl bromide to consider beginning production in that country.

Nueva Granada has consistently made a number of points in support of its refusal to join any of the amendments to the Montreal Protocol. First, it asserts the right to sovereign control over its own resources. Second, it notes the urgent need of its people to lift themselves out of their longstanding poverty and social chaos, brought about by centuries of colonialism and a decade-long civil war financed in large part by certain large industrial nations. Third, Nueva Granada observes that it is free to do as it pleases because no existing international legal rules require it to change its behavior. Thus, while it has attended all the international ozone layer negotiations called by the United Nations Environment Programme (UNEP), Nueva Granada has always strenuously declared that it will not sign or ratify any instruments coming out of the negotiations if they have the potential to limit its freedom to choose its own best path to development. Nueva Granada accuses the developed nations of hypocrisy for having used ozone-depleting technology for their own gain, while now attempting to decree that no one else may do the same.

Nueva Granada's position is, ultimately, that it will not agree to participate in an international phaseout of any ozone-depleting substance unless there are feasible alternatives to that substance, and the developed nations agree to pay developing nations the incremental costs of shifting to the alternative substances. The amendments to the Montreal Protocol, it claims, have added substances for which there are no readily available substitutes. Moreover, there is no guarantee from the developed countries that they will provide the necessary financial and technical resources to implement the amendments. Thus, Nueva Granada indicates that it does not intend to ratify any of the amendments to the Protocol and will participate in international limits on the use of controlled substances only to the extent that it can do so without harming its development. It insists, moreover, that the judgment about what can be done without harming its development is for it alone to make.

In 1993, the U.S. Environmental Protection Agency added methyl bromide to a list of "Class I ozone-depleting substances" under the Clean Air Act. Pursuant to the Act, the EPA scheduled methyl bromide for phaseout by 2001. Although that schedule remains in force, the U.S. Congress is under increasing pressure from methyl bromide producers and from U.S. agricultural interests to modify the schedule or eliminate the phaseout altogether. The Administration's response to the pressure is, in part, to argue to the users of methyl bromide that there are much safer alternatives which can be used without violating U.S. international commitments. However, the producers argue that the refusal of countries like Nueva Granada (a major exporter of fruits and vegetables to the U.S.) to agree to restrictions on the use of methyl bromide means that U.S. producers would be placed at a significant competitive disadvantage if forced to use more expensive and potentially less effective methods of pest control.

The U.S. Administration has decided that it must be seen to be taking effective action against Nueva Granada if its domestic ban on methyl bromide is to survive this political attack. It has decided, therefore, to try and put a stop to the Nueva Granadan "in our own time" ozone policy, which it considers to be an evasion of an international legal consensus that had been achieved after much diplomatic effort and at considerable economic cost to the world. Accordingly, the United States has formally protested to Nueva Granada for flouting this consensus. Breach of this legal consensus, it claims, endangers the future of life on Earth. While conceding that Nueva Granada is a developing country entitled to the deference provided in article 5 of the 1987 Montreal Protocol, the United States requested that Nueva Granada abide by the emission levels that had been established in the 1985 Ozone Convention and *all* of its progeny, and limit and reduce its manufacture of ozone-depleting goods and substances. Nueva Granada, however, adamantly refuses to alter its policy and asserts strongly that it is entitled under international law to pursue its existing policies, in the words of President Valdez, "uninterrupted and without external interference." To date, it has not changed its position and continues to manufacture and use ozone-depleting goods and substances in defiance of the limits and controls imposed by the various amendments to the Montreal Protocol.

You are a lawyer on one of two designated teams in the Office of the Legal Adviser of the United States Department of State. You have been asked by the Legal Adviser to submit a memorandum on the questions presented, arguing for Nueva Granada or the United States according to your designation, in order that he may advise the President of the United States. He instructs you to disregard any specialized international trade rules—e.g., the rules of the W.T.O. agreements—that might apply.

SECTION 2. QUESTIONS PRESENTED

1. Is Nueva Granada violating international law?

2. If so, what rights/remedies does the United States have against Nueva Granada? If not, what lawful political (or practical) steps might the United States take to bring about a change in Nueva Granadan policy?

SECTION 3. ASSIGNMENTS

A. *Reading Assignment*

Study the Readings presented in Section 4, *infra*, and the Discussion Notes/Questions that follow. Also, to the extent possible, consult the accompanying bibliographical references.

B. Recommended Writing Assignment

Prepare a comprehensive, logically sequenced, and *argumentative* brief in the form of an outline of the primary and subsidiary *legal* issues you see requiring resolution for the President of the United States. Also, from the perspective of an independent objective observer, indicate which side ought to prevail on each issue and why. Retain a copy of your issue-outline/brief for class discussion.

C. Recommended Oral Assignment

Assume the U.S. Department of State's Legal Adviser, who is responsible for the legal memorandum to be submitted to the President, has asked you to pose as legal counsel for the United States or Nueva Granada (as designated by your instructor); then, relying upon the Readings (and your issue-outline if prepared), present a 15–20 minute oral argument of "your" government's likely positions before the Legal Adviser.

D. Recommended Reflective Assignment

Consider (and recommend) alternative norms, institutions, and/or procedures that you believe might do better than existing world order arrangements to contend with situations of the kind posed by this problem. In so doing, but without insisting upon *immediate* feasibility, identify the particular transition steps that would be needed to make your alternatives a reality.

SECTION 4. READINGS

1. **John Warren Kindt & Samuel Pyeatt Menefee,** *The Vexing Problem of Ozone Depletion in International Law and Policy,* 24 TEX. INT'L L.J. 261, 262–67 (1989).

Some scientists see the "ozone hole" as only the most recent and worrisome manifestation of a continuing chemical process: the leaching of ozone from the earth's atmosphere. Ozone itself is an unstable form of oxygen, consisting of three oxygen atoms (O_3). At ground level, normal oxygen molecules (O_2) combine with stray oxygen atoms (O_1) found in catalytic trace gases to form ozone. Ironically, this byproduct of automobile exhausts, known as "low-level ozone," is considered a pollutant. Although low-level ozone does contribute to the problems of smog and other air contamination, the "high-level ozone" in the earth's ozone layer is essential to life on earth. This ozone, which occurs naturally in the stratosphere, collects in a layer that extends from six to thirty miles above the earth's surface. In the stratosphere, ozone molecules are formed when solar ultraviolet rays collide with ordinary oxygen molecules. These collisions create free oxygen atoms that recombine with ordinary oxygen molecules to form ozone molecules. Unlike ordinary oxygen molecules, the ozone molecules can absorb solar ultraviolet radiation and thereby keep oxygen molecules at the lower altitudes from being split. The layer further acts as a protective blanket by preventing most ultraviolet radiation from penetrating to the earth's surface. At the same time, ozone, as an unstable molecule, is particularly susceptible to destruction by any one of several chemical reactions. Many of these reactions occur naturally, but some are manmade. Fortunately, the overall natural processes creating and destroying ozone generally appear to balance themselves over time.

The main tropospheric trace gases that have been identified as affecting the ozone layer[1] include:

a. methane (CH_4),

b. nitrous oxide (N_2O),

c. other nitrogen oxides (NO_x),

d. source gases for stratospheric sulfate aerosols (OCS, CS_2),

e. carbon monoxide (CO),

f. carbon dioxide (CO_2), and

g. the halocarbons (e.g., chlorofluorocarbons (CFC_2)).

Methane, for example, is one naturally produced compound that breaks apart in the upper atmosphere, releasing atoms that attack ozone and reduce it to oxygen. Similarly, nitrous oxide rises into the stratosphere, where it is split apart by the same ultraviolet radiation that creates ozone. "The resulting fragments—called radicals—attack and destroy ... ozone molecules."[2]

Mankind has upset the natural balance between ozone creation and destruction by introducing other chemical processes. The apparent culprits in the current ozone depletion problem are a class of manmade compounds, namely "halocarbons," that include chlorofluorocarbons, or "CFCs." First produced in 1928 by chemists at General Motors, CFCs are inert gases: nontoxic, odorless, and nonflammable. They are currently used throughout various industries as: (1) coolants in refrigerators and air conditioners, (2) propellants in spray cans, (3) solvents, (4) components in the manufacture of plastic foam, and (5) agents in medical equipment sterilization. Unfortunately, the very inertness of the CFCs allows these molecules to rise and eventually percolate into the stratosphere. In the stratosphere, the CFCs encounter ultraviolet rays that finally break them down, releasing stray chlorine atoms. Each wandering chlorine atom (Cl) that meets an ozone molecule engages in the following reaction:

$$Cl + O_3 = ClO + O_2$$

The subsequent introduction of a single oxygen atom results in a further reaction:

$$ClO + O = Cl + O_2$$

The net result of this two-step chemical reaction, repeated thousands of times, is an ozone *danse macabre* in which just one chlorine atom may be responsible for the demise of many ozone molecules. According to Sherwood Rowland, a chemist at the University of California at Irvine, "For every chlorine atom ... [released], 100,000 molecules of ozone are removed from

1. For an analysis of the impacts of these compounds on the ozone layer, see WORLD METEOROLOGICAL ORG., REPORT No. 16, ATMOSPHERIC OZONE, GLOBAL OZONE RESEARCH AND MONITORING PROJECT (1985).

2. Lemonick, *The Heat Is On: Chemical Wastes Spewed into the Air Threaten the Earth's Climate,* TIME, Oct. 19, 1987, at 58, 61. *See also* M.O. Andreae, *The Oceans as a Source of Biogenic Gases,* OCEANUS, Winter 1986, at 27, 30.

the atmosphere."[3] The continued use of CFCs is particularly tragic, since alternatives to the utilization of CFCs as refrigerants have existed since 1981. Despite resistance from the CFC industry, these alternatives should be explored thoroughly. The end results of utilizing CFCs are more than mere statistics, and the American public has been alerted to these concerns.

> [I]f the ozone layer diminishes over population areas—and there is some evidence that it has begun to do so, although nowhere as dramatically as in the Antarctic—the consequences could be dire. Ultraviolet radiation, a form of light invisible to the human eye, causes sunburn and skin cancer; in addition, it has been linked to cataracts and weakening of the immune system. Without ozone to screen out the ultraviolet rays, such ills will certainly increase. The National Academy of Sciences estimates that a 1% drop in ozone levels could cause 10,000 more cases of skin cancer a year in the U.S. alone, a 2% increase.[4]

Others have calculated that, between now and the year 2075, ozone depletion could result in "an extra 200 million cases of skin cancer, as well as less specific damage to the body's immune system and to plant and aquatic life."[5]

Theoretically, the complete destruction of the ozone layer would result in the extinction of life on earth. While there is still considerable academic debate over the extent to which a "decreasing" ozone layer would affect life on earth, that impact would definitely be adverse. Some of the predictions include:

> a.   a 2 to 5 percent increase in squamous skin cancer for each 1.0 percent depletion in the ozone layer;

> b.   a 1.0 to 3 percent increase in basal skin cancer for each 1.0 percent depletion of the ozone layer;

> c.   a 1.0 to 2 percent increase in incidence and a 0.8 to 1.5 percent increase in mortality for melanoma skin cancer (which during 1986 killed 5,000 U.S. citizens) for each 1.0 percent depletion of the ozone layer;

> d.   a suppression of the immune system in humans, increasing the number and severity of some diseases (e.g., herpes, leishmaniasis, and other infectious cutaneous diseases);

> e.   a 0.3 to 0.6 percent increase in cataract cases for each 1.0 percent depletion in the ozone layer;

> f.   an alteration in competition between plant species and a reduction in crop yields (e.g., a twenty-five percent reduction in soybean yield given a twenty percent ozone depletion);

> g.   alterations in aquatic ecosystems and possible effects on aquatic food chains;

> h.   a degradation of certain polymers used in industry necessitating expensive economic countermeasures;

> i.   potential increases in low-level ozone;

---

3. Lemonick, *supra* note 2, at 62 (quoting F.S. Rowland, *Stratospheric Sink for Chlorofluoromethanes: Chlorine Atom–Catalysed Destruction of Ozone*, 249 NATURE 810 (1974)).

4. *Id*. at 59–60.

5. G. Taubes & A. Chen, *Made in the Shade?*, DISCOVER, Aug. 1987, at 62.

j. potential increases in hydrogen peroxide, an acid rain precursor; and

k. a contribution to the "greenhouse warming" until the ozone depletion became large, at which point the depletion would start to reduce temperatures.

The United States National Academy of Sciences (NAS) has estimated that a doubling of the amount of carbon dioxide in the earth's atmosphere resulting from a dissipating ozone layer would increase temperatures world-wide by 3 degrees centigrade, plus or minus 1.5 degrees, thus contributing to greenhouse warming.[6] Some results of this global warming could be severe climatic changes and environmental alterations, including the destruction or relocation of water resources. Polar deglaciation could significantly raise the earth's sea level, and by the year 2100, the United States could forfeit fifty to eighty percent of its coastal wetlands.

To highlight some of the problems of a depletion in the ozone layer, a specific scenario may be used as an example. An annual increase of just 2.5 percent in CFCs, 0.6 percent in carbon dioxide, and a continuation of release trends in other gases could result in an additional 40 million cases of skin cancer and 800,000 deaths in the United States by the year 2075. The increase in cases of cataracts could be 12 million. Perhaps more alarming is the fact that ninety percent of the CFCs that have been released to date are still in the troposphere and have yet to work their way up into the ozone layer.

2. **Editors' Note**. In the late 1970s, in response to the scientific findings noted in Reading 1, including initially the work of scientists Sherwood Rowland and Mario Molina of the University of California, as reported in S. Begley, *A Gaping Hole in the Sky*, Newsweek, July 11, 1988, at 21, several countries, including the United States, banned CFC aerosols. However, as Carol Petsonk writes, in *The Role of the United Nations Environment Programme (UNEP) in the Development of International Environmental Law*, 5 Am. U. J. Int'l L. & Pol'y 351, 367–68 (1990), "[g]lobal CFC consumption continued to climb ... as the chemicals were put to other uses. In 1980, the Governing Council [GC] directed UNEP[a] to undertake measures to protect the ozone layer from modifications due to human activities, and in 1981 the GC called for a convention." Thus, Petsonk continues, "[t]he Montevideo Programme [of UNEP][b] gave high priority to the development of a convention on

---

6. *See* Office of Air and Radiation, Envtl. Protection Agency, An Assessment of the Risks of Stratospheric Modification 8 (final draft 1986); *cf.* R. Kerr, *Report Urges Greenhouse Action Now*, 241 Science 23, 23 (1988) (a "worst case scenario" of "unrestrained" emissions of greenhouse gases coupled with a "highly sensitive" climate could cause a 0.8°C global warming). The EPA estimates a 6.0°C increase in global equilibrium temperature in the absence of greenhouse gases. Additionally, if controls are placed on carbon dioxide and methane to decrease global warming to 2.0°C by 2075, ozone depletion would increase three-fold. Protection of Stratospheric Ozone, 53 Fed. Reg. 30,566, 30,570 (1988) (final rule).

a. UNEP stands for the United Nations Environment Programme. It is headquartered in Nairobi, Kenya.

b. *See Montevideo Programme for the Development and Periodic Review of International Law*, U.N. Doc. UNEP/GC.10/5/add.2, Annex, *reprinted in* United Nations Environment Programme, Environmental Law Unit, Montevideo Programme (1982) (available from UNEP and recommending an environmental law agenda for UNEP) [hereinafter Montevideo Programme].

ozone layer protection. Building on its Barcelona Convention model,[7] UNEP sought to obtain simultaneous adoption of a framework convention and a protocol controlling CFCs. There was no scientific consensus, however, on the extent of CFC-catalyzed ozone layer depletion. Several CFC-producing countries, most notably Japan, questioned the need for a CFC protocol. By 1985 UNEP had achieved consensus on only the framework convention [**Basic Document 3.14**]".

3. John Warren Kindt & Samuel Pyeatt Menefee, *The Vexing Problem of Ozone Depletion in International Law and Policy*, 24 TEX. INT'L L.J. 261, 277–82 (1989).

For environmentalists, 1985 began in a promising manner, with forty-one countries in attendance at the UNEP-sponsored Vienna Conference of Plenipotentiaries on Protection of the Ozone Layer. Of the participant countries, eighteen ended the conference on March 22nd by signing the Vienna Convention for the Protection of the Ozone Layer [**Basic Document 3.14**]. Interestingly, in the United States the Convention had the support of both the CFC industry and environmentalists, because of its potential contribution to the development of better scientific data. The Ozone Convention's stated purpose was "to promote exchanges of information, research, and data on monitoring to protect human health and the environment against activities that have an adverse effect on the ozone layer."[8] As the U.S. Department of State noted, "[t]he Convention . . . [was] an important step in protecting the environment and preserving public health from the potential effects of ozone depletion."[9] Furthermore, the State Department had decided that "[d]ue to the nature of the ozone layer, a multilateral undertaking such as the Convention [was] the only way to promote the global coordination and harmonization necessary for protection of stratospheric ozone."[10] The [former] Executive Director of UNEP, Dr. Mostafa Tolba remarked:

> This is the first global convention to address an issue that for the time being seems far in the future and is of unknown proportions. This convention, as I see it, is the essence of the anticipatory response so many environmental issues call for: to deal with the threat of the problem before we have to deal with the problem itself.[11]

* * *

. . . Revised five times, the document embodied not only the view of the attendees, but also the written comments solicited from non-attending states. Despite last-minute efforts, the Ozone Convention did not adopt a protocol for future CFC control measures. . . .

---

7. Barcelona Convention for the Protection of the Mediterranean Sea Against Pollution, Feb. 16, 1976, 15 I.L.M. 285 (1976) (adopting convention and protocols together) [**Basic Document 4.15**].

8. Phillipe Sand, *Protecting the Ozone Layer: The Vienna Convention is Adopted*, ENVIRONMENT, June, 1995, at 18, 19.

9. *Id.*

10. Letter from John C. Whitehead, U.S. Dep't of State, to President Ronald W. Reagan,

submitting the Vienna Convention for the Protection of the Ozone Layer (Aug. 22, 1985), *reprinted in* President's Ozone Message, Treaty Doc. No. 9, at 12, 99th Cong. (1985).

11. Excerpt from statement of Dr. M. Tolba, Executive Director of UNEP, delivered at the Convention for Protection of the Ozone Layer, Vienna, Austria, *reprinted in Sand, supra* note 8, at 20.

Despite this setback in the area of regulatory measures, the Ozone Convention was a success because it provided an umbrella treaty on the ozone problem, along with annexes on "Research and Systematic Observation" and "Information Exchange." Specific accomplishments included:

a.   defining the general obligations of parties to protect human health and the environment from adverse effects "resulting or likely to result" from activities "which modify or are likely to modify" the ozone layer;[12]

b.   calling for research and systematic observations, as well as cooperation in science, technology, law, and data transmission;

c.   establishing a "Conference of the Parties" and a Secretariat to implement the Convention and its protocols; and

d.   providing for the negotiated settlement of disputes concerning interpretation or application of the Convention.

Soon after this success, while the Bonn Economic Summit was in session, the United States strongly urged an international ban on CFC use in aerosols. The Summit resulted in an agreement, based on the December 1984 recommendations of EEC environment ministers, to devise internationally accepted standards to measure environmental changes.

With the Ozone Convention and the Summit agreement, environmentalists began to think that the process for reaching a solution to the problem was well underway, but in May of 1985 there was an alarming report[13] of an "ozone hole" over Antarctica.[14]

* * *

As this information became public, "[e]verything about ... [the hole] seemed ominous.... One scientist, who's not known for hyperbole, compared the hole to 'the canary in the mine.' "[15]

The ozone hole placed the entire ozone problem back on the world's diplomatic agenda. Unfortunately, scientists were unsure of the hole's cause. While many scientists [looked for a chemical culprit (usually chlorine) and] blamed CFCs, others [dubbed "dynamicists"] "thought the effect to be a natural fluctuation, one possibly connected with the solar cycle."[16] ... [Throughout 1986 and much of 1987, and despite numerous reports and publications, it] was still far from clear ... whether the ozone hole was an isolated problem or was symptomatic of a global decline.

4.   Vienna Convention for the Protection of the Ozone Layer, Mar. 22, 1985, U.N. Doc. UNEP/1G.53/5/Rev. 1, 26 I.L.M. 1529 (1987) [Basic Document 3.14].

5.   Editors' Note. As a pure "framework" treaty, the Ozone Convention did not directly control the use or production of ozone depleting sub-

12. Vienna Convention for the Protection of the Ozone Layer art. 2 [**Basic Document 3.14**].

13. *See* National Aeronautics and Space Admn., Present State of Knowledge of the Upper Atmosphere: An Assessment Report 15, 106–07 (1986).

14. *See* U.S. Nat'l Science Found., Press Release No. 86–89, Nat'l Ozone Expedition Statement 1 (Oct. 20, 1986).

15. G. Taubes & A. Chen, *Made in the Shade?*, Discover , Aug. 1987, at 62, 63.

16. R. Hallgren, *Earth Sciences: Meteorology,* 1987 Britannica Book of the Year 175, 176.

stances. Instead, the Convention established a general goal of "protect[ing] human health and the environment against adverse effects resulting or likely to result from human activities which modify or are likely to modify the ozone layer," Ozone Convention, art. 2(1), and created a procedure for the adoption of protocols. *See* Ozone Convention, art. 8, 9, 13, and 17. Efforts to adopt a binding protocol simultaneously with the negotiation of the Convention were unsuccessful. However, the news of the "ozone hole" over Antartica soon convinced world leaders that a framework convention was not enough. Within three years, controls on CFCs and halons had been negotiated as part of the Montreal Protocol.

6. Carol Petsonk, *The Role of the United Nations Environment Programme (UNEP) in the Development of International Environmental Law*, 5 Am. U. J. Int'l L. & Pol'y 351, 367–72 (1990).

A. History

UNEP's most significant environmental law successes have been the [1985] Vienna Convention **[Basic Document 3.14]** and [the 1987] Montreal Protocol **[Basic Document 3.18]**.... Almost immediately after the [Vienna Convention] was adopted, UNEP resumed intensive negotiations on the protocol. Irish reports of a hole in the ozone layer over Antarctica spurred the momentum. Scientific evidence also began to implicate substances other than CFCs. In mid–1987 the Governing Council recommended that the protocol negotiations consider the full range of ozone-depleting substances. Barely three months later, a UNEP-convened diplomatic conference adopted the Montreal Protocol.

B. Legal Strategy

UNEP's strategy in ozone layer protection was to go for a convention directly without getting bogged down in soft law preliminaries. This strategy was aided by the emergence, over the six years of negotiations, of a set of governmental negotiators—scientists and legal/political experts from developing and developed countries—who understood the importance of the issue and were committed to reaching consensus.

UNEP took care to involve not only environmental NGOs, but also industry groups. UNEP recognized that without industry support, CFC production controls would be meaningless. Fortunately for UNEP's efforts, CFC production is concentrated among relatively few countries and companies. The major producers and some of the major consumers are large, publicly held firms and are thus increasingly sensitive to public pressure of the environmental kind.

The constituency that presented the greatest challenge to UNEP's drive for consensus was comprised of Asian and Pacific countries. Many of these had recently joined the ranks of CFC-producing countries and were seeking greater shares of the global market. Japan, a recalcitrant in the Vienna Convention days, finally joined the Protocol. Thailand and Singapore recently became parties, while India and the Republic of Korea have yet to ratify the agreement.[c]

c. As of July 1, 1998, 165 states were party to the Montreal Protocol.

C. RESULTS

Potentially, the Vienna Convention and Montreal Protocol constitute a highly effective regime for reducing—and possibly, in the future, eliminating—emissions of ozone layer-depleting chemicals. Unlike most other environmental agreements, the Montreal Protocol also contains economic incentives to encourage participation and compliance. It further provides for assessment of its efficacy and for readjustment.

The Vienna Convention is the central international mechanism for harmonizing national and international policies and strategies on ozone layer research. The Montreal Protocol is the central international control instrument.

It freezes CFC consumption as of January 1, 1990, requires 50% reductions in CFC production and consumption by mid–1998, and mandates a 1992 freeze on the consumption of halons. The parties have agreed to establish a working group to develop recommendations concerning the determination and consequences of noncompliance.

The Montreal Protocol uses three kinds of provisions as economic incentives to encourage participation in and compliance with the Protocol's control regime: (1) entry into force requirements, (2) controls on trade with nonparties, and (3) research and technology transfer benefits. While the Protocol could have used other types of economic incentives, each of these kinds of provisions aims to make continued production of ozone-destroying CFCs less profitable, while boosting the market for safer substitutes.

Article 16 of the Montreal Protocol provides that eleven countries representing two-thirds of global consumption of controlled substances must ratify the Protocol before it may enter into force. Thus, the Protocol creates a cartel of consumers who control the consumption market, and who have agreed to reduce their consumption. Since most of the major consuming countries are also major producers, the consumption cartel also operates as a production cartel which has effectively agreed to scale back production. Furthermore, as a result of the consumption cutback, this production cartel will face a shrinking market, with correspondingly lower prices and profits, discouraging continued production.

Article 4 of the Montreal Protocol gradually prohibits trade in controlled substances with nonparties. Consequently, nonparty producing states will also face declining demand, with similar effects on prices, profits and production.

As a further result of Article 4's ban on trade with nonparties, nonparty consuming states will face a diminishing legal supply of controlled substances. This could give rise to black markets, were it not for the fact that the Vienna Convention specifically encourages research on the development of substitutes. The Montreal Protocol's consumption controls should accelerate these processes. Nonparty consumer states should therefore find increased availability of safe substitutes, which they can obtain legally from states party to the Protocol. The prices for these substitutes should become competitive as producers in party states shift to producing substitutes instead of producing controlled substances.

The Protocol promotes technology transfer to parties who are developing countries, thereby offering economic incentives for developing countries to join and comply. The benefits of technology transfer should improve the ability of newly industrialized producing countries to penetrate the growing substitutes market. In addition, countries that are located in tropical climates, where demand for coolants is presumably high, should be interested in developing local production of substitutes in order to reduce dependence on expensive imports. The rewards of obtaining technology to develop local production, coupled with the difficulties of obtaining products from other nonparties, should encourage developing countries to join the Protocol.

The Montreal Protocol specifically provides for readjustment of its controls. The parties can undertake such readjustment on the basis of new information about the state of the ozone layer. In light of the preliminary reports of scientific, technical, economic, and environmental assessment panels convened under the Protocol, UNEP has already recommended that the parties amend the Protocol to phase out all protocol-controlled CFCs by 2005.

The parties to the Protocol could also re-evaluate the control measures based on the degree of compliance achieved. Compliance could be measured in terms of reductions in CFC emissions over time, compared against 1986 consumption. In the short term, the relatively concentrated nature of the CFC industry, its susceptibility to the current climate of pro-environment political pressures, and the sense of personal commitment that many negotiators developed over the past ten years, increase the likelihood that compliance will continue with measurable results. Over time, however, if the Montreal Protocol increases competition in the substitutes industry, production may shift to smaller companies less susceptible to these compliance pressures. Hopefully, the Protocol's economic incentives, as well as increased global awareness of the ozone layer problem will continue to foster compliance with these much-needed control measures.

7. Montreal Protocol on Substances That Deplete the Ozone Layer, Sept. 16, 1987, 26 I.L.M. 1550 (1987) (as amended and adjusted by the second Meeting of the Parties (London, 27–29 June 1990); 30 I.L.M. 537 (1991); by the fourth Meeting of the Parties (Copenhagen, 23–25 November 1992); 32 I.L.M 874 (1993); by the seventh Meeting of the Parties (Vienna, 5–7 December 1995), U.N. Doc. UNEP/OzL.Pro.7/12, *available in* **1996 WL806145 (Treaty); and by the ninth Meeting of the Parties (Montreal, 15–17 September 1997), U.N. Doc. UNEP/OzL.Pro.9/12,** *available in* **1998 WL 428304 (Treaty)) [Basic Document 3.18].**

8. Editors' Note. The early effort to control ozone-depleting substances focused on artificial chemicals known as chlorofluorocarbons (CFCs) and halons. CFCs were widely used, especially in developed countries, as propellants in aerosol sprays, as coolants in refrigerators and air conditioners, for the blowing of various foam products (e.g. styrofoam), and as a cleaning agent for various electrical processes and appliances, including computers. Halons were used to extinguish fires. During the 1970s and 1980s, scientists found these chemicals to be an important cause of ozone layer depletion. Thus early diplomatic instruments were directed to the control of the emission of these substances, and, as the evidence of ozone depletion and the role of CFCs and halons became more clear, the controls on emissions of these substances became more strict and more widely accepted. By 1998, 166 nations were party to the Ozone Convention and 165 were party to the Montreal Protocol, which imposes strict controls on CFCs and halons.

In addition to establishing controls over CFCs and halons, the 1987 Montreal Protocol created an innovative process for ratcheting up the level of international control over the production and use of ozone depleting substances. *See* Montreal Protocol, articles 2(9), 2(10), 6. CFCs and halons were listed as "controlled substances" under Annex A of the Protocol. Under the Protocol's procedures, the level of controls imposed on a previously-listed ozone depleting substance can be adjusted as the need arises. The parties must make every effort to reach agreement by consensus on the adjustment of control measures; but if there is no consensus, decisions "shall, as a last resort, be adopted by two-third majority vote of the Parties present and voting representing at least fifty per cent of the total consumption of the controlled substances of the parties." The 1990 London Amendments to the Montreal Protocol substituted for the final sixteen words the words: "a majority of the parties operating under paragraph 1 of Article 5 present and voting and majority of the parties not so operating present and voting." So long as the substance in question has been previously listed as a "controlled substance" in an annex to the Protocol, such adjustments are binding on all parties, even those that vote against them.

Adding new substances to the Protocol's list of controlled substances is more difficult. A 2/3 majority vote of the parties may add substances, but the addition of new substances is treated as an amendment to the Protocol (rather than an "adjustment"), and is subjected to the Ozone Convention's normal procedures for amending protocols. Under those procedures, amendments do not go into effect for parties that do not accept them. *See* Montreal Protocol article 2(10) and Ozone Convention, article 9(5) **[Basic Documents 3.18 & 3.14]**.

The Montreal Protocol has been adjusted and amended several times since 1987. As a result, there is no single definitive version. The Documents Supplement reproduces the Protocol as adjusted and amended by each Meeting of the Parties through September, 1997. If current agreements are observed, the ozone layer should be fully restored by the middle of the 21st century. However, at the time of this writing the most recent amendments were not in effect and prior amendments, though in force, had not been accepted by all of the parties to the Protocol. Because amendments are effective only for those countries that have accepted them, some countries, although party to the Protocol, are not subject to current control measures that relate to substances that were added to the Protocol by an amendment which the country in question has not accepted. Methyl bromide, for example, was not listed as a controlled substance in the original version of the Protocol. It was first listed and controlled by the Copenhagen Amendments in 1992. As of June 1, 1998, fewer than half of the parties to the Protocol had accepted the Copenhagen Amendments. The next three readings describe the three Meetings at which the Parties have approved amendments to the Protocol.

9.   Sylvia Maureen Williams, *The Protection of the Ozone Layer in Contemporary International Law*, 10 INT'L REL. 167, 176–77 (1990).

[T]he second meeting of the parties to the Montreal Protocol was held in London from 27 to 29 June 1990. It was organized by UNEP and hosted by the British government. Nearly all of the sixty states parties to the Protocol were present as well as thirty other countries which attended as observers. One of the highlights of the meeting was the agreement to phase out CFCs by the year 2000 instead of merely reducing their production by half as required in the Montreal Protocol. The meeting also agreed to phase out halons (used in fire extinguishers in computer rooms, ships, aircraft and other related applications), except for essential safety uses.

In both cases, intermediate steps have been established. A fifty per cent cut in the production of CFCs should occur by 1995 and an eighty per cent cut by 1997, with a review of the matter in 1992 to accelerate the reduction schedule. In the case of halons there is an intermediate target calling for a fifty per cent cut by 1995. It should be noted that both these products form part of Annex A of the 1987 Montreal Protocol **[Basic Document 3.18]** listing the substances subjected to control measures. These changes apply automatically to all parties, with immediate effect.

As to hydrochlorofluorocarbons (HCFCs), the substitute product for CFCs (for refrigeration, plastic foams and aerosols), no restrictions were imposed. Instead, the parties issued a Declaration [in Helsinki on May 2, 1989]—outside the Protocol—recommending that they should be used cautiously and phased out between 2020 and 2040. HCFCs had not been submitted to control under Annex A of the Montreal Protocol.

The 1990 London meeting also agreed to phase out two other less destructive chemicals, namely carbon tetrachloride (a chemical foodstock for CFCs solvent in pharmaceuticals, pesticides and some paints) and methyl chloroform (a solvent used in the electronics industry) by the years 2000 and 2005 respectively. In the first case, an eighty five per cent cut is established for 1995 and in the second, a seventy per cent cut by 2000. Neither of these products had been included in Annex A to the Montreal Protocol. These amendments will have to be ratified by the states parties before they come into force, which is not the case for CFCs and halons where the new measures apply automatically following the 1990 London meeting.

Another striking feature of the 1990 London meeting was the question of the transfer of technology. A compromise was reached on this point, after some tough arguing from the Indian Environment Minister, Maneka Gandhi. It was agreed that if developing countries were to run into difficulties in acceding to the new technology and were thus unable to comply with their commitment to phase out CFCs, then a meeting of the parties to the Montreal Protocol could be convened to consider the situation. In this connection, it should be recalled that article 5 of the Protocol includes special provisions for developing countries. Any such country which has a calculated annual level of consumption of the controlled substances (listed in Annex A) of less than 0.3 kg per capita at the time of the entry into force of the agreement for that country, or at any time thereafter within ten years of the entry into force of the Protocol shall, in order to meet its domestic needs, have the right to delay its compliance with the control measures by ten years. Moreover, the parties to the Protocol undertook to facilitate access to environmentally safe alternative substances and technology for parties which are developing countries and to assist them to make expeditious use of such alternatives (article 5, paragraph 2). The provisions of subsidies, aid, credits, guarantees or insurance programmes to parties which are developing countries for the use of alternative technology and for substitute products shall be facilitated, bilaterally or multilaterally, by the parties (paragraph 3). It would appear that, should the substitute product not be available on equitable terms, to parties which are developing countries, these would have the possibility of denouncing the Protocol and would have a strong case for article 8, dealing with non-compliance, to cease to operate in their respect.

Furthermore, the 1990 meeting of the parties to the Montreal Protocol decided to set up a fund for the assistance of developing countries in dealing with the incremental costs of phasing out or substituting ozone-depleting substances. This fund will be administered by the World Bank.

A noteworthy result of this last meeting of the parties was agreement on the need to amend the Montreal Protocol in order to encourage the transfer of technology concerning substitute products to developing countries while, at the same time, preserving the rights of the companies involved with the development of these new products. It was also agreed to review the Protocol in 1992 instead of 1994 as originally decided.

10. *Nations Agree to Cuts in Production of Methyl Bromide, Faster CFC Phase-Out*, **15 Int'l Env't Rep. (BNA) No. 24, at 769 (Dec. 2, 1992).**

Copenhagen—Environment ministers and other officials from more than 80 countries November 25 formally agreed to stricter measures to protect Earth's stratospheric ozone layer.

The new controls include listing methyl bromide as a controlled substance in the Montreal Protocol on Substances that Deplete the Ozone Layer **[Basic Document 3.18]**. Production and consumption of this chemical, based on 1989 levels, will be reduced by 25 percent by 1995.

Negotiators also agreed to an accelerated phase-out of chlorofluorocarbons, moving the deadline for this action from 2000 to the end of 1995.

In addition, the Montreal Multilateral Fund was established to replace an interim fund to help developing countries in meeting the cost of switching from the use of ozone-depleting substances.

Also adopted on the final day of the three-day conference of ministers was a timetable for the phase-out of hydro-chlorofluorocarbons [HCFCs]. This will start in 1996 and will conclude in 2030. HCFCs are chemicals used mainly as substitutes for CFCs. HCFCs contribute to ozone depletion but are far less damaging than the substances they replace.

The HCFC phase-out is based on a formula weighted on the ozone depletion potential of both CFCs and HCFs. The HCFC phase-out starts in 1996 with a 3.2 percent cap on the amount of CFCs and HCFCs produced in 1989.

Manufacturing of HCFCs is to be reduced by 35 percent by 2004, 65 percent by 2010, 90 percent by 2015, and 99.5 percent by 2020.

Along with the accelerated CFC phase-out production and use of carbon tetrachloride—a solvent, grain fumigant and fire-fighting agent—will be prohibited by 1995. Methyl chloroform, mostly used as a metal degreaser, will be banned by 1996, moving up an earlier deadline of 2005 on this substance.

Also included in the agreement was an accelerated phase-out of halons, which are used in fire-fighting equipment, from 2000 to the end of 1994.

Tolba: Not Far Enough

Mostafa Tolba, [former] executive director of the United Nations Environment Program, called the agreement "progress" but acknowledged it did not go far enough.

"The measures agreed here are the strongest package of global environmental laws ever enacted," Tolba said. "The question remains, however: Is this enough? We are in the hands of scientists. From them—and we have sought advice from the best in the world—we know that the answer is 'no.' This package is not enough."

Tolba added, "We have made progress but we have far to go ... we cannot rest until the ozone layer is safe."

Scientists from the Montreal Protocol secretariat estimated the new agreements would reduce worldwide the number of people who would suffer from blindness due to exposure to ultraviolet rays by 400,000. They also estimated the number of skin cancer cases would be reduced by 40,000. Stratospheric ozone blocks harmful ultraviolet rays from reaching the earth, so ozone loss increases exposure.

U.S. Environmental Protection Agency Administrator William Reilly said he was pleased with the outcome of the fourth meeting of the parties to the Montreal Protocol.

"There were four main objectives we came here with," Reilly said. "We got 3.5 of those. The fund was important, the CFC accelerated phase-out was important, the HCFC schedule was what we wanted."

The setback for the U.S. delegation, Reilly reiterated, concerned methyl bromide, a chemical used in some developing countries as a grain fumigant.

11.   Roland Blassnig, *Methyl Bromide Phaseout, CFC Export Licensing Only Gains at Montreal Meeting,* Int'l Env't Daily (BNA), Sept. 24, 1997, *available in* Westlaw BNA–IED Database.

MONTREAL (BNA)—A phaseout plan for methyl bromide and a new chlorofluorocarbons licensing system to track trade in CFCs represented the only significant gains at the Ninth Meeting of the Montreal Protocol on Substances that Deplete the Ozone Layer. These achievements offset the failure of negotiators to advance an HCFC phaseout or reach an agreement for the treatment of process agents.

The meeting, which was held Sept. 15–17, attracted 800 participants representing some 110 governments, including environment ministers, scientists, environmentalists, and industry representatives from around the world. "We have succeeded in maintaining the Montreal Protocol's momentum by adding important new protections for the ozone layer," said the meeting's president, Dr. Won–Hwa Park of Korea, in a communique Sept. 17. Park was referring to the methyl bromide phaseout dates that had been achieved after days of wrangling between the developed and developing countries on just how quickly the fumigant could be retired from service without unduly affecting agricultural trade.

New Phaseout Dates

Developed countries agreed to move up their phaseout date, previously set at 2010, to 2005 with interim reductions of 25 percent by 1999, 50 percent by 2001, and 70 percent by 2003. Developing countries, which committed to a freeze in consumption by 2002, agreed to a 20 percent reduction by 2005 and a total phaseout by 2015. The 20 percent reduction level will be calculated using a four-year average of consumption use during 1995–98 for calculating the base year.

The parties also agreed that the Montreal Protocol Multilateral Fund would earmark $25 million a year in 1998 and 1999 for efforts to phase out methyl bromide in developing countries. Christian Patterson, a spokesman for Ozone Action, told BNA, "That $25 million is not going to go very far." "Definitely it is a very, very positive step, not as much as we would have hoped, but definitely the danger is out," K. Madhava Sarma, executive director of the Ozone Secretariat, the agency that administers the treaty, told BNA.

The United States and Canada had wanted developed countries to phase out methyl bromide by 2001, but opposition from southern European countries could only allow for the phase out to be total four years later. "I'm not satisfied, I'm no way near satisfied," Beatrice Olivastri, the CEO for Friends of the Earth (Canada) told BNA Sept. 17. "The fact that we have a 2005 phaseout for industrialized countries is embarrassing. It easily could have been 2001, it should have been that. I would suggest that Spain and Italy have a bit to account for in that blockage."

Fear Of Backsliding

Olivastri also warned that since the United States, which is the biggest user of methyl bromide in the world, did not achieve the 2001 total phaseout date, industries in that country are now free to engage in backsliding on their phaseout schedules since they do not have to phase out until four years further down the road. Under the federal Clean Air Act, U.S. industries are obligated to phase out methyl bromide use in 2001. "Because they did not get the equivalent date that they had–2001–I would expect some backsliding to happen," Olivastri said. Developing countries, on the other hand, will be able to begin to move ahead with their phaseout plans earlier due to the promised infusion of $25 million from the Multilateral Fund, Olivastri said.

Licensing

Negotiators at the meeting also approved a system for licensing the import and export of new, used, recycled, and reclaimed controlled substances in Annex A–Chlorofluorocarbons (CFC–11, CFC–12, CFC–113, CFC–114, CFC–115) and Halons (halon 1211, halon 1301, halon 2402), in Annex B–other CFCs (CFC–13, CFC–111, CFC–112, CFC–211, CFC–212, CFC–213, CFC–214, CFC–215, CFC–216, CFC–217), in Annex C–HCFCs, and in Annex E–methyl bromide. The licensing system requires parties to the treaty to assist in preventing illegal traffic of these controlled substances and to allow for the cross-checking of information between exporting and importing countries.

The system, which will be in effect in 2000, will allow customs and police officials to track trade in CFCs and to detect unlicensed trade. Sarma told BNA, "Basically, each country has agreed to issue licenses for import and export and to exchange information amongst themselves so that the illegal trade could be curbed." Patterson of Ozone Action told BNA that creation of the licensing system was an attempt to induce greater accountability in the export of CFCs. But licensing merely adds a layer of bureaucracy for exports and imports, Patterson said. Smugglers may still forge licenses and required documentation, he said. Stemming illegal trade in these chemicals will require phasing out consumption and production of CFCs, Patterson said....

CFCs

Meanwhile, the parties also failed to institute a firm regime on the continuing availability of CFCs in developing countries....

HCFCs

* * *

While the EC was convinced that the new cap and the accelerated phaseout date would be of considerable environmental benefit, others, including the United States, took the position that the economic and social costs did not warrant a change in an already agreed-to phaseout schedule. The current phaseout schedule reduces the cap by 65 percent by 2010, 90 percent by 2015, 99.5 percent by 2020, and total reduction by 2030.

Stirpe of the Alliance For Responsible Atmospheric Policy said, "We are pleased that the parties have signaled that HCFCs are a viable alternative to CFCs, that their use is justified to achieve a CFC phaseout, and that any further controls on HCFCs are environmentally insignificant."

A declaration by 38 countries concerned about the absence of any movement on HCFCs at the meeting managed to put the issue on the agenda for the Eleventh conference of the parties in 1999.

12. Editors' Note. As the previous readings suggest, the imposition of international controls on the production and use of methyl bromide has been controversial. Only about half the parties to the Montreal Protocol have agreed to the Copenhagen Amendments, which added methyl bromide as a controlled substance. In addition, many environmental groups are gravely disappointed with the phaseout schedules that have been negotiated for methyl bromide among those parties that have acceded to the Copenhagen Amendments. In 1995, the parties concluded a further adjustment to the Montreal Protocol aimed at the elimination of methyl bromide use in industrialized countries by 2010. Developing countries, however, only agreed to freeze methyl bromide consumption in 2002, thus permitting them to increase their use in the interim. In 1997, the agreed phase-out date for developed countries was accelerated to 2005. Developing nations were required to freeze their consumption in 2002 and to phase-out consumption completely by 2015. One hopeful sign is that current legislation in both the United States and the

European Community (which are the two largest users of methyl bromide in the world, accounting for nearly 70% of total global use) calls for the complete phaseout of methyl bromide by 2001. (U.S. law will ban production and importation, but not use of the chemical. Existing stocks, therefore, could still be exported or used in the U.S. EC law bans both the production and use of the chemical, though there is no significant EC production in any event.) *See* Environmental Protection Agency, *Europe Ends the Era of Ozone Depleting Substances: Commission Adopts Proposal for a New EU Regulation* (visited Sept. 5, 1998) <http://www.epa.gov/docs/ozone/mbr/eu2001.html>. The following reading provides more detail about methyl bromide and the issues surrounding efforts to ban its use and production.

13. Sondra Goldschein, Note, *Methyl Bromide*: *The Disparity Between the Pesticide's Phaseout Dates Under the Clean Air Act and the Montreal Protocol on Substances that Deplete the Ozone Layer*, 4 ENVTL. LAW. 577, 577–607 (1998).

Methyl bromide is an odorless, colorless gas used as a pesticide on more than one hundred crops. Since the early 1930s, methyl bromide has been used effectively for soil fumigation, postharvest treatment, and structural fumigation. Manufactured mainly in the United States and Israel, world production of methyl bromide totaled 140 million pounds annually as of 1993. In 1990, methyl bromide consumption totaled sixty-four million pounds in the United States alone, primarily in California and Florida.

When methyl bromide is released into the atmosphere, it depletes the ozone layer. The Clean Air Act (CAA) regulates methyl bromide production and consumption domestically, whereas the Montreal Protocol on Substances that Deplete the Ozone Layer (Montreal Protocol) regulates production internationally. The CAA phases out production and consumption of methyl bromide by 2001; however, the parties to the Montreal Protocol agreed in September 1997 to a phase-out date of 2005 for developed countries....

The ozone-depletion potential (ODP) of methyl bromide is calculated at approximately 0.6.[d] This number reflects the potential of a substance to deplete the ozone layer compared to the potential of chlorofluorocarbon–11. Bromine, the chemical in methyl bromide that depletes the ozone layer, is at least fifty times more lethal than chlorine in destroying ozone on a per atom basis. The current scientific knowledge of methyl bromide's atmospheric activity, however, is incomplete. The relative levels of methyl bromide contribution from natural and anthropogenic sources, the mechanism by which methyl bromide reacts to form hydrogen bromide, the atmospheric lifetime of methyl bromide, and the amount of methyl bromide emissions from agricultural uses remain uncertain....

Methyl bromide is [also] an acute neurotoxin. Exposure to high levels of methyl bromide can lead to death, birth and inheritable defects, and damage to the central nervous, respiratory, and gastrointestinal systems. Limited exposure can cause throat and eye irritation, skin injuries, shortness of

---

d. The June 23, 1998, Scientific Assessment of Ozone Depletion, a UNEP/WMO/NASA/NOAA consensus document, revised the estimate of methyl bromide's ODP downward to 0.4.

breath, nausea, fatigue, and muscle spasms. The ability of methyl bromide to drift several miles from a fumigation site compounds its danger. . . .

The [Clean Air Act] authorizes the Administrator of the United States Environmental Protection Agency (EPA) to promulgate regulations to phase out the production and consumption of ozone-depleting substances, which are divided into two classes. Class I substances, which have a higher ODP, face an earlier phaseout date than class II substances. * * * On March 18, 1993, EPA proposed to list methyl bromide as a class I substance and added it to the list on December 10, 1993. The petition was supported by contemporary scientific findings, a private petition, and the Montreal Protocol's identification of methyl bromide's 0.7 ODP. The final rule scheduled a freeze on methyl bromide production at 1991 levels in 1994, and the elimination of methyl bromide production and importation by January 1,2001. The rule required no interim reductions. . . .

The United States suggested the addition of methyl bromide as a controlled substance at the April 1992 meeting of the Open–Ended Working Group of the Parties (OEWG) [to the Montreal Protocol]. In response, the OEWG requested additional information on the scientific and economic issues regarding methyl bromide. The resulting Montreal Protocol Assessment Report estimated the ODP of methyl bromide at 0.7. At the Fourth Meeting of the Parties in Copenhagen in 1992, delegates agreed to freeze methyl bromide's use in developed countries in 1995 at 1991 levels, with an exemption for quarantine and preshipment applications, as well as to satisfy the basic domestic needs of developing countries. The parties also unanimously adopted a nonbinding resolution that encouraged nations to reduce methyl bromide use further and to reach a comprehensive agreement on methyl bromide phaseout at the Sixth Meeting. As of December 1997, however, only seventy-four countries have ratified the Copenhagen Amendments.[e]

The parties established a complete methyl bromide phase-out schedule for developed nations at the Seventh Meeting in Vienna. Although the United States advocated a phaseout in 2001 with significant exemptions and no interim phaseout, the parties agreed to a twenty-five percent reduction by 2001, a fifty percent reduction by 2005, and phaseout by 2010. For developing countries, the adopted schedule freezes methyl bromide use in 2002 based on the average use between 1995 and 1998, but the parties did not decide on a phase-out date. At the Eighth Meeting, the parties delayed discussion of methyl bromide regulation until 1997 because it was "not considered urgent under the terms of the ozone-protection treaty."

The parties made important decisions about the international phaseout of methyl bromide at the Ninth Meeting of Parties to the Montreal Protocol. After "days of wrangling," the parties determined two separate phase-out schedules for developing and developed nation's consumption of methyl bromide. The parties approved a four-step phase-out schedule for developed countries, subject to the following reductions: (1) twenty-five percent by 1999; (2) fifty percent by 2001; (3) seventy percent by 2003; and (4) one hundred percent by 2005. The phase-out schedule for developing countries is more lenient. Developing countries must freeze their consumption levels by 2002 at the average of their 1995 to 1998 consumption levels. A twenty percent

e. By July 1, 1998, the number of ratifications had increased to seventy-nine.

reduction must occur by 2005, and the complete phaseout must take place by 2015. The Parties allocated an additional twenty-five million dollars of the Multilateral Fund, which provides capital to help developing nations meet the requirements of the Montreal Protocol, to be specifically directed towards facilitating the phaseout of methyl bromide in developing countries in 1998 and 1999.

The second accomplishment at the Ninth Meeting in Montreal was the agreement to ban trade of methyl bromide with nonparties. The parties also accomplished a third goal by identifying criteria to determine critical use exemptions of methyl bromide after the phase-out date. The Montreal Protocol allows critical use agricultural exemptions for most regulated ozone-depleting chemicals....

A. U.S. Government Reaction

The disparity between the phase-out dates under the Montreal Protocol and the CAA has sparked reaction in the legislative and executive branches. EPA, the USDA, and members of Congress adopt different approaches to prepare farmers for the methyl bromide phaseout in 2001.

1. Environmental Protection Agency

Because of the four year disparity between the international and domestic phase-out dates for methyl bromide, EPA has directed its focus toward the development of economically viable and environmentally sound alternatives. EPA does not doubt that a combination of alternative techniques will replace a significant amount of methyl bromide's functions. EPA views the problems encountered with methyl bromide substitutes as part of the scientific process of developing an effective pest control tool and is confident that this phase-out deadline will successfully spur development as others have in the past. EPA established a Methyl Bromide Alternatives Task Force with representatives from the Office of Pesticide Programs and the Office of Air and Radiation. In addition to coordinating FIFRA, CAA, and Montreal Protocol obligations, the Task Force will also work with interested groups in the research and development of methyl bromide substitutes.

EPA supports a limited number of exemptions for critical agricultural uses that have no available alternatives. In July, EPA representatives testified before Congress that EPA would be willing to work with Congress to amend the CAA to allow exemptions to the methyl bromide ban. However, "[t]he Administration has not settled on any position and is consulting with Congress.... [T]he Administration is considering only the possibility of amending the [CAA] to address methyl bromide and would not support any other changes."[17]

2. Department of Agriculture

The USDA believes that the CAA's early phase-out date will create a competitive disadvantage for American farmers in domestic and international markets, thereby having a detrimental effect on the U.S. economy. A USDA

17. CHEM. MKT. REP., ADMINISTRATION MULLING EXTENSION OF METHYL BROMIDE PHASEOUT DATE 22 (1997), *available in* 1997 WL 8498135.

report[18] stated that "a unique fumigant like methyl bromide, when withdrawn from use, can result in progressively increasing economic losses for several years, and may culminate in the total destruction of the commodity and its allied industry." If no alternatives are found, the USDA estimates that a methyl bromide ban could cause a $1.3 to $1.5 billion annual loss to producers and consumers. The ban would also affect the agricultural export industry. When importing countries require the treatment of produce with methyl bromide as a condition of entry, a ban on methyl bromide could close those markets to American farmers.

The USDA is unsure if any commercially viable alternatives will be available for use in 2001. Although a gradual phaseout of methyl bromide will provide time to develop alternatives, "the likelihood of developing new effective fumigant alternatives to methyl bromide appears very remote." In the event that marketable substitutes cannot be developed in time, the USDA "is willing to work with Congress and other stakeholders to craft a reasonable solution that will assure the continued availability of methyl bromide where it is needed in the United States because of the lack of acceptable alternatives."

3. Congress

On October 6, 1997, Representative Dan Miller (R–Fla.) introduced a bill into the House to extend the CAA's methyl bromide phase-out date.[19] The bill prevents EPA from controlling the production, importation, export, consumption, or use of methyl bromide for a specific farming or postharvest function unless "viable, cost-effective substitutes or other alternatives" exist or the Montreal Protocol specifically requires such actions of all parties. Representative Miller unsuccessfully introduced an essentially identical bill in 1995. Miller reintroduced the current version of the bill in 1997 based on his findings that there are "no safe, effective, commercially viable alternatives to methyl bromide," the ozone layer will repair itself even without the ban on methyl bromide, and the phaseout will cost $1.5 billion in five states given the current alternatives.[20] At this time, the bill has been referred to the House Committee on Commerce and to the Committee on Agriculture. Cosponsor Gary Condit (D–Cal.), in a letter to President Clinton, stressed the competitive disadvantage American farmers would face if the CAA phase-out date remains intact. Methyl bromide users support Miller's regulatory intervention bill.

In February 1996, the Senate went on record in support of USDA research efforts for cost-effective alternatives to methyl bromide when it approved a "Sense of the Senate" resolution submitted by Senator Barbara Boxer (D–Cal.).[21] The resolution urged the USDA and EPA "to work together with Congress and members of the agricultural and environmental communities to evaluate the risks and benefits of extending the methyl bromide phase

18. United States Dairy Assoc., Nat'l Agric. Pesticide Impact Assessment Program, The Biologic and Economic Assessment of Methyl Bromide 5 (1993).

19. H.R. 2609, 105th Cong. § 2 (1997). As of November 1997, 61 Representatives cosponsored the bill. *Bill Summary and Status for the 105th Congress* (visited Jan. 20, 1998) <http://thomas.loc.gov./cgi-bin>.

20. H.R. 2609, 105th Cong. § 1 (1997). The five states are Florida, Georgia, California, North Carolina, and South Carolina.

21. 142 Cong. Rec. S1150 (daily ed. Feb. 7, 1996) (proposed Boxer Amendment No. 3458 to S.1541, 104th Cong. (1996)).

out date." In explanation, Boxer acknowledged the importance of an international effort led by the United States to repair the ozone layer, "but in order to lead, others must follow.... We must not put our farmers at a competitive disadvantage with other nations."

B. Industry Reaction

According to the Methyl Bromide Working Group (MBWG), a coalition of methyl bromide producers, the CAA phaseout causes a variety of problems because of the lack of safe, effective, and approved alternatives to methyl bromide. MBWG determined that recommended alternatives are not commercially feasible. Problems include insufficient development, a lack of information, regulatory obstacles, market conditions, ineffective solutions, environmental side effects, and application problems. The industry group posits that farmers would already have discovered feasible alternatives if they existed.

In addition, a disparity between the phase-out dates of the developing and developed world will cause chemical companies to increase their sales artificially to create a high baseline date for the developing nation methyl bromide freeze. Moreover, because obtaining a critical use exemption under the Montreal Protocol cannot be relied upon as a way to escape the detrimental effects of a ban, MBWG believes that these problems will "draw a swift congressional response."[f]

C. Agricultural Community Reaction

Representatives of growers utilizing methyl bromide, including the American Farm Bureau Federation (AFBF),[22] the Crop Protection Coalition,[23] and the Western Growers Association,[24] oppose the 2001 phase-out date because of the large disadvantage American farmers will face against international competitors. Although American farmers will have phased out methyl bromide by 2001 under the CAA, no other nation will have eliminated its production and consumption of the pesticide by that time. U.S. farmers will lose their position in the world marketplace due to the increased costs associated with problematic methyl bromide alternatives. In California[25] and Florida,[26] a ban will cause farmers to decrease or cease production of crops dependent on methyl bromide. In addition, farmers will lose the export markets of those countries, including Japan, that require methyl bromide as a condition of entry for agricultural products. The harsh economic consequences of a methyl

f. *Methyl Bromide Working Group* (visited Sept. 12, 1998) <www.methylbromide.org>.

22. With 4.7 million members, the American Farm Bureau Federation is the largest general farming organization in the United States. *See Property Rights, Tobacco, Trade on Farmers' Agenda*, ASSOCIATED PRESS, Jan. 10, 1998, *available in* 1998 WL 7375120.

23. The Crop Protection Coalition is made up of trade associations and commodity groups. *See* Brian Broderick, *Industry Official Expects Help from Hill on Methyl Bromide Ban*, Daily Env't Rep. (BNA) No. 183, Sept. 22, 1997, at AA–1.

24. The Western Growers Association is an agricultural trade association with members

that pack and ship a large majority of the fresh fruit, fresh vegetables, and nuts in Arizona and California. *See WGA Calls for Lawmakers to Save Methyl Bromide from Accelerated Phase-Out Period* (visited Jan. 20, 1998) <http://www.wga.com/pages/Methyl4.html> [hereinafter *WGA Calls for Lawmakers*].

25. The economic impact on California is estimated to be $117,559,110 annually.... Numerous crops including strawberries, lettuce, grapes, and cherries will be affected.

26. The economic impact on Florida is expected to total $330,981,937 annually.... Crops affected include tomatoes, eggplant, and melons.

bromide phaseout will provide incentives for farm production to migrate to Mexico.[27] According to AFBF, the phaseout of methyl bromide could cost one billion dollars annually from the combined effects of growers' net revenue and consumer cost. The Crop Protection Coalition estimates a forty percent average yield loss to farmers.

The agricultural community also claims that the 2001 methyl bromide phaseout will not decrease the amount of ozone-depleting substances released because all other countries will continue some level of use. AFBF stresses that "while the [United States] tries to correct this perceived problem singlehandedly, natural sources and other countries make [U.S.] efforts completely meaningless." In addition, eliminating methyl bromide may cause an increase in overall pesticide use. Because no single replacement exists for methyl bromide use and many proposals suggest multiple pesticide substitutions, farmers will have to double or quadruple pesticide use, often creating serious risks to food and groundwater that were not associated with methyl bromide.

Thus, to prevent the onset of economic losses, most growers oppose a complete phaseout of methyl bromide until the development of alternatives. In contrast, the United Farm Workers support a phaseout of methyl bromide because of the enormous human health implications to the field farm workers who assist in the application of the chemical and frequently reside close to the areas where methyl bromide is applied.[28]

D.   Public Interest Reaction

Environmental organizations oppose any extension of the CAA phaseout date and the vague granting of any exemptions. Any delay to the methyl bromide phaseout will cause increased UV radiation exposures, decimation of fisheries, and damage to agricultural and forest industries. In a letter to President Clinton, environmental organizations, as well as labor, public interest, and health groups, stated their opposition to any CAA exemption to the methyl bromide ban. Claiming that it is premature to discuss a critical use exemption, the groups stressed that efforts should instead focus on the development of economically and technically feasible alternatives. A July 29, 1997 letter from thirty environmental and public interest organizations to the House Committee on Commerce claimed that a critical use exemption would doom the Montreal Protocol and CAA goals to failure.

14.   Editors' Note. Developing countries generally have insisted that their right to develop trumps any obligation they might have to participate in global action to protect the environment. Current global environmental problems, they correctly observe, were caused primarily by actions in industrialized countries. Moreover, industrialized countries continue to be the leading contributors to those problems. As a partial response to these claims, the current ozone regime allows developing countries (called "Article 5 parties") to delay participation in international controls placed on ozone-depleting

---

27. . . . In 1996, growers in southern states threatened to move to Latin America if the United States phased out methyl bromide by 2001. *See* Cheryl Hogue, *Scientists Urge United States to Retain 2001 Deadline for Methyl Bromide Phase Out*, DAILY ENV'T REP. (BNA) No. 31, Feb. 15, 1996, at A–2.

28. *See* Cheryl Hogue, *Advocacy Groups Seeking Earlier Bans for Methyl Bromide, Halons, CFC Inhalers*, DAILY ENV'T REP. (BNA) No. 173 (Sept. 8, 1997) at A–7.

substances and to be assisted in their efforts to implement such controls and compensated for their costs in doing so. *See* Ozone Convention, article 4. Montreal Protocol, articles 2, 2A, 2B, 4, 5, 9, 10. Nevertheless, some developing nations continue to refuse to participate at all in these regimes, and many developing nations have refused to join the Copenhagen Amendments, which added methyl bromide as a controlled substance. The remaining readings address the law and policy issues involved in the apparent clash between the right to development and the need for a global solution to the problem of ozone depletion.

15. Richard Benedick, Ozone Diplomacy—New Directions in Safeguarding the Planet 148–52 (1991).

Industrialized nations with less than 25 per cent of the world's population, were consuming [as of 1989] an estimated 88 per cent of CFCs; their per capita consumption was more than 20 times higher than that of the developing nations. For China, the world's most populous country, the disparity was even greater: its per capita CFC consumption was only about one-fortieth that of the European Community and the United States.[29]

In effect, use of these chemicals had for decades contributed to the well-being of the industrialized countries, but at the same time inadvertently built up a threat to the entire planet in the form of long-lasting CFCs in the stratosphere. Developing-country governments, in statements at the 1989 London and Helsinki conferences, stressed that the problem was not of their making. They sought assurances that their populations would neither be deprived of the benefits of these substances nor have to pay more for the equivalent products and technologies. They were increasingly worried that the drive towards rapid phaseout could add new burdens to their economies and adversely affect their standard of living. They argued that additional technical and financial assistance was essential to enable developing nations to contribute to the [Montreal Protocol's] **[Basic Document 3.18]** objectives.[30]

There are several ways in which developing countries might incur incremental burdens through accepting the treaty obligations. In the short term, as CFCs were phased out they might become more expensive to countries dependent on imports. The replacement chemicals and the products made with them were also expected to be costlier. Those developing countries that were themselves current or prospective producers of CFCs and their related products would face problems of access to new substitute technology and the attendant costs of royalties and licenses. In addition, there would be costs associated with converting existing CFC facilities, including the purchase of new capital equipment and possible premature abandonment of old. Operating costs might also rise, including possibly higher-priced raw materials and retraining of workers. Some developing countries also felt that the protocol unfairly excluded them from potentially lucrative trade in products made with or containing CFCs.

---

29. *See* James T.B. Tripp, *The UNEP Montreal Protocol: Industrialized and Developing Countries Sharing the Responsibility for Protection of the Ozone Layer,* 20 J. Int'l L. & Prac. 744 (1988).

30. *See* Editorial, *The Hole in the Ozone Logic,* South, No. 102, at 9 (Apr. 1989); Jonathan C. Randal, *Third World Seeks Aid Before Joining Ozone Pact,* Wash. Post, Mar. 7, 1989, at A16.

It was very difficult to assess the degree of hardship that might be occasioned by these factors. Near term upward pressure on CFC prices in producer countries could be offset by the protocol provisions that forced consumption in those countries to decline at a faster pace than production, thereby creating excess capacity (article 2). The economic assessment panel believed that this effect would ensure "reasonable prices" for exports to supply the anticipating small transitional needs of developing countries.[31] Other analysts, however, questioned the validity of this conclusion.

The extent of incremental costs associated with the new substances and replacement technologies was also uncertain. There would be conversion costs up front, but there would be a tendency for costs to fall over time as research outlays were recovered and economies of scale and competitive forces came into play. It was conceivable that some substitutes and technologies could yield offsetting savings or could turn out to be cheaper and more efficient than CFCs, as had been the case with alternative aerosol sprays. There were no guarantees, however, whether and when this would occur, and developing countries insisted that the imprecise promises of the Montreal Protocol regarding external assistance be given more substance. The *Synthesis Report* confirmed that such assistance would definitely be required.[32]

A relevant consideration in this regard was the extent of damage to the ozone layer that could be caused by future demand for CFCs and halons in the developing nations—whether inside or outside the protocol. If many large developing nations were actually to expand consumption in 10 years from existing insignificant levels to the 0.3 kilogram per capita limit allowed by the treaty, the resultant increases could dwarf cutbacks by industrialized countries. But it was questionable whether such an enormous growth in demand was attainable, and developing-country governments themselves characterized this prospect as "extremely unrealistic."[33]

China's CFC consumption had been rising by 20 percent annually in recent years, and the number of its refrigerators reportedly increased by over 80 per cent in 1988 alone. However, the technology assessment panel determined that growing refrigeration needs in developing countries would consume fewer CFCs than had originally been expected. Although refrigeration, air conditioning, and heat pumps together accounted for 25 percent of global CFC consumption, household refrigeration was only 1 percent, and developing countries accounted for only a small fraction of that. Therefore, the panel estimated that even a 30 per cent annual increase in domestic refrigerators in all developing countries by the year 2000 would generate a demand for CFCs equivalent to less than 2 percent of total worldwide 1986 consumption.

The longer-term potential for developing countries to undermine the effectiveness of the Montreal Protocol could not, however, be dismissed. The science panel had calculated that a 15–year lag in phasing out CFCs by countries accounting for 10 to 20 percent of total consumption would not materially affect peak chlorine concentrations, and would result in only a minor delay in attaining the target level of 2 parts per billion. But if 20

31. UNEP, Synthesis Rep. 11, UN Doc. UNEP/OzL.Pro.W.G.II(1)4, Nairobi (Sept. 4, 1989).

32. *Id.*

33. UNEP, Open–Ended Working Group of the Parties to the Montreal Protocol, Second Session of the First Meeting, *Final Report*, UNEP/Ozl.Pro.W.G.1(2)/4 (Sept. 1989).

percent of 1986 CFC consumption were to continue indefinitely, chlorine loading would never fall below 2ppb [i.e., parts per billion]. And even long-term non-compliance by countries consuming as little as 10 percent of the world's 1986 total could delay elimination of the ozone hole until the end of the twenty-second century, with imponderable risks for the planet.

Developing countries accounted for over 75 percent of the world's population [as of 1989], and this proportion was growing. Moreover, CFC technology was inexpensive and uncomplicated; plants could be small in scale and rapidly constructed and could achieve a relatively fast payback. Therefore, some developing nations could be tempted to build their own CFC facilities if the only alternative was to purchase more-expensive substitute technology or products from Europe, Japan or the United States. The treaty's trade restrictions became irrelevant against the sheer size of the potential domestic markets in some countries. Furthermore, to the extent that populous nations stayed outside the protocol and were therefore not bound by the trade restrictions, new producers in developing countries might try to supply CFCs and CFC products to Africa, Asia and Latin America even as industrialized-country manufacturers were phasing down.

The potential for large-scale nonaccession to the Montreal Protocol or noncompliance with its objectives did not appear entirely academic to some observers. A 1987 Rand Corporation study predicted that the 13 developing countries with the highest demand for CFCs by the year 2000 would be, in order of potential use, China, India, Brazil, Saudi Arabia, South Korea, Indonesia, Nigeria, Mexico, Turkey, Argentina, Venezuela, Algeria and Iran.[34] When the Open–Ended Working Group began its negotiations in August 1989 to revise the protocol, only 3 of these countries—Mexico, Nigeria and Venezuela—had ratified. Moreover, only 14 developing nations had become parties of the protocol by that date; an additional 7 had signed but not yet ratified. In contrast, virtually every industrialized nation, large and small, had joined the protocol.

However, governments of developing countries could not regard continued emissions of CFCs and halons with indifference—they also had a stake in protecting the ozone layer. Even though harmful ultraviolet radiation would cause relatively greater incidence of skin cancer among lightly pigmented populations, all people are susceptible to suppression of the immune response system and to eye cataracts. Indeed, poorer general health conditions and medical facilities increase the risk for populations in developing countries from these prospective health threats. Similarly, productivity declines in agriculture and fisheries would have a disproportionate impact on the developing world, where many already subsist at the margin and food shortages are common. In addition, damage to materials, plastics, paints, and buildings from increased ultraviolet radiation would be more severe in the tropics than elsewhere. The physical threats were real enough.

But there was another, less tangible factor that might motivate otherwise hesitant governments to join the international effort to repair the ozone layer. A new wave of ecological consciousness was uniting populations and governments from every region in common concern for protecting the environment.

---

34. *See* D. Kohler, J. Haaga, & F. Camm, *Projections of Consumption of Products Using* *Chlorofluorocarbons in Developing Countries* (Rand Corp., 1987).

Scientists, political leaders, international organizations, and ordinary citizens were all part of this phenomenon. UNEP itself, led by an Egyptian [Mostafa Tolba] and the only major UN organization headquartered in a developing country, represented in many ways the aspirations and dignity of the South; as the creator of the Montreal Protocol, UNEP had a strong institutional interest in its success. And the United Nations system could be a powerful source of moral suasion. In short, failing to accept a share of responsibility and opting actively to threaten the ozone layer would not be an easy course for a government to follow.

16. Charter of Economic Rights and Duties of States, Dec. 12, 1974, art. 30, G.A Res. 3281, 29th Sess., Supp. No. 31, at 50, U.N. Doc. A/9631 (1975), 14 I.L.M. 251 (1975) [Basic Document 7.2].

17. Rio Declaration on Environment and Development, June 14, 1992, Principles 2, 7, 14, 15, UNCED Doc. A/CONF.151/5/Rev. 1, 31 I.L.M. 874 (1992) [Basic Document 1.29].

18. Sylvia Maureen Williams, *A Historical Background on the Chlorofluorocarbon Ozone Depletion Theory and Its Legal Implications, in* TRANSBOUNDARY AIR POLLUTION 267, 274–77 (C. Flinterman et al. eds., 1986).

The well-known principle underlying the *Trail Smelter* arbitration **[Basic Document 8.4]** and later, the *Corfu Channel* judgment **[Basic Document 8.5]**, that no state has the right to allow its territory to be used for acts contrary to the rights of other states is, without doubt, applicable to the ozone depletion problem except that conditions are somewhat different. Whereas in the *Trail Smelter* and *Corfu Channel* cases the responsibility of the state causing the damage arises *vis-à-vis* another specific country and, therefore, indemnities are more easily determined, in the present instance, the damage affecting the ozone layer–perhaps irreversible and, certainly, retarded–would be reaching the whole international community. The state would, therefore, be responsible *erga omnes* for environmental damage. It necessarily follows that the assessment of the damage and the obligation to restore to the *status quo ante* become far more complex. However so, there exists today a rule of general international law prohibiting states to allow the use of their territory in a way that affects the rights of other states. This rule–which clearly covers the possibility of ozone depletion by the use of CFCs–is binding upon all states and its breach entails the international responsibility of the state causing the injury.

Of no small importance in the discussion of the legal aspects of ozone depletion is, next to the principle of state responsibility, the role played by the principles relating to abuse of rights and good neighborliness with, of course, the limitations [posed by] the global nature of the ozone protection issue. We should be equally aware, however, of the difficulty of drawing a clear line between an abuse as distinct from a harsh but justified use of a right under international law. It is sometimes extremely difficult to determine when a legitimate right is overstepped. Similarly, one ought to bear in mind that, in this assumption, the concept of good neighborliness would include all nations of the world irrespective of their geographic proximity.

The United Nations Stockholm Declaration on the Human Environment of 1972 **[Basic Document 1.12]** has, conversely, provided a number of principles concerning damage to the environment in general and not only damage from one state to another. Principle 6 is of special significance: it calls for the halting of the release of toxic substances in quantities to exceed the capacity of the environment to render them harmless. Principle 21 recognizes the rights of states to exploit their resources under international law provided they ensure that these activities do not cause damage to the environment of other states or to areas beyond national jurisdiction. Principle 22 stresses the need for progressive development of international law in connection with liability and compensation for the victims of pollution or other environmental damage. The [1985 Vienna] Convention for the Protection of the Ozone Layer **[Basic Document 3.14]**—where the recurring note is the need for scientific and technological co-operation—has embodied some of these principles in its context, such as Principle 21 to which express reference is made in the preamble. . . .

19. *International Environmental Wrongs*, Chapter 5, *supra*, at 335.

20. Stockholm Declaration of the United Nations Conference on the Human Environment, Adopted by the U.N. Conference on the Human Environment at Stockholm, June 16, 1972, Preamble & Principles 1–3, 6, 11–13, 21–24, Report of the U.N. Conference on the Human Environment, June 15–16, 1972, U.N. Doc. A/CONF.48/14/ Rev.1 at 3 (1973), U.N. Doc. A/CONF.48/14 at 2–65, and Corr. 1 (1972), 11 I.L.M. 1416 (1972) [Basic Document 1.12].

21. World Charter for Nature, Oct. 28, 1982, Principles 1–4, 6–9, 11, 12, 14, 16, 19, 20, 24, G.A. Res. 37/7, U.N. GAOR, 37th Sess., Supp. No. 51, at 17, U.N. Doc. A/37/51, 22 I.L.M. 455 (1983) [Basic Document 1.21].

22. Noralee Gibson, *The Right to a Clean Environment*, 54 SAS-KATCHEWAN L. REV. 7, 14, 16–17 (1990).

Human rights are but one type of right, namely those rights one holds by virtue of being a person. Not all rights held by human beings are human rights. Contractual and constitutional rights are held by human beings and are not necessarily human rights. They are rights of persons without being "human rights." The right to a clean environment is an important right, but it does not amount to a "human" right.

* * *

It is submitted that a right to a clean environment is an essential condition for the fulfillment of all human rights. It may be considered a precondition for the enjoyment of human rights. This is called the "indispensability" theory. The satisfaction of collective rights, such as the right to a clean environment, is a prerequisite for the materialization of individual human rights. A clean and healthy environment is essential to the enjoyment of basic human rights–even the right to life itself. We are confronted by the need for humans and all other species to survive. The international community must aim at saving all members of the ecosystem. Part of that aim will be the protection of the most basic human right, the need to survive. To talk of protecting other human needs is academic unless that need is met.

In conjunction with the broader international goal of saving the ecosystem, one can formulate an international right to a clean environment. This right would be extended to all members of the ecosystem including humans. It is a right based on need. This right would be viewed as the most basic need of all living organisms. It is even more fundamentally important than individual human rights; it is concerned with the collective survival of all human beings. It is this most important objective to which the right to a clean environment should be linked and not to individual human rights. Granting of rights to the environment as a whole is a recognition of its value, not to us as consumers of environmental amenities, but as an integral part of life itself. This is consistent with the philosophy of deep ecologists.

Also, if the right to a clean environment can be viewed as a survival *need*, it is truly a "universal" right since the cultural aspect of legitimization is not a factor. The *need* for survival is universal due to every organism's inherent need and desire to survive. This need is not linked to notions of culture, therefore, cross-cultural analysis is not required to determine the legitimacy of such a right.

What is required to realize this international right to a clean environment? To speak of a universal right is to speak of a universal duty. As part of the universe, all humans have a right to a clean environment, but to say they have this right is to also impose on all humans the duty of respecting the environment. Discharging this duty and realizing this right will require international acceptance of a right to benefit individuals, peoples, animals and plant life in a holistic and interconnected manner. It can be realized only through the concerted efforts of all actors: the individual, the state, public and private bodies and the international community. In defining this right, one would have to consider the responsibilities it imposes on nongovernmental groups and individuals in addition to the responsibilities of the state. Finally, a specific definition of this right would have to be conceived. "The right to a clean environment" is much too vague. Concrete rights, duties and responsibilities have to be defined in order to begin the process of implementing and enforcing such a right.

The right to a clean environment has not formally been recognized as an international human right. Nor should we recognize it as such without following a procedure that would ensure adequate debate and definition of the right. Moreover, in the course of the debate, we must keep in mind what makes a "human right" unique. If this is done, the conclusion may well be that the right to a clean environment is more properly seen as a universal right and not a "human right". This conceptualization is based on a more realistic view of our ecosystem and would be more congenial to, and less disruptive of, existing human rights.

23. Editors' Note. As observed in Chapter 2, *supra*, some norms of international law are more important than others. Not all are of equal legal force. Some are so basic that nations are not at liberty to enter into treaties not to follow them. Depending on a host of conditioning variables, there exists, in short, a hierarchy of norms.

To be sure, there is disagreement among publicists about which principles fall within the category of fundamental norms. But there is general agreement that such a category exits, and it goes by the name of the doctrine of *jus cogens*, the doctrine of peremptory norms, expressed as follows in Article 53 of the Vienna Convention on the Law of Treaties [**Basic Document 1.7**]:

> A treaty is void if, at the time of its conclusion, it conflicts with a peremptory norm of general international law. For the purposes of the present Convention, a peremptory norm of general international law is a norm accepted and recognized by the international community of States as a whole as a norm from which no derogation is permitted and which can be modified only by a subsequent norm of general international law having the same character.

In *An Introduction to International Law* at 54 (9th ed. 1984), Joseph Starke analogizes to domestic law: "There is undoubtedly some analogy between *jus cogens* and the principles of public policy which at common law render a contract void if it offends against these, such as the principle that parties cannot by agreement between them oust the ordinary courts from their jurisdiction." And in *Principles of Public International Law* 513 (4th ed. 1990), Ian Brownlie identifies the international norms that are considered to be *jus cogens* norms: the prohibition on the aggressive use of force, the principle of nondiscrimination on grounds of race, and rules against the slave trade, piracy, and genocide.

Permanent sovereignty over natural resources may also be included, although it is both uncertain and contentious as to how far the doctrine of *jus cogens* extends. Article 64 of the same Vienna Convention provides that "[i]f a new peremptory norm of general international law emerges, any existing treaty which is in conflict with that norm becomes void and terminates." Thus, there exists within that text both flexibility and scope for dynamic development of principles to meet changing circumstances. While the idea appears to have been developed in the context of treaty law, particularly as a way of restricting the means by which States can by bilateral treaty avoid general rules, it is not logically restricted to that. Indeed, in the rapidly developing area of international environmental law, it is possible that the doctrine of *jus cogens* may be capable of wider development. There conceivably may be some norms of good environmental behavior so basic and fundamental to the future of the planet that nations cannot do as they please about following them.

In Barcelona Traction, Light & Power Company, Ltd. (Belg. v. Spain) (Second Phase), 1970 I.C.J. 3, the International Court of Justice spoke of obligations owed towards the international community *as a whole* (obligations *erga omnes*), stating that "[s]uch obligations derive ... in contemporary international law, from the outlawing of acts of aggression, and of genocide, as also from the principles and rules concerning the basic rights of the human person, including protection from slavery and racial discrimination." *Id*. at 32. Similarly, in *International Law–A Textbook* 76–77, published in the U.S.S.R. in 1986, Professor Grigorii I. Tunkin, a highly respected Russian international lawyer, takes the following expansive view of *jus cogens*:

The basic cause for the emergence of peremptory norms is the growing internationalization of various aspects of social life, especially economic life, and the increasing role of global international problems. This serves to increase the number of issues whose uncontrolled regulation on a local multilateral or bilateral basis may harm the interests of other States. Similarly, the increasing role and influence of the forces of socialism and of progress in the world and the correspondingly greater role of moral principles of international relations also encourage the development of peremptory principles and norms.

And in *An Introduction to International Law* 53 (1988), Mark Janis writes that "*[j]us cogens* is a norm thought to be so fundamental that it invalidates rules consented to by states in treaties *and custom* [emphasis added]. . . . *Jus cogens* postulates an international public order potent enough to invalidate some norms that particular states might otherwise establish for themselves."

As yet, regrettably, there is no authoritative exposition or application of the *jus cogens* doctrine to the problems of the global environment. The scope for development is obvious, however, in situations where the state of scientific knowledge advances rapidly and the cumbersome machinery of multilateral negotiation, agreement, and subsequent ratification lags behind.

Discussion Notes/Questions

1. The first CFCs were produced in 1928. Their impact on the ozone layer did not come to public attention, however, until the publication of M. Molina & F. Rowland, *Chlorofluorocarbons: Chlorine Atom–Catalyzed Destruction of Ozone*, 249 Nature 810 (1974). Even then, however, skepticism about the existence and seriousness of the threat meant that effective efforts to address the problem were still several years away. How do the Ozone Convention and the Montreal Protocol seek to overcome the problems of scientific uncertainty and skepticism about environmental risks? *See* Ozone Convention, articles 2, 3, 6; Montreal Protocol, articles 6, 9.

2. As observed in Reading 1, *supra*, the complete destruction of the earth's ozone layer would mean the extinction of life on earth as we know it. For details, see the report of the U.S. Academy of Sciences, Committee on Impact of Stratospheric Change, entitled *Halocarbons: Environmental Effects of Chlorofluorocarbons*, released in 1976. See also, inter alia, *Ozone Depletion, The Greenhouse Effect, and Climatic Change: Hearings Before the Subcomm. on Environmental Pollution of the Senate Comm. on Environment and Public Works*, 99th Cong. 155 (1986); Nat'l Aeronautics and Space Admin. (NASA), *Present State of Knowledge of the Upper Atmosphere: An Assessment Report* (1986); *Chlorofluorocarbon Effects and Regulations: Hearing Before the Subcomm. on the Upper Atmosphere of the Senate Comm. on Aeronautical and Space Sciences*, 84th Cong. 6 (1976); and Office of Air and Radiation, Envtl. Protection Agency, *An Assessment of the Risks of Stratospheric Modification* (final draft 1986). This latter draft report predicted that a sustained ten percent decrease in ozone will be associated with between 1.6 and 1.75 million additional cases of cataract world wide.

3. In *The Evolution of Policy Responses to Stratospheric Ozone Depletion*, 29 N.R.J. 793 (1989), Peter M. Morrisette, argues that the approach to ozone can best be understood as a two-stage process. The first stage involved ozone depletion as a domestic issue in the United States and several other countries in the 1970s. The second stage was its transformation to an international issue in the 1980s.

Morrisette maintains that factors critical to building international consensus on the need for strong measures controlling the production and use of CFCs were: the evolving scientific understanding of the problem, increasing public concern based on the threat of skin cancer, the perception of potential global catastrophe associated with the discovery of the Antarctic ozone hole (the "dread" factor), and the availability of acceptable substitutes.

Ozone depletion is seen as a test case for the ability of the international community to deal with other global environmental problems. What does Morrisette's analysis mean for other environmental issues, like the loss of biodiversity, climate change, and deforestation?

4. The ozone layer as a global commons is a classic case of what Garrett Hardin calls, in his seminal article, the *Tragedy of the Commons*. *See* Garrett Hardin, *The Tragedy of the Commons*, 162 Science 1243 (1968). The ozone layer is a "pasture open to all," and is therefore likely to be "overgrazed," without international accord. Hardin suggests the privatization of the commons as a solution. This is not a feasible approach for the ozone layer. Reversing the current destruction of our global commons requires a rethinking of the traditional concepts of State sovereignty, national security, and international law. Hardin recognized more than twenty years ago that "[t]he law, always behind the times, requires elaborate stitching and fitting to adapt it to this newly perceived aspect of the commons." *Id*. at 1245.

As noted earlier, adjustments to the Montreal Protocol **[Basic Document 3.18]** go into effect even for those countries that voted against them. What does this mean for the rule of unanimous consent? Why was it necessary? Are there other environmental issues where a similar approach would be justified?

Nations, unhappy with the adjustments made under the foregoing rule, still have a way out. Any party can withdraw from the Protocol at any time after four years of assuming the obligations of reducing the consumption of controlled substances. The withdrawal takes effect one year after giving notice. Should nations be able to withdraw? If they withdraw, will they be caught by similar restrictions in customary law? When might state practice under a treaty become customary law?

Why does the ozone regime make designations of new controlled substances effective only against nations that accept the necessary amendment? Given the seriousness of the threat to the ozone layer, the nearly universal acceptance of the Ozone Convention/Montreal Protocol regime as the proper means to address it, the regime's acknowledgment of the need to abandon the rule of unanimous consent to enable quick action to control ozone-depleting substances, and the regime's reliance on scientific evidence to support its control decisions, might one argue that *any* revisions in the regime necessary to address the threat of ozone depletion, including new designations of controlled substances, are binding on all nations, whether they consent or not? In short, is there now a general consensus that the international community has the right and power to control ozone-depleting substances? Is that consensus strong enough to warrant a conclusion that the traditional rule of *pacta tertiis* has been modified in this context?

5. The World Commission on Environment and Development, also known as the "Brundtland Commission" (after Prime Minister Gro Brundtland of Norway), proposed the principle of sustainable development. *See* The World Commission on Environmental Development, *Our Common Future* (1987). In view of the ozone depletion problem, has humanity reached the point where if development is to be

sustainable it must be rationed? How might this be done? What role can international law play, if any, in dealing with these questions?

6. In Annex I of World Commission on Environmental Development, *Our Common Future* (1987) is set forth a "Summary of Proposed Legal Principles for Environmental Protection and Sustainable Development Adopted by the WCED Experts Group on Environmental Law" **[Basic Document 1.22]**. Principle 1 ("Fundamental Human Right") states that "[a]ll human beings have the fundamental right to an environment adequate for their health and well-being." This principle is also found in the 1989 Declaration of the Hague **[Basic Document 1.24]**, which begins by recognizing that "the right to live is the right from which all other rights stem. Guaranteeing this right is the paramount duty of those in charge of all states throughout the world." Do these communications represent a new or emerging principle of customary law in the environmental field? Are the 1972 Stockholm Declaration of the United Nations Conference on the Human Environment **[Basic Document 1.12]**, the 1985 Vienna Convention for the Protection of the Ozone Layer **[Basic Document 3.14]**, the 1987 Montreal Protocol **[Basic Document 3.18]**, and other treaties of a global nature regulating the global commons like the marine pollution treaties, evidence of such an emerging principle? What might this mean for the present problem? What would Noralee Gibson (Reading 22, *supra*) say?

7. With respect to the ozone depletion problem, the industrialized countries appear to have taken seriously their responsibility to protect the environment. As a result, concentrations of ozone-depleting substances in the atmosphere appear to be declining, and the latest scientific forecast is for a gradual recovery in the ozone layer, *assuming full compliance with the Montreal Protocol, as amended and adjusted. See WMO and UNEP Issue Summary of Scientific Assessment of the Ozone Layer: 1998* (visited Sept. 11, 1998) <http://www.wmo.ch/web/Press/execu-summary.html>.

However, although the Montreal Protocol has been highly successful in reducing the production and consumption of ozone-depleting substances in industrialized countries, it is not yet clear that it will be similarly successful in developing countries. The Protocol does not require developing countries even to freeze their consumption or use of ozone-depleting substances until 1999, and no reductions are required until 2003. As a result, production of CFCs in developing countries rose by 177 percent between 1985 and 1995. *See* Cheryl Hogue et al, *NAFTA Partners, Far East Face Challenges on Tenth Anniversary of Montreal Protocol*, Int'l Env't Daily (BNA), Sept. 9, 1997, *available in* 9/9/97 IED d2. However, as deadlines near for developing nations to take action, signs are emerging that they are taking their obligations seriously and beginning to implement plans to control their use and consumption of the most dangerous substances. *Id.*

8. Like other global environmental issues, ozone depletion is closely linked to issues of industrial development and the international economy. Developing countries, embarking on large-scale expansion of their refrigeration, air conditioning, plastics, and electronics industries, are asked to substitute more expensive chemicals for the cheaper ozone-depleting substances previously used by developed countries. Developing countries must not go through the evolutionary process of previous industrialization, but, rather, must "leapfrog" directly from a state of underdevelopment to efficient, environmentally benign technologies. In this way, ozone protection measures may impact adversely on the emerging "right to development," claimed by all nations. The U.N. Declaration on the Right to

Development, adopted in December 1986, emphasizes the well-being of the human person. *See* Declaration on the Right to Development, G.A.Res. 41/128, Annex, U.N. GAOR, 41st Sess., Supp. No. 53, at 186, U.N. Doc. A/41/53 (1987), *reprinted in* 3 International Law and World Order: Basic Documents (Burns H. Weston ed., 1994). The Declaration is vague and undefined, and the concept remains an amorphous one, but it is worth considering how it intersects with the demands of environmental protection. Can the "right to development" be reconciled with the principle of sustainable development proposed by the World Commission on Environment and Development? What are the limits to this claimed right to development? Should developing countries be expected to follow a different development path from the one taken by developed countries? Why? Why not?

9. At the 1990 meeting of the Parties to the Montreal Protocol, the developing nations successfully argued that they should not have to pay for this move from cheaper to more expensive technologies. The London Amendments to the Montreal Protocol authorized the creation of a Multilateral Fund to facilitate compliance by developing countries. According to its Chief Officer, Dr. Omar E. El–Arini, the Fund has so far disbursed over $450 million. *See The Ozone Secretariat, The Financial Mechanism* (visited Aug. 31, 1998) <http://www.unep.ch/ozone/finance2.htm>. India and China made creation of the Fund a condition of their ratification of the Montreal Protocol, and both countries did, in fact, become Parties to the Protocol after the Fund was established.

10. What if the incentives provided for developing countries to participate in international environmental protection are insufficient or do not work? What is likely to happen then? Developing country participation in efforts to limit use and production of ozone-depleting substances has been facilitated to a certain extent by the Multilateral Fund. This Fund has been used to support the conversion of industry away from the use of ozone-depleting substances; to support necessary technology transfer, technical assistance and other projects designed to slow the use of ozone-depleting substances in developing countries; and to promote future reductions. But the Fund is not a panacea. In 1998, the Protocol's Implementation Committee reported that 14 Parties to the Protocol, which had received a total of $18 million from the Fund to reduce consumption of ozone-depleting substances, had actually increased their CFC consumption over the three years prior to the report. *See U.N Environmental Programme, Report of the Seventeenth Meeting of the Open–Ended Working Group of the Parties to the Montreal Protocol*, ¶ 98, U.N. Doc. UNEP/O_2L.Pro/WG.1/17/3 (1998). Who should determine issues of access to the Fund? Should Fund monies be denied to countries that continue to increase their production of ozone-depleting substances? Or do continued increases simply establish the need for more financial support for that country's efforts? Given that many developing nations continue to refuse to ratify some of the amendments to the Montreal Protocol, should access to the Fund's resources be limited to countries that have ratified *all* the Protocol amendments? Should the United States, a major contributor to the Fund, refuse to contribute if the resources are extended to countries that have not agreed to control production and use of methyl bromide?

11. A continuing question is how to manage trade in ozone-depleting substances and in products containing those substances. Trade controls currently in force require Protocol parties to ban trade with non-parties in controlled substances and in certain products containing controlled substances. Should the trade bans be extended to products "produced" with controlled substances, as an incentive to induce nations to join the Copenhagen Amendments relating to methyl bromide? If such a ban were imposed, could it be determined whether

methyl bromide had been used in the production, for example, of strawberries imported into the U.S. from Nueva Granada?

Two serious problems have also emerged in connection with trade between the Parties to the Montreal Protocol. First, a significant black market has developed for international trade in virgin CFCs. While the production and use of new CFCs is essentially banned in most industrialized countries, it is not yet banned in most developing countries. Moreover, the ban is not adequately enforced in some of the emerging market economies. As a result, newly-produced CFCs are being smuggled into industrialized countries in apparently huge quantities. The new CFCs are frequently sold in the industrialized country as legal "recycled" or "previously-stockpiled" CFCs. The large differential between the price of CFCs in developing countries and the (much higher) price in industrialized countries encourages this trade. *See generally Environmental Investigating Group Finds Widespread Trade of CFCs in Europe*, Int'l Env't Daily (BNA) (Sept. 12, 1997) 9/12/97 IED d3. This phenomenon is likely to repeat itself with other ozone-depleting substances as severe restrictions are implemented in industrialized countries ahead of restrictions in developing countries. Industrialized countries and the Montreal Protocol Parties are only beginning to address the problem seriously. *See* Montreal Protocol, articles 4A and 4B (not yet in force) [**Basic Document 3.18**]. How do those amendments help? The United States has brought successful criminal prosecutions against smugglers. What other solutions can you think of?

A second problem relates to the transfer of outmoded technology from industrialized countries to developing countries. Some developing countries contend that their efforts to reduce the use of CFCs by their industries is hurt by Western companies which "dump" their outmoded CFC-using technology in developing countries at artificially low prices. As a result, developing country industries are attracted to technology which uses CFCs at the same time that developing country governments are undertaking long-term obligations to reduce CFC use. The developing countries contend, moreover, that international trade rules forbid them from banning such imports and that they lack the resources to do so in any event. *See Report of the Seventeenth Meeting of the Open–Ended Working Group of the Parties to the Montreal Protocol*, U.N. GAOR U.N. Doc. UNEP/OzL.Pro/WG.1/17/3, para. 77 (1998). Should the industrialized countries forbid the sale of CFC-using technology to developing countries? Only if the country requests such a ban? What if the developing country allows its own industries to build new CFC-using equipment? Should imports of cheap equipment from industrialized countries still be banned?

12.   The development of CFC and halon substitutes is progressing rapidly. Hydrochlorofluorocarbons (HCFCs), which replace most existing uses of CFCs, are an example of low ozone-depleting substances which have been brought within the ambit of the ozone instruments. In many cases, there are existing alternatives. The problem is that some replacements for ozone-depleting CFCs and halons could themselves become a threat. If used in large quantities over a long period, they too could prevent the ozone layer from returning to its natural state. Many are potent greenhouse gases.

The availability of alternatives to methyl bromide is a hotly-debated issue in the U.S. Even the U.S. government does not appear to have a consistent view. The Environmental Protection Agency insists that adequate alternatives are available; the Department of Agriculture is more skeptical. *See* Goldschein, *supra* Reading 13.

13. Related to the problem of ozone depletion is the problem of global warming, also known as the greenhouse effect. *See* Chapter 12, *infra*. A dissipating ozone layer results in an increase in the amount of carbon dioxide in the earth's atmosphere, and this, in turn, increases temperatures worldwide, thereby contributing to global warming. Some consequences of global warming could be severe climatic changes and other large-scale environmental alterations. The melting of the ice caps could significantly raise the earth's sea level. By the year 2100, according to some assessments, the United States could lose 50–80 percent of its coastal wetlands. However, in part because of considerable scientific uncertainties, global warming is a much more complex problem than ozone depletion. The ozone hole, while admitting more heat, allows for the escape of heat, and this means that CFCs are not treated as greenhouse gases (GHGs). What lessons may be drawn from the problem of ozone depletion that might help with global warming, if any?

14. *Bibliographical Note.* For further discussion concerning the principle themes addressed in this problem, consult the following specialized materials:

(a) *Specialized Books/Monographs.* R. Benedick, Ozone Diplomacy: New Directions in Safeguarding the Planet (1991); D. Brack, International Trade and the Montreal Protocol (1996); J. Brunnée, Acid Rain and Ozone Layer Depletion: International Law and Regulation (1988); The Economics of Managing Chlorofluorocarbons: Stratospheric Ozone and Climate Issues (J. Cumberland et al. eds. 1982); D. Fisher, Fire and Ice: The Greenhouse Effect, Ozone Depletion, and Nuclear Winter (1990); J. Fishman, Global Alert: The Ozone Pollution Crisis (1990); H. French, Clearing the Air: Global Agenda (1990); J. Gribbin, The Hole in the Sky: Man's Threat to the Ozone Layer (1988); A. Makhijani & K. R. Gurney, Mending the Ozone Hole: Science, Technology, and Policy (1995); K. Litfin, Ozone Discourses: Science and Politics in Global Environment Cooperation (1994); S. Roan, Ozone Crisis: The 15–Year Evolution of a Sudden Global Emergency (1989); Ozone Depletion: Health and Environmental Consequences (R. Russell & T. Wigley eds. 1989); C. Shea, Protecting Life on Earth: Steps to Save the Ozone Layer (1988); R. Twum–Barima & L. B. Campbell, Protecting the Ozone Layer Through Trade Measures: Reconciling the Trade Provisions of the Montreal Protocol and the Rules of the GATT (1994).

(b) *Specialized Hearings/Reports. Scientific Integrity and Public Trust: The Science Behind Federal Policies and Mandates: Case Study 1, Stratosphere Ozone, Myths and Realities: Hearing Before the Subcomm. On Energy and Environment of the Comm. On Science,* 104th Cong., 1st Sess. (1996); *Stratospheric Ozone Depletion: Hearings Before the Ad Hoc Subcomm. On Consumer and Environmental Affairs of the Comm. On Governmental Affairs,* 102nd Cong., 1st & 2nd Sess. (1994); *Ozone Depletion, The Greenhouse Effect, and Climatic Change: Hearings Before the Subcomm. on Environmental Pollution of the Senate Comm. on Environment and Public Works,* 99th Cong., 2d Sess. 155 (1986); Nat'l Aeronautics and Space Admin. (NASA), Present State of Knowledge of the Upper Atmosphere: An Assessment Report (1986); *Chlorofluorocarbon Effects and Regulations: Hearing Before the Subcomm. on the Upper Atmosphere of the Senate Comm. on Aeronautical and Space Sciences,* 84th Cong., 2d Sess. 6 (1976); Office of Air and Radiation, Envtl. Protection Agency, An Assessment of the Risks of Stratospheric Modification (final draft 1986); UNEP, The Ozone Layer: Proceedings of the Meeting of Experts Designated by Governments, Intergovernmental and Nongovernmental Organizations on the Ozone Layer Organized by the United Nations Environment Programme in Washington, DC, Mar. 1–9, 1977 (1979); U.S. Academy of Sciences,

Committee on Impact of Stratospheric Change, Halocarbons: Environmental Effects of Chlorofluorocarbons (1976).

(c) *Specialized Articles/Book Chapters.* N. Adams, *Title VI of the 1990 Clean Air Act Amendments and State and Local Initiatives to Reverse the Stratospheric Ozone Crisis: an Analysis of Preemption,* 19 B. C. Envtl. Aff. L. Rev. 173 (1991); J. Bales, *Transnational Responsibility and Recourse for Ozone Depletion,* 19 B.C. Int'l & Comp. L.Rev. 259 (1996); R. Benedick, *The Montreal Ozone Treaty: Implications for Global Warming,* 5 Am. U. J. Int'l L. & Pol'y 227 (1990); B. Blegen, *International Cooperation in Protection of Atmospheric Ozone: The Montreal Protocol on Substances that Deplete the Ozone Layer,* 16 Denv. J. Int'l L. & Pol'y 413 (1987–88); D. Bryk, *The Montreal Protocol and Recent Developments to Protect the Ozone Layer,* 15 Harv. Envtl. L. Rev. 275 (1991); A. Capretta, *The Future's So Bright, I Gotta Wear Shades: Future Impacts of the Montreal Protocol on Substances That Deplete the Ozone Layer,* 29 V.J.I.L. 211 (1988/89); D. Caron, *Protection of the Stratospheric Ozone Layer and the Structure of International Environmental Lawmaking,* 14 Hastings Int'l & Comp. L. Rev. 755 (1991); A. Chase, *Barriers to International Agreements for the Adaption and Mitigation of Global Climate Change: A Law and Economics Approach,* 1 Touro. Entl. L.J. 14 (1994); C. Davidson, *The Montreal Protocol: the First Step Toward Protecting the Global Ozone Layer,* 20 N.Y.U. J. Int'l L. & Pol. 793 (1987–88); D. Doolittle, *Underestimating Ozone Depletion: The Meandering Road to the Montreal Protocol and Beyond,* 16 Ecology L. Q. 407 (1989); I. Elrifi, *Protection of the Ozone Layer: A Comment on the Montreal Protocol,* 25 McGill L. J. 387 (1990); T. Faries, *Clearing the Air: An Examination of International Law on the Protection of the Ozone Layer,* 28 Alberta L. Rev. 818 (1990); A. Gallagher, *The "New" Montreal Protocol and the Future of International Law for Protection of the Global Environment,* 14 Houston J. Int'l L. 267 (1992); J. Granat & J. Weig, *Present Efforts Will Not Make the Holes Disappear: International Efforts to Protect the Ozone Layer,* 5 Fla. Int'l L. J. 135 (1989); H. Heimsoeth, *The Protection of the Ozone Layer,* 10 Envtl. Pol'y & L. 34 (1983); J. K. Holmes & J. Hugh Ellis, *Potential Environmental Impacts of Future Halocarbon Emissions,* 30 Envtl. Sci. & Tech. 348A (1996); D. Hurlbut, *Beyond the Montreal Protocol: Impact on Nonparty States˙and Lessons for Future Environmental Protection Regimes,* 4 Colo. J. Int'l Envtl. L. & Pol'y 344 (1993); P. Jain, *Proposal: A Pollution Added Tax to Slow Ozone Depletion and Global Warming,* 26 Stanford J. Int'l L. 549 (1990); K. Jestin, *International Efforts to Abate the Depletion of the Ozone Layer,* 7 Geo. Int'l Envtl. L.Rev. 829 (1995); R. A. Kerr, *Ozone-Destroying Chlorine Tops Out,* 271 Science 32 (1996); J. Kindt & S. Menefee, *The Vexing Problem of Ozone Depletion in International Environmental Law and Policy,* 24 Tex. Int'l L. J. 261 (1989); J. Lammers, *Efforts to Develop a Protocol on Chlorofluorocarbons to the Vienna Convention for Protection of the Ozone Layer,* 1 Recueil des Cours (Hague Acad. Int'l L.) 225 (1988); J. Lang, *The Ozone Layer Convention: A New Solution to the Question of Community Participation in "Mixed" International Agreements,* 23 C.M. L. Rev. 157 (1986); W. Lang, *Is the Ozone Depletion Regime a Model for an Emerging Regime on Global Warming?,* 9 U.C.L.A. J. Envtl. L. & Pol'y 161 (1991); P. Lawrence, *International Legal Regulation for Protection of the Ozone Layer: Some Problems of Implementation,* 2 J. Envtl. L. 17 (1990); P. Lawrence, *Technology Transfer Funds and the Law—Recent Amendments to the Montreal Protocol on Substances that Deplete the Ozone Layer,* 4 J. Envtl. L. 15 (1992); B. Ling, *Developing Countries and Ozone Layer Protection: Issues, Principles and Implications,* 6 Tul. Envtl. L.J. 91 (1992); M. Lobos, *Thinning Air, Better Beware: Chlorofluorocarbons and the Ozone Layer,* 6 Dickinson J. Int'l L. 87 (1987–88); G. Mattei, *Chlorofluorocarbon and its Effects on the Ozone Layer: Is Legislation Sufficient to Protect the Environment?*, 19 N.C. Central L. J. 88 (1990); J. Mintz, *Keeping Pandora's Box Shut: A Critical Assessment of the Montreal Protocol on Substances that Deplete the Ozone Layer*, 20 U. Miami Inter–American L. Rev. 565 (1989); J. Mintz, *Progress Toward a Healthy Sky: An Assessment of the London Amendments to the Montreal Protocol on Substances that Deplete the Ozone Layer*, 16 Y.J.I.L. 571 (1991); P. Morrisette, *The Evolution of Policy Responses to Stratospheric Ozone Depletion*, 29 Nat. Resources L. J. 793 (1989); V. Nanda, *Stratospheric Ozone Depletion: A Challenge for International Environmental Law and Policy*, 10 Mich. J. Int'l L. 482 (1989); O. Nangle, *Stratospheric Ozone: United States Regulation of Chlorofluorocarbons*, 16 B. C. Envtl. Aff. L. Rev. 531 (1989); A. Noble–Allgire, *Depletion of the Ozone Layer: Global Dimensions*, 25 Trial 92 (Nov. 1989); A. Noble–Allgire, *The Ozone Agreements: A Modern Approach to Building Cooperation and Resolving International Environmental Issues*, 14 S. Ill. U. L. J. 265 (1990); D. Ogden, *The Montreal Protocol: Confronting the Threat to Earth's Ozone Layer*, 63 Wash. L. Rev. 997 (1988); L. Oliva, *The International Struggle to Save the Ozone Layer*, 7 Pace Envtl. L. Rev. 213 (1989); E.A. Parson & O. Greene, *The Complex Chemistry of the International Ozone Agreements*, Mar. 1995, at 16; M. Pinkham, *The Montreal Protocol: An Effort to Protect the Ozone Layer*, 15 Suffolk Transnat'l L. J. 255 (1991); G. Raiczyk, *Montreal Protocol on Substances that Deplete the Ozone Layer: Conference Calling for Accelerated Phase–Out of Ozone–Depleting Chemicals is Planned for 1992*, 5 Temple Int'l & Comp. L. J. 363 (1991); L. A. Shapiro, Note, *The Need for International Agreements Concerning the Ozone Depleting Effects of Chemical Rocket Propulsion*, 4 S.Cal. Interdisciplinary L.J. 739 (1995); S. Shimberg, *Stratospheric Ozone and Climate Protection: Domestic Legislation and the International Process*, 21 Envtl. L. 2175 (1991); W. Simpson, The Problem of Ozone Depletion—Is There an International Legal Solution?, 12 N.C. J. Int'l Law & Com. Reg. 433 (1987); H. Slaper et al., *Estimates of Ozone Depletion and Skin Cancer Incidence to Examine the Vienna Convention Achievements*, Nature, Nov. 21, 1996, at 256; S. Solomon & J. S. Daniel, *Impact of the Montreal Protocol and its Amendments on the Rate of Change of Global Radiative Forcing*, Climatic Change, Jan. 1996, at 7; M. Somerset, *An Attempt to Stop the Sky from Falling: The Montreal Protocol to Protect Against Atmospheric Ozone Reduction*, 15 Syracuse J. Int'l L. & Com. 39 (1989); H. Sorensen, *International Agreements— Montreal Protocol on Substances that Deplete the Ozone Layer, opened for signature* Sept. 16, 1987, 26 I.L.M. 1550 (1987), 29 H.I.L.J. 185 (1988); L. Talbot, *Recent Developments in the Montreal Protocol on Substances that Deplete the Ozone Layer: The June 1990 Meeting and Beyond*, 26 Int'l Law. 145 (1992); P. Tourangeau, *The Montreal Protocol on Substances that Deplete the Ozone Layer: Can It Keep Us All from Needing Hats, Sunglasses, and Suntan Lotion?*, 11 Hastings Int'l & Comp. L. Rev. 509 (1987–88); J. Trask, *Montreal Protocol Noncompliance Procedure: The Best Approach to Resolving International Environmental Disputes?* 80 Georgetown L. J. 1973 (1992); J. Tripp, *The UNEP Montreal Protocol: Industrialized and Developing Countries Sharing the Responsibility for Protecting the Stratospheric Ozone Layer*, 20 N.Y.U. J. Int'l & Pol. 733 (1987–88); B. Tsamenyi & J. Bedding, *The Australian Legislative Framework for the Protection of the Ozone Layer*, 7 Env't. & Planning L. J. 3 (1990); C. Turley, *Ozone Depletion: International Protective Strategies and Implications*, 12 U. Ark. Little Rock L. J. 301 (1989–90); V. Vukasovic, *The Montreal Protocol on Substances that Deplete the Ozone Layer*, 35 Jugoslav Rev. za Medunar. Pravo 84 (1988); S. Williams, *The Protection of the Ozone Layer in Contemporary International Law*, 10 Int'l Rel. (London) 167 (1990); V. Williams, *Ozone Depletion, Developing Countries, and Human Rights: Seeking Better Ground on Which to Fight for*

Protection of the Ozone Layer, 10 J. Nat. Resources & Envtl. L. 83 (1995); P. Zurer, *Ozone Monitoring Shows Ozone Treaty is Working*, Chemical & Engineering News, July 1, 1995, at 7.

    (d) Useful Internet Sites. UNEP Ozone Secretariat (visited Sept. 12, 1998) *<www.unep.org/unep/secretar/ozone/>; World Meteorological Organization* (visited Sept. 12, 1998) *<www.wmo.ch/>; Ozoneaction* (visited Sept. 12, 1998) *<www.ozone.org/>; EPA: Methyl Bromide* (visited Sept. 12, 1998) *<www.epa.gov/docs/ozone/mbr>; Methyl Bromide Working Group* (visited Sept. 12, 1998) *<www.methylbromide.org/methyl.htm>.*

Problem 7-3

THE ATOMIC STEEL MILL

SECTION 1. FACTS

Naerok, once a part of the former Soviet Union, is now an independent republic. The southern plains of Naerok enjoy a temperate climate and are densely populated, while the more mountainous north has an arctic climate, and possesses abundant reserves of iron ore and other natural resources. Whilst part of the Soviet Union, Naerok embarked on the extensive extraction of iron ore and these mining and extraction industries generated economic growth. In the last decade, a nationally growing population, economic expansion, and frigid near-arctic temperatures in the north have given rise to very high energy demands that Naerok has been unable to meet.

After attaining independence, Naerok privatized its iron mines to stimulate economic development. Dunac Ltd. emerged as one of the largest initial investors and operators, and purchased the right to develop the Tal Mine, the largest and most remote of the Naerokian iron mines. One of the challenges facing Dunac was the cost of transporting and shipping raw iron ore through the frozen Lunnes river, and difficult terrain in northern Naerok to Port Kabo at the mouth of the Lunnes. From Port Kabo the iron ore was shipped for processing to the neighboring country of Salep, which had stringent environmental regulations controlling industrial wastes. After a year of operations at the Tal mine, Dunac, which faced heavy transport and environmental costs, decided in 1995 after a thorough study of the alternatives, to invest in a steel processing plant adjacent to the Tal Mine.

One of the obstacles to this proposed course of action was that Naerok lacked sufficient electric power resources to support the addition of an energy intensive steel mill. In fact, northern Naerok had been experiencing a number of brown- and black-outs because of inadequate power generation at the Naerokian state-owned nuclear power plants located near Port Kabo, and heavy electric use during an exceedingly cold winter.

In order to overcome this problem, Dunac proposed to build and operate a nuclear power plant that would meet the new steel mill's electricity needs and also provide additional power in northern Naerok. The proposal was quickly approved by the Naerokian government. Within weeks, an agreement was reached with the current Russian government for the purchase of a mothballed nuclear-powered ice breaker from the cash-strapped Pacific Fleet so that its two pressurized water reactors could be removed from the ship and refitted for this energy project. The ice breaker was delivered from Russia's ports near Vladivostok. Dunac paid Russian scientists for their assistance in the design of the northern Naerok–Dunac nuclear power development project. Naerok is a member of the International Atomic Energy Agency (IAEA), and the Dunac plant as it was built complied with the Naerokian safety and licensing programs that, according to Naerok, also complied with the 1994 Convention on Nuclear Safety and IAEA guidelines.

The power installations, completed very quickly to meet a deadline of August 1996, were located near the northern reaches of the Lunnes River, separated by many hundred miles from a group of conventional "western-style" reactors that Naerok purchased from Canada in the early 1990s. The two Dunac reactors, however, were not fitted with "western-style" containment or cooling structures. Specifically, the new reactors lacked a tertiary—or third—backup cooling water supply, and they had no steel and concrete containment structure.

Instead, Dunac engineers designed a unique emergency system that was hailed by Naerok licensing inspectors as "foolproof" because it provided another means for containing any releases of radioactivity that might result from an accident. Further, Dunac engineering documents provided to the IAEA and Naerok showed that a Loss of Coolant Accident (LOCA) had less than a one–in–one billion chance of occurring when the plants are operated within normal parameters. For these reasons and because of the remote location of the Dunac power plant, the lack of western-style safety structures was not deemed to be a problem by either Dunac or Naerok. The Dunac reactors passed Naerokian safety and licensing tests in late 1996.

The Dunac steel mill, on which construction had already commenced, was completed later in the same year, and the power plant and steel mill came into operation in January 1997. The additional electric power from the Dunac reactors provided power to indigents who could not afford to pay for their heating, and also avoided the otherwise forbidding toll of another exceptionally harsh winter that year. The plant operated at nearly maximum power for long periods of time, and demonstrated an excellent safety record that won awards from the Naerokian licensing authority. The success of this project has spurred Naerok to embark upon other privatization ventures.

At the beginning of February 1999, Naerok was caught in the grip of an unrelenting freeze. All of the power plants—nuclear and otherwise—on the Lunnes River were taxed to the limit of their capacity. While working at full capacity, a series of small cracks in the cooling systems of both Dunac reactors resulted in the escape of some coolant to the atmosphere. Plant operators attempted to remedy this by using the coolant from the secondary system to "make up" the losses in the first. The plant operators became aware of these cracks in the fall of 1998 through standard maintenance procedures, but did not have enough time to repair them. At the next maintenance review, the plant engineers decided that the rugged design of the plant, coupled with its excellent operating and safety record precluded the reasonable expectation of any adverse operational occurrence. Another harsh winter had been forecast and getting the plants ready to provide power during the winter of 1998–99 was the priority.

Disaster struck on the 13th of February, 1999. The two coolant systems in the Dunac Unit 1 were depleted, and failed to keep the reactor within temperature guidelines. Confronting this emergency, plant operators who had dealt with the original leaks by transferring coolant from the secondary system, were slow to recognize or respond to the dreadful peril. At approximately 2:00 a.m. north Naerokian time, Dunac Unit 1 experienced a "melt down" and released a large cloud of radioactive gasses and dust that passed over the Sea of Oshtok, the island nation of Sakhalin and then over north-eastern regions of Russia and China.

The Naerokian Energy Ministry, alerted to the disaster by the plant operators at 11:00 a.m. on the 14th, confirmed the report, and alerted the IAEA and all neighboring countries at 6:00 p.m. Naerokian time on the 14th of Feburary. The radioactive cloud dispersed only minimally as it moved on a swift and unvarying wind that brought it over Russia's coast at Magadan at 1:00 p.m. on the 14th. A Magadan hospital monitoring station measured high concentrations of radioactivity in the cloud. By 9:00 p.m. Naerokian time the cloud passed over the northern tip of Sakhalin, a non-nuclear state, then over Russia at a more southernly point, reaching the city of Quin in China at 6:00 a.m. on the 15th.

When the Sakhalin government received notification that an accident had occurred it quickly moved to evacuate all inhabitants from the area and to destroy all locally grown food supplies. The Russian and Chinese governments proceeded to act in a like manner. All three countries mobilized their health care and military services to check their population and livestock for contamination. Additionally, large quantities of iodide tablets were issued to combat some of the possible health effects.

Russian and Sakhalin fishermen were particularly hard-hit because the warnings reached them only after the concentrated cloud passed over their boats. A fishing moratorium was imposed in the entire north-western portion of the Sea of Oshtok, severely crippling the fisheries. The Sakhalin government was forced to support fishermen whose livelihoods were jeopardized. Finally, expensive measures were instituted to monitor the health of the populations for exposure to radiation in each of the affected countries.

The lack of emergency staff at the Dunac plant significantly slowed the emergency response, and Naerok requested assistance from all its neighbors, but no help was forthcoming. These countries were preoccupied protecting their own citizens, while the extreme cold had made emergency mobilization difficult. Dunac Unit 1 was eventually contained in a concrete, stainless steel, and gravel casing by 6:00 p.m. on the 16th. Until that time, a steady stream of radioactive materials was released, with the last of the "fallout" passing over Quin and out to the Pacific Ocean on the 18th. Radioactivity from the accident was measured in sheep as far away as Vermont in the United States.

In the months immediately following the accident Sakahalin, China, and Russia protested strongly to Naerok, and demanded compensation for the cost of preventive and decontamination measures taken in response to the accident. Sakahalin, China, and Russia, sought to recover their costs and demanded compensation. Naerok countered that the costs incurred were at least partially the fault of each of these countries for failing to come immediately to the rescue of the Dunac reactor. In any event, Naerok asserted that these countries were overreacting to the accident because only minimal portions of sparsely inhabited territory were affected. Finally, Naerok stated that it was "under no legal obligation" to meet these "outrageous" demands. Confronting these Naerokian positions, only Sakhalin sought to enforce its claims for compensation, demanding U.S. $1 billion.

Consultations were entered into by the two countries, but the talks between Naerok and Sakhalin eventually broke down. A judicial settlement was proposed, and the parties agreed to bring the dispute before the International Court of Justice (ICJ) at The Hague, by entering into a special *compromis*, without prejudice to either party's procedural and legal rights under international law. The case is now pending. Both countries are members of the United Nations, and have ratified 1) the 1994 Convention on Nuclear Safety; 2) the 1986 IAEA Convention on Early Notification of a Nuclear Accident; and 3) the 1986 IAEA Convention on Assistance in the Case of a Nuclear Accident or Radiological Emergency. Both parties are signatories to the Rio and Stockholm Declarations. Naerok is a member of the IAEA, and has ratified the 1963 Vienna Convention on Civil Liability for Nuclear Damage and the 1997 Protocol to Amend the Vienna Convention on Civil Liability for Nuclear Damage. Sakhalin has ratified the 1992 Convention on the Transboundary Effects of Industrial Accidents while Naerok has signed but not yet ratified it.

SECTION 2. QUESTIONS PRESENTED

1. Has Naerok violated international law, and if so, what damages or other relief is Sakhalin entitled to?

2. Has Sakhalin violated international law, and if so, what damages or other relief is Naerok entitled to?

SECTION 3. ASSIGNMENTS

A. *Reading Assignment*

Study the Readings presented in Section 4, *infra,* and the Discussion Notes/Questions that follow. Also, to the extent possible, consult the accompanying bibliographical references.

B. *Recommended Writing Assignment*

Prepare a comprehensive, logically sequenced and *argumentative* brief in the form of an outline of the primary and subsidiary *legal* issues you see requiring resolution by the ICJ. Also, from the perspective of an independent objective judge, indicate which side ought to prevail on each issue and why. Retain a copy of your issue-outline/brief for class discussion.

C. *Recommended Oral Assignment*

Assume you are legal counsel for Naerok or Sakhalin (as designated by your instructor); then, relying upon the Readings (and your issue-outline if prepared), present a 15–20 minute oral argument of your government's case before the ICJ.

D. *Recommended Reflective Assignment*

Consider (and recommend) alternative norms, institutions, and/or procedures that you believe might do better than existing world order arrangements to contend with situations of the kind posed by this problem. Why did only Sakhalin press its claim in this case? In so doing, but without insisting upon *immediate* feasibility, identify the particular transition steps that would be needed to make your alternatives a reality.

SECTION 4. READINGS

1. **Editors' Note**: On April 26, 1986 a chemical explosion occurred in one of the four reactors of the state-run Chernobyl nuclear power plant near Kiev in the former Soviet Union. Over the following days, a fire in the damaged reactor caused the release into the atmosphere of radioactive elements. The radiation fall-out caused considerable concern and damage in many continental European countries. Scandinavia also experienced increased radiation levels. Reactions by nations to radiation levels varied. Some nations took preventive actions, such as banning the pasturing of cows and forbidding children in some regions to drink milk. A number of countries intervened in the import and sale of food. Some iodine 131 was detected in rainwater samples in the United States and the State of Oregon advised people not to drink rainwater.

The effects in the then Federal Republic of Germany were described in *Legislative and Regulatory Activities, Federal Republic of Germany*, 38 NUCLE-AR L. BULL. 7, 21 (Dec. 1986) as follows:

> The widespread radioactive contamination of the air, water and soil entailed direct damage to spring vegetables; milk-producing cattle had to be kept from grazing; the consumption of milk and other foodstuffs had to be supervised; import restrictions became necessary; the fixing of state intervention levels led to a change in consumers' eating and buying habits; travel agencies and transport undertakings specializing in Eastern European business lost their clientele; and finally, seasonal workers in agriculture lost their jobs.

In 1987, there were reports that the clean-up in the Chernobyl area involved the decontamination of 60,000 buildings and 500 villages, and the building of a special subterranean concrete wall to prevent groundwater from penetrating into nearby rivers. This concrete wall surrounded the nuclear power station to a depth of fifteen meters. Radioactive topsoil from several square miles was carted away. A "quite small" increase in cancer deaths in the future was predicted. And those evacuated from the area were re-housed elsewhere. It now is clear, however, that the extent of the damage is much greater than was known or predicted at that time and that there is a greater need for effective international control in this realm than previously was realized.

Three major international governmental organizations operate in the nuclear field: the International Atomic Energy Agency (IAEA), established under the aegis of the United Nations; the Nuclear Energy Agency (NEA) of the Organization of Economic Cooperation and Development (OECD); and the European Atomic Energy Community (EURATOM). The IAEA is both a regulator and a promoter of nuclear energy worldwide. The NEA represents the industrialized market economy countries with the most advanced nuclear programs. And EURATOM represents certain European countries only.

Critics argue that the IAEA's dual role as both a regulator and a promoter of nuclear energy results in conflicts that reduce the Agency's effectiveness. The Agency has been particularly criticized for its impotence in the first few days following the Chernobyl explosion. The Soviet Union was a member of the IAEA, yet for three days after the accident the U.S.S.R. remained silent, a fact that caused additional damage to its own people and to its European neighbors that could have been avoided had Moscow disclosed the mishap without delay. It was only later, after radioactivity spread throughout much of Europe and beyond, that the Soviet authorities, in a report to a "Post Accident Review Meeting" called by the IAEA in Vienna, described in detail the causes and circumstances of the accident, its evolution, the emergency actions taken by the Soviet authorities, and their efforts at site decontamination and rehabilitation during August 25–29, 1986. *See* IAEA, Summary Report on the Post Accident Review Meeting on the Chernobyl Accident (1986). While the IAEA moved quickly to negotiate a notification convention and an assistance convention, respectively, the 1986 Convention on Early Notification of a Nuclear Accident **[Basic Document 3.16]** and the 1986 Convention on Assistance in the Case of a Nuclear Accident or Radiological Emergency **[Basic Document 3.17]** these instruments have shortcomings (discussed in the later readings). There is a serious question as to whether an organization like the IAEA can even hope to resolve the issues involved in preventing and dealing with the consequences of transboundary nuclear pollution. While the IAEA has responsibility for establishing health and safety standards to protect health and minimize danger to life and property, there are no mandatory international safety standards applicable to all nuclear installations. A large number of member States oppose binding standards. Opponents maintain that mandatory standards would decrease worldwide nuclear safety because they would reflect the lowest common denominator of safety. Some also argue that such standards would not be sensitive to local conditions and that the objectives of nuclear safety are better served if each state assumes responsibility for nuclear safety. It needs to be considered whether these objections are convincing when weighed against the need for states to be globally accountable for their nuclear safety practices. In this connection, see Gunther Handl, *Transboundary Nuclear Accidents: The Post-Chernobyl Multilateral Legislative Agenda,* 15 ECOLOGY L.Q. 202 (1988).

Another major problem for the IAEA is monitoring compliance with safety standards. On-site inspections are essential. However, as the case of Iraq makes clear, this is likely to meet resistance from states inasmuch as an erosion of their territorial sovereignty is involved, particularly where there is nuclear power in military installations. The IAEA currently undertakes voluntary nuclear and radiological safety assessment services; and, as the number of countries using these services grows, political pressure is likely to increase on holdout states to allow such services. States may find that there is political advantage in allowing such services, both domestically and in their relations with neighboring states.

The exchange of information on nuclear safety incidents is another important need. The IAEA has set up an incident reporting system, but there are problems with it. One difficulty is that not all countries with nuclear power plants participate. There also is debate over whether there should be a principle that nuclear-supplier states have a responsibility to provide recipient states with up-to-date safety information throughout the operational life of the nuclear technology supplied.

Mandatory technical safety standards for plant design and operation, safety audits and independent inspections, and information exchange obviously will enhance nuclear safety. But a major contributing factor to the Chernobyl catastrophe was human error and poor judgment. No amount of legal regulation can eliminate such factors. Thus, it is important to consider how the international community might minimize the risk.

It is important to note that there have been a number of other nuclear plant accidents at earlier times. In England, the Windscale plant experienced an accident that released radioactivity in the 1950s. Near Detroit, the Fermi plutonium breeder reactor experienced an accident that melted four of its fuel assemblies in the 1960s. Determinations of the risk that nuclear power reactors may truly pose have been severely challenged, and there may not be any real data on these issues. The IAEA reported: "[i]n 1996, [that] 59 countries provided information on 66 events. Three incidents were classified as serious incidents (Level 3): one involved a spread of contamination in a nuclear power plant and two concerned radiation exposure over the dose limit in non-reactor installations."[a] These accidents, and some of the uncertainties that are built into the operation of these complex systems serve to emphasize the importance of multiple safety systems. For more discussion of these issues, you might consult the recent issues of *Nuclear Physics*, the current set of the Encyclopedia Britannica or RALPH NADER & JOHN ABBOTS, THE MENACE OF ATOMIC ENERGY (1977). At the least, many levels of safety systems and increasingly rigorous operator training have reduced the risk of a nuclear accident. The safety systems are first designed to moderate the "chain reaction" of neutrons that split the fissionable Uranium (or other nuclear fuel) and release heat. These moderating devices, or "control rods" made of neutron-absorbing materials can be quickly lowered into place between rods of fissionable Uranium so that the production of energy in the reactor can be slowed, reducing the amount of heat that the reactor produces. A backup electric generator is used to supply power to the plant in the case of an emergency where electric power to the plant is interrupted, and plant operators would otherwise be unable to control the plant.

In addition to the control rods and the backup power supply, more than one cooling system is installed, ensuring that the reactor core is kept from melting, losing its structural integrity and then fissioning uncontrollably— "melting down." They are designed to provide enough coolant to bring the core under control, and to stop the plant from generating electricity, allowing repairs to be undertaken.

Finally, the reactor cores of most western style nuclear power plants are surrounded by a steel and concrete containment enclosure that is designed to withstand the force of any explosions that might accompany a "melt down." This last level of containment is aimed at lessening the environmental effects of an accident.

a. *See* Safety of Nuclear Installations: 1996 Annual Report (visited Aug. 28, 1998)<http://www.iaea.or.at/worldatom/inforesource/annual/anrep96/sni.html#two>.

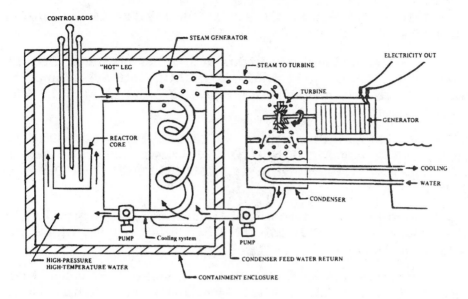

Adapted from Ralph Nader and John Abbots, The Menace of Atomic Energy (1977).

With the implementation of these technologies, the U.S. Nuclear Regulatory Commission (NRC) issued the 1977 Rassmussen Report which found there was only a remote possibility of a nuclear reactor accident in a U.S. commercial power plant that could have serious environmental effects. Less than two years later, Three Mile Island (TMI) Unit 2 experienced a serious accident with some significant releases of radioactive material beyond the containment structure. The ability of these systems to totally prevent accidents is still uncertain. It is known, however, that the containment structure around the reactor core at TMI kept the accident from having much worse environmental effects. In 1986, as is described above, the Chernobyl nuclear power plant experienced a severe accident. Because it lacked a containment dome like that found on the TMI reactor, and because its moderating system contained graphite which burned out of control, the fallout spread throughout Europe and the world.

As you work through the following readings you may want to learn more about the International Atomic Energy Agency. The simplest way to get information about the IAEA is from its web site (assuming that you have a computer with Internet access). Point your browser to *http://www.iaea.org.* Notice that the IAEA keeps its yearly reports on this page as well as fact sheets and a great deal of information regarding the world's use of nuclear power.

2. Section B & D.3. ("Arbitral and Judicial Decisions" & "Exhaustion of Local Remedies"), Chapter Five, *supra,* at 346, 370.

3. Stockholm Declaration of the United Nations Conference on the Human Environment, Adopted by the UN Conference on the Human Environment at Stockholm, 16 June 1972, Report of the UN Conference on the Human Environment, June 15–16, 1972, UN Doc. A/CONF.48/14/Rev.1 at 3 (1973), UN Doc. A/CONF.48/14 at 2–65, and

Corr. 1 (1972), Principles 1–4, 6, 8, 9, 11, 12, 18, 21, 22, 24, *reprinted in* 11 I.L.M. 1416 (1972) [Basic Document 1.12].

4. **Charter of Economic Rights and Duties of States**, Dec. 12, 1974, art. 30, G.A.Res. 3281 (XXIX), U.N. GAOR, 29th Sess., Supp. No. 31, at 50, U.N.Doc. A/9631 (1975), *reprinted in* 14 I.L.M. 251 (1975) [Basic Document 7.2].

5. **World Charter for Nature**, Oct. 28, 1982, Principles 1–5, 11, 12, 20, 21, 24, G.A. Res. 37/7, U.N. GAOR, 37th Sess., Supp. No. 51, at 17, U.N. Doc. A/37/51, *reprinted in* 22 I.L.M. 455 (1983) [Basic Document 1.21].

6. **Statute of the International Atomic Energy Agency (IAEA)**, 26 Oct. 1956, arts. II, III, XII, 276 U.N.T.S. 3, 8 U.S.T. 1093, T.I.A.S. No. 3837 [Basic Document 1.5].

7. **1997 Vienna Convention on Civil Liability for Nuclear Damage**, arts. I, IA, II, III, 36 I.L.M. 1454 (1997) [Basic Document 3.23].

8. **IAEA Convention on Early Notification of a Nuclear Accident**, Sept. 26, 1986, arts. 2, 5, 8, IAEA INFCIRC 335, *reprinted in* 25 I.L.M. 1370 (1986) [Basic Document 3.17].

9. **IAEA Convention on Assistance in the Case of a Nuclear Accident or Radiological Emergency**, Sept. 26, 1986, arts. 2, 3, IAEA INFCIRC 336, *reprinted in* 25 I.L.M. 1377 (1986) [Basic Document 3.16].

10. **Treaty on the Non–Proliferation of Nuclear Weapons**, July 1, 1968, art. III, 729 U.N.T.S. 161, *reprinted in* 7 I.L.M. 811 (1968) [Basic Document 7.29].

11. **Rio Declaration on Environment and Development**, June 13, 1992, Principles 2, 3, & 4, A/CONF.151/5/REV/REV., *reprinted in* 31 I.L.M. 874 (1992) [Basic Document 1.29].

12. **Convention on the Transboundary Effects of Industrial Accidents**, arts. 2, 12, & 13, 31 I.L.M. 1330 (1992) [Basic Document 3.20].

13. **IAEA Convention on Nuclear Safety**, of July 5, 1994, arts. 1, 4, 7, 9, 10, 13, 14, 17, 18, & 19, 33 I.L.M. 1514 (1994) [Basic Documents 3.22].

14. **Convention on Supplementary Compensation for Nuclear Damage**, (adopted Sept. 12, 1997), arts. II, III, & V, *available on the Internet* <http://www.iaea.or.at/worldatom/updates/annex2> [Basic Document 3.24].

15. **Antonia Layard**, *Nuclear Liability Damage Reform After Chernobyl*, 5 Rev. Eur. Community & Int'l Envtl. L. (RECIEL) 218–19, 222 (1996).

* * *

Format of the Liability Regimes

The [Paris and Vienna Convention] regimes have the same broad outline: first, liability is strict. The victim need not demonstrate fault or negligence although exceptions for war, natural disaster or negligence of the victim may be allowed. Secondly, liability is channeled exclusively to the operator of the nuclear installation or ship, although in certain cases a carrier or handler of nuclear material may be treated as an operator. Thirdly, limitations are imposed on the amounts of compensation available and the time in which claims can be brought. Fourthly, the operator must hold compulsory insurance or security up to the prescribed amount which is guaranteed by the state of installation or registry. Only under the Paris Convention are additional public funds available for compensation. Fifthly, jurisdictional rules apply; for land based nuclear plants, the installation state is the designated forum for claims.

Limits

The Paris and Vienna Conventions have two objectives: to compensate the victims of nuclear harm while ensuring the commercial viability of the nuclear industry. Nevertheless, whenever compensation is limited in amount, it will only be partial, and the polluter will not fully pay. Under the Vienna Convention, the installation state may limit liability to not less than US $5 million for any one nuclear incident, where the United States dollar in terms of gold on 29 April 1963, was approximately US $35 per one troy ounce of fine gold (about US $45 million). This complicated formula should not obscure the fact that these limits are wholly inadequate: after Chernobyl, Austria, Germany, Norway, Sweden and the UK alone paid out an estimated US $390 million in compensation. Even under the Paris Convention funds may be insufficient. Here, an operator may be liable to a minimum of 5 million and a maximum of 15 million SDR (between approximately US $7 and US $22 million).

Quickly realizing that supplementary funding was necessary, the parties to the Paris Convention concluded the 1963 Brussels Supplementary convention establishing a system of mutual financial assistance among contracting parties. Under this system, compensation for nuclear damage is to be provided in three stages: first, by the operator of the nuclear installation concerned, up to the liability limit established by legislation; then by the state where the nuclear installation is located; and finally by the contracting parties on a collective basis. Under a 1982 protocol, the Brussels and Paris Conventions provide for compensation of up to 300 SDR (approximately US $440 million). While this figure might have recompensed transboundary damage suffered by neighboring states, both the Vienna and Paris Conventions aim to compensate both installation state and neighboring state victims. It is impossible to estimate how much compensation might have been due to victims within the then USSR, but certainly their losses would in general be expected to exceed those of victims in neighboring states.

The nuclear liability debate is dominated by one overriding reality: liability provisions are only as valuable as the assets available to cover them and the *leitmotif* of the nuclear liability regime has been to fix the maximum amounts of liability within limits which are insurable. In the major markets insurers have responded by establishing "nuclear pools" to underwrite risks, paralleled by exclusions of cover for radioactive contamination for power station operators in their non-pool portfolios. They are also influential in the discussions on reform, submitting that liability limits of 150 SDR are the maximum feasible, limits which are by no means set in stone. In the US the insurance market has responded to higher liability requirements by making more cover available, although sometimes at a higher price. In addition as material damage cover the operator typically exceeds third party liability provision by up to a factor of 10, the extent of under-insurance of third party liability claims remains contentious.

In any case, as Pelzer notes, this "turns things upside down, because liability ought to be based on the risk, independent of the financial security available".[1] Certainly, even if such protection was warranted when nuclear power was a fledgling industry in the 1950s and 1960s, it is unlikely that such an ultra-hazardous activity would receive the same level of political support if it were being developed today. Consequently, while inertia overhangs the process of reform, this should not be overestimated. With the increasing trend towards the privatization of energy generation and the globalization of markets, subsidies both hidden and overt are coming under attack from pressure groups and industry alike. Reform, albeit limited is on the way.

* * *

State Responsibility

Even when nuclear power production is in private hands, the state retains residual responsibility. This principle was confirmed by the signatories to the 1994 Nuclear Safety Convention **[Basic Document 3.22]** who reaffirmed in a preambular paragraph that "responsibility for nuclear safety rests with the state having jurisdiction over a nuclear installation" confirming that they wish to promote "an effective nuclear safety culture"[2] although prime responsibility rests with the operator.[3] Consequently, while the liability regimes prohibit nationals of signatory states from bringing civil proceedings except under the terms of the conventions, the possibility of [states] pursuing claims for breach of state responsibility under public international law is expressly left open.

In any case, it is axiomatic to commentators that states accept their responsibility to minimize harm to other states. While the International Law Commission has proposed a theory of "liability for risk" conflating the primary obligation of responsibility with the secondary obligation of liability, this has been roundly criticized. Certainly, even France during the Nuclear Tests dispute of 1974 acknowledged "its duty to ensure that every condition was met and every precaution taken to prevent injury to the flora and fauna of the world".[4] Nevertheless, the International Court of Justice (ICJ) has never had an opportunity to confirm this responsibility or its scope. In 1974 it held that it was the French assurance to Australia and New Zealand that it

---

1. Norbert Pelzer, *Concepts of Nuclear Liability Revisited: A Post–Chernobyl Assessment of the Paris and Vienna Conventions*, in NUCLEAR ENERGY AFTER CHERNOBYL 97 (P. Cameroon et al. eds., 1988).

2. Convention on Nuclear Safety, preamble para's 3 & 4 **[Basic Document 3.22]**.

3. Convention on Nuclear Safety, Art. 9 **[Basic Document 3.22]**.

4. Nuclear Test Cases **[Basic Document 8.6]**.

would conduct no further atmospheric tests which determined the issue and [the Court] refrained from proscribing the testing itself. Subsequently, in 1995, the ICJ held that as the French tests were now underground, and not atmospheric, New Zealand could not now require the Court to re-open the 1974 proceedings, again avoiding the substantive question.

Consequently, the debate has revolved around two alternative forms of responsibility. The first, the theory of strict liability, is intuitively attractive in the case of "ultra-hazardous activities". These, it is argued, constitute a distinct category for which strict or absolute responsibility is an exceptional principle. The principle has been incorporated into certain conventions: the 1972 Space Objects Liability Convention in the case of terrestrial damage, and to a limited extent, from the nuclear liability regimes themselves.... Nevertheless, state practice provides little support for any one standard of responsibility and demonstrates the lack of consensus on the point. Indeed, Alan Boyle has argued that the failure to demand or offer compensation after Chernobyl points to the conclusion that responsibility is limited to a failure of due diligence and for causing avoidable loss only.[5] Others, (such as Sands) consider that the failure to press a claim reflects a political desire to avoid establishing precedents.[6]

Certainly, the conclusion of the 1994 Nuclear Safety Convention by representatives of 84 states reinforces the view that while countries accept that they have a responsibility to minimize nuclear harm, they believe that this responsibility can be discharged by taking certain prescribed measures. Were an accident to occur, installation states would certainly defend their record of compliance with safety procedures and any claimant state would face enormous practical difficulties in establishing a breach of due diligence. This is a practical hurdle which could be overcome: in the *Corfu Channel* case **[Basic Document 8.5]** the ICJ held that although the fact of the mines in the water did not shift the burden of proof or involve prima facie responsibility, the fact of exclusive territorial control has a bearing upon the methods of proof available to establish the state's knowledge of such events. Here, "a state should be allowed a more liberal recourse to interferences of fact and circumstantial evidence".[7] Due diligence appears to be substantially preferred by states and procedurally feasible.

16. Devereaux F. McClatchey, *Chernobyl and Sandoz One Decade Later: The Evolution of State Responsibility for International Disasters, 1986–1996*, 25 Ga. J. Int'l & Comp. L. 659 (1996).

In two of the worst environmental catastrophes of all time, the Chernobyl explosion in the former Soviet Union and the Sandoz spill in Switzerland, neither of the offending states were held liable for failing to protect, assist, or otherwise notify any of their neighboring states. Both of these incidents took place in 1986, and both produced devastating consequences in the international community. As a result, the past decade has witnessed a concerted effort among international declarations, scholars in international law, and states as reflected in international treaties to impose more duties upon states to assist and notify other states in the event of environmental catastrophes.

---

5. *See infra* Reading 19.
6. *See infra* Reading 21.

7. Corfu Channel Case **[Basic Document 8.5]**.

But how far do these duties extend . . .? Ten years after the Chernobyl and Sandoz disasters rocked the European continent, the threat of chemical and biological transboundary harm looms larger than ever before. Nuclear reactors built thirty and forty years ago continue to deteriorate with age, while depressed economies around the world provide scant funding for the swelling costs of maintenance and repair. Third-world countries move with unchecked haste toward more industrialized modes of commerce and business, while international watercourses are forced to absorb increasing and sometimes deadly levels of chemical waste and pollution. With the potential for large-scale environmental catastrophes at an all-time high, does international law now prescribe a set of obligations for states in which the transboundary harm originates? Has international law progressed to a point where offending states can expect to be held accountable?

* * *

A.   Chernobyl

On April 26, 1986, a reactor exploded at a nuclear power plant located in Chernobyl, U.S.S.R. As a result of the explosion, a devastating amount of radioactive emissions were released into the atmosphere, spreading quickly throughout the Soviet Republic and eventually across the entire face of Europe. While no one will ever know exactly how many people died as a result of the explosion at Chernobyl, the official number of thirty-one listed by Soviet authorities is almost certainly a gross misrepresentation. Estimates as to the number of long-term cancer deaths that resulted from the nuclear accident range from 14,000 to 475,000 worldwide. Scientists estimate that up to 600,000 people outside of the Soviet Union have been adversely affected by the nuclear fallout.

Despite the tremendous impact of the explosion, the government of the Soviet Union failed to make a public statement regarding the explosion until fifteen days after the explosion took place. By that time, all of Europe had been affected; even Wales was forced to halt its dairy production as a result of the nuclear fallout. A ban on the sale of leafy vegetables in Italy was expected to impose losses of up to $100 million on Italian farmers. Reindeer in Sweden that had eaten lichen contaminated with radioactive fallout were declared unfit for human consumption, and the subsequent loss of 100,000 reindeer threatened the continued survival of the country's Lapp population. By June of 1987, the West German government had paid 291 million West German marks for injuries to German nationals resulting from the Chernobyl incident.

Scholars have speculated why no countries brought claims against the Soviet Union. Several countries indicated that they did not initiate any proceedings against the Soviet Union because they did not believe there was any legal basis for securing damages from the Soviet government. Other factors might have also contributed to the reluctance of states to bring claims, such as the difficulty in quantifying the damages, the problem of identifying a direct causal link between the fallout and the harm, and the potential for negative political implications.

B.   Sandoz

[*See* State Responsibility, Chapter Five, *supra* at 344.]

* * *

[I]n 1986 ... a handful of international cases and conventions did exist ... in the area of state responsibility. First, in the famous Corfu Channel case decided by the International Court of Justice in 1949, the Court held that every state has a duty "not to allow knowingly its territory to be used for acts contrary to the rights of other states." The case focused on whether Albania was liable for damages when two British ships exploded after running into mines that were planted in Albanian waters. The Court devoted most of its opinion to the issue of whether Albania either planted the mines or knew about the existence of the mines, and the majority of the Court held that Albania should have known about the existence of the mines. Thus, Albania was held liable for failing to warn the British ships about the mines in its territory.

[T]he Court [may have] espoused a general "duty to warn" in this case. [Or it may] have ... only [pronounced] a duty to warn when the danger was located within the negligent state's own territory. International law has never recognized the common law principle of *stare decisis* so the Corfu Channel case could not be considered, in and of itself, binding ... law. Nevertheless, this decision continues to be cited today as a source for state responsibility, and it has undoubtedly served as a building block for documents such as the International Law Commission's Draft Articles[b] [**Basic Document 1.9**] and the Rio Declaration [**Basic Document 1.29**], which both include a general duty to warn [of extraterritorial environmental dangers].

* * *

While the Corfu Channel case involved the issue of whether a state has a duty to warn another state in the event of impending harm, the Torrey Canyon case dealt more specifically with the issue of whether a state owes any obligations to another state in the event of a transboundary disaster. In that case, one of Great Britain's ships leaked considerable amounts of crude oil onto the shores of Ireland. In an effort to minimize the leakage, Great Britain bombed its own tanker and sank it. The [ICJ] absolved Great Britain of liability because of its affirmative action, thereby intimating that Great Britain owed a duty to Ireland to mitigate the damages.

In another case of transboundary harm, the well-known Trail Smelter Arbitration, the governing tribunal found Canada liable for damages which a private smelting company in British Columbia had caused to property in the United States. In granting an injunction against Canada, the tribunal stated in dicta, "Under the principles of international law, ... no state has the right to use or permit the use of its territory in such a manner as to cause [environmental] injury ... in or to the territory of another or the properties of persons therein, when the case is of serious consequence and the injury is established by clear and convincing evidence."[8] This sentence has provided the basis [in the] opinion that after the Trail Smelter decision, states were

---

b. Note that the ILC's Draft Articles on the Non–Navigational Uses of Watercourses were developed into a treaty: United Nations Convention on the Law of the Non-Navigational Uses of International Watercourses, 36 I.L.M. 700 (1997) [**Basic Document 4.30**].

8. Trail Smelter Arbitration (United States v. Canada), 3 R.I.A.A. 1911 (1941) [**Basic Document 8.4**].

under an affirmative duty to prevent any type of harm occurring within their borders from crossing into the territory of another country.

* * *

The Chernobyl explosion and the Sandoz spill brought to the forefront a number of legal issues which had not been previously addressed in international law. While the issue of transboundary harm had been [debated] for decades, it ... was lacking a definitive standard within the international legal community, and Chernobyl and Sandoz exposed the disharmony among international tribunals and scholarly works regarding standards of liability for transboundary harm. Thus, while the 1986 disasters wreaked devastating consequences upon a number of European states, they also served the purpose of kickstarting a campaign ... to establish more clearly defined procedures and standards which could govern state responsibility in the event of an international disaster.

* * *

Two of the most influential bodies of work which have addressed the issue of state responsibility for international disasters since the Chernobyl and Sandoz incidents have been 1) the International Law Commission's (ILC) Draft Articles on the Law of the Non–Navigational Uses of International Watercourses, submitted to the General Assembly in 1994, and 2) the Rio Declaration on Environment and Development, issued at the United Nations Conference on Environment and Development (UNCED) in 1992.

* * *

[T]hese documents are rather characterized as "soft law", i.e., recommendations or advisory statements which espouse what the drafters of the documents believe the law should be. Customarily documents such as these serve as "suggestive law" and the principles may, through time, evolve to the level of binding customary international law if enough states adopt them in their practice. Nevertheless, certain principles contained in the Draft Articles and the Rio Declaration represent, in the opinion of some scholars, a codification of pre-existing, binding customary international law.

* * *

A.   The ILC Draft Articles[c]

* * *

Articles 27 and 28 deal specifically with a state's responsibility for disasters occurring within its borders which might affect neighboring states. Article 27, entitled "Prevention and mitigation of harmful conditions," requires states to prevent or mitigate conditions of a disaster which might affect any other state. Article 28, entitled "Emergency situations," requires states to notify other states of an emergency originating within its territory, to prevent, mitigate and eliminate any harmful effects of an emergency, and to develop contingency plans for responding to emergencies.

c. *See supra* note b.

B. The Rio Declaration

The Rio Declaration was first issued at the United Nations' Conference on Environment and Development in 1992. Over 170 nations were represented at the conference, and over 100 heads of state attended. Like its predecessor, the Stockholm Conference of 1972, a number of preparatory meetings took place prior to the conference in Brazil. At a meeting in March of 1992, representatives from seven developed and seven developing nations agreed upon the final text. This final text was accepted without alteration at the conference in Brazil.

Principles 18 and 19 of the Rio Declaration respond directly to a number of the problems that were presented in the Chernobyl and Sandoz disasters. Principle 18 requires states to "immediately notify other States of any natural disasters or other emergencies that are likely to produce sudden harmful effects on the environment of those States." Principle 19 demands, "States shall provide prior and timely notification and relevant information to potentially affected States on activities that may have a significant adverse transboundary environmental effect and shall consult with those States at an early stage and in good faith."

In contrast to the ill-defined, if not neo-natal status of international law regarding state responsibility for international disasters in 1986, the Draft Articles and the Rio Declaration explicitly articulate a course of conduct for states in the event of an international disaster. First, both documents expressly mandate a duty of notification. It is beyond reasonable dispute that the duty to notify potentially affected states of a transnational disaster has reached the level of customary international law. There is now "substantial support for such a duty as a matter of general international law."

* * *

Thus, the provisions regarding notification requirements in [Article 12] and Article 28, section 2 of the Draft Articles and Principles 18 and 19 of the Rio Declaration may be seen as codifications of pre-existing, customary international law.

Aside from the notification requirement, the Draft Articles articulate several other duties for states which the Rio Declaration does not include. First, the Draft Articles prescribe an affirmative duty on the part of a state within whose territory an emergency originates to "immediately take all practicable measures necessitated by the circumstances to prevent, mitigate, and eliminate harmful effects of the emergency." This duty to prevent and mitigate the damage of a disaster is not included in the Rio provisions. It has, however, been incorporated into a number of treaties and conventions since the catastrophes of 1986.[9] Additionally, the Draft Articles articulate a duty to develop contingency plans with other states and international organizations in order to respond more effectively to emergencies, but again, this duty is not mentioned in the Rio Declaration. Like the duty to mitigate, a number of

---

9. *See* IAEA Convention on Assistance in the Case of a Nuclear Accident or Radiological Emergency, 25 I.L.M. 1377 (1986) **[Basic Document 3.17]**; IAEA Convention on Early Notification of a Nuclear Accident, 25 I.L.M. 1370 (1986) **[Basic Document 3.16]**.

treaties and international conventions exist in which a duty to develop contingency plans has been included.[10]

* * *

[A]pplying current customary international law to the Soviet Union's response to the explosion in 1986, it is clear that the Soviet government would have violated its duty to notify potentially affected states about the nuclear accident. As dictated by the Rio Declaration, the Soviet Union should have informed all potentially affected states of the accident as soon as the reactor exploded and the radioactive material was launched into the atmosphere. Additionally, the Convention on Early Notification of a Nuclear Accident requires that all states must "notify, directly or through the International Atomic Energy Agency ... those States which are or may be physically affected."

[However], even today no treaty or convention exists which requires "source states" to assist other states in the event of a nuclear accident. Although the Soviet Union signed the Convention on Assistance in the Case of a Nuclear Accident or Radiological Emergency in September of 1986,[11] the articles in this Convention never actually obligate a state to render assistance. They merely allow Member States to request assistance in the event of a nuclear accident. Additionally, while certain international instruments such as the ILC Draft Articles require offending states to assist injured states in mitigating the damages and in developing contingency plans, duties such as these have not been specifically articulated in relation to nuclear accidents and radioactive fallout.

* * *

A.   Standard of Liability

In the wake of both the Chernobyl and Sandoz disasters, one of the most pressing concerns among the European Community was how, and under what standard of liability, damages could be recovered against the Soviet Union and Switzerland. No claims were brought against the two countries because, at least in part, injured states did not believe they could recover any damages against the offending states.

* * *

... [I]n revisiting the two disasters of 1986 and comparing the legal regimes which existed at the time with the current established standards

---

10. *See, e.g.*, Convention on the Trans-boundary Effects of Industrial Accidents, at art. 8 (calling for emergency preparedness) **[Basic Document 3.20]**; International Convention on Oil Preparedness, Response and Co-operation, arts. 3, 6 (requiring oil pollution emergency plans and national regional systems preparedness and response); Agreement on Co-operation for the Protection and Improvement of the Environment in the Border Area, U.S.-Mex., July 18, 1985, Annex II, T.I.A.S. No. 11,269, *reprinted in* 31 Int'l Env't Rep. (BNA) 1403 (addressing pollution of environment along the inland international boundary by discharges of hazardous substances) **[Basic Document 3.12]**; United Nations Convention on the Law of the Sea, art. 199 (establishing obligation to develop contingency plans for responding to environmental emergencies) **[Basic Document 4.20]**; David Wirth, *The Rio Declaration on Environment and Development: Two Steps Forward and One Back, Or Vice Versa?*, 29 Ga. L. Rev. 599, n.108 (1995).

11.   [Basic Document 3.17].

which exist one decade later, the most glaring deficiency that remains today is the lack of firmly incorporated liability standards for transboundary harm.

In 1972, Principle 22 of the Stockholm Declaration set forth a standard which has been followed over the course of the last two decades with frustrating repetition in innumerable conventions and treaties. It provides:

> States shall co-operate to develop further the international law regarding liability and compensation for the victims of pollution and other environmental damage caused by activities within the jurisdiction or control of such States to areas beyond their jurisdiction.

Even the recent Rio Declaration and the ILC Draft Articles avoid prescribing any specific standard of liability for transboundary harm. Principle 13 of the Rio Declaration copies, almost verbatim, the supplication enunciated in Stockholm 20 years earlier to "develop further international law regarding liability and compensation. . . ." While the ILC Draft Articles mark a slight improvement over Stockholm and Rio in that they articulate a standard of care for activities which could affect other watercourse states, they nevertheless abstain from delineating any specific standard of liability for transboundary harm. Article 7 reads, "Watercourse states shall exercise due diligence to utilize an international watercourse in such a way as not to cause significant harm to other watercourse States." It continues that if a state exercises due diligence but nevertheless causes significant harm to another state, the offending state shall consult with the harmed state regarding "(a) the extent to which such use is equitable . . .; [and] (b) the question of ad hoc adjustments to its utilization, designed to eliminate or mitigate any such harm caused, and where appropriate, the question of compensation."

Other important conventions and treaties have also elected to circumvent the issue of liability for transboundary harm. The Convention on Transboundary Effects of Industrial Accidents sidesteps the issue when it states in Article 13, "The Parties shall support appropriate international efforts to elaborate rules, criteria and procedures in the field of responsibility and liability." Similarly, neither of the two Conventions which were created in the wake of the Chernobyl explosion, the Convention on Early Notification of a Nuclear Accident and the Convention on Assistance in the Case of a Nuclear Accident, contain any provisions which specifically address the issues of compensation or standards of liability. While the International Atomic Energy Agency (IAEA) has recognized the lack of global nuclear liability standards and has established a Standing Committee on Liability for Nuclear Damage, the Committee has thus far made little practical progress in establishing nuclear liability standards.

* * *

C.   Strict Liability vs. Negligence

* * *

A negligence standard for transboundary harm seems to be the recognized standard in international law. Several scholars advocate a traditional tort analysis to international transboundary harm, where a complaining state must prove 1) that the offending conduct is attributable to the defendant state, 2) that the offending state breached an international duty, 3) that a causal connection exists between the conduct and the injury, and 4) that material damages took place.[12] Under this type of standard, the crucial inquiries are 1) whether the offending state owed a duty to the injured state, and 2) whether the offending state caused the harm.

* * *

Since most of the conventions and treaties which address international disasters and transboundary harm have failed to provide any uniform standards of liability or any compensation schemes, should it be assumed that damages may never be recovered even if binding international duties are violated?

* * *

[T]he scant attention given to the issues of liability and compensation in international conventions and treaties does not preclude an injured state from recovering an award for damages. It rather suggests that publicists and governments are hesitant to commit to any uniform standards for recovery, and it requires courts and governing bodies to determine for themselves what standards of liability should be appropriate in each individual case.

One question that inevitably arises when the issue of liability is presented is the issue of whether a strict liability or a negligence standard should be applied. Many scholars point to Principle 21 of the Stockholm Declaration as evidence of strict liability for any type of transboundary harm. Principle 21 reads: "States have, in accordance with the Charter of the United Nations and the principles of international law ... the responsibility to ensure that activities within their jurisdiction or control do not cause damage to the environment of other states or of areas beyond the limits of national jurisdiction." While "damage" is not qualified by words like "substantial" or "significant," and while "activities" is not limited to activities within the state's control, the Principle nevertheless refrains from mentioning strict liability. Some scholars believe that the spirit of the Principle endorses a strict liability standard, while others believe that the absence of the term "strict liability" indicates that the drafters of the declaration did not intend for strict liability to apply. Regardless of what the drafters intended, states in the international community have not usually recognized strict liability as the appropriate standard for state responsibility for transboundary harm. Only a small number of treaties have recognized strict liability as the appropriate standard of liability.

* * *

The previously-mentioned Trail Smelter Arbitration has been used by scholars in both camps of the strict liability/negligence debate. Those that endorse the strict liability standard focus on the part of the tribunal's decision which says, "Under the principles of international law, ... no state has the right to use or permit the use of its territory in such a manner as to cause injury ... in or to the territory of another or the properties of persons

---

12. *See, e.g.*, Tamara C. Gereghian, *Medzamor: Weighing the Reopening of Armenia's Unstable Nuclear Power Plant and the Duties of the International Community*, 5 VILLA. ENVT'L. L.J. 163, 170 (1994); L.E. Goldie, *International Responsibility for Manmade Disasters*, SOC'Y OF INT'L L. PROC. 320, 339 (1987).

therein. . . ." These scholars hold fast to the Roman Law principle of *sic utere tuo ut alienum non laedas*, which means "One should use his own property in such a manner as not to injure that of another." However, other scholars who believe that Trail Smelter stands for a negligence standard of liability point out that both parties (the United States and Canada) had already agreed to a compromise which stipulated Canada's wrongdoing in the case, so fault was, in fact, a critical element of the decision.

* * *

Chernobyl and Sandoz highlight the critical role that politics play in determining a state's conduct in the wake of an international disaster. Because of strong diplomatic coercion from states which were harmed by the Sandoz spill, Switzerland agreed to take responsibility for the accident, and it made substantial concessions in subsequent negotiations. The Soviet Union, on the other hand, conceded nothing to the international community, in large part because the international community [did not] exert meaningful political pressure. Diplomatic measures [may] carry with them a real and effective capacity to influence the conduct of states.

17. Paul C. Szasz, *Introductory Note to the 1994 Convention on Nuclear Safety*, 33 I.L.M. 1514 (1994).

The International Atomic Energy Agency is charged, by Art. III.A.6 of its Statute, to "establish or adopt . . . standards of safety for protection of health and minimization of danger to life and property", an activity it has for many years carried out with considerable diligence and technical expertise in promulgating dozens of "safety standards", including "safety fundamentals", "basic safety standards", "operational standards" ("specialized regulations" and "codes of practice"), "safety guides", "safety practices", and "safety reports". However, it has no power to impose these standards on any operations except its own and those which it has in any way assisted. Consequently members of the Agency, and a fortiori other states, have been free to decide whether or not to adopt and apply any or all of the Agency's standards relevant to their nuclear operations. This was consequent on the view that nuclear safety is principally a matter of national concern.

However, in the wake of the Chernobyl disaster (and to a lesser extent the earlier Three Mile Island incident) the actual and potential international aspects of nuclear accidents were sharply brought to the attention of the IAEA and its members. In September 1991 the Agency convened in Vienna an International Conference on the Safety of Nuclear Power, which concluded inter alia that "while safety should primarily be enforced at national levels" consideration should be given to developing a "framework convention" under which the parties would commit themselves to a step-by-step strengthening of nuclear safety and perhaps also create a mechanism for developing substantive protocols making more precise particular facets of that obligation.

Each state party is obliged to entrust to a regulatory body, which must be effectively separated from any body concerned with the promotion of nuclear energy, the implementation of the legislative and regulatory framework that it adopts. Operators of nuclear installations must be licensed, and it is they who remain primarily responsible for the safety of their installations.

Although the Convention sets out a number of general and specific safety considerations that must be taken into account in the operation of nuclear installations, parties are not obliged to adopt any of the relevant Agency safety standards—but presumably if they fail to do so they would have to explain to the periodic review meetings why they did so and how the standards they did adopt protect safety as well or better than the Agency's standards.

Although the Convention on Nuclear Safety thus fails to create a clearly binding international regime for the conduct of what many consider to be an ultra-hazardous activity that may result in significant damage to the international environment as well as to persons outside the state responsible for an accident, it does establish for the parties a system of accountability which may gradually impose the necessary substantive international safety standards on the nuclear industry. These standards may gradually come to constitute the basis for international liability should a party fail to observe the weak substantive provisions of the Convention or its procedural requirements, or even if it should without adequate reason resist critical observations as to its procedures made at the review meetings. The Convention is not a framework instrument as originally envisaged, the substantive provisions of which are to be added gradually by protocols.

18. Alan Boyle, *Nuclear Energy and International Law: An Environmental Perspective*, 60 BRIT. Y.B. INT'L L. 257, 261–65 (1989).

IAEA standards, regulations, codes of practice, guides and other related instruments cover such subjects as radiation protection, transport and handling of radioactive materials and radioactive waste disposal. The Nuclear Safety Standards Programme, revised in 1988, sets basic minimum safety standards and guiding principles for the design, construction, siting and operation of nuclear power plants. The important point is thus that the Agency has competence over a wide range of safety and health issues relating to all aspects of the use of nuclear energy: what it lacks is the ability to give these standards obligatory force.

(C) THE LEGAL EFFECT OF IAEA HEALTH AND SAFETY STANDARDS

Nothing in the Statute confers any binding force on IAEA standards, or requires member States to comply with them.

* * *

[Existing] safeguards agreements and safeguards inspections relate only to non-proliferation; they give the IAEA no power over health and safety. Only where the Agency supplies materials, facilities or services to States does the Statute give it the power to ensure, through project agreements, that acceptable health, safety and design standards are adopted.[13] In such cases, but only in such cases, it also has the right to examine the design of equipment and facilities to ensure compatibility with its standards, and the right to send inspectors to verify compliance.[14] If these are not met, further assistance may

---

13. Statute of the International Atomic Energy Agency, arts. III(6), XI, XII [**Basic Document 1.5**].

14. *Id.* art. XII. . . .

be terminated and membership of the Agency withdrawn.[15] Considerable latitude is normally allowed, however, provided national practices meet the minimum criterion of offering an "adequate" means of controlling hazards and ensuring effective compliance.[16]

These powers over safety relate only to materials or facilities supplied by or through the IAEA; States cannot be required to place their other facilities or materials under its standards merely because they seek its assistance, although they may do so voluntarily.[17] Where assistance is supplied under bilateral agreement without IAEA involvement, even these limited powers are lost, and the practice in such cases has been to provide only for safety consultations with the supplier State.

* * *

(D) Assessing the Role of IAEA Standards

Despite their non-binding character, IAEA health and safety standards are a significant contribution to controlling the risks of nuclear energy. Governments are consulted during the formulation stage and in some cases drafting is carried out in co-operation with specialist bodies, such as the International Committee on Radiological Protection. The Agency's standards thus reflect a large measure of expert and technical consensus, and it is for this reason, and not because of their legal status, that they have been influential and do serve as important guidelines for most States in regulating their nuclear facilities.

(E) The IAEA as an International Inspectorate

The IAEA has very limited power to act as an international nuclear safety inspectorate. Compulsory inspections are possible only where an assistance agreement is in force, and in practice this power is rarely used. The Agency can, if requested, provide safety advice and a review of safety practices at nuclear power stations, through its OSART programme, but up to 1987 only 23 such reviews had been carried out. The [former] Soviet Union has ... sought a review of safety provisions at reactors of the Chernobyl type. Nevertheless, if unsafe practices are found, the Agency can only recommend, not enforce, changes.

19. *IAEA Safety Standards: Code on Safety of Nuclear Power Plants*, *Safety Series No. 50–C–G, reprinted in* The International Law of Nuclear Energy: Basic Documents 593, 651–52, 654, 673, 685–86 (M. ElBaradei et al. eds., 1993).

2. Safety Philosophy

* * *

Defence in Depth

204. A major contribution to the safety philosophy is provided by the defence in depth concept. This concept shall be applied to all safety activities, whether organizational, behavioural or design related, to ensure that they are subject

---

15. *Id.*

16. *Id.* paras. 2, 4.

17. *Id.* arts. III(6), XII A.

to overlapping provisions so that if a failure should occur it would be compensated for or corrected.

205.   The design process shall incorporate defence in depth such that multiple levels of protection are provided. Examples of ... multiple means for ensuring each of the basic safety functions [include] reactivity control, heat removal and the confinement of radioactivity.

* * *

209.   A second application of the defence in depth concept is as follows. A nuclear power plant is designed, constructed and operated in such a manner that the radioactive materials are contained within a succession of physical barriers. These physical barriers usually include the fuel itself, the fuel cladding, the reactor coolant system boundary and the containment envelope. The [plant] design shall provide for the appropriate effectiveness and for the protection of each of these barriers.

* * *

3.   General Design Criteria

* * *

Quality of [the] plant

* * *

320.   Wherever possible, the equipment shall be designed according to applicable approved standards, shall be of a design proved in previous equivalent applications and shall be selected to be consistent with the plant reliability goals required for safety.

* * *

9.   Containment System

Purpose of [the] containment system

901.   To keep release of radioactivity below acceptable limits in accident conditions a system of confinement shall be provided unless it can be demonstrated that the release of radioactivity can be limited by other means. This system may include leaktight buildings or boundaries, pressure suppression subsystems, and cleanup installations. Such a system is usually called a containment system and can have different engineering solutions, depending on its design requirements.

902.   [C]onsideration should be given to the provision of features for the mitigation of consequences of severe accidents.

* * *

Containment leakage

904.   The reactor Containment system shall be designed so that the prescribed maximum leakage rate is not exceeded during accident conditions. The primary, pressure holding, containment may be partially or totally surround-

ed by a secondary confinement for the collection and controlled release or storage of primary containment during accident conditions.

* * *

2.4   Operation

* * *

2.   Surveillance by the Operating Organization[18] and by the Regulatory Body

201.   The operating organization shall have overall responsibility with respect to the safe operation of the nuclear power plant. However, the direct responsibility shall rest with plant management,[19] and therefore the operating organization shall delegate to plant management all necessary authority for the safe operation. Plant management shall ensure that the plant is operated in a safe manner, and in particular in accordance with the operational limits and conditions. The operating organization shall ensure that there is adequate surveillance of the established provisions enabling plant management to discharge its responsibilities. It shall also monitor the effectiveness of overall plant management activity. This surveillance shall be performed by means of inspections and audits at various levels in the headquarters and plant organizational structure.

202.   The operational safety of a nuclear power plant shall be subject to surveillance by a regulatory body independent of the operating organization

203.   It is essential in the achievement of their common objective—safe operation—that the relationship between the regulatory body and the operating organization be based on mutual understanding and respect.

20.   Philippe Sands, CHERNOBYL: LAW AND COMMUNICATION-TRANSBOUNDARY NUCLEAR AIR POLLUTION-THE LEGAL MATERIALS 40–42, 44–47, 51 (1988).

The failure of the USSR to provide immediate information [following the Chernobyl accident] led to prompt action. Under the auspices of the IAEA the Notification Convention **[Basic Document 3.17]** was drawn up and opened for signature within six months of the Chernobyl accident.

The Convention incorporates many of the recommendations set out in the Information Guidelines and applies in the event of any "accident involving facilities or activities of a State Party or of persons or legal entities under its jurisdiction or control".[20] In the event of such an accident States Parties are required to notify, directly or through the IAEA, those States which are or may be physically affected with details of the accident, its nature, time of occurrence and exact location. They are also to promptly provide the States, directly or through the IAEA, and the IAEA with such available information as relevant to minimize the radiological consequences in those States. This includes the cause and foreseeable development of the accident, the general characteristics of the radioactive release (including its nature, form, quantity, composition and effective weight), current and future meteorological and

---

18. The code uses the term "operating organization" which is the plant operator, in this case Dunac.

19. In our fact pattern, Dunac also is the plant manager.

20. Notification Convention Article 1(i) **[Basic Document 3.16]**. The [Notification Convention] only applies to certain "facilities and activities": see Article 1(2).

hydrological conditions, planned or taken protective measures, and the predicted behavior over time of the release.[21] Such information is to be supplemented at "appropriate intervals" by the provision of relevant information including the foreseeable or actual termination of the emergency situation. States should also respond "promptly" to a request for further information or consultations sought by an affected State.[22]

According to one writer the substantive provisions of the Notification Convention, imposing a clear obligation on States to provide immediate, regular and detailed information relating to the actual or potential transborder release of radioactive material, merely reflect pre-existing customary international law and in some parts are less stringent.[23] The significance of the Convention is that it is the first multilateral agreement to provide a detailed framework for the application of clearly identified rules requiring the provision of information in emergency situations, involving a role for the national authorities of States Parties and the IAEA, as well as a binding dispute settlement mechanism.

It is not, however, exhaustive, nor immune from a number of important criticisms. First, the Convention applies only to non-military nuclear accidents.[24] Second, certain of the recommendations contained in the Information Guidelines were not included. In particular, the recommendation in Chapter III that "intervention levels for the introduction of protective measures such as sheltering and evacuation be set in advance by competent national authorities" has not been included in the Convention.[25] In addition the whole of Chapter V, on "Integrated Planning" has been excluded. Third, the reference in Article 1(l) to an accident that "could be of radiological safety significance for another State" leaves it to the discretion of the State in whose territory or under whose jurisdiction or control the accident has occurred to determine what is or is not of radiological safety significance and what are the chances that another State would be affected.[26] Given the dangers of radioactivity it would have been preferable that all radioactive releases be notified to the IAEA. Failing that, there should be an agreed level which would trigger the obligation to provide information. Fourth, a number of States have entered reservations restricting the application of the Convention. Most relate to the non-applicability of the dispute settlement provision, but some relate to the substantive provisions. Thus, the Government of the People's Republic of China stated that the Convention did not apply to cases caused by "gross negligence".

Finally, the Convention does not establish any obligation on States giving or receiving information to make [the information] available to members of the public. The 1985 IAEA Guidelines noted that:

21. Article 5(1).

22. *Id*. art. 6.

23. *See* Silagi, *Volkerrechtliche Verpflichtungen des Genehmigungsstaates bei Stor- und Unfallen, in* FRIEDLICHE KERNENERGIENUTZUNG UND STAATSGRENZEN IN MITTELEUROPA (Pelzer ed. 1987).

24. The five [declared] nuclear weapons States have declared that they will voluntarily apply the convention to all nuclear accidents, irrespective of origin.

25. INTERNATIONAL ATOMIC ENERGY AGENCY, GUIDELINES ON REPORTABLE EVENTS, INTEGRATED PLANNING AND INFORMATION EXCHANGE IN TRANSBOUNDARY RELEASE OF RADIOACTIVE MATERIALS (INFORMATION GUIDELINES) (1985).

26. *Id*. para. 3.5.

Dissemination of information to the public is an important responsibility of the appropriate authorities in each State. Particular arrangements ensuring the necessary co-ordination across international borders should be established.[27]

Desirable as it may be, there is no obligation under international law for a State to provide assistance in the event of a major disaster, nuclear or otherwise. States may, of course, offer assistance on humanitarian grounds, as was the case after the Chernobyl accident. The provision of such assistance nevertheless raises certain legal questions. The most important relate to the direction and control of the assistance: the reimbursement of any costs incurred; the attribution of liability in the event of damage being suffered by the assisting State in the course of assistance: and the liability of the assisting State for damage it might cause during the course of assistance, including any privileges and immunities attaching to the assisting State. These questions require clear answers if the provision of assistance is to be encouraged.

* * *

The IAEA has recognized for some time that "the speed of initial response to a nuclear accident or radiological emergency could be crucial in minimizing the extent of the physical damage and the subsequent release of radioactive material".[28] In 1977 the IAEA concluded an agreement with the UNDRO (United Nations Disaster Relief Agency) for close coordination of their activities in providing assistance in connection with nuclear accidents;[29] and in 1984 it drew up the Guidelines for Mutual Emergency Assistance Arrangements in Connection with a Nuclear Accident or Radiological Emergency (Assistance Guidelines) [IAEA Doc. INFCIRC/310]. These are designed for use as the basis for the negotiation of bilateral or regional arrangements to encourage the provision of assistance and contain very similar provisions to the Nordic Assistance Agreement, including the establishment of channels for communication and, if appropriate, the designation of working languages.

The Chernobyl accident gave fresh impetus for the further development of a legal framework for assistance. Within six months a new multilateral instrument had been drawn up and opened for signature. The 1986 Assistance Convention **[Basic Document 3.16]**, which is closely modeled on the Assistance Guidelines, seeks to facilitate prompt assistance in the event of a nuclear accident or radiological emergency

to minimize its consequences and to protect life, property and the environment from the effects of radioactive releases.

The Convention applies whether or not the accident occurred within the requesting State's territory or jurisdiction and it extends to the provision of assistance in relation to medical treatment or the temporary relocation of displaced persons.

Requesting States are required to specify the scope and type of assistance they require and, where practicable, to provide any necessary information. A State receiving such a request is under an obligation to

27. *Id.* para. 4.5.1.
28. *Id.* Technical Annex, para. 4.

29. INTERNATIONAL ATOMIC ENERGY AGENCY BULLETIN, No. 3, at 79 (1986).

promptly decide and notify the requesting State Party ... whether it is in a position to render the assistance requested, and the scope and terms of the assistance that might be rendered.[30]

States Parties are under an obligation

within the limits of their capabilities [to] identify and notify the [IAEA] of experts, equipment and materials which could be made available ... as well as the terms, especially financial, under which such assistance could be provided.[31]

The IAEA is to make available appropriate resources allocated for emergency purposes, to transmit information relating to resources and, if asked by the requesting State, to coordinate available assistance at the national level.

The Convention contains provisions for the establishment of the direction and control of assistance, the competent national authorities and points of contact and the reimbursement of costs. It also requires the assisting State to maintain the confidentiality of certain information, and establishes rules on privileges and immunities and claims and compensation relating to persons or property injured or damaged in the course of providing the assistance requested. It also sets out a binding dispute settlement provision.

The Convention is a significant contribution to international cooperation in the event of a nuclear accident. Significantly, it establishes an important role for the IAEA, as a channel for the provision of information and assistance to the States Parties or Member States. However, the Convention can be criticized on a number of grounds. It clearly emphasizes the protection of the assisting State. As the Argentinean representative at the Special Session noted, under Article 10(2) the State receiving assistance is to be held responsible for all damage suffered by the assisting State, but the assisting State apparently assumes no responsibility for any damage which it might cause. Furthermore Article 7, on the reimbursement of costs, has the result that a State which has caused a nuclear accident and which agrees to provide assistance to another affected State has the right to require reimbursement of assistance costs. This seems most unsatisfactory, and led the representative from Luxembourg to conclude that the fundamental question of responsibility had not been properly resolved. Moreover, a number of States have entered reservations and declarations restricting the application of the provisions relating to dispute settlement, privileges and immunities, and claims and compensation.

21. Edith Weiss, *Environmental Disasters in International Law*, 1986 ANN. JUR. INTERAM. 141, 145–50 (1986).

The duty to minimize damage and to provide emergency assistance [in the event of environmental disaster] applies both to the State in which the accident occurs and to those States that are in a position to help alleviate the damage. Many bilateral and multilateral agreements contain these obligations. Certain obligations of States in responding to major environmental disasters exist as customary international law.

---

30. Assistance Convention, article 1(1)   **31.** *Id.* art. 2(4).
[Basic Document 3.16].

A State in which a major environmental disaster occurs has the duty to minimize the damage to the human environment. At a minimum this requires that a State promptly notify countries that may be affected, provide available information about the course of the accident, and inform affected States of measures it is taking to reduce the damage. States must also take necessary and practicable steps to prevent or reduce injury to other States from the accident. They must do so for both natural and man-induced disasters, although the State may bear no responsibility for injury caused by the natural disaster. Those States potentially affected by an environmental disaster have an obligation to cooperate in minimizing the damage. The failure to do so on their own territory may be a defense available to the State in which the accident occurred, if claims for reparation are made against it. . . .

The duty to minimize damage from environmental disasters derives from the principle of State responsibility. Principle 21 of the Stockholm Declaration on the Human Environment **[Basic Document 1.12]** . . . reflects customary international law. Support for it is contained in the resolution of earlier disputes, such as the Trail Smelter Arbitration **[Basic Document 8.4]**, and in the multitude of international agreements which implement it. The U.S. Restatement on Foreign Relations Law confirms this obligation of States to "reduce and control" injury to the environment of other States and areas beyond national jurisdiction.[32]

There are four aspects to the duty to minimize damage: the duty to notify promptly; the duty to provide information to potentially affected States; the duty to develop contingency plans; and the duty to cooperate in minimizing damage, as by providing emergency assistance.

1. THE OBLIGATION TO NOTIFY

As early as 1949, the International Court of Justice in the Corfu Channel case **[Basic Document 8.5]** affirmed the obligation of a State to warn other countries exposed to dangers in its territory which could cause serious injury or death. The Court cited a State's duty not to permit knowingly the use of its territory in such a way as to violate the rights of others and "elementary considerations of humanity" as bases for this duty. The same considerations underlie the extension of the duty to notify the other States of major environmental disasters which may affect them.

The duty to notify appears in many treaties concerned with environmental disasters and in Sec. 602 of the Restatement of Foreign Relations Law on the Law of the Environment **[Basic Document 1.23]**, Article 9 of the Montreal Rules of the International Law Association [ILA] **[Basic Document 1.20]**, and Article 19 of the Legal Principles proposed in the report of the World Commission on Environment and Development **[Basic Document 1.22]**.

Treaties concerned with international waterways, marine pollution, nuclear accidents, forest fires, and other environmental catastrophes embody this duty. The provisions normally call for immediate notification when the State becomes aware that an emergency exists which could affect other

---

32. 2 Restatement (Third) of the Foreign   (1987).
Relations Law of the United States, § 601

countries or territories.... Several agreements for forest fires and nuclear emergencies call for parties to designate national authorities to receive the notification. The duty to notify promptly and in good faith is firmly established in international law.

2. THE OBLIGATION TO PROVIDE INFORMATION

There is also an obligation in international law to provide timely and relevant information to the potentially affected States. This has several aspects. The first is the need to provide relevant information about the accident to enable States to take their own measures to minimize the damage; the second is to inform States of measures that the host State is taking to prevent or reduce damage. Both aspects of this obligation appear in the Montreal Rules of the ILA and in the Legal Principles proposed by the World Commission on Environment and Development. Many of the international agreements which provide for notification specifically refer to one or both aspects. The 1986 IAEA Convention [on Early Notification of a Nuclear Accident] **[Basic Document 3.17]** provides in Article 5 a detailed list of information to be provided, if available, which includes information relevant to forecasting the scope and effects of the accident and the off-site protective measures planned. It is important for States in which an environmental disaster occurs to provide both kinds of information to enable potentially affected State[s] to take appropriate preventive or mitigating measures. If notice is to be effective, it must include relevant and appropriate information.

3. THE OBLIGATION TO DEVELOP CONTINGENCY PLANS

There is arguably a duty in customary international law to develop contingency plans for responding to marine pollution disasters in nearby areas, which may soon extend to other kinds of disasters.... Certainly the development of contingency plans is essential for effective responses to environmental disasters and should be part of customary international law applicable to major environmental disasters, particularly those that may be ultrahazardous. It is, however, doubtful that international law as yet requires States in the absence of an international agreement to develop such national contingency plans for disasters other than marine pollution.

4. THE OBLIGATION TO COOPERATE IN MINIMIZING DAMAGE

As part of the duty to minimize damage from environmental disasters, there is an emerging duty in international law which requires States to cooperate with each other in combating environmental disasters and preventing damage. This duty is reflected in the increasingly large number of bilateral and multilateral agreements which provide for emergency assistance and for mutual cooperation with mitigating damage. The details of this obligation are, however, by no means clear. For example, do all States have a duty to provide emergency assistance if requested? Must they be potentially affected by the disaster or is it sufficient that they have the capability to render assistance? What kinds of assistance must be provided? Who is responsible for paying the cost of the emergency assistance? The existing agreements address these issues in different ways.

22. Gunther Handl, *Transboundary Nuclear Accidents*: *The Post–Chernobyl Multilateral Legislative Agenda*, 15 ECOLOGY L.Q. 203, 222–28 (1988).

A. THE PRINCIPLE THAT TRANSBOUNDARY COSTS OF NUCLEAR ACCIDENTS BE FULLY INTERNALIZED

A first and fundamental question concerning accidental transboundary nuclear harm is whether the maxim "a nuclear accident anywhere is a nuclear accident everywhere" might apply to the issues of liability and compensation as well. That is, might the traditional international legal principle that a source state is fully accountable for trans-boundary harm be replaced by the idea of international solidarity cost sharing between source and victim states in the context of catastrophic nuclear accidents?

Although Chernobyl prima facie does not appear to raise questions about the justifiability of shifting away from the traditional principles of liability and compensation, closer examination suggests that resistance in the traditional entitlement rule may have affected the course of events. The Soviets, it is true, explained their refusal to pay compensation for transboundary damage by arguing that there was no legal basis for such claims. Specifically, they claimed that demands for compensation were fatally inadequate because those demands failed to establish clearly the requisite causal relationship. Nevertheless, the Soviet Union's *a priori* rejection of possible claims for compensation implied that such claims were inappropriate in light of the extent and nature of the calamity suffered by the source state itself.

Similarly, it is quite possible that the "East–West factor" played a role in discouraging victim states from pressing international claims against the Soviet Union. Inspired by analogy to relations between developed and developing countries, the "East–West factor" connotes the perception that as between polluting East European and polluted West European countries, states' traditional international entitlements should be suspended. The underlying premise of this perception is that economically better off victim states should contribute to the costs of reducing transnationally harmful pollution and, in the case of accidents, should bear—or at least share—the costs of dealing with the transboundary impacts.

Finally, at least one Western observer called for a limit on Soviet liability "as a matter of practical politics and common sense." He urged victim countries to absorb part of their damage costs as an expression of international solidarity in a world that utilizes nuclear power. Thus, the choice between full accountability and cost sharing as the basic international principle for allocating transboundary costs in the event of major nuclear accidents has been raised at least implicitly in the debates about compensating damage allegedly caused by the Chernobyl accident.

In the context of accidental transboundary nuclear harm, it is unpersuasive to invoke the principle of international solidarity for the purpose of mitigating a perceived harshness of positive international law on reparation. The view that a major nuclear accident is the product of nuclear technology that victimizes both the source state and injured neighboring states and that, in this sense, binds states together in a community of necessity, correctly recognizes that the world is environmentally interdependent. This view, however, is misleading as a conceptual framework for allocating nuclear damages between source and victim states.

The concept of solidarity connotes social recognition of the existence of a community that is aware of an important element of sameness among its members. By contrast, the criteria of "sameness" underlying the notion of worldwide environmental interdependence—a community of necessity—refer to the fact that human beings share the "same" physical reality. This latter sense of sameness fundamentally informs international environmental law and policy, but it is of little significance to the issue of distributing accidental losses. Indeed, factual indicia of a functional global community of loss-bearing states are absent.

* * *

Nuclear disasters [are] intrinsically human caused, but some states utilize nuclear power notwithstanding its obvious risks, whereas many other states choose not to.

In the absence of the necessary quality of sameness, fairness and justice militate against any across-the-board application of the principle of international solidarity to the issue of compensating transboundary damage from nuclear accidents. Otherwise, victim states that have foregone the nuclear energy option domestically would be forced to subsidize foreign nuclear energy production—probably without offsetting benefits and certainly without any basis for expecting reciprocal assistance in the future.

General international cost sharing remains objectionable even as a purely subsidiary loss allocation rule. The rationale for limiting the ability of private operators of nuclear power plants is not generally applicable to the process of internalizing transboundary accident costs at the international level. At the national level, consensus frequently can be found that encouragement of nuclear power production lies in the national interest and, accordingly, that potential liabilities exceeding a certain threshold should be borne by the community at large rather than by the individual private operator. This consensus, however, has no counterpart on the international plane. In sum, it is difficult to make a principled argument for substituting cost sharing for full accountability as the general international allocative principle for transboundary nuclear damage.

23. Antonia Layard, *Nuclear Liability Damage Reform After Chernobyl*, 5 REV. EUR. COMMUNITY & INT'L ENVTL. L. (RECIEL) 222 (1996).

Damage

Both the Vienna and Paris Conventions define "nuclear damage" to include physical injury, death and damage to or loss of property resulting from a nuclear incident, although the Vienna Convention allows states to permit a broader definition. While this is arguably consistent with existing customary international law under the *Trail Smelter* arbitration [**Basic Document 8.4**] both impairment of the environment and the cost of preventive measures are included in the current draft of the Vienna revisions. Nevertheless, although measures of reinstatement may go hand in hand with remediation activities, reparations for ecological harm will be a low priority in any allocation of limited funds. As the allocation of funds will take place in the installation state, it would be a brave court which granted extensive funds for clean-up of another state's environment, unless equal measures were being taken in their own.

Given the diverse legal systems operating in states signatories to the Conventions, discussions over what constitutes "damage" will always be contentious. While the USSR was reluctant to accept that other states had suffered damage after Chernobyl (thereby maintaining that no compensation was due), other states compensated broadly. In Switzerland, the Federal Court compensated market gardeners for their loss of profits, finding an unbroken causal link, and their German Government compensated growers of spring vegetables, dairy and seasonal workers in agriculture and food industries, transport enterprises and travel agencies specializing in Eastern European business. In the U.S., courts compensated for economic losses after the Three Mile Island incident where the applicant could prove physical or property damage. The UK, however, has conventionally taken a more restrictive approach, refusing to compensate for a reduction in property values caused by contamination. In practice, the dividing line between economic loss and physical damage is not always clear, and uniformity is thus difficult to achieve.

One way to minimize such dispute is to introduce agreed international standards of intervention linked to monitoring levels. This possibility has been supported by the Director General of the IAEA who has confirmed that "harmonized international norms would provide an objective threshold both for triggering claims for damage and for determining whether they were justified". Guidelines for intervention have been formulated by the IAEA, the World Health Organization, the European Community and the International Commission on Radiological Protection; and following Chernobyl, research has been undertaken to consider how to extend these intervention levels to account for the effect of radioactive pollution on foodstuffs and the environment. Indeed, Philippe Sands has argued that while these intervention levels would almost certainly be introduced in evidence were a claim ever brought at state level, it would be far more effective for them to be incorporated into the Conventions, a possibility recognized by the IAEA. So far these recommendations have not, however, been taken on board.

24. PATRICIA BIRNIE & ALAN BOYLE, INTERNATIONAL LAW AND THE ENVIRONMENT 158 (1992).

It should be briefly noted here that international claims involving responsibility for injury to aliens, or violation of human rights norms, have been conditional in international judicial and arbitral practice on the prior exhaustion of local remedies, which usually entails resort to the relevant national legal system as a preferred means of redress. Only if justice is effectively denied, or if no redress is available will an international claim then be admissible.

The application of this rule to international claims involving state responsibility for environmental injury is not clearly established. It was not applied in the Trail Smelter Arbitration because no local remedies were available to the transboundary litigants, but the development of equal access schemes and civil liability treaties which facilitate transboundary proceedings may have altered the picture since then. These can afford adequate and effective remedies for pollution damage suffered by individuals, and insistence on exhaustion of local remedies of this kind would be consistent with a policy emphasizing the direct liability of the polluter for environmentally harmful activities. . . .

* * *

[I]f it is accepted that the rule should apply to injury to individuals or their property, it may still be thought inappropriate [to apply it] to claims involving direct injury to the state's environment, or a fortiori in cases concerning the global commons, because these are too far removed from the original justification for the rule and its application could require states to submit themselves to foreign jurisdiction.

Discussion Notes/Questions

1. What should be the standard of care for any obligation to avoid harmful increase in levels of transboundary radioactivity? The possibilities are fault (intention or negligence), strict liability (basically a *prima facie* liability with various defenses or qualifications), and absolute liability (for which there is no exculpation). See L. Goldie, *Liability for Damage and the Progressive Development of International Law,* 14 INT'L & COMP. L.Q. 1189, 1202–20 (1965) for a discussion of the distinction between strict and absolute liability in the context of environmental damage. The dangers of nuclear activity mean that the standard of care should be a high one. The national laws of many countries have a standard of strict liability for ultra-hazardous activities. Some treaties regulating nuclear activities and other ultra-hazardous activities establish a principle of absolute liability. However, the use of the word "absolute" is misleading, as many of these treaties provide exceptions to the rule, e.g. Article 3 of the 1960 Paris Convention on Third Party Liability in the Field of Nuclear Energy (as amended) **[Basic Document 3.1]** and Article IV(1) of the 1962 Brussels Convention on the Liability of Operators of Nuclear Ships **[Basic Document 4.5]**. By contrast the 1972 Convention on International Liability for Damage Caused by Space Objects **[Basic Document 3.5]** provides for objective responsibility for space objects falling on the ground irrespective of fault and has no ceiling or limit on possible compensation. In this context also see Chapter 5.

In 1981, the U.S.S.R. paid $3 million compensation in final settlement for damage incurred in locating and cleaning-up after the disintegration of a nuclear-powered satellite, Cosmos 954, on Canadian territory in 1978. In its statement of claim, Canada relied on Article 2 of the 1972 Convention on International Liability for Damage Caused by Space Objects and maintained that the principle of absolute liability applies to fields of activity having in common a high degree of risk in international law. Is absolute liability a principle in customary law for abnormally dangerous activities? Should it be?

What standard of care would be most likely to achieve the objective of preventing nuclear accidents? There is an argument that strict or absolute liability might make it impossible for operators to obtain financial security (insurance) coverage. Should this be a consideration when dealing with questions concerning global environmental security?

2. What about a principle of individual responsibility applicable to nuclear energy operators and administrators, similar to the kind established at Nuremberg after World War II? Or for exporters of nuclear technology? *See, e.g.,*

Anthony D'Amato & Kristen Engel, *State Responsibility for the Exportation of Nuclear Power Technology*, 74 VA. L. REV. 1011 (1988). Who would apply and enforce such a principle? What about the abolition of nuclear power altogether? Is this desirable? Possible? *See, e.g.*, Richard Falk, *Nuclear Policy and World Order: Why Denuclearization*, 3 Alternatives—J. WORLD POL'Y, 321 (1978). What type of reparation would be best for pollution from a nuclear power plant? Indemnity in the form of monetary compensation? Restoration (if possible)? Satisfaction? Which is the most likely to achieve the objective of prevention? Should there be different criteria for determining reparations for activities with a higher-than-normal likelihood of causing substantial injuries within the territory of another state? Is the "polluter pays" principle appropriate to nuclear pollution given its wide-spread, long-lasting, and serious effects on the environment? Are there other possible ways of handling the question of reparation?

Taking the compensation route raises the issue of how to quantify the value of damage caused in monetary terms. Some losses cannot be quantified. For example, what value would be placed on the destruction of the traditional Lapp way of life, alleged to be a casualty of the effect of radioactivity from Chernobyl on lichen which reindeer eat. States are unlikely to agree on any monetary value, given that it reflects a different set of cultural assumptions. One possible measure of damages would be the cost of making the environment whole. This approach finds support in traditional international law, which provides that "reparation must, as far as possible, wipe out all the consequences of the illegal act and establish the situation which would in all probability have existed if the act had not been committed." Chorzow Factory Case (Ger. v. Pol.), 1928 P.C.I.J. (ser. A) No. 17, at 47.

3. The consequences of a nuclear accident are difficult to establish. There are major problems in proving damage and loss over the long term. Could Sakhalin succeed with a claim based on an alleged infliction of a moral injury? Is material damage required? Would the psychological impact of radioactive fallout on the state's people suffice as a basis for a claim? Gunther Handl, *Territorial Sovereignty and the Problem of Transnational Pollution*, 69 AM. J. INT'L L. 50 (1975) concludes that moral injury is not enough. International law requires proof of material damage, but this could include psychological impact.

The *Nuclear Tests Cases* [**Basic Document 8.6**] raised these issues; but the International Court of Justice did not deal with them because France undertook to stop nuclear testing. Australia and New Zealand argued that radioactive fallout from the French tests on their territory and its dispersion within their airspace without their consent violated their territorial sovereignty. They claimed also that it impaired their independent right to determine what acts should take place within their territories and, in particular, whether each State and its people shall be exposed to radiation from artificial sources. If the International Court of Justice had considered these issues, how do you think it might have decided? Why?

In its Advisory Opinion on the *Legality of the Threat or Use of Nuclear Weapons* [**Basic Document 8.10**], the ICJ took a significant step toward recognizing an obligation to achieve nuclear disarmament. In delivering its Opinion, at the request of the General Assembly of the United Nations, the Court felt it did not have "sufficient elements to enable it to conclude with certainty that the use of nuclear weapons would necessarily be at variance with the principles and rules of law applicable in armed conflict in any circumstance." (Para 95).

However, the Court recognized "the full importance of the recognition by Article VI of the Treaty on the Non–Proliferation of Nuclear Weapons of an obligation to negotiate in good faith a nuclear disarmament." This provision is worded as follows:

> Each of the Parties to the Treaty undertakes to pursue negotiations in good faith on effective measures relating to cessation of the nuclear arms race at an early date and to nuclear disarmament, and on a treaty on general and complete disarmament under strict and effective international control.

It opined that the "legal import of that obligation goes beyond that of a mere obligation of conduct; the obligation involved here is an obligation to achieve a precise result—nuclear disarmament in all its aspects—by adopting a particular course of conduct, namely, the pursuit of negotiations on the matter in good faith." (Para 99).

4. What if Dunac supplied the proper containment structures and the radiation releases still occurred? What if there were a Calvo-type clause in the contract which stated that Sakhalin exempted Naerok from any responsibility? Would Sakhalin be liable to the injured populations under the law of state responsibility? Is there a human rights argument? For a discussion of these questions, see Anthony D'Amato & Kristen Engel, *State Responsibility for the Exportation of Nuclear Power Technology*, 74 Va. L. Rev. 1011 (1988).

5. Where to with the law now? There have been two views on the best approach to handle the law on international liability for nuclear damage. The first considers the Paris and Vienna Conventions [**Basic Documents 3.1 & 3.23**], with wider acceptance, the way to proceed. This approach would harmonize, and perhaps simultaneously apply, the two conventions. The second view believes that there is a need for a new instrument on state liability for nuclear damage. The conventions deal with liability primarily under civil law. They address the liability of individuals or juridical persons for damage resulting in loss or life or damage to the property of individuals. They do not deal with damage to the environment or to claims between states. Such a multilateral instrument would take full account of the work of the International Law Commission on international liability. Which view does the 1994 Convention on Nuclear Safety fit into? Would a "framework" agreement have been better or worse?

6. At the time of Chernobyl, there were no international standards on what constitutes harmful levels of radioactivity. This caused problems. The U.S.S.R. claimed that states took unjustified action in placing restrictions on trade in agricultural products. There were allegations that some states took action for reasons other than the threat of nuclear contamination, such as for trade advantage. The U.S.S.R. has suggested that a new instrument could deal with material, moral, and political damage caused by unwarranted action taken under the pretext of protecting against the consequences of nuclear accidents (the spreading of untrue information, introduction of unjustified restrictive measures, etc). What would such an instrument look like? How would it work?

7. What should Naerok have done prior to the development of the nuclear facility? What is a state's responsibility under international law for transboundary environmental risks and potential harm? Does international law recognize the principle of international liability for risk? Is the source state under a legal obligation to take certain procedural steps, e.g., providing prior information, offering or accepting a request for consultation, and undertaking a transboundary impact assessment designed to minimize the risk? Does such a duty raise practical problems of implementation and enforcement? How might these problems be

overcome? *See* Roda Mushkat, *The Daya Bay Nuclear Plant Project in the Light of International Law,* 7 UCLA PAC. BASIN L.J. 87 (1990).

Should neighboring states have a substantive right of veto or co-decision in respect of the development of a nuclear facility? Should the people and local authorities affected in the neighboring state have the same procedural rights as those enjoyed during a public inquiry by general public and local authorities in the constructing state? Should the constructing state be obliged to include the observations made by the affected people and local authorities of the neighboring state in its decision-making? Should the mere risk of a major accident be regarded as damage to the other state? What about the possible psychological effects of a nuclear power plant on the inhabitants of a region, or any effect on aesthetics and tourism? *See* Koen Lenaerts, *Border Installations*, *in* NUCLEAR ENERGY LAW AFTER CHERNOBYL 49 (P. Cameron et al. eds., 1988). How can states decide what constitutes neighboring territories when distance does not always equate to danger of transboundary pollution?

8.   After Chernobyl, some countries abandoned plans for developing new nuclear power plants. Others looked at phasing-out nuclear power. This would mean the use of alternative sources of power (sun, wind, water, biomass, etc.), which also could have undesirable environmental consequences. In China for example, greater use of coal-fired and oil-fired power plants has the potential to increase emissions of carbon dioxide, increasing the potential effect on global warming. Nuclear power generation involves the release of negligible quantities of carbon dioxide, acidifying gases, and other air pollutants associated with fuel combustion. However, nuclear power has health, safety, and security risks. And there are problems regarding the safe disposal of nuclear waste and the de-commissioning of nuclear plants. What implications do these questions have for the treatment of nuclear technology in international law?

9.   Not to be overlooked either is the nexus between nuclear power and the spread of nuclear weapons. Despite many pressures and blandishments, it has been argued, nuclear weapons proliferation is not likely to be halted until there is a total renunciation of nuclear power for whatever purpose, on the part of the nuclear weapons states especially, and its substitution with other less centralized, less costly, and pollution-free sources of energy such as sun, wind, water, and biomass. Writes Richard Falk:

> The history of civilian nuclear power is a twisted one. It is closely associated with the sense of guilt felt by those who first developed the atomic bomb, and who subsequently tried to make partial atonement by putting the atom to constructive use. Their hope was that the civilian nuclear spin-offs, once perfected, could be lifted from their military context, put to good domestic use, and then transferred abroad through the [1968] Non–Proliferation Treaty,[d] which would yield lucrative foreign markets for US industry in the process. However, the hope that atomic power could serve peace without being tarnished by the horror of Hiroshima fostered an artificial separation between the military and civilian nuclear programs. The catch, and it is a catch–22, is that there is no way to spread nuclear technology around without inevitably spreading the weapons capability right along with it.

Richard Falk, *Nuclear Policy and World Order: Why Denuclearization*, 3 Alternatives—J. WORLD POL'Y 321, 338–39 (1978). In any event, is it feasible to eliminate commercial nuclear power from the world scene? For powerful, seminal advocacy

d. Treaty on the Non–Proliferation of Nuclear Weapons, [**Basic Document 7.29**].

in the affirmative, see Amory Lovins, *Energy Strategy: The Road Not Taken?*, 55 FOREIGN AFFAIRS 65 (1976). *See also* AMORY LOVINS, SOFT ENERGY PATHS: TOWARD A DURABLE PEACE (1977).

10. *Bibliographic Note.* For further discussion concerning the principle themes addressed in this problem, consult the following specialized materials:

(a) *Specialized Books/Monographs.* A. Adede, The IAEA Notification and Assistance Conventions in Case of a Nuclear Accident: Landmarks in the Multilateral Treaty-making Process (1987); McGEORGE BUNDY, WILLIAM J. CROWE, JR., AND SIDNEY D. DRELL, REDUCING NUCLEAR DANGER. THE ROAD AWAY FROM THE BRINK (1993); V. Chernousenko, Chernobyl–Insight From Inside (1991); JOHN H. DOWNS, NEGOTIATING WITH THE RUSSIANS ON NUCLEAR ARMS-LAWYERS MAKING A DIFFERENCE (1997); JOHN H. DOWNS, A CASE STUDY IN TWO-TRACK DIPLOMACY: THE LAWYERS ALLIANCE FOR NUCLEAR ARMS CONTROL: NEGOTIATING WITH THE RUSSIANS ON NUCLEAR ARMS: LAWYERS MAKING A DIFFERENCE (1997); C. Flavin, Reassessing Nuclear Power: The Fallout from Chernobyl (1987); T. Gadkowski, International Liability of State for Nuclear Damage (1989); R. Gale, Final Warning: The Legacy of Chernobyl (1988); MICHAEL B. GERRARD, WHOSE BACKYARD, WHOSE RISK: FEAR AND FAIRNESS IN TOXIC AND NUCLEAR WASTE SITING (1994); D. Gumprecht & A. Kindt, Impact of the Chernobyl Nuclear Power Plant Accident on the Federal Republic of Germany: Recommendations of the Commission on Radiological Protection: Assessment, Limitation and Valuation (1988); J. Helgerson, Nuclear Accidents (1988); A. Kanner, Understanding and Addressing the Consequences of a Nuclear Accident (1981); KENNETH F. MCCALLION, SHOREHAM AND THE RISE AND FALL OF THE NUCLEAR POWER INDUSTRY (1995); GRIGORI MEDVEDEV, NO BREATHING ROOM: THE AFTERMATH OF CHERNOBYL (1993); G. Medvedev, The Truth About Chernobyl (1991); Z. Medvedev, The Legacy of Chernobyl (1990); W. Megaw, How Safe?: Three Mile Island, Chernobyl and Beyond (1987); R. Mould, Chernobyl-The Real Story (1988); Nuclear Energy Law After Chernobyl (P. Cameron et al. eds., 1988); F. Pohl, The Chernobyl Accident and its Consequences (1987); MITCHELL REISS, BRIDLED AMBITION: WHY COUNTRIES CONSTRAIN THEIR NUCLEAR CAPABILITIES (1996); P. Sands, Chernobyl: Law and Communication: Transboundary Nuclear Air Pollution–The Legal Materials (1988); B. Segerstahl, Chernobyl: A Policy Response (1991); L. Scheinman, The International Atomic Energy Agency and World Nuclear Order (1987); ; I. Shcherbak, Chernobyl: A Documentary Story (1989); ALLA YAROSHINSKAYA, CHERNOBYL: THE FORBIDDEN TRUTH (1995);

(b) *Specialized Hearings/Reports.* M. Horn, Nuclear Energy Safety–Convention on Early Notification of a Nuclear Accident, *opened for signature* Sept. 26, 1986, *entry into force* Oct. 27, 1986, *in* Final Document Resolutions and Conventions, Spl. 1 U.N. Int'l Atom. Energy Agency Gen. Conf. (8th plen. mtg.), at 5, U.N. Doc. IAEA/GC(SPL.I) (1986), *reprinted in* 25 I.L.M. 1370 (1986); Convention on Assistance in the Case of a Nuclear Accident or Radiological Emergency, *opened for signature* Sept. 26, 1986, *entered into force* Feb. 26, 1987, *in* Final Document Resolutions and Conventions, Spl. 1 U.N. Int'l Atom. Energy Agency Gen.Conf. (8th plen. mtg.), at 13, U.N. Doc. IAEA/GC(SPL.I) (1986), *reprinted in* 25 I.L.M. 1377 (1986), 28 H.I.J.L. 558–67 (1987); International Nuclear Safety Advisory Group, Summary Report on the Post-accident Review Meeting on the Chernobyl Accident (1986); United Nations, Survey of State Practice Relevant to International Liability for Injurious Consequences Arising out of Acts Not Prohibited by International Law: Study (1984); Watt Committee on Energy, Five Years after Chernobyl, 1986–1991: A Review (1991).

(c) *Specialized Articles/Book Chapters.* Jason Aamodt, *Regulating the Standard of Care Owed to the Public During an Accident at a Nuclear Power Plant* 16 ENERGY L. J. 181 (1995);Chris Addicott, Note & Comment, *Double Indemnity For Operators of Nuclear Facilities? In re Hanford Nuclear Reservation Litigation, The Price–Anderson Act, And The Government Contractor Defense* 72 WASH. L. REV. 505 (1997); A. D'Amato & K. Engel, *State Responsibility for the Exportation of Nuclear Power Technology,* 74 Va. L. Rev. 1011 (1988); J. Asselstine, *The Future of Nuclear Power After Chernobyl,* 6 Va. J. Natural Resources L. 239 (1987); Lila. Bakke, *Are International Institutions Doing Their Job? Nuclear Non-proliferation and Weapons Control* 90 Am. Soc'y Int'l L. Proc. 565 (1996); Craig Barr, *A Practical Guide to Proving And Disproving Causation in Radiation Exposure Cases: Hanford Nuclear Site And Radioactive Iodine* 31 GONZ. L. REV. 1 (1996); Louis Beres, *Israel, The "Peace Process," And Nuclear Terrorism: a Jurisprudential Perspective* 18 LOY. L.A. INT'L & COMP. L.J. 767 (1996);Louis Beres *After the "Peace Process:" Israel, Palestine, and Regional Nuclear War* 15 DICK. J. INT'L L. 301 (1997); A. Boyle, *Nuclear Energy and International Law: An Environmental Perspective,* 60 B.Y.B.I.L. 257 (1989); D. Brown, *Chernobyl: Its Implications for International Atomic Energy Regulation,* 9 Mich. Y.B. Int'l Legal Studies 369B384 (1988); Chuck Broscious, *Gaining Information on the Legacy of Nuclear Weapons Production* 31 GONZ. L. REV. 137 (1996); Robert Busby, Note, *The United States's Failure to Establish a High-level Nuclear Waste Storage Facility Is Threatening Its Ability to Effectively Support Nuclear Nonproliferation* 30 GEO. WASH. J. INT'L L. & ECON. 449 (1997); P. Cameron, *Nuclear Safety after Chernobyl: The Role of International Law,* 1 Leiden J. Int'l L. 121 (1988); Robert Chesney, *National Insecurity: Nuclear Material Availability And The Threat of Nuclear Terrorism,* 20 LOY. L.A. INT'L & COMP. L.J. 29 (1997); J. Downey, *International Pollution: The Struggle Between States and Scholars over Customary Environmental Norms: The Hazy View After Chernobyl and Basil,* 12 S. Ill. U. L. J. 247 (1987); Charles Dunlap, Jr., *Taming Shiva: Applying International Law to Nuclear Operations* 42 A.F. L. REV. 157 (1997); Dirk Dunning, *Federal Sovereign Immunity: How Self-regulation Became No Regulation at Hanford And Other Nuclear Weapons Facilities* 31 GONZ. L. REV. 83 (1996); Robin Dusek, Note, *Lost in Space?: The Legal Feasibility of Nuclear Waste Disposal in Outer Space* 22 WM. & MARY ENVTL. L. & POL'Y REV. 181 (1997); Richard Falk, *Nuclear Weapons, International Law And The World Court: a Historic Encounter* 91 AM. J. INT'L L. 64 (1997); Richard Falk, *The Nuclear Weapons Advisory Opinion And The New Jurisprudence of Global Civil Society* 7 TRANSNAT'L L. & CONTEMP. PROBS. 333 (1997); Eugene R. Fidell, *Maritime Transportation of Plutonium And Spent Nuclear Fuel* 31 INT'L LAW. 757 (1997); John Gleason, *The Decision to Reactivate a First-generation Soviet Nuclear Power Plant: Conceptual and Decision-analytic Frameworks* 8 RISK: HEALTH SAFETY & ENV'T 39 (1997).

More Specialized Articles/Books or Chapters include Stephen Gordon, Comment, *The Prospects For Challenging U.S. Nuclear Weapons Policy in Light of The World Court's Advisory Opinion on The Legality of The Threat or Use of Such Weapons* 28 ST. MARY'S L.J. 665 (1997); David Goren, Note, *Nuclear Accidents in Space And on Earth: an Analysis of International Law Governing The Cosmos–954 And Chernobyl Accidents* 5 GEO. INT'L ENVTL. L. REV. 855 (1993); Seth Grae, *The Nuclear Non-proliferation Treaty's Obligation to Transfer Peaceful Nuclear Energy Technology: One Proposal of a Technology* 19 FORDHAM INT'L L.J. 1985 (1996); Tamara Gureghian, Comment, *Medzamor: Weighing The Reopening of Armenia's Unstable Nuclear Power Plant And The Duties of The International Community* 5 VILL. ENVTL. L.J. 163 (1994); C. Haar, *Foreword: A Report on the Bellagio Conference* on *U.S.-U.S.S.R. Environmental Protection Institutions,* 19 B. C. Envtl. Aff. L. Rev. 481 (1991–92); G. Handl, *Transboundary Nuclear Accidents: The Post Chernobyl Multilateral Legislative Agenda,* 15 Ecology L. Q. 203 (1988); V. Hartke, *The International Fallout From Chernobyl,* 5 Dickinson J. Int'l L. 319 (1987); M. Heller, *Chernobyl Fallout: Recent IAEA Conventions Expand Transboundary Nuclear Pollution Law,* 23 Stanford J. Int'l L. 651 (1987); Horn, *Recent International Developments in the Law of Nuclear Liability,* 5 K.O.I.G. (Helsinki, Finland) 210 (1989); T. Howland, *Chernobyl and Acid Deposition: An Analysis of the Failure of European Cooperation to Protect the Shared Environment,* 2 Temple Int'l & Comp. L. J. 1 (1987B88); S. Kaplan, *Compensating Damage Arising from Global Nuclear Accidents: The Chernobyl Situation,* 10 Loyola of Los Angeles Int'l & Comp. L. J. 241 (1988); James Kuntz, *Nuclear Incidents on Indian Reservations: Who Has Jurisdiction? Tribal Court Exhaustion V. The Price–Anderson Act* 21 AM. INDIAN L. REV. 103 (1997); Barbara Kwiatkowska, *New Zealand V. France Nuclear Tests: The Dismissed Case of Lasting Significance* 37 VA. J. INT'L L. 107 (1996); K. Lenaerts, *Nuclear Border Installations: A Case–Study,* 13 European L. Rev. 159 (1988); Louis Leonard, III, Comment, *Sovereignty, Self-determination, And Environmental Justice in The Mescalero Apache's Decision to Store Nuclear Waste* 24 B.C. ENVTL. AFF. L. REV. 651 (1997); Michael Lettrich, *Popowsky V. Pennsylvania Public Utility Commission: The Supreme Court Holds That The Costs of Decommissioning TMI–2 May Be Classified as "Operating Expenses" Properly Chargeable Consumers* 5 WIDENER J. PUB. L. 865 (1996); R. Levy, *International Law and the Chernobyl Accident: Reflections on an Important but Imperfect System,* 36 U. Kansas L. Rev. 81 (1987); Mark M. Lewis, Note, *In re TMI: Junk Science Meltdown* 19 Thomas Jefferson L. Rev. 305 (1997); Lofstedt Ragnar, *Fairness Across Borders: The Barseback Nuclear Power Plant* 7 RISK: HEALTH SAFETY & ENV'T 135 (1996); D. Magraw, *The International Law Commission's Study of International Liability for Nonprohibited Acts as it Relates to Developing States,* 61 Wash. L. Rev. 1041 (1986); L. Malone, *The Chernobyl Accident: A Case Study in International Law Regulating State Responsibility for Transboundary Nuclear Pollution,* 12 Colum. J. Envtl. L. 203 (1987); S. McBrayer, Chernobyl's Legal Fallout–The Convention on Early Notification of a Nuclear Accident (Sept. 26, 1986, ___ U.S.T. ___, T.I.A.S. No. ___), 17 Georgia J. Int'l & Comp. L. 303 (1987); Saul Mendlovitz & Merav Datan, *Judge Weeramantry's Grotian Quest* 7 TRANSNAT'L L. & CONTEMP. PROBS. 401 (1997); Michael J. Matheson, *The ICJ Opinions on Nuclear Weapons* 7 TRANSNAT'L L. & CONTEMP. PROBS.353 (1997); Michael J. Matheson, *The Opinions of The International Court of Justice on The Threat or Use of Nuclear Weapons* 91 AM. J. INT'L L. 417 (1997); Patsy Mink, *Nuclear Waste: The Most Compelling Environmental Issue Facing The World Today* 8 FORDHAM ENVTL. L.J. 165 (1996); Elena Molodstova, *Nuclear Energy and Environmental Protection: Responses of International Law* 12 Pace Envtl. L. Rev. 185 (1994); Kristin Moody–O'Grady, *Nuclear Waste Dumping in the Oceans: Has the Cold War Taught Us Anything?* 35 NAT. RESOURCES J. 695 (1995); Ellen Moynagh, *The Legacy of Chernobyl: Its Significance For The Ukraine And The World* 21 B.C. ENVTL. AFF. L. REV. 709 (1994); R. Mushkat, *The Daya Bay Nuclear Plant Project in the Light of International Environmental Law,* 7 U.C.L.A. Pacific Basin L. J. 87 (1990); C. O'Keefe, *Transboundary Pollution and the Strict Liability Issue: The Work of the International Law Commission on the Topic of International Liability for Injurious Consequences Arising Out of Acts Not Prohibited by International Law,* 18 Denver J. Int'l L. & Pol'y 145 (1990); Kazuomi Ouchi, *The Threat or Use of Nuclear Weapons: Discernible Legal Policies of The Judges of The International Court of Justice* 13 CONN. J. INT'L L. 107 (1998); J. Perritano, *International Liability for Nuclear Pollution,* 11 Suffolk Transnat'l L. J. 75 (1987); N. Pelzer,

The Impact of the Chernobyl Accident on Nuclear Energy Law, 25 Archiv des Völkerrechts 294 (1987); Raul Pedrozo, *Transport of Nuclear Cargoes by Sea* 28 J. Mar. L. & Com. 207 (1997); Dr. A. Rohan Perera, *French Nuclear Tests in the Pacific–New Zealand's Request for "An Examination of the Situation"—a Retreat into Formalism by the International Court of Justice?,* Sri Lanka J. Int'l L. 115 (1995), *reprinted in,* Fernando Rivero, Georgetown International Environmental Law Review 9 Geo. Int'l Envtl. L. Rev. 246 (1996); Antonio Perez, *To Judge Between The Nations: Post Cold War Transformations in National Security And Separation of Powers–Beating Nuclear Swords Into Plowshares in an Imperfectly Competitive World* 20 Hastings Int'l & Comp. L. Rev. 331 (1997); W. Reilly, *International Cooperation on the Environment: The Cleanup of Eastern Europe,* 19 B. C. Envtl. Aff. L. Rev. 501 (1991/92); P. Riley, *The Legal Control of Nuclear Energy Between States,* 21 Cal. W. Int'l L. J. 303 (1990/91); Nicholas Reynolds & Robert L. Draper, *The Future of Nuclear Power* 8–WTR Nat. Resources & Env't 9 (1994); Jean–Robert Tyran & Peter Zweifel, *Environmental Risk Internalization Through Capital Markets (ERICAM): The Case of Nuclear Power* 13 Int'l Rev. L. & Econ. 431 (1992); Nicholas Rostow, *The World Health Organization, The International Court of Justice, and Nuclear Weapons* 20 Yale J. Int'l L. 151 (1995); Jessica Sanchez & Joanna Burger, *Hunting And Exposure: Estimating Risk And Future Use at Nuclear Production Sites* 9 Risk Health Safety & Env't 109 (1998); Leonard Schroeter, *Human Experimentation, The Hanford Nuclear Site, And Judgment at Nuremberg* 31 Gonz. L. Rev. 147 (1996); *Selected Bibliography on The ICJ Nuclear Weapons Cases* 7 Transnat'l L. & Contemp. Probs. 487 (1997); Keith Siskin, Note, *Does International Law Reflect International Opinion? French Nuclear Testing in the Twentieth Century* 26 Ga. J. Int'l & Comp. L. 187 (1996); Lennart Sjoberg & Britt–Marie Drottz–Sjoberg, *Physical And Managed Risk of Nuclear Waste* 8 Risk: Health Safety & Env't 115 (1997); David Sloss, *It's Not Broken, So Don't Fix It: The International Atomic Energy Agency Safeguards System And The Nuclear Nonproliferation Treaty* 35 Va. J. Int'l L. 841 (1995); P. Slovic, *Perception of Risk and the Future of Nuclear Power,* 9 Ariz. J. Int'l & Comp. L. 191 (1992); Stacy Stanely, *Environmental Impact Statement Not Required For Importation of Nuclear Fuel Rods* 5 S.C. Envtl. L.J. 104 (1996); Martin Strahan, Comment, *Nuclear Weapons, The World Health Organization, and the International Court of Justice: Should an Advisory Opinion Bring Them Together?* 2 Tulsa J.Comp. & Int'l L. 395 (1995); D. Stuckey, *Early Notification of a Nuclear Accident: The Response to Chernobyl,* 14 Brooklyn J. Int'l L. 687 (1988); Prudence Taylor, *Testing Times For The World Court: Judicial Process And The 1995 French Nuclear Tests Case* 8 Colo. J. Int'l Envtl. L. & Pol'y 199 (1997); Grace Thorpe, *Our Homes Are Not Dumps: Creating Nuclear-free Zones* 36 Nat. Resources J. 715 (1996); J. Tomain & C. Burton, *Nuclear Transition: From Three Mile Island to Chernobyl,* 28 William & Mary L. Rev. 363 (1987); Michael Trebilcock and Ralph A. Winter, *The Economics of Nuclear Accident Law* 17 Int'l Rev. L. & Econ. 215 (1997); James Waczewski, Comment, *Legal, Political, and Scientific Response to Ocean Dumping and Sub-Seabed Disposal of Nuclear Waste* 7 J. Transnat'l L. & Pol'y 97 (1997); Monica J. Washington, Note, *The Practice of Peer Review in The International Nuclear Safety Regime* 72 N.Y.U. L. Rev. 430 (1997); Peter Weiss, *The World Court Tackles The Fate of The Earth* 7 Transnat'l L. & Contemp. Probs. 313 (1997); Burns H. Weston, *Nuclear Weapons And The World Court: Ambiguity's Consensus* 7 Transnat'l L. & Contemp. Probs. 371 (1997); M. Widoff, *Accident at Three Mile Island,* 4 W. New Eng. L. Rev. 223 (1981); J. Woodliffe, *Chernobyl: Four Years On,* 39 I.C.L.Q. 461 (1990).

Chapter Eight

PROBLEMS IN PROTECTING THE HYDROSPHERE

As land-based creatures, we easily overlook our heavy dependence on the wetter parts of our physical environment. The fact is, however, that the oceans cover seventy percent of the Earth's surface; that human beings utilize them in fulfillment of sustenance, transportation, recreation, and spiritual needs; and that fresh water supplies, too, are imperative for daily survival.

Yet all too characteristically, humanity shows an astonishing disregard for maintaining the health of the hydrosphere–seemingly oblivious to the fact that the total amount of water in the world is constant, neither to be increased (like timber or fish) nor to be diminished (like petroleum or coal). The oceans and inland streams and rivers are deliberately used for waste disposal, made to bear the residue of industrial and domestic life: oil, sewage, manufacturing effluents, agricultural run-off. Most of the world's wastes– some twenty billion tons a year–end up in the sea, commonly without preliminary processing, usually to remain for years in coastal waters where they impair productive breeding grounds and pollute beaches. Despite international efforts to reduce pollutant sources, pathways, exposures, and risks; careless shipping efforts, legally disguised under "flags of convenience," lead to environmentally damaging oil spills. Inefficient irrigation practices upstream force downstream users to demineralize their water before using it for their crops or for drinking. And so on and so forth. To be sure, it is desirable that the costs of exploitation be weighed against the benefits; to some extent, a balancing act is required. Additionally, causal links are not always easy to establish. Nevertheless, in an interconnected and interpenetrating environment, it is more or less inevitable that the very economic and domestic arrangements that have caused damage will in some way come to bear the consequences.

It is indeed the shared nature of the world's water resources that renders hydrospheric pollution an international issue. As the first two problems in this chapter illustrate, such pollution does not only occur within State boundaries. The demands of inland agriculture and the profusion of shipping both within and outside national frontiers exposes coastlines and coastal cities to many pollution risks originating elsewhere. The sea itself acts as a transporter of pollution from one jurisdiction to another. And as the third problem demonstrates, the shared nature of fresh water resources–here in the form of subterranean aquifers–make it an issue of international environmental law also. Many underground water supplies are accessible to more than one nation, and the usage by one impacts on both the quantity and quality of that which is available to others.

There is much uncertainty, however, regarding the legal regime that deals with these issues. Treaty negotiations are dominated by the economic and development priorities that exploiting the hydrosphere is considered to serve. Marine dumping is viewed, according to a narrow reference frame, as a cheap way to dispose of waste. The dredging that often precedes it facilitates economic activity. Double-hulled ships, offering protection to oil carriers in times of trouble are an expensive option, the carriage itself being a solid source of revenue. Groundwater extraction provides irrigation and fresh water supplies for the populations involved in extended economic projects. And so on. Considerations such as these go a long way to explain the weakness of existing regulation, as do also legal principles that originated in times that preceded both the seriousness of today's environmental problems and contemporary knowledge as to their impacts. Still, traditional principles of State responsibility and evolving notions such as good neighborliness offer sound potential for the ability of international environmental law to protect the hydrosphere effectively.

In the ensuing three problems, these and related issues are addressed.

Problem 8–1

Land–Based Pollution in the Indian Ocean
SECTION 1. FACTS

Originating in the Karakush Mountains in the central Himalayas and fed by frequent year-round rains in the Kushani foothills, the Shivaputra River flows some 1,200 miles southwest through the plains of Rajapur—a large developing nation with a population of over 150 million–to Rajapur's principal port city, Vishnugar, on the Indian Ocean (see Figure 8–1.1).

The Shivaputra is central to Rajapur's state-run economy. In the wide Brahma Valley through which the river flows and which extends northward some 200 miles from the Shivaputra's estuary, Rajapur has established large irrigated cotton and rice cooperatives. Also, the Shivaputra serves as a key transportation route for immense quantities of timber that are harvested in the Kushani region north of the Brahma Valley and that later find their way to the largest paper and pulp mills in Southeast Asia, located close to the Shivaputra's estuary.

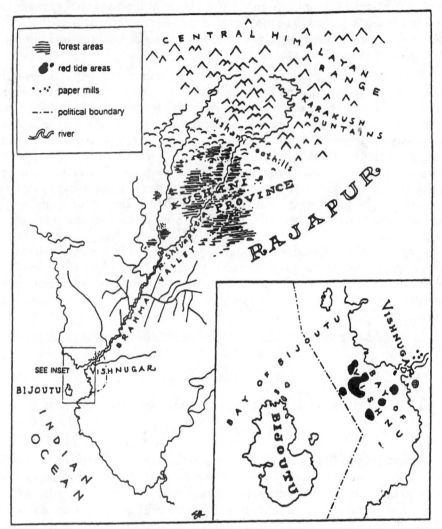

Figure 8-1.1

As a consequence of all this economic activity, Rajapur often is considered a model of economic success in the developing world. Its success, however, has not come entirely without cost. The Shivaputra has become heavily polluted, so much so that its estuarian area, formally known as the Bay of Vishnu, now poses severe threats to human health and marine life. The primary pollutants are DDT (banned in 1996, but persisting in the marine environment all the same), nutrients, and many types of industrial waste, including dioxin[a] and

a. A. Schecter, *Dioxin*, MCGRAW-HILL ENCYCLOPEDIA OF SCIENCE AND TECHNOLOGY 312–13 (7th ed. 1992), defines and describes dioxins as follows:

Any of a family of chlorinated aromatic hydrocarbons, also known as polychlorinated dibenzo-*para*-dioxins. Dioxins are highly toxic, lipophilic contaminants found in a number of chemical products; they are also found

in the food chain in fish, meat, eggs, poultry, and milk. Dioxins are chemically and toxilogically similar to the chlorinated dibenzofurans and polychlorinated biphenyls (PCBs)....

PCDDs are found as impurities or contaminants in chlorinated phenols, which are frequently used as wood or paper preservatives, in the herbicide 2,4,5–trichlorophenoxy-ace-

PCBs (i.e., polychlorinated biphenyls). In recent years, the Shivaputra's estuary and the Bay of Vishnu have been plagued with large algal blooms, or "red tides." These "red tides" especially are thought to be threatening to the health of Rajapur's citizens and responsible for the low level of marine life in the Bay. In the light of these threats, the Rajapuran government recently banned the sale or consumption of fish or other marine life caught in the Shivaputran estuarine area.

Beginning in 1994, the Government of Rajapur constructed a vast network of irrigation canals that tripled agricultural production in the Brahma Valley. Also, at about the same time, it addressed the poor sanitation and consequent public health problems in the area by building a new sewage system there. Both the irrigation outflow and the untreated sewage were directed into the Shivaputra River. Meanwhile, the river bed was dredged, from the Bay of Vishnu to a distance one hundred miles upstream, to facilitate a better flow, to prevent silting, and thereby to facilitate commercial transport of its timber and related uses of the River. Additionally, and likewise to facilitate shipping and prevent possible accumulation of pollutants, Rajapur began a practice of dredging its harbor once every year. The dredge spoils from both the river and the harbor were dumped approximately ten miles away from the Shivaputra's estuary but within Rajapur's territorial waters.

Rajapur showcased these projects to other less developed countries (LDCs) as prototypes of needs-oriented development. It claimed successfully to have used irrigation to increase food production dramatically, to have built sewage systems that reduced the incidence of dysentery and other sanitation-related public health diseases, and to have imaginatively employed dredging technology in its development strategy. Proclaiming that such projects demonstrated the importance and practicability of "sustainable development," Rajapur offered to sell its expertise to other LDCs.

Forty miles to the southwest of Rajapur, in the Indian Ocean, lies the poor but beautiful island nation of Bijoutu, population 4,000,000, whose economy depends on fishing and tourism. Surrounded by expansive coral reefs, the seas around this small island nation abound with a variety of marine life and support hundreds of family fisheries that utilize traditional fishing methods and small boats. The beauty and simplicity of Bijoutu has resulted in a booming tourist trade; and commencing from the late 1980s and intensifying in the 1990s, its coastal areas have become heavily built up with hotels and other tourist amenities. Shell collecting, snorkeling, and scuba diving have become very popular, and Bijoutu's principal harbor has become full of pleasure boats of various makes and sizes. Because of its poverty,

tic acid (2,4,5–T), and in hexachlorophene, an antibacterial agent. These compounds have also been reported in fly ash as well as in stack effluent from municipal incinerators....

As a result of exposure to dioxins, a transient skin rash may be seen; on some occasions, a lesion known as chloracne, a type of acne, is found on the face, especially the nose and cheeks; and in more severe cases, on the neck, back of ears, chest and back, and rarely, genitalia or legs. Chloracne, which is also produced by other chlorinated chemicals may resolve with time or persist for years.... Signs and symptoms of nerve damage such as weakness and pain in the lower extremities with difficulty in coordinating movement have been reported after exposure to dioxins, as have alterations in nerve conduction velocities. Arthritis, hyperirritability, sleep disorders, and decreased libido have also been reported, and psychiatric pathology is frequently observed.

however, Bijoutu has been unable to invest in sewage treatment plants. Thus, it discharges its sewage directly into the Indian Ocean, as well as into the Bay of Bijoutu in which its principal harbor is located.

The mid–1990s saw a severe decline in fish catches, and Bijoutu fishermen (women in Bijoutu do not fish commercially) reported an increase in large fish kills at sea. By the summer of 1997, fish catches had declined nearly 60%, and divers along the reef reported similar declines in non-game species. Fishermen also noticed an increase in "fin rot" and other diseases. About a year and a half later, in the winter of 1998 (the height of the tourist season), a large toxic algae bloom occurred on the continental shelf just outside the Bay of Bijoutu, killing many fish. At the same time, an epidemic of gastrointestinal disorders was reported and linked by Bijoutu's Department of Public Health to bacterial infection caused by the consumption of contaminated shellfish.

The Bay of Bijoutu algal bloom of 1998 was followed by yet another such bloom in the same area in 1999. Also, at about the same time, large slicks of gray matter and thousands of dead fish washed up on the nearby beaches. Following an immediate investigation of these events by the Bijoutu Department of Public Health, scientists discovered that the Bay of Bijoutu was almost completely de-oxygenated. They also reported that the coral reefs near the Bay were severely damaged and that they were in danger of being destroyed by sediment, DDT, dioxin, and lack of oxygen.

Distressed by these developments and facing a severe deterioration in its tourist and fishing trade, the Government of Bijoutu commissioned an interdisciplinary group of eminent Bijoutu scientists (the Commission of Eminent Scientists, or CES) to conduct an extensive study of the causes of the algal blooms, the fish kills, and the damage to the coral reefs and Bay of Bijoutu. The Commission concluded its assignment after six months of intensive work and arrived at a number of critical findings.

First, it determined that the algal blooms, fish kills, and damage to the coral reefs and Bay were caused by chemicals, nutrients, and sediments found in the dredge spoils dumped by Rajapur, which included dioxins and PCBs at many times the levels known to be harmful to human health. These pollutants, they held, were carried by the strong offshore Rajapuran Current (known to affect water temperatures along the coasts of Rajapur and Bijoutu) and deposited on the shallow continental shelf and Bay of Bijoutu. Finally, they determined that Bijoutu's problems began soon after Rajapur commenced its dumping of dredge spoils.

Several complaints by the Government of Bijoutu to the Government of Rajapur yielded no results. Rajapur denied that pollution or waste originating from within its borders was responsible for Bijoutu's problems. Rajapur claimed, on the basis of its own studies, that most of the dredge spoils settled as sediment on the bed of the sea where they remained sequestered. They further asserted that, according to their studies, the Indian Ocean was more than capable of absorbing the dredge spoils dumped into it. Moreover, they pointed out, Rajapur had stopped using DDT as a pesticide in 1996. Finally, they argued that Bijoutu's pollution incidents were caused by Bijoutu's increasing discharge of raw sewage into its coastal waters.

The condition of the marine environment surrounding Bijoutu continued to deteriorate, however, and international attention became focused on the situation. Rajapur's larger trading partners, concerned at the international attention the problem was receiving, encouraged Rajapur to enter into a judicial settlement. Both Bijoutu and Rajapur have signed and ratified the 1982 United Nations Convention on the Law of the Sea [**Basic Document 4.20**], although Rajapur filed reservations regarding the Convention's deep seabed mining provisions. Both parties, by written declarations under Article 287 of the Convention, have selected the International Tribunal of the Law of the Sea (hereinafter Tribunal), located in Hamburg, as the dispute settlement forum under the Convention. By joint agreement, and pursuant to international urging, both parties have now referred all questions arising from their dispute *ex aequo et bono* under Article 293 of the Convention. Both countries are party also to the 1985 Montreal Guidelines on Land–Based Pollution [**Basic Document 4.21**], and the 1995 Washington Declaration on the Protection of the Environment from Land-Based Activities [**Basic Document 4.29**].

Bijoutu seeks damages for lost fishing income and for research and action to restore its fisheries and the ecosystem of the Bay of Bijoutu. Rajapur denies responsibility and, assuming though not admitting to responsibility, states that it can be responsible only for cleanup and not restoration measures.

SECTION 2. QUESTIONS PRESENTED

1. Did Rajapur violate international law by its actions and, if so, is it liable for the environmental damages sustained by Bijoutu?

2. What principles *ex aequo et bono*, if any, should the Tribunal apply in this case?

SECTION 3. ASSIGNMENTS

A. *Reading Assignment*

Study the Readings presented in Section 4, *infra*, and the Discussion Notes/Questions that follow. Also, to the extent possible, consult the accompanying bibliographical references.

B. *Recommended Writing Assignment*

Prepare a comprehensive, logically sequenced, and *argumentative* brief in the form of an outline of the primary and subsidiary *legal* issues you see requiring resolution by the Tribunal. Also, from the perspective of an independent objective judge, indicate which side ought to prevail on each issue and why. Retain a copy of your issue-outline/brief for class discussion.

C. *Recommended Oral Assignment*

Assume you are legal counsel for Bijoutu or Rajapur (as designated by your instructor); then, relying upon the Readings (and your issue-outline if prepared), present a 15–20 minute oral argument of your government's likely positions before the Tribunal.

D. Suggested Reflective Assignment

Consider (and recommend) alternative norms, institutions, and/or proce-dures that you believe might do better than existing world order arrange-ments to contend with situations of the kind posed by this problem. In so doing, but without insisting upon *immediate* feasibility, identify the particular transition steps that would be needed to make your alternatives a reality.

SECTION 4. READINGS

1. John Warren Kindt, *Ocean Dumping*, 13 DEN. J. INT'L L. & POL'Y 335, 335–38 (1984).

As important as the oceans are to mankind, it seems irrational that human enterprise would abuse them. Man's dumping of wastes into the ocean has always occurred. However, due to accelerating industrial development and population growth, the quantities and concentrations of wastes dumped have begun to tax the assimilative capacity of the oceans.

The reasons for the growing use of the ocean as a dump site are readily observable because mankind tends to "regard the oceans as a convenient, limitless receptacle for wastes."[1] "But as problems of waste disposal on land multiply, pressures to use the oceans as a dumping ground become stronger."[2] Ocean dumping often provides the least expensive method of disposal. Since the sites are far removed from land, the adverse effects are less noticeable and therefore less objectionable. However, experience and research have revealed that despite its vastness, the ocean's natural ability to accept, decompose, and recycle wastes is limited. Once saturation levels of waste assimilation develop, irreversible consequences may result, for the "deep sea has a turnover rate measured in thousands of years."[3]

Of the pollutants entering the world's oceans, approximately 10 percent are due to direct ocean dumping. * * * Of the 10 percent of ocean dumped materials, dredged spoils[b] constitute 80 percent of this total.[4] Approximately 1 to 10 percent of the dredged sediment taken from waterways and harbors has been contaminated to potentially unacceptable levels because of industrial, urban, and agricultural activities.[5] Even non-toxic dredged spoils can physical-ly damage marine organisms in ways ranging from inhibiting the penetration of light (due to suspended sediments) to smothering organisms on the ocean floor when large quantities are dumped.

1. COUNCIL ON ENVIRONMENTAL QUALITY, ENVTL. QUALITY–980, 15 (1980).

2. *Id.*

3. Michael Waldichuk, *Control of Marine Pollution: An Essay Review*, 4 OCEAN DEV. & INT'L L. 269, 291 (1977).

b. According to the U.S. Council on Envi-ronmental Quality, "dredge spoils" consist of "the solid materials removed from the bottom of water bodies generally for the purpose of improving navigation: sand, silt, clay, rock, and pollutants that have been deposited from mu-nicipal and industrial discharges." COUNCIL ON

ENVTL. QUALITY, REPORT TO THE PRESIDENT, OCEAN DUMPING iv (1970).

4. *Id.* at 3.

5. *Ocean Dumping: Hearings on H.R., 6112, H.R. 6113, and H.R. 6324 Before the Subcomm. On Oceanography and the Sub-comm. On Fisheries and Wildlife Conservation and the Environment of the House Comm. On Merchant Marine and Fisheries*, 97th Cong., 2d Sess. 126 (1982) (statement of Brig. Gen. For-rest T. Gay III) [hereinafter 1982 Ocean Dumping Hearings].

The dumping of dredged material, sewage sludge, and other wastes has had a measurable impact on ecosystems ... and has led to cadmium and PCB [polychlorinated biphenyl] concentrations that have approached intolerable levels. Toxic pollutants dumped into the ocean, either industrial wastes or municipal sewage sludge, enter into the tissue of marine organisms. As larger forms feed on contaminated organisms, toxic substances accumulate and reach concentration where immediate physical harm can occur to marine mammals, birds, and man. For example, biomagnification[6] of PCB's in marine food chains has been reported, and levels involving birds and mammals have been magnified "by a factor on the order of 10 to 100 at each step."[7]

Pollutants may be highly biodegradable and have only a locally adverse effect, whereas less or non-biodegradable pollutants may have long-term effects on both local and global marine environments. Pollutants can be classified into several scientific categories: (1) hydrocarbons (basically oil and gas); (2) hydrocarbon compounds utilized as organic contaminants, inhibitors, and poisons; (3) heavy metals; (4) radioactive wastes; and (5) solid wastes (including particulate pollution). Of these, heavy metals, poisons, and radioactive wastes are especially hazardous because they tend to bioaccumulate[8] in marine organisms.

The adverse effects of these hazardous wastes are numerous. High levels of pollutants which bioaccumulate have led to "bioconcentration" that kills marine organisms or anything which feeds on them. This phenomenon has killed marine stocks and made surviving stocks inedible, thus causing severe economic losses to the fishing industry.

Most serious is the long-range impact of pollutants on the marine environment. First, pollutants affect some species more than others. The resulting diminution of species variety is known to upset the ecobalance. Secondly, organic wastes, particularly sewage sludge, require oxygen for decomposition. When organic wastes are dumped, they deplete the oxygen in adjacent waters to the extent that some organisms cannot survive. The cycle is accelerated when deceased organisms decompose and further deplete oxygen concentrations in that process. A vicious cycle of death, decay and depletion ensues which threatens the hardiest marine organisms. The oxygen deficiency may continue for years–long after the dumping has ceased.

* * *

2. GESAMP (IMO/FAO/UNESCO/WMO/IAEA/UN/UNEP JOINT GROUP OF EXPERTS ON THE SCIENTIFIC ASPECTS OF MARINE POLLUTION), STATE OF THE MARINE ENVIRONMENT 9–25, 66–81, 90 (1990).

Human Activities Affecting the Sea

In discussing the state of the oceans it is appropriate to focus on those human activities that are likely to affect the marine environment....

6. "Biomagnification refers to the increase in toxicant concentration which occurs in successively higher trophic level organisms in an ecosystem." *Dredge Spoil Disposal and PCB Contamination: Hearings Before the House Comm. On Merchant Marine and Fisheries*, 96th Cong., 2d Sess. 512 (1980) (statement of Frank G. Wilkes).

7. *Id.*

8. "Bioaccumulation refers to those processes by means of which organisms take up chemicals from the physico-chemical environment and incorporate them into some or all of their tissues." 1982 Ocean Dumping Hearings, *supra* note 5, at 449 (submission of the International Association of Ports and Harbors).

1.1 *Development of Coastal Areas*

The coastline is a complex region comprising bays, estuaries and large semi-enclosed areas where human populations and industrial development are concentrated.... [However,] [a]lthough a relationship between human population increase and environmental change has long been recognized, attempts have been made only recently to assess the cumulative impacts of land development in the coastal zone by recording their physical, chemical and biological consequences....

The development and maintenance of ports and harbours is of prime concern to human populations. Water exchange in these areas is often limited and shipping activities introduce contaminants, including oily wastes, cargo escapement and human wastes released from shipboard. These are subject to national and international regulations, but contamination at ports is difficult to control since it enters the sea by many routes, including discharges from pipes, run-off from streets, roofs and parking areas, and inputs from the atmosphere. Also, harbours are the first point of contact with the sea for many rivers, which add a wide variety and large quantity of land-derived material.

After release or discharge to the sea, many contaminants become associated with sediments and may remain sequestered until resuspended by waves and currents or until the sediments are disturbed by dredging to maintain shipping channels. This dredging not only stirs up contaminated material and reintroduces it into the water column, it also brings the problem of dredge spoil disposal, and may give rise to changed patterns of water circulation. In general, harbour sediments carry particularly large chemical contaminant loads, significantly greater than in adjacent areas. Fish or shellfish harvested from these locations are usually tainted by petroleum, which affects their flavour adversely, and levels of contaminants in edible tissues may be high, and fail to meet health standards.

The recreational use of coastal waters for various leisure activities such as bathing, diving, boating and fishing is increasing. In some areas this represents the major, or even the only, industry.... As well as structural engineering alterations to beaches themselves, the immediate hinterland is built up with hotels and support infrastructure. The resulting restructuring along the coastline disrupts traditional fisheries, interferes with marine life and eliminates important habitats. Ironically, this environmental degradation and congestion may destroy the main natural assets on which the tourism development is based.

An intrinsic feature of such developments is the influx of large numbers of people, at least seasonally, resulting in an increase of sewage outflow such that locally available means of treatment and disposal may be overtaxed.... Not surprisingly, inhabitants of coastal areas identified for development often support schemes that they see as enhancing their income and standard of living. Local authorities and national governments also tend to encourage the influx of foreign currency.

* * *

1.2 Discharge of Wastewaters

Contaminants from land reach the marine environment by a variety of pathways. Coastal outfalls discharge directly to estuaries, in-shore waters, bays and open coastal areas.... Rivers act as large-scale collectors and carriers of wastewaters from diverse sources within their drainage basins and offload them to the sea. Thus, rivers can be regarded as major point sources of mixed contaminants, the inputs of which depend on the contaminant load of the rivers and on the physico-chemical and biological transformations taking place in the river itself, and especially in the estuaries and the near-shore zone.

Non-point sources draining to coastal waters include surface run-off from agricultural areas, wash-out of agrochemicals and transport of sediment due to coastal erosion or to deforestation and desertification in the hinterland. Land management practices largely determine these various influxes.

* * *

Noticeable algal blooms in coastal waters are often an early sign of excessive nutrient inputs, and their decay adds to the problem of the oxygen demand due to organic materials from domestic sewage, livestock wastes and various agro-industries (e.g. pulp and paper mills, fish and food processing, sugar refineries). Effects are most severe where the effluents from densely populated industrial areas discharge to semi-enclosed or shallow receiving waters with reduced circulation, long residence times and hence limited scope for self-cleansing.

Major sources of industrial chemical discharges are pulp and paper mills, iron and steelworks, petroleum refineries, petrochemical industries, fertilizer factories, leather tanning and finishing, and other chemistry-based production installations, including pharmaceutical plants. These discharges are complex and, without appropriate treatment and properly sited outfalls, may be harmful to a variety of marine targets and, indirectly, to man. Localized fish kills (e.g. in fish farms), altered benthic communities, and accumulated chemical residues, are often the first warning of chemical pollution.

* * *

1.3 Disposal of Dredged Material, Industrial Wastes and Sewage Sludges

1.3.1 Dredged material and mine tailings

About 80 to 90% of all material dumped at sea results from dredging.... Of the total material dredged, about two-thirds are associated with operations to keep harbours, rivers and other waterwaste from silting up; the remainder represents new works. Future dredging operations are expected to show the same proportions.

* * *

About 10% of dredged materials is contaminated from a variety of sources, including shipping, industrial and municipal discharges, and land run-off. Typical contaminants include oil, heavy metals, nutrients and organo-chlorine compounds. Dumped dredged material has liquid and suspended particulate phases, but the greatest potential for impact generally lies with the settleable or solid-phase material which may affect benthic organisms by smothering and physical disruption of habitats; bioaccumulation and toxicity from both soluble and suspended phases may also occur.

Contaminated dredged material may slowly release its absorbed burden and result in long-term exposure of local habitats to one or more contaminants. However, laboratory and field studies show that leaching into the water column of chlorinated hydro-carbons, petroleum and metals is slight. Nutrients are released at concentrations much greater than background, but mixing processes tend to mitigate effects. The major impact at disposal sites with small current velocities and low wave-energy is the physical mounding of the material. Benthic recolonization of these mounds is relatively rapid on fine-grained sediments and slower on coarse-grained material.

* * *

1.6   Land–Use Practices

While water diversion and dam building in inland areas have profound effects on the coastal zone by altering inputs of fresh water and sediments and by changing the physical characteristics of the coastline, a number of other activities conducted well in-land also affect the sea and its resources. One of the most important of these is the intensive use of persistent agrochemicals, but deforestation, afforestation, irrigation and several other land-use practices are also significant. Their impact on the coast should be taken into consideration at the planning stage.

* * *

The world-wide pressure to increase irrigation in arid areas has often led to adverse effects and will also have consequences in the long term for the marine environment. For example, irrigation water is often entirely consumed before reaching the coast, and any drainage from irrigated soils may be highly saline and contaminated by excess nutrients and pesticide residues.

* * *

BIOLOGICAL EFFECTS

This [section] discusses some of the most critical topics for the assessment of the state of marine ecosystems and of human health in relation to the marine environment....

3.1   Human Health Effects

Although the ₁ sea provides an important source of human food and an attractive environment for recreation, sea water contains a wide variety of agents, biological as well as organic and inorganic, all of which can be a hazard to human health. Use the of the sea and its living resources determines the extent to which health is affected.

* * *

3.1.1   Microbial agents

These can affect human health as a consequence of sea bathing or consumption of seafood. The impact on health during bathing and related recreational beach activities arises from two broadly classified cause/effect mechanisms:

- Contact with microbially polluted sea water which may result in ear, eye and skin infections or respiratory diseases....

- Ingestion of sea water contaminated with pathogens from domestic sewage.... Most of the diseases associated with the ingestion of enteric pathogens affect the gastro-intestinal tract, but some are respiratory in their effects or involve other body systems.

Gastro-intestinal infection due to swimming in sewage-polluted sea water is the most widespread health effect in estuarine and other coastal areas with high population densities. Seasonal population increases at tourist resorts add considerably to the problem, causing increased sewage influx as well as much higher exposure rates due to crowding. As visitors may have low levels of immunity to the local endemic diseases they are especially susceptible. Recent epidemiological studies in the USA and in the Mediterranean have cast a new light on the causal relationship between bathing in sea water contaminated with pathogens of faecal origin and disease among the bathers. The relationship is particularly strong in the case of children under five.

* * *

The same urban sewage which leads to bathing problems is also often responsible for acute gastro-intestinal disorders following the consumption of contaminated seafood. Mollusks and other seafoods are particularly susceptible to contamination by pathogens carried to sea in wastewater flows, since their growing sites are often in highly polluted areas near urban centres. More important, bivalves filter large volumes of sea water and retain pathogenic bacteria and viruses. The fact that these shellfish are popularly eaten raw or only partially cooked greatly increases their disease-causing potential. [A] 1973 cholera epidemic in Naples, Italy, was initiated by contaminated mollusks. Infectious hepatitis is the most important viral infection transmitted by sea-food, and numerous outbreaks of hepatitis demonstrate that mollusks grown in sewage-contaminated water are very effective carriers of the viruses.

* * *

3.3 Eutrophication

In freshwater lakes the impacts of unnaturally large additions of nutrients are well known–changes in primary production and species composition, intense algal blooms and generally deleterious effects, such as oxygen depletion, with consequent effects on water quality and living resources. For some time, similar events were thought to be unlikely in the marine environment which, being larger and more dynamic, would have the capacity to absorb nutrient inputs. It is recognized, however, that enhanced productivity does occur naturally in the sea, for example as a result of upwelling and seasonal river discharges or land run-off. None the less there is evidence of increased frequency and scale of exceptional algal blooms in the sea in recent years at the same time as nutrient inputs have increased.

* * *

In the Baltic Sea, systematic monitoring since 1980 has produced evidence of eutrophication, as seen in progressively decreasing oxygen concentrations and increasing levels of nutrients. Recorded biological effects over the same period indicate higher summer rates of primary production and, since 1980, of increased productivity, including that of fish, but exceptional and unwelcome blooms of plankton algae have also occurred. . . .

Possibly related to higher nutrient inputs was the unusual bloom that occurred along the coasts of Denmark, Norway and Sweden in 1988. The algae responsible was the small flagellate *Chrysochromulina polylepis*. . . . The bloom did great damage to seaweeds, invertebrates and fish in coastal waters between 0 and 12 m depth along a 200 km stretch, and, through an unidentified toxin, also affected farmed salmon, costing the Norwegian fishing industry over US$10 million. Although the toxin does not accumulate in fish flesh, it has been found in blue mussels (*Mytilus edulis*) but there were no reports of illnesses in man. The remarkable feature was that this species had not been recorded previously as producing large blooms in these waters and was not known to be toxic.

* * *

3.4 *Ecological Effects*

* * *

In the nearshore waters of southern California municipal sewage is a major input. In 1971 Orange County diverted its marine outfall from a position at around 18 m depth to a deeper one further offshore at 53 to 60 m. Prior to the change, the benthos close to the outfall was dominated by a few species of small, opportunistic polychaete worms and the fish fauna was sparse. Within three months of the discharge terminating, organic carbon and sulphide concentrations in the sediments had returned to background levels with significant increases in the diversity of fish and benthos and the disappearance of the previous dominants. Many further examples show that the adverse ecosystem changes resulting from nutrient enrichment by sewage both in the water column and in the sediment are reversible, sometimes very rapidly.

3.   K. A. GOURLAY, POISONERS OF THE SEAS 119–122, 140–143 (1988).

Sewage Good and Bad

The basic fact is that sewage reaching the sea through outfalls or dumping as sewage sludge is a heterogeneous mess. In industrialized countries it contains not only domestic human waste but discharges from industry, storm water and surface run-off. Even in Third World countries, when limited to human waste alone, its contents include both a large amount of organic matter and nutrients such as phosphates and nitrates–the gardener's or farmer's delight–and numerous bacteria and viruses, some of them harmful, together with parasitic worms–the bather's nightmare. . . . When industry adds its contribution of oil, metals and chemicals, they bring varied forms of toxicity. . . .

The problem is complicated by the state in which sewage reaches the sea. In developed countries [sewage] may undergo primary treatment–the physical removal of solids, and settlement of the remaining particles to produce a less offensive effluent–and even secondary chemical or biological treatment, which breaks down the organic matter and so reduces its demand for oxygen. The resulting effluent, rich in basic nutrients but still containing what GESAMP[c] calls "soluble contaminants" is discharged through short or long outfalls into the sea in the hope that natural processes and water movement will complete dispersal and degradation.[9]

Most of the world's sewage, however, especially among coastal communities of Third World countries with growing populations, is simply deposited in the sea as "raw" or "untreated" sewage, nutrients and poisons alike. It is here that the greatest danger lies–to both humanity and the seas–as not only the poisons but even the nutrients take their revenge.

Sewage in the Sea

* * *

The seas have a natural method for dealing with organic wastes–decomposition, the breaking down of wastes into inorganic elements. This requires taking oxygen from the water; but as plants are fertilized in the decomposing process, they produce oxygen which replaces that lost. In a balanced ecosystem new production of oxygen compensates for its removal. Introducing large quantities of matter ready for decomposition upsets the cycle by increasing the demand for oxygen–hence eutrophication, the process of over-fertilization that results in mass slaughter of plants and animals, and BOD [biological oxygen demand], the amount of oxygen required for decomposition to take place, as a means of measuring the process.

In the natural cycle fish and other creatures feed on plant life in the water. Removing too much oxygen makes it impossible for animals and fish to survive; in consequence the plants increase in number. As the animals and fish die off, they add more matter for decomposition to existing stocks, further increasing the BOD. The diversity of species on which the whole system depends is now thrown out of gear. The new plant life rarely survives more than a few days; its death brings more material awaiting decomposition, and the ultimate result is an area from which all life is eliminated. In effect, sewage acts as a catalyst, for the BOD of the dead plants can be five or six times as great as that of the untreated sewage. The only survivors are anaerobic (non-oxygen-needing) bacteria responsible for decomposition.

Another unpleasant aspect is the appearance of "red tides" in coastal areas of the sea caused by a population explosion of red species of phytoplankton. So dense are these tides that they have been known to clog the gills of fish and the filters of shellfish, which, if not killed outright, can accumulate poisons and so endanger human consumers. Even sea-spray from the tides can cause harm and lead to irritations of the skin, mouth and throat. First recorded on the Gulf coast of Florida in 1916, the tides occurred again in 1932 and 1948. This 16–year cycle was broken in the 1950s when they appeared in three successive years from 1952 and then annually from 1957 onwards. Nor

c. *I.e.,* the (Joint) Group of Experts on the Scientific Aspects of Marine Pollution. *See, e.g., supra,* reading 2,

9. GESAMP, The Review of the Health of the Oceans: Reports and Studies No. 15, at 59 (1982) [hereinafter GESAMP]; Times Atlas of the Oceans 173 (Alastair Couper ed., 1983). . . .

have other parts of the world escaped. The tides off Brazil, Sri Lanka and Spain may differ in colour but they have the same causes and effects; off Japan, red and other algae, products of industrial and municipal waste, have choked much of the life in the sea around the shores; in 1976 a spectacular explosion occurred off the east coast of the United States in which hundreds of square miles were affected with "massive mortality" of commercially exploitable fish. And, if this appears unduly alarmist, GESAMP's sober account of "plankton blooms" offers a warning that cannot be ignored:

> Several genera and species of marine algae can give rise to toxic blooms, and several specific toxins have been identified. Some of these are lethal to marine organisms, whereas others are simply accumulated by them but can cause distress or death to the human consumer of affected fish or shellfish. Such blooms have been recorded from many parts of the world, and indeed in some places they occur regularly, following a seasonal pattern which can be predicted for a given coastal area.... Unfortunately, however, prior warning is often impossible so that illness from this cause is not infrequent and death sometimes results.[10]

* * *

These effects come from the "beneficial" aspects of sewage; there are also the "soluble contaminants" of the effluent which even treatment does not remove–disease-causing bacteria, viruses and parasites, which survive for hours or days. Viruses tend to remain longer than bacteria, especially if they become attached to organisms at the bottom of the sea....

In the 1950s there were scares in the West that contact with sewage in the sea led to poliomyelitis and typhoid fever. In 1959 the Medical Research Council of the UK published a report which did much to allay these fears by concluding that there was no risk of contracting poliomyelitis from bathing and that only a few cases of typhoid and paratyphoid fevers were due to "grossly contaminated waters". These results should not have been surprising.... Sewage does not generate the viruses; it merely carries them.

In concentrating on major diseases, the Medical Research Council neglected the minor. We now know that there is a connection between sewage in the sea and milder digestive ailments such as "traveller's diarrhoea", that children may be more at risk than adults, and that infections of the eyes or of cuts and abrasions can result. Even without direct contact danger remains. Viruses can contaminate shellfish beds or find their way into fish and so reach the human beings who eat them.[11]

* * *

Since humanity is responsible [for sewage in the sea], only those areas nearest to humanity–the immediate coastal regions with large populations lacking proper sanitation–are most in danger. As GESAMP would say, the effects are "local". Even when dumped in deeper waters, sewage rarely affects more than the immediate area. Benthic organisms are smothered, sediments disturbed and a patch on the ocean bed made barren. But whales and

10. GESAMP, *supra* note 9.

11. ROYAL COMMISSION ON ENVIRONMENTAL POLLUTION, 10TH REPORT: TACKLING POLLUTION-EXPERIENCE AND PROSPECTS 86–87 (1984).

porpoises are unlikely to suffer the fate of human beings on shore. We must not overestimate the dangers–or underestimate them. Sewage remains a poison; in the sea it is a peripheral poison. . . .

* * *

Parade of Poisons

Of the poisonous chemicals entering the sea the most notorious are the chlorinated hydrocarbons or organochlorines known by their initials DDT [dichloro-diphenyl-trichloro-ethane] and PCB [polychlorinated biphenyl].

* * *

[T]he major effects of DDT on life in the sea are undisputed. We know that it enters plankton through their porous cell walls and is stored in their fat, which dissolves the poison more readily than water, and that, as one progresses up the food chain,[d] concentrations increase. Predatory birds that eat fish-eating birds have higher concentrations than the birds or fish eaten at intermediate stages in the process. Yet the effect on even lesser creatures can be disastrous. The eggs of copepods fail to develop into adults so that the population declines. Shrimps continuously exposed to low levels die off, and the growth of mollusks such as oysters is retarded. Fish continue to die off, even when transferred to clean water; eggs and fry are particularly in danger because of the fat-loving properties of DDT. Seabirds are affected when the shells of eggs become so thin that they break while being hatched.

As for human beings, the case remains unproven. The scare caused by the discovery that milk in the breasts of American mothers contained higher quantities of DDT residues than those allowed in bottled milk has died with the imposition of restrictions. And GESAMP is sanguine that "it is unlikely that tolerance levels for man will generally be exceeded by consuming marine food".[12] "Unlikely", we note, but not "impossible"; and "generally" implies that there may be exceptions; GESAMP admits "there is the risk that in some coastal zones residue levels are being reached in some marine organisms which might make them unacceptable as human food".[13] Provided, of course, the human beings are given warning of their "unacceptability" and it is not considered necessary for men, women and children to die before "proof" can be established.

* * *

Polychlorinated biphenyls (PCBs) are less familiar to the non-scientist who at least knows an insecticide when s/he sees one, but fails to find GESAMP's explanation that "PCBs consist of a large number of homologues and isomers of chlorinated biphenyls"[14] particularly helpful, though, from its glossary, we may conclude that these are chlorine-based compounds with different structures. Chlorine, we know, is unpleasant.

* * *

d. *See supra* Figure 6.2 in Chapter 6.   **13.** *Id.*

12. GESAMP *supra* note 9, at 44.   **14.** *Id.* at 41.

PCBs are even more persistent than DDT so that, whatever governments have now done to stop their use, those already in the sea will be around for a long time. Scientists have shown that micro-organisms can actually break them down but the process is so slow that, for practical purposes, we can disregard it. Once they enter the sea PCBs collect on the sediments at the bottom and are gradually released into the water above. This poses a double danger to marine life, which is poisoned both by taking in water and by eating lesser creatures already infected. Like DDT, PCBs are attracted to fatty tissue, where they remain, so that concentrations increase as one passes up the food chain. Their effects vary according to the type of PCB and the extent of their concentration. While they have spread worldwide, research now shows that they are most common in coastal areas near industrialized countries, where they can kill fish, particularly young ones and fish fry.... Similarly, PCBs can affect that ultimate mammal, humanity; in developed countries supplies of seafood are now checked for their presence and, where "safe" limits are exceeded, consumption is banned. In 1971 the US Food and Drug Administration were [sic] forced to destroy 50,000 turkeys and 80,000 chickens fed on PCB-poisoned fishmeal, together with 60,000 eggs. What happens elsewhere is unknown-or fails to appear in the Western press. GESAMP reports complacently that "there appear to be no confirmed records of illness from this source"[15]....

4.   A. Charlotte de Fontaubert, David R. Downes, and Tundi S. Agardy, *Biodiversity in the Seas*: *Implementing the Convention on Biological Diversity in Marine and Coastal Habitats*, **10** Geo. Int'l Envtl. L. Rev. 753, 811–12 (1998).

Practical Examples: Defining Conservation
Priorities—The Case of Coral Reefs

Found in over one hundred countries, coral reefs are biodiversity-rich ecosystems that are highly valuable to tropical coastal communities for food and ecological services such as storm buffering. They are increasingly threatened by a range of human activities, including fishing, coral mining, tourism, sediment and pollution from land-based activities, and global warming. By some estimates, ten percent of coral reefs have already been lost, and another sixty percent may disappear in the next twenty to forty years. Coral reefs are part of larger ecosystems including other habitat types, such as seagrass beds and mangrove forests. Because of the range of threats, and the dependence of coral reefs on other parts of their ecosystem, protective action cannot be limited to the reefs alone.

Coral reefs are massive marine structures formed by the accretion of the limestone skeletons of successive generations of huge numbers of polyps, which are tiny, anemone-like animals. The true reef-building corals are the stony corals, composed of hermatypic polyps containing symbiotic algae (zooxanthellae) within their bodies. The algae process the coral's wastes, recycling vital nutrients and contributing to the ecosystem's high productivity. Reef-building corals form three distinctive types of structures: fringing reefs close to the shore; barrier reefs separated from the mainland by lagoons; and atolls, which are circular reefs formed on the base of islands long since submerged.

15.   *Id.* at 42.

The total area of all coral reefs is about 600,000 square kilometers, or slightly more than 0.1 percent of the Earth's surface.

Coral reefs are the mega-diversity areas of the oceans. They are biologically rich and highly productive systems, endowed with a great diversity of species that display an equally impressive variety of organic form and color. Scientists have identified about 93,000 species of organisms found in coral reefs, and by some estimates there may be as many as one million species yet to be identified.

Human communities, especially in coastal areas of the tropics, depend heavily on intact, productive coral reefs and their resources. Reefs are crucial sources of food for many coastal communities, providing fish, molluscs and crustaceans, and they function as breeding grounds for many commercial species upon which even inland peoples depend. Reefs are especially important for maintaining subsistence and artisanal fisheries in island nations. Reef-related tourism can be a very important source of foreign currency and local employment.... Reefs buffer coastal communities against storms and wave erosion, and an increasing number of biochemicals with medicinal and other valuable applications are being discovered in species from coral reefs.... In addition, some recent studies suggest that reefs may counter global warming by sequestering carbon (i.e., removing carbon dioxide, a greenhouse gas, from the atmosphere).

While coral reefs are highly adaptive to natural disturbances, they are extremely sensitive to human-induced environmental change. Their fragility is compounded by their rate of regrowth, which is slow in comparison to the rate of damage. Reefs grow no more than twelve meters (and often much less) in 1000 years. They have strict environmental requirements, requiring a great deal of light, oxygen, water temperatures between twenty-two and twenty-eight degrees Celsius, and low loads of suspended sediments.

This sensitivity renders coral reefs vulnerable to a wide range of stresses. Land-based activities pose some of the most serious threats. Many corals are killed by sediment runoff due to deforestation, agriculture and loss of mangroves, which act as sediment traps. Pollution from sewage originating from coastal settlements causes eutrophication, stimulating the growth of algae and smothering corals. Run-off from agricultural development on coasts can have a similar over-fertilizing effect. Mining of live coral for use as building material also causes significant harm in some places. Destructive fishing gear such as pole nets and dynamite, or fishing with poisons like cyanide, causes widespread, lasting and sometimes irreversible damage. Diving and boating are damaging some heavily visited reefs. Human activity can have devastating indirect repercussions. For example, overfishing of algae-grazing fishes not only depletes the target species but can trigger the spread of harmful algae on the surface of the corals, causing widespread degradation by smothering.

* * *

What is needed to conserve coral reefs and their valuable resources? Areas of reef that are highly productive or harbor a wide diversity of species are obvious targets for conservation. Many less obvious areas are ecologically linked to reefs; they are equally important and must also be protected. These typically include soft-bottom communities adjacent to the reefs, seagrass meadows where many reef organisms feed and breed, mangrove forests that provide nutrients and nursery areas for many species, and the major migration corridors that link these diverse critical habitats. Any coral reef protection program will have to conserve all these critical areas to some degree in order to be effective. Necessary measures will include control of land-based sources of pollution, designation of protected areas in which uses are restricted and regulation of resource uses to ensure sustainability.

* * *

5. David A. Ring, *Sustainability Dynamics*: *Land–Based Marine Pollution and Development Priorities in the Island States of the Commonwealth Caribbean*, 22 COLUM. J. ENVTL. L. 65, 73, 78–79 (1997).

[C]oral reef systems are "extremely susceptible to sewage and industrial wastes, oil spills, siltation and water stagnation brought about by dredging and filling, thermal pollution and flooding with low salinity or silt-laden water resulting from poor land management."[16] Sewage outfall is "likely to kill coral in the vicinity of the outlet because of reduction in light caused by the sediment."[17] Outfall from nitrogen-rich fertilizers, upon which Caribbean agriculture is increasingly dependent, is also a principal source of coral reef eutrophication.

Development related to tourism is one of the greatest threats to coral reefs.... Offshore from virtually every major resort area, algae fed by nutrients from sewage are choking the coral reefs. The burgeoning tourist industry thus widely degrades the very resources upon which it depends.

* * *

5. Tourism and LBMP

* * *

Environmental degradation related to the tourist industry includes the disappearance of coral through illegal harvesting or the careless management of pleasure craft, the denudation and erosion of beaches from illegal or uncontrolled sand mining [for construction] ... the destruction of wildlife and their habitats by deforestation and illegal dumping of solid wastes in wetlands, the growing incidence of scenic decay and atmospheric pollution from the proliferation of solid waste dumps, the accumulation of garbage in resort areas and on the seabeds of harbors and marinas, the increasing threat to the integrity of the customarily high quality of potable water supplies, impairment of the quality of the coastal waters from the discharge of untreated sewage and other land-based pollutants....

Foreign-backed construction programs nonetheless continue to accelerate throughout the region, the majority of which take place without environmental assessments having been prepared.

---

16. Peter C. Underwood, *The Marine Environment and Ocean Development in the Eastern Caribbean, in* A NEW LAW OF THE SEA FOR THE CARIBBEAN: AN EXAMINATION OF MARINE LAW AND POLICY ISSUES IN THE LESSER ANTILLES 116, 126 (Lecture Notes on Coastal and Estuarine Studies No. 27) (Edgar Gold ed., 1988).

17. DAVID L. MCKEE & CLEM TISDELL, DEVELOPMENTAL ISSUES IN SMALL ISLAND ECONOMIES 134 (1990).

... [T]ourism markets the natural environment.... [I]t is in the immediate interest of all regional tourist industries to maintain the environment. Economic expediency may best account for tourism's relative carelessness. In the interest of sustainability, the local tourist industry should evolve at a proper pace and with due concern for the "commodity" it markets. Given its direct linkage between economics and environmental quality, properly managed tourism may provide a key component for sustainable development....

6. United Nations Convention on the Law of the Sea (UNCLOS), Oct. 7, 1982, Arts. 192–195, 197–210, 213, 229, 230, 232, 242–244 and Annex V, U.N. Doc. A/Conf.62/122, *reprinted in* 21 I.L.M. 1261 (1982). (Basic Document 4.20).

7. Montreal Guidelines for the Protection of the Marine Environment Against Pollution From Land–Based Sources, Adopted at Montreal, May. 24, 1985, UNEP/GC.13/9/A-dd.3, UNEP/GC/DEC/13/1811,UNEP ELPG No. 7, *reprinted in* 14 Envtl. Pol'y & L. 77 (1985) (Basic Document 4.21).

8. *International Environmental Wrongs,* Chapter 5, *supra* at 335.

9. David Ring, *Sustainability Dynamics: Land–Based Marine Pollution and Development Priorities in the Island States of the Commonwealth Caribbean,* 22 Colum. J. Envtl. L. 65, 81–98, 112–13 (1997).

* * *

B. The Role of International Law in LBMP [Land–Based Marine Pollution] Control

1. Obstacles to International LBMP Control

Pollution from LBS [land-based sources] has been considered a major problem in the ocean environment for over twenty years.... However, the complexity of LBMP renders identification and attribution of cause and effect extremely problematic; virtually every human activity on land, especially those connected with economic development, poses some threat to the marine environment. LBMP is often overlooked because it is largely invisible and accumulative. Apportioning responsibility thus presents a dizzying task, particularly to the extent that LBS may interact in the marine environment.

While technical obstacles to LBMP control are substantial, political considerations will present the most serious hurdle in achieving local or international solutions. The nature of LBS is such that they are usually located within one state's sovereign territory. A sovereign state generally has full jurisdiction to deal with its own nationals, within its own territory, so long as its actions do not interfere with its international legal obligations. If sources and impacts occur within the same jurisdiction, marine pollution under traditional international law constitutes a purely domestic matter.

Sovereignty questions thus pervade international LBMP negotiations. Any state commitment in a relevant instrument will generally affect its national economic policies and development priorities. Sovereignty is of particular concern to developing countries, where priorities driven by poverty and debt servicing may favor development at the expense of environmental management. Moreover, the equity concerns that inform the North–South debate broadly implicate LBMP controls. International agreements limit the traditional right to pollute at self-determined levels, but in practice, "states that were able to industrialize first, or those that have vast territories, have been able to establish pollution levels quite independently of other countries."[18] Developing states might be expected to resist legal obligations on this basis, but international environmental law has to some degree overcome perceived inequities by virtue of the concept of differentiated responsibility.

2. Legal Bases for International LBMP Control

The primacy of state actors in international law limits the conceptual bases for global or regional LBMP control. Of those bases, the prevention and control of transboundary pollution is most cognizable given its state sovereignty orientation and arguable customary law development. A second basis, the protection and preservation of shared resources and common interests, suggests some normative ingress on State sovereignty. In all, however, international LBMP law is in a state of infancy.... However, because LBMP is recognized as an international problem, recent multilateral agreements, based in part on evolving customary international law, have directly addressed LBMP.

a. Customary International Law and LBMP. The normative basis for transboundary LBMP control derives from the Roman maxim *sic utere tuo ut alienum non laedas*, or "use your property not to injure that of another." In 1972, the Stockholm Declaration [**Basic Document 1.12**] crystallized this norm with respect to the global environment, thus suggesting tension between sovereign rights and international responsibility. This "good neighborliness" principle may comprise the sole substantive norm of customary international law applicable to LBMP. Moreover, the seminal Trail Smelter arbitration [**Basic Document 8.4**] restricted this duty to cases where the damage was of serious consequence, established by clear and convincing evidence. The nature of LBMP renders this standard nearly impossible to meet with respect to state liability for transboundary effects.

The 1982 Convention on the Law of the Sea ("CLOS") [**Basic Document 4.20**] goes some distance in codifying the *sic utere tuo* principle and reduces the Trail Smelter standard to mere "damage," which would seem to include chronic, low-level degradation characteristic of LBMP. The CLOS also suggests a much broader "obligation to protect and preserve the marine environment,"[19] defining states' responsibilities toward their own environment and the global marine environment. Such a norm would reach the commons aspect of LBMP....

b. The Stockholm Conference. In response to a general rise in global environmental awareness ..., the 1972 United Nations Conference on the Human Environment ("Stockholm Conference") became the "first international forum to consider the protection of the environment on a comprehensive

18. Edith B. Weiss, *International Environmental Law: Contemporary Issues and the Emergence of a New World Order*, 81 Geo. L.J. 675, 704 (1993).

19. United Nations Convention on the Law of the Sea, [**Basic Document 4.20**], art. 192.

basis."[20] The twenty-six principles of its declaration constitute "soft law" that, without creating binding obligations, provide a basis for more precise, legally compelling obligations.

Principle 21 of the Stockholm Declaration articulates the *sic utere tuo norm*, but also, by referring to "areas beyond the limits of national jurisdiction," contributes to the legitimacy of the more general norm regarding protection and preservation of the marine environment. Moreover, under Principle 7, "[s]tates shall take all possible steps to prevent pollution of the seas by substances that are liable to create hazards to human health, to harm living resources and marine life, to damage amenities or to interfere with other legitimate uses of the sea." This indicates an intention to extend the basic norm regarding state responsibility for environmental protection to common spaces such as the high seas....

c. Early Regional Seas Agreements. Regional agreements for the protection of the marine environment began to develop in the wake of the Stockholm Conference. States have preferred to adopt specific obligations with respect to prevention, monitoring, and assessment of marine pollution at the regional level. Various rationales support this general preference, including (1) the encouragement of "maximum participation by the regional nations, especially less developed countries which might otherwise stay away from a globally organized and technologically advanced system," and (2) generally, cost-effectiveness.

The first regional seas agreements arose through direct negotiations between interested parties outside the United Nations system. [T]he Convention for the Prevention of Marine Pollution from Land–Based Sources ("Paris Convention") **[Basic Document 4.14]** ... stood for many years as the sole international legal instrument specifically designed to control LBMP. Success in establishing this early initiative may be attributed in part to relative sociopolitical homogeneity among represented states. The establishment of a commission with the power to adopt—by unanimous vote—provisions that bind parties not objecting formed a basis for further implementation measures. The Paris Convention has spawned the ongoing North Seas Conferences, including the Third International North Sea Conference in 1990, which promulgated a declaration on the control of pollution from, inter alia, nutrients and pesticides.

The 1974 Convention on the Protection of the Marine Environment of the Baltic Sea Area ("Helsinki Convention") **[Basic Document 4.13]** takes a comprehensive approach. LBS control forms part of an overall scheme to protect and enhance the area's marine environment. Considerable political and economic differences exist between parties, but the strategic location and particular sensitivity of this shallow sea help explain this Convention's successful conclusion. The Helsinki Convention is unique in its coverage of sources of pollution rather than pollutants; it governs LBS under a comprehensive listing. The agreement also features an ongoing commission, but all amendments to the convention or its annexes require unanimity. The moder-

20. REVIEW OF DEVELOPMENT AND ACTIVITIES SINCE 1985, MONTREAL MEETING OF THE GOVERNMENT-DESIGNATED EXPERTS FOCUSING ON THE 1985 MONTREAL GUIDELINES FOR THE PROTECTION OF THE MARINE ENVIRONMENT FROM LAND-BASED SOURCES OF POLLUTION 2, U.N. Doc. UNEP/MG/IG/1/2 [hereinafter Montreal Meeting of Experts].

ate overall successes of both the Baltic and North Seas regimes owe much to ongoing improvements in institutional effectiveness. Such effectiveness largely derives from continuing high-profile international meetings which deter recalcitrant countries from opposing environmental measures and provide a forum for domestic groups to assess their governments' activities. These regimes also amplify domestic concern through institutional monitoring and information circulation.

* * *

e.   The Montreal Guidelines. The 1985 Montreal Guidelines for the Prevention of Pollution from Land–Based Sources ("Montreal Guidelines"), **[Basic Document 4.21]** ..., represent the international community's first attempt to address LBMP at the global level. Purely recommendatory in nature, the guidelines provide a checklist of provisions suitable for inclusion in future bilateral and multilateral agreements and national programs. The guidelines also "provide guidance to Governments in areas not covered by any regional agreements, and potentially for the preparation of a global convention." [21]

* * *

The Montreal Guidelines may soon assume a more significant role in developing a global LBMP regime. Chapter 17, Paragraph 25 of UNCED's Agenda 21 states:

> In carrying out their commitment to deal with degradation of the marine environment from land-based activities, States should take action at the national level, and, where appropriate, at the regional and subregional levels, ... and should take account of the Montreal Guidelines for the Protection of the Marine Environment from Land–Based Sources.

f.   The 1982 Convention on the Law of the Sea. The most significant development to date in building a global regime to protect and preserve the marine environment was the entry into force of the Convention on the Law of the Sea ("CLOS") in November 1994. This comprehensive instrument attempts to develop global standards for LBMP control, but political volatility has reduced pertinent provisions to general duties, with clear priority for municipal law.... [However], [g]iven their constitutive character, they may play a significant part in future LBMP regimes.

One primary CLOS objective is to establish a "legal order for the seas and oceans which will ... promote ... protection and preservation of the marine environment." To that end, Part XII of the CLOS defines states' responsibilities toward their own and the global environment....

Article 192 of the CLOS "contains the first explicit statement, in a global treaty, of the general [state] obligation to protect and preserve the marine environment." This obligation extends beyond that part of the environment which is within a state's jurisdiction or control. Article 192, by referring to (1) "states" rather than "state parties," and (2) "the marine environment," apparently codifies a customary norm not to degrade the marine environment.

Article 193 of the CLOS declares each state's sovereign right to exploit its natural resources pursuant to its own environmental policies—qualified, how-

---

21. *Id.* at 5.

ever, by the duty set forth in Article 192. This represents the essential compromise "between the interests of individual states in their economic development and the universal interests in the protection and preservation of the marine environment."[22]

Under Article 194 of the CLOS, states must exercise due diligence in ensuring that their activities do not cause pollution damage to other states' environments, and that any pollution for which such states are responsible does not spread beyond their area of sovereign rights. "Damage" implicitly includes chronic, low-level environmental degradation. LBS is one of four source categories covered by Article 194, which requires that states use "the best practicable means at their disposal and in accordance with their capabilities."

Article 197 of the CLOS directs states to cooperate on a global and regional basis, taking into account regional characteristics. Cooperation includes formulating and elaborating international rules, standards, and recommended practices and procedures.

Articles 192, 193, 194, and 197 provide a policy basis for more specific obligations under Section 5 of Part XII of the CLOS, entitled "International Rules and National Legislation to Prevent, Reduce and Control Pollution of the Marine Environment." Section 5 does not set out international rules or standards; rather, it assumes their existence and requires states to consider and make efforts to develop such law....

Article 207, one of two specific LBS provisions, reflects the implicit dichotomy of sustainable development: environmental protection and development. Paragraph 1 requires states to enact laws to prevent, reduce and control LBMP, "taking into account internationally agreed rules, standards, and recommended practice and procedures." Under this weakest of mandates, states need not adopt international standards, and "such regulations as are adopted need not conform to any particular pattern, whether of minimum standards or otherwise." Paragraph 1 therefore essentially acknowledges the primacy of state LBMP control. Paragraph 2 requires states to "take other measures as may be necessary to prevent, reduce and control such pollution." Paragraph 3's call for regional harmonization of state policies may reflect unresolved issues rather than real commitment. States "shall endeavor to establish global and regional rules" under Paragraph 4, "taking into account characteristic regional features, the economic capacity of developing states and their need for economic development." Cautious language again reflects the impact of territorial sovereignty.

Article 207 is so vague that it may prove useless. Given limited existing LBMP law and the resistance to more exacting measures, the drafters apparently sought to provide constitutive law that could evolve concomitantly with international standards.

Article 213 requires states to enforce their laws and regulations adopted under Article 207, and to "adopt laws and regulations and take other measures necessary to implement applicable international rules and standards

22. UN Convention on the Law of the Sea, **[Basic Document 4.20]** art. 194 (requiring states to take measures to "deal with all sources of pollution of the marine environment" and to "take all measures necessary to ensure that activities are so conducted as not to cause damage.")

established through competent international organizations or diplomatic conferences to prevent, reduce and control [LBMP]." Here the obligation to implement international standards is considerably stronger than that of Article 207. One might argue in this respect that the more specific duty should prevail as a general principle of statutory interpretation.

Arbiters acting under Section 2 of Part XV (Compulsory Dispute Resolution) of the CLOS could potentially create a body of law informing the treaty itself. Article 297(1)(c) of the CLOS defines the type of dispute subject to "Compulsory Procedures Entailing Binding Decisions" under Section 2:

> [W]hen it is alleged that a coastal State has acted in contravention of specified international rules and standards for the protection and preservation of the marine environment which are applicable to the coastal State and which have been established by this Convention or through a competent international organization or diplomatic conference in accordance with this Convention.

Section 2 thus governs disputes arising under Part XII of CLOS. Arbiters apparently may determine the "internationally agreed rules, standards and recommended practices and procedures" of which a state party—accused of insufficient efforts to regulate LBMP—has failed to "take account."[23] This resembles the "arbitrary and capricious" standard which U.S. courts apply to agency actions.

The compulsory dispute resolution ("CDR") regime may be especially significant for disputes arising out of coastal state enforcement measures taken under Part XII. Arbiters may reach the issue of due diligence in implementing "applicable international rules and standards," but also rule on abuse of discretion by a state in enforcing its own pertinent laws. Under Article 293, "[a] court or tribunal having jurisdiction under [CDR] shall apply this Convention and other rules of international law not incompatible with this Convention."

With extension of coastal state jurisdiction come complementary duties to protect and preserve the marine environment. Article 207 describes states' duties with respect to LBMP: implementing national legislation, harmonizing such legislation at the regional level to meet international standards, and creating global standards.... The CLOS LBMP provisions are designed to expand with time to incorporate subsequent international LBMP standards. In this way, the CLOS provides a mechanism for legislation on a global basis. Moreover, CDR may clarify the international standards to which Part XII refers, therefore broadening responsibilities and inducing wider compliance. While the vague textual language of the CLOS renders enforcement difficult, it invites evolution and expansion. Commitment to the CLOS encourages commitment to developing international and regional LBMP law.

* * *

B.   LBMP and Integrated Coastal Management

* * *

---

23. UN Convention on the Law of the Sea, art. 297 **[Basic Document 4.20]**.

Agenda 21 reveals a revolutionary approach to protection of the marine environment. Instead of relying on regulation of individual pollutants and point sources, Agenda 21 advocates the integrated management of activities along entire coastal areas as not only appropriate but essential. The management areas include a nation's exclusive economic zone—the waters extending 200 miles from its shores, as set out by the Convention on the Law of the Sea. . . .

Agenda 21 stresses the need to identify existing and projected uses and their interactions, and to promote compatibility and balanced uses. Chapter 17B, entitled "Marine environment protection," directly addresses LBMP and stresses a precautionary and anticipatory approach to prevent marine environment degradation. Sewage effluents, synthetic organic compounds, sediments, and anthropogenic inputs of nitrogen and phosphorus, all significant problems . . . are given priority. Watershed management practices to prevent, control and reduce marine degradation are also emphasized. Chapter 17F, entitled "Strengthening international, including regional cooperation and coordination," stipulates that states agree to "promote institutional arrangements necessary to support the implementation of the program areas in this chapter." . . .

In summary, Agenda 21 calls for direct action at the regional level to replace inflexible regulations with integrated coastal environmental management areas which encourage cooperation between developers and environmentalists to maximize the maritime environment's capacity for sustainable development.

C.   The Special Case of Small Island Developing States

Chapter 17.128 of Agenda 21 cites the unique obstacles to the "[s]ustainable development of small islands"—limited resources, geographical dispersion, market isolation, ecological fragility, extensive biodiversity, and political marginalization—and pledges assistance to "enable these states to address environmental change, mitigate impacts, and reduce the threats posed to marine and coastal resources." International organizations are encouraged to recognize the special development requirements of small island developing states ("SIDS") and give them priority in the provision of assistance.

The coastal marine resources of SIDS are of critical importance given the islands' limited natural resources, which are often stretched by overpopulation. The problem is usually compounded by limited human, technical and financial resources. While some SIDS may be able to solve their own environmental problems, by limiting development in proportion to their resources, other SIDS will require outside help—regional cooperation supported by international financial and technical assistance.

* * *

Agenda 21's greatest success may have been its linkage of sustainable island development, integrated management of coastal areas, and LBS-induced marine pollution. . . . Sustainable development projects could be tested relatively cheaply on the island states, and the industrialized world could be encouraged to invest in the projects as a "pilot case for sustainable development."[24] Ultimately, if the projects worked, the industrialized world might consider sustainable development projects more plausible, even at home.

* * *

10. Qing-nan Meng, Land–Based Marine Pollution: International Law Development 105–106, 169–170 (1987).

(iii) Technical assistance. Technical assistance [to prevent, reduce, and control pollution of the marine environment] is provided for in Articles 202 and 203 [of the 1982 United Nations Convention on the Law of the Sea **[Basic Document 4.20]**. The main purpose of these articles is to help developing countries obtain the technology they need to take proper measures, so that international control will be more effective. Whether these articles create new obligations or are only a declaration of intention will remain unclear until actual steps have been taken. Nevertheless, the kind of assistance required is indicated.[25] Assistance in dealing with accidents and environmental assessment is included, and preferential treatment for developing countries is urged.

* * *

(v) Responsibility and liability. Article 235 of UNCLOS enunciates the principle of responsibility for the fulfillment of obligations concerning the protection of the marine environment. In the event that states are found liable for causing damage by means of pollution, they are obliged to ensure that appropriate forms of compensation are available within their national legal systems. The Convention also requires cooperation in the further development of international law on responsibility and liability.

* * *

The Montreal Guidelines

* * *

(b) The Relationship With Existing International Agreements

The Introduction [to the Guidelines] emphasizes that the guidelines were prepared "on the basis of the common elements and principles drawn from relevant existing agreements ... drawing upon experience already gained through their preparation and implementation". This statement contains two messages: first the guidelines were not intended to contradict existing internationally agreed principles, rules and standards, a point that was emphasized by many participants;[26] and second, they are not merely a restatement of existing agreements but a further elaboration as well. The principal agree-

---

24. Arthur L. Dahl, *Land-based Pollution and Integrated Coastal Management*, 17 Marine Pol'y 561, 571 (1993), *citing* Strategy for the Reduction of the Degradation of the Marine Environment from Land-based Sources of Pollution and Activities in Coastal Areas, U.N. Doc. UNEP(OCA)/WG.14/3 (1991)[hereinafter Strategy].

25. UN Convention on the Law of the Sea, art. 202 **[Basic Document 4.20]**.

26. Statements Regarding the Relationship of the Draft Guidelines Principles for the Protection of the Marine Environment against Pollution from Land–Based Sources with the 1982 United Nations Convention on the Law of the Sea, Annex 1, UNEP WG. 92/4 **[Basic Document 4.20]**.

ments which were used as the basis of the guidelines are the Law of the Sea Convention [**Basic Document 4.20**], the Paris Convention on Land–Based Marine Pollution [**Basic Document 4.14**], the Helsinki Convention [**Basic Document 4.6**], and the Mediterranean Protocol on Land-based Marine Pollution [**Basic Document 4.19**]. . . .

* * *

(d) The Nature of the Guidelines

The nature of the guidelines is stated in straightforward fashion in the Introduction [to the Guidelines]: "These guidelines are of a recommendatory nature. They are presented as a checklist of basic provisions rather than a model agreement, from which governments may select, adopt or elaborate, as appropriate, to meet the needs of special regions".[27] Although of limited legal force in a formal sense, the recommendatory nature of the guidelines does not necessarily reduce the significance of the document at the present time: the fact is that this is the first globally-agreed legal instrument specifically on land-based marine pollution control. . . .

11. R. Michael M'Gonigle, *"Developing Sustainability" and the Emerging Norms of International Environmental Law: The Case of Land–Based Marine Pollution Control*, 28 Can. Y. B. Int'l L. 169, 194–205 (1990).

General Obligation

Under the existing agreements [appertaining to land-based marine pollution], the parties undertake a general obligation, the most common wording being that they will "take all appropriate measures" to "prevent, reduce and control"[28] or "prevent, abate and combat"[29] pollution from land-based sources. . . .

This general obligation itself means little unless concrete standards for implementation are also set out but, even so, the obligation has not been accepted without compromise. . . .

[G]uideline 4 of the Montreal Guidelines [**Basic Document 4.21**] qualifies the basic obligation to adopt "all measures necessary" (in itself stronger wording than "all appropriate measures") with the phrase "in accordance with their capabilities." In short, the wording in each instrument varies according to the degree of action being demanded–that which is "appropriate" being likely weaker than that which is "necessary", a requirement to "minimize" being more far-reaching than a requirement to "abate." But in no agreement is the obligation clear and unequivocal.

Categorical Obligations

In these agreements, implementation obligations are of both the positive and negative kind. . . .

27. *Id.*

28. United Nations Convention on the Law of the Sea (UNCLOS) art.207 [**Basic Document 4.20**].

29. Barcelona Convention [**Basic Document 4.19**], Art. 8, 15 I.L.M. 285 (1976); Kuwait Convention, art. 7 [**Basic Document 4.18**]; Jeddah Convention, art. 6, UNEP Reg. p. 201; The Athens Protocol, Art. 1, 19 I.L.M. 869 (1980), refers to "prevent, reduce, combat and control"; as does of the Abidjan Convention Art. 7[20 I.L.M. 746 (1981)].

Monitoring

The existing agreements provide for the carrying out of monitoring activities to assess the nature and extent of pollution in the areas covered by those agreements, as well as activities to assess the effectiveness of measures taken pursuant to the agreements to reduce pollution of the marine environment. The Montreal Guidelines list a number of specific goals for monitoring and data management activities, including the collection of data on natural conditions of the region as regards its physical, biological and chemical characteristics,[30] the collection of data on inputs of substances or energy that cause or potentially cause pollution emanating from land-based sources,[31] and the evaluation of the effectiveness of measures in meeting the environmental objectives for specific marine environments.[32]

* * *

Provisions of this type are rarely controversial. In the Mediterranean context, for example, all states accepted the provisions relating to monitoring and scientific co-operation (Articles 8 and 9) with little discussion. However, the lack of controversy may reflect a failure to give sufficient consideration to the provision of the funds necessary to ensure that effective action can be taken. Without these funds, the obligations are largely hortatory....

Control Strategies

The Montreal Guidelines, in Guideline 13, incorporate a general obligation to develop programs and measures for the prevention, reduction, and control of pollution from land-based sources. The development of this basic categorical obligation in all the existing agreements has been beset by controversy on both the method (or procedure) for setting standards, and the substance of these standards.

* * *

[I]n the Montreal Guidelines, paragraph (c) of Guideline 13 provides that where appropriate, states should undertake to establish priorities for action along the lines of a "black list/grey list" approach.... The lists may be modified through agreement of the parties; typically, they undertake to eliminate pollution from land-based sources by substances listed in the black list (usually annex I), considered particularly hazardous because of toxicity, persistence and bioaccumulation. The parties undertake to "strictly limit" pollution from substances listed in the grey list (usually annex II) which, though hazardous, are less noxious or seen to be rendered harmless more readily by natural processes.

The control of black list substances is undertaken jointly by the parties, while the release of grey list substances is left more to the discretion of national authorities taking into account, among other factors, the ambient environmental quality of the receiving marine environment. Discharges of grey list substances are usually subject to the issuance of an authorization by competent national authorities....

---

30. Montreal Guidelines, Guideline 11, para. (a) **[Basic Document 4.21]**.

31. *Id*. para. (b).

32. *Id*. para. (c).

Integrated Management

As part of the concern to have both a comprehensive overview of the problem of regional marine pollution and a coordinated response to it, several provisions in these agreements seek to encourage the adoption of an integrated planning and management approach. Guideline 10 of the Montreal Guidelines stipulates that states "should undertake" such an approach, with other provisions setting out specific components of the obligation.

Guideline 15 provides for a duty of immediate notification whenever releases originating from land-based sources within the territory of a state are likely to cause pollution to the marine environment of other states or of areas beyond the limits of national jurisdiction. The duty is to notify the other state or states, as well as competent international organizations, whereupon information exchange and consultations should be undertaken with a view to preventing, reducing, and controlling the pollution. In addition, Guideline 12 provides for impact assessments of the potential effects of proposed major projects that may cause pollution from land-based sources, so that measures may be taken to prevent or mitigate it.

These guidelines embody more specific and comprehensive obligations than those of existing agreements (though they remain guidelines). In the UNCLOS Convention **[Basic Document 4.20]**, requirements are set out for the assessment of potential polluting effects of activities (Articles 204 and 206) and notification (Articles 198 and 205), but there is no discussion of a duty of prior consultation except in the context of dumping. Commentators have pointed out that it is important that all these elements be treated jointly, "since the absence of any of them may lessen the effect of the other two."[33] The International Law Commission's Rules on Transfrontier Pollution treat the principles of prior notification and consultation as existing parts of international law, while environmental impact assessment is viewed as a developing rule.

National Enforcement

Enforcement of international pollution controls can occur on either a state-to-state or person-to-person basis....

Guideline 16, paragraph (c), of the Montreal Guidelines provides that each state should grant "equal access to and non-discriminatory treatment in its courts, tribunals and administrative proceedings to persons in other States who are or may be affected by pollution from land-based sources under its jurisdiction or control." These principles of non-discriminatory access are well-established in other environmental conventions as well....

Liability and Compensation

The above four elements–monitoring, a control strategy, integrated management, and national enforcement–constitute a positive implementation obligation. To a great degree, however, the limited achievements in implementation under agreements concluded to date result from the absence of serious penalties for failure to act–that is, the absence of negative obligations, especially categorical obligations of state responsibility, liability, and compen-

33. Barbara Kwaitkowska, *Marine Pollution from Land–Based Sources: Current Problems and Prospects*, 20 Ocean Dev. & Int'l L. 315, 328 (1984).

sation. As one scholar put it, the law is "a series of statements without redress."[34]

[I]n general, however, state responsibility for harm caused by pollution from national land-based sources is limited to instances of pollution "derived from the conduct of its agencies or when it is permitted by the state in some other way, and when the discharge is prohibited by international law"[35] . . . .

In light of the seemingly narrow scope of this approach where liability attaches only for unlawful conduct, it is of importance to determine exactly what constitutes a breach of an international obligation. With the increase in international treaties committing states to a duty of "good neighbourliness," the "trend in international law is to impose an obligation on states to take all measures necessary"[36] to prevent extraterritorial damage from activities under their jurisdiction or control. To hold the state liable, "a victim state would have to prove either that the state did not take any such measures or that the measures taken were inadequate."[37] This is certainly the implication of the International Law Commission's attribution of liability to a state "provided that it knew or had means of knowing that an activity referred to in Article 1 was being, or was about to be carried out in its territory or in other places under its jurisdiction or control."[38]

This interpretation of the current law implies the emergence of an important new norm of international environmental law which renders a state publicly liable for the damaging activities of its industries and citizens outside the national territory. This norm is, however, by no means universally accepted, but even if it were, it requires further specificity for it to have great practical effect. That the development of norm is incomplete is not surprising, considering the serious economic implications that the implementation of a principle of public (or state) responsibility would have for a country's industrial activities. Instead, existing agreements dealing with land-based sources tend to limit reference to these issues to an obligation to "further develop" rules and procedures, without laying down any concrete provisions for the determination of liability.

12.   A. Charlotte de Fontaubert, David R. Downes, and Tundi S. Agardy, *Biodiversity in the Seas: Implementing the Convention on Biological Diversity in Marine and Coastal Habitats*, 10 GEO. INT'L ENVTL. L. REV. 753, 767 (1998).

The Pros and Cons of Ecotourism

Nature-based tourism or "ecotourism" can offer a sustainable alternative to the over-exploitation of living resources and destructive consumptive uses that have devastated coral reefs and other marine habitats and living resources. Outside attention to the resource can spark both local and national interest in protecting it, opening the door for marine protected areas, coastal

34. Judith Perritano, *International Liability for Nuclear Pollution*, 11 SUFFOLK TRANSNAT'L L. J. 75, 78 (1987).

35. QING-NAN MENG, LAND-BASED MARINE POLLUTION: INTERNATIONAL LAW DEVELOPMENT 201 (1987).

36. *Id.*

37. SACHIKO KUWABARA, THE LEGAL REGIME OF THE PROTECTION OF THE MEDITERRANEAN AGAINST POLLUTION FROM LAND-BASED SOURCES 115 (1984).

38. Report of the International Law Commission on the Work of Its 42nd Session, May 1–July 20, 1990, UNGAOR, Supp. No. 10 (A/45/10) art. 3.

management plans and effective resource management. Revenues generated by tourism can support local development and create incentives for conservation. Revenues can be used to finance conservation and management, in the form of monitoring and enforcing regulations, establishing permit systems, and installing or constructing devices such as mooring buoys. In turn, these measures and amenities thus provide a "draw" for ecotourism.

Coral reefs are typical marine sites for ecotourism. Often, ecotourism is associated with scuba diving on coral reefs. Although diving activities will inherently affect the reefs and irresponsible or ignorant divers can cause serious damage, a number of cases have shown that dive operators and reef managers can work together to support conservation. Other tourism activities that utilize coral reef resources directly include snorkeling, swimming and boating, "seascape" viewing, and collecting. Less direct are the activities that depend on the existence of a healthy, intact reef system, even when tourists do not come into contact with the reef itself,, such as some forms of beach tourism and landscape viewing in general. Development is typically more sustainable if it capitalizes on a diversity of visitor interests, reducing pressure on the primary target resources. However, ecotourism is not a panacea and can lead to both unsustainable development and user conflicts. Some of the potential problems include the following:

(1) By attracting attention to the resource, ecotourism development can create ever greater demand for access and use; even the tourism focused on nature that is the essence of ecotourism may become unsustainable if visitors become more numerous and the effects of their visits are not monitored and managed;

(2) Ecotourism can create an elitist situation, providing access only to those who can afford it;

(3) Inappropriate ecotourism development can disrupt self-regulating traditional systems of use;

(4) Continuing ecotourism development can spur local population expansion, increasing pressure on resources;

(5) Ecotourism, when coupled with the formation of a recreational use-oriented marine park, can lead to an increase in resource exploitation outside boundaries of core areas;

(6) Successful ecotourism can create a false sense of security that coastal management throughout the country or region is being effectively addressed;

(7) Tourist attraction to one area can deflect attention from other deserving areas;

(8) Economic growth may take precedence over ecological sustainability;

(9) The presence of foreign tourists can lead to the incursion of foreign value systems at the expense of local value systems;

(10) Tourist visits can open the door for alien species introduction that subsequently undermines native biodiversity; and

(11) Sharing of benefits with local communities may be inadequate, particularly in the case of international ecotourism.

There must be a balance between the benefits that ecotourism can provide and the dangers of tourism development. Ecotourism development must take place within the framework of integrated coastal area management (ICAM). Before ecotourism activities start, there should be assessments of the likely effects on ecosystems and local societies. Assessments should consider the carrying capacity of the environment for tourism use, including infrastructure, services to the tourism industry, direct exploitation of living resources and indirect cumulative degradation of the resource base. Involving local stakeholders as early as possible in the planning process is perhaps the most important step that can be taken to ensure that ecotourism development is suitable in the long run.

13. Washington Declaration on Protection of the Marine Environment from Land-Based Activities [Basic Document 4.29].

Discussion Notes/Questions

1. Given the difficulty of determining causation, the importance of monitoring becomes self-evident. In its report *The State of the Marine Environment*, GESAMP states that:

> The difficulty of monitoring biological change, given its long-term and extensive geographic variation, and the problem of interpreting these observations in the light of the results of experimental exposures of a few species to a few known contaminants, are not easily resolved. Where changes are expected, for example, in areas receiving discharges, monitoring programmes may be initiated, but they may involve an expensive and long-term commitment of resources.... In addition, it is often charged that irreversible damage will ensue before the results of long-term programmes are accumulated and analyzed.

> It follows that long-term field observations seldom provide early warning of significant effects at population level, nor do they by themselves identify the principal or even important causative agents. Aside from catastrophic events, it is usually difficult to distinguish between natural and man-made causes of biological change....

GESAMP, *State of the Marine Environment* 83–84 (1990).

In the instant case of *Rajapur v. Bijoutu*, describe the kind of monitoring that might have helped solve the problem of causation.

2. The World Bank has instituted new guidelines for funding projects:

> First, the "mutually reinforcing roles" of sustainable development and environmental protection "must be vigorously exploited through sound macroeconomic policies that will promote growth and reduce poverty".... "The fight against poverty helps to preserve the environment".

> Second, developing countries need to implement policies that discourage waste and overuse of natural resources.

> And third, people and institutions in developing countries must be provided with incentives to engage in activities that are less damaging to the environment.

Special Report: The World Bank, The Environment, and Development, World Bank News 42 (1991).

Is the World Bank's lending policy consistent with international law? As an international agency can the World Bank be held responsible if its policies lead to environmental consequences which otherwise would not occur? For example, if Rajapur were able only to build its irrigation and sewage system through a World Bank loan and these activities resulted in harm to Bijoutu, does the World Bank have any responsibility to Bijoutu? To the world community? Why? Why not?

3. Conceptually, it is preferable to analyze dumping as a *method* of disposing of pollutants rather than as a *source* of pollution. The 1972 Convention for the Prevention of Maritime Pollution by Dumping of Wastes and Other Matter [**Basic Document 4.11**] defines dumping as "any deliberate disposal at sea of wastes or other matter...." It becomes evident on reflection that the sources of any wastes dumped at sea are land-based or vessel-based activities. The fact that international conventions, which usually deal with the sources of pollution, also deal with dumping ought not confuse us into thinking that dumping, too, is a source of marine pollution. Of course, in a very broad sense, methods that seek to neutralize or treat pollutants so as to render them less harmful, such as incineration, burial, scrubbing, or conversion become sources if they lead to pollution. One way of determining if something is a source of pollution, rather than a polluting method, is to ask what happens if we ban the activity in question. If the ban removes the pollution problem, we are dealing with a source of pollution. If it does not, we probably are dealing with a method of pollution control. In the case, say, of nuclear reactors dumped in the oceans by the former Soviet Union (see Discussion Note/Question 4, *infra*), we might ask: "What if the dumping of spent nuclear reactors is banned?" The answer is that we still are left with the problem of disposing or decommissioning spent nuclear reactors. If, however, we ask "what if nuclear power is not used?", the answer is that we have dealt with the problem of reactors at source, and would not therefore, have a further problem.

4. News reports dealing with the Russian dumping of radioactive wastes, discussed more extensively in the introduction to Part I (pages 1 to 14) raise sharp questions about the extent to which land-based pollution can be distinguished from vessel pollution and dumping. In *Nuclear Material Dumped Off Japan*, N.Y. Times, Oct. 19, 1993, A1, col. 1, David E. Singer points out that "Moscow has admitted disposing of large amounts of highly radioactive waste at sea since the 1950s, and Russian officials have said they have run out of places to store liquid and solid nuclear waste on land." Furthermore, the following newspaper account of how the former Soviet Union dumped entire reactors into the Kara Sea raises profoundly disturbing questions about the received wisdom. Tragically, it also confirms a worst case scenario for high level nuclear waste. Writes W. Broad, *Russians Describe Extensive Dumping of Nuclear Waste*, N.Y. Times, April 27, 1993, A1 & B8:

> The dumping of highly radioactive wastes at sea has been banned worldwide for more than three decades.... Now a Russian report has detailed how the Soviet Union repeatedly broke those rules, making it clear that Moscow lied in asserting that it had never dumped radioactive waste into the oceans.
>
> The document paints a picture even darker than the rumors and half-truths about ocean dumping that began to swirl as the Soviet Union collapsed. It turns out that a vast amount of highly radioactive waste was dumped by the Soviet Union: twice the combined total of 12 other nuclear nations. But the threat to marine life is unclear since no records are yet available on the exact composition of the radioactive refuse and no one knows for sure if containment vessels are intact or leaking.

Early in the nuclear age, spent fuels from nuclear reactors, laden with cesium–137 and other deadly isotopes, were judged too dangerous to oceanic life and ultimately to man to be dumped, and a decade ago the ban was extended to all other forms of nuclear waste, including low-level ones like uranium mill tailings. The oceans, by global consensus, were ruled off limits to mankind's most pernicious toxins.

18 Nuclear Reactors Dumped

The team of 46 experts that reproduced the new report of Soviet violations was headed by Dr. Aleksei V. Yablokov, the top environmental advisor to the Russian President, Boris N. Yeltsin. * * * The Yablokov report says the Soviet Union dumped 2.5 million curies of radioactive wastes, including 18 nuclear reactors from submarines and an icebreaker. Sixteen of these power plants were cast into the shallow waters of the Kara Sea, six of them heavy with radioactive fuel, turning this Arctic site near major northern fisheries into the world's largest known nuclear dump.

* * *

Debate Over Health Risks

Debate is beginning to build over the potential health risks of the newly disclosed oceanic dumping and what, if anything, to do about them. Although uncontained liquid wastes dispersed long ago, solid and liquid wastes in sunken reactors and steel drums appear to be localized although the Russians say they have almost no direct observational data about whether such containers are intact, corroding or breached.

* * *

In theory, the powers of the ocean to dilute such material can make radioactive wastes essentially harmless. But localized releases of high concentration can do real damage when picked up by marine life.

[T]he Russian oceanic wastes appear to have a level of radioactivity roughly akin to the long-lived isotopes thrown into the atmosphere by the Chernobyl explosion in 1986, the world's worst nuclear accident [see Problem 7–3, supra]. If ocean wastes were similarly dispersed, he said, they could, in theory contaminate fish or food.

* * *

For related concerns, see Problem 7–3, supra at 538, and Problem 9–1, infra, at 692 along with the Introduction and Chapters 1–3.

5. In 1995, in Washington, D.C., the Intergovernmental Conference to Adopt a Global Programme of Action for the Protection of the Marine Environment from Land–Based Pollution adopted the Washington Declaration on Protection of the Marine Environment from Land–Based Activities (Washington Declaration) [**Basic Document 4.29**] as well as the Global Programme of Action for the Protection of the Marine Environment from Land–Based Activities (Global Programme) UNEP(OCA)/LBA/IG.2/7 (5 Dec. 1995). [**Basic Document 4.28**]. The Washington Declaration is linked to the Global Programme which itself is "designed to be a source of conceptual and practical guidance to be drawn upon by national and/or regional authorities in devising and implementing sustained action to prevent, reduce, control and/or eliminate marine degradation from land-based activities." Global Programme, para. 14. The Global Programme sets forth extensive guidelines including sections on actions at the national level, regional and international

cooperation methods, and recommended approaches based on different sources of pollution (e.g. sewage, persistent organic pollutants, radioactive substances, nutrients, sediment, etc.). *See* Global Programme, paras. 94–99 "Sewage," 100–06 "Persistent Organic Pollutants," 133–39 "Sediment Mobilization," and 149–51 "Physical Alteration and Destruction of Habitats." How might adherence to the Global Programme by Rajapur change its methods of waste disposal and/or dredging practices? What about Bijoutou? Would the Global Programme make a difference in the methods it chooses to deal with waste disposal, fishing practices, and/or tourism?

6. *Bibliographical Note.* For further discussion concerning the principle themes addressed in this problem, consult the following specialized materials:

(a) *Specialized Books/Monographs.* J. Cuisine & J. Grant, The Impact of Marine Pollution (1980); GESAMP 15, The Review of the Health of the Oceans; Reports and Studies No. 15 (1982); J. Kindt, 1 & 2 Marine Pollution and the Law of the Sea (1986); C. Moorcraft, Must the Seas Die? (1972); R. Soni, Control of Marine Pollution in International Law (1985); P. Sand, Marine Environment Law in the United Nations Environment Programme (1988); Times Atlas of the Oceans (A. Couper ed. 1983); H. Windom & R. Duce, Marine Pollutant Transfer (1976).

(b) *Specialized Hearings/Reports.* World Bank News, Special Report: The World Bank, The Environment, and Development (1991).

(c) *Specialized Articles/Book Chapters.* M. Belsky, *Management of Large Marine Ecosystems: Developing a New Rule of Customary International Law*, 22 San Diego L. Rev. 733 (1985); A. Boyle, *Marine Pollution Under the Law of the Sea Convention*, 79 A.J.I.L. 347 (1985); J. Grolin, *The Future of the Law of the Sea: Consequences of a Non–Treaty or Non–Universal Treaty Solution*, 13 Ocean Dev. & Int'l L. 1 (1983); L. Guruswamy, *Environmental Protection and the United Nations Convention on the Law of the Sea*, Lloyd's Mar. & Com. L. Q. 705 (1983); ___, *Laws Controlling Mercury Pollution: Issues and Implications for the United Kingdom*, Lloyd's Mar. & Com. L. Q. 611 (1982); B. Kwiatkowska, *Marine Pollution from Land–Based Sources: Current Problems and Prospects*, 14 Ocean Dev. & Int'l L. 315 (1984); J. Kindt, *The Effect of Claims by Developing Countries on LOS International Marine Pollution Negotiations*, 20 V.J.I.L. 315 (1980); ___, *Special Claims Impacting Upon Marine Pollution Issues at the Third U.N. Conference on the Law of the Sea*, 10 Cal. W. Int'l L. J. 397 (1980); ___, *International Environmental Law and Policy: An Overview of Transboundary Pollution*, 23 San Diego L. Rev. 583 (1986); R. Lotilla, *The Efficacy of the Anti–Pollution Legislation Provisions of the 1982 Law of the Sea Convention: A View From South East Asia*, 41 I.C.L.Q. 137 (1992); R. M'Gonigle, *"Developing Sustainability" and the Emerging Norms of International Law: The Case of Land–Based Marine Pollution Control*, 28 Can. Y. B. Int'l L. 169 (1990); L. Schenke, *The Marine Protection, Research, and Sanctuaries Act: The Conflict Between Marine Protection and Oil and Gas Development*, 18 Hous. L. Rev. 987 (1981); A. Springer, *Towards a Meaningful Concept of Pollution in International Law*, 26 I.C.L.Q. 531 (1977); L. Teclaff & E. Teclaff, *Transfer of Pollution and the Marine Environment Conventions*, 31 N.R.J. 187 (1991); M. Waldichuck, *Control of Marine Pollution: An Essay Review*, 4 Ocean Dev. & Int'l L. 269 (1977).

Problem 8–2

An Oil Tanker Spill in Angloboer's Coastal Waters

SECTION 1. FACTS

The *Petrol Mariner*, an eighteen-year-old single-hull ship weighing 98,000 tonnes (deadweight), is an oil tanker owned by SuperMar, Inc., a Delaware corporation. It is registered in the Grain Coast, a West African republic, and sails under that nation's flag.

In July of last year the *Petrol Mariner* was steaming southwestward from Saudi Arabia to Brazil around the Cape of Good Hope carrying 84,000 tonnes of unrefined heavy crude oil within its single hull. The crude had been loaded following a vessel seaworthiness inspection at Ras Tanura, Saudi Arabia, an inspection similar to the inspection performed by the *Petrol Mariner's* classification society just two months earlier.

The captain had charted a course that would take the *Petrol Mariner* through the South Narrows, a 22–mile wide channel located in southernmost Angloboer, a relatively prosperous former British colony situated in southern Africa and fringed on its southernmost coast with saw-edged reefs and sunken rock islands. The South Narrows is one of Angloboer's most important breeding grounds for seabirds—albatrosses, gannets, gulls, penguins, petrels, shearwaters, white stocks, and diverse migratory species from the Northern Hemisphere—and marine mammals, including many thousand seals. It also is home to extensive fish stocks, from which most of the residents of the area derive their livelihoods as fishers, fish processors, or fish farmers.

Powerful southern hemispheric winter storms had created rough seas in the channel that July, and the *Petrol Mariner's* captain, making his first voyage as head of the vessel, had to decide whether to take the ship through the South Narrows or chart a safer course around Angloboer's southernmost cluster of reefs and submerged rock islands. Noting that this latter route would add sixty miles to the journey, several more hours of transit time, and several thousand dollars to the cost of the voyage, he elected the South Narrows route. Consulting with maritime authorities and acting on their suggestion, the captain charted a course through the middle of the South Narrows that left at least ten miles of sea on either side of his ship.

In the early morning, when the *Petrol Mariner* entered the South Narrows, weather conditions deteriorated amid hurricane-force winds. At about 4:45 a.m., as the ship sailed southwestward, high waves flooded the ship's fuel system, shutting down its engines and some electrical power as well as its communications system. Pushed by wind and waves, the ship began to drift north, toward Angloboer's saw-edged and rocky coastline.

At 5:19 a.m., after electrical power was restored, the *Petrol Mariner* contacted Angloboer's coastal authorities, and at 6:30 a.m., amid further drift,

614

the coastal authorities called for several tugs. One-half hour before the first tug's arrival at 9:30 a.m., the *Petrol Mariner*'s captain and his Filipino and Greek crew abandoned the vessel and were escorted to Angloboer by rescue helicopters. By the time the first tug arrived, there was no one aboard the *Petrol Mariner* to help attach a tow line. Efforts to land people aboard the tanker failed in the face of violent winds, and the ship soon struck ground, rocks piercing the *Petrol Mariner*'s single hull. Eventually all of the 84,000 tonnes of heavy crude spilled into the highly sensitive South Narrows channel environment, damaging one of Angloboer's most important ecological areas.

Despite Angloboer's use of dispersants and bioremedial agents to break up the oil slicks, the effects of the spill were extensive. Environmental impacts included the killing of thousands of seals and sea birds, while albatrosses, gannets, gulls, penguins, petrels, shearwaters, white stocks, and other species returning to their breeding grounds became mired in an "oily mousse." A frothy oil residue washed into coves and inlets, killing local land vegetation, damaging beaches, and defacing the pristine scenery that had lured several thousand tourists each year to the area. Additionally, entire albacore tuna, anchovy, herring, and mackerel stocks, among others, were destroyed, thus eliminating the only source of income for many of Angloboer's fishers and fish processors. Given the extent of the damage, Angloboer was convinced that the limited damages recovery authorized under the International Convention on Civil Liability for Oil Pollution Damage, 1992 ("the Liability Convention") and the International Convention on the Establishment of an International Fund for Compensation for Oil Pollution Damage, 1992 ("the Fund Convention") were inadequate.

Citing violation of its Pollution Control Act (PCA), Angloboer instituted proceedings in its courts against the captain of the *Petrol Mariner*, SuperMar, Inc., and the Grain Coast. Under the PCA, all three parties can be held jointly and severally liable for all costs incurred in the clean-up and for damage caused to ecosystems. None of the defendants having submitted to the jurisdiction of Angloboer's courts, however, Angloboer has also instituted judicial proceedings against SuperMar in the United States. SuperMar has raised numerous jurisdictional objections.

Thus, frustrated by its inability effectively to pursue legal proceedings and spurred by a slide in the public opinion polls because of its alleged helplessness, the Government of Angloboer temporarily suspended the passage of all single hull ships in a specified ecologically sensitive zone (ESZ) surrounding and including the South Narrows. After giving due notice of this action, including notice to the International Maritime Organization [IMO], it ordered its navy to intercept and head off any single hull tankers attempting to enter the ESZ. Angloboer claims that it is exercising its legal rights as a coastal state to take preventive action against further disasters. Moreover, it argues that such actions are consistent with its rights to protect its security. It has asked the IMO to adopt this ban as a mandatory "ship routeing system" for the South Narrows, forcing all single-hull oil tankers to avoid the area completely. It has also asked the IMO to designate the South Narrows as a "particularly sensitive sea area" in which special protection against oil pollution is warranted. The IMO has so far declined to act on either request.

Alarmed by the impact that Angloboer's actions might have on maritime shipping, a number of maritime states have persuaded Angloboer, the Grain Coast, and SuperMar to refer their claims to a Special Arbitral Tribunal under Article 287(1)(d) of the 1982 United Nations Convention on the Law of the Sea (LOS). All parties have agreed to be bound by international law as determined by the arbitral tribunal, and consented to abide by its decision.

Angloboer claims that SuperMar's actions and those of the Grain Coast violated international law, first by authorizing the use of single-hulled tankers in the ecologically sensitive and notoriously treacherous South Narrows, and second by virtue of the *Petrol Mariner's* captain taking the *Petrol Mariner* through the South Narrows despite full knowledge of an impending major storm. The use of single hulls in such circumstances is manifestly dangerous and negligent, Angloboer claims, and contrary to current trends in state practice, as evidenced by, for example, new, stricter sea-vessel legislation in the United States in the wake of another massive oil spill in Alaska and, in addition, the International Maritime Organization's requirement that all new oil tankers must have double hulls. Angloboer demands damages for actual clean-up costs and consequential damages for harms done to its fishing and tourist industries and to its ecosystems.

SuperMar contends, on the other hand, that there is no international consensus on the need for double hulls because they offer no significant protection against oil spills in accidents caused by ships running aground on rocks in violent storms. It also claims that double-hulled ships would not be safe alternatives because of the potential for a buildup of dangerous gases between the hulls. Moreover, it argues, the cost of retrofitting its older ships with double hulls is prohibitively expensive. Finally, SuperMar denies any negligence on the part of the tanker captain.

The Grain Coast, for its part, has stated that the demand for double-hull retrofitting is being made by wealthy "traditional maritime powers" who can afford the expense of retrofitting. The Grain Coast, like other flag-of-convenience states, is unable to make ship retrofits without threatening fledgling development efforts. If the Grain Coast is to be expected to retrofit, it must have financial assistance from the wealthy countries who benefit from its registry.

Both SuperMar and the Grain Coast claim that the action of Angloboer in proclaiming and preventing entry into the ESZ violated international law.

Angloboer and the Grain Coast are both parties to the 1982 United Nations Convention on the Law of the Sea; the 1973 International Convention for the Prevention of Pollution from Ships, With Annex I, along with its 1978 Protocol (MARPOL 73/78); the International Convention on Civil Liability for Oil Pollution, 1992 and the International Convention on the Establishment of an International Fund for Compensation for Oil Pollution Damage, 1992.

The case is now before the Special Arbitral Tribunal and is awaiting argument.

SECTION 2. QUESTIONS PRESENTED

1. Has either SuperMar or the Grain Coast violated international law; and, if so, to what damages is Angloboer entitled?

2.   Has Angloboer violated international law?

SECTION 3. ASSIGNMENTS

A. *Reading Assignment*

Study the Readings presented in Section 4, *infra*, and the Discussion Notes/Questions that follow. Also, to the extent possible, consult the accompanying bibliographical references.

B. *Recommended Writing Assignment*

Prepare a comprehensive, logically sequenced, and *argumentative* brief in the form of an outline of the primary and subsidiary *legal* issues you see requiring resolution by the Special Arbitral Tribunal. Also, from the perspective of an independent objective judge, indicate which side ought to prevail on each issue and why. Retain a copy of your issue-outline/brief for class discussion.

C. *Recommended Oral Assignment*

Assume you are legal counsel for Angloboer or the Grain Coast and SuperMar (as designated by your instructor); then, relying upon the Readings (and your issue-outline if prepared), present a 15–20 minute oral argument of your client's likely positions before the tribunal.

D. *Recommended Reflective Assignment*

Consider (and recommend) alternative norms, institutions, and/or procedures that you believe might do better than existing world order arrangements to contend with situations of the kind posed by this problem. In so doing, but without insisting upon *immediate* feasibility, identify the particular transition steps that would be needed to make your alternatives a reality.

SECTION 4. READINGS

1.   **David M. Dzidzornu & B. Martin Tsamenyi**, *Enhancing International Control of Vessel–Source Oil Pollution Under the Law of the Sea Convention*, 1982: *A Reassessment*, 10 UNIV. OF TASMANIA L. REV. 269, 271 (1991).

Sea pollution by oil is a major phenomenon capable of making our seas virtually biological deserts. The biological devastation of ocean oil pollution is not yet fully known. The emerging evidence, however, shows that the ability of the oceans to tolerate continued pollution is not interminably elastic. The real danger is that whilst there may seem to be an ebb and flow to their ability to neutralise pollutants, persistent fouling by oil and other substances disposes the oceans to reach a point of sudden biological collapse. The ecological and socio-economic effects of vessel-source oil pollution have been well documented.

2. Sally A. Meese, *When Jurisdictional Interests Collide*: *International, Domestic, and State Efforts to Prevent Vessel Source Oil Pollution*, 12 OCEAN DEV. & INT'L L. 71, 74–81 (1982).

OIL IN THE MARINE ENVIRONMENT

Marine pollution, as recognized by most legal and scientific scholars, may be defined as:

> [T]he introduction by man, directly or indirectly, of substances or energy into the marine environment (including estuaries) resulting in such deleterious effects as harm to living resources, hazards to human health, hindrance to marine activities including fishing, impairment of quality or use of sea water, and reduction of amenities.[1]

The sea, covering about two-thirds of the earth's surface, helps maintain the vital biological and ecological balance by supplying much of the world's oxygen and determining its climate. The world's seas are not homogenous in nature, however. Their vulnerability to oil pollution varies depending on their geography, depth, temperature, salinity, currents, and age.

* * *

A. The Fate of Oil in the Marine Environment: Physical, Chemical, and Microbiological Processes

The ultimate effects that petroleum hydrocarbons and the resultant products have in the marine environment are partially dependent upon the changes that take place within the sea-water medium. Oil is naturally dispersed and diluted and is subject to a variety of physical, chemical, and microbiological processes. The changes are in part dependent on the type of oil which undergoes the transformation. The original oil, the interim and end products can all affect an environment differently.

Transported petroleum consists of hydrocarbons as well as small amounts of oxygen, sulphur, and nitrogen. It is carried in a variety of states: from light to heavy crude (unrefined), to refined light distillates and residual refined oils. These compounds vary with respect to viscosities, densities, and boiling temperatures (as well as other properties) which affect their behavior and destructiveness in the marine environment.

The lighter oils contain a higher percentage of aromatic compounds. Consequently, these oils are more toxic than the relatively inert heavy crude and residual products of distillation. The aromatic compounds are more volatile and are thus rapidly distributed through organisms via ingestion and respiration. Their high volatility, however, makes them less stable in the marine environment, and they are more easily evaporated and weathered. Thus, their initial contribution to marine pollution is great, but this effect diminishes relatively rapidly with time. The more inert and heavier oils resist dispersion and evaporation, and while they are subject to alteration, they persist in one form or another for much longer periods of time. An "average" crude oil will lose about fifty percent of its hydrocarbons via evaporation. Heavy crude oil and fuel oil, however, will probably lose less than ten percent,

---

1. JAMES BARROS & DOUGLAS JOHNSTON, THE
INTERNATIONAL LAW OF POLLUTION 6 (1974).

while diesel and light fuel oil will rapidly lose seventy-five percent or more of its hydrocarbons.

* * *

B. *Ecological Effects of Oil in the Marine Environment*

The main focus of recent scientific investigation remains on the potential for ecological damage. At an international meeting held in 1979 on oil pollution control, it became apparent to those in attendance that only limited generalizations regarding the environmental effects of oil could be drawn. Major areas of concern among scientists today include spill effects on nekton and plankton and the effect of petroleum hydrocarbons on benthic organisms, bottom sediments, and enclosed and semi-enclosed seas.

Scientists are also uncertain as to the long-term effects of ocean oil spills. A well-documented study of the short and long-term effects of coastal spills was conducted by the Woods Hole Oceanographic Institution:

> In 1969, a relatively small spill of 4,000 barrels from the barge *Florida* contaminated several miles of coastline, which included salt marsh and shellfish flats, in West Falmouth, Massachusetts. While the oil was visible on the surface for only a short time, sediment contamination has kept shellfish flats closed for nearly 10 years. New areas have been contaminated as oil and the subtidal sediments have spread seaward over the years.[2]

Scientists do not yet fully understand the effects of the slow release of hydrocarbons over a period of years. In addition, not enough is known about oil in the benthos environment once it is forced down from the surface by turbulence.

> The benthos is a vital part of our marine ecosystem where finfish spawn and shellfish, such as scallops and ocean quahogs, live. Oil in the benthos contaminates these niches, possibly reducing fish populations vital to commercial fisheries.[3]

Oil which is discharged into the water tends to disrupt the food chain by forming an oil slick which poisons algae, plankton, and other intertidal organisms. The initial source of food for larger creatures, and eventually man, comes from these small organisms, and their deaths have repercussions throughout the entire ecosystem. Moreover, scientists have theorized that organisms which are not killed immediately may absorb oil and introduce the toxins into the food chain at other stages and produce long-term sub-lethal genetic effects.

C. *Damage to Fisheries, Kelp, Birds, and Marine Mammals*

Seabirds are the only group of marine organisms known to be affected greatly enough by oil pollution to have world populations threatened. Death is attributed to smothering, removal of protective natural oils (and thereby death by exposure and loss of buoyancy), and uptake of toxic contaminants.

---

2. Statement of Dr. Evelyn P. Murphy, in Oil Pollution of the Oceans: A Tanker Owner's Perspective, Sea Grant Report No. MITSG 79–1 (1978).

3. *Id.*

Planktonic eggs and larvae numbers can be greatly affected proximate to a spill; however, the total effect on morbidity to a pelagic (mid-water) fishery is not normally measurable. Some investigators assume the overall effects to be small.

Benthic organisms are susceptible to oil pollution by fouling of feeding and respiratory apparatus by oil droplets, and by smothering. Oil spills can have disastrous effects on specific benthic fisheries which are important as a source of food for humans. Intertidal and shallow subtidal benthics (e.g., mollusks, barnacles, tubeworms) may remain relatively unharmed if spilled oil is not too thick and has lost most of its toxic components. They can often survive a coating of heavy inert oil. In deeper water, benthics will be affected if a spill settles directly to the bottom and some toxic components are intact.

Edible crabs and lobsters live offshore and are therefore more subject to oiling by weathered products than by other pollution. It has been claimed that low concentrations of kerosene actually attract lobsters.

Marine mammals appear to be almost unaffected by oiling. Some destruction of thermal proofing fur can occur, but hairless marine mammals (dolphins, whales) seem to be able to avoid spills, and proof of increased mortality has not been established. There are reports of irritation to the eyes and nostrils of fur seals, which would be of particular concern in sub-Arctic and Arctic environments where populations are large and the effects persistent.

* * *

D.   Aspects of a Spill's Location

One of the most unfortunate aspects of oil pollution is that most pollution occurs in the coastal and estuarine areas which are of greatest ecological and economic importance and which are most vulnerable to the harmful effects of pollution. Again, this is an area where our knowledge of the total extent and source of oil discharges is imperfect. There is general agreement among scientists that the environment appears better able to cope with oil spills from large tankers in the comparatively deep water of the ocean than spills in shallow estuaries.

The ecological damage done by a specific quantity and type of oil is dependent upon the section and environment in which the spill occurs, and the concentration of the oil when it impinges on the ecosystem. For instance, a more rapid evaporation and breakdown of toxic compounds occur with higher temperatures. A spill in the Arctic or sub-Arctic would persist much longer than one in a tropical region. Spills become more dangerous as they progress from the open ocean through near-shore, and into the enclosed estuaries and rivers. In the open ocean, the increased turbulence by waves and the vastness of space allow a large proportion of the oil to degrade or disperse before any harm can be done. The open sea is relatively immune to inputs of oil, especially in diffuse concentrations (as allowed presently by ballasting and tank cleaning operations). Closer to the coast aesthetics also begin to play a role, and spills may curtail tourism in some areas. The proximity to land allows more oil in a more toxic state to reach benthic organisms more rapidly so that damage can be severe. Beaches and rocky coastlines can be smothered under a layer of persistent oils. Waterways, estuaries, and rivers are even more susceptible to damage because they are enclosed, and because they have a high productivity. They are often the site for intense fishing of invertebrates for human consumption.

Unfortunately where there is a greater risk posed by oil pollution, we normally also see the greatest amounts of spillage. Since the great bulk of maritime activity occurs in the coastal zone, these systems are subjected to a constant threat of pollution and degradation.

3.   Stockholm Declaration of the United Nations Conference on the Human Environment, Adopted by the UN Conference on the Human Environment at Stockholm 16 June 1972, Report of the UN Conference on the Human Environment, June 15–16, 1972, UN Doc. A/CONF.48/14/Rev. 1 at 3 (1973), UN Doc. A/CONF.48/14 at 2–65, and Corr. 1 (1972), *reprinted in* 11 I.L.M. 1416 (1972): Principles 2, 6, 7, 21 [Basic Document 1.12].

4.   World Charter for Nature, Oct. 28, 1982, G.A. Res. 37/7, U.N. GAOR, 37th Sess., Supp. No. 51, at 17, U.N. Doc. A/37/51, *reprinted in* 22 I.L.M. 455 (1983): Principles 1–4, 11, 12, 13, 24 [Basic Document 1.21].

5.   David M. Dzidzornu & B. Martin Tsamenyi, *Enhancing International Control of Vessel–Source Oil Pollution Under the Law of the Sea Convention*, 1982: *A Reassessment*, 10 Univ. of Tasmania L. Rev. 269, 272, 275–76, 278–79, 281–82 (1991).

The Pre-1982 Arrangement

Juridical control of oil pollution from vessels at the international level has operated in the overall context of the legal rules determining the use of the seas by all States without let or hindrance. Since Hugo Grotius' concept of *mare liberum* won the day in the debate over the juridical nature of the sea, the only restraint on national conduct in the maritime realm has been the concept of *abuse of rights* which seeks to ensure that States use the seas reasonably in due consideration of the interests and rights of other users. Thus, when, following the work of the International Law Commission, the Geneva Conference 1958 sought to codify the Law of the Sea, jurisdiction over pollution control by States was barely recognized.

The Geneva Conventions

The *Convention on the High Seas* 1958 **[Basic Document 4.2]** assured every State freedom of navigation and the right to extend its nationality to ships duly registered under its laws. It gave each State absolute jurisdiction over the construction, design, equipment and manning (CDEM standards) of its flag vessels. It left to each State the discretion to ensure that the CDEM standards it adopts conform to generally accepted international standards and to ensure that its flag vessels observe those standards. As a corollary, the flag State is given sole jurisdiction to institute any legal and disciplinary process against its vessels in the event that any incident of navigation on the high seas may involve them. . . .

* * *

The IMO Conventions

When the Geneva regime was concluded the *Intergovernmental Maritime Consultative Organization*, now the *International Maritime Organization* (IMO), had come into existence. It was to this organization the Geneva system looked to develop the applicable rules and standards, and the jurisdiction of States regarding the prevention of pollution of the marine environment from vessel-source oil. Even though it was not [until] 1975 when the Convention establishing IMO was amended to give it the task of laying down anti-pollution measures, the technical rules (CDEM standards) it has laid down in its Conventions from 1954 have been aimed at preventing, minimizing and, if possible, eliminating marine pollution from vessel oil.

The IMO's 1954 *Convention for Prevention of Pollution of the Sea by Oil* (OILPOL 54), which was amended a number of times, was eventually super-seded by the 1973 *Convention for the Prevention of Pollution by Ships* (MARPOL 73) together with its 1978 amending Protocol (MARPOL 78) **[Basic Document 4.12]**[a]. . . .

The aim of MARPOL 73/78 is to eliminate intentional oil pollution of the marine environment and to minimize accidental discharges of oil. To this end, it gives the flag States the duty to ensure that their flag vessels comply with the technical standards of construction, design and equipment set out in Annex I, and requires them to issue a certificate of verification of compliance with the standards. The certificate is to be, *prima facia*, admissible as valid by every Party to the Convention. This explains why a port State has jurisdiction only to inspect a ship for the sole purpose of verifying that it has on board a valid certificate.[b] However, if it has clear grounds to believe that the ship's condition does not correspond substantially with the particulars of the certifi-cate, or if the ship does not have a valid certificate on board, the port State is authorized to take steps to ensure that the ship can proceed to sea without posing an unreasonable threat of harm to the marine environment. As part of this obligation, it may permit the ship to go the nearest repair yard.

* * *

The first of the "compensation" Conventions is the *Convention on Civil Liability for Oil Pollution Damage 1969 (Civil Liability Convention)*.[c] This Convention adopts uniform international rules and procedures for determin-ing questions of liability and to provide compensation where "pollution damage" occurs, or where costs are incurred in the attempt to prevent, or minimize any such damage. Under its scheme, the flag States are obliged to ensure that their vessels carry insurance as provided for under the Conven-tion, and port States have the right to verify the validity and currency of such insurance in respect of vessels entering their ports. By virtue of the 1984 Protocol to this Convention, compensation is now available to State parties for pollution damage caused within the Exclusive Economic Zone (EEZ). A correlative supplementary scheme, the 1971 *Convention on the Establishment of an International Fund for Compensation for Oil Pollution Damage (Fund*

---

a. *See infra* Reading 8.

b. Port state authority has been signifi-cantly expanded in the 8 years since this arti-cle was published. *See infra* Reading 15.

c. *See infra* Reading 24.

Convention),[d] offers extra compensation to cover pollution damage beyond the limit of compensation available under the 1969 Civil Liability Convention scheme. By a similar amending Protocol in 1984, the Fund Convention also extends its coverage to damage within the EEZ. Once again, it is the port State which is the beneficiary of an "inspection of insurance certificate" jurisdiction under these schemes.

... In response to a series of grave maritime casualties involving oil tankers, the 1969 *Convention Relating to Intervention on the High Seas in Case of Oil Pollution Casualties* **[Basic Document 4.7]** was concluded. This Convention is limited in terms of its control. It only gives the coastal State the right to take measures necessary to "prevent, mitigate or eliminate grave and imminent danger" to its "coastline or related interests from pollution or threat of pollution ... by oil." The exercise of this right must follow—as in the *Torrey Canyon* incident 1967, which directly gave birth to the Convention—"upon a maritime casualty or acts related to such casualty, which may reasonably be expected to result in major harmful consequences." The right is further curbed, in deference to the freedom of unimpeded navigation and flag State jurisdictional supremacy, by the obligation to consult and take measures proportionate to the nature of the threat, in default of which the coastal State is required to pay compensation for any damage resulting from the adoption of an excessive measure.

6.   Convention on the High Seas, Apr. 29, 1958, 13 U.S.T. 2312, T.I.A.S. No. 5200, 450 U.N.T.S. 82: arts. 1,2, 4–6, 10, 24 [Basic Document 4.2].

7.   Convention on the Territorial Sea and the Contiguous Zone, Apr. 29, 1958, 15 U.S.T. 1606, T.I.A.S. 5639. 516 U.N.T.S. 205: art. 1, 3, 5, 10, 14–17, 19, 24 [Basic Document 4.4].

8.   MARPOL 73/78: Protocol of 1978 Relating to the International Convention for the Prevention of Pollution From Ships 1973, *done at London*, Feb. 17, 1978, 1341 U.N.T.S. 3 **(consolidated text)** [Basic Document 4.12].

9.   *Marine Affairs: IMO Provisions Requiring Double Hulls on New Ships Takes Effect, Agency Announces*, 16 INT'L ENVTL. REP. (BNA) 514 (1993).

All oil tankers now have to be fitted with double hulls or use another method that provides the same level of protection, according to the United Nations agency responsible for maritime issues.

The requirement for double hulls or alternatives became effective July 6, [1993], the U.N. Maritime Organization said. This provision and others dealing with oil tanker pollution were adopted in March 1992 as changes to the 1973 Convention on the Prevention of Pollution by Ships.

Other amendments adopted to MARPOL 73/78 **[Basic Document 4.12]** at that time will require existing tankers to be fitted with double hulls or an equivalent design when they reach the age of 25 years. This requirement, however, [did] not take effect until July 6, 1995.

d.   *See infra* Reading 25.

The design standards for new ships are included in a new regulation 13F of Annex I of the convention that deals with oil pollution, the IMO said. The regulation applies to tankers ordered after July 6, 1993, whose keels were laid on or after January 6, 1994, or which are delivered on or after July 6, 1996. The standard applies to new tankers of 5,000 dead weight tons (dwt) or more.

The measure on existing tankers (regulation 13G), which [came] into effect July 6, 1995, covers crude oil vessels of 20,000 dwt and product carriers of 30,000 dwt and above.

10. Committee on Tank Vessel Design, Marine Board, Commission on Engineering and Technical Systems, National Research Council, Tanker Spills: Prevention by Design 1–2, 4, 7, 8, 33, 46, 47, 50, 51 (Pre–Publication Copy, 1991).

The threat of pollution exists wherever tank vessels travel.... [While] [i]mproved tank vessel design is one way to reduce the risk of oil pollution ..., the risk cannot be eliminated entirely. [Of course,] to assure some risk reduction, tank vessels of any design must be properly constructed, operated, inspected, and maintained. [But] [w]hether adequate risk reduction can be achieved at reasonable cost through design changes is a controversial question; opinion varies widely.... [N]aval architects traditionally have not designed tank vessels ... to withstand collisions and groundings. Design based on the possibility of accidents, a practice common in many industries, should be considered for tank vessels....

* * *

The paucity of data on tank vessel accidents and oil outflows, gaps in knowledge concerning vessel structural behavior in accidents, and uncertainties concerning the quantification of environmental benefits resulting from design improvements make any but the most primitive conclusions subject to conditional scenarios, assumptions, and judgments ranging from the informed to the intuitive.

The following conclusions are adequately supported with facts:

● Double hull vessels in low-energy (typically low velocity) accidents should not pollute.

● Vessels that carry cargo in contact with a single skin (with the sea on the other side) will cause some pollution in any accident where a cargo tank is penetrated. However, certain design alternatives will minimize the amount of pollution in some specified scenarios.

● High-energy accidents nearly always result in pollution. The relative advantages of design alternatives in reducing pollution from particular scenarios are highly dependent on the assumptions made in the scenarios.

* * *

A total of 17 design concepts, as well as 3 combination concepts, were evaluated by the committee.... The committee did not identify any design as superior to the double hull for all accident scenarios.

* * *

Various issues related to . . . double hulls (or any design incorporating large void spaces) have caused considerable controversy. Increased risk of fire and explosion, possible vessel instability after an accident, perceived salvage difficulties, and increased personnel hazards are cited by critics of these designs. . . .

Void spaces involve risk of fires and explosions due to the potential accumulation of hydrocarbon vapors, which can enter through cracks or pits in bulkheads adjoining cargo tanks or through a defect in the cargo piping system. Although double hulls have significantly increased void spaces compared to single-hull tankers, there is no reliable evidence of increased incidence of fires or explosions in existing double bottom or double-hull ships.

* * *

Double-hull designs have large void spaces exposed to potential damage, flooding, and additional weight, which implies possible instability following an accident. However, tankers designed to international (MARPOL) standards tend to be exceptionally stable and generally exceed current damage stability requirements. Double-hull vessels can be designed not only to meet requirements for damage stability, but also to survive more severe accident damage than currently required.

* * *

Retrofitting double hulls on existing tank vessels is possible, but potential difficulties could result from combining new and old structural members. Furthermore, retrofitting would be . . . expensive.

* * *

There is some evidence of a link between vessel age and serious casualties: Older vessels have more accidents, particularly fires/explosions and structural/machinery damage. . . .

* * *

Tankers must satisfy a substantial number of design requirements when initially constructed for purposes of safety and pollution prevention. . . . Regulation of ship design for safety and pollution prevention is achieved primarily through three international conventions:

● The International Convention on Load Lines (1966), or ICLL [640 U.N.T.S. 133];

● The International Convention for the Safety of Life at Sea (1974) and its 1978 Protocol (SOLAS) [T.I.A.S. Nos. 9700 & 10009], and

● The International Convention for the Prevention of Pollution from Ships (1973) and its 1978 Protocol (MARPOL).

The ICLL establishes the deepest draft to which a ship can be safely loaded. . . . The overall objective of SOLAS is to assure safety of the crew, ports, passengers, ships, and cargo, and, indirectly, the environment. . . . Both ICLL and SOLAS have the indirect effect of preventing oil spills and consequently marine pollution. The MARPOL convention seeks to prevent pollution directly, both from normal operational discharges and accidents. MARPOL specifies design, equipment, and procedural requirements to prevent pollution of the seas from oil. . . .

* * *

The IMO Conferences of 1973 and 1978 together produced fundamental changes in the way tankers are designed and operated. . . . Most important is the fact that the "MARPOL vessel" represents the current standard, against which any further design changes should be measured. MARPOL also set a precedent by establishing major retrofitting requirements for tankers, applying new equipment requirements to existing tankers for the first time.

* * *

Implementation of IMO conventions is not straightforward because the procedures—and their effectiveness—can vary. Requirements are imposed on a vessel through its flag state. Each tankship therefore is governed in design, arrangements, and construction by the international agreements ratified by its flag state.

11. Tammy Alcock, *"Ecology Tankers" and the Oil Pollution Act of 1990*: *A History of Efforts to Require Double Hulls on Oil Tankers,* 19 ECOLOGY L.Q. 97, 107–08 (1992).

Every report of which the author is aware has concluded that double hulls and bottoms are effective in preventing accidental spills or lessening their severity. In single-skin vessels, the cargo tanks are located just inside the outer hull (with the ocean on the other side). Any accidental breaching of the hull will result in oil outflow (unless the breached tank happens to be empty or carrying water as ballast on a return trip). . . .

Studies have concluded that many oil spills, including the one by the *Exxon Valdez*, could have been prevented . . . or their severity lessened by some type of double-skin construction. In one early study, thirty tank vessel casualties occurring between January 1969 and April 1973 were examined to determine whether double bottoms would have prevented the resulting oil outflow.[1] . . . [I]n twenty-seven of the thirty cases, a double bottom would have reduced oil outflow. This means that in the cases studied (mostly small to medium size tankers, not VLCCs[e]), a double bottom . . . would have been effective in ninety percent of the incidents "in reducing oil outflow. . . ."[5] One report following the grounding of the *Valdez* speculated that if that tanker, with a beam of 166 feet, had been fitted with a double bottom or hull . . ., the space between the bottom and the cargo tanks would have been eleven feet. . . . [T]he rocks of Bligh Reef penetrated an estimated five feet into the *Valdez's* hull.

More recently, the National Research Council found that no pollution occurred in fifty-four groundings of double-bottomed ships between 1977 and 1987. The NRC study concluded that ships with double bottoms or double hulls would spill no oil in eighty-five percent of the groundings, while single-

---

4. *See, e.g.,* James C. Effectiveness of *Double Bottoms in Preventing Oil Outflow from Tanker Bottom Damage Incident,* 12 MARINE TECH. 60 (1975).

e. *I.e.,* Very Large Crude Carriers.

5. Committee on Tank Vessel Design, National Research Council, Tanker Spills: Prevention by Design 30 (1991).

skinned ships would almost always lose at least some oil. Further, the spillage reduction benefits of double hulls were found to be greater in VLCCs than in smaller ships. . . .

12.   L. F. E. Goldie, *Environmental Catastrophes and Flags of Convenience—Does the Present Law Pose Special Liability Issues?*, 3 PACE Y. B. INT'L L. 63, 63, 66, 67, 81, 86–90 (1991).

INTRODUCTION

Maritime flags are a symbol of nationality. As such, they are generally thought to be important in determining when a relationship exists between a state and a ship and, thus when a vessel is subject to the law of that state. The flag of a vessel serves two different functions: it is a symbol of the nationality of the ship, which consequently designates the national law governing the affairs of the vessel, and it identifies the location of those responsible for the vessel.

For at least the last thirty years, the practice of some shipowners registering their ships under the flags of states with less stringent manning and safety requirements than states which traditionally have set the standards of safety, has led to controversies. Some states offer vessel registration under conditions that impose fewer financial and administrative burdens than those which are imposed by other states. Economic rather than political considerations usually account for an owner's decision to flag . . . a vessel. . . .

* * *

States have two responsibilities in the flagging of ships. The first responsibility arises in the decision whether or not to flag the vessel. Since international law places so few restrictions on the right to grant nationality to ships, this responsibility is fulfilled easily. Thereafter, other states are obliged to recognize the ship's nationality as being that of the flag granting state.

The second responsibility arises when the flagged vessel sails. The flag state has a general obligation to insure that its flagged vessels neither impede nor endanger other states in their use of international waters.

* * *

Over the years, transnationally operating agreements and international agencies have developed, at least in part, to restrain pollution damage to the oceans, enhance the rational use of resources, and to protect the mammal life of the sea. As a result, the arbitrary and individualistic interests which resort to flags-of-convenience may be seen as increasingly anachronistic. These interests resist the circumambient development of a legal consciousness by remaining a legal device for circumventing the law. This paradox is still possible because there remains in this modern world, where state sovereignty survives, the constantly eroding ancient principle of the exclusivity of the sovereignty of the flag state, regardless of the flag or the state's actual relation to the ship or the relevancy of its laws to the rational use of the oceans from the point of view of international community values.

* * *

II. *Flags of Convenience as Responsibility–Avoiding Devices*

The great weakness of the present international law governing jurisdiction over ships and shipping stems from its present naive invitation to engage in legal fictions and responsibility-avoiding devices. Indeed, international law clearly encourages the avoidance of its own values, rules, policies and prescriptions as embodied in the concept of "genuine link" while it evades the obligation of making those rules and presumptions effective. For as long as shipowners find certain laws objectionable, they will feel encouraged to seek legal devices to evade the laws to which they object provided that no disagreeable consequences will result.

* * *

III. *Flags of Convenience and the IMO Civil Liability Convention*

A number of coastal countries have become signatories to the International Convention on Civil Liability for Oil Pollution Damage (CLC) **[Basic Document 4.25]**.... The CLC was designed to "adopt uniform international rules and procedures for determining questions of liability and providing adequate compensation for vessel source oil pollution". Note should be taken of the CLC's selection of the owner of the ship as the party to be made liable under article three. The owner has been defined as "the person or persons registered as the owner of a ship, or in the absence of registration, the person or persons owning the ship." ... In the conduct of ships and shipping enterprises one frequently finds that the charterer (the "operator" of a ship) is more in control of her than is the owner. (There are various kinds of charter parties or agreements between the owner and the charterer of a ship.) Under bareboat or demise charters, for example, the manning, operation, provisioning and navigation of a ship are in the hands of the charterers—who are thus the parties who exercise control over the ship. The owner has effectively passed control to them. The restriction of liability to the "owner" may look suspiciously like the creation of a straw man to answer for major maritime pollution catastrophes in light of the practice of owners of flags-of-convenience ships.

* * *

Although, in a flags-of-convenience situation, the owner may be a judgment-proof straw man, the CLC's limitation of the party to be made liable to the "owner" may be salvaged by another provision. The Convention requires that the parties to it should issue a certificate to each tanker it registers, which indicates that she carries a form of insurance or guarantee adequate to compensate persons harmed by oil pollution casualties. The convention also provides for a right of direct action against the insurer or other guarantor.

Conclusion

The use of flags-of-convenience could render the owners of giant tankers (of ever-increasing tonnage and risk to the environment) effectively judgment proof, as a matter of fact, from liability for harms they cause. Also, as the world's giant tanker fleet continues to age, more and more ships become less and less safe. This development is an inevitable consequence of tanker economics. As ships age they tend to become the property of less scrupulous owners, who, in order to glean their profits, make cuts in their ship's maintenance and so in their environmental protection costs. Thus, in order to earn a precarious living, these vessels will increasingly become menaces on the high seas, creating disasters afloat and on the shoreline. Hence, the privilege of registering ships under permissive flags-of-convenience will increasingly create more severe problems. . . .

* * *

The owners of such shipping vessels operate on the joint assumptions of: (1) the existence of a regulatory system (for example an anti-dumping or an anti-pollution convention) that ties the hands of the maritime nations that honor it; and (2) the effectiveness of the anomalies inherent in the flags-of-convenience system to permit the flags-of-convenience owners to be loosened from the restriction of such a regulatory system. They can thus directly profit from that system's restraints on others. . . . In this way, the anomalies created by resort to flags-of-convenience can undermine the effectiveness of international conventions directed to preventing, or at least greatly reducing, the incidents of the pollution of the sea by ships. Resort to flags-of-convenience thus exacerbates the tragedy of the already polluted common high seas and creates the condition for undermining any regulatory attempts to rationalize the use of that common resource.

13. Editors' Note. The rule of flag state control, "derived from the fundamental rule that, except in certain extraordinary situations, a merchant ship on the high seas is subject only to the jurisdiction of the flag state," is mirrored by the "duty [of the flag state] to ensure maritime safety and the protection of the marine environment." Ademuni Odeke, *Port State Control and UK Law*, 28 J. Mar. L. & Com. 657–59 (1997). Ideally, flag states would fulfill this duty by ensuring that ships on their registries meet international standards on safety and pollution controls. The reality, however, has been that some flag states lack the resources or the will to enforce international standards, with the result that "many of the vessels registered in them are old and substandard . . . [and] have been involved in many of the major pollution incidents of the past thirty years." *Id.* at 657.

Although coastal states have traditionally exercised very little authority over foreign-registered vessels, checking them only for evidence of necessary flag state certifications, a coastal state which is also a port state has, in theory, a wider authority. *See* John Hare, *Port State Control: Strong Medicine to Cure a Sick Industry*, 26 Ga. J. Int'l & Comp.L. 571 (1997). Except under limited circumstances, "a coastal state enjoys full sovereignty over its internal waters. As such, no right of innocent passage exists through such waters. . . . Foreign merchant ships in internal waters are, in principle, under the complete civil and criminal jurisdiction of the coastal state." Odeke, *supra* at 657. Consequently, when foreign-flagged vessels pass through internal waters to call at a local port, they are under the sovereignty of the port state authorities. Nevertheless, "the practice of the majority of ports, at least until the last decade, was to give scant inspection to calling vessels." Hare, *supra at* 571.

During the 1990s, there was an explosion in the use of port state control to address the problem of substandard ships created by the growth of flags of convenience (FOC) and the failure of the authorities of FOC states to adequately police their vessels. The emergence of port state control as an antidote to the problems of flag state control began with the signing of the so-called Paris MOU On Port State Control in 1982. *See* Memorandum of Understanding on Port State Control in Implementing Agreements on Maritime Safety and Protection of the Marine Environment, Jan. 26, 1982, 21 I.L.M. 1 (1982). The Paris MOU was a regional agreement under which the maritime authorities of a number of Western European port states agreed to cooperate to increase the level of port state inspection and control exercised to ensure that the standards under which ships were operated (including standards relating to ship quality, pollution control and working conditions) satisfied the requirements set out in various international instruments dealing with issues of ship safety and avoidance of marine pollution. The Paris MOU has been followed by the adoption of a number of other regional MOUs, including agreements among maritime authorities in Asia, in Latin America, and in the Caribbean. Hare, *supra.* Work is underway on the development of port state control regimes for the Indian Ocean and for West and Central Africa.

The International Maritime Organization has played an important role in the development of port state control. First, most of the international instruments which establish applicable international standards are the result of the work of the IMO. Moreover, the IMO has continued to enhance safety and pollution control standards by taking actions to supplement or amend the relevant international conventions and to establish standards that are generally binding on all IMO member states. Those Conventions frequently give powers of inspection to the port state, and have been amended from time to time to increase those powers. Second, IMO assists states in establishing port state control measures and it participates as an observer in the regional groups discussed above. Third, the IMO has adopted a resolution that endorses port state control and sets out procedures to guide port states in applying port state control measures. *See* IMO Resolution A787(19). The combination of port state control measures and pressure from the IMO upon flag states themselves to enforce international safety measures means that the problem of substandard ships is increasingly being seen as a problem of bad shipowners rather than as a consequence of ships flying under flags of convenience. *See* Roulston, *Distinctions becoming more blurred*, Lloyd's List Int'l 6, February 11, 1997; Roulston, *Fightback Starts Against Flags of Convenience*, Lloyd's List Int'l 8, Sept. 19, 1997. *See generally* Speech by William A. O'Neil, Secretary–General of the International Maritime Organization, to the First Joint Ministerial Conference of the Paris and Tokyo Memoranda on Port State Control (24–25 March 1998), accessed on September 2, 1998 at <www.imo.org/imo/speech-1/pscontro.htm>.

14. Alan E. Boyle, *Marine Pollution under the Law of the Sea Convention*, 79 Am. J. Int'l L. 347, 347–51, 357–62 (1985).

Protection of the marine environment had not been given much attention at the Geneva Conference on the Law of the Sea in 1958 and the Geneva Conventions had little to say on the subject. States were required by Articles 24 and 25 of the Convention on the High Seas **[Basic Document 4.2]** to regulate oil pollution from ships, pipelines and seabed operations, to prevent nuclear pollution and to cooperate with international organizations in preventing pollution; but these obligations fell a long way short of constituting a general duty to control and regulate all sources of marine pollution or to protect the marine environment, and their content was uncertainly defined, leaving states much discretion in their application. In practice, states enjoyed a substantial measure of freedom to pollute the oceans, and the existing law did not provide for the full range of forms and sources of marine pollution.

By 1973, when the Third United Nations Conference on the Law of the Sea began work, general multilateral conventions had been concluded to regulate vessel-source pollution, dumping at sea, intervention in cases of maritime casualties and civil liability for vessel-source pollution. These did much to refine and develop the sketchy provisions of the Convention on the High Seas, but states were not obliged to adopt them, and their record of ratification and enforcement left much to be desired.... Essentially, the deficiencies of the existing legal regime stemmed from the lack of a generally accepted framework or structure of legal principles capable of dealing with the full range of marine pollution problems and defining comprehensively and with greater particularity the powers and duties of states in all matters of marine environmental protection.

Those general principles which did exist were increasingly seen to be unsatisfactory and ineffective in their operation. The traditional principle of exclusive flag state jurisdiction over vessels beyond the territorial sea had not succeeded in eliminating vessel-source pollution or in protecting coastal states from the threat to their environment posed by the rapid increase in the transport of oil and other noxious substances by sea. Coastal states could respond to this problem by claiming greater jurisdiction over pollution beyond their territorial sea, but this solution, a deeply controversial inroad on the freedom of navigation, was resisted by many. In the absence of widespread recognition of such claims, only the law of state responsibility afforded some general protection and rights of redress for states affected by pollution emanating from sources outside their jurisdiction. But here, uncertainty and doubt over the applicable principles were highlighted by the Torrey Canyon disaster, which quickly prompted the adoption of the 1969 Conventions on intervention on the high seas [Basic Document 4.7] and civil liability [See Basic Document 4.25]. These were useful clarifications of the rights of states to take preventive action or seek compensation from national courts when threatened or affected by oil pollution from vessels, but even when extended to other forms of vessel-source pollution, they still dealt only with a relatively limited and specific problem. Wider principles of state responsibility for damage to the marine environment or to other states continued to rest on inference from a handful of arbitral and judicial decisions concerned only incidentally with marine pollution and formulated at a high level of generality.

* * *

[I]t is the Law of the Sea Convention [Basic Document 4.20] that represents perhaps the most concrete and extensive manifestation of the desire of states to realize the principles and recommendations of the Stockholm Conference and to bring about more effective control of marine pollution. The articles on the protection and preservation of the marine environment that finally emerged as part XII of the Convention represent the first attempt to set out a general framework for a legal regime that establishes on a global, conventional basis the obligations, responsibilities and powers of states in all matters of marine environmental protection. Save for those articles dealing with the deep seabed and the settlement of disputes, no other part of the Convention differs so radically from the Geneva Conventions of 1958 or more fully exemplifies an altered sense of priorities. The articles on this subject are thus of the greatest general significance.

Building on the codification and development of the existing structure of customary law and general and regional conventions relating to pollution, the marine pollution regime is both general, in its application throughout the marine environment, and comprehensive, in including all forms and sources of marine pollution. Articles 192 and 194 place on states a basic duty to protect and preserve the marine environment and an obligation to take all measures necessary to prevent, reduce and control marine pollution and to ensure that activities under their jurisdiction or control do not cause pollution damage to other states or otherwise spread beyond the seas where they exercise sovereign rights. . . .

This structure, and it is only a general framework of powers and duties, not a code of specific standards for particular forms of pollution, reflects a fundamental shift from power to duty as the central controlling principle of the legal regime for the protection of the marine environment. Whereas previously states were to a large degree free to determine for themselves whether and to what extent to control and regulate marine pollution, they will now in most cases be bound to do so on terms laid down by the Convention. For the first time, they are obliged to cooperate globally and regionally in controlling pollution, formulating rules and standards, giving notification of imminent or actual damage and undertaking research and the exchange of information. Again for the first time, there are obligations to provide technical and scientific assistance, especially to developing states, to conduct monitoring and environmental assessments. These obligations serve also to define and elaborate the customary obligation of responsibility for causing environmental damage, which is now placed on a conventional basis. Against this background, it is no longer a power to control, still less a freedom to pollute, that characterizes the legal regime of the marine environment, but a new framework based on obligations of control, regulation, enforcement, cooperation and responsibility.

* * *

Coastal State Powers of Regulation

Faced with the inadequacy of contemporary arrangements for controlling pollution at sea, a strong lobby of states, including notably Canada and Australia, exerted considerable pressure at the conference for a general extension of coastal state legislative powers in the territorial sea and in an extended zone beyond it. Some states, especially Canada, had already begun to claim pollution control zones beyond the territorial sea, but these claims were strongly opposed by major maritime powers who feared that the extension of coastal state legislative control would interfere with the freedom of navigation and might lead to the application of a variety of standards affecting vessels.

There was general agreement at the conference that coastal states should continue to have jurisdiction over pollution in the territorial sea and that, in principle, they should be given jurisdiction to protect and preserve the marine environment within the exclusive economic zone. ... But the extension of coastal state powers over vessels remained controversial; thus, it is not possible to characterize the result of the conference as a straightforward extension of coastal state power at the expense of the flag state. Instead, the creation of the exclusive economic zone involved a compromise between the competing claims of flag states and coastal states: on the one hand, the EEZ regime conferred regulatory jurisdiction over all sources of pollution including vessel pollution on the coastal state; on the other, that regulatory jurisdiction in respect of vessels was limited to the application of international rules for enforcement purposes only.

Thus, although the Convention leaves untouched the exclusive responsibility of the flag state for the regulation of vessel pollution on the high seas, the new EEZ regime does involve a significant redistribution of power to the coastal state in pollution matters over a geographically much larger area. In other respects, however, this change is considerably less radical than some states had hoped. The real debate at the conference on extending coastal state jurisdiction over vessels was not about whether coastal states should have authority over a wider area of sea, but about who should be entitled to set applicable regulations and what these rules and standards should include. Should they be international rules and standards or should coastal states have the power to determine their own national regulations? Should there be limitations on the range of matters the coastal state would be entitled to regulate? Both of these questions were of particular concern to maritime states, whose clear preference for international rules and standards and for excluding construction, design, equipment and manning from the purview of coastal state power the Convention substantially recognizes.

For the territorial sea, the final compromise was not in any sense an extension of coastal state regulatory jurisdiction but a clarification and definition of its limits. Article 17 of the Convention on the Territorial Sea and the Contiguous Zone had merely required foreign ships exercising the right of innocent passage to comply with the laws of the coastal state, insofar as these were in conformity with the Convention and other rules of international law and did not hamper innocent passage. Although the coastal state's regulatory power was therefore not unlimited, it was nevertheless a power to adopt national, rather than international, rules, a power exercisable within relatively broad and imprecise limits. The Law of the Sea Convention contrasts strongly with this by specifying the matters on which the coastal state may legislate, including under Article 21, the safety of navigation, the preservation of the environment of the coastal state, and the prevention, reduction and control of pollution. The Convention retains the basic preference for national rules and standards in the territorial sea, however, and in effect allows the coastal state to adopt its own pollution discharge rules for foreign vessels; there is no requirement that these conform to international standards, whether those contained in the 1954 or 1973 Conventions or otherwise.

There are two important limitations on this power of the coastal state to legislate for pollution control in the territorial sea. The obligation not to hamper, deny or impair the right of innocent passage remains, and the right of innocent passage is itself defined in much more detailed and specific terms by Article 19. Vessels causing pollution will only cease to be in innocent passage if the pollution is "wilful and serious," which probably excludes most typical operational discharges of oil because, though they may be "wilful," they are more rarely "serious." The effect of these provisions thus seems to strengthen the hand of flag states in resisting intrusive legislative inroads on their vessels' right of passage, despite the apparent power of the coastal state to set its own standards for pollution control.

Maritime states were also successful, after much debate, in securing the exclusion of coastal state regulation of the design, construction, manning and equipment of foreign ships unless such rules give effect to "generally accepted international rules or standards." This provision and the reference in Article 23 to special precautions established by international agreement for nuclear-powered ships and ships carrying inherently dangerous or noxious substances are the only places in the Convention where coastal state power in the territorial sea is confined to the adoption of international standards. Although Article 22, which permits the use of sea lanes and traffic separation schemes, requires the coastal state to "take into account" the recommendation of the "competent international organization," this formulation, like other similar ones, seems to leave the coastal state broad discretion to draw up its own national routing schemes. That interpretation appears to be consistent with state practice in the territorial sea.

The territorial sea regime envisaged by the Convention is thus a compromise: it offers coastal states power to control navigation and pollution, while preserving rights of passage and international control of the construction, design, equipment and manning standards for vessels. This result, in substance, endorses the position that had prevailed in practice before the Convention, but by substituting more precise definitions for formerly vague limitations, the Convention preserves the rights of maritime flag states more securely from future erosion.

The extension of coastal state legislative jurisdiction to cover vessel pollution in the exclusive economic zone is more clearly controlled by and limited to the application of international standards. Here the coastal state has jurisdiction over the protection and preservation of the marine environment, but it must have due regard for the rights and duties of other states, which include the right of navigation. Article 211(5) specifies that coastal state regulations for the control of pollution from vessels should conform and give effect to "generally accepted international rules and standards established through the competent international organization or general diplomatic conference." This formulation seems to leave the coastal state no discretion in the adoption of rules and standards. Clearly, it is not entitled to set more onerous rules or standards for vessel pollution than those accepted internationally, but it does not seem able to apply lower standards either, since these would not "conform to or give effect to" international rules and standards. Paradoxically, since regulation of vessel pollution in the economic zone is not obligatory, the coastal state may simply refuse to adopt any rules or regulations. The difficulty of deciding what constitutes "generally accepted international rules and standards" applies here as well, but most delegations at the conference appear to have had the 1973 marine pollution Convention in mind.

Special circumstances in the economic zone are provided for in two ways. Zones of special mandatory measures for the prevention of vessel pollution may be authorized by the IMO ("the competent international organization"). The coastal state may then adopt international rules and standards for special areas promulgated by the IMO, or adopt its own national laws, provided these relate only to discharge or navigation and not to construction, design, equipment or manning. Only within ice-covered areas does the coastal state have a general power to apply national standards to EEZ pollution control, provided they have due regard for navigation and are nondiscriminatory. This exception was a concession to Canadian interests in the Arctic Ocean, but its limited application does not seriously affect the general conclusion that for vessel pollution in the zone, the Convention favors the application of international, rather than national, rules and standards.

All told, this compromise scheme does not add up to the dramatic extension of coastal state legislative jurisdiction over vessel pollution that some states had originally sought. Apart from concessions over special areas and ice-covered zones, the Convention serves the interest of maritime states in ensuring uniformity of standards in the economic zone and, above all, in preserving their ability to influence the formulation of those standards through the IMO. Herein lies the importance of the distinction between coastal state legislative power over vessels in the territorial sea and in the exclusive economic zone. Only in the territorial sea is the coastal state in most respects the sole judge of its interests, within the limits imposed by the Convention. In the economic zone it has no such discretion over the rules it may apply. Not only does that power lie primarily with the states that make up the IMO, but the international regulations adopted through that institution are an expression of compromise and common interest among the various groups represented there, and not merely of the interests of coastal states. For this reason, the articles on vessel pollution in the economic zone are better understood not as an attempt to give the coastal state more power at the expense of the flag state, but as part of a policy of strengthening and making more effective the primary duty of flag states to control their own vessels. In this sense, the coastal state's legislative role in the zone is a secondary or subsidiary one, more important for enforcement purposes than as an example of legislative jurisdiction.

15. United Nations Convention on the Law of the Sea (UNCLOS), Dec. 10, 1982, U.N. Doc. A/CONF 62/122, *reprinted in* 21 I.L.M. 1261 (1982): arts. 1–3, 8, 17–25, 36, 55–58, 86–92, 94, 192–97, 211, 216–21, 233 [Basic Document 4.20].

16. David M. Dzidzornu & B. Martin Tsamenyi, *Enhancing International Control of Vessel–Source Oil Pollution Under the Law of the Sea Convention*, 1982: A Reassessment, 10 Univ. of Tasmania L. Rev. 269, 281–82 (1991).

As a general principle, the LOSC [the 1982 United Nations Convention on the Law of the Sea] **[Basic Document 4.20]** gives coastal States powers to control pollution in their territorial seas in accordance with laws and regulations they may adopt. Similarly, they are accorded jurisdiction in the EEZ to protect and preserve the marine environment. These broad powers are not absolute. In the territorial sea they are subject to the right of innocent passage for all states.

* * *

Coastal states retain their sovereign right to enact legislation to control vessel-source oil pollution in the territorial sea. Even though it would seem that Article 211(1) [of the LOSC] envisages the adoption by States of international anti-pollution rules and standards applicable in all sea areas, including the territorial sea, the coastal State's prescriptive right in Article 211(4) is not required to conform to any such standards and rules. Thus the coastal State's discretionary jurisdiction for this purpose could be used to adopt more stringent discharge standards than may exist under such international Conventions as MARPOL 73/78 [**Basic Document 4.12**]. The context of Article 211 suggests that a coastal state that generally adopts lax anti-pollution legislation would contravene its obligations for pollution control in the territorial sea, under Part XII [of the LOSC].

17. Brian D. Smith, State Responsibility and the Marine Environment: The Rules of Decision 188–89, 198–203 (1988).

The territorial definition bestowed upon the marginal sea of up to twelve miles vests the coastal state with the same expansive prescriptive and enforcement competence enjoyed over any region within the bounds of the state. The Hague Conference reports observed "that the power exercised by the State over this belt is in its nature no way different from the power which the State exercises over its domain on land. Most states have in fact [endeavored] to prevent conduct in territorial waters injurious to the marine environment."

The significant distinction between the coastal state's environmental authority in internal and territorial waters turns, of course, on foreign vessels' right of "innocent passage"....

II. Innocent Passage

a. Evolution

It was not until the middle of the nineteenth century that the concept of a *right* of "innocent passage" in the marginal sea was articulated. Prior to that period, there was some recognition in the literature that non-threatening passage ought to be tolerated by the coastal state. Nevertheless, the [then] contemporary absolutist definition of sovereign prerogative dictated that passage in territorial waters remain subject to coastal state discretion.

The "bundle of rights" alternative to the territorial definition of the marginal sea provided the first theoretical foundation for a right of passage. Proponents of this view simply argued that authority to interfere with vessels in innocent passage was not among the limited jurisdictional rights vested in the coastal state. With the advent of the doctrine of relative sovereignty, however, recourse to a non-territorial definition was no longer required. The acknowledgement of navigational rights as a qualification to state authority even in a territorial sea was not inconsistent with the relativist perspective of the character of sovereignty....

The consensus at the 1930 Hague Conference on the territorial definition of the marginal sea rested precisely on the premise of relativism. The conferees emphasized that "[o]bviously, sovereignty over the territorial sea, like sovereignty over the domain on land, can only be exercised subject to the conditions laid down by international law".[6] Principal among the identified conditions was the right of innocent passage. Article 4 of the Conference text prohibited the imposition by the coastal state of obstacles to the exercise of innocent passage. "Passage is not *innocent* when a vessel makes use of the territorial sea of a Coastal State for the purpose of doing any act prejudicial to the security, to the public policy or to the fiscal interests of that State."

* * *

Even vessels exercising the right of innocent passage were not ... to be immune from coastal authority. To the contrary, the Conference text specifically provided (*a*) that coastal states may verify a vessel's innocence and take steps to protect against prejudicial acts and (*b*) that vessels exercising innocent passage must nevertheless comply with "laws and regulations enacted in conformity with international usage". Among the several species coastal state regulations specifically enumerated as conforming with international practice were laws related to "the protection of the waters of the Coastal State against pollution of any kind caused by vessels" and "the protection of the products of the territorial sea". Implicitly, vessels violating such regulations forfeited some measure of the immunity from local authority otherwise conferred by innocent passage; the extent and import of such forfeiture were nowhere clarified in the text.

[The author next discusses three events in the period intervening between the 1930 Hague Conference and the 1958 United Nations Conference on the Law of the Sea, among them the *Corfu Channel Case* [**Basic Document 8.5**]. The author continues:]

Following this decision, there could be little question that a right of innocent passage had risen to the dignity of a rule of international law. Yet, the decision only directly affirmed the existence of a right with respect to passage in international straits—zones of crucial navigational significance. Moreover, the analysis engaged by the Court raised a subsidiary set of questions as to the criteria of "innocence." Certain commentators ascribed the Court's inquiry into the manner of the vessels' passage to the conclusion that manner is the determinant of innocence. Others voiced the broader perspective that the Court only defined otherwise patently threatening warship passage as innocent due to the unique facts with respect to motivation; but for the evidence that the British intent was only to test the right, the manner of the passage would not have been deemed innocent. The *Corfu Channel* decision, then, illuminated, without solution, certain of the basic uncertainties in the definition and interpretation of the right of innocent passage.

b. *The 1958 Geneva Convention*

The first multilateral forum for the resolution of such uncertainties was the 1958 Geneva conference; having confirmed a regime of sovereignty, the conferees were compelled to define the qualifications to that regime. Article 14

---

6. Observations to Art. 1, Second Comm. Rpt., Final Act, Conference for the Codification of International Law: The Legal Status of the Territorial Sea, League of Nations Pub. No. C. 228 M. 239 (1930).

of the [Territorial Sea] Convention **[Basic Document 4.4]** sets forth the basic rule that "ships of all States, whether coastal or not, shall enjoy the right of innocent passage through the territorial sea." "Passage" is then defined as "navigation through the territorial sea for the purpose either of traversing that sea without entering internal waters, or of proceeding to internal waters, or of making for the high seas from internal waters." Passage is to be conferred the privileges of "innocence" "so long as it is not prejudicial to the peace, good order or security of the coastal State."

Notably, the language of the 1930 draft requiring a "use" of the sea with the "purpose" committing a "prejudicial act" was not incorporated in the definition of innocence.... Presumably ..., the rationale of the deletion of "purpose" was to codify the propriety of the inquiry into *both* manner and purpose of passage suggested, under its most persuasive interpretation, by the *Corfu Channel* decision. Furthermore, by deletion of the references to "use" and "prejudicial act", the Geneva text had the apparent intent to expand the bounds of the analysis of innocence even beyond consideration of actual conduct and its purpose engaged by the ICJ. Activity was no longer a requisite component of the definition of "prejudice" to the coastal state. Hence, the broad language of the Convention generally has been interpreted as establishing the relevance of, and the legitimacy of an inquiry into, additional passive characteristics such as species of cargo and destination.

Article 15 supports the preceding general grant of a right of innocent passage with the statement that "[t]he coastal State must not hamper innocent passage." As with the parallel 1930 provisions, this prohibition was not intended to suggest the absence of coastal state regulatory authority. To the contrary, Article 16 clearly acknowledges the state's authority to take any action to prevent non-innocent passage. Moreover, Article 17 recognizes the coastal state's right to regulate the passage of even innocent vessels with the admonition that "vessels exercising the right of innocent passage shall comply with the laws and regulations of the coastal State enacted in conformity with these Articles and other rules of international law."

One of the principal drafting objectives of these provisions was to disassociate the idea of non-innocence of passage from that of infringements of local laws. In other words, the intent of the participants, not expressed in the text, was to establish an objective definition of innocence. In the words of Fitzmaurice:

> If a vessel infringes such a [local] law or regulation, she may indeed be liable to a fine or other penalty. But her passage does not, merely on that account, cease to be innocent, or become liable to be prevented or denied entirely.... To render a passage non-innocent, there must be something more than a mere infringement of a local law or regulation. There must really be something going beyond the existence of local laws and regulations as such—something that could be considered as tainting the passage even if there happened not to be any specific domestic law or regulation under which it was logically illegal.[7]

7. Gerald Fitzmaurice, *Some Results of the Geneva Conference on the Law of the Sea,* 8   I.C.L.Q. 72, 94–95 (1979).

A violation of law, therefore, justifies prohibition of passage only to the extent that the coastal state law or regulation which has been transgressed reflects the objective definition. McDougal and Burke have succinctly summarized the object and effect of the disassociation:

> For violation of coastal prescriptions ... relating to interests broadly formulated as "peace, good order, or security," the coastal State would be competent to prohibit passage as non-innocent. For failure to comply with other coastal laws, however, passing vessels could not be excluded from the territorial sea but they could be subject to other forms of coastal authority.[8]

The basic issues unresolved by the Convention's approach relate precisely to the character of authority retained by the coastal state with respect to matters which do not rise to the level of implicating innocence itself. With respect to environmental matters, it is quite clear, from the comments prepared in conjunction with the Convention itself and the predecessor 1930 text, that coastal state authority to prescribe and enforce regulations designed to protect the environment against vessels in innocent passage was indeed contemplated by the Geneva participants. Yet, that competence, together with all other coastal state authority, is expressly subject to the rule that innocent passage shall not be "hampered." The interpretative problem, of course, is that any exercise of coastal state legal authority may, to some degree, hamper passage. The very existence of a prescription which requires compliance of all actors within the territorial sea may have a chilling effect on the exercise of the right of innocent passage. This is true even in the absence of any enforcement action taken by the coastal state which physically interferes with innocent passage itself. The penalty for a violation of a coastal regulation may be enforced at another opportunity by methods or actions other than direct physical interference with the navigation of an offending vessel. Hence, the simple presence of rules subject to such subsequent enforcement would constitute an impediment to the exercise of innocent passage by any vessel that might anticipate a violation; the threat of incurring liability may effectively impede the exercise of navigational rights.

The utility of the restriction against hampering passage may be found, however, in its logical implication: a test of proportionality or reasonableness. It is submitted that the object of the "hampering" language must be to strike an appropriate balance among (a) the significance of the interest which the coastal state seeks to protect or advance, (b) the threat to such interest in the absence of prescriptive authority and (c) the character and magnitude of the attendant interference with the exercise of innocent passage. Expressed in its most abstract form, the rule of decision that will lead to such a balance must be one of "reasonableness." Coastal state prescriptions designed to protect minor interests which materially impair navigational rights ... ought not to be tolerated. Such regulations would not survive scrutiny under a test of reasonableness. As unreasonable prescriptions, they must be deemed to "hamper" the exercise of innocent passage. On the other hand, the same degree of hindrance to foreign vessels might well be defined as reasonable in connection with the application of a prescription designed to safeguard a seriously threatened interest of greater significance. Notwithstanding their practical

---

8. MYRES MCDOUGAL & WILLIAM BURKE, THE   PUBLIC ORDER OF THE OCEANS 254 (1972).

effect, such prescriptions should not be viewed as impermissibly "hampering" to passage.

* * *

The reconciliation of the coastal state's right to regulate vessels in innocent passage and the imperative not to hamper such passage is even more difficult in the context of enforcement authority. Even a minor enforcement action, such as detention for inspection, taken against a vessel in innocent passage, directly interferes with the course of its navigation. Indeed, McDougal and Burke, in a critique following the 1958 Convention, persuasively argue that denial of entry to the territorial sea represents a far less intrusive or hampering exercise of enforcement authority than do other acts such as arrest, seizure, or judicial sale.[9] They submit, therefore, that the 1958 provisions which preclude only prohibitions of innocent passage fail to impose limits on enforcement actions of even greater detriment to the enjoyment of navigational rights.

The latter conclusion, however, fails to recognize the applicability of the provision forbidding acts which hamper innocent passage to the exercise of coastal state enforcement authority. The subsumed test of reasonableness would dictate that the degree of interference attendant to any enforcement act must be proportionate to the interests of the coastal state, including the importance of the interest protected, the nature of the prescription violated, the risk of harm in the absence of enforcement, etc. It may indeed be appropriate to immunize a vessel from direct interference with passage caused by the enforcement of a rule forbidding the introduction of pollution, when the violation consists of the discard of a small bin of garbage. On the other hand, a discharge of oil, although perhaps not rising to the level of "serious" pollution, may merit a limited enforcement response such as inspection and brief detention. The prohibition against "hampering" thus provides a flexible rule of decision for determining the reasonableness, i.e. legality, of any exercise of enforcement authority.

Abuse of enforcement, however, represents such a threat to innocent passage that the 1958 [Territorial Sea] Convention text set forth a series of guidelines as to when a coastal state may take any action to enforce a prescription against a vessel in passage. Article 19 first provides that a state "should not" conduct an arrest or investigation on board such a vessel for the commission of a crime during passage unless: (a) "the consequences of the crime extend to the coastal State"; (b) "the crime is of a kind to disturb the peace of the country or the good order of the territorial sea"; (c) requested to do so by the captain or the flag state's consul; or (d) "it is necessary for the suppression of illicit traffic in narcotic drugs." Article 20 then states that a passing vessel "should not" be stopped or diverted in innocent passage for the exercise of civil jurisdiction over a person on board and "may not" be so interfered with for the exercise of civil jurisdiction over the vessel itself for liabilities not related to the current passage. Finally, coastal states are precluded from enforcing extraterritorial prescriptions against vessels in innocent passage not on their way to internal waters; no arrest may be made for crimes committed prior to entry into the territorial sea. It is noteworthy

---

9. *Id.* at 260–61.

that only the text regarding arrest for prior or extraterritorial crimes and civil jurisdiction is unequivocally mandatory. Although the conclusion is not without its critics, most commentators have concluded that the "should not" language in the balance of Articles 19 and 20 was "intended to reflect the fact that the rule enunciated represents standard international practice rather than strict international law."[10]

c. The LOS III Regime

1. Definition of "Innocence"

In basic structure, the regime of innocent passage defined in the 1982 LOS Convention [**Basic Document 4.20**] closely parallels that described in the provisions of the 1958 [Territorial Sea] Convention [**Basic Document 4.4**]. Article 17 commences with a statement of the affirmative right of innocent passage through the territorial sea. Article 18 recites, with certain expansion, the definition of "passage" articulated in 1958. Article 19(1) continues with the familiar language as to the meaning of "innocence": "Passage is innocent so long as it is not prejudicial to the peace, good order or security of the coastal State." The Convention then seeks to reduce the level of abstraction of this definition. Article 19(2) provides:

> Passage of a foreign ship shall be considered to be prejudicial to the peace, good order or security of the coastal State if in the territorial sea it engages in any of the following activities: ... *(h)* any act of wilful and serious pollution contrary to the Convention; ... *(l)* any other activity not having a direct bearing on passage.

... [T]his elaboration represents a deviation from custom and the 1958 text.... Article 19 would deny to the coastal state the legal authority to prohibit passage or exercise plenary authority with respect to vessels discharging pollution unless that discharge is "wilful." There would seem little question that the 1958 Convention contemplated coastal competence to prevent passage to polluting vessels as non-innocent. Indeed, it is difficult to comprehend an argument that the preservation of aesthetic and recreational amenities, resource productivity, related general economic welfare, and the physical well-being of the population does not constitute a core interest embraced in the language "peace, good order or security." The Convention's introduction of a standard of intent is, therefore, perplexing. The polluter's state of mind would not seem relevant to the issue of the magnitude and character of the threat to the coastal state. As one commentator has succinctly put it: "[t]he consequences, including harm to marine resources, amenities, and other coastal resource interests, can be just as prejudicial if a foreign ship 'with gross negligence,' or merely 'accidentally' or 'inadvertently,' causes them."[11] In short, the *mens rea* component of the Convention's definition of innocence is consistent with neither the underlying logic nor the current state of the customary regime.

* * *

10. Gerald Fitzmaurice, *supra* note 12, at 104.

11. Jan Schneider, World Public Order of the Environment 158 (1975) (unpublished Ph. D. dissertation, Yale Law School).

The harm with which a vessel with inherently hazardous cargo or inadequate CDEM[6] threatens the coastal state may occur, on the other hand, absent any intentional activity or even any human agency whatsoever. Accidents do happen. The prejudice to coastal state interests occurs, therefore, merely with presence. Hence the only opportunity the coastal state has to prevent the threat or the actual harm is to deny the right to such presence.

* * *

2. *Prescriptive Authority*

The LOS Convention treats the issue of the prescriptive authority of the coastal state over vessels in innocent passage in substantially the same fashion as the 1958 text. Article 21(1) recites the authority of the coastal state to prescribe laws and regulations in connection with the exercise of innocent passage with respect to a substantial list of matters, including "the preservation of the environment of the coastal State and the prevention, reduction and control of pollution thereof." The provision of the text relating exclusively to the protection of the marine environment underscores this prescriptive right: "Coastal States may, in the exercise of their sovereignty within their territorial sea, adopt laws and regulations for the prevention, reduction and control of marine pollution from foreign vessels, including vessels exercising the right of innocent passage." Finally, the Convention states explicitly the correlative: "[f]oreign ships exercising the right of innocent passage through the territorial sea shall comply with all such laws and regulations."

As in the 1958 text, the basic qualification to this grant of coastal state prescriptive authority is the prohibition against "hampering" innocent passage. With one exception, no provision either elaborates on the definition of hampering or suggests any limitation to environmental prescriptions. That exception is a requirement that coastal state laws applicable to vessels in innocent passage "shall not apply to the design, construction, manning or equipment of foreign ships unless they are giving effect to generally accepted international rules or standards."[12]

18. Editors' Note. Coastal states have always had the authority to control ships and shipping within their internal waters and, to some extent, their territorial seas. Their rights with regard to the territorial sea and the exclusive economic zone are, however, limited by the international navigation rights of other states. In recent years, "a number of states ... have shown themselves prepared to depart from the strict provisions of [UNCLOS] in order to protect their coasts from ship-source pollution. The means used include: establishing regulatory 'traffic' measures that purport to bind foreign transiting vessels in adjacent areas extending beyond territorial waters, although mandatory systems are generally permissible only within them; or requiring such vessels to notify, or even, in extreme cases, seek permission from their authorities before entering the territorial sea, EEZ or other jurisdictional waters." Glen Plant, *The Relationship between International Navigation Rights and Environmental Protection: A Legal Analysis of Mandatory Ship Traffic Systems, in* Competing Norms in the Law of Marine

---

6. *I.e.*, Construction, Design, Equipment, and Manning.

12. LOS Convention, art. 21(2).

Environmental Protection (Ed. Henrik Ringbom, 1997). *See generally* Sixty–Seventh Conference of the International Law Association, Report of the Committee on Coastal State Jurisdiction Relating to Marine Pollution, Helsinki, Finland (London 1996). The legality of mandatory ship routeing measures is questionable, even within the territorial sea, as they could be viewed as hindering the right of innocent passage, especially if they seek to exclude certain kinds of vessels (e.g. single-hulled oil tankers) from particular areas. Nevertheless, three recent amendments to the Convention on Safety of Life at Sea (SOLAS), purport to authorize the International Maritime Organization to adopt (at the request of governments) "state-designated [ship reporting systems] which are mandatory for foreign ships *even beyond the responsible state's territorial waters,*" *id.* at 15 (emphasis added), *see* IMO Res. MSC 31(63), 23 May 1994; SOLAS Regulation V/8–1, mandatory routeing systems, *see* IMO Res. MSC 46(65), 16 May 1995); SOLAS Regulation V/8, **[Basic Document 4.27]** and mandatory (within territorial waters) traffic management systems, SOLAS Regulation 8–2. The IMO regulations specifically note that nothing contained in them "shall prejudice the rights and duties of Governments under international law or the legal regime of international straits," but there is a perceived ambiguity in the failure to mention "freedom of navigation in high seas/exclusive economic zone areas." *See* Plant, *supra* at 15–22.

Article 211(6) of UNCLOS permits coastal states to establish heightened controls on maritime activities to protect the environment in areas of the exclusive economic zone which require special protection. The designation of an area as a "specially protected area" is to be made by the International Maritime Organization, the "competent international organization," on request of the coastal state. The MARPOL Convention defines a "special area" as "a sea area where for recognized technical reasons in relation to its oceanographical and ecological condition and to the particular character of its traffic the adoption of special mandatory methods for the prevention of sea pollution by oil is required." MARPOL, Annex I, Regulation 1(10). **[Basic Document 4.12]**. Agenda 21 seeks to promote this concept by directing "States acting ... within the framework of the IMO" to consider the need for additional environmental protection measures "in particularly sensitive areas identified by IMO." Agenda 21, Chapter 17, para. 17.30(a)(iv) **[Basic Document 1.30]**. In 1991, the IMO passed a *Resolution on Guidelines for the Designation of Special Areas and Identification of Particularly Sensitive Sea Areas,* IMO Res. A.720(17), and has convened several meetings on the concept since then. *See generally* Patricia Birnie, *The Status of Environmental 'Soft Law': Trends and Examples with Special Focus on IMO Norms, in* Competing Norms in the Law of Marine Environmental Protection 31, 54–55 (Henrik Ringbom, ed. 1997). IMO guidelines allow areas to be designated as "particularly sensitive sea areas" when they satisfy a number of criteria. Ecological criteria include whether the area is a unique or rare ecosystem, the diversity of the ecosystem in the area, and the vulnerability of the ecosystem to degradation. Social criteria include the importance of the area for recreation, tourism, science or education. The Great Barrier Reef in Australia and the Sabana-Camaguey Archipelago in Cuba are currently designated as particularly sensitive sea areas by the IMO.

19. International Maritime Organization, Maritime Safety Committee, Resolution MSC.46(65), Adoption of Amendments to the International Convention for the Safety of Life at Sea, 1974, with Annex Containing Regulation V/8–Routeing, adopted 16 May 1995, entered into force 1 January 1997 [Basic Document 4.27].

20. Alan E. Boyle, *Marine Pollution under the Law of the Sea Convention*, 79 Am. J. Int'l L. 365–67 (1985).

In traditional customary international law, responsibility for loss or damage represented the only significant general principle mitigating the freedom to pollute the seas. Although the Law of the Sea Convention exemplifies the transition to a legal regime with an altogether wider foundation, emphasizing obligations of regulation and control, state responsibility remains instrumental in defining obligations to compensate for injury to other states or to the environment caused by pollution. The Convention has made some important changes in these respects and in the related issue of coastal state rights to notification of and self-protection from threatened or imminent pollution.

Injury to Other States or to the Environment

Principles of state responsibility for pollution damage in customary law are usually derived from the Trail Smelter arbitration,[g] the Corfu Channel[h] case and the Lake Lanoux arbitration.[i] These decisions appear to put states under an obligation not to use or permit the use of their territory to cause loss or damage to another state, and it has been assumed that this principle is applicable by extension to damage caused by marine pollution emanating from another state or from activities under another state's jurisdiction or control. These customary principles are expressed at a high level of generality and as regards marine pollution are supported by little evidence of state practice. It has thus been difficult to determine with any degree of particularity the scope and content of primary obligations for whose default states may be held liable to make reparation. In addition, it is uncertain to what extent responsibility in customary law is strict or requires fault, and views differ over the circumstances in which a state should be held responsible for the actions of its nationals. The availability at the international level of declaratory or injunctive relief for environmental damage is also a controversial issue.

Many of these problems derive from uncertainties about the principles of state responsibility in general, and they can only be resolved in the wider context of a review of those principles as a whole. The International Law Commission is at present conducting such a review; the Law of the Sea Convention merely urges cooperation in the further development of the subject. But the Convention does provide that states are responsible for fulfilling their international obligations concerning the protection and preservation of the marine environment, and it now follows that, potentially, they may be held responsible for default of any of their environmental obligations under the Convention. By declaring those obligations expressly and in rather wider terms than hitherto, the Convention offers a surer foundation for the

g. Basic Document 8.4.   i. Basic Document 8.3.
h. Basic Document 8.5.

future development of the law of state responsibility on environmental matters.

Articles 194 and 198 reiterate the basic customary obligations to avoid causing pollution damage to other states or their environment and to notify them of imminent or actual damage, but the Convention has a broader emphasis, concerned with the protection and preservation of the marine environment as such.[13] States are thus required to take all necessary measures to prevent, reduce and control pollution of the marine environment,[14] to prevent pollution from spreading beyond the areas where they exercise sovereign rights,[15] to prevent the transfer of pollution damage or hazards from one area to another or the transformation of one type of pollution into another,[16] and to prevent, reduce and control pollution from the use of technology or the introduction of new or alien species.[17] It is for breach of these provisions that Article 235 seems to contemplate the novel possibility of state responsibility for causing damage to the marine environment unconnected to loss or damage to the interests or environment of other states. This notion represents a considerable departure from arbitral awards like the Trail Smelter or Lake Lanoux decisions, and it is altogether more difficult. The Convention does not reveal how the concept of responsibility, expressed in its customary form as an obligation to make reparation, could usefully be applied to the causing of general environmental pollution when no state has suffered loss as a result. How would the damages be assessed and who would claim them? The Convention offers no guidance on these points and, as with other aspects of the subject, further development in state practice will be needed if effect is to be given to these still rather general principles.

21. *International Environmental Wrongs*, Chapter 5, *supra*, at 323.

22. Alexandre Kiss & Dinah Shelton, International Environmental Law 350, 351, 354–56, 367–71 (1991).

Among the various elements required to establish liability—causality, identifying the wrongdoer, proof and measurement of harm—an issue common to domestic and international environmental law is determining the *legal basis or degree of fault necessary to impose liability*. Traditionally, international responsibility is founded on fault imputable to the acting state. Fault should not be confused with intent; it is not necessary to show that a state intentionally or maliciously violated an international obligation. However, it is generally necessary to show that an obligation was violated and that harm resulted from the violation. Fault therefore exists when the actor fails to perform a duty or observe a standard. However, in general the applicable international rules and standards do not hold a state responsible when it has taken necessary and practicable measures (i.e., exercises due diligence), although . . . some international agreements provide for responsibility regardless of preventive efforts undertaken by the state.

13. Convention, arts. 192, 194(1).   16. *Id*. art. 195.
14. *Id*. art. 194(1).
15. *Id*. art. 194(2).   17. *Id*. art. 196.

One of the requirements that arises from breach of a rule of international law is that the activity causing environmental harm should be abated. However, certain activities which cause or risk causing harm are not deemed illegal, because their benefits outweigh the risks of harm. In such a case, compensation still must be provided the victims of any substantial harm that occurs. The risk-creating conduct is permitted, but the victim does not bear the risk of the injury which results. Instead, a social responsibility is imposed upon the actor to compensate the victims for harm which occurs even though the activity is legal. . . .

* * *

[I]n the *Chorzow Factory* case, the Permanent Court of International Justice, finding the obligation to make reparations to be a principle of international law and even resulting from a general conception of law, indicated the scope and purpose of reparations:

> reparation must, in so far as possible, wipe out all the consequences of the illegal act and re-establish the situation which would, in all probability, have existed, if that act had not been committed. Restitution in kind, or, if that is not possible, payment of a sum corresponding to the value which a restitution in kind would bear, the award, if need be, of damages for loss sustained which would not be covered by restitution in kind or payment in place of it. . . . [18]

Of course, damage suffered must be measurable in the absence of restitution in kind, application of which is still more problematic in environmental matters than in other domains. In international practice, various conventions and drafts state that harm to the environment requires that the state of origin restore the environment to its *status quo ante* and that anyone who carries out the necessary work is entitled to reimbursement if the operation is reasonable. . . .

In evaluating or measuring damages a great deal of uncertainty exists because the elements of the environment often are not viewed as having economic value when they remain outside the marketplace. For example, there may be wide divergences in valuing seabirds killed by an oil spill or the aesthetic value of a clean coastline. In other cases, damages may be estimated according to accepted case law from other fields, including such items as lowered property values due to pollution or lost business due to smoke or noise.

A case of private liability illustrates the problems that arise in measuring environmental damage. The *Amoco Cadiz* case was brought by France and other injured parties as a result of extensive damage to the coast of Brittany from the oil tanker spill. The United States District Court where the case was brought examined in detail the question of damages after rendering an initial decision on issues of liability, discussed below. In awarding the plaintiffs $85.2 million, the court's 435–page opinion[19] addresses the claims made by France, the harmed cities and towns, individuals, farmers, fishermen and environmen-

---

18. Chorzow Factory (Indemnity) Case, P.C.I.J. (ser. A), No. 17, at 29.

19. *In re* Oil Spill by Amoco Cadiz off the Coast of France on March 16, 1978, No. MDL 376, 1988 WL 2796 (N.D.Ill.1988).

tal protection groups. The decision discusses the following categories of damages:

—Clean up operations made by public employees: the claim for costs of the cleanup was accepted to the extent that public employees took time from their regular duties or put in overtime to assist. This extended beyond municipal employees to all public employees, including elected officials and the military. Travel costs incurred in the cleanup also were reimbursed. The time of volunteers was not compensated because their efforts were donated, but the proven costs of transportation, food and lodging could be claimed.

—Gifts made by local communities in money or goods to volunteers or military officials were found to be inappropriate for inclusion in the damage claim, being in the nature of recognition of and gratitude for the services rendered.

—Costs of material and equipment purchased for the cleanup. The Court allowed recovery, less the residual value of purchased items, provided the acquisition was reasonable and the equipment was used, in fact, during the cleanup and that a residual value could be proven. As for previously owned equipment, depending on the evidence the claimants were found entitled to recover either the difference between the value of the equipment before its use commenced and the value thereafter, or a reasonable rental value for the equipment during the term of its use.

—Costs of using public buildings. The damage suffered by buildings during the cleanup operations was compensated. The extra costs arising from use of the building during the cleanup were reimbursed, such as increased water, power, and telephone usage.

—Coastline and harbor restoration. The expenses for these purposes were taken into consideration.

—Lost enjoyment. Viewed as a claim for damage to the quality of life and public services afforded by French towns, the Court applied French law and rejected this claim.

—Los[s] of reputation and public image of the towns. This claim assumed that tourists who would normally have visited the communes for vacation and other recreational purposes went elsewhere due to the deterioration of the beaches. The Court rejected the claim, finding that it was more precisely covered and measurable in individual claims brought by hotels, restaurants, campgrounds and other businesses.

—Individual claims. The Court accepted some of the numerous individual claims, applying as a general rule the loss of income for one year. . . .

—Ecological harm. . . . The Court did not award damages for injury to the biomass, the totality of life in the sea and on the bottom in the affected zone, deeming it complex, attenuated, speculative and based on a chain of assumptions. . . .

* * *

Given the myriad uncertainties and risks of litigation, a plaintiff could become involved in a legal steeplechase where one hurdle after another must be overcome in order to receive compensation for environmental harm. States have introduced special procedures in an effort to reduce the hurdles in two fields where the effects of environmental harm may be the most serious: the production of nuclear energy and the transportation of oil by sea.

The most important of these conventions is the 1969 International Convention on Civil Liability for Oil Pollution Damage [*See* **Basic Document 4.25**], amended for the first time by a protocol signed in London in 1976, and to a greater extent by a second protocol in 1984. There also must be added the 1971 Convention on the Establishment of an International Fund for Compensation for Oil Pollution Damage [*See* **Basic Document 4.26**], also modified by the 1976 and 1984 protocols.[j]

[C]ompensation for environmental deterioration is limited [under the Civil Liability Convention] to reasonable measures of restoration.... Article 3, as amended in 1984, channels responsibility onto the owner of the ship at the moment of the accident, expressly excluding any action against any other person, unless such person acted intentionally to cause such damage or knew that such damage would result from his or her action....

The Convention thus establishes strict liability; it is not necessary to prove fault to obtain compensation....

Article 9 provides that the exclusive forum for actions for compensation is the state or states where the pollution damage has occurred. Any enforceable judgment given by a court with jurisdiction and not subject to further appeal must be recognized in all contracting states, absent specified irregularities in the proceedings.[20]

23.   International Convention on Civil Liability for Oil Pollution Damage, 1992, *adopted on* Nov. 27, 1992, *reprinted in* Civil Liability for Oil Pollution Damage, at 47 (IMO 1996) [Basic Document 4.25].[k]

24.   International Convention on the Establishment of an International Fund for Compensation for Oil Pollution Damage, 1992, *adopted on* Nov. 27, 1992, *reprinted in* Civil Liability for Oil Pollution Damage, at 67 (IMO 1996) [Basic Document 4.26].[l]

25.   Mans Jacobsson & Norbert Trotz, *The Definition of Pollution Damage in the 1984 Protocols to the 1969 Civil Liability Convention and the 1971 Fund Convention*, 17 J. Mar. L. & Com. 467, 467–72, 476–77, 479–81 (1986).

---

j. The 1984 protocols to the Liability and Fund Conventions never entered into force. They were replaced by 1992 protocols which have entered into force. *See* notes k and l, *infra*.

20.   Article 10.

k. This document reproduces the consolidated text of the International Convention on Civil Liability for Oil Pollution Damage, *concluded at Brussels on* Nov. 29, 1969, 973 U.N.T.S. 3, 9 I.L.M. 45 (1970), as amended by the 1976 and 1992 Protocols to that Convention. The 1992 Protocol provides that the 1969 Liability Convention and the Protocol shall be "read and interpreted together as one single instrument" and that the consolidated text shall be known as the "International Conven-

tion on Civil Liability for Oil Pollution Damage, 1992."

l. This document reproduces the consolidated text of the International Convention on the Establishment of an International Fund for Compensation for Oil Pollution Damage (without annex and protocols), *concluded at Brussels,* 1971 U.N.J.Y.B. 103, as amended by the 1976 and 1992 Protocols to that Convention. The 1992 Protocol provides that the 1971 Fund Convention and the Protocol shall be "read and interpreted together as one single instrument" and that the consolidated text shall be known as the "International Fund for Compensation for Oil Pollution Damage, 1992."

Questions of liability and compensation for pollution damage caused by oil spills from tankers are governed by two international instruments: the 1969 Convention on Civil Liability for Oil Pollution Damage (Civil Liability Convention) [*See* **Basic Document 4.25**] and the 1971 Convention on the Establishment of an International Fund for Compensation for Oil Pollution Damage (Fund Convention) [*See* **Basic Document 4.26**]. The Civil Liability Convention lays down the principle of strict liability for the shipowner in respect of oil pollution damage and provides for a system of compulsory insurance. In the absence of "actual fault or privity" the shipowner's liability is limited to an amount which depends on the tonnage of the ship. The Fund Convention is supplementary to the Civil Liability Convention. The main function of the Fund convention is to provide supplementary compensation to those who cannot obtain full and adequate compensation for oil pollution damage under the Civil Liability Convention.... The Fund Convention sets up an intergovernmental organization, the International Oil Pollution Compensation Fund (IOPC Fund), to administer the regime set up by the Convention. The IOPC Fund has its headquarters in London.

The Civil Liability Convention entered into force in 1975 and the Fund Convention in 1978. The Civil Liability Convention was in force in [71] States as of [December 31, 1992].[m]

* * *

APPLICATION OF THE CONVENTIONS TO DIFFERENT TYPES OF
DAMAGE THAT ARISE FROM POLLUTION INCIDENTS

(a) General Remarks

Every year there are many incidents causing oil pollution damage in States Parties to the Civil Liability Convention. As most of the cases are settled out of court by the P & I clubs,[n] there are very few court decisions on the interpretation of the Civil Liability Convention and its definition of "pollution damage."[o] However, from the time it was set up in October 1978,

---

m. For details concerning the States Parties to the Civil Liability Convention and the Fund Convention, see Appendix I ("Status of Basic Documents in International Environmental Law and World Order") in the documentary supplement to this coursebook.

n. The insurance of shipowners' oil pollution liabilities through TOVALOP (a voluntary industry agreement) or CLC is provided in virtually all cases by the Scandinavian and British Protection and Indemnity Associations (P & I Clubs), with their associated pooling and collective reinsurance arrangements. These currently provide a maximum limit of cover, for oil pollution, of $500 million, for any one accident or occurrence. The major risks against which shipowners are indemnified include loss of or damage to cargo, loss of life and injury to crew, passengers and stevedores, collisions and dock damages, and oil pollution liability.

The P & I Clubs are among the most powerful members of the marine insurance industry. These organizations, along with the London-based Lloyd's insurance syndicates, have virtually controlled the setting of marine insurance rates. Their representatives have gathered information at intergovernmental meetings and have actively lobbied their individual governments. In 1969 and 1971, according to R. MICHAEL M'GONIGLE & MARK ZACHER, POLLUTION, POLITICS, AND INTERNATIONAL LAW: TANKERS AT SEA 272 (1979), "it was the United Kingdom with its nine P & I Clubs (the "London Group") and its huge underwriting establishment (Lloyd's) that was the omniscient spokesman for the industry. With the huge foreign exchange earnings the business provides, it is not an industry to be taken lightly."

o. Article I(6) reads: " 'Pollution Damage' means loss or damage caused outside the ship carrying oil by contamination resulting from the escape or discharge of oil from the ship, wherever such escape or discharge may occur, and includes the costs of preventive measures and further loss or damage caused by preventive measures."

until 1 June 1986, the IOPC Fund has been involved in the settlement of claims arising out of 29 incidents. The IOPC Fund has thus acquired considerable experience with regard to the admissibility of claims.... [And] for a claim to be accepted by the IOPC Fund, it has to be proved that the claim is based on expenses actually incurred, that there was a link between the expenses and the incident, and that the expenses were incurred for reasonable purposes.

* * *

(c) Damage to Property and Preventive Measures

Pollution incidents normally cause *damage to property*. The oil may contaminate boats, fishing gear, piers and embankments. Beaches and coastlines may be polluted, necessitating clean-up operations at considerable cost. Preventive measures and clean-up operations may cause damage to roads, piers and embankments, and these would have to be repaired. Damage to property caused by oil pollution clearly falls within the notion of "pollution damage" as defined in the Civil Liability Convention.

* * *

The same can be said of *consequential losses* suffered by owners or users of property that has been contaminated or damaged. The owner of a polluted fishing boat may be prevented from using his [sic] boat for some time while the boat is being cleaned, thereby suffering loss of income.

* * *

The costs of so-called *"preventive measures"* constitute a special kind of pollution damage under the Conventions. The notion ... covers measures taken to prevent or minimize pollution damage. If a tanker incident occurs, it may be necessary to take measures to prevent oil from escaping from a damaged ship, for example by the sealing of fractures. In connection with a spill, measures may have to be taken to contain the oil. Measures are often taken to prevent oil that has escaped form a ship from reaching the coastline, by using booms around the vessel itself or along the coast that is threatened. Dispersants may be used at sea at great cost to combat an oil spill. Costs of such operations are, in principle, to be considered as the costs of preventive measures.

* * *

... The measures must be considered "reasonable" from an objective point of view in the light of the information available at the time when the specific measures were taken. The measures taken must be seen in relation to the threat that existed. The costs incurred must not be disproportionate to the results achieved or to the results which could reasonably be expected.

* * *

(e) Pure Economic Loss

Persons whose property has not been damaged may suffer economic loss as a result of oil pollution ("pure economic loss").... Hotel owners and restauranteurs may lose income due to the fact that tourists do not come to the area because the beaches have become polluted. A reduction in income for such persons may result in a loss of tax revenues for the municipalities concerned.

* * *

Both in civil law countries and in common law countries, there is generally a reluctance to recognize claims of this kind. The reason for this attitude is fear of the far-reaching consequences that the acceptance of such claims could have; it has been referred to as the risk of opening "the floodgates for liability in an indeterminate amount for an indeterminate time to an indeterminate class." The problem is that it is very difficult to find criteria for the admissibility of such claims. In most countries, a claim for compensation is generally accepted only if it relates to damage to a defined and recognized right. Claims that do not relate to recognized rights are in principle not accepted for the purpose of compensation....

* * *

(f) Damage to the Environment

Marine pollution incidents very often cause damage of a type which cannot be easily assessed in monetary terms. Apart from damage to persons and property and consequential or pure economic loss, oil may cause damage to the marine environment. The marine environment does not have a market value as such.

[I]f such damage were in principle included, it would be necessary to establish who would be entitled to claim compensation, and how damage to the environment should be assessed in monetary terms. The present definition of the Civil Liability Convention does not give any indication as to whether damage to the environment as such is compensable....

Eds.—Note: The IOPC Fund established under the 1971 Fund Convention has interpreted "pollution damage" to cover economic loss suffered by persons who depend directly on earnings from coastal or sea related activities, including fishermen and hoteliers and damage to property. [IOPC Fund, Annual Report 1988]. Note that this interpretation does not extend to ecological or environmental damage. The 1984 and 1992 Protocols to the 1969 Liability Convention do provide limited compensation for impairment of the environment and ecological harm "limited to costs of reasonable measures of reinstatement actually undertaken or to be undertaken.... "[p]

Discussion Notes/Questions

1. State practice is one of the components of the emerging international law. States sometimes take unilateral action in defiance of established international norms in an effort to contribute to the development of an international law. Has the United States contributed to the development of a global environmental regime regarding vessel-source pollution by passing the Oil Pollution Act of 1990, Pub. L. No. 101–380, 104 Stat. 484? That act ultimately will require that only double-hulled tankers call at U.S. ports. In addition, the Act imposes strict liability for removal costs and damages upon each responsible party for discharges

p. *See* **Basic Document 4.26**, art. 1(6).

of oil from vessels and facilities into navigable waters, onto adjoining shorelines, or into waters within the exclusive economic zone of the United States.

The double hull and unlimited liability provisions of the U.S. legislation received editorial scrutiny in the Financial Times, Jan. 7, 1993, at 11, in the context of the wreck of the *Braer* in the Shetland Islands. It stated:

> The wreck of the Braer on the Shetlands is likely to become the worst pollution disaster the UK has ever experienced. It has already produced calls for tougher controls on ships in British waters.... An obvious model for the UK to follow would be the US, which passed tough new legislation in the form of the 1990 Oil Pollution Act in the wake of the Exxon Valdez disaster. This sets the toughest standards yet in existence: it required ships to have double hulls for added strength, and imposed unlimited liability on them for the costs of cleaning up any pollution they caused.

* * *

> In acting unilaterally, the US has also complicated efforts to create common international regulations under the auspices of the International Maritime Organization.... IMO regulations will require all new ships built from next July to have double hulls, and all existing ships to be upgraded by 1995. There are also moves within IMO to oblige shipowners to put safety on a par with profits in the management of their operations.

> The problem with the IMO, however, is that enforcement of its regulations is up to the signatory states—there is no international police force. If the Braer disaster leads to stricter policing, that would be welcome. A second weakness of the current approach is the emphasis on the responsibilities of the shipowner rather than the owner of the cargo.

> Under present IMO arrangements, a compensation fund financed by oil-importing countries (excluding the US) will pay up to £54m for environmental liabilities over and above the vessel's own insurance. This is shortly to be increased to £120m. The IMO believes, probably rightly, that this arrangement is preferable to unlimited liability since it provides much stronger guarantee of a pay-out within a reasonable period of time.

> Any significant change in the existing arrangements would have to strike a careful balance between the requirements of safety and the environment, and the commercial need to ship oil....

Are the provisions of the U.S. law dealing with double hulls contrary to Part XII of the 1982 United Nations Convention on the Law of the Sea ("Protection and Preservation of the Marine Environment") [**Basic Document 4.20**]? If so, does the fact that the U.S. is not a party to the LOS Convention make it harder or easier for U.S. practice to generate customary international law?

What about Angloboer? Is its unilateral action to protect its South Narrows consistent with emerging international practice, as evidenced by the IMO's approval of ship routeing systems? *See* Reading 19. Or do international norms require Angloboer to await IMO authorization for its actions?

And what about IMO authorizations? The relevant IMO Regulations [**Basic Document 4.27**] provide that ship routeing systems must be consistent with the rights of other nations under international law, especially rules dealing with international straits. Can Angloboer ban single-hull tankers from the South Narrows consistently with international law? Would it matter whether the South Narrows was designated a "particularly sensitive sea area?" Look again at the provisions of UNCLOS referenced in Reading 15. *See generally* Glen Plant, *The Relationship between International Navigation Rights and Environmental Protection: A Legal Analysis of Mandatory Ship Traffic Systems*, in Competing Norms in the Law of Marine Environmental Protection (Henrik Ringbom, ed. 1997).

2.   The interest of coastal states in controlling the movement of oil tankers and other ships near their shores seems evident from the Readings. But what of the interests of maritime nations in free navigation? Avoiding international straits and other areas within other states' EEZs or territorial waters can add significantly to the length, expense, and risks of a voyage. Do maritime states or states which receive goods from overseas have an interest in maintaining international navigational freedoms? Does the United States, for example, have an interest in the free navigation through international straits of oil tankers carrying mideastern oil to U.S. oil refineries? (Examine a map.) Does the U.S. have an interest in the free navigation of its warships? Even if those ships are carrying potentially dangerous nuclear materials on board? Is the U.S. likely to accede to unilateral claims of right to control navigation where that control hinders the right of innocent passage? If unilateral claims are asserted only against maritime commerce from states too weak to protest, can the claims nevertheless create a new international rule as a result of the lack of protest? Are the U.S. and other maritime nations more likely to view restraints on free navigation as tolerable if they have been approved by an international body like the IMO? Why? *See generally* Stephen J. Darmody, *The Law of the Sea: A Delicate Balance for Environmental Lawyers*, 9 NAT. RESOURCES & ENV'T 24 (1995).

3.   Centrally positioned in the struggle against abusive ocean practices, especially as regards marine pollution, has been, as may be inferred from the above Readings, the International Maritime Organization (IMO), a specialized agency of the United Nations established in 1958 (as the International Maritime Consultative Organization, or IMCO) and since then an important force in the development of international pollution control law. As noted in the Readings, the IMO has sponsored such conventions as: the 1969 International Convention Relating to Intervention on the High Seas in Cases of Oil Pollution Casualties [**Basic Document 4.7**]; the International Convention on Civil Liability for Oil Pollution Damage, 1992 [**Basic Document 4.25**]; the International Convention for the Establishment of an International Fund for Compensation for Oil Pollution Damage, 1992 [**Basic Document 4.26**]; the 1972 Convention on the Prevention of Marine Pollution by Dumping Wastes and Other Matter [**Basic Document 4.11**]; and MARPOL 73/78 [**Basic Document 4.12**].

The IMO's function, which has expanded over the years to meet the increasingly complex needs of maritime activity, is essentially to facilitate intergovernmental cooperation and exchange of information on technical matters affecting shipping and to ensure high standards of maritime safety and efficient navigation. With a membership of 156 nations as of 1998, the IMO has its headquarters in London. It operates through an Assembly (the policy-making organ of the agency), a Council and Secretariat (which perform the administrative and normal operational functions of the agency), and the Maritime Safety and Marine Environment Protection Committees (which serve the needs of their respective specialized interests). As a central force in international pollution control and maritime rule and standard setting, the IMO is likely to play an increasingly important role in the future development of the Law of the Sea. In this connection, see Articles 197–212 of the 1982 LOS Convention [**Basic Document 4.20**].

On the IMO's work on pollution, *see, Competing Norms in the Law of Marine Environmental Protection* (Henrik Ringbom, ed. 1997); Cleopatra E. Henry, *The Carriage of Dangerous Goods by Sea: The Role of the International Maritime Organization in International Legislation* (1985); David W. Abecassis, *IMO and Liability for Oil Pollution from Ships: A Retrospective*, 1983 Lloyd's Mar. & Comm. L. Q. 45; Alan E. Boyle, *Marine Pollution Under the Law of the Sea Convention*, 79 Am.J.Int'l L. 347 (1985); Note, *Environmental Law—A Survey of International Maritime Controls: Prelude to Geneva*, 8 Vand. J. Transnat'l L. 477 (1975); Mario Valenzuela, *IMO: Public International Law and Regulation, in* The Law of the Sea and Ocean Industry: New Opportunities and Restraints 141 (Douglas M. Johnston & Norman G. Letalik eds. 1984). For more detailed discussion of the IMO in general, *see* 1–2 Samir Mankabady, *The International Maritime Organization* (2d rev. ed. 1986).

4.   The IMO Resolution on ship routing systems, **[Basic Document 4.27]**, was adopted pursuant to the tacit amendment/opt out procedure in the International Convention for the Safety of Life at Sea. Under this procedure, amendments to the convention which have been adopted by the appropriate IMO Committee go into force automatically unless a stated number of states representing a high proportion of world merchant fleet tonnage explicitly rejects them. The amendments, moreover, are binding on all Convention parties which do not expressly reject them. What are the benefits of this procedure? Could a similar tacit amendment/opt out procedure be adopted for amendments to UNCLOS? Why might the procedure be less acceptable in that context?

5.   Examine the Liability Convention **[Basic Document 4.25]**. Upon what party does it impose liability? Given that substandard ships are often owned by shell corporations with no significant assets other than the ship itself, what good does the Convention do? What provisions of the Convention ensure that there will be funds to satisfy the owner's liability?

6.   What about the Fund Convention? **[Basic Document 4.26]**. Who pays for the compensation provided by this Fund? Can shipowners receive compensation from the Fund to cover liabilities they incur pursuant to the Liability Convention? In general, who should bear the costs of oil spills: the states through which oil tankers pass on their journey? The states which flag the oil tankers? The states which would have consumed the oil? The ship owners? The owners of the cargo? Someone else?

7.   "In addition to the statutory regimes for liability and compensation," writes Hugh Bryant, *Legal Regimes for Oil Pollution*, 2 Eur. Envtl. L. Rev. 69, 70–71 (1993):

> two very important voluntary plans, to which shipowners and cargo owners respectively subscribe, operate to provide comprehensive compensation and liability regimes, broadly speaking, where the CLC and Fund Convention do not apply. These are TOVALOP, the Tanker Owners' Voluntary Agreement Concerning Liability for Oil Pollution (signed Jan. 7, 1969, reprinted in 8 I.L.M. 497 (1960)) and CRISTAL, the Contract Regarding a Supplement to Tanker Liability for Oil Pollution (signed Jan. 14, 1971, reprinted in 10 I.L.M. 137 (1971)).
>
> TOVALOP and CRISTAL came about as a result of the determination of shipowners and the oil industry to take constructive action to encourage prompt and effective clean-up and to ensure proper and adequate compensation....

Although TOVALOP and CRISTAL are described as voluntary agreements, they are voluntary only in the sense that a shipowner or cargo owner makes a voluntary decision whether or not to subscribe to the contract involved, but once having subscribed, he is under a contractual obligation to carry out that plan stipulated by the agreements.

TOVALOP applies when persistent oil threatens to escape or does escape from a tanker entered in the scheme. The tanker is not required to be loaded with cargo and no spill need actually occur for TOVALOP to apply. This should be contrasted with the regime under CLC, which does not apply if the tanker is empty of cargo or if no oil is actually spilled. The only major exception to this application of TOVALOP is if the spill occurs in a jurisdiction where CLC applies. In those circumstances CLC will operate and TOVALOP will not come into play. TOVALOP [currently, 3/93] provides the limit of liability of $160 per limitation ton, which is about $147 per gross ton, up to a maximum of $16.8 million.

Under TOVALOP, it is not necessary in order to obtain compensation to prove that a shipowner was at fault, and the owner of the participating tanker which spills or threatens to spill oil, either cargo or fuel, is contractually bound to organize spill prevention or clean-up measures. . . .

[I]n practice nearly all the world's tanker tonnage is currently entered in TOVALOP. This comes about because of the understanding between the principal insurers of shipowners' oil spill liabilities, the P & I clubs, and TOVALOP, according to which any tanker entered in one of the International Group of P & I clubs will automatically be entered in TOVALOP as part of the process of obtaining P & I coverage. Under TOVALOP the tanker owner remains responsible for settling his liabilities, and therefore TOVALOP will only accept the entry of a tanker if it is entered in one of the International Group of P & I clubs so that there is certainty that it has adequate insurance to meet those liabilities.

CRISTAL is the counterpart of TOVALOP, devised so that all cargo owners such as the major oil companies, or indeed any company which is engaged in the production, refining, marketing, storing or trading of oil which receives oil in bulk for its own consumption or use, can provide supplementary compensation for oil spills over and above that provided by a shipowner under the CLC regime. At present [3/93] it is estimated that about 80 per cent of the total volume of oil transported by sea is owned by parties to the CRISTAL agreement.

CRISTAL applies when damage has been caused by an oil spill, or the threat of one, which exceeds the limits provided by CLC. In addition, where a CRISTAL cargo is carried, there is a special supplement available to the TOVALOP agreement, which provides for additional voluntary compensation by shipowners entered in TOVALOP, which applies worldwide, i.e., irrespective of whether or not CLC applies, and provides for a further fund up to a total of $70 million. CRISTAL itself provides up to $135 million. However it should be noted that the TOVALOP supplement and CRISTAL do not provide amounts in addition to the total of the CLC and Fund Convention limits, and are themselves related to the ship's tonnage, so that it will only be in cases involving the very largest ships where TOVALOP and CRISTAL will provide funds additional to those available through the CLC and the IOPC Fund.

Do we require legally binding conventions if voluntary agreements can achieve the same objectives? After all, TOVALOP preceded the Civil Liability Convention

[Basic Document 4.25] and CRISTAL preceded the Fund Convention **[Basic Document 4.26].** To what extent are voluntary agreements like TOVALOP and CRISTAL "harder" than traditional "soft" law? *See generally* Steven J. Hazelwood, *P & I Clubs: Law and Practice* (2nd Ed. 1994).

8. In addition to its efforts to develop international standards that contribute to the prevention of oil pollution, the IMO has developed a convention designed to facilitate international cooperation in combating oil spills (or the threat thereof) when they occur. The International Convention on Oil Pollution Preparedness, Response and Cooperation was adopted in 1990 and entered into force in 1995. States party to the Convention are required to establish plans and procedures for dealing with oil pollution incidents. The IMO will develop oil pollution emergency plans for ships, which ships will be required to carry. Ships must report oil accidents to coastal authorities, and coastal authorities must maintain stores of equipment to combat spills and must undertake periodic training exercises. International Convention on Oil Pollution Preparedness, Response and Cooperation, 1990, and Final Act of the Conference, 30 I.L.M. 733 (1991).

9. The disputants in the problem have elected to resolve their differences via a special arbitral tribunal under Article 287(1)(d) of the 1982 U.N. Convention on the Law of the Sea **[Basic Document 4.20]**, and to consider themselves to be bound by international law as determined by the arbitral tribunal. Pertinent in this connection is John Warren Kindt, *Dispute Settlement in International Environmental Issues: The Model Provided by the 1982 Convention on the Law of the Sea*, 22 Vanderbilt J. of Transnat'l L. 1097, 1099–1100, 1105, 1111–1112, 1117 (1989):

> In the context of the United Nations Charter and its concomitant United Nations system, states adhering to the [1982] LOS convention are obligated to utilize the Convention's dispute settlement mechanisms regarding disputes that arise within the purview of the Convention.... [A] unique aspect of the LOS Convention is that instead of being found in an annex as in all similar multilateral treaties of the modern era, the dispute settlement provisions constitute part of the Convention's main text.

> * * *

> [I]t should be emphasized that, with perhaps the debatable exception of part XI, substantial authority exists that the LOS Convention constitutes customary international law.

* * *

III. THE DISPUTE SETTLEMENT PROVISIONS OF THE LOS CONVENTION

[T]he LOS Convention is a well-recognized and widely acceptable mechanism for settling disputes between a multitude of countries. The very size and scope of the Convention argues its authoritativeness in this regard. It stands as the culmination of a vast international effort regarding the law of the sea.... UNCLOS III constituted the largest convocation of nations in history that had as its premise the drafting of an international treaty.... Since the substantive parts of the Convention are the result of "painstakingly" negotiated compromises, the final rules have been widely accepted among states belonging to various regional groups and representing different political, economic, and ideological approaches. Of course, this type of "general acceptance" constitutes one of the major attributes of customary international law and consequently serves to further the acceptance of part XV as binding international settlement procedure.

* * *

The dispute settlement mechanisms of part XV are particularly relevant to multilateral treaties involving marine pollution. The varying sources of marine pollution, the different methods by which it is transported, and the importance placed on activities that cause such pollution, all indicate the potential for disputes and the need for a system of dispute resolution that is both flexible and compulsory. The dispute settlement provisions of the LOS Convention provide these essential elements and should be used as an authoritative reference to guide future negotiations....

See also Alan E. Boyle, *UNCLOS, the Marine Environment and the Settlement of Disputes, in* Competing Norms in the Law of Marine Environmental Protection 241 (Henrik Ringbom, ed. 1997).

In October 1996, the Secretary General of the United Nations swore in the first twenty-one justices elected to serve on the International Tribunal for the Law of the Sea. The Tribunal has authority to adjudicate issues arising under UNCLOS, including issues relating to pollution control and navigation rights. The Tribunal issued its first decision on December 4, 1997, in the case of *Saint Vincent and the Grenadines v. Guinea (The M/V Saiga), reprinted in* 37 I.L.M. 362 (1998).

10. *Bibliographical Note.* For further discussion concerning the principle themes addressed in this problem, consult the following additional specialized materials:

(a) *Specialized Books/Monographs.* D. Abecassis, The Law and Practice Relating to Oil Pollution from Ships (1978); P. Birnie & A. Boyle, International Law and the Environment (1992); D. Boesch, C. Hershner, & J. Milgram, Oil Spills and the Marine Environment (1974); R. Churchill, M. Nordquist, S. Lay, & K. Simmonds, New Directions in the Law of the Sea (1986); R. Clark, Marine Pollution (1986); E. Gold, GARD Handbook on Marine Pollution (2nd Ed. 1997); J. Kindt, Marine Pollution and the Law of the Sea (1986); J. Merrills, International Dispute Settlement (2d ed. 1991); M. M'Gonigle & M. Zacher, Pollution, Politics, and International Law (1979); C. Okidi, Regional Control of Ocean Pollution: Legal and Institutional Problems and Prospects (1978); J. Schneider, World Public Order and the Environment: Towards an International Ecological Law and Organization (1979); R. Shinn, The International Politics of Marine Pollution Control (1974).

(b) *Specialized Reports.* IMCO/FAO/UNESCO/WMO/WHO/IAEA/UN Joint Group of Experts on the Scientific Aspects of Marine Pollution (GESAMP), *Impact of Oil on the Marine Environment*, Rep.Stud.GESAMP (6) (1977); *Safer Ships, Cleaner Seas* (Report of Lord Donaldson's Inquiry into the Prevention of Pollution from Merchant Shipping) London, Her Majesty's Stationery Office (1994). *In the Matter of Oil Spill by the Amoco Cadiz Off the Coast of France on March 16, 1978*, 954 F.2d 1279 (7th Cir.1992); U.S. House of Representatives, *Exxon Valdez Oil Spill Cleanup*: Hearings Before the Subcommittee on Coast Guard and Navigation of the Committee on Merchant Marine and Fisheries (1989); U.S. House of Representatives, Oil Pollution and Compensation: Hearings Before the Subcommittee on Coast Guard and Navigation of the Committee on Merchant Marine and Fisheries (1989); *Implications of the United Nations Convention on the Law of the*

Sea for the International Maritime Organization, study by the Secretariat of IMO, IMO Doc. LEG/MISC/1 of 28 July 1987.

(c) *Specialized Articles/Book Chapters.* R. Becker, *Marpol 73/78: An Overview in International Environmental Enforcement*, 10 Geo. Int'l Envtl. L. Rev. 625 (1998); B. Boxer, *Marine Environmental Protection in the Seas of Japan and Okhotsk*, 20 Ocean Dev. & Int'l L. 193 (1989); Collins, *The Tanker's Right of Harmless Discharge and Protection of the Marine Environment*, 18 J. Mar. L. & Com. 275 (1987); S. J. Darmody, *The Law of the Sea: A Delicate Balance for Environmental Lawyers*, 9–SPG Nat. Resources & Env't 24 (1995); P. Dempsey, *Compliance and Enforcement in International Law—Oil Pollution of the Marine Environment by Ocean Vessels*, 6 Nw. J. Int'l L. & Bus. 459 (1984); P. Dempsey & L. Helling, *Oil Pollution by Ocean Vessels—An Environmental Tragedy: The Legal Regime of Flags of Convenience, Multilateral Conventions, and Coastal States*, 10 Den. J. Int'l L. & Pol. 37 (1980); D. M. Dzidzornu, *Coastal State Obligations and Powers Respecting EEZ Environmental Protection Under Part XII of the UNC-LOS: A Descriptive Analysis*, 8 Colo. J. Int'l. Envtl. L. & Pol'y 283 (1997); P. Edelman, *The Oil Pollution Act of 1990*, 8 Pace Envtl. L. Rev. 1 (1990); E. R. Fidell, *Maritime Transportation of Plutonium and Spent Nuclear Fuel*, 31 Int'l. Law 757 (1997); W. P. Glenn, Jr., *Maritime Commerce: Reducing Environmental Losses*, 9–SPG Nat. Resources & Env't 40 (1995); E. Gold, *Marine Pollution Liability After "Exxon Valdez": The U.S. All or Nothing Lottery!*, 22 J. Mar. L. & Com. 423 (1991); L. Goldie, *Transfrontier Pollution—From Concepts of Liability to Administrative Conciliation*, 12 Syracuse J. Int'l L. & Comm. 185 (1985); J. Hare, *Port State Control: Strong Medicine to Cure a Sick Industry*, 26 Ga. J. Int'l & Comp. L. 571 (1997); M. Jarman, *Marine Pollution: Injury Without A Remedy?*, 24 San Diego L. Rev. 603 (1987); Kindt, *Vessel–Source Pollution and the Law of the Sea*, 17 Vand. J. Transnat'l L. 287 (1984); A. Odeke, *Port State Control and UK Law*, 28 J. Mar. L. & Com. 657 (1997); J.A. Perkins, *Ship Registers: An International Update*, 22 Tul. Mar. L.J. 197 (1997); G. W. Poulos, *Legal Implications of the ISM Code: New Impediments to Sea Fever*, 9 U.S.F. Mar. L.J. 37 (1996); L. C. Sahatjian, *The ISM Code: A Brief Overview*, 29 J. Mar. L. Com. 405 (1998); B. Smith, *Innocent Passage as a Rule of Decision*, 21 Colum. J. Transnat'l L. 49 (1982/83); M. Stephenson, *Vessel–Source Pollution Under the Law of the Sea Convention—An Analysis of the Prescriptive Standards*, 17 U. Queensland L. J. 117 (1992); W. Tetley, *Shipowner's Limitation of Liability and Conflicts of Law: The Properly Applicable Law*, 23 J. Mar. L. & Com. 585 (1992); W.M. Von Zharen, *Environmental Governance of the Seas, the Coastal Zone and their Resources*, 9 SPG Nat. Resources & Env't 3 (1995).

(d) *Useful Internet Sites:* United Nations Division for Ocean Affairs and the Law of the Sea, *Oceans and Law of the Sea Homepage*, (visited Sept. 18, 1998) <www.un.org/Depts/los>; International Maritime Organization, *Safer Ships and Cleaner Oceans* (visited Sept. 18, 1998) <www.imo.org>; Faculty of Law of the University of Cape Town, South Africa, *Marine and Shipping Law*, (visited Sept. 18, 1998) <www.uct.ac.za.depts/shiplaw>.

Problem 8–3

Groundwater in the Middle East

SECTION 1. FACTS

Tiferias and Josiam, once part of two different ancient civilizations, are two developing countries in the Middle East. Josiam is a long, narrow country bordered by the Mediterranean Sea on the west. Isarek–a slightly more developed coastal country also bordering the Mediterranean–and Tiferias, which lies east of Isarek, together form Josiam's southern border. Isarek has attracted increasing numbers of tourists due to its coastal position, while Josiam, although possessed of some livestock, relies upon tourism to supplement its industrial base that is primarily located in the north. Tiferias on the other hand remains predominately dependent upon livestock and some farming.

The western half of Tiferias lies in the Kirbalah Desert, which extends a short distance into Isarek and also into the extreme southern portion of Josiam. An unconfined aquifer lies under the Kirbalah along the border of Tiferias and Josiam. This aquifer is recharged by water percolating through the soil during the region's seasonal rains and also by stream systems which flow from the Hannuk River. The Hannuk itself flows only through Josiam on its way to the Mediterranean Sea, while several of its outcropping streams flow into Tiferias. The river's level and flow fluctuate drastically depending upon the season, and the stream systems in Tiferias are often completely dry. *See* Figure 8.3.

Josiam's once prosperous coastal tourist industry has recently suffered a drastic decline because of rioting and civil disorder, primarily in the north, following political unrest and economic instability. It finds its industrial base unable to support the required economic growth without help from tourism. Since the Hannuk River area is almost exclusively dominated by large industrial companies, making it incompatible with tourism, Josiam has recently begun to look at the desert aquifer as a potential boost to tourist growth in southern Josiam. Up until recently, Josiam's coastal position and the presence of the Hannuk River made it unnecessary for Josiam to utilize the aquifer except for a few wells used by the country's sparse shepherd population.

Tiferias, on the other hand, has always relied heavily on the aquifer to support the water needs of the vast number of shepherds who live in this arid region. Spurred by the growth of tourist trade in neighboring Isarek, the government of Tiferias has recently decided to draw some of those tourists from the coast into Tiferias. To this end, the government of Tiferias, commencing four years ago, embarked upon its Historical Restoration Project near the ancient desert city of Tewbid involving the construction of living museums each depicting different phases of Tiferias' rich cultural heritage.

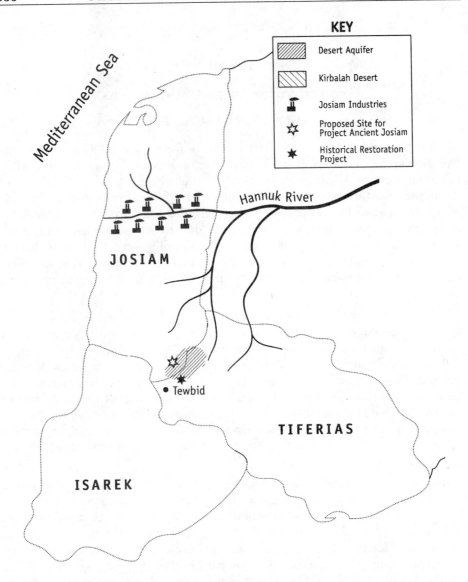

These living museums were constructed around existing historical markers and places, so as to make them both attractive and accessible to discerning tourists. A modest hotel, several restaurants and small gift shops, as well as numerous concession stores were planned. Except for the hotel that is scheduled for construction this year, all other facilities have been completed; and the Tiferian government has built a new well field containing nearly 150 wells to serve as a source of water.

The Historical Restoration Project was an immediate success, and to prepare for future growth, the government of Tiferias has recently made provisions for three further well fields. In taking these steps, Tiferias concluded that it would be cheaper to build more well fields than to develop and enforce a regional water conservation plan. Pumping in the first Tiferian well field coincided with the waning of the seasonal rains, and the three new fields are scheduled to come into flow shortly.

In Josiam, however, shepherds have become increasingly concerned about the effects of Tiferias's extensive pumping of the shared desert aquifer and the falling water levels of their lakes used as watering holes for their livestock. The problem has become aggravated by the influx of shepherds to the south due to Josiam's political and economic problems. Furthermore, the government of Josiam, seeing the success of Tiferias's Historical Restoration Project, has initiated steps to implement a similar project called Project Ancient Josiam. Although Project Ancient Josiam is still in the planning stages, the Josiam government wants to ensure a sufficient water supply for the project.

Aware that the lake water levels rise and fall according to the amount of rainfall, Josiam was nonetheless worried by Tiferias's excessive pumping, and initiated hydrological tests a year ago. The tests determined through the use of dyes and tracers that Tiferias's new well field did indeed contribute to the decline of the lake levels.

Josiam accused Tiferias of using the common desert aquifer in an unreasonable, wasteful manner; and of failing to notify or consult with Josiam before beginning the Historical Restoration Project. Tiferias maintains that its use of the desert aquifer is reasonable, and that its own research studies showed that the well field would have no significant adverse effect on the desert aquifer. Therefore, Tiferias asserts that it was under no duty to notify or consult with Josiam. Additionally, Tiferias claims that as a developing country it is using its resources in the best practicable manner; and that Josiam has not extensively used the aquifer in the past and should not be able to interfere with Tiferias's continuous use.

Even prior to this dispute, both Josiam and Tiferias became concerned about possible disputes involving their common water resources; and recognized the potential for similar disputes in the future, especially due to the scarcity of water at certain points in the year. After negotiations the two countries created a Transboundary Water Commission (TWC) that depends for its jurisdiction on the consent of State parties, and is authorized to apply applicable treaty law and general international law. In light of the seriousness of the present dispute, both parties have referred the matter to the TWC, and agreed to accept and implement the findings of the TWC. Both parties have signed but not ratified the Convention on the Law of the Non-navigational Uses of International Watercourses [**Basic Document 4.30**]. Both parties have signed and ratified the Vienna Convention on the Law of Treaties [**Basic Document 1.7**].

SECTION 2. QUESTIONS PRESENTED

1.   Has Tiferias violated international law?

2.   Has Josiam violated, or will its planned development, violate international law?

SECTION 3. ASSIGNMENTS

A. *Reading Assignment*

Study the Readings presented in Section 4, *infra*, and the Discussion Notes/Questions that follow. Also, to the extent possible, consult the accompanying bibliographical references.

B. *Recommended Writing Assignment*

Prepare a comprehensive, logically sequenced, and *argumentative* brief in the form of an outline of the primary and subsidiary *legal* issues you see requiring resolution by the Josiam–Tiferias ad hoc tribunal. Also, from the perspective of an independent objective judge, indicate which side ought to prevail on each issue and why. Retain a copy of your issue-outline/brief for class discussion.

C. *Recommended Oral Assignment*

Assume you are legal counsel for either Josiam or Tiferias (as designated by your instructor); then, relying upon the Readings (and your issue-outline if prepared), present a 15–20 minute oral argument of your government's likely positions before the ad hoc tribunal.

D. *Recommended Reflective Assignment*

Consider (and recommend) alternative norms, institutions, and/or procedures that you believe might do better than existing world order arrangements to contend with situations of the kind posed by this problem. In so doing, but without insisting upon *immediate* feasibility, identify the particular transition steps that would be needed to make your alternatives a reality.

SECTION 4. READINGS

1. **Stephen McCaffrey, *The Coming Fresh Water Crisis*: *International Legal and Institutional Responses*, 21 Vt. L. Rev. 803, 804–05, 807–09, 810–21 (1997).**

* * *

I. WATER SCARCITY: THE NATURE OF THE PROBLEM

A. The World's Water Supply

The absolute quantity of water on Earth does not change. It is thought to have been the same for billions of years. However, ninety-seven percent of all water is salt water while only three percent is fresh. Of that amount of fresh water, most is locked in polar ice caps and deep underground aquifers—effectively beyond human reach. Only .3 percent of total fresh water reserves on Earth is found in rivers and lakes. The largest share of fresh water that is available to humans takes the form of groundwater, which constitutes about thirty percent of global fresh water reserves. While the quantity of fresh water does not change on an absolute basis, the amount available to each individual does change with the growth of the human population.

B.   Population

While it took all of human history up to the year 1950 for the population to reach two and a half billion, it took fewer than forty years for it to double. And by the year 2000 it will have topped the six billion mark. If present trends continue, the United Nations estimates that after 2100 the world's human population will stabilize at around twelve billion. What does this mean in terms of the availability of fresh water? "In 1850, the average amount of water available per person worldwide was 43,000 cubic meters per year; today it is under 9,000—a change brought about only by increases in population...."[1]

* * *

E.   Water Stress and Scarcity

What does all this mean in terms of the availability of water to humans in the coming decades? Let us take as a yardstick the generally accepted definitions of water "scarcity" as one thousand cubic meters of fresh water or less available to each person per year and water "stress" as between one thousand and seventeen thousand cubic meters of available fresh water per capita. Experts believe that: "By the year 2025, over 30 countries will be unable to provide 1,000 [cubic meters] per person per year, simply because of population growth."[2] That is, in thirty years over thirty countries will be under water scarcity. In some countries the situation is much worse. In 1990, there were twelve countries in which water availability was fewer than five hundred cubic meters per person per year. This number is projected to increase to nineteen by 2025. By the year 2025, thirty-two percent of the global population will live in some fifty-two countries suffering from water stress or chronic water scarcity. By contrast, in 1990, a mere six percent of the world's population were living under these conditions.

F.   Human Use of Water

... We use about eight percent of the world's fresh water supplies for health and sanitation purposes. Agriculture consumes about sixty-seven percent of the available supply. In developing countries the figure is closer to seventy percent. Industrial uses account for roughly twenty percent of the global water supply. This leaves precious little for freshwater ecosystems that nourish countless species of plants and animals and constitute a vital part of the human life-support system.

Human consumption of fresh water is escalating at alarming rates. On a worldwide basis, demand is doubling every twenty-one years. Agricultural use is increasing most rapidly. It is projected to double in the forty years from 1960 to 2000, from about 1500 to 3000 cubic kilometers per year.... The result of all this is that within the lifetime of a person living in regions as arid

1. Peter H. Gleick, *Water Resources: A Long–Range Global Evaluation*, 20 ECOLOGY L.Q. 141, 143 (1993).

2. Peter H. Gleick, *Water in the 21st Century*, in WATER IN CRISIS, 105–06 (Peter H. Gleick ed., 1993).

as the Middle East or North Africa, the amount of available water per capita will have decreased by eighty percent by the year 2025.

* * *

G. Water Quality

Another factor that reduces the amount of usable water is degradation of water quality. While the focus of this paper is upon the quantity of water available to meet human needs, water may not be usable by humans if it is polluted. In fact, contamination of fresh water resources—whether by industrial discharges, inadequate sanitation facilities, or saltwater intrusion—strikes directly at vital human needs such as water for food and drinking. Therefore, considerations of water quality play an important role in determining whether water of adequate quantity is available for human use.

H. The International Dimension

Some forty percent of the world's population live in the 250 drainage basins that are shared by more than one country. These international watersheds make up nearly half the Earth's surface, excluding Antarctica, and some sixty percent of Africa and Latin America. . . .

II. STRATEGIES TO ALLEVIATE WATER SCARCITY

. . . What, if anything, can be done to alleviate these problems? Just make more fresh water, one might suggest, through desalination. But while this is technically possible, it is not a practical alternative for the vast majority of the countries of the world because of the extremely high amounts of energy the desalination process requires. It is thus not surprising that half the world's installed desalination capacity is in the Gulf countries. Instead, it seems likely that the solutions—to the extent that there are any—are much less direct and dramatic. They will have to address the pervasive and diffuse problems identified above, through such strategies as comprehensive water planning, education, integrated management, enhancing the role of women, and increased efficiency in irrigation. These are in fact the very kinds of techniques that are being applied by agencies within the United Nations system and by individual countries as a result of United Nations action. . . .

A. Water Scarcity and the United Nations

The United Nations has been active in this field for some time. . . .

The latest United Nations-based effort to address fresh water problems is found in Chapter 18 of Agenda 21, the program of action in the field of environment and development adopted at the United Nations Conference on Environment and Development (UNCED) in June 1992. To avoid confusion, it should be noted at the outset that Agenda 21 is not a binding legal instrument, as is sometimes thought. It was, however, unanimously adopted by 178 states participating in UNCED, indicating a broad measure of support for its programs. Agenda 21 is already being applied and implemented widely, both by states and by international organizations.

Chapter 18 is entitled "Protection of the Quality and Supply of Freshwater Resources: Application of Integrated Approaches to the Development, Management and Use of Water Resources." The ambitious "general objective" of the program contained in Chapter 18 is stated as follows: "to make certain that adequate supplies of water of good quality are maintained for the entire population of this planet, while preserving the hydrological, biological and chemical functions of ecosystems, adapting human activities within the capacity limits of nature and combating vectors of water-related diseases."[3] With regard to water scarcity, the Chapter states in its introductory paragraphs that "widespread scarcity, gradual destruction and aggravated pollution of freshwater resources ... demand integrated water resources planning and management" that "must cover all types of interrelated freshwater bodies, including both surface water and groundwater, and duly consider water quantity and quality aspects."[4]

* * *

The United Nations Commission on Sustainable Development (CSD) was established by the General Assembly on the recommendation of UNCED to oversee the implementation of Agenda 21. At its second session in 1994, the CSD noted "with great concern that many countries are facing a water crisis, with rapid deterioration of water quality, serious water shortages and reduced availability of freshwater, which severely affect human health, the ecosystem and economic development...."[5] It recognized "that the crisis needs urgent and concrete action by national Governments as well as international organizations in order to implement Chapter 18 of Agenda 21, particularly by supporting developing countries...."[6]

B. The Role of Law

* * *

1. Agenda 21

We start from the premise that Agenda 21 does not contain legally binding obligations. But its recommendations in each of the seven program areas are intended to be taken into account by states in enacting or updating water-related legislation. In this sense, Agenda 21, and Chapter 18 in particular, is a blueprint for legislative action in the field of the protection and management of fresh water resources.... [W]e do know that a wide array of international organizations in the United Nations system—including, importantly, international financial institutions such as the World Bank—are actively implementing Agenda 21, including its fresh water programs, and are assisting states with their own implementation efforts. Thus, it appears that the fresh water program of Agenda 21 is being gradually implemented—not because it has the force of law, but because governments realize that it is in their own self-interest to do so....

3. Agenda 21: Programme of Action for Sustainable Development, Rio Declaration on Environment and Development, State of Forest Principles, the Final Text of Agreements Negotiated by Governments at the United Nations Conference on Environment and Development (UNCED), June 3–14, 1992, introduction at 3, Rio De Janeiro, Brazil, U.N. Doc. A/CONF. 151/5. **[Basic Document 1.30].**

4. *Id.* para. 18.3.

5. Commission on Sustainable Development, U.N. ESCOR, 2d Sess., Supp. No. 13, para. 133, U.N. Doc. E/CN.17/1994/20/Rev.1 (1994).

6. *Id.* para. 135.

2.   Institutional Approaches to Water Scarcity

It is widely recognized by experts in the field that any strategy to address water scarcity must employ basin-wide, integrated planning and management. On the international level, this is difficult to achieve without a mechanism for ongoing communication between the countries concerned, such as a joint commission. On both the national and international levels, water resources are best protected and managed as a unit, that is, by the drainage basin as a whole, rather than parts thereof. . . .

3.   Water Scarcity and Sustainable Development

The concept of sustainable development plays a pervasive role in strategies to avoid and alleviate water scarcity; development that exacerbates conditions of water scarcity cannot be sustainable. And development is virtually guaranteed to be unsustainable unless it is based upon basin-wide, integrated planning and management of fresh water resources.

As far as legal principles for sustainable development are concerned, efforts have been, and are being made, to define such principles. . . . About the most that can be said at this stage is that general principles such as those of prevention, precaution, environmental impact assessment, polluter pays (in the sense at least of cost internalization), and citizen participation should be included among the principles of international law for sustainable development. However, it is not yet entirely clear whether these principles operate on the inter-state or the national level, or both. For problems of water scarcity to be addressed effectively, it is essential that the principles be implemented on both levels.

4.   Water Scarcity and International Human Rights Law

. . . While the international community, as well as individual states, have an obligation to come to the assistance of these deprived individuals, it does not appear that as a practical matter human rights law presently offers much hope to the vast majority of those in grave need of access to potable water and adequate sanitation services.

The purported "controversy" between those who would treat water as an economic good and those urging that water is a human right has not been helpful. There is broad agreement that users should be charged appropriately for water lest it be overconsumed, especially by economic activities such as industry and agriculture. But what is "appropriate" will, of course, vary with the ability of the user to pay. Those below the poverty line should not have to pay for water required for basic needs, which means that governments will have to subsidize their water from fees paid by other users who are better off.

5.   The Law of International Watercourses

It may happen, of course, that one country's use of the waters of an international watercourse is at least partly responsible for water scarcity in another country. This problem is likely to arise with increasing frequency due to the large number of international drainage basins in the world as well as the location of many of them in water-short regions. In the absence of an applicable treaty between the states concerned, the situation would be governed by rules of general international law. In 1994, the International Law

Commission of the United Nations (ILC) completed work on a set of draft articles on the Law of the Non–Navigational Uses of International Water-courses.[a] In short, the draft would require a state to notify other potentially affected states of any planned activity that might be harmful to those other states, and to consult and negotiate with them in good faith concerning the plans. It also requires states to use international watercourses in an equitable and reasonable manner, and to refrain from uses that would cause other states significant harm. . . .

These general rules—many of which are undoubtedly part of customary international law—are already being cited and relied upon by governments in disputes over international watercourses. . . . Rules of international law cannot by themselves alleviate the scarcity of water, but they can both prevent one state from causing another to suffer needlessly from it, and promote cooperative efforts by states in managing their shared water resources to avoid conditions of water scarcity to the extent permitted by natural conditions.

III. OUTLOOK

There is really no need to wait until the next century for a glimpse of things to come. Fantastic schemes have already been proposed, and even tried, for bringing water to areas under water stress or scarcity. . . . The legal questions raised by these schemes are manifold, difficult, and important. But a fundamental question that will have to be addressed as water resources continue to dwindle is who "owns" the water in constant motion in the hydrologic cycle? Is this not a classic "common pool resource" that should be shared equitably by the international community? More concretely, is an iceberg floating in the sea beyond the limits of national jurisdiction res nullius, so that it is subject to appropriation? Or is it res communis, subject to allocation only by the international community?

These questions lead me to inquire whether the day is far away when water-short states begin to assert a "right" to a portion of the water that evaporates from areas of the sea beyond the limits of national jurisdiction. While such a claim might seem far-fetched at first blush, this would not be the first time international law recognized rights of states in natural resources located in "the commons" because those states were geographically disadvantaged. As is well known, somewhat similar rights were conferred upon landlocked and geographically disadvantaged states in respect to the living resources of the sea by the United Nations Convention on the Law of the Sea (UNCLOS) [Basic Document 4.20]. For example, article 70, paragraph 1 of UNCLOS provides:

> Geographically disadvantaged States shall have the right to participate, on an equitable basis, in the exploitation of an appropriate part of the surplus of the living resources of the exclusive economic zones of coastal States of the same subregion or region, taking into account the relevant economic and geographical circumstances of all the States concerned and in conformity with the provisions of this article and of articles 61 and 62.[7]

a. These Draft Articles provided the basis for the Treaty of the Law of the Non-navigational Uses of International Watercourses [Basic Document 4.30].

7. The Law of the Sea, United Nations Convention on the Law of the Sea, at 24–25

The expression "geographically disadvantaged states" is defined as:

[C]oastal States ... whose geographical situation makes them dependent upon the exploitation of the living resources of the exclusive economic zones of other States in the subregion or region for adequate supplies of fish for the nutritional purposes of their populations or parts thereof, and coastal States which can claim no exclusive economic zones of their own.[8]

... It is clear ... that the above-quoted provisions recognize rights in states for which geography has caused hardships, which is precisely the case with regard to the arid states of the world. And the rights the articles recognize are in fact entitlements to an equitable share of natural resources that would otherwise be under the jurisdiction of other states. The fact that the international community has accepted such rights represents a recognition that states should not have to suffer geographically-caused hardships alone. Rather, other states that are more fortunate may be called upon to share their resources, on an equitable basis, with those that are disadvantaged, as a matter of international solidarity. The same principles would seem to apply with equal or greater force to the sharing of fresh water.

* * *

2. JOSEPH L. SAX ET AL, LEGAL CONTROL OF WATER RESOURCES: CASES AND MATERIALS 448–50 (2d ed. 1991).

I. THE CONNECTION OF GROUNDWATER AND SURFACE FLOWS

Modern hydrogeology has established the fact that much groundwater and surface water is related. Depending on local geologic conditions, groundwater can feed streams or drain them. Streams that gain water from groundwater are called "effluent streams"; streams that leak water into the underlying aquifer where it eventually becomes a part of the stored stock of groundwater are called "influent streams." [Many] legal disputes ... arise because of the longstanding practice of assigning water rights to groundwater and surface water separately without taking full account of the fact that the water involved is part of a single hydrologically integrated source.

In a major article on the subject, Professor Davis ... summarizes the relationship between groundwater and streamflow:

Groundwater will return to the surface at any point where the water table reaches the level of the surface, as at springs, or where it is higher than the level of a stream. Such a stream, which is fed by groundwater flow, is designated an effluent stream.... [T]here is a hydrologic relationship between the stream and the percolating groundwater supply.[9]

The understanding of how groundwater and surface water is linked has not always been so well defined, and that difference in understanding of natural processes accounts for some of the doctrinal development of groundwater law.... Just as the lack of detailed knowledge of hydrogeology shaped

[Basic Document 4.20] (addressing these rights specifically as the "Right of land-locked States" and the "Right of geographically disadvantaged States").

8. *Id.* Articles 61 and 62 concern, respectively, conservation and utilization of living resources. *See id.*

9. P. Davis, *Wells, and Streams: Relationship at Law,* 37 Mo.L.Rev. 189, 196–97 (1972).

groundwater law in its assignment of liability for harms done to other groundwater users, that lack of knowledge also helps to explain why the law of groundwater emerged as an independent body of law, unconnected to the law of surface waters.

With the establishment of independent bodies of groundwater and surface water law, it was inevitable that cases of conflict over the use of hydrologically linked water would arise in which the respective groundwater and surface water users would each claim their use to be legal under the body of law governing their water source.... Taking as a typical case dewatering of an influent surface stream in a riparian jurisdiction caused by groundwater withdrawals made pursuant to the absolute ownership doctrine, the conflict is patent. If the case is judged under surface water law, the riparian is entitled to at least a proportioned use of the stream that would require the other users of the stream to curtail their use. If the case is decided according to groundwater precepts, the groundwater user is privileged to withdraw the water without liability or curtailment. By choosing reparianism as the surface water law and absolute ownership as the groundwater law, the example ... highlights the conundrum, but the choice of those legal doctrines is not essential. The same problem of dis-integration of governing law can arise in the case of a prior in time surface water senior being displaced by a newly initiated groundwater user taking water lawfully under any of the five groundwater doctrines, even an independently administered prior appropriation system for groundwater.

Historically, the courts did not resolve these conflicts in a consistent manner. In his study of the reported cases from the East and Midwest, Professor Davis found courts roughly equally divided in their choice of whether to apply groundwater law or surface water law to define the rights of the affected parties. To address the arbitrariness inherent in such mixed results, Professor Davis felt that improvement in understanding of hydrogeology ought to be reflected in the law. He described the advances in measurement of groundwater movement:

> The two methods that have been developed to measure groundwater movements are clearly expensive. The first method involves putting in a pattern of test wells. Groundwater is pumped from one of the centrally located wells at a constant rate and the fall in the water table in the other observation wells is measured at intervals, in time. The correlation of the pumping rate and the fall in the water table at the various observation wells, which reveals the dimensions of the cone of depression, allows computation of the effective transmissibility of the aquifer and its coefficient of storage, and reveals the hydrogeologic boundaries, impermeable discontinuities and potential recharge boundaries of the aquifer. The second method involves the injection into groundwater of a slug of tracer, often a fluorescent dye, which is carried along with the moving groundwater to observation wells below. Within the limits imposed by the diffusion, dispersion, dilution and absorption of the tracer, this method allows the determination of the direction and rate of flow of groundwater.[10]

To put that knowledge to work, Professor Davis advocated making the groundwater user liable for foreseeable interference with surface water users

---

10. *Id.* at 235.

and outlined the situations in which the groundwater user ought to have knowledge of the likely consequences of intended actions:

> Since information about groundwater movement can now be made available by routine methods, the assumption that it is unknown can no longer justify the absolute ownership and reasonable use rules of groundwater. However, the contention that the groundwater user should not be subject to liability when he cannot predict in advance the injurious consequences of groundwater use still has validity. The reason is that the tests necessary to determine groundwater movements and injurious consequences are expensive. It would seem unjust to impose liability on a landowner who cannot afford to make these tests, when he has not made them, by charging him with constructive knowledge of what he would have learned. But it also seems ludicrous to presume that a landowner does not know the results of such tests when, in fact, he has made them. There are decisions of this kind, and some courts have wisely balked at denying relief in this situation. The high-capacity well pumping situation is typical. No competent man is going to put in an extremely expensive large well, for municipal purposes for example, unless he has first made hydrologic tests to determine whether there is enough groundwater available to feed the well.[11]

3. DAVID H. GETCHES, WATER LAW IN A NUTSHELL 237–41, 272 (3d. ed. 1997).

I. BASIC HYDROLOGY

A. How Groundwater Occurs

1. *Permeability of Rock Formations*

Occurrence and movement of groundwater are governed by the laws of physics and local geological conditions. Although groundwater can occur in the form of underground streams, most groundwater is percolating water stored in the pores, or interstices, of rock formations....

Porosity is the measure of the amount of open space within rock. It is defined as the percentage of the rock's total volume occupied by pore space. Other factors being equal, the greater the porosity, the more freely water can move through the rock and the more water that can be stored within.

... The porosity of a volume of [a particular ground substance] may equal that of [a different type of ground substance], but the *permeability* (... ability to transmit water) [may be different].... Groundwater is often in permeable formations that are bounded and contained by impermeable formations.

* * *

3. *Aquifers*

Aquifers may be thought of as underground reservoirs. They are rock formations that yield water in significant quantities. Thus, a formation with low permeability may not be an aquifer, even if porous and saturated with

11. *Id.* at 233–34.

water, because the water is liberated at a rate too slow to be of use. Aquifers may be confined or unconfined. Most common are *unconfined aquifers*, in which the water exists under normal atmospheric pressure. Unconfined aquifers must be pumped to withdraw the water. *Confined* or *artesian aquifers*, by contrast, are under a pressure greater than that of the atmosphere. This pressure is generated when the aquifer is squeezed between overlying and underlying impermeable strata. If the positive pressure is great enough, the water in a well may rise to the surface without pumping, but any pressure sufficient to raise the water above the top of the zone of saturation (water table) is sufficient to make the aquifer artesian.

* * *

Aquifers are initially filled with water either by geological processes occurring when the rock was created (*connate water*) or by subsequent sources such as rainfall (*meteoric water*). Typically, an aquifer is recharged by precipitation falling or flowing where the aquifer outcrops on the surface; it may also be recharged by surface or underground streams. The rate of recharge, like the rate of water movement, varies greatly and is a function of geologic conditions. Some aquifers get no recharge; others recharge so slowly that it takes millions of years to fill them.

Geologists call the amount of water an aquifer will yield without depletion the *"safe yield."* The term has also been used by economists, courts, and legislatures to describe rates of depletion in excess of recharge, but which are viewed as reasonable in light of current demands for the water. When withdrawals from any aquifer exceed its recharge, an overdraft or *mining* condition is said to exist.

* * *

III. CONJUNCTIVE USE

A. Regulation of Groundwater Connected With Surface Sources

1. Interaction of Groundwater and Surface Water

Groundwater is often hydrologically connected to surface streams. For example, seepage from a stream may charge an underlying aquifer. The surface flow of a stream may "ride piggyback" upon the groundwater contained in the aquifer beneath the stream. Or, a stream may be fed by seepage from aquifers.... In these situations, stream water use may diminish water in the aquifer and withdrawals of groundwater may diminish surface flow. Some states call such interconnected groundwater sources "tributary."

4. GEORGE A. GOULD & DOUGLAS L. GRANT, CASES AND MATERIALS ON WATER LAW 318–19 (5th ed. 1995).

1. Under natural conditions, water in an aquifer moves slowly from areas of recharge to areas or points of discharge. Over millennia, an aquifer undeveloped by wells reaches a state of equilibrium in which average natural recharge over a climatic cycle approximately equals natural discharge. The introduction of wells into the aquifer disrupts the natural equilibrium in one or more of three ways, as explained by the following definition of the hydrologic term "capture": "Water withdrawn artificially from an aquifer is

derived from a decrease in storage in the aquifer, a reduction in the previous discharge from the aquifer, an increase in the recharge, or a combination of these changes. The decrease in discharge plus the increase in recharge is termed capture. [. . .]'' [citation omitted]. Capture is a crucial concept in the management of groundwater storage: withdrawals by wells in excess of capture will reduce storage.

* * *

2.   One adverse consequence of groundwater level decline is an increase in the cost of withdrawing water as wells need to be deepened. Other physical problems that may accompany declining water levels, depending on the physical conditions, are the following: land surface subsidence; aquifer compaction, resulting in loss of transmissivity and storage capacity; intrusion into the aquifer of oceanic saltwater or poor quality water from a neighboring aquifer; and depletion of surface lakes, streams, and wetlands. In addition, economic and social dislocations may result from the eventual physical or economic depletion of an aquifer.

* * *

3.   Absent controls of some sort, overdepletion or overrapid depletion of storage is likely because of the usual "common pool" nature of groundwater. If a groundwater pool is shared by users, as it usually is, there is little incentive for individual users to conserve the water in storage for future use because water not pumped now will be taken by someone else. This results in the parties undervaluing and overusing water presently.

5.   Stockholm Declaration of the United Nations Conference on the Human Environment adopted by the UN Conference on the Human Environment at Stockholm, June 16, 1972, Principles 1–3, 5, 8, 13, 21, 22, Report of the UN Conference on the Human Environment, June 15–16, 1972, U.N. Doc. A/CONF.48/14/Rev. 1 at 3 (1973); UN Doc. A/CONF.48/14 at 2–65 and Corr. 1 (1972), 11 I.L.M. 1416 (1972). [Basic Document 1.12].

6.   Rio Declaration on Environment and Development, June 13, 1992, Principles 1–9, 12, 13, UNCED Doc. A/CONF.151/5/Rev. 1, 31 I.L.M. 874. [Basic Document 1.29].

7.   Julio Barberis, *The Development of International Law of Transboundary Groundwater*, 31 Nat. Resources J. 167, 169–72, 175–78, 186, (1991).

The harm that one State may cause another in connection with a given aquifer could affect the quantity or quality of the water or its geological structure. The quantity of water in an aquifer can be adversely affected by exploitation in excess of its rate of recharge or by a modification of its sources of supply. Supply modification may occur, for example, if any artificial alteration is made in the volume of flow of a river feeding the aquifer or if any modification occurs in the terrain in the natural recharge area. . . .

Deterioration in water quality, or pollution of water, includes any impairment in composition or content due to human agents. . . .

International law obligates each State not to cause harm to another.[12] This obligation includes direct State action within its own territory and each State's duty to insure that its territory is not used in a manner injurious to other countries. This rule is reaffirmed in principle 21 of the Stockholm Declaration **[Basic Document 1.12]**, which reads:

> States have, in accordance with the Charter of the United Nations and the principles of international law, the sovereign right to exploit their own resources pursuant to their own environmental policies, and the responsibility to ensure that activities within their jurisdiction or control do not cause damage to the environment of other States or of areas beyond the limits of national jurisdiction.

Recommendation 90 of the U.N. Water Conference stresses the need to apply this principle to shared water resources. With particular reference to groundwater, this same principle is stated in article 3 of the agreement of February 27, 1974, between Czechoslovakia and the German Democratic Republic. It is clear that the damage should be of certain magnitude and not a mere inconvenience. This rule has developed through general and constant practice, and is accordingly recognized as a customary rule. Doctrine also shares this view.

Resolution 2995 (XXVII) of the United Nations General Assembly [U.N.Doc. A/8730 (1973)] also acknowledges this principle and states:

> The General Assembly ... emphasizes that, in the exploration, exploitation and development of their natural resources, States must not cause significant harmful effects in zones situated outside their national jurisdiction.

Where groundwater is concerned, a number of treaties make express reference to the rule which requires that no appreciable harm should be caused.

* * *

Hence international law prohibits States from causing appreciable damage to other States. Current doctrine extends this prohibition by including not only cases of actual appreciable harm but also those involving serious risk, for example, the siting of a nuclear power station close to international boundaries which endangers boundary aquifers with radioactive pollution.

* * *

... This customary [obligation not to cause appreciable harm] applies to the conduct of the State that exploits a resource in neighboring territories. The other basic rule governing the use of shared natural resources is that such use must be equitable and reasonable. This idea is commonly expressed in terms of "equitable utilization" or "equitable apportionment." The rule enjoys wide acceptance today and is part of general international law.

The concept of equitable/reasonable use for international aquifers should be considered from two standpoints: from the use itself and from the way in which the derived benefits are to be apportioned between States. In other

---

12. Island of Palmas Case (U.S. v. Neth.), 2 U.N.R.I.A.A. 829, 839 (1928); Trail Smelter Case (U.S. v. Can.) **[Basic Document 8.4 and Chapter 5(A) at 340, *supra*]**.

words, the use made of groundwater must be reasonable and equitable, and so must the apportioning of the benefits.

In recent decades, the increasing demand [for] groundwater, and the adverse effects of excessive withdrawals in certain aquifers, have made States aware of the need to manage and regulate their use according to predetermined needs. In this sense, reasonable use of an aquifer means to preserve the resource by adapting withdrawals to the recharge regime. Likewise, reasonableness is linked to a certain order in the exploitation according to differing requirements. For example, it would be unreasonable to use an aquifer mainly to supply ornamental fountains or boating ponds to the detriment of people who need drinking water.

The general rule of reasonable use can be found in principle 2 of the Stockholm Declaration **[Basic Document 1.12]**:

> The natural resources of the earth including air, water, land, flora and fauna and especially representative samples of natural ecosystems must be safeguarded for the benefit of present and future generations through careful planning or management, as appropriate.

Recommendation 51, c, v of the same Conference also refers to the "rational use of water resources."

The African Convention on the Conservation of Nature and Natural Resources **[Basic Document 6.4]**, which includes groundwater, establishes "rational utilization" as one of its objectives. Among the bilateral agreements dealing with groundwater, the one between the German Democratic Republic and Czechoslovakia (1974) prescribes, in article 5, specific measures tending to secure reasonable use (rationelle Nutzung) of transboundary waters. However, the most complete document on the subject of present study is unquestionably the "Declaration of Principles on the Rational Use of Water" adopted by the Economic Commission for Europe in 1984 in decision C (XXXIX).

Reasonable use of a natural resource also implies securing the maximum possible yield. This is referred to as "optimization." Article 3 of the Charter of Economic Rights and Duties of States **[Basic Document 7.2]** makes express reference to it. The bilateral agreement on groundwater between the German Democratic Republic and Poland[13] also requires that the users secure maximum yield through optimization.

The apportionment of the benefits between countries sharing an aquifer must also be equitable and reasonable. The distribution must be carried out so that each country obtains the maximum satisfaction for its needs with non-existent or minimum harmful effects. This does not require a mathematically equal distribution of benefits among the sharing countries, but instead requires distribution according to the needs of each State.

When the equitable utilization rule is applied, the respective States' total benefits and inconveniences caused by groundwater withdrawals must be considered. Thus, an application of the rule may result in an aquifer use that will yield noticeable benefits for several States in terms of water supply for people and livestock, yet will result in appreciable disadvantages to irrigation in a given area of one of those States. Benefits and disadvantages are not

---

13. Bilateral Agreement on Groundwater Between German Democratic Republic and Poland, art. 3(2) (Gesetzblatt der Deutschen Demokratischen Republik, 1967, I. No. 11, 95).

assessed separately for the respective uses of water, but rather are done jointly. In this case, allowances must be made not only for economic but also for social and cultural factors ..., such as education, customs, lifestyle of the population, and their own scale of values.

The Stockholm Conference on the Environment refers to the equitable utilization rule, in its recommendation 51(b)(iii), which states that: "the net benefits of hydrologic regions common to more than one national jurisdiction are to be shared equitably among the nations affected." In turn, the World Water Conference confirmed this rule in recommendation No. 91:

> In relation to the use, management and development of shared water resources, national policies should take into consideration the right of each State sharing the resources to equitably utilize such resources as a means to promote bonds of solidarity and cooperation.[14]

For the equitable apportionment of shared aquifers, it is necessary to consider the volume of the aquifer in the territory of each State. Where two States share an aquifer, an equitable solution would be that the volume that each may withdraw should be proportionate to the segment of the aquifer lying within its territory. This rule is usually applied in the exploitation of shared mineral resources, such as gas or oil deposits, extending on either side of an international boundary.

* * *

[The author concludes:] The protection of groundwater is a relatively recent development in international law, but it is following the same general rules applicable to other shared resources. The relevant applicable principles include the obligation not to cause appreciable harm, the duty of equitable and reasonable use, the obligation to provide prior notice, and the duty to negotiate. All these principles are generally accepted customary rules which are now being applied in the context of shared aquifers to ensure their maintenance and protection.

8. Albert E. Utton, *International Groundwater Management*: *The Case of The U.S.–Mexican Frontier,* **in** INTERNATIONAL GROUNDWATER LAW **157, 161–64 (Ludwik A. Teclaff & Albert E. Utton eds., 1981).**

II. THE ECONOMIC CONTEXT

Under the common law doctrine, each owner's right to the water itself, or the right to use the water, is insecure because other pumpers may take possession of the mobile resource at any time. Accordingly, the individual surface owner is encouraged to exploit the groundwater resource as quickly as possible, so that the fluid and mobile water resource will not be captured by others.... It has also been noted that

> in the absence of effective social institutions to guide resource use, private groundwater use can be predicted eventually to generate excessive investment and extraction costs; induce a pumping rate which is greater than socially optimal, and which may lead to irreversible depletion;

---

14. Report of the United Nations Water Conference, Mar del Plata, March 14–25, 1977, U.N. Doc. E/Conf. 70/CBP/1, at 53 (1977).

dissipate economic rent or producer surplus, and in general create economic waste and resource inefficiency.[15]

This situation thus leads to great insecurity for all existing users of water from an aquifer, although the concepts of "security" and "flexibility" are essential criteria for an adequate water rights system. Underlying the concept of physical security is the premise that holders of groundwater rights must have a reasonable degree of certainty—the supply of water must not be unreasonably uncertain. Ordinarily, the physical supply of groundwater is more secure than surface water, since the aquifer frequently stores water in seasons and years of heavy rain and above average recharge. This stored water can then be used in seasons and years of lower rain fall and lower recharge.

In addition, however, there is the factor of "tenure security." Tenure security does not refer to reliability of supply, but to the effect of human actions on the reliability of supply, that is, the security of the land owner from the unreasonable use or export of groundwater by his neighbor. The common law rule of absolute ownership obviously increases tenure insecurity because it countenances the unrestrained right of one's neighbor to pump all the water he may need, without restraint or liability to other overlying owners for any adverse effects of his pumping. This has the economic effect of stimulating investment in groundwater development because of the uncertainty of one's property right over this "fugitive resource." There is an incentive to each land owner to protect himself against his neighbor's lawful acts by capturing as much of the resource as quickly as possible. Therefore, there is an economic incentive for over-investment and for depletion, rather than for conservation of the resource.

This conceptual approach has been elaborated on by Kelso, Martin, and Mack:

> Two aspects of water rights most significant for an understanding of men's behavior relative to water and to one another over water are: (1) ... that whatever rights they hold to water and its use will be stable and dependable over time, and (2) the flexibility permitted to them to effect changes in use and allocation of use of the water covered by their rights, and to acquire and transfer water rights from and to others.... Security and flexibility are the twin essences of socially efficient property relations.[16]

Thus, the twin concepts of flexibility and security require that owners of groundwater rights have security in their use and that groundwater rights be readily transferable between uses and users. As Veeman points out, "the indefiniteness of property rights associated with a fugitive resource such as groundwater leads to its rapid development and, perhaps, depletion."[17]

* * *

15. T. Veeman, *Water Policy and Water Institutions in Northern India: The Case of Groundwater Rights*, 18 N.R.J. 569, 576–77 (1978).

16. MAURICE M. KELSO ET AL, WATER SUPPLIES AND ECONOMIC GROWTH IN AN ARID ENVIRONMENT: AN ARIZONA CASE STUDY 52, 54 (1973).

17. T. Veeman, *supra* note 15, at 20.

The legal situation encourages overdevelopment; overdevelopment results in over-investment in developing the resource and, therefore, both economic waste and resource waste are likely due to the insecurity arising from inadequate institutional controls. Moreover, the increase in use by one pumper can lead to increasing the marginal costs of the second pumper. In cases in which overdraft occurs,

> the private pumper who, through extraction of water, causes draw-down in nearby wells, bears only his private costs of additional withdrawal. Part of the cost of additional pumping is imposed on neighboring users whose conditions of pumping are adversely affected. In these circumstances, the private marginal costs of pumping by the individual user are less than the social marginal cost in a classic case of technological external diseconomy.[18]

In addition to the depletion of the aquifer, the extraction of groundwater can affect the quality of the water by lowering the water table or hydrostatic pressure "so as to allow adjoining, contaminated waters to flow into the reservoir."[19] The following possible economic ramifications of deteriorating groundwater conditions have been projected:

> Crop yields will decrease; there will be efforts to shift to other crops or activities in the zone, and abandonment of formerly productive economic activity. There will be increased costs to industry to treat water prior to use, or it will be necessary to bring in acceptable water from elsewhere. As the water table is lowered, there is increased consumption of energy for the additional lifting by pumps, and wells will need to be deepened, or new wells sunk, to tap the same aquifer. Outmigration of the affected population and changes in gainful activities will result in dislocations affecting economic planning.... Finally, it is likely that there will be important impacts on the development and conservation of other resources resulting from deteriorated ground water conditions, where dependence on that source for water is significant.[20]

The history of groundwater development presents a "general picture ... of more recent resort to ground water ... without an adequate understanding of the physics of the resource and without regard, generally speaking, for the future."[21] ... A system should be devised which will reduce the likelihood of water users on one side of the international boundary adversely affecting water users on the other side of the boundary, thereby causing conflict between the two countries.

9. D. Caponera, *The Role of Customary International Water Law*, *in* WATER RESOURCES POLICY FOR ASIA 365, 367–68, 372, 380–81 (Mohammed Ali et al. eds., 1985).

18. *Id.* at 24.

19. W. Fischer, *Management of Interstate Groundwater,* 7 NAT. RESOURCES LAW. 521, 522 (1974).

20. R. Hayton, *The Ground Water Legal Regime as Instrument of Policy Objectives and Management Requirements, in* 2 ANNALES JURIS AQUARUM 272, 286 (2d Int'l Conf. on Water Law & Admin., Caracas, Venezuela, Feb. 8–14, 1976).

21. *Id.* at 286.

Role of Custom in International Water Resource Law

General principles and rules of customary international law of fresh water resources play a very important role when there is no agreement governing the relations of states sharing an international river, lake, or drainage basin. In fact, they also play an important role when such agreement exists.

When an international river agreement is recorded in writing, problems of interpretation of general clauses, of reservations, or of ambiguous provisions may arise for which the treaty does not provide a solution. In the practice of applying specific treaty provisions, recourse may thus be necessary to general principles underlying the treaty, or rules which are extraneous to the operative text of the treaty. Questions may also arise as to whether an agreement ever came into force or, indeed, is still in force. Here, rules of international law regulating the formulation, modification, termination, and construction of treaties must be brought into play.[d]

More important still from the standpoint of customary rules of international water resources law, states sharing an international river or drainage basin may be confronted with problems which are beyond the reach of existing agreements among them. Most international "river treaties" have tended, and will probably tend, to deal only with certain water use or management issues. As the utilization of the waters of international rivers or drainage basins increases in quantity and complexity, however, the rules agreed to in the "river treaties" in force may become inadequate or simply insufficient. In the absence of treaty coverage on such matters, recourse must be made to the unwritten rules, if any exist, governing the development, conservation, and use of shared rivers and drainage basins.

The important point is that any international drainage basin treaty is not something standing alone, but is supported by, limited by, and tested against a set of general international law standards, the content and the validity of which are not determined by the agreement in question. The conventional law of any international drainage basin can be effectively applied only with the aid of principles and rules drawn from the larger international legal system, including any sub-system of the region or basin community.

Finally, for those international streams without even a partial treaty regime with respect to water use, there is no immediate alternative but to fall back on the applicable rules of customary international law.

* * *

Evolution of Customary Rules

The integrating tendencies which call for more efficient use of water within the national borders operate also within the politically divided basin. Here the pull of geographical unity has been reinforced by the realization that damage caused by a beneficial use or a harmful effect of water does not stop at the political boundary. The steadily, though slowly, growing capacity to inflict damage at ever-increasing distances through water use and exploitation

---

d. For the canons of treaty interpretation, see Part III of the 1969 Vienna Convention on the Law of Treaties [**Basic Document 1.7**]. *See also* Subsection 6 of Chapter 2(A) at 91, *supra.*

has forced a cooperation between co-basin states and may eventually lead to the obliteration of differences between the rules that govern water use and exploitation within state borders, and those that pertain to the transfrontier effects of such use.

* * *

SUMMARY STATEMENT OF KEY PRINCIPLES

The present state of general international law on shared water resources development, conservation, and use can be summed up by the three key principles as follows:

1. *Duty Not to Cause Substantial Injury.* States sharing an international watercourse or basin are under obligation not to cause each other substantial injury, in regard to both water quantity and quality aspects. This principle stems from the broader proposition that a state may not use or allow the use of its territory in such a way that harm is caused to the territory or interests of another state. The effect or harm, however, must be appreciable, that is, it must have an impact of some consequence in order to constitute transgression of an interest protected at international law. The complementary doctrine of good neighborship, in fact, requires states to tolerate inconsequential, or minor interferences.

2. *Right to an Equitable and Reasonable Share in the Utilization of the Waters of an International Watercourse or Basin.* Subject to the overreaching principle mentioned above, states sharing an international watercourse or basin have the right to use the waters therein. This right being an attribute of sovereignty, each sharing state's own right is equal to the right of the other sharing states. When the circumstances are such that all the sharing states' equal rights cannot be satisfied to their full extent, some adjustment or accommodation is necessary. In the absence of specific conventional rules, such adjustment is done on the basis of equity. In sum, there is probably no more widely accepted principle of international water resources law than that each state "is entitled, within its territory, to a reasonable and equitable share of the beneficial uses of the waters" of an international river, lake, or basin.[22]

3. *Duty to Inform, Consult, and Engage in Good Faith Negotiations.* The fundamental duty of states to refrain from using the waters of an international river, lake, or basin in such a way as to cause appreciable harm to another state on the same watercourse or in the same basin entails in practice that states must inform one another in advance of water development plans and projects which may have an appreciable detrimental impact on their respective interests. Whereas one state cannot claim a veto power over another state wishing to alter the status quo in an international river, lake, or basin, it must nevertheless be afforded access to information and opportunities to evaluate the situation and to suggest adjustments if the proposed alteration may harm appreciably its legitimate interests. In turn, the state proposing the alteration must give proper consideration to the objecting state's representations,

---

22. This is the formulation used in Article IV of the [1966] Helsinki Rules on the Use of the Waters of International Rivers [**Basic Document 4.6**].

and both proposing and objecting state are under a duty to engage in good-faith negotiations with a view to finding a suitable accommodation of their respective interests.

It is fair to state, in sum, "that the duty to inform and to consult, and then to work out a solution that obviates the expected appreciable harm is now cardinal in the field of shared water resources."[23]

10.   United Nations: Convention on the Law of the Non–Navigational Uses of International Watercourses, Report of the Working Group of the Sixth Committee, arts. 1–33, 36 I.L.M. 700, UN Document (A/51/869) (1997) [Basic Document 4.30].

11.   Stephen McCaffrey, *The 1997 United Nations Convention on International Watercourses*, 92 Am. J. Int'l L. 97, 99–103, 106 (1998).

The Convention on the Law of the Non–Navigational Uses of International Watercourses **[Basic Document 4.30]** was adopted by the United Nations General Assembly on May 21, 1997.

* * *

In part I, Article 2, Use of terms, defines the key expressions "watercourse," "international watercourse" and "watercourse State." The most important of these is the definition of "watercourse," which is defined broadly as "a system of surface waters and groundwaters constituting by virtue of their physical relationship a unitary whole" (paragraph (a)). This definition not only accords with hydrologic reality, but also calls the attention of states to the interrelationships among all parts of the system of surface and underground waters that makes up an international watercourse. Thus, it should be clear immediately that an effect on one part of the system will generally be transmitted to other parts. Two states cited the inclusion of groundwater in the Convention as a reason for abstaining from the vote on it. . . .

Part II is introduced by Article 5, Equitable and reasonable utilization and participation. This article sets forth what many regard as the cornerstone of the law in this field. . . . [A] fair number of delegations urged that the ILC's draft articles as a whole be updated to reflect contemporary developments in international environmental law. Article 5 was one of the articles for which concrete changes in this regard were proposed. In the end, the only such change made by the working group was the addition of the words "and sustainable" after "optimal" in the first paragraph. This addition has the beneficial effect of making the objective of equitable and reasonable utilization the attainment of "optimal and sustainable utilization" of an international watercourse. However, even this objective, with all the balancing of interests implied in the words "optimal" and "sustainable," must be pursued in a manner that is "consistent with adequate protection of the watercourse" and that "tak[es] into account the interests of the watercourse States concerned."
. . .

23. S. Schwebel, Special Rapporteur, United Nations Int'l L. Comm'n, Third Report on the Law of the Non-navigational Uses of International Watercourses para. 154, U.N. Doc. A/CN.4/348 (1981).

A final point with regard to Article 5 is that the working group, and ultimately the General Assembly, accepted the new concept of equitable participation, which is embodied in paragraph 2. The basic idea behind this concept is that, to achieve the goals laid down in paragraph 1 of the article, riparian states must often cooperate with each other by taking affirmative steps, individually or jointly, with regard to the watercourse.... [I]t had not been included per se in attempts to codify the law in this field until the ILC made it a part of Article 5. Its acceptance ... helps to convey the message that a regime of equitable utilization of an international watercourse system, together with the protection and preservation of its ecosystems, cannot be achieved solely through action by each riparian state in isolation; cooperation is necessary.

Article 6, Factors relevant to equitable and reasonable utilization, contains a nonexhaustive list of factors to be taken into account by a state to ensure that its utilization of an international watercourse is equitable and reasonable. Of course, these factors may also be looked to by riparian states in negotiations concerning whether their respective uses of the watercourse are equitable, or by a third party called upon to make such a determination. Several delegations suggested various additions to the ILC's text, including the ultimately unsuccessful proposals to add references to the contribution to the watercourse by each watercourse state (India), the availability of other water resources (Egypt), and sustainable development and the needs and interests of future generations (Finland)....

Article 7, Obligation not to cause significant harm, was perhaps the most controversial provision of the entire Convention. Agreement on its language was achieved only at the end of the working group's second session. Article 7 was treated as being closely linked with Articles 5 and 6 throughout the negotiations. The working group finally adopted the three-article package by a vote of 38 to 4, with 22 abstentions. Changes were made in both paragraphs of the ILC's text. The most significant change in paragraph 1 was the replacement of the phrase "exercise due diligence" with "take all appropriate measures"—which appears to be nothing more than another way of saying the same thing. The point of both phrases is that the obligation is not a strict one: it is an obligation of conduct rather than an obligation of result. The working group also made it explicit that this obligation of watercourse states is to "prevent" the causing of harm. While this meaning may have been implicit in the ILC's text, the addition of the express reference to prevention removes any doubt and underlines the anticipatory nature of the obligation.

Paragraph 2 of Article 7 was the focal point of the contention in the working group.... [T]he language finally adopted represents an attempt to strike a balance between the equitable utilization and "no-harm" rules. Upstream states generally favored the equitable utilization rule of Article 5 on the theory that it gives them more flexibility in making new uses of their watercourses. Conversely, downstream states on the whole preferred the no-harm rule of Article 7 on the ground that it affords them, and especially their established uses, greater protection.... The facts and circumstances of each case, rather than any a priori rule, will ultimately be the key determinants of the rights and obligations of the parties. Difficult cases, which are bound to proliferate in the future, will be solved by cooperation and compromise, not rigid insistence on rules of law. In its own way, the final text of paragraph 2 acknowledges as much (although not as clearly as the ILC's text had) by requiring a state causing harm to take measures, "in consultation with the affected State," to eliminate or mitigate the harm.

Paragraph 2 essays a difficult balancing act with regard to the relationship between the equitable utilization and no-harm rules.... [A]s compared with the version adopted by the ILC on first reading in 1991, it seems reasonable to conclude that the no-harm rule would not automatically override that of equitable utilization if they should come into conflict. The very existence of a second paragraph implicitly acknowledging that harm may be caused without engaging the harming state's responsibility supports this conclusion. Also indicating recognition that significant harm may have to be tolerated by a watercourse state are the numerous mitigating clauses referred to above, especially the phrase "having due regard for the provisions of articles 5 and 6." Finally, the proposition that the no-harm rule does not enjoy inherent preeminence is supported by Article 10, which provides that any conflict between uses of an international watercourse is to be resolved "with reference to articles 5 to 7." Thus, if state A's hydroelectric use conflicts with state B's agricultural use, the conflict is not to be resolved solely by applying the no-harm rule of Article 7 but, rather, through reference to the "package" of articles setting forth the principles of both equitable utilization and no harm.

... The report of the working group to the General Assembly contains "statements of understanding" concerning certain provisions. One of those statements relates to the requirement of paragraph 2 that the state causing the harm "eliminate or mitigate" it. According to the statement, "In the event such steps as are required by article 7(2) do not eliminate the harm, such steps as are required by article 7(2) shall then be taken to mitigate the harm."

* * *

Consequently, among the conclusions that may be drawn from the working group's statement of understanding are (1) that the harming state must endeavor, in the way required by paragraph 2, to eliminate the harm and, to the extent that the harm is not so eliminated, to mitigate it, and (2) that the harming and the harmed states must, in resolving the situation, be guided by the provisions of Articles 5 and 6—i.e., by the duty to ensure that, overall, each state's utilization is equitable and reasonable vis-a-vis the other's.

The position of Article 9, Regular exchange of data and information, in the General Principles part of the Convention underlines its importance. The short of the matter is that it will be virtually impossible for a state to satisfy itself that its utilization of an international watercourse is equitable and reasonable vis-a-vis other watercourse states unless it receives data and information from them on a regular basis concerning the condition of the watercourse....

Article 10, Relationship between different kinds of uses, deals with the question of an inherent hierarchy of uses.... Article 10 makes clear that ... [no] other kind of use (e.g., irrigation, production of hydroelectric power, domestic consumption) automatically takes precedence over others. It recognizes, however, that an agreement or custom to the contrary would change this result. The expression "vital human needs" in paragraph 2 of Article 10 was discussed at some length in the working group, . . . [and] [t]he final text maintains the ILC's language, but a "statement of understanding" indicates that, "[i]n determining 'vital human needs', special attention is to be paid to providing sufficient water to sustain human life, including both drinking water and water required for production of food in order to prevent starvation." Although this is no doubt right, some countries may fear that the concept of "vital human needs" could become a loophole, enabling a state to justify its use on this ground even when the involvement of vital needs is highly debatable. . . .

Part III of the Convention contains a set of procedures to be followed in relation to a new activity in one state that may have a significant adverse effect on other states sharing an international watercourse. The fact that the basic obligation to provide prior notification of such changes was accepted as a part of the Convention by most delegations is, in itself, important: it provides further evidence that the international community as a whole emphatically rejects the notion that a state has unfettered discretion to do as it alone wishes with the portion of an international watercourse within its territory. . . .

Several delegations attached great importance to part IV of the Convention. Various proposals were made with a view to strengthening these "environmental" provisions, but in the end only minor changes were made in the ILC's text. . . . In a "statement of understanding," the working group indicated that Articles 21–23 "impose a due diligence standard on watercourse States." This interpretation is consistent with the ILC's commentary and general international law.

* * *

OUTLOOK

[The Convention] was based on, and hews closely to, a draft prepared by the International Law Commission, the United Nations body responsible for the "progressive development of international law and its codification." As is its practice, the ILC did not indicate which of the provisions codify, and which progressively develop, the law. But it seems clear that the most important elements of the Convention—equitable utilization, "no harm," prior notification—are, in large measure, codifications of existing norms. . . . Even the provisions of the Convention that do not reflect current law are likely to give rise to expectations of behavior on the part of riparian states that may, over time, ripen into international obligations.

12. Rio Declaration on Environment and Development, June 14, 1992, Principles 2–5, 14, 15, UNCED Doc. A/CONF.151/5/Rev. 1, 31 I.L.M. 874 (1992). [Basic Document 1.29].

13. Legal Principles for Environmental Protection and Sustainable Development Adopted by the Experts Group on Environmental Law of the World Commission on Environment and Development, June 1986, Principles 9–18, *in* Expert Group on Environmental Law of

THE WORLD COMMISSION ON ENVIRONMENT AND DEVELOPMENT, ENVIRONMENTAL PROTECTION AND SUSTAINABLE DEVELOPMENT (1987). [Basic Document 1.22].

Discussion Notes/Questions

1. Water disputes have become one of the most dangerous flash points in the water scarce areas of the world, particularly in the Middle East. In the present problem, the situation has not escalated to the point of warfare. However, what if Josiam decided to argue that Tiferias was guilty of environmental modification contrary to international law for having drastically reduced Josiam's water supply? What if Tiferias decided to argue the same about Josiam's proposed use? How would you respond to these allegations? Environmental warfare has been treated in Problem 11–4 in Chapter 11, *infra*. Consider the facts of this problem in light of the 1976 Convention on the Prohibition of Military or Any Other Hostile Use of Environmental Modification Techniques (ENMOD) [**Basic Document 7.30**] discussed in Problem 11–4. Article 2 of the ENMOD Convention defines the term "environmental modification techniques" as "any technique for changing–through the deliberate manipulation of natural processes–the dynamics, composition or structure of the earth, including its biota, lithosphere, hydrosphere and atmosphere...." Might the alteration of the use of an international watercourse, such as was done by Tiferias and proposed by Josiam in the present problem, serve as an illustration of prohibited environmental modification? Why? Why not? Does the motive behind the modification make a difference?

2. International cooperation efforts are increasing as a whole, and the area of water scarcity issues is not an exception. For example, an on-going research project involving the environmental protection of Israeli–Palestinian shared aquifer resources is funded by the United States Agency for International Development–Middle East Regional Cooperation program.[24] Another example of cooperation efforts can be found in the Israel–Jordan–Palestine Liberation Organization: Declaration on Cooperation on Water–Related Matters, which was signed by the three parties in February of 1996, in recognition of their common need to develop effective water resources management systems. *See* 36 I.L.M. 761.

Additionally, some authors believe that the idea of water wars is not as impending as once thought. See the following excerpts from Tony Allan, *Why Middle East Powers Aren't Warring Over Water*, Middle East Economic Digest: The Middle East in 1997, Jan. 1997, at 14–16:

> Miraculously, and above all silently, Middle East governments have been able to avoid the apparently inevitable consequences of their inherited water deficits, despite the fact that this is a life-and-death economic issue for them and their peoples.
>
> Analysis based on watersheds has led to the misleading conclusion that water deficits will be the cause of major armed conflict in the Middle East. Yet water has not been even a minor element in a regional conflict scenario for over a quarter of a century.
>
> Nevertheless, those suffering from water paranoia have cause for their concern. In the past 25 years the status of the region's water resources has significantly worsened. In 1970, the water needs of the Middle East and North African countries could be met from within the region. Until then, regional governments and their engineers had been able to mobilize supply-managing

24. For a description of some of the scientific goals of the project, see *The Environmental Protection of the Water Resources of the Shared Israeli–Palestinian Mountain Aquifer* (visited Nov. 13, 1998) *http://atar.mscc.huji.ac.il/truman/water1.html.*

techniques to deliver new water to meet the requirements of municipal, industrial and agricultural needs. The demographically driven increased demands of the past 50 years have been unprecedented and forced the region into water deficit. Yet there has been no water war.

Ideally each individual needs a cubic meter of water (a ton) for drinking each year, about 100 cubic meters for other personal needs and 1000 cubic meters to grow the food that person consumes. Industry and especially services, are relatively minor users of water.

Every additional mouth, however, needs over 1100 cubic meters of new water every year and it is agricultural water needs that present the impossible challenge for Middle Eastern economies. The watersheds, including groundwater, of the region cannot meet the irrigation requirements.

There is also, however, an extremely important hidden source of water: "virtual water." Virtual water is the water contained in the food that the region imports. More water flows into the area as virtual water each year than flows down the Nile for Egypt's agriculture. The use of this virtual water obtained in the global trading system has enabled the political leaderships of the region to augment their respective inadequate water resources.

The global trade in food staples has proved to be a very accessible and effective system. Politicians and resource managers find this source far more attractive than stressful, even potentially disastrous, wrangling over local water with hostile neighbors. The strategic imperative of providing food for citizens has been met through access to politically stress free virtual water.

* * *

The global trade in food staples has been particularly accessible for the past 50 years, even to poor economies, because competition by the generators of the global grain surplus–the United States and the European Community–brought down the global price of grain until the beginning of 1995.

. . . Intelligence on the status of the global capacity to meet future virtual water needs at affordable prices is an enormously important economic issue for Middle Eastern governments.

. . . Great is the frustration for the staffs of international agencies such as the World Bank who believe that many countries underestimate the importance of trying to influence global trade in staple foods. This author has been urging for some years that Middle East importers should act together as the pivotal force in the global grain trade.

. . . The second water policy priority as seen from outside is the allocative efficiency of water use. In water-short circumstances, according to basic economic principles, water should be allocated to uses which bring the best return to water supplies. In agriculture, water should be allocated to crops which bring a sound return to water as well as sound economic returns to the economy. . . . At sector level, industrial use is more efficient than agricultural use. This policy is commonly referred to as demand management.

. . . The third water policy priority is productive efficiency which means achieving better returns to existing water uses. Investment and changes in management and technology are means by which improvements in productive efficiency can be achieved.

Middle Eastern governments prioritize water policy in exactly the reverse order despite the fact that productive efficiency requires investment but far less political risk. Allocative efficiency on the contrary, especially at the sector level, can only be very politically stressful. It involves shifting a crucial input–water–from an agricultural sector which brings a poor economic return to industry or services, where it brings a higher return. Governments have proved very reluctant to handle the politics associated with such reallocation. In Israel, where the policy has been successfully implemented it took over 20 years of debate to achieve sectoral water re-allocation.

Addressing the global virtual water priority by focusing on market intelligence and a regionally coordinated approach to trading in food staples has not gained a place on the water policy agenda in the region. The politics of water in the Middle East are driven by very deeply held belief systems. Water is central to a traditional agricultural way of life which is of direct importance to significant proportions of the populations of individual economies. More important it is perceived by influential majorities and key constituencies to be of crucial strategic significance.

Recent rises in the price of grain, and consequently of virtual water, should force a re-examination of the beliefs. But change will be slow and will take decades rather than years. Adjustments will be sufficient, however, to avoid water wars.

Do you agree or disagree with Tony Allan's approach to the water scarcity problems in the Middle East? With his determination that the water wars will not come to pass? Can you think of any additional options for the governments and citizens of countries facing water scarcity?

See also Muhammad R. Shatanawi's *Capacity Building and Research Needs in Water Resources in the Arab Regions Towards the 21st Century* (visited Nov. 13, 1998) <http://www.unesco.org.eg/ prog/science/ihp/7th/shatanaw.htm>. Shatanawi, Professor of Water Resources and Irrigation at the University of Jordan, discusses the concept of "capacity building," listing the basic elements of "capacity building" as well as reasons for the ineffectiveness of existing national and local institutions in dealing with the Middle Eastern water problems.

Some of the author's reasons for institutional inefficiency include the following:

● Inadequate funding and human resources;

● Inadequate working environment for those people in implementing positions;

● Inadequate or completely lacking education and training opportunities; and

● Lack of public awareness programs to ensure community involvement and support.

The author's vision for correcting the problems listed above stems from four elements found in Agenda 21 which together comprise the concept of "capacity building":

● An implementing environment which includes the appropriate policy and legal framework;

● Institutional strength at all levels;

● Human resources development; and

● Increased awareness and education on every level of society.

Shatanawi goes on to suggest action to be taken in the area of capacity building, as well as human resource development, and research and development.

3. Might either of the parties involved have canvassed the legality of the other party's reduction of the desert aquifer water in their respective domestic courts? Domestic forums, as we have seen in Chapter 3, are sometimes able to apply international law, and a question that arises in this context is the extent to which transnational water disputes might be litigated in domestic as opposed to international tribunals. Stephen McCaffrey, in *Background and Overview of the International Law Commission's Study of the Non–Navigational Uses of International Watercourses*, 3 Colo. J. Int'l Envtl. L. & Pol'y 17 (1992), discusses this question at 25–27:

> [T]wo additional [items] that had been proposed to the Commission were not included in the draft articles as finally approved. One of these chapters was titled "Implementation," and contained a set of articles on the following subjects: private remedies, provision of information to the public, jurisdictional immunity, a conference of the parties, and amendment of the draft articles. The other part was titled "Fact–Finding and Settlement of Disputes." It contained an article on fact-finding, as a means of implementation of the provisions of the draft and of dispute avoidance, and four articles on the settlement of disputes (viz., obligation to settle disputes by peaceful means; consultations and negotiations; conciliation; and arbitration).
>
> All that remains of these two chapters at this stage of the Commission's work is article 32, "Non-discrimination," which is based on article 4, "Equal Right of Access," of the proposed chapter on implementation.[e] The Commission's Drafting Committee had, in fact, forwarded to the full Commission for its consideration an article titled "Recourse under Domestic Law," which provided as follows: "A watercourse State shall ensure that recourse is available in accordance with its legal system for compensation or other relief in respect of appreciable harm caused in other States by activities related to an international watercourse carried on by natural or juridical persons under its jurisdiction."
>
> This article, which was a slightly modified version of article 3, paragraph 1 of the chapter on implementation proposed in the sixth report, had originally been modeled upon article 235, paragraph 2 of the 1982 United Nations Convention on the Law of the Sea (UNCLOS) [**Basic Document 4.20**]. Despite the striking similarity of the article to that provision of UNCLOS, which had been generally acceptable to States, the Commission was unable to reach consensus on the acceptability of such a provision in the context of international watercourses. While some members supported the provision, and even argued that it together with article 32 as finally adopted did not go far enough, others feared that it might result in interference by private individuals in matters that primarily concerned relations between States. That the article on recourse under domestic law gave rise to such controversy is somewhat puzzling in light of both the similar provision in the Law of the Sea Convention and the acceptance by the Commission of article 32 on non-discrimination, which could prove to be more onerous in some circumstances than a requirement to ensure the availability of recourse under domestic law.

As reported to the Commission in plenary session, the article concerned only the elimination of any substantive or procedural obstacles to obtaining relief for extraterritorial harm. It did not deal with the question of access to the applicable

e. The principle of non-discrimination is now embodied in Article 32 of the Convention on the Law of the Non–Navigational Uses of International Watercourses, Reading 10 [**Basic Document 4.30**].

procedures, the subject of article 32. The possibility that recourse may be available for domestic, but not extraterritorial, harm is a real one, as demonstrated by the facts leading up to the well-known Trail Smelter arbitration [**Basic Document 8.4**]. There the injured citizens in the US state of Washington could not bring an action directly against the smelter in the Canadian city of Trail, British Columbia because of a common law doctrine known as the "local action rule," which required that actions to recover for injury to land be brought in the jurisdiction where the land was located. Since jurisdiction could not be obtained over the smelter in the state of Washington, the plaintiffs were compelled to request that the US Government take up their claims. The continuing vigor of this doctrine has prompted the respective uniform law organizations in Canada and the United States to promulgate draft provisions dealing with the problem. It is unfortunate that the Commission was not prepared to do the same.

4. *Bibliographical Note*. For further discussion concerning the principle themes addressed in this problem, consult the following specialized materials:

(a) *Specialized Books/Monographs*. J. Bulloch & A. Darwish, Water Wars: Coming Conflicts in the Middle East (London: Gollance) (1993); D. Caponera, FAO 36: Water Law in Moslem Countries (1973); Desertification and Development: Dryland Ecology in Social Perspective (B. Spooner ed. 1982); Environmental Protection and the Law of War: A "Fifth Geneva" Convention on the Protection of the Environment in Time of Armed Conflict (G. Plant ed. 1992); J. Krutillo, The Columbia River Treaty (1967); J. Lammers, Pollution of International Water-courses (1984); C. Meyer et al., Water Resource Management: a Casebook in Law and Public Process (3d ed. 1988); J. Starr, A Shared Destiny (1983); Water in the Middle East: Conflict or Cooperation? (T. Naff & R. Matson, eds. 1984); Water in the Middle East: Legal, Political and Commercial Implications (J.A. Allan & C. Mallat, eds. 1995); Water Resources Policy for Asia (M. Ali et al. eds. 1985); The World Bank, Striking a Balance: The Environmental Challenge of Development (1989).

(b) *Specialized Hearings/Reports*. The Encroaching Desert: The Consequences of Human Failure, A Report of the Independent Commission on International Humanitarian Issues (1986); Report of the International Law Commission on the 39th Session, UN GAOR, 42nd Sess., Supp. No. 10, at 52, UN Doc. A/42/10 (1987); Third Report on the Law of the Non-navigational Uses of International Water-courses (S. Schwebel, Special Rapporteur), U.N. Doc. A/CN.4/348 (1981) and Corr. 1; The Law of the Non–Navigational Uses of International Watercourses, U.N.Doc. A/CN.4/406 (1987) and Add. 1 and Add. 2, *reprinted in* 2(1) Y. B.Int'l L. Comm'n 15, at 39, U.N.Doc. A/CN.4/SER.A/1987/Add.1 (1987); Treaty of Friend-ship and Neighbourly Relations Between Iraq and Turkey, March 29, 1946, 37 U.N.T.S. 281; United Nations Conference on Environment and Development, Adoption of Agreements on Environment and Development, Agenda 21, U.N. Doc. A/conf.151/4 (parts I–IV) (1992); United Nations Conference on Environment and Development, Adoption of Agreements on Environment and Development, Rio Declaration on Environment and Development Note by the Secretary–General of the Conference U.N. Doc. A/conf.151/5 (1992); U.N. Dept. of Int'l Econ. & Soc. Aff., Management of International Water Resources UN Doc. ST/ESA/5, U.N. Sales No. E.75.II.A2. (1975).

(c) *Specialized Articles/Book Chapters*. A. Adede, *United Nations Efforts To-ward the Development of an Environmental Code of Conduct For States Concern-ing Harmonious Utilization of Shared Natural Resources*, 43 Alb. L. Rev. 488 (1979); R. Bilder, *The Role of Unilateral State Action in Preventing International*

Environmental Injury, 14 Vand. J. Transnat'l L. 51 (1981); ___, *International Law and Natural Resources Policies*, 20 N.R.J. 451 (1980); C. Bourne, *Procedure in the Development of International Drainage Basins*, 22 U. Toronto L. J. 172 (1972); A. Boyle, *State Responsibility for Breach of Obligations to Protect the Global Environment, in* Control Over Compliance with International Law 69 (W. Butler ed. 1991); J. Chipmin, *Third World Politics & Security in the 1990's*, 14 Wash. Q. 148, (1991); D. Chenevert, Comment: *Application of the Draft Articles on the Non–Navigational Uses of International Watercourses to the Water Disputes Involving the Nile River and the Jordan River*, 6 Emory Int'l L. Rev. 495 (1992); J. Cohen, Note: *International Law and the Water Politics of the Euphrates*, 24 N.Y.U. J. Int'l L. & Pol. 502 (1991); R. D'Arge and A. Kneese, *State Liability for International Environmental Degradation: An Economic Perspective*, 20 N.R.J. 427 (1980); J. Dellapenna, et al., *Water Resources in the Middle East: Impact on Economics and Politics*, 80 Proceed.Am. Soc'y Int'l L. 249 (1986); N. Hilmy, *Some Legal Questions About Irrigation from the River Nile as an International River*, 34 Rev. Egyptienne de Dr. Int'l 123 (1978); C. Klein–Chesivoir, Note: *Avoiding Environmental Injury: The Case for Widespread Use of Environmental Impact Assessments in International Development Projects*, 30 V.J.I.L. 517 (1990); S. McCaffrey, *The Law of International Watercourses: Some Recent Developments and Unanswered Questions*, 17 Denv. J. Int'l L. & Pol'y 505 (1989); V. Nanda, *Emerging Trends*, 6 Denv. J. Int'l L. & Pol'y 239 (1976); L. O'Keefe, *Transboundary Pollution and the Strict Liability Issue: The Work of the International Law Commission on the Topic of International Liability for Injurious Consequences Arising Out of Acts Not Prohibited by International Law*, 18 Denv. J. Int'l L. & Pol'y (1990); D. Parton, *The "Duty to Inform" in International Environmental Law*, 6 B. U. Int'l L. J. (1988); J. Starr, *Water Wars*, Foreign Pol'y 17 (Summer 1991); A. Teclaff, *Fiat or Custom: The Checkered Development of International Water Law*, 31 N.R.J. 45 (1991); P. Vesiland, *Water: The Middle East's Critical Resource*, 183 Nat'l Geographic 38 (May 1993); M. Whiteman, *International Rivers and River Basins*, 3 Dig. Int'l L. 920 (1964).

Chapter Nine

PROBLEMS IN PROTECTING
THE LITHOSPHERE

The three problems in this chapter identify two fundamental truisms. In the first two we see how different human activities, ranging from those that cater to the prodigal life styles of the rich industrial countries to those that are necessary for the agricultural development of poor nations, almost inexorably end up fouling our nest, i.e., the global environment we inhabit. In Problems 9–1 and 9–3, we see especially vividly the interpenetrating, interconnected, and indivisible nature of the global environment and therefore the manifest artificiality of dividing it into its component parts—the atmosphere, the hydrosphere, the lithosphere, and the biosphere. While necessary for pedagogical and analytical purposes, such fragmentation does not faithfully mirror nature. The extent to which, for example, lakes and rivers and the ocean—significant parts of the hydrosphere—are interwoven ecologically and geographically to form a bio-region within the lithosphere is striking; lakes and rivers and the ocean, it is clear, are an integral part of nature's design for the lithosphere.

In rich countries, pollution results from a staggering array of household, commercial, and industrial uses that maintain abundant and wasteful life-styles. The natural resources required to satisfy modern living standards—extravagant by any historical criterion—include, but are not limited to, the energy we consume to heat and cool and to move ourselves and our goods in speedy fashion by air, land, and water; the pesticides, fungicides, insecticides and other chemicals upon which we have become dependent to produce our food; and, of course, the luxurious materials we assemble to build and furnish our homes, cars, and boats, and to attire ourselves from head to foot. All of which puts enormous pressure on our natural resources, particularly the nonrenewable kind, and on the fragile ecosystems that support them.

In addition to imposing severe strains upon our natural resources and the ecosystems that support them, however, is the fact that the entire process of exploitation, involving renewable and nonrenewable resources alike, gives rise to enormous quantities of wastes, residuals, and pollutants. Goods are dispensed with and quickly replaced by new and different goods, long before the expiry of their use life. The matter and energy that is necessary to satisfy our life styles are neither created nor destroyed; they are merely transformed, so that massive quantities of wastes or residuals become the unavoidable and

690

punishing by-products of today's living. In short, in addition to depleting non-renewable resources, we today appear to be—in advanced industrial societies certainly, but also in some developing countries—inescapably locked into a profligate cycle of waste.

Unfortunately, the world community has yet to act upon the simple truth that these wastes, residuals, and pollutants will not go away until we stop demanding and embracing the life-style and end-products that produce them. Tampering with our standard of living and "quality of life" is not easy to accept because growth in gross domestic product (GDP) is holy writ and because economic regression is anathema. Demanded products and services, even when accepted as the cause of waste and pollution, are not abandoned because to abandon them, it is popularly believed, is to diminish our life-styles, not to enhance them.

And so, the threats to the lithosphere remain and grow. While we try to resolve the self-created impasse of building bigger and better nests even while knowing that the act of doing so only spoils them, what do we do with the huge quantities of toxic and hazardous wastes that are created? "NIMBY" (Not In My Back Yard) has become a familiar refrain. But developed countries seem nevertheless unwilling to pay the high price of waste treatment that is necessary to dispose of toxic and hazardous substances, not to mention everyday waste and residuals, safely. With the encouragement of some economists (see Chapter 4, *supra*), it is sometimes sought to dispose of these materials in less developed countries (LDCs) despite the perils posed thereby.

And what about the chemical wastes that result from the production and overuse of toxic agricultural chemicals? It is correct that agricultural chemicals are necessary for LDCs to become more productive in their agriculture and to feed their exploding populations. But how do we prevent their overuse, which is responsible for harm to human health and damage to the environment? How might international law pragmatically assist in arresting the damage caused by such chemicals?

Finally, it is important to appreciate that rivers and streams, though they constitute less than one-half percent of the water in the hydrosphere, are critical to the proper maintenance of the lithosphere and therefore to human habitation. It is true that the use of river water for irrigation purposes, accepted as desirable since time immemorial, has made deserts bloom. Yet the overuse of river water by upper riparian states can reduce the volume of water available to lower riparian states in such a way as to increase substantially the salinity of the soils and even to create deserts. In the water-deprived areas of the world, such as the Middle East, this sort of thing can realistically lead to war, which, in turn, can and usually does lead to rapid further deterioration of the natural environment, including of course the lithosphere.[a]

In the ensuing three problems, these and related issues are addressed.

a. For consideration of the impact of war on the natural environment, see Problem 11–3 ("Environmental Warfare in Khalifan").

Problem 9.1

Scuttling the *SS Roli*

SECTION 1. FACTS

Seran is a developed, industrialized country in Southeastern Asia located between the Philippines and Indonesia. It is approximately the size of the state of New Mexico, U.S., with a growing population of nearly 20 million people who are primarily of Chinese, Indian and Malaysian descent.

Yarbon Island, a small island nation, is a less developed country (LDC) with a population of about 250,000, located 300 miles southeast of Seran in the Pacific Ocean. The Kien channel, a well used shipping route, forms part of the seas separating the two countries. Yarbon Island is very sparsely populated, primarily because its predominantly rocky desert terrain does not support agricultural subsistence. Yarbon Island is surrounded by shallow reefs rich in biodiversity and species that are found nowhere else in the world. These coral reefs are also home to an important fishery resource from which more than two hundred and fifty thousand tons of fish are harvested each year, accounting for seventy five percent of Yarbon's gross national product (GNP).

Seran has been acclaimed for fostering an environmentally friendly recycling industry that assembles battery operated electric vehicles (EVs). These EVs are used in many of the world's largest cities, and have reduced vehicle emissions and smog in urban areas. The leading Seranian EV manufacturer Electra-car, has gross international sales exceeding US $50 billion yearly, and employs more than 100,000 workers.

Electra-car has developed a competitive edge over its trading rivals primarily by using recycled materials in its vehicles. The great bulk of these materials are acquired by Electra-car from its recycling subsidiary, Enviro Recycling Corp (Enviro) which has collection depots all over the world. Enviro also owns and operates a large lead and steel smelting facility, for reprocessing recycled materials which is located on the southeastern tip of Seran, in the village of Banei.

Enviro uses large barges to transport recycling materials from its worldwide collection facilities to its smelter in Seran. One of Enviro's oldest and smallest vessels the 100 meter *SS Roli* has been in operation for the past 40 years. Flying the Seranian flag, the ship has been in regular service between China and Seran, frequently plying the Kien Channel en route to Hong Kong with cargoes of lead and acid from used batteries, scrap metal, and salvaged lubricants.

Because of its age and increasing operating costs, Enviro decided to retire the *SS Roli* by scuttling it. At first Enviro had planned on putting the ship into a large waste dump for nonrecyclable material that it operated near its smelting facility. However, the dump was scheduled to be shut down by Seran, pursuant to its strict new environmental laws, and Enviro had to look elsewhere for a site to bury the *SS Roli*.

In January 1997, Enviro negotiated a deal with the government of Yarbon Island, whereby the *SS Roli* would be sunk and made into an artificial reef that would replace and supplement some of the recent reef losses around Yarbon.

The Yarbonian reefs had suffered from damage and erosion over the past decade because of intense fishing, increased shipping traffic through the Kien Channel, and large volumes of waste and toxic pollution generated by the region's expanding population. Yarbonian officials were convinced that sinking a number of retired ships near the damaged areas were a cost effective way of restoring the coral reefs.

Enviro and Yarbon Island officials concurred that using the ship to create an artificial reef did not constitute dumping as defined in international environmental law. Enviro agreed that the *SS Roli* would be emptied of any cargo, stripped of its engines, fuel and lubricants, and then partially filled with gravel and other inert debris to aid in the sinking. On March 11, 1997, the *SS Roli* was submerged at a site designated by Yarbon, fifty miles due west of its coast, in nearly 25 meters of water above one of the severely eroded Yarbonian reefs. Pursuant to their agreement, Enviro also paid Yarbon US $1 million.

Late in November, 1998, both the Yarbonian and Seranian Fishery Services reported that the total fish catch was far below expectations, and that fish along the southern tip of Yarbon Island often exhibited peculiar maladies, including central nervous system disorders, skin lesions and unusually low weight. Fearing possible damage to their prosperous fishing industries, the two countries jointly commissioned a team of international scientists to study the problem. In their report, the scientific team warned that overfishing had resulted in a serious decline of fish, and that fishing harvests had to be curtailed to facilitate species recovery and restore ecological stability.

The scientific team also concluded that many of the fish exhibited diseases that might result from lead contamination. Subsequently, a special Yarbonian inquiry quickly arrived at two findings about the possible sources of lead contamination. First, effluent discharged into the sea by Enviro's lead smelting facility in Banei was being swept over the seas into Yarbon waters by prevailing winds. Second, a plume of acidic water with a high lead content identified near the site of its scuttling implicated the *SS Roli* as a source of lead pollution.

A Yarbonian-sponsored dive team visited the *SS Roli* and reported that they were unable to visually identify any containers or wastes in the ship because of highly turbid water, but that samples of the water indicated sharply heightened lead levels near the ship which decreased with increased distance from the ship. Acting upon these findings, Yarbon indefinitely closed fishing around the reefs on the southern tip of its territory. Shortly thereafter, traces of lead were reported in the water further north, along Yarbon's coast.

The government of Yarbon Island immediately demanded that Enviro remove the scuttled ship which had become a serious danger to the health of the Yarbon people and the environment. The company declined to do so, noting that it had sunk the ship as required by Yarbon according to their agreement, and had paid Yarbon US $1 million. As there was no Enviro property on the island, Yarbon Island had little recourse against the company within its own court systems.

The government of Yarbon Island then lodged a formal complaint with the government of Seran, which assured Yarbon that it had absolutely no knowledge of the events or of Enviro's activities. The Seranian government investigated the scuttling of the *SS Roli*, and found Enviro shipping records showing that when the *SS Roli* was sunk its holds were filled with "clinker" and other detritus from Enviro's lead smelter.

The two countries entered into consultations with a view to mitigating or eliminating the environmental harm posed by Enviro's smelters and the *SS Roli* to Yarbon fisheries, and obtaining Seranian help in restoring the damaged fishing resource. The consultations proved unfruitful, and the two countries agreed to refer this matter to the International Court of Justice (I.C.J.), accepting the courts jurisdiction under Article 36(2) of the Statute of the I.C.J., to which both Seran and Yarbon Island are parties.

Neither Seran nor Yarbon Island have any domestic laws directly prohibiting Electra-car's actions in the instant case. Both states are parties to the United Nations Convention on the Law of the Sea (UNCLOS), and are members of the United Nations. Additionally, both states have signed and ratified the 1992 Convention on Biological Diversity, the 1989 Basel Convention on the Control of Transboundary Movements of Hazardous Wastes and Their Disposal. Both countries have ratified the 1995 amendment and annexes VIII & IX to the Basel Convention. Yarbon Island is also a member of the Convention for the Protection of the Natural Resources and Environment of the South Pacific Region and has previously included the seas ten miles from its coast in the "Convention Area" under article 3.

SECTION 2. QUESTIONS PRESENTED

1. Has Seran violated international law?
2. What remedies is Yarbon Island entitled to under International Law?

SECTION 3. ASSIGNMENTS

A. *Reading Assignment*

Study the Readings presented in Section 4, *infra*, and the Discussion Notes/Questions that follow. Also, to the extent possible, consult the accompanying bibliographical references.

B. *Recommended Writing Assignment*

Prepare a comprehensive, logically sequenced, and *argumentative* brief in the form of an outline of the primary and subsidiary *legal* issues you see requiring resolution by the I.C.J. Also, from the perspective of an independent objective judge, indicate which side ought to prevail on each issue and why. Retain a copy of your issue-outline/brief for class discussion.

C. *Recommended Oral Assignment*

Assume you are legal counsel for Yarbon Island, on the one hand, or Seran on the other (as designated by your instructor); then, relying upon the Readings (and your issue-outline if prepared), present a 15–20 minute oral argument of your government's likely positions before the I.C.J.

D. Recommended Reflective Assignment

Consider (and recommend) alternative norms, institutions, and/or procedures that you believe might do better than existing world order arrangements to contend with situations of the kind posed by this problem. In so doing, but without insisting upon *immediate* feasibility, identify the particular transition steps that would be needed to make your alternatives a reality.

SECTION 4. READINGS

1. Editors' Note. Industrialized countries export a significant amount of their hazardous waste. The wastes involved cover a wide spectrum and include municipal solid wastes, incinerator ash, asbestos wastes, sewage sludge, old tires, and radioactive wastes. Exported waste is dumped, buried, and burned in the country of receipt. The extent of the hazardous waste trade is not known accurately, and the facts are controversial. The second reading, see infra, Andrea Marcus, *Transboundary Toxic Waste Disposal: Understanding the Gravity of the Problem and Addressing the Issue through the Human Rights Commission*, 1–Fall Int'l Dimensions (1997), provides some specific accounts of the international waste trade.

The international trade in waste has grown in response to strong legal and economic incentives. Businesses face strict and costly regulations for waste disposal at home. There often is a shortage of disposal sites within industrialized nations. The "not in my backyard" (NIMBY) philosophy of nearby residents exacerbates this problem. For some countries, there are geological, topographical, and other factors that can create difficulties for building adequate disposal facilities. Third World countries often have minimal or no hazardous waste disposal regulations and, even where there are regulations, there often is no enforcement mechanism. The costs of transportation and disposal overseas are therefore less than disposing of hazardous wastes at home. See Hao–Nhien Q. Vu, *The Law of Treaties And The Export of Hazardous Waste*, 12 UCLA J. Envtl. L. & Pol'y 389 (1994)(discussing the numerous reasons for the transfrontier movements of hazardous wastes from industrialized nations to the Third World).

Third World countries for their part face a dilemma. Hazardous waste disposal can provide major revenue. For example, "in 1992, Italian and Swiss companies took advantage of the confused political situation in war-torn, famine-stricken Somalia to secure an $80 million, twenty-year contract for dumping toxic wastes there. The contract was supposedly signed by the Somali Minister of Health, but at the time none of the warring factions in Somalia truly held power." *Id.*

2. Andrea Marcus, *Transboundary Toxic Waste Disposal: Understanding the Gravity of the Problem and Addressing the Issue Through the Human Rights Commission*, 1 INT'L DIMENSIONS 11–13 (1997).

What may be called recycling, may actually be dumping hazardous waste, or processing it in ways that create additional toxic waste hazards. This often results from the receiving countries' lack of resources or technology to safely deal with the waste, or extractions from the waste which can create toxic by-products. The Basel Convention creates this loophole through the exception from Basel's requirements for shipments of waste to be "recycled." Waste labeled "For Recycling" is not subject to the same restrictions and bans as other toxic waste under The Basel Agreement. Some figures estimate that toxic waste destined for "recycling" may constitute as much as 90% of all toxic waste shipments. This ... severely undermin[es] the Basel Convention's resolution.

* * *

Taking into account the problems regarding enforcement of the Basel Convention, and the current ineffective status of the Bamako Convention, the illegal export [sic] and disposal of toxic waste continues. Non–Governmental Organizations and individuals who have attempted to stop, or simply investigate continued violations, do so without enforceable UN assistance, and often at the risk of imprisonment and/or death. The following are just a few of the thousands of examples of illegal toxic waste dumping, import, and export, that result in the continuing degradation of the environment, and often fatal violations of human rights:

1. In November of 1994, in South Africa, African National Congress President Nelson Mandela visited victims of the international toxics trade. At Thor Chemicals, the world's largest recycler of mercury wastes, one worker at the Natal plant died, and almost a third of the workforce reportedly suffered some form of mercury poisoning, including one man who had been in a coma for years. Certain types of mercury wastes cannot be legally disposed of in the United States, and Thor's suppliers include at least three U.S. corporations and the U.S. Department of Energy. On February 21, 1994 an ANC inspection team found more than 10,000 barrels of mercury wastes from three U.S. companies stockpiled at the plant.

2. In early 1994, Thor Chemicals returned a shipment of waste mercury to its source, Borden Chemicals and Plastics, in the United States. The documentation for the shipment indicated that it was activated carbon, which is no more hazardous than charcoal. Thor Chemicals spokesman John MacDonald confirmed that the shipment contained mercuric chloride, but said that Thor had the means to dispose of it safely.

3. In 1992, Italian and Swiss companies, who claimed to have agreements with a Somalian government official, planned to dump half a million tons of hazardous waste each year for the next 20 years in Somalia. This prompted the Swiss government to request U.N. help to track down any of its companies involved. During these alleged agreements, Somalia was suffering political turmoil and severe famine, making it particularly vulnerable to corrupt bargaining between impostors claiming to hold authority in Somalia, and opportunistic companies exporting toxic waste. On October 6, 1992, the Executive Director of the United Nations Environment Programme (UNEP), Mostafa K. Tolba, stated that the deal had been aborted, and that UNEP was "pleased to have played a role in heading off an environmental tragedy in Somalia."

4. In 1990, U.S. Customs Officials discovered lead waste in an empty truck returning to the United States. The officials tracked the waste to an

American owned battery "recycling" plant in Mexico, where batteries shipped from the United States were simply opened and their acid dumped on the ground. The extracted lead was then shipped back to the U.S. for resale. In response to felony charges in California for unlawfully transporting hazardous waste across the border, the facility owner pleaded no contest and paid a $25 million fine.

5. In 1991, instead of paying the $300 per ton price for disposal in the U.S., an American corporation sold 1000 tons of dust containing lead and calcium to a waste broker for $45 per ton. The broker sold the dust to another American company which later sold it to Bangladesh as fertilizer. The poisonous quality was discovered only after one third of the "fertilizer" had already been spread on fields, and fifty pound bags of the fertilizer were on shelves in local markets. In July of 1993, after months of pressure from environmentalists, the financier of the scheme, the Asian Development Bank, sent a team of epidemiologists and toxicologists to investigate. It also tentatively agreed to fund the return to the U.S. of the toxic that is still warehoused. No date had been set for the return of the waste because the U.S. government had not yet agreed to accept it. Late in 1992, the company that generated the waste, Gaston Copper, pleaded guilty to violating U.S.-waste export reporting procedures and accepted a $1 million fine.

6. In 1992, a U.S. firm shipped 8,000 tons of contaminated soil from California to be used as landfill for a causeway project in the Marshall Islands. Local protests led by Greenpeace and other green groups prompted the U.S. environmental protection authorities to impound the ship in Guam, and later send it back to the United States.

7. In October 1992, the S.S. United States, after being purchased by a consortium that planned to refurbish it for luxury cruising, was sent to Turkey to have its more than 500,000 square feet of asbestos removed. In Turkey, the asbestos removal was estimated at about $2 million, instead of the $100 million it would have cost in the United States. However, the Turkish government, citing the dangers, refused to allow the asbestos to be removed there. In October of 1993, the ship was hauled to the Black Sea port of Sevastopol in Ukraine, where the government did not object to the hazards of the asbestos removal.

8. In March 1994, Philippine customs officials impounded two 12–meter long containers of computer waste from Australia after a Greenpeace ship intercepted the shipment at sea at night. When this sort of waste lands in China, workers strip the cables for copper wire and the remaining material is either burned or stockpiled. Computer waste contains chlorinated compounds and rare metals which produce dioxins and other toxic substances when burned. For example, computer keyboards emit brominated dioxins, a substance linked to cancer and immune system disorders.

9. Australian laws do not control the export of waste if it is being sent for "recycling and recovery purposes." As a result, Australian exports to Asia include plastic scrap, lead car batteries, metal scrap, and other hazardous wastes, and more recently, computer junk. Between 1992 and 1993, Australia sent hundreds of tons of plastic waste to the following Asian countries: China Hong Kong, India, Kiribati, Malaysia, the Philippines, Singapore, South Korea, Papua New Guinea, Taiwan and Vauatu.

10.   In October 1993, Chinese customs officials discovered that a shipment declared and documented as fuel oil instead contained chemical wastes produced in Korea by the Macao International Limited Corporation.

11.   In November 1993, a train from Germany carrying 239 tons of hazardous pesticides stored in leaking drums, stood unwanted at the northern Albanian border. The pesticides, stored in 17 railroad cars, were ordered from Germany but not admitted to Albania because the new democratic government did not want the cargo and asked the German government to take it back. Environment Minister Klaus Toepfer said he would immediately send 1.4 million marks ($817,000) to ensure the pesticides caused no danger. In the meantime, the leaking toxic pesticides were left waiting at the border. The German train endangered Lake Shkoder, and the water supply of large parts of the Southern Balkans.

12.   In January of 1993, the German waste trading company Rimex, sent 230 tons of various kinds of toxic wastes and chemicals to the Ukranian town of Rovno. The waste included three barrels (about 180 kg) of extremely toxic mercury wastes; chemical reagents (expired in 1976 and 1978); waste paints containing heavy metals; outdated pesticides; wood preservatives; pure DDT; prussic acid (hydro cyanic acid); laboratory chemicals and pharmaceuticals in glass containers and cardboard boxes; and red and white phosphorus which can ignite at any time without outside influence. Except for the mercury, which was not declared at all, Rimex declared the wastes it exported to Ukraine as "building materials" and "consumer goods." In June of 1993, German Chancellor Helmut Kohl, visited the Ukraine, and agreed to send a team of experts to the eastern region city of Rovno to examine and package safely the wastes.

13.   February 6, 1996, Alexandr Nikitin was arrested and charged with espionage and acts of high treason because of his involvement in the production of a Bellona Foundation report on atomic safety in Russian Northern Fleet installations and submarines based on the Kola peninsula. The charge carried a penalty from ten years of imprisonment up to and including the death sentence. The Norwegian Minister of Foreign Affairs stated, in response to the arrest of Nikitin, that openness regarding environmental and nuclear safety questions and the possibility of citizens and organizations to freely engage in environmental work are among the most important changes the new times have brought to Russia. Regrettably, many countries still do not permit their citizens to engage freely in environmental work. Nikitin's arrest and imprisonment is only one of many examples of people being imprisoned or executed for their attempts to bring their countries environmental hazards to light.

These incidents illustrate that industrialized countries can easily unload their toxic waste in lesser developed countries due both to economic incentives and the lack of sufficient regulatory mechanisms in lesser developed countries. Not only does this harm the receiving countries, but it greatly reduces incentives for countries to regulate and reduce the amount of toxic waste they produce.

3.   Editors' Note. There are a number of risks posed by the hazardous wastes trade. Many developing countries have totally uncontrolled hazardous waste disposal practices. Others do not have the technical expertise or means of enforcement to properly handle these dangerous substances. Sometimes nations do not know what they are receiving due to mislabeling and the deliberate mixing of hazardous material with harmless material. Often waste brokers handle the transaction, which increases the risks of mishandling and subterfuge.

The risks for the receiving country are not only contaminated air, soil, water, and foodstuffs. Rates of cancer, birth defects, and other health problems can be alarmingly high in areas contaminated by hazardous wastes. Many hazardous wastes have a long life span in the environment. The effects of poorly managed wastes may take generations to show up. There can be direct, physically harmful effects on neighboring states. Of major concern is the possible effect on the biosphere.

The transboundary shipment of waste is also not in the interests of the exporting industrialized nations inasmuch as there is no guarantee that the wastes will then be properly managed. Industrialized nations may experience a "boomerang effect." Most developing nations have agricultural economies. Food-importing countries could find, therefore, that the poisons end up on their dining room tables.

There are yet other risks involved in exporting hazardous wastes. For four consecutive years, French officials have discovered illegal waste mixed together with legally imported waste from Germany. Twenty-five tons of illegal plastic waste from Germany was discovered by French customs officials on January 18, 1994 near the town of Laon. Included with the plastics were hospital waste and heavy metals, such as lead and zinc. See *Environment Minister Hails Controls on Waste Imports in Wake of Latest Discovery*, 17 Int'l Env't Rep. (BNA) 118 (Feb. 9, 1994). Prosecutors in Frankfurt alleged that in 1993 several waste management companies, including one that is part of the Thyssen group, mixed hazardous electronic and automobile scraps with recyclable material, labeled the mix "tradeable goods," and then shipped the consignment to a landfill in France. See *More Waste Trouble Ahead for Germany as DSD Brings Rates Back Up*, 2 Env't Watch W. Eur. (Cutter Info. Corp.) No. 116, at 4 (Aug. 6, 1993). Christopher J. Foreman, *a Comparative Analysis of Internal Controls on the Transfer of Waste Within The E.U. And U.S.* 3 Cardozo J. Int'l & Comp. L. 251, at n.6 (1995). Not surprisingly, the *Khian Sea* ferried its cargo of municipal ash from Philadelphia around the world for several years as successive countries refused to let it dispose of the waste, before the waste was finally dumped in the Indian Ocean. *Ship Operators Accused of Lying*, Wash. Post, July 15, 1992, at A4.

4. Stockholm Declaration on the Human Environment of the United Nations Conference on the Human Environment Adopted by the UN Conference on the Human Environment at Stockholm, 16 June 1972, Report of the U.N. Conference on the Human Environment, Stockholm, 15–16 June 1972, U.N. Doc. A/CONF.48/14/Rev.1 at 3 (1973), U.N. Doc. A/CONF.48/14 at 2–65, and Corr. 1 (1972), *reprinted in* **11 I.L.M. 1416 (1972): Preamble & Principles 1–3, 6, 11–13, 21–24** [Basic Document 1.12].

5. **Charter of Economic Rights and Duties of States, Dec. 12, 1974, art. 30 U.N.G.A.Res. 3281 (XXIX), 29 U.N. GAOR, Supp. (No. 31) 50, U.N. Doc. A/9631 (1975),** *reprinted in* **14 I.L.M. 251 (1975):** [Basic Document 7.2].

6. **World Charter for Nature, Oct. 28, 1982, G.A. Res. 37/7, U.N. GAOR, 37th Sess., Supp. No. 51, at 17, U.N. Doc. A/37/51,** *reprinted in* **22 I.L.M. 455 (1983): Principles 1–4, 6–9, 11, 12, 14, 19, 19, 20, 24** [Basic Document 1.21].

7. **Organization for Economic Co–Operation and Development: Council Decision–Recommendation on Exports of Hazardous Wastes From the OECD Area (1986)** [Basic Document 5.2].

8. **Basel Convention on the Control of Transboundary Movements of Hazardous Waste, Done at Basel, Mar. 22, 1989,** *reprinted in* **28 I.L.M. 649 (1989): Preamble & arts. 1, 2, 4, 6, 9, Annex 1, 3, 7, 8, 9 (As amended)** [Basic Document 5.6].

9. **Marguerite M. Cusack,** *"International Law and the Transboundary Shipment of Hazardous Waste to the Third World: Will the Basel Convention Make a Difference?"*, 5 Am. U. J. Int'l L. & Pol'y. 393, 395, 397–412, 414–16 (1990).

Today, several national, regional, and international agreements exist which restrict the transboundary shipment of toxic wastes. . . .

* * *

I. International Regulation of Transfrontier
Movements of Hazardous Wastes

A. *The United States*

1. Historical Development

In 1969, the United States passed the National Environmental Policy Act (NEPA) in an effort to establish environmental protection policies. Because NEPA does not apply extraterritorially, however, President Carter issued Executive Order No. 12,264 which established, inter alia, procedures for the export of hazardous substances. Although President Reagan revoked Order No. 12,264 in 1981, the Resource Conservation and Recovery Act (RCRA) had been passed in 1980.

Initially, RCRA only established regulations regarding domestic generation, treatment, transport, storage, and disposal of solid wastes. Consequently, factors such as the increase in the domestic generation of toxic waste and disposal costs, the decrease in the number and capacity of domestic disposal sites, and the public opposition to the location of disposal sites known as "Not In My Backyard" (NIMBY) compelled American businesses to view exportation of toxic wastes as a viable alternative. As a result, pressures from environmental interest groups and several foreign policy embarrassments compelled Congress to address the exportation of hazardous waste and pass the Hazardous and Solid Waste Amendments of 1984 (HSWA) to RCRA in 1984.

Pursuant to HSWA, the exporter must notify the United States Environmental Protection Agency (EPA) of its proposed shipment of hazardous waste to another country. Within thirty days thereafter, the EPA and the State Department must inform the importing government that the law of the United States prohibits the exportation of hazardous waste without consent from the importing nation. Following the receipt of consent or objection from the importing nation, the EPA must notify the exporter within thirty days. HSWA also requires that the primary exporter report annually to the EPA a summary of the types, quantities, frequency, and final destinations of all toxic wastes exported during the previous year. HSWA's specific notification, consent, and annual report provisions are waived if the United States and the importing government have a formal bilateral agreement regarding the transfer of toxic waste.

HSWA broadly defines "hazardous wastes" as substances that cause significant illnesses, an increase in mortality, or harm to individuals' health or to the environment. Accordingly, the EPA has listed specific solid wastes and characteristics of waste that HSWA regulates. Concerning liability, however, HSWA lacks the requisite clear legislative intent to enable it to have extraterritorial effect. Although private citizens and the United States government may bring suit regarding the noncompliance of HSWA's notification and consent requirements, foreign nations can only seek redress through the American tort system when imported toxic wastes cause injury within their borders.

* * *

C. *Organization for Economic Cooperation and Development*

1. *Historical Development*

In 1974, the OECD[1] established the Waste Management Policy Group (the Group) to address international waste problems on three fronts: first, source reduction; second, material reclamation; and, third, transportation and disposal of toxic waste. In 1984, however, the OECD focused exclusively on the transfrontier movement of toxic waste when it adopted the Decision and Recommendation on Transfrontier Movements of Hazardous Waste (1984 Final Decision).[2] The 1984 Final Decision required member nations to notify the countries involved of any transboundary movement of hazardous waste.

The OECD also recommended principles for member nations to follow in the implementation of the 1984 Final Decision. First, any party involved in the export of toxic waste must obtain authority from the nations of origin, transit, and final destination. Second, the nation of generation must apply its domestic laws of toxic waste exportation as stringently to exports as to domestic movements. Third, the exporter must provide the exporting, transit, and importing nations with adequate and timely information regarding the

---

1. [T]he OECD is exclusively composed of industrialized democracies: Australia, Austria, Belgium, Canada, Denmark, Finland, France, the Federal Republic of Germany, Greece, Iceland, Ireland, Italy, Japan, Luxembourg, the Netherlands, New Zealand, Norway, Portugal, Spain, Sweden, Switzerland, Turkey, the United Kingdom, and the United States. [Iberia is a member of the OECD also].

2. Decision and Recommendation on Transfrontier Movements of Hazardous Wastes, OECD Doc. C(83)180 (Feb. 13, 1984), *reprinted in* 25 I.L.M. 1010 (1986) [hereinafter 1984 Final Decision].

origin, composition, and quantities of waste; any environmental risks involved in transport; the conditions of carriage; and the identity of all parties. Fourth, an importer may object to a toxic waste shipment if the objection is in accordance with its own domestic law. Fifth, if the importer cannot complete safe disposal, the generator must reassume responsibility for the waste, or alternatively, re-import it.

The OECD improved the 1984 Final Decision by adopting the Decision–Recommendation on Exports of Hazardous Wastes in 1986 (1986 Export Decision).[6] In addition to the notification requirements imposed on exporting countries, the 1986 Export Decision requires member nations to prohibit exports unless the importing nation consents to the exports. Furthermore, an OECD member country must provide prior notification to any transit country involved. Finally, according to the 1986 Export Decision, a member nation must ensure that the importing country has adequate disposal facilities.

* * *

[In 1989,] the OECD finally adopted a number of resolutions and decisions designed to control the transboundary movement of hazardous waste to developing countries. The OECD will use the EC's core list of hazardous chemicals to resolve the most contentious issue which is the definition of "hazardous waste." Moreover, a member nation must prohibit any export of hazardous waste if there is reason to believe that the waste will not be disposed of in an environmentally sound manner. The OECD, however, fails to require exporting nations to receive consent from a transit country before shipping the waste. Moreover, the OECD decided to leave the issue of liability for a future international meeting.

II.   The Basel Convention on the Control of Transboundary Movements
        of Hazardous Wastes and Their Disposal, Final Act

* * *

C. The Basel Convention on the Transboundary Movements
        of Hazardous Wastes and Their Disposal

On March 22, 1989, after two years of intense and divisive debate, thirty-four nations signed the Basel Convention **[Basic Document 5.6]**. The purpose of the Basel Convention is to enhance the control of the transfrontier movement of toxic wastes in order to encourage safe management and reduction in volume of transboundary shipments. The Basel Convention has yet to be implemented, however, because the required twenty nations have not ratified its provisions. Many nations view the Basel Convention as signaling the international community's commitment to protect both human health and the world environment. Proponents suggest that the Basel Convention ... envelops a larger global community than previous international agreements, thereby resulting in implementation on a larger economic and political scale. Supporters further contend that the Basel Convention qualitatively expands and improves on the presently existing international and regional agreements which attempt to control the transfrontier movements of

---

6. Council Decision–Recommendation on   Area ... [hereinafter 1986 Export Decision]
Exports of Hazardous Waste from the OECD   **[Basic Document 5.2]**.

hazardous waste. Several international environmental organizations and most developing countries, on the other hand, believe the Basel Convention is laden with ambiguities and loopholes. Opponents point to the Convention's ambiguous language and the exclusion of fundamental and important concepts. They assert that the Basel Convention does not restrict the transboundary shipment of hazardous waste; instead, it merely provides a global tracking system for toxic waste movement. Accordingly, critics contend the Basel Convention grants industrialized nations formal permission to use developing nations as dumping grounds for their hazardous wastes. Finally, critics charge that the Basel Convention simply reiterates the existing, yet inadequate international toxic waste agreements. As evidence, opponents note that the Basel Convention does not include important amendments proposed by several Third World countries.

    10. Jason L. Gudofsky, *Transboundary Shipments of Hazardous Waste For Recycling And Recovery Operations,* 34 Stan. J. Int'l L. 219, 272–85 (1998).

V.   Implications for Recovery, Recycling, and Re-use

    [B]ilateral and multilateral agreements ... impose varying degrees of control on transboundary movements of hazardous wastes. At one end of the spectrum, the Bamako Convention seeks to limit trade in wastes between African countries and to eliminate it altogether between African and non-African countries. It accomplishes this objective by prohibiting all shipments into Africa, regardless of whether wastes are destined for recovery or final disposal operations, and by imposing strict requirements on transboundary shipments of wastes within Africa. Furthermore, by establishing an extremely wide definition of wastes, the Parties to the Bamako Convention have ensured that the Convention covers virtually every potentially dangerous substance or material.

    At the other end of the spectrum are the Decisions of the OECD Council. Rather than limiting trade in hazardous wastes, the Decisions impose requirements intended to ensure that transboundary shipments proceed in an environmentally sound manner. For wastes destined for recovery, the 1992 Decision establishes general consent and, similar to the Basel Convention, general notification procedures. The purpose of these procedures is to lower the transaction costs associated with shipping wastes. Rather than indiscriminately labeling wastes as hazardous and thus increasing related costs, the 1992 Decision creates a three-tiered system, organized by color (green, amber, or red), which imposes increasingly stringent levels of control in accordance with the risk that a particular material poses to human health and the environment.

    Finally, in the middle (if it may be called that) lies the Basel Convention. The Convention suffers because it seeks to accommodate the needs of countries with widely divergent views regarding the appropriate levels of controls that should be imposed on transboundary shipments. On one hand, many Lower–Income Countries (LICs) and some Higher–Income Countries (HICs) support a total ban on shipments from OECD to non-OECD Member countries, while other countries, mainly the HICs (including non-OECD Members), favor controlled trade. The Parties to the Basel Convention ultimately agreed to permit trade, but only if waste shipments meet stringent requirements such as prior written informed consent and environmental soundness.

Many of the Parties to the Basel Convention, particularly the LICs, have become increasingly disenchanted with the level of control offered by the Basel Convention. Much of this concern derives from a lack of definitional clarity of many of the key terms (such as the terms "waste" and "disposal"). These Parties have successfully mobilized support for wholesale changes to the Basel Convention. Particularly important among such changes are those regarding transboundary shipments of hazardous wastes destined for recycling and recovery operations.

It is generally accepted that recycling and recovery of hazardous wastes can be both environmentally and economically beneficial. At the same time, however, if wastes are mislabeled and are in fact destined for final disposal, or if the process or the by-products produced from the recycling process are not managed in an environmentally sound manner, then recycling can have an adverse effect on human health and the environment. The goal, therefore, is to establish an appropriate regulatory scheme that encourages recycling and recovery while also guarding against related adverse consequences.

The following [sic] examines far-reaching changes to the Basel Convention instituted at a recent Conference of the Parties to the Convention. These changes are particularly important, since the Basel Convention is the only truly global agreement concerning transboundary movements of hazardous wastes. The subsequent Subpart discusses some of the benefits and drawbacks of a variety of regulatory approaches.

A. Recent Initiatives Concerning the Regulation of Transboundary Shipments of Hazardous Wastes for Recovery Operations

Article 15 of the Basel Convention established a Conference of the Parties and provided that meetings of the Conference would be held at regular intervals starting no later than one year after the Convention's entry into force. The first Conference was held in 1992; three additional Conferences have been held since that time. During the two most recent Conferences, held September 18–22, 1995, in Geneva, Switzerland, and February 23–27, 1998, in Kuching, Malaysia, the Parties unanimously adopted and affirmed Decision III/1, which provides for a far-reaching amendment to the Convention. The amendment requires that countries enumerated under a newly created annex to the Convention—Annex VII—shall immediately refrain from transporting to non-Annex VII countries any hazardous wastes destined for final disposal. This requirement was to be extended to hazardous wastes destined for recovery by December 31, 1997. The amendment will have a tremendous impact on recycling efforts generally and on the recycling industry specifically.

* * *

2. Historical Background of Decision III/1

Although the Basel Convention was initially proposed and signed in 1989, it did not officially enter into force until May 5, 1992, three months after Australia became the twentieth country to ratify the Convention under its domestic law. In accordance with Article 15, the Parties held their first Conference of the Parties in Piriapolis, Uruguay, on December 3–4, 1992. At that first Conference, the Parties adopted a substantial number of Decisions covering a broad range of matters; Decisions I/16 and I/22 are the most significant with respect to shipments destined for recovery operations.

In Decision I/16, the Parties requested the Conference's Technical Working Group to consider criteria for determining whether a particular waste is suitable for recovery and recommend control procedures to ensure that all shipments of hazardous wastes occur safely. Interestingly, in Decision I/22 the Parties seemed to acknowledge that different obligations should apply to wastes destined for disposal and wastes destined for recovery operations. Decision I/22 requests that the "industrialized countries" prohibit transboundary shipments of hazardous and other wastes "for disposal" to "developing countries." Decision I/22 further notes that, until the Technical Working Group has completed its report pursuant to Decision I/16, the Parties should ensure that any shipments destined for recovery purposes "be handled in an environmentally sound manner."

Rather than seeking innovative solutions, the second Conference of the Parties, held March 21–25, 1994, in Geneva, was dominated by Parties who effectively lobbied for a total ban on all shipments of hazardous wastes from OECD to non-OECD countries. These Parties argued that any such shipments violated prima facie the Convention's environmental soundness requirement. In response to this claim, the Conference adopted Decision II/12, which urges OECD Member countries to immediately prohibit shipments destined for final disposal to non-Member countries, and to extend this requirement, by December 31, 1997, to wastes destined for recovery operations.

Although Decision II/12 was adopted by consensus, there seemed to be some disagreement among the Parties as to exactly what the Decision covered and how it affected shipments destined for recovery purposes. The Report of the Second Meeting of the Conference thus noted:

> Many representatives strongly supported a total ban on export of hazardous wastes from OECD to non-OECD countries, not only for final disposal but also for recovery and recycling operations. Some representatives were, however, of the opinion that under the strict control of the Basel Convention and when the importing country possessed the technological capability to recover raw materials from hazardous wastes, the transboundary movements of such wastes should be allowed.[7]

The official statements made by the Parties demonstrate the differences in opinion. The representative of Sri Lanka, on behalf of the G–77 and China, asserted that as a result of Decision II/12, the only hazardous wastes traded from an OECD country to a non-OECD country after December 31, 1997, will be the former's "know-how." Representatives from other countries, such as Austria and Australia, expressed their concern over whether prohibiting shipments for recovery activities was in the best interest of the environment. The Austrian representative of Austria noted that "he would have preferred to see a flexible system which would have given room for well specified exceptions in the field of recycling and recovery."

---

7. Report of the Second Meeting of the Conference of the Parties to the Basel Convention on the Control of Transboundary Movements of Hazardous Wastes and their Disposal, at 7, U.N. Doc. UNEP/CHW.2/30 (1994).

In the meantime, in accordance with paragraph 2 of Decision II/14, the Technical Working Group developed a draft paper, Guidance Document on Transboundary Movements of Hazardous Wastes Destined for Recovery Operations, to be considered by the Parties at the next Conference. Among other things, the paper outlined some of the benefits and drawbacks of recovery operations and established criteria for determining whether a recovery operation is environmentally sound. The Technical Working Group ultimately recommended that more resources and time, including the production of case studies, be devoted for examining the potential benefits of recovery and, if prudent, suggested possible future regulatory protections.

Instead of moving forward, the Parties proposed Decision III/1, which, except for a few exceptions, essentially incorporates Decision II/12. At the Third Meeting of the Conference of the Parties in 1995, Decision III/1 was adopted as an amendment to the Convention.

3.   Decision III/1

Decision III/1 amends Article 4 of the Basel Convention and adds a new annex, Annex VII, to the Convention. The amendment, which is incorporated into the Convention as Article 4A, provides:

> 1.   Each Party listed in Annex VII shall prohibit all transboundary movements of hazardous wastes which are destined for operations according to Annex IV A, to States not listed in Annex VII.
>
> 2.   Each Party listed in Annex VII shall phase out by 31 December 1997, and prohibit as of that date, all transboundary movements of hazardous wastes under Article 1(i)(a) of the Convention which are destined for operations according to Annex IV B to States not listed in Annex VII. Such transboundary movement shall not be prohibited unless the wastes in question are characterized as hazardous under the Convention.[8]

Annex VII covers "Parties and other States which are members of OECD, EC, Liechtenstein." **[Basic Document 5.6]**. Implementation of paragraph 1 of Article 4A should not be problematic. Most, if not all, of the OECD Member countries have generally abided by the request to ban shipments of hazardous wastes destined for final disposal to non-OECD countries, as required by Decision II/12. Further, although the definition of hazardous wastes is far from clear, the amendment at least adopts the one provided for under Article 1(1). Thus, any waste already treated as hazardous under the Convention continues to be considered hazardous under the amendment. Finally, there seems to be wide support for such a ban. The Report of the Third Meeting of the Conference of the Parties noted that the Parties at the Third Meeting gave their "unanimous approval of the decision that transboundary movements of hazardous wastes to developing countries for final disposal should cease immediately."

The amendment in paragraph 2 concerning hazardous wastes destined for recovery operations is much more contentious. One of the main difficulties lies in the amendment's differentiating between hazardous wastes in para-

---

8. Decisions Adopted at the Third Meeting of the Conference of the Parties to the Basel   Convention, U.N. Doc. UNEP/CHW.3/35 (1995).

graphs (a) and (b) of Article 1(1). To begin, it is unclear exactly what wastes "are characterized as hazardous under the Convention." The problem is that Annex III of the Basel Convention provides that each Party must use its own national tests to determine whether a waste exhibits any of the enumerated hazardous characteristics. Hence, it does not prescribe any uniform methods for determining whether a waste falls under the Convention. This problem is compounded since Annex III does not prescribe quantitative standards for determining if a hazard exists and does not provide clear definitions and descriptions of the characteristics enumerated—particularly sections H10 to H13.

As a result of such deficiencies, a number of Parties indicated that they would not ratify and implement the amendment until the Technical Working Group completes its study and presents a satisfactory proposal for clarifying Annex III (and thus the amendment as well).[9] For example, Canada's representative to the Third Meeting attached the following statement to Decision III/1: "[Canada] will be unable to consider ratification of this amendment prior to an outcome on definitional terms from the technical working group, from which Canada can draw the assurance that trade in non-hazardous recyclables will not be jeopardized." The representative of the Russian Federation announced that the Federation "cannot accept the proposed amendment and does not consider itself bound thereby." According to the Russian Federation, the scope of paragraph 2 of the amendment is much broader than initially agreed upon, while the time-frame for negotiating clarification and changes is too short.

While the lack of definitional clarity is certainly a major problem and, for the time-being, will relegate paragraph 2 of the amendment to no more than a general statement of concern, it is uncertain even whether the Parties agree on requirements prescribed by Decision III/1. Some Parties asserted that "[m]any representatives strongly supported the adoption of an amendment to the Convention which would ban all exports of hazardous wastes from OECD to non-OECD countries, not only for final disposal but also for recovery and recycling operations." In this vein, Malaysia indicated that it considered Decision II/12, including the provisions concerning hazardous wastes destined for recovery, as binding; while Costa Rica indicated that it felt that by excluding paragraph (b) of Article 1(1), Decision III/1 did not go far enough. On the other hand, some Parties believed the amendment should only extend to hazardous wastes destined for final disposal. This concern represents the trepidation felt by some Parties who are weary of placing excessive limits on recycling and recovery activities. Canada asserted:

> Canada is committed to the wise utilization of all resources. As such, Canada believes that environmentally sound recycling is required to ensure the availability of such resources for use by future generations. Environmentally sound recycling is a necessary and integral part of sustainable development. There will be a need for recycling of hazardous wastes today, tomorrow, and for many years to come.[10]

---

9. The COP4 to the Basel Convention adopted two new annexes that list and exempt wastes from Basel application. *See* [**Basic Document 5.6, Annexes 7 & 9.**]

10. *Id.*, Annex II at 20.

Australia also indicated that it read the amendment as excluding "such commodities as ferrous scrap and unmixed paper, and the majority of wastes on the OECD Green List which pose no threat to public health or amenity."[11]

Although Decision III/1 was accepted by consensus of the Plenary, it will not be fully implemented until it is ... accepted [and ratified] by all of the Parties. In order for this to happen, from both a legal and practical perspective, the Parties must first agree upon a common interpretation of the amendment, and then decide upon criteria for membership in Annex VII. With respect to the first issue, the Technical Working Group's listing of hazardous wastes into categories "A" and "B" has been accepted. This should bring some definitional clarity to the question of what constitutes a hazardous waste. The Parties to the Convention are still debating the second issue. Accordingly, at the Fourth Meeting of the Conference of the Parties, the Parties agreed to cooperate with the Subgroup on Legal and Technical Experts to consider, among other things, whether other countries will be permitted to join Annex VII.

Some of the Parties are not willing to impose a blanket prohibition against shipments of hazardous wastes from Annex VII to non-Annex VII countries. Hence, in addition to adopting the Guidance Document on Transboundary Movements of Hazardous Wastes Destined for Recovery and Operations, Decision III/14 calls upon the Technical Working Group to prepare case studies and guidelines for constructing and improving recovery facilities in non-OECD countries. More work will have to be done before the amendment is made part of the Convention. Although not a positive step, this represents the likely direction in which the Convention is headed.

4.   Fourth Meeting of the Conference of the Parties

The Fourth Meeting of the Conference of the Parties was held in February 1998. At this meeting, the Parties agreed first to incorporate lists A (wastes characterized as hazardous under Article 1(1)(a) of the Basel Convention) and B (wastes that will not be covered by Article 1(1)(a) of the Convention unless they contain Annex I materials to an extent causing them to exhibit Annex III characteristics). This should bring some additional clarification as to what constitutes a hazardous waste. More controversial, however, was the debate over the proper scope of Decision III/I and Annex VII thereto. The debate is now focused on whether the list of countries enumerated in Annex VII is a closed or open list. Monaco, Israel, and Slovenia have asked to be included in that list. This proposal has been fiercely rejected by many of the LICs, most notably the Arab States, who fear that opening up the list of countries included in Annex VII will be a slippery slope towards making the Basel Convention a mere voluntary agreement between the Parties. Other Parties, most notably Canada, support the right of countries to join Annex VII. Presumably, this is based on both an acknowledgment of the principle of territorial sovereignty and recognition of the potential benefits of recovery and recycling operations. For the reasons already canvassed, the position taken by the latter group of countries, namely to open Annex VII to any countries which wish to join, or at least to countries satisfying certain minimum criteria, is the preferable one.

11. *Id.*, Annex II at 22.

The Parties have further reserved the application of Decision III/1 to the next meeting, the Fifth Meeting of the Conference of the Parties. At that time, the Parties will once again consider whether Annex VII should be closed to only those countries that were originally included on the list, or whether to allow other countries to freely join. With respect to the latter proposition, the Parties have agreed, through the Subgroup of Legal and Technical Experts, to consider criteria for joining Annex VII.

B. The Future of Recycling and Recovery: On the Verge of "Throwing the Baby Out with the Bath Water"

Instead of proposing innovative ways to establish a regulatory scheme that both allows the non-Annex VII countries to capture the economic and environmental benefits of recycling and guards against abuses and illegal traffic in hazardous waste, the Parties to the Basel Convention have accepted an amendment that presumes that all transboundary shipments from HICs to LICs, regardless of the type or nature of the process to be used for disposing or treating wastes, must be prohibited. As a result, future negotiations will likely center around developing a common interpretation of the substantive elements of the amendment, rather than on possible schemes for permitting hazardous waste shipments destined for recovery operations. Indeed, this proved to be the case at the Fourth Meeting, where the debate centered on membership to Annex VII.

According to the Guidance Document, permitting transboundary movements of hazardous wastes for recycling or recovery:

- could, in some instances, "result in a transportation distance that is less than would be the case for movement to domestic facilities";
- has "the potential to reduce the size and generally reduces the hazard potential of waste streams," provided that the recovery complies with the requirement of "environmentally sound management";
- "should promote energy savings and/or act to reduce the demand for increased exploitation of natural resources";
- can produce materials which are fungible; and
- "normally reduces the quantity of residuals which would otherwise go to final disposal, even considering the need for disposal of residual materials from the recovery process."[12]

From an environmental perspective, the prime advantage of recycling is the resulting decrease in both demand for virgin resources and production of hazardous wastes. Aside from either preventing or minimizing the production of hazardous wastes, recycling is generally the most favorable method of "disposal."

There are, of course, a number of potential drawbacks to encouraging global programs of waste recovery and recycling. First, some countries do not have the capability for assessing the nature of wastes being imported and/or the capacity to treat them in an environmentally sound manner. Second, even if a country can suitably assess and recycle its imported hazardous wastes,

12. Report of the Secretariat and Guidance Document on Transboundary Movements of Hazardous Wastes Destined for Recovery Oper- ations, Third Meeting of the Conference of the Parties to the Basel Convention, at 17, U.N. Doc. UNEP/CHW.3/17 (1995).

that does not necessarily mean the country can deal with potential emergencies, such as spills or fires, or provide the infrastructure necessary to continually monitor and control the byproducts produced during the recycling process. Third, because unscrupulous waste traders sometimes mislabel wastes destined for final disposal, the likelihood of potential emergencies may be even greater. Fourth, very few studies have analyzed in detail the environmental effects of recovery and recycling in LICs. Most existing studies have been conducted in the HICs, where the climatic and ecological conditions are often very different than in the LICs. Finally, it is possible that by focusing on recycling and recovery, countries will not pay enough attention to the more important objectives of waste prevention and minimization.

Although recycling and recovery present some dangers, these potential dangers do not justify a total ban on transboundary shipments in and of themselves. Failure to provide a relatively open system of trade in secondary materials may stunt the development of a strong recycling and recovery industry. Recycling operators require an ample supply of material in order to be productive and profitable. Without guaranteed sources of supply, which can only result from greater international cooperation and a clarification of the terms of the Basel Convention, there will be less incentive for prospective and existing facilities to increase their capital expenditures. Furthermore, by creating artificial barriers to trade (i.e., barriers based on income level rather than technological capacity), countries are given neither the ability to capture the benefits of economies of scale nor the ability to develop a competitive advantage in recycling operations. It is only through the development of a strong waste management industry that the international community might thwart illegal trafficking and pursue environmentally efficacious waste management policies.

11. Muthu S. Sundram, *Basel Convention on Transboundary Movement of Hazardous Wastes: Total Ban Amendment*, 9 PACE INT'L L. REV. 1, 31–34, 36–37, 42 (1997).

DEVELOPMENT OF LIABILITY PROTOCOL

The Ad Hoc Working Group of Legal and Technical Experts (LTE) is a subsidiary body of the COP charged with the development of Model National Legislation and preparation of a draft Protocol on Liability and Compensation for damages resulting from transboundary movements of hazardous wastes and their disposal.

* * *

GENERAL OBJECTIVES OF THE PROTOCOL

The Protocol attempts to provide for "comprehensive regime for liability and for adequate and prompt compensation"[13] for damage which results

---

13. Draft Articles of a Protocol on Liability for Damage Resulting from the Transboundary Movements of Hazardous Wastes and Their Disposal, Report of the Ad Hoc Working Group on the Work of its Third Session, Annex, Article 1, Geneva, Feb. 20–24, 1995, art. 2, P 2(b), U.N. Doc. UNEP/CHW.1/WG.1/3/2 (March 17, 1995)

Damage means:

(i) loss of life or personal injury;

(ii) loss or damage to property other than property held by the person liable for the damage in accordance with the present Protocol;

"from the transboundary movement and disposal of hazardous wastes and other wastes due to incidents occurring during the time from the transboundary movement has commenced until completion of the disposal of *26 the wastes [including aftercare of disposal sites]."[14] These issues are not new to the Basel Convention. Similar issues were successfully dealt with during the negotiations of European Council Convention on Civil Liability for Damage Resulting from Activities Dangerous to the Environment, known as the Lugano Convention.[15] The deliberation in the development of Liability Protocol for Basel Convention are, however, more complicated than the Lugano Convention for several reasons:

- Basel Convention has larger number of participants which has been ratified by one hundred countries as of August 16, 1996;

- the Basel waste chain consists of a number of insufficiently capitalized countries;

- extra sensitivity is attached to a number of liability issues because of special considerations for the needs of developing countries; and

- greater political awareness is required in setting up the parameters partly due to the suspicion with which the developing countries look upon developed countries.

* * *

LIABLE PERSONS

A broad objective of the Basel Convention is to promote global environmental protection through minimization of production of hazardous wastes and other wastes, rather than find ways to impose liability upon persons after a harm is caused from such substances. Another objective is to manage the wastes covered under the Convention within the country that generated the waste, if it can do so in an "environmentally sound" manner and in an efficient way.

The Basel Convention attempts to accomplish these goals by placing greater obligations on generators/exporters, i.e., the supply side of the scale, by controlling the transboundary movement of hazardous wastes and other wastes, and thus providing for an elaborate control mechanism which includes both (i) notice to and consent from importing and transit countries and also (ii) a requirement that an exporting country may not export covered wastes, if there is a reason to believe that the exported waste will not be handled in an environmentally sound manner in the importing country. In this sense, the Basel Convention is far different from the liability provisions of [the U.S.] Comprehensive Environmental Response, Compensation, and Liability Act

(iii) loss of profit from impairment of the environment;

(iv) impairment of the environment, in so far as this is not considered to be damage within the meaning of sub-paragraphs (i), (ii), and (iii) above;

(v) the cost of preventive measures;

(vi) any loss or damage caused by preventive measures, to the extent that the damage arises out of or results from the transboundary movement and disposal of hazardous wastes and other wastes under the Convention.

14. *Id.* art. 3, P 1.

15. Lugano Convention, Europ. T.S. No.150, June 21, 1993.

(CERCLA) which imposes liability upon "owners and operators" of a "facility" from which there is a "release."

Though CERCLA, a backward looking statute, is primarily intended to be a "compensation and liability act" for past harms, and the Basel Convention is a forward looking statute and is, therefore, more akin to [the U.S.] Resource Conversation and Recovery Act (RCRA) which, through an elaborate permit system, requires that "hazardous waste be properly managed in the first instance thereby reducing the need for corrective action at a future date," a close inspection reveals that the Basel Convention is a hybrid of both CERCLA and RCRA. For example, an important provision of RCRA is that it establishes a permit system for "treatment, storage, and disposal" of all regulated hazardous wastes. To obtain a permit, a "facility operator," must comply with a vast amount of regulations that deal with a number of different aspects of "treatment, storage, and disposal" pertaining to incineration, landfills, chemical treatment, liquid disposal restrictions, siting of facilities, groundwater and leachate monitoring, fencing and warning signs, special employee training, emergency procedures and site closures. The Basel Convention shifts this burden to generators/exporters themselves, rather than placing the onus on importers who would, in a strict sense, be "facility operators," because the clientele that the Basel Convention intends to protect is mainly from developing countries who lack the sophisticated knowledge and technical know-how of "environmentally sound management" of hazardous wastes and other wastes.

As a result, an objective definition of "persons" liable under the Basel Convention has not been easy and is still elusive. The PWG discussed numerous definitions and exemptions, and at one point, a delegation even suggested introduction of fault-based liability either as an alternative or as supplement to strict liability proposals. Though this suggestion was quickly rebuffed by most of the delegates on the ground that a "subjective" fault-based liability would be a far cry from the Convention's goals to set "objective" strict liability standards, it is a clear example of the enormous complexity faced by the PWG which is obligated to "consider" every proposal advanced by the parties. The PWG, in its Third session, took up three alternatives for consideration, and ran out of time to consider a fourth alternative proposed by a delegation. In the end, as discussed below, the alternatives still remain unresolved.

FIRST ALTERNATIVE

In the first alternative, "the generator; the exporter; and any person, including the disposer, who at the time of the incident is in [possession and/or] control of the hazardous wastes or other wastes shall be liable for damage."[16]

Though the drafters may have meant broad coverage of persons under "any person," for example, waste brokers and arrangers, the text does not convey that meaning. First, the Protocol defines neither the term "person" nor the term "disposer". Second, the phrase "any person" in the draft is,

16. Report of the Third Meeting of the Conference of the Parties to the Basel Convention on the Control of Transbsoundary Movements of Hazardous Wastes and Their Disposal, U.N. Environment Programme at 29, U.N. Doc. UNEP/CHW.3/34 (1995).

indeed, modified by "who at the time of the incident is in possession and/or control" where an "incident" is "any occurrence or series of occurrences having the same origin in relation to the transboundary movement and disposal of hazardous wastes and other wastes under the Convention, that causes damage or creates a grave and imminent threat of causing damage." Third, what sort of "occurrence or series of occurrences" would be deemed to have "relation to" the transboundary movement is not clear. Finally, the draft defines neither the term "imminent" nor the phrase "imminent threat of causing damage." Do the drafters actually mean "threat of" "imminent endangerment?"

What if an "arranger," through appropriate "notice and consent," and, pursuant to Article 11 of the Basel Convention which allows transboundary movement of hazardous wastes and other wastes under a "bilateral, multilateral, or regional agreement," transfers the ownership of Basel-covered waste to a Basel-importer and an "incident" occurs because of the negligence of, rather than intentional conduct of, but, "at the time of ownership" of the importing Basel party? What is the status of the "arranger" who in this case is not a generator? Is he or she a "person?" or, an "exporter?" or, a "disposer?" Would a distinction in the classification of liable "persons" have any bearing in a claim for contribution which, as will be discussed later, is an action in equity?

A most disturbing aspect of this alternative is the language "who at the time of the incident is in [possession and/or] control of the hazardous wastes or other wastes." Almost always, the contemplated incident, e.g., damage to the environment from the disposal of hazardous waste or other wastes, will happen at the time the hazardous waste and other wastes is in the possession, control or custody of the importing party or a facility operator. In other words, an innocent importer or facility operator, whom the Convention intends to protect, will now become strictly liable for the damages to the same extent as the generator or the exporter of the hazardous waste and other wastes. Because the Liability Protocol also establishes "joint and several liability" regimes, any protection to an innocent importing State is only illusory.

* * *

Third Alternative

Under the third alternative of the draft, "any person who at the time of the incident has operational control of the wastes, shall be liable for damages."[17] Among all the three alternatives, this provides the broadest coverage. The coverage under this alternative is joint, strict and several. However, clarification of what is an "operational control" is needed as well as an unambiguous definition for "incident."

One delegation which supported this alternative, also recommended that the PWG consider giving some weight to fault-based concept of liability that could apply to other persons who did not have "operational control of the wastes," but were involved in the transboundary movement of hazardous wastes. A number of delegates supported this view. A number of other

17. *Id.*

delegations, however, opposed the introduction of any fault-based liability into the Protocol because they were concerned that it would divert the Protocol's declared goal of developing a "comprehensive regime of liability."[18] These delegations argued that because the PWG is charged with making a "special law with objective and not subjective liability," developing a Protocol that would enable examining fault liability on a case-by-case basis would be difficult.

Another delegation proposed to expand the existing joint and several liability provisions of Article 4 by adding a right of contribution from other liable parties and including a set of "permissive factors" that the courts may consider in resolving contribution claims:

> [E]ach Contracting Party shall ensure that any person who shall be liable in accordance with Article 4(1) and, as a result, is defending a claim for compensation in its courts, shall have the ability in the same action to seek contribution from any other person who shall be liable thereunder.

> 4(2) It is further proposed to include a number of permissive factors that may be considered by the competent courts of the Parties in resolving contribution claims as follows:

> a) In resolving claims for contribution among those who are liable pursuant to Article 4(1), above, the competent court of a contracting Party may allocate damages among such liable Parties using such equitable factors as the court determines are appropriate....[19]

* * *

CONTRIBUTION

The Draft Protocol, in a bracketed text, provides for joint and several liability against all liable persons and states:

> [Each contracting Party shall ensure that any person who shall be liable in accordance with Article 4, paragraph 1, and is defending a claim for compensation in its courts, is entitled to seek contribution from any other person who shall be liable thereunder.][20] Thus, "a claim for compensation" is technically divorced from "determination of liability." This is similar to the case law on contribution claims in Superfund cases. A bracketed text of the draft allows the court to take into consideration a number of equitable factors in allocating damages which may include the following:

> (i) the amount of hazardous wastes and other wastes contributed by each liable person;

> (ii) the degree of hazards of hazardous wastes and other wastes contributed by each liable person;

> (iii) the degree of fault borne by each liable person for the inability to determine (i) and (ii) above;

18. *Id.*

19. *Id.* at 41(4)(2)(bis).

20. Draft Articles of a Protocol on Liability for Damage Resulting from the Transboundary Movements of Hazardous Wastes and Their Disposal, Report of the Ad Hoc Working Group on the Work of its Third Session, Annex, Article 1, Geneva, Feb. 20–24, 1995, art. 4, P 2(bis), U.N. Doc. UNEP/CHW.1/WG.1/3/2 (March 17, 1995).

(iv) the mobility of hazardous wastes and other wastes contributed by each person;

(v) the degree and nature of involvement of each liable person in the generation, transportation, treatment, storage, or disposal of the hazardous wastes and other wastes;

(vi) the degree of care exercised by each liable person with respect to hazardous wastes and other wastes taking into the characteristics of the hazardous wastes and other wastes;

(vii) the cooperation of each liable person in providing complete and timely information during the allocation process; and

(viii) the relative degree of fault borne by each liable person with respect to the incident giving rise to the damage.

Indeed, these are similar to what is known as "Gore Factors" debated in Congress as part of superfund reform. In relation to the right of recourse, one delegation presented the following proposal for contribution claims:

Each Contracting Party shall ensure that any person who shall be liable in accordance with Article 4(1) and, as a result, is defending a claim for compensation in its courts, shall have the ability in the same action to seek contribution from any other person who shall be liable thereunder. (emphasis added)

Under this proposal, one who seeks contribution has the option of initiating a separate contribution action or have it heard in the same action at the conclusion of the liability phase of the trial, as provided under CERCLA S 113(f). Several delegations expressed reservation related to the phrase "shall have the ability in the same action" and recommended that it be replaced with the phrase "is entitled to seek contribution."

Though the contribution provisions are at present included in Article 4 of the draft that deals with liability, it is felt that it would be more appropriate to move it to Article 10 governing "Competent Courts." Regardless of at which point of the Protocol the contribution provision is inserted, the draft seems to be somewhat ambiguous with respect to persons from whom contribution may be sought.

The draft permits a person already found liable "to seek" contribution only from another person "who shall be liable thereunder." It appears that "thereunder" refers to the contribution claim itself. Though "shall be liable" would imply that a liable person may not be able to "obtain" contribution from another person unless the latter person is also found liable, there appears to be some confusion between "seeking" contribution and actually succeeding in "obtaining" contribution. In other words, a liable person should be able "to seek" contribution merely by being able to haul any other "liable-party" or a "potentially liable party" into a court of law; and if the court determines that the once-potentially-liable-party is indeed liable, it may allocate damages on equitable considerations.

* * *

DEFENSES TO LIABILITY

As would be expected in a comprehensive liability regime considered under the Protocol, the defenses to liability are minimal. The Draft Protocol provides that:

There shall be no liability if the damage is exclusively:

a) a result of armed conflict, hostilities, civil war or insurrection which was not reasonably foreseeable;

b) a result of a natural phenomenon of an exceptional, inevitable and irresistible character provided that all reasonable safety measures have been taken to prevent the damage;

c) a result of the wrongful intentional conduct of a third person provided that all reasonable safety measures have been taken, to prevent the consequences of such conduct;

d) a result of compliance with a compulsory measure of a public authority; or

(e) a result of a negligent or other wrongful act of any government or other authority.

12. Mark A. Montgomery, *Banning Waste Exports: Much Ado about Nothing*, 1 BUFF. J. INT'L L. 197, 203–05, 208–10, 216–18 (1994).

What seems to have become a common type of illegal waste trade is the importation of what a buyer perceives to be a good-quality, usable product, but upon delivery, the buyer discovers that he has received useless, contaminated, or even dangerous materials. This is fraud. It can occur in any kind of trade, and its victims have no socio-economic boundaries—they can be rich importers and poor importers alike. One often cited incident occurred in Bangladesh, in 1991; importers bought fertilizer that they later discovered had been mixed with dust from a copper smelter. It is interesting to note that this transfer would have been considered illegal under the terms of the Basel Convention, had it been in force. Furthermore, the United States government prosecuted and convicted the South Carolina company that exported the waste and agreed to take back the remaining toxic fertilizer even though the United States was under no formal, legal obligation to do so. Similar incidents have taken place in Haiti, Zimbabwe, Sierra Leone, and Poland. However, once again, without a systematic, empirical study of the quantity and direction of illegal waste movements, it is difficult to say with any certainty that non-OECD countries are subject to greater environmental damage from this sort of trade than OECD countries.

Greenpeace and others stress the possibility that these cases of fraud represent the "tip of the iceberg" of illegal waste transfers to developing countries. This may be true, but it remains only a possibility because of the anecdotal nature of these reports; it is not an established fact. A number of anecdotes seem to support the idea that developing countries have become the "global dumping ground" through fraud. But a number of "anecdotes" is not the logical equivalent to "data". It could be that Greenpeace's anecdotes are only exceptions to an otherwise unexciting rule: most waste traders operate legally and openly. While theories of waste trade icebergs are logically coherent and conceivably possible, these theories have not yet been systematically tested through empirical observation. The fact is that no one knows how big the illegal trade really is. Furthermore, as will be argued below, the size of the illegal waste trade will remain unaffected by the new waste export ban.

Taking a justifiably conservative, skeptical view of the best available data on waste transfers to non-OECD countries, it becomes apparent that the evidence is inconclusive: it is difficult to gauge the effectiveness of the Basel Convention, with or without the new export ban.

* * *

Trade in Non-hazardous Waste Will Continue

The Basel Convention purports only to regulate the international trade in hazardous waste. It is important to keep in mind that not all exported waste is hazardous, yet non-hazardous waste can still pose risks to human health and the environment. A recent proposal to export waste from the United States to Suriname illustrates the problem. The government of the Suriname reported to the government of the United States that it had learned of two separate plans to import waste into the South American country. The government of Suriname did not want to import either the municipal waste or sludge mentioned in the two proposals. The U.S. government expressed its support of the Surinamese government position, but replied that the U.S. government had no legal authority to restrict these waste exports unless they were defined under U.S. law as hazardous. Since neither the Basel Convention, nor U.S. law regards these materials as "hazardous," the Surinamese government could restrict their import under the Basel Convention only if it declared the waste "hazardous" and refused to import it under the prior informed consent rules of the Convention. Otherwise, even with the new ban, the transfer of waste to Suriname would be perfectly legal, despite its possible negative environmental consequences. In the end, the importing country is responsible for ensuring that its own environmental standards are upheld: in short, only Suriname can protect Suriname.

Non-OECD Countries May Become Complacent

One of the arguments in favor of the ban on waste exports is that it makes exporting countries responsible for whatever leaves their borders. Countries that have outlawed hazardous waste imports—103 in all—may believe that the export ban now relieves them of their own responsibility to ensure that no waste enters their borders. Yet, the illegal trade will continue to cause problems—perhaps even greater ones than that of the legal trade. Cases like the one in Bangladesh could become even more common if non-OECD countries now relax their efforts to keep out unwanted waste.

Moreover, by placing responsibility for waste trade problems on the shoulders of OECD countries, some non-OECD countries may think it unnecessary to develop their own waste control laws, or to worry about creating effective environmental institutions. This thinking undermines the Basel Convention because the Convention encourages governments to create "focal points" and "competent authorities" responsible for hazardous waste import policies. Some non-OECD countries may believe themselves rid of the annoyance and expense of developing these mechanisms now that a waste export ban has been imposed. Ironically, while it may have been intended as an "additional protective measure" for developing countries, a waste export ban may actually retard the creation of environmental awareness and responsibility among some non-OECD governments. Specifically, the ban may hinder efforts of non-OECD countries to improve their own hazardous waste management systems.

* * *

Legitimate Recycling Will Be Undermined

Environmental activists, among others, have been telling us for years that recycling is good. Recycling slows the consumption of non-renewable resources, decreases waste, and makes good economic sense. Even recovery operations that specialize in handling hazardous waste are perceived as helpful, even though they do not solve every problem associated with the hazardous waste generation. No form of recycling is cost-free or risk-free. Yet, even the most deleterious of waste materials, like lead-acid car batteries, can be profitably and safely recycled. The new waste export ban, however, will make it illegal to export waste to non-OECD countries for the purpose of recycling at the end of 1996. The waste export ban may actually impede global recycling efforts that are otherwise environmentally wise and economically sensible.

One particular subcategory of waste trade fraud is what is known as "sham recycling". This occurs when importers buy certain waste products, like metal or electronic scrap, with the intention of recycling or reprocessing this waste to extract usable materials for profit, but they discover that the shipment they bought is useless, and then must be dumped domestically. This sort of fraud is classified as illegal under the Basel Convention, and its victims would be justified in requiring the exporting state to re-import the bogus recyclables.

"Sham recycling" is not the same thing, however, as legitimate recycling activities that are done poorly, or that harm people or the environment. Some governments permit waste imports for recycling or recovery, but make little effort to ensure that these activities are carried out safely. It is deplorable when people die in connection with poorly managed recycling facilities abroad, as has occurred at a notoriously dangerous mercury recovery facility in South Africa. But two things must be kept in mind about these facilities. First, the majority of materials being treated at these facilities are of domestic origin. Second, it is only the governments of these countries which have the capability and the authority to protect the local environment and human health. While one may argue that industrialized countries should champion worker rights in developing countries, this issue should not be confused with legitimate waste recycling.

Moreover, just because recycling or recovery operations are carried out in a non-OECD country does not necessarily mean that the environment or human health will be at risk. Greenpeace has condemned the government of Singapore for permitting the importation of scrap aluminum (including aluminum cans) and then "dumping" it. The Ministry of Environment responded with the assertion that the aluminum processing facilities in question were approved by the Ministry and met Singapore's environmental standards. The Ministry has also argued that the waste export ban on recyclables will hinder legitimate, cross-border recycling. Some non-OECD countries are, in fact, able to ensure the safety of recycling and recovery operations.

The new ban will permit a non-OECD country to import hazardous waste for recycling after 1997, as long as its government informs the Secretariat of the Basel Convention that it would allow imports from an OECD country, and provided that the government specifies the categories and quantities of hazardous waste permitted, the specific recycling or recovery process to be used, and the final destination of the residues remaining at the end of the recycling process. These requirements will encourage governments to increase their oversight of domestic recycling operations. However, given that some OECD countries do not carefully regulate these operations themselves, one wonders.

* * *

Rich Countries May Become the "Environmental Nannies" of the Poor

Perhaps the worst thing about a waste export ban is that it sets up the OECD countries as "protectors" of developing countries. This has sweeping implications because as "environmental nannies", rich countries will be able to make decisions that will affect not only the environment, but the economies of other countries. The OECD countries will be able to decide whether a non-OECD country should or should not receive a certain kind of waste. If a waste fits any of the descriptions of "hazardous" found in the Annexes to the Basel Convention, or is defined as hazardous under the domestic law of the exporting country, the exporting government could refuse to export that waste—even if the non-OECD country indicated its consent to receive the shipment. In effect, the rich country will be able to decide whether the poor country is able to handle the waste effectively, resulting in a "new form of paternalism."

Many developing countries have bitterly fought "environmental imperialism" on the part of industrialized countries who seek to impose their environmental standards upon them. Developing countries have sought to assert their sovereignty over their own environmental resources as provided for in the Stockholm Declaration of 1972. Malaysia's Prime Minister Datuk Seri Mahathir Mohamad has been one of the most vocal critics of "imperial pressures" on environmental issues. Unfortunately, this contradiction between sovereignty and international management of hazardous waste disposal has not been seriously addressed in academia.

The politically-correct thing to do would be to allow states to assert their sovereignty and choose for themselves. Of course, this would permit states to make bad decisions. Ultimately, however, the responsibility for providing a clean, healthy environment rests with individual governments. Rather than creating a system in which "nanny states" act as environmental custodians for the rest of the world, it is more desirable to let all countries decide for themselves how to manage their environment, including whether or not to import hazardous waste. If they decide to refuse the waste imports, the original terms of the Basel Convention protect their right to do so, and the Convention empowers them to force the exporting state to take back unwanted, illegally imported waste.

13.   **African, Caribbean and Pacific States–European Economic Community Convention (LOMÉ IV), Dec. 15, 1989, 1990 arts. 33–41, E.C. 96,** *reprinted in* **29 I.L.M. 809 (1990)** [Basic Document 1.26].

14.   **Draft Code of Conduct on Transnational Corporations, Adopted by the U.N. Economic and Social Council, Feb. 1, 1988, U.N. Doc. E/1988/39/Add.1 (1988): paras. 43–45** [Basic Document 7.3].

15.   **Organization of African Unity: Council of Ministers, Resolution on Dumping of Nuclear and Industrial Waste in Africa, May 23, 1988,** *reprinted in* **28 I.L.M. (1988)** [Basic Document 5.5].

16.   **Bamako Convention on the Ban of Import Into Africa and the Control of Transboundary Movement and Management of Hazardous Wastes Within Africa, Jan. 30, 1991, arts. 1, 4, 9** *reprinted in* **30 I.L.M. 775 (1991)** [Basic Document 5.7].

17.   **Rio Declaration on Environment and Development, June 14, 1992, UNCED Doc. A/CONF.151/5/Rev. 1,** *reprinted in* **31 I.L.M. 874 (1992): Principles 2, 3, 12, 14** [Basic Document 1.29].

18.   **Agenda 21, Ch. 20 of the United Nations Conference on Environment and Development, ("Environmentally Sound Management of Hazardous Wastes Including Prevention of Illegal International Traffic in Hazardous Wastes"), June 13, 1992, Report of the U.N. Conference on the Environment and Development at Rio de Janeiro, June 3–14, 1992, U.N. Doc. A/CONF.151/26 (1992): paras. 20–1 to 20–8; 20–39 to 20–46** [Basic Document 5.3].

19.   *See generally* **Chapter 5 ("International Environmental Wrongs"), at 335,** *supra.*

20.   **Convention on Biological Diversity, June 5, 1992, arts. 3, 8, 14, 20** *reprinted in* **31 I.L.M. 818 (1992)** [Basic Document 6.11].

Discussion Notes/Questions

1.   As Andrea Marcus in Reading 2 makes clear, there are many waste dumping incidents that illustrate the problem of the international waste trade. A particularly graphic example not cited by Marcus comes from the small coastal town of Koko, Nigeria, where a farmer leased residential land for $100 a month to an Italian importer for storage of nearly 10,000 drums containing misdescribed substances. Koko people stole the substance and spread it on their crops, believing it was fertilizer. Distillers of a local gin stole drums to hold their product. The Nigerians requested the assistance of the United States to determine the contents of the drums, after newspaper reports raised questions about the drums, a number of which were leaking. The drums contained chemical toxins, including PCBs. The Nigerian government evacuated the town and demanded that the Italian government clean up the site and retrieve the waste, even though it was not involved in the shipment. Finally, heavy pressure from Nigeria, including detaining an Italian ship not involved with the waste, resulted in the Italian government ordering the retrieval of the waste. The wastes were loaded back onto the *Karin B*, which thereafter was refused port in Spain, the Netherlands, Denmark, and the United States before finally making port in Italy.

Incidents like this one resulted in the 1988 resolution by the Organization of African Unity condemning the disposal of hazardous wastes in Africa and demanding that those responsible clean up the mess [**Basic Document 5.5**]. Will the Basel Convention [**Basic Document 5.6**] stop incidents such as this? Greenpeace argues that it will not. Greenpeace points to the reaction of a prominent waste trader who says that obtaining the signature of one government official required by the Convention is not a problem compared to the other hurdles he faces in shipping wastes to developing countries. As further evidence, Greenpeace maintains that none of the long-term plans to build incinerators, landfills, and other waste-import facilities in developing countries has been withdrawn following the signing of the Basel Convention. *See* Vallette, The International Trade in Wastes: A Greenpeace Inventory 7 (1989).

Will the "Total Ban Amendment" change this reasoning? If it is not ratified by a substantial number of countries? Do the OECD countries have other (non-Basel) obligations that might cause them not to export hazardous wastes to Less Developed Countries? *See infra* Reading 11.

The Basel Convention provides for a Secretariat to oversee its implementation? Will this allow monitoring? Without monitoring, will countries comply? How adequate are the enforcement provisions? Are arbitration and the International Court of Justice likely to be successful means of dealing with disputes arising under the Convention? Should there be a "super-enforcement" agency? Might the United Nations Environment Programme (UNEP) take this role? Environmental groups? Should they have standing before the International Court of Justice?

2. In the present problem, what about dangers to the health of inhabitants of nearby island nations caused by eating polluted fish? What if the problem dealt with disposal within the territorial waters of a coastal state that shared a common seafront with a number of other nations?

3. Transboundary shipments of hazardous waste present a different legal and philosophical situation from the typical transboundary pollution problem which involves one state's involuntary invasion of another. Here, in theory, willing sellers and willing buyers of risk are involved. Should the law interfere with voluntary agreements? Does the lack of informed consent invalidate a voluntary agreement?

Is the consent of a developing country really voluntary? Do developing countries actually have a choice? Often the choice is between accepting hazardous waste imports and starvation. Who is informed about the risks? Generally not the local community that ends up with the waste. Should informed consent require a process whereby the people affected have the opportunity to make a decision on the risks? How can they be represented in the decision-making?

See generally, e.g., Panel Discussion (Robert E. Lutz, Ved P. Nanda, David A. Wirth, Daniel Magraw, & Günter Handl), *International Transfer of Hazardous Technology and Substances: Caveat Emptor or State Responsibility? The Case of Bhopal, India*, 79 Proceed. Am' Soc'y Int'l L. 303 (1985).

4. The hazardous waste disposal trade is an example of the North–South conflict on environmental issues. In *The Role of the United Nations Environment Programme (UNEP) in the Development of International Environmental Law*, 5 Am. U. J. Int'l L. & Pol'y 325, 375–377 (1990), Carol Petsonk describes the major stumbling blocks in developing the Basel Convention [**Basic Document 5.6**]. Contrast the handling of the ozone issue in this connection. *See* Problem 7–2 ("Nueva Granada Versus the Ozone Layer") in Chapter 7, *supra*. The Basel

Convention contains no economic incentives to encourage compliance, spur waste reduction, or combat the rumored corruption on both sides of North–South trade. Petsonk suggests that a world market in tradable waste-import rights could provide the economic incentive. Would a world market be feasible? Would it improve the practices of waste-disposing states? Would it prevent the illegal waste trade?

5.   Industrialized nations have found that the best way to control waste is to control what goes into the "waste stream." The first place to start in dealing with hazardous waste problems is to stop the production of the waste at its source. Changes to in-plant processes and raw materials can mean clean production. UNEP is currently developing a database of clean technology, which will eventually be cheaply available to industries and governments worldwide. Hazardous waste can be recycled. It can also be treated before disposal to render it less hazardous.

Does the international hazardous waste trade work against environmentally sound and long-term solutions to the problem? Does the export of wastes mean there is less incentive to develop or use technologies which minimize waste at its source? Is there an ethical issue here too? When wastes are exported, the populations and environments of the receiving countries suffer for the unsustainable production processes of the industrialized world. Should international law permit this?

6.   Some environmentalists argue that none of the current technologies for destroying hazardous substances is safe. Therefore toxic and hazardous substances should be put into safe, long term stores. The problem with this suggestion is that nothing on Earth is permanent. Earthquakes or other natural events, or corrosion of the containers, can destroy such a store and release the hazardous materials into the environment. Water-borne contamination from this type of disposal also can cause problems, as occurred with Mururoa Atoll in French Polynesia (France's nuclear weapons testing site in the South Pacific). *See, e.g.,* Request for the Indication of Interim Measure of Protection Submitted by the Government of New Zealand (N.Z. v. Fr.), 1978 I.C.J. Pleadings (Nuclear Tests). Also there is the question of how long it will be before the development of the disposal method is perfected. Should we leave future generations with this heritage? Some of these wastes have been described as toxic time-bombs.

7.   Some newly industrialized countries may generate more hazardous waste per square kilometer than the United States. In some countries, liquid hazardous wastes discharge straight into sewers or alleyways. In many places human scavengers pick through dumps containing hazardous wastes looking for food or recyclable materials. Do industrialized nations have a duty to assist developing countries with hazardous waste management programs? What form should this assistance take? *See, e.g.,* Susan E. Bromm, *Creating a Hazardous Waste Management Program in a Developing Country,* 5 Am. U. J. Int'l L. & Pol'y 325 (1990).

8.   In the present problem, Electra-car is a multinational corporation. What are the responsibilities of multinational companies under international environmental law? What should their responsibilities be? What is the status of codes of conduct in international law? Should they include undertaking environmental impact and risk assessments before undertaking hazardous waste disposal? Should their obligations involve monitoring the facility and undertaking remedial action into the future?

Nations where multinational companies tend to be based are more likely to have stronger traditions of environmental regulation than other countries. Extra-territorial regulation of transnational businesses by the industrialized nations in which they are based is one way to address environmental problems. Is it likely to be the most effective way? Should transnationals have a special status in international law?

United States environmental laws do not apply to the foreign operations of U.S. businesses. American businesses must comply with the laws of the countries in which they operate. Often these laws do not contain the same standards. Some U.S. businesses voluntarily adopt high standards, but others do not. Should legislation require U.S. businesses to comply with U.S. environmental protection statutes in their overseas operations? Is it shortsighted to allow lower standards of conduct for operations in other countries given that the by-products of these activities may return through the biosphere to injure the economy and environment of the home country. *See* Alan Neff, *Not in Their Backyards, Either: A Proposal for a Foreign Environmental Practices Act,* 17 Ecology L. Q. 477 (1990).

If waste disposal becomes more costly and difficult, will there be a tendency to dispose of wastes illicitly, perhaps at sea? What will this mean for the global environment? Alternative waste disposal methods also have problems. Increased at-sea incineration of hazardous wastes poses a threat to the marine environment from ash disposal at sea. There are limited enforcement mechanisms available to ensure the proper disposal of ship wastes. What is to be done about these practices? Can they be banned? Regulated? How?

9. *Bibliographical Note.* For further discussion concerning the principle themes addressed in this problem, consult the following specialized materials:

(a) *Specialized Books/Monographs.* American Bar Association, Brownfields: a Comprehensive Guide to Redeveloping Contaminated Property (Todd S. Davis, Kevin D. Margol eds. 1997); Jackson B. Battle & Maxine I. Lipeles, Hazardous Waste 2nd ed. 1994); Dr. Benjamin A.Goldman and Laura Fitton, Toxic Wastes and Race Revisited: an Update of the 1987 Report on the Racial and Socioeconomic Characteristics of Communities with Hazardous Waste Sites (1994); John A. Hird, Superfund: the Political Economy of Environmental Risk (1994); Gayle Woodside, Hazardous Materials and Hazardous Waste Management : A Technical Guide (1993); British Medical Association, Hazardous Waste and Human Health (1991); C. Henry, The Carriage of Dangerous Goods by Sea: The Role of the International Maritime Organization in International Legislation (1985); C. Hilz, The International Toxic Waste Trade (1992); E. Louka, The Transnational Management of Hazardous and Radioactive Wastes (Occasional Paper No. 1, Orville Schell Center for International Human Rights, Yale Law School, 1992); B. Moyers, Global Dumping Ground: The International Traffic in Hazardous Waste (1991); Transboundary Movements and Disposal of Hazardous Wastes in International Law: Basic Documents (B. Kwiatkowska & A. Soons eds. 1992).

(b) *Specialized Hearings/Reports.* Great Britain Dept. Transport, Regulations Concerning the International Carriage of Dangerous Goods by Rail (1990); International Maritime Organization, International Maritime Dangerous Goods Code (1990); OECD, Transfrontier Movements of Hazardous Wastes: Legal and Institutional Aspects (1985); U.N. Committee of Experts on the Transport of Dangerous Goods, Recommendations on the Transport of Dangerous Goods (7th rev. ed. 1991); U.N., E.C.E. et al., European Agreement Concerning the International Carriage of Dangerous Goods By Road (ADR) (1985); U.N.E.P., Basel Convention on the Control of Transboundary Movements of Hazardous Wastes and Their Disposal (1990).

(c) *Specialized Articles/Book Chapters.* D. Abrams, *Regulating the International Hazardous Waste Trade: A Proposed Global Solution,* 28 Colum. J. Transnat'l L. 801 (1990); B. Bailey & V. Nanda, *Export of Hazardous Waste and Hazardous Technology: Challenge for International Environmental Law*, 17 Den. J. Int'l L. & Pol'y 155 (1988); D. Barr & K. Anderson, *Natural Resources Defense Council, Inc. v. Nuclear Regulatory Commission: Environmental Reviews and Nonproliferation Policy in the Licensing of Nuclear Exports*, 16 Geo. Wash. J. Int'l L. & Econ. 579 (1982); Gerrit Betlem & Michael Faure, *Environmental Toxic Torts in Europe: Some Trends in Recovery of Soil Clean-up Costs and Damages for Personal Injury in the Netherlands, Belgium, England and Germany*, 10 Geo. Int'l Envtl. L. Rev. 855 (1998); Gonzalez et al., *Environmental Aspects of Maquiladora Operations: A Note of Caution for U.S. Parent Corporations*, 22 St. Mary's L. J. 659 (1991); R. Benedick, *The Environment on the Foreign Policy Agenda*, 13 Ecology L. Q. 171 (1986); M. Bothe, *International Regulation of Transboundary Movements of Hazardous Waste*, 33 German Y. B. Int'l L. 422 (1990); M. Boethe, *UNEP's Environmental Law Activity on International Transport and Disposal of Toxic and Dangerous Wastes*, 6 Ind. 6 Indus. & Env't. 3 (1983); S. Bromm, *Creating a Hazardous Waste Management Program in a Developing Country*, 5 Am. U. J. Int'l L. & Pol'y 325 (1990); T. Burck, *Is Foreign Hazardous Waste Really the Same as Domestic Hazardous Waste When Imported into the U.S.?*, 17 N.C. J. Int'l L. & Comm. Reg. 401 (1992); J. Cargas, *Extraterritorial Jurisdiction of the Proposed Federal Waste Export Control Act*, 7 Am. U. J. Int'l L. & Pol'y 397 (1992); A. Chircop, *The Marine Transportation of Hazardous and Dangerous Goods in the Law of the Sea*, 11 Dalhousie L. J. 612 (1988); M. Crithariss, *Third World Nations Are Down in the Dumps: The Exportation of Hazardous Waste*, 16 Brooklyn J. Int'l L. 311 (1990); M. Cusack, *International Law and the Transboundary Shipment of Hazardous Waste to the Third World: Will the Basel Convention Make a Difference?*, 5 Am. U. J. Int'l L. & Pol'y 393 (1990); C. Douglas, *Hazardous Waste Export: Recommendations for United States Legislation to Ratify the Basel Convention*, 38 Wayne L. Rev. 289 (1991); M. Dowling, *The International Regulation of Hazardous Waste: Problems of Definition and Classification*, 8 Zeitschrift für Umweltpolitik 141 (1985); J. Downey, *International Pollution: the Struggle Between States and Scholars Over Customary Environmental Norms: the Hazy View After Chernobyl and Basel*, 12 S.Ill. U. L. J. 247 (1987); M. Feeley, P. Gilhuly & R. Ammons, *W(h)ither Goes the EC Proposed Directive on Civil Liability for Waste*, 15 B.C. Int'l & Comp. L. Rev. 241 (1992); M. Forster, *Hazardous Waste—Toward International Agreement*, 12 Envtl. Pol'y & L. 64 (1984); ___, *The 1984 Protocols to the Oil Pollution Compensation Conventions*, 13 Envtl. Pol'y & L. 42 (1984); B. Gentry, *Environmental Regulation in Europe: Hazardous Waste and Contaminated Sites*, 10 Nw. J. Int'l L. & Bus. 397 (1990); L. Gilmore, *The Export of Non–Hazardous Waste*, 19 Envtl. L. 879 (1989); Jason L. Gudofsky, *Transboundary Shipments of Hazardous Waste For Recycling And Recovery Operations*, 34 Stan. J. Int'l L. 219 (1998); E. Gold, *Legal Aspects of the Transportation of Dangerous Goods at Sea*, 10 Mar. Pol'y 185 (1986); D. Hackett, *An Assessment of the Basel Convention on the Control of Transboundary Movements of Hazardous Wastes and Their Disposal*, 5 Am. U. J. Int'l L. & Pol'y 291 (1990); F. Halter, *Regulating Information Exchange and International Trade in Pesticides and Other Toxic Substances to Meet the Needs of Developing Countries*, 12 Colum. J. Envtl. L. 1 (1987); G. Handl & R. Lutz, *An International Policy Perspective on the Trade of Hazardous Materials and Technologies*, 30 H.I.L.J. 351 (1989); A. Helfenstein, *U.S. Controls on International Disposal of Hazardous Waste*, 22 Int'l Law. 775 (1988); Bruce Howard, *a New Justification for Retroactive Liability in Cercla: an Appreciation of the Synergy Between Common and Statutory Law*, 42 St. Louis U. L.J. 847 (1998); K. Howard, *The Basel Convention: Control of Transboundary Movements of Hazardous Wastes and Their Disposal*, 14 Hastings

Int'l & Comp. L. Rev. 223 (1990); B. Huntoon, *Emerging Controls on Transfers of Hazardous Waste to Developing Countries*, 21 Law & Pol'y Int'l Bus. 247 (1989); M. Jarman, *Disposal of Waste & Right of Passage,* Law Sea Inst. Proceed 92 (1992); S. Johnson, *The Basel Convention: The Shape of Things to Come for United States Waste Exports?*, 21 Envtl. L. 299 (1991); D. Judy, *Hazardous Substances in Developing Countries: Who Should Regulate Foreign Corporations?*, 6 Va. J. Nat. Resources 143 (1986); M. Kelly, *International Regulation of Transfrontier Hazardous Waste Shipments: A New EEC Environmental Directive*, 21 Tex. Int'l L. J. 85 (1986); Madeline June Kass, Pamela J. Bridgen, Valerie Ann Lee, *Brownfields: Where The Market Makes Green*, 13–SUM Nat. Resources & Env't 345 (1998); R. Klingaman, *The European Community and Liability for Cleaning Up Abandoned Hazardous Waste Sites: Should the EC follow the United States' example?*, 9 Wis. Int'l L. J. 125 (1990); G. Kratz, *Implementing the Basel Convention into U.S. Law: Will it Help or Hinder Recycling Efforts?*, 6 B.Y.U. J. Public L. 323 (1992); K. Kummer, *The International Regulation of Transboundary Traffic in Hazardous Wastes: the 1989 Basel Convention*, 41 I.C.L.Q. 530 (1992).

Other Specialized Articles/Books Chapters include H. Leonard & D. Morell, *Emergence of Environmental Concern in Developing Countries: A Political Perspective*, 17 Stan. J. Int'l L. 281 (1981); Z. Lipman, *The Convention on the Control of Transboundary Movements and Disposal of Hazardous Wastes and Australia's Waste Management Strategy*, 7 Envtl. & Plan. L. J. 283 (1990); D. Maes, *Transboundary Waste Dumping: The United States and Mexico Take a Stand*, 27 N.R.J. 941 (1987); C. Mahalu, *The O.A.U. Council of Ministers' Resolution on Dumping of Nuclear and Industrial Waste in Africa and the Basel Convention of 1989*, 2 Afr. J. Int'l & Comp. L. 61 (1990); K. McCrory, *The International Exportation of Waste: The Battle Against the Path of Least Resistance*, 9 Dick. J. Int'l L. 339 (1991); M. Montgomery, *Traveling Toxic Trash: An Analysis of the 1989 Basel Convention*, 14 Fletcher Forum Wld. Aff. 313 (1990); A. Moskowitz, *Criminal Environmental Law: Stopping the Flow of Hazardous Waste to Mexico*, 22 Cal. W. Int'l L. J. 159 (1991/92); A. Neff, *Not in Their Backyards, Either. A Proposal for a Foreign Environmental Practices Act*, 17 Ecology L.Q. 477 (1990); ___, *The Waste Export Control Act: Proposed Legislation and the Reagan–Era Legacy to International Environmental Protection*, 10 Nw. J. Int'l L. & Bus. 479 (1990); M. Núñez–Muller, *The Schoenberg Case: Transfrontier Movements of Hazardous Waste*, 30 N.R.J. 153 (1990); P. Obstler, *Toward a Working Solution to Global Pollution: Importing CERCLA to Regulate the Export of Hazardous Waste*, 16 Y.J.I.L. 73 (1991); William E. O'Neil, *Marine Pollution Liability of Directors And Officers: Insurance Coverages*, 32 Rev. Jur. U.I.P.R. 491 (1998); Rozelia S. Park, *An Examination of International Environmental Racism Through the Lens of Transboundary Movement of Hazardous Wastes*, 5 Ind. J. Global Legal Stud. 659 (1998); P. Passman, *Japanese Hazardous Waste Policy: Signaling the Need for Global and Regional Measures to Control Land–Based Sources of Pollution*, 26 V.J.I.L. 921 (1986); E. Rose, *Transboundary Harm: Hazardous Waste Management Problems and Mexico's Maquiladoras*, 23 Int'l Law. 223 (1989); R. Rosenthal, *Ratification of the Basel Convention: Why the United States Should Adopt the No Less Environmentally Sound Standard*, 11 Temp. Envtl. L. & Tech. J. 61 (1992); S. Rublack, *Fighting Transboundary Waste Streams: Will the Basel Convention Help?*, 22 Verfassung & Recht in Ubersee 364 (1989); ___, *Controlling Transboundary Movements of Hazardous Waste: The Evolution of a Global Convention*, 13 Fletcher Forum Wld. Aff. 113 (1989); J. B. Ruhl, *The Seven Degrees of Relevance: Why Should Real–World Environmental Attorneys Care Now About Sustainable Development Policy?*, 8 Duke Envtl. L. & Pol'y F. 273 (1998); J. Scagnelli, *International*

Hazardous Waste Management–Emerging Trends?, 9 Int'l Construction L. Rev. 394 (1992); A. Schmidt, *Transboundary Movements of Waste Under EC law: the Emerging Regulatory Framework*, 4 J. Envtl. L. 57 (1992); R. Scott, *The Toxic Time Bomb in the Borderland: Can the "Emergency Planning and Community Right to Know Act" Help?*, 30 N.R.J. 969 (1990); M. Semenoff, *Foreign Trade in Trash? Exporting Hazardous Waste*, 4 Nat. Resources & Env't 14 (1989); Symposium, *The Regulation of Hazardous Exports*, 12 Colum. J. Envtl. L. 1 (1987); Lucia Ann Silecchia, *Pinning the Blame & Piercing the Veil in the Mists of Metaphor: The Supreme Court's New Standards for the Cercla Liability of Parent Companies And a Proposal for Legislative Reform*, 67 Fordham L. Rev. 115 (1998); Symposium, *Maritime Transport, Control, and Disposal of Hazardous Waste*, 14 Mar. Pol'y 183 (1990); C. Uram, *International Regulation of the Sale and Use of Pesticides*, 10 Nw. J. Int'l L. & Bus. 460 (1990); J. Van Dyke, *The United States and Japan in Relation to the Resources, the Environment, and the People of the Pacific Island Region*, 16 Ecology L.Q. 217 (1989); M. Vilcheck, *The Controls on the Transfrontier Movement of Hazardous Waste from Developed to Developing Nations: The Goal of a "Level Playing Field"*, 11 Nw. J. Int'l L. & Bus. 643 (1991); P. Vint, *The International Export of Hazardous Waste: European Economic Community, United States, and International Law*, 129 Mil. L. Rev. 107 (1990); J. Williams, *Trashing Developing Nations: The Global Hazardous Waste Trade*, 39 Buff. L. Rev. 275 (1991); D. Worrell, *Issues and Policy Considerations Regarding Hazardous Waste Exports*, 11 Hous. J. Int'l L. 373 (1989); J. Isaacs, *U.S. Hazardous Waste Exports: Regulations and Proposals*, 15 Md. J. Int'l L. & Trade 69 (1991).

Problem 9–2

Toxic Pollution in Yoribo and Bamileko

SECTION 1. FACTS

In 1985, PanAfrica AgChem (PAAC) was incorporated under the laws of
Yoribo, an industrializing yet largely underdeveloped country in sub-Saharan
West Africa. The company's goal was to promote sub-Saharan agricultural
products and productivity. In 1987, PAAC began construction of an agricultural chemical plant at Khasa, a small city near Yoribo's river boundary with
Bamileko, a neighboring agricultural producer to Yoribo's southeast. The new
plant produced insecticides, herbicides, and rodenticides. These pesticides
included DDT, as well as other organochlorines: aldrin, dieldrin, heptachlor,
chlordane, and endrin.[a]

International pressures quickly mounted on the Yoribon government to
ensure the safe treatment and disposal of the wastes that would result from
the Khasa plant's production process. Thus, in the late 1980s, the government
called upon PAAC to incorporate into its plans the construction of underground hazardous waste treatment units (WTUs) and the implementation of a
waste treatment and disposal strategy (WTDS) to be monitored by Yoribon
officials. PAAC complied and acquired both the WTUs and a WTDS which
were designed to meet the hazardous waste disposal standards of the United
States. The design and operation standards for the WTUs were aimed at
preventing pollution and groundwater contamination. The WTDS dealt with
inter alia, various kinds of pre-treatment to prevent the formation of leachate.[b] Specifications for liners and leachate collection systems were intended to
minimize the migration of any leachate into the adjacent subsurface soil and
groundwater. Each WTU was estimated to cost $US 7 million to construct and
a half million US dollars per year to maintain.

After a comprehensive resource allocation study in the late 1980s, PAAC
embarked upon a plan to construct ten WTUs, phased in at the rate of one per
year so as to avoid maintaining empty units. Lacking sufficient capital to
undertake this program in its entirety, it sought a subsidy from the Yoribon
government. The country's economy was enjoying a petroleum boom, and the
Yoribon government agreed, for a "reasonable period," to subsidize two-thirds
of the cost of building the WTUs. During the first six years of the ten-year
plan (1988–1998), six WTUs were built and operated on schedule.

The chemicals produced at the Khasa facility sold well throughout sub-
Saharan Africa. Neighboring Bamileko became one of PAAC's principal customers, purchasing agricultural chemicals from PAAC in bulk in order to get

a. Organochlorines are insecticides that
contain carbon (hence "organo"), chlorine, and
hydrogen. They are sometimes referred to by
other names: chlorinated hydrocarbons, chlorinated organics, chlorinated insecticides, and
chlorinated synthetics. The waste streams

from these chemicals are considered "hazardous" under Annex I of both the Basel and
Bamako conventions [**Basic Documents 5.6
& 5.7**], specifically under categories Y4 and Y5.

b. A product or solution, usually containing
contaminates, formed by the leaching of soil.

727

lower prices and then selling them to farmers at subsidized rates. DDT and other organochlorines were shipped to a Bamilekon government distribution point in large metal drums that carried warnings and instructions in English and in pictograms, and were re-packaged in various receptacles by largely illiterate day laborers who simply glued paper labels on the containers that said in English—not Bamilekon—"agriculture chemicals." The Government of Bamileko then dispatched the receptacles to small-scale farmers in various parts of the country. Bamileko did not request, and PAAC did not provide, suitable packaging for small-scale farmers.

In the mid–1990s, oil prices began a drastic decline that caused the Yoribon economy to stall and retreat. This decline prompted a successful coup attempt by Army officers who withdrew Yoribo's WTU subsidy and dramatically reduced public sector employment, including that of officials charged with monitoring PAAC's activities. Concurrently, there was a slump in demand for agricultural chemicals from neighboring countries that faced similar economic difficulties.

Without the subsidy PAAC felt unable to build the remaining four WTUs, but it bowed to the new government's pressures to maintain full production of its agricultural chemicals. Faced with the new reality, PAAC began to look for less expensive ways to store its toxic wastes. After a lengthy search, in which the Yoribon government chose not to participate, PAAC found an off-plant location several miles away.

The new site was at Yoribo's Mt. Mandara, a 3,000–feet high ridge located in an unpopulated stretch of land adjacent to the Mimbu, the river that separates Yoribo and Bamileko. Without government consultation, PAAC hired local laborers to tunnel 150 feet through the ridge and into a large "dead" cavern.[c] Work crews deposited directly on the floor of the cavern four years of accumulated waste from the Khasa facility, sealed in fifty-five-gallon drums and labeled in chalk. Many drums were stacked on top of one another with little regard for the chemical compatibility of their contents. The crews closed the site with earth, rock, and a cement "seal" over the opening they had made. PAAC maintained general records of the types of waste and waste byproducts being stored at the Mandara site, but a precise inventory of the number of fifty-five-gallon drums and the exact contents of each was neither kept nor supplied to the Yoribon government. No provision was made for follow-up analysis of the waste dumped at the site or for groundwater monitoring by either PAAC or Yoribo.

Two years ago, a wetter than usual rainy season in Yoribo and its surrounding region caused considerable erosion around Mt. Mandara. The rains soaked the land surrounding the Mandara cavern and water migrated into the cavern. The intrusion of water caused the drums to rot and disintegrate which led to the escape of various toxic and hazardous substances into the soil. Eventually, the toxins leached through the soil at Mt. Mandara and into the Mimbu. At the same time, the heavy rains led to unprecedented runoffs from the maize, millet, peanut, and sorghum fields that border the Mimbu on the Bamilekon side of the river. Upon entering the water, the toxic compounds rapidly worked their way through the food chain, accumulating in

c. A "dead" cavern is one through which water is no longer flowing and contributing to calcitic growths such as stalactites and stalagmites.

the livers and fatty tissues of carp, trout, and various tilapia. Some of the toxins bonded with other organic matter, and various algae in the water, and were carried downstream. Other toxins settled on the riverbed as sediment.

Downriver, in Douaundé, Bamileko's largest metropolitan area, the impact of these toxins gradually became apparent. Thousands of Bamilekon citizens who consumed riverbed feeding fish, such as carp and tilapia, complained of joint pain, extreme muscular weakness, anxiety, vomiting, mild jerking, dizziness, and convulsions. Textile factories that traded with Europe and the United States had to cut production by forty percent due to worker illnesses, and lost new contracts as a result. Local hospitals reported a significant increase in the number of babies born with birth defects.

Alarmed by these events, Bamilekon authorities set up a commission of inquiry (the Commission) consisting of biology, zoology, and medical experts from Douaundé University who were teamed with public health care officials from the local office of the World Health Organization (WHO). During its two-month inquiry the Commission sampled fish, mollusks, plankton, and other life from the Mimbu, and found much higher traces of organochlorines, including DDT, heptachlor, and chlordane than might be expected even for a country, like Bamileko, that extensively used these chemicals in its own agricultural programs. After sampling drinking water drawn from wells fed by the river, the Commission found levels of pesticides 1,500 times in excess of Bamilekon and WHO standards. It also discovered that toxic concentrations in river water increased steadily as samples were drawn further upriver, but then abruptly dropped to lower though still abnormally high levels immediately after passing Yoribo's Mt. Mandara. The Commission reported accordingly to the Bamilekon government.

After considering the report, the Government of Bamileko accused the Government of Yoribo of violating international law by secretly dumping hazardous waste that damaged the environment and people of Bamileko. Bamileko argued that Yoribo had violated the 1991 Bamako Convention on Transboundary Movements of Hazardous Wastes and the 1989 Basel Convention on the Control of Transboundary Movements of Hazardous Waste. Beyond these breaches of conventional international law, Bamileko asserted that Yoribo had violated customary international law as reflected in the principles of good neighborliness and the 1985 Cairo Guidelines and Principles of Environmentally Sound Management of Hazardous Waste.

Yoribo refuted these allegations, asserting that the production of agricultural chemicals and the disposal of their wastes in the best practicable manner within its own borders constitutes equitable and reasonable use of its territory. Assuming, though not admitting to some leaching at Mt. Mandara, Yoribo stated first that the use of Mt. Mandara was both equitable and reasonable, and amounted to good management. Additionally, Yoribo argued that Bamileko was primarily responsible for the chemical levels in the Mimbu and the harm the chemicals might have caused. In support of this allegation, Yoribo cited its own studies which revealed high toxicity levels caused by runoff directly upstream from Mt. Mandara in an area of intensive Bamileko agriculture. Furthermore, Yoribo asserted that Bamileko had negligently used higher than recommended doses of the agricultural chemicals it imported from Yoribo, in clear violation of the instructions and warnings on the drums PAAC had supplied.

Troubled that the international publicity given to these incidents might damage its delicate negotiations with various OECD nations for substantial development assistance, the new Government of Yoribo proposed that the two countries submit their dispute to an ad hoc tribunal established under Article 20(2) of the Bamako Convention, which had been signed and ratified by both countries.[d] Bamileko has agreed to submit to the jurisdiction of such an ad hoc tribunal, and both parties agree that the tribunal should resolve their dispute according to international law.

SECTION 2. QUESTIONS PRESENTED

1. Has Yoribo violated international law?
2. If so, is Bamileko entitled to any damages?

SECTION 3. ASSIGNMENTS

A. *Reading Assignment*

Study the Readings presented in Section 4, *infra*, and the Discussion Notes/Questions that follow. Also, to the extent possible, consult the accompanying bibliographical references.

B. *Recommended Writing Assignment*

Prepare a comprehensive, logically sequenced, and *argumentative* brief in the form of an outline of the primary and subsidiary *legal* issues you see requiring resolution by the Yoribo–Bamileko ad hoc tribunal. Also, from the perspective of an independent objective judge, indicate which side ought to prevail on each issue and why. Retain a copy of your issue-outline/brief for class discussion.

C. *Recommended Oral Assignment*

Assume you are legal counsel for Yoribo, on the one hand, or Bamileko on the other (as designated by your instructor); then, relying upon the Readings (and your issue-outline if prepared), present a 15–20 minute oral argument of your government's likely positions before the ad hoc tribunal.

D. *Recommended Reflective Assignment*

Consider (and recommend) alternative norms, institutions, and/or proce-

---

d. Yoribo and Bamileko are parties also to the 1989 Basel Convention on the Control of Transboundary Movements of Hazardous Wastes [**Basic Document 5.6**]. In addition, the two governments have issued statements of accession to the 1987 Cairo Guidelines and Principles for the Environmentally Sound Management of Hazardous Wastes [**Basic Document 5.3**], the 1985 London Guidelines for the Exchange of Information on Chemicals in International Trade [**Basic Document 5.4**], and the FAO Code of Conduct on the Distribution and Use of Pesticides [**Basic Document 5.1**]. Neither party has signed nor ratified the Rotterdam Convention on Prior Informed Consent Procedures for Certain Hazardous Chemicals and Pesticides in International Trade [**Basic Document 5.9**].

dures that you believe might do better than existing world order arrangements to contend with situations of the kind posed by this problem. In so doing, but without insisting upon *immediate* feasibility, identify the particular transition steps that would be needed to make your alternatives a reality.

SECTION 4. READINGS

1.   JOHN M. JOHNSON & GEORGE WHITAKER WARE, PESTICIDE LITIGATION MANUAL 1–2, 11–2 to 11–4 (1992).

Pesticides are chemicals used to kill or control pests. These chemicals are typically manmade synthetic organic compounds, but there are a few exceptions in the form of naturally occurring compounds that are derived from plants.

To the grower, pests could include insects and mites that damage crops; weeds that compete with field crops for nutrients and moisture; aquatic plants that clog irrigation and drainage ditches; diseases of plants caused by fungi, bacteria, and viruses; nematodes, snails, and slugs; rodents that feed on grain, young plants and the bark of fruit trees; and birds that eat their weight every day in young plant seedlings and grain from fields and cattle feedlots as well as from storage.

* * *

DDT is probably the best known and most notorious [organochlorine] of this century. It is also fascinating, and remains to be acknowledged as the most useful insecticide developed.[e]

* * *

How does DDT kill? The mode of action has never been clearly worked out for DDT. In some complex manner it destroys the delicate balance of sodium and potassium within the neuron, thereby preventing it from conducting impulses normally.

Let us consider a few salient points concerning DDT in order to understand some of the well-documented evils attributed to it. The first point is DDT's chemical stability. DDT and TDE are *persistent*, that is, their chemical stability gives the products long lives in soil and aquatic environments and in animal and plant tissues. They are not readily broken down by microorganisms, enzymes, heat, or ultraviolet light. . . .

Second, we note that DDT's solubility in water is only about six parts per billion parts (ppb) of water. DDT has been reported in the chemical literature to be probably the most water-insoluble compound ever synthesized. However, it is quite soluble in fatty tissue, and, as a consequence of its resistance to metabolism, it is readily stored in fatty tissue of any animal ingesting DDT alone or DDT dissolved in the food it eats, even when it is part of another animal.

Since DDT is not readily metabolized and thus not excreted, and it is freely stored in body fat, it accumulates in every animal that preys on other

e. DDT, banned for use in the United States by the U.S. Environmental Protection Agency in 1973, can be considered the pesticide of greatest historical significance–affecting human health, agriculture, and the environment.

animals. It also accumulates in animals that eat plant tissue bearing traces of DDT. For example, a dairy cow excretes (or secretes) a large share of the ingested DDT in its milk fat. Humans drink milk and eat the fatted calf, and thereby ingest DDT. The same story was repeated in food chains ending in the osprey, falcon, golden eagle, sea gull, pelican, and so on.

The principle of these food chain oddities is this: Any chemical that possesses the characteristics of stability and fat solubility will follow the same biological magnification (biomagnification) as DDT. The polychlorinated biphenyls (PCBs), a group of chemicals that have no insecticidal properties, are stable and fat soluble and have climbed the food chain just as DDT has. Other insecticides incriminated to some extent in biomagnification, belonging to the organochlorine group, are TDE, DDE (a major metabolite of DDT), dieldrin, aldrin, several isomers of HCH, endrin, heptachlor, and mirex.

2. ROBERT BOARDMAN, PESTICIDES IN WORLD AGRICULTURE: THE POLITICS OF INTERNATIONAL REGULATION 133, 135–36 (1986).

* * *

Estimates of crop destruction by pests vary from the specific to the general. A 1981 study calculated that the sugar industry in Tanzania was losing approximately $1.23 million annually because of sugar cane smut. Losses for 25 crops in India in the 1960s were put at 25 per cent for vegetables, 20 per cent for potatoes, 20 per cent for cotton, and 20 per cent for rice. Reductions in losses through the use of control measures were expected to be on the order of 50 per cent for castor and chilies, 25 per cent for sugarcane, and 30 per cent for tobacco. The cost of pest damage in Arab countries has been estimated at around $2 billion annually, with losses for particular sectors ranging from 25–72 per cent in the case of vegetables and 23–71 per cent in the case of various field crops. Aggregating these kinds of figures has given estimates of total worldwide damage to agriculture of about $66 billion annually. The US National Academy of Science published a study in 1977 which suggested that a reduction of only 20 per cent in losses resulting from pests attacking major food crops would be required to feed an additional 476 million or more people. Worldwide post-harvest losses alone due to pests have been put at between 10–20 per cent, and estimates for pre-and post-harvest totals are approximately 45 per cent.

* * *

Generally speaking, pesticide use has beneficial effects if it can stabilize crop yields on a year-to-year basis, and in addition if this allows a more effective allocation of resources between the agrochemical and other sectors. There are, of course, various drawbacks associated with pesticide use. Balancing these against the advantages is not an easy task. But as one FAO expert group noted in 1970: "While deaths from the misuse of pesticides in developing countries will undoubtedly be higher than in developed countries, they still may not be of primary importance to a health ministry which is stretched to capacity in attempting to deal with preventable and major causes of death, e.g., starvation and non-potable water supplies."[f]

f. FAO WORKING PARTY OF EXPERTS ON THE OFFICIAL CONTROL OF PESTICIDES, SECTION A (LEGIS- LATION), A MODEL SCHEME FOR THE ESTABLISHMENT

3. Margo Brett Baender, *Pesticides and Precaution: The Bamako Convention as a Model for an International Convention on Pesticides Regulation*, 24 N.Y.U. J. INT'L L. & POL. 557, 559–60, 562–66 (1991).

Modern agriculture relies extensively on the use of agrichemicals [sic] such as pesticides and synthetic fertilizers in both developing and developed countries. This reliance results from agricultural policies which have encouraged intensive production in the short term with little regard for long-term environmental effects.

* * *

1. PESTICIDES IN THE DEVELOPING WORLD

* * *

c. Misuse of Pesticides

Pesticides are misused in the developing world due to lack of official controls, resources, and information. Many countries have insufficient legislation to ensure safe use of pesticides. Where appropriate legislation does exist, many developing countries do not have the resources necessary for its implementation. Because of urgent demands for extremely limited government funds, capacity to staff environmental ministries and research centers is seriously constrained. International guidelines on pesticides have been adopted to compensate for the paucity of adequate domestic regulatory mechanisms, but the resources for implementation are still lacking. According to a 1989 FAO[g] survey, eighty-four developing countries had insufficient resources to conform to FAO pesticide guidelines.[1]

As a result of inadequate regulation and enforcement, many pesticides reach farmers without the information necessary for safe application. Pesticides are often imported into developing countries in large containers and then repackaged into smaller containers for individual sale. These new containers, often unmarked or labeled only with the name of the product, may not carry the original safety information....

Even safety information that does reach farmers may be useless. Many farm workers in the developing world are illiterate or unable to read the foreign language in which labels and other accompanying literature are printed....

d. Pressures to Use Pesticides

Pesticides are frequently over-applied in developing countries by up to forty percent above the recommended amount, thus compounding the safety and environmental problems. Excessive or unnecessary use of pesticides may result from governmental pressure to maximize cash crops for export to gain the foreign currency needed for debt repayment. Farmers seek to increase their incomes by using pesticides more extensively on cash crops than on subsistence crops grown to feed the local population. They often use pesticides

OF NATIONAL ORGANISATIONS FOR THE OFFICIAL CONTROL OF PESTICIDES 12–13 (AGP:CP 28) (1970).

g. I.e., United Nations Food and Agriculture Organization.

1. *See* Charlotte Uram, *International Regulation of the Sale and Use of Pesticides*, 10 NW. J. INT'L L. & BUS. 460, 471 (1990).

as "insurance," applying them in amounts far in excess of what is necessary to maximize crop yields, under the mistaken impression that more pesticides mean more profits....

Governments in developing countries use subsidies to promote greater use of pesticides on crops grown for export to the developed world. These subsidies reduce the cost of pesticides to the farmer by twenty to eighty percent. * * * The reduced financial costs made possible by subsidies can influence a farmer to use more pesticides because the cost-benefit analysis usually does not include the health and environmental risks involved in pesticide use. A farmer who compares the costs of heavily subsidized agri-chemicals to that of more time-consuming, labor-intensive agricultural techniques that use fewer pesticides will usually adopt the chemical approach. Pesticide subsidies thus accelerate environmental damage and act as a barrier to the adoption of cleaner farming practices.

International development projects also contribute to the over-use of pesticides in the [T]hird [W]orld. The World Bank, for example, has encouraged [T]hird [W]orld development modeled on [F]irst [W]orld development without conducting adequate environmental assessments of the impact of [F]irst [W]orld technology in a [T]hird [W]orld setting. This policy has resulted in pesticide abuses in World Bank-supported agricultural projects. * * *

4. J. Allen et al., *Comparative Toxicology of Chlorinated Compounds on Mammalian Species*, in DIFFERENTIAL TOXICITIES OF INSECTI-CIDES AND HALOGENATED AROMATICS 469, 474–75 (Fumio Matsumura ed., 1984).

2.1. TOXICITY [OF DDT] TO HUMANS

Severe cases of accidental poisoning of humans with massive amounts of DDT have been reported. The main symptoms are extreme muscular weakness, joint pain, extreme nervous tension, anxiety, confusion, inability to concentrate and depression. Other than the incidents of acute poisoning, it appears that DDT is generally not very toxic to man.

* * *

3.1. TOXICITY [OF CYCLODIENE INSECTICIDES] TO HUMANS

The chlorinated cyclodienes can be classified as neurotoxins, and many of the signs and symptoms of poisoning resemble those produced by DDT. Unlike DDT, however, these compounds tend to produce convulsions before other less serious signs of illness have appeared. Persons who have been exposed to cyclodiene insecticides report headaches, nausea, vomiting, dizziness and mild chronic jerking. On the other hand, patients occasionally have convulsions with no previous symptoms. There have been a number of fatalities resulting from acute poisoning by the cyclodiene insecticides.

Davies and Lewis[2] reported 14 case histories of acute endrin poisoning. The syndrome associated with these poisonings was referred to as "fits" and

---

2. G. Davies & I. Lewis, *Outbreak of Food Poisoning from Bread Made of Chemically* *Contaminated Flour*, 2 BRIT. MED J. 393 (1956).

consisted of several, and in some cases sudden and unforewarned, convulsions. The clinical character of dieldrin poisoning in man was well documented by Patel and Rao[3] in 20 cases involving males aged sixteen to forty years. The symptoms showed a definite graduation, starting with giddiness, headache, and twitching of muscles proceeding to convulsive attacks occurring up to several times a day, with loss of consciousness for periods of up to two hours. The convulsions were similar to epileptic seizures, but they were never preceded by any sensory disturbance of aura. The convulsions occurred at any time of the day or night, and were not associated with emotional or other disturbances. These convulsions were characterized by violent tonic contractions of the body muscles, rolling up of the eyeballs, clenching of the teeth, and occasional tongue-biting. Psychic disturbances ranging from loss of memory for recent events to serious disturbances such as mania have been observed.

5. FUMIO MATSUMURA, TOXICOLOGY OF INSECTICIDES 496 (2d ed. 1985).

In man, the signs of dieldrin poisoning ... include headache, nausea, vomiting, dizziness, and general malaise. In severe cases, convulsions are the only symptom observed. A coma may or may not follow a convulsion. Hyperexcitation and irritability are common. However, all these symptoms do not always appear in human poisoning. In some spray operators with repeated exposure, a condition similar to epilepsy has resulted. Laboratory tests have shown the presence of dieldrin in the tissues and urine after poisoning, but this finding is not proof of poisoning, for dieldrin has been found in the blood and urine of spraymen who showed no symptoms. Workers who had convulsions and other signs of poisoning tended to show a high concentration of dieldrin in the blood. . . .

6. Elizabeth B. Baldwin, *Reclaiming Our Future: International Efforts to Eliminate the Threat of Persistent Organic Pollutants*, 20 HASTINGS INT'L & COMP. L. REV. 855, 855–62 (1997).

Evidence is mounting that certain types of chemicals known as persistent organic pollutants ("POPs") are causing increasingly detrimental health and environmental effects around the world.[1] The international community has become concerned in recent years about the severity of the adverse effects of POPs and their continued global distribution. . . . Because POPs are transported by wind, ocean currents, and by migrating wildlife, the potential effects of POPs are global in scope.

POPs are produced or released during industrial processes which utilize chlorine, or the combustion of waste and certain fuels, or by the manufacture, use, and storage of chemicals such as organochlorine pesticides. Examples of POPs include DDT, chlordane, toxaphene, endosulfan, and various other pesticides, as well as industrial products (PCBs) and byproducts (dioxins and furans).

* * *

3. T. Patel & V. Rao, *Dieldrin Poisoning in Man: A Report of 20 Cases Observed in Bombay State*, 1 BRIT. MED. J. 919 (1958).

4. Persistent organic pollutants are toxic organic compounds that break down very slowly in the environment and accumulate in the tissues of living organisms. . . .

II. Persistent Organic Pollutants

A. Evidence of Pops' Global Effects

POPs are synthetic chemicals that resist breakdown and accumulate in human body fat. Once absorbed by a living organism or sprayed on a crop, these chemicals quickly pass through the food chain, increasing their concentration in each transfer. Pesticides in particular are a "special class" of POPs in that they are designed to poison and kill and are intentionally dispersed into the environment. Many POPs are highly toxic, cause certain forms of cancer, or disrupt hormonal development.[5] Years ago, scientific studies linked synthetic chemicals to cancer in wildlife and humans. More recent animal research has revealed an even greater variety of detrimental effects that POPs cause within the environment. These effects include: (1) sterility in bald eagles; (2) altered nesting patterns and population declines in birds exposed to DDT; (3) severe deformities of chicks exposed to dioxin; (4) reproductive failures of mink, whales, and other wildlife; (5) decline in otter population; (6) genital abnormalities in alligators; and (7) a plague among Mediterranean dolphins exposed to PCBs. These harmful effects are not limited to wildlife but can harm the human species as well, as indicated by studies documenting genital abnormalities and decreases in fertility among humans.

POPs have been known to cause harm from one generation to the next (e.g., a woman who is exposed to POPs may not suffer any symptoms but her exposure may affect the hormonal development of her child before it is born). This ability to disrupt the human endocrine system has led to POPs being labeled "endocrine disrupters." Endocrine disruption caused by synthetic chemical residues in humans has been shown to lead to the following: (1) low fertility rates and sperm counts; (2) behavioral changes; (3) impairments in learning ability; (4) disrupted neurological development; (5) genital abnormalities; (6) certain hormone-related forms of cancer, including breast, testicular, and prostate cancers; (7) immune system disruption; (8) skewed hormone ratios; (9) internal reproductive organ disruption; (10) inadequate levels of thyroid hormone, which plays a role in reproduction and the development of healthy offspring; (11) ectopic (tubal) pregnancies; (12) endometriosis (a disease which is a leading cause of infertility in women); and (13) miscarriages.

* * *

Scientists have discovered that numerous chemicals are hormone disrupters. The difference between natural and synthetic hormone disrupters lies in their persistence. Natural hormone disrupters, such as plant estrogens, may be eliminated from the body within one day. However, the human body cannot break down synthetic hormone disrupters; they accumulate in body tissue, ensuring long-term exposure.

* * *

C. Areas of Controversy

. . . [S]ome critics argue that synthetic POPs pose no danger to humans because humans have adapted to certain natural (non-synthetic) hormone

---

5. For a recent and comprehensive narrative regarding connections between synthetic chemicals and cancer, see generally Sandra Steingraber, Living Downstream: An Ecologist Looks at Cancer and the Environment (1997).

disrupters. A leading scientist responds that "while we may have evolved ways to coexist with [natural hormone disrupting] compounds, this does not mean they are harmless.... Even naturally occurring hormone mimics can disrupt development of the unborn or young children."[6] Furthermore, as noted above, synthetic POPs pose an even greater hazard than natural compounds because they can persist in the body for years, while plant estrogens might be eliminated within a day.

* * *

Finally, critics question the accuracy of using animal studies to forecast dangers posed to humans. Opponents note that it is well established that similarities in endocrine systems have existed across many species throughout evolution. Therefore, the link between animals and humans in this area cannot be ignored. As Rachel Carson noted over thirty years ago, "in nature nothing exists alone.... Man, however much he may like to pretend the contrary, is part of nature."[7]

* * *

7. London Guidelines for the Exchange of Information on Chemicals in International Trade (UNEP–Guideline, as Amended 1989), Introduction to the Guidelines, Guideline 13. [Basic Document 5.4].

8. FAO International Code of Conduct on the Distribution and Use of Pesticides 1989, Arts. 1–3, 5–11, FAO Conference Resolution 10/85 (as amended in 1989). [Basic Document 5.1].

9. Charlotte Uram, *International Regulation of the Sale and Use of Pesticides*, 10 Nw. J. Int'l L. & Bus. 460, 469–71 (1990).

In 1985, the United Nations Food and Agricultural Organization (FAO) adopted an International Code of Conduct on the Distribution and Use of Pesticides (the "Code") **[Basic Document 5.1]** to reduce the hazards associated with the use of pesticides.

* * *

The Code sought to provide a way to reduce the risks of pesticide use, particularly in those countries without adequate pesticide registration and control schemes. The Code established voluntary standards, relying on cooperative efforts. At its adoption, "[i]t [was] designed to be mainly an interim measure until adequate national regulations [were] instituted."

* * *

The Code establishes voluntary, legally non-binding standards of conduct for all governmental, public, and private entities associated with the distribution and use of pesticides. Its language is general and wide-ranging.

Article 3, for example, on pesticide management, states that "Governments have the overall responsibility and should take the specific powers to

---

6. Theo Colborn et al., Our Stolen Future: Are We Threatening Our Fertility, Intelligence, and Survival? A Scientific Detective Story 82 (1996).

7. Rachel Carson, Silent Spring 51, 188 (1962).

regulate the distribution and use of pesticides in their countries." The same article directs governments of exporting countries to adhere to the Code provisions in the manufacture, distribution and advertising of pesticides, especially in countries without legislation or regulation, and to take special care to ensure safe and effective use of the product worldwide. It requests that all entities and organizations, including public sector groups, provide information and disseminate educational materials on pesticides and their use. Under Article 3 of the Code, everyone bears and shares broad responsibility.

* * *

Article 10, on labelling, packaging, storage, and disposal ... directs most of its standards to industry. It states that "Industry should use labels that" show the appropriate hazard classification of warnings, use appropriate symbols or pictograms, whenever possible, in addition to written warnings and instructions; warn against reuse of the containers; and provide product batch or lot information. . . .

The Code also establishes in Article 12 a general prescription that "Governments should monitor the observance of the Code and report on progress made to the Director–General of FAO." In accordance with Article 12 of the Code, the FAO issued a questionnaire designed to indicate the extent to which countries were observing the Code. Seventy-three percent of the countries responded to the questionnaire in 1988. Of the 115 responding countries, 84 developing countries stated that they did not have adequate governmental resources to control pesticides and comply fully with the Code. Africa had the greatest number of countries with difficulty observing the Code.

10.   Margo Brett Baender, Note, *Pesticides and Precaution: The Bamako Convention as a Model for an International Convention on Pesticides Regulation*, 24 N.Y.U. J. INT'L L. & POL. 557, 579–80, 582–83 (1991).

The [FAO] Code of Conduct **[Basic Document 5.1]** establishes voluntary, non-binding standards for governments and industry to follow in the development, packaging, labeling, advertising, disposal and storage of pesticides. Governments have "overall responsibility" for regulating the distribution of pesticides in their countries,[8] and pesticide manufacturers and distributors are called on to adhere to the provisions of the Code of Conduct in order to reduce health hazards associated with pesticides.[9] Manufacturers are expected to evaluate pesticides in terms of safety to human health and the environment prior to marketing.[10] The Code urges industry to try to reduce hazard by "introducing" products in ready-to-use packages that are not attractive for reuse.[11] Labels should be clear and concise, printed in an "appropriate language" and accompanied by explanatory symbols and pictures.[12] The Code of Conduct exhorts governments to introduce pesticide registration and control schemes,[13] and governments of exporting countries are asked to provide technical assistance to countries that lack the resources

---

8. Code of Conduct [**Basic Document 5.1**], art. 3.1.

9. *Id.* arts. 3.2, 5.2, 6.2, 10, 11.

10. *Id.* art. 8.1.1.

11. *Id.* arts. 5.2.2.2, 5.2.2.3.

12. *Id.* arts. 5.2.2.5, 10.2.4, 10.2.2.

13. Code of Conduct, arts. 5.1, 6.1.

or expertise to assess data on pesticides.[14] As a non-binding document, the Code of Conduct has no enforcement provisions, although Article 12 states that it should be observed through "collaborative action" by the parties concerned.[15]

* * *

WEAKNESSES OF THE CODE OF CONDUCT, OLD AND NEW

[T]he FAO Code of Conduct remains inadequate to address the hazards of pesticide use. The primary weakness of the Code of Conduct is that it is purely voluntary.... The FAO has no enforcement power and can only monitor compliance.... Because of its voluntary nature, the Code of Conduct must resort to vague, hortatory language, which is subject to interpretation (and thus evasion) by government and industry. Article 5.2.3, for example, states that industry should "halt sale and recall products when safe use does not seem possible under any use directions or restrictions." The Code of Conduct does not, however, define safe use, what level of risk or harm is acceptable, or how much evidence of unavoidable harm is necessary to justify recall. Furthermore, NGO reports from sixteen developing countries indicate that the Code of Conduct's standards are routinely violated. For example, the pesticide industry often violates standards for advertisement of pesticides. In Indonesia, advertisements made safety claims for pesticides in violation of Article 11.1.8 of the Code of Conduct. In addition, advertisements in the Philippines, Colombia, and Paraguay depict unsafe practices (e.g., a television commercial shown in Paraguay which portrays a man mixing pesticides with his bare hands). This is a violation of Article 11.1.2, which calls on industry to refrain from using advertisements containing representations of dangerous practices.

Furthermore, the Code of Conduct does not adequately address the widespread lack of resources available for implementation of its guidelines in developing countries. It notes that exporting countries should assist developing countries as much as possible in training personnel to assess data on pesticides, yet it makes no provision for technical assistance for monitoring or enforcement of its guidelines on use of pesticides within national boundaries....

11. J. Wylie Donald, *The Bamako Convention as a Solution to the Problem of Hazardous Waste Exports to Less Developed Countries*, 17 COLUM. J. ENVTL. L. 419, 422–24 (1992).

Improper storage, treatment, or disposal of hazardous wastes can lead to serious human health effects. These effects can be particularly severe in LDCs that are incapable of dealing with hazardous wastes in an environmentally sound manner. Dumpsites can be hazardous to the public through fire or explosion. Solvents leaking from dumps can contaminate groundwater supplies. Disease and infection can spread from hospital waste, fecal material, and rotting garbage. Many hazardous materials are carcinogens (e.g., benzene, polychlorinated biphenyls ("PCBs")) or neurotoxins (e.g., lead, mercury). Workers, as well as people scavenging at dumpsites, can expose themselves

---

14. *Id*. arts. 3.3, 4.4.   **15.** *Id*. art. 12.1.

and their families to these poisons. People living next to the dump site or whose water supply is contaminated by the waste are likely to be injured. Crops planted on these poisoned lands are likely to fail.

The improper disposal of hazardous wastes can also cause substantial changes in the local environment. Careless disposal of persistent chemicals can contaminate the food chain, threatening both sensitive species and human health. Leachates and sewage sludges can cause massive fish kills or oxygen depletion in marine environments. Furthermore, the majority of research done on the effects of hazardous wastes on the environment has been limited to the temperate climates of the industrialized nations; hazardous waste effects in tropical regions may be significantly different.

12. Jennifer R. Kitt, *Waste Exports to the Developing World: A Global Response*, 7 GEO. INT'L ENVTL. L. REV. 485, 488, 491–92 (1995).

[M]any LDCs do not have the technological capabilities to dispose of hazardous wastes. Improper disposal of hazardous waste leads to serious health problems in countries poorly equipped to remedy them. In addition, waste disposal schemes by private waste traders can pose foreign relations problems for industrialized countries. This diplomatic tension may lead to a breakdown in international cooperation on other transnational or global issues. Despite these problems, the economic incentives to import and to export hazardous wastes are strong on both sides of the waste trade.

* * *

[T]he natural environment and climate of many LDCs make toxic wastes more dangerous than in the developed world. For example, heavy rainfall in sub-Saharan Africa causes landfilled waste to leach into the groundwater supply quickly. This is dangerous because most people in LDCs drink untreated water and are therefore susceptible to even low levels of contaminants. Human contact with dump sites is also more likely in LDCs than in the industrialized world. Landfills are often located near the poorest people, many of whom search landfills for possible items to use or sell.

In addition, many LDCs do not have the administrative or political infrastructure to regulate hazardous waste disposal properly. Many do not even have adequate disposal facilities for their own municipal garbage. For example, the city of Accra, Ghana collected only ten percent of its municipal garbage in 1989. Eighty-one percent of collected waste was landfilled and nine percent was burned. Researchers found 100 official, communal refuse dumps and 100 unauthorized dumps, many along water courses. Without proper control and enforcement mechanisms, wastes imported from the industrialized world will simply be dumped as well.... To combat this problem, some countries have gone so far as to impose the death penalty for dumping. However, without strict enforcement of environmental laws, the developing world will remain susceptible to illegal dumping.

Another potential problem is that LDCs often lack the technical capabilities for disposing of hazardous waste. Wealthy countries have technology and expertise to control certain dangers. Lower workforce expertise and limited financial resources in LDCs may increase the risk of accidents. The developing world does not create many industrial wastes; thus, it has had little opportunity to develop proper disposal techniques. Lack of experience with the industrial world's products may result in safety risks. For example, Greenpeace witnessed factory workers pulling batteries apart with their bare hands in a Philippine lead recovery facility. This practice stands in dramatic contrast to the U.S. practice, where law requires workers in lead recycling facilities to wear full-body protection and to shield themselves from the hazardous fumes.

13. Cairo Guidelines and Principles for the Environmentally Sound Management of Hazardous Wastes, Guidelines 2, 4, 5, 7, 9, 12–14, 17, 19, 22, 28, Decision 14/30 of the Governing Council of UNEP (June 17, 1987). [Basic Document 5.3].

14. Basel Convention on the Control of Transboundary Movements of Hazardous Wastes and Their Disposal, Mar. 22, 1989, Preamble & arts. 1–4, 9, 10, 13, 18, 20, 28 I.L.M. 657 (1989). [Basic Document 5.6].

15. Bamako Convention on the Ban of Import Into Africa and the Control of Transboundary Movement and Management of Hazardous Wastes Within Africa, Jan. 30, 1991, Preamble & arts. 1, 2, 4(3), 10, 13, 20, 30 I.L.M. 775 (1991). [Basic Document 5.7].

16. Howard S. Kaminsky, *Assessment of the Bamako Convention on the Ban of Import Into Africa and the Control of Transboundary Movement and Management of Hazardous Wastes Within Africa,* 5 GEO. INT'L ENVTL. L. REV. 77, 77, 81–87 (1992).

The Bamako Convention **[Basic Document 5.7]**, a regional agreement among several African states, provides, *inter alia,* for a complete ban on the import of hazardous wastes into Africa, and the management of hazardous wastes produced within Africa. It endeavors to redress the shortcomings observed by the OAU in the Basel Convention on the Control of Transboundary Movement of Hazardous Wastes and Their Disposal **[Basic Document 5.6].**

* * *

C. ENVIRONMENTALLY SOUND MANAGEMENT

An important obligation found throughout the Bamako Convention is that parties must ensure that hazardous wastes are managed in an environmentally sound and efficient manner. The parties must ensure that the transboundary movement of hazardous waste is reduced to a minimum, and neither exports nor imports are permissible if the respective states have reason to believe that the wastes will not be disposed of in an environmentally sound and efficient manner....

Like the Basel Convention, the Bamako Convention defines environmentally sound management of hazardous wastes as "taking all practicable steps to ensure that hazardous wastes are managed in a manner which will protect human health and the environment against the adverse effects which may result from such wastes." This definition, because it is phrased in general terms, fails to specify the necessary criteria for compliance with the standard. Different countries may disagree as to what constitutes the obligation of environmentally sound management, and the Bamako Convention does not make the violation of these standards an illegal transboundary movement.

D. INSTITUTIONAL FRAMEWORK: IMPLEMENTATION AND ENFORCEMENT

The Bamako Convention provides for a Secretariat to oversee implementation of the Convention by facilitating the flow of information. Enforcement is the responsibility of individual parties and a conference of the parties.... Neither the Secretariat, nor the conference of the parties, nor any other parties have the power to undertake independent inspections. These deficiencies make enforcement inadequate under the Convention....

However, the Bamako Convention dispute settlement provisions are considerably stronger than those in the Basel Convention. Bamako directs the parties to seek settlement through negotiation, or any other peaceful means of their choice. Upon failure, the parties must submit their dispute to an ad hoc arbitration organ or to the International Court of Justice (ICJ). In contrast, the Basel Convention provisions are feeble, because the disputing parties must accept the jurisdiction of the ICJ or the arbitration organ before such bodies can intervene. Despite the improvement of the dispute settlement provisions of the Bamako Convention, its institutional framework as a whole remains weak.

* * *

II. PROGRESSIVE INTERNATIONAL CONCEPTS EMANATING FROM THE CONVENTION

A. Precautionary Approach

Although the precautionary approach has been included in numerous international documents, the Bamako Convention is the first treaty which explicitly contains the precautionary approach in its operative parts. Article 4(3)(f) defines the precautionary approach....

The precautionary approach is a shift away from scientific proof and economic analysis. It emphasizes the vulnerability of the environment, the limitations of accurately predicting threats to the environment and the measures required to prevent such threats, the availability of practical alternatives which enable the termination or minimization of inputs into the environment, and the need for long term holistic economic consideration accounting for environmental degradation and the costs of waste management....

The Bamako Convention is unique in that it is the only international document that allows for preventive action without waiting for scientific proof.[16]

* * *

B. Strict Liability

Another progressive international concept is embodied in the Bamako Convention's requirement that parties impose "strict, unlimited liability as

16. Prior, that is, to the 1992 Rio Declaration on Environment and Development [**Basic Document 1.29**].

well as joint and several liability on hazardous waste generators."[17] The vast majority of international treaties impose only an obligation of due diligence for the prevention of harm, rather than strict liability. Strict liability often spreads the burden of prevention more equitably between signatory states and their industries ... or places the burden solely on the shoulders of the operator or generators without holding the state liable....

* * *

The OAU's rationale for imposing strict liability in the Bamako Convention is that strict liability relieves the African courts of the obligation to set standards of reasonable care, and relieves plaintiffs of the difficult task of proving the breach of these standards. Imposing strict unlimited liability as well as joint and several liability on hazardous waste generators has the advantages of simplifying the plaintiffs choice of defendant and establishing a clear line of responsibility. The decision to impose strict liability on the generator rather than other defendants is based on the assumption that the generator is usually in the best position to exercise effective responsibility for the shipment, and secure insurance.

A flaw of the Bamako Convention is that despite imposing strict liability on generators, it fails to require the parties or the importing, exporting, or transit states to serve as guarantors. This could pose a serious problem if a generator becomes insolvent, or if the harm does not occur until many years after disposal has taken place and the generator no longer exists.

17. Ibrahim J. Wani, *Poverty, Governance, the Rule of Law, and International Environmentalism: A Critique of the Basel Convention on Hazardous Wastes*, 1 KAN. J.L. & PUB. POL'Y 37, 40–45 (1991).

THE BASEL CONVENTION'S NOTICE AND CONSENT REQUIREMENTS
AND REGULATORY INADEQUACIES IN DEVELOPING COUNTRIES

The reporting, consent, and tracking approach of the Basel Convention [Basic Document 5.6] presumes that participating nations have an effective legal system, a functioning administrative structure and regulatory scheme, and a reasonably open political system based on the rule of law. Obviously, these are elements that are absent in most developing countries. For that reason, the Basel Convention is unlikely to achieve its objective of environmentally sound hazardous waste management and disposal.

The EPA [United States Environmental Protection Agency] hazardous waste disposal regulations, from which the Basel Convention borrows, are supported by a legal and regulatory environment that is conducive to achieving its objectives. First, the EPA has the capability and necessary expertise to adopt appropriate regulations to deal with the hazardous waste problem. More specifically, the EPA was created as an independent executive agency to ensure that sound environmental quality, rather than extraneous political and other considerations, would remain its focus. In addition, the agency was equipped with the expertise and technical capability to perform the complex task of environmental policymaking and implementation.

---

17. Bamako Convention [Basic Document 5.7], art. 4(3)(b).

[C]ompared to developing countries, the EPA is ... a good model. Most developing countries do not even have functioning administrative structures capable of sound policymaking or sophisticated regulation of serious problems such as hazardous waste disposal.

The Basel Convention itself recognizes this deficiency, but it merely urges the developing countries to establish appropriate regulatory agencies. Without the proper political and legal infrastructure, however, it is highly unlikely that these countries will establish functional and effective regulatory agencies. To be effective, regulatory agencies need some measure of political autonomy so that they may utilize their expertise to formulate and implement policies with minimal interruption from other branches of government. It is imperative that such autonomy be recognized and respected by the executive, legislative, and judicial branches of the government.[8]

In countries with highly centralized and autocratic governments, environmental agencies, where they exist, typically have minimal autonomy and are frequently subject to political caprice. Although the tendency of politicians to tamper with expert scientific studies exists in the developed countries too, it is far more pronounced in the developing countries where there are no effective legal and political restraints on such excesses. In addition to their small number, experts in developing countries are largely excluded from policymaking.

* * *

The law in most developing countries is either unpublished or poorly organized. Agency regulations in particular are virtually inaccessible to the public. It is elementary that without access to the text of regulations, it is almost impossible to challenge agency action. Agencies are provided a protective shield that breeds arbitrariness, hampers policy enforcement, impedes institutional accountability, and encourages secrecy, which in turn breeds corruption and abuse of authority. These are all characteristic features of governments in developing countries, which undoubtedly have profoundly adverse effects on their environmental policies and programs.

* * *

Governance and the rule of law also influence environmentalism and the effectiveness of environmental policy. The experience of countries with more effective environmental policies indicates that a public constituency for the environment is indispensable to successful environmental protection and that public environmentalism is enhanced by a democratic political climate. Environmental policy regulation is more effective where regulatory agencies have a measure of autonomy to utilized their expertise. To be successful, however, the regulatory process must also promote discourse and public participation, demand external accountability by the regulatory agencies, and ensure objective and consistent enforcement of environmental regulations. For the most part, these conditions do not exist in the poorer countries.... [T]he Basel Convention is fundamentally flawed because it fails to address the legal and political deficiencies in the developing countries, yet, adopts a complex report-

---

8. Many countries do not possess these forms of clearly distinguishable governmental branches.

ing, consent, and tracking scheme that is simply not viable in most developing countries.

18. Rio Declaration on Environment and Development, June 14, 1992, Principles 2–5, 14, 15, UNCED Doc. A/CONF.151/5/Rev. 1, 31 I.L.M. 874 (1992). [Basic Document 1.29].

19. Legal Principles for Environmental Protection and Sustainable Development Adopted by the Experts Group on Environmental Law of the World Commission on Environment and Development, June 1986, Principles 9–18, *in* **Environmental Protection and Sustainable Development (by an Expert Group on Environmental Law of the World Commission on Environment and Development, 1987).** [Basic Document 1.22].

20. Charles Odidi Okidi, *"Preservation and Protection" Under the 1991 ILC Draft Articles on the Law of International Watercourses,*[h] **3 Colo. J. Int'l Envtl. L. & Pol'y 143, 144–45, 149, 155–72 (1992).**

The central subject before the ILC is water, in particular its quality and quantity as it exists in international courses. The significance of water derives from the uses to which it is put by nature. To man the obvious significance of water arises from the fact that it sustains human life. . . .

Thus, water is indispensable for sustenance of life of all living things, including plants. Agriculture, on which human life depends for food, relies on water and there are still no substitutes. Therefore, water must exist in certain quantities to sustain life today and for all future times.

To sustain life, water must be of a certain quality. . . . [T]he ILC task is concerned with a limited but invaluable resource amounting to about three percent of the water on earth. . . .

Of critical significance is the quality of the water, despite whether the quantities are diminishing or an equilibrium between utilization and replenishment through the hydrologic cycle is maintained. . . .

A. General Principles

A pioneering work by Anthony Lester on the legal basis of the protection of international drainage basins identifies and examines three concepts as the doctrinal basis of the obligation not to cause transboundary pollution.[18] The three concepts are international servitude; abuse of rights; and neighbourship.

* * *

In [his] analysis Lester confines himself primarily to the consumptive use of international waters, finding the notion of "permanence" as the basis of objection to application of servitude at the international plane. However, the notion of permanence may have some value to the ideals of preservation and protection. . . . Pollution . . . should be unacceptable—permanently. There-

---

h. Now *see* Convention on the Law of the Non-Navigational Uses of International Watercourses **[Basic Document 4.30].**

18. Anthony Lester, *Pollution, in* The Law of International Drainage Basins 89 (Albert H. Garretson et al. eds., 1967).

fore, watercourse States would properly bind themselves to one another to ensure that they desist from introducing substances or energy which may have detrimental impacts on the water. Thus it seems that there may be some limited application of the rule of servitude to the international watercourses, but only in one respect; to protect the water quality from any substances or energy which might have a detrimental effect on the watercourse or its ecosystem.

The second doctrine is that of abuse of rights. Within the present context the doctrine suggests that pollution of an international watercourse by a riparian or watercourse State is an abuse of rights. This would be subsumed under the rules of state responsibility for activities which a State has a right to do in its own territory even though these activities may have adverse consequences in the territory or interests of other States. But Lester also argues that wherever the doctrine of abuse of rights is applied, there must also be the right that can be forfeited as a consequence of the abuse. In the present instance, there are no rights to be forfeited. Lester concludes that the doctrine of abuse of rights, as such, is inappropriate with respect to obligations to preserve and protect the ecosystem of an international watercourse because sovereignty over a territory cannot be thus forfeited.

The third doctrine is that of neighbourship, implying reciprocity in the conduct of States which share a neighbourhood. Lester submits that neighbourship derives from physical interdependence of contiguous States.... There is an additional idea of neighbourhood created by being in a community of States which are riparian to a given international watercourse.... [F]or ... [the] riparian to pollute the body of water [it shares] or otherwise cause harm to its ecosystem is deemed to be unacceptable conduct among neighbours.

The fundamental point here is that the very fact of being neighbours creates an obligation to the effect that actions taken by one party on its side of the fence should not harm or annoy the other. This is not based on being a good neighbour; rather, if one does no wrong to a neighbour, one does not expect a wrong in return. At the very least, the neighbourship doctrine breeds a situation of co-existence, even if there is no active cooperation. The implication is a recognition of the obligation to preserve and protect the watercourse and its ecosystem individually, where there is no joint or cooperative action by the watercourse States.

It may be submitted ... that the neighbourship doctrine obliges a State to preserve and protect the ecosystem, not out of goodness, but out of self-interest and reciprocity. That is, if one causes harmful effects to the ecosystem in a manner that injures the interests of the other party, then a similar measure may be meted against it.

This neighbourship doctrine also finds expression in the age old Roman maxim *sic utero tuo ut alienum non laendas*, or so use your own that it does not injure the interests of your neighbour....

[I]t seems that a state obligation to ensure that activities within its territory or its jurisdiction should not cause injuries to others is well founded. It expresses the reason why most commentators reject the theory of absolute territorial sovereignty enunciated in 1895 by Judson Harmon, an Attorney General of the United States who saw no obligation on the part of the United

States when it came to diverting the waters of the Rio Grande in a manner that would harm the interests of Mexico.

Within the foregoing discussion it is established that there are principles of international law which can be applied to the preservation and protection of international watercourses in the absence of bilateral and multilateral agreements.

B. CASE LAW

Instances of international water disputes involving preservation and protection are hard to come by. In fact, the two arbitral decisions, *Trail Smelter Arbitration* **[Basic Document 8.4]** and *Lac Lanoux Arbitration* **[Basic Document 8.3]** (only by analogy and by way of dictum, respectively), have become the celebrated examples. What they have in common is the direct expression that there is an international obligation not to cause transboundary environmental injuries. . . .

The emphasis [in the *Trail Smelter Arbitration*] is on the responsibility of the Dominion to reduce or otherwise control pollution, even though Trail Smelter was a private firm. This is the point which brings the jurisprudence of the *Trail Smelter* case close to that of the *Corfu Channel* case **[Basic Document 8.5]**. In the latter case the International Court of Justice (ICJ) found Albania responsible for the placement of the mines at *Corfu Channel* even though there was no proof that Albania, the State, had actually performed the wrongful act. Responsibility was based on the fact of sovereignty. In a separate concurring opinion, Judge Alvarez put forth the point forcefully that "[e]very State is considered as having known, or as having a duty to have known, of prejudicial acts committed in parts of its territory where local authorities are installed; that this is not a presumption, nor is it a hypothesis, it is the consequence of sovereignty." Then he added in the same lines that "[e]very State is bound to take preventive measures to forestall the execution in its territory of criminal or prejudicial acts to the detriment of other States or of their nationals."

Clearly, then, the *Corfu Channel* case and the *Trail Smelter* decision seem to articulate rather forcefully the rule of state responsibility to prevent environmental pollution which may injure the interest of other States.

[The] *Lac Lanoux* arbitration was between France and Spain. . . . France proposed to construct a dam on the River Carol to raise the capacity of Lac Lanoux and create a head for hydroelectric power generation. . . . Spain objected plainly to the very fact of the construction of the dam and control of the flow because it introduced human discretion into the regime of international drainage systems, possibly jeopardizing Spanish interest in irrigation.

The Tribunal rejected [this] argument . . . , specifically because no harm to Spanish interests was actually established. . . . [But] [i]t is this reference to possible change in quality or composition of the water which makes the *Lac Lanoux* decision significant as evidence of international obligation not to cause harm to an international watercourse. It also offers support to the provisions of the ILC draft articles on preservation and protection of the quality of such watercourses.[9]

9. For a differing position on these cases, see Charles B. Bourne, *The International Law*

C. Treaty Law

* * *

The trend is definite towards a new generation of drainage-basin agreements that are [broad], seeking the integrated management of the basins' resources for development. But in each case, they seem to stress the imperatives for preservation and protection; reduction, control and prevention of pollution; and the protection of biodiversity including the control and prevention of the introduction of alien species of flora and fauna. Specific instances such as the Zambesi Action Plan provide for protection of the marine environment.

Without exhausting the analysis of treaties on the African drainage basins, we observe that treaty making within the Organization of African Unity (OAU) has shown deference to environmental preservation and protection generally, and water resources in particular. Within the first decade of independence of most African countries, they adopted the African Convention on the Conservation of Nature and Natural Resources at Algiers on September 15, 1968 [Basic Document 6.4]. Under article V the contracting parties undertook an obligation to manage their water and air resources so as to maintain them in the highest possible quantitative and qualitative levels. Furthermore, the parties would establish and implement policies which maintain air-and water-based essential ecological processes, including prevention of pollution. Paragraph 2 is particularly pertinent to international watercourses as it obligates States to ensure conservation, management, utilization, and development of underground and surface water. In points of detail, the paragraph requires the study of water cycles and investigation of catchments, conservation of catchment areas, control of utilization, and the prevention and control of pollution as well as the establishment of emission and water-quality standards....

The sensitivity to environmental protection and natural resources management is, once more, evinced in the Treaty Establishing the African Economic Community [30 I.L.M. 1241 (1991)] adopted by the fifty one OAU member States at Abuja, Nigeria on June 3, 1991. Article 46(2)(b) specifically requires the member States to cooperate in "the development of river and lake basins," while sub-paragraph (c) requires "the development and protection of marine and fishery resources...." The general issue of cooperation in the management and/or protection of water resources is included in a number of articles.

D. Learned Societies

Learned societies have made notable contributions to the development of the law of international drainage basins or watercourses.... The ILA [International Law Association], more than any organization of its kind, has had the biggest impact on the development of the law of international drainage basins. For this ... we cover only the Dubrovnic Resolutions of 1956 to the Belgrade report in 1980.

Commission's Draft Articles on the Law of International Watercourses: Principles and *Planned Measures*, 3 Colo. J. Int'l Envtl. L. & Pol'y 65, 65–92 (1992).

According to paragraph IV of the Resolution of Dubrovnic, States are responsible for any act on a river which causes injury to another State, but only if the injury is preventable. This limitation is further applied specifically to pollution in paragraph VII. This cautious formulation is a distinct departure from the position of strict liability suggested above in the analysis of the *Trail Smelter* arbitration and the *Corfu Channel* case.

The parties to the Dubrovnic Resolutions agreed on the necessity for integrated and harmonious basin management, a principle which is also reflected in paragraph 1 of the New York Resolution of 1958. The latter resolution was explicit in enjoining co-riparians "to prevent further pollution" and to reduce all existing pollution. . . .

It was in 1966 at Helsinki that the ILA adopted its rules, popularly known as the Helsinki Rules **[Basic Document 4.6]**, which have had a major impact on the law of international water resources. Chapter 3 of the Helsinki Rules deals with "pollution," which is defined as "any detrimental change resulting from human conduct in the natural composition, content, or quality of the waters of an international drainage basin." . . .

The obligation to prevent any form of pollution or any increase in the existing pollution is qualified only by reference to substantial injury or damage. . . . [S]uch a qualification is problematic and misleading because most pollution problems which become acute result from bioaccumulation over time. Secondly, it is a basic presumption that law does not concern itself with trivia.

The Helsinki Rules were elaborated at the August 1972 New York session which adopted "Articles on Marine Pollution of Continental Origin." . . .

The extent to which the Helsinki Rules had influenced the thinking of other learned societies is testified to by the immediate adoption of its formulations by the Asian–African Legal Consultative Committee (AALCC). At its 1973 session the AALCC adopted a set of provisions on "The Law of International Rivers." Proposition VIII on pollution is identical to the provision on pollution under the Helsinki Rules.

It is clear that there is ample support for preservation and protection in the legal commentaries of distinguished legal societies. But there is, admittedly, some degree of variation as to the clarity and firmness of the statements of obligations which States ought to assume.

21. United Nations: Convention on the Law of the Non–navigational Uses of International Watercourses, Report of the Working Group of the Sixth Committee, arts. 7–9, 11–21, 23, 36 I.L.M. 700, UN Document (A/51/869) (1997). [Basic Document 4.30].

Discussion Notes/Questions

1. As noted in John M. Johnson & George Whitaker Ware, *Pesticide Litigation Manual* 1–1 (1992):

> Historians have traced the use of pesticides to the time of Homer around 1000 B.C. By 900 A.D., the Chinese were using arsenic as an insecticide in their gardens. The chemistry at their disposal was certainly more primitive, but they faced precisely the same challenge which confronts pesticide makers today: the development of substances that would kill unwanted insects,

weeds, plant diseases, and other pests without harming desired plants, beneficial insects, wildlife, and, most importantly, humans.

Why has it taken so long to regulate the use of pesticides harmful to the desired natural environment? Has the international community made significant progress in this regard since the days of Homer and the ancient Chinese? Marginal progress? What more, if anything, needs to be done?

2. In an omitted passage of Reading 17, *supra*, Ibrahim J. Wani states that "poverty affects the priority that a government gives to environmental policy." "Until very recently," he notes, "international environmental efforts were resisted by governments in developing countries who viewed them as a form of 'ecoimperialism' and as a conspiracy against economic progress in developing countries. This suspicion resulted from a common perception in developing countries that environmental degradation is an inevitable by-product of economic development."

These suspicions were apparently behind developing countries' opposition at the 1992 UNCED Conference in Rio de Janeiro to developed country initiatives to negotiate a new forestry convention that *inter alia*, would protect tropical rain forests. Given such concerns, what are the prospects for the further development of international environmental law? Do vast differences of wealth among States mean that an international environmental law that is acceptable to both developed and developed States can exist only if development efforts bring national comparative wealth closer together? Do such development efforts invariably demand that environmental considerations be given lesser priority?

3. Graciela Chichilnisky in her essay: Sustainable Development and North South Trade, in *Protection of Global Biodiversity: Converging Strategies* 101 (Lakshman Guruswamy & Jeffrey McNeely, eds., 1998) argues that the present acceleration of environmental destruction can be linked to the economic trading strategies that came into vogue after World War II. The theory of comparative advantages of trade, which recommends that developing countries emphasize resource exports and exports of labor-intensive products, has proven devastating to both the economies and environment of Latin America and Africa. In contrast, the Asian tigers approach based on external economies of scale, has generated knowledge-intensive products where benefits spread across whole industries and whole economies, leading to more economic growth with much less environmental degradation. Such an approach, she argues, should be promoted throughout the world trading system instead of resource intensive patterns of growth that continue to threaten our global environment. This is particularly important because other resource conserving strategies such as green accounting and property rights regimes remain politically unattainable. If Chichilnisky is right might an international law restricting economic growth based on natural resource exploitation, while apparently preventing development, in reality serve the best interests of less developed countries?

4. The hazards caused by a number of chemicals have become evident many years after their development. The lead time before the dangers of DDT were revealed was considerable. For many years before its use was banned in the United States, DDT was a highly recommended agricultural pesticide. How should emerging international environmental law deal with such situations? Are States liable for the harms caused by activities that were thought to be safe at the time? Should they be? What are the arguments for making States retrospectively liable for activities that were not known to be harmful at the time they occurred? If the environmental harm caused by such activities were considered as the opportunity

costs of international development, should compensation and damages be funded by a massive, general international insurance fund? If so, where would the insurance money come from? Additionally, to what extent might environmental impact assessments anticipate and foresee harm to health and the environment?

Even in the most recent international instruments, dangerous chemicals such as DDT continue to be tolerated. However the concerns over persistent organic pollutants (POPs)–such as DDT and others–are mounting, and efforts to regulate and eliminate these dangers are increasingly pursued in international forums. For example the Basel Convention was amended in 1995 at the Third Meeting of the Conference of Parties to the Basel Convention on the Control of Transboundary Movements of Hazardous Wastes and Their Disposal, UNEP/CHW.3/35 (Decision III/1) to "prohibit ... all transboundary movements of hazardous wastes under Article 1(i)(a) of the Convention" from industrialized to developing countries. Article 4A. The amendment also created a new paragraph in the preamble of the Convention: "[r]ecognizing that transboundary movements of hazardous wastes, especially to developing countries, have a high risk of not constituting an environmentally sound management of hazardous wastes as required by this Convention." The hope for the amendment is that the export ban will bolster the impact of developing countries current import bans and encourage more effective management of hazardous wastes at their sources. *See Basel Convention Adopts Amendment Banning Hazardous Waste Exports From Developed to Developing Countries* (visited Sept. 21, 1998) <http://www.uenp.ch/basel/sbc/pr9–95a.htm>.

Another example is the United Nations Economic Convention for Europe's Draft Protocol to the Convention on Long–Range Transboundary Air Pollution on Persistent Organic Pollutants, which was adopted at a special session in June of 1998. EB.AIR/1998/2. The objective of the Protocol is "to control, reduce or eliminate discharges, emissions and losses of persistent organic pollutants." Article 2. While the Protocol does ban the production and use of some substances (DDT not being one of them) immediately, others are scheduled to be eliminated from production and use at a later date. Article 3. However, limited exemptions in specific circumstances and under specific conditions are allowed. Article 4. Repeated references are made throughout the text of the Protocol to "tak[e] into consideration" the Basel Convention "in particular." For additional facts see the United Nations press release, *Negotiators Reach Agreement on Heavy Metals and Persistent Organic Pollutants* (Feb. 17, 1998) <http://www.unece.org/press/98env4e.htm>. Also, the Global Programme of Action [**Basic Document 4.28**], presents suggestions for dealing with persistent organic pollutants in paragraphs 100–06.

Even more recently, in Rotterdam on September 11, 1998, representatives from fifty-seven countries and the European Community signed the Convention on the Prior Informed Consent Procedure for Certain Hazardous Chemicals and Pesticides in International Trade [**Basic Document 5.9**]. The Convention, which presently covers twenty-two pesticides and five industrial chemicals, mandates that these chemicals (which include DDT) not be exported unless the importing country explicitly agrees to such after receiving information on the health and environmental hazards of importation. *See* FAO Press Release, *Rotterdam Convention on Harmful Chemicals and Pesticides Adopted and Signed* (visited Sept. 21, 1998) <http://www.fao.org/WAICENT/OIS/PRESS_NE/PRESSENG/1998/ prenU-NEP.htm>; *see also, Legally Binding Convention to Control Trade in Hazardous Chemicals Adopted in Rotterdam* (visited Sept. 21, 1998) <http://www.fao.org/NEWS/1998/980904–e.htm>.

The Convention on the Non–navigational Uses of International Watercourses [**Basic Document 4.30**] is another recent convention not signed by either Yoribo or Bamileko. Read the provisions dealing with cooperation (arts. 8–10), prevention of harm (art. 7), and prevention and reduction of pollution (art. 21). Are these provisions restatements or codifications of customary law? If so, what impact do they have on the conduct of the parties to this case?

How, if at all, would Yoribo and Bamileko have acted differently had they been parties to one or more of these new international environmental instruments?

5. In the era of "global money," there are large transnational corporations (TNCs) whose gross revenues exceed the gross national products (GNPs) of dozens of countries. For example, in 1984 Exxon Corporation had gross sales larger than the GNP of Switzerland and only slightly less than the GNP of Sweden. The fiftieth largest TNC, Proctor and Gamble, had gross sales exceeding the GNP of Bangladesh. *See* Bruce M. Russett & Harvey Starr, *World Politics: The Menu for Choice* 71 (1989). General Motors is a bigger economic unit than all the less developed countries except China and India. Such revenues, along with a sometimes global presence, give businesses tremendous sway over the policies of countries through formal and informal contacts in the governmental policy-making establishments in their home countries as well as their host countries. Some commentators perceive TNCs as a growing international political force strong enough to undercut the sovereignty of even some developed countries. *See, e.g.*, Barry B. Hughes, *Continuity and Change in World Politics: The Clash of Perspectives* (1990). *See also* Richard J. Barnet & Ronald E. Muller, *Global Reach: The Power of the Multinational Corporations* (1974). Given this reality, is the international community correct to place liability for environmental harms on States that may or may not possess the real power to exercise sovereignty over what occurs as a result of corporate activity within their borders?

6. Simple and complex trading relationships among States have become a prominent feature of the modern international community. Some countries with export-driven economies depend on other States for a major portion of their export revenues. For example, thirty-nine percent of Guatemala's and fifty-four percent of Trinidad and Tobago's exports are to the United States, while 65 percent of Niger's exports are to France. *See* United States Central Intelligence Agency, *Handbook of Nations* (12th ed. 1992). Does this state of affairs suggest that a country's major trading partner might, for example, influence its decision to build a facility that produces toxic chemicals? Is it possible that such decisions are influenced by major aid donors? Should a more onerous duty of care to prevent environmental harm be placed on developed or more powerful countries? If so, what are the possibilities for international law to develop doctrines that transfer State responsibility and/or delineate contributory negligence? Under existing international law, to what extent, if any, would State responsibility be affected if Yoribo previously met with Bamileko and several other countries who were to be the principal customers, and on the basis of their commitments to purchase the Khasa plant's chemicals, decided to build the plant, whereas a lack of interest might have led Yoribo not to build? If existing law does not allow it, to what extent should liability be transferred to these other States?

7. *Bibliographical Note.* For further discussion concerning the principle themes addressed in this problem, consult the following specialized materials:

(a) *Specialized Books/Monographs.* J. Belfiglio, Hazardous Waste Disposal Sites: A Handbook for Public Input and Review (1981); Beyond Dumping:

New Strategies for Controlling Toxic Contamination (B. Piasecki ed. 1984); British Medical Association, Hazardous Waste and Human Health (1991); ___, Pesticides, Chemicals, and Human Health (1991); M. Brown, Laying Waste: The Poisoning of America by Toxic Chemicals (1980); R. Carson, Silent Spring (1962); J. Cashman, Management of Hazardous Waste: Treatment/Storage/Disposal Facilities (1986); M. Chatterji, Hazardous Materials Disposal: Siting and Management (1987); S. Epstein, L. Brown & C. Pope, Hazardous Waste in America (1992); Hazardous Waste and Toxic Wastes: Technology Management and Health Effects (S. Majumdar & E. Miller eds. 1984); Hazardous Waste Management Engineering (E. Martin & J. Johnson, Jr. eds. 1987); E. Hodgson, R. Mailman & J. Chambers, Dictionary of Toxicology (1988); S. Khan, Pesticides in the Soil Environment (1980); J. Kindt, 2 Marine Pollution and the Law of the Sea (1986); J. Lammers, Pollution of International Watercourses (1984); L. Lave & A. Upton, Toxic Chemicals, Health and the Environment (1987); L. Louden, Toxicity of Chemicals and Pulping Wastes to Fish (1979); J. Leonard, Pollution and the Struggle for the World Product: Multinational Corporations, Environment and International Comparative Advantage (1988); F. Matsumura, G. Boush, & T. Misato eds., Environmental Toxicology of Pesticides (1972); E. Miller & R. Miller, Environmental Hazards: Toxic Waste and Hazardous Material (1991); L. Morales, Toxic Dumping in the Third World: A Bibliography (1989); M. Sittig, Handbook of Hazardous Chemicals and Carcinogens (1985); Toxic and Hazardous Materials: A Sourcebook and Guide to Information Sources (J. Webster ed. 1987); Toxicology: The Basic Science of Toxicology (L. Casarett & J. Doull eds., 2d ed. 1980); M. Vance, Chemical Plant Wastes: A Bibliography (1989).

(b) *Specialized Hearings/Reports.* GESAMP, The State of the Marine Environment (1990); United States Environmental protection Agency, Office of Solid Waste and Emergency Response, Hazardous Waste Bibliography (1987); House of Lords Select Committee on Science and Technology, Hazardous Waste Disposal (1981); K. Jager, Aldrin, Dieldrin, Endrin, and Telodrin: An Epidemiological and Toxicological Study of Long–Term Occupational Exposures (1970); D. Pimentel, Ecological Effects of Pesticides on Non–Target Species, Executive Office of the President, Office of Science and Technology, Supt. of Documents, U.S. Govt. Printing Office, Stock No. 4106–0029 (1971); World Health Organization, Principles and Methods for Evaluating the Toxicity of Chemicals, Pt. I (1978).

(c) *Specialized Articles/Book Chapters.* A. Bevenue, The Bioconcentration Aspects of DDT in the Environment, 61 Residue Reviews 37 (1976); T. Brennan, Causal Chains and Statistical Links: The Role of Scientific Uncertainty in Hazardous–Substance Litigation, 73 Cornell L. Rev. 469 (1988); P. Capel, Accidental Input of Pesticides into the Rhine River, 22 Envtl. Sci. & Tech. 992 (1988); J. Dunoff, Reconciling International Trade with Preservation of the Global Commons: Can We Prosper and Protect?, 49 Wash & Lee L. Rev. 1407 (1992); V. Engfer, G. Partida, T. Vernon, A. Toulet & D. Renas, By–Products of Prosperity: Transborder Hazardous Waste Issues Confronting the Maquiladora Industry, 28 San Diego L. Rev. 819 (1991); J. Meagher, Environmental Protection and Industries in Developing Countries: The Case of India Since Bhopal, 3 Georgetown Int'l Envtl. L. Rev. 1 (1990); D. Miller, Courtroom Science and Standards of Proof, Lancet 1283 (Nov. 29, 1987); D. Mossman, Predicting the Effects of a Pesticide Release to the Rhine River, 60 J. Water Pollution Control Federation 1806 (1988); V. Nanda, International Preventive Law Needed to Halt Irreparable Damage to Earth, 8 Preventive L.

Rep. 11 (1989); V. Nanda & B. Bailey, Challenges for International Environ-mental Law–Seveso, Bhopal, Chernobyl, the Rhine and Beyond, 21 Law–Technology 1 (1988); ——, Export of Hazardous Waste and Hazardous Tech-nology: Challenge for International Environmental Law, 21 Land Use & Environment Law 657 (1990); B. Piagen, Prevalence of Health Problems in Children Living Near Love Canal, 2 Hazardous Waste Mat. 23 (1985); J. Riley, No Haven from Harm in the Fields: Pesticides, 8 Nat'l L. J. 1 (1986); J. Scagnelli, International Hazardous Waste Management—Emerging Trends?, 9 Int'l Constr. L. Rev. 394 (1992); T. Schoenbaum, AGORA: Trade and Environment: Free International Trade and Protection of the Environment; Irreconcilable Conflict?, 86 A.J.I.L. 700 (1992); L. Stickel, Pesticide Residues in Birds and Mammals, in Environmental Pollution by Pesticides 254 (C. Edwards ed. 1973); M. Traylor, Dangerous Chemicals in International Per-spective: The Developing United Nations Role, 15 Envtl. L. Rep. 10,156 (1985); A. Upton, T. Kneip & P. Toniolo, Public Health Aspects of Toxic Chemical Disposal Sites, 10 Ann. Rev. Pub. Health 1 (1989); E. Wagner, Bhopal's Legacy: Lessons for Third World Host Nations and for Multinational Corporations, 16 N.C. J. Int'l L. & Comm. Reg. 541 (1991).

Problem 9–3

Desertification in Africa

SECTION 1. FACTS

Cleoganda is a poor, developing, land-locked country in the semi-arid eastern part of the North African continent. The Dingu province of Cleoganda is located in a bio-region that sits over an aquifer. The soil underlying the aquifer consists almost entirely of compressed, low permeability clay. The aquifer was naturally replenished and recharged through its subterraneous hydrologic connection to the Bakoba River, creating a groundwater reservoir and a dozen shallow wells. Fed by the Zanegal Tributary, the Bakoba River forms the border between Cleoganda and Lukyna.

The Bakoba River once flooded frequently, creating wetlands and supporting adjacent fertile lands within its watershed, however, Cleoganda is now completely arid, even hyper-arid in some places, and suffers from desertification. A number of factors contributed to Cleoganda's present plight, including a period of prolonged drought and climatic change in the 1980s and 1990s, as well as over-cultivation, over-grazing, deforestation, and poor irrigation practices.

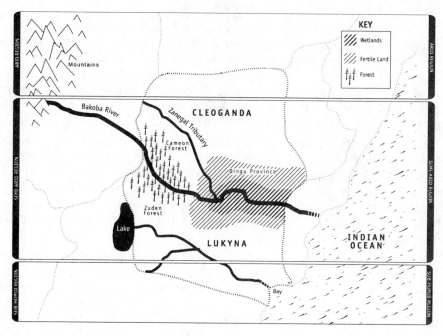

Located southwest of the Bakoba River, Lukyna is a coastal state with a small port on the Indian Ocean to the east and the Zuden Forest located at the semi-arid northwestern border along the Bakoba River. Lukyna lies mostly in a semi-arid region, but is sub-humid in parts. As a coastal state, Lukyna enjoys more trade than Cleoganda, including the exportation of cotton and tobacco as cash crops, and grows only a small fraction of the food it requires. Lukyna receives substantial foreign developmental aid from the U.S. which it uses to grow cash crops for exportation. See Figure 9.3–1 on previous page.

The Ajoenya Tribe, numbering 100,000 and originally located in the Dingu province of Cleoganda, are an ancient people who previously lived and farmed as their ancestors did centuries ago. They communally owned and cultivated the land, producing most of their own food while raising herds of cattle, sheep, and goats which they grazed in available pasture lands. In the 1980s, Cleoganda's population experienced an exponential annual growth rate of five percent, resulting in an increased need for food and livestock.

In order to ensure and enhance crop yields more land was brought under the plough, and irrigation methods were used more extensively. Poor irrigation practices led to salinization—an accumulation of salts that created desert-like conditions—in the once fertile area. Prolonged drought caused the shallow wells to dry up and also reduced the volume of water in the Bakoba River to a fraction of its original volume. Also, the increase in livestock led to over-grazing of pasture land, which in turn led to the destruction of natural plant species. Faced with the shortage of food caused by the failure of irrigation and ground water, the Ajoenya deforested the land adjoining the Bakoba for fuel wood which they traded.

The once fertile soil flood plains of the Bakoba became desert with no adequate water supply, while the Cameon Forest—as the forested area straddling the Cleoganda–Lukyna border is denominated on the Cleoganda side—disappeared in the face of clear-cutting and deforestation. Many people in the region died from famine and disease, including thousands of the Ajoenya. Facing starvation in 1995, the remaining members of the Ajoenya Tribe migrated across the river to Lukyna without permission or documentation.

Lukyna protested the Ajoenya's migration from Cleoganda, claiming that the migration violated Lukyna's sovereignty, and caused transboundary harm. Lukyna further alleged that Cleoganda had violated the Convention to Combat Desertification in Those Countries Experiencing Serious Drought and/or Desertification, Particularly in Africa (Desertification Convention) [Basic Document 5.8], which entered into force in December, 1996. Cleoganda did not respond to Lukyna's protests.

Pursuant to a lucrative commodity trading agreement in the mid–1990s with Albion, a developed European nation, Lukyna's need for cheap labor increased dramatically. Unlike the communal property system in Cleoganda, property in Lukyna is privately owned, and the private land owners of Lukyna began a system of sharecropping land in Lukyna to accommodate and use the foreign tribes that migrated into Lukyna. Private landowners allowed foreign tribes to live on and farm sixty percent of the sharecropped land for their own food requirements and for grazing their herds of sheep, cattle, and goats. The remaining forty percent of the land was used to produce the tobacco and cotton cash crops for export.

The Ajoenya Tribe, who now live on a settlement in the region, sharecrop land in Lukyna. The Ajoenya Chief negotiated an agreement with private landowners, on behalf of 50,000 members of the Tribe who migrated to Lukyna. The land they sharecrop was barren and inhospitable, and the migration of the Ajoenya has allowed the landowners to open up land that would otherwise be fallow. The Tribe receives no state assistance or education on how to farm or care for the land, and they are farming the land without implementing any conservation or crop and soil management measures. They have begun deforestation of the Zuden Forest for grazing and to increase production of food crops.

Within Lukyna, the presence of the Ajoenya Tribe has created ethnic hostility between native Lukynans who are antagonistic toward some of Ajoenya's cultural norms. They are repelled by the Ajoenya practice of venerating their Chief, treating him as part of the Pantheon of gods, and accepting his word as law within the Tribe. In contrast, Lukyna, formerly under colonial rule, is now a democratic republic having held two successful democratic elections, including a relatively peaceful change of government.

Lukynan hostility toward Ajoenya is aggravated by the fact that the Ajoenya consider women to be property in their society and even sell some of them as slaves. By contrast, Lukynan women have been recognized as equals with full voting rights, legal status, and the right to own property. There have been several incidents of sabotage in the Ajoenya's settlement, including the destruction of crops, for which a group of Lukynans claim responsibility.

The Green Party in Lukyna has urged the Lukynan government to implement the Desertification Convention and applicable conservation measures to the sharecropping agreements within the borders of Lukyna. The Green Party insists that Lukyna create a National Action Plan (NAP) as specified under the Convention as well as implement educational programs directed toward women who play a key role in farming. The Green Party has also argued that avaricious landowners are using Ajoenya to decimate biodiversity and promote the spread of desertification, and urge that the Lukyna negotiate a regional action program with Cleoganda per the African Annex of the Convention.

The Opposition Party in Lukyna, on the other hand, claims that the desertification problem is a direct result of the mass migration into Lukyna and asserts that the answer is to return the Ajoeyna to Cleoganda, rather than spending Lukynan resources on foreigners. The Opposition Party is suspected of stirring up the ethnic hostility between Lukynans and the Ajoenya. Opinion polls taken in Lukyna indicate that a clear majority of the population agree with the Opposition Party and want the Ajoenya removed or expelled from Lukyna.

Bowing to political pressure, Lukyna has ordered the expulsion of the Ajoenya Tribe, but Cleoganda refuses to accept their return. It argues a lack of resources to sustain the return of the Ajoenya, further asserting that the Tribe's sharecropping agreement is evidence of Lukyna's responsibility for the Ajoenya. Cleoganda also claims that Lukyna is obligated to the Ajoenya as migratory workers under the International Convention on the Protection of the Rights of All Migratory Workers and Their Families. Moreover, Cleoganda requests enforcement of Lukyna's duties under the Desertification Convention to implement education and conservation measures within Lukyna with respect to migratory workers from Cleoganda.

The Desertification Convention was signed and ratified by Lukyna in 1994 and Cleoganda in 1995, and entered into force in December of 1996. Pursuant to Article 28, 2(b), both parties have filed instruments accepting the compulsory jurisdiction of the International Court of Justice. Both parties have also signed and ratified the International Convention for the Protection of the Rights of All Migrant Workers and their Families (1990). They are both parties to the Charter of the United Nations, the Stockholm Declaration and the Vienna Convention on the Law of Treaties. Neither party has signed or ratified the Convention on Biological Diversity.

Following an escalation of diplomatic exchanges between Cleoganda and Lukyna, both countries tried to negotiate a settlement of their dispute, under Article 28, 1 of the Desertification Convention, but failed to reach agreement. Both countries have subsequently referred the matter to the International Court of Justice.

SECTION 2. QUESTIONS PRESENTED

1. Is Cleoganda responsible/liable for the migration of the Ajoenya Tribe to Lukyna and for subsequent environmental damage caused by the Tribe?

2. Is Lukyna responsible/liable to Cleoganda for violating international law applicable to the Ajoenya Tribe?

SECTION 3. ASSIGNMENTS

A. *Reading Assignment*

Study the Readings presented in Section 4, *infra*, and the Discussion Notes/Questions that follow. Also, to the extent possible, consult the accompanying bibliographical references.

B. *Recommended Writing Assignment*

Prepare a comprehensive, logically sequenced, and *argumentative* brief in the form of an outline of the primary and subsidiary *legal* issues you see requiring resolution by the ICJ. Also, from the perspective of an independent objective judge, indicate which side ought to prevail on each issue and why. Retain a copy of your issue-outline/brief for class discussion.

C. *Recommended Oral Assignment*

Assume you are legal counsel for Lukyna, on the one hand, or Cleoganda, on the other (as designated by your instructor); then, relying upon the Readings (and your issue-outline if prepared), present a 15–20 minute oral argument of your government's likely positions before the ICJ.

D. *Recommended Reflective Assignment*

Consider (and recommend) alternative norms, institutions, and/or procedures that you believe might be more effective than existing world order arrangements in resolving situations of the kind posed by this problem. In so doing, but without insisting upon *immediate* feasibility, identify the particular transition steps that would be needed to make your alternatives a reality.

SECTION 4. READINGS

1. ALAN GRAINGER, THE THREATENING DESERT 1–6 (1990).

INTRODUCTION

Desertification is one of the most serious problems facing the world today. Large parts of the dry areas that cover more than one-third of the earth's land surface are being degraded, with serious effects on the environment, food production, and the lives of millions of people. Desertification, characterized by the degradation of soil and vegetative cover, can occur in any dry area, not just on the fringes of natural deserts. It is a global phenomenon, affecting both developed and developing nations, and is a particular problem in Africa, the Middle East, India and Pakistan, China, Australia, the USSR, the USA, Latin American countries such as Brazil and Chile, and European countries such as Greece, Spain and Portugal.

* * *

Desertification has been occurring for millennia, but became a matter of worldwide concern in the early 1970s when a major drought in the Sahel region of West Africa, which in the opinion of most experts continues to this day, killed between 50,000 and 250,000 people, about 3.5 million cattle, and countless sheep, goats and camels. This prompted the United Nations to convene a Conference on Desertification (UNCOD) in Nairobi in 1977 to agree on a Plan of Action to combat desertification and bring it under control by the year 2000.

The extensive scientific investigations which preceded UNCOD showed that the Sahel tragedy was not just a natural disaster caused by lack of rainfall, but the result of a chronic process of land degradation in which people had a key role. The four main direct causes of desertification ... were identified as overcultivation, overgrazing, deforestation and the mismanagement of irrigated cropland. However, while poor land use can simply be the result of bad management, it is greatly influenced by periods of drought, during which cropping and grazing become more intensive in order to maintain overall food production.

* * *

2. UNITED NATIONS ENVIRONMENT PROGRAMME, STATUS OF DESERTIFICATION AND IMPLEMENTATION OF THE UNITED NATIONS PLAN OF ACTION TO COMBAT DESERTIFICATION 1–5 (1991).

A. CONCEPT OF DESERTIFICATION

* * *

10. Whether the process of desertification or its end result is considered, its most obvious symptoms include:

—Reduction of yield or crop failure in irrigated or rainfed farmland;

—Reduction of perennial plant cover and biomass produced by rangeland and the consequent depletion of food available to livestock;

—Reduction of available woody biomass and the consequent extension of distance to sources of fuelwood or building material;

—Reduction of available water due to decreasing of river flow or groundwater resources;

—Encroachment of sand that may overwhelm productive land, settlements or transport and communications systems;

—Increased flooding, sedimentation of water bodies, water and air pollution;

—Societal disruption due to the deterioration of life-support systems that calls for outside help (relief aid) or that prompts people to seek haven elsewhere (the phenomenon of environmental refugees).

11. The causes of these various forms of ecological degradation and corresponding socio-economic disruption stem from a combination of (a) human exploitation that overburdens the natural carrying capacity of the land resource system, as well as occasional increased negligence and abandonment of land due to the out-migration of people, (b) the inherent ecological fragility of the resources system, and (c) adverse climatic condition, in particular severe recurrent droughts. The high degree of land degradation plays a large part in increasing the susceptibility of farming systems to the shocks of drought, as the Sudano–Sahelian region of Africa has so clearly shown in the last three decades. Land resource exploitation results from such land use operations as irrigated farming, rainfed agriculture and pastoralism, with other contributive factors such as excessive wood cutting, the extraction of mineral resources, excessive tourism and the hunting of game animals. Excessive human pressures on natural resource systems relate to: (a) increase of population and escalation of human needs; (b) socio-political processes that exert pressures on rural communities for orienting their production towards national and international markets; (c) socio-economic processes that reduce the market value of rural products and raise the prices of the basic requirements of rural people; (d) processes of national development, especially programmes for expansion of farmlands for production of cash crops, that exacerbate land and water use conflicts and often reduce areas available to marginalized communities. An overriding socio-economic issue in desertification is the imbalance of power and access to strategic resources among different groups within a given society.

* * *

13. The urgency of addressing this problem stems from the fact that desertification has alarming socio-economic and environmental consequences.

Socio-economically,

—It is the main cause of global loss of productive land resources and thus reduces the world's capability to provide sufficient food and shelter to growing populations;

—It causes economic instability and political unrest in the affected areas, exacerbates the struggle for scarce land and water resources, and spurs outward migration in search of relief and refuge;

—It exerts enormous pressures on the economy and stability of societies outside the affected areas by escalating the need for food aid, as well as the influx of environmental refugees;

—It prevents the achievement of sustainable development in the countries and regions affected and through them, the world as a whole;

—It directly threatens the health and nutrition status of the affected populations, particularly children.

Environmentally,

—It is an increasing element of planetary environmental degradation that plays a vital role in water, air and soil pollution; deforestation; soil loss; and climate change;

—It contributes heavily to loss of global biodiversity, particularly in the areas that are centres of origin of major crop species of the world, such as wheat, barley, sorghum and maize;

—It increases the loss of biomass and bioproductivity of the planet and the exhaustion of the global humus reserve, thus disrupting normal global bio-geochemical turnover and, in particular, reducing the global carbon dioxide sink;

—It contributes to global climate change by increasing land surface albedo, increasing the potential of such change and decreasing the current evapo-transpiration rate, changing the ground surface energy budget and adjoining air temperature, as well as adding dust and CO_2 to the atmosphere.

* * *

3. Convention to Combat Desertification in those Countries Experiencing Serious Drought and/or Desertification, Particularly in Africa, June 17, 1994, arts. 1–5, 7–11, 19, 28, Annex I, arts. 1–4, 7–8, 33 I.L.M. 1328 (1994) [Basic Document 5.8].

4. William C. Burns, *The International Convention to Combat Desertification: Drawing a Line in the Sand?*, 16 MICH. J. INT'L L. 831, 832–48 (1995).

INTRODUCTION

The process known as desertification, which can be broadly characterized as degradation of land, resulting in decreased productivity, is not a new phenomenon. 4200 years ago, the world's first empire, the Akkadian in Mesopotamia, collapsed after only a century of prosperity as a result of severe drought that induced desert-like conditions throughout what is now Iraq, Syria, and parts of Southern Turkey.

In the sixth century B.C., the capital of the Kingdom of Kush, Napata, was abandoned because of overgrazing by herds, resulting in erosion and advancement of the desert. More recently, in the latter part of the 19th

Century and early part of the 20th, desertification seriously denuded the productivity of large portions of rangelands in the United States and Australia.

However, in the past three decades the rate of desertification has increased dramatically in the forty percent of land surface classified as arid or semi-arid, dealing particularly harsh blows to the besieged inhabitants of developing nations. During the present decade, the amount of land degraded by desertification will be double that of the past two decades. This translates into the staggering loss of about 58 thousand square kilometers of once productive land annually, an aggregate area about the size of the state of West Virginia. By 1993, more than 3.6 billion hectares of the total area of the drylands was [sic] subject to some degree of desertification, representing nearly one quarter of the global land mass. On the African continent, eighty percent of sub-Saharan drylands and rangelands, or about 1.5 billion hectares show significant signs of desertification, as well as seventy-two percent of the drylands in South America and seventy percent in Asia.

Several nations in the developing world are suffering disproportionately. In China, desertification is advancing by 2100 square kilometers per year, with over one-sixth of the nation's total land mass subject to some degree of degradation. In India, forty percent of the land is desertified, encompassing about 120 million hectares. An astounding eighty-five percent of the landmass of Kenya is experiencing some degree of desertification, with almost twenty percent currently severely degraded.

The United Nations has estimated that "desertification threatens the future of more than 785 million people, or 17.7 percent of the world's population who live in ... drylands ... Of this number between sixty and one hundred million people are affected directly by decreases in productivity associated with the current desertification process."[1] Moreover, the United Nations Environment Program has estimated that if trends continue unabated, about eight billion acres of grazing land, irrigated zones, and croplands will be in jeopardy by the end of the century, threatening the livelihoods of 1.2 billion of the world's 5.5 billion people.[2]

* * *

I. DESERTIFICATION: CAUSES AND CONSEQUENCES

The term "desertification" is defined in the Convention as "land degradation in arid, semi-arid and dry sub-humid areas resulting from various factors, including climatic variations and human activities."[3] As this definition implies, desertification is attributable to both human and natural factors.

* * *

1. Charles L. Amuyunzu, Desertification in the East and Southern African Sub–Regions: Lessons For the Desertification Convention 1 (Aug. 16–20, 1993) (paper presented at the International NGO Conference on Desertification at Bamako, Mali) (on file with author).

2. David E. Pitt, *Nations Mobilize To Limit Deserts*, N.Y. TIMES, Dec. 12, 1993, at 25.

3. The Convention defines "land degradation" as:

[R]eduction or loss, in arid, semi-arid and dry sub-humid areas, of the biological or economic productivity and complexity of rainfed cropland, irrigated cropland, or range, pasture, forest and woodlands resulting from land uses or from a process or combination of processes, including process-

A.   Causes of Desertification

1.   Human Factors

Human-induced desertification is caused primarily by four activities: overcultivation, overgrazing, deforestation, and poor irrigation practices.

a.   Overcultivation

Overcultivation occurs when farmers crop lands more intensively than is sustainable by the land's natural fertility. Drylands are particularly susceptible to overcultivation. Soils in arid and semi-arid regions are formed by processes where water is extremely limited. As a consequence, the soils are not leached and the evaporative process produces an accumulation of soluble salts near the land surface. This results in a severe shortage of important nutrients, especially nitrogen and phosphorous. The paucity of these nutrients in turn results in low soil organic matter (humus) content, rendering the soil highly susceptible to erosion.

Soil and wind erosion are primary causes of desertification in the world's drylands. Erosion results in exposed topsoil becoming crusted, which reduces its ability to absorb water or causes it to be blown away by wind or washed away by water. The subsoil that remains after the valuable nutrient layer of topsoil is removed is largely infertile and is characterized by reduced water absorption properties.

Erosion also wreaks havoc with vegetation; wind carrying soil particles can "sand-blast" plants, shredding leaves through abrasion, killing them outright, or burying them under sand and dust. The loss of surface vegetation results in an acceleration of the desertification process, exposing topsoil to further erosion and destabilizing its composition. Vegetation that does subsequently grow under such conditions will usually respond less well to rain, produce less biomass, and die at increasingly earlier stages of drought. The impoverishment of the soil also leads desperate farmers to expand into more marginal rangelands, which quickly become degraded, exacerbating the desertification cycle.

Overcultivation in dryland areas can be primarily attributed to two factors: population pressures necessitating increased crop production and the expansion of cash cropping.

In areas where desertification is of particular concern, such as sub-Saharan Africa and the Middle East, population growth rates of more than three percent are severely taxing food resources.

* * *

Reduction in fallow periods is particularly harmful to the viability of agricultural lands. Fallow periods permit a land's fertility to regenerate naturally. Additionally, farmers often plant trees on land lying fallow, which provide nitrogen fixing nutrients for the soil and help prevent erosion. Fallow

es arising from human activities and habitation patterns, such as:

(i) soil erosion caused by wind and/or water;

(ii) deterioration of the physical, chemical and biological or economic properties of soil; and

(iii) long-term loss of natural vegetation[.] Convention art. 1(f).

lands also often provide grazing resources for livestock, which, in turn, provide fertilizer for the fields.

At one time, dryland farmers could shift cereal cultivation from field to field, with fallow periods ranging from a few years up to a few decades. Increased population densities now preclude this in many dryland regions, and fallow periods have been severely reduced or eliminated. In some nations, fallowing is actively discouraged by law. For example, in Senegal, a farmer who does not plough her land within a three-year period can be stripped of ownership.

As commodity prices have plummeted in recent years, many developing nations have turned to the cultivation of monocultural cash crops, such as cotton and groundnuts, to obtain revenue for development and to service foreign debt. Many developed nations have actively encouraged this strategy by tying aid to cash crop production.

* * *

Cash crops are particularly stressful on drylands. Groundnut cropping in the Sahelian region of Africa, for example, has substantially reduced the productivity of dryland soils and has reduced the area used for food crops and fallow time, which further exacerbates soil deterioration. Similarly, the decision of farmers in Thailand to switch from cultivation of rice to tapioca has resulted in deforestation and overcultivation of soil, important precursors of desertification.

b.   Overgrazing

Overgrazing occurs when livestock density becomes excessive and too many animals are grazed on the same area of rangeland. It is a major cause of desertification in the drylands, the site of one-half of the world's cattle, one-third of its sheep, and two-thirds of its goats.

In recent years, population pressures have substantially increased the size of livestock herds in dryland areas while the area available for grazing has declined as pastoralists are displaced by farmers. This has resulted in the concentration of high volumes of livestock in extremely limited areas, contributing to desertification in several ways. First, livestock overgrazing results in the loss of vegetation, which is consumed or trampled, contributing to soil erosion.... Overgrazing also may result in the displacement of desirable species of plants, such as palatable grass species, which help to hold soil together, by drought-resistant shrubs, which do little to maintain soil viability or prevent erosion.

Second, the trampling of soil, particularly at places where livestock congregate, such as watering holes, results in the pulverization of the soil, contributing to erosion. In addition, pounding by livestock hooves can result in the compaction of soil. This results in surface crusting, which reduces infiltration of water into the soil and accelerates the process of water erosion.

c.   Deforestation

Deforestation is proceeding at a tragic rate in many parts of the developing world, including dryland regions in Africa, Asia, and the Middle East. According to the Food & Agriculture Organization, four million hectares of land are deforested every year in arid lands. On the African continent, ten times more wood is harvested annually than is produced in the continent's forests. Two particularly disheartening examples in Africa are in Ethiopia, where ninety percent of the vegetation has been stripped away since the beginning of the century, and in Uganda where forest cover has declined from thirty-one thousand square kilometers to less than six thousand square kilometers in the last ninety years.

* * *

The pressure on forests in drylands comes from two directions. First, the desperate need to expand food production has resulted in the clearing of large areas of forestland for crop cultivation. For example, in the Senegalese Mbegue forest, over seven hundred kilometers of forest was [sic] cleared for cultivation in less than one month.... Overall, it has been estimated that seventy to eighty percent of ongoing deforestation can be attributed to clearance of land for crop production.

A second primary cause of deforestation is demand for fuel wood. About one-third of the world's population, and ninety percent in the developing world, rely exclusively on wood and woody materials as a source of heat for cooking and warmth. As supplies of farmland trees and the scrubby woodlands of unfarmed areas have been depleted, poaching has increased in ecologically critical national forests. This has resulted in the diminution or elimination of natural growths of forest and steppes in many dryland regions.

* * *

The loss of tree cover is often the first step in the process of desertification. "[T]rees play a vital role in protecting and retaining soils."[4] Tree and plant roots help to anchor soil down, preventing wind and water erosion.... In Ethiopia, where national forest cover has fallen from sixteen percent a few decades ago to just three percent currently, soil is washed away in some areas by rains at the rate of twenty tons per hectare per year.

Diminution of tree cover also diminishes the water retention capacity of soil, contributing to the buildup of silt deposits and impairing the effectiveness of irrigation schemes and water reservoirs. Finally, trees provide a hospitable microclimate for grasses and supply important nutrients through stem flow to soil.

d. Irrigation/Salinization

One of the primary constraints to increasing food production in dryland regions is a shortage of water. Controlled application of water can help expand production in the short-term in the drylands. However, the construction of irrigation schemes that direct the flow of water to root zones in optimum quantities is critical for long-term gains.

Unfortunately, poor-planned irrigation projects can lead to desertification. When irrigated land is not properly drained, the soluble salts contained in irrigation water accumulate in the system and contiguous soil because the outflow of saline water is prevented or hindered. Additionally, expansion of irrigation schemes may cause the ground water table to rise, bringing salts up

---

4. Mengiste Deste, *The Ethiopian Situation*, RESOURCES, 1993–II, at 28–29.

to the soil profile. The accumulation of salts in soils creates desert-like conditions because its constituent elements, including sodium chlorides and sodium sulfates, reduce soil fertility, stunt plant growth, and impair the metabolism between the compounds of soil, atmosphere, and hydrosphere that supply the biosphere with nutrients.

* * *

Overall, the environmental organization Earth Action reports that 1.25 million acres are desertified each year because of improper irrigation practices. Recent research pegs the annual loss of farmland from salinization at almost one percent. If current trends continue, nearly thirty percent of the world's presently irrigated acreage will be lost by 2025, rising to nearly fifty percent by 2050.

2.   Climatic Factors

The role of climatic factors in contributing to the desertification process has been a constant source of controversy.

* * *

Climate clearly plays a role in the desertification process, though its precise contribution is hard to calculate. Rainfall variations are a primary cause of variations in forage production and decisions as to how to utilize rangelands. Moreover, a substantial amount of the year-to-year variation in vegetation cover in arid and hyper-arid areas can be attributed to changes in rainfall. As indicated earlier, sparse vegetation cover leads to erosion, which accelerates the process of desertification.

B.   Impact of Desertification
1.   Productivity Losses: Agricultural

In contradistinction to the popular image of dryland regions as barren, hostile expanses of land, arid regions are a critical source of food production, accounting for at least one-fifth of the world's supply.[5] Unfortunately, desertification has substantially denuded food production in the drylands in the past two decades, and this process threatens to accelerate cataclysmically as this decade closes.

Approximately eighty percent of the agricultural land in arid regions suffers from moderate to severe degrees of desertification. Over sixty million acres of agricultural land are directly affected by decreases in productivity associated with desertification, and an additional fifty to seventy thousand square kilometers of useful land go out of production annually.

The degradation of agricultural lands translates directly into a decline in crop production. For example, in Africa, soil fertility losses linked to desertification has reduced dryland crop yields by twenty-five to fifty percent in severely desertified areas. Per capita grain production on the continent has plummeted twelve percent since 1981 and twenty-two percent since 1967.

Burgeoning population rates make future declines in food production potentially catastrophic. The world population, currently at 5.8 billion, is

---

5.   R.L. HEATHCOTE, THE ARID LANDS: THEIR
USE AND ABUSE 27 (1983).

increasing by ninety-three to ninety-five million annually, the fastest rate in history.

* * *

The United Nations recently averred: "If the process of desertification is not arrested in the near future, the world shortage of food will increase dramatically within a few decades."[6] Perhaps the most chilling portent of this conclusion is on the African continent where desertification is contributing to stagnating or even declining levels of agricultural production.

* * *

3. Urban Unrest/Environmental Refugees

Faircloth recently observed, "environmental issues now have major political and security implications."[7] Land degradation powerfully demonstrates the regional and global implications of environmental crises in the last part of this century. Desertification has created millions of dryland "environmental refugees," people who are compelled to abandon the land because it can no longer support them.[8] For example, in Burkina Faso, desertification has caused the migration of almost one million men and women, one-sixth of the nation's population. Similarly, one-sixth of the population of Niger has been uprooted as a consequence of desertification. The pace of desertification-induced migration has increased substantially in recent years, with two to three thousand individuals joining the ranks every day.

Beyond the personal tragedy that forced migration inflicts on its victims, it is also a major cause of unrest and political strife in many dryland region nations. Environmental refugees often migrate to urban areas in search of jobs and social services. Urbanization is increasing at the startling rate of eight to ten percent annually in developing countries affected by desertification. The urban population of nations in the Sahelian region of Africa quadrupled between 1969 and 1980, largely attributable to migration induced by land degradation.

Rapid and uncontrolled migration to urban areas often results in social revolt and political unrest. For example, four separate uprisings occurred in Sahelian urban centers in Northern Nigeria between 1980 and 1985, all triggered by migrants who had been displaced by desertification and drought.[9] Frustrated by their inability to obtain employment or housing in areas ill-equipped to absorb them, "they gave vent to their feelings of anger, economic powerlessness and frustration which had haunted them for a very long time."[10] Similarly, the rapid influx of Hindu settlers fleeing degraded lands

---

6. *Status of Desertification and Implementation of the United Nations Plan of Action to Combat Desertification: Report of the Executive Director,* U.N. Environment Programme, 3rd Special Sess., at 3, U.N. Doc. UNEP/GCSS.111/3 (1992).

7. A.J. Faircloth, *Global Environmental and Natural Resource Problems–Their Economic, Political, and Security Implications,* WASH. U. L.Q. 78, 79 (1991). *See also* Norman Myers, *Environmental Refugees in a Globally Warmed World,* 43 BIOSCIENCE 752 (1993).

8. John Madeley, *For Millions, Life is a Battle Against the Sand,* GAZETTE (Montreal), June 26, 1993, at 16.

9. *See* E.E. Okpara & O.A. Salau, *Desertification Dynamics in West and North Africa,* 4 RESOURCES 1993–II, at 26.

10. *Id.; see also* Arthur H. Westing, *Population, Desertification, and Migration,* 21 ENVTL. CONSERVATION, Summer 1994, at 110, 112.

into the Sikh-predominated Punjab region exacerbated tensions between the two groups in the 1970s and 1980s.

In a perverse twist of fate, massive migration by refugees fleeing environmental degradation begets yet more environmental damage. Refugees often settle in fragile ecosystems, depleting resources such as woody biomass and beginning the desertification cycle over again. Additionally, mass migration reduces the pool of rural manpower, delaying efforts to rehabilitate dryland areas.

* * *

5. Kyle W. Danish, *International Environmental Law and the Bottom–Up Approach: A Review of the Desertification Convention*, 3 IND. J. GLOBAL LEGAL STUD. 133 (1995).

II. DESERTIFICATION: A BACKGROUND ON THE PROBLEM

A. The Definition and Extent of Desertification

* * *

Mismanagement of drylands has had disastrous consequences throughout world history. Improper irrigation practices played a significant role in the collapses of the Sumerian and Babylonian empires. Overcultivation in the American Great Plains precipitated the "Dust Bowl" conditions of the 1930s, during which an estimated 3.5 million people left their farms.[11]

* * *

A persisting image of the problem of desertification is that of deserts encroaching upon formerly productive lands. This common depiction is a distortion. The regions threatened by desertification encompass a far greater area than merely the fringes of the world's deserts. Moreover, the oscillation of desert fringes seems to be a distinct phenomenon, related almost entirely to climate variation and of a smaller magnitude than historically assumed.

Though dryland regions exist on nearly each of the continents, there is a strong correlation between poverty and drylands. Consider the total land area of the world's developing countries. The poorest, least developed countries—in which annual per capita income averages under $500—make up twenty percent of that total land area. These same countries, however, contain sixty-three percent of all the drylands in developing countries.[12] The Sahelian region of Africa, which includes Cape Verde and portions of Senegal, Mauritania, Mali, Burkina Faso, Niger, Chad, and the Sudan, consists largely of drylands. Severe drought, extensive poverty, rapid population growth, and political instability have exacerbated the consequences of desertification in this region. The concentration of the world's poorest people on inherently ecologically fragile lands drives the need for an effective international response to desertification.

* * *

11. DAVID S.G. THOMAS & NICHOLAS J. MIDDLETON, DESERTIFICATION: EXPLODING THE MYTH 22–23 (1994).

12. *See* Robert W. Kates & Viola Haarman, *Where the Poor Live*, ENVIRONMENT, May 1992, at 5, 7.

IV. THE DESERTIFICATION CONVENTION

A. Overview

At [United Nations Conference on Environment and Development] UNCED, African countries pressed for an international convention on desertification. They cited the failure of the [Plan of Action to Combat Desertification] PACD and emphasized that no problem better captured the crisis of the environment and development. Delegates to UNCED officially requested the U.N. General Assembly to establish an intergovernmental negotiating committee on desertification. UNCED participants also agreed to include a chapter on desertification in Agenda 21, the non-binding international action plan for sustainable development. The chapter contains detailed recommendations for national, regional, and international initiatives. [13]

* * *

1. Overview of the Text: Principles and General Obligations

The first paragraph in the article on "principles" articulates four of the principal themes of the Convention: (1) local participation in planning and implementing desertification programmes; (2) improved coordination and utilization of financial and other resources; (3) the enhancement of cooperation among governments, [non-governmental organizations] NGOs, and land users to improve understanding of the problem; and (4) recognition of the special needs and vulnerability of affected developing countries.

Article 4 sets out a number of "general obligations" that all the Parties undertake. Among these are duties to adopt an integrated approach to combating desertification; the Parties must address the physical, biological, and socio-economic aspects of the problem. The Parties also agree that eradicating poverty and improving international economic conditions are elements of efforts to combat desertification.

Article 5 contains a set of obligations specifically for affected country Parties. To the extent that national circumstances allow, preventing desertification must be a priority in national policies. The affected country Parties must also agree to promote awareness among citizens and citizen groups.

* * *

5. Overview of the Text: The Regional Annexes

* * *

The African Annex contains the most detailed measures and strongest commitments. Unlike the Convention text and the three other regional annexes, the African Annex lists several specific measures that should be included in African country action programmes. African countries also undertake to execute these programmes without waiting for the Convention to enter into force. Acknowledging the priority of assisting Africa, the developed country Parties agreed to concrete commitments for transferring financial

---

13. *See* Agenda 21, adopted June 13, 1992,   I, II, III) (1992).
ch. 12., U.N. Doc. A/CONF. 151/26/Rev.1 (vols.

resources to the affected countries of Africa; they pledged to maintain the current level of assistance or to increase that level.

* * *

C. Analysis: Micro–Level Obligations: The "Bottom–up" Approach

The hallmark of the Desertification Convention is its elaboration of a bottom-up approach for combating desertification.

* * *

1. The "Bottom–Up" Approach: Participation in Desertification Action Programmes and in Sustainable Development Programmes

The Convention says that the national action programmes—the "central element of the strategy" to combat desertification—should consist of local development programmes that are based on participatory mechanisms. The national action programmes therefore shall:

> [P]rovide for effective participation at the local, national and regional levels of non-government organizations and local populations, both women and men, particularly resource users, including farmers and pastoralists and their representative organizations, in policy planning, decision-making, and implementation and review of national action programmes.

Notably, the Parties are obligated to provide for "effective participation" of local stakeholders and NGOs. A duty to provide merely for their "participation" arguably could be discharged by making only modest attempts to keep local stakeholders and NGOs informed and involved. The Parties must provide participation not only in implementing the programmes but also in deciding on the content of the programmes. Participation is required during continuing elaboration and revision; the plans "shall be updated through a continuing participatory process...." This paragraph also gives identity to the land users and land user groups of central importance—women as well as men, pastoralists as well as farmers, and NGOs.

* * *

The African Parties agreed to obligations not only to enhance participation of land users in desertification action programmes, but also to develop a process which can maximize their participation in planning national sustainable development programmes generally. In Article 6, concerning the "[s]trategic planning framework for sustainable development," these Parties agree to undertake a "consultative and participatory process" involving local populations and NGOs to "provide guidance on a strategy ... to allow maximum participation from local populations and communities." This language seems to create a binding obligation of decentralized development planning within the African country Parties. Such obligations should help to alleviate the political marginalization of rural land users. As noted earlier, this marginalization is one of the socio-economic conditions at the root of desertification.

2. The "Bottom–Up" Approach: Capacity–Building

Additional evidence of the bottom-up process' centrality in the Desertification Convention is its extensive section on "Capacity building, education, and public awareness." Though the language in this section more closely approximates policy recommendations than strictly binding obligations, one should not conclude that the parties are placing little emphasis on this aspect of the response to desertification.

* * *

The article defines capacity-building as "institution building, training and development of relevant local and national capacities." In addition to some measures aimed at institutions, the Parties agree to promote capacity-building through a range of activities involving the key local actors identified in earlier articles.

* * *

The section on educational awareness programs contains strictly binding obligations for the Parties. They are obligated to create and support programs to educate the public in affected countries about the causes and effects of desertification. To meet these objectives the Parties "shall" among other things, organize awareness campaigns and "promote" permanent public access to "relevant information."

* * *

4.   The "Bottom–Up" Approach: Special Roles for NGOs

NGOs were an important element of the negotiations and the text reflects their central role in the bottom-up process created by the Convention.

* * *

In the last few decades, the role of non-governmental organizations in developing, implementing, and enforcing international environmental initiatives has increased substantially. Non-governmental organizations are participating in the drafting of international agreements, sometime as members of the delegation of state parties. They monitor the performance of state parties. They shame and expose those parties that do not comply with their obligations. NGOs also are playing a major role in carrying out environmental initiatives both in tandem with state agencies and independently.

Nonetheless, according to the majority view, NGOs do not have legal personality in international law. Arguably, some legal personality attaches to those NGOs with which intergovernmental organizations and convention secretariats have established formal relationships.

* * *

Given this current state of international law, the Desertification Convention represents a significant leap forward. In the text of the Convention itself, there are twenty-two separate references to NGOs. These references do not merely establish that a future desertification secretariat or intergovernmental organization should create a formal relationship with an NGO. The text obligates the state parties themselves to work with NGOs. According to the international law established under the Convention, non-governmental organizations shall be an integral element of the international and national-level policy responses to desertification.

The Convention acknowledges two important roles of NGOs in the bottom-up process. Because of their special links to the grass-roots, NGOs are recognized as effective conduits through which the international community can channel resources, information, and power to local populations. Thus, within the text, they are consistently grouped among the key local actors— women, farmers, pastoralists, local communities, local populations, etc.

The other role of NGOs recognized by the Convention is that of expert bodies. Implicitly, NGOs are placed on equal footing with intergovernmental organizations as organizations with whom Parties should consult and coordinate. In fact, the Convention consistently refers to intergovernmental organizations and non-governmental organizations in tandem. The Parties agree to develop national and field-level operational mechanisms to coordinate the efforts of developed country Parties, developing country Parties, and "relevant intergovernmental and non-governmental organizations." ... In undertaking educational and awareness-building programs, the Parties "shall" cooperate with "competent intergovernmental organizations, as well as non-governmental organizations." Any financial mechanisms developed by the Conference of the Parties shall provide information on available sources of funds "to interested Parties and relevant intergovernmental and non-governmental organizations" in order to promote cooperation among them.

* * *

6.   William C. Burns, *The International Convention to Combat Desertification: Drawing a Line in the Sand?*, 16 Mich. J. Int'l L. 831, 872–74, 876–80 (1995).

IV.   THE CONVENTION TO COMBAT DESERTIFICATION: OASIS OR MIRAGE?

* * *

1.   Land Tenure

Many dryland nations are characterized by land tenure arrangements antipathetic to private ownership and transfer of land interests. This includes state ownership with accordance of leasehold rights for a limited period of time, communal ownership by members of a designated group, and open access tenure, in which no one owns the land or can control access. These methods of allocating property interests are counterproductive from the standpoint of engendering sound land management practices. Tenant farmers, for example, have little interest in the long-term productivity of the soil since they often are compelled to vacate the land they occupy after a few years. Thus, they are usually chary to make the capital or labor commitments necessary to protect the land from factors such as wind and water erosion. Communal land arrangements often result in the "tragedy of the commons," which again obviate the incentive of implementing conservation practices:

> [I]f ownership is not defined and security of tenure assured, land owners do not have the incentive to conserve and improve communal land [e.g. soil erosion control]. However, they impinge on each other on the basis of pursuing long term economic interests that, collectively, they might be better off if they could be restrained, but no one gains individually in self-restraint. ... This scenario, which Hardin so vividly characterised as the

'tragedy of the commons,' is often presented as the classic illustration of the predator form of human behaviour and the core of the problem of degradation on common property resources which is enshrined in traditional tenurial systems.[14]

* * *

2. The Role of Women in Land Conservation

As the drafters of both Agenda 21 and the Convention recognized, women play a critical role in land management in developing nations. Women play a predominant role in the production of food crops, producing ninety to ninety-five percent of the crops in Africa, are responsible for a large proportion of animal husbandry, and collect the vast majority of fuelwood. Thus, any effort to address the root causes of desertification must actively engage women in the process. As one commentator noted, "the energy and skills of women as natural resource managers may be a decisive factor in the battle against land degradation."[15]

Unfortunately, many developed nations actively degrade the role of women in the context of land, denying them security of tenure, access to credit, and educational services. Affected Parties to the Convention should strive to improve the lot of women in several ways. First, the laws in many developing nations need to be reformed to permit women to inherit land, and to provide for daughters and single women to hold title to land. Second, credit policies which often deny women access to capital, or exact exorbitant interest payments, need to be eliminated. The [Food and Agricultural Organization] FAO has estimated that women receive ten percent or less of all agricultural credit, even when they are the sole breadwinners.[16] As a consequence, women are unable to invest in sounder agricultural practices, purchase technologies to reduce demand for fuelwood, or gain access to timesaving equipment, which would make it easier to them to concentrate on sound land management. Third, efforts should be made by dryland governments to target land management training programs to women. This will require the reorientation of extension agencies in many nations which almost exclusively direct their services at men.

* * *

4. Population Control

Population pressures in dryland nations have contributed substantially to the desertification crisis. Moreover, with population growth rates of three percent to 3.5 percent annually, many dryland nations can expect their populations to double in just twenty-three years, exacerbating land degradation trends.

* * *

14. Kwasi Nsiah-Gyabaah, Environmental Degradation and Desertification in Ghana 90 (1994) (citations omitted).

15. *Reiterating the Role of Women in Desertification*, Eco, June 10, 1994, at 2.

16. *See* World Resources Institute, World Resources 43 (1994).

Unfortunately, two out of three women in the developing world who would like to avail themselves of family planning have no access. The number denied access is at least 120 million.

* * *

Second, research consistently indicates that raising educational levels for women lowers reproductive rates by "affecting the age at which unions first form and the number of children they have."[17] According to the World Bank, women denied a secondary education have an average of seven children; this figure drops to three if they receive secondary instruction. Higher education rates also reduce infant mortality rates, which can ultimately contribute to lowered birth rates. The United Nations estimates that each year of education received by a young mother reduces the death rate of her children by seven percent.

Unfortunately, women's educational levels are abject in many developing nations. Of the 960 million illiterate individuals in the world (most of whom are in the developing world) two-thirds are women.[18] In many developing nations, religious customs and patriarchal institutions deny women educational opportunities and ensure unchecked population growth. Thus, the prospects for enhancing the status of women is contingent on a meaningful commitment by affected Party governments to achieve gender equity.

Finally, increasing security of land tenure, discussed earlier in this article, might yield the ancillary benefit of reducing population growth rates. A recent study indicates that in nations where private land rights are weak there is an incentive to have more children because they can be sent out to "capture" open-access resources such as firewood, animal fodder, grazing, and fish.[19]

* * *

E. Emphasis on Local Decisionmaking and Empowerment

A final significant aspect of the Convention is its recognition of the importance of participation by groups and individuals at the local level in affected nations. Implicit in the Convention's approach is a commitment to decentralization, defined as:

> [T]he transfer of responsibility for planning, management, and the raising and allocation of resources from the central government and its agencies to field units of central government ministries or agencies, subordinate units or levels of government, semi-autonomous public authorities or corporations, area-wide, regional or functional authorities, or nongovernmental private or voluntary organizations.[20]

17. *Recommendations of the Latin American and Caribbean Regional Conference on Population and Development,* 19 POPULATION & DEV. 885 (1993).

18. *See* Storer H. Rowley, *Population Forum Criticized for Overemphasizing Abortion; Other Important Issues Slighted,* CHICAGO TRIBUNE, Sept. 8, 1994, at 7. In China, 70% of all illiterate adults are women. Yojana Sharma, *China-Education: State Firms' Debts Spell Troubles for Schools,* INTER PRESS SERVICE, Dec. 22, 1994, *available in* LEXIS, News Library, Inpres File.

19. *See Population Misconceptions,* ECONOMIST, May 28, 1994, at 84.

20. Harlan Hobgood, Sahel Decentralization Policy Rpt. (Vol. 11): Facilitating Transitions from Centralized to Decentralized Poli-

[P]rograms reflecting the "top down" concept, whereby programs are formulated at an aggregate decisionmaking level (such as a government ministry or donor organization), often fail "because local circumstances vary greatly over time and space. The informed, key decision-makers are the farmers and pastoralists themselves."[21]

* * *

Failure to apprise local residents and groups of the rationale for development and conservation programs also engenders resentfulness and misunderstanding of program objectives. For example, in the 1940s in Zimbabwe, the government's Natural Resources Board sought to mandate that local people build contour ridges to protect the soil. While this may have been a sound program to combat desertification, it encountered substantial resistance because it was viewed as an imperialistic edict of the colonial government. The failure of the program was primarily attributed to a failure to develop local conservation committees and to educate the public as to the objectives of the program. Similarly, in Burkina Faso, a large-scale anti-erosion project failed abjectly because farmers neither understood the objectives of the project nor were educated on how to participate.

By contrast, projects that emphasize the active participation of local people in the planning and implementation of conservation programs have proven to be far more successful. For example, the [Organization of Rural Associations for Progress] ORAP initiative in Zimbabwe, a mass movement of over half a million rural people, has contributed positively to anti-desertification efforts in that nation. ORAP educates local populations about environmental issues, including soil and water resources, through culturally appropriate means, including drama troops. It also emphasizes self-reliance and community-based programs to facilitate local control of development activities.

* * *

7. **Alastair Iles, *The Desertification Convention: A Deeper Focus On Social Aspects of Environmental Degradation?*, 36 HARV. INT'L L.J. 207, 209-13, 216-17 (1995).**

III. A FEMINIST CRITIQUE: THE PUBLIC/PRIVATE DICHOTOMY

* * *

The many disparate strands of feminist legal theory contend that gender is not used as a category of analysis in international law and that traditional theorists assume that international law norms invariably treat women identically to men. In reality, however, women are frequently unequal and subordinate to men in their social and economic power. By failing to take account of the ways in which a society's structures and practices produce inequalities, traditional international law fails to recognize the possibility that its norms may affect men and women within a state unequally.

tics 1–2 (Apr. 1992) (on file with the *Michigan Journal of International Law*).

21. JOHANNES KOTSCHI ET AL., TOWARDS CONTROL OF DESERTIFICATION IN AFRICAN DRYLANDS: PROBLEMS, EXPERIENCES, GUIDELINES 28 (1986); *see also* MICHAEL CARLEY & IAN CHRISTIE, MANAGING SUSTAINABLE DEVELOPMENT 26 (1993).

Of particular relevance to the desertification context, feminist legal theorists have identified strict doctrinal divisions between the "public" and the "private" lives of legal actors.[22] Having divided life activities into separate public and private realms, legal practitioners have associated each realm with a complex array of particular social meanings. The public sphere relates to rational thought, participation in civic affairs, knowledge, and productive work. By contrast, the private space is concerned with family life, personal relationships and reproduction. The distinction is a gendered one because the public space is viewed as "male" while the private space is identified as "female". The public/private distinction is also value-weighted. Greater importance is ascribed to the public sphere than the private sphere. Those gendered oppositions, such as the ones between activity and passivity or between intellect and culture, reflect established beliefs about gender.

Feminist criticism shows how the public/private distinction operates, in part, to maintain the social and economic inequalities of women.

* * *

IV. TRADITIONAL INTERNATIONAL LEGAL STRUCTURES: AN IMPEDIMENT

While international environmental law is developing rapidly in the 1990s, it remains bound within older conceptions of how international law ought to operate. Yet desertification eludes solutions that originate from those traditional conceptions, and demands a more radical focus on the internal organization of states as a way to combat the poverty that causes desertification. A public/private analysis of two important norms highlights this disjuncture between desertification and traditional solutions.

The norms of legal personality and sovereignty pervasively shape international law. Identified by Antonio Cassese as "constitutional norms," they are fundamental to the operation of the international law framework[23] and underpin the modern United Nations institutional system. As it is commonly understood, legal personality embodies the idea that states are identically equal in their legal character and rights and that they exist as subjective and morally equal persons. Sovereignty, as it is often defined, refers to the capacity of states to exert their own political and juridical power within their territories. Sovereignty implies that states are entitled to control freely their internal organization, such as the choice of political system or the distribution of societal wealth, as this is within their domestic jurisdiction. These norms encourage the liberal idea that a state exists as a singular, unified, bounded entity.

International legal scholarship has often attributed "personhood" to states.[24] That is, states are generally perceived as actors in the international community, with other bodies or individuals within their structures being denied full participation in international law-making. Although there are also

22. *See, e.g.,* Hilary Charlesworth, *The Public/Private Distinction and the Right to Development in International Law*, 12 Austl. Y.B. Int'l 190, 102 (1992).

23. *See* Antonio Cassese, International Law in a Divided World 395 (1986).

24. *See, e.g.,* T.J. Lawrence, Principles of International Law 60 (1895). "The Sovereign States which are Subjects of International Law are regarded as units in their dealings with other states. They are corporate bodies, acting through their governments." *Id.*

criticisms of the theoretical equation of states to persons, this equation remains influential in guiding national and international practices. Until recently, the international community has been reluctant to create norms directly interfering with national policies and practices. Despite the fact that some international legal instruments, such as conventions covering various aspects of international human rights, purport to intrude into the national sphere, the frequent inefficacy of such instruments demonstrates that national institutions and practices are still affected by the philosophical momentum of traditional international legal theory.

Traditionally, the concept of sovereignty precluded criticism or even investigation of a state's internal organization. The "interior" of a state is unknown and strange to international law; as a "private" zone, it transcends rational legal analysis and intervention. In other words, the abstraction of a state creates a kind of corporate veil between international and internal activities. The lingering perception that the policy choices and structural arrangements which promote desertification are purely "private" matters impedes the prevention of desertification from the international level.

* * *

The lack of participation of local communities in national and international policy-making leads to technocratic "public" solutions to "private" concerns. In yet another layer of the public/private distinction, governance occurs within the public realm, while the needs and experiences of many social groups exist in the private sphere. Their problems, such as a lack of access to healthcare or water, were formerly seen as matters of individual suffering, and not as widespread patterns of inequality affecting large numbers of people.

Urban centers, the loci of policy-making power, routinely discount the potential contributions of the rural communities. Seen as fragmented and provincial, rural communities are traditionally not considered by national authorities as participants in national policy-making processes.

Because of its reliance on traditional norms of sovereignty and legal personality, the international community has tended to adopt solutions that are state-centered and highly technocratic. These "top-down" solutions of international institutions and national governments determine how desertification will be tackled within their own framework of priorities. Traditionalist solutions would leave untouched concerns about the distribution of socio-economic power within a society.

* * *

The African Annexure is, however, probably the most interesting part of the Convention. It contains a list of specific actions that African nations should take to address the social dimensions of desertification. Article 3 specifies that parties must take into account some particular conditions of Africa, including the widespread poverty prevalent in most African countries, the heavy reliance of populations on natural resources, and the difficult socio-economic conditions which induce internal or regional migrations. Under article 4, African parties agree to combat desertification "as a central strategy in their efforts to eradicate poverty." They also agree to strengthen reforms towards greater decentralization and participation of local communities. Article 6 requires African nations to use "a consultative and participatory process involving ... local populations, communities and non-governmental organizations" to plan anti-desertification efforts. Importantly, article 8 requires states to adopt a national action program, which contains measures to improve the economic environment and eradicate poverty. Even though the contents of such programs are subject to qualifications, African states have explicitly committed themselves to socio-economic measures which will enhance the position of local peoples.

As far as the Convention takes into account the social dimensions of desertification, it is a promising development in international environmental law. But the apparent focus of the Convention on socio-economic factors and on the role of local communities is only a beginning. This focus is in no sense a direct intervention into the domestic jurisdiction of states but merely requires states to take notice of those considerations while formulating national plans. There is no firm obligation imposed on states to change their internal social organizations to give priority to the needs of local peoples. For example, much attention was devoted to the question of whether land tenure should be referred to specifically in the Convention. It seems that this question was ultimately rejected in favor of the vague statements used in article 5 and in article 8(3)(2)(a)(ii) of the African Annexure.

8. **International Convention for the Protection of the Rights of All Migrant Workers and Their Families**, May 2, 1991, arts. 1–9, 15, 22–23, 55–56, 79–83, 92, G.A. Res. 45/148, U.N. GAOR, 45th Sess., Supp. No. 49, U.N. Doc. A/45/49, 30 I.L.M. 1517 (1991) [Basic Document 7.23].

9. **Linda S. Bosniak, *State Sovereignty, Human Rights and the New UN Migrant Workers Convention*, 86 AM. SOC'Y INT'L L. PROC. 623, 634–38 (1992).**

[T]he line between refugees and the broader class of international migrants has been notoriously difficult to draw.

... [T]he present period is characterized by massive transnational population movements, both controlled and uncontrolled, both regular and irregular. One of the most pressing international legal issues posed by these migrations concerns the nature of the human rights obligations that the receiving states (the states of immigration) owe to the migrants present in their territory. The issue, specifically, is this: To what degree is the treatment of these migrants properly subject to international human rights standards, and to what extent does that treatment fall within states' largely unfettered domain of territorial sovereignty? Is it realistic for the international community to set forth detailed standards governing states' treatment of aliens in their own territory, and will the states in which these aliens reside accept the legitimacy of such efforts?

* * *

The Migrant Workers' Convention was formally conceived in 1979, when the UN General Assembly called for the establishment of an international working group to draft a convention on the subject of the general human rights of migrant workers and their family members in the countries of employment and residence.

* * *

The major substantive debates that occupied members of the working group concerned the Convention's scope of coverage. How broadly or narrowly the terms "migrant worker" and "family member" were drawn would, of course, determine the real effect of the instrument. In this context, the most troublesome question was whether and to what extent irregular migrants (more often called undocumented migrants) would be protected. Undocumented migrants, to define the term, are ordinarily migrants who have entered a state of employment or residence without authorization, or who entered with permission but remained after the expiration of their visas, or who are employed there without permission. In many countries, asylum-seekers whose applications have been denied but who remain in state territory constitute an important part of the undocumented migrant population. Many Convention sponsors presumed from the beginning that undocumented migrants would be part of the protected class, but several states of immigration, including Germany, Australia, and to a lesser extent, the United States, opposed their inclusion for all but the most minimal protections.

Article 2 of the Convention broadly defines "migrant worker" as "a person who is to be engaged, is engaged or has been engaged in a remunerated activity in a State of which he or she is not a national." Irregular or undocumented migrants are, by definition, covered under this formulation, and they were not excluded under any other provision (although ... they are entitled to a lesser degree of protection than are migrants "in a regular situation"). Notably, however, another provision specifically excludes legally recognized refugees and stateless persons from coverage.

The scope of the term "family member" was less controversial; Article 4 defines family members as including spouses of migrant workers, common law spouses if recognized by the law of the state of employment, their dependent children, and other dependent persons recognized under the laws of a ratifying state or under multilateral or bilateral agreements between the states concerned.

The effect of these spacious definitions is striking; despite the nominally limited purpose of The International Migrant Workers Convention, the protected class includes the great majority of persons who reside, legally or illegally, in countries of which they are not nationals. This is so because the Convention covers not only persons who migrated for the purpose of employment, but also most people who entered for reasons entirely unrelated to employment, if they have worked at any point. In addition, the Convention covers most persons closely related to these individuals.

* * *

The Convention contains two major substantive sections according rights to migrants. The first, Part III, enumerates an extensive array of protections applicable to "all migrant workers and members of their families." Among these are employment-related rights, including the rights to enforce employment contracts against employers, to participate in trade unions, and to enjoy the protection of wage, hour and health regulations in the workplace; basic civil rights, including the rights to due process of law in criminal proceedings, freedom of expression and religious observance, domestic privacy, and equality with nationals before the courts; social and cultural rights, including access to emergency medical care, access to education for children, and "respect for cultural identity"; and process rights in the contexts of immigration enforcement, detention and deportation.

The second major substantial section according rights, Part IV, sets forth rights limited to migrant workers and members of their families who enjoy "regular" immigration status. These include rights to family unity, to liberty of movement within the state of employment, to participation in the public affairs of that state, to further employment-related rights, and to equality with nationals in the area of social benefits, including housing, education and health services.

While Parts III and IV represent the heart of the Convention, several other provisions scattered throughout the document enumerate what we might call "states' rights" in the migration area. These provisions were clearly inserted as a kind of warranty for states, which might otherwise think the Convention asks them to give up too much. One key article reaffirms states' authority to pursue the immigration control and admission policies they see fit (Article 79); another requires them to undertake control measures to end the process of clandestine migration and the presence and employment of irregular migrants including, "whenever appropriate," employer sanctions (Articles 68 and 69). Another provision explicitly emphasizes that states are not obliged to regularize the status of irregular migrant workers or members of their families in their territories (Article 35), even if they are required to extend to them the panoply of rights previously mentioned. Yet another underlines that migrants are not exempt from "the obligation to comply with the laws and regulations of ... the State of employment" (Article 34), including, by implication, states' laws against unauthorized entry, employment or residence.

* * *

To state it simply, the Convention's commitment to universal human rights runs head-on into states' special protectiveness of their sovereignty in matters of migration and immigration.

The Convention's viability is particularly threatened by its coverage of undocumented migrants, notwithstanding the "states' rights" clauses. Most states view the presence of undocumented aliens as a violation of their recognized authority to govern the admission and incorporation of foreigners into their national communities. However much actual effort a state expends on immigration control measures, "illegal aliens," as they are often called, are treated as symbols of the state's violated sovereignty. It is one thing to require that these migrants be provided with basic procedural protections in the deportation context, and to ensure that they are protected by those limited rights recognized as customary under international law.

* * *

[T]he UN General Assembly adopted the [Migrant Workers Treaty] instrument in December 1990....[a] Germany, Australia and Japan, as well as the United States ... indicated their unwillingness to sign the Convention, even though each participated in the working group that drafted it. This is due in large measure either to the Convention's inclusion of undocumented migrants in the protected class or to the breadth of protections it provides them. For these states and others, establishing internationally mandated state obligations with respect to undocumented aliens simply goes too far in ceding national sovereignty.

* * *

The social condition of undocumented immigrants represents an enormous problem in many immigrant-receiving countries. Briefly put, these are people who are exceptionally powerless due to their vulnerability to expulsion and other punishment related to their irregular immigration status. They invariably constitute one of the most socially and economically marginal populations in the societies in which they live. In light of the international human rights regime's commitment to universality and to the protection of especially vulnerable social groups, it is entirely appropriate that the United Nations has turned its attention to this population. What is more, a powerful case can be made that providing protections to undocumented migrants will help to curtail the process of irregular migration, since such protections would mitigate the characteristic exploitability of these workers that is so attractive to some employers.

However compelling the arguments in favor of protection, states of immigration are unlikely to cooperate. The Migrant Workers Convention may come to serve as a kind of normative benchmark for groups working to improve the status of migrants, but at the level of positive law, the Convention is an instrument whose time has not yet come.

* * *

10. Jean–Marie Henckaerts, *The Current Status and Content of the Prohibition of Mass Expulsion of Aliens*, 15 Hum. Rts. L.J. 301, 306–10 (1994).

III.   Mass Expulsion of Migrant Workers

A.   International Conventions on Migrant Workers

It goes without saying that the universal prohibition of mass expulsion of aliens applies with equal vigor to migrant workers. Generally, the conventions specifically applicable to migrant workers offer special protection in light of their particular situation. The precarious predicament of migrant workers has been a constant concern, first and foremost, of the International Labour Organisation (ILO). Pursuant to its aim to provide a framework for assistance and protection for migratory workers, the ILO has elaborated several conventions and recommendations to improve the recruitment and working conditions of migrant workers.... Because the ILO mandate concentrates on

---

a. As of August, 1998, Mexico, Morocco, Chile, Sri Lanka, Bosnia, and Herzegovina have signed the treaty and Colombia, Egypt, Phillipines, Seychelles and Uganda have signed and ratified it, but as of September, 1998, the Migrant Workers Treaty has not entered into force. *See* [Basic Document 7.23].

working conditions of migrant workers, none of these Conventions or Recommendations deal with the issue of expulsion, let alone mass expulsion, in great detail. But according to Ricca, these ILO documents "convey the message that collective expulsion is, by its very nature, so liable to infringe individual rights that the authors thought it pointless to condemn it in so many words, as if they took the condemnation for granted."[25] ... The ILO Conventions have not been characterized by a high degree of ratification....

* * *

The singular most important characteristic of the Migrant Workers Convention's genesis is that it was purposely elaborated within the framework of the UN and not within the ILO. Third World countries wanted a Convention that was friendly towards their illegal immigrants in the West and reckoned they had better chances to push their ideas through in the UN where they enjoy an "automatic majority."[26] As expected, the result is a document that is friendlier towards illegal immigrants than any previous convention; more so probably than countries can bear to sign up for. With respect to "all migrant workers and members of their families" (i.e. legal or illegal), Article 22(1) of the Convention provides that [m]igrant workers and members of their families shall not be subject to measures of collective expulsion. Each case of expulsion shall be examined and decided "individually." By treating legal and illegal aliens on an equal footing with respect to mass expulsion, the Migrant Workers Convention adopts the only possible approach.... The UN Manual on Human Rights Reporting specifies that:

> Although the guarantees of article 13 protect only aliens who are lawfully within the territory of a State, reports should also describe the procedures leading to the expulsion of illegal entrants. In particular, reports should describe the procedures for reaching the decision on the legality or illegality of a person's entry or stay in the country. The Committee has pointed out that such a decision must comply with the requirements of article 13.[27]

As a result, undocumented migrant workers, because they are protected by the prohibitions of arbitrariness and discrimination, are also covered by the prohibition of mass expulsion. This has clearly been laid down in Article 22 of the Migrant Workers Convention.

* * *

B. Mass Expulsion of Migrant Workers in Practice: An Issue of Illegal Immigration

If one looks at the major cases of mass expulsion of migrant workers in recent decades, one notices that the problem has been the illegal status of most expellees making them liable to expulsion without much question, which does not mean that they should not get an individual review of their case.

25. Sergio Ricca, International Migration in Africa: Legal and Administrative Aspects 64, 65 (1989).

26. Roger Bohning, *The ILO and the New UN Convention on Migrant Workers: The Past and Future*, 25 Int'l Migration Rev. 698, 699 (1991).

27. Fausto Pocar, *The International Convention on Civil and Political Rights, in* Manual on Human Rights Reporting 100 (U.N. Centre for Human Rights & UNITAR 1991), U.N. Doc. HR/PUB/1991/1, U.N. Sales No. E.91.XIV.1 (1991).

Usually, however, the illegal status of many migrant workers is tolerated by the government at an initial stage but is always readily available in case the government wants to get rid of its illegal aliens. Quite importantly, the ILO Conventions ... address the issue of undocumented workers and, in general, urge countries to elaborate policies, strategies and cooperation plans to deal effectively with this serious and destabilizing matter. Immigration control, regularization and carrier and employer sanctions are the principal weapons in the war against undocumented migrants.... [B]ecause of their duty to act in good faith, states cannot knowingly condone illegal immigration or fail to adopt measures and policies to combat it or to rectify the status of illegal immigrants and later invoke this illegal status to justify a mass expulsion of illegal migrant workers. Recourse to mass expulsion under such circumstances would be diametrically opposed to what the ILO Conventions and Recommendations envisaged. According to Goodwin–Gill, "even so-called irregular migration is often tolerated by reviewing States for political and economic purposes; such knowledge and omission to effect control have a direct bearing upon the issue of State responsibility."[28]

* * *

C. African Cases of Mass Expulsion of Migrant Workers

With respect to Africa in particular, it should be noted that the free movement of persons has enjoyed a long tradition. These movements were most often confined to areas of cultural and ethnic proximity, unrestricted by formal regulations.... [S]ubstantial but undocumented streams of economically-motivated movements continued and have persisted.

* * *

In what is present day Ghana, "aliens" had started to pour in during the 19th century at the time of the establishment and consolidation of the colonial regime. Initially, no attempt was made to halt the large scale immigration of workers. Immigrants were welcomed to perform manual labor local residents scorned. When Ghana became independent. "the alien community had become an important, if not indispensable factor in the process of the economic development of Ghana. [President] Nkrumah, in the furtherance of his policy of African brotherhood, encouraged the migration of other Africans into Ghana to participate in the accelerated pace of economic growth of the new country."[29] Although immigration laws were passed requiring all aliens residing in Ghana to possess immigration documents, the hospitable regime of Nkrumah could and would not effectively enforce these laws.... The actual expulsion created scenes of panic and fear. Except for Nigeria, which vigorously protested the manner of the expulsion other affected countries acquiesced to the Ghanaian measure: the matter was not brought before the OAU or the UN.

The Nigerian mass expulsion of 1983, like that of 1985, was the result of a complex interplay between various factors.... [Nigeria's] neighbors were

28. Guy S. Goodwin–Gill, *The Collective (Mass) Expulsion of Non–Nationals is Prohibited* 2 (1993).

29. Lamin Jalamang Sise, Expulsion of Aliens in International Law: Some African Case Studies 246 (1975) (unpublished Ph.D. dissertation, Johns Hopkins University) (on file with author).

suffering from natural disaster (Sahelian drought), social conflict (internal strife in Chad), and deteriorating economies (especially Ghana). In terms of pull and push factors, a perfect setting was created to induce millions of people to leave their ordinary dwellings in search of a better existence. "Its large porous borders, virtually uncontrolled and often lacking any physical landmark" did not contribute to the enforcement of immigration laws.[30] The establishment of the Economic Community of West African States (ECOWAS) in 1975[b] and especially the coming into force of the Protocol on free movement in 1980 also contributed to the flows of migrant workers to Nigeria. Article 27 of the ECOWAS Treaty provides that:

1. Citizens of Member States shall be regarded as Community citizens and accordingly Member States undertake to abolish all obstacles to their freedom of movement and residence within the Community.

2. Member States shall by agreements with each other exempt Community citizens from holding visitors' Visas residence permits and allow them to work and undertake commercial and industrial activities within their territories.

The Protocol on free movement made this provision operational. It provided that a community citizen visiting any member state can do so, free of visa requirements, provided he enters through an official entry point and the stay does not extend beyond 90–days. Possession of a valid travel document and an international health certificate were, nevertheless, required. If a migrant wanted to stay beyond the initial 90–day period, he had to request and obtain permission for extension. The Protocol left the issue of employment authorization to national legislation.

* * *

Ushered in by rapidly declining oil revenue, Nigeria fell prey, however, to a grave economic recession and an attendant unemployment rise. The Federal government was forced to impose a hiring stop and private employers were compelled to retrench their workers on a large scale. Against this backdrop, anti-alien sentiments built up and on January 17, 1983, the government announced that all aliens who were illegally living or working in Nigeria would be required to leave the country within the next two weeks. As in other cases of mass expulsions in Africa, and maybe everywhere, the events leading to the expulsion were gradual whereas the actual expulsion was sudden and dramatic. Estimates about the number of persons affected lie around 1.5 million. . . .

* * *

[G]eneral expulsion orders may raise more hopes than they can possibly satisfy: Economically a mass expulsion is a serious miscalculation. None of the . . . economies recovered to any significant degree after the expulsions; unemployment remained. An already weak economy cannot absorb the shock of million-consumers leaving, a million people trained in the trade or profession they are carrying out. As for the crime rate, proportionally it did not drop

30. *Id.* at 429.

b. The Economic Community of West African States (ECOWAS): Revised Treaty was completed July 24, 1993, reaffirming the 1975 Treaty establishing ECOWAS, 25 I.L.M. 660 (1996).

either. Finally, in all instances, a large number of aliens have returned which really shows how unsuitable the measure is in the long run.

* * *

11. Arthur C. Helton, *The Legal Dimensions of Preventing Forced Migration*, 90 AM. SOC'Y INT'L L. PROC. 545, 546–48 (1996).

Population displacements are caused by a wide variety of factors. Some are in the nature of emergencies. Armed conflicts and widespread violations of fundamental human rights often precipitate mass population movements. Environmental catastrophes and natural disasters frequently produce forced movements of people. Other factors are chronic in character. Economic underdevelopment and disparity, environmental degradation, deforestation, desertification and failures of governance can promote population movements. Often, involuntary displacements result from a complex interaction of numerous causes for which the identification of solutions is sometimes elusive.

An international legal regime is emerging that may contribute to preventing or ameliorating the causes of forced migration. It includes the development of normative standards concerning such matters as refugees, migrant workers, human rights, humanitarian need, peace, development and environmental protection. This emerging regime, however, is characterized by conceptual lacunae, uneven institutional capacities, inadequate remedies and operational fragmentation.

* * *

Migrant Workers

Economic causes. Discussions of forced migration have tended to center on asylum-seekers who have fled state persecution or armed conflict. To a large extent, international migration is an economic phenomenon. Global economic restructuring has been a significant factor in prompting movement. People have sometimes been forced to migrate for economic survival, and this movement has been largely unregulated.

International standards concerning migrant workers have evolved on such matters as working conditions, social security and protection of employment rights. These labor standards find their origin in broader human rights concepts. Human rights norms underscore the particular vulnerability of migrant workers, whose rights have been addressed and amplified in several international documents, particularly the International Labour Organization's conventions and recommendations concerning migrant workers. The 1990 UN International Convention on the Protection of the Rights of All Migrant Workers and Members of their Families also establishes standards. The Convention defines a "migrant worker" by acknowledging his or her status as engaged in economic activity outside of the country of origin. The Convention sets out general entitlements enjoyed by migrant workers that are also guaranteed to all other persons under human rights law, modeled on the International Covenant on Civil and Political Rights. It also extends an additional set of rights on behalf of migrant workers and their family members who are "documented." The Convention includes, as well, provisions applicable to particular categories of migrant workers and members of their families, including cross-border or "frontier" workers, seasonal workers, and so forth. Protections are weaker for undocumented workers.

* * *

Environmental causes. Environmental reasons for involuntary movements are varied. Populations may be displaced through natural or anticipated disasters or environmental emergencies. For example, drought emergencies that generate poor agricultural yields are major causes of migration. Still others are affected by the lure of economic prosperity. Environmental disasters have caused increased levels of environmental damage over the years, compounded by the effects of high population versus land ratios. Deforestation is intimately linked to the global economy. Often, there are few alternatives available other than market activities that deplete natural resources. Development projects, in order to be effective, must take into account issues of biodiversity, wildlife conservation, deforestation and the appropriate resettlement of indigenous people who may be affected by such projects.

* * *

12. Maria Stavropoulou, *The Question of a Right Not to Be Displaced*, 90 Am. Soc'y Int'l L. Proc. 545, 551–52 (1996).

Noncitizens may be subjected to expulsion, although this measure must conform with relevant provisions of peremptory international law and obligations incurred through the adoption of relevant human rights instruments. ... [T]he expulsion of migrants and migrant workers is regulated under a number of special instruments, including the Migrant Workers Convention (not yet in force), certain ILO Conventions, and regional instruments.

Forced movements of persons are also illegal if they are discriminatory. The prohibition of invidious discrimination forms a cornerstone of all human rights conventions and declarations. In addition, certain provisions, such as Article 26 of the [International Convention on Civil and Political Rights] ICCPR, guarantee equality before the law and freedom from discrimination in the equal protection of the law in general, and provide protection from forced movement on discriminatory grounds, such as race or religion. Expulsion of aliens, while not discriminating against them vis-a-vis nationals, may nevertheless constitute discrimination among different aliens. In addition, the rebuttable presumption of discriminatory action in the case of collective expulsions may also exist.

If, however, the forced movement of persons is not targeted on any specific group or person on invidious discriminatory grounds, it may or may not be prohibited. The decisive question is whether a specific distinction between various persons or groups of persons, who find themselves in a comparable situation, is based on unreasonable criteria. The principle of proportionality, given the specific circumstances, will also have to be taken into account.

* * *

In addition, the forced movement of persons may be indirectly prohibited by a number of provisions within human rights law that protect life and personal security, subsistence, property, the family, participation in cultural life, work and participation in public affairs. Where the forced movement of persons has the purpose or effect of genocide, torture, inhuman or degrading treatment, slavery, or apartheid or violates other principles of jus cogens, it is prohibited even in situations where derogation from certain human rights obligations is permitted.

* * *

When interpreted and drawn together, human rights standards provide that evictions, transfers, relocations or expulsions cannot be invidiously discriminatory and may be undertaken only in the specific circumstances provided for in international law and on the basis of a specific decision by a state authority expressly empowered by law to do so. It should normally be expected that individual reviews of each case are conducted and individual administrative actions issued, with the limited exception of genuine emergencies where immediate evacuation may be unavoidable or even imperative. In the absence of such guarantees, such measures would be arbitrary and therefore unlawful. Questions of state responsibility arise in the case of illegal forced movements attributable to the state.

13. *International Environmental Wrongs*, **Chapter Five,** *supra,* **at 335.**

Discussion Notes/Questions

1. Desertification is a problem in all semi-arid regions of the world, as well as parts of North America. Desertification in Africa is exacerbated by the prolonged periods of drought, which create the need for irrigation and inhibit the recharge of natural water supplies. The present problem is located in the eastern section of North Africa; however, the Middle East also suffers from desertification. Peter Beaumont, *The Middle East—Case Study of Desertification, in* THE THREATENED DRYLANDS: REGIONAL AND SYSTEMATIC STUDIES OF DESERTIFICATION 45, 45–47, (J. Mabbutt & S. Berkowicz eds., 1980), describes the nature of desertification in the Middle East:

> The Middle East is made up of a wide variety of environments, ranging from high snow-clad mountains in Turkey and Iran to some of the most arid sand deserts in the world in southern Arabia and Egypt. For convenience it is possible to divide the region into two zones: in the north there are a series of high mountain ranges, upland plateaux and intermontane valleys, while to the south the landscape is dominantly composed of alluvial lowlands and gently sloping terrain. Climatically there are great variations as well, at least in terms of temperature, though nearly all areas are subject to marked water deficiencies at certain times of the year.

> Population in the Middle East is concentrated in areas which have access to water resources, whether in the form of precipitation or as water brought by rivers from areas of water surplus. It is in these areas too that the effects of desertification tend to be greatest, although the complexity of the differing environments and land-use impacts makes it difficult to put forward broad generalizations.

> Of all the world's arid zones, the Middle East possesses the longest history of human settlement. It is in this region that the cultivation of cereals first began, though the exact date remains uncertain. We do know however that by about 12,000 BP [sic: Before Present?] Mesolithic hunters and

gatherers were reaping wild barley and oats for use as food. By 8000 BP numerous village communities were in existence, growing wheat and barley and raising sheep and goats, in southern Turkey, the uplands of Palestine, the Zagros Mountains, on the interior plateau of Iran and along the foothills south of the Caspian Sea. By 6000 BP the traditional crops of Mediterranean agriculture, the olive, vine and fig, had been domesticated in the eastern Mediterranean region.

These early settlements were located mainly in regions where rainfed agriculture was possible and where the wild ancestors of wheat and barley were growing. In the periods between about 8000 and 6000 BP there occurred a significant change in the location of the agricultural communities in the Middle East, with movements from the wetter foothill zones to the arid floodplains of the Tigris–Euphrates lowlands. This move was only possible with the development of complex irrigation networks which became a characteristic feature of these lowlands.

* * *

What this information shows is that many of the present-day cultivated areas within the Middle East have been utilized for agricultural activities for at least 5500 years. The net effect has been widespread degradation of the natural vegetation, and in some cases removal of topsoil over large areas. So great have some of these changes been that it is often difficult to reconstruct in detail the nature of the landscape when man first moved into it.... An examination of the long history of land use in the Tigris–Euphrates lowlands reveals a number of periods of desertification separated by intervals of prosperity. Some of this land abandonment seems to have been the result of natural, though nearly always man-induced causes, such as salinization or silt accumulation, while at other times socio-political instability appears to have played a dominant role.

Three periods when salinity severely hampered cultivation in Mesopotamia have been recognized as the result of archaeological research. The most important one, which was also the earliest, occurred between 4400 and 3700 BP and affected much of southern Iraq. This progressive increase in soil salinity is witnessed by a fall in cereal yields over the period, together with an increase in the use of the more salt-tolerant barley compared with wheat. Another and less severe phase of salinization occurred in central Iraq between 3300 and 3900 BP, whilst a final period can be identified in the area east of Baghdad, which became progressively more salty after 1200 AD.

* * *

A second physical environmental problem, which was also man-induced, was siltation. This had a two-fold effect. First, the deposition of silt in the fields following irrigation meant that the level of these fields increased over time, making them too high to receive water by gravity flow from the adjacent canals. Evidence from some areas of Iraq suggests a rise of 1 [meter] in about 500 years. Deposition of silt in the major canals also reduced their water-carrying capacity and necessitated costly cleaning operations. By about 1100 AD siltation of the canals and deposition of silt on the land was making it difficult to cultivate the area to the southeast of Baghdad. As a result the depopulation of formerly cultivated areas occurred.

* * *

These examples illustrate clearly that periods of land abandonment and desertification followed by the recolonization of certain lands have occurred for thousands of years in areas such as the Tigris–Euphrates lowlands. Even today, with the high technology available, the development of these lowlands for agricultural purposes still present very severe difficulties.

* * *

[A]n added difficulty [is] caused by the high dissolved solids content of the irrigation water. These waters, with TDS [total dissolved solids] of between 300 and 500 ppm [parts per million], can lead to rapid salinity build-up in the soil. In the future it seems likely that this problem will intensify. Both Turkey and Syria are proposing to use large volumes of water from the Euphrates for major new irrigation projects. The result will be that the discharge of the River in Iraq will be smaller and water quality reduced as the result of field drainage. An inevitable consequence would seem to be that some of the irrigated lands of Iraq will be forced out of cultivation, as has happened so often in the past.

2.   According to the 1998–99 Report from the World Resources Institute, soil erosion, caused by wind and water is occurring 16–300 times faster than it can be replaced. Further, ten to fifteen percent of irrigated land suffers from salinization or waterlogging. "[S]oil degradation between 1945 and 1990 lowered world food production some 17 percent ... in Africa," production losses from soil erosion alone are estimated at just over 8 percent.[c] What types of alternatives to current agricultural and/or logging practices would successfully decrease soil degradation? Does it make a difference if the proposed alternatives are to be implemented in the United States or Africa? Why or why not? For some examples of proposed alternatives for agricultural practices, see Discussion/Notes and Questions, in Problem 11–2 ("Environmental Standards in Vinland and Tierrasol"), Note 2.

3.   The development of international environmental law evidences a trend toward enhancing the role of women in society and recognizing the integral part women play in conservation. Desertification is, in part, a result of women's subordination and lack of power: population explosions result from the lack of birth control means available to women in undeveloped countries, in addition to the fact that women are often less educated than their male counterparts. However, the lack of female involvement in politics, particularly in underdeveloped countries further inhibits efforts to combat desertification. Consider the holistic approach employed by the Desertification Convention which requires education and local action to combat desertification and its potential effects on the role of women in undeveloped societies. Will the causes of desertification be impacted if women are excluded from the picture? There is potential for exponential impacts if women are educated, in terms of farming techniques, economic, political and social issues. Perhaps the Desertification Convention is a pivotal point in equality and environmental awareness for the added value placed on traditional feminine roles. Do you agree or disagree with the suggested link between desertification problems and lack of input by and education for women? Why or why not? What are some specific ways in which the voices of women would make a difference in combating desertification? Other environmental problems?

c. WORLD RESOURCES INSTITUTE, 1998–99   RONMENT 157 (1998).
WORLD RESOURCES: A GUIDE TO THE GLOBAL ENVI-

An article, *Education of Girls Shows Increase Around the World*, ASSOCIATED PRESS (Washington), Oct. 19, 1998, notes the increased enrollment for girls in schools across the world:

> The world has made striking gains in increasing school enrollment of girls during the past 10 years, with the most progress in some unexpected places such as the Middle East and sub-Saharan Africa.
>
> A new report says girls now actually outnumber boys in secondary schools in 18 countries, mostly in Latin America. But 51 countries still have serious gender gaps, with 75 million fewer girls than boys in their schools, says a report released Sunday by Population Action International.
>
> Researchers and government officials credit the decade's gains to factors that include a spreading awareness of the importance of women, as well as general economic growth.
>
> In Malawi, where the gap has been sharply reduced, pregnant girls are no longer automatically expelled from school. In Egypt, an aggressive school-building program increased enrollment of girls by 60 percent in rural primary schools.
>
> A project involving training of female teachers and other initiatives in Pakistan increased girls' enrollment in villages of the province with the largest gender gap, Baluchistan, by 87 percent, the report said.
>
> But in Pakistan and many other countries the gap remains wide and obstacles are great.
>
> "Educating a girl is like watering your neighbor's garden," said Shanti Conly, a co-author of the study, in describing a prevalent attitude in India. There, girls often are valued most for the help they do at home.

* * *

> The 51 countries with serious gender gaps have a total school enrollment estimated at 600 million. The study estimates that the additional cost of educating as many girls as boys in those countries would be about $5.8 billion—and could nearly double in 10 years.
>
> Despite the increase in the proportion of girls educated, when compared with boys, the number of girls in the gap continues to grow because of rapid growth in the number of school-age children.
>
> The study ranked 132 countries according to the extent to which girls and boys differ in access to schooling. To cover as many countries as possible, it used figures from 1995 and compared them to 1985.
>
> More than half the countries have no gender gap.
>
> Ten countries—Nepal, Oman, Algeria, Saudi Arabia, Togo, Lebanon, Congo, Egypt, Iran and Malawi—are cited as making the most progress in closing the gap.

How, in your view, will greater access to education for girls help to resolve environmental problems in the developing world?

3. *Bibliographical Note.* For further discussion concerning the principle themes addressed in this problem, consult the following specialized materials:

(a) *Specialized Books/Monographs.* Y. Ahmad, & M. Kassas, Desertification: Financial Support for the Biosphere (1987); R. Baker, Desertification: Cause and Control, A Study of the U.N. Plan of Action and Its Possible Application (1980); Desertification and Development: Dryland Ecology in

Social Perspective (B. Spooner ed. 1982); Environmental Protection and the Law of War: A "Fifth Geneva" Convention on the Protection of the Environment in Time of Armed Conflict (G. Plant ed. 1992); A. Grainger, Desertification: How People Make Deserts, How People Can Stop and Why They Don't (1982); J. Walls, Land, Man and Sand: Desertification and its Solution (1980); The World Bank, Striking a Balance: The Environmental Challenge of Development (1989); David S.G. Thomas, & Nicholas J. Middleton, Desertification: Exploding the Myth (1994); Lloyd Timberlake, Africa in Crisis (1985); Paul C. Stern et al (Eds.), Global Environmental Change, Understanding the Human Dimensions (1992); Valentine Udoh James, Africa's Ecology: Sustaining the Biological and Environmental Diversity of a Continent (1993), 1998–99 World Resources: A Guide to the Global Environment (World Resources Institute 1998), World Atlas of Desertification (United Nations Environment Program 1998).

(b) *Specialized Hearings/Reports.* The Encroaching Desert: The Consequences of Human Failure, A Report of the Independent Commission on International Humanitarian Issues (1986); Report of the International Law Commission on the 39th Session, UN GAOR, 42nd Sess., Supp. No. 10, at 52, UN Doc. A/42/10 (1987); United Nations Conference on Environment and Development, Adoption of Agreements on Environment and Development, Agenda 21, U.N. Doc. A/conf.151/4 (parts I–IV) (1992); United Nations Conference on Environment and Development, Adoption of Agreements on Environment and Development, Rio Declaration on Environment and Development Note by the Secretary–General of the Conference U.N. Doc. A/conf.151/5 (1992); Widespread Migration: The Role Of International Law and Institutions, 86 American Society of International Law Proceedings 623 (April 1–4, 1992); Forced Movement of Peoples, 90 American Society of International Law Proceedings 545 (March 27–30, 1996).

(c) *Specialized Articles/Book Chapters.* A. Adede, *United Nations Efforts Toward the Development of an Environmental Code of Conduct For States Concerning Harmonious Utilization of Shared Natural Resources,* 43 Alb. L. Rev. 488 (1979); R. Bilder, *The Role of Unilateral State Action in Preventing International Environmental Injury,* 14 Vand. J. Transnat'l L. 51 (1981); ___, *International Law and Natural Resources Policies,* 20 N.R.J. 451 (1980); J. Chipmin, *Third World Politics & Security in the 1990's,* 14 Wash. Q. 148, (1991); R. D'Arge and A. Kneese, *State Liability for International Environmental Degradation: An Economic Perspective,* 20 N.R.J. 427 (1980); C. Joyner, *Towards Transnational Management of Desertification: The Ecopolitics of Global Concern,* 16 Int'l L. 67 (1987); C. Klein–Chesivoir, *Note: Avoiding Environmental Injury: The Case for Widespread Use of Environmental Impact Assessments in International Development Projects,* 30 V.J.I.L. 517 (1990); V. Nanda, *Emerging Trends,* 6 Denv. J. Int'l L. & Pol'y 239 (1976); L. O'Keefe, *Transboundary Pollution and the Strict Liability Issue: The Work of the International Law Commission on the Topic of International Liability for Injurious Consequences Arising Out of Acts Not Prohibited by International Law,* 18 Denv. J. Int'l L. & Pol'y (1990); Alastair Iles, *The Desertification Convention: A Deeper Focus on Social Aspects of Environmental Degradation?* 36 Harv. Int' Law J. 207 (Winter 1995); William C. Burns, *The International Convention to Combat Desertification: Drawing A Line in the Sand?,* 16 Mich. J. Int'l Law 831 (Spring 1995); Kyle W. Danish, *International Environmental Law and the Bottom–Up Approach: A Review of the Desertification Convention,* Ind. J. Global Legal Studies 133 (Fall 1995); Jean–Marie Henckaerts, *The Current Status and Content of the Prohibition of Mass Expulsion of Aliens,* 15 Human Rights Law Journal 301 (1994).

Chapter Ten

PROBLEMS IN PROTECTING
THE BIOSPHERE

In pursuit of human needs and wants, the living resources of the seas are being plundered, the grandest species are being endangered, and life-supporting rain forests are being destroyed. Each of these developments, reflecting humanity's mounting demands upon the natural environment, represents a threat to biodiversity, to the intricately differing varieties of genes, species, and ecosystems that inhabit planet Earth. The pressures of contemporary economic and social reality, combined with increased technological ability, press the boundaries of environmental exploitation to their limits and beyond. To some degree, the loss of biodiversity is a natural process; species extinction has always existed. But the incredibly increased and accelerating rate at which humanity is decimating other species suggests that controls are needed—tough ones. And especially is this the case in respect of the world's tropical forests, the so-called "lungs of the world"—jungles, rain forests, cloud forests, and swamp and mangrove forests. Together these forests, covering about twenty percent of the Earth's land surface, contain nearly half the world's species of plants and animals, including many from which modern crops and medicines are derived. They are, however, fast disappearing and, with them, the large percentage of biotic wealth that is stored in them.

Historically, international policies and programs designed to conserve and otherwise protect the biosphere, most of them of relatively recent origin, have foundered on the shoals of state sovereignty or, in the case of sea life, on derivations of the time-honored principle of freedom of the high seas. Invoking the *Lotus* doctrine of plenary state sovereignty,[a] States rely on their claimed right to pursue independent action within their jurisdictional boundaries so that the consensus needed to establish binding legal restraints becomes difficult to achieve. Under the state-centric principle of *res nullius*[b], conflicts of interest in the global commons between protective regimes and economic needs become oftentimes impossible to reconcile. Moreover, differing cultural values, as well as economic and political realities, mitigate against widespread compliance with agreed-upon protective measures. In addition, policing assaults upon the biosphere—as in driftnet fishing, elephant poach-

a. *See* S.S. "Lotus" (Fr. v. Turk.), 1927 P.C.I.J. (ser. A.) No 10, at 4.

b. Property owned by no one, but capable of being acquired through certain unilateral acts.

ing, or tropical rainforest destruction—requires substantial enforcement resources, which many states do not have readily at hand. Thus, it should come as no surprise, international law and policy have so far responded to threats to biodiversity with only limited success.

Where success has been achieved, of course, the contributing factors demand to be analyzed, as they may be instructive for other settings. But given the interconnectedness and interdependence of the Earth's biosphere, fully comprehending that one state's behavior may ultimately affect the world community at large is, on final analysis, the most crucial lesson to be learned. Precisely because of its interpenetrating character, biodiversity is a source of global security; the adaptability it provides cannot be replaced by the most ingenious of synthetic alternatives. And so it seems wrong that its intrinsic values should be allowed to be overridden by the artificial boundaries of state territory or the short-term reference frames of the decision-makers within them. If we are serious about protecting and enhancing the biosphere, we must entertain at least the possibility that a vision or philosophy of sovereignty for our time must have a larger frame of reference than the state and human society alone, and that the old ideas built around the primacy of space must give way, at least in part, to perspectives that emphasize time and community. Time is a crucial factor with biodiversity; each day that goes by there is a significant loss of the Earth's biotic riches.

Problem 10–1

Driftnet Fishing in the South Pacific

SECTION 1. FACTS

With few other resources to develop, and relying heavily upon the rich ocean ecosystems that surround it, New Polynesia, a small South Pacific island nation, was an early supporter of the 1982 United Nations Convention on the Law of the Sea. Early on, it ratified the Convention, simultaneously declaring the existence of a 200–mile exclusive economic zone (EEZ), and thereupon assuming exclusive control over an ocean area eight times larger than its entire land mass. Also, optimistic about the future prospects these actions would create, it invested heavily in its domestic trolling and long-line fishing fleet, built new shore-based processing facilities, and entered into several joint venture arrangements, granting other nations access to the fisheries within its claimed EEZ. To protect New Polynesia's new resource, the New Polynesian legislature passed strict marine resource conservation laws and supported efforts that resulted in a ban on driftnet fishing in many of the EEZs in the region.

Despite New Polynesia's efforts, recent scientific studies have revealed a steep decline in the albacore tuna population which migrates through New Polynesia's EEZ. The decline appears to be due to overfishing on the high seas and in the EEZs of other nearby island nations. The studies also report alarming declines in the population of other species in the area, particularly marine mammals and sea turtles. The scientists believe this is due to the widespread use of large pelagic driftnets by vessels fishing on the high seas in the region. Such driftnets often catch and kill species other than those targeted, sometimes in volumes exceeding the volume of the targeted catch itself.

The New Polynesian government quickly realized that it could not adequately protect its fishery without increased cooperation from other fishing nations, and it promptly invited all the neighboring island nations, as well as all distant states whose vessels traditionally fished in the region, to a diplomatic conference to discuss the problem. The Conference heard reports from experts indicating that the tuna fishery in the region was seriously depleted and would be irreparably damaged if steps were not taken to restrict severely the tuna catch. Because albacore tuna are a highly-migratory species, the experts indicated that coordinated and comprehensive restrictions on fishing throughout the region were essential to ensure the sustainability of the fishery.

As a result of the Conference, the island nations of the region, joined by some distant water fishing nations, entered into an agreement creating the "Polynesian Area Albacore Tuna Commission" or PAATCO. Article I of the Agreement recited that PAATCO was formed as a regional fisheries organization within the framework of the Food and Agricultural Organization of the United Nations and for the purpose of regulating fisheries in a defined area, "the AREA," of the Southern Pacific Ocean. The Agreement further stated in Article I that PAATCO's objectives were "(a) to preserve the tuna fishery and other marine life in the AREA," and "(b) to ensure implementation of i) the fisheries conservation and management provisions of UNCLOS, ii) the 1995 Fish Stocks Agreement[c], iii) the Agreement to Promote Compliance with International Conservation and Management Measures by Fishing Vessels on the High Seas, iv) the Code of Conduct for Responsible Fisheries, contained in the Kyoto Declaration and Plan of Action, adopted at the International Conference on the Sustainable Contribution of Fisheries to Food Security (Kyoto, Japan, 4–9 December 1995), and v) other relevant international conservation and management measures."

Under the Agreement, membership in PAATCO is open to coastal states situated wholly or partially in the covered ocean Area and to any other state whose vessels engage in fishing in the Area. The PAATCO Commission is given the power, acting by unanimous vote and on the basis of reports of its Scientific Committee, to set yearly total allowable catch levels for the Area and to allocate the catch among the parties. Allocations are to take account of "the precautionary principle, the principle of maximum sustainable yield, the interest of parties in exploiting fisheries within their EEZs, and the interest of parties with historical fisheries in the Area." The Commission is also given the power to adopt any other fishing regulations "necessary to the conservation of marine resources in the Area."

As to enforcement, the Agreement provides that each party will adhere to the Agreement and, in addition, will apply all the other fishing agreements mentioned in Article I, applying on a provisional basis any agreements not otherwise in force. Each party also agrees to enforce the Commission's rules

c. *Agreement for the Implementation of the Provisions of the United Nations Convention on the Law of the Sea of 10 December 1982 relating to the Conservation and Management of Straddling Fish Stocks and Highly Migratory* Fish Stocks, U.N. G.A.O.R., 6th Sess., U.N.Doc. A/CONF.164/37, *reprinted in* 34 I.L.M. 1542, 1567 (1995) [**Basic Document 6.14**].

against its own vessels and against vessels fishing within its EEZ. Finally, each party is obliged to "take appropriate action, consistent with international law, to deter fishing activities by nationals, residents or vessels of non-party States where such activity could affect the attainment of the objectives of the Agreement."

At its first meeting the PAATCO Commission, acting on the basis of a preliminary report from its Scientific Committee of "significant depletion in Area tuna stocks," unanimously agreed to limit the total allowable catch of albacore tuna in the Area to 25% of the previous year's catch. Quotas were set for each party to the Agreement, and a complete ban was announced on tuna fishing in the Area by any non-party state. The Commission indicated that the ban on non-party fishing was "a necessary measure to ensure the effectiveness of the adopted conservation measures." The Commission also "noted" that "large-scale driftnet fishing for any species invariably results in excessive catches of that target species and poses an exceptional threat to non-target species and to ships in the Area." It therefore called upon all states, including non-party states, to ensure that their vessels complied with the international ban on the use of driftnets, as well as with the Commission's regional ban on tuna fishing.

A month after this action was taken, New Polynesia received a report from the international environmental group Save Our Planet (SOP) that their research vessel, the *Earth Warrior*, had spotted and videotaped a vessel driftnetting on the high seas just outside New Polynesia's EEZ. The vessel bore the flag of Kuroshio, an East Asian country that had participated in the conference that created PAATCO, but that had refused to sign the Agreement and had indicated its objection to any effort to control its "freedom to fish on the high seas."

After confirming the *Earth Warrior's* report, the authorities in New Polynesia contacted the Kuroshio maritime authority and asked it to send naval support to stop the illegal fishing by the ship bearing its flag. Kuroshio's maritime authority replied that it did not accept that its vessel was fishing illegally, that it objected to any interference with its vessel by New Polynesia or any other state, and that it certainly would not interfere with lawful fishing by its fleet. Furthermore, Kuroshio noted that it was an extremely poor nation and that the annual catch of its fishing fleet provided a critical part of the food supply of the poorest members of its population. Any interference with its fishing fleet would jeopardize the food security of its population.

After receiving this message, New Polynesia's authorities immediately dispatched one of their two navy frigates to intercept, arrest, and impound the Kuroshio ship and its catch of tuna. The evidence from both the videotape and the naval vessel is that the Kuroshio vessel was, in fact, engaged in a large-scale driftnetting operation for albacore tuna. It appears that it was fishing exclusively on high seas areas, although those areas were within the "Area" covered by the PAATCO Agreement.

Kuroshio protested the arrest and impoundment of its vessel and demanded its immediate release. However, alleging that Kuroshio had violated international law by driftnetting and by fishing for tuna within the regulated Area, and therefore claiming every right to arrest and impound the vessels,

New Polynesia refused. To which Kuroshio countered that it "[did] not recognize the claimed driftnet fishing ban or the PAATCO tuna catch restrictions as comprising enforceable norms of international law." Furthermore, it claimed that New Polynesia had no authority to interfere with a foreign vessel on the high seas, even if that vessel was fishing in violation of international law. Finally, Kuroshio observed that both the driftnet fishing ban and PAATCO's restrictions on the tuna catch were based on "cursory and inadequate pseudo-scientific guesswork" that did not warrant any interference with Kuroshio's efforts to feed its growing population.

The full videotape of the *Earth Warrior's* research team had by this time reached the world's electronic media, and the international community was outraged at the horrific footage it saw: of not only tuna, but dolphins, seals, sea-turtles, and many other species of fish, as well as seabirds and even a young whale, that had been caught and died in the driftnets. The videotape also clearly showed that more than half of the fish entangled in the nets were lost as the nets were retrieved, leaving a trail of dead creatures in the ship's wake.

Thus, after several rounds of tense negotiations, Kuroshio was pressured by the international community to resolve the dispute with New Polynesia through arbitration. Three arbitrators expert in international law have been appointed (one chosen by Kuroshio, one by New Polynesia, and the third presiding arbitrator chosen by the other two), and a *compromise* has been agreed to, requiring the arbitral panel to decide the dispute in accordance with international law. Both countries are parties to the 1982 UN Convention on the Law of the Sea. Both countries are also members of FAO and both voted in favor of the FAO's Code of Conduct for Responsible Fisheries when that Code was adopted at an FAO Conference in 1995. New Polynesia is party, in addition, to the 1989 Langkawi Declaration on Environment, the 1989 Wellington Convention for the Prohibition of Fishing with Long Driftnets in the South Pacific, the 1995 Fish Stocks Agreement, and the Agreement to Promote Compliance with International Conservation and Management Measures by Fishing Vessels on the High Seas. Kuroshio is party to none of these additional agreements. The case is now pending.

SECTION 2. QUESTIONS PRESENTED

1. Is Kuroshio in breach of international law for allowing vessels flying its flag to engage in high seas driftnet fishing and in tuna fishing in violation of the conservation and management measures adopted by PAATCO?

2. Is New Polynesia in breach of international law for seizing and impounding a vessel flying Kuroshio's flag when that vessel's allegedly unlawful fishing activities were confined to high seas areas?

SECTION 3. ASSIGNMENTS

A. *Reading Assignment*

Study the Readings presented in Section 4, *infra*, and the Discussion Notes/Questions that follow. Also, to the extent possible, consult the accompanying bibliographical references.

B. Recommended Writing Assignment

Prepare a comprehensive, logically sequenced, and *argumentative* brief in the form of an outline of the primary and subsidiary *legal* issues you see requiring resolution by the ad hoc international arbitral panel. Also, from the perspective of an independent objective judge, indicate which side ought to prevail on each issue and why. Retain a copy of your issue-outline/brief for class discussion.

C. Recommended Oral Assignment

Assume you are legal counsel for Kuroshio or New Polynesia (as designated by your instructor); then, relying upon the Readings (and your issue-outline if prepared), present a 15–20 minute oral argument of your government's likely positions before the ad hoc international arbitral tribunal.

D. Recommended Reflective Assignment

Consider (and recommend) alternative norms, institutions, and/or procedures that you believe might do better than existing world order arrangements to contend with situations of the kind posed by this problem. In so doing, but without insisting upon *immediate* feasibility, identify the particular transition steps that would be needed to make your alternatives a reality.

SECTION 4. READINGS

1. *Large Scale Pelagic Driftnet Fishing and Its Impact on the Living Marine Resources of the World's Oceans and Seas: Report of the Secretary General*, U.N. GAOR, 45th Sess., Agenda Item 79, ¶ ¶ 26–33, U.N. Doc. A/45/663 (1990).

* * *

26. A driftnet is a fishing gear made of a single or several rectangular panels of net webbing linked together and suspended vertically in the water by floats on the top of the panels and sinkers at the bottom. They drift with the winds and the currents, thus creating a webbing curtain in which the fish are enmeshed. By adjusting the size and the weight of the floats and sinkers it is possible to modify the buoyancy of the net and to suspend it at various depths in the water column. Driftnets belong to a broader category of nets called gillnets. The other types of gillnets include set-gillnets, encircling gillnets and fixed gillnets.

27. Until the 1950s the size of driftnets was necessarily limited by the weight of the natural fibres (hemp or cotton) of which they were made. The introduction of synthetic fibres and the growing utilization of hydraulic winches allowed fishermen to fish with longer sets of nets, thus increasing the fishing power of the gear, but also increasing the incidental catches of non-targeted species, in particular marine mammals.

28. The gear is now used both by modern industrial fleets operating on the high seas (with nets from 5 to 50 km in length) and by artisanal and semi-

industrial fishermen of developing countries in coastal areas (with nets from a few hundred metres up to more than 10 km in length). The focus of this report is on the use of large-scale driftnets by fishing fleets operating on the high seas, since the Assembly in resolution 44/225 expressly did not address the question of small-scale driftnet fishing traditionally conducted in coastal waters, especially by developing countries. There is no internationally agreed definition of what should be considered as a "large" driftnet and state practice is not uniform. Several States have adopted laws and regulations on the maximum length of the gear: New Zealand 1 km, Australia 2.5 km, USSR 3.7 km (see also para. 148). The Convention for the Prohibition of Fishing with Long Drift Nets in the South Pacific set the limit at 2.5 km. The member countries of the Indian Ocean Fishery Commission recently considered that for socio-economic reasons it was felt that the solutions being contemplated in other regions of the world (for example, the South Pacific), in particular with regard to the maximum size of driftnets, might not be *mutatis mutandis* applicable to the Indian Ocean.

29. It should be noted, however, that high-seas driftnet fishery presents unique problems in terms of management and data collection since that depends on the co-operation of the States concerned. By comparison, according to the submission from the Government of Australia dated 11 July 1990, it is much more likely that driftnet fisheries based on the exclusive economic zone will be regulated or at least monitored than those on the high seas.

30. Japan has conducted modern large-scale driftnet fishing for salmon in the North Pacific since the 1950s under agreements with the Soviet Union, Canada and the United States of America. In the late 1970s, the high incidental catches of squid in this fishery prompted fishermen to develop a new gillnetting technology to exploit squid during the closure of the salmon season. This led to a great expansion of effort into the new driftnet fishery for squid in the central northern North Pacific. An albacore driftnet fishery using large meshed nets originated in the coastal waters of Japan and expanded into the North Pacific in the mid–1970s and into the South Pacific from the mid–1980s.

31. The magnitude of the impact of those high seas driftnet fisheries may be assessed from the levels of their annual yields. With a total driftnet catch in the North Pacific in 1988 of about 300,000 tons of squid, this fishery accounts for an appreciable part of the total squid landings from the Pacific for that year, which were estimated at about 850,000 tons. The driftnet fishery for albacore in the North Pacific represented, with a catch of about 9,000 tons in 1986/87, only about 20 per cent of the total yield of this stock, whereas for the South Pacific albacore the total catches greatly increased in 1989, owing to driftnet fishing, and exceeded by far the level of exploitation suggested to be safe by scientists from all interested countries.

32. A new driftnet fishery for albacore by French vessels has operated in the Bay of Biscay since 1986. A large-mesh driftnet fishery for swordfish and albacore has been operated in the central Mediterranean by an Italian fleet (see para. 147). In addition, there exists a number of smaller driftnet fisheries in various parts of the oceans mainly operated in waters under national jurisdiction. More detailed accounts of those fisheries are given under section VI below.

33. It was the effectiveness of this type of gear and the ease with which very large amounts of nets could be and were deployed in recent years in the South Pacific which raised serious concern in the first instance among the coastal States of the region, whose economies are linked to and in some cases dependent on the effective management and conservation of the fisheries resources within their exclusive economic zones. According to the submission of the Government of New Zealand dated 7 September 1990, the sudden increase of driftnet vessel effort was seen as a threat to the long-term sustainability of some of the important fish resources, in particular albacore, as well as representing a serious environmental threat with respect to the by-catch of marine mammals and other living resources taken by the gear. That situation prompted the South Pacific Forum States to adopt the Tarawa Declaration and subsequently the Wellington Convention banning the use of driftnets longer than 2.5 km.

2. **Editors' Note**. As the U.N. Report indicates, large-scale pelagic driftnets, which are suspended in the water like giant curtains and strung out as a wall for many miles, drift across the open ocean and indiscriminately catch everything in their path. In one sense, driftnetting of this type is very efficient. A single boat, suspending a number of nets in a long line simultaneously, can have up to 40 miles of such nets going down to a depth of about 48 feet below the surface of the ocean in a single positioning, and typically several vessels of a driftnet fleet will work together to fish in this manner. At its height in any given fishing season, driftnetting on the part of Japan, South Korea, and Taiwan, countries long and principally engaged in the practice because of the huge quantities of fish needed by their large populations for whom fish is a traditional and staple part of the diet, resulted in up to 22,500 miles of deep nets being drifted through the waters of the Pacific and Indian oceans each night—enough to stretch more than once around the Earth.

In an environmental or ecological sense, however, large-scale pelagic driftnetting is very inefficient and is sometimes called "wall of death" fishing because it kills most living things in its path. Whatever they catch, driftnets kill or maim. Marine creatures in search of food, and lured by fish already caught in the net, swim or dive into the webbing where they become entangled. If they do not drown or manage to escape they may suffer for several months before dying from injury, starvation, or both. Tuna species other than those being sought by the fishers, marlin, swordfish, and sharks are common victims. The nets are also dangerous for marine mammals and sea birds that must return to the surface to breathe because the nylon mesh often used in the nets is so sheer that it is invisible to mammals and birds and undetectable by dolphin sonar. People have been alerted to the dangers of driftnetting by graphic photographs of fur seals, sea lions, dolphins, and small whales all becoming entangled and dying.

Although the scientific evidence is not clear on the extent or persistence of the problem,[d] lost driftnets may continue to drift in the oceans and continue to entangle not only fish but marine mammals, turtles, and seabirds. These "ghost nets" are a hazard also to shipping and other seafaring activities. Fouling propellers and intakes, they can cause severe damage to

---

d. *See* William T. Burke, *Regulation of Driftnet Fishing on the High Seas and the New* *International Law of the Sea*, 3 Geo. Int'l Envtl. L. Rev. 265, 269 n. 23 (1990).

vessels and pose a danger to human life because divers must submerge to cut them free.

But because the marine life of the open sea is not inexhaustible the real threat of driftnetting is to the marine ecosystems that are essential to life on Earth. Many of the victims of driftnetting are especially endangered because the reproductive rates of their species are very low and because we now are technically capable of catching fish faster than they can breed. Large-scale driftnetting is not the only fishing technique that can result in overfishing. But its rapid growth during the last two decades, its indiscriminate impact on a variety of species, and its incredible efficiency as a means of catching huge quantities of fish, have brought it under special criticism and attack. The near collapse of the albacore tuna fishery in the South Pacific has been blamed on the increase of large-scale driftnetting in the area. Driftnetting is also alleged to have contributed greatly to the serious decline of North Pacific salmon fishery. In the North Pacific driftnet fishery, the target species have been albacore tuna, salmon, and squid; and while the salmon would normally return to their streams of origin to spawn, they have been taken in large numbers by driftnet fishing boats on the open seas, before they can begin their breeding cycle.[e]

In addition to threatening stocks of individual fish species, driftnetting has repercussions throughout the marine ecosystem, endangering the diversity of marine life in our oceans. The survival of any one species in a marine ecosystem depends upon the existence of others—species rely upon each other as elements of the same food chain, predator populations keep other populations in balance, and certain species rely on others as "hosts." In the North Pacific, driftnetters have taken heavily from albacore tuna and squid stocks, which are an essential part of the ocean food chain. If the practice continues unabated, there is a real possibility of damaging the entire marine ecosystem of the region.[f]

It was not until the late 1980s, however, when driftnetters began to work the South Pacific albacore tuna fishing grounds, between latitude 30° and 40° south, and among the richest in the world, that high levels of political and diplomatic concern began to generate over this type of fishing. From this time forward, as demonstrated in part by two resolutions adopted by the U.N. General Assembly in 1989 and 1991–GA Res. 44/225 on Large-scale Pelagic Driftnet Fishing and Its Impact on the Living Marine Resources of the World's Oceans and Seas of December 22, 1989 **[Basic Document 6.9]** and GA Res. 46/215 on Large-scale Pelagic Driftnet Fishing and Its Impact on the Living Marine Resources of the World's Oceans and Seas of December 20, 1991 **[Basic Document 6.10]**—many nations came to question whether,

---

e. The Devastating Effects that Uncontrolled Large–Scale Driftnetting has had on the Marine Resources of the Northern Pacific Ocean: Hearings Before the Subcomm. on Fisheries and Wildlife Conservation and the Environment of the House Comm. on Merchant Marine and Fisheries, 102d Cong., 1st Sess. 95 (1991)(prepared statement of Alan Reichman, Ocean Ecology Campaigner, Greenpeace U.S.A.).

f. As Burke points out, however, there has not been much serious study of the particular impact of large-scale driftnetting on the general problem of depletion of marine resources. "With the possible exception of the effects of driftnet gear on salmon populations in the North Pacific, there does not appear to be an accepted body of knowledge about the effects of driftnets on particular target species, on incidentally affected species, or on the marine ecosystem as a whole." Burke, *supra* note d at 266.

with most driftnet fishing done in international waters, the principle of freedom of the high seas should be allowed to be invoked on behalf of what increasingly is seen as a systematic assault upon, and depredation of, the marine ecosystem. Still, for a variety of reasons, the legal situation remains somewhat cloudy, and accordingly more of the story must be told.

From the 1987–88 fishing season to that of 1988–89, the number of driftnet fishing vessels, each equipped with dozens of driftnets, grew from 20 Japanese and seven Taiwanese vessels to over 60 Japanese and up to 130 Taiwanese vessels, and all at a time when the South Pacific island countries with few resources were in various stages of developing longline fisheries for the albacore tuna (of great economic importance to these small countries notwithstanding its highly migratory nature).[g] Prior to the 1988–89 fishing season, the South Pacific Albacore Research Group (SPAR), an informal organization of researchers from various countries,[h] had estimated that continued fishing by driftnets at the levels then occurring would seriously deplete the entire stock of albacore tuna within two years, in large part because juvenile tuna, which swim near the surface and therefore are caught and killed by driftnets long before maturity, were being heavily depleted. It also was reported that the more traditional and therefore less exploitative troll fishers of the region, primarily from New Zealand and the United States, were finding it increasingly prohibitive to fish in the area because of their need to carry divers on their voyages to clear driftnets from the propellers of their vessels. Accordingly, a major economic resource—and with it the prospect of vigorous economic development—was seen by the otherwise resource-poor South Pacific countries to be slipping quickly from their grasp at the hands of distant water fishing nations plundering the available stocks.

At about the same time, several nongovernmental environmental organizations took up the issue. Earthtrust was able to film pictures of dolphins caught in driftnets and to produce a television documentary on the subject containing films that evoked a strong emotional response against driftnetting wherever shown. A big campaign was organized by the NGOs, particularly Earthtrust and Greenpeace. They provided information to public officials and otherwise lobbied governments as well as making the case directly to the world's public.

The NGO campaign was run with a "piracy on the high seas" approach.[i] The "wall of death," it was claimed, killed fish that never could be recovered; spelled death for marine mammals, seabirds, and fish other than those being pursued; posed hazards for navigation; and otherwise was a recipe for envi-

---

g. It is estimated that at least 1,200 vessels worldwide are outfitted for driftnetting. Driven by economic demand and reward, such fisheries have developed also in the Indian Ocean and the Caribbean Sea.

h. "SPAR is an informally constituted group of researchers from various countries who are interested in South Pacific albacore; it meets at intervals, usually in response to changes, or likely changes, in the fishery." Judith Swan, *International Regulation of Driftnet Fishing Activities, in* Growing Demands On A Shrinking Heritage: Managing Resource–Use

Conflicts 216, 221–22 n. 24 (M. Ross & J. Sanders eds. 1992).

i. In Burke's analysis of the issues he notes that "principles about piracy at sea have been frequently mentioned in public statements by some public officials but will not be discussed here because they have no relevance to any of the problems of high seas driftnet fishing. ... Statements of this kind are made for political effect and internal national consumption...." Burke, *supra* note d, at 270.

ronmental degradation generally. People should not eat tuna caught by driftnets, it was argued.

The response of nations interested in defending driftnetting was no less adamant: no scientific evidence existed, they said, that the method was reducing stocks of fish to unsustainable levels or endangering the survival of particular species of fauna. But the intensive NGO campaign was highly successful. The issue had popular appeal. The alleged lack of scientific evidence was not persuasive.

The issue was closely studied by the Fisheries Agency of the South Pacific Forum, which was established by the Forum in 1979 with headquarters in Honiara in the Solomon Islands. The Forum Fisheries Agency (FFA) reported to the Heads of Government of the Forum after it had convened a meeting of interested countries in November 1988 at which it was concluded that the southern albacore fishery probably would collapse should the projected expansion of driftnet fishing in the South Pacific occur. Plans were put in place to collect data on landing, use of port facilities, and transhipment, and otherwise to secure as much information as possible using the resources of the governments involved. In March 1989, another meeting was convened by the FAA when it was clear that the situation was serious and that wider support was needed to pursue the issue. A review of the relevant law concluded that high sea driftnet operations were not being conducted in accordance with Part V of the 1982 United Nations Convention on the Law of the Sea [**Basic Document 4.20**], particularly Articles 87, 116–119, and 300 thereof.

In June 1989, a further consultation was held in Suva with members of the FFA, the distant water fishing nations engaged in the fishery, and scientists. While concern was clearly expressed about the sustainability of the present albacore tuna stocks, no agreement was reached. The South Pacific nations took the view that action was required while the distant water fishing nations contended that there was no proof that action was required. In any event, the distant water fishing nations certainly would not agree to stop.

The Heads of Government of the South Pacific Forum took up the issue at their annual meeting in Tarawa, Kiribati in July 1989. In the Tarawa Declaration, adopted by the FFA, the Forum resolved, "for the sake of future generations of Pacific peoples,"

> to seek the establishment of a regime for the management of albacore tuna in the South Pacific that would ban driftnet fishing from their region; such a ban might then be a first step to a comprehensive ban on such fishing.[j]

Also resulting from the Tarawa meeting was a commitment to establish a convention to create a "driftnet free zone," with New Zealand agreeing to host the treaty-drafting meeting and to take up the issue in other international organizations.

In October, the Prime Minister of New Zealand told the U.N. General Assembly that "[f]reedom of the high seas cannot be invoked to protect what is in effect a systematic assault on the regional marine ecosystem."[k] In the

---

j. *Tarawa Declaration*, adopted July 10–11, 1989. *Quoted in* Regulation of Driftnet, *supra* note b, at 31; *reprinted in* 14 Law of the Sea Bull. 29 (1989).

k. Provisional Verbatim Record of the Fif-

same month, the Commonwealth Heads of Government, meeting at Lang-kawi, Malaysia, stated in their Langkawi Declaration [**Basic Document 1.25**] that they were committed to "seek to ban ... pelagic drift-net fishing".[1] With most the South Pacific Forum countries being members of the Common-wealth and with a total of 42 countries in the Commonwealth, there now was something of an international bandwagon rolling against driftnet fishing.

Thereafter, a big diplomatic effort was made to inform governments of what a ban against driftnet fishing involved and to seek their support for a United Nations General Assembly resolution. The United States, New Zea-land, and all the Forum countries co-operated in promoting General Assembly Resolution 44/225 [**Basic Document 6.9**] in 1989, which, in the end, was adopted without a vote although it was clear that Japan was unhappy with the course that developments had taken. Language was included sufficient to avoid Japanese objection, and Japan agreed to phase out driftnet fishing in the South Pacific.

But pressure for further action remained into late–1989 and 1990. The Forum countries worked fast in negotiating a convention, and it was signed in Wellington, New Zealand on November 24, 1989, about four months after it was called for in the Tarawa Declaration. The purpose of the Wellington Convention [**Basic Document 6.8**], which entered into force on May 17, 1991, was to prohibit driftnet fishing on the high seas and in the exclusive economic zones of countries lying within a large area of the Pacific defined by the Convention—a novel way of dealing with the problems of a particular fishery, by agreeing to an international convention to deal specially with it. Relating to "driftnet fishing activities" and not merely the act of fishing, parties to it were required to take specific measures, although the legal effects of the Convention are perhaps not as significant as its political and diplomatic consequences. It was a signal to the world that the South Pacific really cared about the practice of driftnet fishing and that it would go to considerable lengths to stop it. In the world of international diplomacy, this was equivalent to a regional full court press.

United Nations efforts hardened over the years as well, such that Japan, in July 1990, announced that it was ceasing driftnetting in the South Pacific a year earlier than it had undertaken to do in General Assembly Resolution 44/225 of 1989. Taiwan, not being a member of the United Nations was harder to reach, but finally it too announced its intention to stop. Additional-ly, the U.N. General Assembly, in Resolution 46/215 of 1991 [**Basic Document 6.10**], called for "a global moratorium on all large-scale pelagic driftnet fishing ... by 31 December 1992."

But what if nations elect not to follow Resolution 46/215? It is not self-executing and theoretically not considered binding. True, driftnet fishing is to be seen as primarily an environmental, economic, and diplomatic problem. But even while, like most transnational environmental problems, it reflects a heady mix of environmental science, economics, and diplomacy, so must it also be understood to be, fundamentally, a legal problem. As will be seen as you review the law and commentary in the following readings, not everyone was

teenth Meeting, UN GAOR, 44th Sess., 15th mtg., at 75, U.N. Doc. A/44/PV.15 (prov. ed. 1989).

1. *Langkawi Declaration* [**Basic Document 1.25**], para. 8.

happy with the manner in which the "law" on driftnetting was made: there is room to challenge its legitimacy and its consistency with other principles of international environmental law.[m]

3. *Resolution on Large–Scale Pelagic Driftnet Fishing and Its Impact on the Living Marine Resources of the World's Oceans and Seas*, G.A. Res. 44/225, U.N. GAOR, 44th Sess., Supp. No. 82 (*f*), U.N. Doc. A/C.2/44/L.81 (1989), *reprinted in* 29 I.L.M. 1555 (1990). [Basic Document 6.9].

4. *Resolution on Large–Scale Pelagic Driftnet Fishing and Its Impact on the Living Marine Resources of the World's Oceans and Seas*, G.A. Res. 46/215 U.N. GAOR, 46th Sess., Supp. No. 77, U.N. Doc. A/46/645/Add.6 (1991), *reprinted in* 31 I.L.M. 241 (1992). [Basic Document 6.10].

5. **Convention for the Prohibition of Fishing With Long Driftnets in the South Pacific, Nov. 24, 1989, *reprinted in* 29 I.L.M. 1449 (1990).** [Basic Document 6.8].

6. **William Burke, Mark Freeberg and Edward Miles, *The United Nations Resolutions on Driftnet Fishing: An Unsustainable Precedent for High Seas and Coastal Fisheries*, 25 OCEAN DEV. & INT'L L. 127, 128, 144, 170–72 (1994).**

This paper examines the international and national implications of United Nations General Assembly Resolutions 44/225 (1989) **[Basic Document 6.9]** and 46/215 (1991) **[Basic Document 6.10]** recommending a moratorium on the use of large-scale pelagic driftnets in high seas fishing. Because of its pivotal role, special attention is given to the campaign in support by the United States. The United States position, and by necessary extension the conclusion of the General Assembly as a whole in following the United States lead, was based primarily on emotion and hyperbole rather than scientific data and interpretations. In addition, as will be shown, significant systematic observations of relevant driftnet fisheries were not taken into account.

As a consequence, the General Assembly disregarded the most basic canons of sound fisheries management, the use of the best available scientific data and the conscious assessment of alternative means to achieve the conservation objective. This approach laid the basis for the use by the United States of coercive economic diplomacy to terminate all high seas fishing with large pelagic driftnets by Japan, Korea, and Taiwan, and by all other nations anywhere in the world ocean. The only scientific support cited for this action prohibiting the use of a certain fishing gear anywhere in the ocean beyond national jurisdiction is a single review of one high seas fishery in a particular part of the North Pacific Ocean. No other scientific or fisheries data were considered, although revealing observational data were known to be available showing that complete termination of driftnet gear was highly questionable.

---

m. It should be noted that, quite apart from the efforts to regulate large-scale driftnet fishing for conservation reasons, there are pre-existing international agreements pertaining to the disposal or loss of driftnets at sea. These include the London Dumping Convention [Basic Document 4.11] and the 1973/78 Convention on the Prevention of Pollution from Ships (MARPOL), Annex V [Basic Document 4.12].

Thus the termination of the use of large high seas driftnets was achieved not only at high cost in principle but also abruptly ended the acquisition of information necessary for effective management of high seas fisheries. Of equal or greater import, the United Nations General Assembly action potentially puts at risk extensive artisanal and subsistence driftnet and other fisheries within national jurisdiction, especially in Asia and South America. If the levels of bycatch proscribed by the resolutions are an acceptable basis for prohibitive action on the high seas, continuation of other fisheries is subject to serious question.

* * *

Had this issue been handled by fisheries managers, the South Pacific would have been recognized as a special case, given the limited nature of the southern albacore resource, the extreme dependence of South Pacific island states on fisheries, the extensive involvement of Japanese and Korean fishing industries in the region, and the diplomatic/political significance of the region for Japan. Severe limits on the level of effort by Japan and Korea would therefore have been imposed. The case of Taiwan is more complicated because Taiwan linked response to South Pacific demands on driftnets to diplomatic recognition of Taiwan by South Pacific island states, a step which would have considerably complicated their relations with China. In the North Pacific, the most probable response would have been reductions in fishing effort combined with the use of time and area closures on all three fleets. That the final policy outcome was complete termination of all fishing operations by all three fleets can be explained only in terms of the role played by the United States.

* * *

At the level of decision process, the United States, New Zealand, Australia and the Pacific Island states were aware of the lack of a suitable international mechanism for coping with activities on the high seas. Motivated by quite different considerations, as noted above, they invoked the broad jurisdiction (and very public forum) of the United Nations General Assembly. While it is accustomed to conducting broad political debates and generating political pressure, the Assembly is poorly suited for dealing with complex scientific and technical details. The lack of understanding about fishery matters must weaken the authority to be accorded recommendations resulting from such a process.

An initial indication of the defective workings of the General Assembly on this matter may be seen by comparing provisions of the 1989 and 1991 resolutions and observing the actions taken by the Assembly.

First, it is at least strange that the 1989 Resolution recognized in preambular paragraph 6 that regulations for conservation and management of high seas resources "should take account of the best available scientific data and analysis," but two years later Resolution 46/215 was rushed through the General Assembly without any account being taken of the available scientific data on the largest driftnet operations in the North Pacific Ocean.

Second, operative paragraph 2 in the 1989 Resolution called for driftnet fishing states to cooperate in "enhanced collection and sharing of statistically sound scientific data." Two years later, after cooperating to produce data which showed high seas bycatch rates and amounts lower than in many fisheries inside national jurisdiction, these states were rewarded by passage of a Resolution to eliminate their fisheries.

Third, in the same vein, the 1989 Resolution urged the collection of data "in order to assess the impacts of such fishing methods." But, two years later, the cooperative effort and the resulting data were simply ignored and, instead of assessing what they showed about the impacts of driftnets in the circumstances, the fisheries were terminated on the basis of impacts alleged to have occurred in some other fishery.

Fourth, as this misfeasance was occurring, so far as is known, few coastal states have paid any attention to the operative paragraph in Resolution 44/225 encouraging them to collect and submit scientific information on driftnet fishing in their own EEZs. The United States has legislatively prohibited use of large driftnets within and outside its EEZ, but has thus far neither collected nor submitted any information on the many driftnet fisheries operating within its EEZ. Meanwhile, both driftnets within the EEZ and other gear continue to have higher relative bycatch rates.

Fifth, in further illustration of unprincipled decision-making, operative paragraph 3 of the 1989 Resolution called for review, "particularly within regional organizations" by June 30, 1991, of impacts of driftnet fishing and for those concerned to "agree upon further cooperative regulation and monitoring measures as needed." Instead of allowing time for such reviews, or a decent interval thereafter to design appropriate regulations, or itself taking into account available and relevant scientific data, the General Assembly hurriedly took action on the basis of a partial review and immediately recommended terminating all the high seas driftnet fisheries in the world. As already noted, disregarded in this process were not only its own injunctions to take account of the best available scientific data and analysis but also its own invitation to all interested members of the international community to agree on cooperative regulation and monitoring measures.

Sixth, 1989 Resolution preambular paragraph 8 affirmed the obligation of states, in accordance with the 1982 Convention on the Law of the Sea, to cooperate in taking conservation measures "as may be necessary for the conservation of the living resources of the high seas." A few paragraphs later, with speedy inconsistency, the resolution called for a moratorium on high seas driftnet fisheries even if it were not shown that conservation measures were necessary. The 1991 Resolution emphasized this incongruity by calling for termination of all high seas driftnet fisheries without consulting any data related to the necessity for conservation measures, except for dubious reliance on a review of one of the several high seas driftnet fisheries in the North Pacific Ocean.

Finally, 1989 operative paragraph 4 clearly anticipated removal of the moratorium and the continuation of high seas driftnet fishing when effective conservation measures were introduced. In contrast, the 1991 Resolution appears to leave no room for a driftnet fishery for which effective conservation measures were later devised and applied, apparently on the assumption that such measures were inconceivable. No evidence supporting such an assumption was ever mentioned.

This review of the contradictions and inconsistencies of the two resolutions amply documents the results of a hasty politically driven process. The preconceptions and presumptions about high seas driftnet gear were so ingrained or so eagerly accepted that evidence to the contrary could not be imagined. Although multi-national efforts were underway in the North Pacific to gather data on the harvest by driftnets, none were available in 1989 (and little in 1991) to inform the decision-makers at the United Nations. Instead the opponents of driftnets acted upon presumptions which took the place of evidence.

This paper shows that the presumptions were very likely incorrect and that data were available to be assessed for this purpose but were never used. A decision process so badly flawed and executed should not be permitted to determine or to influence the current or future content of international law for high seas fisheries.

In sum, this record of defective performance, coupled with the fact that the United Nations system has a specialized agency (the Food and Agriculture Organization) with a considerable range of expertise in fisheries affairs, creates a serious issue about how to extend governance over living resources in the ocean beyond national jurisdiction. Here was the use of a decision process ill-suited to presentation, analysis and informed consideration of detailed data, necessarily of a complex and technical nature. Given the general lack of expertise and professional competence in fisheries matters, it is not surprising that the participants could so easily be misled by partial and selective reporting and by clever manipulation of the reported data. No hearing process was employed or even available, yet those who decided on recommended action were asked to assess scientific information for which they were poorly prepared.

The significance of regulatory process is that the conservation problems of ocean fishing are complicated matters whose governance requires, *inter alia*, at a minimum, some degree of scientific understanding for meaningful analysis and decision. If international institutions are required for avoiding and resolving conflicts over these problems, and few doubt that they are, resort should be had to mechanisms with the requisite capabilities. These will very likely be below the high political level involved in the driftnet situation. Failure to establish and employ adequate decision-making entities ought to invalidate decisions resulting from the defective processes actually used. At the least, recommendations from such entities will have little continuing credibility.

* * *

In addition to lacking support in established law of the sea principles, the General Assembly adoption of the extreme form of the precautionary principle is dubious on other grounds. The Rio Declaration on Environment and Development **[Basic Document 1.29]** recommended the precautionary approach in Principle 15:

> In order to protect the environment, the precautionary approach shall be widely applied by States according to their capabilities. Where there are threats of serious or irreversible damage, lack of full scientific certainty shall not be used as a reason for postponing cost-effective measures to prevent environmental degradation.

The General Assembly process scarcely resembles this recommendation. The assembly made no effort to consider scientific information regarding the severity of the expected harm in specific fisheries, failed to review systematic observational data from fisheries outside the North Pacific, did not calculate the risk of occurrence of the apprehended harm, took no account of possible alternative approaches, and gave no consideration to the costs of the moratorium being recommended. In light of the probable catastrophic social and economic consequences of the abrupt termination recommended by the Assembly, reasonable prudence and fairness certainly should have warranted adherence to an approach such as that subsequently embodied in Rio Principle 15.

Fairly considered, the North Pacific data available in 1991 on the Japanese squid driftnet fishery might have been sufficient to warrant additional restrictions on some driftnet fishing, rather than outright termination. On the other hand, the data on the Taiwan and South Korean fisheries might have been assessed differently, justifying less intervention, if any at all. In any event, the blunderbuss approach of an absolute global moratorium was not only not indicated, but also missed a genuine opportunity to establish an effective high seas conservation scheme.

7.   Editor's Note. As the principal problem suggests, the protection of fisheries is not simply a matter of banning driftnetting. Excessive and unregulated fishing, whether by driftnetting or otherwise, on the high seas or in the exclusive economic zone of a particular nation, can seriously deplete migratory species and straddling stocks of species upon which other nations depend. Whether existing international law is adequate to deal with this problem is an open question. The following readings illustrate some of the relevant principles and problems.

8.   Stockholm Declaration on the Human Environment of the United Nations Conference on the Human Environment Adopted by the UN Conference on the Human Environment at Stockholm, 16 June 1972, Report of the UN Conference on the Human Environment, Stockholm, 15–16 June 1972, UN Doc. A/CONF.48/14/Rev.1 at 3 (1973), UN Doc. A/CONF.48/14 at 2–65, and Corr. 1 (1972), *reprinted in* 11 I.L.M. 1416 (1972): Principles 2–4, 11, 13, 24, 25. [Basic Document 1.12].

9.   *World Charter for Nature*, G.A. Res. 37/7, U.N. GAOR, 37th Sess., Supp. No. 51, at 17, U.N. Doc. A/37/51 (1982), *reprinted in* 22 I.L.M. 455 (1983): Principles 1–4, 6, 7, 9–11, 14, 19, 24. [Basic Document 1.21].

10.   Rio Declaration on Environment and Development of the United Nations Conference on Environment and Development, June 14, 1992, UNCED Doc. A/CONF.151/5/Rev.1, *reprinted in* 31 I.L.M. 874 (1992): Principles 1, 2, 4, 6. 7, 8, 12, 15. [Basic Document 1.29].

11.   Cyril De Klemm, *Migratory Species in International Law*, 29 N.R.J. 935, 938–39 (1989).

States have sovereign rights over all animals which happen to be present on their territory at any moment in time. This generally recognized principle of law is, however, not embodied in any specific international instrument. It is merely a consequence of the universal recognition of the sovereignty of States over their natural resources. With regard to animals occurring in the EEZ of a State, the sovereignty of the State concerned has been explicitly established by article 56 of the United Nations Convention on the Law of the Sea [**Basic Document 4.20**].

The fact that a State has sovereign rights over all wild animals on its territory and in its EEZ does not, however, necessarily mean that it is the owner of these animals. This is a matter which is dealt with by national legislation as a consequence of these sovereign rights. In some countries, wild animals continue to be *res nullius* as they were in Roman law. Increasingly, however, national legislation tends to provide for state or public ownership of such animals unless they have been lawfully obtained by private persons by hunting, trapping, fishing, or collecting.

The consequence, however, of the existence of sovereign rights over wild animals is that States have exclusive jurisdiction *ratione* over them in all areas under their jurisdiction and no jurisdiction outside their national jurisdictional limits. As a result, animals that migrate from one jurisdiction to another are subject, in succession, to the sovereign rights and jurisdiction of all the States along their migration route. Conversely, where no State has sovereign rights, [for example] in the high seas, animals become international *res nullius* that anybody may exploit, overexploit, or destroy as he [sic] pleases. This latter principle is embodied in international law under the name of freedom of fishing on the high seas.

As long as conservation and management problems did not arise, the absurdity of the system was of little or no importance. It became apparent as early as the beginning of this century, however, that certain species, particularly marine species, would disappear, at least as economic resources, if no conservation measures were taken throughout their ranges, irrespective of jurisdictional zones.

In the absence of a rule of international law conferring upon migratory species a special legal status in recognition of their international nature, restrictions to the exercise of sovereign rights may only be voluntary, through the conclusion of treaties whereby Range States of particular species, as States exploiting these species on the high seas, agree to accept certain conservation obligations.

Although existing principles of international law cannot be affected by the conclusion of such treaties and, therefore, the legal status of migratory species remains unchanged, it is nonetheless significant that many States have now accepted to limit the effects of these principles in the interest of conservation and, in doing so, to provide practical solutions to complex problems.

The very fact that a relatively large number of treaties have now been concluded in many parts of the world to provide a certain degree of protection to an increasing number of migratory species is a clear proof that the particular requirements of these species together with the necessity of concerted action for their conservation and management is now broadly recognized. One may, however, wonder whether more effective conservation action could not result from the development and adoption by the world community of a specific legal status for migratory species from which rules could be derived that would be binding upon all States. Three possibilities seem to be open in this respect: internationalization, nationalization, and the use of the shared resources concept.

12.   William Burke, *The Law of the Sea Concerning Coastal State Authority Over Driftnets on the High Seas*, in U.N. Food and Agriculture Organization (FAO) Legislative Study 47, at 13, 14–27 (1991).

[T]he following obligations of fishing states [are] owed to the general international community of states:

- to take the necessary measures to conserve the living resources of the high seas;[1]

- to cooperate with other states in taking measures to conserve such resources;[2]

- to enter into negotiations with other states fishing the same or different resources in the same area "with a view to taking the measures necessary for the conservation of the living resources concerned";[3]

- to contribute and exchange scientific information, catch and effort statistics and other data regarding conservation of stocks on the high seas;[4]

- to take measures "designed, on the best scientific evidence available to the states concerned, to maintain or restore populations of harvested species at levels which can produce the maximum sustainable yield, as qualified by relevant environmental and economic factors . . .";[5]

- to ensure that the measures adopted are non-discriminatory against the fishermen of any state;[6] [and]

- to observe treaty obligations they have undertaken.[7]

An issue involving each of the above substantive principles (except the last) is whether it is also a principle of customary international law.

An additional principle relating to all of the above is the obligation not to abuse the rights and freedoms of the high seas while in the exercise of those rights and freedoms. Flag state activities on the high seas are protected only to the extent that they are reasonable in relation to others' use, similar or otherwise.

High seas fishing states also have obligations (whether by explicit agreement or by customary law or both) to coastal states concerning animal populations that are subject at some phase of their life cycles to coastal state jurisdiction. Assertions have been made invoking the principle that high seas fishing states are obliged by agreement[8] and perhaps by customary law to

---

1.   *See* Article 61 of the U.N. Convention on the Law of the Sea [**Basic Document 4.20**] [hereinafter "LOS Convention" or "UNCLOS"].

2.   *Id.*, art. 118.

3.   *Id.*

4.   *Id.* at art. 119(2).

5.   *Id.* at art. 119(1)(a).

6.   *Id.* at art. 119(3).

7.   *Id.* at art. 116.

8.   *Id.* at art. 118; *see also* Convention on Fishing and Conservation of the Living Resources of the High Seas [**Basic Document 6.3**] [hereinafter "1958 Resources Convention"].

observe coastal state conservation regulations affecting high seas fishing for particular species. The coastal state regulations potentially or actually applicable include those addressed to shared stocks, particularly those that are common to coastal state jurisdiction and to the high seas (straddling stocks), anadromous species and highly migratory species. The provisions applicable in these instances are in Parts V, VII and XV of UNCLOS.

States fishing on the high seas may also be bound by specific commitments undertaken by agreement with other states (on a bilateral or multilateral basis).

* * *

Rights of High Seas Fishing States
Freedom of Fishing on the High Seas

Article 2 of the 1958 Convention on the High Seas **[Basic Document 4.2]** embodies the general understanding, also considered to be part of customary law of the sea, that the freedoms of the high seas include the freedom of fishing in this area. This freedom, as all others on the high seas, must be conducted with reasonable regard to the interests of others in their exercise of the same or other freedoms of the high seas. Freedom of fishing has traditionally extended to all types of fishing gear, without exception.

Article [1] of the 1958 Convention on Fishing and Conservation of the Living Resources of the High Seas **[Basic Document 6.3]** contains a more qualified formulation of the rights of states to fish on the high seas, declaring:

"1. All States have the right for their nationals to engage in fishing on the high seas, subject (a) to their treaty obligations, (b) to the interests and rights of coastal States as provided for in this Convention, and (c) to the provisions contained in the following articles concerning conservation of the living resources of the high seas.

2. All States have the duty to adopt, or to cooperate with other States in adopting, such measures for their respective nationals as may be necessary for the conservation of the living resources of the high seas."

Although Article [1] is in a treaty that has not been widely adopted, paragraph 2 at least is now considered to be part of customary law. As noted more fully below, the International Court of Justice in the Fisheries Jurisdiction Case (the United Kingdom vs. Iceland) declared that a high seas fishing state must take full account of necessary conservation measures in conducting its operations.[9]

The most recent multilateral agreement dealing with freedom of fishing on the high seas affirms it once again and also confirms that states generally are agreed on obligations that burden this right. Part VII of UNCLOS **[Basic Document 4.20]** deals with the high seas and Article 87 entitled "Freedom of the high seas" provides:

"1. The high seas are open to all States, whether coastal or land-locked. Freedom of the high seas is exercised under the conditions laid down by the Convention and by other rules of international law. It comprises, *inter alia*, both for coastal and landlocked States: . . .

---

9. Fisheries Jurisdiction (U.K. v. Ice.), 1974 I.C.J. 3 [hereinafter "Fisheries Case"].

(e) freedom of fishing, subject to the conditions laid down in Section 2."

In Section II, Article 116 [of the LOS Convention] repeats Article 1 of the 1958 Geneva Fishing Convention **[Basic Document 6.3]** in declaring that "all States have the right for their nationals to engage in fishing on the high seas ...", but adds significant new conditions that are relevant, *inter alia*, to high seas pelagic driftnets, as will be noted below.

While it is evident that the principle of freedom of fishing on the high seas continues to protect this activity, it is also evident that conditions burden the exercise of this right and need to be considered in relation to the use of driftnets (or the use of other fishing gear) on the high seas.

Obligations of High Seas Fishing States to the General Community of States

Obligation to Conserve the Living Resources of the High Seas

The decision in the Fisheries Jurisdiction Case (United Kingdom vs. Iceland)[10] establishes the principle that states fishing on the high seas have the duty to attend to the needs of conservation of the living resources affected. In a passage directly relevant to issues involved with high seas driftnet fishing, the International Court of Justice ... declared in reference to fishing in an area the majority of the Court considered part of the high seas:

"It follows that even if the Court holds that Iceland's extension of its fishery limits is not opposable to the Applicant [United Kingdom], this does not mean that the Applicant is under no obligation to Iceland with respect to fishing in the disputed waters in the 12–to 50–mile zone. On the contrary, both States have an obligation to take full account of each other's rights and of any fishery conservation measures the necessity of which is shown to exist in those waters. It is one of the advances in maritime international law, resulting from the intensification of fishing, that the former *laissez-faire* treatment of the living resources of the sea in the high seas has been replaced by a recognition of a duty to have due regard to the rights of other states and the needs of conservation for the benefit of all. Consequently, both Parties have the obligation to keep under review the fishery resources in the disputed waters and to examine together, in the light of scientific and other available information, the measures required for the conservation and development, and equitable exploitation, of those resources, taking into account any international agreement in force between them ...".[11]

Although this duty was first enunciated in the 1958 Geneva Convention on Fishing and Conservation of the Living Resources of the High Seas **[Basic Document 6.3]**, it is no longer considered to be only a treaty obligation binding the parties to that agreement, but is rather a general obligation owed to the community of nations as a whole. Elaborating on the Court's pronouncement quoted above, Judge Dillard's concurring opinion in the Fisheries Jurisdiction Case observed that "although Iceland was not a part to this (1958 Fishing) Convention, it is yet possible to surmise that, in light of the practice of States and the widespread and insistent recognition of the need for

---

10. *Id.*   11. *Id.* at 31.

conservation measures, the principle it announces may qualify as a norm of customary international law . . .".[12]

Since the Fisheries Jurisdiction Case decision in 1974, the negotiations in the Third United Nations Conference on the Law of the Sea produced still further evidence of the general acceptance of the obligation to conserve high seas living resources. Article 117 [of the 1982 U.N. Convention on the Law of the Sea or UNCLOS] **[Basic Document 4.20]** provides that "all States have the duty to take, or to cooperate with other States in taking, such measures for their respective nations as may be necessary for the conservation of the living resources of the high seas". Thus, irrespective of another state's involvement in a high seas fishery, a state whose nationals fish on the high seas is obliged to adopt conservation measures for its own nationals. These obligations are now embodied in customary international law.

The state or states to whom the high seas fishing state is obliged are not specifically identified in the provisions of the various treaties. However, the injunction to have due regard to the interests of other states appears to establish that another state (not necessarily another fishing state) with an interest may secure redress for non-observance of the obligation involved. In the Fisheries Jurisdiction Case, the Court found that the United Kingdom's interests had been infringed upon by Iceland as a coastal state in exercise of its freedom of fishing, but indicated that "due regard" extended also to the interests of other states.[13]

* * *

UNCLOS **[Basic Document 4.20]** contains important innovations in its provisions for the conservation of living resources, including those for high seas living resources. Article 119 provides:

"1. In determining the allowable catch and establishing other conservation measures for the living resources in the high seas, States shall:

(a) take measures which are designed, on the best scientific evidence available to the States concerned, to maintain or restore populations of harvested species at levels which can produce the maximum sustainable yield, as qualified by relevant environmental and economic factors, including the special requirements of developing States, and taking into account fishing patterns, the interdependence of stocks and any generally recommended international minimum standards, whether subregional, regional or global;

(b) take into consideration the effects on species associated with or dependent upon harvested species with a view to maintaining or restoring populations of such associated or dependent species above levels at which their reproduction may become seriously threatened.

2. Available scientific information, catch and fishing effort statistics, and other data relevant to the conservation of fish stocks shall be contributed and exchanged on a regular basis through competent international organizations, whether subregional, regional or global, where appropriate and with participation by all States concerned.

12. *Id.* at 69.   **13.** *Id.* at 68–69.

3. States concerned shall ensure that conservation measures and their implementation do not discriminate in form or in fact against the fishermen of any State."

The most significant innovation in Article 119 is that departure from the maximum sustainable yield as the goal of conservation measures is permitted. Such departure is the intent of providing that relevant environmental and economic factors may be used to determine the level of abundance to be maintained in a fishery. In practice this enables the adoption of measures that provide for a higher level of abundance of stocks than might otherwise have to be maintained in order to produce the maximum sustainable yield. The resulting increased stock density permits a higher catch per unit of effort, which translates into lower costs and greater net returns for the harvester. The price of this achievement is a lower total catch. In the case of a high seas fishery, this means there are less fish to be shared among the fishing states concerned. The overall returns might be greater, but because of different costs to different national fleets the net returns might be less to some. It should be emphasized that in this context, as well as in others, there may be sound environmental or economic reasons for measures that seek a level of abundance that will produce the maximum sustainable yield. Nonetheless, there may be disputes about the alternatives allowed by Article 119.

Article 119 does not require that the states concerned with high seas conservation determine an allowable catch for the stocks of interest, although it does not exclude this form of regulation either. The article leaves it to the states concerned to determine the nature of the conservation measures, if any, that should be employed in the fishery. It is apparent that prohibiting any use of driftnet gear is not directed by this article, nor is it excluded.

It is also clear from Article 119 that high seas driftnet fishing states must make an effort to acquire information about species associated with or dependent upon harvested species and must take into consideration the effects on such species. Driftnet technology is known to kill substantial quantities of marine mammals, therefore this obligation is an important one.

The substantive conservation obligation that must be considered for associated or dependent species is the obligation to maintain or restore populations "above levels at which their reproduction may become seriously threatened". Although this obligation permits substantial takings, it also may require considerable research effort since population abundance of high seas species, as well as the effects of the driftnet gear on such populations, may be difficult to determine.

Obligation to Cooperate With Other States in Taking Conservation Measures

The previous discussion also shows that the obligation to cooperate is now clearly spelled out in UNCLOS **[Basic Document 4.20]**, most particularly in Article 117, and is probably considered also to be a customary law of the sea principle. In the Fisheries Jurisdiction Case, the International Court found that due to their respective rights in the high seas areas involved, beyond 12 miles (as the Court held), the parties were required "to examine together, in the light of scientific and other available information, the measures required for the conservation and development, and equitable exploitation, of those resources ..."[14]. In addition to this specific form of cooperation flowing from the simultaneous rights in the high seas, the Court found that the parties were to engage in negotiations to resolve the dispute between them and directed them to do so.

Cooperation can obviously take many forms and is not exhausted by any single activity, whether parallel or joint or coordinated. In the case of driftnets, there has already been significant cooperative activity of various kinds between the various states concerned at bilateral, regional and global levels, which might be taken as evidence of a perceived obligation to do so. Japan, in particular, has long been involved in research regarding its salmon driftnet fisheries in the North Pacific, in discussions regarding this research and in negotiations to deal with the impacts of this fishery on various stocks. More recently, several North Pacific states have reached bilateral agreements with the United States on a variety of measures to develop scientific information regarding the squid driftnet fishery in this region.

Elsewhere, the South Pacific albacore tuna fishery has recently attracted considerable attention, including meetings between Pacific island nations among others, and the states using driftnet gear. At a meeting in June 1989 attended by Japan, the Republic of Korea and Taiwan (Province of China), the Pacific island nations called for a cessation of the use of driftnet gear in the South Pacific until a satisfactory management regime was established. The Republic of Korea reportedly agreed to such termination, but Japan and Taiwan (Province of China) did not. However, they did agree to various cooperative actions over the following season, including in the case of Japan a freeze on the number of boats at the 1988/89 level, the dispatch of a patrol vessel to the region and efforts to collect such relevant fishery data as coastal statistics.

* * *

Obligation to Negotiate Conservation Measures

Article 118 of UNCLOS [Basic Document 4.20] sharpens the expression of the duty to cooperate in conservation, specifying that high seas fishing states must negotiate "with a view" to taking the necessary conservation measures. This duty arises both where the nationals of different states take identical living resources or where they take different resources in the same area. Specifying an obligation to negotiate is a different burden than simple cooperation, which might be shown by other activities, and is more demanding. An obligation to negotiate does not require an agreement, but it does mandate good faith in the attempt to remove differences and reach substantive agreement.

* * *

Obligation to Generate and to Contribute Scientific Information About Stocks Being Fished on the High Seas

The obligation to conserve fisheries exploited on the high seas seems necessarily to imply that the flag state has the corresponding responsibility of undertaking the requisite scientific investigation to inform an adequate con-

14. *Id.* at 34–35.

servation programme. Unless this state also has the duty to develop the scientific basis for such a programme, including knowledge of the significant effects of such fishing on species and stocks caught incidentally to the target fishery, it could hardly carry out the basic obligation to conserve.

The evidence is overwhelming that conservation measures for living marine resources are formulated to take account of scientific investigations carried out by individual nation states involved in the use of such resources. Many coastal and fishing states have entered into limited multilateral agreements on the conservation of fisheries and marine mammals. The agreements often provide for an institutional mechanism for cooperation among the states concerned and specifically call for scientific undertakings by the member states in order to provide a basis for conservation measures to be recommended by the agency thus established. In a few instances states have created independent scientific staffs to carry out the necessary scientific work, but this has been the exception. The standard approach to international cooperative activity has been to have the necessary scientific investigation performed by scientific entities within the member states, followed by consultations and discussions regarding the results of the research and, sometimes, by joint recommendations to the nations involved.

* * *

UNCLOS [**Basic Document 4.20**] unequivocally places the responsibility for fisheries research on coastal states within the exclusive economic zone where they have sovereign rights and upon high seas fishing states (in addition to coastal states) for fishing on the high seas. It not only provides that the coastal state has sovereign rights for the purpose of conservation of the living resources in the exclusive economic zone, which limits authority for the purpose to the coastal state, but it also specifically provides that only the coastal state has the authority to regulate and to conduct fishery research in the zone. A state fishing in the exclusive economic zone may be required to do fishery research in the zone, but Article 62(4) declares that this is subject to the authority and control of the coastal state. In short, there is no question that the obligation to conduct research in the zone rests with the coastal state, which has the duty to carry out conservation of the resources there.

The situation is analogous to that in the high seas. The responsibility for conservation measures is placed on high seas fishing states. Article 117 requires such states to take the measures necessary for conservation. Unless words have lost their meaning, this enjoins a high seas fishing state to produce or acquire the data, perhaps requiring direct research, that is necessary for conservation action.

Article 119 is similarly unequivocal in requiring the production and distribution of scientific information concerning high seas fisheries: "Available scientific information, catch and fishing effort statistics and other data relevant to the conservation of fish stocks shall be contributed and exchanged on a regular basis through competent international organizations, whether subregional, regional or global, where appropriate and with participation by all States concerned."

As the Court remarked in the Fisheries Jurisdiction Case, it is obvious that the relevant information would be in the hands of those harvesting the living resources.

* * *

The Scientific Basis for High Seas Conservation Measures

The standard of scientific evidence relating to conservation measures on the high seas is found in Article 119 of UNCLOS [**Basic Document 4.20**]: "1. In determining the allowable catch and establishing other conservation measures for the living resources of the high seas, states shall: (a) take measures which are designed, on the best scientific evidence available to the States concerned, to maintain or restore populations of harvested species at levels which can produce the maximum sustainable yield, as qualified by relevant environmental and economic factors...." This language is similar but not identical to that in Article 61(2), which spells out the authority of coastal states within their exclusive economic zone. In both instances the decision-maker is to employ the best scientific evidence available.

This formula is clearly relative, demanding only the best available evidence, not the "fullest" or "complete" or the best that can be conceived. Accordingly, this standard does not necessarily place a great or imposing burden that must be discharged before the necessary conservation measures can be taken by coastal or high seas fishing states. Taking action to conserve does not require these states to produce definitive studies or assessments of the data on particular fishery problems that allegedly involve excessive exploitation. It has long been recognized that in particular contexts information about catch statistics, population structures, characteristics of life history, population abundance, relationships to other species, interaction with the marine environment as a whole and long-term cycles, as well as other crucial data, is difficult to come by. Relevant information is sometimes scarce and may be produced by uncertain methods. It may be of variable quality and subject to divergent interpretations. As a result, an absolute standard of scientific verity would inevitably mean a non-existent regulatory system, leaving fisheries open to continued exploitation no matter how probable it was that excessive harvests were being taken.

The "best available" standard even permits the use of poor evidence to justify conservation measures concerning a specific fishery, if that evidence is the best available. This may have some special importance in connection with high seas driftnet fisheries, which may be found in remote areas where the preceding investigations may be sketchy and doubtfully representative and where the coverage of investigations may be thin in relation to the size of the area of exploitation. Even this information, as poor as it may be, might be superior in quality relative to the initial efforts by regularly constituted scientific teams brought in for hurried studies. However, the "best available" standard may trigger regulatory activity that would otherwise have awaited more systematic or complete investigation.

* * *

Obligations of High Seas Fishing States to Coastal States

UNCLOS [Basic Document 4.20] contains provisions that establish obligations for states fishing on the high seas for certain living resources that also occur in areas subject to coastal state jurisdiction and therefore are shared with the coastal state. Articles 63(2), 64 and 66 set out obligations for conservation on the high seas and would be applicable to fishing with driftnets if applicable at all. Article 63(2) requires the high seas fishing state and the coastal state to seek agreement where the stocks being fished on the high seas are also found within the exclusive economic zone. The obligation is to seek agreement on the conservation of the shared stock in the adjacent area, i.e. the high seas.

Article 64 refers to another specific instance of shared stocks: highly migratory species that are fished within the exclusive economic zone as well as outside. Under Article 64, the high seas fishing state and the coastal state in a region are to cooperate "with a view to ensuring conservation . . . of such species throughout the region". The last three words suggest that conservation measures here would be applicable on the high seas and also in areas subject to national jurisdiction, although the measures perhaps need not be identical.

Article 66 concerns anadromous species and provides, inter alia, that the state of origin has primary interest in and responsibility for such stocks. The state of origin is to establish regulatory measures for fishing within its exclusive economic zone and on the high seas beyond, including those regulating total allowable catches. The high seas fishing state and the host state of the anadromous species shall maintain consultations "with a view to achieving agreement on terms and conditions of such fishing giving due regard to the conservation requirements and the needs of the State of origin in respect of these stocks".

An obligation of the high seas fishing states under these several articles in Part V of UNCLOS differs from those previously discussed because it is owed to specific states rather than to the general community of states. Furthermore, these articles, coupled with those on high seas, provide that the high seas fishing state is not competent to decide alone on conservation measures for high seas fishing under the circumstances set out in these articles. A coastal state is a necessary associate of the high seas fishing state when it takes species subject to the coastal state's rights, duties and interests.

These various articles concerning shared stocks might be considered supplemental in nature, because if the high seas driftnet states and the coastal states cooperate and negotiate successfully, i.e. adopt and implement an effective regime of conservation measures, there is no need to resort to any other principles of international law to resolve conservation difficulties. However, if these states are unable to take measures necessary for the conservation of living resources on the high seas by acting together, coastal states might invoke these other principles in UNCLOS to justify unilateral imposition of conservation measures on harvesting stocks on the high seas. At the present stage of affairs this seems unlikely, but it is not beyond the realm of possibility. Accordingly, the following discussion examines the purport of the articles mentioned in relation to possible coastal action to achieve conservation of the high seas stocks involved.

Article 63(2): Straddling Stocks

Although Article 63(2) [of UNCLOS **[Basic Document 4.20]**] establishes that the high seas fishing state has the duty to seek agreement with the coastal state, it is Article 116 which provides that "the right ... to engage in fishing on the high seas is subject to ... (b) the rights and duties as well as the interests of coastal states provided for, *inter alia*, in Article 63, paragraph 2, and Articles 64 to 67".

Article 87 in part VII of UNCLOS declares that the freedom of fishing on the high seas is subject to several provisions, including Articles 116 to 120. Thus, Article 116 goes beyond requiring action to seek agreement to declare that the right to fish on the high seas is subject to the rights and duties of coastal states with respect to straddling stocks.

Because Article 56 establishes the sovereign rights of the coastal state over the living resources of the exclusive economic zone, Article 116 means that the right to fish on the high seas is subject to the sovereign rights, as well as the interests, of coastal states as provided in the articles of Part V of UNCLOS. Accordingly, UNCLOS might be interpreted to provide that the use of high seas driftnets upon stocks that also occur within a coastal state's exclusive economic zone is subject to the sovereign right of that coastal state.

The question that remains to be answered regarding Article 116 is how the apparently superior right of the coastal state might be implemented in the specific context of straddling stocks, the situation where high seas fishing takes stocks also occurring within the exclusive economic zone of the coastal state. Assuming the states concerned have not been able to conclude an agreement on conservation in the high seas area, one interpretation of Article 116 is that the coastal state be considered authorized to establish conservation measures applicable to the stock as a whole, including the high seas portion, and to demand compliance with those measures by high seas fishing states. Refusal to comply with genuine conservation measures by the high seas fishing states would constitute a violation of the treaty if it were in force or, otherwise, of its customary international law obligation to join in conserving the living resources of the high seas. Appropriate enforcement of that customary law obligation could take the form of disruption of the driftnet operation by disabling the nets sufficiently to accomplish the conservation purpose. There would be no boarding or arrest of a foreign fishing vessel on the high seas, therefore no interference with the driftnet fishing vessels would be involved nor any claim to exercise jurisdiction over that vessel. The sole jurisdiction claimed would be to achieve compliance with conservation measures directed at and affecting the gear being used.

In accordance with UNCLOS, objections to this enforcement effort could be resolved by submitting the dispute to a third party dispute settlement whose decision would be binding on those concerned. Under the treaty, the coastal state and the high seas fishing state would be bound to submit to such a settlement procedure. Even apart from the treaty, the coastal state taking this course of action should consider itself bound to submit to such settlement. Conservation measures should remain in effect pending a decision.

* * *

Article 64: Highly Migratory Species

Among the principal stocks that appear to be affected by driftnet fishing is albacore tuna, both in the South Pacific and in the North Pacific. It is now generally agreed that the UNCLOS [**Basic Document 4.20**] articles on these species reflect or embody existing customary international law. In the case of tuna, nearly all states in the world consider that this species falls within coastal state jurisdiction while present within the exclusive economic zone and that this is consistent with Article 64 of UNCLOS. As noted above, under Article 64 coastal states and other states fishing for tuna in a region are to cooperate to ensure conservation throughout the region, including the high seas.

The South Pacific states are clearly on record regarding their general views about the obligations of high seas fishing states concerning the harvest of tuna by driftnets. The Tarawa Declaration of 11 July 1989 by the South Pacific Forum states in relevant part:

... recalling the relevant provisions of the 1982 Convention on the Law of the Sea, and in particular Articles 63, 64, 87, 116, 117, 118 and 119;

... recognizing that the use of driftnets as presently employed in the Southern Pacific Albacore Tuna Fishery is not consistent with international legal requirements in relation to rights and obligations of high seas fisheries conservation and management and environmental principles;

... resolves for the sake of this and succeeding generations of Pacific peoples to seek the establishment of a regime for the management of albacore tuna in the South Pacific that would ban driftnet fishing from the region; such a ban might then be a first step to a comprehensive ban on such fishing.

These statements appear to mean that any driftnet fishing on the high seas for albacore tuna is inconsistent with some principle or principles of international law, but the suggested principles are not elaborated upon in this statement. The subsequently adopted Convention for the Prohibition of Fishing with Long Driftnets in the South Pacific [**Basic Document 6.8**], discussed below, also does not further identify these principles.

The states fishing for tuna on the high seas with driftnets would appear to be subject also to the "rights, duties and interests" of the coastal state within whose waters those tuna also occur. As a straddling stock, tuna may differ from coastal species in the sense that tuna may be caught on the high seas in areas much further removed from the coastal areas in which they also occur, making the relationship in stocks and fishing activities more difficult to establish. Assuming that relationship is established, however, the legal relationship of dominant right would otherwise seem the same.

The South Pacific Convention does not assert any jurisdiction by South Pacific Forum states over high seas driftnet fishing by other states on the high seas. These states obviously oppose this fishing and demand its termination, but other than the possible implications of the general language in the Tarawa Declaration they have not suggested that they have jurisdiction over the fishing itself on the high seas. The Convention is limited to an agreement by the states of the region, other states adjacent to it and states fishing in it to prohibit their nationals or registered vessels from conducting a driftnet fishery for tuna in the region defined in the treaty. It does not claim jurisdiction directly to prohibit that fishing and to enforce that prohibition. There seems to be no other evidence of such a claim to jurisdiction.

Article 65: Marine Mammals

Marine mammals under UNCLOS [**Basic Document 4.20**] are subject to coastal state sovereign rights within the exclusive economic zone in the same sense as any other living resources of the zone. However, in accordance with Article 65, the other provisions of the treaty regarding coastal state obligations to provide access to a surplus of such species do not apply to marine mammals. Although there may be mammals available for exploitation in the exclusive economic zone, because there is little or no local take allowed, there is no obligation to permit foreign harvesting. It is well-known that some marine mammals found within coastal state jurisdiction are also found on the high seas and are often taken in driftnet operations there. The analysis above regarding stocks subject to Article 116 and its provision for the superior right of the coastal state also appears to apply here. Article 120 makes Article 65 applicable to the conservation and management of marine mammals on the high seas.

[Professor Burke's discussion of UNCLOS Articles 66 and 300 are omitted.]

13. *United Nations Convention on the Law of the Sea*, Dec. 10, 1982, arts. 2, 3, 8, 55–75, 87, 89, 94, 110, 116–20 U.N. Doc. A/CONF.62/122 (and corr.) (1982), *reprinted in* 21 I.L.M. 1261 (1982) [Basic Document 4.20].

14. Agenda 21, Ch. 17 on *Protection of the Oceans, All Kinds of Seas, Including Enclosed and Semi–Enclosed Seas, and Coastal Areas and the Protection, Rational Use and Development of Their Living Resources: Report of the United Nations Conference on the Environment Development*, U.N. Doc. A/CONF.151/26 (Vol. II) (13 August, 1992) [Basic Document 1.30].

15. Geoffrey Palmer, *Towards a New Ocean World Order*, **Address to Oceans Day at the Global Forum, Rio de Janeiro, June 8, 1992.**

The issue of driftnet fishing has opened up afresh the whole question of the legal regime to be applied to the high seas.

There is little in Chapter 17 of Agenda 21 [**Basic Document 1.30**] which even addresses the problem. The high seas have been recognized as global commons, but there are no measures there to control industrial fishing. Expansion at the levels which have occurred in recent years will bring what it has brought everywhere else where there have been inadequate conservation measures—the end of the resource. I can see nothing in Chapter 17 which will save the high seas from massive environmental pressure. We have no experience which suggests that the regulation which has been found so necessary to conserve the resources within EEZs are not necessary upon the high seas. None. The proposition cannot stand serious scrutiny. What is lacking is not evidence of the need or the ability to save the resource. What is lacking is the political will of nation states.

A great deal has been said about sustainability at this conference and there is no doubt sustainability is the key. But it is not clear what sustainability means in each context in which it arises. It has to be worked through in detail on the basis of the available evidence in light of the circumstances.

Sustainability attempts to resolve the tension between development and conservation. That is why everyone is in favour of it. When it has been teased out into a legally operative set of definitions, they may not be quite so happy.

When it comes to the oceans, what does sustainability mean? I do not see as much specificity as is needed to make a real impact in Part A or C of Chapter 17: "Integrated management and sustainable development of coastal areas, including exclusive economic zones"; and "Sustainable use and conservation of marine living resources of the high seas". We can all be in favour of what is there. The question is what difference will it make? I can suggest a set of principles which would give sustainability in the fisheries area some substance:

- management and development of marine fisheries must be conducted using a multi-species approach, conserving whole eco-systems;

- all fishing techniques determined nondiscriminatory or harmful to the marine environment must be eliminated;

- all existing technologies which reduce by-catch and serve to protect the marine environment be implemented as quickly as possible and the development of others encouraged;

- all agreements involving management of fisheries incorporate self-implementing enforcement provisions which establish and fund effective monitoring and reporting programmes;

- complete international compliance with the United Nations Driftnet Resolution 46/215 **[Basic Document 6.10]** be adopted and provisions for monitoring and compliance also be adopted;

- the development of new fisheries targeted towards a greater variety of marine species particularly those occurring at lower trophic levels should be encouraged;

- the development of research and information gathering programmes related to increasing biological knowledge and determining sustainable fisheries yields;

- greater emphasis on selective fishing methods;

- greater support for smaller scale fishers around the world;

- much more emphasis on precautionary principle generally in managing the oceans in a time of uncertainty, particularly in the absence of reliable data on sustainability of fish yields;

- concern for and research into the effects of ozone depletion and increased ultra violet penetration with decreases in fish numbers and other unpredictable consequences;

- the development of requirements to use the resource caught and not waste it.

It has been decided here at Rio only two days ago, in an amendment to Agenda 21, that there will be further negotiations on questions which arise concerning sustainability of fisheries on the high seas after UNCED. The Conference will deal with:

- migratory species;
- straddling stocks; and
- means of improving cooperation on fisheries among states.

This agreement, while welcome, is too restricted.

It was made evident at the recent International Conference on Responsible Fishing at Cancun, Mexico, and the Declaration made there, that the international legal framework needs considerable development within the framework of UNCLOS [**Basic Document 4.20**]. The Santiago Principles discussed earlier by some nations and proposed by 40 nations at Prep. Comm. [Preparatory Committee] IV also deserves attention. I am of the opinion myself that these issues cannot easily be dealt with in piecemeal fashion. A new convention altogether appears to be needed to deal with conservation and use of living marine resources on the high seas. Such a convention ought to be firmly based on the ecosystem approach to assessing the impact of high seas fisheries on the marine environment.

16. Giselle Vigneron, *Compliance and International Environmental Agreements: A Case Study of the 1995 United Nations Straddling Fish Stocks Agreement*, 10 Geo. Int'l Envtl. L. Rev. 581 (1998).

A. The Need for the 1995 U.N. Agreement

In 1992, participants in the U.N. Conference on Environment and Development (Rio Summit) held in Rio de Janeiro, Brazil, expressed serious concern about the state of world fisheries, in particular the mismanagement of straddling and highly migratory fish stocks in the high seas. Participants expressed this concern by adopting Agenda 21, Chapter 17, Programme Area C, which addressed the sustainable use and conservation of marine living resources of the high seas [**Basic Document 1.30**]. In this program, the Rio Summit called for an intergovernmental conference under U.N. auspices as soon as possible, in order to promote effective implementation of the provisions of the U.N. Convention on the Law of the Sea on straddling fish stocks and highly migratory fish stocks. Thus, the issue of conservation and management of those fish stocks was recognized as an urgent matter to be dealt with through international cooperation. The same year, the U.N. General Assembly decided that in 1993 it would convene an intergovernmental conference on straddling fish stocks and highly migratory fish stocks. The U.N. Conference was able to adopt the final version of the 1995 U.N. Agreement at its last session on August 4, 1995 [**Basic Document 6.14**].

The 1995 U.N. Agreement proved necessary for world fisheries. The UNCLOS failed to provide specific measures by which to conserve world fisheries. As a result, the global stock of straddling and highly migratory fish continued to decline precipitously and finally spurred coastal states and distant-water-fishing states to settle their longstanding differences. For these reasons, the international community cooperated with a sense of urgency.

1.   The Insufficient Legal Framework of the UNCLOS

As indicated in its title, the 1995 U.N. Agreement **[Basic Document 6.14]** intends to implement UNCLOS provisions, **[Basic Document 4.20]** which include only general obligations relating to the conservation and management of the living resources of coastal states' exclusive economic zones (EEZs) and of the high seas. For areas under national jurisdiction, the UNCLOS provisions are weak on states' obligations to cooperate for the conservation of straddling and highly migratory fish stocks. The language used is very general and does not reflect stringent obligations. For instance, the UNCLOS advises that states fishing for straddling fish stocks should "seek . . . to agree upon the measures" necessary for their conservation, whereas states fishing for highly migratory fish stocks must only "cooperate . . . with a view to ensuring conservation" of those species.

Similarly, in the area of high seas fishing, the UNCLOS only provides for a general obligation to cooperate for the conservation and management of living resources and does not offer any guidance on how to fulfill these obligations. Due to its ambitious scope, the UNCLOS was not intended to contain detailed provisions on the specific topic of fishing resources conservation and management. Thus an implementing agreement was needed to bolster the few general provisions in the UNCLOS. The 1995 U.N. Agreement provided this needed supplemental structure.

The legal structure of the UNCLOS is only one reason that states promptly adopted the 1995 U.N. Agreement. The sense of necessity also arose out of nations' realization that most straddling and highly migratory fish stocks were threatened by overexploitation.

2.   Worldwide Stock Depletion

In 1994, the U.N. Food and Agriculture Organization (FAO) published a report on the state of highly migratory and straddling fish stocks and confirmed the trend of stock depletion worldwide. The FAO established that total catches of straddling fish stocks in the 200–mile EEZ and the high seas were declining since 1989, when they reached a peak of 13.7 million tons. Stock depletion and overfishing also struck highly migratory fish stocks. The FAO reported that out of twenty existing stocks of principal market tuna species, fourteen were depleted. For example, the Southern Bluefin tuna found in the Atlantic, Indian and Pacific Oceans appears to have been overexploited in the Indian, Pacific and South Atlantic Oceans: a continuous decline of its biomass has occurred from 1979 to at least the early 1990s. The Northern Bluefin tuna was also reported to be overfished in the Western Atlantic, with its biomass only 10%–23% of its 1970 level.

This trend of fish stock depletion, mainly caused by unregulated high seas fishing practices, created some tensions between coastal states and distant water fishing nations (DWFNs). Those states sought to resolve their conflicts through the 1995 U.N. Agreement.

3.   Tensions Between Coastal States and DWFNs

Tensions between coastal states and DWFNs; are best understood in light of the behavior of straddling fish stocks. Straddling fish stocks swim into the high seas out of a coastal state's EEZ, or out of the high seas into areas of national jurisdiction. Because of the straddling nature of those stocks, their mismanagement on the high seas will have an impact on fisheries in the EEZs of coastal states. Thus, depletion of those fish stocks on the high seas can only adversely affect the abundance level of those stocks fished in EEZs and render ineffective national conservation and management efforts imposed by coastal states within their zone of national jurisdiction. Such lack of cooperation from DWFNs explains the tensions between them and coastal states.

One of the most famous cases of conflict between coastal states and DWFNs involved Canada and the European Union (EU) on the Newfoundland Grand Banks in Canada. As a member of Northwest Atlantic Fisheries Organization (NAFO) and a coastal state with direct interests in the Northwest Atlantic Fishery, Canada wanted to ensure compliance with NAFO's measures, particularly by the EU, a distant water fishing party to NAFO. To ensure that the EU would respect NAFO's quotas, Canada secured a diplomatic agreement with the EU in December of 1992. However, the unregulated high seas fishing was not contained and Canadian fishing industries pressured their government for stronger enforcement beyond the 200–mile limit to protect the fish stocks. This claim for an extension of governmental authority beyond 200 nautical miles and similar claims by Colombia, Peru, Mexico, Argentina, and Chile threatened the freedom of high seas fishing and the economic interest of DWFNs.

Such tensions on both sides needed to be resolved. For this reason, negotiations of the 1995 U.N. Agreement were welcomed by coastal states and DWFNs. Both recognized the urgent need to address the issues of conservation and management of high seas living resources.

B. Key Provisions of the 1995 U.N. Agreement

The 1995 U.N. Agreement **[Basic Document 6.14]** is the first multilateral agreement seeking to improve the conservation and management of straddling and highly migratory fish stocks on a global scale and in a comprehensive manner. If properly implemented by its various parties, this agreement would revolutionize the management and conservation of world straddling and highly migratory fish stocks.

* * *

2. The Role of Regional Fisheries Organizations

While the Agreement lays down the basic legal framework and general standards, it calls for regional fisheries organizations to adopt the detailed conservation and management measures (such as allocations of allowable catches or levels of fishing efforts). By giving members of regional fisheries organizations strong enforcement powers, recognized as binding by all parties to the agreement, the 1995 U.N. Agreement thus empowers regional organizations with a prominent role.

a. The Duty to Cooperate With Regional Organizations

To ensure effective conservation and management of the straddling and highly migratory fish stocks, all States party to the 1995 U.N. Agreement must pursue cooperation "either directly or through appropriate ... regional fisheries management organizations" This obligation is confirmed in Article

8–3, under which states are to implement this duty by either becoming a member of a regional organization or by agreeing to apply the conservation and management measures established by such an organization. To enforce Article 8–3, Article 8–4 restricts access to the fishery resources under the regulation of regional organizations to those states which are members of such an organization or which apply its conservation measures. Article 8–5 takes the duty to "pursue cooperation" even further. Where no regional organization exists, relevant coastal states and states fishing on the high seas for straddling and highly migratory fish stocks must establish such an organization and participate in its work.

b.   The Strong Enforcement Powers of Members of Regional Organizations

The 1995 U.N. Agreement grants states the unprecedented authority to board foreign ships. Under customary law and the UNCLOS, the "flag state principle" subjects a fishing vessel on the high seas to the exclusive jurisdiction of the state under whose flag it is registered. Thus, only representatives of a vessel's flag state are empowered to board and inspect it. However, the UNCLOS allows some exceptions to this principle. In particular, Article 21 of the 1995 U.N. Agreement represents a far-reaching exception to the flag state principle. Under this enforcement mechanism, a state member of a regional organization is allowed to board and inspect the vessel of any other state, whether or not a member of such an organization, as long as this vessel is fishing in any high seas area covered by that organization. The inspecting state does not need to receive the consent of the flag state. However, it may board and inspect the vessel only for the purpose of pursuing compliance with regional conservation and management measures. The inspecting state may investigate further and eventually bring the vessel to the nearest port only if there are "clear grounds for believing that a vessel has committed a serious violation."

* * *

c.   Increased Duties of Flag States

The 1995 U.N. Agreement has fleshed out the existing rules of the UNCLOS concerning duties of flag states towards their vessels. While the UNCLOS does not provide to flag states provisions regarding the fishing conduct of its vessels, the Agreement does contain such provisions. Such provisions include a flag state's obligation to control its fishing vessels on the high seas by means of fishing licenses, authorizations, or permits in accordance with any regionally or globally agreed-upon procedures. A flag state must establish a national record of authorized fishing vessels and mark fishing vessels and fishing gear for identification in accordance with internationally recognizable vessel and gear marking systems. Furthermore, a flag state must record and report in a timely manner vessel positions, catch of target and non-target species, and other relevant fisheries data. A flag state must also verify the catch of target and non-target species by establishing observer programs, inspection schemes, and vessel monitoring systems such as satellite transmitter systems. Finally, one of the most remarkable duties of a flag state lies in its obligation to ensure compliance of its fishing vessels with subregional, regional, or global conservation and management measures relating to straddling and highly migratory fish stocks.

17. *Agreement for the Implementation of the Provisions of the United Nations Law of the Sea of 10 December 1982 Relating to the Conservation and Management of Straddling Fish Stocks and Highly Migratory Fish Stocks*, adopted 4 August 1995, U.N.Doc. A/CONF. 164/37 (1995), *reprinted in* 34 I.L.M. 1542 (1995), arts. 5, 6, 8, 17, 18(1)-(2), 19(1), 20(1), 20(6), 20(7), 33(2) [Basic Document 6.14].

18. **Food and Agriculture Organization,** *Agreement to Promote Compliance with International Conservation and Management Measures by Fishing Vessels on the High Seas*, Nov. 24, 1993, *reprinted in* 33 I.L.M. 968 (1994), arts. II(1), III(1)(a), VI(9), VII, VIII(2) [Basic Document 6.13].

19. **Food and Agriculture Organization,** *Code of Conduct for Responsible Fisheries*, adopted by FAO Conference on 31 October 1995, arts. 6.1, 6.2, 6.6, 6.11, 6.12, 6.14, 7.1, 7.2, 7.5, 7.6, 8.1, 8.2, 8.5, 11.2 [Basic Document 6.15].

Discussion Notes/Questions

1. Article 2 of the 1995 Fish Stocks Agreement (Reading 17) recites that the objective of the Agreement is "effective implementation of the relevant provisions" of UNCLOS. Does this mean that the powers granted to coastal states by the Agreement are powers that those states would have in any event under a proper reading of UNCLOS? Do the FAO documents (Readings 18 and 19) suggest expanded coastal state powers? Does the coastal state's right to protect EEZ resources extend to the high seas?

2. The South Pacific region is largely water, with about 10,000 small islands scattered throughout. Most of the inhabited islands have small land areas and small populations. The establishment of 200–mile zones in the South Pacific by twenty-two self-governing South Pacific nations and island territories was a significant development. It created a set of adjoining EEZs and fishery zones that bring approximately 40% of what was open South Pacific ocean under the control of the island nations. The island states have capitalized on this fact, by negotiating a number of regional agreements concerned with the use of ocean resources in the South Pacific. These regional arrangements include treaties on fisheries, the environment and natural resources, and nuclear activities. The new regional ocean regime means that the South Pacific island nations set the rules in a way that ensures that the benefits of the use of ocean resources increasingly remain in the region. It also means that large parts of the region are no longer available as a dumping ground for waste and the testing of nuclear weapons by developed countries.

What might be the consequence if other ocean regions were to follow this lead? It might be copied, for example, in other ocean areas where distant water fishing fleets seek access to EEZs under the control of developing nations. What might the implications be for the law of the sea? Does it pose a threat to free navigation and other high seas freedoms in the world's oceans? For a discussion of the South Pacific Ocean regime and some of the wider questions it raises, *see* Biliana Cicin–Sain, *The Emergence of a Regional Ocean Regime in the South Pacific*, 16 Ecology L. Q. 171 (1989).

3. What if the present problem were situated elsewhere in the world, e.g., the North Pacific, the Caribbean, or the Indian Ocean? Would it make any difference to many of the arguments made in the present South Pacific problem?

There is a longer history of regulation of high seas driftnet fishing in the North Pacific. However, as intimated in the above readings, the South Pacific moved more quickly on the issue than did the North Pacific. For an excellent analysis by one who was involved in the driftnet fishing issue relative to the North Pacific, *see* Judith Swan, International Regulation of Driftnet Fishing Activities (Oceans Institute of Canada 1991).

Banning driftnet fishing by *developed* countries in the Mediterranean Sea and the northeast Atlantic proved to be one of the harder tasks facing international conservation groups. Until the summer of 1998, the EU allowed the use of driftnets up to 2.5 kilometres long, a length restriction that was widely reported to be ignored by EU fishing vessels in the region. Finally, under intense international pressure, the EU Council agreed to ban all driftnet fishing in its waters or by its vessels by January 1, 2002.

4. With regard to the general problem of preventing overfishing on the high seas or in EEZs, there are several intergovernmental fisheries management organizations and arrangements, many of them well-established, which are currently considering how to implement the conservation provisions of UNCLOS and the 1995 Fish Stocks Agreement [**Basic Document 6.14**]. These organizations include the Inter–American Tropical Tuna Commission, the Northwest Atlantic Fisheries Organization, the Permanent South Pacific Commission, the South Pacific Forum Fisheries Agency, the Asia–Pacific Fisheries Commission, and others. *See* Report of the Secretary–General to the 52nd Session of the United Nations General Assembly, *Oceans and the Law of the Sea: Agreement for the Implementation of the Provisions of UNCLOS Relating to the Conservation and Management of Straddling Fish Stocks and Highly Migratory Fish Stocks*, U.N. Doc. A/52/555, 31 October 1997.

5. Korea, Japan, and Taiwan, major driftnetting countries, had agreed to stop the practice as of this writing, and accordingly large-scale pelagic driftnetting may be a thing of the past. However, illegal use of driftnets will continue under any ban. The reality is that some individuals and larger fishing interests will take no notice of a ban. For example, fishery associations in some countries have said that they will not comply with the U.N. moratorium.

What kind of strategy might the U.N. need to formulate to deal with illegal driftnetting? Will a monitoring program be required? If so, what kind? Will multinational jurisdiction and sanctions be required? What nations have an interest in enforcing the ban? In particular, how do the two FAO documents cited in the Readings address the enforcement problem? How does the 1995 Fish Stocks Agreement deal with the issue?

Even if all nations cooperate in combatting driftnetting, pirate driftnetting is likely to continue. The DriftNetwork, an alliance of conservation and marine scientific organizations, was formed to collect information on unlawful driftnetting and pass it along to government authorities for use in combatting the practice.

6. World leaders have referred to large-scale driftnet fishing as "piracy." Burke describes such claims as empty rhetoric with "no relevance" to a considered legal analysis of this problem. *See* Burke, *supra* note d, at 270. Is he correct? Professor Ian Brownlie, in Principles of Public International Law 239 (4th ed. 1990), observes that a definition of piracy must include any act of depredation "committed for private ends." Article 15 of the 1958 Convention on the High Seas [**Basic Document 4.2**] and Article 101(a)(ii) of UNCLOS [**Basic Document 4.20**] define piracy as, *inter alia*, "any act of depredation, committed for private ends by the crew . . . of a private ship . . . and directed . . . against . . . property in

a place outside the jurisdiction of any State." Might driftnetting be properly classified as piracy? If so, it then would be subject to "universal jurisdiction." What does this mean?

7. Might trade sanctions be used to stop driftnetting in a driftnet-free zone or elsewhere in the world? The U.S. Marine Mammal Protection Act, 16 U.S.C.A. § 1371 (1988) requires a ban on the importation of commercial fish, or products from fish, which have been caught with commercial fishing technology that results in the incidental kill or serious injury of ocean mammals in excess of U.S. standards. *See also* Driftnet Act Amendments of 1990, Pub. L. 101–627, Title I, § 107(a), Nov. 28, 1990, 104 Stat. 4441, 16 USCA § 1826 (1988). These measures were further strengthened by the High Seas Driftnet Fisheries Enforcement Act of 1992, Pub. L. 102–582, Nov. 1992, 106 Stat. 4900, 16 U.S.C.A. §§ 1362, 1371, 1826(a) (1993). Among other things this legislation provides for denial of access to United States ports by driftnet vessels; fish caught by the method are banned from importation into the United States. There is an expanded power to extend the embargo to non-fish products. The legislation explicitly relies upon the United Nations resolutions on driftnetting.

In 1991, a GATT (now World Trade Organization) dispute settlement panel determined that a U.S. embargo on Mexican tuna imports under the Marine Mammal Protection Act was inconsistent with U.S. GATT obligations [**Basic Document 7.1**]. *See United States/Mexico Tuna Imports Dispute*, 30 I.L.M. 1594 (1991). The United States imposed a trade embargo on tuna caught by the Mexican tuna fishing fleet in an area beyond the EEZ of the United States. The ban was imposed because the fishing technique being used (not driftnetting) resulted in very high "by-catches" of certain species of dolphin. In 1998, a WTO panel ruled that a similar U.S. ban on shrimp imports, designed to induce fishing nations to take steps to protect endangered sea turtles, was also a violation of GATT. *See* World Trade Organization, Report of the Panel, *United States—Import Prohibition of Certain Shrimp and Shrimp Products*, WT/DS58/R (15 May 1998). These rulings could be read as endorsing a general principle that countries may not use trade sanctions to protect resources beyond their territorial limits.

What does this mean for environmental laws and treaties? Environmental treaties to protect shared global resources rely on trade sanctions to punish violators. Trade sanctions are an effective way to discourage free-riders, countries that would like to enjoy a treaty's benefits without conforming to its requirements. For example, the U.S. threat of a trade embargo on Taiwan's seafood products was a powerful incentive for Taiwan to comply with the U.N. moratorium on driftnetting. Trade sanctions might also be employed in laws to protect the oceans, biological diversity, fisheries, whales, migrating birds and endangered species. They are also used in national laws implementing international treaties that employ trade measures, like the Montreal Protocol on Substances which Deplete the Ozone Layer [**Basic Document 3.18**] and the Convention on International Trade in Endangered Species of Wild Fauna and Flora [**Basic Document 6.5**].

Should international trade agreements trump national environmental laws which use trade measures to achieve conservation goals?

If you favor the use of trade sanctions in this way, consider what international *environmental* law has to say on the subject. Does not the Rio Declaration clearly disfavor, as a matter of international *environmental* law, unilateral trade sanctions of the sort imposed by the U.S. in the tuna and shrimp cases? *See* Rio Declaration, Principle 12 [**Basic Document 1.29**]. *See* Marc Pallemaerts, *Inter-*

national Environmental Law in the Age of Sustainable Development: A Critical Assessment of the UNCED Process, 16 J.L. & Comm. 623 (1996).

For further discussion pertinent to GATT and the environment, *see* Problem 11–1 ("The Environment and GATT Collide in Albion") in Chapter 11, *infra*.

8.   Suppose a driftnet contains, as its "by-catch," wildlife species that are the subject of international wildlife conventions protection. The known "by-catch" of the North Pacific driftnet fisheries includes, for example, three species of turtles listed in the Convention on International Trade in Endangered Species of Wild Fauna and Flora Appendix I and 15 species of cetaceans listed in Appendix II **[Basic Document 6.5]**. What if the "by-catch" included a whale and the flag state was a party to the International Whaling Convention **[Basic Document 6.2]** which imposes a moratorium on catching whales for other than scientific purposes? What if the present problem had been sited in an area subject to the 1979 Berne Convention on the Conservation of European Wildlife and Natural Habitats [E.T.S. 104]? The Berne Convention lists the strictly protected species and they include a large number of cetaceans and seabirds. Parties to the Convention must prohibit the use of all indiscriminate means of killing and the use of all means capable of causing serious disturbance to populations of the species. The Convention lists prohibited killing methods, including nets used on a large-scale or in a non-selective manner.

Other applicable conventions might be the 1979 Bonn Convention on the Protection of Migratory Species of Wild Animals (19 I.L.M. 15 (1979)) **[Basic Document 6.7]** and the 1957 Fur Seal Convention (314 U.N.T.S. 105). The purpose of the Bonn Convention is to protect populations of migratory wild animals that regularly traverse national boundaries. Article 5(a) requires state parties to prohibit flag vessels operating outside national jurisdiction from the taking of listed species. The Fur Seal Convention prohibits the taking of fur seals in the North Pacific Ocean. Japan, the former Soviet Union, Canada and the United States are parties.

9.   The decision by the main driftnetting countries—Korea, Japan, and Taiwan—to stop driftnetting was heavily influenced by political and trade considerations highlighted, in part, by nongovernmental organizations (NGOs) that played a major part in mobilizing public opinion. The NGOs did this by undertaking grass roots campaigning, confrontations (such as sending the *Rainbow Warrior II* to the South Pacific in the 1989–90 fishing season), and political lobbying. "[The] driftnet fishing issue," writes Judith Swan, Discussion Note/Question 3, at 13, "was a natural for the NGOs to espouse. It has the recipe for a prominent public relations, and fundraising campaign—high seas adventure, marine mammals, seabirds, threats to navigation, potentially wasteful drop-out rates and environmental degradation." What are the advantages and disadvantages of NGO involvement in this realm? What effect might NGOs have on other international environmental issues? Should they have a role in the making of international law? Should they have legal status to bring violations of international law before the International Court of Justice? Why? Why not?

In this connection, consider the complaint of Burke, et al., in Reading 5, that international action against driftnetting was taken without proper scientific study and on the basis of inaccurate perceptions of the problem created, in part, by NGOs. Earthtrust, an NGO which played a prominent role in promoting the driftnet ban, describes its activities on its website. *See Earthtrust and Driftnets: A Capsule History,* <www.earthtrust.org> accessed August 28, 1998. Among other accomplishments noted on the website is Earthtrust's role in stopping a planned

U.S. driftnet research cruise. Earthtrust apparently argued that using driftnets for research purposes would violate the U.S. driftnet ban and send an inappropriate message that "scientific driftnetting is defendable."

10.   The approach to driftnetting in the South Pacific shows that sometimes it is possible to resolve an international environmental issue quite quickly. What are the techniques for marshalling support for this sort of campaign? What did the Langkawi Declaration by the Commonwealth Heads of Government (quoted in Reading 2, at note 1) add to the matter? Do soft law solutions have a place in dealing with environmental issues?

11.   Driftnet fishing raises ethical issues concerning animal rights. It brings up the question of the appropriate relationship between human activity and nature. What parallels do you *see* with the problems revealed in this chapter and those of land based species which are threatened by people—for example, elephants or rhinoceroses?

12.   *Bibliographical Note.* For further discussion concerning the principal themes addressed in this problem, consult the following additional specialized materials:

(a) *Specialized Books/Monographs.* W. T. Burke, The New International Law of Fisheries: UNCLOS 1982 and Beyond (1994); W. Burke, M. Freeberg and E. Miles, The United Nations Resolutions on Driftnet Fishing: An Unsustainable Precedent for High Seas and Coastal Fisheries (1993); D. Bowett, The Law of the Sea (1979); Center for Environmental Education, Plastics in the Ocean: More Than A Litter Problem (1987); D. Johnston, The International Law of Fisheries (1965); A. Koers, International Regulation of Marine Fisheries (1973); Marine Policy and the Coastal Community (D. Johnston ed. 1976); M. McDougal & W. Burke, The Public Order of the Oceans (1962); G. Palmer, Environmental Politics (1990); F. Orrego Vicuna, The Exclusive Economic Zone (1989).

(b) *Specialized Reports.* FAO, FAO Legislative Study 47: The Regulation of Driftnet Fishing on the High Seas—Legal Issues (1991); FAO, Report of the Expert Consultation on Large–Scale Pelagic Driftnet Fishery, UN Doc. No. FIPL/R434 (Fisheries Rep. No. 434) (1991); Panel, *Emerging Legal Regimes in the Pacific: a Panel,* 82 Am. Soc. Int'l L. Proc. 351 (1988); C. Stewart, Report on the Laws Relating to Gillnet and Driftnet Fishing in Papua New Guinea (1990); UN COFI, Large–Scale Pelagic Driftnet Fishery, UN Doc. No. C89/INF./17 (Nov. 1989); *Large Scale Pelagic Driftnet Fishing and its Impact on the Living Marine Resources of the World's Oceans and Seas: Report of the Secretary General,* U.N. GAOR, 45th Sess., Agenda Item 79, U.N. Doc. A/45/663 (1990).

(c) *Specialized Articles/Book Chapters.* D. K. Anton, *Law for the Sea's Biological Diversity,* 36 Colum. J. Transnat'l L. 341 (1997); D. S. Aradia, *Does the Emperor Have No Clothes? Enforcement of International Laws Protecting the Marine Environment,* 19 Mich. J. Int'l L. 497 (1998); H. L. Brown, *The United Nations Conference on Straddling Fish Stocks and Highly Migratory Fish Stocks: An Analysis of International Environmental Law and the Conference's Final Agreement,* 21 Vt. L. Rev. 547 (1996); K. R. Bryan, Note, *Swimming Upstream: Trying to enforce the 1992 North Pacific Salmon Treaty,* 28 Cornell Int'l L.J. 241 (1995); W. T. Burke, *Implications for Fisheries Management of U.S. Acceptance of the 1982 Convention of the Law of the Sea,* 89 Am. J. Int'l L. 792 (1995); W. Burke, *Regulation of Driftnet Fishing on the High Seas and the New International Law of the Sea,* 3 Georgetown Int'l Envtl. L. Rev. 265 (1990); C. C. Carr, *Recent Developments in Compliance and Enforcement for International Fisheries,* 24 Ecology L.Q. 847 (1997); D. Cass, *The Quiet Revolution: The Development of the*

Exclusive Economic Zone and Implications for Foreign Fishing Access in the Pacific, 16 Melbourne U. L. Rev. 83 (1987); A. C. de Fontaubert et al., *Biodiversity in the Seas: Implementing the Convention on Biological Diversity in Marine and Coastal Habitats*, 10 Geo. Int'l Envtl. L. Rev. 753 (1998); L. Guruswamy, *The Promise of the United Nations Convention on the Law of the Sea (UNCLOS): Justice in Trade and Environment Disputes*, 25 Ecology L.Q. 189 (1998); G. J. Hewison, *High Seas Driftnet Fishing in the South Pacific and the Law of the Sea*, 5 Geo. Int'l Envtl. L. Rev. 313 (1993); G. J. Hewison, *The Convention for the Prohibition of Fishing With Long Driftnets in the South Pacific*, 25 Case W. Res. J. Int'l L. 449 (1993); G. J. Hewison, *The Legally Binding Nature of the Moratorium on Large–Scale High Seas Driftnet Fishing*, 25 J. Mar. L. & Com. 557 (1994); K. Holland, *Exploitation on Porpoise: the Use of Purse Seine Nets by Commercial Tuna Fishermen in the Eastern Tropical Pacific Ocean*, 17 Syracuse J. Int'l L. & Comm. 267 (1991); M. Islam, *The Proposed "Driftnet–Free Zone" in the South Pacific and the Law of the Sea Convention*, 40 I.C.L.Q. 184 (1991); J. K. Jenkins, Comment, *International Regulation of Driftnet Fishing: The Role of Environmental Activism and Leverage Diplomacy*, 4 Ind. Int'l & Comp. L. Rev. 197 (1993); D. Johnston, *The Driftnetting Problem in the Pacific Ocean: Legal Considerations and Diplomatic Options*, 21 Ocean Dev. & Int'l L. 5 (1990); C. Kelly, *Law of the Sea: The Jurisdictional Dispute Over Highly Migratory Species of Tuna*, 26 Colum. J. Transnat'l L. 475 (1988); L. A. Kimball, *Whither International Institutional Arrangements to Support Ocean Law?*, 36 Colum. J. Transnat'l L. 307 (1997); R. J. McClaughlin, *UNCLOS and the Demise of the United States' Use of Trade Sanctions to Protect Dolphins, Sea Turtles, Whales, and Other International Marine Living Resources*, 21 Ecology L.Q. 1 (1994); C. Mizukami, *Management of Highly Migratory Species and Fisheries Relations Between Japan and South Pacific States*, 24 U. Brit. Colum. L. Rev. 127 (1990); C. Park, *The U.S.-Korean Fishing Rights Dispute in the North Pacific Ocean*, 16 Ecology L. Q. 259 (1989); M.J. Picard, *The International Law of Fisheries and Small Developing States: A Call for the Recognition of Regional Hegemony*, 31 Tex. Int'l L. J. 317 (1996); H. Scheiber, *Origins of the Abstention Doctrine in Ocean Law: Japanese–U.S. Relations and the Pacific Fisheries, 1937–1958*, 16 Ecology L. Q. 23 (1989); S. Sugarman, *The Failure to Achieve a High Seas Driftnet Ban*, 3 Int'l Legal Persp. 5 (1992); J. Swan, *International Regulation of Driftnet Fishing Activities, in* Growing Demand on a Shrinking Heritage: Managing Resource–Use Conflicts 216 (M. Ross & J. Saunders eds. 1992); A. Szkely, *Yellow-fin Tuna: A Transboundary Resource of the Eastern Pacific*, 29 Nat. Resources J. 1051 (1989); B. Tsamenyi, *The Treaty on Fisheries Between the Governments of Certain Pacific Island States and the Government of the United States of America: The Final Chapter in United States Tuna Policy*, 15 Brooklyn J. Int'l L. 183 (1989); Giselle Vigneron, *Compliance and International Environmental Agreements: A Case Study of the 1995 United Nations Straddling Fish Stocks Agreement*, 10 Geo. Int'l Envtl. L. Rev. 581 (1998); D. Vice, *Implementation of Biodiversity Treaties: Monitoring, Fact–Finding, and Dispute Resolution*, 29 N.Y.U. J. Int'l L. & Pol. 577 (1997).

(d) *Useful internet sites.* Earthtrust: <http://www.earthtrust.org>; Food and Agricultural Organization: <www.fao.org>; United Nations Law of the Sea: <www.un.org/Depts/los/>; Greenpeace: <www.greenpeace.org>.

Problem 10–2

Poaching Elephants in Usambara

SECTION 1. FACTS

Located in central East Africa, the small nation of Bawanda was once a haven for wildlife, its wide savannahs home to immense herds of elephant, gazelle, and numerous other species. However, twelve years of violent civil war and a long period of drought devastated the countryside. The once abundant herds slowly vanished and were displaced by tens of thousands of homeless human refugees, expanding deserts, and guerrilla warfare. Hardest hit were the elephants—the entire population decimated by hunting, both for food, which the refugees desperately needed, and for ivory, which could be sold on the black market for a small fortune by soldiers and refugees alike. Indeed the proceeds of the ivory trade were an important factor in the purchase of arms by the combatants.

Despite the recent arrival of peace and the establishment of a new coalition government in Bawanda, however, little attention has been given to Bawanda's wildlife or to its natural resource base in the wake of the war, although the government of Bawanda did enter into and ratify a number of relevant international instruments. Almost all of Bawanda's time has been spent trying to feed and relocate its suffering population, and, as a result, a black market in ivory has been thriving, which, in turn, has driven poachers in Bawanda into neighboring Usambara in search of elephant tusks.

Unlike its less fortunate neighbor to the north, the government of Usambara long ago set aside a 60,000 square kilometers park to protect its indigenous wildlife, including elephants. There, the once endangered elephant population has risen from 10,000 to 40,000 over the past fifteen years, and this turn of events has resulted in a booming tourism industry that provides substantial revenue to the Usambara government and supports a generally stable economy. Indeed, Usambara elephants have increased in numbers to such a degree that Usambara recently has begun to allow hunters, at a very high cost and on government-sponsored safaris, actually to kill selected animals so as to maintain an appropriate ecological balance in its elephant population.

The poachers coming from Bawanda, it now appears, have begun to have a serious negative impact on Usambara's ecologically driven tourism industry. Despite many appropriately addressed formal complaints by Usambara to Bawanda, however, no steps have been taken to remedy the poaching problem, either through enforcement action or legislation. The Government of Bawanda has explained politely that it simply does not have the resources necessary to provide the protection Usambara requests. Additionally, it claims that Usambara is partially to blame for the problem, as its official safaris have the effect of providing an incentive to poach in its park.

This dispute reached a climax when, in May of last year, Usambaran troops surprised and pursued a band of poachers who had been in the midst of butchering elephants three and one half kilometers into Usambaran territory. When they were surprised by the Usambaran troops, the poachers took off in their vehicles and made for the Bawandaan border. The troops pursued the poachers and, with the help of helicopters, were eventually able to apprehend them. However, the arrest of the poachers took place two kilometers into Bawandaan territory. Moreover, before entering Bawandaan territory to arrest the poachers, the Usambaran troops had sought and obtained permission to do so from the highest levels of the Usambaran government. Following the poachers' surrender, the Usambaran forces seized eleven elephant tusks (thought to be worth about $1 million), took the poachers into custody, transported them back to detention in Usambara, and eventually tried, convicted, and imprisoned each of them for breach of Usambara's laws protecting elephants.

All the poachers in question, as it turned out, were Bawandaan nationals, and they had launched their raid from Bawandaan territory. Indeed, there is evidence to suggest that such was their usual mode of operation. Nevertheless, Bawanda demanded their immediate return and the return of the tusks to its custody; and when Usambara refused, a war of increasingly hostile words ensued. Usambara claims that it had every right to enter Bawandaan territory because Bawanda's lack of action on the issue had created an ongoing violation of international law which Usambara took steps to remedy. Bawanda denies any legal responsibility to act, and, in turn, claims that Usambara's safari policy is itself a violation of international law. Distressed by these developments, the Director–General of the United Nations Environment Programme (UNEP) intervened, and has persuaded both governments that the appropriate way to deal with the dispute is to submit it to her mediation since UNEP was headquartered in Africa and since both disputants were African nations. Both countries agreed and accepted that her mediation should be guided by the relevant doctrines, principles, and rules of international law.

Both countries are signatories to the 1972 Stockholm Declaration on the Human Environment, the 1982 World Charter for Nature, the 1992 Rio Declaration on Environment and Development, and Agenda 21 of the 1992 United Nations Conference on Environment and Development. Also, both have signed and ratified the 1973 Convention on International Trade in Endangered Species of Wild Fauna and Flora (CITES) and the 1968 African Convention on the Conservation of Nature and Natural Resources. Additionally, both have signed, although not yet ratified, the 1992 Convention on Biological Diversity.

You are head of UNEP's Legal Division and you are asked by UNEP's Director–General to prepare a comprehensive outline of the legal issues present in this dispute. She specifically asks for an evaluation of each side's arguments in respect of each issue and the likely result were the dispute to be submitted to the Permanent Court of Arbitration at The Hague as set out in Article XVIII of the 1973 CITES Convention.

SECTION 2. QUESTIONS PRESENTED

1. To what extent, if any, is Bawanda in breach of its obligations under international law and, assuming such breach, to what extent, if any, can Usambara claim reparation therefor?

2. Was Usambara entitled under international law to pursue the poachers across its border into Bawanda, to arrest them, and to take them back to Usambara for trial and punishment?

SECTION 3. ASSIGNMENTS

A. Reading Assignment

Study the Readings presented in Section 4, *infra*, and the Discussion Notes/Questions that follow. Also, to the extent possible, consult the accompanying bibliographical references.

B. Recommended Writing Assignment

Prepare a comprehensive, logically sequenced, and *argumentative* brief in the form of an outline of the primary and subsidiary *legal* issues you see requiring clarification for the Director–General of the United Nations Environment Programme. Also, from the perspective of an independent objective judge, indicate which side ought to prevail on each issue and why. Retain a copy of your issue-outline/brief for class discussion.

C. Recommended Oral Assignment

Assume you are legal counsel for Bawanda or Usambara (as designated by your instructor); then, relying upon the Readings (and your issue-outline if prepared), present a 15–20 minute oral argument of your government's likely positions before the Director–General of UNEP.

D. Recommended Reflective Assignment

Consider (and recommend) alternative norms, institutions, and/or procedures that you believe might do better than existing world order arrangements to contend with situations of the kind posed by this problem. In so doing, but without insisting upon *immediate* feasibility, identify the particular transition steps that would be needed to make your alternatives a reality.

SECTION 4. READINGS

1. John B. Heppes & Eric J. McFadden, *The Convention on International Trade In Endangered Species of Wild Fauna and Flora: Improving the Prospects for Preserving Our Biological Heritage*, 5 Boston U. Int'l L.J. 229, 229–32 (1987).

The Convention on International Trade in Endangered Species of Wild

Fauna and Flora (CITES)[a] has been characterized as "perhaps the most successful of all international treaties concerned with the conservation of wildlife." As of 1987, ninety-six nations had become parties to the agreement, "making it the world's most widely accepted international treaty." While it is undeniable that CITES has exerted a salutary influence on international wildlife trade, there is a compelling need to strengthen further the treaty's framework. Policymakers must confront the reality that illegal international trade in endangered species has continued to boom despite the existence of the CITES framework.

Illegal trafficking in wildlife species and products has been one of the primary contributing factors to the precipitous decline of wildlife species in recent years. The U.S. Department of Interior has estimated that as many as 300 species now face extinction each decade. An even less sanguine assessment estimates that the current rate of extinction may be as high as several species per day. Hundreds of mammal, reptile, and bird species are in imminent danger of extinction, as well as 20,000–25,000 species of plants. Many experts calculate that species extinction is now occurring at a greater rate than at any time since the last great extinction cycle at the end of the Pleistocene era more than 65 million years ago, when dinosaurs gradually disappeared.

Species diminution has several adverse consequences. First, utilitarian benefits that can be derived from flora and fauna species, both currently known and potentially discoverable, are lost irretrievably when a species is rendered extinct by over-exploitation. If preserved, rare species of animals and plants ultimately may help to alleviate the world's food crisis. For example, scientists in recent years discovered that Zea diploperennis, a rare Mexican tall grass, may be crossed with corn through techniques of genetic engineering to create a perennial, virus resistant hybrid which could substantially increase the world's food supply in the future. In recent years, water shortages have proven to be the primary constraint against expansion of food productivity. The crossing of commercial tomatoes with a rare wild tomato from the Galapagos Islands has yielded a hybrid that can be irrigated with 70% sea water, helping to alleviate pressures on irrigation systems in developing countries.

Wildlife species also yield important pharmacological benefits. Extracts from certain marine species show promise as anti-cancer agents. Marine sponges have yielded a large number of important antibiotics in recent years. Additionally, pharmacologically active ingredients in other species of fauna and flora are utilized in a wide range of heart drugs, analgesics, anticoagulants, and hormones.

Wildlife species also perform obscure yet critical functions in the regulation of the ecosystem. For example, certain species of wild birds eat water plants and other green water contaminants, ensuring clean reservoirs essential for the survival of other species. Certain species of flora also help to regulate rainfall, recycle matter, and resist soil erosion. Wild species of flora and fauna also protect watersheds and coastal areas from floods and droughts by acting as a buffer. Impoverishment of biodiversity threatens to upset the delicate balance of nature that supports life on earth as we know it. Several

a. [Basic Document 6.5].

members of the National Academy of Sciences view the ramifications of a loss of biodiversity "as second only in severity to the consequences of large scale nuclear warfare."

Wildlife is also a significant source of economic benefits for many nations. For example, a survey conducted by Statistics Canada in 1982 estimated that Canadians spent an estimated $4.2 billion on wildlife-related activities in 1981 alone. This figure does not include the additional foreign exchange that is earned from tourist expenditures on wildlife-related activities.

The diminution of wildlife species also threatens to deny society the aesthetic and spiritual benefits of nature. Throughout history, mankind has celebrated its bond with animal and plant life in art, music, and literature. In recent years, society has begun to accept its role as protector of nature for its own sake:

> [T]his non-humanistic value of communities and species is the simplest of all to state: they should be conserved because they exist and because this existence itself is but the present expression of a continuing historical process of immense antiquity and majesty.[1]

The Preamble to CITES embodies this belief in the intrinsic value of wildlife species, "recognizing that wild fauna and flora in their many beautiful forms are an irreplaceable part of the natural systems of the earth which must be protected for this and the generations to come...."

2. Michael Glennon, *Has International Law Failed the Elephant?*, 84 Am. J. Int'l L. 1, 1–4 (1990).

If, as Lao-tse said, nature is not anthropomorphic, some fellow creatures nonetheless seem to share the better angels of our character; among these animals, none is grander than the African elephant.[3] Elephants live in close-knit "families" of about ten members that seem to do just about everything synchronously—feeding, walking, resting, drinking or mud wallowing.[4] Each unit has a matriarchal structure: it is headed by the oldest female and consists of younger females and their calves, as male calves tend to leave the family and strike out on their own when they reach sexual maturity between the ages of 10 and 15. Fighting is rare.

Elephants are the largest land animals on earth. They grow for their entire life, weighing up to 6 tons and eating up to 300 pounds of food a day, consisting primarily of grasses and bark. Left alone, they can live past 60. They seem able to communicate with low-frequency calls that carry for 6 miles, which may explain the coordinated movement and behavior of separate groups. On the same day that the culling of elephants began in Hwange National Park in Zimbabwe, elephants 90 miles away fled to the opposite corner of the reserve.

---

1. Ehrenfeld, The Arrogance of Humanism 207–08 (1978).

3. This article deals with the African elephant, *Laxodonta africana*. The Asian elephant, *Elephas maximus*, is somewhat smaller and more often tuskless. *A Program to Save the African Elephant*, World Wildlife Fund Letter, No. 2, 1989, at 1–2 [hereinafter *To Save the Elephant*].

4. The following text draws heavily on C. Moss, Elephant Memories: Thirteen Years in the Life of an Elephant Family (1988).

Elephants are quite tactile. They often touch each other with their trunks, and tend to stand and even walk bunched together, leaning on or rubbing each other. After being apart for a while, they greet each other by intertwining trunks, clashing tusks and flapping ears, exhibiting great excitement even if the separation has lasted for only a few days. They aid other members of the group that are threatened or disabled.

Elephants have a haunting sense of death. When a member of the family dies, they touch the carcass gently with their trunks and feet, and cover it with loose earth and branches. They do not react to the remains of other species but are fascinated by those of their own:

> When they come upon an elephant carcass they stop and become quiet and yet tense.... First they reach their trunks toward the body to smell it, and then they approach slowly and cautiously and begin to touch the bones, sometimes lifting them and turning them with their feet and tusks. They run their trunk tips along the tusks and lower jaw and feel in all the crevices and hollows in the skull [probably] trying to recognize the individual.[5]

Observers noticed one 7–year old male lingering at such a site long after the others had gone, "repeatedly feeling and stroking the jaw and turning it with his foot and trunk." It was the remains of his mother. Females whose calves have died have seemed lethargic and depressed for many days afterwards. When the matriarch dies, the entire family can disintegrate, its former members seemingly becoming asocial and aggressive.

Elephants have no natural enemies; threats come entirely from man [sic]. Licensed hunting continues to account for several hundred deaths per year. The Governments of South Africa and Zimbabwe conduct culling programs aimed at maintaining their elephant populations at a level the available habitat can support. As with many other species, loss of habitat to human encroachment is a major problem. Elephants and cattle compete for some of the same food, and as Africa has become increasingly agricultural, the natural range of the elephant has diminished. Certain native groups have engaged in random killing of elephants: the Masai, for example, spear elephants as proof of their bravery and even as a form of political protest. As the Masai began to grow crops, their harassment of elephants increased.

Tourism, too, has had its effect. Tourist lodges in the parks have garbage pits that attract various animals, including elephants. Plastic bags and gloves, medicine bottles, broken glass, metal, wrappings and containers have all turned up in elephant dung. A psychiatrist has concluded that these environmental pressures may drive the elephant to increased feeding on fermenting food: "environmental stress can be an important variable in the self-administration of alcohol [from fermented fruits and grains] in these natural habitats. Elephants drink, perhaps, to forget ... the anxiety produced by shrinking rangeland and the competition for food. And I think that we can see a little bit of ourselves in this kind of behavior."[6]

---

5. *Id.* at 270.

6.   R. Yaeger & N. Miller, Wildlife, Wild Death: Land Use and Survival in Eastern Africa 115 (1986).

By far the greatest threat to the elephant's survival is poaching. The elephant is killed for its ivory tusks, which are carved and used for dice, jewelry, trinkets, ornaments, billiard balls, piano keys and knife handles. A principal use is for *hanko*, personalized signature seals considered status symbols in Japan. International conservation groups estimate that the illegal killing of elephants for their ivory has reduced Africa's elephant population from 1.5 million to fewer than 500,000 in the last decade. By some estimates, the poachers kill two to three hundred a day; at this rate, the African elephant could be extinct by the end of the century....

Numbers, however, do not tell the whole story. They do not convey the brutality of the killing, sometimes by paramilitaristic poachers who spray bullets from semiautomatic weapons over entire herds. They do not disclose the horror burned in the memories of survivors that have witnessed the hacking of parents and siblings they have lived with for decades and afterwards wander aimlessly in despair. Numbers—and dispassionate references to "ivory" and "offtake"—do not reveal what really is at issue:

> The word *ivory* disassociates it in our minds from the idea of an elephant. One tends to lump it with jade, teak, ebony, amber, even gold and silver, but there is a major difference: The other materials did not come from an animal; an ivory tusk is a modified incisor tooth. When one holds a beautiful ivory bracelet or delicate carving in one's hand, it takes a certain leap of understanding to realize that piece of ivory came from an elephant who once walked around using its tusk for feeding, digging, poking, playing and fighting, and furthermore that the elephant had to be dead in order for that piece of ivory to be sitting in one's hand.[7] "Every 10 minutes, another elephant is slain and its tusks wrenched or cut from its face by poachers intent on delivering more ivory to the marketplace."[8]

3. Edwin M. Smith, *The Endangered Species Act and Biological Conservation*, 57 S. CAL. L. REV. 361, 367–68 (1984).

Habitat destruction is the most important contemporary source of human-caused extinction both within the United States and around the world. Throughout history, human culture has been responsible for massive ecological change in many regions. Within the United States, more intensive uses of land for agriculture, urban expansion, forestry, hydroelectric power development, and mineral and petroleum exploration have increased the risk of extinction for many species. Particularly threatened are predators needing large areas of wilderness for hunting, and species highly adapted to specific habitats.

The destruction of tropical moist forests places large numbers of species in jeopardy, creating the greatest threat to global biological diversity. Growing populations and underdeveloped economies generate pressure to clear jungles in Africa, Asia, and South America and threaten more than one third of the world's living species. Much of the forest destruction reflects the developing nations' agricultural and industrial efforts to serve consumer demand in developed nations. Tropical jungles are also cleared for domestic cooking fuel

---

7. C. Moss, *supra* note 4, at 291. This book is the authoritative work concerning the life and plight of the elephant.

8. P. Brennan, *Ivory Wars; Fighting to Save the Elephants*, WASH. POST, Sept. 24, 1989, at Y7.

because these developing nations cannot compete with industrialized nations in the world market for petroleum and its byproducts. Unfortunately, the productivity of the soil after the clearing of these forests is quite limited. As a result, the period of efficient agricultural use of the land is frequently very short. Conservation of the biological diversity of tropical moist forests is a problem fraught with social, political, and economic difficulties; nevertheless, the urgency of protecting tropical rain forests necessitates immediate efforts toward an appropriate solution.

   4. Editors' Note. A frequent complaint about international policy concerning the elephant is that it is unduly influenced by the sentimental and unrealistic views of the elephant held by animal protectionists in developed nations. There is a tendency to overlook or underestimate the hazards of large elephant populations to the people of the developing countries in which the elephant resides. Elephants are difficult to support and can do tremendous destruction to the natural environment and human settlements. The average elephant eats 18 hours a day, consuming up to 300 pounds of vegetation. It takes a minimum of 4 square kilometers per elephant to support a healthy population. During a drought elephants compete with other species, including humans, for limited food. As they roam, they can strip entire areas clear of vegetation, leading to the demise of other species. In the past, this has led governments to undertake efforts to exterminate elephants as pests. Paul and Anne Ehrlich describe some of the history:

> Humanity has also attempted to exterminate populations and species of herbivores that attack domesticated plants. A major source of mortality for African Elephants has been control programs implemented to keep them from molesting farms. Entire populations have been exterminated in those programs. A large animal on an overpopulated island, the Ceylon Elephant has been pushed into the endangered category by hunting both for sport and for predator control. The elephants' depredations of plantations led the government to institute a bounty programme in 1831. One celebrated hunter of the time, a Major Rogers, promptly killed more than fourteen hundred elephants, and the number of kills in general reached the point where the government had to cut the bounty from ten to seven shillings to save money. Today a couple of thousand individual elephants remaining in Sri Lanka are dependent on a few inadequate reserves for survival—which [survival] seems unlikely in the face of the expanding human population and expanding agriculture.

Paul Ehrlich & Anne Ehrlich, *Extinction—The Causes and Consequences of the Disappearance of Species* 128 (1981).

   Although government extermination programs aimed at elephants are probably a thing of the past, concern over human-elephant conflict is not. Elephants often raid and destroy crops of poor African farmers, and no effective mechanisms to confine them to particular areas (or to fence them out of cropland) have been developed. Elephants are also dangerous to humans whose paths they cross (and vice versa, of course). Reports of elephants killing people are common and regular in Africa, and human-elephant conflict can only escalate as populations of both species grow.

In short, preservation of the elephant imposes significant costs on the peoples and countries in which elephants live. Consideration of this reality has prompted efforts to develop approaches to conservation that make it pay, not only for the world at large, but also for the directly-affected human populations. The next reading explores some of the policy issues.

5. FRANCES CAIRNCROSS, COSTING THE EARTH—THE CHALLENGE FOR GOVERNMENTS, THE OPPORTUNITIES FOR BUSINESS 131–41 (1992–93).

... Conservation is a sort of investment: and like all investments, it carries costs.... [The trick is not just to draw attention to the many values of biological diversity.] Conservation, for those who actually undertake it, is a matter of setting benefits against costs. If the benefits, as perceived by those who do the conserving, are smaller than the costs, then species will continue to vanish. In theory, the benefits may look promising: the countries with the greatest natural health are frequently the poorest, their people struggling to survive on subsistence agriculture. Surely it should be possible to live off all those valuable natural resources? In reality, the problems are often immense.

Some of the problems are created by governments. Many countries offer subsidies, set prices, or give tax reliefs in ways that positively encourage the destruction of a country's natural heritage. But even without perverse government intervention, it is often hard to devise effective incentives for conservation.

One of the most important things that has dawned on conservationists in recent years is that, while governments have tremendous powers to encourage the destruction of natural resources, the cooperation of local people is usually essential to conserve them. As Jeffrey McNeely's excellent study *Economics and Biological Diversity*[10] points out,

> Biological resources are often under threat because the responsibility for their management has been removed from the people who live closest to them, and instead transferred to government agencies located in distant capitals. But the costs of conservation still typically fall on the relatively few rural people who otherwise might have benefitted most directly from exploiting these resources. Worse, the rural people who live closest to the areas with greatest biological diversity are often among the most economically disadvantaged—the poorest of the poor.

Schemes to encourage conservation increasingly shy away from non-use. Instead, attempts are made to find sustainable uses that will bring in revenue for local people. When national parks are set up, people may find themselves driven out of land that they have traditionally harvested, while revenues from tourism go to the faraway government. In Zimbabwe's Matobo National Park, for instance, villagers are crammed on overgrazed lands around the park boundaries. Some villagers lived on the park lands until the mid–1950s, and their descendants regard the land as still theirs. Thatch is Zimbabwe's main roofing material, but overgrazing has damaged supplies. In the park, thatching grass grows so well that managers periodically burn it off to prevent a dangerous fire. In 1962 the park authorities agreed to let local villagers cut

---

10. JEFFREY McNEELY, ECONOMISTS AND BIO-   SERVE NATURAL RESOURCES xi (1988).
LOGICAL DIVERSITY, DEVELOPING INCENTIVES TO CON-

grass in the park, in exchange for agreeing not to poach wildlife or graze cattle illegally. A group of villagers is allowed to cut an annual quota of thatch. One bundle in ten goes to the park authorities (on the principle that people tend to undervalue "free" goods) and is used by them to thatch park buildings. A valuable crop of thatch has been cut by local people each year. Trespassing by cattle herders has been reduced and poaching minimized.

A more recent Zimbabwean experiment, in the dirt-poor northern district of Nyaminyami, began in 1988. Central government handed over to local people the right to manage the region's wildlife—and to keep the profits. In 1989 the district council hoped to make some Z$500,000 ($220,000) from sales of surplus game and licences for safari hunting. Within five years, it is hoped that sum will double. Meat from culling impala is sold cheaply to villagers, or used to rear crocodiles whose skins are exported lucratively to France and whose tails are served up in local restaurants.

There have been attempts to bribe people more directly. Tile Wolong nature reserve in China is an important habitat of the giant panda. To try to reduce human pressure on the area, the government provided some $770,000– worth of food rations to 3,400 local people in return for carrying out one of a number of activities, including patrolling the reserve to feed starving pandas, [building] new free houses to resettle families from the most important parts of the reserve, and [planting] abandoned farm land with varieties of bamboo that pandas [are known to like].

Can the concept of sustainable use, rather than conservation, save two of the world's most endangered and precious natural resources, the large mammals and the tropical rain forests? Perhaps, though old-fashioned conservationists are skeptical. Take the example of the African elephant, whose numbers have been halved by poaching, falling from about 1.2m in 1981 to just over 600,000 by 1989. In some countries [see Table 10–2.1] the decline has been even more appalling: Kenya's elephant population fell by two-thirds between 1981 and 1989, Zambia's and Tanzania's by almost three-quarters. The beasts have been killed for their ivory. So, in the hope of stemming the slaughter, a decision was taken in October 1989 to ban trade in ivory. The richest of the final consumers of ivory—the United States, the EC and Japan—all banned imports.

Splendid, said conservationists. In the wake of the ban, the price of ivory plummeted and poaching fell sharply. The elephant, it seemed, might possibly have been saved. Since trade in the skins of wild cats, including leopards, was banned, their numbers have greatly revived. On the other hand, since the black rhino was given the same protection in 1975 . . ., its numbers have dropped from 500,000 to fewer than 40,000.

Which fate awaits the elephant? The most convincing answer comes from a group of economists at the London Environmental Economics Centre (LEEC) in a study[11] they carried out in 1988–89 as part of the groundwork for the conference that eventually banned the ivory trade [see Table 10–2.1]. They argue powerfully that a ban may eventually speed up the disappearance of the elephant from the wild, because it destroys one of the main ways in which governments could—if they chose—earn back the costs they incur in

11. E. BARBIER ET AL., ELEPHANTS, ECONOMICS
and Ivory (1990).

conserving the species. They suggest that the ivory trade has not caused the elephant's decline. The key factor has been the failure of African governments to use the world ivory market to their best advantage. A ban on the trade will not help, for two reasons. First the effect will initially be to cause a sharp drop in ivory prices. That will encourage a new demand for ivory among potential importers previously priced out of the market, such as South Korea, Taiwan and African countries themselves. This trade will be unmonitored, because these new importers have not subscribed to the international convention that governs trade in endangered species.

Table 10–2.1 Elephant Numbers: Regions and Selected Countries		
Country/Region	1981	1989
Zaire	376,000	103,000
Central African Republic	31,000	27,000
Congo	10,800	25,000
Gabon	13,400	92,000
Central Africa total	**436,200**	**278,100**
Kenya	65,000	18,000
Tanzania	203,900	75,000
Sudan	133,700	21,000
West Africa total	**429,500**	**125,600**
Botswana	20,000	58,000
South Africa	8,000	8,200
Zambia	160,000	45,000
Zimbabwe	47,000	49,000
Southern Africa total	**309,000**	**203,300**

Source: African Elephant and Rhino Specialist Group.

Secondly, a ban destroys a possible incentive to preserve elephants. If elephants are to survive, they must be seen in Africa as an immensely valuable source of foreign exchange. The problem for the elephant is not that it lacks value. If it did, then arguments for saving it would be harder to maintain. Its trouble is that it is too valuable, and that it is, in effect, available to anybody who wants to risk killing it.

But conserving elephants [has huge costs]. Even if the ivory trade were indeed to be stopped effectively by the ban, elephants might still continue to vanish. "If they are not killed for their ivory, they will be killed for the land they occupy," argue the LEEC economists. Conserving elephants not only means forgoing the use of the land on which they forage. . . . It also means spending hugely on preventing poachers. Zimbabwe reckons that it costs $200 per square km to protect wild elephants from illegal hunting. For Africa as a whole an effective war against poachers might well cost $80m–100m a year.

With a ban in place, only a few countries have an incentive to conserve, and they are the ones whose tourist trade has been built on showing wildlife to visitors. Elephants are one of the mainstays of the Kenyan tourist trade. Properly exploited, they might bring in even more than they do. A back of an envelope survey of tourists in Kenya, by Gardner Brown of the University of Washington in Seattle, found that the average tourist was happy to pay a $100 surcharge to protect the elephant. Even allowing for exaggeration, that suggests Kenya's 1m game park tourists could bring in an extra $20m a year in revenues, one-third as much as all Africa gets from killing the beasts.

The elephant's best hope of survival in other countries still lies mainly in its tusks. The aim should be to cull elephants at a sustainable rate and use the revenue to help to pay for conservation. One intriguing study [see Table 10–2.2] in Botswana compared the value of managing elephant herds just for the enjoyment of tourists wanting to view wildlife, with the value if tourism is combined with elephant cropping. The cropping reduces yields from tourism by about 10%, but leads to other gains, such as tanning elephant hides, ivory carving and producing meat for crocodile farming. The extra benefits almost double the total economic value of a herd.

Even larger revenues may be raised by selling hunters from rich countries the right to kill their own big game. The value of an elephant to a party of German sportsmen [sic] exceeds . . . its value to an ivory poacher. Zimbabwe has long found big-game hunting a lucrative use for its elephants. A group of European or American hunters stalking one of the 100–200 elephants a year that are allowed to be killed this way can easily spend $15,000 all told, some of it going to local people who work as guides and bearers. That is perhaps five times as much as those same people could make by poaching an elephant themselves. Some hunters argue that their very presence, armed to the teeth with guns and field glasses, is a deterrent to poachers. They are probably right.

Table 10–2.2

Economic benefits of different elephant management options, Botswana ($1 = 1.8 pula)
Net Present value @ 6% (m pula, 1989)

Option	After 5 years	After 10 years	After 15 years
1. Game viewing with no consumptive uses	34.7	98.1	160.6
2. Game viewing with elephant cropping	91.2	198.4	288.9
Difference 2–1	56.5	100.3	128.3
Net benefits from consumptive uses*	60.0	110.1	144.4

* The difference between options 1 and 2 is only an approximate indicator of the net benefits from consumptive uses, as the introduction of elephant cropping reduces the benefits from game-viewing tourism by 10%. By allowing for this reduction, the net benefits from consumption uses can be calculated.

Source: J. Barnes, Department of Wildlife and National Parks, Botswana; *quoted in* E. Barbier et al., *Elephants, Economics and Ivory, Earthscan Publications* (1990).

Above all, local people need to see the elephant as a source of income. As the LEEC economists argue:

The history of wildlife conservation efforts in Africa has been dominated by a universal approach of divorcing local communities from any control or rights of exploitation of their wildlife. Wildlife utilisation, except perhaps for tourism and limited safari hunting, has been discouraged, and any safari and tourist revenues have gone to the state, not to local communities. The state's objective is to manage elephants and other wildlife for the benefit of the whole nation, whereas the local communities are denied access to protected areas and even to the right to hunt in areas neighbouring them. The incentives for the local population to engage in or assist in poaching increase, while their incentives to cooperate in reducing poaching or aiding conservation efforts decrease.

The best hope for conservation is to try to make sure that more of the gains from conservation come to local people. To achieve that, it is important to try to create clear ownership rights over elephants, preferably giving a big share in them to local communities. Up to now, conservation efforts have cut links between local people and the wildlife they once hunted; restore some of those links, and hunting may return to sustainable levels. If local people have the promise of hard currency from the tusks of some of their elephants in future, they have less incentive to kill them before they reach maturity and breed. Better still, if governments can turn potential poachers into effective game-keepers, they save some of the cost of game-keeping.

Because the African elephant is being driven to extinction by an international trade, its conservation needs an international solution. Many of the people who put the highest value on the elephant's survival, at least metaphysically, do not live in Africa. But with elephants, as with other wildlife valued by foreigners, there arises the question of sovereignty. If the world regards elephants as something whose preservation is important to the whole human race, then a [tussle] may arise between the individual African countries and the world at large. Richer countries may say, in effect: "If they [the elephants] are a public good—we will accept a duty to help meet the costs of conserving them. If they are just your elephants, you cannot expect us to help."

Something of this emerged in the discussions over the ban on the ivory trade. Those countries that have been most successful in conserving their herds, South Africa, Botswana, Malawi and Zimbabwe, opposed a ban. They argued that their herds are not declining, and that one reason is that they are able to pay for conservation partly from the revenue they earn from exporting ivory and elephant hides from periodic culls....

The LEEC economists vigorously support these countries [that] have made a large investment in conservation, and now see the return on it [under threat]. To raise the yield from elephants further requires not the banning of the ivory trade, but its control. African countries are lucky enough to have a product for which demand in some rich countries is highly inelastic: in other words, even if the price rises, people will continue to buy enthusiastically. Exporting countries could easily increase their takings even without selling more ivory.

It would make sense for African governments to join together to form a sort of ivory OPEC, a cartel which closely controlled the offtake of ivory. They would gain a number of advantages. They could drive up the price, taking advantage of the inelastic demand. They could eliminate middlemen, who now take a large share of the profits of illegally exported ivory. They would have a new source of cash to help to pay for conservation. And they would make sure that the elephant survived, to earn money for future generations. Such a cartel might stand a better chance than OPEC of surviving, because it is not in the long-term interest of consumers of ivory to exterminate the elephant. On the contrary, consumers may be happy to ensure the survival of the elephant by helping to make controls on the ivory trade watertight, if they receive a constant but restricted flow of ivory in exchange. Only those who carve ivory, who make more money the more tusks they handle, have little interest in making constraints work.

With the ban, however, the elephant's future is uncertain. Temporarily, the collapse of demand in the rich industrial countries will discourage poaching. The price of ivory within Africa has fallen dramatically. Large new dollops of aid from the West are helping to improve the pay and equipment of park guards. The danger is that poaching will revive. New markets will be developed. Some people who in the past bought ivory legally will now buy it illegally. [Some of the legal demand, in other words, will overflow into the illegal market]. That will drive up the black market price, raising the profitability of poaching and increasing the risks that poachers are willing to take.

6. Editors' Note. Conservationists and the international legal community have largely embraced the notion that protection of species is most effective when local human communities derive benefits from that protection.[a] Thus, there is little objection to policies like eco-tourism, which seeks to generate revenue to local communities from conservation efforts, but which does not involve any trade in the endangered species or its parts. When "sustainable use" policies go further, however, and propose that human exploitation of an endangered species should include taking, trade or, indeed, any use of the animal, so long as species existence is not threatened, then serious disagreements emerge. One of the most intense conflicts has been over the question whether to permit commercial trade in elephant parts, especially ivory.

Despite the predictions and concerns expressed in the preceding Reading, the African elephant was listed in Appendix I of the Convention on International Trade in Endangered Species of Wild Fauna and Flora (CITES) **[Basic Document 6.5]** in 1989, leading to a ban on commercial trade in ivory. Arguably, the ban worked. While the population of African elephants fell from an estimated 1.3 million in 1979 to about 600,000 in 1989, current estimates suggest that the population has stabilized, or even increased, since the ban on ivory trade was implemented. Poaching, although it continues, appears to be a much less severe problem than it was in the 1970s and 1980s. *See* Michael J. Glennon, *New Developments in International Environmental Law*, 85 Am. Soc'y Int'l L. Proc. 401, 418 (1991). Groups that support the ban offer this as

a. For a discussion of efforts to involve local communities in wildlife management programs, including efforts by African countries which explicitly affect elephant conservation, *see* Gregory F. Maggio, *Recognizing the Vital Role of Local Communities in International Legal Instruments for Conserving Biodiversity*, 16 UCLA J. Envtl. L & Pol'y 179, 196–200 (1998).

proof of its success. *See generally*, David Harland, *Killing Game: International Law and the African Elephant* 102 (1994).

On the other hand, most of the improvement in elephant numbers may be due to increases in elephant populations in those countries that were doing an adequate job of protecting them even before the elephant was listed in CITES Appendix I, and the ban on ivory trade, while a factor, is not the only reason population numbers have stabilized overall. Zimbabwe, Namibia and Botswana, all of which were protecting the elephant before the ban, now find that their elephant populations are too large and growing. In other countries, ineffective protection before the ivory ban has remained ineffective protection after. As for the future, those countries with effective elephant conservation policies argue that the limits on their exploitation of the elephant is contributing to resource shortages which threaten their ability to continue their preservation efforts.

And so the debate over policy continues. It is a debate over absolute protection versus sustainable use and, more critically, over which uses are sustainable. It is a debate that is often stated explicitly in North/South terms, with Northern countries accused of ecological imperialism for their insistence that the South's profitable ivory trade be brought to an end. At the 10th meeting of the Conference of the Parties to CITES in June 1997, the next chapter in the story was written when Namibia, Botswana and Zimbabwe successfully sought to have their elephant populations downlisted from Appendix I to Appendix II. (Elephant populations in other countries are still listed in Appendix I.) The decisions taken at that meeting also permit limited trade in ivory to begin, provided certain conditions are met. *See* Reading 16, *infra*.

7. African Convention on the Conservation of Nature and Natural Resources, Sept. 15, 1968, 1001 U.N.T.S. 3 [Basic Document 6.4].

8. Stockholm Declaration on the Human Environment of the United Nations Conference on the Human Environment, Adopted by the UN Conference on the Human Environment at Stockholm, 16 June 1972, Principles 2–4, 11, 13, 21, 24, 25, Report of the UN Conference on the Human Environment, Stockholm, 15–16 June 1972, UN Doc. A/CONF.48/14/Rev.1 at 3 (1973), UN Doc. A/CONF.48/14 at 2–65, and Corr. 1 (1972), *reprinted in* **11 I.L.M. 1416 (1972)** [Basic Document 1.12].

9. Convention on International Trade in Endangered Species of Wild Fauna and Flora (CITES), March 3, 1973, arts. I–III, VII–IX, XIV, XXIII, XXIV, 27 U.S.T. 1087, T.I.A.S. No. 8249, *reprinted in* **12 I.L.M. 1085 (1973)** [Basic Document 6.5].

10. Draft Principles of Conduct in the Field of the Environment for Guidance of States in the Conservation and Harmonious Utilization of Natural Resources Shared by Two or More States, February 7, 1978, Principles 1–5, 7–8, 10, 12.1, 13 U.N. Doc. A/RES/3129, UNEP/ IG.12/2, at 11–14, *reprinted in* **17 I.L.M. 1098 (1978)** [Basic Document 1.18].

11. World Charter for Nature, Oct. 28, 1982, Principles 1–4, 6, 7, 9–11, 14, 19, 24 G.A. Res. 37/7, U.N. GAOR, 37th Sess., Supp. No. 51, at 17, U.N. Doc. A/37/51, *reprinted in* 21 I.L.M. 1261 (1982) [Basic Document 1.21].

12. Rio Declaration on Environment and Development, June 14, 1992, Principles 4, 12, 14 UNCED Doc. A/CONF.151/5/Rev. 1, *reprinted in* 31 I.L.M. 874 (1992) [Basic Document 1.29].

13. Convention on Biological Diversity, *reprinted in* 31 I.L.M. 822 (1992) [Basic Document 6.11].

14. *International Environmental Wrongs*, Chapter 5, *supra*, at 335.

15. Michael Glennon, *Has International Law Failed the Elephant?*, 84 Am. J. Int'l L. 1, 10–18, 20–23, 26–27, 28, 30–33 (1990).

II. THE CURRENT STATE OF THE LAW

International law has developed a system, of sorts, directed at the preservation of species such as the African elephant. Although customary international law now requires states to protect endangered species, the norm has received virtually no attention, perhaps because of its acknowledged indeterminacy in application. Rather, discussion has focused on conventional norms—specifically, those set out in CITES.

The Convention on International Trade in Endangered Species of Wild Fauna and Flora [CITES **[Basic Document 6.5]**] was signed in Washington, D.C., on March 6, 1973, and entered into force on July 1, 1975. By October 1989, 103 states were parties. CITES establishes a straightforward, three-tiered structure. Levels of protection are a function of the degree of threat to the survival of a species, which corresponds to the appendix in which the species is listed.

Appendix I provides the highest level of protection; it includes "all species threatened with extinction which are or may be affected by trade."[12] It applies to specimens of those species, whether dead or alive. Export is allowed solely pursuant to permit, which is only issued, inter alia, when "a Scientific Authority of the State of export has advised that such export will not be detrimental to the survival of that species."[13] The import of such specimens is allowed only pursuant to a similar permit.[14] In addition, the Convention contains provisions governing the re-export of Appendix I specimens: a "re-export certificate" is required, which may be granted only when the re-exporting state is satisfied that the specimen was imported into that state in accordance with the Convention.[15] The most restrictive provisions, those governing the trade in species listed in Appendix I, thus apply to producer states, middleman states and consumer states. In net effect, these provisions are intended to close down international trade in the species listed in Appendix I.[16]

12. CITES, art. II(1).
13. *Id.* art. III(2)(a).
14. *Id.* art. III(3)(a).

15. *Id.* art. III(4)(a). *But see* art. I(b)(ii).
16. An exception is allowed only in "exceptional circumstances." *Id.* art. II(1).

Appendix II provides an intermediate level of protection; it includes "all species which although not necessarily now threatened with extinction may become so unless trade in specimens of such species is subject to strict regulation."[17] Thus, trade in species found in Appendix II is permitted, but regulated. The principal distinction between its regime of protection and that accorded Appendix I specimens is that, while the limitations applicable to export and re-export are similar, the limitations governing import are far less rigorous. No import permit is required with respect to Appendix II specimens, and imports for commercial purposes are allowed. Appendix II covers tens of thousands of species.[18]

Appendix III provides the least protection; it includes "all species which any Party identifies as being subject to regulation within its jurisdiction for the purposes of preventing or restricting exploitation."[19] Limitations applicable to Appendix III specimens are much narrower than those pertinent to Appendix I or II specimens and derive primarily from the laws of the exporting state; unlike species listed in the first two appendixes, Appendix III species are unilaterally designated by the exporting state.

CITES permits any party to enter a specific reservation with regard to any species included in any one of the appendixes.[20] Thus, Japan, although a party, has entered reservations with respect to four different species of whales.

CITES provides that the parties will meet every 2 years. At the 1985 meeting, the parties adopted a system directed at controlling the international trade in raw ivory, which operated as follows:

[E]ach African country first sets a quota establishing the number of elephants that can be killed within its orders during the following year. All tusks and large pieces of unworked ivory taken within each country must be marked with that country's identification number. The export of those tusks or pieces must be accompanied by an export permit, and a copy of the permit must be sent to the CITES Secretariat. The Secretariat then tallies the number of tusks that are exported from each African country to ensure that its quota is not surpassed. Before an importing country accepts a shipment of ivory, it must first receive notification from the Secretariat that the permit is in order and that the quota has not been reached.[21]

Because CITES defines "specimen" as "any readily recognizable part or derivative thereof,"[22] CITES has been construed as governing only raw ivory, not worked ivory.[23]

---

17. *Id.* art. II(2)(a).

18. However, nearly all are plants; 303 are mammals, 618 are birds, and 340 are reptiles. In 1986 Appendix I contained 179 mammals, 133 birds and 52 reptiles.

19. CITES, art. II(3).

20. *Id.* art. XXIII(2)(b).

21. H. REP. NO. 827, 100th Cong., 2d Sess. 7 (1988) (Endangered Species Act Amendments of 1988) 9–10 [hereinafter 1998 HOUSE REPORT].

22. CITES, art. I(b)(ii). This definition applies with respect to species listed in Appendixes I or II; a different definition applies with respect to species listed in Appendix III.

23. The terms "readily recognizable" and "derivative" are not defined by CITES. Consequently, trade in certain parts and derivatives is regulated by some parties but not by others. S. LYSTER, INTERNATIONAL WILDLIFE LAW 242 (1985).

One central function of the biennial meeting is to review the species listed in each appendix and to determine whether to add, delete or transfer species from one appendix to another.[24] Such amendments to Appendixes I and II require the approval of a two-thirds majority of those parties present and voting.[25] The amendment enters into force 90 days after the meeting.[26]

* * *

[From 1977–1989, the African elephant was listed in Appendix II of CITES. During that same period, legal and illegal trade in ivory soared, as did poaching of elephants.] [A]s poaching accelerated, public awareness grew. In late 1988, Kenya's President Daniel arap Moi ordered that poachers (many of them Somalis) be shot on sight. Richard Leakey, the newly appointed Director of the Kenya Wildlife Service, said that he favored a flat-out ban: "If we can get some of the big consumer countries behind this, it will be very positive."[27] "The poaching is as bad as it has ever been," Leakey said. "We are losing the elephant."[28] Shortly afterwards, the U.S. Department of the Interior announced that it supported a ban on the ivory trade, and the Kenyan Government reversed its previous position and announced that it, too, favored a worldwide ban. On May 23, 1989, Britain joined the call for a ban. As governmental support mounted for moving the elephant from CITES Appendix II to Appendix I, key non-governmental wildlife organizations feared that, in anticipation of a total ban at the CITES meeting in October, poaching would increase dramatically. These organizations urged immediate unilateral bans to preempt "what could become an elephant holocaust."[29] An "orgy" of killing, they warned, could occur before a CITES ban would take effect.

The dominoes then began to fall. France announced that it was banning the import of ivory as of June 5, 1989. On the same day, President George Bush announced a ban by the United States. Interior Secretary Manuel Lujan, Jr., said on June 6 that the United States (which in 1988 had imported about 12 percent of the world's raw and worked ivory) was imposing the moratorium on all ivory imports before the October meeting because a new review had found that there was no way to distinguish between legal and illegal ivory. "We believe the current international system for controlling ivory trade has failed to protect the elephant, and we have no choice but to halt commercial ivory shipments into the United States," Secretary Lujan said.[30] On June 6, West Germany announced an immediate ban. And on June 9, the environment ministers of the European Community's 12 member nations voted to impose such a moratorium. (The European Community has accounted for about 20 percent of ivory imported from Africa.) The senior vice president of the World Wildlife Fund thereupon declared victory: "The ivory trade has

24.   CITES, art. IX(3)(b).

25.   *Id.* art. XV(1)(b).

26.   *Id.* art. XV(1)(c).

27.   Press, *Africans Back Ban on Ivory Sales*, Christian Sci. Monitor, Apr. 26, 1989, at 6.

28.   J. Perlez, *Poachers in Kenya Killing Elephants*, N.Y. Times, Apr. 23, 1989, § 1, pt. 1, at 5, col. 1.

29.   C. Clover, *Poaching Epidemic "May Wipe Out Elephant in 15 Years,"* Daily Telegraph (London), June 2, 1989, at 9; Reuters (June 1, 1989).

30.   *U.S. Trying to Protect Elephants, Declares Ban on All Ivory Imports*, N.Y. Times, June 7, 1989, at A18.

been shut down," said Curtis Bohlen. "The African elephant is now in far less danger of extinction than it was only a week ago."[31]

The unilateral bans, however, turned out to be less than universal. Hong Kong banned only imports of raw ivory; Japan banned imports of raw and worked ivory, but not raw ivory from African countries that are parties to CITES. The Japanese also announced their intent to continue to trade with "managed" states such as South Africa, which refused altogether to join the ban. Southern African producer states, led by Zimbabwe and including South Africa and Botswana, similarly announced their intent to continue to export ivory to the Far East.

In October, the parties to CITES met in Lausanne and moved the elephant to Appendix I.[32] They rejected a "split-listing" proposal by southern African states that would have permitted the continued lawful sale of ivory by southern African states. Not surprisingly, five of those states refused to be bound by this outcome, entered reservations, and announced that they would continue to sell ivory.

III. THE SHORTCOMINGS OF CITES

It is [perhaps] too soon to assess the impact of the 1989 Lausanne decision to move the elephant from CITES Appendix II to Appendix I, or of the unilateral national bans that preceded that action.... What is clear is that the international system in effect before Lausanne permitted the trade in illegal ivory to flourish to the point of resulting in the slaughter of almost half of all elephants. As *The Economist* concluded, CITES had proven "utterly powerless" to control the ivory trade.[33] Without examining how and why that happened, it is difficult to predict whether the elephant is now safe under Appendix I, or to consider what further steps might be indicated.

* * *

Why the Ivory Trade Flourished Under CITES

However incomplete our current picture of the international ivory trade, it nonetheless seems fair to conclude that throughout the 1980s, the trade boomed despite the CITES protective regime for a fairly obvious reason: CITES did not sufficiently diminish the incentives of producers, middlemen or consumers.

Producer states faced a variety of problems. The vast profits available from poaching, or merely looking the other way, made the corruption of enforcement personnel a recurrent difficulty.[34] Game wardens, *The Economist* observed, "can make more from a couple of contraband tusks than they do in a year's honest work. Fat profits made government officials fairly easy to suborn."[35] Grinding poverty, as noted above, also has played a major role.

31. D. Hawkins, *For the Elephants' Sake, A Quick Ban on Ivory*, N.Y. TIMES, June 11, 1989, 1, at 6.

32. ...However, a resolution was passed establishing a set of criteria, based on the African Elephant Conservation Act, that would allow a country to be removed from Appendix I if it were able to comply with the criteria.

33. *Saving the Elephant: Nature's Great Masterpiece*, ECONOMIST, July 1, 1989, at 16.

34. *To Save the Elephant, supra* note 3, at 7.

35. *The Slaughter of Elephants*, ECONOMIST, Apr. 15, 1989, at 49, 50.

Even producer states that purposefully undertook the task of protecting their elephant populations from poachers faced a shortage of resources. Their game wardens frequently were overwhelmed by the poachers' firepower, to the extent that Kenya—a nation that has come to take wildlife conservation seriously—asked Britain for helicopter gunships, spotter planes transports and automatic weapons for its new, paramilitary Anti–Poaching Unit. By one estimate, the cost of surveillance, fencing and support equipment needed to halt poaching entirely in Kenya's Tsavo National Park was $200 per square mile per day—which worked out to $1.6 million a day.

Producer states seemed little affected by the quota system they established under CITES. The system has been entirely voluntary and had no binding effect on the parties. Consequently, if a producer state exceeded its quota or even declined to supply a quota to the CITES Secretariat, other CITES parties had no legal basis under CITES for refusing entry to that producer state's ivory. Moreover, the quotas have been based on ridiculously high estimates of sustainable yields provided by the producing countries. "The quota system," the World Wildlife Fund concluded, "has proved to be little more than a procedure for ivory-producing states to notify the CITES Secretariat of the number of tusks they plan to export in a given year."[36]

Entrepôt states thrived on the ivory trade under CITES. Burundi, which was not a party to CITES until 1987, and the United Arab Emirates, the only state to sign CITES and then withdraw, operated free of constraints. As conservationist pressures increased, individual middlemen stored raw ivory within Africa in the hope that those pressures would someday ease.

Consumer states faced little incentive to cut back on ivory importation. There is no requirement in CITES that worked ivory be identified by country of origin when imported. Consequently, the worked ivory trade has not been controlled; the U.S. Fish and Wildlife Service has not required that the country of origin be declared. In the past, this loophole has been exploited by intermediary countries that are parties to the Convention to avoid the CITES restrictions on raw ivory. "Traders in Hong Kong, for example, imported ivory from Dubai, a free-trade zone in the United Arab Emirates, where the tusks were superficially carved. This allowed Hong Kong traders to import 'ivory artwork' from Dubai...."[37] A report by the United Nations Environment Programme observed: "Already ivory carvers are being moved to places such as the United Arab Emirates, Dubai and Taiwan—where there are few import controls on even raw ivory—so that the partly worked products can then be freely imported into the major centers."[38]

* * *

IV. Making CITES Work

Two Models of Protection: Management and Embargo

When the Lausanne Conference began, two very different models of wildlife protection were competing for acceptance. The two approaches had

---

36. *To Save the Elephant, supra* note 3, at 8.

37. W. Booth, *Africa Is Becoming an Elephant Graveyard*, 243 Science 732 (1989).

38. UNEP, UNEP/GEMS Environment Library No 3, The African Elephant 7 (1989).

earlier split the conservation community, and set southern Africa against East Africa. One I will call the "embargo" model; the other, the "management" model.

The embargo model derived from the practical impossibilities inherent in distinguishing illegal ivory from legal ivory. It would attempt to close down the trade in ivory by completely prohibiting it. Its proponents reasoned that the more legal ivory is traded, the easier it will be for poachers to place illegal ivory into the trade stream. "By keeping the ivory trade going," one expert said, "there is no question that illegal trading will go on."[39] Kenyan President Moi, a leader of the proembargo forces, thus set fire to 2,500 ivory tusks, worth $3 million: "We could sell the ivory, and use the money for conservation," his conservation minister said, "but we believe that that is only fueling the market."[40]

The management model would attempt to limit and control the ivory trade, rather than banning it altogether. Proponents of management would permit the sale of ivory from several sources: (1) supplies of confiscated poached ivory; (2) elephants that die a "natural death"; and (3) culling operations in states where elephant populations exceed the available habitat. They argued that such ivory is best placed on the market to provide revenues for stricter enforcement efforts. A ban would simply drive the trade underground and propel the price of ivory ever upwards. Thus, ivory should be marketed to relieve supply pressures created by the black market. Moreover, management proponents contended, the *people* in these (largely) underdeveloped countries should not be left to starve while convertible "white gold" was being accumulated by their governments.

* * *

The matter is not free from doubt, but the most reasonable conclusion is that the elephant would be better protected by the embargo approach than by the management approach. The management model works best in protecting nonendangered or formerly endangered animals, such as the American alligator and beaver, under a "sustainable use" regime. Earlier arguments against a prophylactic ban on ivory trading were more plausible when developed countries would have had to initiate the ban over African opposition. Now that African states have taken the lead, the situation has changed. Among other things, their leadership role may lessen the possibility that enforcement difficulties will prove insurmountable. The knowledge that *all* ivory in international commerce is there illegally would make effective control easier. Prior to the Lausanne Conference, the U.S. Fish and Wildlife Service announced that it would oppose a move at the sessions to allow countries to trade in ivory. It gave this reason: "It is very doubtful that legal trade of ivory stocks could be accomplished without providing cover for illegal trade."[41] That position was correct then, and it is correct now.

Nevertheless, that is not the solution that emerged from Lausanne. The solution that did emerge is a hybrid of the two models, and therein lies its defect. Although in principle a listing under Appendix I represents a CITES

---

39. N.Y. TIMES, June 22, 1989, at A8.

40. SUNDAY TELEGRAPH (London), July 16, 1989, at 14.

41. 54 Fed. Reg. 37,027 (1989).

endorsement of the embargo model with respect to a certain species, in reality no bona fide embargo is put in place since CITES permits parties to enter reservations. Thus, under the post-Lausanne CITES regime, notwithstanding the elephant's Appendix I listing, it remains legal for ivory-producing states to sell ivory, and six have indicated their intent to do so—even though a majority of the CITES parties recognized that termination of the trade is essential to protecting the elephant and major consumer states have agreed to ban imports.

* * *

Global Environmental Resources, Rights and Obligations

* * *

It is now possible to conclude that customary international law requires states to take appropriate steps to protect endangered species. Customary norms are created by state practice "followed by them from a sense of legal obligation."[42] Like highly codified humanitarian law norms that have come to bind even states that are not parties to the instruments promulgating them, wildlife protection norms also have become binding on nonparties as customary law. Closely related to this process of norm creation by practice is that of norm creation by convention: customary norms are created by international agreements "when such agreements are intended for adherence by states generally and are in fact widely accepted."[43] Several such agreements are directed at wildlife protection, and CITES is one of them. It is intended for adherence by states generally and is accepted by the 103 states that have become parties. In addition, some nonparties comply with certain CITES documentary requirements so as to trade with parties. CITES is not "rejected by a significant number of states";[44] only the United Arab Emirates has withdrawn from the agreement. In such circumstances, the International Court of Justice has observed, international agreements constitute state practice and represent law for nonparties.

Moreover, customary norms are created by "the general principles of law recognized by civilized nations."[45] Because CITES requires domestic implementation by parties to it, and because the overall level of compliance seems quite high, the general principles embodied in states' domestic endangered species laws may be relied upon as another source of customary law. Even apart from the CITES requirements, states that lack laws protecting endangered species seem now to be the clear exception rather than the rule. That there exists *opinion juris* as to the binding character of this obligation is suggested by the firm support given endangered species protection by the UN General Assembly and various international conferences.

While the existence of a norm requiring the protection of endangered species thus seems likely, its scope remains uncertain. To the extent that the norm derives from CITES and laws implementing CITES, that scope would be fairly narrow, for the norm would cover only species in international trade,

---

42. Restatement (Third) of the Foreign Relations Law of the United States, pt. VI (1987), 102(2).

43. *Id.* § 102(3).

44. *Id.* § 102 comment i.

45. I.C.J. Statute [Basic Document 1.4], Art. 38(1)(c).

not those taken for domestic consumption or those endangered by threats to their habitat. Even if it could be shown that major legal systems generally comprise endangered species legislation, more work needs to be done to determine exactly what elements those laws have in common. What constitutes an "endangered species," for example, is debatable. Is it one that is endangered in *every* state, or only in the state making the assessment? And to what lengths must a state go in protecting a species it finds "endangered"? Must it do everything necessary to protect that species, notwithstanding the cost or the ecological significance of the species?

As to the elephant in particular, it is hard to argue under customary international law that states such as South Africa and Zimbabwe are prohibited from selling ivory by a new customary norm, corresponding generally to the CITES restrictions. In the *North Sea Continental Shelf* case, the International Court of Justice said:

> Although the passage of only a short period of time is not necessarily, or of itself, a bar to the formation of a new rule of customary international law on the basis of what was originally a purely conventional rule, an indispensable requirement would be that within the period in question, short though it might be, State practice, including that of States whose interests are specially affected, should have been both extensive and *virtually uniform* in the sense of the provision invoked.... [46]

The nonparticipation of southern African states suggests that any such custom is not "virtually uniform." In fact, the southern African elephant "excess" states might be seen as partaking in a regional custom of the sort considered in the *Asylum* case.[47] Or they might be seen as "persistent objectors" to an emerging norm during the inchoate stages of its development.

It thus appears doubtful that a customary norm concerning the elephant or any other endangered species can yet play any significant role in its protection. But the trend cannot be doubted; and once its contours are more clear, the customary norm requiring states to protect endangered species ought to take on the character of an obligation *erga omnes*. Ordinarily, claims for the violation of an international obligation may be made only by the state to which the obligation is owed. Obligations *erga omnes*, however, run to the international community as a whole; thus, their breach is actionable by any state since such matters are "[b]y their very nature ... the concern of all States.... [T]hey are obligations *erga omnes*."[48]

16.   Editors' Note. The listing of the African elephant in Appendix I of CITES was regarded as a major victory by Glennon and others who favored the embargo approach to the ivory trade as the most effective means to discourage the poaching that was decimating the species during the 1970s and 1980s. They regarded the earlier attempt to regulate the ivory trade, the "Ivory Export Quota System of the late 1980's," as an unmitigated disaster. *See generally* Philippe J. Sands & Albert P. Bedecarre, *Convention on International Trade in Endangered Species: The Role of Public Interest Non–Governmental Organizations in Ensuring the Effective Enforcement of the Ivory*

---

46. 1969 I.C.J. 3, 43 (emphasis added).

47. Asylum (Colom./Peru), 1950 I.C.J. 266 (Judgment of Nov. 20).

48. Barcelona Traction, Light & Power Co., Ltd. (Belg. v. Spain), Second Phase, 1970 I.C.J. 3, 32 (Judgment of Feb. 5).

Trade Ban, 17 B.C. ENVTL. AFF. L. REV. 799 (1990). Furthermore, as noted earlier, the ban seemed to work. Although several Southern African nations initially indicated that they would defy the ban and continue to trade in ivory, widespread adherence to the ban by importing states caused the Southern African states eventually to comply. Although they renewed their assertion of defiance in 1992, the ban is widely regarded as having effectively shut down the ivory trade. *See* DAVID HARLAND, KILLING GAME: INTERNATIONAL TRADE AND THE AFRICAN ELEPHANT 99–103, 158 (1994).

Since Rio, however, the developing countries have increasingly argued that the concept of sustainable development, and the related concept of sustainable use of resources, counsels against Appendix I listings of endangered species. Appendix I listings forbid any commercial trade in listed species and their parts, and thus severely restricts the commercial use of species. Developing countries have been increasingly successful in arguing that commercial exploitation should be allowed, so long as it does not threaten the existence of the species.

In June 1997, the Conference of the Parties to CITES held its 10th meeting in Harare, Zimbabwe. The elephant topped the agenda. As they had before, Botswana, Namibia and Zimbabwe all sought to move the elephant populations within their countries from Appendix I to Appendix II, a move which would allow commercial trade in elephants and ivory. They offered to limit the downlisting so that only government sales could be made (no private market), sales could be made to Japan alone, and governments would sell only from their (considerable) ivory stockpiles. Strong opposition to the proposal was offered by countries and NGOs that feared that any resumption of the ivory trade would prompt renewed poaching and that illegal sales could not be adequately policed.

In the end, "a confusing compromise was reached." Elephant populations in the three countries were downlisted, but the sale of raw ivory was approved only subject to extensive conditions. Moreover, a provision (of questionable legality) called for relisting of the relevant elephant populations on Appendix I in the event that either elephant poaching or the illegal ivory trade increase. *See* Conference of the Parties, Decisions 10.1 & 10.2, *Convention on International Trade in Endangered Species of Wild Fauna and Flora. See also* David Favre, *International Environmental Law: Convention on International Trade in Endangered Species: International Legal Developments in Review: 1998*, 32 INT'L LAWYER, 515, 519–521 (1998). At this writing, the outcome (or legal effect) of this conditional downlisting is not yet certain.

17.   Frederick A. Mann, *Reflections on the Prosecution of Persons Abducted in Breach of International Law*, in INTERNATIONAL LAW AT A TIME OF PERPLEXITY 407, 407–20 (Y. Dinstein ed., 1989).

A State which authorizes the abduction of a person from the territory of another sovereign State is guilty of a violation of public international law. This principle is supported by considerable State practice, numerous decisions of municipal courts and a large body of doctrinal opinion. Its basis is the incontrovertible rule that exercise of physical force by one State in the territory of another State without the latter's consent constitutes an excess of international jurisdiction or a violation of the "principle of respect for State sovereignty", which is guaranteed by not only Article 2 of the Charter of the United Nations **[Basic Document 1.3]** and other texts, for these "merely respond to firmly established and longstanding tenets of customary international law".[49]

Notwithstanding the almost elementary character of the rule, some of its implications require comment.

1. The rule presupposes that the abduction is carried out by agents instructed or authorized by the State or by private volunteers whose acts have been adopted or ratified by the State.

* * *

2. A breach of international law occurs only in the absence of consent by the State whose sovereignty the abduction affects.

* * *

3. The normal and generally accepted remedy in the event of a wrongful abduction is the return of the victim, i.e., restitution in kind. There are numerous cases in which the injured State has demanded, and the wrongdoing State has agreed, to the return of the victim.

It is important to stress the unanimity of practice and doctrine on this point, for it has often been doubted whether international law recognizes the remedy of restitution in kind: some scholars have asserted the rule that international law knows no remedy other than damages. This view is clearly without foundation, and it is satisfactory to notice that a Committee of the Federal Constitutional Court of the Federal Republic of Germany rendered an important decision on the point, which quite clearly assumes that if France— whence the accused person was removed by fraud—had demanded it, the Federal Republic would have been duty-bound to return him.

4. On the other hand if, as has already been pointed out, the return of the abducted person does not eliminate the initial wrong (as is shown by the fact that a claim for damages may be pursued by the injured State even after the return), the failure to comply with a request for the return of the abducted person is a separate wrong which is quite independent of the original one.

* * *

During the greater part of the last 150 years or so, this problem has been seen as one of jurisdiction: does the State have criminal jurisdiction in respect of the abducted person? It would be idle to deny that such jurisdiction exists, and it exists however abhorrent the circumstances of the abduction may be. *Mala captus bene detentus,* as the old adage teaches. The matter was exhaustively considered by the Israeli courts, when in 1961 and 1962 they had to decide *Eichmann's* case.[50] It would be almost disrespectful to the most learned judgment by eight Israeli Judges sitting in the District Court of Jerusalem and the Supreme Court of Israel if an attempt were made to review once again the ample material from many countries that led them to the conclusion

49. *Nicaragua v. United States of America,* [1986] I.C.J. 110, 212.

50. 36 Int'l L. Rep. 5 (District Court) and 277 (Supreme Court).

that the abduction of Eichmann from Argentina did not in any way prejudice Israel's jurisdiction over him.

* * *

Since then, at least two supreme tribunals have affirmed the established rule that, irrespective of the circumstances in which the accused has been brought within the country, a court has jurisdiction to try him for any offence he may have committed: the accused stands before the court and this fact alone confers jurisdiction *ratione personae* upon it.[b]

* * *

Finally, in England and the Commonwealth, there is no doubt about the jurisdiction of their courts in respect of an abducted person, though there as well as in the United States of America, as will appear later, much uncertainty surrounds the real problem.

* * *

With rare unanimity and undeniable justification the courts of the world have held that the manner in which an accused has been brought before the court does not and, indeed, cannot deprive it of its jurisdiction, of its right to hear the case against the person standing before it.... In so deciding the courts of the world have, however, failed to face the decisive question. This is not whether jurisdiction exists, but whether jurisdiction should be exercised.

* * *

... [T]he ideas expressed in ... international documents [such as the European Convention for the Protection of Human Rights and Fundamental Freedoms (213 U.N.T.S. 221) and the International Covenant on Civil and Political Rights **[Basic Document 7.14]**] are also included in many constitutions where they are described by such principles as the dignity of the person, the rule of law, due process of law and many similar headings. These universally recognized principles of municipal law constitute important evidence of State practice and, therefore, supplement the international texts to which reference has been made. One cannot possibly agree, therefore, with an astonishing dictum in a German decision:

> In several States, it is true, there have been decisions which seem to be founded upon the view that the illegality created by the abduction could justify an obstacle to judicial proceedings. This practice, however, is neither sufficiently broad to qualify as a firm practice restricting jurisdiction nor does it sufficiently clearly express the conviction of criminal proceedings against an abducted person abducted in a manner inconsistent with public international law; in some decisions there is in fact an express statement that principles of municipal law (rule of law, due process of law) were preventing the proceedings.

b. The established rule was given further support by *United States v. Alvarez–Machain,* 504 U.S. 655 (1992). In that case, the U.S. Supreme Court held that a criminal defendant who was abducted to the United States from a country with which the U.S. had an extradition treaty (Mexico) did not thereby acquire a defense to the jurisdiction of U.S. courts and could be tried in those courts for violations of U.S. law. Trial of defendant was proper, said the Court, even if the abduction of the defendant was "shocking" and "in violation of general international law principles." *Id.* at 669.

This discloses a curious view of the sources of public international law:[51] they most certainly include State practice, in particular judicial practice of municipal courts and principles of constitutional law.

* * *

... [I]n a large number of cases [in the United States] beginning in 1961, the general rule was laid down according to which the government could not realize directly 'the fruits of its own deliberate and unnecessary lawlessness in bringing the accused to trial' Consequently courts should 'decline to exercise jurisdiction over a defendant whose presence has been secured by force or fraud.' It is interesting to observe that in laying down the new rule, the Court invoked not only 'the underlying principle that the government should be denied the right to exploit its own illegal conduct', but also international law as represented by Article 2(4) of the United Nations Charter and Article 17 of the Charter of the Organization of American States according to which the territory of a State "is inviolable" and "may not be the object ... of ... measures of force taken by another State, directly or indirectly, on any ground whatever".[c]

* * *

... As a matter of legal reasoning—words, phrases, formulations—verbiage can be found for either or any solution of the problem discussed in these pages. Even if it is approached from the point of view of legal policies, the ambivalence of the possible attitudes is obvious; in these days of terrorism, violent crimes, traffic in drugs and consequent dangers to the public, one can understand and sympathize with the tendency of the authorities to pursue and combat the wrongdoers by any means, fair or foul, and to treat them as outcasts who have forfeited any right to consideration or indulgence. This is a great danger, and it is believed that, for this reason alone, neither society nor the law must allow a departure from the great principle that no illegality must ever bear fruit.... The wrongful abduction from a foreign State's territory is bound to lead to international anarchy and friction, both in law and in fact. In particular, it will undermine the system of extradition treaties with its carefully elaborated provisions, including its exceptions such as that relating to political crimes.... Just as extradition treaties provide for reciprocity, their disregard or their replacement by unauthorized snatching of individuals from one Party's territory would tempt the other Party to reciprocate in kind.

18. Mark Gray, *The United Nations Environment Programme: An Assessment*, 20 ENVTL. L. 292, 294–96 (1990).

The mandate to further the principles underlying UNEP was [as] vague as the principles themselves. The General Assembly Resolution creating UNEP **[Basic Document 1.13]** instructed the Executive Director to review the world environmental situation and to act as a focal point for environmental action and coordination within the United Nations system. Essentially,

---

51. *Cf.* art. 38 of the Statute of the International Court of Justice **[Basic Document 1.4]**.

c. Shortly after Mann wrote this analysis, the U.S. Supreme Court held that U.S. courts should take jurisdiction even when the defendant was brought before the court by an abduction that violated international law. *See United States v. Alvarez-Machain*, 504 U.S. 655 (1992).

this meant taking overall responsibility for the implementation of the Action Plan's recommendations, including environmental assessment, environmental management, and supporting activities.

UNEP was designed as a catalyst—promoting, encouraging and guiding government action rather than [as an] implementer or enforcer. It would ensure that governments gave emerging environmental problems of wide international significance appropriate and adequate consideration by identifying environmental hazards, promulgating solutions, and providing a framework for the creation of national and multilateral agreements and institutions. UNEP can plead for and initiate action, mobilize support for a particular approach, and even issue demands. Ultimately, however, it must look to states for execution.

UNEP began with no formal mandate to develop international environmental law. Some considered its development a necessary component of UNEP's existence. Others saw it as implicit in Principle 22 of the Stockholm Declaration [**Basic Document 1.12**], which calls for state cooperation to develop international environmental law. Various decrees have since assigned UNEP a quasi-legislative role, such as General Assembly Resolution 3129, calling for the establishment of international standards regarding shared resources. UNEP's Governing Council has authorized the Executive Director to initiate legal consultations between experts and participate in developing principles.

IV. STRUCTURES AND PROCEDURES

General Assembly Resolution 2997 [**Basic Document 1.13**] sets out UNEP's institutional and financial structure. The Governing Council (Council), the Executive Director (Director) and his Secretariat, and the Environmental Fund are all located in Nairobi, Kenya. UNEP is unique among U.N. agencies in that it finances all programs with direct, voluntary contributions from U.N. member states. Only Council and Secretariat administrative expenses come from the general U.N. budget.

The Council is a policymaking body composed of fifty-eight member states elected by the General Assembly according to a geographical distribution. Through the Economic and Social Council (ECOSOC), which has an overlapping mandate, the Council reports annually to the General Assembly. In particular, UNEP reports on the relationship between the environmental policies and programs and the economic and social programs within the U.N. system. By instructing and guiding the Council, the General Assembly controls the interrelated issues of development and the environment, and ECOSOC reviews the scientific and technical aspects.

The Director and his Secretariat provide substantive support to the Council and administer the Environmental Fund under its direction. The Director also advises intergovernmental and U.N. bodies on the formulation and implementation of programs and assists in their coordination. As well, he helps to assess the programs' effectiveness. At the Council's request, or on his own initiative, the Director consults with governments and U.N. agencies and convenes informal meetings with scientific and legal experts. These interactions often produce reports, studies, recommendations, and planning proposals.

In sum, UNEP, through its programs and coordination efforts, identifies problems and trends. It determines priorities by evaluating the urgency and universal importance of a matter, the efforts already expended on it, the possibility of significant results within a decade, and the prospects for thus improving international environmental cooperation.

19. Agenda 21, Chapter 38, International Institutional Arrangements, ¶ ¶ 38.9–38.28 [Basic Document 1.30].

20. Governing Council Decision on the Role, Mandate and Governance of the United Nations Environment Programme, U.N.E.P., 19th Sess., 7th mtg., U.N. Doc. GC19/1/1997 (1997) [Basic Document 1.38].

Discussion Notes/Questions

1. It is difficult to obtain reliable estimates of elephant populations in Africa as a whole. The size of poached ivory is becoming smaller and smaller as younger elephants are being killed. In some areas there are apparently no elephants of over thirty years of age (elephants can live for sixty years). This is a major threat to the social structure of the elephant herds, since elephants have a long childhood during which survivorship knowledge is passed on. *See* Cyrille de Klemm, *Migratory Species*, 15 ENVTL. POL'Y & L. 81 (1985).

2. The problem facing the elephant is as much a problem of human encroachment on elephant habitat as it is of illegal ivory poaching. Furthermore, setting aside game preserves does not solve the problem. As noted earlier, elephants leave reserves and deprecate bordering cropland. Moreover, the land set aside for game land is often good land as it must support vegetation. This means that the land cannot be farmed or used to support human populations. In this connection, it may be asked whether there is a human right to food? *See* Penny Overby, *The Right to Food*, 54 SASKATCHEWAN L. REV. 19 (1990). If so, and assuming that it is an important human right, what does this signify for elephants? Should elephants or other wildlife be required to justify economically the allocation of land and resources that are necessary for their protection? Is it worth the cost to the human population to save elephants?

On the other hand, as the above readings make clear, there are pressures also on the elephant's traditional territory. Expanding human populations take over more and more of their habitat, and the elephants become increasingly confined to sanctuaries where they are easy targets for poachers. How much of this problem is, in the end, really attributable to human overpopulation, and how does one address that? *See* Problem 11–3 ("Population Control Meets Human Rights in Hanguo"), *infra*. Regardless, what does it all signify for elephants? Do they have legal rights? *See* Christopher Stone, *Should Trees Have Standings Toward Legal Rights for Natural Objects*, 45 S. CAL. L. REV. 450 (1972). Three U.S. Supreme Court justices, in a dissenting judgement in *Sierra Club v. Morton*, 405 U.S. 727, 741 (1972), accepted that natural objects could have legal rights.

3. In addition to the threats posed by international trade and resource conflicts between human populations and wildlife populations, non-human species face threats of extinction from competition from other non-human species (often introduced to an area by humans) and from local consumption of endangered species. Yet these problems are not addressed adequately, or at all, by international law. For example, CITES "does not address the issue of local community harvesting and consumption . . . for domestic subsistence or commercial purposes,

despite the extensive documentation that local consumption of species [including the elephant] otherwise protected under CITES is a significant conservation issue." *See* Gregory Maggio, *Recognizing the Vital Role of Local Communities in International Legal Instruments for Conserving Biodiversity*, 16 UCLA J. ENVTL. L. & POL'Y 179, 206–07 (1998). Indeed, of the four main threats to species survival—international trade in endangered species, conflicts with introduced species, resource conflicts (including habitat destruction) with humans, and local consumption of the species—international law provides a well-developed response only to the international trade problem, which may actually be the *least* significant threat to species survival. Is there anything that the international community can do about threats that are local in origin? If so, what? Or are local threats of local concern only? If the elephant is destroyed in a country because of local consumption of the animal for food and ivory, is that a matter of no concern to the international community so long as the ivory is not exported? Could the profits from international trade in ivory be used to discourage local consumption (by raising standards of living)? Or is that an apologist's pipedream?

4.   Why save the elephant? Is there an obligation on States to preserve global environmental resources? What might this involve for the States that have the elephant within their boundaries? What might it mean for other countries? Do non-elephant countries have an obligation to help elephant countries meet their custodial obligations to elephant populations? What would these support obligations involve? Should they apply to the opportunity cost of forgoing the sale of ivory as well as the cost of conservation programs? Should all who benefit from elephant protection share the cost? How might this be done? *See* Michael Glennon, *Has International Law Failed the Elephant?*, 84 AM. J. INT'L. L. 1, 34–43 (1990). Is there a role for UNEP through an international aid program to African countries? What role is there, if any, for the other UN agencies? What about debt for nature swaps? How about debt for ivory? Debt for nature swaps have been arranged for Bolivia, Costa Rica, Madagascar, the Philippines, Zambia, and elsewhere, often with support from non-governmental organizations like the World Wide Fund for Nature (WWF), and debt for ivory swaps have been proposed as a means of allowing governments to use the stockpiles they've seized from poachers or accumulated from ailing large populations or gathering ivory from animals that have died naturally. *See generally* Amanda Spitler, *Exchanging Debt for Conservation*, 37 BIOSCIENCE 781 (1987); *A Debt to Nature*, ECONOMIST, Aug. 19, 1989, at 35.

5.   In a protected environment, elephants thrive and multiply quickly. This consequence leads to biodiversity problems of its own making, as they choke out other species and, then, the species that fed on them. In other words, the laws protecting elephants can help make them a nuisance.

What is to be done about this dilemma? Should we allow the thinning of the populations by governments? They harvest the weak, old, and dying, sell the ivory on the legal market, and give the food to local persons (elephant meat dries to a sturdy jerky which will preserve for up to one year). What about a hunting season, much like the United States has with deer or elk? Shouldn't these countries be allowed to profit from the excess elephants their strong management system produces by "selling" the right to take a controlled number of surplus animals?

6.   The 1989 conference of parties to the CITES Convention [**Basic Document 6.5**] in Lausanne included the African elephant on Appendix I. That meeting also agreed to establish an experts panel to review the elephant stock and the management and enforcement measures undertaken by range countries for

consideration at the 1992 meeting. The experts panel found that the elephant populations of Botswana, South Africa, and Zimbabwe no longer met criteria for Appendix I listing. It found that South Africa and Zimbabwe had met all other criteria and therefore satisfied the conditions to resume the elephant trade. However, other Southern African range countries were found not to meet the criteria. Anti-poaching programs were deemed not uniformly effective.

At the 1992 Conference of the Parties the Southern African states of Botswana, Malawi, Namibia, South Africa, Zambia, and Zimbabwe proposed downgrading the classification of the African elephant to Appendix II. In deference to international concern over illegal poaching for ivory tusks, they modified their proposal to allow only for trade in elephant hide and meat gathered during regulated culling programmes. A number of African countries, the East African countries especially, as they are the hardest hit by poaching, responded by stressing that any trade in elephant hide and meat would be an incentive for poaching and stockpiling of ivory until the lifting of a ban in ivory trade. The Southern African States then withdrew their proposal. Efforts to find a compromise that would accommodate the Southern African concerns and give effect to the panel report were unsuccessful. There was strong pressure from animal welfare groups, conservation groups, and governments. The United Kingdom announced a contribution equal to US $1 million to support elephant conservation and enforcement programs in range States.

As noted earlier, the search for a compromise culminated in a partial lifting of the Appendix I listing for elephants by the 1997 Conference of the Parties. But what if elephants had not been downlisted for those countries with successful conservation programs? Would the governments of the States in Southern African have been justified in withdrawing from the Convention and trading in elephant products with countries not party to CITES? What if CITES loses the membership of countries because they see its protectionist philosophy as inconsistent with sustainable development? The proposals by Southern African states concerning the elephant are a response to this underlying issue.

7. SIMON LYSTER, INTERNATIONAL WILDLIFE LAW 240 (1985), considers that CITES is "perhaps the most successful of all international treaties concerned with the conservation of wildlife." This is true in terms of the numbers of States that are signatories. But just how effective is CITES? The illegal trade in endangered species continues. National record-keeping is poor. Many countries do not have inspection personnel trained to identify CITES species. Trade regulation is poor with respect to non-parties. Countries opt out of certain species protection (as provided for in Article XIII). Critics point to its failure to prevent the decline of rhino populations, despite the listing of rhinos on Appendix I since the inception of CITES. (Although others observe that non-listed rhino populations have recovered nicely, as the commercial trade in rhino parts has created an incentive for farming and conservation efforts.)

CITES is subject, moreover, to a number of pressures and challenges. There is the problem of block voting, where different geographic areas vote together for political or economic rather than scientific reasons. A country with a species at issue receives no extra votes on a listing issue. This means that range States have decisions imposed on them by countries distant from the associated local social and economic problems. This exacerbates the emerging North–South division over environmental protection versus sustainable development and sustainable use of wildlife. Is there a need for a reassessment of the protectionist philosophy and approach of CITES? Can the principle of the sustainable use and sustainable development of wildlife for the economic benefit of local populations be reconciled with CITES's more protectionist approach to conservation? If so, how?

8. The attitude of nongovernmental organisations, like the World Wide Fund for Nature, will have a major bearing on the future of CITES. To date domestic animal welfare groups and conservation groups in developed countries have been highly effective in mobilising governments. Would it be helpful for nongovernmental organisations to put their weight behind a review of CITES to integrate the principles underlying sustainable use and development?

The issue is also affected by the consumer demand for carved ivory. In some cultures ivory is in demand for medical, fertility, or religious purposes, including powdered ivory. There is already an environmental backlash taking its toll on ivory sales, even in Japan which for many years has been the world's biggest importer of ivory. Traders are experimenting with ram and water buffalo horns, hippopotamus teeth and trying other substitutes. What can individuals do to save the elephant? How can you change public opinion worldwide?

Would domestic legislation help? The African Elephant Conservation Act, 16 U.S.C.A. §§ 4201–4245 gives the United States Secretary of the Interior considerable powers. It is a criminal act in the United States to import raw or worked ivory in violation of the CITES Ivory Control System. The control system considers all intermediate forms of ivory between the whole tusk and the final retail product as raw ivory. The system is designed to make forgery and illegal permits much more difficult to use. However, once carved or powdered, there are practical problems of tracing and identification of illegal ivory. Should other countries integrate the Ivory Control System into their domestic law?

Some developing countries object vehemently to certain provisions of U.S. law which forbid trade in ivory, even if it is not detrimental to elephant populations, unless it can be shown to be of *benefit* to the elephant. Is this a case, as some poor nations charge, of the United States favoring animals over the poor peoples of the South, even when the animals are not endangered?

9. What if Bawanda wanted to raise elephants on farms and trade in ivory. Would this be permitted by CITES? *See* Hubertus Welsch, *Trade in Appendix I Species*, 13 ENVTL. POL'Y & L. 100 (1984). At COP–10 in Harare in June 1997, significant decisions were taken with the aim of encouraging ranching activities aimed at threatened species (albeit aimed at species other than the elephant).

10. The question of saving the elephant is part of a much bigger international environmental law issue: conserving biodiversity. Biological diversity encompasses three concepts—genetic diversity within each species, species diversity, and ecosystem diversity. The most effective way to conserve biodiversity is to prevent the destruction or degradation of habitat.

Why conserve biodiversity? That is the theme of the *Global Biodiversity Strategy* developed by the World Resources Institute, the World Conservation Union, and the United Nations Environment Programme in a cooperative effort and published in 1992. Consider the following statement from its Introduction (§ V):

Earth's plants, animals, and microorganisms—interacting with one another and with the physical environment in ecosystems—form the foundation of sustainable development. Biotic resources from this wealth of life support human livelihoods and aspirations and make it possible to adapt to changing needs and environments. The steady erosion of the diversity of genes, species, and ecosystems taking place today will undermine progress toward a sustainable society. Indeed, the continuing loss of biodiversity is a telling measure of the imbalance between human needs and wants and nature's capacity.... The human race had 850 million members when it entered the industrial age, sharing Earth with life forms nearly as diverse as the planet has ever possessed. Today, with population nearly six times as large and resource consumption proportionately far greater, both the limits of nature and the price of overstepping them are becoming clear. A turning point is upon us. We can continue to simplify the environment to meet immediate needs, at the cost of long-term benefits, or we can conserve life's precious diversity and use it sustainably. We can deliver to the next generation (and the next) a world rich in possibilities or one impoverished of life; but social and economic development will succeed only if we do the first.

11. The Japanese have argued, with respect to whaling, that preservation concerns are motivated by culturally specific values; the imposition of these values on countries and cultures that do not share them, is a form of imperialism. *See* Kazuo Sumi, *The "Whale War" Between Japan and the US: Problems and Prospects*, 17 DEN. J. INT'L L. & Pol'y 317 (1989); S. Holt, *Whale Mining, Whale Saving*, 9 MARINE POL'Y 192 (1985). Consider, also, the following Japanese newspaper report:

> Whale meat fans, munching chewy chunks of blubber in the raw fish bars and restaurants of Japan, are worried that their whale hunters will be forced by international pressure to hang up their harpoons.
>
> "Is whale meat really going to disappear from restaurants?" asked businessman Keita Kurosaki in between mouthfuls of dark red whale meat.
>
> Just about every Japanese hopes not. Whale meat, they say, is not only delicious, it's good for you.
>
> "It's low in calories, rich in protein, and taste," said a slender female college student in a restaurant specialising in whale meat. "Whale meat is a health food, isn't it?"
>
> A man in his late 20s said; "It's great to eat whale meat as regular meal, or as a light snack after work."
>
> "It's so good—just try it," added a middle-aged businessman.
>
> Japanese people react emotionally to western demands that whale killing be stopped to help save many species which western experts say are facing extinction.
>
> The Minister of Agriculture, Forestry and Fisheries, Mr. Mutsuki Kato, summed up the opinion of most of his countrymen in a speech to Parliament last month.
>
> "A large number of Japanese feel it ridiculous that it's all right to kill cows but not whales," Mr. Kato said.
>
> "We feel a statement saying it is barbaric to eat whales is racially prejudiced, and we are not convinced when we are told not to hunt whales in our own waters." ...

Eriko Sugita, *Japanese are Still Eating Whales Despite Protests*, BUSINESS TIMES (Tokyo), Sept. 3, 1987, *as reprinted in* TOM MILLIKEN, DECIMATION OF WORLD WILDLIFE: JAPAN AS NUMBER ONE, app. VIII (1988).

The Japanese argue that since some whale stocks, the minke particularly, have recovered well, they should be free to resume whaling on a commercial basis.

In protected areas, the elephant too is recovering to the point of creating problems. Why should countries like Japan be condemned for importing ivory when situations like this exist? Is it another incidence of cultural imperialism? It certainly appears that cultural attitudes inform our response to the eating of whale meat. In Japan the principal use of ivory is for hanko, personalized signature seals which are considered status symbols. To what extent do Western cultural ideals inhibit the reasonable culling of elephants that exceed their available habitat?

Japan is one of the countries that readily imports ivory. In 1989, Japan's unilateral bans did not include raw ivory from African countries that are CITES parties. It announced its intention to trade with "managed" States that refused to join the ban. Such states cull their elephant populations and purport to use the proceeds for conservation. *See* Michael Glennon, *Has International Law Failed the Elephant?*, 84 Am. J. Int'l L. (1990). With elephants it can be argued that legal trade provides a cover for illegal trade from truly endangered elephant populations. With whaling there is a problem with enforcement; exactly what whales and how many are being taken? The question remains, however: should the cultural values of some regulate the conduct of all?

12. Elephants are by no means the only large mammals on the list of endangered species. For example, tigers are being hunted to a point which they are now reaching extinction. There is a flourishing market in tiger bones in some Asian countries, and it seems that the "few remaining wild tiger populations may not survive beyond the end of this decade." *See Tiger Bone Survey—Undercover Survey of Markets Reveals Tons of Tiger Bone For Sale*, Earth Trust Chronicles 14 (Summer, 1993). Similarly the rhinoceros is in trouble, as well as some species of dolphin and whales. As is pointed out by Patricia W. Birnie and Alan E. Boyle in International Law and the Environment 240 (1993):

> The threats to wildlife arise from a wide variety of sources. Various species have been captured throughout the centuries not only for food, but for their skins, feathers and other products used or traded by man [sic], for display in zoos, for scientific research, as pelts, and for medicinal, cultural, religious, and artistic purposes among others. Such activities, if extensive, are now seen not only as threats to the existence of individual species or habitats but also to the biodiversity represented by such species, which provides, *inter alia*, a gene pool of immense present and future value to humankind as well as having value for its own sake.

13. Do "common heritage" arguments override cultural arguments? *See* Eugene Hargrove, *An Overview of Conservation and Human Values: Are Conservation Goals Merely Cultural Attitudes?*, *in* Conservation for the Twenty-First Century 227 (David Western & Mary Pearl eds. 1989). *See also* Bryan Norton, *The Cultural Approach to Conservation Biology, in id.*, at 241.

14. Can species and/or ecosystems really be managed? When elephants are protected, they place disproportionate demands on the available ecosystem. Does this indicate that by focusing on species rather than adopting an ecosystem approach, management attempts are necessarily rendered ineffective? What has been the outcome of other instances of attempted management? Is an ecosystem approach possible? *See* Anne Batchelor, *The Preservation of Wildlife Habitat in Ecosystems: Towards a New Direction Under International Law to Prevent Species' Extinction*, 3 Fla. Int'l L.J. 307 (1988). *See also* Sarah Fitzgerald, International Wildlife Trade: Whose Business Is It? (1989).

15. What about the law enforcement issues in the problem? Reading 17 suggests that Usambara may well have violated international law in allowing its troops to enter Bawandaan territory in pursuit of poachers. But what choice did it have, given Bawanda's refusal to cooperate in combatting poaching? Should some sort of exception to the usual rules be invoked to permit Usambara to take action in a situation of this sort? What general rule might justify crossing the border? What limits should be imposed? Is an analogy to the Law of the Sea doctrine of "hot pursuit" appropriate? The doctrine of "hot pursuit" permits a coastal state to pursue foreign ships into international waters and seize them there when it has good reason to believe that the foreign ship has violated its laws and the pursuit begins within the pursuing state's territorial sea or contiguous zone. *See* United Nations Convention on the Law of the Sea, art. 111 [**Basic Document 4.20**].

16. Reading 18, *supra*, shows how the United Nations Environment Programme (UNEP), set up in the aftermath of the 1972 Stockholm conference, does not really have authority to protect the environment. It can encourage ecologically wise practices. It can warn against ecologically unwise ones. But it cannot alone accomplish much; it is not even a full-fledged United Nations agency. Could a differently constituted organization achieve more? Is it realistic to expect nations to consent to an international agency that would have real power and authority to protect the environment? How would such an agency work?

Glennon suggests that UNEP could be responsible for arranging assistance to game wardens. He envisages that this could involve some form of paramilitary or police training and that UNEP should be able to call upon countries in the manner of the Security Council under Chapter VII of the U. N. Charter [**Basic Document 1.3**]. *See* Michael Glennon, *Has International Law Failed the Elephant?*, 84 Am. J. Int'l L. 1, 38 (1990). Are suggestions such as these consistent with UNEP's existing powers and resources? What are UNEP's limitations? What extra powers does it need? *See* Mark Gray, *The United Nations Environment Programme: An Assessment*, 20 Envtl. L. 291 (1990); Carol Petsonk, *The Role of UNEP in the Development of International Environmental Law* 5 Am. U. Int'l L. & Pol'y 217 (1990); Nicholas Robinson, *Introduction: Emerging International Environmental Law*, 17 Stan. J. Int'l L. 229 (1981).

17. Far from expanding UNEP's authority, the trend during the 1990s has been to reduce UNEP's role and to locate some environmental policy-making responsibilities elsewhere. The 1992 Rio Conference on Environment and Development established a new agency, the Sustainable Development Commission, to monitor the implementation of the output of the Rio Conference. *See* **Basic Document 1.31**. By the mid–1990s, responsibility for developing and implementing international environmental policy was spread among a patchwork of agencies:

Several United Nations bodies currently operate to address environmental concerns, either directly, as do the United Nations Environment Programme (UNEP), the United Nations Development Programme (UNDP), and the United Nations Commission on Sustainable Development (CSD); or peripherally, as the United Nations Educational, Scientific and Cultural Organization (UNESCO), the International Maritime Organization (IMO), and the Organization for Economic Co-operation and Development (OECD). Following the Rio Conference, cooperative environmental action was revitalized within the UN system, and the UNDP, in conjunction with the CSD, has taken a coordinating role in promoting environmentally sound development practices. The CSD actively gathers information and promotes follow-up on the Rio

Conference, and it recommends prudent environmental and development policies.

Melanne Andromecca Civic, *A New Conceptual Framework for Jordan River Basin Management: A Proposal for a Trusteeship Commission*, 9 COLO. J. INT'L ENVTL. L. & POL'Y 285, 324–25 (1998). As other agencies began to strengthen their role in addressing environmental problems, some governments began to suggest that UNEP might be superfluous. In 1997, UNEP survived a major assault on its existence, an assault led by the United States. *See Dowdeswell Defends UNEP Credentials to Increasingly Skeptical Governing Council*, BNA Int'l Envtl. Daily (Feb. 5, 1997). In the end, UNEP's central role in international environmental affairs was confirmed by the Nairobi Declaration **[Basic Document 1.38]**, although UNEP was somewhat restructured by the creation of a High–Level Committee of Ministers and Officials in Charge of Environment, essentially a body of government representatives established to keep regular tabs on UNEP's functioning. After the implementation of this change, UN Secretary–General Kofi Annan also emphasized the central role of UNEP (not insignificantly, the only UN agency headquartered in a developing country) in his 1997 report on UN Reform. *See Secretary General's Report on Reforms Gives New Support for Continuing UNEP*, BNA Int'l Envtl. Daily (July 22, 1997).

18. Throughout negotiations for the 1992 Convention on Biological Diversity **[Basic Document 6.11]**, concerns were expressed regarding intellectual property and free trade. Though the United States has now endorsed the Convention, the chief of the U.S. delegation said that the Convention was "flawed" because it failed to provide adequate protection of intellectual property and that it would have a dampening affect on free trade in genetically engineered organisms. It was perceived that the treaty's language allows countries that are the source of raw materials for biotechnology to pass laws that reduce the intellectual property rights of companies involved. Such concerns pose yet another barrier to protection for biodiversity. How can such concerns be resolved? How do they fit with the "common heritage" principle. Who should benefit from biodiversity? Who should control it?

19. On final analysis, is concern for the elephant misguided? Consider the following extract:

> Biotic diversity is not linked to the distribution of elephants, rhinos, and other so-called charismatic megaherbivores. The massive investment in conservation campaigns directed at these species does more for the souls of the donors and the egos of the elephant experts than it does for biotic diversity, which is centered on less exciting communities of montane, forests, Mediterranean heathlands, wetlands, lakes and rivers.

Brian Huntley, *Conserving and Monitoring Biotic Diversity: Some African Examples*, in BIODIVERSITY 248, 259 (E. Wilson ed. 1988).

20. *Bibliographical Note.* For further discussion concerning the principal themes addressed in this problem, consult the following additional specialized materials:

(a) *Specialized Books/Monographs.* Biodiversity (E. Wilson ed., 1988); F. Cairncross, Costing the Earth (2d ed. 1992); S. Colb, The Ivory Trade and the Future of the African Elephant (1989); P. Ehrlich & A. Ehrlich, Extinction: The Causes and Consequences of the Disappearance of Species (1981); D. Favre, International Trade in Endangered Species: A Guide to CITES (1989); S. Fitzgerald, International Wildlife Trade: Whose Business Is It? (1989); D. Harland,

Killing Game: International Law and the African Elephant (Praeger Publishers, 1994); S. Lyster, International Wildlife Law (1985); R. Martin, J. Caldwell & J. Berzdo, African Elephants, CITES, and the Ivory Trade (1986); N. Myers, A Wealth of Wild Species (1983); I. Parker & M. Amin, Ivory Crisis (1985); E. Wilson, The Diversity of Life (1992).

(b) *Specialized Hearings/Reports*. Environmental Investigation Agency, A System of Extinction: The African Elephant Disaster (1989).

(c) *Specialized Articles/Book Chapters*. A. Batchelor, *The Preservation of Wildlife Habitat in Ecosystems: Towards a New Direction Under International Law to Prevent Species' Extinction*, 3 Fla. Int'l L. J. 307 (1988); W. Booth, *Africa Is Becoming an Elephant Graveyard*, 243 Science 732 (1989); M. Bowman, *The Protection of Animals Under International Law*, 4 Conn. J. Int'l L. 487 (1989); J. Cheung, Comment, *Implementation and Enforcement of CITES: An Assessment of Tiger and Rhinoceros Conservation Policy in Asia*, 5 Pac. Rim L. & Pol'y J. 125 (1995); T. Dobson, *Loss of BioDiversity: An International Environmental Policy Perspective*, 17 N.C.J. Int'l L. & Com. Reg. 277 (1992); D. Favre, *Tension Points Within the Language of the CITES Treaty*, 5 B.U.J. Int'l L. 247 (1987); D. Favre, *The Risk of Extinction: A Risk Analysis of the Endangered Species Act as Compared to CITES*, 6 N.Y.U. Envtl. L.J. 341 (1998); W. Flevares, *Ecosystems, Economics, and Ethics: Protecting Biological Diversity at Home and Abroad*, 65 S. Cal. L. Rev. 2039 (1992); M. Gray, *The United Nations Environment Programme: An Assessment*, 20 Envtl. L. 291 (1990); A. Heimert, *How the Elephant Lost his Tusks*, 104 Yale L.J. 1473 (1995); C. Kripes, *Sustainable Use of Endangered Species Under CITES: Is it a Sustainable Alternative?*, 17 U. Pa. J. Int'l Econ. L. 461 (1996); C. Kripes, *Sustainable Use of Endangered Species Under CITES: Is it a Sustainable Alternative?*, 17 U. Pa. J. Int'l Econ. L. 461 (1996); K. Liwo, *The Continuing Significance of the Convention on International Trade in Endangered Species of Wild Fauna and Flora During the 1990's*, 15 Suffolk Transnat'l L. J. 121 (1991); G. Maggio, *Recognizing the Vital Role of Local Communities in International Legal Instruments for Conserving Biodiversity*, 16 UCLA J. Envtl. L. & Pol'y 179 (1997–1998); G. Meyers, *Surveying the Lay of the Land, Air, and Water: Features of Current International Environmental and Natural Resources Law, and Future Prospects for the Protection of Species Habitat to Preserve Global Biological Diversity*, 3 Colo. J. Int'l L. & Pol'y 479 (1992); N. Myers, *Endangered Species*, in the North–South Dialogue in Economics of Ecosystem Management (D. Hall, N. Myers & N. Margolis eds. 1985); B. Padgett, *The African Elephant, Africa, and CITES: The Nest Step*, 2 Ind. J. Global Legal Stud. 529 (1995); C. Petsonk, *The Role of UNEP in the Development of International Environmental Law*, 5 Am. U. J. Int'l L. & Pol'y 217 (1990); R. Shaw, Note, *Nabbing the Gourmet Club: Utilizing RICO Enforcement and Punitive Provisions to Curb the International Trade of Endangered Species*, 42 N.Y.L. Sch. L. Rev. 283 (1998); D. Vice, Note, *Implementation of Biodiversity Treaties: Monitoring, Fact–Finding, and Dispute Resolution*, 29 N.Y.U. J. Int'l L. & Pol'y 577 (1997); D. Woodruff, *The Problems of Conserving Genes and Species*, in Conservation for the Twenty–First Century 83 (D. Western & M. Pearl eds., 1989).

(d) *Useful Internet Sites. United Nations Environment Programme*, (visited Oct. 27, 1998) <www.unep.org>; *World Wildlife Fund*, (visited Sept. 16, 1998) <www.wwf.org>; *Wildnet*, (visited Oct. 26, 1998) <www.wildnetafrica.com>; *CITES*, (visited Oct. 27, 1998) <www.wcmc.org.uk/CITES>.

Problem 10–3

A Rainforest and the Guahibo Are Threatened in Amazonia and Caribia

SECTION 1. FACTS

The South American countries of Amazonia and Caribia share a highly biodiverse rainforest, the boundaries of which extend across the political borders of both nations. In addition to potentially supporting over ten percent of the Earth's remaining unknown or non-described gene pool, this nearly pristine rainforest is home to an indigenous people known as the Guahibo. Utilizing the resources of this rich biotic zone to support their traditional lifestyle and culture, the Guahibo reside on both sides of the modern Amazonia-Caribia border.

The Guahibo people live throughout the rainforest in small communal villages, which are periodically moved as food resources are depleted through consumption and seasonal change. While the Guahibo of Amazonia and Caribia rarely move their entire villages across the national border, sections of both populations do so frequently. These movements take the form of social visitations, marriage exchanges, ceremonial festivals, and trading ventures.

The political organization of the Guahibo is focused at the village-household level; however, a "headman" is often vested with the power to make "economic" decisions for a coalition of three to four villages. These decisions typically involve designating the hunting and gathering resource areas an individual village may access, how resources are to be divided between villages, and when it is time for a village to relocate to a new location. Although other factors are considered, the ability to maintain a steady flow of resources is the primary quality an individual must possess to be a headman.

In the late 1980s, the Government of Caribia created an "Equatorial Reserve" in Caribia's portion of the rainforest. The reserve was initiated to protect the unique Guahibo culture from outside economic practices and to safeguard the rainforest's resources. Fearing non-native practices would adversely impact the Guahibo and the biotic resources, outsiders such as missionaries, miners, hunters, and traders were restricted from entering the rainforest sanctuary.

Accomplished through a so-called debt-for-nature swap engineered by the Nature Conservancy (NC)[a] and the World Bank, the Equatorial Reserve is administered, according to the debt-for-nature agreement, by a Governing

---

a. The Nature Conservancy is an international nongovernmental organization (NGO) with forty years of experience, and approximately 650,000 members worldwide that has as its objective, the purchase of land for the preservation of biological diversity by saving plants, animals, and their habitats from extinction. Its Latin American division, a principal player in trying to save Latin America's rain forests, reefs, grasslands and groves, already has helped to protect more than 20 million

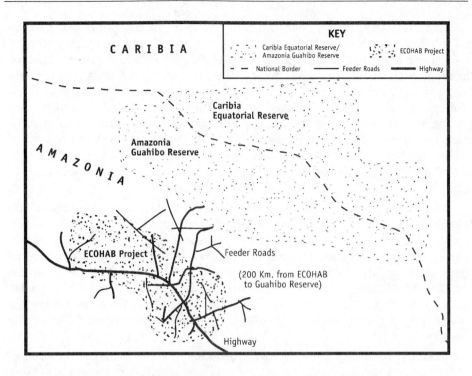

Board composed of members of the NC's local Caribian chapter, officials of the Caribian government, and members of the Guahibo tribe. Thus far the principal difficulty faced by the Board has been preventing encroachment into the Reserve by self-proclaimed "settlers" from the outside, especially miners, squatters and poachers. Many of these so-called settlers have occupied, slashed and burned parts of the "medicine valley" where many of the herbal and medicinal plants of the Guahibo are found to grow. Through strict penalties and stepped-up patrols, however, the Board has gradually reduced the violations by its own nationals to an acceptable level. The greater problem has been the encroachment of non-native people from the adjacent Guahibo reserve across the border in Amazonia.

In an attempt to protect indigenous communities from the effects of a vast state-sponsored development project, the Amazonian government formed a number of tribal reservations for indigenous peoples. Encompassing the portion of rainforest adjacent to the Caribian Equatorial Reserve, the Amazonian Guahibo Reserve was one of these protected regions. The project, financed by the World Bank and called Eco–Habitacion (ECOHAB), originally envisioned the widespread colonization of the northern Amazonian province of Matorral. To reduce population pressures in the eastern cities and to begin what was foreseen as a hugely profitable exploitation of Matorral, ECOHAB included an ambitious road building project and settlement plan. First, a federal highway was constructed which traversed the province along with a system of feeder roads. Next, ranching was introduced as well as "sustainable" tree farming.

acres of tropical habitat in Latin America and
the Caribbean.

Unfortunately, as has been the case elsewhere in the rainforest, neither the ranching nor the tree farming proved successful. Ranching quickly became unproductive due to the mineral leaching of rangeland; while sustainable tree farming, because of incentive mismanagement and poor soils, made little headway against traditional "slash and burn" practices. To compound the problem, small quantities of gold and tin have been found in the region, leading to a surge of new immigrants. In response, the Amazonian government has proposed a second phase of ECOHAB that includes the introduction of charcoal-burning pig-iron smelters and large scale tin mining, as well as a secondary system of feeder roads to open up new land—and to these ends it again has sought financing from the World Bank.

Due to its long distance from the locus of project activities (about 200 kilometers), the Amazonian Guahibo Reserve remained relatively undisturbed during the early stages of ECOHAB. In recent years, however, a nearly lawless environment has emerged in Matorral, with the Amazonian government showing little ability or inclination to protect the Reserve from encroachment. Among other developments, settlers have extended the feeder roads to the Reserve's boundaries. Encouraged by several Guahibo headmen a steady flow of miners and traders have used these feeder roads to enter the Reserve.

Seeking what they believed would benefit the eleven villages they represented, three Guahibo headmen invited gold and cassiterite[b] miners into their territory. In exchange for allowing the miners to prospect for gold and tin within the reserve, the cooperating headmen and their people would receive annual payments of western goods. While the majority of these villagers welcomed the useful items brought by the miners, as well as the traders who followed in their wake, a few of them were angered by the presence of these outsiders on their lands. Some of the dissatisfied villagers, along with a considerable number of Guahibo from other communities, fled to Caribia's Equatorial Reserve because they feared the miners' practices and the increase in illnesses that appeared soon after their arrival.

Understandably, the government of Caribia and the NC see a threat to their conservationist and protective efforts. In particular, Caribia and the NC are concerned that the Amazonian miners will extend their operations into the Caribian Equatorial Reserve. Furthermore, there is a fear that the Reserve will be jeopardized by the strain refugee Guahibos will place on its biotic resources. Repeated demands by Caribia for Amazonia to halt the flow of Guahibo refugees into their country have been ignored. As a consequence, Caribia has become increasingly strident in international circles. With approximately one-half of the Guahibo tribe residing in the contiguous Amazonian reserve, Caribia previously believed that the immediate problem could be contained if Amazonia would simply protect its Guahibo Reserve with proper diligence under Amazonian law. However, seeing the considerable dangers that lie ahead, Caribia now demands that the vast Amazonian development projects to the south of its Guahibo Reserve be stopped or, at least, sharply cut back. Amazonia refuses to entertain such a demand, claiming the right to develop according to its own policies, and the parties remain deadlocked.

b. Native stannic acid, the most common ore of tin.

In light of this impasse, Caribia has referred its dispute with Amazonia to arbitration under the 1992 Convention on Biological Diversity. In its notification under article 1 of Annex II of the Convention, Caribia alleges violation by Amazonia of articles 3–5 and 8(j) of the Convention, stating that Amazonia's actions have threatened the conservation of biological diversity both in Caribia and Amazonia. Both countries have signed and ratified the Convention, and both have accepted arbitration as their chosen means of dispute settlement under article 27(3)(a) of the Convention. The Arbitral Tribunal has called for written memorials from each of the parties.

In addition, Caribia has filed a "complaint of non-observance" against Amazonia at the headquarters of the International Labour Organization (ILO) in Geneva, Switzerland. The complaint alleges multiple violations of the 1989 ILO Convention (No. 169) Concerning Indigenous and Tribal Peoples in Independent Countries, which both Amazonia and Caribia have signed and ratified, as they have also all other potentially relevant human rights treaties.[c] Under article 26 of the ILO Constitution, the complaint has been referred to an independent Commission of Inquiry which has called for written arguments from both countries.

With the concurrence of the parties, both the Biodiversity Convention's Arbitral Tribunal and the ILO's Commission of Inquiry have decided to sit together, as one joint tribunal, and have announced that they will not entertain arguments relating to remedies until they have heard arguments on the alleged breaches of international law.

SECTION 2. QUESTIONS PRESENTED

1. Has Amazonia violated international obligations within the competence/jurisdiction of the Biodiversity Convention's Arbitral Tribunal?

2. Has Amazonia violated international law within the cognizance of the ILO's Commission of Inquiry?

SECTION 3. ASSIGNMENTS

A. *Reading Assignment*

Study the Readings presented in Section 4, *infra,* and the Discussion Notes/Questions that follow. Also, to the extent possible, consult the accompanying bibliographical references.

B. *Recommended Writing Assignment*

Prepare a comprehensive, logically sequenced, and *argumentative* brief in the form of an outline of the primary and subsidiary *legal* issues you see requiring resolution by the Biodiversity Arbitral Tribunal and the ILO's

---

c. In addition to ILO Convention No.169, Amazonia and Caribia are parties to the United Nations Charter, the 1948 Convention on the Prevention and Punishment of the Crime of Genocide, the 1966 International Covenant on Economic, Social and Cultural Rights, the 1966 International Covenant on Civil and Political Rights, and the 1969 American Convention on Human Rights. In addition, they are signatories to the 1948 Universal Declaration of Human Rights.

Commission of Inquiry. Also, from the perspective of an independent objective judge, indicate which side ought to prevail on each issue and why. Retain a copy of your issue-outline/brief for class discussion.

C. Recommended Oral Assignment

Assume you are legal counsel for Caribia or Amazonia (as designated by your instructor); then, relying upon the Readings (and your issue-outline if prepared), present a 15–20 minute oral argument of your government's likely positions before the Biodiversity Arbitral Tribunal and the ILO Commission of Inquiry.

D. Recommended Reflective Assignment

Consider (and recommend) alternative norms, institutions, and/or procedures that you believe might do better than existing world order arrangements to contend with situations of the kind posed by this problem. In so doing, but without insisting upon *immediate* feasibility, identify the particular transition steps that would be needed to make your alternatives a reality.

SECTION 4. READINGS

1. **Convention on Biological Diversity,** *reprinted in* **31 I.L.M. 822 (1992)** [Basic Document 6.11].

2. **Peter H. Raven & Jeffrey A. McNeely,** *Biological Extinction: Its Scope and Meaning for Us, in* PROTECTION OF GLOBAL BIODIVERSITY: CONVERGING STRATEGIES 13, 13–30 (Lakshman D. Guruswamy & Jeffrey A. McNeely eds., 1998).

INTRODUCTION

We are confronting an episode of species extinction greater than anything that the world has experienced for the past 65 million years. To understand species extinction in the broadest possible terms, consider this fundamental fact: the Earth, our planetary home, is finite. Since the Earth is limited, and everything in it is limited, the economic formulas developed over the past few hundred years to keep track of the values involved in human transactions cannot make it any larger, nor give us any more of the productive systems and commodities on which we depend. It does not matter what conversions may be possible: no matter how clever we may be, the Earth remains the same. Contrary to the wishful thinking embodied in some cornucopian scenarios, the Earth and its systems can either be used in such a way as to provide a sustainable context for our operations, or we shall destroy them. We are currently losing the biological diversity on which we depend at a rate that will greatly limit our future options.

* * *

FUTURE EXTINCTION RATES

How do we project rates of species loss reasonably into the future? First, the 1.4 million species that have been named and classified probably represent no more than 15 percent of the world's total species. This number is currently estimated by many scientists at about 10 million species, approximately 85 percent of them terrestrial; some scientists consider far higher numbers to be credible. Probably at least 7 million of them occur in the tropics and subtropics, with 1.5–2 million in the better-known temperate regions. These estimates refer to species of eukaryotic organisms only (organisms with cells that have a contained nucleus); current methods are unable to estimate the numbers of distinct kinds of bacteria or viruses. The insects have an especially interesting history.... [I]nsects possess an extensive fossil record which demonstrates that their diversity at the family level exceeds that of preserved vertebrate tetrapods through 91 percent of their evolutionary history. The great diversity of insects was achieved not by high origination rates but rather by low extinction rates comparable to the low rates of slowly-evolving marine invertebrate groups. The great radiation of modern insects began 245 million years ago and was not accelerated by the expansion of angiosperms—flowering plants—during the Cretaceous period. The basic trophic machinery of insects was in place nearly 100 million years before angiosperms appeared in the fossil record, so the loss of these ancient life forms seems especially tragic.

The geological record suggests that despite recent depredations, we share the Earth now with the largest number of species that have ever existed at one time, with the communities and ecosystems of the tropics the richest in number of species and most complex that have ever occurred.

Judging from the fossil record, the average life span of a species is about 4 million years, and of a mammal is about 2 million years. If the total number of species in the world is about 10 million, then the background rate of extinction can be calculated at about 4 species per year. This appears to be a reasonable order-of-magnitude estimate, even though extinction rates (and the longevity of species) vary widely between groups. At such a rate, approximately 40,000 species of organisms would have become extinct during the first 10,000 years following the appearance of agriculture. For the approximately 250,000 species of plants, it would amount to the disappearance of one species every 10 years; for the 4,500 mammals, one every 275 years; and for the 9,000 bird species, one every 275 years (assuming an avian species lifespan of 4 million years).

In fact, at least 115 species of birds and 58 species of mammals have become extinct during the past 400 years, during which the number of human beings in the world has increased 11-fold to its current level of 5.5 billion people. This documents a rate of extinction for these groups more than 50 times the base level. Since 1930, when the global human population reached two billion people, at least 19 species of birds and 14 species of mammals have become extinct, with more extinctions probable but not yet finally documented. The rates for the past 64 years, therefore, can be documented to be roughly 100 times the base level for these groups, and are probably considerably higher—despite intensive efforts to conserve species of birds and mammals.

In temperate regions, for groups that are well known, such as plants, butterflies, and vertebrate animals, it is generally the case that about 10 percent of the species in a given area are currently regarded by specialists as threatened or endangered. The figures are much higher for freshwater organisms than for terrestrial ones; thus, more than 70 percent of the 297 native freshwater mussels in the United States are considered threatened, endangered, or of special concern. Although some industrialized countries, such as the United States, are in a position to put substantial resources into the preservation of biodiversity, other nations are not so fortunate. Thus, the losses in temperate countries such as Chile and South Africa, with very large numbers of species found nowhere else, are likely to be great.

Predictions of extinction rates in the future have been based largely on the demonstrated relationship between species number in a given group of organisms and area. The relationship between species number and area is expressed by the formula $S = CAz$, where S is the number of species, A is the area of the place where the species live, and C and z are constants. For purposes of calculating rates of species extinction, C can be ignored, and z is what counts. Generally, the value of z varies between 0.15 and 0.35, with the exact value depending on the kind of organism being considered and the habitats in which those organisms are found. As Wilson has pointed out, when species are able to disperse easily from one place to another, z is low; when they do not have this ability, z is high. Thus, birds have a low z value, orchids a high z value.

The rule of thumb, which corresponds to the commonly-observed z value of 0.3, is that when an area is reduced to one-tenth of its original size, the number of species eventually drops to half. The word "eventually" is used because some species may disappear immediately when the forest is cleared, while others decline slowly and constitute what Janzen called "the living dead." Also, for as many as half of the original species to persist in a habitat that has been reduced to a tenth of its original size assumes that what remains is an undivided block of the original habitat in optimal condition. Even now, about two-thirds of the surviving tropical rain forests are highly fragmented. Large blocks of individual forests rarely persist, so that the rate of survival at equilibrium is likely to be very much lower, with as few as 30 percent, 20 percent, or even 10 percent of the original species surviving. When the last forest patches are cleared in a given area, the rate of survival suddenly may drop to near zero.

* * *

The relationship between species number and the area the species inhabit has been clearly demonstrated for hundreds of different habitats and situations throughout the world. Obviously, exceptional situations exist that prove the rule, but it is time to stop picking at the general pattern with individual exceptions to try to argue to a conclusion that defies the very substantial body of information that exists in this area. We therefore apply these principles to an analysis of what extinction rates are likely in the coming decades.

The rate of clearing of all tropical forests in the 1980s was estimated by the United Nations' main agency dealing with forests, the Food and Agriculture Organization (FAO), at 0.8 percent per year. For tropical rain forests and other moist tropical forests, they calculated the rate for the 1980s at 1.5 percent per year, reaching 1.8 percent by the end of the decade. In other words, an area of the biologically richest and most poorly-known ecosystem on Earth equal in size to the state of Florida is clear-cut each year. A problem with forest-loss data, important though it certainly is, is that it is not able to pick up other types of negative impacts on the habitat, such as the plowing of grasslands, overgrazing of rangelands, draining wetlands, damming streams, pollution of soils and water, introduction of exotic organisms, hunting pressures, and so forth. In all forests, at least an equivalent amount is grossly disrupted each year through such practices as selective logging and slash-and-burn agriculture, but let us accept only clear-cutting as a basis for our calculations here. Following his careful review of the data, Wilson has calculated that for the area occupied by tropical rain forest alone, and using the most conservative projection of the relationship between species number and area, 2.7 percent of the species in the tropical rain forest are being lost per decade, a rate of extinction well over 10,000 times the background extinction rate for this area—and doubtless a minimum estimate; alarming as is such a rate, Smith et al. have arrived at a similar extinction rate, based on their global analysis of several lines of evidence. Furthermore, rates of forest destruction are accelerating throughout the world, and roughly doubled for tropical rain forests during the 1980s; consequently, rates of extinction can logically be expected to increase rapidly in the future. As mentioned earlier, the global population is not expected to stabilize until it has doubled or tripled, and 90 percent of that growth is projected to take place in the tropics.

On the basis of similar projections, Simberloff has calculated that by the end of the next century about two-thirds of all plant and bird species in South America will have become extinct. His calculations are conservative, because they unrealistically assume a constant rate of forest clearing similar to that experienced in the 1980s. Although the actions that we may take can still affect the situation profoundly, it is difficult to imagine any area of the tropics persisting with more than a tenth of its original vegetation undisturbed by the end of the next century, so that very conservatively a quarter of global biodiversity will have disappeared by that time for reasons of the clearing of tropical rain forest alone.

We can summarize the current situation as follows. Assuming a total of 10 million species in the world, and a current extinction rate of 5 percent per decade, which is a moderate estimate of the loss as estimated by people competent to deal with the field, we would be losing an average of 50,000 species per year over the next several decades—of which only 7,000, on the average, would have been recognized and named. These losses would include about 20 species of mammals, 40 species of birds, and 1,250 species of plants per year—staggering figures, but ones consistent with the rates of loss of habitat that are currently observed, and likely to occur in the future if we simply ignore them and get on with "business as usual." Even at the most conservative level ever calculated for extinction rates, we are in the process of losing a fifth that many species per year—no less than 250 species of plants, for example.

Throughout the world, rates of extinction will depend to a very great extent on the way in which we treat individual areas. For example, areas of high biological diversity and threat, which Myers has termed "hot spots," contain an estimated 20 percent of the world's plant species in about 0.5 percent of the world's total land surface. Taking these and other factors into account, those scientists who have attempted to estimate species extinction over—the people who are competent and active specialists in the field, and understand the factual and theoretical basis of dealing with it—have arrived at extinction rates centering around 5 percent of the world's total species per decade, with some estimates as low as 1 percent (2,500 times the background rate of extinction for the past 65 million years) and others as high as 11 percent per decade (nearly 30,000 times the background rate). As Wilson has pointed out succinctly, "Clearly we are in the midst of one of the great extinction spasms of geological history."

If two-thirds of living species are indeed lost over the course of the next century, the proportion will be more or less equivalent to that which disappeared at the end of the Cretaceous Period, 65 million years ago—one of the several great extinction events of Earth history. It took more than 5 million years for the world to regain its ecological equilibrium after that event, a sobering period of time to contemplate since it is more than 10 times the length of history of our own species.

WHY DOES IT MATTER?

Why is the loss of biodiversity important? The answers to this question are not generally well understood by the general public, or even by policy-makers. For example, a study commissioned in 1993 by Defenders of Wildlife showed clearly that most Americans are unaware of the scope or importance of biodiversity, instead regarding many more local and less threatening problems, such as pollution, as more serious. Viewed appropriately, the loss of species and their genetic diversity is not a matter of the decimation of rhinos or elephants, or of the northern spotted owl, the Tennessee snail darter, or the Furbish lousewort—icons that convey very different messages to people who approach them from different standpoints. Instead, the loss of biodiversity should be viewed as a ripping apart—desecration, in the literal sense—of the fabric of our living world, and the destruction of the machinery that makes our unique planetary home function. Only someone unaware, or unwilling to become aware, of the way in which living systems function could conceivably view this destruction with indifference, because it will profoundly affect the future of each of us, of our children and their children, and of our planet for as long as our species exists.

The reasons for being concerned with the loss of biodiversity fall into three basic classes: ethical; economic; and ecological.

The Ethical and Aesthetic Values

As Paul Ehrlich and Edward O. Wilson put it in their acceptance of the Crafoord Prize, the Royal Swedish Academy's equivalent of the Nobel Prize for ecology, in 1990 the first reason is ethical and aesthetic.

> Because *Homo sapiens* is the dominant species on Earth, we and many others think that people have an absolute moral responsibility to protect what are our only known living companions in the universe. Human responsibility in this respect is deep, beyond measure, beyond conventional science for the moment, but urgent nonetheless. The popularity of ecotourism, bird-watching, wildlife films, pet-keeping, and gardening attest that human beings gain great rewards from those companions [and generate substantial economic activity in the process].

A related view, strongly supportive of a reverence for life, was presented by Charles Darwin in the concluding paragraph of his classic of 1859, "On the Origin of Species...."

> It is interesting to contemplate a tangled bank, clothed with many plants of many kinds, with birds singing on the bushes, with various insects flitting about, and with worms crawling through the damp Earth, and to reflect that these elaborately constructed forms, so different from each other, and dependent upon each other in so complex a manner, have all been produced by laws acting around us. These laws, taken in the largest sense, being Growth with reproduction; Inheritance which is almost implied by reproduction; Variability from the indirect and direct action of the conditions of life, and from use and disuse; a Ratio of Increase so high as to lead to a Struggle for Life, and as a consequence to Natural Selection, entailing Divergence of Character and the Extinction of less improved forms. Thus, from the war of nature, from famine and death, the most exalted object which we are capable of conceiving, namely, the production of the higher animals, directly follows. There is grandeur in this view of life with its several powers, having been originally breathed by the Creator into a few forms or into one; and that, while this planet has gone circling on according to the fixed law of gravity, from so simple a beginning endless forms most beautiful and most wonderful have been, and are being evolved.

Aldo Leopold's (1949) words put the matter poetically:

> It is a century now since Darwin gave us the first glimpse of the origin of species. We know now what was unknown to all the preceding caravan of generations: that men are only fellow-voyagers with other creatures in the odyssey of evolution. This new knowledge should have given us, by this time, a sense of kinship with fellow-creatures; a wish to live and let live; a sense of wonder over the magnitude and duration of the biotic enterprise.

Above all we should, in the century since Darwin, have come to know that man, while now captain of the adventuring ship, is hardly the sole object of its quest, and that his prior assumptions to this effect arose from the simple necessity of whistling in the dark. Many sensitive human beings find the ethical argument for the preservation of life implied by these authors compelling.

The Economic Values

The second class of reasons for being concerned with the loss of biodiversity are economic, in relation to the properties of individual kinds of organisms. Individually, we use organisms as sources of food, medicines, chemicals, fiber, clothing, structural materials, energy (biomass), and for many other purposes. For example, about 100 kinds of plants provide the great majority of the world's food, but there are tens of thousands of kinds of other plants, especially in the tropics, that have edible parts and might be used more extensively for food, and perhaps brought into cultivation. Incidentally, our collective investment in the development of appropriate agricultural systems or new crops in the tropics is disgracefully small, despite the extreme importance of such advances for the welfare of a large proportion of our fellow human beings, and their consequences for global stability.

The fundamental relationship involved here is that sustainable productivity is essentially biological productivity. Plants and other organisms are natural biochemical factories, and can provide many products of importance for human welfare. More than 60 percent of the world's people depend directly on plants for their medicines, with more than 5,000 species used in China and 1,300 in northwestern Amazonia, for example. In the global drug markets that supply the needs of the remaining people, some 119 drugs in international commerce are derived directly from plants, and the great majority of western medicines owe their existence to research on the natural products that organisms produce.

For example, of the top 20 pharmaceutical products sold in the United States in 1988, a $6 billion market, two are taken directly from natural sources, three are semi-synthetics, eight are synthetics with their chemical structure modeled on previously used natural compounds, and seven had their pharmacological activity defined by natural products research. Natural products research, therefore, played a role in the derivation of each one of them. Since there are some 250,000 kinds of plants in the world, and relatively few have been examined for their secondary compounds, it stands to reason that the remaining species contain many unknown compounds of probable therapeutic importance. Against such a background, the projected loss of something like 12,500 plant species per decade seems particularly threatening: why have we no intervention scheme to preserve all plants, something that is both feasible and highly desirable?

It is worth considering why these natural products are so important in the development of drugs. Gordon Cragg, chief of the Natural Products Branch of the National Cancer Institute, put it this way, "I still maintain that no chemists can 'dream up' the complex bioactive molecules produced by nature, but once the natural lead compounds have been discovered then the chemists can proceed with synthetic modifications to improve on the natural lead."

A few examples will illustrate the point. Artemisin, the only drug effective against all of the strains of the *Plasmodium* organisms that cause malaria, has a chemical structure totally different from that of quinine and the other chemicals used against this disease, which afflicts 250 million people annually. It was discovered because the Chinese people have for 2,000 years used an extract of annual wormwood, *Artemisia annua*, to treat fevers.

Taxol, derived initially from the western yew, *Taxus brevifolia*, was found in a random collection by a joint USDA–NIH program screening plants for anti-cancer activities. The taxol molecule is structurally unique, and it is highly unlikely that it could have been visualized if it had not been discovered in nature. To date, it is the only drug that shows promise against breast cancer and ovarian cancer, two of the major diseases of women in the United States and throughout the world. From a scientific point of view, taxol's novel mechanism of action is especially interesting. It *promotes* the polymerization of tubulin to form microtubules, which it then stabilizes, thereby preventing cell division and the spread of the cancer. Other antimitotic agents interfere with mitosis by *inhibiting* the polymerization of tubulin; taxol is unique in this respect. Biochemists are now trying to determine the site of action of taxol on tubulin and microtubules, which may then permit the rational design of other drugs through molecular modeling. The point here is that the natural product led to the discovery of this new mechanism of action; until one determines such mechanisms and sites of action, one cannot proceed with molecular modeling.

A final example concerns Michellamine B, a novel compound from the African vine *Ancistrocladus korupensis*, which was discovered by Missouri Botanical Garden scientists working under contract with the National Cancer Institute to collect random samples of plants for screening as anti-cancer and anti-HIV activity. Subsequently, the Garden has assisted the government of Cameroon in establishing a plantation for this valuable plant, which is rather rare in nature, since it is now to be tested widely in laboratory animals because it shows a remarkable range of anti-HIV activity. Even though Michellamine B may be too highly neurotoxic to be valuable directly as a drug, this discovery will have considerable value. The reason is that this compound does not work in the same way as AZT and other anti-HIV drugs, which affect the reverse transcriptases and proteases that have been found to play key roles in the viral replication. When its method of action is understood, it may well prove to be a useful molecular probe, and assist in the discovery of other drugs that will be effective against AIDS.

Against this background, it is easy to understand why the major pharmaceutical firms are expanding their programs of exploration for new, naturally-occurring molecules with useful properties. In contrast, it is almost impossible to understand how any intelligent and reasonably sensitive individual could view the disappearance of a major proportion of the biodiversity on Earth with equanimity, or why the world's nations have not already united in a major effort to explore and conserve the biodiversity on which so much of our common future will clearly depend.

Considering plants generally, we are just starting to develop the techniques that will enable us to transfer genes and complexes of genes between unrelated kinds of organisms directly, and thus do a much more precise job of improving crops than has been possible earlier. Several important considerations relate to this ability. First, the world agricultural system is overly-dependent on the close relatives of particular crops; the ability to interbreed strains will recede rapidly in importance as the years go by. Second, we must find ways to overcome our almost mystical distrust of genetically engineered organisms—especially when we are ready to use the same techniques immediately for medical purposes. By not doing so, we are foregoing a significant part of our ability to promote global sustainability for no perceptible gain.

Summarizing, the direct economic values of biodiversity are real and significant: values in crop production, medicines, and so forth. Prescott–Allen and Prescott–Allen carried out a detailed analysis of the contribution wild species of plants and animals made to the American economy, concluding that some 4.5 percent of GDP is attributable to wild species. The combined contribution to GDP of wild harvested resources averaged some $87 billion per year over the period 1976 to 1980; the value undoubtedly has increased substantially since then. In general, the exact magnitude of these values is uncertain and new discoveries occur frequently, so that "option values" are considerable. Many values are not readily captured in the marketplace due to lack of property rights, public good problems, open access, and externalities. For these and other reasons, too little is invested in exploring and protecting biodiversity.

It is just 41 years since Watson and Crick first postulated a plausible structure for DNA, a postulate that led to the universal acceptance of this molecule as the genetic material which governs heredity. Although we have been pursuing molecular biology and its applications to the understanding of biological phenomena at all higher levels of complexity ever since, the hundreds of articles that appear monthly in journals throughout the world provide ample evidence that we still have much to learn. It is an even shorter time, only 21 years, since scientists first successfully transferred a gene from one unrelated kind of an organism to another, giving rise to genetic engineering. We are just starting the task of sequencing entire genomes and beginning to understand them; at present, we cannot really estimate reliably the genetic difference between a corn plant and a human being, or what the differences signify. Clearly, we are at the dawn of a new era of biological understanding. We are just learning how to screen for most useful properties of organisms to transfer, the technology for gene transfer, so we must be deeply worried about the disappearance of a major proportion of our planet's organisms.

Sadly, many non-biologists think about individual species as if they were simply packages of commodities on the supermarket shelf. As soon as an economic value is assigned to a species, it becomes a commodity which can be exploited. Economic arguments may therefore encourage consumption of nature. As Aldo Leopold has put it, "A system of conservation based solely on economic self-interest is hopelessly lopsided. It tends to ignore, and thus eventually eliminate, many elements in the land that lack commercial value but that are essential to its healthy functioning. It assumes that the economic parts of the biotic clock will function without the uneconomic parts." Even ignoring the moral and aesthetic dimensions mentioned above, each species is in fact the unique product of more than 3.5 billion years of evolution, superbly adapted to its individual habitat, and with an expectable life span perhaps ten times that which our own species, *Homo sapiens*, has already experienced. Each species possesses a unique combination of genes—how many or in what proportion we do not know—controlling all of its characteristics. These genes are now capable of being transferred from one system or species to another, but only if we face the problem of extinction and take action so that they still exist when we have developed the technology to use them intelligently. To paraphrase Aldo Leopold, "The first rule of intelligent tinkering is to save all of the bits and pieces."

The Ecological Values

The third class of reasons that people should be concerned with the loss of biodiversity pertains to the array of essential services provided by natural ecosystems. Such services include protecting watersheds, regulating local climates, maintaining atmospheric quality, absorbing pollutants, and generating and maintaining soils. Ecosystems, functioning properly, are responsible for the Earth's ability to capture energy from the Sun and transform it into chemical bonds, a form in which it is used to provide the energy necessary for the life processes of the fewer than 300,000 species of photosynthetic organisms and all of the other 10 million or so species, including ourselves, which depend on them.

It could be argued that the existence or health of a forest or of a population of fish depends on a system of ecological processes, relationships, and species; and that many if not most of these, have no instrumental, aesthetic, or inherent value, at least as perceived by society at large. Perhaps one of the most important things that ecological economists can do is to identify how these ecosystem functions are in fact valuable to people. Norton used the term "contributory value" to express the indirect benefits that species involved in predator-prey relationships essential to population stability of harvested species, and that species diversity in general, confers to ecosystems. He argued that all species have contributory value, and that the loss of any species represents an incremental decrease in the overall utility value of ecosystems.

Ecosystems are also responsible for regulating the recycling of nutrients, derived from the weathering of minerals in the soil and from the atmosphere, and making them constantly available for the maintenance of life. The populations of organisms that control pests on adjacent crops are often maintained in natural or semi-natural ecosystems nearby, as are many of the insects and other animals that pollinate these crops and ensure the production of their crops of fruits and seeds. People are not very aware of these ecosystem services, nor of the role of biodiversity in their lives, as can be illustrated by the "debate" about logging that has been going on in the Pacific Northwest, far western Canada, and the Alaska Panhandle for several decades. It is presented as a confrontation between lumbermen, who want to "preserve" their jobs by cutting down the remaining 10 percent of the irreplaceable forests that are still available to them on public lands, a process that would take less than five years—where would the jobs be then?—and the environmentalists' concern with a poorly-differentiated race of a widespread western bird, the northern spotted owl. What of the beauty and majesty of these forests? What of the reasons that people choose to live in these regions, and enjoy them, and visit them as tourists? Tourism contributes more to the economy of the states involved than the lumber industry, but how do we deal with the direct negative relationship between these two economic forces? What of the role of the forests in protecting tens of thousands of species of other organisms, including the source of the only effective drug against breast cancer and ovarian cancer? How about the watersheds, the soils, the clear streams with their annual salmon runs—all dependent on the forests? We badly need a regional and national attitude that could really address the important questions, such as these, and not, by virtue of endless litigation, treat only a couple of its factors to reach a clumsy compromise that really suits no one.

This more comprehensive view is essentially the attitude that Secretary of the Interior Bruce Babbitt has espoused in many of the actions that the Department of the Interior has taken under his direction, including the formation of the National Biological Survey; the resulting controversy largely reflects society's incomplete understanding of sustainability, or perhaps our unwillingness to put what we know in our hearts to be true into practice for the benefit of our children and grandchildren. But the times are changing, and if those of us who understand something about the ecological systems that support us all are generous enough with our time and effort, they will change even more rapidly.

Cairns and Pratt point out that simple communities are not capable of the same responses to stress as more complex communities. This may be a result of fewer redundant species in the species pool capable of exploiting changing conditions or of biological differences in the taxa found in early successional or immature comma found in later successional (more mature) stages. The result of these differences, the underlying biology of which is poorly known, is the inability of communities to disperse propagules to new habitat, to respond to toxic chemicals, or, in the case of simple communities, to exclude invaders. Continual erosion of biological diversity may result in the loss of key species that regulate numbers of other taxa and allocation of resources to biomass.

Ecosystems of all kinds are what make the world look as it does, and function as it does, but we know next to nothing of the degree to which those individual organisms can be substituted from one ecosystem into another—the very principles by which we shall need to use the survivors of the holocaust we are precipitating now to re-stabilize the world once our numbers have become stable and "sustainability" becomes more than a kind of hopeful ideal, used to justify boundless expansionism. All of these inorganic and mechanical strategies tend to end in failure, because they do not have the self-sustaining qualities of the living systems into which our ancestors evolved, and which we are now destroying so rapidly. As we modify ecosystems, we use ever-increasing amounts of pesticides, herbicides, fertilizers, chlorination, water control measures such as dams and irrigation, and other strategies that require large energy subsidies, based primarily on finite supplies of fossil fuels. Organisms are generally highly adapted to their roles in particular ecosystems, and in ways that we understand poorly. Clearly, much of the quality of ecosystem services will be lost if the present episode of extinction is allowed to run unbridled for much longer, and the rebuilding of these systems in which our descendants will necessarily be engaged is likely to be seriously impaired by our neglect.

WHAT SHOULD BE DONE?

The preservation of biodiversity can be accomplished only as a part of an overall strategy to promote global stability.... Since about 80 percent of the world's biodiversity is confined to tropical developing countries, it is obvious that international assistance on a massive scale will be necessary to stabilize our common management of our planetary home and to provide hope for the future of most of the world's animals, plants, fungi, and microorganisms. Building technical competence in nations around the world so that they can manage their own biodiversity for their own benefit, and thus for ours, is one of the best investments that we can make in our common future. It is only from the organisms that we are able to save that we shall be able to build the productive systems and ecological communities of the future, and the new Convention on Biological Diversity is an important international initiative toward this end.

Concerning the fate of biodiversity, it is obvious that land conversion and habitat destruction are often carried too far as the result of subsidies to ranching, logging, farming, and other activities that result in biodiversity loss. Too little is spent to protect biodiversity and too much is spent to destroy it, so that—from an economics perspective—what is happening is far from efficient or "optimal." Much effort must be devoted to converting a business press that is largely ignorant of this reality, or chooses to ignore the facts, to one that addresses sound economic development as what it is: sound ecological development.

More specifically, and in the context indicated above, the preservation of selected natural and semi-natural areas is the major strategy that will result in the preservation of the greatest amount of biodiversity at the lowest cost. Managing ecosystems everywhere for maximum biological diversity, and limiting to the extent possible further human incursions into relatively undisturbed natural areas, would be important aspects of such a strategy. Human cultural diversity must also be taken seriously into account if biological diversity is to be preserved: the two are intimately connected. The use of primary forests should always be avoided when disrupted communities provide alternatives. In addition, many organisms will be preserved only if they are brought into cultivation, into zoos, type culture centers, or similar facilities, deep frozen, or otherwise preserved in a living condition outside of their natural habitats. A world scheme for accomplishing the preservation of the maximum amount of biodiversity possible would be the most important single contribution that the people of our generation could make to the future.

At the same time, it is clearly important to encourage national and international efforts to learn more about biodiversity, so that it can be managed—in all senses of that word, including conservation—more effectively. The efforts of the National Biodiversity Institute in Costa Rica provide an outstanding example of the methods whereby a nation can take possession of its own biodiversity, conserve it, and use it for its own benefit; analogous efforts have been initiated elsewhere, in Taiwan, Mexico and the United States. Electronic data processing provides the tools necessary for the efficient handling of information about biodiversity, and should be utilized fully in this area of human knowledge.

In conclusion, quantifying the precise rate of extinction and determining a precise figure for the number of species on earth is of only minor relevance to the extinction crisis facing the world today. Policy makers and the public may like to assess the magnitude of the extinction crisis, and thus the priority to be given to the issue, on the basis of an absolute rate, but the investment of time and effort in refining such predictions contributes little to tackling the root causes of the problem. Indeed, obsession with an absolute extinction rate may give an unrealistically optimistic impression in that no allowance is made for the genetic impoverishment of the multitude of species brought to the verge of extinction through the progressive loss of discrete sub-populations.

* * *

3. A. Dan Tarlock, *Exclusive Sovereignty Versus Sustainable Development of a Shared Resource: The Dilemma of Latin American Rainforest Management*, Tex. Int'l L.J. 37, 38–42, 55–57 (1997).

THE NEED FOR SUSTAINABLE DEVELOPMENT

Rainforest destruction is one of the most studied but intractable global environmental problems. We no longer view tropical forests simply as commodities to be exploited to the maximum extent possible. Contrary to earlier thinking, rainforests are biologically rich but extremely fragile and complex ecosystems with limited regeneration potential. Their biological wealth is in the canopy not in the soil, and thus intensive development effectively converts rainforests into nonrenewable resources. Thus, science counsels that these resources should be conserved and managed to sustain a variety of commodity and non-commodity uses, but the economics and culture of underdevelopment propel the host countries toward rapid exploitation.

The immediate roots of the current unsustainable levels of exploitation began in the 1960s when South and Central American counties began to use foreign loans to develop their forests for mineral extraction, cattle ranching, export crops such as cotton, sugar, fruits and flowers, as well as for ambitious population resettlement programs. Logging also increased as superior Southeast Asian and West African hardwood forests were consumed. In the 1980s and early 1990s, rainforest destruction was widely publicized in both the developed and developing worlds as a major example of international degradation. Some host countries became more sensitive to the problem and took steps to discourage conversion to more intensive uses and to develop new management strategies to balance forest use and conservation.

* * *

Rainforest destruction is the product of national policies driven by internal as well as external forces. The main determinants of forest exploitation are population pressures and national development and settlement policies. The creation of counter[-]incentives to the historic pattern of under-regulated exploitation involves the highly politically sensitive issues of population control and distribution, economic growth rates, and property entitlement regimes. For example, Brazilian rainforest destruction is the direct result of government decisions during the military dictatorship, supported by multinational development banks and aid programs that subsidized cattle ranching as one of the several strategies to break the country's historic reliance on monoculture and encouraged population resettlement to relieve poverty in the populous but drought-prone adjoining Nordeste (Northeast) region. . . .

The history of the causes of rainforest destruction teaches that effective remedies to modify forest management practices cut to the core of national civilian and military prerogatives. For this reason, rainforest destruction must be approached indirectly through principles and institutions that are superimposed on classic international law sovereignty principles—although this is still a radical reorientation of the role of international law. Unlike the objective of classic international law, international environmental law—along with human rights law—seeks to influence internal national decisions. In economic terms, law must help rainforest nations to find a way to capture the positive externalities of rainforest conservation. A recent estimate of the annual value of rainforest destruction is $10 billion. The creation of internal incentives must be undergirded, however, by legal principles which provide some promise of penalizing unsustainable management.

Despite all its weaknesses, the best hope for this project is to use the emerging international principle of sustainable development as a benchmark against which both indirect incentives and prohibitions to better manage rainforest resources can be measured. Only the concept of sustainable development holds out the possibility of addressing the legitimate development needs of the rainforest host nations within an international environmental legal framework. Sustainable development has the potential to evolve into a binding legal principle that applies to both external and internal management decisions, and it can support the modification of existing principles of international law which hinder rainforest conservation. Sustainable development is superior to the developing countries' post-Stockholm argument that they are entitled to exploit their resources for their own benefit as compensation for the legacy of the political or economic dependence in the nineteenth century. It is equally superior to the romantic "green" ethics of subsistence existence.

* * *

Debt-for-Nature

Sustainable development supports new biodiversity conservation concepts such as debt-for-nature swaps. These swaps are attempts to create financial incentives for rainforest nations to preserve biodiversity. The basic rational is simple. Rainforest nations are burdened with debt that was incurred to buy oil or finance inefficient public infrastructure in the 1970s. In 1987, a Washington D.C. based NGO purchased $650,000 worth of Bolivian debt for $100,000 in return for a government commitment to preserve 3.7 million acres of tropical rainforest. The experiment was not an initial success because the government failed to fund the management account for two years and did not enact the promised reserve protection legislation. The enforcement problem was partially cured by the next swap. Ecuador issued $10,000,000 worth of bonds. NGOs were invited to purchase debt on the secondary market and then repay the bonds. The interest was assigned to Fudacion Natura for the purchase and management of reserves, and $10,000,000 of discounted debt was purchased. Debt-for-nature swaps involve foreign government debt purchases, debt forgiveness, or government grants to NGOs.

Debt-for-nature swaps are usually hailed as creative market solutions to biodiversity protection that result in voluntary surrender of a country's sovereign right to develop. Some host countries are happy to turn unexploited natural areas into a source of needed cash, but to some countries, debt-for-nature swaps represent an unacceptable forced sale of the country's patrimony. Brazil has a long history of resistance to debt-for-nature swaps because they interfere with sovereignty. This objection can be mitigated by the principle of sustainable development. . . .

Toward an Ethic of Stewardship Sovereignty

The ethic of sustainable development can be implemented in international law by modifying the concept of exclusive territorial sovereignty to make clear that nations have primary but not exclusive control over resource decisions with extraterritorial impacts and that nations owe duties to the international community. . . .

The idea of limited rather than absolute sovereignty is now widely accepted by developed and developing nations. The Tasmanian Dam Case (where the Australian High Court accepted the World Heritage Convention as a restraint on its internal resource use) and the constitutional protection of rainforests in the 1988 Brazil Constitution are both examples of the acceptance of stewardship obligations by rainforest countries. Stewardship sovereignty applies a basic principle of post-modern environmental ethics to international law. There is currently a lively debate about the source and scope of environmental ethics, but, at a minimum, there is also an emerging global consensus that we must replace the Greco–Judeo–Christian tradition that man is a despot over nature with the principle that we are stewards of the earth. Thus, we must approach all exploitation decisions with much more caution than we have in the past.

* * *

4. Roger W. Findley, *Legal and Economic Incentives for the Sustainable Use of Rainforests*, 32 Tex. Int'l L.J. 17, 19–21, 27–30 (1997).

II. Economic Analysis of Sustainable and Unsustainable Uses

The erosion of biodiversity is attributable in large part to the divergence between the private and social costs and benefits of biodiversity use and conservation. Private costs and benefits accrue to the immediate user of the environment: the farmer, the miner, and the logger. Social costs and benefits accrue to society as a whole—local, national, and international. For example, if biodiversity is conserved through sustainable use of a tropical forest, it yields benefits to people in other countries, either because they simply want it to be there or because it helps sustain basic biogeochemical cycles on which human survival depends. But if the country in which the forest is located receives neither financial nor other resources in return for these global external benefits, they provide the country no incentive to conserve the biodiversity.

Economic benefits from unsustainable use of forests tend to be heavily short-term, local, and internal to the users. Thus, if a landowner cuts and sells timber and then converts the land to pasture or crops, he immediately realizes the value of the logs and soon realizes the value of the cattle or crops. The landowner does not have to share those values with anyone else, and the external benefits that accrue to others from his activity tend to favor the local economy rather than the national or global economy.

By contrast, the economic costs of unsustainable uses tend to be heavily long-term, discounted, and external (borne by the national and global communities). If such uses are subsidized financially by the national government or by multilateral development banks (the World Bank and the Interamerican Development Bank), but sustainable uses are not subsidized, there are even stronger incentives for landowners and local communities to favor unsustainable uses.

Among the long-term costs of deforestation are the loss of biodiversity and the increase of global warming. For example, the loss of unique plant species means the permanent loss of medicinal plants and of genetic resources for agriculture. Plant species are used medicinally as both major commercial products and traditional medicines. In the developed world, perhaps twenty-five percent of all medical drugs are based on plants and plant derivatives. In poor countries, the proportion is closer to "seventy-five percent." Genetic and species diversity provides important benefits to agriculture, including yield increases concomitant to plant improvements and natural insurance against yield variability of nondiversified systems.

* * *

With respect to sustainable uses of forests (conservation), the costs (short-term profits foregone) tend to be largely internal and local, while the benefits are heavily external, long-term, and subject to discounting. As a result, the returns from conservation, such as preservation of biodiversity and avoidance of global warming, accrue mainly to parties other than the landowner and the local community.... Unless the landowners and the local community are able to capture (through reimbursement) some of the national and global gains from conservation, there is little local incentive to conserve.

* * *

COMPENSATORY PAYMENTS FROM OTHER NATIONS

[T]he costs of sustainable uses (conservation) of rainforests—short-term profits foregone—tend to be largely internal and local, while the benefits—preservation of biodiversity and avoidance of global warming—are heavily external and long-term. Such benefits accrue to a great extent to the global community, that is, to parties beyond the boundaries of the nation in which the forest is located. As recognized by the 1992 Convention on Biological Diversity and Convention on Climate Change, it is appropriate that the global community—especially wealthier northern counties—compensate tropical nations for their protection of the rainforests as sources of biological resources and as carbon "sinks."

Article 8 of the Biodiversity Treaty provides that each contracting party shall, "as far as possible and as appropriate," regulate or manage "biological resources important for the conservation of biological diversity whether within or outside protected areas, with a view to ensuring their conservation and sustainable use." In return for this consideration by developing countries, the developed counties agree, in Article 20, to provide "new and additional financial resources to enable developing country Parties to meet the agreed full incremental costs to them of implementing measures which fulfill the obligations of the Convention." These financial resources may be provided through the Global Environment Facility (GEF), a joint undertaking of the United Nations Development Programme, the United Nations Environment Programme, and the World Bank, or through bilateral, regional, and other multilateral channels. Early in 1994, the United States and other developed countries promised to give the GEF $2 billion over three years to help the developing countries fulfill their commitments under the Biodiversity and Climate Change Conventions. The total cost of the United States' share was $430 million.

Other commitments also have been made, but the developed nations have not rushed to satisfy their obligations. For example, in mid–1994, the government of Brazil had spent more than $1 million preparing small-scale, local participation projects for the Amazon region. These projects were to be financed by a Pilot Program for the Amazon established by the G–7 (the world's seven richest nations). However, none of the $1.5 billion promised by the G–7 had been received by Brazil from the Rain Forest Trust, a special fund administered by the World Bank to receive and disburse money.... By late 1996, the G–7 had provided a total of $280 million to the Rain Forest Trust, but only $10 million had been disbursed for Pilot Program Projects....

If and when compensatory payments begin to flow to rainforest countries, the need remains to assure that some of the funds are passed through the recipient national governments to local landowners and governments, who otherwise would bear most of the costs (profits foregone) of sustainable uses and whose support for conservation is crucial to its success. Article 11 of the Biodiversity Treaty commits each contracting party, "as far as possible and as appropriate, [to] adopt economically and socially sound measures that act as incentives for the conservation and sustainable use of components of biological diversity." Without positive incentives, local interests are unlikely to opt for sustainable rather than more profitable, unsustainable uses.

5. **Rio Declaration on Environment and Development, June 14, 1992, Principles 1, 3–6, 8, 9, 13, 14, 22 UNCED Doc. A/CONF.151/5/Rev. 1,** *reprinted in* **31 I.L.M. 874 (1992)** [Basic Document 1.29].

6. *International Environmental Wrongs,* **Chapter 5** *supra* **at 335.**

7. **United Nations Charter, June 26, 1945, Preamble, arts. 2(7), 55, 56, 59 Stat. 1031, T.S. No. 993, 3 Bevans 1153, 1976 U.N.Y.B. 1043** [Basic Document 1.3].

8. **Convention on the Prevention and Punishment of the Crime of Genocide, Dec. 9, 1948, 78 U.N.T.S. 277** [Basic Document 7.10].

9. **Universal Declaration of Human Rights, Dec. 10, 1948, arts. 1– 3, 7, 17, 27, 30, G.A. Res. 217A, U.N. GAOR, 3d Sess., pt. 1, Resolutions, at 71, U.N. Doc. A./810 (1948)** [Basic Document 7.11].

10. **UNESCO Declaration on the Principles of International Cultural Cooperation, 14th Sess., Nov. 4, 1966,** *reprinted in* United Nations, Human Rights: A Compilation of International Instruments **409, U.N. Doc. ST/HR/l/rev. 3 (1988)** [Basic Document 7.12].

11. **International Covenant on Economic, Social and Cultural Rights, Dec. 16, 1966, arts. 1, 2, 15, 25,** *reprinted in* **6 I.L.M. 360 (1967)** [Basic Document 7.13].

12. **International Covenant on Civil and Political Rights, Dec. 16, 1966, arts. 1, 2, 6, 27, 47, 999 U.N.T.S. 171,** *reprinted in* **6 I.L.M. 368 (1967)** [Basic Document 7.14].

13. **American Convention on Human Rights, Nov. 22, 1969, arts. 1, 4, 16, 21, O.A.S. Treaty Series No. 36, at 1, O.A.S. Off. Rec. OAE/Ser.L./V/II.23, doc. 21, rev. 6 (1979),** *reprinted in* **9 I.L.M. 673 (1970)** [Basic Document 7.16].

14. International Labour Organization Convention (No. 169) Concerning Indigenous and Tribal Peoples in Independent Countries, June 27, 1989, arts. 1–8, 12–20, 24–31, Int'l Labour Conf., Draft Rep. Comm. on Convention, No. 107, Appendix I, C.C. 107/D.303 (June 1989), *reprinted in* 28 I.L.M. 1382 (1989) [Basic Document 7.21].

15. Draft Declaration on the Rights of Indigenous Peoples, as Agreed upon by the Members of the Working Group on Indigenous Populations at its Eleventh Session, Geneva, Switzerland, August 23, 1993, U.N. Doc. E/CN.4/Sub.2/1993/29 [Basic Document 7.24].

16. S. James Anaya, Indigenous Peoples in International Law 47–51, 53, 98–107, 109–12 (1996).

ILO Convention No. 169 of 1989

The basic theme of Convention 169 [**Basic Document 7.21**] is indicated by the convention's preamble, which recognizes "the aspirations of [indigenous] peoples to exercise control over their own institutions, ways of life and economic development and to maintain and develop their identities, languages and religions, within the framework of the States in which they live." Upon this premise, the convention includes provisions advancing indigenous cultural integrity, land and resources rights, and nondiscrimination in social welfare spheres; and it generally enjoins states to respect indigenous peoples' aspirations in all decisions affecting them.

Upon adoption of Convention No. 169 by the International Labour Conference in 1989, several advocates of indigenous peoples' rights have expressed dissatisfaction with language in Convention No. 169, viewing it as not sufficiently constraining of government conduct in relation to indigenous peoples' concerns. Criticism was leveled at several of the convention's provisions that contain caveats or appear in the form of recommendations, and at the underlying assumption of state authority over indigenous peoples. Much of this criticism, however, was couched in highly legalistic terms and worst-case scenario readings of the convention without much regard to overall context....

New and Emergent Customary International Law

ILO Convention No. 169 is significant to the extent it creates treaty obligations among ratifying states in line with current trends in thinking prompted by indigenous peoples' demands. The convention is further meaningful as part of a larger body of developments that can be understood as giving rise to new customary international law with the same normative thrust. Since the 1970s, the demands of indigenous peoples have been addressed continuously in one way or another within the United Nations and other international venues of authoritative normative discourse. The extended multilateral discussion promoted through the international system has involved states, nongovernmental organizations, independent experts, and indigenous peoples themselves. It is now evident that states and other relevant actors have reached a certain new common ground about minimum standards that should govern behavior toward indigenous peoples, and it is also evident that the standards are already in fact guiding behavior. Under modern theory, such a controlling consensus, following as it does from widely shared values of human dignity, constitutes customary international law.

Norms of customary law arise—or to use the now much favored term crystalize—when a preponderance of states and other authoritative actors converge on a common understanding of the norms' contents and generally expect future behavior in conformity with those norms. As Professors McDougal, Laswell, and Chen describe it in their important study, customary law is "generally observed to include two key elements: a 'material' element in certain past uniformities in behavior and a 'psychological' element, or *opinio juris*, in certain subjectivities of 'oughtness' attending such uniformities in behavior."[4] The traditional points of reference for determining the existence of a customary norm are patterns of communicative behavior involving physical episodic conduct.... Under traditional analysis, the content of the emergent rule and the required subjectivities of normative expectation (the so called *opinio juris)* are inferred from the episodic conduct.

Today, however, interactive patterns around concrete events are not the only—or necessarily required—material elements constitutive of customary norms. With the advent of modern international intergovernmental institutions and enhanced communications media, states and other relevant actors increasingly engage in prescriptive dialogue. Especially in multilateral settings, explicit communication of this sort may itself bring about a convergence of understanding and expectation about rules.... It is thus increasingly understood that explicit communication among authoritative actors, whether or not in association with concrete events, is a form of practice that builds customary rules. Of course, conforming conduct will strengthen emergent customary rules by enhancing attendant subjectivities of expectation.

There has been a discernible movement toward a convergence of reformed normative understanding and expectation on the subject of indigenous peoples; under the theory just sketched, this movement is constitutive of customary international law. Relevant normbuilding international practice, which has been substantially driven by indigenous peoples' own efforts, has entailed information gathering and evaluation, discussion and articulation of policies and norms, and the reporting of domestic initiatives against the backdrop of the developing norms.

* * *

Since the convention **[Basic Document 7.21]** was adopted in 1989, government comments directed at developing an indigenous rights declaration in the U.N. subcommission working group, the subcommission itself, and the U.N. Commission on Human Rights generally have affirmed the basic precepts set forth in the convention, and indeed the comments indicate an emerging consensus that accords even more closely with indigenous peoples' demands. The Draft United Nations Declaration on the Rights of Indigenous Peoples **[Basic Document 7.21]**—developed by the working group and adopted by the full body of independent experts who comprise the subcommission—stands in its own right as an authoritative statement of norms concern-

---

4. Myres McDougal et al., Human Rights and World Public Order: The Basic Policies of an   International Law of Human Dignity 269 (1980).

ing indigenous peoples on the basis of generally applicable human rights principles; and it is also a manifestation of the movement in a corresponding consensual nexus of opinion on the subject among relevant actors. The extensive deliberations leading to the draft declaration, in which indigenous peoples themselves played a leading role, enhance the authoritativeness and legitimacy of the draft.

The draft U.N. declaration goes beyond the Convention No. 169, especially in its bold statements in areas of indigenous self-determination, land and resource rights,[5] and rights of political autonomy.[6] It is clear that not *all* are satisfied with *all* aspects of the draft declaration developed by the subcommission working group. Some indigenous peoples' representatives have criticized the draft for not going far enough, while governments typically have held that it goes too far. Nonetheless, a new common ground of opinion exists among experts, indigenous peoples, and governments about indigenous peoples' rights and attendant standards of government behavior, and that widening common ground is in some measure reflected in the subcommission draft.

Cultural Integrity

Affirmation of the world's diverse cultures was the central concern of a resolution by the Fourteenth General Conference of the United Nations Educational, Scientific and Cultural Organization [UNESCO]. The 1966 UNESCO Declaration of the Principles of International Cultural Cooperation **[Basic Document 7.12]** proclaims in its first article:

1. Each culture has dignity and value which must be respected and preserved.

2. Every people has the right and duty to develop its culture.

3. In their rich variety and diversity, and in the reciprocal influence they exert on one another, all cultures form part of the common heritage belonging to all mankind.

Article 27 of the International Covenant on Civil and Political Rights **[Basic Document 7.14]**, the U.N. Minority Rights Declaration, and the UNESCO Declaration are each framed by preambular language establishing their derivation from the human rights principles of the United Nations Charter. A number of other human rights instruments also have provisions upholding rights of cultural integrity.

While rights of cultural integrity outside the specific context of indigenous peoples have been associated with "minority rights," indigenous rights advocates have frequently rejected calling indigenous groups minorities in their attempts to establish indigenous peoples within a separate regime with greater legal entitlements.... International practice has not endorsed such as formalistic dichotomy but rather has tended to treat indigenous peoples and minorities as comprising distinct but overlapping categories subject to common normative considerations....

The cultural integrity norm, particularly as embodied in article 27 of the covenant, has been the basis of decisions favorable to indigenous peoples by the U.N. Human Rights Committee and the Inter–American Commission on

5. **Basic Document 7.24**, arts. 23, 25–30   6. *Id.* at arts. 31–38.
31–38.

Human Rights of the Organization of the American States. Both bodies have held the norm to cover all aspects of an indigenous group's survival as a distinct culture, understanding culture to include economic or political institutions, land use patterns, as well as language and religious practices....

In its 1985 decision concerning the Yanomami of Brazil, the commission again invoked article 27 and held that "international law" in its present state ... recognizes the right of ethnic groups to special protection on their use of their own language, for the practice of their own religion, and, in general, for all those characteristics necessary for the preservation of their cultural identity.[7] The commission viewed a series of incursions into Yanomami ancestral lands as a threat not only to the Yanomami's physical well-being but also to their culture and traditions. Significantly, the commission cited article 27 to support its characterization of international law even though Brazil was not a party to the International Covenant on Civil and Political Rights, thus indicating the norm's character as customary international law.

A similarly extensive view of the cultural integrity norm as applied to indigenous peoples has been taken by the U.N. Human Rights Committee, although clearly in the context of applying treaty obligations assumed under the covenant. In *Ominayak v. Canada*[8] the committee construed the cultural rights guarantees of article 27 to extend to "economic and social activities" upon which the Lubicon Lake Band of Cree Indians relied as a group. Thus the committee found that Canada, a signatory to the covenant and its Operational Protocol, had violated its obligation under article 27 by allowing the provincial government in Alberta to grant leases for oil and gas exploration and for timber development within the aboriginal territory of the Band. The committee acknowledged that the Band's survival as a distinct cultural community was bound up with the sustenance that it derived from the land.

* * *

Conversely, and as more clearly expressed by article 27, the individual human being is in his or her own right an important beneficiary of cultural integrity. The relationship of the individual to the group entitlement of cultural integrity was signaled by the U.N. Human Rights Committee in the case of Sandra Lovelace.[9] Lovelace, a woman who had been born into an Indian band residing on the Tobique Reserve in Canada, challenged section 12(1)(b) of Canada's Indian Act, which denied Indian status and benefits to any Indian woman who married a non-Indian. The act did not operate similarly with respect to Indian men. Because she had married a non-Indian, section 12(1)(b) denied Lovelace residency on the Tobique Reserve. She alleged violations of various provisions of the covenant, including articles proscribing sex discrimination, but the committee considered article 27 as "most directly applicable" to her situation. In ruling in her favor, the

---

7. Case No. 7615 (Brazil), Inter–Am. Commission Res. No. 12/85 (March 5, 1985), *Annual Report of the Inter–American Commission on Human Rights*, 1984–1985, O.A.S. Doc. OEA/ Ser.L/V/II.66, doc. 10, rev. 1 at 24, 31 (1985).

8. Ominayak, Chief of the Lubicon Lake Band v. Canada, Communication No. 267/1984, *Report of the Human Rights Committee*, U.N. GOAR, 45th Sess., Supp. No. 40, Vol. 2, at 1,

U.N. Doc. A/45/40, Annex 9 (A) (1990) (views adopted March 26, 1990).

9. Lovelace v. Canada, Communication No. R.6/24, *Report of the Human Rights Committee*, U.N. GOAR, 36th Sess. No. 40, at 166, U.N. Doc. A/36/40, Annex 18 (1977) (views adopted Dec. 29, 1977).

committee held that "the right of Sandra Lovelace to access to her native culture and language 'in community with the other members' of her group, has in fact been, and continues to be interfered with, because there is no place outside the Tobique Reserve where such a community exists."

While the Lovelace case emphasizes the rights of the individual, the Human Rights Committee's decision in *Kitok v. Sweden*[10] demonstrates that the group interest in cultural survival may take priority. Ivan Kitok challenged the Swedish Reindeer Husbandry Act, which reserved reindeer herding rights exclusively for members of Saami villages. Although ethnically a Saami, he had lost his membership in his ancestral village, and the village had denied him re-admission. The Human Rights Committee acknowledged that reindeer husbandry, although an economic activity, is an essential element of the Saami culture. The committee found that, while the Swedish legislation restricted Kitok's participation in Saami cultural life, his rights under article 27 of the covenant had not been violated. The committee concluded that the legislation was justified as a means of ensuring the viability and welfare of the Saami as a whole.

International practice related to articulating standards in the field of indigenous rights is in accord with the foregoing interpretations of the norm of cultural integrity, and the practice is probative of the norm's status as customary law.... The same cultural integrity theme is at the core of the Draft United Nations Declaration on the Rights of Indigenous Peoples and previous drafts that were produced by the chair of the U.N. Working Group on Indigenous Populations pursuant to that body's standard-setting mandate. States have joined indigenous rights advocates in expressing widespread agreement with that essential thrust even while diverging in their views on particular aspects of drafts.

* * *

As the international community has come to consider indigenous cultures equal in value to all others, the cultural integrity norm has developed to entitle indigenous groups to affirmative measures to remedy the past undermining of their cultural survival and to guard against continuing threats in this regard. It is not sufficient, therefore, that states simply refrain from coercing assimilation of indigenous peoples or abandonment of their cultural practices. ILO Convention No. 169 provides: "Governments shall have the responsibility for developing, with the participation of the peoples concerned, coordinated and systematic action to protect the rights of these peoples and to guarantee respect for their integrity."[11] The draft U.N. declaration **[Basic Document 7.24]** echoes the requirement of "effective measures" to secure indigenous culture in its many manifestations. Comments by governments to the working group and other international bodies, as well as trends in government initiatives domestically, indicate broad acceptance of the requirement of affirmative action to secure indigenous cultural survival.

10. Communication No. 197/1985, *Report of the Human Rights Committee,* U.N. GOAR, 43rd Sess., Supp. No. 40, at 207, U.N. Doc. A/43/40, Annex 7(G) (1988) (views adopted July 27, 1988).

11. Art. 2(1).

Lands and Natural Resources

The Inter–American Commission on Human Rights and the U.N. Human Rights Committee in the cases previously mentioned acknowledged the importance of lands and resources to the survival of indigenous cultures and, by implication, to indigenous self determination. That understanding is a widely accepted tenet of contemporary international concern over indigenous peoples. It follows from indigenous peoples' articulated ideas of communal stewardship over land and a deeply felt spiritual and emotional nexus with the earth and its fruits....

* * *

Indigenous land and resource—or territorial—rights are of collective character, and they include a combination of possessory, use, and management rights. In its article 14(1), Convention No. 169 affirms:

> The rights of ownership and possession of [indigenous peoples] over the lands which they traditionally occupy shall be recognized. In addition, measures shall be taken in appropriate cases to safeguard the right of the peoples concerned to use lands not exclusively occupied by them, but to which they have traditionally had access for their subsistence and traditional activities.

* * *

Thus Convention No. 169 affirms the notion promoted by the Inter–American Commission on Human Rights and the U.N. Human Rights Committee that indigenous peoples as groups are entitled to a *continuing* relationship with lands and natural resources according to traditional patterns of use or occupancy. Use of the words "traditionally occupy" in article 14(1), as opposed to use of the past tense of the verb, suggests that the occupancy must be connected with the present in order for it to give rise to possessory rights. In light of the article 13 requirement of respect for cultural values related to land, however, as sufficient present connection with lost lands may be established by continuing cultural attachment to them, particularly if dispossession occurred recently.

* * *

The essential aspects of Convention No. 169's land rights provisions are strongly rooted in an expanding nexus of international opinion and practice. In responding to a questionnaire circulated by the International Labour Office in preparation for the drafting of the new convention, governments overwhelmingly favored strengthening the land rights provisions of ILO Convention No. 107 of 1957, including governments not parties to that convention. Although Convention No. 107 is generally regarded as flawed, it contains a recognition of indigenous land rights that has operated in favor of indigenous peoples' demands through the ILO's supervisory machinery. The discussion on the new convention proceeded on the premise that indigenous peoples were to be accorded greater recognition of land rights than they were in Convention No. 107. Convention No. 169's land rights provisions were finalized by a special working party of the Labour Conference committee that developed the text of the convention, and the committee approved the provisions by consensus.

Government statements to the U.N. Working Group on Indigenous Populations and other international bodies confirm general acceptance of at least the core aspects of the land rights norms expressed in Convention No. 169. The statements tell of worldwide initiatives to secure indigenous possessory and use rights over land and to redress historical claims.... It is evident that certain minimum standards concerning indigenous land rights, rooted in otherwise accepted precepts of property, cultural integrity, and self-determination, have made their way not just into conventional law but also into customary law.

Self Government

While the norm of indigenous self-government upholds the development of autonomous institutions for indigenous peoples, it also upholds their effective participation in the larger political order. The draft U.N. declaration affirms the overwhelmingly accepted view that "indigenous peoples have the right to participate fully, if they so choose, at all levels of decisionmaking which may affect their rights." Similarly, ILO Convention No. 169 requires effective means by which indigenous peoples " 'can freely participate ... at all levels of decision-making" which may affect them."

* * *

The dual thrust of the normative regime concerning indigenous peoples' self-government—on the one hand autonomy and on the other participatory engagement—reflects the view, apparently held by indigenous peoples themselves, that they are not to be considered *a priori* unconnected from larger social and political structures. Rather, indigenous groups—whether characterized as communities, peoples, nations, or other—are appropriately viewed as simultaneously distinct from yet parts of larger units of social and political interaction, units that may include indigenous federations, the states within which they live, and the global community itself....

17. Faisal H. Naqvi, *People's Rights or Victim's Rights: Reexamining the Conceptualization of Indigenous Rights in International Law*, 71 IND. L.J. 673, 714–16 (1996).

Article 27 and the Norm of Cultural Integrity

To determine whether Article 27 of the International Covenant on Civil and Political Rights [Basic Document 7.14] is part of customary international law, we must first examine whether the "material element" exists in the shape of "patterns of communicative behavior involving physical episodic conduct" and whether this element is supported by the required *opinio juris* In examining the existence of the "material element," what we must address first is whether these patterns must be deduced solely from the actions of states, or whether other actors can also be seen as authoritative. Anaya, for example takes an extremely aggressive view on this point:

> [I]nteractive patterns around concrete events are no longer considered the only—or even necessarily required—material elements constitutive of customary norms. With the advent of modern international intragovernmental institutions and enhanced communications media, states and other relevant actors increasingly engage in dialogue to come to terms on

international standards. It is now understood that express communication, whether or not in association with concrete events, is a form of practice that builds customary rules, and that communication may itself bring about a convergence of understanding and expectation about rules even in advance of a widespread corresponding pattern of physical conduct.[12]

This view is excessively deferential in its attitude towards the authoritative effect of the pronouncements of scholars and other nongovernmental actors and is logically flawed. It is one thing to admit that in an age of instantaneous global telecommunications, agencies may function as authoritative actors in the constitutive process of customary international law. However, agencies and other nongovernmental actors fulfill this role precisely because they act as governmental representatives (or because states choose, in certain circumstances, to defer to their authority) and not as authoritative actors in their own right. . . .

This is not to deny that international agencies or even nongovernmental agencies on occasion serve as originators and framers of customary law. However, such nonstate actors function only as reliable indicators of state practice or of normative rules and provisions that states consider binding. A nonstate actor, such as an NGO, acting independently in its own right, is not a source of international law. . . . Anaya's dismissal of state practice as unnecessary for the formation of customary international law, is therefore, considerably overstated.

18. Constitution of the International Labour Organization, Oct. 9, 1946, 15 U.N.T.S. 35, 62 Stat. 3480, T.I.A.S. 1868, *as amended through 1991*, arts. 22, 24–34, 37 [Basic Document 1.2].

19. Virginia A. Leary, International Labour Conventions and National Law: The Effectiveness of the Automatic Incorporation of Treaties in National Legal Systems 6–9 (1982).

Lord McNair described the international labour convention as "one of the most striking innovations in the field of treaty-making which has occurred during the present century."[13] Since 1919, more than [160] labour conventions have been drafted and adopted by the annual Conference of the International Labour Organization. Although they concern different subject matter, these conventions (hereinafter referred to as "ILO conventions") share certain common features. Anumber of the innovative features of this large body of conventions result from the effort to regulate the internal law and practice of states through the device of the treaty.

[The author next notes some of the innovative features contained in ILO labor conventions, made necessary to ensure the adoption of appropriate standards in a realm traditionally considered a matter of domestic concern: employer and worker representatives participating "on an equal basis with government delegates in the elaboration of international labour conventions"; "the omission of the practice of governmental signature to the text of drafted conventions"; "an understanding that no reservations may be made to the

12. S. James Anaya, *Indigenous Rights Norms in Contemporary International Law*, 8 Ariz. J. Int'l & Comp. L. 1, 9 (1991).

13. Arnold McNair, The Expansion of International Law 29 (1962).

conventions"; and "a requirement that Member States submit conventions to their legislative bodies." She then continues:]

ILO conventions have not only been innovative but they have also been precursors of an ever-growing group of treaties, such as human rights treaties, which are intended to regulate national social and economic policy. Multilateral international agreements laying down general norms—so called "law-making" treaties—existed prior to international labour conventions but they largely concerned such inter-state matters as postal regulations, river and railroad communications and protection of the wounded in time of war. International labour conventions were virtually the first multilateral treaties primarily intended to improve the lot of individuals within states.

* * *

1. The Norms of ILO Conventions

More than 130 ILO conventions are presently in force. They cover a wide variety of subjects: conditions of employment, occupational health and safety, social security, employment of women and children, migrant workers, forced labour, freedom of association and employment policy. Rather than drawing up a limited number of conventions which cover a broad spectrum of social and labour matters the International Labour Conference has, with a few exceptions, drawn up separate conventions on specific subjects [e.g., the rights of indigenous and tribal peoples].

* * *

The norms of ILO conventions vary greatly in specificity, precision and detail. Some ... standards are expressed in precise, negative proscriptions such as "women, without distinction of age, shall not be employed during the night in any public or private industrial undertaking."[14] ... A number of conventions require ratifying states to "undertake" a certain course of action: "Each Member of the International Labour Organization which ratifies this Convention undertakes to suppress the use of forced or compulsory labor."[15] ... In recent years, the International Labour Conference has adopted a small group of conventions referred to as "promotional conventions", which by their very nature differ in form and purpose from most of the other instruments adopted.... Instead of laying down precise standards ..., these conventions set objectives of a more general character [that] require programmes of action which can generally be achieved only by concerted and gradual measures over a period of time, involving therefore promotional methods appropriate to national conditions.[16]

An example of such a provision is Article 1 of ILO Convention No. 122 concerning Employment Policy: "[e]ach Member shall declare and pursue, as a major goal, an active policy designed to promote full, productive and freely chosen employment." The majority of conventions, however, are drafted in such a way as to afford the maximum amount of flexibility consonant with the assumption by a State of a real measure of obligation. Consequently, the

---

14. Article 3 of Convention (No. 41) Concerning Employment of Women During the Night (revised 1934). The term "night" is defined in Article 2 of the Convention.

15. Article 1 of Convention (No. 29) Concerning Forced or Compulsory Labour, 1930. "Forced Labour" is defined in Article 2.

16. 1973 R.C.E. 8–9.

convention is often short in form and restricted to the formulation of a few broad obligations. It is not encumbered by unnecessary details which might only serve to impede ratification and may be dealt with more appropriately in the form of a recommendation. The normal convention is composed of a brief preamble, a few general obligations, a number of exceptions, implementing provisions which allow wide discretion to the national authority and the final clauses concerning ratification, denunciation, duration and revision.[17]

[The intention has been] to regulate labour and social conditions in countries with widely varying climatic conditions as well as economic and social development. This aim has had an important influence on the drafting of the provisions of ILO conventions. A number of "flexibility devices" [e.g., vague and accommodating terms] have been included in conventions for this purpose. . . .

Some conventions which contain precise rules or proscriptions also contain exemption clauses which permit exceptions from the rules or proscriptions in particular circumstances. Others permit wide latitude on the part of the "competent national authority" in applying and interpreting the rules of the convention. Some conventions permit a ratifying state to exclude certain parts of a convention when accepting the convention.

Occasionally states which have ratified or are considering ratifying a convention raise questions concerning the interpretation of a provision of the convention. Article 37 of the ILO Constitution provides:

> Any question or dispute relating to the interpretation of this Constitution or of any subsequent convention concluded by the members in pursuance of the provisions of the Constitution shall be referred for decision to the International Court of Justice.

Only one case involving the interpretation of an international labour convention has been referred to the International Court.[18] A procedure has, however developed whereby the International Labour Office upon a request from a state will provide an interpretation of an ILO convention based on the language, the preparatory work and subsequent practice. This interpretation is transmitted to the state with a reservation "that the Constitution of the International Labour Organization confers no special competence upon the International Labour Office to give an authentic interpretation of the provisions of conventions adopted by the International Labour Conference." The interpretation is communicated to the Governing Body of the ILO and published in the ILO Official Bulletin.

* * *

20. EBERE OSIEKE, CONSTITUTIONAL LAW AND PRACTICE IN THE INTERNATIONAL LABOUR ORGANISATION 161–64 (1985).

(B) OBLIGATIONS OF MEMBERS OF THE ILO WITH RESPECT TO RATIFIED CONVENTIONS

The ILO Constitution imposes two major obligations on Member States with respect to Conventions which they have ratified. First, they are required

---

17. J. F. McMahon, *Legislative Techniques of the International Labour Organization*, 41 BRIT. Y. B. INT'L L. 1, 37 (1965–66).

18. Advisory Opinion on the Interpretation of the Convention of 1919 Concerning Employment of Women During the Night, 1932 P.C.I.J. (ser. A/B) No. 50, at 4.

to take necessary action to give effect to the Convention: and secondly, to submit annual reports on the Convention to the ILO. These two questions will be examined separately.

(i) Obligation of Members of the ILO to Give Effect to Ratified Conventions

It has been noted that Members of the ILO are not under an obligation to ratify a Convention. If, however, they do ratify one, the ILO Constitution imposes an obligation on them to "take such action as may be necessary to make effective the provisions of such Convention."[19]

The nature of the action to be taken by the member State in order to fulfil this obligation is not specified in the ILO Constitution. However, various bodies and organs in the ILO have had occasion to comment on the nature and scope of this obligation. According to an interpretation given by the International Labour Office in 1950, "the nature of the action required in the particular country to make effective the provisions of the Convention is left to be determined in the first instance by that country.... From an international point of view, what is essential is that the provisions of a Convention should be fully applied; in regard to the manner of application, both the Constitution of the Organisation and the terms of the individual Conventions deliberately leave a wide measure of discretion to each country."[20]

It has, however, been emphasized that the discretion left to each country cannot be considered to be absolute, and that account must be taken of the need for member States, in most cases, to introduce the provisions of ratified Conventions into their domestic law. The way in which this is done will vary according to the constitutional system in each State. Certain constitutional systems provide that a Convention which has been ratified and published (or promulgated) becomes, *ipso facto*, binding in domestic law. But in countries where this is not the case, the provisions of the Convention should be introduced into the national legislation in the widest sense of the term (laws, regulations, ordinances, decrees, etc.) according to the nature of the country's legal system and the matters covered by the Convention.

Commenting on the nature of the obligation of a Member of the ILO to give effect to a Convention which it has ratified, the Committee of Experts on the Application of Conventions and Recommendations stated in 1978 that "such action as may be necessary" is not limited to measures of a legislative nature in the broad sense of the term. According to the provisions of each Convention, the action necessary includes—and sometimes essentially comprises—other types of measures: administrative, economic and financial, the establishment of action programmes, the creation of appropriate bodies, including labour inspection services, the establishment of judicial, administrative or other procedures, joint or tripartite bodies, etc. These measures, which are generally called for to supplement legislative provisions, and sometimes even constitute the fundamental obligation of governments, are intended to guarantee the effective implementation and the application in practice, of ratified Conventions.

Similarly, in 1962, the Commission of Inquiry appointed to examine the complaint submitted by Ghana against Portugal pointed out that the mere

19. ILO Constitution, art. 19(5)(e) **[Basic Document 1.2]**.

20. 38 ILO Official Bull. No. 5, at 305–06 (1950).

enactment of legislation which conforms with the provisions of the Convention does not, *ipso facto*, constitute a discharge of the obligations which arise under the provisions of the Constitution for Members which ratify a convention. According to the Tribunal:

> While only the International Court of Justice can pronounce authoritatively on the matter, the Commission construes this obligation as being an obligation to make the provisions of the Convention effective in law and in fact. It is herefore necessary, but not sufficient, that the provisions of the law should comply with the requirements of the Convention.... Full conformity of the law with the requirements of the Convention is therefore essential but taken alone is not enough.[21] ...

The Tribunal then concluded that Members are under a further obligation to apply the provisions of the relevant national legislation effectively. "There should be adequate penalties for infractions which are, and is known will be, strictly enforced."[22]

Again, the Commission of Inquiry appointed in 1962 to examine the complaint submitted by Portugal against Liberia rejected the argument of Liberia that under Liberian Law the provisions of a Convention prevailed over inconsistent provisions of national legislation, and therefore operated as an implied repeal of all such provisions prior in date to the ratification of the Convention; and concluded that an implied repeal of legislation inconsistent with the requirements of the Convention was not, and in the nature of the case could not be, a sufficient fulfillment of the obligations embodied in the Convention.

In 1969, the Commission of Inquiry appointed to examine the complaint against Greece also rejected the argument of the Greek Government that the proclamation, or existence, of a state of emergency, constituted justification for the non-observance of the provisions of a Convention which it had ratified. The Tribunal took the view that it was an accepted principle of international law that a State could not rely on the terms of its national law, or otherwise invoke the concept of national sovereignty to justify non-performance of an international obligation, and that any doubt concerning the extent of such obligation should be determined by exclusive reference to the relevant principles of international law, whether made express by the parties to a treaty or derived from another source of international law, in particular custom and general principles of law.[23]

The Commission then emphasized that the position of pleas of emergency or necessity in international custom could be said to correspond essentially to the place given to pleas of *force majeure* in national systems of law. Such a plea generally required a showing of "irresistible force of circumstances," and both the general principles of law derived from national practice and international custom were based on the assumption that the non-performance of a legal duty could be justified only where there was impossibility of proceeding by any other method than the one contrary to the law. It should be shown

21. *Report of the Ghana–Portugal Commission of Inquiry*, para. 716, 45 ILO Official Bull., Supp. II, at 231 (1962).

22. Id.

23. *Report of the Commission of Inquiry appointed to examine the Complaint against Greece*, 54 ILO Official Bull. Special Supp., at 24–26 (1971).

also that the action sought to be justified under the plea was limited, both in extent and in time, to what was immediately necessary.

The Commission concluded that there was no evidence or information on the basis of which it could be said that there existed in Greece in 1967 a state of emergency, or such exceptional conditions as would justify temporary non-compliance with the Conventions.

In the light of these pronouncements, it may be permissible to state that, on the basis of the jurisprudence of the Commissions of Inquiry, and the Committee of Experts on the Application of Conventions and Recommendations, supported by the practice of the ILO, members of the ILO are under an obligation to enact laws to give effect to the provisions of Conventions which they have ratified and to take administrative or other necessary action to ensure that the provisions of the law are effectively applied and complied with in their territories. Unless the Conventions contain express provisions to the contrary, national constitutional provisions or other national laws may not be relied upon as justification for failure to carry out the provisions of Conventions, and such failure will not, *ipso facto*, be justified by the claim of a state of emergency, *force majeure*, or necessity.

* * *

[Subsequently, in his "general conclusions," Professor Osieke writes:]

... [T]he ILO was created by a Constitution which lays down its objects and purposes, defines its functions and powers and those of its main organs, and creates rights and obligations for its members. This means that the ILO Constitution possesses a dual character—that of a multilateral treaty, and of a constitution. The consequence of its treaty character is that a question or situation which is not expressly provided for in the constitution may be resolved or dealt with by reference to general international law—in particular, the Law of Treaties as contained in the Vienna Convention on the Law of Treaties, 1969 **[Basic Document 1.7]**, or even customary international law. One of the consequences of the constitutional character of the ILO Constitution is that all the functions and powers of the Organisation and its organs are derived from the Constitution, and this instrument provides the parameter or yardstick for determining the proper or improper exercise of those functions and powers. In this regard, the Constitution represents the supreme law of the ILO and ensures that its functions and powers are exercised for the general good of the organisation and not used arbitrarily in flagrant disregard of its objects and purposes. Thus, the Constitution of the ILO occupies a central position in the concept of constitutionalism in that body.

Discussion Notes/Questions

1. A decision-maker in the present problem is the Commission of Inquiry of the International Labour Organization (ILO), the oldest continuous intergovernmental organization in the world. The ILO is conveniently described in Joseph G. Starke, *Introduction to International Law*, 658–61 (10th ed. 1989), as follows:

The International Labour Organisation (ILO) was originally created under Part XIII of the Treaty of Versailles 1919, but subsequently, to dissociate the Organisation as far as possible from the League of Nations and from the treaty itself, this section of the Treaty was detached, and its clauses renumbered, and it emerged with the new title of the "Constitution of the International Labour Organisation". This Constitution was amended in 1945, 1946, 1953, 1962, and 1964. Formerly the International Labour Organisation had some organic connection with the League of Nations but that was altered by the constitutional amendments of 1945 and 1946, and in the latter years it became a specialised agency linked with the United Nations by a special relationship agreement.

From the outset, the main object of the Organisation has been to promote international co-operation in the sphere of industry and labour so that economic competition between states or other like conditions shall not militate against the realisation of minimum as well as uniform labour standards throughout the world. The Organisation's efforts are principally directed to bringing the legislation and practice of each state into line with the most enlightened modern conceptions as to the treatment of Labour, and with changing economic and social conditions in each such country. The idea of social justice underlying its work has been made more manifest in the amendments to the Constitution of 1945 and 1946, and was given particularly solemn expression in the Declaration of Philadelphia adopted by the International Labour Conference in 1944 and annexed to the Constitution. That Declaration reaffirms the principles that labour is not a commodity, that freedom of expression and association are essential to international progress, and that poverty is a danger to prosperity, and it also recognises that the obligation of the Organisation is to further among nations world programmes designed to achieve full employment, higher standards of living, the provision of facilities for the training and transfer of labour, and the extension of social security measures.

The outstanding feature of the International Labour Organisation is its tripartite character, as it is representative in its organs of governments, employers, and employees.

The three main organs of the Organisation are: (1) the International Labour Conference; (2) the Governing Body; (3) the International Labour Office.

The International Labour Conference is a policy-making and legislative body, being in effect a "world industrial Parliament". It consists of four representatives in respect of each member state, two representing the government and one each labour and management respectively in that country. Delegates speak and vote independently. Voting is by a two-thirds majority. The Conference promotes labour legislation in each state, by adopting: (a) Recommendations; and (b) Conventions. A Recommendation enunciates principles to guide a state in drafting labour legislation or labour regulation, and for this reason has been termed a "standard-defining instrument". States, however, are under no binding obligation to give effect to a Recommendation, although they are duty bound to bring it before the appropriate national legislative authority. A Convention is in the nature of a treaty, although it is adopted by the Conference and not signed by delegates of the member states. Primarily, it is conceived as a model for domestic legislation. Member states are under an obligation to bring the Convention before the competent authorities for the enactment of legislation or other action (article 19 of the Constitution). If a member state obtains approval for a Convention, it is bound to ratify it, and thereupon assumes the obligation of applying its provisions. Also that member state is bound to report annually on the measures it has taken to bring its legislation into accord with the Convention.

The Governing Body, which meets several times a year, is more or less the executive organ of the Organisation. It has similar tripartite character to that of the Conference, being composed of 56 members, 28 representing governments, 14 representing management and elected by the employers' delegates to the Conference, and 14 representing labour and elected by the workers' delegates to the Conference. The Governing Body appoints the Director–General of the International Labour Office, proposes the Budget of the Organisation and supervises the work of the Office and of the various Committees and Commissions.

The amendments of 1945 and 1946 to the Constitution were made principally with a view to strengthening the provisions for the application of Conventions adopted by the Conference, to make the Organisation completely independent of League of Nations machinery, and to enable it to co-operate more fully with the United Nations and other international institutions. This involved a thorough redrafting of article 19 of the Constitution concerning the obligations of member states with reference to Conventions and Recommendations, including the addition of an obligation for member states to report from time to time on their relevant law and practice even where the competent authorities had not approved of the instruments submitted to them for approval and other action, and including also more specific provisions as to the application of these instruments within federal states....

Besides Conventions and Recommendations (so far more than 160 Conventions and more than 170 Recommendations have been adopted) the Organisation has through its organs adopted less formal instruments to express its policies; for example, resolutions, conclusions, observations, codes of guidelines, and reports. Collectively all these instruments form an International Labour Code embodying world standards of labour policy. At the date of writing, there have been more than 5,000 ratifications of ILO Conventions. Other important features of the Organisation's machinery are the provisions in articles 24–25 of the Constitution conferring industrial associations of employers and workers the right to make a representation to the Governing Body that a member state has failed to observe effectively a Convention binding it; several such representations have been made. Then there is the procedure of complaint by member states set out in articles 26 to 34; this may lead to the appointment of a Commission of Inquiry and action against the state not fulfilling its obligations, to induce it to comply therewith. Supervision of the implementation of ILO instruments is carried out by a Committee of Experts on the Application of Conventions and Recommendations.

The third organ of the International Labour Organisation, the International Labour Office, represents the administrative or civil service staff of the Organisation, discharging very similar functions to those of the United Nations Secretariat and acting as a publishing house.

In the last two decades the International Labour Organisation has moved strongly into the field of expert advice and technical assistance, manpower [sic] organisation, productivity and management, education and development, the working environment, occupational health and safety, social security, and workers' education.

2. In *International Labour Conventions and National Law: The Effectiveness of the Automatic Incorporation of Treaties in National Legal Systems*, a portion of which is extracted above (Reading 19, *supra*), Virginia A. Leary, at 17–18, outlines the "supervisory system" of the ILO:

Reciprocity has traditionally been the most important enforcement mechanism in international law. It fails to function, however, when states do not perceive their own immediate interests as threatened by another state's noncompliance with international law. Thus, inter-state complaints, either before judicial or quasi-judicial bodies, have not proved highly effective in regard to enforcement of treaties laying down social and humanitarian norms which consist of parallel rather than reciprocal or contractual obligations.

The most effective present methods of enforcement of such treaties are supervisory systems by an international organization or procedures for individual complaints at the international level. States have been more willing to accept the development of supervisory systems involving reporting to an international body, and fact-finding by such bodies, than procedures for complaints by individuals. The phenomenon of the increasing adoption of treaties on social and economic matters has thus been paralleled by the increasing importance of international supervisory systems. The ILO supervisory system is one of the oldest and most successful of such systems. Landy has pointed out the need for supervisory systems:

> It is hardly surprising that, with this steady extension of the treaty as the main-stay of international organization, the question of actual performance should also have been raised with increasing insistence. For the adoption of international legislation and its formal acceptance by a growing number of countries cannot, by themselves, add to the stability of inter-State relations, unless there also exists some degree of assurance that the contracting parties really comply with their treaty obligations. This concern that governments respect their pledged word thus emerges as a crucial problem of the contemporary world.... [P]rocedures have had to be developed in order to verify governmental compliance with ratified treaties.[24]

The ILO supervisory system consists of (1) procedures provided for in the ILO Constitution, (2) a special procedure instituted in collaboration with the United Nations for investigating allegations of violations of freedoms of association, and (3) the "regular supervisory procedure."

* * *

The special procedures under the ILO Constitution [which are relevant to the present problem] have been used only to a limited degree. Article 26 of the Constitution provides that a state which has ratified a particular convention may file a complaint that another ratifying state is not effectively observing the provisions of the convention. The same Article provides for the ILO Governing Body to appoint a Commission of Inquiry to investigate the complaint if it sees fit. The Governing Body may also adopt the same procedure on its own motion or on receipt of a complaint from a delegate to the Conference. States have rarely filed complaints under this Article although in recent years several complaints have been filed by Conference delegates. Thus inter-state complaints in the ILO system, as is the case with enforcement procedures of other similar treaties, have not played an important role.

---

24. Ernest A. Landy, The Effectiveness of International Supervision—Thirty Years of ILO Experience 1–2 (1966).

3. "Under the ILO Constitution," writes Professor Ebere Osieke, at page 204 of *Constitutional Law and Practice in the International Labour Organization,* a portion of which is extracted above (Reading 20, *supra*), "responsibility for the interpretation of [ILO] Conventions is assigned to the International Court of Justice and a tribunal which may be established for that purpose. However," he continues, "the practice of the Organisation shows that the International Labour Office also interprets Conventions in certain circumstances." Professor Osieke then goes on, at pp. 204–33, to detail "[t]he various parts played by the [ILO] organs in the exercise of this function" as follows:

(a) Interpretation of Conventions by The International Court of Justice

The powers of the Court to interpret Conventions are laid down in Article 37(1) of the ILO Constitution, which provides that "any question or dispute relating to the interpretation of . . . any subsequent Convention concluded by the Members in pursuance of the provisions of this Constitution shall be referred for decision to the International Court of Justice."

* * *

(b) Complaints against Members of the ILO

Complaints constitute the second category of actions that may be taken against Members for the breach of their obligations under Conventions.

(i) Initiation of complaints

Article 26(1) of the ILO Constitution grants a right to any Member "to file a complaint with the International Labour Office if it is not satisfied that any other Member is securing the effective observance of any Convention which both have ratified"; and Article 26(4) authorises the Governing Body to adopt the complaints procedure "either of its own motion or on receipt of a complaint from a delegate to the Conference." Here again, an effect of the provisions of Article 26(4) is to grant a right of complaint in respect of international agreements to entities which are not parties to them; though, as Members are not under an obligation to implement Conventions which they have not ratified, a complaint cannot be validly initiated against a Member under Article 26 with respect to a Convention to which it is not a party. The use of the phrase "if it is not satisfied" in Article 26(1) suggests that the test to be applied for determining the question of breach of a Convention is subjective.

* * *

(ii) Determination of complaints

The first action that may be taken on a complaint is prescribed by Article 26(2) of the ILO Constitution which provides that "the Governing Body may, if it thinks fit . . . communicate with the government in question in the manner described in Article 24." It seems clear from these provisions that although the complaint is to be filed with the Office, only the Governing Body is competent to deal with it. Its powers in this respect are discretionary: it may communicate the complaint to the Member against which it is made, and it may invite such Member to make such statement on the subject as it may think fit.

The alternative action that may be taken on a complaint is to refer it to a Commission of Inquiry. As most of the complaints received so far have been dealt with in this manner, Commissions of Inquiry appear to play an important part in the determination of complaints, and it is necessary to examine their more important characteristics.

Appointment of a commission of inquiry. Article 26(3) of the ILO Constitution provides that "if the Governing Body does not think it necessary to communicate the complaint to the government" against which it is made, "or if, when it has made such communication, no statement in reply has been received within a reasonable time which the Governing Body considers to be satisfactory, the Governing Body may appoint a Commission of Inquiry to consider the complaint and to report thereon."

* * *

Composition of a commission of inquiry. The composition of a Commission of Inquiry is not regulated by the ILO Constitution, nor by any Standing Orders, but by the practice of the Organisation....

* * *

Procedure of a commission of inquiry. The ILO Constitution does not contain any provisions on the procedure to be followed by a Commission of Inquiry. The matter was considered by the Officers of the Governing Body in 1961 as a result of the complaint filed by the Government of Ghana against the Government of Portugal, after which they recommended that the Commission of Inquiry, if appointed, should determine its own procedure, but should "begin its work by examining the particulars furnished by the Government of Ghana and the observations of the Government of Portugal with a view to determining on what matters it needs fuller information. The Commission will then, through the Director–General, consult the Governments of Ghana and Portugal, but without being bound by the views of either of them, concerning the arrangements necessary to ensure that it has at its disposal thorough and objective information concerning the questions at issue ...".[25]

This proposal was approved by the Governing Body, and the Commission of Inquiry, at its first sitting, laid down its procedure, which was designed to give every opportunity to the governments concerned, the governments of neighbouring countries and some governmental international organisations, to submit information about the complaint. At its second sitting, the Commission heard the arguments of the representatives of the governments concerned, and the evidence given by their witnesses, who were examined and cross-examined by the agent and counsel of the Members involved in the complaint. The members of the Commission afterwards visited the territories of Mozambique, Angola and Guinea, "in order to ascertain whether reasonably specific allegations were supported by current or recent facts."[26] The foregoing procedure has been consistently followed in the consideration of complaints by subsequent Commissions of Inquiry, and may now be regarded as an established practice.

25. Report of the Ghana–Portugal Commission of Inquiry, para. 716, 45 ILO Off. Bull., Supp. II, at 7 (1962).

26. Governing Body, Minutes (150th Sess., Nov. 1961), at 96.

Jurisdiction of a commission of inquiry. An indication of the nature of the jurisdiction of a Commission of Inquiry may be found in Article 28 of the ILO Constitution which provides that:

> When the Commission of Inquiry has fully considered the complaint, it shall prepare a report embodying its findings on all questions of fact relevant to determining the issue between the parties and containing such recommendations as it may think proper as to the steps which should be taken to meet the complaint and the time within which they should be taken.

* * *

Development of law and precedent. The provision of Article 28 that a Commission of Inquiry should prepare a report embodying its findings "on all questions of fact" suggests that it is not expected to deal with questions of law and politics. While it is possible, and indeed desirable, that a Commission of Inquiry will not concern itself with political questions, it seems difficult to distinguish findings of fact from those of law in these cases. In order to establish whether a Member is in breach of its legal obligations, a Commission of Inquiry will have to examine the facts on which the complaint is based, as well as the nature of the Member's obligations under the relevant Convention. In doing so, the Commission will be dealing with questions both of fact and of law.

* * *

Binding effect of recommendations of a commission of inquiry. The final duty of a Commission of Inquiry is to prepare a report embodying its findings and recommendations, where appropriate, as to the steps which should be taken to meet the complaint and the time within which they should be taken. A question arises, however, as to the binding effect of these recommendations. An answer to it may be found in the ILO Constitution. Article 29(1) requires the Director–General to communicate the report of the Commission of Inquiry to the Governing Body and to each of the governments involved in the complaint, and to publish the report. Article 29(2) provides that each of these governments must inform the Director–General "within three months" whether or not it accepts the recommendations contained in the report, and, if not, whether it proposes to refer the complaint to the International Court of Justice.

4. *Environmental Assessment.* Nongovernmental Organizations (NGO's) and international lending institutions are playing an increasingly important role in global environmental protection. In the present problem, it was open to the Nature Conservancy or Caribia to have adopted another route to address the problem. They could have lodged official complaints with the World Bank stating that at least the second phase of ECOHAB demanded to be assessed under the Bank's Environmental Assessment Operational Directive (EAOD).

In a dramatic turn around of its lending policies it now appears that development institutions such as the World Bank appear to have committed to environmentally sustainable development, as against development *per se*. Pursuant to its adoption of sustainable development, the Bank has introduced a variety of instruments into its lending and advisory activities. Environmental Assessment (EA) is one of the most important of these tools. The objectives of an EA is to prevent, minimize, mitigate or compensate for any adverse environmental and social impacts of the project under consideration.

In 1989 the Bank adopted Operational Directive (OD) 4.00, which is in the process of becoming an operational policy, and EA has become standard procedure for Bank-financed investment projects. EA is designed to be a flexible process which makes environmental considerations an integral part of project preparation and which allows environmental issues to be addressed in a timely and cost-effective way during project preparation and implementation.

Between October 1989 and May 1995, more than one thousand projects subject to the requirements of the EA–OD have been presented to the Board of Directors. Over fifty percent (50%) required some form of environmental analysis, and ten percent (10%) needed a full EA. The EA itself requires that adverse environmental impacts be identified and assessed, along with feasible mitigation measures. It further obligates a systematic exploration of the alternatives accompanied by a comparative cost benefit analysis. The EA is then reviewed by the Bank, and the project in question is appraised only if the EA is found satisfactory. The Bank then supervises the implementation of the EA as part of overall project supervision. The EA process is more fully described in, *Introduction: EA at the World Bank* (visited Nov. 24, 1998) <http://www-esd.worldbank.org.>.

Even without the intervention of Caribia or the Nature Conservancy, do you think that the second stage of the ECOHAB project, as proposed, could have survived scrutiny under the EA requirements of the World Bank?

5.   The cultural rights of indigenous peoples, including rights to land, form an integral part of the discourse on human rights. Initiatives like "debt for nature" may be seen, therefore, as merging the human rights of indigenous peoples with the protection of the environment. The "debt for nature" merging process, however, is not without its difficulties, as is made clear in the following remarks by Robert A. Williams, Jr., *Comments on Energy and the Environment: Intersecting Global Issues*, 9 ARIZ. J. INT'L & COMP. L. 199, 202–203 (1992):

> The problem for human rights law and policy in addressing indigenous peoples' demands for self-determination over the territories and resources they claim—whether in the rainforest or the Arctic—is the same in many fundamental ways as it is for nation states. The question becomes: How do you create sustainable development? This perspective places indigenous peoples' claims within the same emerging context and intellectual framework used by modern human rights advocates. The emerging framework accepts the idea of a right to develop all territories under a peoples' control as a critical component of the right to self-determine. Development in this context aims at the improvement of the welfare of the entire population of a state, including its indigenous peoples.
>
> This right to self-determination is tempered by a recognition that environmental rights must compliment development rights. These environmental rights recognize that all human beings including indigenous peoples have the right to an environment adequate for their health and welfare, and also have the responsibility to protect that environment for the benefit of present and future generations. Development, therefore, must occur in an environmentally sensible and sustainable context within the nation state and within boundaries of indigenous peoples' territories.

> * * *

> My only fear is that indigenous peoples may lose out as non-indigenous environmentalists groups seek to link indigenous peoples' human rights to deforestation and the issue of global warming. Indigenous peoples may be

denied an equal right to participate and consult in a global dialogue on the rights and responsibilities of all self-determining peoples with respect to the challenges of global warming. They may also be denied the responsibility to control their own destiny in responsible fashion. History bears witness to these denials. For the past 500 years people have hypothesized and identified what indigenous' peoples rights should be from a non-indigenous western perspective. Preventing similar denials in the future will only result if we begin listening to indigenous peoples and encouraging their contributions to a dialogue about the sources, nature and parameters of human rights for all human beings.

In *The Growing Voice of Indigenous Peoples: Their Use of Storytelling and Rights Discourse to Transform Multilateral Development Bank Policies*, 8 ARIZ. J. INT'L & COMP. L. 117, 142–48 (1991), H. Elizabeth Dallam critiques the emerging discourse which proclaims indigenous peoples to be guardians of fragile ecosystems as follows:

> The successes won by environmentalist groups acting in connection with pro-indigenous groups and indigenous peoples deserve enormous praise. However, pro-indigenous activists, scholars and indigenous peoples themselves have begun to question the discourse emerging out of this coalition. In their struggles against World Bank policies, indigenous peoples and environmentalist groups have been natural allies. Environmentalists have vast resources, and "[t]he indigenous in return have networks and information of great value for international projects."[27]

> According to the emerging discourse, "native populations and national resource managers are appropriate allies, ... [g]iven ... the close union of the goals of native people to preserve the environment in perpetuity with the goals of the advocates of protected areas, alliance is a logical step."[28] According to James Clad, who has reported on the subject of conservation and indigenous peoples for the World Conservation Union ("IUCN"), "[t]he argument that indigenous peoples and conservationists are 'natural allies' is made with particular force when strategies to preserve tropical forests ... are discussed."[29] His point is well-taken given the amazing successes of indigenous groups of the Amazon rainforest.

* * *

The discourse proclaims that indigenous people know how to live in harmony with the forest and will protect it, thereby, protecting the rest of the world from the damaging effects of global warming. Indeed, several of the indigenous groups themselves adopt this language. Recall Davi Kopenawa Yanomami's interview with Terence Turner. Davi stated:

> The whites have dirty spirits, the Indians, too. There are, however, places in this world that are not dirty, where nature is still clean, as *Omame* directed. The shamans know these places, they understand this cleanness, they can teach it to others.[30]

27. S. Schwartzman, *Indigenists, Environmentalists and the Multilateral Development Banks*, 8 CULTURAL SURVIVAL Q. 74, 75 (Dec. 1984).

28. James Clad, *Conservation and Indigenous Peoples: A Study of Convergent Interests*, 8 CULTURAL SURVIVAL Q. 68 (1984), *quoting* L. Brownrigg, Native Cultures and Protected Areas: Management Options (Amaru IV Cooperative/World Wildlife Fund, USA, n.d.).

29. *Id.*

30. Terence Turner & Davi Kopenawa Yanomami, *I Fight Because I am Alive*, 15 CULTURAL SURVIVAL Q. 46, 62 (1991).

The Moxo Indians of the Chimane Forest Reserve in Amazonian Bolivia who are protesting commercial lumbering activities have stated, "We have learned to take care and maintain the ecology because we know that it guarantees our existence."[31] Thus, some indigenous groups are binding themselves to fragile ecosystems, and those indigenous groups that do not inhabit such areas cannot access the discourse or environmentalist support.

The nature of this discourse is troubling. Though the coalition between environmentalist and indigenous groups has been very successful in the past decade, it may be advertently closing doors for the future. Moreover, the discourse primitivizes indigenous peoples. Clad illustrates this point with the following quote from a 1981 International NGO Conference on Indigenous Peoples and the Land, held in Geneva:

> In the world of today there are two systems, two different irreconcilable "ways of life." The Indian world—collective, communal, human, respectful of nature and wise—and the western world—greedy, destructive, individualist and enemy of mother nature.[32]

The truth of these statements is questionable. As Clad asserts, "[s]uch statements not only ignore past adoption of biologically disruptive technology by aboriginal peoples, but also in a curious way buttress the fallacy of the 'noble savage,' a uniquely European concept."[33] For instance, thirteen out of fourteen Kayapo tribes, who worked so hard at blocking the Altamira–Xingu dam, were reported in May of this year to be allowing logging and gold mining on their land.[34] Paiakan, the leader who traveled seven countries to ask for international support to stop the destruction of the rainforest, has been marginalized from the tribe because he does not support its exploitation of the land.

* * *

Moreover, indigenous peoples may oppose the initiatives of environmentalists. For instance, Evaristo Nugkuag of COICA has stated that he opposes debt-for-nature swaps proposed by environmentalists.[35] The swaps involve "purchase of debt by a non-profit environmental organization in return for environmental concessions by the debtor country."[36] Conservationists have heralded the swaps as an innovative way to save "what remains of the rich flora and fauna and natural systems of debt-burdened countries."[37] Under these plans, conservation groups such as the Worldwide Fund for Nature ("WWF") and Conservation International ("CI") define and participate in the management environmental programs for debtor countries.[38] The conserva-

---

31. Quoted in K. Redford, The Ecologically Noble Savage, 15 CULTURAL SURVIVAL Q. 46, 47 (1991).

32. J. Clad, supra note 28, at 69.

33. Id.

34. M. Kepp, Trouble With the Techno Tribe: Are the Amazonian Kayap's Turning Pro-development?, THE SAN FRANCISCO CHRONICLE, May 12, 1991, at 4.

35. Amazon Indians Protest Exclusion From Decisions, Financial Report, Oct. 19, 1989 (Domestic Money: Money Report).

36. H. McGee, Jr. & K. Zimmerman, The Deforestation of the Brazilian Amazon: Law,

Politics, and International Cooperation, 21 IN-TER-AM. L. REV. 513, 547 (1990).

37. W. Reilly, Debt–for–Nature Swaps: The Time Has Come, 1990 INT'L ENVTL. AFF. 135.

38. For a discussion of the level of involvement of conservationist organizations in specific projects, see D. Page, Debt–for–Nature Swaps: Experience Gained, Lessons Learned, 1989 INT'L ENVTL. AFF. 275; P. Borrelli, Debt or Equity?, 1998 AMICUS J. 42; J. Rosebrock & H. Sondhoff, Debt–for–Nature Swaps: A Review of the First Experiences, 1991 INTERECONOMICS, 82.

tionists' plans may include setting up reserves or initiating better maintenance of existing reserves.

By November, 1989, groups such as WWF and CI had undertaken debt-for-nature swaps in five countries, relieving $20 million of third world debt. Nukuag of COICA, however, opposes the swaps because of the disastrous effects of a forest preservation plan that CI arranged in Bolivia. The Chimanes Indians who inhabit the Bolivian forest to be preserved offered their own conservation proposal, yet CI simply ignored it. Instead CI designated a "Permanent Production Zone" for logging of the forest. The logging practices have "wreaked havoc across the land," and "[l]ogging roads have opened up the forest to colonization, with disastrous consequences for the forest wildlife on which the Indian depend."[39] Moreover, the Chimanes do not even have title under Brazilian law to their lands. In August, 1990, 2,000 Indians marched for one month across Bolivia in opposition to the destruction of their lands under the debt-for-nature swap. Thus, debt-for-nature swaps are a good idea in theory, yet may ignore indigenous rights to gain title to their ancestral homelands and to exercise their own development plans.

* * *

In situations where indigenous peoples have not already been forced off their traditional lands and are using their lands in an environmentally sound manner, the alliance between indigenous activists and environmentalists makes sense in the short run. Indigenous peoples may need to draw on the resources of environmentalist groups and the power of environmental fears in order to gather international attention. Indeed, indigenous groups of the Amazon rainforest have been the most successful in getting World Bank loans halted probably due to growing awareness of the importance of preserving the rainforest in order to slow global warming. Other indigenous peoples living in less precious environments may be ignored by environmentalists because while groups such as the Kayapo are marshalling international attention, "less-flashy" indigenous peoples are losing their lands and cultures to World Bank projects.

The danger in the emerging discourse that credits indigenous groups as being the best keepers of areas, such as rainforests, that are environmentally valuable, is that indigenous peoples without such lands may be excluded from the discussion. An important addition to the discourse is Nugkuag's notion that indigenous peoples should not merely be consulted about development plans but should be participants in the planning process. Moreover, indigenous peoples should explicitly bring their rights to cultural survival and self-determination established at the Working Group to discussions about development plans. The right to self-determination includes the right to develop or to have control over one's resources. In particular, those indigenous groups who cannot claim to be "stewards" of their lands should enter into these conversations.

6. The skepticism expressed by Williams and Darrell about the fusion of environmental protection with the rights of indigenous peoples, was confirmed by the imbroglio surrounding the Kyapo in Brazil between 1993 and 1995. The Kyapo leaders had made headlines in late 1993 by arriving at the capital to lobby the Brazilian federal government for permission to sell mahogany that logging companies, at the invitation of the Kyapo, had harvested in their reserve. They also

39. D. Lewis, *Conflicts of Interests*, Geographical Mag. 18, 21 (Dec. 1990).

demanded compensation from the Brazilian government which had ordered that non-indigenous miners be removed from their reserve. The mining practices of these non-indigenous gold miners had caused mercury pollution that created grave health hazards and environmental dangers within the Kyapo reserve. In order to stop this, the Attorney-General of Brazil obtained a court order expelling both miners and loggers from the Kayapo reserve. Although a divided Kayapo finally agreed to the expulsion they did so only after highlighting their right to take the developmental path of their choice, even if it happened to be environmentally unfriendly. This chapter of the story of the Kayapo is more fully described in: Linda Rabben, *Kayapo Choices: Short–Term Gain vs. Long–Term Damage* 19 CULTURAL SURVIVAL Q. 11 (1995).

7. On the weaknesses of the Convention on Biological Diversity see, Editors' Note, Reading 23, Chapter 11.2, *infra*, at 985.

8. *Bibliographical Note.* For further discussion concerning the principle themes addressed in this problem, consult the following specialized materials:

(a) *Specialized Books/Monographs.* J. Brunnée, Acid Rain and Ozone Layer Depletion: International Law and Regulation (1988); International Union for Conservation of Nature, et al., Conserving the World's Biological Diversity (1990); A. Kiss & D. Shelton, International Environmental Law (1991); D. Mahar, Government Policies and Deforestation of Brazil's Amazon Region (1989); N. Valticos, International Labour Law (1979); E. Wilson, Biodiversity (1988); ___, The Diversity of Life (1992). Lakshman D. Guruswamy & Jeffrey A. McNeely,(eds) Protection of Global Biodiversity: Converging Strategies (1998); A. Akerele, V. Heywood, and H. Synge, (eds) The Conservation of Medicinal Plants (1989); P.R. Ehrlich and E.H. Ehrlich, Extinction: The Causes and Consequences of the Disappearance of Species (1981); N Myers, The Primary Source: Tropical Forests and Our Future (1984); D Pearce and D. Moran, The Economic Value of Biodiversity (1994).

(b) *Specialized Hearings/Reports.* Congressional Research Service, Debt for Nature Swaps: A Brief Overview (1988); Hague Report, Sustainable Development: From Concept to Action (Dutch Ministry of Development Cooperation, UNDP & UNCED, March 1992); Note by the Secretary–General of the Conference on Environment and Development, Rio Declaration on Environment and Development, U.N. Doc. A/conf.151/5 (May 7, 1992); ___, Non-legally Binding Authoritative Statement of Principles for a Global Consensus on the Management, Conservation and Sustainable Development of All Types of Forests, U.N. Doc. A/conf. 151/6 (Apr. 21, 1992); United Nations Conference on Environment and Development, Adoption of Agreements on Environment and Development, Agenda 21 Note by the Secretary–General of the Conference, U.N. Doc. A/conf.151/4 (pt. I) (Apr. 22, 1992); ___, U.N. Doc. A/conf.151/4 (pt. II) (May 1, 1992); ___, U.N. Doc. A/conf.151/4 (pt. III) (Apr. 24, 1992); ___, U.N. Doc. A/conf.151/4 (pt. IV) (Apr. 27, 1992); U.S. Congress, Office of Technology Assessment, Combined Summaries: Technologies to Sustain Tropical Forest Resources and Biological Diversity (1992); World Bank, Operational Directive 4.00, Annex A: Environmental Assessment (1989); World Commission on Environment and Development, Our Common Future (1987); World Resources Institute, et al., Global Biodiversity Strategy (1992); World Resources Institute, et al., Global Biodiversity Strategy: A Policy–Makers' Guide (1992).

(c) *Specialized Articles/Book Chapters.* D. Alheritiere, *Settlement of Public International Disputes on Shared Resources*, 25 N.R.J. 701 (1985); Comment, *Debt for Nature Swaps in Latin American Countries: The Enforcement Dilemma*, 7

Conn. J. Int'l L. 123 (1991); T. Dobson, *Loss of Biodiversity: An International Environmental Policy Perspective*, 17 N.C. J. Int'l & Comm. Reg. 277 (1992); L. Goldie, *Equity and International Management of Transboundary Resources*, 25 N.R.J. 665 (1985); T. Hamilton, *Debt for Nature Swaps: A New Strategy for Protecting Environmental Interests in Developing Nations*, 16 Ecology L. Q. 1065 (1989); J. Starke, *Implementation and Enforcement of ILO Conventions and Standards*, 64 Austl. L. J. 511 (1990); E. Wilson, *Threats to Biodiversity*, Scientific American 108 (Sept. 1989); J. Wood, International Labour Organization Conventions—Labour Code or Treaties?, 40 I.C.L.Q. 149 (1991); N. Myers, *Threatened Biotas:"Hotspots" in tropical forests*, 8 Environmentalist 1 (1988).

Chapter Eleven

PROBLEMS IN PROTECTING AGAINST PARTICULAR HUMAN BEHAVIORS

Preceding chapters have identified transnational environmental problems with reference to the earth-space environments in which we live: the atmosphere, the hydrosphere, the lithosphere, and the biosphere. But some threats to our natural heritage cannot be so categorized or characterized because they bear consequences for more than one "sphere"—potentially, indeed, for the entirety of the global environment. Three such threats, each of which pose a diffuse range of challenges to effective environmental protection, are free trade agreements, population growth, and military conflict.

Free Trade Agreements. The pressures and incentives of international trade are major factors in the destruction of species and ecosystems. At the same time, they afford a powerful means for enforcing environmental standards. The problem is, however, that the manipulation of trade barriers and market access, even if in the name of environmental protection, is in direct conflict with the policy of trade liberalization that underlies the principal charters of the international trading system, to wit, the General Agreement on Tariffs and Trade (GATT) **[Basic Document 7.1]** and associated free trade agreements. Problem 11–1 raises important questions about GATT and it progeny. Does the GATT Agreement on Technical Barriers to Trade (TBT) continue to obstruct environmental protection, or on the contrary, does it open the door to limited environmental protection? And how might the TBT be interpreted by WTO judicial tribunals whose jurisdiction is limited to GATT law?

In contrast to GATT the North American Agreement on Environmental Cooperation (NAAEC), an environmental side agreement of the North American Free Trade Agreement (NAFTA), has shown greater awareness of the need for environmental protection, and instituted innovative procedures for doing so. The extent to which environmental protection may be pursued through such procedures is examined in Problem 11–2.

Population Growth. Population growth stretches environmental resources to their limits and unsustainable usage occurs as short-term human needs become paramount. To some extent, of course, population growth can be considered a natural phenomenon. On final analysis, however, human society is responsible for its control, and for this reason there is much debate about the true nature of the problem and about how it should be addressed. Some contend that there simply are too many people. Others argue that it is a problem essentially of resource distribution. Further explanations blame the irresponsible exploitation of resources by environmentally destructive technology. In addition, there are those who advocate increased population growth on the grounds that more people will compel better technological solutions. Often neglected in these debates, however, is the human rights dimension of the population problem, a neglect that some population theorists argue leads not only to gross abuses of such rights but also to the continuation of the population problem itself. Human rights abuses certainly do exist relative to the curbing of population growth and consequently provide an added complexity to the difficult issue of population control.

Military Conflict. In warfare, where human life is treated as dispensable, the natural environment can equally become the victim of hostile action. Of course, the environment usually suffers indirectly as a consequence of the methods of warfare employed. But it can be severely damaged as a result of deliberate, direct assaults as well—as a consequence of any one of a number of hostile manipulations that hold out the potential to weaken the enemy by disrupting the enemy's physical surroundings. Natural phenomena such as landslides or rainfall can be artificially triggered. Human-controlled environments such as dams or waterways can be blown up or altered. Air, water, soil, and animal and plant life can be poisoned or otherwise degraded. Even outer space and celestial bodies—potentially through, say, the diversion of asteroids via nuclear weapons—are not immune. True, within a context of mass killing, in which all semblance of law appears to have vanished, it must seem incongruous to consider the illegality of such actions. Any assessment of right and wrong is complicated, if not altogether confused, by the coercive circumstances. Yet the law of war—*jus in bello* especially, but *jus ad bellum* as well—is precisely concerned with standards of acceptable albeit warring behavior. Military necessity is weighed against humanitarian concerns and, as evidenced by the Nuremburg trials following World War II, progressive judgments can be made. Still, international law as applied to environmental warfare does not provide a sure-footed guide for such judgments. Despite a smattering of treaty provisions and a relatively rich heritage of customary law norms and general principles, the standards are not fully defined and their applicability is ambiguous. Despite the mediative role of the principle of proportionality, the principle of military necessity is seen commonly to override the principle of humanity. Without a well defined rule of environmental protection to contest it, environmental well-being remains, in warfare, a somewhat illusive goal.

Problem 11–1

The Environment and Gatt Collide in Albion

SECTION 1. FACTS

Responding to overwhelming international public concern about depletion of forests and species habitat, the Parliament of the Kingdom of Albion, a European nation, enacted legislation called "the Forest and Habitat Protection Act" (the FHPA). The relevant objectives of the FHPA were, inter alia:

1.   "to prevent harvesting of mature Albion forests that are the habitat of numerous valuable and irreplaceable endangered species."

2.   "to encourage the sustainable management of global forests and their forest habitats."

3.   "to join similar developed countries in implementing the Convention on the International Trade in Endangered Species (CITES)."

The FHPA empowered Albion's Minister for the Environment (Minister) to take the national and international administrative and legal action necessary to implement its provisions.

Persuaded of the need to take appropriate action after attending an international conference on endangered species, the Minister undertook a close examination of Albion's conservation policies and practices. Upon discovering that a number of species within Albion's forests were endangered and close to extinction, the environmental Minister, acting under the FHPA, banned the harvesting of trees in seventy percent of Albion's forests, containing the bulk of Albion's high quality softwoods. Despite governmental promises to the contrary, the ban resulted in the near closing of many businesses within Albion's once prosperous timber industry. Home furnishings, construction trades, and logging enterprises were severely damaged from the lack of timber supply available in Albion.

Cascadia, a developing South American country with a growing timber industry, filled the gap created by the environmental restrictions by contracting with companies in Albion to supply timber and products built with high quality softwoods from Cascadia.

Reacting to widespread pressure from national businesses and trade unions, the Government of Albion began a national campaign advocating the use of "plastic wood" substitutes, manufactured by its large petrochemical industry, for the construction of homes and the making of furniture. The strategy failed because consumers preferred old fashioned wooden homes and furnishings. Consequently, plastic wood sales remained sluggish while Cascadian soft wood imports surged. In response, Albion created tax incentives that encouraged the building and purchasing of homes and furniture made with plastic wood.

A short time later, the Minister investigated a timber trade union's complaint that Cascadia was violating the FHPA and CITES. After an inquiry required by the FHPA, the Minister determined that clear-cutting timber-harvesting methods in Cascadia's forests endangered the habitats of such wildlife as the Northern Spotted Owl and the Grizzly Bear, listed in the CITES annexes. Also, the Minister determined that Cascadia's harvesting methods threatened endangered plant species, including the Pacific Yew used by several large pharmaceutical companies to produce cancer-fighting drugs. Although the Cascadian government had decided not to award new contracts for the harvesting of mature forests, the large number of existing contracts permitted the continuation of such harvesting for many years. However, the environmental Minister further decided that Cascadia was in violation of the FHPA as well as CITES, and classified it as an "offending nation" until it took "significant steps to protect these wildlife, plant species, and their corresponding habitats."

Having classified Cascadia as an offending nation, Albion's Minister exercised her further powers under the FHPA and prohibited the importation of timber products from Cascadia. Authorized to impose restrictions to prevent offending nations from exporting banned products through third parties, she also prohibited imports of all softwood products from Pandanao, an emerging nation and new trade partner of Cascadia. She was doing so, she stated in her official capacity, because a large number of Pandanaoan products used softwoods from Cascadia.

Purporting to act under the GATT Agreement to Technical Barriers to Trade (TBT), the Minister gave notice of new product standards for imports and domestic products. These standards prohibited products made from wood harvested in mature forests that supported endangered species. Acting to enforce these standards, the Minister prohibited the importation of timber from Cascadia. Consequent upon the Minister's decisions, Albion's imports of lumber products were substantially reduced. At the same time, "plastic wood" sales in Albion began to boom with several celebrity endorsements of futuristic home furnishings.

Among the companies affected by the import prohibition were Furniture–In–The–Raw, a Pandanao-based corporation which employed native carpenters to expertly carve up-scale home furnishings. Without the opportunity to export products to a large consumer like Albion, the Pandanao's timber business quickly dropped and many workers were laid off. Acting together, Cascadia and Pandanao filed a complaint against Albion with the Dispute Settlement Body of the World Trade Organization of the 1994 General Agreement on Tariffs and Trade (GATT), to which all three countries are Parties. They asked that a panel be constituted to decide the matter. All parties consented, and a panel was commissioned from the WTO Secretariat's list of trade experts.

Cascadia and Pandanao argued that Albion's actions constituted a violation of Articles I, III, IX, XI, and XX of the GATT and imposed an undue burden on international trade. Albion responded that its actions were appropriate under the GATT's Agreement on Technical Barriers to Trade (TBT) which lists protection of the environment as a legitimate objective for placing limitations on product standards. Albion further argued that these restrictions are permitted because they do not discriminate between domestic or imported products, in accordance with Article 2.1 and Article 4. Finally, Albion argued that its actions were authorized by CITES.

The GATT panel ruled in favor of Cascadia and Pandanao, holding that Albion's FHPA required executive actions in clear violation of the GATT. Albion was duly informed of the decision and asked to amend its laws in compliance with the WTO body's decision. However, claiming that its actions were within the terms of the TBT and CITES, Albion refused to lift its import restrictions. Cascadia and Pandanao consequently filed an action with the GATT Appellate Body for enforcement of the earlier GATT ruling against Albion, and the Appellate Body has set a date for pleadings and oral arguments.

All three countries are party to the Charter of the United Nations [**Basic Document 1.3**], the 1969 Vienna Convention on the Law of Treaties [**Basic Document 1.7**], and the GATT of 1994 [**Basic Document 7.1**]. Albion and

Pandanao have signed and ratified the 1973 Convention on International Trade in Endangered Species (CITES) **[Basic Document 6.5]**. However, Cascadia has signed but not yet ratified the Convention.

SECTION 2. QUESTIONS PRESENTED

1. Were Albion's actions justified under international environmental law?

2. Were Albion's actions prohibited under the GATT?

SECTION 3. ASSIGNMENTS

A. *Reading Assignment*

Study the Readings presented in Section 4, *infra*, and the Discussion Notes/Questions that follow. Also, to the extent possible, consult the accompanying bibliographical references.

B. *Recommended Writing Assignment*

Prepare a comprehensive, logically sequenced, and argumentative brief in the form of an outline of the primary and subsidiary legal issues you see requiring resolution by the GATT Appellate Body. Also, from the perspective of an independent objective judge, indicate which side ought to prevail on each issue and why. Retain a copy of your issue-outline/brief for class discussion.

C. *Recommended Oral Assignment*

Assume you are legal counsel for Cascadia and Pandanao, on the one hand, or Albion, on the other (as designated by your instructor); then, relying upon the Readings (and your issue-outline if prepared), present a 15–20 minute oral argument of your government's likely positions before the GATT Appellate Body.

D. *Suggested Reflective Assignment*

Consider (and recommend) alternative norms, institutions, and/or procedures that you believe might do better than existing world order arrangements to contend with situations of the kind posed by this problem. In so doing, but without insisting upon immediate feasibility, identify the steps that would be needed to make your presentation.

SECTION 4. READINGS

1. International Convention on International Trade in Endangered Species of Wild Fauna and Flora (CITES) (with appendices I & II and annexes and as amended), Mar. 3, 1973, arts. I–IV, VIII–X, XIV 27 U.S.T. 1087, T.I.A.S. No. 8249, 993 U.N.T.S. 243, *reprinted in* 12 I.L.M. 1085 (1973) [Basic Document 6.5].

2. William C. Burns, *Cites and the Regulation of International Trade in Endangered Species of Flora: A Critical Appraisal*, 8 DICK. J. INT'L L. 203, 207–11 (1990).

CITES regulates international trade in wild animals and plants through a permit system. Endangered species and specimens of these species are listed in one of three appendices which reflect the different levels of protection required to maintain their viability.

A. The CITES Framework

Each party to the treaty is required to designate one or more "Management Authorities" to regulate the granting of permits or certificates on behalf of that party. Also, one or more "Scientific Authori[ties]" are designated to monitor the status of species that are contained in the Appendices. The treaty also contains provisions to add or delete species from the Appendices, as appropriate, as well as for moving a species from one appendix to another. At least once every two years, the Parties convene to review implementation of the Convention and to make recommendations to improve the Convention's effectiveness.

1. Appendix I Threatened Species. Appendix I of CITES is reserved for "all species threatened with extinction which are or may be affected by trade." International trade in specimens of species contained in Appendix I is subject to strict regulatory requirements in both exporting and importing states. Exportation of an Appendix I species requires the "prior grant and presentation of an export permit." CITES mandates that an export permit for an Appendix I species shall only be granted after:

1. a Scientific Authority designated by the State of export has certified that exportation of the species or specimen will "not be detrimental to the survival of that species;"

2. a Management Authority designated by the State of export is satisfied that the species or specimen has not been obtained "in contravention of the laws of that State for the protection of fauna and flora;"

3. a Management Authority of the State of export is satisfied that living specimens have been prepared for shipment in such a manner as to minimize injury or cruel treatment of the species; and

4. the Management Authority of the exporting State is satisfied that an import permit has been granted by competent authorities in the state of destination.

A party wishing to import an Appendix I species must obtain an import permit and an export permit. CITES provides that an import permit will be granted when the following conditions are met: a Scientific Authority designated by the importing State has certified that importation of the species will not be detrimental to the survival of the species in question; a Scientific Authority of the importing State is satisfied that the prospective recipient of living specimens is properly equipped to house and care for the specimen; and a Management Authority of the importing state is satisfied that specimen is "not to be used for primarily commercial purposes."

2. Appendix II Prospective Threatened Species. Specimens of flora and fauna species are included in Appendix II of the treaty when the species "although not necessarily now threatened with extinction may become so unless trade in specimens of such species is subject to strict regulation in order to avoid utilization incompatible with their survival." A party contemplating the exportation of an Appendix II species must first obtain an export permit. The criteria that officials must follow in determining whether an export permit should be granted are identical to those outlined in Article III for Appendix I species. Importation of Appendix II species is permitted only upon the presentation of an export permit.

3. *Appendix III.* Appendix III of the treaty is reserved for species that are designated for protection by domestic legislation and which require "the cooperation of other parties in the control of trade." Trade in Appendix III species is only permitted in cases where the Management Authority of the exporting state has granted an export permit. The permits must specify that the specimen was not obtained illegally and that living specimens are being shipped in a manner that will minimize health risks or cruelty to the species.

4. *Flora Species Provisions.* Two provisions of CITES specifically focus on international trade in endangered species of flora. Article I(b)(iii) provides that trade in "any recognizable part or derivative thereof" of a plant species included in Appendix I, or any "readily recognizable part or derivative" specified by the parties for an Appendix II or III species in relation to that species shall also be subject to treaty regulation. In construing this provision, the parties to the Convention interpret the term "readily recognizable part or derivative" to exclude trade in seeds, flasked seedling cultures, pollen, spores, tissue culture, and cut flowers of artificially propagated orchids.

Article VII(4) provides that Appendix I plant species that are artificially propagated for commercial purposes, shall be classified as Appendix II species for the purposes of international trade. The Parties interpret the term "artificially propagated" to refer to plants "grown by man from seeds, cuttings, callus tissue, spores or other propagules under controlled conditions." Trade in an artificially propagated flora stock is permitted only if the stock is "established and maintained in a manner not detrimental to the survival of the species in the wild." Further, the stock must be "managed in a manner designed to maintain the artificially propagated stock indefinitely." The Management Authority of the state of export may issue a certificate based on requirements that are acceptable to an importing state in lieu of other exporting state requirements.

3.   Vienna Convention on the Law of Treaties, Jan. 27, 1980. arts. 27, 30, U.N.Doc. A/CONF.39/27 at 289 (1969), 1155 U.N.T.S. 331, *reprinted in* 8 I.L.M. 679 (1969) [Basic Document 1.7].

4.   General Agreement on Tariffs and Trade (GATT), Oct. 30, 1947, T.I.A.S. No. 1700, 61–V Stat. All, 4 Bevans 639, 55 U.N.T.S. 18: arts. I, III, IX, XI, XX [Basic Document 7.1].

5.   Final Act Embodying the Results of the Uruguay Round of Multilateral Trade Negotiations: Understanding on Rules and Procedures Governing the Settlement of Disputes, Apr. 15, 1994, Annex 2, Legal Instruments-Results of the Uruguay Round vol. 1, 33 I.L.M. 1125 (1994): paras. 2.1, 11.1, 16.4, 17.1, 17.14, 21.1 [Basic Document 7.8].

6. Paul S. Kibel, *Reconstructing the Marketplace: the International Timber Trade and Forest Protection*, 5 N.Y.U. ENVTL. L.J. 735, 736, 737, 759, 780–781 (1996).

* * *

If we have instituted sustainable forestry in our own backyard—but have done so through exporting the ecological effects of our demands for forest products to nations with fewer environmental safeguards on timber harvesting—have we truly achieved sustainability?

* * *

The internationalization of the timber trade has been made possible in large part by the free trade regime established under the General Agreement on Tariffs and Trade (GATT). Under GATT, national governments may not condition the import of products on adherence to environmentally responsible production standards, such as the practice of sustainable forestry.

* * *

The General Agreement on Tariffs and Trade (GATT), and other regional trade agreements such as the North American Free Trade Agreement (NAFTA) and the European Union (EU), are based largely on the principle of comparative advantage. Because each nation is endowed with different natural resources, different levels of industrialization, and different labor forces, each nation is particularly suited to a different type of economic activity. If imports and exports are allowed to move freely across national borders, each nation will focus its economic activity in areas where it enjoys a comparative advantage. It will concentrate on economic sectors where it can produce a product or service at a lower marginal cost than competing nations.

* * *

As of 1995, over 113 nations have signed the 1973 Convention on International Trade in Endangered Species of Wild Fauna and Flora (CITES). CITES does not seek to directly protect endangered species or the development practices that destroy their habitats. Rather, it aims to reduce the economic incentive to kill endangered species by closing off the international market. The primary objective of CITES is to restrict or prevent international commercial trade in endangered species or products derived from such species.

CITES regulates by means of an international permit system. For plant and animal species threatened with extinction, international import or export is generally forbidden. For plant and animal species suffering decline, but not yet facing extinction, international permits must be secured before importation or exportation can occur. In theory, CITES permits the endangered species trade to be monitored and controlled, so that the trade does not cause species extinction or decline.

In recognizing the connection between conservation of natural resources and international trade, CITES is rightfully credited as a breakthrough agreement. By restricting or eliminating the international market for certain products, the treaty aims to reduce the poaching of many endangered species. As such, CITES represents an acknowledgment by the international commu-

924 PROBLEMS IN INT'L ENVIRONMENTAL LAW Pt. II

nity that, at least in certain instances, there are justifiable environmental exceptions to the principle of unregulated trade.

Unfortunately, the exception CITES establishes is very narrow. Most significantly, the CITES exception does not include products made possible by the destruction of endangered species' critical habitats. Because the destruction of natural habitat plays a much larger role in global species extinction than hunting, CITES has not improved the condition of most endangered species.

For example, many lumber and paper products are obtained from the unsustainable logging of native forests containing endangered species. CITES does not require nations to ban or restrict the import of such lumber or paper products, only the import of endangered plants or animals that happen to rely on the native forest for their existence.

CITES serves as an important example of how the regulation of international trade can positively impact environmental protection. In its present form, however, CITES is too narrow in scope to reform the timber trade and protect native forests.

7. Agreement on Technical Barriers to Trade, Apr. 15, 1994, Marrakesh Agreement Establishing World Trade Organization, Annex 1A, LEGAL INSTRUMENTS-RESULTS OF THE URUGUAY ROUND vol. 1, 33. I.L.M. 1125 (1994); arts. 1–5, 13, 14 [Basic Document 7.7].

8. Lakshman Guruswamy, *The Promise of the United Nations Convention on the Law of the Sea (UNCLOS): Justice in Trade and Environmental Disputes*, 25 ECOLOGY L. Q. 189, 196, 197–206 (1998).

* * *

Despite a rhetorical reference to environmental protection in the preamble of the WTO, GATT/WTO calls for the advance of free trade effectively unrestrained by environmental concerns.

* * *

B. Substantive Law

In order to overcome GATT prohibitions against trade restrictions, it is necessary to find justification under GATT 1947 Article XX [hereinafter Article XX], which provides:

> Subject to the requirement that such measures are not applied in a manner which could constitute a means of arbitrary or unjustifiable discrimination between countries where the same conditions prevail, or a disguised restriction on international trade, nothing in this Agreement shall be construed to prevent the adoption or enforcement by any contracting party of measures ... (b) necessary to protect human, animal or plant life or health [or that are] ... (g) relating to the conservation of exhaustible natural resources if such measures are made effective in conjunction with restrictions on domestic production or consumption. [1]

1. *See* General Agreement on Tariffs and Trade, Oct. 30, 1947, 61 Stat. A–3, 55 U.N.T.S. 187 [annexed to the Final Act adopted at the Conclusion of the Second Ses-

The extensive jurisprudence dealing with the nature and ambit of these exceptions will not be explored in this discussion. Instead, this Article takes a functional look at the application of these exceptions in three recent cases that offer a baseline for interpreting Article XX exceptions. According to these decisions, the very narrow basis on which environmental action can be justified does not provide a satisfactory basis for justifying, much less vindicating, environmental protection.

GATT Dispute Settlement Panel Report on United States Restrictions on Imports of Tuna,[2] [hereinafter Tuna I] was a case in which the United States Marine Mammal Protection Act (MMPA) required the relevant authorities to ban the importation of yellow tuna that had been caught with dolphin-killing nets. After years of fruitless negotiation between the U.S. and Mexico to establish rules for dolphin mortality, the U.S. prohibited the importation of yellow tuna caught with dolphin-killing rather than dolphin-friendly nets. The GATT Panel held that the U.S. ban violated GATT and did not fall within the exceptions in Article XX (b), (d) or (g).

Three years after Tuna I, in United States–Restrictions on Imports of Tuna (Tuna II),[3] the European Economic Community challenged the secondary embargo provisions of the MMPA that required any intermediary nation exporting yellowfin tuna to the United States to provide the relevant authorities with proof that such yellowfin tuna had not been caught with dolphin-killing nets. Once again the GATT panel held against the United States. According to the Panel such action was not "necessary" under Article XX(b), and was not "primarily aimed at" the conservation of natural resources under Article XX(g).

The Report of the Appellate Body in United States–Standards for Reformulated and Conventional Gasoline (Venezuela Gasoline Appeal)[4] was an appeal by the U.S. from a WTO Dispute Settlement Panel requested by Venezuela and Brazil to review pollution standards imposed on gasoline imports by the United States Environmental Protection Agency (EPA) under the Clean Air Act (CAA). The EPA calculated these standards from 1990 baselines, and the dispute essentially revolved around whether domestic refiners were given an unfair and preferential advantage over foreign refiners in the formulation and setting of such standards. The Appellate Body ruled that the manner in which the United States determined the 1990 baselines, and the consequent pollution standards for gasoline under the CAA, could not be justified under Article XX(b), (d) or (g).

In these three cases, the United States took action to protect the environment but did not specifically argue that it was obliged to do so by treaty. In light of the apparently "unilateral" nature of the U.S. action, a preliminary question is whether GATT/WTO permits environmental action

---

sion of the preparatory Committee of the United Nations Conference on Trade and Employment, as subsequently rectified, amended or modified][hereinafter GATT 1947][**Basic Document 7.1**].

2. *See* GATT Dispute Settlement Panel Report on United States Restrictions on Imports of Tuna, Aug. 16, 1991, 30 I.L.M. 1594 (1991)[hereinafter Tuna I] [**Basic Document 8.7**].

3. United States Restrictions on Imports of Tuna, June 16, 1994, *available in* 1994 WL 907620, para. 3.4 [hereinafter Tuna II]. [**Basic Document 8.8**].

4. 35 I.L.M. 603 (May 20, 1996), [**Basic Document 8.9**].

that has been authorized and mandated, but is not obligatory, by a multilateral treaty that did not include all GATT contractual parties.

In fact, Tuna II addressed that question. While not claiming that its actions were obligated by CITES, the U.S. did offer treaty justification for its actions by arguing generally that they "were consistent with and directly furthered the objectives"[5] of CITES and other environmental treaties. More specifically, the U.S. argued that the actions were authorized and empowered by CITES. According to the U.S.:

> All species of dolphins involved in the fishery of the eastern tropical Pacific were listed in CITES Appendix II. Moreover, while the United States was not obliged under CITES to adopt the measures at issue, CITES specifically provided for these measures in providing for "stricter domestic measures" in order to further the objectives of that agreement. The Unites States' measures were stricter domestic measures, as explicitly contemplated under CITES, taken to protect species of dolphins that CITES protects. These measures were in addition to the restrictions on trade in specimens of the dolphins themselves that are required under CITES . . .[6]

The U.S. relied upon CITES and other international environmental treaties to contend that these treaties should, according to international law, be taken into account as general or special rules for interpreting Article XX of GATT. The U.S. also argued that the actions taken by the parties to these multilateral environmental treaties constituted "subsequent practice" under general international law and under Article 31(3)(b) of the Vienna Convention on Treaties. The Panel made short shrift of these arguments. It asserted that the CITES and the other environmental treaties were not subsequent agreements, regarding the interpretation or application of Article XX, which had been signed by all the parties to the GATT. The Panel bluntly declared that CITES and the other treaties "did not apply to the interpretation of the General Agreement or the application of its provisions."[7]

As this Article will demonstrate, by so holding the Panel was acting in conformity with GATT law and jurisprudence. The recognition that environmental treaties affect the interpretation or application of GATT in any way would require judicial lawmaking that the GATT/WTO panels are forbidden from undertaking. This particular aspect of the decision in Tuna II was just one of the ways in which GATT, and the decisions of GATT/WTO tribunals, have obstructed the implementation of environmental treaties. Five of them merit mention.

First, the word "necessary" (to protect human, animal or plant life and health) in Article XX(b) has been restrictively interpreted to mean that a government may not employ a necessary measure if it could use an alternative and less trade-offensive measure. Even where a measure is required to protect human, animal or plant life or health, it may well be held to be unnecessary in the view of the GATT/WTO tribunal. Import and export restrictions under CITES could well be struck down on the basis that they are not the least trade-restrictive measures available to the country concerned.

---

5. *Supra* note 3, paras 3 & 4.   **7.** *Id*. para. 5.19.

6. *Id*.

Second, Tuna II interpreted "relating to" (the conservation of exhaustible natural resources) in Article XX(g) to allow extra-territorial conservation efforts which had been prohibited by Tuna I. However, the Appellate Body in Venezuela Gasoline Appeal reconfirmed that the extraterritorial rule asserted in Tuna II should be "primarily aimed" at the conservation of exhaustible natural resources, as determined by GATT/WTO. This means that a GATT/WTO tribunal can impune any action taken under the Basel Convention or Montreal Protocol on the basis that the action is, in the tribunal's view, not primarily aimed at conservation even if the concerned states assert a contrary view.

Third, GATT/WTO tribunals have assumed a disturbing interventionist character. Oblivious of their appellate status, they seem eager to override the judgment of nation states with which they disagree and make their own decisions on the facts. They seem unaware of judicial restraint, of the need for deference to the decisions of national fact finding bodies, or of the standards of review that restrain an appellate body from interfering in an executive action unless it is arbitrary, capricious or an abuse of discretion.

Fourth, Tuna I reiterated the rule that Article XX could only be directed at products and not at process or production methods. It concluded that measures aimed at reducing dolphin mortality were a production method and were not covered by Article XX(g). According to this interpretation, the Montreal Protocol would clearly be contrary to GATT.

Finally, the Appellate Body in the Venezuela Gasoline Appeal created another formidable hurdle against states seeking to claim the environmental exemptions under Article XX. In summary, the Appellate Body found that the burden placed on states that sought to come within Article XX was not confined to satisfying the narrow health, environment, and natural resource exemptions found within paragraphs (a) to (j). States must also prove that the measures taken do not violate the "chapeau" (introductory or preambular provisions) of Article XX, which prohibit "arbitrary" or "unjustified" discrimination or a "disguised restriction" of free trade. In holding that the United States had violated the chapeau, the Appellate Body demonstrated no hesitation to overrule decisions and rules made by the United States Environmental Protection Agency—the administrative agency that makes decisions affecting national environmental policy. In doing so, the Appellate Body showed scant regard for the ordinary and well recognized principles of deference accorded primary decisionmakers.

The law applied by GATT/WTO is confined to that found in its own treaties and does not recognize any broader corpus of general international law, let alone IEL. Because there is no distinction made in the language of Article XX between treaty and non-treaty justification, it is a mistake to argue that unilateral decisions are more difficult to justify than those based on multilateral treaties. Since environmental protection has never been a GATT/WTO objective, covered agreements do not deal with environmental protection apart from the exceptions found in Article XX. A plethora of provisions make it abundantly clear that the GATT/WTO Panels and Appellate Bodies must restrict themselves to the Understanding and the Covered Agreements, which should be strictly construed not to add to or diminish the rights and obligations provided by the treaties.

DSU Article 3(2) is an interesting provision that has all the hallmarks of an unresolved disagreement. It reiterates that the dispute settlement system should first, preserve the rights and obligations of Members under the Covered Agreements, and, second, clarify the existing provisions of those agreements in accordance with customary rules of interpretation of public international law. Having stated this, it proceeds immediately to attenuate future interpretation by prohibiting any tribunal from adding to or diminishing rights and obligations provided in the Covered Agreements. This flies in the face of judicial lawmaking and assumes a set of precise, tailor made, predetermined and inflexible rights and duties that can be mechanically dispensed without any judicial intervention.

Such an approach is untenable for a number of reasons. First, the Understanding and the Covered Agreements were made by humans not gods and could not anticipate every fact, contingency, and circumstance that could give rise to controversies about rights and duties. Second, the Understanding and Covered Agreements cannot anticipate the law that should be applied in every situation. Each set of rights and duties ought to be applied to the particular, variegated fact situation; the scope of each right and duty could not possibly be ordained in advance. The need for this flexibility is the reason why international instruments are couched in various degrees of generality and indeterminacy. Third, while duties and rights are correlative concepts, they are "institutions" and tools of judicial reasoning for deriving and assigning benefits and burdens. It has been persuasively argued that institutional concepts consist of three sets of rules: 1) a set of constitutive rules specifying situations to which they might be applied; 2) a set of rules specifying the legal consequences; and 3) terminative rules specifying outcomes. Each step involves judicial analysis, reasoning, discretion, and power within a continuing time frame to ascertain the nature, scope, and applicability of indeterminate rights and duties.

The Understanding attenuates judicial discretion to adapt the law to new situations. It defies reality by assuming that an initial expression of law in a treaty freezes both time and content. In fact, any expression of law is intended to be applied to future events over an indefinite period of time during which its initial meaning is subject to change.

The customary international rules of interpretation, as restated in the Vienna Convention on the Law of Treaties (Vienna Convention), assume there can be no expression of rights and obligations that can be applied automatically with dogmatic immutability. Instead, the Vienna Convention calls for any treaty to be interpreted according to its ordinary meaning in "[c]ontext and in the light of its object and purpose." The Vienna Convention also states that any applicable rules of international law should be taken into account.

The Understanding has apparently rejected the Vienna Convention criteria by asserting that the rights and obligations set out in the covered agreements are sufficient for all purposes and earlier references to rules of interpretation in the Understanding must be understood as aspirational and decorative rather than obligatory. The emerging profile of an inward looking, even blinkered, judicial system that shuts out the broader corpus of international law becomes evident when compared to the jurisprudence of the ICJ. ICJ decisions apply international conventions, international custom, the general principles of law recognized by civilized nations, judicial decisions, and the teachings of "the most highly qualified publicists."[8] The law applied by GATT/WTO is confined to its own agreements.

* * *

10.   Christine M. Cuccia, *Protecting Animals in the Name of Biodiversity: Effects of the Uruguay Round of Measures Regulating Methods of Harvesting*, 13 B. U. INT'L L. J. 481, 500–502 (1995).

* * *

VI.   Enlarging the Context of Article XX: Can the TBT Agreement Save the Dolphins?

The GATT and the TBT Agreement share some similar provisions. For example, both agreements prohibit discrimination between like products. Trade measures must be applied equally to domestic and imported products to ensure that imported goods receive treatment "no less favourable" than similar domestic goods. There are also some important distinctions. As discussed above, past GATT panels limited the GATT's application by concluding that Article III does not encompass process methods, and that Article XX does not apply extraterritorially. By contrast, the TBT Agreement applies to both products and "related processes or production methods." Moreover, while Article XX recognizes a country's right to adopt measures "necessary to protect human, animal or plant life or health," or those measures "relating to the conservation of exhaustible resources which are made effective in conjunction with restrictions on domestic production or consumption," the TBT extended the language of Article XX to specifically include the environment. Thus, because the TBT Agreement also applies to environmental measures related to product standards, the Agreement may in effect enlarge the scope of Article XX to reach some forms of extraterritorial production processes. If this is the case, countries may be able to regulate trade of imported animal products on the basis of method of production.

* * *

With the changes made in the TBT, however, similar measures may be justified. In order for a government to satisfy the requirements of the TBT Agreement, it must make sure that all imported products are treated the same as similar domestic products. Thus, a ban that puts heavier burdens on producers in a particular region, such as the U.S. ban on tuna harvested in the Eastern Tropic Pacific, would not be appropriate. The language of the treaty seems to suggest that a blanket prohibition of such behavior may be acceptable if other requirements are met. Therefore, in order to adopt a ban on imported tuna caught in purse seines, a country would have to prohibit domestic producers as well as all foreign producers from using purse seines.

Second, the government must have a legitimate objective supported by a narrowly tailored measure which is not more trade-restrictive than necessary to achieve the objective. Legitimate measures include protecting animal life or

---

8. *See* Statute of the International Court of   **[Basic Document 1.4]**
Justice, June 26, 1945, 59 Stat. 1031, art. 38.

health. Protecting the environment is also a legitimate objective. Conserving wildlife, which is necessary to maintaining biodiversity, falls under both of these categories. Therefore, under this interpretation, the United States prohibition on tuna captured in purse seine nets, has a legitimate interest because its objective is to conserve dolphins. The United States recognized that if capturing tuna incidentally killed a large number of dolphins, the dolphin population could not sustain itself.

Under the TBT Agreement, a protection measure must not be more trade-restrictive than necessary to achieve its stated objective. Although the United States argued that an extraordinary conservation measure was "necessary" to conserve dolphins, the "United States had not demonstrated to the Panel—as required of the party invoking an Article XX exception—that it had exhausted all options reasonably available to it to pursue its dolphin protection objectives through measures consistent with the General Agreement, in particular through the negotiation of international cooperative arrangements...."[9]

The TBT shifts the burden of proving a measure's necessity to the complaining party. In order to show that another government's trade measures violate this provision, a complaining government must show that another measure is reasonably available, that the alternative fulfills the same objective, and that the alternative is significantly less trade-restrictive.

* * *

11. Mark Edward Foster, *Trade and Environment: Making Room for Environmental Trade Measures Within the GATT*, 71 S. CAL. L. REV. 393, 397–398, 400–407, 410–413 (1998).

* * *

II. ENVIRONMENTAL TRADE MEASURES

The use of trade measures to pursue environmental objectives has been part of the international landscape for almost 100 years. As early as 1906, an international conference adopted a treaty to stop the production and importation of matches made with white phosphorous. This treaty proved effective in allowing manufacturers to switch to alternative methods of production without the fear of being undercut by competitors. This use of a trade measure as a policy-changing device, and many like it since, illustrate the important role that trade measures have played in the historical interaction between states. Trade sanctions, for example, have repeatedly been used by the international community to force a state to alter some form of its domestic or international policies. Given the historical use of trade measures as legitimate international tools, there is some hope that environmental trade measures ("ETMs") can also be used "legally" and effectively to protect the environment.

An ETM is a unique style of trade-oriented device. An ETM "is a restriction on international trade with the announced purpose of promoting

9. United States Restrictions on Imports of Tuna, GATT Doc. D/S21/R (Sept. 3, 1991)(report of the Panel), *reprinted in* General Agreement on Tariffs and Trade, Basic Instruments and Selected Documents 155, para. 5.28 (Supp. XXXIX 1993).

an environmental objective"[10] and has "an actual or potential impact on international trade."[11] Whether or not there is any room within the GATT for ETMs remains unsettled, and the conclusion of the Uruguay Round has only raised more questions as to their acceptability. The November 1996 Report of the WTO Committee on Trade and Environment stated:

> there is already scope under the WTO provisions to use trade measures for environmental purposes. These provisions aim to ensure that WTO Members may adopt and enforce measures in pursuit of important public policy objectives for the protection of their environmental resources, while safeguarding Members' WTO rights against arbitrary or unjustifiable discrimination and disguised restrictions on trade. [12]

What the WTO Report gave with one hand, however, it took away with the other. The next paragraph stated:

> Most of the delegations which intervened in the debate ... stated that they consider the provisions of GATT Article XX to not permit a Member to impose unilateral trade restrictions that are otherwise inconsistent with its WTO obligations for the purpose of protecting environmental resources that lie outside its jurisdiction. For them, a renewed commitment needs to be taken by WTO Members to avoid using trade measures unilaterally for that purpose....[13]

In light of these statements, and because "the practice and rhetoric of the GATT/WTO system are predicated on the general undesirability of using trade restrictions not permitted under the existing GATT rules to pursue environmental objectives,"[14] it is useful both to examine the characteristics of ETMs (both multilateral and unilateral) and to identify what it is about their nature that creates so many headaches for the international trading community.

* * *

2. Restricting Trade With an External Reach

The utility of a trade measure as an environmental device is a function of both its form and its external reach. Interrelated attributes, form and external reach consistently prove to be the most critical aspects of environmental trade measures.

a. Restrictiveness: The degree to which an environmental trade measure restricts the free flow of goods between states is determined by its form. Its form ultimately reflects the nature of the environmental problem being

---

10. Steve Charnovitz, *A Taxonomy of Environmental Trade Measures*, 6 GEO. INT'L ENVTL. L. REV. 1, 3 (1993) [hereinafter Charnovitz, Taxonomy].

11. *Id.* at 5.

12. Report of the WTO Committee on Trade and Environment, WT/CTE/1, para. 6 (Nov. 8, 1996)[hereinafter 1996 CTE Report].

13. *Id.* para. 7. The Committee on Trade and Environment will undoubtedly play an important role in any integration of trade and environment in the GATT. The recent report of the CTE to the Singapore Conference demonstrates a heightened recognition of the need for further integration; however, it failed to establish any concrete rules or recommendations. *See generally id.*; Singapore Ministerial Declaration, Dec. 13, 1996, 36 I.L.M. 218 (1997).

14. BENEDICT KINGSBURY, ENVIRONMENT AND TRADE: THE GATT/WTO REGIME IN THE INTERNATIONAL LEGAL SYSTEM, IN ENVIRONMENTAL REGULATION AND ECONOMIC GROWTH 189, 199 (A.E. Boyle, ed., 1994).

addressed. Essentially, an ETM takes a specific form because a regulating state has determined that a certain type of trade restriction is critical to realizing its environmental goals.[15]

An ETM's form is most often derived from the level of priority a given state assigns to an environmental interest. An environmental interest that a state regards as only a minimal priority, or that necessitates only minimal safeguards to achieve the desired goal, requires only a minimal ETM—for example an eco-labeling requirement. Eco-labeling requirements, when not imposed for protectionist goals, impose a minimal restriction on trade. On the other hand, for an environmental interest in which a state has expressly stated a "vital" interest, a more severe form of an ETM may be enacted. The most severe ETM that a state may choose to impose is a trade sanction. For example, a state may impose an embargo on all goods from another state so long as that second state continues to destroy its rainforests. Thus, the restrictive form of an ETM will theoretically mirror the persuasion necessary to achieve its announced objective.

Beyond restrictiveness, the ease with which a regulating state can administer a given ETM also affects an ETM's form. For example, in Reformulated gasoline, the United States attempted to justify the use of different gasoline standards between domestic and foreign refiners based in part on the administrative challenges associated with testing foreign gasoline. Its rationale: the data available on foreign refiners was less reliable or less readily available, thus mandating the EPA's use of bifurcated baselines. Consequently, a state may choose one form of trade measure over another if administrative or logistic concerns facilitate the enactment and enforcement of the measure.

Although an ETM's restrictive qualities and a state's ability to enforce an ETM ultimately should determine its form, there are other considerations that may in practice affect its form as well. One such consideration of greatest concern, is hidden protectionism. According to Ved Nanda, "[t]he controversy surrounding the use of [ETMs] centers on the possibility of a state imposing an ETM as a protectionist measure."[16] Like the bifurcated standard of Reformulated Gasoline, one could assert, much as Venezuela and Brazil did, that the EPA's disparate standards embodied an attempt to protect domestic refineries. Because protectionist or discriminatory considerations may in fact be hidden under the guise of environmental protection, the form of an ETM, in particular, its suitability for environmental protection, must be closely examined in order to avoid unjustifiable trade measures. However, the potential for abuse should not nullify the use of ETMs entirely. Restrictions on trade, if based on legitimate environmental concerns, are capable of fostering further environmental protection.

b.   External reach: The "external reach" of an ETM refers to the extent to which the trade measure is designed to affect behavior beyond a home state's borders. While it is true that all trade measures possess a primary external

---

15.   *See* e.g., Tuna I, **[Basic Document 8.7]** (embargo on Tuna); Tuna II, **[Basic Document 8.8]** (same); WTO panel Dispute Report on U.S. Standards for Reformulated Gasoline, **[Basic Document 8.11]**.

16.   Ved P. Nanda, International Environmental Law & Policy 44 (1995).

effect in that they force importers to alter the number of quality goods imported, the secondary external effect of an ETM dictates its external reach.

* * *

Similar to form, the external reach of an ETM depends on the priority assigned to an environmental concern by the regulating state. From the example above, it is clear that if the United States desired to use trade as a tool to stop deforestation in Brazil it would be forced to enact a measure with a great external reach. Without this external reach the ETM would fail to serve its purpose: the cessation of Brazilian clear-cutting. "The rationale for using an ETM for such [a] purpose ... [is that] the country employing the trade measure believes that it has a significant interest in foreign life or health, or in a foreign country's use of 'its' resources." [17]

ETMs consistently possess an external reach because some states conclude that extraterritorial environmental concerns are worthy of trade restraints. The problem, however, is that the environmental resources these states are striving to protect either exist in part or in whole outside the regulating state's borders. Thus, some ETMs, out of necessity, possess extraterritorial features in the form of external reach. In this sense, environmental trade measures are fairly site specific in that ETMs, in order to be truly related to a clear environmental concern, must be directed exclusively at remedying a specific environmental problem—whether inside or outside the state. The form which an ETM takes—a standard, a tariff, a restriction, or a sanction—will at least in part reflect the location of the focus.

i.   The need for external reach: The trade and environment conundrum is frustrated by the reality that the effective pursuit of environmental goals frequently mandates extraterritorial effects. As discussed briefly above, the need for environmental measures to have extraterritorial effects is due for the most part to the nature of environmental concerns. The sources of environmental concern, specifically pollutants and wildlife, are not constrained by political boundaries, and thus, effective environmental measures designed to remedy such concerns necessarily must not be so constrained either. For example, the protection of marine mammals can only be effectively realized through measures that are directed at the waters of all states where marine mammals are located as well as at the high seas. The following section reviews the impact that the variant location of environmental resources and of potential harms has on effective environmental regulation.

The locations of environmental harms are commonly separated into five possible categories: (1) domestic, (2) transboundary, (3) global, (4) foreign resulting in a loss of global "positive externalities," and (5) foreign.[18] While trade measures designed to remedy environmental harms that exist within a state's territory (category (1) above) are usually considered legitimate, the remaining four categories require some degree of external reach to remedy the environmental harm in question. Moreover, the failure of an environmental measure to apply extraterritorially will often render environmental protection

---

17. Charnovitz, Taxonomy, *supra* note 10 at 9.

18. *See* DANIEL C, ESTY, GREENING THE GATT: TRADE, ENVIRONMENT, AND THE FUTURE 121–26 (1994).

ineffective. The fact that some environmental harms pose a serious enough threat to states to warrant the enactment of environmental legislation creates a host of issues worthy of discussion on the extraterritorial application of environmental measures.

ii.   Extraterritoriality and extrajurisdictionality: Extraterritoriality is an essential aspect of ETMs. Whether or not such an "external reach" is justified under the eyes of international law turns on the jurisdictional basis of the measure. A measure that affects behavior outside a state's borders may sometimes be justified when the enacting state has jurisdiction to prescribe such regulations. Although international law does not control international trade, the question of jurisdiction, and of a state's ability to prescribe extraterritorial laws, does impact the legitimacy of ETMs under the GATT/WTO.

International law has always recognized that regulations taken within one state can have clear effects outside of its borders. From the regulation of nationals abroad to limits on foreign subsidiaries, extraterritorial effects have given rise to unique questions regarding the appropriate scope and limits of such regulations. Although certain extraterritorial effects of regulations are permitted under international law, there is serious doubt as to where such effects begin to inhibit the sovereignty of another state.

International law has attempted to address the issue of extraterritoriality by creating a standard of reasonableness—weighing the effects and justifications of a regulating state's actions against the foreign interests being compromised. Obviously such an inquiry does not lend itself to clear line drawing, but it does illuminate the basic considerations that the international community reviews in determining the validity of regulations with extraterritorial effects.

International law has consistently been forced to deal with extraterritorial regulations. It has done so by assessing the reasonableness of allowing the regulating state to exercise jurisdictional control. For example, it is well established in international law that a state's emission of transboundary pollution is not reasonable when such conduct is weighed against another state's right to be free from such an encroachment. But an inquiry into whether another state's interference is justified, however, almost by definition requires a value assessment between countries. Unfortunately, an objective balancing of subjective interests is nearly impossible without imposing some other value assessment on the analysis. For this reason, international law has limited its analysis to asking whether an extraterritorial regulation is "reasonable" in light of both the interest being advanced and the interest being infringed upon.

The ability of one nation to control or influence the affairs of parties outside its borders, and the limit of this ability, remains a resilient problem in international affairs due in part to the power disparities that exist between nations as well as to the inherently expansive/proscriptive nature of certain states. This Note does not attempt to resolve the issue of extraterritoriality and extrajurisdictionality under international law, but it does mean to suggest that certain trade regulations with extraterritorial effects may be legitimately employed to achieve a given objective. The GATT framework itself suggests that regulations with extraterritorial effects are acceptable, or at least possible, because trade measures—extraterritorial by definition—are permitted in specific situations.

iii.   Justifications: The ability of a state to prescribe laws that have an extraterritorial impact has been, and remains, context dependent. The traditional demarcation used by the international community when determining whether or not a state has jurisdiction over a matter turns on the location of the activity the regulation is attempting to control. Customary international law provides that jurisdiction to prescribe a regulation exists if the subject regulation is (1) aimed at an activity that occurs within the state's territory, (2) aimed at the conduct of its nationals, or (3) aimed at an activity that has a "substantial effect" on the regulating state.[19] It is this third category—granting jurisdiction to prescribe laws over activities that have "substantial effects" on the home country—that remains the most nebulous. Unlike the determination of a national border or the citizenship of a person or corporation, demonstrating that some activity results in "substantial effects" on the regulating country can be much more tenuous.

The problem of course is determining how substantial the effects must be to justify extraterritorial legislation. Regulations that are merely an extension of rightful jurisdiction are usually acceptable under international law because of the "substantial effects" nexus. They most often prevent nationals from committing espionage, or corporations from paying bribes to foreign public officials, and are usually considered within the purview of a nation-state's jurisdiction. For example, the Foreign Corrupt Practices Act ("FCPA"), enacted in 1977, is designed to regulate U.S. nationals and U.S. corporate entities in their business conduct abroad. Because its extraterritorial effects are limited in scope to U.S. entities, such measures are justified due to their close relationship with the regulating country.

Regulations that are justified because they are attempting to render effective international norms in which the regulating state has a "vital interest" give rise to a unique set of additional problems. Under such measures, the proximity of the activity being regulated relative to the regulating country dictates whether such a measure can be justified on the basis of jurisdiction. For example, the United States, for a variety of reasons, maintains an embargo against Cuba. Although there is international disagreement on whether an embargo is the appropriate means through which to demonstrate disapproval of another state, the unilateral measures against Cuba can at least in theory be justified because of Cuba's proximity to the United States and the impact that its current government has had on U.S. nationals—namely the expropriation of the property of Cuban–Americans when the Castro regime came to power in 1958. Such regulations represent a unilateral effort to affect change abroad, and their acceptability is dependent upon the nexus between the activity being regulated and the regulating country.

The lesson to be drawn from international law and extraterritoriality is that extraterritorial measures are usually discouraged unless there is a sufficient nexus between the measure's focus and the regulating state. This nexus can be created in one of two ways: (1) the measure's focus has "substantial effects" upon the state, or (2) the measure's focus is of "vital

---

19.   *See* RESTATEMENT (THIRD) OF FOREIGN RE-
LATIONS LAW § 402 (1987).

importance" to the domestic policies of the state. This is not to say that jurisdiction exists every time one of these two factors is present, but it is clear that the presence of these factors can in certain contexts create a basis for jurisdiction.

B. The Source of ETMs: Environmental Valuations, Conflicts, and Consensus

1. The Sources of Conflict

The tension that exists between the contending goals of environmental protection and trade liberalization stems from three sources: (1) different valuations of environmental priorities between states, (2) the extraterritorial nature of global environmental problems and the extraterritorial nature of measures designed to remedy them, and (3) the perceived incompatibility of free-trade goals and trade measures directed at the environment.

In order to assess accurately why ETMs have not found a home within the GATT/WTO regime, it is essential to recognize these three factor as "unique" to environmental protection. It is precisely because environmental standards and goals transcend the traditional limits of international activity that they are perceived as threats to the modern free-trade regime. Any reforms designed to accommodate environmental concerns in the WTO must also accommodate the "unique" problems associated with environmental protection.

* * *

2. Multilateral Versus Unilateral Environmental Trade Measures

Increasingly, the legal source of an ETM is crucial to an assessment of its legality under the GATT. Environmental trade measures are commonly divided into two categories—multilateral environmental trade measures and unilateral environmental trade measures. Although the source of an ETM has little to do with whether or not it violates another state's rights under the GATT, this distinction has been made in part because of the perception that "multilateral" ETMs (usually based on multilateral agreements) are somehow more legitimate than their unilateral counterparts. While it is rarely crystal clear why this distinction per se should control a trade measure's acceptability under the GATT, the GATT and WTO favor the use of multilateral ETMs over their unilateral implementation.

Modern multilateral environmental agreements are the best examples of consensus in the international framework and they seemingly legitimize a given objective. Principle 12 of the Rio Declaration states that nations:

> should cooperate to promote a supportive and open international economic system that would lead to economic growth and sustainable development in all countries, to better address the problems of environmental degradation.... Unilateral actions to deal with environmental challenges outside the jurisdiction of the importing country should be avoided. Environmental measures addressing transboundary or global environmental problems should ... be based on an international consensus.[20]

20. Rio Declaration on Environment and Development, June 14, 1992, 31 I.L.M. 874,

International consensus supporting a particular environmental priority provides a strong foundation for action. According to a report by the Center for International Environmental Law ("CIEL"), more than 800 bilateral and multilateral agreements contain provisions dealing with one or more aspects of the environment. In fact many of these principles are evolving into customary international law.

a.   Multilateral environmental trade measures: At this point it is important to differentiate between unilateral and multilateral environmental trade measures. There is strong evidence that the use of ETMs pursuant to a multilateral environmental agreement will survive GATT scrutiny. Multilateral ETMs are those taken pursuant to some international consensus—the most common sources of such consensus being multilateral environmental agreements. MEAs "based on international consensus are viewed by the international community as the best way of coordinating policy action to tackle global and transboundary environmental problems cooperatively."[21] Some states feel that "[w]hen account is taken of the limited numbers of MEAs that contain trade provisions, and the fact that no trade dispute has arisen over the use of those measures to date, ... there is no evidence of a real conflict between the WTO and MEAs."[22]

Several multilateral environmental agreements authorize the use of trade measures to pursue an agreed upon environmental objective. The GATT Secretariat has identified nineteen international environmental agreements that contain trade provisions. The most notable of these MEAs include: the Convention on International Trade in Endangered Species of Wild Fauna and Flora ("CITES"), the Montreal Protocol on Substances That Deplete the Ozone Layer, and the Basel Convention on the Control of Transboundary Movement of Hazardous Wastes and Their Disposal.

Whether or not the "authorization" of the use of trade measures prescribed by these agreements is legal under the GATT is unclear. Some commentators have argued that CITES "authorizes" parties to take "stricter domestic measures regarding the conditions for trade" for species listed under CITES and "domestic measures restricting or prohibiting trade" for species not listed under CITES.[23] Steve Charnovitz, Director of the Global Environment and Trade Study at Yale University, argues alternatively that "what CITES actually says is that '[t]he provisions of the present Convention shall in no way affect the right of Parties to adopt: stricter domestic measures.' "[24] Although MEAs seem to permit (and even promote) the use of trade measures, the reality is that multilateral ETMs are legitimized by the fact that there is some consensus associated with their use. The GATT legality of MEAs remains uncertain, but there is little question that they are the preferred device through which to pursue environmental goals. When consen-

---

878 (1992)[hereinafter Rio Declaration]. [Basic Document 1.29]

21. Report of the WTO Committee on Trade and Environment, WT/CTE/1, para. 8, (Nov. 8, 1996)[hereinafter CTE Report].

22. *Id.* para. 10. Some commentators suggest adding to article XX an exception which would explicitly include trade measures taken pursuant to MEAs.

23. Charnovitz, Taxonomy, *supra* note 10 at 8 (quoting CITES, 27 U.S.T. at 1108, 993 U.N.T.S. at 253). *See also* Montreal Protocol, 26 I.L.M. 1541 [**Basic Document 3.18**].

24. Charnovitz, Taxonomy, *supra* note 10 at 8 (quoting CITES, 27 U.S.T. at 1108, 993 U.N.T.S. at 253).

sus does not exist, however, states lack the ability to pursue an environmental objective, even if that objective is considered a "vital" national interest.

It is important to point out, however, that trade measures taken pursuant to MEAs are not free from controversy. While the signing of an MEA frequently is considered to constitute a waiver of the signatories' GATT obligations/rights with respect to a particular MEA, it is not clear whether a state can impose an ETM, even if it is authorized by a MEA, against non-signatories. ETMs taken against a state that is not a signatory of a particular MEA will likely be treated much like unilateral ETMs under the GATT because, like unilateral ETMs, they constitute an unsolicited infringement upon another state's trade rights. The only distinction between the two as far as the GATT is concerned remains the legal source of the measure. An in-depth review of the GATT legality of trade restrictions taken pursuant to MEAs is not appropriate here and can be found elsewhere, but it is important to note the distinction between multilateral and unilateral ETMs. In this sense, certain MEA-authorized ETMs may very well be subjected to the same scrutiny as unilateral ETMs.

12. General Agreement on Tariffs and Trade: Dispute Settlement Panel Report on United States Restrictions on Imports of Tuna, submitted to the Parties, Aug. 16, 1991, *reprinted in* 30 I.L.M. 1594 (1991) [Tuna I] [Basic Document 8.7].

13. General Agreement on Tariffs and Trade (GATT) Secretariat, Report of the Panel, United States–Restriction on Imports of Tuna, June 16, 1994, *reprinted in* 33 I.L.M. 839 [Tuna II] [Basic Document 8.8].

14. Mike Meier, *GATT, WTO and the Environment: To What Extent Do GATT/WTO Rules Permit Member Nations To Protect the Environment When Doing So Adversely Affects Trade*, 8 Colo. J. Int'l Envtl. L. & Pol'y 241, 244, 277–280 (1997).

I. INTRODUCTION

The Uruguay Round of the General Agreement on Tariffs and Trade (GATT)[25] has expanded international trade rules and established new dispute settlement procedures,[26] turning the GATT into the World Trade Organization (WTO). Despite its success in expanding international trade, the GATT has been criticized for its failure to protect the environment. In the context of international trade, the desire to liberalize and expand trade and the desire to protect health and the environment sometimes conflict. Among the examples are US attempts to protect dolphins from being caught in tuna fishing nets, US attempts to increase the fuel efficiency of automobiles, and US clean air requirements regarding gasoline. Each of these attempts to protect the

25. Final Act Embodying the Results of the Uruguay Round of Multilateral Trade Negotiations, Apr. 15, 1994, Legal Instruments-Results of the Uruguay Round vol. 1 (1994), 33 I.L.M. 1125 [hereinafter Final Act] [Basic Document 7.1].

26. *See* Understanding on Rules and Procedures Governing the Settlement of Disputes,

Apr. 15, 1994, Agreement Establishing the World Trade Organization, Annex 2, Legal Instruments-Results of the Uruguay Round, vol. 31 (1994), 33 I.L.M. 1226 [hereinafter Procedures Governing the Settlement of Disputes]. [Basic Document 7.8].

environment was challenged under the GATT/WTO framework on the grounds that it interfered with international trade. The basic analysis used in reviewing those disputes within the GATT/WTO framework is, first, whether the national measure is inconsistent with the GATT/WTO provisions and, second, whether the measure, if inconsistent with the GATT/WTO, can be otherwise justified.

* * *

II.   Article 20 Exceptions to GATT/WTO Trading Principles

Currently, there are four health and environment specific exceptions to the general principles of the GATT that GATT/WTO Dispute Settlement Panels (Panels) must consider when reviewing national measures: Article 20(b), Article 20(g), the Agreement on the Application of Sanitary and Phytosanitary Measures, and the Agreement on Technical Barriers to Trade.

* * *

IV.   THE AGREEMENT ON TECHNICAL BARRIERS TO TRADE

The Agreement on Technical Barriers to Trade[27] (TBT Agreement), another ancillary agreement within the GATT/WTO framework, is intended to prevent technical standards from being used for protectionist ends. The TBT Agreement covers processing and production methods related to characteristics of the product itself, such as automobile emission standards. The scope is broadly defined to include "product characteristics or their related processes and production methods."[28] The TBT Agreement recognizes that members have the right to establish protection at levels that they consider appropriate but requires that technical regulations not be "prepared, adopted or applied with a view to or with the effect of creating unnecessary obstacles to international trade."[29] The principles of national treatment and nondiscrimination must be respected; technical regulations and standards cannot be applied less favorably to imported products than to domestic products.

The TBT Agreement establishes a six-part test to review national environmental measures. A national technical measure that has been challenged within the GATT/WTO framework will be reviewed to see: (1) whether the national measure is within the definition of "technical regulation" (the TBT Agreement applies to all products, including industrial and agricultural products, except sanitary and phytosanitary matters, which fall under the SPS Agreement); (2) whether, with respect to the terms of the national measure, products imported from another member receive treatment no less favorable

---

27. Agreement on Technical Barriers to Trade, Apr. 15, 1994, Agreement Establishing World Trade Organization, Annex 1A, *reprinted in* Uruguay Round Trade Agreements, Text of Agreements, Implementing Bill, Statement of Administrative Action, and Required Supporting Statements, H.R. Doc No. 103–316, vol.1, 103d Cong., 2d Sess. 1427 (1994)[hereinafter TBT Agreement] **[Basic Document 7.7]**.

28. Annex 1 § 1 of the TBT Agreement defines a "technical regulation" as a "[d]ocu-

ment which lays down product characteristics or their related processes and production methods, including the applicable administrative provisions, with which compliance is mandatory. It may also include or deal exclusively with terminology, symbols, packaging, marking or labeling requirements as they may apply to a product, process or production method." TBT Agreement, *id.*, annex 1, § 1.

29. *Id.* art. 2.2.

that the treatment received by similar domestic products and by similar products imported from other countries; (3) whether the national measure has been prepared, adopted, or applied to create unnecessary obstacles to international trade (for this purpose, national measures shall be only as trade restrictive as necessary to fulfill a legitimate objective, taking into account the risks of nonfulfillment); (4) whether circumstances that originally necessitated the national measure have changed so that the measure is no longer necessary; (5) whether the national measure is based on international standards, unless special conditions, such as climatic or geographical factors, require otherwise; and (6) whether the importing member considered whether a similar technical regulation of the exporting member could be accepted as equivalent.[a]

The interpretation advice in the TBT Agreement states that the Agreement supersedes other GATT/WTO rules in case of conflict.[30] A national measure would be proper if it met the requirements of the TBT Agreement, even if it failed to qualify for an exception under Article 20. Strangely, however, the Panel in the Gasoline Case did not discuss the TBT Agreement. The Panel found it unnecessary to consider the TBT Agreement because the Gasoline Rule, in the Panel's view, did not qualify for an exception under Article 20. But because the TBT Agreement is arguably more generous than Article 20 in allowing exceptions to the GATT,[31] and because the TBT Agreement purports to supersede Article 20 in cases of conflict, one would have expected the Panel to at least consider whether the Gasoline Rule might have qualified for an exception under the Agreement, despite having not qualified for one under Article 20. By failing to consider the TBT Agreement, however, the Appellate Body implied either that the TBT Agreement does not supersede Article 20 in cases of conflict or that the Agreement has a scope as narrow or narrower than Article 20. Arguably, the Gasoline Case indicates that the TBT Agreement actually imposes additional requirements on top of the general GATT rules, the interpretative provision notwithstanding, and that it may defeat an Article 20 defense.

* * *

Second, the SPS Agreement does not accept "legitimate" purposes to the same extent that the TBT Agreement does. Under the SPS Agreement, for a member to have a national measure that results in a higher level of sanitary or phytosanitary protection, the member must essentially prove the necessity of the measure by way of a scientific "risk assessment." By comparison, the TBT Agreement accepts a national measure as being necessary to protect human health and the environment where the measure represents the "appropriate level" of protection, even though that level may be above the average level established by other members.

a. In support of his argument the author references the TBT Agreement, Annex 1 § 1, articles 1.3, 1.5, 2.1, 2.2, 2.3, 2.4, & 2.7.

30. *See* General Interpretive Note to Annex 1A, Apr. 15, 1994, Agreement Establishing World Trade Organization, Annex 1A, reprinted in Uruguay Round Trade Agreements, Texts of Agreements, Implementing Bill, Statement of Administrative Action, and required

Supporting Statements, H.R. Doc. No. 103–316, vol. 1, 103d Cong., 2d Sess. 1338 (1994)[hereinafter General Interpretive Note].

31. Article 2 of the TBT Agreement expressly accepts "legitimate" reasons for a national measure as justifying the measure, whereas Article 20 does not. See TBT Agreement, *supra* note 27.

At this point, one cannot say how the TBT Agreement will be applied in practice and how it will differ from the GATT Article 20. Although the TBT Agreement is supposed to prevail over the GATT in case of conflict, and although the TBT Agreement contains very specific requirements for the review of national measures, the Panel in the Gasoline Case did not reach the TBT issue because it was able to decide the issue based on Article 20. The Gasoline Case would have been an appropriate subject for the TBT Agreement, but the Panel avoided the issue. The United States, in its appeal, did not appeal the Panel's failure to consider the TBT Agreement, instead it focused its argument on Article 20. The Appellate Body gave the TBT Agreement only cursory mention, leaving the significance of the Agreement unclear.

* * *

15. World Trade Organization Appellate Body: Report of the Appellate Body in United States–Standards for Reformulated and Conventional Gasoline, May 20, 1996, *reprinted in* **35 I.L.M. 603 (1996)** [Basic Document 8.9].

16. World Trade Organization, Report of the Appellate Body in Unites States–Import Prohibition of Certain Shrimp and Shrimp Products, Oct. 12, 1998, *reprinted in* **1998 WL 720123 (1998)** [Basic Document 3.11].

17. Steve Charnovitz, *Green Roots, Bad Pruning: GATT Rules and Their Application to Environmental Trade Measures*, 7 TULANE ENVTL. **L. J. 299, 303, 304, 305, 310–315, 323–324, 326–328, 330, 332–338 (1994).**

* * *

I.   PRODUCT STANDARDS

Product standards are qualitative and quantitative benchmarks. They relate to factors such as purity (for example, in meat), safety in use (for example, in cocaine), or pollution emitted (such as catalytic converters). Such standards are applied to both domestic products and imported products.... It is important to recognize that product standards focus on consumption of the object itself. A product standard must be differentiated from another type of environmental standard, known as a process standard. Process standards ...focus on production rather than on consumption.... Product standards can be divided into two types: design and performance. Design standards relate to the physical characteristics of a product or how it is constructed.... On the other hand, performance standards relate to how well a product works or how it complies with specific operational tests.

* * *

A.   GATT Article III

The GATT applies a discipline to product standards known as "national treatment." Under GATT Article III:4, imported products must be accorded treatment no less favorable than that accorded to like domestic products of national origin in respect of all laws, regulations, and requirements affecting their internal sale, offering for sale, purchase, transportation, distribution, or use.

* * *

C. GATT Article XX

Recognizing that the Article III discipline can interfere with health measures, the GATT provides for General Exceptions in Article XX. Article XX provides as follows:

Subject to the requirement that such measures are not applied in a manner which would constitute a means of arbitrary or unjustifiable discrimination between countries where the same conditions prevail, or a disguised restriction on international trade, nothing in this Agreement shall be construed to prevent the adoption or enforcement by any contracting party of measures:

(b) necessary to protect human, animal or plant life or health;

(g) relating to the conservation of exhaustible natural resources if such measures are made effective in conjunction with restrictions on domestic production or consumption.

* * *

In summary, many environmental product standards are likely to be GATT legal under Article III. But when a standard has the effect of treating an imported product less favorably than a "like" domestic product, the standard will violate Article III. Standards that fail Article III may qualify as exceptions under Article XX, although this never has been explicitly addressed in the context of product standards. The existing GATT Standards Code adds more rules on product standards, but so far these have had limited influence. The new TBT Agreement written in the Uruguay Round is far more stringent than the current Code, and even than the GATT itself, because it mandates a "least trade restrictive" test. The new agreement will supersede GATT Articles III and XX.

II. PROCESS STANDARDS

Process standards are the most complex kind of ETM. They are concerned with how a product is manufactured, prepared, harvested, or extracted. In contrast to product standards, which relate to observable, or at least testable, characteristics of the product, process standards relate to aspects of production that cannot be ascertained by inspection. While this product versus process distinction is useful, it should be recognized that considerable ambiguity exists. After all, process standards can only be implemented when they are applied to a product. The critical distinction is that while process standards and product standards are both concerned with quality, process standards look beyond the quality of the product itself to the quality of the production process.

There are two types of process standards. One concerns processes which change, or may change, product characteristics.

* * *

But for the fact that the regulatory concern is undetectable in the product itself, the regulation of these practices could be viewed as product standards. If the concerns become detectable, a process standard can be rewritten as a product standard. The current GATT Standards Code refers to such regulations as "processes and production methods" (or PPMs), and exempts them from international discipline. The new Uruguay Round Agreement and TBT Agreement would apply the new disciplines to such PPMs.

The other type of process standards are far more controversial. They involve issues which do not affect the product itself, except perhaps in a metaphysical sense.

* * *

In regulating processing methods, the concern is usually not that a product itself is harmful to consumers. Instead, the concern is that the production process is harmful or wasteful either to particular groups, such as dolphins swimming near tuna, or to the ecosystem as a whole. Environmental damage might arise directly from the act of taking an animal or plant, or indirectly from the negative externalities of the production process. Such externalities might harm a foreign environment, a domestic environment, the global commons (for example, the incidental killing of dolphins), or they might spill over into the environment (as do chlorofluorocarbons (CFCs)).

* * *

Process standards, and import prohibitions, can be written in three different ways. First, a nation could enact a measure aimed at defiled items. Defiled items are those products made using environmentally damaging methods.... Second, a country could have a measure aimed at items from nations engaging in environmentally damaging production practices.... Third, a nation could enact a measure aimed at items from countries whose governments fail to adopt environmentally sound government policy.

* * *

[A] restriction is a process standard if the environmental concern has a connection to the product being regulated or taxed. When the connection becomes tenuous or indirect, a process standard turns into a trade sanction. Although all ETMs are sometimes accused of being protectionist, it is probably process standards that stand the greatest danger of being manipulated for that purpose.

* * *

C.   GATT Article XX

Some commentators have suggested that Article XX(b) and (g) cannot be invoked to justify import bans relating to the production process. But it is hard to reconcile this view with the fact that Article XX(d) and (e) are invoked to justify import bans relating to the production process. Article XX(d) is used to justify import bans against goods made without the legal acquisition of intellectual property rights. Article XX(e) is used to justify import bans against goods made with prison labor. The provision relating to the "products of prison labor" would have little meaning unless it can apply to process standards and process-related prohibitions.

No one has pointed to any drafting history demonstrating that GATT's authors intended subsections (b) and (g) to be narrower than subsections (d) and (e). The legitimacy of applying Article XX(b) and (g) to production practices is further buttressed by the fact that environmental trade restrictions tied to the production process were in use long before the GATT was contemplated. There is no evidence that GATT's authors sought to disallow them.

The view that Article XX does not extend to process standards is often attributed to the Dolphin Panel. But this seems a misreading of the Panel's report which objects to "extrajurisdictionality" in Article XX, not to process-based ETMs. It should also be noted that GATT Article VI permits discriminatory tariffs based on the production process used in a foreign country. This provision applies principally when the producer receives a government subsidy or sets its price too low.

* * *

[W]hat if a nation declares that it will no longer admit wood or wood products from forests inhabited by the northern spotted owl? Since the national treatment and nondiscrimination prerequisites would be automatically met for spotted owls, perhaps a nation's solicitude for other species, or for other environmental issues, could be a factor in determining whether such an import ban is a "disguised" restriction.

Article XX(b) requires that trade measures be "necessary" to protect life or health. The GATT preparatory history suggests that this meant "necessary" in a scientific sense. Yet this subject received little attention at that time. Recent GATT adjudication has focused on whether an ETM under Article XX(b) is "necessary" in a theoretical rather than a scientific sense. The Thai Cigarette Panel ruled that a measure would be considered "necessary" only if it "entails the least degree of inconsistency with other GATT provisions."[32] This is often referred to as the least-GATT-inconsistent test.

* * *

Nevertheless, there is no reason to read "necessary" in Article XX(b) as meaning "absolutely necessary" in the sense that without the action, achievement of the policy goal would be impossible. The GATT does not require that tariffs, subsidies, internal taxes or other measures be screened as to their necessity. Thus, it is illogical that the one part of GATT called "General Exceptions" should be the one subject to the most stringent "necessary" test. Moreover, as Justice Marshall pointed out in his famous disquisition on the word "necessary" in *McCulloch v. Maryland,*

> to employ the means necessary to an end is generally understood as employing any means calculated to produce the end, and not as being

---

32. Thailand: Restrictions on Importation of Internal Taxes on Cigarettes, GATT BISD 37S/200 (Nov. 1990)[hereinafter Thai Cigarette Report].

confined to those single means, without which the end would be entirely unattainable.[33]

Like Article XX(b), Article XX(g), concerning the conservation of exhaustible natural resources, has suffered serious impairment in the course of being interpreted by GATT panels. Although the authors of the GATT saw a clear need for this exception, they wanted to prevent it from being used as a restriction on market access or as protectionism. To guard against such abuses, the GATT required parallel restrictions on domestic production or consumption.

* * *

III.   IMPORT BANS

Import bans can be carried out in several ways. They can be aimed at the item itself (for example, a turtle), products made from the item (for example, tortoise shell eyeglasses), or products derived from a process that entails the item (for example, shrimp caught in ways that kill turtles).

* * *

A.   GATT Article XI

Import bans, and export bans, violate GATT Article XI which disallows "prohibitions or restrictions other than duties, taxes or other charges."[34] In other words, GATT members cannot use import bans because they are tantamount to a quantitative restriction of zero. Article XI does provide for three exceptions, but none of them are applicable to typical ETMs.

This disallowance of import bans by GATT has great significance for ETMs. Under CITES, trade in "specimens" (living or dead) of endangered species must be carried out in accordance with regulations requiring both import and export permits (or re-export certificates). The treaty lists several criteria for the granting of such import permits by national governments including advice from a "Scientific Authority" that the import will be for purposes which are not "detrimental to the survival of the species involved."[35] Strictly speaking, CITES does not prohibit imports. But it does mandate a licensing system under which commercial trade will regularly be prohibited. Therefore, actions under CITES would be inconsistent with GATT Article XI.

Because CITES is a convention on "International Trade," the Article III defense would seem inapplicable. Since CITES imposes no requirements on domestic sales or consumption (for example, it does not regulate domestic trade in endangered species), the treaty can hardly be an internal regulation enforced at the border. But even if CITES did mandate comparable domestic restraints, there would still be a GATT problem with the contingent import approach. This approach is used in other environmental agreements and laws, and involves tying imports to the approval of the exporting nation. The problem is that any discrimination between "like" products based on certain situations in the country of origin would violate GATT Article I. Of course, an

---

33. 17 U.S. 316, 413–14 (1819).

34. GATT, *supra* note 24 art XI:1.

35. Convention on International Trade in Endangered Species of Wild Fauna and Flora,

Mar. 3, 1973, art. III:3 (a), 12 I.L.M. 1085. [hereinafter CITES][**Basic Document 6.5**].

exporting nation which does not grant approval is unlikely to complain in the GATT. Nor do consumers in the country banning the import have a right to complain to the GATT. So for practical purposes, contingent import provisions will not be ruled GATT-illegal.

* * *

B. GATT Article XX

Import prohibitions that are inconsistent with GATT Articles I or XI may nevertheless be allowable under the General Exceptions in Article XX. It is generally agreed that under Article XX(b), GATT members may "give priority to human health over trade liberalization."[36] For instance, a country might ban the importation of hazardous waste even though similar waste is produced domestically. The country could try to justify the ban under Article XX(b) on the grounds that transporting waste over populated areas is too dangerous.

Article XX(b), however, requires that such measures be "necessary." It is important to understand that what may be perceived as "necessary" to ban in one country may be perceived quite differently in another.

* * *

Whether Article XX(b) permits governments to give priority to animal or plant health over trade liberalization is in dispute. One view is that Article XX(b) applies equally to all forms of life. Yet it is sometimes argued that an animal has to be endangered to be covered by Article XX(b). Since Article XX(b) is not generally perceived as requiring that humans be endangered before a trade-related health measure can be justified, it is unclear how a different requirement for animals might have come about.

Some commentators suggest that Article XX(b) is too limited to cover many important environmental trade measures. This view can be challenged, however, when one considers the fact that anything which affects the health of a living organism could be reached by Article XX(b). While there may be some environmental concerns, such as recreational opportunities, that are not addressed by the life and health standards of Article XX(b), every critical international environmental issue would seem to be incorporated in the Article.

Furthermore, the scope of Article XX(g) is as broad as that of Article XX(b). Most of the world's serious environmental issues, such as climate change, ocean pollution, disappearing forests, driftnet fishing, recycling, and biodiversity, can be characterized as a natural resource lacking conservation. Only the last of these issues, however, was specifically considered in writing the GATT.

* * *

To qualify for either of GATT's environmental exceptions, however, an ETM would have to meet the two prerequisites in Article XX's headnote: the discrimination and the disguised restriction tests. As noted above, there is no

---

36. Thai Cigarette Report, *supra* note 31, para. 73, at 222–23. But the panel also points out that measures must be "necessary" in order to be covered under Article XX(b). *Id.* at 223.

"like product" requirement in Article XX. Discrimination is allowed so long as it is not arbitrary or unjustifiable. For example, the U.S. import regulations implementing CITES distinguish between species that are captivebred and those caught in the wild. Such discrimination is justifiable because trade in captive-bred species does not diminish the population in the wild.

18. *See generally, supra* Chapter 5 "International Environmental Wrongs", at 335.

Discussion Notes/Questions

1. The Appellate Body (AB) of the World Trade Organization or GATT handed down another defeat for the international environmental protection laws of the U.S. in *United States–Import Prohibition of Certain Shrimp and Shrimp Products* [**Basic Document 8.11**]. At issue was the action taken by the U.S. under the Endangered Species Act (ESA), [Public Law 93–205, 16 U.S.C.1531 *et seq*] requiring all U.S. shrimp trawlers to use approved Turtle excluder Devices (TED's) in areas where shrimp harvesting could lead to the trawling of certain species of endangered sea turtles. The ESA also imposed an import ban on shrimp harvested with commercial fishing technology which may adversely effect sea turtles. The ban did not apply to countries certified by the U.S. as harvesting shrimp without the incidental taking of turtles.

India, Malaysia, Pakistan and Thailand whose shrimp were banned from U. S. markets because they did not use turtle excluders challenged the ban imposed on them. The Panel set up by the Dispute Settlement Body (DSB) of the GATT held that the U.S. actions violated article X1.1 of the GATT and could not fall within the exceptions in article XX. The AB upheld that decision though some of their reasons for doing so were different to those advanced by the panel.

The Panel reasoned that any measure which undermined the WTO s multilateral trading system must necessarily be prohibited by article XX. Overruling the Panel, the AB found that article XX does in fact embody exceptions to free trade and that the chapeau cannot, *ab initio,* be interpreted as to strike down every measure that amounted to a violation of free trade (para 121). Having established that it was possible to come within the exceptions created by article XX, the AB examined the law and practice of the ESA to ascertain if indeed it could be justified under article XX. Pursuant to its examination, the AB held that the U.S. measures did not comply with the requirements of he chapeau, and did not, therefore, fall within the exceptions created by article XX. The AB saw the task of applying the chapeau as one of "locating and marking out a line of equilibrium between the right of a member to invoke an exception under article XX and the rights of other members under varying substantive provisions (e.g. article XI) of GATT 1994 . . ." (para 159).

The AB decided that the ESA had been implemented and applied by the U.S. in a manner that constituted a means of "unjustified discrimination" and "arbitrary discrimination" contrary to the chapeau, and was therefore in violation of GATT. It ordered the U.S. to bring its laws and administration into compliance with GATT.

This is a far reaching decision that purports to pass judgment on the conduct of the foreign policy of the U.S. The AB found that the U.S. had engaged in unjustified discrimination by not entering into serious multilateral negotiations to protect sea turtles. The fact that the U.S. had successfully negotiated an international agreement to protect sea turtles with a group of other southern hemispheric countries was viewed by the AB as discrimination against the countries bringing this action. The AB asserted an equally wide jurisdiction over the domestic affairs of the U.S. It held that the actions of the U.S. amounted to arbitrary discrimination because the internal administrative procedures of the U.S. pertaining to certification did not comply with the minimum standards of transparency and procedural fairness established by X: 3 of GATT 1994.

In this decision AB has taken the unusual step of asserting the power of judicial review over the actions of the U.S., and substituting its own judgement on questions of foreign policy and internal administration. These are two areas that fall quintessentially within the internal power and authority of a sovereign state. The circumstances in which the U.S. should engage in negotiation with other nations cannot be stipulated by international tribunals unaware of the full facts or the complexities of foreign policy. Similarly, the internal administrative procedures of a country are not subject to review by international tribunals. If a international tribunal purports to review such actions, it should at least exercise great deference, and not intervene unless the actions being reviewed are palpably arbitrary and capricious.

Does this decision generate greater confidence in the DSB of the GATT?

2. Was Albion restricted to the adjudicatory system of the GATT, or are there other international forums that can decide claims such as this? In light of what he considers are endemic weaknesses of the GATT adjudicatory system, Professor Guruswamy, argues in his article: *The Promise of the United Nations Convention on the Law of the Sea (UNCLOS): Justice in Trade and Environmental Disputes*, 25 ECOLOGY L. Q. 189 at 191–193, 206–211 & 222–226 (1998), another part of which is excerpted in reading 8, *supra*, that GATT is not the exclusive forum for adjudicating environmental disputes with trade ramifications. He contends that tribunals established under the United Nations Convention on the Law of the Sea (UNCLOS), and in specified circumstances even the International Court of Justice, are possessed of jurisdiction to hear such cases.

* * *

[I]t is not necessary for IEL to be forced into the procrustean bed of trade law. GATT/WTO tribunals now adjudicate a significant number of issues that could be heard in more impartial fora that could recognize and uphold, rather than diminish or marginalize IEL. This Article points out that, within key areas of potential conflict, the substantive international environmental obligations and the dispute settlement procedures of the UNCLOS overcome GATT/WTO concerns over free trade. UNCLOS incorporates substantive principles of IEL and creates a binding system of adjudication and dispute resolution that confers upon its legal forums the jurisdiction and adjudicatory authority to hear trade and environment disputes. Even where states are not parties to UNCLOS, but nevertheless accept its provisions as codifications of customary IEL, the International Court of Justice (ICJ) can adjudicate trade and environment disputes in limited circumstances.

* * *

II

THE ENVIRONMENTAL PROMISE OF UNCLOS

Those concerned with fairness and justice in trade and environment disputes should look instead at UNCLOS, which came into force on November 16, 1994. UNCLOS, as former U.S. Secretary of State, Warren Christopher, pointed out in a letter of submittal to the President, "[i]s the strongest comprehensive environmental treaty now in existence or likely to emerge for quite some time,"[37] and can be the foundation of a "Constitution for the Oceans." Its 59 provisions obligating environmental protection and conservation, out of 320 in all, possess a fundamental and over-arching character. UNCLOS deals with conservation and the management of living resources, pollution prevention, reduction and control, vessel pollution, and environmental management. It can be asserted that UNCLOS is not only a treaty but a codification and articulation of the present state of the rules applicable to oceans, and it has ascended to the status of customary IEL, binding on both signatories and non-signatories.

In this context, it is worth remembering that the oceans occupy over seventy percent of the earth and are in many ways a proxy for the global environment. The fact that most pollution finds its way into the oceans through direct and indirect pathways from land requires control of "land-based pollution" with measures directed at air, land, and water pollution. Furthermore, notable areas of oceanic governance, including the conservation of wetlands, coastal areas, and biodiversity, are among the most critical issues confronting international environmental protection in general. As former Secretary of State Christopher noted, UNCLOS is the strongest and most comprehensive environmental treaty now in existence.

While UNCLOS does not create a World Oceanic Organization, its dispute resolution provisions are stronger and more binding than those of the GATT/WTO. Even if the primacy of UNCLOS's dispute resolution is in issue, the undoubted jurisdiction of an UNCLOS tribunal—as opposed to a GATT/WTO tribunal—could be invoked to settle disputes involving environmental actions that are sanctioned by UNCLOS but contrary to GATT/WTO trade law.

One of the dominant characteristics of UNCLOS is that it is an umbrella agreement that brings other international rules, regulations and implementing bodies within its canopy. Many of UNCLOS's provisions are of a constitutional or general character and will be augmented by specific regulations, rules and implementing procedures formulated by other international agreements and by nation states.

Article 197 illustrates the inclusive core of UNCLOS. It commands that:

> States shall co-operate on a global basis and, as appropriate, on a regional basis, directly or through competent international organizations, in formulating and elaborating international rules, standards and recommended practices and procedures consistent with this Convention, for the protection and preservation of the marine environment, taking into account characteristic regional features.[38]

When Article 197 is read in conjunction with Articles 237 and 293, UNCLOS's encompassing extent is clear beyond a doubt. Article 237 deals with obligations under other conventions that protect and preserve the environment and elucidates that the provisions of UNCLOS themselves are "[w]ithout prejudice to the specific obligations assumed by states under special conventions and agreements concluded previously which relate to the protection and preservation of the marine

---

37. Warren Christopher, Letter of Submittal of the Secretary of State to the President of the United States, in Message from the President of the United States and Commentary Accompanying the Nations Convention on the Law of the Sea and the Agreement Relating to the Implementation of Part XI upon their Transmittal to the United States Senate for its Advice and Consent, *reprinted in* 7 Geo. Int'l Envtl. L. Rev. 77, 81 (1994)[hereinafter Letter of Submittal].

38. *See* Third United Nations Conference on the Law of the Sea, art. 197, **[Basic Document 4.20]**.

environment and to agreements which may be concluded in furtherance of the general principles set forth in this Convention."[39] Having made this point, it goes on to clarify that: "[s]pecific obligations assumed by States ... should be carried out in a manner consistent with the general principles and objectives of this Convention."[40] It is worthy of note that Article 237 covers both past and future agreements, holding that they should be implemented in a manner consistent with UNCLOS' general principles.

Significant IEL treaties—antithetical to GATT as it transpires—are an important part of the design, environmental objective, and architecture of UNCLOS. Not only are many of the specific obligations assumed in these IEL treaties "consistent" with UNCLOS, they are an integral and necessary part of UNCLOS's environmental umbrella. Pursuant to this legal scheme, Article 293 declares that an UNCLOS tribunal shall "[a]pply this Convention and other rules of international law not incompatible with this Convention."[41]

A scenario is emerging that is remarkably different from the GATT/WTO. It appears that UNCLOS tribunals will be interpreting and applying a formidable number of environmental provisions whose objective is to advance international environmental protection and not to liberalize trade. In dramatic contrast, GATT/WTO dispute settlement bodies—set up to implement a regime of liberal trade—are uncertain about IEL and diminish environmental protection even where it is recognized.

* * *

IV

ADJUDICATING TRADE AND ENVIRONMENT DISPUTES

Very few international disputes lead to adjudication because the international community has generally avoided the compulsory judicial settlement of disputes. There is little doubt that the absence of compulsory judicial settlement is a serious weakness in the embryonic legal system prevailing in international society. It is in this context that GATT/WTO has assumed prominence as a unique system of compulsory and binding dispute settlement. The attention given to GATT/WTO appears to have ignored the equally compulsory and binding dispute settlement procedures under UNCLOS, as well as the more limited, but nonetheless significant jurisdiction of the ICJ.

* * *

C. UNCLOS and the ICJ

[T]he United States has been challenged on numerous occasions under GATT/WTO for taking action to protect the international environment in violation of GATT. While UNCLOS mandates the protection of the international environment, the United States will not be able to avail itself of UNCLOS jurisdiction. The refusal of the United States to ratify UNCLOS precludes access to those dispute settlement procedures. Even the fact that the ICJ may have been elected as a judicial forum under Article 287(1)(b) of UNCLOS will not give the ICJ jurisdiction over non-parties to UNCLOS such as the United States.

The time may be ripe for the United States to revisit a prescient and creative suggestion made by Louis Sohn. This suggestion might give the United States an

---

39. *See id.* art. 237, para.1.   **41.** *See id.* art. 293, para. 1.
40. *See id.* art. 237, para. 2.

opportunity to defend its actions in a neutral forum. The path suggested by Sohn assumes the United States has not ratified UNCLOS, and is therefore, denied access to UNCLOS dispute settlement procedures. He also assumes that the United States accepts the environmental provisions of UNCLOS as a codification or restatement of customary international law. Arising from these premises he suggests a course of action that opens the door for the International Court of Justice to interpret and apply such law. Sohn proposed that the United States, which does not presently accept the compulsory jurisdiction of the ICJ, might sign a supplementary declaration under Article 36 of the Statute of the International Court of Justice, accepting the jurisdiction of the Court with respect to those rules of customary international law codified in UNCLOS, if necessary with an exception for deep sea bed mining.

Under Article 36(2) the United States may declare that it recognizes as "compulsory ipso facto and without special agreement, in relation to any other State accepting the same obligation, the jurisdiction of the Court in all legal disputes concerning . . . any question of international law" relating to the rules of customary IEL codified in UNCLOS. Such a declaration would confer jurisdiction on the ICJ, on law of the sea matters, over those states that similarly have accepted its jurisdiction. However, the Unites States' acceptance of Article 36(2) jurisdiction would need to avoid the kind of crippling reservations made under the "optional clause."

This course of action would confer compulsory jurisdiction on the ICJ under Article 36, independent of the dispute settlement provisions of UNCLOS. The jurisdiction of the ICJ would arise from the fact that the states involved have agreed to it under Article 36. This will enable the ICJ to decide whether, for example, the rules of customary international law, as codified in UNCLOS, may or may not prevail over GATT/WTO.

The course that Sohn advocates is admittedly of limited application. It would be confined to those countries that have accepted the Article 36 jurisdiction of the ICJ and have not effectively negated their acceptance with crippling reservations of the "self judging" kind. Nonetheless, it appears to be a felicitous way of overcoming some obstacles, bringing the United States within the customary environmental law umbrella of UNCLOS, and possibly persuading the United States to ratify the treaty. The existence of an impartial tribunal and the possibility that IEL can be reaffirmed in a non-GATT/WTO judicial context, will restore confidence in international adjudication and help strike the balance between free trade and environmental protection.

* * *

Bibliographical Note. For further discussion concerning the principal themes addressed in this problem, consult the following specialized materials:

(a) *Specialized Books/Monographs.* W. Baumol, Environmental Protection, International Spillovers and Trade (1971); H. Daly & J. Cobb, For the Common Good: Redirecting the Economy Toward Community, the Environment, and a Sustainable Future (1989); B. Johnson, Responding to Tropical Deforestation: An Eruption of CrisisCAn Array of Solutions (1991); S. Lyster, International Wildlife Law (1985); D. Favre, International Trade in Endangered Species: A Guide to CITES (1989); J. Jackson, The World Trading System: Law and Policy of International Economic Relations (1989); E. Leamer, Sources of International Comparative Advantage: Theory and Evidence (1984); J. Leonard, Pollution and the Struggle for the World Product (1988); D. Mahar, Government Policies and

Deforestation in Brazil's Amazon Region (1989); C. Pearson, Implications for the Trade and Investment of Developing Countries of US Environmental Controls (1976); C. Pearson, Environmental Policies and Their Trade Implications for Developing Countries, With Special Reference to Fish and Shellfish, Fruit and Vegetables (1982).

(b) *Specialized Hearings/Reports.* C. Arden Clarke, The General Agreement on Tariffs and Trade: Environmental Protection and Sustainable Development, A Report Prepared for the World Wildlife Fund International, (1991); German Bundestag, Protecting the Tropical Forests: A High Priority International Task, Report of the Enquete Commission "Preventive Measures to Protect the Earth's Atmosphere," 11th German Bundestag (1990).

(c) *Specialized Articles/Book Chapters.* A. Anderson, *Smokestacks in the Rainforest: Industrial Development and Deforestation in the Amazon Basin,* 18 World Development 1191 (1990); P. Anderson, *The Myth of Sustainable Logging: The Case for a Ban on Tropical Timber Imports,* 19 The Ecologist 166 (1989); S. Barrett, *The Problem of Global Environmental Protection,* 6 Oxford Rev. Econ. Pol'y 68 (1990); H. Bingswanger, *Brazilian Policies that Encourage Deforestation of the Amazon,* 19 World Development 821 (1991); R. Blackhurst, *International Trade and Domestic Environmental Policies in a Growing World Economy,* in International Relations in a Changing World 9 (R. Blackhurst et al. eds. 1977); S. Brown, *International Trade and the Environment: Interdependent Goals or Irreconcilable Conflict? Introduction,* 49 Wash. & Lee L. Rev. 1219 (1992); G. Castle, *The Need for an International Dispute Panel: Position, Consensus and Interdependent Goals,* 49 Wash. & Lee L. Rev. 1403 (1992); S. Charnovitz, *International Environmental Law Colloquium, Green Roots, Bad Pruning: GATT Rules and Their Application to Environmental Trade Measures,* 7 Tulane Envtl. L.J. 299 (1994); C. M. Cuccia, *Note: Protecting Animals in the Name of Biodiversity: Effects of the Uruguay Round of Measures Regulating Methods of Harvesting,* 13 B.U. Int'l. L.J. 481 (1995); M.E. Foster, *Trade and Environment: Making Room for Environmental Trade Measures Within the GATT,* 71 Cal. L.Rev. 393 (1998); R. de C. Grey, *The Decay of the Trade Relations System,* in Issues in World Trade Policy: GATT at the Crossroads (R. Snape ed. 1986); M. Glennon, *Has International Law Failed the Elephant?,* 84 A.J.I.L. 1 (1990); L. Guruswamy, *The Promise of the United Nations Convention on the Law of the Sea (UNCLOS): Justice in Trade and Environmental Disputes,* 25 Ecology L.Q. 189 (1998); M. Hurlock, *Note: The GATT, U.S. Law and the Environment: A Proposal to Amend the GATT in Light of the Tuna/Dolphin Decision,* 92 Colum. L. Rev. 2098 (1992); P. Goldman, *Resolving the Trade and Environment Debate: In Search of a Neutral Forum and Neutral Principles,* 49 Wash. & Lee L. Rev. 1279 (1992); J. Heppes & E. McFadden, *The Convention on International Trade in Endangered Species of Wild Fauna and Flora: Improving the Prospects for Preserving our Biological Heritage,* 5 B. U. Int'lL. J. 229 (1992); R. Housman, *A Kantian Approach to Trade and the Environment,* 49 Wash. & Lee L. Rev. 1373 (1992); R. Housman & D. Zaelke, *Trade, Environment, and Sustainable Development: A Primer,* 15 Hastings Int'l & Comp. L. Rev. 535 (1992); __, *The Collision of the Environment and Trade: The GATT Tuna/Dolphin Decision,* 22 Envtl. L. Rep. 10268 (1992); J. Jackson, et al., *Implementing the Tokyo Round: Legal Aspects of Changing International Economic Rules,* 81 Mich. L. Rev 267 (1982); A. Jansson, *On the Significance of Open Boundaries for an Ecologically Sustainable Development of Human Societies,* Ecological Economics (R. Constanza ed. 1991); F. Kirgis, Jr., *Environment and Trade Measures After the Tuna/Dolphin Decision,* 49 Wash. & Lee L. Rev. 1221 (1992) ; K. Komoroski, *The Failure of Governments to Regulate the Industry: A*

Subsidy Under the GATT?, 10 Hous. J. Int'l L. 189 (1988); M. Meier, *GATT, WTO and the Environment: To What Extent Do GATT/WTO Rules Permit Member Nations to Protect the Environment When Doing So Adversely Affects Trade,* 8 Colo. J. Int'l Envtl. L. & Pol'y 241 (1997); R. Lucas, D. Wheeler, & H. Hettige, *Economic Development, Environmental Regulation and the International Migration of Toxic Industrial Pollution: 1966B1988,* Paper presented at the Symposium on International Trade and the Environment, World Bank, Washington D.C. (1991); M. Ritchie, *GATT, Agriculture and the Environment: The Double Zero Plan,* 6 The Ecologist 214 (199); T. Schoenbaum, *Agora: Free Trade and Environment: Free International Trade and Protection of the Environment: Irreconcilable Conflict?,* 86 A.J.I.L. 700 (1992); S. Shrybaum, *International Trade and the Environment: An Environmental Assessment of the GATT,* 20 The Ecologist 30 (1990); J. Smith, *Some Current Environmental Issues in Forestry,* 68 N. Dak. L. Rev. 345 (1992); H. Southworth, *GATT and the Environment-General Agreement on Tariffs and Trade, Trade and the Environment, GATT Doc. 1529,* 32 V.J.I.L. 1997 (1992); R. Stewart, *International Trade and Environment: Lessons from the Federal Experience,* 49 Wash. & Lee L. Rev. 1329 (1992); J. Trachtman, *Decision: GATT Dispute Settlement Panel,* 86 A.J.I.L. 142 (1992); J. Trask, *Note: Montreal Protocol Noncompliance Procedure: The Best Approach to Resolving the International Environmental Disputes?,* 80 Geo. L. J. 1973 (1992); J. Whalley, *The Interface between Environmental and Trade Policies,* 101 Economic Journal 180 (1991); D. Wirth, *The International Trade Regime and the Municipal Law of Federal States: How Close a Fit?,* 49 Wash. & Lee L. Rev. 1389 (1992).

Problem 11–2

Environmental Standards in Vinland and Tierrasol
SECTION 1. FACTS

Vinland, a wealthy Western Hemispheric nation, shares a common border with Tierrasol, a mid-size developing country. Vinland's constitutional and governmental system parallels that of the United States, and Vinland has accepted United States' decisions interpreting constitutional issues as persuasive authority on numerous occasions. Both Vinland and Tierrasol have recently joined an expanded North American Free Trade Agreement (NAFTA), which includes the North American Agreement on Environmental Cooperation (NAAEC). In the years following these agreements, a number of differences relating to the enforcement of their environmental laws have emerged. Generally, while both states subscribe to similar environmental standards, Vinland has maintained a better record of enforcement than Tierrasol, which has downplayed the enforcement of environmental standards in its pursuit of economic development. Tierrasol's lower standards, coupled with the NAFTA's removal of trade barriers between the states, has created new challenges to Vinland's industries that are forced to compete with Tierrasol's industries which spend comparatively less on environmental regulation.

Both Vinland and Tierrasol engage in poultry farming. The poultry industry in Vinland recently has consolidated on large, integrated poultry farms in an attempt to maintain viability in the face of cheaper competition from Tierrasol in the wake of the NAFTA. These farms, consisting of confined poultry operations, are located along Vinland's Eulynne River to ensure adequate water for their processing plants, and discharge large volumes of animal waste into Vinland's waterways. One of the largest integrated poultry plants managed by Vinland corporation, Meyer, has recently expanded. The resulting waste, although not exceeding Meyer's discharge limits under Vinland's water pollution laws, has caused serious environmental threats to numerous endangered species located directly downstream to the Meyer operations within the Vinland Nature Reserve. These species have been declared endangered species under Vinland's Endangered Species Act.[a]

Environmental non-governmental organizations (NGOs) in Vinland became concerned about the potential threat to the endangered species found only within the Nature Reserve, and initiated scientific studies of the Eulynne River as well as the several small lakes in the Nature Reserve which are fed by the river. These studies showed excessively high levels of nutrients such as phosphorus, nitrogen, and potassium in the water due to the poultry waste. The NGOs reported these findings to the Vinland government, but nearly a year elapsed, and no action was taken. During this interim, the attentions of

---

a. Vinland's Endangered Species Act is copied *verbatim et literatim* from the U.S. Endangered Species Act of 1973 as amended [**Basic Document 6.6**].

Vinland's NGOs were drawn to an oil tanker spill along the coast of another Western Hemispheric state. The Vinland NGOs, rapidly opted to focus their time and concerns on this area, in preference to the less-visible problem of excessive nutrients which they placed on the back burner.

The South Fork of the Eulynne River splits from the main Eulynne River at Vinland's eastern border and flows southward to form Tierrasol's eastern border. In addition, a number of creeks and streams branch westward from the South Fork in the course of its southward passage. Tierrasol's poultry farmers who are located throughout Northern Tierrasol, do not directly discharge poultry waste into the waterways as do Vinland's poultry operators. Instead, the Tierrasol farmers spread the animal waste over their land as a method of both fertilization and disposal. During periods of heavy rain, some of this waste runs-off into the surrounding creeks and streams which branch from the South Fork of the Eulynne River and continue to flow into the waterways of the Vinland Nature Reserve.

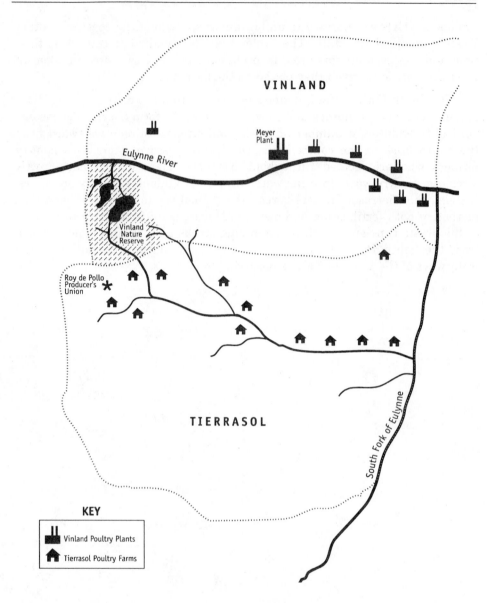

Prior to the consolidation, Vinland imported most of its poultry from Roy de Pollo, a mid-sized poultry producers union in Tierrasol, to whom many small farmers sold their poultry at very low prices. The Vinland consolidation resulted in a recognizable decrease in poultry imports from Tierrasol; and Roy de Pollo has faced numerous complaints from its members, who claim that their livelihood is threatened by Vinland's new consolidated poultry plants.

Additionally, the national environmental agency of Tierrasol has recently instituted a crack-down on improper sanitation at Roy de Pollo's poultry shipment plant, in order to meet with the terms of the NAFTA. Poultry producers in Tierrasol who are bearing the cost of improving environmental standards in addition to the decrease in exports to Vinland, face a bleak prospect.

Not long after Vinland NGOs had presented their reports on the excessive nutrient levels in the Nature Reserve waters to the Vinland government, members of the Environmental Front of Tierrasol (EFT), a Tierrasol NGO, read reports of this problem in the *Tierra Club Weekly* (a periodical devoted to environmental issues) and decided to investigate the problem by sending observers to the Nature Reserve. These observers, through a casual survey of the Nature Reserve, confirmed the suspicions of the EFT, and alleged that the Vinland Environmental Standards Agency (VESA), the agency charged with protecting endangered species on the reserve under Vinland's Endangered Species Act, had abdicated its duties by refusing to enforce the provisions of that law against Meyer.

According to the Tierrasol NGOs, the VESA relaxed its enforcement of Vinland's environmental laws after Vinland joined the NAFTA agreement, because of the VESA's new policy that the economic benefits from a flourishing poultry industry outweighed any costs resulting from damage to the environment. The limited financial resources of the EFT, however, prevents them from mounting a publicity campaign against Vinland and Meyer; while the Government of Tierrasol is unwilling to "rock the boat" by upsetting Vinland for fear of jeopardizing the increased economic prosperity that could arise from the full implementation of the NAFTA.

Roy de Pollo's president, an ardent environmentalist and frequent vacationer at Vinland's Nature Reserve, learned about the report of the EFT and decided to institute action against Vinland under the North American Agreement on Environmental Cooperation (NAAEC) for violation of Vinland national environmental law. Roy de Pollo invited the EFT to join in a suit under the NAAEC, and after discussion; both parties agreed that their private party suit under the NAAEC could also work to enforce the provisions of the 1992 Convention on Biological Diversity (CBD)[b] and the Western Hemisphere Convention.

Vinland has signed and ratified the CBD, but has yet to take further action to implement the Convention. Tierrasol has signed but not ratified the CBD. Additionally, both Vinland and Tierrasol have signed and ratified the 1940 Convention on Nature Protection and Wildlife Preservation in the Western Hemisphere (Western Hemisphere Convention). The only action taken by Vinland thus far under the Western Hemisphere Convention was the creation of the Nature Reserve itself. Tierrasol has yet to take action under this convention.

Although dubious about the alleged rights of Roy de Pollo and the EFT, Vinland is eager to maintain its domestic and international reputation as a leading environmental advocate within the Western Hemisphere; and has agreed to take any legal and administrative actions required of it by the NAAEC Commission. Vinland views this as a politically preferred way of remedying any environmental problems without negative public reaction, and without the need for NAAEC enforcement measures. The Secretariat has already indicated that the Roy de Pollo–EFT submission meets the criteria

b. At the Second Meeting of the Conference of the Parties of the CBD, the Ministers adopted the Jakarta Ministerial Statement on the Implementation of the Convention on Biological Diversity (Jakarta Mandate) **[Basic Document 6.16]** which amounts to little more than reaffirmations of the CBD provisions.

under article 14(1) of the NAAEC. However, in light of Vinland's cooperation and citing exceptional circumstances, the Secretariat decided to allow oral arguments before the NAAEC Commission to address all of the legal issues involved including article 14(1) standing, and Vinland's alleged violation of international law.

SECTION 2. QUESTIONS PRESENTED

1. To what extent can Roy de Pollo or the EFT seek to enforce Vinland's obligations under the Biodiversity Convention and the Western Hemispheric Convention?

2. Can Roy de Pollo or the EFT challenge Vinland's alleged failure to enforce its own national law?

SECTION 3. ASSIGNMENTS

A. *Reading Assignment*

Study the Readings presented in Section 4, *infra,* and the Discussion Notes/Questions that follow. Also, to the extent possible, consult the accompanying bibliographical references.

B. *Recommended Writing Assignment*

Prepare a comprehensive, logically sequenced, and *argumentative* brief in the form of an outline of the primary and subsidiary *legal* issues you see requiring resolution by the NAAEC Commission. Also, from the perspective of an independent objective judge, indicate which side ought to prevail on each issue and why. Retain a copy of your issue-outline/brief for class discussion.

C. *Recommended Oral Assignment*

Assume you are legal counsel for Vinland or Roy de Pollo and the EFT (as designated by your instructor); then, relying upon the Readings (and your issue-outline if prepared), present a 15–20 minute oral argument of your government's likely positions before the NAAEC Commission.

D. *Suggested Reflective Assignment*

Consider (and recommend) alternative norms, institutions, and/or procedures that you believe might do better than existing world order arrangements to contend with situations of the kind posed by this problem. In so doing, but without insisting upon *immediate* feasibility, identify the particular transition steps that would be needed to make your alternatives a reality.

SECTION 4. READINGS

1. Stockholm Declaration of the United Nations Conference on the Human Environment adopted by the UN Conference on the Human Environment at Stockholm, June 16, 1972, Report of the UN Conference on the Human Environment, June 15–16, 1972, Principles

1–3, 5, 8, 13, 21, 22 UN Doc. A/CONF.48/14/Rev. 1 at 3 (1973), UN Doc. A/CONF.48/14 at 2–65, and Corr. 1 (1972), *reprinted in* 11 I.L.M. 1416 (1972) [Basic Document 1.12].

2. Rio Declaration on Environment and Development, June 13, 1992, Principles 1–9, 12, 13 UNCED Doc. A/CONF.151/5/Rev. 1, *reprinted in* 31 I.L.M. 874 [Basic Document 1.29].

3. North American Agreement on Environmental Cooperation, 32 I.L.M. 1480 (1993) [Basic Document 7.4].

4. World Charter for Nature, Oct. 28, 1982 Principles 1–12 G.A. Res. 37/7, U.N. GAOR, 37th Sess., Supp. No. 51, at 17, U.N.Doc.A/37/51, *reprinted in* 22 I.L.M. 455 (1983) [Basic Document 1.21].

5. *See generally* Chapter 5 ("International Environmental Wrongs"), at 335, supra.

6. Henry J. Steiner, et al., Transnational Legal Problems: Materials and Text, 556–60 (4th ed. 1994).

Note on Self-Executing Treaties

(1) A self-executing treaty has been defined as one "which prescribes by its own terms a rule for the Executive or for the courts or which creates obligations for individuals enforceable without legislative implementation." Evans, *Self-Executing Treaties in the United States of America*, 30 Br. Ybk. Int. L. 178, 185 (1953). Compare Section 141 of Restatement (Second), Foreign Relations Law of the United States, which states that a treaty "that manifests an intention that it shall become effective as domestic law of the United States at the time it becomes binding on the United States (a) is self-executing in that it is effective as domestic law of the United States...."[1] Note the relationship between the concept of a self-executing treaty and the status of "supreme law" that is accorded the treaty under the Supremacy Clause.

When inquiring into the "intention" of the treaty's drafters, a court will of course look carefully at the text of the agreement. It will consider the verbs used–"does hereby" versus "shall undertake"–as well as other textual indications. Having exhausted such data, it may examine the broader context of the agreement, including the feasibility of construing a treaty to be self-executing in the light of the administrative and political problems inherent in creating operative rules without implementing or reinforcing legislation.

United States v. Postal, 589 F.2d 862 (5th Cir. 1979), held that the 1958 Geneva Convention on the High Seas was not self-executing. Its analysis of the parties' intent stressed that multilateral treaties have many parties not recognizing the self-executing character of treaties, and that the United States

---

1. The equivalent Section in Restatement of the Foreign Relations Law of the United States (Revised) (Tent. Draft No. 6, 1985) is § 131. One could point towards a number of legislative or constitutional analogies in the United States. Section 1 of the Fourteenth Amendment, for example, is "self-executing" in the sense that courts apply the Due Process Clause or the Equal Protection Clause without legislative implementation. But note, on the other hand, that Section 5 of that amendment gives Congress the power to enforce it "by appropriate legislation." That is, the same text at once constitutes applicable "law" upon which private parties may rely in litigation, and provides a basis for federal legislation.

does not have mutuality of obligation to such states if it views the treaty as self-executing.

(3) The question of a plaintiff's standing to assert rights under a treaty is often linked to that of the treaty's self-executing character. For example, in *Pauling v. McElroy* [164 F.Supp. 390 (D.D.C. 1958), aff'd, 278 F.2d 252 (D.C.Cir.1960)], the court rebuffed a suit based in part on the U. N. Charter, to enjoin the Atomic Energy Commission and the Secretary of Defense from detonating nuclear devices in the Marshall Islands for test purposes. Both grounds for seeking dismissal of the complaint were available to defendants. Indeed the opinions in the district and circuit courts considered a third, related, problem–whether plaintiff's claim was "justiciable" or within the realm of political questions and thus immune from judicial consideration on the merits.

Problems of standing and of a treaty's self-executing quality interact in a variety of ways. For example, the Nuclear Test Ban Treaty with the Soviet Union could be considered self-executing, in the sense that it imposes an obligation on the Executive to cease certain tests. But the question on standing of a private plaintiff to prevent a violation of the Treaty raises distinct and decisive issues. Of course, many self-executing treaties are intended to confer rights upon individuals, particularly treaties defining rights or duties of aliens in the territory of a signatory. For example, many clauses in treaties of Friendship, Commerce and Navigation have long been considered self-executing.

(4) Whether the purpose of the treaty is to regulate conduct of or towards private persons may not be decisive in determining whether the treaty is self-executing. Treaties that are not principally directed at activities of private persons may be found to be self-executing and may thus be invoked by private parties. For example, an agreement between two countries settling a boundary dispute might be relevant to later litigation in either affecting real property in the disputed area. On the other hand, drafters of a treaty may primarily intend to benefit private parties but at the same time make clear that Congressional implementation is required. Thus a treaty with Guatador might state that the United States "undertakes to enact legislation enabling nationals of Guatador to own land for agricultural purposes."

* * *

(6) Comparable problems arise under the constitutional law or practice of foreign countries of determining the effect of a treaty as internal law, the extent to which it creates rights or duties enforceable by or against individuals without implementation by domestic statutes. Such problems are apt to be particularly acute in the case of multilateral treaties which are intended to create similar or identical legal situations within each of the contracting parties. One prominent example is the European Convention on Human Rights [1950 European Convention for the Protection of Human Rights and Fundamental Freedoms, 213 U.N.T.S. 221, Eur.T.S. No. 5]. The question has been posed before courts of several parties whether individuals can directly invoke the Convention to challenge governmental action which allegedly violates it. Similar issues have arisen under the Rome Treaty creating the European Common Market, and of course under numerous bilateral treaties to which European countries were parties.

7. *Sei Fujii v. State*, 242 P.2d 617 (1952).

[Fujii, a Japanese man who was ineligible for U.S. citizenship under the United States' laws for naturalization at that time, filed suit to determine whether land he had purchased had escheated under the provisions of the California Alien Land Law. The applicable law (1 Deering's Gen. Laws, Act 261, as amended in 1945) stated in part:

§ 1. All aliens eligible to citizenship under the laws of the United States may acquire, possess, enjoy, use, cultivate, occupy, transfer, transmit and inherit real property, or any interest therein, in this state, and have in whole or in part the beneficial use thereof, in the same manner and to the same extent as citizens of the United States, except as otherwise provided by the laws of this state.

§ 2. All aliens other than those mentioned in section one of this act may acquire, possess, enjoy, use, cultivate, occupy and transfer real property, or any interest therein, in this state, and have in whole or in part the beneficial use thereof, in the manner and to the extent, and for the purposes prescribed by any treaty now existing between the government of the United States and the nation or country of which such alien is a citizen or subject, and not otherwise.

§ 7. Any real property hereafter acquired in fee in violation of the provisions of this act by any alien mentioned in section 2 of this act, ... shall escheat as of the date of such acquiring, to, and become and remain the property of the state of California.

The Superior Court of Los Angeles County determined that the property in question had escheated to the state. Subsequently the District Court of Appeals, Second District reversed that decision, holding that the Alien Land Law was unenforceable because it conflicted with the Charter of the United Nations, which as treaty was the supreme law of the land. The California Supreme Court reversed that decision in an opinion by Chief Justice Gibson, excerpts of which follow.]

It is first contended that the land law has been invalidated and superseded by the provisions of the United Nations Charter pledging the member nations to promote the observance of human rights and fundamental freedoms without distinction as to race. Plaintiff relies on statements in the preamble and in articles 1, 55 and 56 of the Charter, 59 Stat. 1035.

It is not disputed that the charter is a treaty, and our federal Constitution provides that treaties made under the authority of the United States are part of the supreme law of the land and that the judges in every state are bound thereby. U.S. Const., art. VI. A treaty, however, does not automatically supersede local laws which are inconsistent with it unless the treaty provisions are self-executing. In the words of Chief Justice Marshall: A treaty is "to be regarded in courts of justice as equivalent to an act of the Legislature, whenever it operates of itself, without the aid of any legislative provision. But when the terms of the stipulation import a contract–when either of the parties engages to perform a particular act, the treaty addresses itself to the political, not the judicial department; and the Legislature must execute the contract, before it can become a rule for the court." *Foster v. Neilson*, 2 Pet. 253, 314, 7 L.Ed. 415 (1829).

In determining whether a treaty is self-executing courts look to the intent of the signatory parties as manifested by the language of the instrument, and, if the instrument is uncertain, recourse may be had to the circumstances surrounding its execution. [I]n order for a treaty provision to be operative without the aid of implementing legislation and to have the force and effect of a statute, it must appear that the framers of the treaty intended to prescribe a rule that, standing alone, would be enforceable in the courts.

* * *

It is clear that the provisions of the preamble and of Article 1 of the charter which are claimed to be in conflict with the alien land law are not self-executing. They state general purposes and objectives of the United Nations Organization and do not purport to impose legal obligations on the individual member nations or to create rights in private persons. (5) It is equally clear that none of the other provisions relied on by plaintiff is self-executing. [A]lthough the member nations have obligated themselves to cooperate with the international organization in promoting respect for, and observance of, human rights, it is plain that it was contemplated that future legislative action by the several nations would be required to accomplish the declared objectives, and there is nothing to indicate that these provisions were intended to become rules of law for the courts of this country upon the ratification of the charter.

The language used in articles 55 and 56 is not the type customarily employed in treaties which have been held to be self-executing and to create rights and duties in individuals. For example, the treaty involved in *Clark v. Allen,* 331 U.S. 503, 507–508, 67 S.Ct. 1431, 1434, 91 L.Ed. 1633, relating to the rights of a national of one country to inherit real property located in another country, specifically provided that "such national shall be allowed a term of three years in which to sell the [property] ... and withdraw the proceeds ..." free from any discriminatory taxation. See, also, *Hauenstein v. Lynham,* 100 U.S. 483, 488–490, 25 L.Ed. 628. In *Nielsen v. Johnson,* 279 U.S. 47, 50, 49 S.Ct. 223, 73 L.Ed. 607, the provision treated as being self-executing was equally definite. There each of the signatory parties agreed that "no higher or other duties, charges, or taxes of any kind, shall be levied" by one country on removal of property therefrom by citizens of the other country "that are or shall be payable in each State, upon the same, when removed by a citizen or subject of such state respectively." In other instances treaty provisions were enforced without implementing legislation where they prescribed in detail the rules governing rights and obligations of individuals or specifically provided that citizens of one nation shall have the same rights while in the other country as are enjoyed by that country's own citizens.

* * *

It is significant to note that when the framers of the charter intended to make certain provisions effective without the aid of implementing legislation they employed language which is clear and definite and manifests that intention. [Quotations omitted.] In *Curran v. City of New York,* 191 Misc. 229, 77 N.Y.S.2d 206, 212, these articles were treated as being self-executory.

* * *

The provisions in the charter pledging cooperation in promoting observance of fundamental freedoms lack the mandatory quality and definiteness which would indicate an intent to create justiciable rights in private persons immediately upon ratification. Instead, they are framed as a promise of future action by the member nations. Secretary of State Stettinius, Chairman of the United States delegation at the San Francisco Conference where the charter was drafted, stated in his report to President Truman that article 56 "pledges the various countries to cooperate with the organization by joint and separate action in the achievement of the economic and social objectives of the organization without infringing upon their right to order their national affairs according to their own best ability, in their own way, and in accordance with their own political and economic institutions and processes." [Citation omitted.] The same view was repeatedly expressed by delegates of other nations in the debates attending the drafting of article 56. [Citation omitted.]

The humane and enlightened objectives of the United Nations Charter are, of course, entitled to respectful consideration by the courts and Legislatures of every member nation, since that document expresses the universal desire of thinking men for peace and for equality of rights and opportunities. The charter represents a moral commitment of foremost importance, and we must not permit the spirit of our pledge to be compromised or disparaged in either our domestic or foreign affairs. We are satisfied, however, that the charter provisions relied on by plaintiff were not intended to supersede existing domestic legislation, and we cannot hold that they operate to invalidate the alien land law.

* * *

8. Endangered Species Act of 1973, as amended, 16 U.S.C. §§ 1531 & 1537 (1976 & Supp. V 1981) [Basic Document 6.6].

9. Convention on Nature Protection and Wildlife Preservation in the Western Hemisphere, Oct. 12, 1940, 161 U.N.T.S. 229, U.S.T.S. 981, 56 Stat. 1374, 3 Bevans 630: arts. 1–10 [Basic Document 6.1].

10. Simm Lyster, International Wildlife Law 97–102, 105–08 (1985).

* * *

The Western Hemisphere Convention **[Basic Document 6.1]** was a visionary instrument, well ahead of its time in terms of the concept it espouses. . . . [A]lthough the Convention has stimulated the establishment of some protected areas, the enactment of some national conservation legislation and the development of some international cooperative programs, it has become a "sleeping Convention" which, with a few notable exceptions, is now of limited practical value in most Party countries.

1. *Objectives [of the Western Hemisphere Convention]*

The Parties had two main objectives in signing the Western Hemisphere Convention. The first was to protect all native animals and plants from extinction through means within man's control. . . . The preamble to the Convention states that it is the desire of the Parties to

[p]rotect and preserve in their natural habitat representatives of all species and genera of native flora and fauna, including migratory birds, in sufficient numbers and over areas extensive enough to assure them from becoming extinct through any agency within man's control.

This objective is especially significant in light of the fact that a) the combined territories of the Parties to the Convention probably contain over 25% of all species on earth and b) between 1–2% of tropical forest (the richest of all habitat types in terms of species diversity) in South and Central America may be disappearing each year. Such a rate of deforestation clearly threatens the survival of, if it has not already extinguished, thousands of native species. The Parties have therefore committed themselves to the ambitious goal of conserving the natural diversity of the largest and one of the most threatened "reservoirs" of species in the world.

A second objective of the Convention, also stated in the preamble, is to

[p]rotect and preserve scenery of extraordinary beauty, unusual and striking geologic formations, regions and natural objects of aesthetic, historic or scientific value, and areas characterized by primitive conditions in those cases covered by this Convention.

3. *Conservation of habitat*

The Western Hemisphere Convention was one of the first international agreements to emphasize the need to conserve habitats as a means of protecting species, and its primary focus is on the establishment of "national parks, national reserves, nature monuments and strict wilderness reserves". **[Definitions have been omitted. *See* Basic Document 6.1, article I.]**

b) *Establishment of protected areas*

Article II of the Convention requires its Parties to

[e]xplore at once the possibility of establishing in their territories national parks, national reserves, nature monuments and strict wilderness reserves as defined in the preceding article. In all cases where such establishment is feasible, the creation thereof shall be begun as soon as possible.

Where such establishment is impractical, it shall be done "as soon as ... circumstances will permit." Parties are required to notify the OAS of any national parks, national reserves, nature monuments and strict wilderness reserves which they have established, and of the legislation and methods of administrative control adopted in connection therewith.

Each of the four categories of protected area described by the Western Hemisphere Convention has been established by one or more Parties. National parks are the most widespread. The majority of Parties have at least one and some have considerably more.... "National reserves" are less common, and where the term "national reserve" has been used it has not always had the same meaning. In Peru, for example, national reserves denote an area set aside for the protection and propagation of species such as vicuna (*Vicugna vicugna*) where the intention is to promote controlled exploitation of the animal, whilst in Argentina they denote buffer zones between national parks and surrounding farmland. However, the practice of setting aside areas for the purpose of rational use of their natural resources, which is the basic concept behind the Convention's definition of national reserves, is widespread even if the terminology varies. The "national forests" of Brazil, Peru and the U.S.A., the "fiscal forests" of Uruguay and the "forest reserves" of Venezuela all have this kind of management objective.

Argentina, Chile, Paraguay and Venezuela all use the term "nature monument" or "natural monument" to describe an object or area which is strictly protected in much the same sense as is intended by the Western Hemisphere Convention. They are generally smaller than national parks, although the U.S. government's designation of 22.7 million hectares in Alaska as a "national monument" in 1978 is a major exception to this rule. Chile has also used the term to protect individual species—all specimens of Chilean false larch (*Fitzroya cupressoides*) and araucaria (*Araucaria araucana*) have been declared "natural monuments" under Chilean law.

The term "strict wilderness reserve" is not used by any Party *per se,* although the scientific zones of national parks that are closed to the public and many of the scientific and biological reserves of Brazil, Chile and Ecuador are all designed to protect remote and primitive land, which is the basic objective of a strict wilderness reserve. The U.S.A. comes closest to using the terminology of the Western Hemisphere Convention. The Wilderness Act of 1964 [16 U.S.C.A. § 1131 (1964)] establishes a National Wilderness Preservation System in the U.S.A. and defines wilderness as "an area where the earth and its community of life are untrammelled by man, where man is himself a visitor who does not remain". To qualify as wilderness, an area must, among other things, be under the control of the U.S. government and be at least five thousand acres in size. Wilderness areas may be established within national parks or national forests or as separate units.

In conclusion, a point of caution should be noted. There are many factors which may have influenced the decisions of Party governments to set up national parks, national reserves, nature monuments or strict wilderness reserves, and a desire to implement the Western Hemisphere Convention may or may not have been of practical significance. It is impossible to be certain how important the Convention has been to the establishment of protected areas in Party countries because Parties have never submitted reports to the OAS on measures they have taken to implement the Convention, and only a few of the domestic legislative or administrative instruments used by Parties to create protected areas refer back to the Convention as a source of legal authority or command. Nevertheless, correspondence with bureaucrats in national parks departments in Party countries indicates that the Convention has been of considerable value both in the conceptual development of habitat protection since 1940 and as a leverage to support their efforts to get protected areas established.

* * *

6. *Cooperation*

Article VI requires Parties "to cooperate among themselves in promoting the objectives of the present Convention" and, in particular, to assist each other with scientific research and field study, to "enter in to agreement with one another ... in order to increase the effectiveness of this collaboration" and to "make available to all the American Republics equally through publication or otherwise the scientific knowledge resulting from such cooperative effort."

Article VI is one of the most important articles of the Western Hemisphere Convention. So many of the species found in the Western Hemisphere are either migratory or are found in more than one country that mutual cooperation between Parties is essential if efforts to protect them are to succeed. In addition, the financial resources and technical expertise in wildlife management are so heavily weighted in favor of a few countries in the region that assistance to the poorer countries is vital if the latter are to be able to carry out sound scientific conservation policies. In 1976, after many years of relative inactivity in the field of cooperation, the General Assembly of OAS unanimously agreed

> [t]o urge the implementation of the Convention by the member states through mutual cooperation in activities such as scientific research and technical cooperation and assistance relating to wild flora and fauna, the creation, planning and training in the management of parks and reserves, the adoption of measures to conserve wild flora and fauna, and to protect species which are in danger of extinction.[2]

Whether as a result of the OAS resolution or not, there has unquestionably been an expansion in cooperative activities under the aegis of the Western Hemisphere Convention since the mid 1970s. . . .

11. Greg Block, *Independent Review of the North American Agreement for Environmental Cooperation (NAAEC)*, SB 79 ALI–ABA 291, May 15, 1997.

* * *

A. PRIORITY ENVIRONMENTAL ISSUES

* * *

A survey of critical environmental concerns expressed by government and nongovernmental organizations during the NAFTA debate that drove the creation of the NAAEC **[Basic Document 7.4]** shows that a number were linked directly or indirectly to expanded North American economic integration.

* * *

Biodiversity continues to play an important role in the environmental agenda of North America, in part, because it is so integral to the state of the environment, given the vast number of species which inhabit Canada, Mexico, and the United States. In North America, protecting biodiversity and habitats must be a shared responsibility, given the number of mammals, bird and even insect populations that straddle boundaries and migrate across borders.

2. *See* C. Freese & C. Wetterberg, *Cooperative Action under the Aegis of the Western Hemisphere Convention,* Final Report of Technical Meeting on Legal Aspects Related to the Convention on Nature Protection and Wildlife Preservation in the Western Hemisphere (March 1980), OAS Doc. OEA/Ser. J./XI, CICYT/Doc. 199, at 69.

Protecting the habitats of migratory species frequently implies protection for resident species as well.

* * *

One means of protecting biological diversity is by acceding to and enforcing various international conventions. All three North American countries have signed the United Nations Convention on Biological Diversity (the Biodiversity Convention) **[Basic Document 6.11]**. Its main objective is the conservation of biological diversity, the sustainable use of its components, and the fair and equitable sharing of the benefits arising out of the utilization of genetic resources. Other key commitments under the agreement include obligations to identify important components of biodiversity and monitor these components and the activities which are likely to have adverse effects on it and to establish laws to protect threatened species, and develop systems of protected areas to conserve biological diversity.

National strategies to safeguard biodiversity include protecting the most threatened and vulnerable species and their habitats. North America is responsible for 11 percent of the world's threatened species. Of this, Canada accounts for 0.8 percent, Mexico 4.7 percent, and the United States 5.5 percent.

* * *

One means of doing this is by protecting species' habitats. Overall, North America includes at least 190 million hectares of land and marine areas under national protection. This amounts to more than 9 percent of the total land area, which is significantly more than the 5 percent protected globally. The Biodiversity Convention encourages national targets for protected areas at 12 percent of total area.

* * *

B.   Some Linkages Between the Environment and Trade

* * *

Among the most important concerns of some environmentalists associated with NAFTA and trade agreements more broadly are: that increased competition will encourage countries to lower their environmental standards in order to attract investment, thereby creating so-called "pollution havens"; that increased industrial activity will lead to increased pollution and increased consumption of natural resources including fossil fuels thereby adding to an already overwhelming burden on an environment already under stress in many locales; that domestic and international environmental laws will be challenged as creating unnecessary trade barriers thereby threatening the integrity of multilateral agreements such as the Montreal Protocol or the Convention on the International Trade in Endangered Species (CITES) that include trade-restrictive provisions in order to facilitate their enforcement by parties; and, that countries would maintain high levels of environmental protection in theory, but in practice would reduce their emphasis on the enforcement of environmental laws, thereby providing domestic industry with a competitive advantage in an open market.

* * *

12. Raymond MacCallum, *Evaluating the Citizen Submission Procedure Under the North American Agreement on Environmental Cooperation*, 8 COLO. J. INT'L ENVTL. L. & Pol'y 395, 396-99, 401-02 (1997).

* * *

II. ENVIRONMENTAL CONCERNS WITH THE NAFTA

Although the NAFTA has been hailed as the "greenest" trade agreement ever, this claim is largely based on the fact that sustainable development and environmental protection get a few cursory mentions in the NAFTA, where such considerations are unprecedented in the history of trade agreements. In reality, it was the perceived failure of the NAFTA to seriously address the substantial concerns of environmentally conscientious critics that forced the development and adoption of the NAAEC **[Basic Document 7.4]**.

The primary concern with the NAFTA stemmed from the disparities between the environmental enforcement capacities of Mexico and the more effective regulatory regimes of the other parties.

* * *

Another concern . . . was that the NAFTA would prevent the use of unilateral trade measures to achieve positive environmental objectives. A related concern was that certain established environmental and human health standards could be successfully challenged as nontariff barriers under the NAFTA.

* * *

A final concern is that NGOs were generally dissatisfied with the degree of public participation and opportunity for input. . . . As NGOs had been responsible for putting environmental concerns on the NAFTA agenda, they arguably deserved a continued role in the oversight of trade and environment issues.

III. THE COMMISSION FOR ENVIRONMENTAL COOPERATION AND THE ARTICLE 14 PROCEDURE

* * *

Anyone residing or established in North America (including individuals, NGOs, and businesses) can bring a submission against any of the Parties to the NAAEC, alleging that that Party "is failing to effectively enforce its environmental laws."[3] Besides providing for documentary details, such as the requirement that the submitter be properly identified[4] and that the Party have been given prior notice of the matters alleged in the submission,[5] Article

---

3. NAAEC, [Basic Document 7.6] art. 14(1).   **5.** *See id.* art. 14(1)(e).

4. *Id.* art. 14(1)(b).

14(1) establishes discretionary criteria. Subsection (1)(c) requires that sufficient factual matters be alleged to allow the Secretariat to review the submission. Subsection (1)(d) requires that the submission have the purpose of promoting enforcement rather than of harassing industry.

If the Secretariat determines that the submission meets the subsection (1) criteria, it will then decide whether to request a response from the Party, based on factors enumerated in subsection (2).

* * *

The Party's response has the potential to halt the proceeding if the matter is currently the subject of a domestic "judicial or administrative proceeding."[6] Similarly, if in the discretion of the Secretariat the matter has been adequately explained, or if more appropriate domestic remedies exist, the submission can be dismissed. However, if the Secretariat determines that a Factual Record is warranted, and the Council exercises a two-thirds vote in support of the recommendation, then a Factual Record will be prepared by the Secretariat.

A Factual Record will merely be an objective evaluation and description of the matters asserted by the submitter and the Party. No judgment of wrong doing is contained in the Factual Record. Neither do any direct remedies flow from the preparation and publishing of a Factual Record. Any remedial power of the procedure lies only in its ability to shame the truant Party.

* * *

13.   Christopher N. Bolinger, *Assessing the CEC on its Record to Date*, 28 Law & Pol'y Int'l Bus. 1107, 1118-30 (1997).

* * *

B.   The Endangered Species Act Petition

In response to the first petition under article 14's citizen submission process, the Secretariat established its first precedent: a "failure to effectively enforce" a Party's environmental law cannot arise "from the enactment of a law which suspends the implementation of certain provisions of another statute."[7]

In July 1995, Earthlaw, a legal clinic at the University of Denver College of Law, filed an article 14 submission on behalf of one Mexican and four U.S. environmental groups alleging that the United States was failing to effectively enforce the Endangered Species Act (ESA). The allegation arose from lan-

---

6. *Id.* art. 14(3)(a). This is a reasonable safeguard against any potential interference with the sovereignty of judicial and administrative bodies. It is important to note that "judicial or administrative proceeding" is defined for purposes of Article 14(3), as:

(a) a domestic judicial, quasi-judicial or administrative action pursued by the Party in a timely fashion and in accordance with its law. Such actions comprise: mediation; arbitration; the process of issuing a license, permit, or authorization; seeking an assurance

of voluntary compliance or a compliance agreement; seeking sanctions or remedies in an administrative or judicial forum; and the process of issuing an administrative order; and

(b) an international dispute resolution proceeding to which the Party is a party.

7. Letter from Victor Lichtinger, Executive Director, Secretariat, to Earthlaw, University of Denver College of Law 2, 4 (Sept. 21, 1995) [hereinafter ESA Decision].

guage in a rider ... known as the "Hutchison Amendment," [which] rescinded $1.5 million from fiscal year 1995 funds used to determine whether species are "threatened" or "endangered" or whether a habitat is a "critical" one under the ESA. In addition, the Rescissions Act proscribed any compensation from other programs for the loss of funds.

Petitioners recognized that the NAAEC [**Basic Document 7.4**] explicitly preserves "the right of each Party to establish its own levels of domestic environmental protection and environmental development policies and priorities, and to adopt or modify accordingly its environmental laws and regulations."[8] However, petitioners complained that the Hutchison Amendment was neither a repeal nor a modification of the ESA, but rather the suspension of the ESA's enforcement ability.

Upon determining that the submission met the threshold criteria of NAAEC article 14(1), the Secretariat had to decide whether to request a response from the U.S. government and was guided by whether the goals of the NAAEC would be advanced by considering the matter under articles 14 and 15. The Secretariat concluded that the submission did not merit a response from the U.S. government and terminated the submission process.

The Secretariat reasoned that the NAAEC, read as a whole, "strongly suggest[s] that a failure to enforce environmental law applies [only] to the administrative agencies or officials charged with implementing laws and regulations."[9] The Secretariat pointed to several passages in the NAAEC that imply that legislative acts were not envisioned as failures to enforce. First, article 45(1) reads that "[a] Party has not failed to 'effectively enforce its environmental law' ... in a particular case where the action or inaction in question by agencies or officials of that Party" is a reasonable exercise of prosecutorial discretion or resource allocation.[10] The Secretariat opined that ascribing action or inaction to "agencies or officials" suggests that article 14 is directed at "administrative breakdowns (failures) resulting from acts or omissions of an agency or official charged with implementing environmental laws."[11]

* * *

Ultimately, the Secretariat viewed the Rescissions Act as a modification of the ESA, explicitly guaranteed by article 3 of the NAAEC.

* * *

C. THE TIMBER PETITION

In August 1995, while the ESA petition was pending, another citizen submission was filed challenging a different legislative act by the United States. [P]etitioners stated, the logging rider "provides that whatever environmental analysis is produced and whatever procedures are followed by federal agencies for such timber sales 'shall be deemed to satisfy the require-

---

8. Article 14 Submission, Endangered Species Act Enforcement, at 3 (filed on behalf of Biodiversity Legal Foundation) (SEM–95–001) (June 30,1995) [hereinafter ESA Submission] <http://www.cec.org/templates/registry-text.cfm? & varlan=english & documentid=1 & format=2> (visited Nov. 18, 1997).

9. ESA Decision, *supra* note 7, at 3.

10. NAAEC, art. 45 (1).

11. ESA Decision, *supra* note 7, at 3.

ments' of several specifically listed and 'all other applicable Federal environmental and natural resources laws.' "[12] Accordingly, timber sales affected by the logging rider were "not subject to challenge for violations of such laws."[13]

As in its response to the ESA submission, the Secretariat again considered the logging rider to be a legislative modification of preexisting environmental law that "becomes a part of the greater body of laws and statutes on the books."[14] Applying the precedent set forth in its ESA decision, the Secretariat could not "characterize the application of a new legal regime as a failure to enforce an old one" under article 14.[15] Accordingly, the Secretariat declined to request a response from the United States and terminated the petition process.

* * *

D. The Cozumel Pier Petition

The third citizen submission for discussion was the first to move the Secretariat to request a response from any Party. In January 1996, three Mexican groups submitted an article 14 petition which alleged a failure by Mexican environmental authorities to effectively enforce a law requiring the presentation of an Environmental Impact Assessment (EIA) in regard to the development of a port terminal and related works on the resort island of Cozumel, Mexico.

Under Mexico's General Law of Environmental Protection and Ecological Balance (General Ecology Law), an environmental impact review by the National Ecology Institute is required of projects that could cause ecological imbalance or could exceed statutorily prescribed environmental conditions.[16] Though developers of Cozumel pier had an EIA approved by the government, the submitters argued that ... [among other allegations] the pier project is located within ... a natural area safeguarded under Mexican law.

The Cozumel petition met the threshold requirements of article 14(1). In determining whether to request a response from Mexico under article 14(2), the Secretariat noted—in considering the "harm prong" of the article 14(2) analysis–"the importance and character of the resource in question," the "magnificent" Paradise Coral Reef just off Cozumel in the Caribbean.[17] Significantly, the Secretariat "recognized that the submitters may not have

---

12. Emergency Supplemental Appropriations for Additional Disaster Assistance, for Antiterrorism Initiative, for Assistance in the Recovery from the Tragedy that Occurred at Oklahoma City, and Rescissions Act, 1995, § 2001(i)(1)-(8), Pub. L. No. 104–19, 109 Stat. 194 [hereinafter Rescissions Act II].

13. Article 14 Submission, Rescissions Act and Environmental Enforcement (filed by the Sierra Club et al. with The Commission For Environmental Cooperation, (SEM–95–002) (Aug. 30, 1995) at 3 (visited Nov. 16, 1997) <http://www.cec.org/cgi-shl/dbml.ex ...rytex & varlan-english & documentid–6> [hereinafter Timber Submission].

14. Determination Pursuant to Article 14 & 15 of the North American Agreement on Environmental Cooperation: Submission I.D. SEM–95–002, (Dec. 8, 1995) at 3 [hereinafter Timber Decision].

15. Id.

16. Law of Environmental Protection and Ecological Balance (General Ecology Law), in Diario Oficial de la Federacion, Jan. 28, 1988, at 24–57, tit. 1, ch. V, arts. 28 & 32, at 33 [hereinafter General Ecology Law].

17. Recommendation of the Secretariat to Council for the Development of a Factual Record in Accordance with Articles 14 & 15 of the North American Agreement on Environmental Cooperation: Submission I.D. SEM–96–001 (June 7, 1996) at 3 [hereinafter Cozumel Recommendation].

alleged the particularized, individual harm required to acquire legal standing to bring suit in some civil proceedings in North America," but found that the "especially public nature of marine resources [brought] the submitters within the spirit and intent of [a]rticle 14...."[18] Furthermore, the submitters had exhausted their local remedies, primarily by making use of the "denuncia popular" (public denunciation) administrative procedure.[19] Finally, the Secretariat determined that further study of the Cozumel pier situation " 'would substantially promote' the objectives of the NAAEC."[20] As a result, the Secretariat requested a response from the Mexican government in February 1996.

In its March 1996 response to the Secretariat, Mexico primarily claimed that an EIA for pier-related off-shore works was premature pending authorization of the work by the Secretary of Communication and Transportation (SCT). In addition, the government asserted that the submitters had not exhausted their remedies, namely a civil suit to redress environmental harm, which demands actual, individualized harm and is rarely recognized in Mexican courts. A third argument posited that the submitters had failed to show that the alleged failure to enforce Mexican environmental law had caused their organizations to suffer direct harm as a consequence under article 14(2)(a).

Despite Mexico's assertions, in June 1996 the Secretariat indicated the possibility of a failure to enforce environmental law and recommended to the Council that a factual record be prepared.

* * *

At their annual meeting in August 1996, the CEC Council unanimously voted to approve the preparation of a factual record. After voting to move forward, Mexico's Secretary for Environment, Natural Resources and Fisheries, Julia Carabias, agreed to halt further development of the Cozumel Pier project until the Secretariat could complete its investigation.

IV. ANALYSIS

The NAAEC and its implementing institution, the CEC, were much criticized by many in the environmental community as weak political constructs that would fail to adequately address the environmental problems that would stem from the liberalization of trade represented by NAFTA. In the wake of the CEC's activities to date, such criticism has not abated and has indicted the institution on several counts: (1) the CEC is insufficiently independent and therefore has to "pull its punches" when reporting on environmental problems or investigating failures to enforce; (2) it is a "toothless" institution with no power to enforce its recommendations; and (3) its procedures are suspect and provide for inadequate transparency and public participation.

* * *

18. *Id.*

19. *Id.*

20. *Id.* at 3.

A. CRITICISMS

1. The Political Issue

Critics contend that the CEC is "strapped into a political straight-jacket" because its Council is comprised of political appointees who are necessarily limited in their ability to respond to citizen complaints.

* * *

However, by placing full power in political representatives of the Parties, the NAAEC preserves internationally accepted notions of national sovereignty, democratic accountability, and the ability of the institution's creators and fund suppliers to manage their creation. Political accountability need not be considered a weakness in international organizations; rather, the governments of Mexico, Canada, and the United States have ensured their own accountability by establishing the CEC.

* * *

Similarly, the Secretariat's decisions concerning the complaint that U.S. legislative riders to appropriations bills were failures to effectively enforce environmental laws are equally politically accountable and not the disaster that critics contend. Certainly, a strict reading of the NAAEC leaves room for the contention that using legislation to cut off funding for certain enforcement activities is a failure to effectively enforce the underlying law. But the Secretariat laid out reasoning in the ESA and Timber decisions for which it is ultimately politically accountable. Furthermore, the U.S. Congress itself remains accountable for its decision to modify its environmental laws or the funding thereof.

* * *

2. Teeth?

[M]any feel that a lack of enforcement power renders the CEC worthless, and bemoan the fact that if a factual record developed under articles 14 and 15 indicates a failure of effective enforcement, citizens can only depend upon another Party to pursue sanctions against the offending Party. Such criticism ignores the fact that even the formalized moral power of the CEC provides a benefit for the environment and a tool for environmentalists. Never before have U.S. citizens had the opportunity to challenge environmental enforcement activities in Mexico (or vice versa). Perhaps even more important is the fact that Mexican citizens now have an extremely accessible formal means to attack weak enforcement efforts in their own country. . . .

* * *

Furthermore, it is not entirely clear that a CEC with strong enforcement powers would be beneficial for the environment. In fact, it has even been suggested that a strengthened CEC would necessarily alter the complex interaction between the legislature, the executive, and the judiciary behind U.S. regulation and result in a "reduction in agency-and-technology-forcing statutes and a lessening of the substantive scope of environmental legislation."[21] Environmental regulation, it is posited, is an interactive process

---

21. Kal Raustiala, *The Political Implications of the Enforcement Provisions of the NAFTA Environmental Side Agreement: The CEC* as a Model for Future Accords, *25 ENVT'L. L. 31 (1995)*.

whereby "the legislature sets sweeping but ambiguous standards, the executive agencies employ limited and sporadic application of the statutes, and environmental and industry groups challenge the legislation and its enforcement in the courts."[22] If a supernational body such as the CEC were to step into this process with a strong enforcement hand, and, for example, aggressively sanction the United States for a persistent pattern of non-enforcement of air quality standards in Los Angeles, it is feared that environmental statutes would lessen in substantive scope in order to bring regulation in line with actual outcomes and to increase the total degree of enforcement. For the same reasons, Congress might institute lesser regulatory standards, such as "regulating in the public interest," in lieu of more protective ones, and technology-forcing statutes would become less common. Thus, it is possible that sharper teeth for the CEC could actually diminish environmental quality.

3.   Transparency and Public Participation

The environmental NGO community generally believes that public input is important for bringing about political decision-making that will account for the environment. Several factors, including the lack of public input, an inability for NGOs to be heard, secret dispute resolution procedures, and the "unavailability of even basic documentation" have given other international agreements such as the World Trade Organization (WTO) a bad reputation among environmentalists. In this context, NAAEC needed to meet a very high standard of openness. While it succeeds to a great degree and represents a tremendous step forward from prior trade agreements, there is room for further improvement.

The NAAEC provides unprecedented access to international decision-making institutions through the article 13 and 14 mechanisms. A key element to this open scheme is a public registry of submissions and responses. Furthermore, the Council must hold public meetings; the Secretariat's annual report must be made public; and a voice for NGOs is provided by the Joint Public Advisory Committee.

Prior to its enactment, critics contended that article 14 placed strict limitations on citizen complaints. The record to date shows that there is little truth to this contention. No petitioner has yet failed the article 14(1) threshold requirements, and the Cozumel petition indicates that very little is required in terms of standing to petition. It appears that so long as some degree of harm is asserted, the submission is not drawn exclusively from mass media reports, submitters have utilized the legal means available to them, and the claim of a failure to enforce is not derived from a legislative act, the Secretariat shall request a response from the Party alleged to have failed to enforce their environmental laws.

* * *

14. Kal Raustiala, *International "Enforcement of Enforcement" Under the North American Agreement on Environmental Cooperation*, 36 Va. J. Int'l L. 721, 732, 744-45 (1996).

* * *

---

22. *Id.* at 47.

The core issue in an article 14 proceeding is an assertion of a failure to effectively enforce environmental law. Under the NAAEC [**Basic Document 7.4**], a Party has not failed to effectively enforce its environmental law where the

> action or inaction in question by agencies or officials of that Party ... reflects a reasonable exercise of their discretion in respect of investigatory, prosecutorial, regulatory or compliance matters; or ... results from bona fide decisions to allocate resources to enforcement in respect of other environmental matters determined to have higher priorities.[23]

Hence, failure to enforce environmental law appears to be defined, negatively, as unreasonable or arbitrary actions by "agencies or officials" which undermine or otherwise severely diminish enforcement.

II.   SUBMISSIONS, RESCISSIONS, AND RESPONSES

* * *

A.   The NAAEC and Enforcement

The Secretariat's argument, that the NAAEC ... leads to a purely "executive" definition of enforcement and that the legislative riders in question constitute new laws, is a reasonable one.

* * *

The obvious starting point is how the treaty itself defines "enforcement." The enforcement actions enumerated in article 5—appointing and training inspectors, engaging in on-site inspections, providing for search and seizure, using licenses and permits—although not exhaustive, can only be understood as traditional actions of the executive. None of the actions listed are exclusive responsibilities of Congress, while nearly all are typically undertaken solely by the President.... In short, when the NAAEC defines enforcement illustratively it relies on actions which are generally undertaken by the executive branch. The clear implication, and the one inferred by the Secretariat in its response, is that for the purposes of the NAAEC enforcement is an executive rather than a legislative act.

* * *

15.   Noemi Gal–Or, *Private Party Direct Access: A Comparison of the NAFTA and the EU Disciplines*, 21 B.C. INT'L & COMP. L. REV. 1, 3, 4 (1998).

I.   INTRODUCTION: THE RELEVANCE OF LOCUS STANDI
FOR PRIVATE PARTIES IN NAFTA AND IN THE EU

The right to bring an action and have standing (locus standi) in a legal dispute has become increasingly significant.... The territorial state gradually but consistently is making room for supranational entities to partake in a variety of affairs which, for the last three hundred years, were considered to be the state's absolute prerogative. At the same time, numerous voices are demanding that similar rights be accorded to individuals as well. The individ-

---

23. NAAEC, art. 45(1).

ual is understood to be more than a private person. Thus, the individual's welfare is embodied in the notion of "public interest." This broader aspect of communalism needs to be taken into consideration as lawmakers create policies, the effects of which are no longer just local, but regional and international as well. Universally noted ... the drafters of large and complex international economic institution-establishing treaties have largely ignored the role to be played by individuals and non-state actors in general.

* * *

Observations made almost thirty years ago about the shortcomings of the status of the individual person as a subject of international law are still valid today. When considering the individual as an actor in international trade, the following explanation continues to apply:

> [t]he position of the individual as the subject of international law [is] greatly obscured by a failure to distinguish between the recognition of rights enuring to the benefit of the individual and the enforceability of these rights at his instance. The fact that the beneficiary is incapable of taking independent steps in his own name to enforce them does not signify that he is not a subject of the law or that the rights in question are vested exclusively in the agency which possesses the capacity to enforce them.[21]

This contention has been strengthened by the recognition of the intertwining relationship between foreign and domestic policies.... Of great significance, especially concerning representative democracies, is the fact that by creating international legal regimes (e.g., trade, security, culture), governments bind their citizens to laws. The citizens, however, play an extremely limited role in the creation of these laws.... [T]he ensuing weakening of representative democratic institutions is exacerbated by the fact that, in practice, civil rights can be compensated for by the possession of economic might. In this process, economic inequality undermines formal legal equality. "Big business" easily exerts leverage within national and international systems in ways unavailable to ordinary persons, small businesses, and nonprofit, non-governmental organizations (NGOs).

Second, international lawmaking through inter-governmental agreements only unsystematically and partially harmonizes law among the signatory states. Consequently, different domestic laws providing for varying degrees of access to justice bind citizens in different countries belonging to the same international legal regime. This results in varied access to justice.

* * *

16. Kal Raustiala, _The "Participatory Revolution" in International Environmental Law_, 21 HARV. ENVTL. L. REV. 537, 538, 542, 549, 551, 558-61, 565-67 (1997).

* * *

---

24. Nkambo Mugerna, _Subjects of International Law, in_ MANUAL OF PUBLIC INTERNATIONAL LAW 249, 318 (Max Sorensen ed., 1986).

Treaties are by definition interstate compacts, and generally only states may negotiate them and undertake their obligations. But while states have traditionally been the dominant actors in the creation and maintenance of conventional international law, recent changes in international environmental law have afforded a historically unparalleled opportunity for participation by private, nongovernmental organizations ("NGOs"). As has long been the case in domestic environmental law, NGOs are now major actors in the formulation, implementation, and enforcement of international environmental law.

* * *

[N]GOs have been increasingly incorporated into what were previously "states-only" governance activities, and the scope, type, and scale of their activities are much greater today then ever before. This shift in both formal and informal participation represents a notable evolution when contrasted with historical practice.

* * *

Most of the pre–1987 multilateral treaties are either silent on the subject of NGO access or grant only very limited access. The trend over time has been towards greater procedural guarantees for NGOs, and in practice NGOs have become much more active. CITES **[Basic Document 6.5]** stands out as the first major multilateral treaty to incorporate NGOs in an active way, and is clearly a landmark in this regard. Some regional accords are also notable. The recently negotiated environmental side agreement to NAFTA, the North American Agreement on Environmental Cooperation ("NAAEC") **[Basic Document 7.4]** goes further than most multilateral treaties in terms of NGO access and participation. Under the NAAEC, NGOs may submit claims to the treaty Secretariat asserting that a party to the NAEEC is failing to effectively enforce its domestic environmental law. Such claims may trigger an investigation and action by the Secretariat, to which NGOs are encouraged to submit opinions. There is no explicit technical criteria that NGOs must meet. NGO members may also serve on the arbitral panels created to assess the merits of and actions addressing such submissions.

* * *

Overall, there has been a proliferation of opportunities for NGOs to make official statements to state delegations, to present documents, and to receive working government documents as they appear. Legal proposals from NGOs are occasionally introduced by sympathetic national delegations, and NGO members have become part of national delegations, even those of countries of which they are not citizens.

* * *

In short, procedural guarantees of access for private actors have been increasing in international environmental law, but such guarantees have varied in degree and kind both across and within the law. CITES aside, NGO access is not a recognized right, yet the requirements for denial of access are increasingly stringent and in practice denial is a rare event. Nonetheless,

NGOs are often barred from informal meetings, and their access to such meetings is very much at the whim of the delegations involved.

* * *

A. THE BENEFITS OF NGO PARTICIPATION

* * *

1. Policy Research and Development

International environmental law increasingly establishes policies aimed at the alleviation of a number of transboundary and global problems. Many global and regional environmental issues are relatively novel and highly complex, and little experience exists to guide the policy-making process. . . . But large, expertly staffed, and often well-funded NGOs exist that devote considerable effort and resources to policy research and development and often possess substantial international expertise on environmental policy. By involving such NGOs in the policy process, governments gain reasonably accurate, efficacious, and creative policy advice from many independent sources, and are able to move these research costs "off-budget."

[N]GOs provide perspectives and ideas that may not have emerged from a bureaucratic review process. This is particularly important for developing countries, which often lack not only the resources but the intellectual infrastructure and expertise to allow adequate policy evaluation and creation.

* * *

2. Monitoring

a. Of Parties

By increasing the transparency of the lawmaking process through procedural guarantees to private actors, states also increase their own information base about what other states are doing. Governments often resist information-gathering by other governments or by international organizations.

* * *

b. Of Delegations

* * *

NGO participation in international law-making is one means by which governments can create fire alarms and allow outside parties to alert them to delegation actions. NGOs, as interested parties, have an incentive both to monitor delegations and to inform government actors of their findings.

* * *

3. Political Concerns

Ratification and implementation are essential to the effectiveness of international environmental agreements. As noted, the failure to satisfy domestic interests can cause the rejection of a proposed international accord. One strategy to reduce the likelihood of ratification failure is to include important domestic players, including NGOs, in the process of international negotiations. Directly involving societal actors in the negotiations process enhances the flow of information and may win the support of skeptics and opponents. By involving NGOs in the process, governments also gain information about NGO preferences with respect to various policy options.

* * *

B.   INCORPORATING STAKEHOLDERS

* * *

The belief that participation by private sector organizations is good for the environment, promotes sustainable development, and is ethically progressive was first reflected in a major international document in the 1987 report of the World Commission on Environment and Development (popularly known as the Brundtland Commission). The Commission advised that

> [a]t the national level, governments, foundations, and industry should also greatly extend their cooperation with NGOs in planning, monitoring, and evaluating as well as carrying out projects when they can provide the necessary capabilities on a cost-effective basis. To this end, governments should establish or strengthen procedures for official consultation and more meaningful participation by NGOs in all relevant organizations.[25]

The Rio Declaration on Environment and Development **[Basic Document 1.29]** and Agenda 21, **[Basic Document 1.30]** the chief documents that emerged from UNCED, also favor private sector participation. The Rio Declaration states that "[e]nvironmental issues are best handled with the participation of all concerned citizens, at the relevant level."[26] Agenda 21 proposes that the UN system "provide increased financial and administrative support for non-governmental organizations and their self-organized networks, in particular those based in developing countries ... to enhance their partnership role in programme design and implementation."[27] Agenda 21 further advocates that the UN system design open and effective means to achieve the participation of non-governmental organizations, including those related to major groups, in the process established to review and evaluate the implementation of Agenda 21 at all levels and promote their contribution to it; [and t]ake into account the findings of review systems and evaluation processes of non-governmental organizations in relevant reports.[28]

These statements, while legally non-binding, are more than mere rhetoric; they reflect an increasingly common view that Professor Phillipe Sands has stated succinctly: "[s]tates can no longer claim to be the sole holders of the right to participate in the international legal order and its processes, having been joined by a new range of actors."[29]

---

25. WORLD COMMISSION ON ENVIRONMENT AND DEVELOPMENT, OUR COMMON FUTURE 328 (1987).

26. Rio Declaration on Environment and Development, U.N. Conference on Environment and Development, at 3 (principle 10) U.N. Doc. A/CONF.151/5 (1992).

27. Agenda 21, United Nations Conference on Environment and Development, U.N. Doc. A/CONF.151/4 (Part III), at 22 (1992) (¶ 27.12).

28. *Id.* (part IV), at 52 (1992) (¶ 38.43).

29. Phillipe Sands, *Introduction to Lee Kimbal, Environmental Law and Policy in* GREENING INTERNATIONAL LAW 122 (Phillipe J. Sands ed., 1993).

17. RESTATEMENT (THIRD) OF THE FOREIGN RELATIONS LAW OF THE UNITED STATES (1987), § 111.

§ 111. INTERNATIONAL LAW AND AGREEMENTS AS LAW OF THE UNITED STATES

(1) International law and international agreements of the United States are law of the United States and supreme over the law of the several States.

(2) Cases arising under international law or international agreements of the United States are within the Judicial Power of the United States and, subject to Constitutional and statutory limitations and requirements of justiciability, are within the jurisdiction of the federal courts.

(3) Courts in the United States are bound to give effect to international law and to international agreements of the United States, except that a "non-self-executing" agreement will not be given effect as law in the absence of necessary implementation.

(4) An international agreement of the United States is "non-self-executing"

(a) if the agreement manifests an intention that it shall not become effective as domestic law without the enactment of implementing legislation,

(b) if the Senate in giving consent to a treaty, or Congress by resolution, requires implementing legislation, or

(c) if implementing legislation is constitutionally required.

18. RESTATEMENT (THIRD) OF THE FOREIGN RELATIONS LAW OF THE UNITED STATES § 906, comments (1986).

Private Remedies For Violation of International Law

A private person, whether natural or juridical, injured by a violation of an international obligation by a state, may bring a claim against that state or assert that violation as a defense

(a) in a competent international forum when the state has consented to the jurisdiction of that forum with respect to such private claims;

(b) in a court or other tribunal of that state pursuant to its law; or

(c) in a court or other tribunal of the injured person's state of nationality or of a third state, pursuant to the law of such state, subject to limitations under international law.

[Comment:]

a. International remedies available to private persons. International tribunals and other fora are generally not open to claims by private persons. However, the increasing recognition of the rights of private persons, whether natural or juridical, under international law, has led to a variety of remedies and arrangements to protect these rights. A few international agreements have given private persons access to an international forum where the agreement establishing the forum allows such extension of its jurisdiction.

* * *

b.   Domestic remedies for private persons. Private remedies against a state in a domestic forum for violations of international law are subject to the law of the forum and to the limitations imposed by international law.

* * *

19.   RESTATEMENT (THIRD) OF THE FOREIGN RELATIONS LAW OF THE UNITED STATES § 907, comments (1986).

Private Remedies For Violation of International Law: Law of The United
    States

(1) A private person having rights against the United States under an international agreement may assert those rights in courts in the United States of appropriate jurisdiction either by way of claim or defense.

(2) A private person having rights against a foreign state under an international agreement of the United States may assert those rights against that state in courts in the United States of appropriate jurisdiction by way of claim or defense, subject to limitations under international law.

[Comment:]

a.   Claims under international agreements of the United States. This section applies only to claims based on an international agreement to which the United States is a party. In principle this section applies not only to United States nationals but also to foreign individuals and foreign corporations even if they are not resident or doing business in the United States, provided they meet other jurisdictional requirements. However, a plaintiff who is a foreign national without any important link to the United States is likely to face the obstacle of forum non conveniens in a claim against a foreign state. Hence, it would be possible for him to bring a claim against another state, even under a United States treaty, only in exceptional circumstances, such as those discussed in s 453, Reporters' Note 4.

International agreements, even those directly benefiting private persons, generally do not create private rights or provide for a private cause of action in domestic courts, but there are exceptions with respect to both rights and remedies. Whether an international agreement provides a right or requires that a remedy be made available to a private person is a matter of interpretation of the agreement.

* * *

b.   Jurisdiction of federal courts over claims for violations of international law. The remedies indicated in this section may be in either State or federal courts. Federal courts have jurisdiction over cases arising under international law and international agreements of the United States.* * *

20.   Lakshman D. Guruswamy, *The Convention on Biological Diversity: A Polemic*, *in* PROTECTION OF GLOBAL BIODIVERSITY-CONVERGING STRATEGIES 350, 354 (Lakshman Guruswamy & Jeffrey McNeely eds., 1998).

Although the collective obligation to protect biodiversity was seen by the United Nations Environmental Programme, the World Conservation Union, and numerous other nongovernmental organizations as constituting the foundations of the new treaty, the CBD rejects such an obligation, instead proclaiming that states have the "sovereign right to exploit their own resources pursuant to their own environmental policies" (Article 3). In a similar vein, the CBD rejects the principle that biodiversity is the natural heritage of humankind. Accepting biodiversity as our common natural heritage gives rise to the corollary obligation that we protect and preserve such a heritage. Instead, the CBD settles for an effete and legally nonbinding recitation that biodiversity is the common "concern" of humankind. Furthermore, the attenuated affirmation that "biodiversity is a common concern of humankind" is found only in the Preamble, even though it ranked as a fundamental principle throughout the drafting process.

Even when the CBD attempts to protect biological diversity by *in situ* conservation, *ex situ* conservation, and sustainable use in Articles 6–14, it makes sure that every obligation assumed (except those related to research, training, education, and public awareness) yield to the caveat: "as far as possible and as appropriate." Moreover, Article 7, which deals with the key elements of identification and monitoring, allows each contracting party to do such identification. This contrasts with earlier expectations and drafts that provided for the establishment of Global Lists of Biogeographic Areas of Particular Importance for the Conservation of Biological Diversity and of Species Threatened with Extinction on a Global Scale to be internationally, not nationally, determined.

21. James Stephen Carpenter, *Farm Chemicals, Soil Erosion, and Sustainable Agriculture*, 13 STAN. ENVTL. L. J. 190, 201, 216-17, 219-20 (1994).

Nitrogen, phosphorous, and potassium are widely used as fertilizers on the nation's major crops. In 1960, these fertilizers were used at a rate of about seven million tons per year. The annual total is now over nineteen million tons. A significant portion, perhaps about half, of all fertilizers remain unused by the planted crop. The unused fertilizers may contaminate soil and water by attaching to organic matter or by leaching into the soil and groundwater directly. Long-term studies show that significant increases in nitrate concentration in groundwater are strongly correlated with overlying agricultural use.

* * *

C. Wildlife and Modern Farming

Fertilizers, pesticides, and erosion all kill wildlife directly, and perhaps more importantly, alter and destroy habitats. Most extensively studied are the effects of waterway pollution. In a comprehensive study of the off-farm impacts of soil erosion, Clark observed:

> Aquatic ecosystems can be seriously affected by sediment and other erosion-related contaminants in complex ways. Sediment can destroy spawning areas, food sources, and habitat as well as directly damage fish, crustaceans, and other aquatic wildlife. Algal growth stimulated by nutrients also blocks sunlight, and pesticides and other contaminants carried off agricultural lands can be directly toxic to fish. The National Fisheries Survey identified agricultural runoff as chronically affecting fish

communities in thirty percent of the nation's waters, and fish kill reports have identified such runoff as a major cause of acute episodes.[30]

At least half, and perhaps seventy percent, of all land-based nutrients reaching surface waterways come from agriculture. Nutrient runoff levels from fertilizers are sometimes high enough to kill fish directly. Most damage results from eutrophication, the excessive nutrient enrichment of water which causes high rates of plant growth and subsequent decay. Phosphorus and nitrates, the two main nutrients from agriculture, can have a "devastating effect on many lakes, rivers, and bays" by stimulating excessive algal growth.[31] Changes in vegetation growth caused by the unnatural algal growth "can have serious repercussions throughout a food chain."[32] Fish populations, for example, may increase in the early stages of eutrophication, but later decline, since "as algae die and decay, they use oxygen, sometimes reducing the oxygen levels so much that some fish species can no longer survive."[33]

* * *

How should we evaluate this damage to wildlife? Clark observes that "little is known about the overall magnitude of these impacts [on biological communities], and there is no commonly accepted methodology for placing economic values on them."[34] That wildlife generally do not have a readily acceptable market price should not imply that this damage has little value. The several billion dollars spent each year on wildlife conservation suggests the opposite. In fact, surveys demonstrate that many Americans place a high value on wildlife, both as hunters and as nonconsumptive users who, for example, participate in hiking or bird watching. As Clark concludes: "The absence of an estimate of damage costs to biological communities, however, should not be taken as an indication that the impacts are small. They are not. If there were appropriate procedures for placing economic values on these damages, this category might well outweigh any of the others."[35]

D.   Adding Up the Negatives

The social costs of conventional agriculture are significant, and in light of the lack of knowledge regarding some dangers, particularly the health effects of farm chemicals, the costs may be much greater than we know. Both pesticides and fertilizers present health risks for the population as a whole, and even more serious dangers for farmers, farmworkers, and their families. Soil erosion may not literally threaten agricultural productivity over the next few decades, but if ethical issues of generational equity are considered, or if doubts about the market's ability to act as a conserver of soil prove justified, the sustainability of the land may well be in question. Further, in purely economic terms, the off-farm costs to society from pesticides and soil erosion amount to at least three billion dollars annually. Finally, conventional farming causes incalculable damage to fish and wildlife.

* * *

30. Edwin H. Clark et. al., Eroding Soils: The Off-Farm Impacts at xv (1995); *see also* Judith D. Soule & Jon K. Piper, Farming in Nature's Image: An Ecological Approach to Agriculture 15 (1992). . . .

31. National Research Council, Alternative Agriculture 85, at 100 (1989). . . .

32. Clark, *supra* note 30, at 110.

33. *Id.* at 7–8. . . .

34. *Id.* at xv.

35. *Id.*

22.   Convention on Biological Diversity, June 5, 1992, *reprinted in* **31 I.L.M. 818 (1992)** [Basic Document 6.11].

23.   Editors' Note. Five years have elapsed since the coming into force of the much heralded United Nations Convention on Biological Diversity (CBD) **[Basic Document 6.11]** signed at the "Earth Summit" at Rio de Janeiro in June 1992. Despite the warm, even euphoric welcome extended to this treaty by the environmental community, the difficulties of implementing the CBD in the last five years are unmasking and uncovering its flawed environmental foundations. The language of any legal instrument embodies and expresses the considered intentions of its creators, and may contain obligatory provisions that are legally binding. They may also contain hortatory and aspirational commitments that are not legally enforceable. The CBD rejected "hard" environmental obligations that are legally binding for non-legal exhortations, and highly qualified "soft" commitments. Whatever be their value as face-saving strategies for reaching agreement on the CBD, such aspirational expressions do not create a stable foundation for tough decisions in the world of realpolitik.

The implementation of the CBD in the last five years has resulted in a proliferation of bureaucracies and agencies, including a Clearing House Mechanism (CHM), A Subsidiary Body on Scientific Technical and Technological Advice (SBSTTA), a Ad Hoc Working Group on Biosafety (BSWG), and the Global Environment Facility (GEF), the designated interim institutional structure for financial mechanisms. These bodies and their multiplying staff, were created by four major meetings of the supreme decision-making body of the CBD–the Conference of the Parties (COP)–held in 1994 (Bahamas), 1995 (Jakarta), 1996 (Buenos Aires), and 1998 (Bratislava). While many within the expanding bureaucracies and attendees at these large meetings, are showering their projects with lavish praise, a number of objective reviewers examining the achievement of the CBD, are noting the paucity of what has been accomplished in the last five years.[36]

Some of the recent criticisms leveled against the implementation of the CBD include the charges that the truncation of "sustainable use" from "conservation" has impeded the advance of sustainable development, that the different legal obligations imposed on the parties has hampered progress on substantive issues, and that the parties have failed to address forest issues.[37] This comment[38] will argue that these and other problems of implementation stem from fundamental constitutive weaknesses of the CBD.

First, the CBD rejects the concept of sustainable development by prioritizing economic growth over environmental protection, and allows international resources earmarked for the protection of biodiversity to be expended on economic growth that could destroy biodiversity. Second, it denies state responsibility for damage to the global commons. Finally, it repudiates the

---

36. Chris Wold, *The Futility, Utility, and Future of the Biodiversity Convention*, 9 Colo. J. Int'l Envtl. L. & Pol'y 1 (1998); Marc Pallemaerts, *International Environmental law in the Age of Sustainable Development: A Critical Assessment of the UNCED Process*, 15 J. L. & Com. 623 (1996).

37. *See* Wold, *supra* note 36.

38. The criticisms of the CBD are based on, and reproduce portions of: Lakshman D. Guruswamy, *The Convention on Biological Diversity: A Polemic*, in Protection of Global Biodiversity: Converging Strategies 351–359 (Lakshman D. Guruswamy & Jeffrey A. Mc Neely eds., 1998).

idea that the plant, animal, insect, and genetic resources of the world (our biodiversity) are the common heritage of humankind and that it is the responsibility of the community of nations to protect this heritage.

To begin, the Convention rejects the concept of sustainable development—the very *grundnorm* of the Earth Summit. Sustainable development has not been authoritatively defined, but its key attributes are identifiable. In essence, it calls for economic growth that can relieve the great poverty of the less developed countries (LDCs), based on policies that sustain and expand the environmental resource base Consequently, sustainable development becomes environmentally sensitive development that meets the needs of the present generation without compromising the ability of future generations to meet their own needs.[39]

Sustainable development, therefore, gives parity of status to economic growth and environmental protection. It rejects economic development and growth that is not environmentally sensitive or destroys the resource base. It is a new concept precisely because it embraces both development and environmental protection. But, the Convention states both in its Preamble and in critical articles dealing with the financing of the Convention that "economic and social development and poverty eradication are the first and overriding priorities of developing countries" (Preamble; *see* Art. 20(4)). By diminishing environmental protection, the Convention effectively disowns sustainable development. The CBD goes even further than subjugating biodiversity to development, it empowers developing countries subjectively to determine what constitutes development.

This diminishing of biodiversity, and accentuation of development subjectively defined is confirmed by the financial provisions. To enable LDCs to implement the Convention, developed countries agree both to pay the "full incremental costs" of such implementation (Art. 20(2)) and to transfer technology to LDCs (Art.16). An examination of the commitments of developing countries, in exchange for this transfer of money and technology, is revealing. The Convention lucidly states that "economic and social development and eradication of poverty are the first and overriding priorities of the developing country Parties" (Art. 20(4)). Having made the overriding principle clear, it then develops the implementing structure. The institutional structures as well as the "policy, strategy, programme priorities and eligibility criteria relating to" access to those transferred resources and technologies will be determined by the Conference of the Parties to the Convention (Art. 21(1)).

Where does this leave us? In the absence of an explicit commitment to protect biodiversity, any resources transferred under the Convention could be used by a small minority of zealous developing countries to advance their own concept of economic and social development. If, for example, they decide that road building, "reclamation" for beach development and marinas, or even the cutting down of tropical forests is necessary for economic and social development, they would be acting within the powers and privileges granted to them.

A somewhat foreboding omen of the future direction of the Convention is offered by its treatment of tropical rain forests. It is estimated that tropical forests are home to at least fifty percent of plant and insect diversity.[40] Yet all

39. WORLD COMMISSION ON ENVIRONMENT AND DEVELOPMENT, OUR COMMON FUTURE 1—8 (1987).

40. *Id.* at 151; Norman Myers, *Tropical forests and their species: Going, going ...?, in*

references to tropical forests, contained in the earlier drafts of the CBD proposed by conservation organizations, were systematically and deliberately, excised from the Convention.[41]

Second, the Convention tilts against an emerging and developing pattern of regional customary and treaty law that, in the last fifty or so years, has sought to establish the common responsibility of humankind to protect biodiversity.[42] Many involved in the development of international environmental law hoped that the Convention would consolidate these endeavors, and provide an instrument that dealt comprehensively, globally, and more specifically with the nature of the obligation to protect biodiversity. Instead, the Convention contains no substantive obligation to protect biodiversity.

Although the collective obligation to protect biodiversity was seen by the United Nations Protection Agency (UNEP), the World Conservation Union (IUCN), and numerous other non-governmental organizations (NGOs) as constituting the foundations of the new treaty, the Convention rejects such an obligation and instead proclaims that states have the "sovereign right to exploit their own resources pursuant to their own environmental policies...." (Art. 3). In similar vein, the Convention rejects the principle that biodiversity is the natural heritage of humankind.

The natural heritage of humankind is to be distinguished from the "common heritage of mankind" (CHM) that has been applied to the deep sea bed and the ocean floor beyond the limits of national jurisdiction (United Nations Convention on the Law of the Sea, arts. 133, 136, & 156–169, A/CONF.62/122, 10 Dec. 1982, 21 I.L.M. 1261 (1982)), and the outer space regime respectively (Agreement Governing the Activities of States on the Moon and Other Celestial Bodies, art. 11(1), G.A.Res.68, 34 UN GAOR Supp. (No. 46) at 77, UN Doc. A/RES/34/68, 5 Dec. 1979, 18 I.L.M. 1434 (1979)). At its core the CHM involves inclusive enjoyment and sharing of the products of the common heritage, and its thrust remains redistribution, not conservation. By contrast, the "Natural Heritage of Humankind" refers to the biological necessities of the world, necessary for the existence and development of all humankind, that may fall within the national jurisdiction of States.

The acceptance of biodiversity as the common natural heritage would gives rise to a corollary obligation to protect and preserve such a heritage. Instead, the Convention settles for an effete and legally nonbinding recitation that biodiversity is the common "concern" of humankind. Furthermore, the attenuated affirmation that "biological diversity is a common concern of humankind" is found only in the Preamble, even though it ranked as a Fundamental Principle throughout the drafting process.

Even when the Convention attempts to protect biological diversity by in-situ conservation, ex-situ conservation, and sustainable use in Arts. 6–14, it makes sure that every obligation assumed (except those related to research, training, education, and public awareness) yield to the caveat: "as far as

BIODIVERSITY (E.O.Wilson ed., 1988); E. O. WILSON, THE DIVERSITY OF LIFE (1992).

41. UNEP, Fifth Revised Draft Convention on Biological Diversity,20 Feb. 1992, UNEP/bio.div/N7–INC.5/2 [hereinafter Fifth Revised Draft].

42. LAKSHMAN GURUSWAMY & BRENT HENDRICKS, INTERNATIONAL ENVIRONMENTAL LAW IN A NUTSHELL 107–23 (1997) [hereinafter NUTSHELL].

possible and as appropriate." Furthermore, Art. 7, which deals with the key elements of identification and monitoring, allows each Contracting party to do such identification. This contrasts with earlier expectations and drafts that provided for the establishment of Global Lists of Biogeographic Areas of Particular Importance for the Conservation of Biological Diversity and of Species Threatened with Extinction on a Global Scale to be internationally, not nationally, determined.[43]

Any obligations to protect the common heritage of humankind need not fall disproportionately on the poor and the deprived. Given the enormous disparities of wealth amongst nations, equity, fairness[44], and efficiency require that discharging the burden of protection should fall differentially and more heavily on the richer nations. Biological diversity is a public good that is of critical importance to all humanity, and ought to be protected by the entire international community. In the absence of a system of international government that can act to protect public goods for collective benefit, other mechanisms should be found. One fecund suggestion is to give areas of biodiversity a designated value, and pay the owner country an interest or financial allotment for the conservation or preservation of such areas[45]. The burden of such payments should be proportionately heavier for the richer nation.

It is also clear that the duty to preserve huge extents of forest, marsh, or coral reefs rich in biological diversity could entail daunting opportunity costs to LDCs. For example, an obligation to protect rain forests placed on LDCs is tantamount to denying those LDCs the right to cut down and develop such forests, to provide land, housing, and food to their desperately poor populace. Accordingly, it becomes necessary, first, to affirm the responsibility of the entire community of nations and the nations in which it is found *in situ* (in situ nations) to protect biodiversity. Second, measures and mechanisms must be devised to ameliorate the costs borne by LDCs.

This is not at all the same as the "burden sharing" referred to in Art. 21(1) of the Convention. The present arrangements deny the responsibility of the community of nations and in situ nations for protecting and preserving biodiversity while asserting that any commitment by developing countries to protect biodiversity will depend on the extent to which they are bankrolled by developed countries (Art. 20(4)). Unfortunately, by denying that developing states have any responsibility to protect biodiversity, the Convention fails to confirm any tangible responsibility of the community of nations to protect biodiversity. This is a serious defect, and the second flaw of the Convention.

Third, the challenge facing the Convention was to extend state responsibility for extra-territorial harm to damage caused to the global commons.[46] The global commons may include the critical habitats or homes of life-forms physically located within the territorial jurisdiction of nation states. But such an extension of state responsibility was roundly rejected by the Convention, and its application has been strictly confined to extra-territorial damage. The Fifth Revised Draft Convention had asserted the Principle that States are

43. Fifth Revised Draft, *supra* note 41.

44. J. RAWLS, A THEORY OF JUSTICE (1971).

45. R. Sedjo, *Property Rights and the Protection of Plant Genetic Resources, in* SEED AND SOVEREIGNTY: THE USE AND CONTROL OF PLANT

GENETIC RESOURCES (J.R. Kloppenburg Jr. ed., 1988).

46. *See* NUTSHELL, *supra* note 42, at 398–400.

responsible "for the conservation and sustainable use of their biological resources."[47] While a weaker formulation of that Principle is retained in the Preamble (5th para.), it is effectively emasculated by the assertion that States have a sovereign right over their biological resources (4th para.).

What emerges is a deeply flawed Convention that fails at its core to live up to expectations. On the contrary, it very nearly interdicts the obligation to protect biodiversity, fails to institutionalize the principle of differentiated responsibility as hitherto understood, and rejects sustainable development. The conclusion that the Convention flounders in holding the ring between the global need for biological diversity and the sovereign right of states to control and develop their own resources is a somber conclusion that does not bode well for the future.

Discussion Notes/Questions

1.   This problem offers students a window to the innovative provisions of the NAFTA environmental side-accord, the North American Agreement on Environmental Cooperation (NAAEC). The NAAEC is important for jurisprudential and functional reasons. By granting judicial access to private citizens and NGOs, the NAAEC takes a significant jurisprudential step toward overcoming some of the problems confronting international environmental law (IEL). Guruswamy and Hendricks point out in International Environmental Law In a Nutshell, at 409–11:

> We ... are confronted with ... the stubborn political fact that in the absence of strained political relationships, states do not generally take each other to court. Whether based on self-interest arising from the mutual vulnerability of a state to actions by others, or a desire not to offend friendly states, the crop of cases has been meager.

> On the other hand, environmental litigation in national courts is proliferating and it makes sense to use national courts to advance international remedies.

* * *

> It is almost obvious that IEL needs to develop innovative means of overcoming the deficiencies of a sovereignty-based system of international governance. Global environmental problems have to be solved within a consensual legal system of sovereign states who alone are empowered to make legal and political decisions about them. Legal or economic theories support the plain fact that nation states act in their own best interests and not that of the global community. While they might act to save the global commons where their own self-interest is affected, their actions are premised on individual, not community needs. Not surprisingly, there are many situations in which the cries for legal measures to arrest or avert environmental perils are left unanswered.

> Despite attempts to re-conceptualize international legal society along different lines, there is little evidence to support a fundamental change of the present sovereignty-based legal system. The suggestions for reform we propose accept that sovereignty will remain the basis of decision-making, and are of an incremental and functional nature premised on what appears possible.

---

47.   Fifth Revised Draft, *supra* note 41, art. 3(2)(a).

Even so, it is perfectly feasible for the present sovereignty based system to give better status and delegate more functions to NGOs.

As we have seen, NGOs are a fact of international life and they have long played an active role in IEL. As such, it does not take a big leap to institutionalize them as actors entitled to contribute in the law-making and implementing processes. This has already been done by the International Labor Organization (ILO) and it is achievable for the various international organizations to take measures to accord NGOs a similar status in their deliberations. There will, of course, be some problems concerning selection and accountability, but these are not insurmountable obstacles, and could be resolved along the same lines as the ILO. We have also already seen how the Commission on Sustainable Development (CSD) entertains reports from NGOs. Since such a move was based on consensus, it is well within reach to hope that other organizations created by treaty will do likewise. In addition, Agenda 21 envisions a greater role for NGOs and calls on the UN system to give them increased administrative and financial support. [¶ 27.12] It further calls on the UN system to enhance the contribution of NGOs to decision-making, implementation and evaluation of its projects. [¶ 27.9 (a)]. The infusion of people power into the law-making and implementing process will help to reduce the "democratic deficit" in international law-making and implementation.

On a functional level, many students seek careers in the private sector, while few end up working for the government. Of the few that work for the government, even fewer will work directly with the State Department negotiating international issues between states. The majority of students will more likely to be involved in international environmental law as attorneys for corporations, non-governmental organizations, and private parties. The provisions in the NAAEC, by granting private parties the right to challenge government non-enforcement of environmental laws, opens a significant legal field to these students. The proposed expansion of the NAFTA to the entire Western Hemisphere will only increase the opportunity for private attorney involvement in international environmental issues.

The "sluice gate" argument has often been used as a reason why individuals and NGOs should not be admitted as actors in IEL. Their admission into IEL, it can be argued, will open the sluice gates, leading to a flood of litigation which international courts and agencies are unable to adequately process. Do the first few decisions made by the Secretariat of the CEC mean that the CEC will be bombarded by private party claims of governmental non-enforcement regardless of the merit behind the claims? Why or why not? What type of measures could be taken to ensure that such claims are not submitted in order to ensure sufficient time for the claims which have substance?

2.   Much thought is being given to the assessment of current agricultural practices across the globe, and the potential room for improvement of those practices without sacrificing quality, efficiency or profitability. Concerns about agricultural run-off, application and quantities of fertilizers and pesticides, soil erosion, lack of proper crop rotation and agricultural biotechnology comprise some of the issues currently facing the agricultural arena. J. S. Carpenter, in an omitted section of Reading 21, *supra*, writes on the possibility of "Sustainable Alternatives" to environmentally damaging agricultural practices which we reproduce below. As you read it, think of the specific benefits and problems which would arise in implementing these alternatives for the economically and environmentally different countries of the world. Would it be more difficult for developing coun-

tries or developed countries to implement the changes? Would the type of alternative practice make a difference in answering the last question? (Citations have been omitted.)

III. SUSTAINABLE ALTERNATIVES

As early as 1980, the USDA determined that alternative farming practices could be practical. . . . There is strong evidence that many farmers are interested in alternatives that reduce health risks, protect farm resources, reduce environmental harms, and retain long-term profitability. In 1980, USDA estimated that at least 20,000 farmers practiced organic farming techniques. The number has probably doubled or tripled since.

A. Already Existing Alternatives

Forty years ago farmers did not simply let pests attack their crops and animals without any recourse; nor did they sit idly as the soil slowly washed and blew away. At the end of World War II, most farms in the Midwest, Great Lakes, Northeast, and parts of the South were diversified crop-livestock operations. High-density animal confinement was rare. Most farmers produced forage and feed grains for their animals, which required longer crop rotations and less use of some purchased inputs, particularly fertilizers. Most farmers returned manure to the land. Far fewer insecticides and almost no herbicides were used. Pests were controlled through rotations, cultivation, and a variety of cultural and biological means.

After the war, increasingly inexpensive chemical inputs appeared to solve the two most difficult production problems—pests and nitrogen depletion. Chemicals encouraged the shift to "monocropping," the production of the same crop on the same field year after year, which dramatically increased both erosion and chemical pollution of soil and water, albeit with increased production.

Although the old "pre-chemical" insights are often useful, sustainable farming hardly calls for a return to those methods. Instead, sustainable practices combine "traditional conservation minded farming techniques with modern technologies," enabling farmers to use modern methods to reduce reliance on external inputs by enhancing the productivity of internal resources. The following five practices are most closely associated with sustainable agriculture.

1. Crop Choice.

Rather than specializing in a single crop and planting it in the same field year after year, sustainable farmers "increase crop diversity, use multi-year rotations, and develop integrated crop and livestock operations." Crop rotations are used to "mitigate weed, disease, insect and other pest problems; increase available soil nitrogen and reduce the need for purchased fertilizers . . . and reduce soil erosion."

2. Pest and Weed Control.

Sustainable farming replaces pesticides and herbicides with Integrated Pest Management (IPM). IPM employs several different approaches including "natural predators and other biological controls, resistant crops, crop varieties well-suited to agronomic conditions, crop rotations, mechanical cultivation, and intercropping." IPM techniques reduce pesticide use by improving "plant health and the abilities of crops to resist insect pests and diseases."

3.   Soil Fertility and Cultivation.

In place of synthetic fertilizers, farmers use "crop rotations, legumes to fix nitrogen, . . . livestock manures," and other organic materials. Soil erosion and moisture loss can be minimized by year-round soil protection employing plant residues and various winter crops. Meadow rotations, repeated application of animal manures and other organic wastes, and incorporation of green manures into soil "[tend] to conserve or increase soil organic matter."

4.   Livestock Production.

While many farms operate sustainably without livestock, in many parts of the nation, animals provide a key element in sustainable practices. The integration of crops and livestock makes possible sustainable practices such as crop rotations and the production of legumes and grass forage crops. Livestock also provide nutrients in manure while pastures provide an effective use of highly erodible land. Hundreds of livestock farms already experiment with intensive rotational or controlled grazing systems, which permit animals to move in the open air and also require "fewer anti-biotics and hormones than their grain-fed, feedlot counterparts." Erosion and the use of pesticides and inorganic fertilizers are reduced with these systems.

5.   Conservation Tillage.

Conservation tillage is often defined as "any tillage system that leaves thirty percent of the previous crop's residue on the surface after spring planting." At present, conservation tillage is used on roughly a third of the nation's cropland and is "one of the most effective and least expensive methods for controlling soil erosion." Unfortunately, organic farms are unable to employ conservation tillage because it generally requires a significant increase in the use of herbicides.

B.   Evaluating Alternatives

The comparison of these alternatives to conventional farming raises two key questions. First, assuming alternative systems are actually practical, what are the likely benefits to the environment and public health? Second, what are the costs in terms of production efficiency in shifting from conventional farming to alternatives?

* * *

3.   *Bibliographical Note.* For further discussion concerning the principal themes addressed in this problem, consult the following additional specialized materials:

(a) *Specialized Books/Monographs.* N. Brady, The Nature and Property of Soils, 8th ed. (1974); M. Bronckers, Selective Safeguard Measures in Multilateral Trade Relations (1985); The Future of American Agriculture, S. Batie and R. Healy, eds. (1980); D. Getches, Water Law in a Nutshell (1997); J. Jackson, World Trade and the Law of GATT: A Legal Analysis of the General Agreement on Tariffs and Trade (1969); ___, Implementing the Tokyo Round: National Constitutions and International Economic Rules (1984); ___, The World Trading System: Law and Policy of International Economic Relations (1989); T. Miller, On the

Border: Portraits of America's South Western Frontier (1981); F. Powledge, Water (1982);

(b) *Specialized Articles/Book Chapters.* D. Alheritiere, *Settlement of Public International Disputes on Shared Resources: Elements of a Comparative Study of International Instruments,* 25 N.R.J. 701 (1985); D. Caponera, *Patterns of Cooperation in International Water Law,* 25 N.R.J. 589 (1985); S. Charnovitz, *The NAFTA Environmental Side Agreement: Implications for Environmental Cooperation, Trade Policy, and American Treatymaking,* 8 Temp. Int'l & Comp. L.J. 257 (1994); D. Dicke, *Public International Law and a New International Economic Order, in* Legal Issues in International Trade 23 (D. Sarcevic & H. Houtte eds. 1990); J. Dunoff, *Reconciling International Trade with Preservation of the Global Commons: Can We Prosper and Protect?,* 29 Wash. & Lee L.Rev. 1407 (1992); L. Farey, *Toward the Development of Performance Criteria Beyond Best Management Practices,* 48 Okla. L.Rev. 353 (1995); L. Farey, R. Jones & S. Pratt, *Conservation Districts as the Foundation for Watershed-based Programs to Prevent and Abate Polluted Agricultural Runoff,* 18 Hamline L. Rev. 151 (1994); J. Friedkin, *International Water Treaties: United States and Mexico, in* Water Resources Policy for Asia 393 (M. Ali, G. Radosevich & A. Khan eds. 1987); L. Goldie, *Equity and International Management of Transboundary Resources,* 25 N.R.J. 665 (1985); R. D. Hayton & A. E. Utton, *Transboundary Groundwaters: The Bellagio Draft Treaty* 29 Nat.Resources J. 663 (Summer 1989); K. Patton, *Dispute Resolution Under the North American Commission on Environmental Cooperation,* 5 Duke J. Comp. & Int'l L. 87 (1994); J. Owen Saunders, *NAFTA and the North American Agreement on Environmental Cooperation: A New Model for International Collaboration on Trade and the Environment,* 5 Colo. J. Int'l Envtl. L. & Pol'y 273; E. Weiss, *Environment and Trade as Partners in Sustainable Development: A Commentary,* 86 A.J.I.L. 728 (1992).

Problem 11–3

Population Control Meets Human Rights in Hanguo

SECTION 1. FACTS

Hanguo[a] is one of the most populous countries in the world, containing 1.2 billion people spread over seven percent of the world's arable land.

The Government of Hanguo is concerned that its rapidly growing population is lowering the standard of living and economic prosperity of its people. The Government has for many years been convinced that the finite natural resources available in Hanguo, and in the world as a whole, are necessarily strained by ever increasing demands resulting from exponentially growing populations. It therefore considers that, as a matter of environmental and human integrity, it must implement policies which seek to limit population growth, and to this end has instituted a one-child-per-family policy pursuant to which the Government sponsors the use of contraceptives, abortion, and sterilization. It also has provided for a formidable array of economic incentives to ensure that the one child quota is followed. Benefits made available by the Government are rigorously rationed.

Hanguo has pursued this policy over a period of years and has had some success in reducing its birth rate. In recent years, as well, the rate of economic growth in Hanguo has increased.

Hanguo's policy relies to a great extent on financial support from the United Nations Fund for Population Activities. The fund is maintained essentially by large Western countries, including a thirty percent contribution by the major industrialized country of the Federation of Columbia.[b]

There have been grave concerns expressed about the human rights implications of Hanguo's policy and the way it is being implemented. There are, for example, reports that Hanguoan women are being rounded up in the night and taken to 24–hour sterilization clinics. Unauthorized pregnancies are alleged to be compulsorily terminated, unauthorized children lose their rights to free education and healthcare subsidies, and economically-based punishments (such as annual fees representing one-tenth of family income) pose a great burden on some families.

The newly elected President of the Federation of Columbia is particularly concerned about these reports. While she believes that over-population in the developing world is a major problem, she also thinks that population policies should conform to international human rights standards. She insists that both conventional and customary international law prohibit the coercive policies being instituted by Hanguo. At the most recent World Population Conference, she announced that the Federation of Columbia's support was being withdrawn from any population program that involved coercion–citing to the 1948

---

a. Pronounced "Hängwua."

b. Not to be confused with the Republic of Colombia in South America.

Universal Declaration of Human Rights; the 1959 Declaration on the Rights of the Child; the 1966 International Covenant on Economic, Social and Cultural Rights; the 1966 International Covenant on Civil and Political Rights; the 1968 Proclamation of Teheran; the 1969 Declaration on Social Progress and Development; the 1979 Convention on the Elimination of All Forms of Discrimination Against Women; and the 1989 Convention on the Rights of the Child.

The position of the Federation of Columbia's new President was not strengthened by the fact that the Federation of Columbia has not ratified many of the instruments she cited, although it has signed most of them. However, the President argued that the Federation of Columbia's domestic constitutional law gave protection as great if not greater than these instruments do, and that therefore there was no need to ratify them. If they were ratified, she contended, the language of each instrument would have the same legal effect as a domestic statute and this would cause confusion with the guarantees in the Constitution itself. The President argued that the instruments were part of a pattern that established clear customary norms of international law on these matters and that Hanguo is in breach of them.

Except for the 1948 Universal Declaration of Human Rights, Hanguo has neither signed nor ratified any of the instruments in question. Along with the Federation of Columbia, however, it is a member of the United Nations, and at every international negotiation concerned with these human rights instruments—most of them sponsored by the United Nations—Hanguo has vigorously argued that Western concepts of human rights have no application to Hanguo. Such rights are at best aspirational, it contends, and always have been understood to be subject to national historical, social, economic, and cultural conditions. Hanguo has been particularly adamant that such rights should not be used as a pretext for interfering in the internal affairs of another nation.

It came as no surprise, therefore, that the Government of Hanguo saw the Federation of Columbia's initiative as directly attacking not only its policy, but also its sovereign right to regulate its own internal affairs. Hanguoan representatives argued that the human rights provided by international law are not inviolable and that the general standard of living and environmental standards compromised by a burgeoning population must be weighed against individual rights. For the Federation of Columbia to effectively stymie a governmental policy designed for the community good, was an infringement of state sovereignty. Hanguo representatives also strongly argued that the unequal distribution of global wealth and power is what forces countries like Hanguo to be so strict. Factors such as inadequate old age security and poorly funded education contribute greatly to population growth.

The conference erupted into a full-scale ideological debate. The Federation of Columbia stated that Hanguo's drain on environmental resources was due to its increasing use of technologies and practices that are now well-known to be ecologically destructive. Hanguo pointed out that the Federation of Columbia's per capita resource use was outrageously high and that it should be doing everything within its powers to address both that issue as well as aiding the developing world in its attempt to ensure economic and environmental security.

Since both countries had new leadership and there appeared to be no way that the countries could come together at the conference, wiser heads counselled that this unseemly diplomatic wrangle should not continue. On the third day, in a joint statement, both countries announced that they had decided to commence negotiations to sort out their differences. The statement said that they would attempt to agree on the international law applicable to the issues that sparked the debate, and then to act in accordance with that agreement.

SECTION 2. QUESTIONS PRESENTED

1. Is Hanguo in breach of any rule of international law in pursuing the population policies enumerated in the problem?

2. What policy arguments are available to enhance the position taken by each government?

SECTION 3. ASSIGNMENTS

A. *Reading Assignment*

Study the Readings presented in Section 4, *infra*, and the Discussion Notes/Questions that follow. Also, to the extent possible, consult the accompanying bibliographical references.

B. *Recommended Writing Assignment*

Prepare a comprehensive, logically sequenced, and argumentative brief in the form of an outline of the primary and subsidiary legal issues you see requiring resolution in the negotiations between Hanguo and the Federation of Columbia. Also, from the perspective of an independent objective judge, indicate which side ought to prevail on each issue and why. Retain a copy of your issue-outline/brief for class discussion.

C. *Recommended Oral Assignment*

Assume you are legal counsel for Hanguo, on the one hand, or the Federation of Columbia, on the other (as designated by your instructor); then, relying upon the Readings (and your issue-outline if prepared), present a 15–20 minute oral argument of your government's likely positions at the negotiating table where the diplomatic representatives from Hanguo and the Federation of Columbia are meeting.

D. *Recommended Reflective Assignment*

Consider (and recommend) alternative norms, institutions, and/or procedures that you believe might do better than existing world order arrangements to contend with situations of the kind posed by this problem. In so doing, but without insisting upon immediate feasibility, identify the particular transition steps that would be needed to make your alternatives a reality.

SECTION 4. READINGS

1. Nicholas Kristof, *China's Crackdown on Births: A Stunning, and Harsh, Success*, N.Y. TIMES, May 25, 1993, at 1, cols. 4–5.

BEIJING, April 24. She should be taking her two-month old baby out around the village now, proudly nursing him and teaching him about life. Instead her baby is buried under a mound of dirt, and Li Qiuliang spends her time lying in bed, emotionally crushed and physically crippled.

The baby died because under China's complex quota system for births, local family planning officials wanted Ms. Li to give birth in 1992 rather than 1993. So on Dec. 30, when she was seven months pregnant, they took her to an unsanitary first-aid station and ordered the doctor to induce early labor.

Ms. Li's family pleaded. The doctor protested. But the family planning workers insisted. The result: The baby died after nine hours, and 23–year–old Ms. Li is incapacitated.

LOWEST FERTILITY EVER

That episode in Hunan Province, described in a classified Government report and confirmed by the local authorities, is one outgrowth of a major nationwide crackdown by the Chinese family planning authorities. While the crackdown has been under way for two years, information about it is only now emerging as the authorities release population statistics showing a stunning decline in the birth rate.

The latest data suggest that through compulsory sterilization and other measures China has lowered fertility to by far its lowest level ever here. The statistics for 1992—showing many fewer babies even than during the harsh crackdowns of the early 1980's—amazed population experts, for the family planners achieved targets that they had not expected to reach until the year 2010.

PROBLEM FOR CLINTON

Ms. Li's persecutors had a reason for going to such extremes to enforce population quotas: they were protecting themselves under a new "responsibility system" that the Government has introduced as the mechanism for the crackdown. Under this system, central leaders hold local officials personally responsible for reducing births in their jurisdictions, and punish them for failing to do so.

The evidence of a far-reaching crackdown presents a direct challenge to the Clinton Administration. President Reagan had cut off the United States Population Fund because of concerns that its work was intertwined with a coercive family planning program in China, but President Clinton announced last month that he would end the boycott.

Now the new evidence of a crack-down is likely to embarrass Mr. Clinton as he tries to restore funds to the United Nations program. Moreover, criticisms in the United States about forced sterilization in China are likely in turn to inflame Chinese sensitivities and could create new tensions in Chinese–American relations.

To be sure, some Chinese—particularly city-dwellers—support a tough family planning policy. They say the drop in fertility is helping to produce a historic economic boom and a rise in the nation's education and health standards.

By restricting couples to one or two children each, they say, the Government is helping to lead China out of poverty and into a modern, industrialized future. They note that one reason why China's long-term development prospects may be better than Bangladesh's or Kenya's is that Beijing appears to have defused its population bomb.

Peng Pejyun, the 64–year–old minister of the State Family Planning Commission, acknowledged in a rare news conference on Wednesday that it was mainly Government efforts that had brought down the birth rate.

"Why did fertility drop so drastically?" asked Ms. Peng, who two years ago convinced the Politburo to order the crackdown. "Above all because party and Government officials at all levels paid greater attention to family planning and adopted more effective measures."

The indications of a drop in fertility come in a raft of statistics announced by Ms. Peng, printed in the official Population News or disclosed by Chinese officials. Among the figures are these:

The birth rate dropped to 18.2 per 1,000 population in 1992, down from 21.1 in 1990 and 23.33 in 1987.

Based on last year's birth data, each Chinese woman can expect to have an average of 1.8 or 1.9 children in her lifetime—about the same as in the United States or Britain. China's total fertility rate, as this statistic is known, was 2.3 in 1990 and had never before dipped below 2. In, contrast, the average Indian woman has four children.

Only 9.6 percent of all births in 1992 were third, fourth or subsequent children. In 1988, the figure was 15.4 percent.

The proportion of couples of childbearing age who are sterilized or use contraception rose to 83.4 percent in 1992, up from 71.1 percent in 1988.

"It's what would be called saturation contraception in any other country," said Judith Banister, a specialist on China's population at the United States Bureau of the Census. "You can't get much higher than that."

The Methods

Sterilization Made Efficient

China already has 1.17 billion inhabitants, 22 percent of the world's population on 7 percent of its arable land. Even at present fertility levels, the Chinese population will continue to soar because the age structure is very young and many Chinese have yet to enter their child-bearing years.

Some experts believe China's population will peak at almost 1.9 billion in the first half of the next century before stabilizing and then gradually declining again.

To Chinese peasants, who account for nearly one person in five on the planet, almost nothing is so important as bearing children, particularly sons.

Many peasant couples feel that they have failed in life's mission, that they have dishonored their ancestors, if they do not extend the male line.

In the early 1980's, there was a storm of international protest when it became clear that the local authorities sometimes dragged women to abortion clinics if they did not have permission to become pregnant. Interviews in a dozen provinces in the last few years suggest that such use of physical force is now less common.

Instead, the focus of the crackdown has shifted to the more efficient method of compulsory, organized sterilization, so that women do not have the option of becoming pregnant again.

Typically, local cadres swoop down on each village once or twice a year, taking all the women who have already had children to a nearby clinic. There they are fitted with IUD's or else undergo sterilization.

Some women manage to get pregnant again before they are sterilized; others flee the village on the day they are supposed to go to the clinic. When the authorities discover an unauthorized pregnancy, they normally apply a daily dose of threats and brow-beating.

Some women buckle and accept an abortion, while many others simply flee to a relative's village, returning only after the child is born. In such cases, fines equivalent to hundreds or even thousands of dollars—per capita income in the countryside last year, was $135—are imposed. Peasants in many different provinces say homes are routinely knocked down if the fine is not paid.

Worst–Case Abuse

Local Officials Get Carried Away

The report about Ms. Li, who is crippled after the induced labor, is an example of how local officials became carried away in the current crackdown. The three-page account, classified "secret", describes how Ningziang County decreed in September that women should normally be allowed to give birth only after reaching the age of 24.

The problem for local authorities was that they had already given some women "pregnancy permits" even though they were under 24. Some of these women were pregnant. Nine of them—including Ms. Li—would not give birth until 1993, the first full year in which the new age limit took effect.

"Some district and township officials feared that they would be fined for not meeting the family planning targets, or would not receive their bonuses," the report declares.

So at the end of December the family planning officials formed an "early birth shock brigade" to round up all nine women so labor could be induced. When the team showed up at Ms. Li's home, her mother-in-law pleaded with the officials.

"My daughter-in-law's health isn't good, and she may not be able to get pregnant again," the report quotes the woman as saying. "So let her have one baby, someone to look after her and my son when they grow old. It doesn't matter if it's a boy or a girl. After it's born, she'll go get sterilized."

The officials rejected the plea. And at the first-aid station, when the doctor said Ms. Li was too frail to undergo induced labor, they swept his protests aside and ordered him to proceed. She bled severely, fell unconscious and almost died along with the baby.

Her family took her to the township clinic, which saved her life. Now she has returned home, but the report says she is crippled, without specifying the nature of her injuries.

The report deplores the actions of the local officials and calls for Ms. Li to be compensated for her medical expenses. But a county officer, reached by telephone, said that so far nothing had been done, except that the officials responsible for the "early birth shock brigade" have been summoned to a meeting and told not to induce labor in the future.

The Motivations

Insistence on Meeting Targets

In retrospect, it is now possible to piece together how the crackdown came about. Interviews with Chinese and foreign specialists, and examination of materials published in China, indicate that Ms. Peng and other senior officials became increasingly concerned in the late 1980's that enforcement was growing lax and that China would miss its targets.

In early 1991, Ms. Peng convinced Prime Minister Li Peng and the Communist Party General Secretary, Jiang Zemin, that the matter was urgent. The standing committee of the Politburo, the highest decision-making body, unanimously resolved to tighten family planning work.

Most important, the new "responsibility system" galvanized provincial leaders to pass warnings all the way down the chain of command: family planning targets had to be met! Otherwise, those in charge of the area would be fined or even dismissed.

A result was a 25 percent surge in the number of people sterilized in 1991, to 12.5 million. The number declined in 1992 to 6.5 million, apparently because most women of child-bearing age already had been sterilized by then.

The scope of the crackdown became visible only after the State Family Planning Commission released data from a sample survey conducted in October. The data for 1992 startled almost everyone.

"We were very surprised by these numbers," said Sterling D. Scruggs, the China director of the United Nations Population Fund. "We didn't expect statistics approaching these levels for several more years."

Western diplomats said they believed that a crackdown was the only plausible explanation for the new statistics. They said Ms. Peng herself seems willing to take credit for the drop in birth rate.

THE MISSING GIRLS

Some Newborns Seem to Vanish

One prime concern among demographers is that hundreds of thousands of newborn Chinese girls seem to vanish from the statistics each year. Biology dictates that for every hundred female births there should be about 105 or

106 male births. But in 1989 for every 100 reported girl births, there were 113.8 births of boys.

That ratio implies that about 8 percent of newborn girls appear to have vanished from the statistics. In China that amounts to 900,000 missing girls each year.

Ms. Peng refused to release the sex ratio in 1991. An aide in charge of statistics, Zhang Erli, said the 1992 survey did not collect such information.

In fact, experts say the survey did gather the data and found a sex ratio of 118.5. But the sample size was small and the margin of error very high, so it is not clear how meaningful the difference is.

Zeng Yi, a leading Chinese demographer, said that the problem of the missing girls is very serious but that most of them are probably alive and never reported to the authorities. Parents who are allowed only one or two children may not want to use up their limited ration on a girl; instead they do not report the birth and try again.

A second factor, according to Mr Zeng and many other experts, is the growing use of ultrasound equipment in Chinese hospitals. Peasants find out from the doctor—usually with a small bribe—whether a fetus is male or female. If it is female, they get an abortion and start all over.

A final factor, which Mr. Zeng argues is much rarer, is simply infanticide. On instructions from the parents the midwife keeps a bucket of water beside her, and if a girl emerges, she drowns the baby immediately. It is reported as a still birth.

Mr. Zeng and other Chinese experts deplore all such practices. But ultrasound equipment is spreading rapidly, and so many specialists fear that the sex ratio is likely to become increasingly skewed.

Mr. Zeng cautioned that part of the apparent decline in fertility may simply be the result of under-reporting, particularly of girls. The figures were already adjusted upward by 7 percent to compensate for under-reporting, but Mr. Zeng believes that may not have been enough.

To some diplomats, what the new statistics underscore above all else is how little is known of what happens in the Chinese countryside.

"We had almost no idea that this was going on," a Western diplomat said, shaking his head in perplexity. "Even those who follow these things just had no clue."

2.   Reed Boland, *The Environment, Population and Women's Human Rights*, 27 ENVTL. L. 1137, 1142–54 (1997).

[P]opulation policies are [often] imposed as part of a strategy to lower the rate of population growth. As the world's population has increased dramatically since World War II, there has been growing acceptance of this strategy. High rates of population growth have been viewed as outstripping the ability of countries to sustain socioeconomic development, depleting the world's resources and causing major political instability. Stemming or reversing these rates has been judged to be the key to a sustainable and livable future. This strategy has gained widespread acceptance in the international population community, as well as in the planning departments of various governments.

One of the most consistent proponents of this approach has been the government of India, which recognized early in its history the problems associated with high rates of population growth and, in response, adopted one of the first major population policies. In the mid 1970s, the anxiety of the Indian government over the country's demographic prospects reached a fever pitch, leading it to adopt a highly coercive plan to lower the rate of population growth. One major component of the plan was the promotion of widespread sterilization of Indian citizens. To carry out these sterilizations, the Indian government established mass camps where sterilizations were performed in assembly line fashion under unsanitary conditions. At the height of the campaign, millions of people were sterilized within a six-month period. Many of these people were rounded up against their will and taken to the sterilization camps. In some cases, police were called upon to enforce the policy.

The most flagrant excesses of this plan were not long-lived. There was a public outcry over forced sterilizations and Prime Minister Indira Gandhi and her government, which had instituted the plan, were voted out of office in the next election. Nonetheless, the plan left lasting scars. First, it created a precedent for coercive action which has lasted until today. The Government still operates sterilization camps where conditions are unsanitary and women are pressured to be sterilized. Second, it created a population that mistrusts government efforts to deal with increasing population growth. This fact is particularly apparent in the negative reactions of male Indians to the plan. The sterilization program was largely directed at men who were induced to undergo vasectomies. Measures since then have been directed primarily at the sterilization of women, even though it is easier, safer, and more cost effective to perform a sterilization on a man than a woman.

The Chinese government has also engaged in major and well-publicized excesses in the execution of its population policy. The history of China's population policy has been one of broad fluctuations. After the takeover of the government by Communist forces in 1949, the new regime aggressively pursued a policy of encouraging births.... By the mid 1960s, however, China had largely reversed its policy. It began advocating the use of family planning, with a two child per family norm urged in some parts of the country. Despite this promotion of family planning and the continuing drop in the rate of population growth, by the end of the 1970s, the government tightened policy further. Alarmed by predictions that its population would exceed 1.2 billion before the end of the century and worried about the relative scarcity of domestic agricultural land to produce the food to sustain this population, the government adopted the one child per couple policy and instituted a series of strict measures to enforce it. Implicit or explicit threats of force were part of these measures that, on occasion, became real; persons who would not voluntarily comply with the policy were required to be sterilized or obtain an abortion.

Because of the secrecy of Chinese society and the government's denials of responsibility, the extent of the use of actual force is very difficult to gauge. Nonetheless, there are sufficient independent and unbiased reports to leave little doubt that coerced abortions and sterilizations have occurred, including evidence that mass sterilization campaigns have been carried out in various provinces. The government itself has acknowledged as much, although it places much of the blame for these excesses on overzealous local officials.

Indeed, given a population of over one billion people that has never known a democratic regime and in which force has, in recent years, played a prominent role, to suggest otherwise would be, at the least, to ignore human fallibility. Such excesses and the hostility that they generated, particularly in the rural population, were responsible for a major relaxation of the one child policy in the mid to late 1980s. During this time many exceptions to that policy were established for rural couples, ethnic minorities, and various other groups, including families that had given birth only to girls. Moreover, enforcement of existing laws was less stringent than before. However, by the beginning of the [1990s], policy had once again shifted. Results of the 1990 census indicated that population targets had not been met, leading the government to tighten enforcement procedures once again.

C. Non-physical Forms of Coercion

Not all coercive activities carried out in the name of population control have been as obvious as forced sterilization, abortion, or forced motherhood. There are a number of more subtle ways in which governments have tried to enforce their will over citizens' reproductive behavior. One is through the use of incentives or disincentives. The incentives fall into two broad categories: incentives to individuals to adopt various forms of family planning.... India gave monetary rewards to persons who agreed to be sterilized, made the salary of officials contingent on their ability to recruit sterilization acceptors, and imposed fines and imprisonment upon those who failed to meet demographic targets. Since the emergency, India has continued to offer monetary incentives to both acceptors and recruiting officials and, relying heavily on sterilization to implement its policy, sets sterilization targets for villages.

Similarly, a constant feature of China's population policy has been the penalization of couples who have more than the allotted number of children. This has been done by denial of social benefits, demotion at work, and imposition of fines. In contrast, those who adhere to the one child per couple policy have been rewarded with improved housing, access to better medical and educational benefits, and promotion at work. Most recently, China has affirmed its belief in the efficacy of incentives by instituting a family planning responsibility system to enforce its population policy. Under this policy, local officials are given the responsibility for reaching contraception targets set by the national government. If they fail to do so, they are penalized. The use of such incentives has also been commonplace in the implementation of the population policies of a number of other countries, including Vietnam and Bangladesh.

Another coercive method of enforcing population policies is through the application of various psychological pressures to bring about desired conduct. The Chinese government relies extensively on this method. Friends, family members, co-workers, and local officials are all called upon to place pressure on women to use intra-uterine devices (IUDs) which they are forbidden to remove, to be sterilized after the birth of a second child, or to have an abortion if they become pregnant. In some areas, the contraceptive use and pregnancy status of women are now monitored by officials by means of periodic physical examinations, much like those carried out under the Ceaususcu regime. Often threats of more coercive measures accompany this pressure if the desired method of family planning is not adopted.

Pressure of a slightly different nature has been a continuing feature of the Indonesian population policy. "Safaris," caravans of medical personnel, officials, and members of the police or military who enter rural towns have applied this pressure. They gather the populace together, deliver lectures upon the benefits of contraception, usually one favored form, and, sometimes under implicit threat, sign up acceptors and dispense the particular contraceptive being promoted. Indonesia also has relied on a system of village group pressure under which officials and community leaders make efforts to persuade women to accept family planning. Meetings are held periodically at which the women of a village gather together to discuss family planning in terms that utilize collective pressure to strengthen compliance with national policy.

* * *

E.   THE IMPACT OF COERCIVE POLICIES ON EXISTING HUMAN RIGHTS PROBLEMS

1.   Son Preference and Pre–Natal Sex Selection

* * *

Whatever the causes of son preference, the imposition of restrictive population policies has heightened the intensity of its practice. If families are allowed to have only one or two extraordinary measures to achieve this goal, [including] ... infanticide, ... abandonment or physical neglect of girls resulting eventually in death, [and abortion].

* * *

2.   Eugenics

Another problem made worse by the introduction of restrictive population policies is the practice of eugenics. Although the eugenics movement was a powerful force from the late 19th to the mid–20th centuries, in recent years most observers have considered it to be largely a matter of historical record. The discrediting of the scientific theories upon which eugenics was based, as well as the notorious excesses perpetrated in its name by the German National Socialist regime, seemed to sound the death knell of eugenics.

However, eugenic features can be discerned in the population policies of various countries. For example, the government of Singapore, which in recent years has reversed its population policy and adopted a pro-natalist stance, has targeted many of its incentives at the most highly educated parts of its population. Successful female college graduates have been encouraged through various social benefits to give birth to more children in order to maintain the high standard or "quality" of the population, while the poor have been offered nothing. In this case, the policy also has racial overtones, since most of the successful college graduates are ethnic Chinese and most of the poor are not. Such a racially-motivated policy was also promoted by the apartheid government of South Africa and has been suspected in the Indonesian government's implementation of population policies in East Timor.

The phrase "quality of the population" has, in fact, become a euphemism in a number of countries for eugenic theories and practices. The term appears, for example in laws of the Republic of Korea, Indonesia, China, and Japan.

However, in response to recent criticism, the Japanese have removed the word eugenics from their law and revised some of its more objectionable features. The practice of eugenics has seen its greatest implementation in China, where, in the mid–1980s, a number of provinces adopted laws calling for sterilization of the mentally and physically disabled and those suffering from hereditary diseases to prevent them from bearing children. The concern was that scarce resources were being spent on caring for millions of disabled persons, rather than on more productive projects. In 1994, China released a draft law instituting such measures on a country-wide basis. The criticism from abroad was so vociferous that the government withdrew the draft, removed some of its most coercive features, and toned down its language. While the new law is an improvement over the draft version, it nonetheless contains some disturbing provisions....

3. Euthanasia

Another human rights issue of growing concern that is implicated in population policies is euthanasia. In China, serious proposals have already been made to enact legislation authorizing euthanasia. In 1995, deputies to the National People's Congress submitted a draft law that would allow technically advanced hospitals in large cities to perform euthanasia on terminally ill patients. Under the draft, a patient would have to request the procedure, which would have to be approved by two medical experts, and relatives would also need to consent. In 1996, a group of prominent doctors gave its endorsement to the legislation, as did deputies to Shanghai's local legislature who approved a proposal calling for patients "to have the right to live and the right to die." The Chinese Government has not yet taken any action, although there is speculation that it is preparing the way to pass a national law on euthanasia.

* * *

F. THE ROLE OF LAW IN COERCIVE POLICIES

One important point to emphasize, at least from the viewpoint of law, is that all of these population policies are or were supported by a carefully drafted series of laws. They are not simply informal policies implemented sub rosa, or as the government of China would try to convince the rest of the world, isolated excesses carried out by overzealous local officials. The governments sought to give legitimacy through the legal system to what otherwise might seem thoroughly illegitimate.... At the time of the most intense pressure to perform sterilizations in India, the state of Maharashtra enacted legislation to justify its actions. The duty to practice family planning is enshrined in the Chinese constitution, which is one of only two constitutions in the world to contain such a provision. Local family planning laws spell out in detail the sorts of steps to be taken to fulfill this duty. In addition, many local laws make explicit what the government tries to deny—that coercion is endemic and, in fact, a key in the eyes of the government to population policy. Such laws often provide that excess pregnancies must be terminated and that persons who have exceeded targets must undergo operations or, in more euphemistic terms, "measures" must be adopted.

3. Editors' Note. The population policies described in the first two readings are clearly offensive to many people, especially when they result in excesses like those described in Reading 1. Nevertheless, one cannot ignore the possibility that population control may be necessary for human survival on the planet, and that some type of coercive policy (though not necessarily the policies described in these readings) may be the only way to achieve population control. The next several readings present various perspectives on two key questions. First, is population control necessary to protect the environment? Second, what policies are most likely to be effective in reducing population growth? As you read, you will see a range of answers to each of these questions. As to the necessity of population control, some fear that we are on the brink of disaster if governments do not take immediate effective action; others believe the problem will cure itself (more people means more technological innovation to sustain them). Opinions differ equally dramatically on techniques of control. Some policymakers in the developing world, as the first two readings suggest, believe that governments must pursue strong (and sometimes coercive) control policies to achieve results. Others argue that population control will happen on its own—if women are given rights. And what should the developed world do to help the developing world slow population growth? Promote development some say, and people will choose to limit family size. Stop providing assistance to overpopulated countries, others say, and the people will realize that they must control their population themselves. These and other perspectives are examined in the next few readings. We end with a series of readings which address a third question, the central issue of the problem: do coercive population control policies violate human rights?

4. Paul R. Ehrlich & Anne H. Ehrlich, *The Population Explosion: Why We Should Care and What We Should Do About It*, 27 ENVTL. L. **1187, 1188–94 (1997).**

The overriding reason to care about the population explosion is its contribution to the expanding scale of the human enterprise and thus to humanity's impact on the environmental systems that support civilization. The number of people (P), multiplied by per capita affluence (A) or consumption, in turn multiplied by an index of the environmental damage caused by the technologies employed to service the consumption (T), gives a measure of the environmental impact (I) of a society. This is the basic $I = P \times A \times T$ identity, often just called the "I = PAT equation." A useful surrogate for the $A \times T$ of the $I = PAT$ equation is per capita energy consumption (Epc); hence $I = P \times Epc$. Almost all of a society's most environmentally damaging activities involve the mobilization and use of energy at high levels, including the manufacture and powering of vehicles, machinery, and appliances; constructing and maintaining infrastructure; lighting and heating buildings; converting forests into paper, furniture, and homes; producing inputs for, and processing and distributing outputs from, high-yield agriculture; and so on.

The surrogate formula has some drawbacks, however. At the lowest levels of development, energy use probably underestimates environmental impact. For example, very poor people can cause serious environmental damage by cutting down trees for fuelwood. At the highest development levels, energy use probably overestimates environmental impact: a given amount of energy use in Western Europe, Japan, or the United States undoubtedly provides more benefits and does less damage than the same amount used in Poland or Russia because of much greater efficiency and stricter environmental regulation. Yet, despite these imperfections, for comparisons between nations or for intertemporal comparisons, energy use seems to be a priori a reasonable measure that correlates with many types of environmental damage. It certainly is the most readily available statistic with those characteristics.

Employing energy use as the standard, the scale of the human enterprise has grown about twenty-fold since 1850. During that time, per capita energy consumption has risen about five-fold globally, and the population has grown about four-fold. Roughly then, population growth can be considered to be responsible for about 45% of humanity's environmental peril: the combined risks accrued as a result of increasing worldwide environmental impacts. The risks arise from human-caused worldwide changes such as widespread habitat destruction (e.g., deforestation, desertification, urban construction), alteration of the composition and geochemical processes of the atmosphere (e.g. the addition of excess greenhouse gases, depletion of stratospheric ozone, generation of air pollution), overdrafts of groundwater, soil depletion and erosion, water pollution, disruption of the hydrologic, carbon, and nitrogen cycles (among others), and general toxification of the planet. These and many other factors combine into an unprecedented assault on the life-support systems of civilization: the global cycles and natural ecosystems that supply indispensable goods and services to humanity.

These mostly unappreciated but indispensable benefits include the maintenance of the quality of the atmosphere, regulation of the climate, provision of food from the sea, replenishment of soils, control of pests, and other vital underpinnings of agriculture, production of timber, medicines, and myriad other industrial materials, and regulation of freshwater flows (including controlling floods and droughts) and other forms of weather amelioration. Natural ecosystems also maintain a vast genetic library from which humanity has already derived all manner of things, including domesticated plants and animals, and which is essential to their continued usefulness.

The I = PAT equation carries an especially important lesson for Americans. It is customary to think of poor nations as overpopulated compared to rich ones, but in terms of global environmental impact, exactly the opposite is true. It is true that most European nations and Japan have greatly slowed, halted, or even reversed their population growth, while most developing nations continue to expand their population sizes at rates of 1.5% to 3.5% per annum.

But when consumption, the A x T factor (Epc), is considered, an entirely different picture emerges. Thus, around 1990, the average American used some 11,100 watts (11.1 kilowatts, kW) per person, more than ten times as much energy as the average citizen of a developing country. In actuality, the gap between the United States and developing nations is often much wider. For example, the United States in 1990 used 195 times as much commercial energy per capita as Madagascar, 20 times that of Zambia, and 13 times that of China. In other cases, it was narrower: eight times that of Malaysia and six times that of Mexico. Using commercial energy as a measure excludes the use of gathered wood, crop residues, and animal wastes as fuel by poor farmers, so the actual per capita energy consumption in very poor countries is somewhat understated. And in some developing nations such as China, Indonesia, and Malaysia, commercial energy use is growing very rapidly. Nevertheless, the overall picture is quite clear.

The United States already has the world's third largest population, 268 million people. China is number one with 1.24 billion, India number two with 970 million, and Indonesia number four with 205 million. Compared to other industrialized countries, the American population is growing at a record rate of more than one percent per year (if immigration is included). When the population figures are added to energy consumption, it is easy to see why the United States can be called the most overpopulated nation.

By assaulting earth's ecosystems, humanity is, in essence, sawing off the limb on which it perches. Population growth is clearly a major force behind the saw. The chances of successfully feeding and otherwise caring for an expanding population are being continuously diminished. That is why all human beings should care deeply about the population explosion and, because of their own disproportionate environmental impacts, why Americans should show particular concern.

II. WHAT SHOULD BE DONE ABOUT THE POPULATION EXPLOSION?

It is a great deal easier to explain why the population explosion should be a critical issue for all of humanity than it is to find one's way through the manifold issues of what ought to be done about it.

A. Basic Goals

The easiest answer to the question above is move as rapidly as is humanely possible toward an optimum sustainable population size. But this vague answer immediately raises a series of obvious questions: What is an optimum sustainable population size? What steps would move society in that direction? How does one establish what is humane? Science can put theoretical bounds on the answer to the first question, since there is a biophysical upper limit on the number of people that could be supported over the long term with a given set of technologies and social (including political and economic) arrangements.

But most people would probably agree that there is a considerable difference between the largest sustainable population and an optimal sustainable population. Few would find supporting the maximum number of human beings, in a situation somewhat analogous to the way battery chickens are reared, to be optimal. Many would desire varied diets, comfortable homes, opportunities for travel and solitude, uncrowded living conditions, and other amenities, all of which would reduce the number of people that could be sustained. With an approximation of current conditions, it has been estimated that the upper bound of an optimum population, one that would in some sense allow for a maximum quality rather than quantity of human life over the long term, would be in the vicinity of two billion people, about one third the current number.

That estimate is based largely on patterns of energy use. Today, humanity is using roughly 13,000,000,000,000 watts of energy. In more convenient notation, that is 13×10^{12} watts, or 13 terawatts (tW). With that much energy use, humanity has developed a quite unsustainable civilization. Indeed, it is only able to maintain some 5.8 billion people today, with a billion or so undernourished and in desperate poverty, by using up its natural capital.

The most important forms of natural capital are productive agricultural soils, fossil groundwater, and biodiversity. Soils, which normally are generated on a scale of inches per millennium, are in many places being eroded at rates of inches per decade. At least twenty-five billion tons of topsoil are lost annually, and some estimates range far higher. In many areas, groundwater that accumulated during the ice ages is overdrawn. In the southern high plains of the United States, the Ogallala aquifer is naturally recharged at a rate of about one-half inch per year, but is being pumped at a rate of four to six feet per year to irrigate crop fields. This "mining" of the aquifer produces a net withdrawal about equal to the flow of the Colorado River. Similar overdrafts of groundwater are occurring in many areas of the world, including parts of India and China. Depletion and degradation of natural resources is, of course, a story as old as civilization; what is new is the unprecedentedly colossal and planet-wide scale on which it is occurring today.

The loss of populations, species, and communities of plants, animals, and microorganisms that are working parts of our life-support systems (and thus partly responsible for the delivery of ecosystem services) is the most irreversible loss of all. Just one element of biodiversity, species diversity, is disappearing at a rate estimated to be 1000 to 10,000 times the "background" rate, which is the more or less constant extinction rate that biologists presume to occur naturally over time. Populations, another critical element, are disappearing even faster. We are witnessing the greatest biological cataclysm of the last sixty-five million years—since an apparent collision with an extraterrestrial object exterminated the dinosaurs and much of the rest of Earth's flora and fauna.

In short, in a 13 tW world, humanity is unable to maintain itself on its natural "income," the sustainable flow of solar energy and cycles of elements in the biosphere. Like a profligate son, humanity is spending its inheritance of capital, in essence bragging each year that it is writing bigger and bigger checks on its "account" while paying no heed to the plummeting "balance." This behavior is supported by diverse claims that fly in the face of all of environmental science: technology can save humanity because resources are infinite, population growth can continue for another seven billion years, and there is no need to worry about the state of the environment.

All the degradation and depletion of natural resources that should be constantly renewed through solar energy and ecosystem functions, as well as the generation of various forms of pollution and the buildup of greenhouse gases in the atmosphere leading to global climate change, are largely being driven by civilization's use of 13 tW of non-solar energy, mostly from fossil fuels. Thus, it would seem that a 4.5 to 6 tW world, given substantial changes in human behavior, might be sustainable while providing everyone in a moderately large population with a life of reasonably high quality. But will it be possible to get there without wrecking our life-support systems? Since it seems nearly inevitable that the human population will not stop expanding until it has reached at least eight to ten billion people several decades from now, it is clear that one or two additional centuries would be required for a gradual, humane reduction to an optimum population size, assuming that some way is found to support the gigantic overshoot of carrying capacity.

5. Julian L. Simon, *The Population Debate: The Case for More People*, in Environmental Science: Action for a Sustainable Future 110 (D. Chira ed., 3d ed. 1991).

Many technological advances come from people who are neither well educated nor well paid—the dispatcher who develops a slightly better way of deploying taxis in his ten-cab fleet, the shipper who discovers that garbage cans make excellent, cheap containers for many items, the retailer who discovers a faster way to stock merchandise, and so on. Even in science one need not be a genius to make a valuable contribution.

In the past century there have been more discoveries and a faster rate of growth of productivity than in previous centuries, when fewer people were alive. Whereas we develop new materials almost every day, it was centuries between the discovery and use of, say, copper and iron. If there had been a larger population, the pace of increase in technological practice might have been faster.

Classical economic theory concluded that population growth must reduce the standard of living: the more people, the lower the per capital income, all else being equal. However, many statistical studies conclude that population growth does not have a negative effect on economic growth. The most plausible explanation is the positive effect additional people have on productivity by creating and applying new knowledge.

Because technological improvements come from people, it seems reasonable to assume that the amount of improvement depends in large measure on the number of people available. Data for developed countries show clearly that the bigger the population, the greater the number of scientists and the larger the amount of scientific knowledge produced.

There is other evidence of the relationship between population increase and long-term economic growth: an industry, or the economy of an entire country, can grow because population is growing, because per capita income is growing, or both. Some industries in some countries grow faster than the same industries in other countries or than other industries in the same country. Comparisons show that in the faster-growing industries the rate of increase of technological practice is higher. This suggests that faster population growth, which causes faster-growing industries, leads to faster growth of productivity.

The phenomenon economists call "economy of scale"—greater efficiency of larger-scale production where the market is larger—is inextricably intertwined with the creation of knowledge and technological change, along with the ability to use larger and more efficient machinery and greater division of labor. A large population implies a bigger market. A bigger market is likely to bring bigger manufacturing plants, which may be more efficient than smaller ones and may produce less expensive foods.

A bigger population also makes profitable many major social investments that would not otherwise be profitable—railroads, irrigation systems, and ports. For instance, if an Australian farmer were to clear a piece of land far from neighboring farms, he might have no way to ship his produce to market. He might also have trouble finding workers and supplies. When more farms are established nearby, however, roads will be built that link him with markets in which to buy and sell.

We often hear that if additional people have a positive effect on per capita income and output, it is offset by negative impacts such as pollution, resource shortages, and other problems. These trends are myths. The only meaningful measure of scarcity is the economic cost of goods. In almost every case the cost of natural resources has declined throughout human history relative to our income.

Conventional wisdom has it that resources are finite. But there is no support for this view. There is little doubt in my mind that we will continue to find new ore deposits, invent better production methods, and discover new substitutes, bounded only by our imagination and the exercise of educated skills. The only constraint upon our capacity to enjoy unlimited raw materials at acceptable prices is knowledge. People generate that knowledge. The more people there are, the better off the world will be.

6. BETSY HARTMANN, REPRODUCTIVE RIGHTS AND WRONGS: THE GLOBAL POLITICS OF POPULATION CONTROL AND CONTRACEPTIVE CHOICE 20–24, 28–30, 33 (1987).

Ecologists, like any other members of a scientific discipline, are not a homogenous group. On one side are what I call the human racers, people who perceive the battle over the environment as inevitable race between man and nature and who believe the earth is already nearing the limits of its "carrying capacity." Because they view mankind itself as the enemy, the human racers are Malthusians.[c] "In the simplest terms, we are in a race to see if we can slow, and eventually halt, population growth before local life-support systems collapse," warns Lester Brown of the Worldwatch Institute.[1]

On the other side are the structuralists, who view environmental destruction as the outgrowth of inefficient, and often inequitable, forms of social organization, which can and should be reformed. They recognize that in some instances population pressure can contribute to environmental degradation, but ask what are the underlying social dynamics that cause that pressure to come about.

The human racers of course have a point. No one wants a world of standing room only, where every bit of land, drop of water, and unit of energy are pressed into producing sustenance for an endlessly expanding human mass. Other species have a right to inhabit the earth, and our own quality of life is enhanced by respect for the natural environment. However, while limiting human numbers makes sense in the long run, it does not follow that in the short run overpopulation is the main cause of environmental depletion.

c. Writing in the late 1700s and early 1800s, Malthus maintained that, unless restrained by "preventative checks", the human population would double every 25 years. The result would be *geometric* growth—1, 2, 4, 8, 16, 32, 128 etc.—that would outstrip Earth's capacity for food production, which could be expected to increase in an *arithmetic* progression—i.e., 1, 2, 3, 4, 5, 6, 7, etc. According to Malthus, humans were little different from plants and animals in this respect; their numbers would be checked by the limited carrying capacity of the planet.

1. L. BROWN, ET AL., STATE OF THE WORLD 209 (1984).

On the contrary, it is the consumption explosion in the industrialized world rather than the population explosion in the Third World which is putting the most pressure on natural resources. For example, the U.S., with only 5 percent of the world's people, uses one-third of the world's flow of nonrenewable resources and one-quarter of the gross planetary production of goods and services. The average U.S. citizen uses almost 300 times as much energy as the average citizen of Bangladesh. A small rate of population increase in the industrialized countries thus puts much more pressure on resources than a rapid population in the Third World. Within Third World countries too, elites are shifting to the same high consumption patterns, using up far more resources per capita than their poor compatriots whom they accuse of overbreeding.[2]

Moreover, as the structuralists would point out, many of the main ecological crimes being perpetrated on the earth today—chemical and nuclear wastes dumped in the sea, radio-active clouds from faulty reactors and weapon tests, acid rain from dirty smokestacks—have considerably more to do with unregulated and inappropriate patterns of technological development than with the procreative powers of peasants.

What about the serious environmental deterioration which is occurring in many Third World countries, through deforestation and desertification in particular? Although here the Malthusian case would seem more compelling, there is much more to the story than just population pressure.

When the Center for Science and Environment in New Delhi investigated deforestation in India, where millions of hectares of forest land are disappearing each year, it found a very different state of affairs from the official government view that the "population explosion is mainly responsible for depletion of our valuable forests."[3] The Center cites a number of studies which reveal how private contractors, through payoffs to corrupt forest officials, have illegally felled huge sections of India's forests, at the same time as they were declared off limits to the local communities who have long depended on them for a livelihood. Meanwhile, "official" forestry projects, aided by international agencies such as the World Bank, are encouraging the export of India's hardwoods and the destruction of mixed, ecologically sound forests in favor of monoculture plantations of pine, eucalyptus, and teak.[4]

Even the poor's desperate need for firewood may have fewer ecological consequences than is commonly imagined. The wood they collect for cooking fuel is largely composed of branches, twigs, and roots—only the rich can afford logs. A village study by the Indian Institute of Science found that gathered firewood did not contribute in any significant way to deforestation, casting "serious doubts on the widespread belief held by many environmentalists that the firewood demand of the poor is leading to extensive deforestation."[5]

---

2. E. NAFZIGER, THE ECONOMICS OF DEVELOPING COUNTRIES 185, 188 (1984).

3. *See* section on forests in CENTER FOR SCIENCE AND ENVIRONMENT, THE STATE OF INDIA'S ENVIRONMENT 1982: A CITIZEN'S REPORT (1982).... Government view quoted in R. Guha, *Forestry in British and Post-British In-*

dia, A Historical Analysis, ECON. & POL. WKLY., Nov. 5, 1983, at n. 166.

4. B. Dogra, *World Bank vs. The People of Bastar, Reforestation or Deforestation?*, 10 CULTURAL SURVIVAL Q. No. 1 (1986).

5. CENTER FOR SCIENCE AND ENVIRONMENT, THE STATE OF INDIA'S ENVIRONMENT, *supra* note 3, at 152.

Similar processes are occurring in many other Third World countries. The destruction of the Amazon rain forest in Brazil, one of the world's last great tropical forests, is a sad tale of corporate greed. National and multinational corporations, including Goodyear, Volkswagen, Nestle, and Mitsubishi, have stripped millions of acres for lumber and cattle ranching.[6] In the Philippines, before he was deposed, dictator Ferdinand Marcos gave illegal logging concessions worth over a billion dollars to relatives and political cronies, depleting the country's forest reserves from 34.6 million acres in 1965, when Marcos took power, to only 5.4 million acres today.[7]

Like deforestation, desertification, which threatens almost 20 percent of the earth's surface, is frequently attributed to overpopulation. "Excessive population pressure on limited land resources means desertification," claims a United Nations news feature. "That is the bottom line."[8]

But for many peasants there is another bottom line: the monopolization of land resources by the rich. El Salvador is a case in point. Just as the war ravaging this small Central American nation is often blamed on rapid population growth, so is its deteriorating environment. Today El Salvador faces accelerated erosion of an estimated 77 percent of its land. The country is generally steep and mountainous, with fertile lands located in the middle of volcanic slopes, river basins, and coastal plains. These few productive areas belong to large estates growing cotton, sugar, coffee, and cattle for export.

El Salvador's land ownership pattern is highly skewed: Fewer than one in a hundred farms is more than 250 acres, yet these large farms occupy half the total cultivable land in the country. Meanwhile, the peasants have been pushed onto the higher slopes, where in order to survive, they cut down vegetation and grow subsistence crops on land unsuitable for cultivation. Erosion is the inevitable result.

In such a situation, more people do mean more ecological destruction, since they are crowded onto a limited land space. In this sense, rapid population growth is a factor in desertification, but to call it the primary cause is to simplify a much more complex process. El Salvador's peasants are putting pressure on marginal lands not because of their numbers alone but because they themselves have been made marginal by an agricultural system controlled by the rich.

According to demographer John Caldwell, who has studied the delicate ecological zone of the African Sahel, it is impossible to establish a direct relationship between population pressures and desertification. Over the last decade, he reports, there has been very little scientific investigation of the impact of rising population densities on the environment of poor, arid countries, and many demographers are reluctant even to use the term "carrying capacity."[9]

It will be interesting to see if the environmental argument against population growth, like the hunger argument, also passes out of fashion.

6. F. Lappé & J. Collins, Food First: Beyond the Myth of Scarcity 48–52 (1979).

7. G. Jones, *Marcos Profited from Smuggling $1b in Timber, Officials Say*, Boston Globe, May 22, 1986.

8. UNEP, *Population and Desertification in Kenya*, Press Release Feature 84/4, Nairobi, February 1984.

9. J. Caldwell, *Desertification: Demographic Evidence, 1973–1983*, a report to the UNEP Desertification Section (n.p.; n.d.).

Certainly, today more sophisticated Malthusian thinkers are moving away from it, concentrating instead on the deleterious consequences of rapid population growth on the economy at large. For example, in its *World Development Report 1984*, the theme of which was population and development, the World Bank argued that rapid population growth is a "serious brake on development," resulting in "lost opportunities for raising living standards, particularly among the large numbers of the world's poor."[10] The World Bank has slightly altered the previous Malthusian line of causality. While it now admits that poverty, not the sheer weight of human numbers, is responsible for hunger and environmental depletion, it blames poverty on the economic consequences of population growth, thus continuing to hold the poor responsible for their own misery.

* * *

The Cornucopians

In recent years, Malthusian fatalism has met its match in the unrepentant optimism of certain influential New Right economists. In their book *The Resourceful Earth*, Julian Simon and Herman Kahn challenge the "limits to growth" philosophy and claim that "if present trends continue, the world in 2000 will be less crowded (though more populated), less polluted, more stable ecologically, and less vulnerable to resource-supply disruption than the world we live in now."[11]

These conservative Cornucopians believe that free enterprise and nuclear energy can do the trick, just as long as there isn't too much government interference through environmental regulation. According to Simon, temporary shortages of resources simply spur the development of new techniques to find them, so that in the end we are better off than if the shortage had never occurred. Meanwhile, population growth produces the "ultimate resource," "skilled, spirited and hopeful people," who, provided they live in an unfettered market economy, can come up with the new ideas to make the system work.[12]

The Cornucopians, who found a sympathetic ear in the Reagan White House, heavily influenced the drafting of the official U.S. Policy Statement for the 1984 U.N. International Conference on Population. In a major reversal of policy, the document described population growth as a "neutral phenomenon," which has become a problem only because of too much "governmental control of economies" and an "outbreak of anti-intellectualism, which attacked science, technology and the very concept of material progress" in the West.[13]

There are a number of obvious flaws with the Cornucopian approach. The unbridled faith in science, technology, and human inventiveness translates into a lack of concern for the very constraints on the environment we face at the end of the twentieth century and begs the question of appropriate versus

10. World Bank, World Development Report 1984, at 86.

11. J. Simon & H. Kahn, The Resourceful Earth (1984).

12. J. Simon, *Myths of Population*, Wall Street Journal, Aug. 3, 1984, at 16, col. 4.

13. *U.S. Policy Statement For the International Conference on Population, reproduced as* Attachment A, *in* Ford Foundation, The Ford Foundation's Work in Population 45–46 (1985).

inappropriate technologies. Arguably, what is needed is more government environmental regulation, not less. Nor will higher rates of population growth necessarily yield more geniuses if the majority of the world's people remain trapped in poverty. Even the best of brains need food for sustenance and education for development. And before debating the pros and cons of the free market, it is important to point out that the free market simply does not exist, except perhaps in Disney World. Even the Third World countries Simon et al. herald as the great free market successes—South Korea, Taiwan, Singapore—have substantial government involvement in the economy. In the end, the Cornucopians dodge the real issues of power and inequality just as the Malthusians do.

They have performed a great service, however, by opening up the population debate. After more than two decades of hegemony, the Malthusian orthodoxy is on the defensive and has had to cede some ground in order to save the church.

The relaxation of the Malthusian position is reflected in a 1986 U.S. National Academy of Science report, which retreats substantially from past alarmist assessments of population growth, including one issued by the academy fifteen years ago. While concluding that population growth is more likely to impede progress than promote it, the report finds it is not the unmitigated environmental and economic evil it has been portrayed to be. According to the report, there is no "necessary relation" between population growth and resource exhaustion, and the effect of population growth on the economy is mixed. Even when population growth has a negative impact, slower growth alone will not guarantee progress.[14] The report has helped to establish a "middle ground" in the population debate, a middle ground, one might note, already occupied by many demographers and economists who have consistently held a more reasoned view of the issue.

Within the population establishment, the likely effect of the academy's report will be to push the Malthusians into an even more selective application of their logic, as they search out areas of the globe where it is easier to make their case.

* * *

The Malthusians are fundamentally wrong. The solution to the population problem lies not in the diminution of rights, but in their *expansion*. This is because the population problem is not really about a surplus of human numbers, but a lack of basic rights. Too many people have too little access to resources. Too many women have too little control over their own reproduction. Rapid population growth is not the cause of underdevelopment; it is a symptom of the slow pace of social reform.

Two basic sets of rights are at issue. First is the right of everyone on the earth today, not just in the future, to enjoy a decent standard of living through access to food, shelter, health care, education, employment, and social security. Despite present high rates of population growth, most—if not all—societies have the means to guarantee this right to all their people, if wealth

14. For an account of the report, see C. Holden, *A Revisionist Look at Population and*   *Growth*, 231 SCIENCE 1493, 1493–94 (Mar. 28, 1986).

and power were shared more equitably. A fairer distribution of resources between the industrialized world and the Third World is just as necessary.

Once people's physical survival is ensured and children are no longer their only source of security, history shows that population growth rates fall voluntarily. Higher living standards across the board were the motor force behind the demographic transition in the industrialized world. Similarly, those Third World countries, whether capitalist, socialist, or mixed economy, which have made broad-based development a priority have also experienced significant reductions in population growth, often at relatively low levels of per capita income. These include Cuba, Sri Lanka, Korea, Taiwan, and China. Meanwhile, a country like India, where the benefits of substantial economic growth have flowed disproportionately to a small elite, still has high rates of population growth despite the massive amount of resources the government has devoted to population control.

The right to a decent standard of living is necessary but not sufficient. The other critical right is the fundamental right of women to control their own reproduction. The expansion of reproductive choice, not population control, should be the goal of family planning programs and contraceptive research.

7.   Jorgen Randers & Donella Meadows, *The Carrying Capacity of Our Global Environment: A Look at the Ethical Alternatives, in* Western Man and Environmental Ethics: Attitudes Toward Nature and Technology 253, 273–76 (Ian G. Barbour ed., 1973).

Stopping the population explosion is becoming increasingly more accepted as an important task to be accomplished as fast as possible, but what about stopping physical growth? Can we really suggest a deliberate restriction of our production, leaving the world's poor in their present miserable situation?

Striving towards global equilibrium does *not* imply "freezing" the world in its present configuration of rich and poor nations and peoples. It is overall growth which must finally stop, but that does not preclude redistribution of the world's existing wealth. One possibility is that the developed world deliberately stops its growth and possibly even lets itself "shrink" somewhat, while the developing world is allowed (and maybe helped) to grow economically to an acceptable, but not infinitely high level. Thus initially it will be the developed world which has to take the lead in the path towards *economic* equilibrium; however, the developing world will have serious responsibilities in attempting to stop its rapidly growing populations.

Many people believe that we must cling to the goal of maximizing physical growth, simply because we are still so very far from having attained the Utopia where everything is plentiful for everyone. However, we must remember our conclusion above that a continued reliance on short-term objectives and continued growth only makes it certain that there will be no acceptable future—for any country. In other words: such a Utopia does not exist, and striving towards it is futile.

Also it should be made quite clear that economic growth as we have experienced it over the last century in *no* way has resulted in increased equality among the world's people. To the contrary, growth in its present form widens the gap between the rich and poor....

An end to overall economic growth, however, might very well ultimately lead to a more equitable distribution of wealth throughout the world—because no one would accept economic inequalities in the present under the (false) pretence that they would be removed through future growth. Of course the state of global equilibrium will also have its problems—mainly political and ethical. In the words of H. E. Daly,[15] the American economist:

> For several reasons the important issue of the stationary state will be distribution, not production. The problem of relative shares can no longer be avoided by appeals to growth. The argument that everyone should be happy as long as his absolute share of the wealth increases, regardless, of his relative share, will no longer be available.... The stationary state would make fewer demands on our environmental resources, but much greater demands on our moral resources.

But these political problems have solutions, and we are certainly more likely to find those solutions in an equilibrium state than in a collapsing one.

Stopping the overall physical growth on our planet is not an attempt by the rich countries to divert attention from economic development to the protection of "their" environment. Rather global equilibrium is a necessity if mankind wants to have an equitable future on his small, fragile planet.

8. Robert M. Hardaway, *Environmental Malthusianism: Integrating Population and Environmental Policy*, 27 ENVTL. L. 1209, 1209–17 (1997).

I. INTRODUCTION: THE TRADITIONAL MALTHUSIAN DEBATE

When Thomas Malthus warned of the dangers of overpopulation in his 1798 Essay on Population, he was concerned mostly about food. Malthus warned that if the world's population was permitted to expand unchecked, growth would be checked by starvation and disease and humankind reduced to subsistence.

Today, although starvation does serve as a modest check on population expansion in underdeveloped areas of the world, world population continues to expand at an incomprehensible rate. Every one-third of a second, at about the speed a machine gun fires its bullets, the planet earth somehow makes room to accommodate an additional human being. Every eighteen days, the world's population expands by a number equal to the entire human population of the world in 5000 B.C. Every five months the population expands by a number equal to the number of humans living in 1575. Every year from now through the twenty-first century, ninety million people will be added to the world population. The world's population has doubled in only three and one-half decades since 1950. This startling rate of growth is not expected to stabilize for forty to fifty more years.

So was Malthus wrong? Well, yes and no.

Perhaps one-tenth of the world's population suffers from starvation, or at least malnutrition severe enough to affect resistance to disease. Nonetheless, the majority of the five and one-half billion human beings alive today eat, if

---

15. H. Daly, *Toward a Stationary–State Economy, in* THE PATIENT EARTH 226, 236–37 (J. Harte & R. Socolow eds., 1971).

not heartily, at least as much as is needed to fuel the unabated and unprecedented expansion of the human race. Indeed, the rate at which the human population is expanding today is far greater than it was in 1798 when the population was one-fifth its present size.

Certainly Malthus did not take into account the degree to which the opening of the new world would provide resources to support population expansion for many years to come. Nor did he anticipate the extent to which technology, modern farming techniques, and the Green Revolution would spur growth in food production. But have such developments refuted basic Malthusian theory, or have they simply delayed the dreaded day of reckoning when Malthusian theory will be vindicated with full force and virulence?

Frankly, the vindication and broad public acceptance of Malthusian theory has not been aided by the small and vocal group of Malthusian doomsayers who perennially predict eminent disasters of resource depletion or mass starvation. Computer models found in books such as Donella Meadows' 1972 The Limits to Growth and her 1992 I'm-really-serious-now Beyond the Limits have been dismissed by skeptics as just more Malthusian cries of wolf. (Meadows' computer models had predicted, among other disasters, that gold would run out by 1981 and that oil would run out by 1992). Such hyperbole has provided grist for a growing body of increasingly influential anti-Malthusians, who maintain that population growth is not only not a problem, but actually a very healthy phenomenon necessary for continued economic growth and continued increases in the human population's standard of living. Although certainly sincere, much of this work has been counter-productive inasmuch as it has diminished in the public consciousness the integrity of basic Malthusian assumptions. It gives the anti-Malthusians the chance to say again and again "I told you so," and to relegate the Malthusians to the level of the soap box and the religious fanatic carrying the placard "The End is Near."

A group of theorists led by Julian Simon and Simon Kuznets, for example, have argued that when population expansion causes a shortage of resources, human ingenuity is spurred to create substitutes, as when a shortage of ivory in the last century led to the invention of celluloid. They also point out that a large population makes possible the exploitation of economies of scale principles, such as the mass production of automobiles.

Ester Boserup, in her 1981 book Population and Technological Change, observes that it has been overpopulation which historically has led to the creation of a highly developed human civilization. She cites the example of ancient Mesopotamia, which over a period of 8000 years became very densely populated: "Gradually, the population changed from primitive food gatherers to people who applied the most sophisticated systems of food production existing in the ancient world." Thus, overpopulation led to the development of infrastructure, roads, and "the creation of cities [which] allow[ed] for greater specialization and more efficient organization of the economy." The larger population in turn permitted a more efficient division of labor.

These anti-Malthusians further cite the theories of labor postulated by William Petty and Adam Smith. As Petty illustrated, "[i]n the making of a Watch, if one man shall make the Wheels, another a Spring, another shall

Engrave the Dial-plate, and another shall make the Cases, then the Watch will be better and cheaper, than if the whole Work be put upon any one man.''

Adam Smith followed up on this theory with his example of pin production, in which "a single worker might turn out at most twenty pins a day, a factory employing a team of ten workers manages to produce twelve pounds a day, or 48,000 pins, 4800 per worker."

In her 1988 book The War Against Population, Jacqueline Kasun presents a diagram purporting to show that there is no statistical relationship between rates of population growth and rates of economic growth, concluding that "[m]any countries with high rates of population growth have high rates of per capita output growth, while the converse is also true." She also points out that some of the places with the highest population density, such as Hong Kong, Singapore, and the Netherlands, also have some of the highest per capita output growth rates.

The anti-Malthusians have also enjoyed support from organized religion. A gathering of bishops assembled to defend the Pope's ban on birth control has asserted that the earth could feed forty billion people, or eight times the present population.

Views on population that are influenced by religious views on such practices as family planning and birth control are in accord with the classic and traditional view of population as a source of ultimate wealth. As Joseph Schumpeter has noted, with rare exceptions, kings, philosophers, and economists alike have traditionally been enthusiastic about an increasing population:

In fact, until the middle of the eighteenth century, they were as nearly unanimous in this "populationist" attitude as they [had] ever been in anything. A numerous and increasing population was the most important symptom of wealth; it was the chief cause of wealth; it was wealth itself—the greatest asset for a nation to have.

To be sure, traditional Malthusians have their counter-arguments. While conceding the basic point that resource shortages may spur the invention of substitutes, they point out that air, waterways, and soil have a limited capacity to sustain an expanding population, regardless of how many resource substitutes are invented through the application of human ingenuity.

* * *

The debate will continue as long as the Malthusian date of reckoning is postponed; that is, until food production growth and technology fail to accommodate the expansion in population. broad-based starvation, which directly serves to reduce the entire world population. Isolated historical events, such as the Irish potato famine of the 1850s or the current tragedy of half a billion people starving in underdeveloped countries (45,000 children dying every day, and over a billion humans living in squalor), will continue to be chalked up to misallocative economic systems or bad farming methods.

Anti–Malthusians point to the fact that the dire predictions of latter day Malthusian zealots have failed to come true, and point to the failure of Malthusians to envision such developments as the Green Revolution and technological progress as means of accommodating an ever expanding population. Just as pre-Columbian Europeans did not dream of a New World in the western hemisphere to accommodate population expansion, today's short-sighted doomsayers cannot envision the colonization of the solar system or other planets in the galaxy.

In fact, a close look at the Malthusian debate reveals that the protagonists do not disagree as much as they claim. Even the most zealous anti-Malthusian concedes that there are limits to how many people the earth can hold. Presumably these limits will be reached before the earth becomes a ball of flesh expanding at the speed of light.

Likewise, responsible Malthusians concede that human ingenuity has postponed, and probably will continue to postpone, the day of Malthusian reckoning for some time to come. It is not a trivialization of this great debate to suggest that the debate is reducible to a simple disagreement about timing. The current debate also begs the real issue: assuming that there is a limit on the capacity of the earth to support an expanding population, what forces of law or nature should be relied upon to check that expansion short of the dreaded Malthusian consequences of starvation and subsistence? Will human-kind continue to rely upon starvation, disease, wars, and plagues, as it has in the past? Or is civilized human society capable of devising more humane checks which can be imposed consistent with human dignity and compassion? When should the checks be imposed? Is the greater risk in imposing checks too soon, or too late?

9. Elizabeth Spahn, *Feeling Grounded: A Gendered View of Population Control*, 27 ENVTL. L. 1295, 1306–10 (1997).

In population control policies, as Professor Paula Abrams has demonstrated, controlling female fertility is also frequently motivated by dominance competition games. Sometimes it is an anti-natalist policy, as in China today or India under Indira Ghandi, which aims to control female fertility to reduce population and move ahead in the standard of living competition. Other times, as is often the case with fundamentalist religions, or Romania under Ceausescu, or the United States in the late nineteenth century, the competition is to out breed the other side by banning abortion and limiting access to contraceptives.

Still other situations involve selective breeding policies, in which favored populations are forced or encouraged to breed, while disfavored populations are murdered, involuntarily sterilized, or raped into extinction. Eugenics, whether practiced by Nazis, or in Bosnia, or in the U.S. against those of African ancestry present the ultimate slippery slope of the population control game.

Of course population strategies which narrowly focus on controlling female fertility do not actually work very well to reduce fertility rates. Additionally, they do great harm to the women being controlled. Indira Ghandi's policy of involuntary sterilization resulted not only in the topple of her government by popular election, but also in a deep suspicion of family planning programs and clinics and a long period of stagnation in the decline of the birth rate.

A consensus developed at the 1994 United Nations International Conference on Population and Development (ICPD), is that the most effective approach to lowering female fertility involves empowering women rather than attempting to control them. The 1992 World Development Report by the World Bank likewise expressed the view that gender equity, economic development, the environment, and population growth should be approached with an integrated set of policies which will produce a synergistic effect. The United Nations Population Fund (UNPF) report Investing in Women: The Focus of the 90s, also published in 1992, stresses that investments in women include "social investments" such as health and education services, equal economic opportunities, as well as family planning investment.

The problem of limiting population growth while respecting women's human rights is not an either/or dichotomy with the only choice between brutal coercion or massive numbers of births. . . .

A more sophisticated and nuanced approach will achieve the goal of stabilizing or even reducing population levels in terms of new births. Approaching obliquely, at a forty-five degree angle instead of charging straight ahead, is a more sophisticated strategy, redirecting the energy of population policy makers toward creating environments in which lower fertility rates flourish because the women themselves, and their families, flourish with fewer births.

There are four major factors which the more sophisticated analysts have identified as influencing a reduction in births. First, and statistically most significant to lowering female fertility rates, is the increase of secondary education for girls. Even just focusing on basic literacy helps significantly, but secondary education is preferable. Second, ensuring access to a full spectrum of reproductive health care, including family planning, but in particular treatment for reproductive tract infections, is a significant factor in the reduction of births. Third, providing economic opportunities, especially employment for which actual wages are paid directly to the women workers, and land rights directly held by women farmers instead of through male intermediaries, influences birth rates. Fourth, strengthening women's ability to make and implement their own decisions about their education, health, and economic lives (empowerment) in both the private and public aspects of their lives can reduce the number of births. Combining all four techniques is obviously the most effective approach to developing an environment, which will tend to encourage lower female fertility rates.

10. Reed Boland, *The Environment, Population and Women's Human Rights*, 27 ENVTL. L. 1137, 1166–67 (1997).

It is important to note that while improving the education and status of women is crucial to achieving a stable rate of population growth, other changes are necessary. Among these are the satisfaction of the basic needs of society–in particular health care, education, and social security, so that societies will not feel the need for large families to support them in old age. All of the societies that have managed to lower fertility rates have made major strides in these areas. Another factor is making contraceptives available to those persons who desire to use them, as well as safe abortion services when contraception fails. Here the promoters of traditional population polices have been right. Studies consistently show that there are hundreds of millions of persons throughout the world who would like to limit their number of births but do not have effective means to do so other than relying on natural and traditional methods, such as the rhythm method, withdrawal, breast-feeding, and abstinence. Further, the accessibility of contraceptives and the manner and context in which contraceptives are presented can make a significant difference in the willingness of acceptors to continue to use them. Although there is disagreement over the extent to which the greater availability of modern forms of contraception and abortion has been responsible for lowered birth rates in the last few decades, such rates certainly would have been more difficult to achieve without such availability. Unless socioeconomic conditions are as desperate as those prevailing in Romania under the Government of President Ceausescu, people will find it difficult to limit births without contraceptives.

Nonetheless, the importance of improving the education and status of women to this process is vital. While there is no ironclad assurance that adopting this approach will bring about the desired results, there is strong evidence that it will, stronger than the evidence supporting coercive measures. At the least, unlike many of the other measures that have been tried, such an approach will be promoting human rights rather than compromising them.

11.   Robert M. Hardaway, *Environmental Malthusianism: Integrating Population and Environmental Policy*, 27 ENVTL. L. 1209, 1231–41 (1997).

B.   FAMILY PLANNING

The stabilization of the world's population does not require drastic or Draconian measures such as those instituted in India in the 1970s, or in China today. Population could be stabilized without coercive measures if governments provided contraceptives and family planning services to every woman of child-bearing age. Even if nations could not fully achieve such a goal, stabilization might still be attained if nations: 1) expanded their existing family planning programs, 2) fostered liberal policies of free trade and permitted economic growth to raise world incomes, particularly those in developing countries, so that parents would not need children solely for ensuring their economic survival, and 3) reformed their immigration policies so that people-exporting countries would be forced to deal directly with their internal population problems within their own borders rather than simply exporting their excess humans.

A recent study by the Population Council revealed that "100 million couples who want to delay or stop having children have no means of doing so." With over 100 million births a year worldwide, it can readily be seen that voluntary family planning programs, if made widely available, could achieve population stabilization.

* * *

C.   IMMIGRATION

Historically, immigration has been the method of avoiding Malthusian consequences. When a potato famine threatened Ireland in the mid–1800s, thousands of Irish immigrated to America. Today, thousands of people from underdeveloped areas of the globe immigrate, both legally and illegally, to such developed countries as the United States.

Of course, the mere transfer of human beings from one location on the globe to another neither adds to, nor detracts from, the total human population. However, the fact that emigration can serve as an escape valve to avoid population pressures within a country relieves the government of the human-exporting country from the task of making hard choices and adopting policies that address the population problem directly.

For example, as long as a country has the option of simply exporting humans in order to relieve population pressures within its boundaries, it will have no incentive to take on the Church or other groups which resist any kind of population or family planning policy. The export of excess humans, whom the country cannot feed or support, becomes the path of least resistance.

Immigration reform in the developed countries of the world would force human-exporting countries to come to grips with their own population problems, including designing a system of family planning services and providing contraceptives to all of its citizens. Unfortunately, the whole idea of immigration reform is often resisted on purely emotional or political grounds. Like abortion, the history of immigration is often misunderstood.

* * *

D.   ECONOMIC GROWTH POLICIES

Economic growth has a significant environmental impact. It is, however, only one of three components of total environmental impact. Holdren has created a model that measures total environmental impact by multiplying population size by per capita consumption by environmental impact per unit of consumption ($I = P \times C \times U$). Current environmental policy is directed primarily towards the "U" component, that is, toward reducing the environmental impact of individual units. The mandating of emission controls on automobiles and smokestacks are examples of this policy. Such measures have been ineffective in significantly reducing total environmental impact, because the reduction of one type of pollutant often results in the increase of another type. Furthermore, a modest decline in pollutants released by individual units (such as cars) is more than offset by an explosion in the total number of units.

Some environmentalists have suggested an attack on the second component, "C", per capita consumption of units. A large body of academic opinion has taken a position against economic growth, free trade, and a rise in living standards. Professor Benson, for example, at the 1992 Conference on Free Trade and the Environment in Latin America stated that "the costs of traditional economic growth exceed the benefits and will lead to environmental collapse. Therefore, free trade, which promotes that growth, is a fundamentally misguided public policy."

In other words, it would be better if living standards did not rise; the miserable and poverty-stricken third world residents should do their part for the environment by staying poor and miserable. As Professor Daly has put it, "for all 5.4 billion people presently alive to consume resources and absorptive capacities at the same per capita rate as Americans or Europeans is ecologically impossible."

Vice President Albert Gore adopted a similar view in his book Earth in the Balance, stating that "we cannot continue to use the good of the earth as we have in the past.... [S]ociety is given to ... consumerism while remaining indifferent to the damage which [it] causes." This "environmentalism of the spirit," as the Vice President calls it, has a nice, politically acceptable ring to it, and sounds much like Professor Benson's scholarly version which states that costs of economic growth and a rise in living standards will lead to "environmental collapse."

Nevertheless, the notion that not only Americans, but the world's poorest people should cut back their consumption, is not one I recall being touted during the last presidential campaign. Perhaps this skeptic might be forgiven for doubting the fairness, if not the practicality of an environmental program based on convincing people to reduce their standard of living. A dictator such as Ceaucescu in Romania could adopt such a program–he would simply turn off the light and shut down the heat. Democracies would have a much more difficult time accomplishing a similar result.

Such proposals also fail to recognize that technological innovation spawned by economic growth has been the one human development which has delayed the onset of Malthusian consequences. Without the "Green Revolution" millions more humans would be suffering the Malthusian consequences of starvation and disease. Without technologically advanced pollution-control devices and equipment, the environment would be degrading at an even higher rate than it is presently.

This leaves the third component of Holdren's equation, the "P," representing population. Unfortunately, this is the very component that most environmental groups are unwilling to touch with a ten-foot pole.

But environmental programs focusing on the "U" have proven ineffective, costly, and counter-productive. Notions of "environmentalism of the spirit," based on a lowering of living standards, are unfair and impractical in any society other than a dictatorship. This leaves population control as the key component in any realistic environmental program.

12. Virginia Deane Abernethy, *Allowing Fertility Decline: 200 Years After Malthus's Essay on Population*, 27 ENVTL. L. 1097 (1997).

Currently, fertility rates are declining or are already low in most countries. The economic opportunity model presented herein predicts that this trend will continue because it is a response to real economic and environmental signs. The fertility decline can be delayed by either lavish foreign aid or attractive migration opportunities, because these harbingers of opportunity neutralize local signals of scarcity.

Well-meaning environmentalists regard explosive population growth as an enduring dilemma. The frequent target of interventions to stop population growth is the total fertility rate (TFR), an estimate of the number of children to be born to a woman over her lifetime. Here, I propose an economic opportunity model of fertility, to explain why fertility rates rise or fall.

This model puts much new data in perspective.

The economic opportunity model holds that a sense of environmental and economic limits motivates couples to prefer and plan small families. The positive, motivational role for perceived limits may appear to fly in the face of both humanitarian goals for world-wide improvement in the standard of living and the neoclassical value system which equates growth with well-being. The model also raises the concern that it is coercive to let hardship influence behavior. Thus, I pose two questions. First, is the economic opportunity model of fertility empirically correct? Assuming yes, is the process coercive?

* * *

Demographic transition theory (DTT) tells policymakers that economic development, low infant mortality, and education cause a preference for small family size. But this causal explanation arose from correlational data from the 1930s and reflected fertility during a period when western countries were sunk in economic depression. It has little other basis and has been contradicted by in-depth historical studies. Moreover, accumulating data suggests that DTT variables have uncertain power to predict or cause fertility decline. Nevertheless, DTT has been used to rationalize international programs designed to assist Third World development, an enterprise assumed to be not only humanitarian, but also effective for reducing fertility.

I propose a different and much simpler explanation of family size preferences. The premise is that children are desirable among all peoples. It is no large leap to the hypothesis that families ordinarily want as many children as they believe they can successfully raise.

Standards for success and opportunity vary across cultures and socioeconomic sectors; therefore, the following two causal principles of the economic opportunity model are phrased in terms of subjective perception. One, a sense of expanding opportunity causes families to raise their family size target; this usually results in larger actual family size. Two, a perception of scarcity, limits, or contracting opportunity leads to marital and reproductive caution, i.e., smaller family size.

The economic opportunity model of fertility suggests policies which are often diametrically opposed to those prescribed by demographic transition theory. For example, DTT is congruent with generous immigration policies and international economic development aid. But the economic opportunity model suggests that this open-handedness is often problematic, sending the message abroad that local constraints can be discounted because international wealth is abundant and opportunity is beckoning. If people believe that negative signals coming from their own environment and economy can be safely ignored, incentives to exercise marital and reproductive caution are overwhelmed.

* * *

In evaluating models, the reader might keep in mind the following: 1) correlations do not establish causality, 2) a theory should account for either upward or downward movement in the dependent variable here, (the fertility rate), and 3) tests of causal relationships require, as a minimum, that the supposed cause be temporally prior to the supposed effect. These three threshold tests are met in the examples offered here and elsewhere, and they may be considered, if not proof, at least strong support for the economic opportunity model.

Nevertheless, the economic opportunity explanation of fertility has not swept demographic circles. Perhaps the answer lies in most of us wishing to be active in doing good, whereas the economic opportunity model demands a waiting game. It counsels to let people perceive, then believe, that rescue will not happen, that a better life depends upon reproductive restraint and not upon international rescue or a foreign welcome mat for an impoverished country's excess numbers.

Help should be effectively channeled. The economic opportunity model supports micro-loans to individuals that amount to a small leg-up toward productive work and do not falsely raise expectations of a windfall. Assistance with family planning is another useful program because it helps interested families to humanely implement a dependent limiting, saving, capital accumulation strategy which raises family well-being over the long run.

In sum, interventions which give the appearance of international responsibility for improving conditions should be avoided because they encourage disregard of local signs of environmental and economic stress. The result of open-handed immigration and foreign assistance policies is almost sure to be continuing high fertility, so our well-meant policies are not, in fact, a kindness. Only if interventions avoid misleading promises of rescue can one proceed with confidence that worldwide fertility will swiftly fall.

13. Reed Boland, *The Environment, Population and Women's Human Rights*, 27 ENVTL. L. 1137, 1139–40, 1156–59 (1997).

I believe that embracing the doomsday approach without consideration of all the facts has had major harmful consequences, particularly with respect to questions of population control. First, it has led to major excesses and mistakes in the planning and implementation of population policies and programs. There has been a rush to adopt measures to lower the rate of population growth, such as directly inducing people to accept contraception to the point of using force, but the measures have not been thought through either as to their ultimate efficacy or to the impact that they have on the lives of individuals. The result has been practices that seriously implicate human rights, particularly women's human rights since the fertility of women is the target of most population programs. Fear of an unsustainable future for all has created immediate suffering for many.

* * *

III.   HUMAN RIGHTS INSTRUMENTS AND COERCIVE POPULATION POLICIES

Many of the practices carried out in the name of population policy have important human rights implications under both binding international agreements and less formal documents signed by country representatives at international conferences. The issue of human rights in the area of population policy is complex, and has been provided with a theoretical framework only in the last several years. Traditional human rights concerns may seem alien to this field in a number of ways. Historically, human rights activism has largely focused on classic abuses of civil and political rights abuses such as torture, unjust imprisonment, political persecution and disappearances, denial of freedom of speech and correspondence, unfair trials, and similar occurrences. One characteristic feature of these abuses has been their public nature; they have been perceived as involving government action in a public setting. The direct intervention of the government has resulted in individuals being deprived of rights that they would otherwise have.

If considered at all, the rights implicated in population policies—namely reproductive rights–have appeared not to fit this model. They involve private settings, family relations, sexual conduct, and social custom and policy. Demands for reproductive rights seem to belong more to the province of economic and social rights, that is, part of claims for the provision of various generalized social benefits such as health, education, housing, and employment. They have been thought of not as rights inherent to the individual, which only the government could take away, but rights that exist theoretically and cannot be exercised without the intervention of the government to actualize them. Moreover, it certainly is not a coincidence that the human rights aspects of population policies relate to the concerns of women in a far more central way than most classic human rights issues. Indeed, they deal with issues that are, in some sense, unique to women's actual experiences: conception, pregnancy, and childbirth, issues which have often been considered part of the private sphere. Because the human rights community has traditionally been less interested in social, economic, and women's rights than in civil and political rights, reproductive rights have been treated somewhat as a stepchild of the international rights community.

It is important, however, to recognize that the rights implicated in population policies do, in significant ways, fit into a traditional human rights framework. They do involve government action of a highly organized and coercive nature. Population policies are formulated by governments and involve government officials at many levels, from central planners to regional and local officials to medical workers involved with the treatment of specific persons. They represent the intrusion of government into the very core of individual's lives and are not simply a matter of relations between husbands and wives and family members. Further, population policies are often implemented in public settings, such as hospitals, clinics, etc., where operations can be performed and family planning devices dispensed, inserted, or implanted. Enforcement is often achieved through mass meetings or through the public pressure of local officials and work associates, or even the police in extreme situations. As discussed above, these policies are also supported by laws.

Accordingly, there are provisions of civil and political human rights treaties that are highly relevant to reproductive rights. For example, although it does not refer to reproductive rights by name, the Covenant on Civil and Political Rights (the human rights document traditionally regarded with the greatest respect by international human rights groups) contains provisions that are highly applicable. **[Basic Document 7.14]** It guarantees the right to life, the right not to be subjected to medical or scientific experimentation without consent, the right not to be subjected to inhumane or degrading treatment, the right to liberty and security of person, the right not to be subjected to arbitrary or unlawful interference with privacy or the family, and the right to marry and found a family. The Covenant also endorses the general principle that it is to be implemented without discrimination on the basis of sex. It does not require a strained reading of the Covenant to see how many of the activities associated with population policies violate these civil and political rights and discriminate on the basis of sex.

In addition, reproductive rights are the named subject matter of the Convention on the Elimination of All Forms of Discrimination against Women, which was endorsed by the United Nations General Assembly and opened for ratification in 1979. **[Basic Document 7.19]** This Convention had its origin in the international community's perception that although the major human rights conventions all prohibited discrimination on the basis of sex and indicated that their provisions were to be implemented without such discrimination, their statements on this issue were too general. Further attention needed to be devoted to specific aspects of sex discrimination, with an emphasis on some of the particular problems facing women, including reproduction.

The result is a treaty based on the equality of men and women which guarantees a broad array of rights–civil, political, social, and economic. By the end of 1995, the treaty had 151 parties, however, the United States was not among them. The Convention specifically endorses the following rights: 1) access to information on health and to information and advice on family planning, 2) the right to protection of the function of reproduction, 3) the right of access to health care services, including family planning, 4) the right to freely and responsibly decide on the number and spacing of children, and 5) the right to have access to the education and means to exercise this right. It is relatively easy to see the applicability of these provisions to coercive population policies.

The rights to decide freely and responsibly on the number and spacing of children, and to have access to the education and means to exercise these rights are of particular interest. This phrase constitutes what one might call, at this point in the evolution of thinking on population issues, the classic formulation of reproductive rights in an international context. The phrase's first recorded use was in the final document approved by the Teheran Conference on Human Rights in 1968. Since then, in various wordings, it has been a staple of population thinking, taken up by a number of individual governments in population policy statements and laws, and reiterated prominently in the documents adopted by the three international population conferences, held in Bucharest in 1974, in Mexico City in 1984, and, most recently, in Cairo in 1994.

This is not to say that a one-to-one correspondence can automatically be made between various coercive population policy measures and the rights that they violate. Relying on human rights documents is not as simple a matter as connecting dots in a picture. There are a number of issues that must be taken into consideration in examining the human rights aspects of population policies. One is the issue of cultural relativism, the principle that in different countries widely differing customs, religious beliefs, and social and cultural expectations play a significant role in determining how moral elements of a particular action are perceived. Another is the issue of necessity, the principle that actions taken in one context might seem thoroughly inappropriate, but in another might appear to be the only rational choice because of the gravity of the problem.

This latter principle is inherent in the classic formulation of reproductive rights itself, which has been the subject of heated debate and detailed exegesis nearly from the beginning. The primary issue is the interpretation of the contrasting words "freely" and "responsibly," linked together as delimiters of reproductive rights. This linkage has prompted a series of questions. Is there a true "free" reproductive right if it must be exercised "responsibly?" Who is to determine what constitutes responsible action: the individual, the couple, the family, the community, or the government? What are the limits of "responsible" action? For example, does responsibility entail undergoing sterilization and abortion when not desired, bearing children that are unwanted, submitting to contraception (including contraception that may be harmful to health) or, conversely, bearing more children than can be properly cared for? Does a government have a right to impose strict population control measures in the name of responsibility for the purpose of providing a better life for future generations? The answers to these questions have fueled recent debates over population, the environment, and reproductive rights.

14. *Report of the International Conference on Population and Development*, **U.N. Conference on Population and Development, principles 4–11, U.N. Doc. A/CONF./171/13 (1994) Annex, Program of Action of the International Conference on Population and Development,** *adopted on* **13 September 1994 at Cairo, Egypt.**

Principle 4

Advancing gender equality and equity and the empowerment of women, and the elimination of all kinds of violence against women, and ensuring women's ability to control their own fertility, are cornerstones of population and development-related programmes. The human rights of women and the girl child are an inalienable, integral and indivisible part of universal human rights. The full

and equal participation of women in civil, cultural, economic, political and social life, at the national, regional and international levels, and the eradication of all forms of discrimination on grounds of sex, are priority objectives of the international community.

Principle 5

Population-related goals and policies are integral parts of cultural, economic and social development, the principal aim of which is to improve the quality of life of all people.

Principle 6

Sustainable development as a means to ensure human well-being, equitably shared by all people today and in the future, requires that the interrelationships between population, resources, the environment and development should be fully recognized, properly managed and brought into harmonious, dynamic balance. To achieve sustainable development and a higher quality of life for all people, States should reduce and eliminate unsustainable patterns of production and consumption and promote appropriate policies, including population-related policies, in order to meet the needs of current generations without compromising the ability of future generations to meet their own needs.

Principle 7

All States and all people shall cooperate in the essential task of eradicating poverty as an indispensable requirement for sustainable development, in order to decrease the disparities in standards of living and better meet the needs of the majority of the people of the world. The special situation and needs of developing countries, particularly the least developed, shall be given special priority. Countries with economies in transition, as well as all other countries, need to be fully integrated into the world economy.

Principle 8

Everyone has the right to the enjoyment of the highest attainable standard of physical and mental health. States should take all appropriate measures to ensure, on a basis of equality of men and women, universal access to health-care services, including those related to reproductive health care, which includes family planning and sexual health. Reproductive health-care programmes should provide the widest range of services without any form of coercion. All couples and individuals have the basic right to decide freely and responsibly the number and spacing of their children and to have the information, education and means to do so.

Principle 9

The family is the basic unit of society and as such should be strengthened. It is entitled to receive comprehensive protection and support. In different cultural, political and social systems, various forms of the family exist. Marriage must be entered into with the free consent of the intending spouses, and husband and wife should be equal partners.

Principle 10

Everyone has the right to education, which shall be directed to the full development of human resources, and human dignity and potential, with particular attention to women and the girl child.

Education should be designed to strengthen respect for human rights and fundamental freedoms, including those relating to population and development. The best interests of the child shall be the guiding principle of those responsible for his or her education and guidance; that responsibility lies in the first place with the parents.

Principle 11

All States and families should give the highest possible priority to children. The child has the right to standards of living adequate for its well-being and the right to the highest attainable standards of health, and the right to education. The child has the right to be cared for, guided and supported by parents, families and society and to be protected by appropriate legislative, administrative, social and educational measures from all forms of physical or mental violence, injury or abuse, neglect or negligent treatment, maltreatment or exploitation, including sale, trafficking, sexual abuse, and trafficking in its organs.

15. **Agenda 21, Ch. 5 of the United Nations Conference on Environment and Development ("Demographic Dynamics and Sustainability"), June 2–8, 1992, para. 5.1–5.55.** [Basic Document 1.30].[d]

16. **Charter of the United Nations (as amended), June 26, 1945, arts. 55, 56, 1976 Y.B.U.N. 1043.** [Basic Document 1.3].

17. **Universal Declaration of Human Rights, Dec. 10, 1948, arts. 16, 29, G.A. Res. 217A, U.N. GAOR, 3d Sess., pt. 1, Resolutions, at 71, U.N. Doc. A/810 (1948).** [Basic Document 7.11].

18. **Final Act of the United Nations International Conference on Human Rights at Teheran, 13 May 1968, point 16** *in* HUMAN RIGHTS: A COMPILATION OF INTERNATIONAL INSTRUMENTS 43 (1988). [Basic Document 7.15].

19. **Declaration on Social Progress and Development, Dec. 11, 1969, G.A. Res. 2542, U.N. GAOR, 24th Sess., Supp. No. 30, at 49, U.N. Doc. A/7630 (1970).** [Basic Document 7.17].

20. **International Covenant on Economic, Social and Cultural Rights, Dec. 19, 1966, art. 10(1), 993 U.N.T.S. 3.** [Basic Document 7.13].

21. **International Covenant on Civil and Political Rights, Dec. 16, 1966, art. 23(1), 999 U.N.T.S. 171.** [Basic Document 7.14].

22. **Convention on the Elimination of All Forms of Discrimination Against Women, Dec. 18, 1979, art. 12, G.A. Res. 34/180 (Annex), U.N. GAOR, 34th Sess., Supp. No. 46, at 194, U.N. Doc. A/34/830 (1979), 19 I.L.M. 33 (1980).** [Basic Document 7.19].

23. **Convention on the Rights of the Child, Nov. 20, 1989, art. 2(2), G.A. Res. 44/25 (Annex), U.N. GAOR, 44th Sess., Supp. No. 49, at 166, U.N. Doc. A/RES/44/49 (1990), 20 I.L.M. 1448 (1989).** [Basic Document 7.22].

24. **Lisa B. Gregory,** *Examining the Economic Component of China's One–Child Family Policy Under International Law: Your Money or Life,* 6 J. CHINESE L. 45, 60–78 (1992).

B.   HUMAN RIGHTS AS INTERNATIONAL LAW

The question of the legally binding nature of custom, resolutions and declarations, hardly a clear-cut subject under the best of circumstances, becomes even more complex with regard to the highly controversial area of international human rights. The Charter of the United Nations **[Basic Document 1.3]** specifically mandates "respect for, and observance of, human rights and fundamental freedoms."[16] It further provides that "[a]ll members

---

   d. Chapter 5 of Agenda 21 addresses, *inter alia,* the need for "[d]eveloping and disseminating knowledge concerning the links between demographic trends and factors and sustainable development" (including paras. 5.1–5.5). After stating the "Basis for Action" and the "Objectives" of this "Programme Area," it lists specific activities, processes, and actions

that States should implement. None is very specific.

   16. U.N. Charter, art. 55(c). It is interesting to observe that the tension between human rights and development is present even within this article, which states that the United Nations shall promote: "higher standards of liv-

pledge themselves to take joint and separate action in co-operation with the Organization for the achievement of [these] purposes[.]"[17] The Charter is indisputably a treaty, legally binding upon all members of the United Nations, including China. However, even if one accepts the argument that "the legal duty to promote respect for human rights includes the legal duty to respect them,"[18] the scope of human rights is not defined within the Charter.

The Universal Declaration of Human Rights [**Basic Document 7.11**] represents the United Nations' first attempt to articulate this scope. Numerous subsequent United Nations resolutions, Final Acts and Covenants have reaffirmed the provisions of the Declaration, thus re-enforcing the view that "the Universal Declaration of Human Rights constitutes an authoritative interpretation of the Charter of the highest order, and has over the years become a part of customary international law."[19] Subsequent conventions and declarations have further elaborated specific types of "human rights" and how States should go about promoting and observing them. The conventions bind the States Parties by virtue of their treaty status. However, because China is not a signatory to most of these instruments, it becomes necessary when evaluating whether the one-child policy violates international human rights to determine the extent to which China may nonetheless be constrained by the customary international law created by these treaties and declarations.[20]

The Chinese recognize the existence of customary international law, and consider United Nations resolutions a subsidiary means of determining the rules of law. In their view, those General Assembly resolutions adopted by unanimous or overwhelming majorities, while not possessing a formally legal character, do have a certain binding force on those members who voted for their adoption, as well as "general significance in international relations."[21] Furthermore, the People's Republic recognizes the Universal Declaration as "the first international human rights document that has laid the foundation for the practice of human rights in the world arena."[22]

This praise not withstanding, Chinese legal scholars and government representatives have consistently insisted that global human rights standards

ing, full employment, and conditions of economic and social progress and development." *Id.* art. 55(a).

17. *Id.* art. 56.

18. H. LAUTERPACHT, INTERNATIONAL LAW AND HUMAN RIGHTS 152 (1973).

19. MONTREAL STATEMENT OF THE ASSEMBLY FOR HUMAN RIGHTS 2 (New York, 1968). This view is not undisputed. See Lauterpacht, *supra* note 38, at 408–17 for the proposition that the Universal Declaration is no more than "morally binding." Discussing the "grey zone" of legality in which the Universal Declaration exists, Henkin observes that: "[w]ith time, the Universal Declaration has itself acquired significant legal status ... Few [States] claim that any state that violates any provision of the Declaration has violated international law. Almost all would agree that some violations of the Declaration are violations of international law." L. HENKIN, THE AGE OF RIGHTS 19 (1990).

20. Put another way, to what extent does repeated reference in treaties and declarations to, for example, a couple's right to decide the number and spacing of their children constitute evidence of an *opinio juris communis* which binds China despite that State's non-participation?

21. H. Chiu, *Chinese Attitudes Toward International Law in the Post–Mao Era, 1978–1987,* 21 INT'L L. 1127 (1987) (quoting a discussion in GUOJI FA [INTERNATIONAL LAW] 35 (Wang Tieya & Wei Min eds. 1981), the standard textbook on international law used in most Chinese colleges and institutions).

22. Information Office of the State Council, *Human Rights Whitepaper: Human Rights in China,* BEIJING REV., Nov. 4–10, 1991, at 8 [hereinafter *Human Rights Whitepaper*].

are aspirational, and must in practice be subject to national historical, social, economic and cultural conditions.[23] They deny that individuals are subjects of international law. Indeed, they "harbor a skeptical view" of the validity of international human rights law, and generally accuse Western countries of "attempt[ing] to use the pretext of protecting human rights to interfere in China's and other socialist states' internal affairs."[24]

However, by analyzing China's position from the "the practical attitude, the attitude of seeking truth from facts,"[25] it can be argued that China's behavior suggests de facto recognition of international human rights law. Although currently a State Party to very few of the major human rights conventions,[26] the PRC nevertheless has not hesitated to invoke the Charter and generally accepted principles of international law concerning human rights to denounce actions by other States.[27]

With respect to the possible incorporation of certain human rights provisions in the Constitution of the People's Republic, Nathan points out that:

> The Constitution in China is not a "guarantist" document which protects the rights of individuals against the encroachment of the state. It is instead based on the assumption of a harmony between the high interests of the individual (if he can perceive them) and those of the state (provided that the leaders of the state properly understand their duty).[28]

If Nathan's assessment is correct, then the one-child family policy must be evaluated from the standpoint of international standards of human rights, not of China's own constitutionally guaranteed civil liberties.

Although scholars generally agree that certain human rights are *erga omnes* (obligations binding upon all States) and therefore abuses of those rights violate customary international law, there is no consensus regarding whether the right to decide number and spacing of children falls within this category. The Restatement (Revised) § 702 provides that "a state violates international law if, as a matter of state policy, it practices, encourages or condones ... (g) consistent patterns of gross violations of internationally recognized human rights."[29] However, as the previous discussion indicates, there may well be considerable debate as to the extent to which the procrea-

---

23. The Chinese maintain the position expressed by Chen Shiqiu, permanent representative of the PRC to the UN, that "in view of the diversity of social and political systems, degrees of economic development and historical, religious and cultural backgrounds, it was only natural that the concept of human rights should be interpreted in different ways." *Report of the Economic and Social Council*, U.N. GAOR 3rd Comm., 50th mtg. at 7, U.N. Doc. A/C.3/45/SR.50 (1990).

24. *Supra* note 21, at 1139.

25. *Human Rights Whitepaper, supra* note 22, at 9.

26. A. Nathan et al., *Current Chinese Communist Views of Human Rights*, in HUMAN RIGHTS: A SYMPOSIUM, PT. II, at 114, 121 (1978). The United States of America is also not a State party to the majority of international human rights conventions. For comparative information on the United States' record of

participation in international human rights instruments, see *Human Rights—Status of International Instruments*, 31 March 1991, U.N. Doc ST/HR/5, U.N. Sales No. E.87.XIV.2 (1991), at 10–11; L. Henkin, *Rights: American and Human*, 79 COLUM. L. REV. 405, 420–25 (1978).

27. *See* Nathan et al., *supra* note 26, at 121.

28. *Id.* at 115–16.

29. RESTATEMENT (THIRD) OF THE FOREIGN RELATIONS LAW OF THE UNITED STATES, § 702(g). The Restatement notes that § 702(g) does not extend to certain "infringements of recognized human rights" which are "committed singly or sporadically (although they may be forbidden to states parties to the International Covenants or other particular agreements)."

tive rights effected by China's one-child family policy constitute either *lex communalis* or *jus cogens* (norms from which no derogation is permitted). Leaving that theoretical debate to more competent authorities, let us now take up the issue of what is and is not guaranteed as of right under specific human rights instruments.

IV.   The Right to Found a Family in International Law: Scope and Limitations

A.   *Family and Human Rights in the Universal Declaration of Human Rights*

Article 16 of the Universal Declaration of Human Rights [**Basic Document 7.11**] seems concerned primarily with guaranteeing the freedom of individuals to enter into, maintain, and dissolve a conjugal union. Paragraphs (1) and (3) of Article 16 taken together suggest that the international community in 1948 regarded the family unit (i.e., the traditional model of husband-wife-child), rather than simply the spousal relationship, as the natural and desirable state of existence. Couples are guaranteed the right to attain the model status if they wish by bringing some number of children into their homes, either through procreation or adoption, and the State is exhorted to protect the resulting unit.

The Universal Declaration may view the family as a fundamental building block, but does not conceive of it as an end unto itself. The "right" to found a family is expressed in language which suggests neither a mandate to procreate nor a guarantee that couples may have as many children as they wish. The Universal Declaration clearly places the individual and his rights within the broader context of society. Article 29 contemplates man living within a society, responsible to it for conducting his life in a communally non-detrimental manner. Individuals have "duties to the community"—namely that they must abide by the rule of law, respect the rights of others, and comply with the "just requirements" which promote the "general welfare." Article 29(3) suggests that the "just requirements" in Article 29(2) include the principle that no one shall exercise his rights to a degree which unreasonably harms others. In the Chinese context, it is possible to interpret the Universal Declaration to mean that parents have the right to *some* children under Article 16, but, according to Article 29, the number may be subject to legal limitations necessary to ensure the general welfare of the community.

Using the Universal Declaration as a skeletal frame upon which to build, many subsequent international instruments have specifically explored the connection between families, human rights and national development. While the language of these instruments is not identical, there are certain common elements which give the impression that these documents are cross-referential, and that collectively they may articulate an internationally recognized matrix of "laws" relating to familial rights and State duties. The following section will attempt to set forth the uniform aspects of these international instruments and to explore the significant distinctions between them, so that China's policy of economic incentives and disincentives may be measured against a concrete standard.

B.   Articulating the "Law" of Procreative Rights and the Duty to Develop

The legal matrix of individual, familial and societal rights and duties appears to embrace the following principles: (1) the family is the natural and fundamental unit of society; (2) as such, it is entitled to some degree of State protection; (3) all children have, without distinction or discrimination, an explicit right to protection by the family and the State; (4) parents have the right to decide freely and responsibly the number and spacing of their children; (5) States have an affirmative duty to provide parents access to and education about family planning so that they may exercise this right; (6) every human being has the right to an adequate standard of living; and (8) by implication, in order to be successful, State policies may take precedence over certain individual and family rights.

C.   Variations Among the Instruments

1.   Principles 1 and 2: The Family Is the Fundamental Unit of Society and Therefore Entitled to Protection

The Universal Declaration's view that the family is the natural and fundamental unit of society and is therefore entitled to protection by society and the State[30] has been embraced unconditionally and with only slight linguistic variations by all subsequent instruments referring to the family. However, the instruments part company on the degree and character of protection a State must provide. Thus, the International Covenant on Economic, Social and Cultural Rights claims that the family should be afforded "[t]he widest possible protection and assistance" [in Article 10(1)]. The International Covenant on Civil and Political Rights states merely that the family is entitled to "protection" but identifies the source of this protection as "society and the State" [Article 23(1)]. The drafters of the Declaration on Social Progress and Development **[Basic Document 7.17]** appear to have consciously steered a middle course by urging that the family should be "assisted and protected" [in Article 4]. Their approach was modified only slightly under the Convention on the Rights of the Child to provide that this assistance should be given as "necessary" [as stated in the preamble].

The issue of how much and what type of assistance and protection is afforded the family becomes important in the context of parental rights and State duties. If the locus of decision-making regarding number and spacing of children resides primarily with parents, their ability to make these decisions requires that the State assist with (or at least no hinder) access to contraceptive devices. Furthermore, because exercise of family rights is constrained by responsibilities to the community, protection may imply protection of all families collectively, rather than of each discrete family unit.

2.   Principle 3: All Children Have the Right to Parental and State Protection without Distinction or Discrimination

International law appears to afford children heightened protection in certain areas, and to explicitly forbid differentiated treatment for children based upon birth order. The International Covenant on Economic, Social and

---

30. It may also be entitled to protection by international organizations. The Proclamation of Teheran notes in Point 16 that "[t]he protection of the family and of the child remains the concern of the international community." U.N. Doc. A/CONF.32/41 (1968) [hereinafter Teheran Proclamation] **[Basic Document 7.15]**.

Cultural Rights **[Basic Document 7.13]** provides that "special measures" should be taken on behalf of all children without discrimination "for reasons of parentage or other conditions" [Article 10(3)]. The International Covenant on Civil and Political Rights identifies the child's "family, society and the State" as the entities required to give protection and assistance without discrimination as to "birth" [Article 24(1)]. Both the Declaration on the Rights of the Child[e] and the Convention on the Rights of the Child **[Basic Document 7.22]** provide that States shall respect and ensure the rights of all children without discrimination on the basis of "birth or other status" [Declaration on the Rights of the Child Principle I], while the Convention on the Rights of the Child further insists that States shall protect the child from discrimination based upon the "status" or "activities" of the parents [Article 2(2)].

Economic policies which penalize a child solely on the basis of birth order appear to violate the international standard set forth above since they discriminate based upon a factor which is wholly outside the child's control. However, as will be discussed below, this standard is reactive, applying to the child once it is born, and should be distinguished from policies which are primarily aimed at discouraging prospective parents from conceiving and bearing the "additional" child.

3. Principle 4: Parents Have a Right to Decide the Number and Spacing of Their Children

The principle that parents have the right to decide the size of their family and therefore are entitled to access to information and means which will enable them to exercise this right also appears to have gained broad acceptance under international law. The General Assembly formally recognized the "sovereignty of nations in formulating and promoting their own population policies, with due regard to the principle that the size of the family should be the free choice of each individual family[.]"[31]

Yet, the relevant texts do not consistently express the degree to which these family rights are inviolable. The Proclamation of Teheran **[Basic Document 7.15]** asserts that parents have a "basic right" to determine freely and responsibly the number and spacing of their children,[32] while the Declaration on Social Progress and Development **[Basic Document 7.17]** states that this right is exclusive. The Convention on the Elimination of All Forms of Discrimination against Women does not qualify the right, but simply affirms that men and women shall have equal rights regarding decisions as to number and spacing of children.

On its face, the "exclusive right" granted by the Declaration on Social Progress and Development appears to extend isolated family rights beyond the parameters established in the Universal Declaration and other instruments, in which family rights are clearly constrained by duties to the

e. G.A. Res. 1386, UN GAOR, 14th Sess., Supp. No. 16, at 19, U.N.Doc. A/4354 (1960).

31. Population Growth and Economic Development, G.A. Res. 2211, U.N. GAOR, 21st Sess. (1966), *reprinted in* 11 UNITED NATIONS RESOLUTIONS, ser. I, Resolutions adopted by the General Assembly 1966–1968, at 157, 158 (D. Djonovich ed., 1975).

32. Point 16 states that, "[p]arents have a basic right to determine freely and responsibly the number and spacing of their children." Teheran Proclamation, *supra* note 30. **[Basic Document 7.15]**.

community. Indeed, an examination of the "legislative history" of the Declaration reveals that there was considerable disagreement among the drafters as to just how "exclusive" Article 4 was intended to be. Despite the fact that the article was approved unanimously, after the vote several delegates expressed their reservations regarding the word "exclusive," on the grounds that "[a] country's population growth must go hand in hand with economic growth," and making the right "exclusive" would impede government programs.[33] However, only a small portion of the States representatives actually commented on the issue of exclusivity. Therefore, it is difficult to ascertain how high parental rights may have been elevated by the Declaration above the "basic" level. Furthermore, because the Declaration, which does not have treaty status, is the only international instrument which characterizes this right as "exclusive," the degree to which customary international law embraces this right's exclusivity remains unclear, particularly in light of competing and compelling State interests. Nevertheless, post-debate statements, while not constituting a definitive interpretation of the text, do underscore the fact that several delegations regarded an international instrument espousing an "exclusive" parental right as a potentially dangerous trump to State demographic policies.

4.   Principle 5: Parents Have a Right to Practice Family Planning and States Have a Duty to Provide Information and Access

Over the years, family planning has gained the status of a "human right" and States have been assigned a certain degree of responsibility for ensuring this right. The Declaration on Population refers to family planning as a basic human right.[34] The Final Act of the International Conference on Human Rights claims that families have a right to adequate education and information to enable them to practice family planning.[35] The Declaration on Social Progress and Development requires States to formulate and establish, "as needed," population programs which shall include "education, training of personnel and the provision to families of the knowledge and means necessary" to enable them to exercise their rights regarding birth decisions [Article 22(6)]. The Convention on the Elimination of All Forms of Discrimination Against Women **[Basic Document 7.19]** provides that women shall have the same rights as men in the arena of family planning [Article 12].

Among these instruments, the Declaration on Social Progress and Development is most noteworthy because it moves beyond simply articulating the

---

33. Mrs. Galetshoge (Botswana), U.N. GAOR, 3rd Comm., 23rd Sess., 1601st mtg., at 2, U.N. Doc. A/C.3/SR.1601 (1968). Mr. Sanon (Upper Volta) said that "[w]hile his country respected the right of parents to determine the size of their families, it also recognized the right of the State to limit population growth for economic or security reasons." Mrs. Agboton (Dahomey) explained that she voted against the word because, in her view, the smaller and weaker countries should be allowed the right to influence population trends, if necessary, with a view to maintaining a balance between the size of the population and the degree of economic and social development. *Id.* Similarly, Mr. Gherib (Tunisia) was of the opinion that "a Government might find itself forced to furnish guidance to parents, by means of persuasion, in regard to number and spacing of births. That being so, the insertion of the word 'exclusive' could raise difficulties for some Governments." *Id.*

34. The Declaration was signed by 30 Heads of State on Human Rights Day, 10 December 1966. World Population Conference, Bucharest, U.N. Doc. E/Conf. 60/CBP/6, at n.7 (1974).

35. *Human Rights Aspects of Family Planning,* International Conference on Human Rights, Res. XVIII, U.N. Sales No. E.68. XIV.2, at 14; *discussed in* the World Population Conference, Bucharest, U.N. Doc. E/Conf.60/CBP/5, at 3–4 (1974).

family's "rights," to requiring that States actively provide family planning information and means to their citizens. Among the drafters, the idea that national demographic policies and programs should include dissemination of knowledge, training and means necessary to ensure effective implementation proved as controversial as had the term "exclusive." In fact, a separate vote was taken on the words "and means."[36] General Assembly records indicate that the drafters' intent was to ensure individuals access to information about and means to exercise birth control. The issue of coercive birth control was not raised.

5.   Principles 6, 7 and 8: Everyone Has the Right to an Adequate Standard of Living and the State Has a Duty to Formulate Policies Which Will Foster Realization of That Right, Even Though Such Policies May Intrude Upon Specific Family Rights

As was discussed above, the Universal Declaration conceives of the family as an *integrated* unit of society, and individual behavior as being subject to certain socially mandated limitations which will enhance "the general welfare" [Article 24(2)]. The International Covenant on Economic, Social and Cultural Rights calls upon States to "recognize the right of everyone to an adequate standard of living for himself and his family, including adequate food, clothing and housing, and to the continuous improvement of living conditions" [Article 11(1)]. Additionally, this Covenant requires that States placing limitations on specifically protected rights do so only in "so far as this may be compatible with the nature of these rights and solely for the purpose of promoting the general welfare in a democratic society" [Article 4]. However, without more, the Universal Declaration and the Covenants stop well short of addressing acceptable and unacceptable means of balancing procreative rights and community goals, let alone the specifics of the one-child-per-family policy.

The Proclamation of Teheran takes a step toward subordinating isolated parents' wishes to broader social authority by recognizing that "the widening gap between the economically developed and developing countries impedes the realization of human rights" and that it is "imperative for every nation, according to its capacities, to make the maximum possible effort to close this gap" [Point 12]. An examination of the United Nations records reveals that participants of the International Conference on Human Rights at which the Proclamation was drafted recognized that full realization of civil and political rights would be impossible without "sound and effective national and international policies of economic and social development."[37] The Conference ominously observed that unlimited population growth posed a serious threat to world health.

The Declaration on Social Progress and Development attempts to place "exclusive" parental rights within the broader context of communal and national concerns by affirming that each State has the "right and responsibility" to set its own goals and means for achieving social development, "without

36. It passed by 60 votes to 16, with 17 abstentions. U.N. GAOR 3rd Comm., 24th Sess., 1684th mtg., at 185, U.N. Doc. A/C/.3/ SR.1684 (1969).

37. Participants included representatives from the Food and Agricultural Organization

(FAO) and the World Health Organization (WHO) as well as member states. Int'l Conf. on Hum. Rts., 1968 U.N.Y.B. 538 U.N. Sales No. E.70.I.1., 540.

any external interference" [Article 3]. The family unit is to be protected "so that it may fully assume its responsibilities within the community" [Article 8]. Furthermore, the government is assigned "the primary role and ultimate responsibility of ensuring the social progress and well-being of its people," and of developing programs which bring these goals closer to realization [Article 8]. Lastly, the Declaration calls for the formulation of programs, "within the framework of national demographic policies," including education regarding and access to methods of birth control, which will enable families to exercise their rights [Article 22]. It appears that international human rights law leaves individual nations broad discretion with regard to internal demographic policies. Several international documents have explicitly stated that formation of a national demographic policy is an exercise of state sovereignty. However, State exercise of intrusive population control must be measured against other international standards, including human rights.

The Declaration on the Right to Development[38] reiterates some of the language found in prior instruments, first by affirming that States have both the right and the duty to formulate development policies. The text expressly states that "[a]ll human beings have a responsibility for development, individually and collectively" and that individuals must consider "their duties to the community" when exercising their human rights [Article 2]. States are assigned "the primary responsibility" for creating conditions which favor national development, and are required to undertake "all necessary measures" to provide individuals equal access to "basic resources, education, health services, food, housing, employment and the fair distribution of income" [Articles 3 and 8].

Even the Convention on the Rights of the Child gives the State a mandate to ensure that conditions exist under which a child can realize its right to an adequate standard of living, "particularly with regard to nutrition, clothing and housing" [Article 27]. Nevertheless, the Convention provides that children's right shall be promoted by States parties "in accordance with national conditions and within their means," thus carefully bounding these high aspirations within actual resource constraints.

Discussion Notes/Questions

1. The "population explosion" theory argues that the sheer number of human beings and their rate of reproduction amounts to a global crisis. This argument ignores, to some extent, the relative differences in resource use between the developed and developing world. On this basis, the strong focus on population numbers is arguably a specious one. The strongest critics of the population explosion view contend that it stems from racism. In fear of being overrun by "dark hordes," racist elites from the North blame the increasing numbers in the South. It has been suggested that there is remarkable alliance in the eugenics and birth control movements. *See* Betsy Hartmann, Reproductive Rights and Wrongs: The Global Politics of Population Control and Reproductive Choice 95–98 (1987). Chairman Mao referred to birth control as a bourgeois plot to visit "bloodless genocide" upon the Chinese people. *Cited in* Lisa Gregory, *Examining the Economic Component of China's One–Child Family Policy Under International Law:*

---

38. G.A. Res. 41/128, U.N. GAOR., 41st   (1987) **[Basic Document 7.20].**
Sess., Supp. No. 53, at 186, U.N. Doc. A/41/53

Your Money or Your Life?, 6 J. CHINESE L. 45, 48 (1992). What of the suggestions made by Hardaway and Abernethy (limit immigration and foreign aid so as to encourage population control by denying a "safety net" to countries with excess population)? *See* Readings 11 and 12. Does the incredible disparity in resource consumption invalidate the North's calls for population reduction? What right does the North have to dictate population policies while it continues to ineffectively deal with its consumption problem? Is it conceivable to imagine an international forum, or even instrument, which deals with population *as well as* consumption (perhaps climate change) as constituent parts of a two-pronged problem? *See* Reading 14.

2.   The population issue raises starkly the conflict between individual and collective rights. Perhaps the rights of the natural environment are also in competition. *See* P. Elder, *Legal Rights for Nature—The Wrong Answer to the Right(s) Question*, 22 Osgoode Hall L. J. 285 (1984); David Favre, *Wildlife Rights: The Ever–Widening Circle*, 9 ENVTL. L. 241 (1979); Christopher Stone, *Should Trees Have Standing?: Toward Legal Rights for Natural Objects*, 45 S. Cal. L. Rev. 450 (1972). Is the rights framework useful for addressing the complexity of population problems? Does the inherently political and economic nature of the situation render the theoretical notion of rights of academic value only?

3.   It is usually women from the South who are most affected by population policies. First, it is most often their bodies that are the subject of coercive methods of enforcement. Such control raises the classic issues that arise in debates about abortion. On what basis can the State intervene in the private realm of women's bodies? Second, the one-child family limit has been shown to increase domestic violence. When only one child is allowed, men become angry if their partner bears a daughter. A third concern is the increase in female infanticide in response to one-child family policies. Fourth, control over reproductive choice directly influences the ability of women in the developing world to change their role in the family and society: "The experience of controlling her own fertility is directly and concretely empowering." *See* Barbara Stark, *International Human Rights and Family Planning: A Modest Proposal*, 18 Den. J. INT'L L. & POL'Y 59, 78 (1989). What sorts of legal protection should and could be afforded women within the regulatory regimes of population control?

4.   Many policy analysts believe there is a strong correlation between rising wealth and declining birth rates. On this basis the Reagan Administration concluded that a vigorous free market economy is the best way to solve the population problem. Such an economy was predicted to stimulate development, with the consequent wealth influencing family planning choices. An alternative conclusion is that there must be a major redistribution of wealth from North to South. The first conclusion has the obvious advantage of political palatability. Perhaps the difference in conclusions serves merely to highlight the politically motivated nature of the population issue. To what extent is the connection between population and the environment a political one? Is the linking of the two concerns a political tactic for ensuring greater attention to issues of economic distribution? What does Abernethy's analysis suggest about the supposed link between development and declining birth rates, and the policies that are based on that link? *See* Reading 12.

5.   It is often suggested that educating women as to contraception is one of the best ways to address the population issue. It should be noted, however, that cultural constraints in the South limit the effectiveness of such programs. In some studies, male partner acceptance of contraceptive use is one of the greatest

determinants of birth rates. *See* Lori L. Heise, *Freedom Close To Home,* 19 Populi No. 6, at 7 (1992). Such studies point to the cultural and other barriers (such as religion) that any international initiative is required to address. Should rights override cultural and religious norms? Would attempts to do so merely exacerbate the situation?

6.   It has been denied by Chinese officials that coercion is part of official policy. However, the use of physical force has been sufficiently documented to indicate its widespread use. It is reported that after a couple's first child, the mother is required to be fitted for an IUD. If a couple does have a second child, one or both of the parents are sterilized. Alternatively, abortions are performed on unauthorized births. *See* John Aird, Slaughter of the Innocents (1990). Chinese officials have been forced to concede that although "the Chinese Government does not condone forced abortions or sterilizations, . . . coercion, even though counter to official policy, does occur in some instances." *See Is China's Birth Control Program Still Coercive?: Hearings Before the Senate Comm. on Foreign Relations,* 100th Cong., 1st Sess. (1987), *cited in* Note, *Coercive Population Control Policies: An Illustration of the Need for a Conscientious Objector Provision for Asylum Seekers,* 30 VaJ.Int'l L. 1007, 1012 (1990).

It is worth noting, however, that it may be the manner in which child limits are imposed, not the limits themselves, that contravene international human rights law. The United Nations Educational, Scientific and Cultural Organization (UNESCO) has recognized that a "misunderstanding of the proper relations between coercive measures and human rights may doom an otherwise worthy population project . . . ." *See* UNESCO, Human Rights Aspects of Population Programmes 23 (1977). Such policies may arguably be *required* to fulfil obligations under international environmental law. Does Agenda 21 suggest this in any concrete fashion? How should any conflict between environmental and human rights instruments be resolved in the international arena? Through intergovernmental negotiations? Some other way?

7.   In the developing world, environmental concerns are often perceived as a luxury. Without the problems of food shortages and poverty, it is easy to be troubled by the more esoteric concerns of the environment. In the developing world the more pressing issues of human life and death will necessarily take precedence.

Human rights also can be seen as a First World luxury. Indeed, instruments such as the International Covenant on Economic, Cultural and Social Rights **[Basic Document 7.13]** give allowance for the disparate abilities to comply. Consider the following quote by Shen Guozian, director of publicity at China's Family Planning Commission:

> If America had 1.1 billion people, then they would not be so concerned about this humanitarianism they talk about.

As quoted in James Kynge, *China Steps Up Enforcement of 1–Child–Per–Family Law,* L.A. Times, May 6, 1990, at A4. On the other hand, human rights are generally perceived to be universal claims that are recognized as of right, not by love, grace, or charity. *See, e.g.,* Human Rights in the World Community: Issues and Action (Richard Pierre Claude & Burns H. Weston eds. and contribs., 2d ed., 1992). *See also* Myres S. McDougal, Harold Lasswell, & Lung–Chu Chen, Human Rights and World Public Order: The Basic Policies of an International Law of Human Dignity (1980).

With respect to the population issue, what tests and/or mechanisms should be employed to recognize the more limited ability of the developing world to meet standards? Should the developing world be allowed lower human rights or environmental standards at all? Does the developed world have an obligation in law to increase the ability of the developing world to meet standards?

8.   Randers and Meadows, *supra*, state that

it should be quite unnecessary to point out that our environment is finite.... The quantity which is most obviously in limited supply on our earth is arable land. There are about 3.2 billion hectares of land suitable for agriculture on the earth. Approximately half of that land is under cultivation today. The remaining half will require immense capital costs to settle, clear, irrigate, or fertilize before it can produce food.... We are faced with further obvious constraints in connection with natural resources like fresh water, metals and fuels.... Even if we assume that we find the means to generate the energy needed ... we are still faced with the fundamental thermodynamic fact that virtually all energy generated finally ends up as heat.... The heat ... will begin to have worldwide climatic effects when the released amount reaches some appreciable fraction of the energy normally absorbed by the sun.... A third limitation to population and industrial growth is our globe's finite absorptive capacity for pollution.

See Jorgen Randers & Donella Meadows, *The Carrying Capacity of our Global Environment: A Look at the Ethical Alternatives,* in Western Man and Environmental Ethics: Attitudes Toward Nature and Technology 273–76 (I. Barbour ed. 1973).

In contrast, Julian Simon, *supra*, argues that there is no support for the view that resources are finite: "There is little doubt in my mind that we will continue to find new ore deposits, invent better production methods, and discover new substitutes, bounded only by our imagination and the exercise of educated skills."

These passages are reminiscent of the scientific uncertainty problems associated with issues such as climate change. How should decision makers at an international level deal with conflicting interpretations and theories regarding population?

9.   Various United Nations bodies have concerned themselves with the problem of population control. As Reading 14 illustrates, a human rights approach was endorsed by the UN-sponsored International Conference on Population and Development at Cairo in 1994. The progress of the Program of Action adopted at that Conference is reported in Commission on Population and Development, Economic and Social Council, *Activities Conducted by Non–Governmental Organizations and Intergovernmental Organizations in Sexual and Reproductive Health and Rights: Three Years After the International Conference on Population and Development: Report of the Secretary–General,* E/CN.9/1998/5 (1997).

10.   *Bibliographical Note.* For further discussion concerning the principal themes addressed in this problem, consult the following additional specialized materials:

(a) *Specialized Books/Monographs.* 1–17 Annual Review of Population Law (1974–1990); A. Bandarage, Women, Population and Global Crisis: A Political–Economic Analysis (1997); China's One–Child Family Policy (E. Croll, D. Davin & P. Kane eds. 1985); Controlling Reproduction: An American History (Andrea Tone ed., 1996); P. Ehrlich & A. Ehrlich, The Population Explosion (1980); P. Ehrlich et al., The Stork and The Plow: The Equity Answer to the Human Dilemma (1995);

S. Fraser & J. Caldwell, China, Population, Education and People (1987); L. Grant, Juggernaut: Growth on a Finite Planet (1996); B. Hartmann, Reproductive Rights and Wrongs: The Global Politics of Population Control and Contraceptive Choice (1987); W. G. Hollingsworth, Ending the Explosion: Population Policies and Ethics for a Humane Future (1996); J. E. Jacobsen, Population Growth (The Global Change) (1996); J. Kasun, The War Against Population: The Economics and Ideology of Population Control (1988); E. Liagin, Excessive Force: Power, Politics, and Population Control (1996); C. N. Milwertz, Accepting Population Control: Urban Chinese Women and the One–Child Family Policy (1996); C. Wang, Population and Development Planning in China (1991); D. Warwick, Bitter Pills, Population Policies and their Implementation in Eight Developing Countries (1982).

(b) *Specialized Reports.* Council on Environmental Quality, Dep't of State, *Global Future: Time to Act, Report to the President on Global Resources, Environment and Population*, 9 B.C. Envtl. Aff. L. Rev. 261 (1980/81); *Population and Human Rights*, Proceedings of the Expert Group on Population and Human Rights, Geneva, Apr. 3–6, 1989 (1990); *Report of the International Conference on Population and Development*, U.N. Conference on Population and Development, U.N. Doc. A/CONF.171/13 (1994).

(c) *Specialized Articles/Book Chapters.* P. Abrams, *Reservations About Women: Population Policy and Reproductive Rights*, 29 Cornell Int'l L.J. 1 (1996); K. S. Barber, Case Note, *Xin-Chang Zhang v. Slattery: Rejecting China's Coercive Population-Control Policy as Grounds for Political Asylum in the United States*, 41 Vill. L. Rev. 521, n2 (1996); M. Brennen, *International Family Planning*, 8 Hous. J. Int'l L. 155 (1985); J. Clarke, *The Chinese Population Policy: A Necessary Evil?*, 20 N.Y.U. J. Int'l L. & Pol. 321 (1987); C. Cohen, *International Fora for the Vindication of Human Rights Violated by the United States' International Population Policy*, 20 id. 241 (1987); B. Commoner, *Rapid Population Growth and Environmental Stress*, 21 Int'l J. Health Services 199 (1991); B. Conable Jr., *Development and the Environment: A Global Balance*, 5 Am. U. J. Int'l L. & Pol'y 235 (1990); M. H. Cooper, *Population and the Environment*, 8 CQ Researcher 601 (1998); D. Foley, *The Legitimacy of the "Mexico City Policy" in the Context of Human Rights-Based Restrictions on United States' Foreign Aid*, 27 Colum. J. Transnat'l L. 387 (1989); L. Gregory, *Examining the Economic Component of China's One-Child Family Policy Under International Law: Your Money or Your Life*, 6 J. Chinese L. 45 (1992); G. Hardin, *Living On A Lifeboat*, 24 Bioscience 561 (1974); W. Hollingsworth, *World Population: An Unwishful Assessment, A Hopeful Proposal*, 10 B.C. Envtl. Aff. L. Rev. 853 (1983); S. Isaacs, *Reproductive Rights 1983: An International Survey* 14 Colum. Human Rights L. Rev. 311 (1982/83); J. Jacobson, *Gender Bias, Poverty, and the Population Trap*, 19 Populi No. 4, at 12 (1992); J. Jewett, Student Author, *The Recommendations of the International Conference on Population and Development: the Possibility of the Empowerment of Women in Egypt*, 29 Cornell Int'l L. J. 191 (1996); E. Keng, *Population Control Through the One-Child Policy in China; Its Effects on Women*, 18 Women's Rights Law Reporter 205 (1997); M. Marcus, *United States Foreign Population Assistance Programs: Anti-Abortion Propaganda?*, 15 Brooklyn J. Int'l L. 843 (1989); L. Marsden, *Human Rights and Population Growth: A Feminist Perspective*, 3 Int'l J. Health Services 567 (1973); C. Meindersma, *Population Exchanges: International Law and State Practice*, 9 Int'l J. Refugee L. 335 (1997); M. Palmer, *The People's Republic of China: Problems of Marriage and Divorce(1988–1989)*, 27 J. Fam. L. 57; J. Randers & D. Meadows, *The Carrying Capacity of our Global Environment: A Look at the Ethical Alternatives*, in Western Man and Environmental Ethics:

Attitudes Toward Nature and Technology 273 (1973); A. W. Reitze, Jr., *Population, Consumption and Environment Law*, 12 Nat. Resources & Env't 89 (1997); C. E. Schulman, Student Author, *The Grant of Asylum to Chinese Citizens Who Oppose China's One-Child Policy: A Policy of Persecution or Population Control?*, 16 B.C. Third World L.J. 313 (1996); A. Sen, *Fertility and Coercion*, 63 U. Chi. L. Rev. 1035 (1996); J. Simon, *The Population Debate: The Case for More People*, in Environmental Science: Action for a Sustainable Future 110 (D. Chira ed., 3rd ed., 1991); S. Slaton, *Hard Decisions: Asylum Protection as Applied to Aliens Opposing Population Control Policies*, 16 Nova L. Rev. 955 (1992); B. Stark, *International Human Rights and Family Planning: A Modest Proposal*, 18 Den. J. Int'l L. & Pol'y 59 (1989); Symposium on Population Law, 27 Envt'l. L. 1097 (1997); P. Weintraub, *Population Law: Legal Control of Demographic Processes,* 5 Eur. Demographic Info. Bull. 129 (1974); G. Zhang, *U.S. Asylum Policy and Population Control in the People's Republic of China*, 18 Hous. J. Int'l L. 557 (1996).

(d) *Useful internet sites.* Population Action International, <www.population-action.org>; The Population Institute, <www.populationinstitute.org>; U.N. Population Division, *United Nations Population Information Network (POPIN)*, <www.undp.org/popin/>; University of Wisconsin–Madison, *Center for Demography and Ecology*, <www.ssc.wisc.edu/cde/>; Zero Population Growth, <www.zpg.org>.

Problem 11-4

Environmental Warfare in Khalifan

SECTION 1. FACTS

A life-sustaining feature of Southwestern Asia is the Tiphrates River. Originating in the Anatolian Mountains, it flows in a southeasterly direction through Amirabia and Khalifan into the Arabian Gulf (see Figure 11–4.1). Amirabia is a modernizing oil-rich country under the strong military dictatorship of General Ali Mussulman. Its economy is based primarily on the export of oil and, to smaller extent, on agricultural products grown in the irrigated regions adjacent to the Tiphrates River. Khalifan, a two hundred years-old sheikdom, also exports oil, though in lesser quantities than Amirabia, and relies upon the rich soils of the Tiphrates River delta for substantial agricultural production.

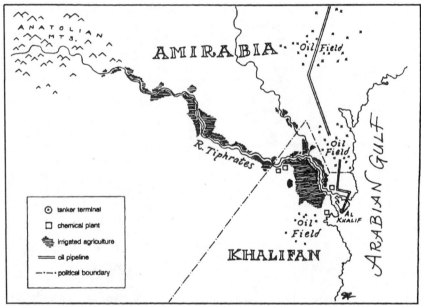

Figure 11-4.1

Both Amirabia and Khalifan have access to the Arabian Gulf and to the open seas beyond. Only Khalifan, however, has a port deep enough to accommodate the huge "supertankers" upon which Amirabia depends to export its oil, which it has done for more than three decades via a pipeline from its coastal storage facilities to Khalifan's deep water port. Thus when Khalifan, never particularly friendly with Amirabia, proposed three years ago a substantial increase in its port taxes "to help upgrade our petroleum and

1044

agricultural industries," Amirabia immediately protested, arguing that the proposed tax increase would severely burden Amirabia's economy. Despite Amirabia's protests, however, Khalifan increased its port taxes as proposed. In addition, after repeated but unsuccessful appeals to Amirabia to renegotiate a treaty governing the Amirabian–Khalifani pipeline and in apparent disregard of a treaty provision requiring "joint consultations" in respect of "any lessening of the [pipeline] flow," it shut down the pipeline.

Shortly thereafter, in a surprise move, General Mussulman ordered his army into Khalifan to repudiate, in his words, "this affront to Amirabia's national sovereignty and to international law." "The economic terrorists who have effectively taken our country hostage," he proclaimed, "must be taught a lesson." Within several days, Amirabia's military forced Khalifan's ruling family into exile, took control of the sheikdom's governmental apparatus, and proceeded to seize Khalifan's banks and businesses in the name of what General Mussulman called "economic equity."

The response of the organized international community was harsh. After many months of fruitless negotiations and unavailing economic sanctions, the United Nations Security Council, citing "unlawful aggression" on Amirabia's part, decided upon military sanctions to force Amirabia out of Khalifan. An international military coalition was assembled, penetrating air strikes began, a land and sea invasion was launched, and within a short while General Mussulman ordered his army back across the Amirabian–Khalifani border.

In retreat, however, concerned to prevent the infliction of threatened major harm upon their armed personnel and weapons systems, the Amirabian forces engaged in widespread destruction of Khalifan's roads, railways, bridges, and anything else that might assist the advancing U.N. coalition. Additionally, they set fire to several Khalifani oil wells and similarly destroyed two large Khalifani chemical plants situated near the Amirabian–Khalifani border alongside the Tiphrates River. Being few in number, the oil well fires, which darkened the surrounding skies for almost three weeks, were subsequently and relatively quickly extinguished in full. The burning of the chemical plants, however, caused a large cloud of toxic smoke to billow into the atmosphere and an estimated two million gallons of agricultural chemicals to spill into the Tiphrates River. By the time the damage to the chemical plants was discovered by the U.N.-sponsored forces, the cloud of smoke stretched for many miles across the Khalifani countryside, leaving sick and dying civilians urgently in need of evacuation and medical care.

In the chaos, it was several days before anyone noticed the extent of the chemical spill in the Tiphrates River. As the chemicals flowed downstream, they eliminated nearly all forms of life in and near the river, especially in the area of the delta. Fish and other marine animals covered the river's surface in many places, aquatic vegetation slowly died, and groves of citrus and other trees along the river perished. Because it was not at first evident that chemicals had been released into the river, no immediate action was taken to prevent the pollution of a large percentage of Khalifan's irrigated fields, killing crops and rendering useless the land until the chemicals could be washed from the soil. Drinking water systems also were affected, and thousands of people suffered a variety of illnesses and death. Children were the hardest hit.

General Mussulman and his military commanders were subsequently captured by a crack squadron of British commandos and are being held in a British prison under U.N. auspices awaiting judgment by an ad hoc war crimes tribunal specially constituted by the U.N. Security Council. The Tribunal has heard arguments from representatives of the U.N. military coalition on the violation of traditional humanitarian rules of armed conflict and now asks to hear arguments on alleged international environmental crimes. Specifically, the Tribunal asks to know whether or not the "torching" of Khalifan's oil wells and the indiscriminate release of chemicals into the Tiphrates River constituted crimes under international law and, if so, what sanctions might be imposed upon General Mussulman and/or his government, if any. The Tribunal has taken judicial notice of the fact that Amirabia is a party to the 1976 Convention on the Prohibition of Military or Any Other Hostile Use of Environmental Modification Techniques and that, while a party to the 1949 Geneva conventions on the laws of war, it has neither signed nor ratified the two 1977 protocols to the 1949 Geneva conventions or any other potentially relevant treaty, including the 1907 Hague Convention (No. IV) Respecting the Laws and Customs of War on Land.

SECTION 2. QUESTIONS PRESENTED

1. Do Amirabia's "torching" of Khalifan's oil wells and its release of chemicals into the Tiphrates River constitute violations of international law?

2. If Amirabia's "torching" of Khalifan's oil wells and/or its release of chemicals into the Tiphrates River may be found to constitute violations of international law, what sanctions, if any, may be imposed upon General Mussulman and/or his governmental associates?

SECTION 3. ASSIGNMENTS

A. Reading Assignment

Study the Readings presented in Section 4, *infra*, and the Discussion Notes/Questions that follow. Also, to the extent possible, consult the accompanying bibliographical references.

B. Recommended Writing Assignment

Prepare a comprehensive, logically sequenced, and *argumentative* brief in the form of an outline of the primary and subsidiary *legal* issues you see requiring resolution by the ad hoc war crimes tribunal. Also, from the perspective of an independent objective judge, indicate which side ought to prevail on each issue and why. Retain a copy of your issue-outline/brief for class discussion.

C. Recommended Oral Assignment

Assume you are legal counsel for Amirabia or Khalifan (as designated by your instructor); then, relying upon the Readings (and your issue-outline if prepared), present a 15–20 minute oral argument of your government's likely positions before the ad hoc war crimes tribunal.

D. *Recommended Reflective Assignment*

Consider (and recommend) alternative norms, institutions, and/or procedures that you believe might do better than existing world order arrangements to contend with situations of the kind posed by this problem. In so doing, but without insisting upon immediate feasibility, identify the particular transition steps that would be needed to make your alternatives a reality.

SECTION 4. READINGS

1. Editors' Note. In late January 1991, Iraqi forces, in retreat from a military coalition authorized by the United Nations Security Council to reverse Iraq's August 1990 invasion of Kuwait, demonstrated a willingness to use the environment as a weapon of war by setting hundreds of Kuwaiti oil wells ablaze and by spilling thousands of gallons of oil into the Persian Gulf. In *Environmental Legal Issues Arising from the Gulf Conflict*, 10 Oil & Gas L. & Tax Rev. 348 (1990), John Salter discusses the air pollution and environmental and ecological effects of these actions and of the counteractions of the U.N.-authorized military coalition:[a]

Air Pollution

The hundreds (estimated to be between 400 and 800 as at 12 March 1991) of well-head fires started by Iraqi soldiers before the Allied ground offensive was launched and continued by such soldiers when later retreating have caused the creation of columns of steam and thick dark clouds forming a vast pall of smoke as toxins poured into the air cutting out light during the day time. Estimated emission of smoke for the first 30 days is some 580,000 tonnes penetrating 0.6 miles into the atmosphere above burning wells and two miles above burning refineries.... Water, which provides pressure for exploitation of wells, is being sucked up through the oil and this may cause permanent damage to future commercial prospects of oil exploration....

Environmental Effects

Environmental effects could arise under at least four heads:

(1) From crude oil from Iraqi/Kuwaiti oil terminals;

(2) From air pollution from burning Iraqi/Kuwaiti installations;

(3) From windborne organisms from Iraqi biological weapons plants;

(4) From radioactive contamination from Iraqi nuclear installations.

The effects of marine oil pollution are reasonably well known following the experience of the *Nowruz*, *Exxon Valdez*, *Torrey Canyon* and *Amoco Cadiz* cases. However, the scale is rather larger in that if the amount of the oil spill for example was actually 11 million barrels as

a. Salter reports, at 348, the first question asked of Iraqi President Saddam Hussein by Mr. Peter Arnett of Cable News Network (CNN) in an interview given January 29, 1991:

I [Arnett] asked what he [Saddam Hussein] had to say about claims by the U.S. that Iraq had opened its spigots in Kuwait and let oil pour into the Gulf. The President responded that the U.S. had used oil as a weapon by attacking Iraqi tankers and oil installations on land. He said it showed that the U.S. is not concerned about the effect on the environment.

originally estimated then this is approximately seven times the size of the *Amoco Cadiz* disaster and 13 times the size of the *Torrey Canyon* disaster. The March 1967 *Torrey Canyon* disaster caused some 119 tons of crude oil to be washed up on [English] West Country beaches. However, by 1972 one could hardly see any signs of pollution. The reason for this could be the surge of the tides with their scouring effect. A team of people had worked on the beaches using various detergents for six to seven days to break up the oil. It could be smelt in the nearby town for some weeks after the event. The cost of the clean-up exercise in those days was $100,000. The cost of the Gulf marine pollution clean-up in 1991 has been estimated at $500 million. The cost of the *Exxon Valdez* clean-up (the ship ran aground in March 1989) was agreed by Exxon Corporation in a settlement on 13 March 1991 at up to $1.1 billion, payable over ten years, including the $100 million criminal fine for environmental damage (believed to be a record).

The effects of the use of or strikes on stores of finished chemical weapons have not been so well studied. Professor Steven Rose of the Open University has stated that there could be a real danger of an epidemic spreading from the Gulf region. The Director of the United Nations Environmental Programme has said that the effects of any biological weapons used in the Gulf conflict could be felt as far away as Europe. Biological organisms such as anthrax live in the atmosphere for between 40 to 50 years and could be pushed by wind as far as Northern Europe. It would be difficult to contain the effects of any such attack. The effects of radioactive fall-out have been studied by the International Atomic Energy Agency who reported on 6 February that there was no evidence that attacks on the Iraqi nuclear installations had released any radioactive contamination. Since the attacks had taken place at least two weeks before the announcement any releases that had taken place would have been detected.... [T]he reason may be that both the Iraqi plants are small research reactors in which the field is immersed in a pool of water at least five metres deep. Such reactors do not contain large quantities of fissile material and are operated only intermittently. Most are surrounded by large earth walls to protect them from the effects of bombing.

The effects of air pollution have also been extensively studied by the European Community. The environmental effects of the firing of well-heads and refineries relate not only to the Gulf States but also to Pakistan and possibly North India. These have so far been identified as covering:

(1) Acid or black toxic rain.

(2) Smog, being persistent air pollution and the reason for Gulf health officials warning people with respiratory problems to stay indoors, because of the increasing sulphur-dioxide levels.

(3) Farm produce and orchard failures (especially crops). Obstruction of sunlight could affect the double-cropping of rice. The first crop (assuming 120–day rice is planted) might not ripen in time for the second crop to be planted.

(4) Grazing herds affected by soot ingestion.

(5) Break up of desert pavement (a shield of pebbles laid down over thousands of years making it difficult for strong winds to dislodge sand) leading to erosion and violent dust and desert storms clogging up, for example, airport runways.

(6) Global warming and ozone effects which are thought probably not enough to cause measurable temperature change.

(7) Possible failure of Asian monsoons, although it is felt at present that the scale is not sufficiently large to affect monsoons.

Ecological Effects

The International Maritime Organisation[b] has already classified the Gulf area as a special area due to its sensitive ecology. Its shallow waters are significant in this connection. That is not to say that the marine life there is not used to oil spills. There have been frequent spills from ships with tank-cleaning and other oil-related activities. In 1983 during the Iran–Iraq War the Iranian Nowruz field was allowed to leak some 30,000 tons of crude oil per day into the Gulf for a period of some nine months. However, it will in the short term have a considerably adverse effect on marine life. Some 600 dead birds have already been counted on a stretch of sand two kilometres long. There are believed to be only some 600 to 3,000 sea-cows still existing in the area. It has already been hunted close to extinction. If they can avoid coming to the surface in polluted waters there is a chance that they may flourish[,] as crude oil, once certain toxins have been taken out, will help the sea-grass beds and the sea-cows' habitats to flourish. Bahrain and other Gulf States are very dependent on fishing and, undoubtedly, such a large spill will affect this activity. Shrimp spawning-grounds are likely to be severely affected off Manifah. Fish nursery areas and fragile coral reefs would also be affected.

The marine life at risk consists of the sea-cows or dugongs, dolphins, turtles, shrimps, cormorants and coral which exist in a highly stressed environment because of the range of temperatures and the high salinity of a substantially enclosed sea area. Extensive breeding-grounds of the hawksbill turtle and the green turtle lie along the coast of the southern Gulf. Among the seabirds threatened are the red-necked phalarope wintering in the Gulf, the Socotra cormorant which breeds in the winter, Audubon's shearwater, the red-billed tropic bird, Jouanin's petrel, the sooty gull, the slender-billed gull, the Caspian tern, the white-checked tern, the bridled tern, the sooty tern, the Saunder's tern, the greater crested tern and the lesser crested tern.

The effect of the firing of well-heads and refineries on ecology is considered to be quite serious, particularly having regard to water pollution by fall-out with its consequential threats to life itself.

These harms, inflicted upon the natural environment by the 1990–91 Persian Gulf War, are part of what motivated the extract that follows.

b. The International Maritime Organization (IMO), formerly known as the International Maritime Consultative Organization (IMCO), is a specialized agency of the United Nations based in London. It was established in 1958 for the purpose of promoting cooperation and encouraging high standards of safety and navigation in the maritime field. For further details, see Discussion Note/Question 3 at 654 in Problem 8–2, *supra*.

2.   Stephen Dycus, National Defense and the Environment 140–45 (1996).

It might seem that the only important consideration in waging war is winning. Once the fighting begins, support for the troops always becomes the first article of political faith. We might expect that rules to protect the environment would simply be ignored. Some have even argued that instead of trying to limit wartime environmental impacts, we ought to make war as terrifyingly unpredictable and destructive as possible, to encourage the enemy to surrender sooner.

However, limits on wartime destruction have been recognized at least since biblical times. For example, the Old Testament provides this instruction: "If you besiege a town for a long time, making war against it in order to take it, you must not destroy its trees by wielding an ax against them.... You may destroy only the trees that you know do not produce food."[1] Such limits were well understood by early scholars of international relations, such as Hugo Grotius . * * * If "trees could speak," Grotius noted, "they would cry out that since they are not the cause of war it is wrong for them to bear its penalties."[2] These ideas inform the modern law of war, a collection of customary practices and formal agreements among nations concerning limitations on the initiation and conduct of armed conflict.

Several international agreements are deliberately aimed at protecting the natural environment from the effects of war. The best known is the 1977 Environmental Modification Convention (ENMOD) **[Basic Document 7.30]**, which was prompted by United States use of chemical defoliants to destroy forests and croplands in Vietnam, and by its efforts to manipulate weather patterns over that country. ENMOD provides in part:

> Each State Party to this Convention undertakes not to engage in military or any other hostile use of environmental techniques having widespread, long-lasting or severe effects as the means of destruction, damage, or injury to any other State Party....

> [T]he term "environmental modification techniques" refers to any technique for changing–through the deliberate manipulation of natural processes–the dynamics, composition or structure of the Earth, including its biota, lithosphere, hydrosphere and atmosphere, or of outer space.[3]

Despite the convention's broad language, its framers understood it to apply only to the creation of phenomena such as earthquakes, tsunami, cyclones, and changes in weather patterns, climate, and ocean currents—all tactics that are probably beyond the capabilities of modern military science.

Another 1977 agreement, Protocol I to the 1949 Geneva Convention **[Basic Document 7.31]**, calls for wide-ranging protections for noncombatants and their property, as well as for the natural environment. It prohibits using "methods or means of warfare which are intended, or may be expected, to cause widespread, long-term and severe damage to the natural environment." It also admonishes belligerents not to so damage the environment as

---

1. 20 *Deuteronomy* 19–20 (New Revised Standard Version).

2. Hugo Grotius, On the Law of War and Peace 747 (Francis W. Kelsey trans., 1964).

3. ENMOD, arts. I.1. and II **[Basic Document 7.30]**.

to "prejudice the health or survival of the population," and it prohibits attacks "against the natural environment by way of reprisals."[4]

Protocol I places the burden on warring nations to analyze the environmental implications of their military operations and to avoid serious environmental harms, just as those nations are bound to avoid injuries to noncombatants. Yet one critic dismisses the protocol as a "vague, impractical, and unworkable ... effort to prevent all collateral ecological damage." He complains that by prohibiting reprisals against noncombatant and environmental targets, it removes the "best deterrent to illegal conduct in war." Worse, in this critic's view, it might forbid the first use of nuclear weapons.[5]

Protocol I has not yet been formally ratified by the United States, although it may reflect a "developing customary international law" which is binding on all nations, regardless of whether they are signatories to any treaties.[6] Indeed, the Army's field manual, "The Law of Land Warfare," recognizes as customary international law some of the very principles set out in Protocol I.[7] For example, the manual defines "permissible objects of attack" as including only combatants and "objects which by their nature, location, purpose, or use make an effective contribution to military action and whose total or partial destruction, capture or neutralization, in the circumstances ruling at the time, offers a definite military advantage."[8] Identical language appears in Protocol 1.[9]

Other international agreements are meant to protect specific geographical areas from the effects of particular weapons or from armed conflict generally. Nuclear weapons are prohibited altogether on the floor of the sea,[10] in outer space,[11] and in Latin America.[12] All weapons of war are banned from Antarctica.[13]

Still other law of war principles are concerned mainly with protection of noncombatants and their property, but their application may also help to protect the environment from needless destruction. A 1907 convention declares that the "right of belligerents to adopt means of injuring the enemy is not unlimited."[14] An even earlier agreement concludes that the only permissi-

---

4. Protocol Additional to the Geneva Conventions of 12 August 1949, and Relating to the Protection of Victims of International Armed Conflict [hereinafter Protocol I] [**Basic Document 7.31**].

5. Guy B. Roberts, *The New Rules for Waging War: The Case Against Ratification of Additional Protocol I*, 26 VA. J. INT'L L. 109, 145, 148, 165 (1986). For a contrasting view from the head of the U.S. delegation to the conference that adopted Protocol I, see G. Aldrich, *Progressive Development of the Laws of War: A Reply to Criticism of the 1977 Geneva Protocol I*, 26 VA. J. INT'L L. 693 (1986).

6. John E. Parkerson, Jr., *United States Compliance With Humanitarian Law Respecting Civilians During Operation Just Cause*, 133 MIL. L. REV. 31, 52 (1991).

7. Department of the Army Field Manual FM 27–10, *The Law of Land Warfare* (1956 and change 1976) [hereinafter FM 27–10].

8. *Id.*, para. 40c (change 1976).

9. Protocol I, *supra* note 4, art. 52(2).

10. Treaty on the Prohibition of the Emplacement of Nuclear Weapons and Other Weapons of Mass Destruction on the Seabed and the Ocean Floor and in the Subsoil Thereof (Seabed Arms Control Treaty), Feb. 11, 1971, 23 U.S.T. 701, 10 I.L.M. 146.

11. Treaty on the Principles Governing the Activities of States in the Exploration and Use of Outer Space, Including the Moon and Other Celestial Bodies [**Basic Document 3.3**].

12. Treaty for the Prohibition of Nuclear Weapons in Latin America (Treaty of Tlatelolco), Feb. 14, 1967, 22 U.S.T. 762, 6 I.L.M. 521.

13. Antarctic Treaty [**Basic Document 2.1**].

14. Hague Convention IV Respecting the Laws and Customs of War on Land [**Basic Document 7.25**].

ble objective of a nation at war is to weaken the military forces of its enemy.[15] The selection of targets is strictly limited by military necessity. In other words, any destruction must be indispensable for securing the prompt submission of the enemy with the least possible expenditure of resources. However, military necessity is no defense for acts that violate the customary or conventional law of war, since that law incorporates the concept of military necessity. In one of the Nuremberg war crimes trials, the court declared that the "rules of international law must be followed even if it results in the loss of a battle or even a war."[16]

Attacks on noncombatants and their property are almost always forbidden, whether deliberate or inadvertent. Injury to noncombatants is permitted only when enemy forces or other military targets are located nearby, and then only when the injury is proportionate to the military advantage gained by the attack. The United States interprets customary international law as providing that civilian property may not be attacked unless it "effectively contributes to the enemy's war-fighting or war sustaining capability."[17]

Just as attacks on noncombatants are usually forbidden, destruction of the environment that supports those noncombatants is also outlawed. Thus, civilian foodstuffs, agriculture areas, livestock, and drinking water supplies are protected from attack, unless they directly support enemy military operations. This principle is accepted by the United States as reflecting customary international law.[18] According to the Army's field manual, the poisoning of water wells and streams, as well as pillage and purposeless destruction, are punishable as war crimes. Facilities dedicated to art, religion, science, or charity, must also be spared, along with hospitals and historic monuments, since their destruction would serve no military purpose.[19]

Installations such as dams, nuclear power plants, and loaded oil tankers may not be attacked, because they contain dangerous forces that could seriously injure the civilian population and the environment if released.[20] The prohibition is waived, however, when such a facility provides "regular, significant and direct support of military operations," and there is no other feasible way to terminate such support.[21]

Weapons that cause superfluous injury or unnecessary suffering, such as biological and chemical weapons, are prohibited. For example, the 1925 Geneva Gas Protocol prohibits the use in war, but not the possession, of

15. So proclaimed in St. Petersburg Declaration Renouncing the Use, In Time of War, of Explosive Projectiles Under 400 Grammes Weight, Dec. 11, 1868, 138 Parry's Treaty Series 297.

16. *United States v. List*, 11 Trials of War Criminals Before the Nuremberg Military Tribunals Under Control Council No. 10 at 1253, 1272 (1950).

17. Protocol I, *supra* note 4, art. 57(2)(b); *see also* Office of the Chief of Naval Operations, United States Department of the Navy, The Commander's Handbook on the Law of Naval Operations, NWP 9 (Rev. A), FMFM 1–10 (1989) [hereinafter NWP 9], Supp. 1989, at 8–2 n. 9.

18. Protocol I, *supra* note 4, art. 56(1); *see, e.g.*, NWP 9, *supra* note 17 at Supp. 1989, 8–4 n. 15.

19. Washington Treaty on the Protection of Artistic and Scientific Institutions and Historic Monuments (Roerich Pact), Apr. 15, 1935, 49 Stat. 3267, T.S. 899; 1954 Hague Convention for the Protection of Cultural Property in the Event of Armed Conflict, May 14, 1954, 249 U.N.T.S. 240 (signed but not ratified by the United States).

20. Protocol I, *supra* note 4, art. 56(1).

21. Protocol I, *supra* note 4, art. 56(2). *See* Department of the Air Force, International Law–The Conduct of Armed Conflict and Air Operations, *AFP* 110–31 at 5–9 to 5–11 (1976).

asphyxiating, poisonous, and other gases, all analogous liquids, materials, and devices, and bacteriological methods of warfare.[22]

There is disagreement about whether the Geneva Gas Protocol covers irritants, such as tear gas, and herbicides like those used extensively by United States forces for defoliation in Vietnam. In 1975, President Ford renounced the first use of riot control agents and chemical herbicides in war, "except in defensive modes to save lives."[23] Moreover, such materials may not be used except upon the express order of the President. The use of tear gas and nausea inducing agents was authorized by President Bush during the Persian Gulf War. But they were never actually directed against Iraqi forces, apparently out of concern that Saddam would retaliate with deadly chemical weapons.

The Biological Weapons Convention of 1972 prohibits the development, production, or stockpiling of biological or chemical toxin weapons.[24] While the United States insists that it holds no offensive biological weapons, it has long conducted experiments with such weapons for defensive purposes. In 1984, for example, the Army asked Congress to fund construction of new facilities for testing biological and toxin agents at its Dugway Proving Ground southwest of Salt Lake City. Fears that the expanded facility would be used for recombinant DNA research and the development of a new type of genetically engineered biological weapon prompted NEPA litigation to force an assessment of the environment risks.[25]

More than 150 nations have now signed the 1993 Chemical Weapons Convention.[26] It expressly prohibits the development, production, possession, or use of chemical weapons, including their retaliatory use, and requires the destruction of existing stockpiles and production facilities. It also forbids the use of riot control agents in warfare. The United States has signed, but not yet ratified, the convention.

Even weapons that are not illegal per se must be used in a way that does not cause unnecessary harm. For example, the 1981 Inhumane Weapons Convention imposes restrictions on the use of certain conventional weapons, such as mines, booby traps, and incendiary devices, that could cause excessive or indiscriminate injuries. That convention also forbids incendiary attacks on forests and other plant cover, unless such vegetation is used to conceal military targets.[27] The United States has signed, but not ratified, the Inhumane Weapons Convention, and does not consider itself necessarily bound by the terms of the convention.

22. Protocol for the Prohibition of the Use in War of Asphyxiating, Poisonous or Other Gases, and of Bacteriological Methods of Warfare, June 17, 1925, 26 U.S.T. 571, 94 L.N.T.S. 65.

23. Executive Order No. 11,850, 40 Fed. Reg. 16,187 (1975); *see also* FM 27–10, *supra* note 7, para. 38c.

24. Convention on the Prohibition of the Development, Production and Stockpiling of Bacteriological (Biological) and Toxin Weapons and on Their Destruction, Apr. 10, 1972, 26 U.S.T. 583, 1015 U.N.T.S. 163.

25. *See* Foundation on Economic Trends v. Weinberger, 610 F.Supp. 829 (D.D.C.1985).

26. Convention on the Prohibition of the Development, Stockpiling and Use of Chemical Weapons and on Their Destruction, Jan. 13, 1993, 32 I.L.M. 800; reproduced with extensive explanation in *Chemical Weapons Convention*, S. Treaty Doc. No. 21, 103d Cong., 1st Sess. (1993).

27. Convention on Prohibitions or Restrictions on the Use of Certain Conventional Weapons Which May be Deemed to be Excessively Injurious or to Have Indiscriminate Effects, 20 I.L.M. 1287 (1981).

There is a long-running debate about the legality of nuclear weapons. On one side, it is argued that the use of such weapons would inevitably cause many unnecessary injuries, in violation of the law of war principles of discrimination, proportionality, and humanity. Some say that such use would cause wide-spread, long-term, and severe damage to the environment as well, which is forbidden by Protocol I. The United States and other nuclear powers insist that since there is no explicit prohibition of nuclear weapons, their use is permitted. It is Army policy that, absent contrary instructions from national command authority, field commanders who utilize nuclear weapons must restrict noncombatant casualties to 5 percent at the margins.[28] As with other weapons, however, even that amount of damage must not be disproportionate to the military advantage gained from their use. In May 1993, the governing body of the World Health Organization asked for an advisory opinion from the International Court of Justice (World Court) about whether the use of nuclear weapons would violate international law. The matter [was decided on July 8, 1996].[c]

The law of war thus furnishes an incomplete and unpredictable bulwark against excessive environmental damages in armed conflict. Some of the law's most important principles have yet to be codified in formal agreements among nations, and there is disagreement about the meaning of some provisions. Many nations are not yet parties to all of the formal agreements. Only about one-third of all countries have ratified the Environmental Modification Treaty, while fewer than 60 percent have approved Protocol I. Some nations have qualified their ratification with weakening conditions. For example, before signing the Chemical Weapons Convention in 1993, the United States had not forsworn the use of chemical weapons in war, as required by the 1925 Geneva Gas Protocol, but only promised that it would not use them first. The agreements that do exist fail to address a number of critical issues, such as the legality of nuclear weapons. And, except for some outright prohibitions, they contain few clear standards to guide military planners or commanders in the field. One commentator sums up the existing authorities this way:

> The legal norms that exist are scattered, and are either very general and vague, as well as subject to "military necessity" exceptions, or more specific and relevant, but not directed at prevailing belligerent practices of the sort most likely to generate environmental harm. Furthermore, the status and relevance of principles of customary international law are quite indefinite, as is the related matter of whether treaty norms reflect and embody customary norms.[29]

These difficulties have led to calls for a "Fifth Geneva" Convention on protection of the environment in wartime.

28. *See* Department of the Army FM 101–31–1, Staff Officers' Field Manual: Nuclear Weapons Employment Doctrine and Procedure (1977). *See also* NWP 9, *supra* note 17 at 10–1.

c. *See* Legality of the Threat or Use of Nuclear Weapons (Advisory Opinion of July 8), U.N. Doc. A/51/218 (1996), *reprinted in* 35 I.L.M. 809 & 1343 (1996). The Opinion is available also at *Legality of the Threat or Use of Nuclear Weapons* (visited Feb. 1, 1998) <http://www.law.cornell.edu/icj/icj1/opinion.htm>. For overview and critical commentary, see Burns H. Weston, *Nuclear Weapons and the World Court: Ambiguity's Consensus*, 7 TRANSNAT'L L. & CONTEMP. PROBS. 371 (1997).

29. Richard A. Falk, *The Environmental Law of War: An Introduction, in* ENVIRONMENTAL PROTECTION AND THE LAW OF WAR 78, 79 (G. Plant ed., 1992).

Even where the law is clear, it is not always followed. Military commanders understandably tend to accumulate and use all the firepower they can, both to accomplish their assigned missions and to protect their troops from harm. Sometimes they use more force than necessary, or miss their targets because of poor planning, flawed intelligence, enemy deception, or equipment failure.

Criminal sanctions for law of war violations (war crimes) may be imposed by special courts convened by the victorious nations to punish serious infractions. The Nuremberg Tribunal at the end of World War II is an example. War crimes trials may also be conducted by representatives of other nations. The International Tribunal for the Former Yugoslavia and the newly created Tribunal for Rwanda are current examples. In addition, war crimes may be tried in United States military courts.[30] There have been numerous calls for war crimes trials of Saddam Hussein and members of his military for their gratuitous pollution of air and waters, for atrocities committed in Kuwait, and for missile attacks on Israeli cities. Thus far, however, such calls have gone unheeded.

In theory, at least, compensation may be exacted from the guilty party. In 1991, the United Nations Security Council adopted a resolution declaring that Iraq was "liable under international law for any direct loss, damage, including environmental damage and the depletion of natural resources ... as a result of Iraq's unlawful invasion and occupation of Kuwait."[31] The International Court of Justice, or World Court, is authorized to hear such claims for damages, but only when the nations involved submit themselves to the jurisdiction of the court.[32]

Rather than relying on threats of punishment for violations, the law of war depends mostly for its influence on the self-interest of nations. Each nation can be expected to refrain from using weapons or tactics that it would consider unjust if used against it, hoping that other nations will follow suit. To encourage uniform respect for the law, however, each nation must discipline members of its own forces who fail to comply.

3. Hague Convention (No. IV) Respecting the Laws and Customs of War on Land, Oct. 18, 1907, Preamble, art. 2, and Annexed Regulations 22, 23, 55, 36 Stat. 2277, T.S. No. 539, 1 Bevans 631 [Basic Document 7.25].

4. Geneva Convention (No. IV) Relative to the Protection of Civilian Persons in Time of War, Aug. 12, 1949, arts. 2, 53, 147, 158, 6 U.S.T. 3516, T.I.A.S. No. 3365, 75 U.N.T.S. 287 [Basic Document 7.26].

5. Stockholm Declaration on the Human Environment of the United Nations Conference on the Human Environment Adopted by the UN Conference on the Human Environment at Stockholm, 16 June 1972, Principles 2, 57, 21, 22, 26, Report of the UN Conference

---

30. Article 18 of the Uniform Code of Military Justice provides for trial of any person accused of violating the law of war. 10 U.S.C. § 818 (1988).

31. S.C. Res. 687, para. 16 [**Basic Document 7.32**].

32. U.N. Charter arts. 36(3), 92 [**Basic Document 1.3**]. The World Court is governed by the Statute of the International Court of Justice [**Basic Document 1.4**].

on the Human Environment, Stockholm, 15 16 June 1972, UN Doc. A/CONF.48/14/Rev.1 at 3 (1973), UN Doc. A/CONF.48/14 at 265, and Corr. 1 (1972), *reprinted in* 11 I.L.M. 1416 (1972) [Basic Document 1.12].

6. **Convention on the Prohibition of Military or Any Other Hostile Use of Environmental Modification Techniques (ENMOD), Dec. 10, 1976, arts. I, II, 31 U.S.T. 333, T.I.A.S. No. 9614, 1976 U.N. JURID. Y.B. 1125,** *reprinted in* **16 I.L.M. 88 (1977)** [Basic Document 7.30].

7. **Protocol I Additional to the Geneva Conventions of August 12, 1949, and Relating to the Protection of Victims of International Armed Conflict, June 8, 1977, arts. 35, 36, 51, 52, 54 58, 85, 1977 U.N. JURID. Y.B. 95,** *reprinted in* **16 I.L.M. 1391 (1977)** [Basic Document 7.31].

8. **World Charter for Nature, Oct. 28, 1982, Principles 5, 11, 12, 20, 24 &** *passim,* **G.A. Res. 37/7, U.N. GAOR, 37th Sess., Supp. No. 51, at 21, U.N. Doc. A/37/L.4 and Add.1 (1982)** [Basic Document 1.21].

9. **Rio Declaration on Environment and Development of the United Nations Conference on Environment and Development, June 14, 1992, Principles 24 &** *passim,* **UNCED Doc. A/CONF.151/5/Rev.1,** *reprinted in* **31 I.L.M. 874 (1992)** [Basic Document 1.29].

10. **Jozef Goldblat,** *The Environmental Modification Convention of 1977: An Analysis, in* ENVIRONMENTAL WARFARE: A TECHNICAL, LEGAL, AND POLICY APPRAISAL **53-57 (A. Westing ed., 1984).**

The Enmod Convention [**Basic Document 7.30**] deals with changes in the environment brought about by deliberate human manipulation of natural processes, as distinct from conventional acts of warfare which might result in adverse effects on the environment. Covered by the Convention are those changes which affect the dynamics, composition or structure of the Earth, including its biota, lithosphere, hydrosphere and atmosphere, or of outer space (article II). The employment of techniques producing such modifications as the means of destruction, damage or injury to another state party is prohibited. (This may be taken to mean that the use of environmental modification techniques to enhance the use of conventional weapons–for example, by dispersing fog covering airfields or other targets to be bombed–is not proscribed so long as the environmental modification technique itself produces no harm.) In the opinion of the USA, the targets alluded to include the enemy's military forces and civilian population, as well as its cities, industries, agriculture, transportation systems, communication systems and natural resources and assets.... Nor is it allowed to assist, encourage or induce other nations to engage in these activities.

* * *

The ban under the Enmod Convention applies to the conduct of military operations during armed conflicts, as well as to hostile use (whether by military or non-military personnel) when no other weapon is being employed or when there is no overt conflict. It is applicable both to offence and defence, regardless of geographical boundaries. In the light of these explanations, which were given by the Soviet ... and US ... sponsors of the text, the term "hostile" alone would have sufficed as a purpose criterion upon which the Convention is based. But not all hostile uses causing harm to others are prohibited by the Convention; only those having "widespread, long-lasting or severe effects" are outlawed [in article I].[d] The meaning of these terms, according to the Understanding relating to article I, is as follows:

1. *widespread* : encompassing an area on the scale of several hundred square kilometres;[33]

2. *long-lasting* : lasting for a period of months, or approximately a season; and

3. *severe* : involving serious or significant disruption or harm to human life, natural and economic resources or other assets.

It is noted in the Understanding that the above interpretation is intended exclusively for this Convention and should not prejudice the interpretation of the same or similar terms used in connection with any other international agreement. That proviso was found necessary in order to forestall an identical interpretation to be given to the terms "widespread, long-term and severe" used in the 1977 Protocol I Additional to the Geneva Conventions of 1949, and Relating to the Protection of Victims of International Armed Conflicts which was then under negotiation [**Basic Document 7.31**]. Indeed, the two documents pursue different aims. Geneva Protocol I . . . is meant to ban the employment in armed conflict of methods or means of warfare which are intended, or may be expected, to cause serious damage to the environment, whatever the weapons used (article 55); to make this ban applicable, the presence of all three of the criteria-widespread, long term end severe-is required. On the other hand, the Enmod Convention forbids the use (or manipulation) of the forces of the environment as "weapons", both during hostilities and when there is no overt conflict; in this case, the presence of only one of the three criteria–widespread, long-lasting, *or* severe–is enough for the environmental modification technique to be deemed outlawed.

Thus, the use of environmental modification techniques is prohibited if two requirements are met simultaneously: (*a*) that the use is hostile; and (*b*) that it causes destruction, damage or injury at, or in excess of, the threshold described above. Exempted from the prohibition are non-hostile uses of the modification techniques, even if they produce destructive effects exceeding the threshold. Equally permissible are hostile uses which produce destructive effects below the [troika] threshold. Assuming, therefore, that hostile intent has been proved (which may not be easy), it would still not be illegal, according to the Understanding, to devastate an area smaller than several hundred square kilometres . . . ; or to cause adverse effects lasting for a period of weeks instead of months, or less than a season; or to bring about disruption or harm to human life, natural and economic resources or other assets, which

---

d. Sometimes referred to as the "troika clause." *See, e.g.*, C. Wunsch, The Environmental Modification Treaty, 4 Am. Soc. Int'l L.J. 113, 115 (1980).

33. According to the interpretation provided by the USA, the entire area would have to experience destruction, damage or injury at approximately the same time to meet the "widespread" criterion. . . . This could result

from a single operation or it could be the cumulative result of a series of operations conducted over a period of months or years. If, over the course of several years, a total are on the scale of several hundred square kilometres were affected, but the area actually suffering destruction, damage or injury at any one time was small, the "widespread" criterion would not be met.

are not "severe", "serious" or "significant", whatever these subjective terms might mean to countries of different sizes, of different population densities or at different stages of economic development. For example, Trinidad and Tobago noted that the definitions of the terms "widespread, long-lasting or severe" do not address themselves to the situation of small entities, such as the islands of the Caribbean.... Moreover, the perpetrator's perception of the gravity of such acts may not coincide with that of the victim.

However, earthquakes, tsunamis (seismic sea waves), an upset in the ecological balance of a region, changes in weather patterns (clouds, precipitation, cyclones of various types, tornadic storms), changes in climate patterns, changes in ocean currents, changes in the state of the stratospheric ozone layer and changes in the state of the ionosphere appear to be definitely prohibited by the Enmod Convention when produced by hostile use of environmental modification techniques. For it is understood that all these phenomena would result, or could reasonably be expected to result, in widespread, long-lasting or severe destruction, damage or injury.... It has been recognized, in the Understanding relating to article II, that the use of techniques producing other phenomena could also be appropriately included, insofar as the criteria of hostility and destructiveness were met. (In this connection, the USA referred to volcanic eruptions, tectonic plate movements, sea-level changes, lightning, hail and changes in the energy balance of the planet.) Nevertheless, only the most fanciful events are enumerated in the Understanding—those which are unlikely to be caused through deliberate action for warlike purposes, that is, in such a way that the effects would be felt only, or primarily, by the enemy....

As a consequence of the threshold approach, the techniques which can produce more limited effects (such as precipitation modification short of changing the "weather pattern") and which are, therefore, more likely to be used to influence the environment with hostile intent in a selected area, especially in tactical military operations, have escaped proscription. As noted earlier, the use of environmental modification techniques not as direct means of destruction, damage or injury, but to facilitate the effectiveness of other weapons in producing destruction, damage or injury, also does not appear to be covered.... Moreover, the imprecise and haphazard definition of the terms "widespread, long-lasting or severe" may generate controversies greater than a ban without any qualification. Thus, no convincing reason has been given as to why any hostile modification of the environment or any amount of damage caused by such modification should be tolerated at all. Even the right to use modification techniques on a state's own territory to forestall or stop foreign invasion (e.g., by opening dams or producing massive landslides) might be legitimately challenged.

Evidently, certain powers preferred not to forswear altogether the possibility of using environmental methods of warfare and to keep future options open. This conclusion can also be drawn from the fact that the Enmod Convention was conceived as a non-use agreement rather than as an arms-limitation measure. Hence, it does not prohibit the development of the prohibited techniques....

11. Richard A. Falk, *Environmental Disruption by Military Means and International Law,* **in** ENVIRONMENTAL WARFARE: A TECHNICAL, LEGAL, AND POLICY APPRAISAL 33, 39-40 (A. Westing ed., 1984).

The 1977 Protocol I Additional to the 1949 Geneva Conventions **[Basic Document 7.31]** is also relevant.... This Protocol carried forward ... earlier general directives on environmental protection against military activities.[e] It elaborates on some of the general thinking embodied in the 1899 and 1917 Hague Conventions[f] and in article 35 sets forth [pertinent] standards of law.... On the face of it, article 35.3 would seem to prohibit weapons of mass destruction, yet this is far from assured. The legal reach of the formulations is restricted, or at least ambiguous, because the US delegate to the negotiations had insisted that this Protocol not be understood as intending to have any bearing on the legal status of nuclear weapons. In question here is whether the formulation in article 35.3 is merely expressive of international customary law, and thus cannot be restricted in its scope by the unilateral declaration of any government. Article 36, dealing with new weapons, is also relevant inasmuch as it implies that a new weapon may be illegal even if not subject to an explicit prohibition either by "this Protocol or by any other rule of international law". At the same time experts on international law mainly agree that the legality of new weapons and tactics cannot be presumed, but depends on establishing compatibility with preexisting general principles of the law of war....

e. Falk is here referring to, *inter alia,* Article 55 of the 1907 Hague Regulations Respecting the Law and Customs of War **[Basic Document 7.25]**, Article 53 of the 1949 Geneva Convention (IV) Relative to the Protection of Civilian Persons in Time of War **[Basic Document 7.26]**, and Principles 21 and 26 of the 1972 Stockholm Declaration on the Human Environment **[Basic Document 1.12]**.

f. *See* International Convention for the Pacific Settlement of International Disputes (Hague I), July 29, 1899, U.S.T.S. 392, 32 Stat. 1779 (superseded by the 1907 Convention for the Pacific Settlement of International Disputes, *infra*); International Convention with Respect to the Laws and Customs of War on Land (Hague II) July 29, 1899, U.S.T.S. 403, 32 Stat. 1803 (superseded by the 1907 Convention Concerning the Laws and Customs of War on Land, *infra*); International Convention for the Adapting to Maritime Warfare of the Principles of the Geneva Convention of Aug. 22, 1864, July 29, 1899, U.S.T.S. 396, 32 Stat. 1827 (superseded by the 1907 Convention for the Adaptation of the Principles of the 1906 Geneva Convention to Maritime War, *infra*); Convention for the Pacific Settlement of International Disputes (Hague I), Oct. 18, 1907, 54 L.N.T.S. 435, 205 C.T.S. 233; U.S.T.S. 537, 36 Stat. 2199; Convention Respecting the Limitation of Employment of Force for Recovery of Contract Debts (Hague II), Oct. 18, 1907, 205 C.T.S. 250, U.S.T.S. 537, 36 Stat. 2241; Convention Relative to the Opening of Hostilities (Hague III), Oct. 18, 1907, 205 C.T.S. 263, 2 AM. J. INT'L L. Supp. 85; Convention Respecting the Laws and Customs of War on Land (Hague IV), Oct. 18, 1907, 205 C.T.S. 277, U.S.T.S. 539, 36 Stat. 2277; Convention Concerning the Rights and Duties of Neutral Powers and Persons in Case of War on Land (Hague V), Oct. 18, 1907, 205 C.T.S. 299, U.S.T.S. 540, 36 Stat. 2310; Convention Relative to the Status of Enemy Merchant Ships at the Outbreak of Hostilities (Hague VI), Oct. 18, 1907, 205 C.T.S. 305, 2 AM. J. INT'L L. (Supp.) 127; Convention Relative to the Conversion of Merchant Ships into Warships (Hague VII), Oct. 18, 1907, 205 C.T.S. 319, 2 AM. J. INT'L L. (Supp.) 133; Convention Relative to the Laying of Automatic Submarine Contact Mines (Hague VIII), Oct. 18, 1907, 205 C.T.S. 331, U.S.T.S. 541, 36 Stat. 2332; Convention Respecting Bombardments by Naval Forces in Time of War (Hague IX), Oct. 18, 1907, 205 C.T.S. 345, U.S.T.S. 542, 36 Stat. 2351; Convention for the Adapting to Maritime Warfare of the Principles of the Geneva Convention (Hague X), Oct. 18, 1907, 15 L.N.T.S. 340, 205 C.T.S. 359, U.S.T.S. 543, 36 Stat 2371; Convention Relative to Certain Restrictions on the Exercise of the Right of Capture in Maritime War (Hague XI), Oct. 18, 1907, 205 C.T.S. 367, U.S.T.S. 544, 36 Stat. 2396; Convention Relative to the Creation of an International Prize Court (Hague XII), Oct. 18, 1907, 205 C.T.S. 381, 2 AM. J. INT'L L. (Supp.) 174; Convention Respecting the Rights and Duties of Neutral Powers in Maritime War (Hague XIII), Oct. 18, 1907, 205 C.T.S. 395, 2 AM. J. INT'L L. (Supp.) 202. All of these agreements are reprinted in 2 Weston (1994).

The 1977 Geneva Protocol I expresses a rule in its article 55 that seems to incorporate the minimum current consensus of international law on military activities in relation to the natural environment.... Note here that [the] formulation [of "widespread, long-term, and severe damage"] does not clearly prohibit the type of tactics relied upon by the USA in the Second Indochina War, which could arguably fall below the damage threshold.... However, it might well be that an impartial tribunal, if convened to assess environmental harm in Indochina, would find US practices incompatible with the standards of article 55. In the so-called Understanding relating to article I of the 1977 Enmod Convention **[Basic Document 7.30]** the terms "widespread", "long-lasting" and "severe" were interpreted as follows by the Conference of the Committee on Disarmament (CCD):

(a) "widespread": encompassing an area on the scale of several hundred square kilometres;

(b) "long-lasting": lasting for a period of months, or approximately a season;

(c) "severe": involving serious or significant disruption or harm to human life, natural and economic resources or other assets.

The CCD stressed that this interpretation was "intended exclusively for this Convention and is not intended to prejudice the interpretation of the same or similar terms if used in connection with any other international agreement".

One must note that these three criteria, as used in the 1977 Geneva Protocol I **[Basic Document 7.31]**, are not subject to any exemption by way of military necessity, nor is the prohibition directed, as in the Enmod Convention **[Basic Document 7.30]**, only at tactics that have as their object environmental destruction. At the same time, the word "and" rather than "or", as in the Enmod Convention, suggests that all three features of environmental harm must be present for the prohibition to be applicable. It would appear, by virtue of the textual language, that most contemplated uses of weaponry of mass destruction fall within the ban.

The general prohibition of article 55 of the 1977 Geneva Protocol I is made more specific in article 56 where "dams, dykes and nuclear electrical generating stations" are legally protected from attack "even where these objects are military objectives". In fact, article 56.1 even forbids attack upon "military objectives located at or in the vicinity of these works or installations ... if such attack may cause the release of dangerous forces". Unfortunately this "special protection against attack" is partially withdrawn in article 56.2 where these installations including dams, dikes and nuclear electrical generating stations, can be attacked if they are being used "in regular, significant and direct support of military operations and if such attack is the only feasible way to terminate such support". Whether this "special protection" will mean much, if anything, in the setting of war remains to be seen, but the recognition of these new environmental dimensions of the law of war is at least a formal acknowledgment of concern that can be acted upon by public pressures. Whether such legal standards were applicable prior to 1977 depends on whether they are regarded as incorporating earlier treaty and customary rules of war, or as establishing something new.[g]

g. Falk continues, at 40: "Note also that the 1981 Convention on Prohibitions or Re-   strictions on the Use of Certain Conventional Weapons [19 I.L.M. 1523 (1980)] confidently

12.   Adam Roberts, *Environmental Issues in International Armed Conflict: The Experience of the 1991 Gulf War*, in PROTECTION OF THE ENVIRONMENT DURING ARMED CONFLICT 227–37 (R. Grunawalt et al. eds., 1996).

[T]he provisions of the laws of war regarding the environment [are] one of the many areas in which the laws of war consist of a very disparate body of principles, treaties, customary rules, and practices, which have developed over the centuries in response to a wide variety of practical problems and moral concerns.

A.   *Underlying Principles of the Laws of War*

In considering what the laws of war have to say about environmental damage, it is necessary to start with their underlying principles, most of which seem to have a bearing on the question of environmental destruction. These principles, though ancient in origin, are reflected in many modern texts and military manuals. They include the principle of proportionality, particularly in its meaning of proportionality in relation to the adversary's military actions or to the anticipated military value of one's own actions; the principle of discrimination, which is about care in the selection of methods, of weaponry and of targets; the principle of necessity, under which belligerents may only use that degree and kind of force, not otherwise prohibited by the law of armed conflict, which is required for the partial or complete submission of the enemy with a minimum expenditure of time, life, and physical resources; and the closely-related principle of humanity, which prohibits the employment of any kind or degree of force not required for the purpose of the partial or complete submission of the enemy with a minimum expenditure of time, life, and physical resources.

Each of these four principles strongly points to the conclusion that actions resulting in massive environmental destruction, especially where they do not serve a clear and important military purpose, would be questionable on many grounds, even in the absence of specific rules of war addressing environmental matters in detail. When the four principles are taken together, such a conclusion would seem inescapable.

It has been suggested by Richard Falk that there are, in addition, two "subsidiary principles" which "seem to be well-grounded in authoritative custom and to have relevance to the array of special problems posed by deliberate and incidental environmental harm." These are the principles of neutrality and of inter-generational equity.[34] The proposition that these are in fact key principles of the laws of war, though it may be unorthodox, is serious. Both these types of consideration do inform certain provisions of the laws of war, and do affect attitudes to environmental destruction. However, since these principles do not add greatly to existing law as reflected in the four

invokes in its preamble these recent legal developments of isolating environmental protection as a distinct concern of the international law of war ... : 'Also recalling that it is prohibited to employ methods or means of warfare which are intended, or may be expected, to cause widespread, long-term and severe damage to the natural environment.' "

34.   Richard A. Falk, *The Environmental Law of War: An Introduction, in* ENVIRONMENTAL PROTECTION AND THE LAW OF WAR 78, 85 (G. Plant ed., 1992).

principles already outlined and in treaties, it is not necessary to pursue the issue here.

There are obvious limits to the value of customary principles as a basis for guiding the policies of States in wartime. As Richard Falk has said, in pessimistic vein:

> there are extreme limitations associated with a need to rely on these customary principles. Their formulation is general and abstract, and susceptible to extreme subjectivity and selectivity in their application to concrete circumstances.[35]

B. Treaties on the Laws of War

Can treaty law, with its more precise texts and its formal systems of adherence by States, overcome any limitations of the framework of principles as outlined above? In treaties on the laws of war, several kinds of prohibitions can be found which have a bearing on the protection of the environment in armed conflicts and in occupied territories:

1. Many general rules protecting civilians, since these rules also imply protection of the environment on which the civilians depend.

2. Prohibitions of unnecessary destruction, and of looting of civilian property.

3. Prohibitions of attacks on certain objectives and areas (e.g., restrictions on the destruction of dikes).

4. Prohibitions and restrictions on the use of certain weapons (e.g., gas, chemical and bacteriological).

5. Prohibitions and restrictions on certain methods of war(e.g., the poisoning of wells, or the indiscriminate and unrecorded laying of mines).

The word "environment" does not occur in any treaty on the laws of war before 1977. This does not mean that there was no protection of the environment, but rather that such protection is found in a variety of different forms and contexts. The pre–1977 treaties on the laws of war relate to protection of the environment obliquely rather than directly: they offer general statements of principle, and also some detailed regulations which may on occasion happen to be relevant to the environment.

Thus, the 1868 St. Petersburg Declaration on explosive projectiles, in ringing words which. were to prove terribly problematic in subsequent practice, declared that "the only legitimate object which States should endeavour to accomplish during war is to weaken the military forces of the enemy."[36]

Several of the Hague Conventions and Declarations of 1899 and 1907 contained provisions with a bearing on the environment. In the 1907 Hague Convention IV on land war **[Basic Document 7.25]**, the preamble refers to the need "to diminish the evils of war, as far as military requirements permit", and goes on to state in the famous Martens Clause:

---

35. *Id.* at 16.

36. Declaration Renouncing the use of in time of War of Explosive Projectiles under 400 Grammes in Weight; St. Petersburg, 1868, 1 Am. J. Int'l L. (Supp.) 95.

Until a more complete code of the laws of war has been issued, the high contracting Parties deem it expedient to declare that, in cases not included in the Regulations adopted by them, the inhabitants and the belligerents remain under the protection and the rule of the principles of the law of nations, as they result from the usages established among civilized peoples, from the laws of humanity, and the dictates of the public conscience.[37]

In the Regulations annexed to the 1907 Hague Convention IV, Article 22 states: "The right of belligerents to adopt means of injuring the enemy is not unlimited." Geoffrey Best has commented: "Post-1945 extensions of that principle from its traditional application to enemy persons and properties to the natural environment are no more than logical, given the novel and awful circumstances that have suggested them."[38] Article 23 (g) of the Hague Regulations is relevant to certain instances of environmental damage when it states that it is especially forbidden "to destroy or seize the enemy's property, unless such destruction or seizure be imperatively demanded by the necessities of war." Also in the Regulations, Section III (which deals with military occupations) contains many provisions having a potential bearing on environmental protection. Article 55 is the most obvious, but not the only, example:

> The occupying State shall be regarded only as administrator and usufructuary of public buildings, real estate, forests, and agricultural estates belonging to the hostile State, and situated in the occupied country. It must safeguard the capital of these properties, and administer them in accordance with the rules of usufruct.

It could be further argued that the rules relating to neutrality in war, as contained in 1907 Hague Convention V (in land war) and 1907 Hague Convention XIII (in naval war), by requiring belligerents to respect the sovereign rights of neutral powers, prohibit environmental damage seriously affecting a neutral State.[39] This is a typical case in which protection of the environment, even where it is not mentioned in existing law, may nonetheless be a logical implication of such law.

The 1925 Geneva Protocol on gas and bacteriological warfare[40] provides one basis for asserting the illegality of forms of chemical warfare having a harmful effect on the environment. The Protocol has been the subject of a number of controversies as to its exact scope, and these controversies have included matters relating to the environment. In 1969, during the Second Indochina War, and following reports of U.S. use of chemicals in Vietnam, a U.N. General Assembly Resolution (which unsurprisingly did not receive unanimous support) addressed the issue, declaring that the 1925 Protocol prohibits the use in armed conflicts of:

---

37. Hague Convention No. IV Respecting the Laws and Customs of War on Land [**Basic Document 7.25**].

38. Geoffrey Best, *The Historical Evolution of Cultural Norms Relating to War and the Environment, in* CULTURAL NORMS, WAR AND THE ENVIRONMENT 18, 85 (A. Westing ed., 1988).

39. Hague Convention No. V Respecting the Rights and Duties of Neutral Powers and Persons in Case of War on Land, 1907, 36 Stat. 2310; T.S. 540; and Hague Convention No. XIII Concerning the Rights and Duties of Neutral Powers in Naval War, 1907, 36 Stat. 2415; T.S. 545.

40. Protocol for the Prohibition on the use in War of Asphyxiating, Poisonous, or Other Gases and of Bacteriological Methods of Warfare, 1925, 26 U.S.T. 571; T.I.A.S. 8061.

(a) Any chemical agents of warfare—chemical substances, whether gaseous, liquid or solid—which might be employed because of their direct toxic effects on man, animals or plants;

(b) Any biological agents of warfare—living organisms, whatever their nature, or infective material derived from them—which are intended to cause disease and death in man, animals or plants, and which depend for their effects on their ability to multiply in the person, animal or plant attacked.

The four 1949 Geneva Conventions say little about the protection of the environment. They are concerned above all with the immediate and important task of protection of victims of war. However, one of these agreements, the 1949 Geneva Convention IV (the Civilians Convention) **[Basic Document 7.26]** builds on the similar provisions of the 1907 Hague Regulations when it states in Article 53, which is in the section on occupied territories:

Any destruction by the Occupying Power of real or personal property belonging individually or collectively to private persons, or to the State, or to other public authorities, or to social or co-operative organizations, is prohibited, except where such destruction is rendered absolutely necessary by military operations.

The International Committee of the Red Cross (ICRC) commentary on this article contains the following assessment on the question of "scorched earth" policies:

A word should be said here about operations in which military considerations require recourse to a "scorched earth" policy, i.e. the systematic destruction of whole areas by occupying forces withdrawing before the enemy. Various rulings of the courts after the Second World War held that such tactics were in practice admissible in certain cases, when carried out in exceptional circumstances purely for legitimate military reasons. On the other hand, the same rulings severely condemned recourse to measures of general devastation whenever they were wanton, excessive or not warranted by military operations.[11]

Article 147 of Geneva Convention IV, and similar articles in Conventions I and II,[12] confirm that grave breaches of the Convention include "extensive destruction and appropriation of property, not justified by military necessity and carried out unlawfully and wantonly."

The 1954 Hague Cultural Property Convention[13] seeks to protect a broad range of objects, including groups of historic buildings, archaeological sites, and centers containing a large amount of cultural property. All such property is to be protected from exposure to destruction, damage, and pillage. In many cases, obviously, action which was wantonly destructive of the environment would also risk violating the provisions of this Convention.

41. Commentary on Geneva Convention IV 302 (Pictet ed. 1958).

42. Geneva Convention for the Amelioration of the Condition of the Wounded and Sick in Armed Forces in the Field, 1949, 6 U.S.T. 3114; T.I.A.S. 3362; and Geneva Convention for the Amelioration of the Condition of Wounded, Sick, and Shipwrecked Members of the Armed Forces at Sea, 1949, 6 U.S.T. 3217; T.I.A.S. 3363.

43. Convention for the Protection of Cultural Property in the Event of Armed Conflict (with Regulations and Protocol), 1954, 249 U.N.T.S. 240.

Environmental matters were addressed by name and directly in two laws of war agreements concluded in 1977. In both cases one important stimulus to new law-making was the Second Indochina War. Although neither of these treaties was formally in force in the 1991 Gulf War, they provide language and principles which may assist in defining and asserting the criminality of certain threats to the environment.

The first of these two 1977 agreements is the U.N. Convention on the Prohibition of Military or Any Other Hostile Use of Environmental Modification Techniques **[Basic Document 7.30]**. This accord (otherwise known as the ENMOD Convention) was concluded mainly in reaction to the use by the United States of forest and crop destruction, and rain-making techniques, in the Second Indochina War. It deals, essentially, not with damage to the environment, but with the use of the forces of the environment as weapons. Article I prohibits all "hostile use of environmental modification techniques having widespread, long-lasting or severe effects as the means of destruction, damage or injury" to the adversary. Article II then defines "environmental modification techniques as 'any technique for changing—through the deliberate manipulation of natural processes—the dynamics, composition or structure of the Earth, including its biota, lithosphere, hydrosphere and atmosphere, or of outer space.' An authoritative U.N. understanding which was attached to the draft text of the Convention in 1976 provides a non-exhaustive list of phenomena which could be caused by environmental modification techniques: these include, among other things, 'an upset in the ecological balance of a region.' "

The second of these 1977 laws of war agreements touching on the environment is the 1977 Additional Protocol 1 **[Basic Document 7.31]**. This accord, which is additional to the four 1949 Geneva Conventions, contains extensive provisions protecting the civilian population and civilian objects. Article 48, entitled "Basic Rule", states:

> the Parties to the conflict shall at all times distinguish between the civilian population and combatants and between civilian objects and military objectives and accordingly shall direct their operations only against military objectives.

Article 52, on "General Protection of Civilian Objects", similarly provides a framework for protecting civilian objects, and thus has obvious implications for protection of the environment.

* * *

C. Case Law

In addition to treaties, past cases are an important guide to the law. In the Second World War there was much general devastation, on many fronts in both Europe and Asia. Some of this resulted in charges of wanton destruction at post-war trials.

The Charter of the International Military Tribunal at Nuremberg did not specifically mention the environment, but it did include in its catalogue of war crimes "plunder of public or private property, wanton destruction of cities, towns, or villages, or devastation not justified by military necessity." In the Tribunal's trial of the major German war criminals in 1945–46, there was a great deal of evidence about such destruction. One of the defendants, General Alfred Jodl, was *inter alia* found guilty of war crimes including scorched earth destruction in respect of North Norway, Leningrad, and Moscow.[44]

Many post-Second World War cases before national tribunals related to environmentally damaging abuse of natural resources in occupied territories. In respect of one Polish case, the United Nations War Crimes Commission was asked to determine whether ten German civilian administrators, each of whom had been the head of a department in the Forestry Administration in occupied Poland in 1939–44, could be listed as war criminals on a charge of pillaging Polish public property. It was alleged that the accused had caused "the wholesale cutting of Polish timber to an extent far in excess of what was necessary to preserve the timber resources of the country." The U.N. War Crimes Committee agreed that *prima facie* evidence of the existence of a war crime had been shown, and nine of the ten officials charged were listed as accused war criminals.

On the other hand, in one post-war case, scorched-earth policies by a retreating occupying power were not ruled to be necessarily illegal. In the case of United States v. Wilhelm List (also called the *Hostages Case*), a U.S. military tribunal at Nuremberg found one of the defendants, General Lothar Rendulic, not guilty on a part of the charge against him based on scorched earth. In the winter of 1944–45, he had been in charge of retreating German forces in northern Norway. As a precautionary measure against a possible attack by advancing Soviet forces, he had destroyed housing, communication and transport facilities in the area. The court said that the defendant "may have erred in the exercise of his judgement but he was guilty of no criminal act." This part of the judgment was intensely controversial in Norway, and was discussed in the Storting on several occasions. It was widely felt that these German devastations, which had continued up to 6 May 1945, went far beyond the demands of military realism.

[*Eds.*—Professor Roberts continues his analysis of the legal protection of the environment by acknowledging recent developments in this area of the law. Following the 1991 Gulf War, proscription of military conduct that had deleterious effects on the environment became a matter of widespread discussion. Among the various proposals for further action was a fifth Geneva Convention dealing with environmental damage caused specifically by warfare. However, this idea was considered imprudent and has not been earnestly pursued in recent years. Rather, work has continued in a more nuanced fashion. International organizations have encouraged states to ratify and comply with agreements that provide for the protection of the environment in wartime, if they have not already done so. In particular, the U.N., through the International Committee of the Red Cross (ICRC), has admonished states to comply with existing law and, most tangibly, promulgated model guidelines for military manuals relative to the environment during armed conflict.

---

44. Charter of the International Military Tribunal, concluded in London in August 1945, Article 6(b)–extract. Full text in *The Trial of German Major War Criminals: Proceedings of the International Military Tribunal Sitting at Nuremberg Germany*, Part 22, London, HMSO, 1950, at 412–13. The section of the judgment dealing with Jodl's responsibility for destruction is at 517. *See also* the numerous references to scorched earth in Part 24 (the index volume) at 620.

In the next reading, Harry Almond describes the tension between competing state interests that serve to hinder the efforts of organizations like the ICRC in drafting and implementing policies of substance regarding environmental protection.]

13. Harry Almond, Jr., *Weapons, War and the Environment*, 3 GEO. INT'L ENVTL. L. REV. 117, 118–19, 121–23, 125, 129–30, 133 (1990).

[R]egulation of activities that might have adverse affects on the environment remains at a rudimentary stage.... One reason for this is the presence of competing policies. For example: environmental regulation may deny progress and development when embodied in anti-weapon regulation that may impair national security, self-defense capabilities, or even maintenance of public order under a deterrence regime. Since this competition among policies prevails during peacetime, it is likely that attempts to protect the environment during armed hostilities will be far more difficult to implement.

* * *

Protection of the environment is probably at best a peripheral factor under present conditions.... [In situations involving the intentional use of violence] damage [to the environment] is not subject to compensation unless that remedy is compelled by the community at large (the United Nations) or the victorious belligerent. States presently hold that environmental damage is to be avoided, and states are said to have "responsibility" for protecting the damage. But arrangements among states—primarily international treaties or conventions—provide for only a limited amount of regulation and do relatively little to impose corrective relief or damages upon those states. Moreover, the context of this environmental harm—the interaction among states—is such that they must unite in efforts to provide research into its prevention and to provide restorative relief if damage does occur.

Environmental responsibilities are often laid down in documents or declarations of national intent ... [hortatively] calling upon states to behave according to certain proposed norms of conduct while providing no means for enforcement.... One should note ... that the law of war ... [has] expectations extending to regulation or prohibition of environmentally harmful conduct. Thus, the fundamental principle [of proportionality] in the law of war contains a complementary interplay of two things: regulation concerning what states may do in view of the necessities of war, and what they must refrain from doing under the "humanitarian principle" of protecting civilians and civilian objects.... [But] [t]he practice of states during hostilities shows a relatively limited tolerance with regard to protecting the environment, and a wide degree of freedom in resorting to violence.

The limitations adopted in the [1977] Geneva Protocols Supplementary to the Geneva Conventions of 1949 **[e.g., Basic Document 7.31]** ... failed to limit environmental damage during wartime.... [T]he language of the articles relating to the environment is hortatory—that is, the Protocol adopts protection as a desired goal instead of establishing protection under the rule of law. Moreover, notwithstanding the adoption of standards of some precision for limiting damage, the provision is ambiguous. Because states are unlikely to impose limits upon themselves during armed combat—particularly limits upon damage they may cause to such an abstract entity as the "environment"—measures must be taken to provide precisely how much damage would be tolerated, against what standards, applied by what entity, and subject to what liability. Thus, there are no provisions here, or under the sanctions and enforcement procedures of the world global order, for enforcing the provision. It might be enforced by belligerents when the conflict is over, but such enforcement depends largely upon actions taken by those who win the conflict, as the Nuremberg decisions have shown.[45]

The language of Article 55 is ambiguous; it is not a clear directive to states or to their military commanders to say that they must refrain from certain actions or they will be subject to measures relating to breach of state responsibility ..., [although it is] strengthened by other provisions in the Geneva Protocols as well as by the law of war, including its customary international law ..., [which] are aimed at reducing ... damage in general, that is, to the targets, to protecting or avoiding attack on those that are not legitimate objects of attack, and to protecting the non-combatant population at large. Strengthened state practice in fulfilling these other provisions will strengthen expectations about protecting the environment under Article 55.... [But] treaty instruments made in peacetime are unlikely to be applied among states or control their activities during hostilities.... The possibilities for more effective international regulation under treaties are open once states have fully established their policies.... [In the meanwhile,] enforcement of law to protect the environment ... will depend upon control asserted [by states] over their own territories or over the entities or individuals responsible for violation of that law.

14. Editors' Note. It has long been accepted under traditional international law that self-defense is justified only when the necessity for action is "instant, overwhelming, and leaving no choice of means, and no moment for deliberation." Letter from Mr. Webster, Secretary of State to Lord Ashburton (Aug. 6, 1842), *reprinted in* 2 JOHN BASSETT MOORE, A DIGEST OF INTERNATIONAL LAW 409, 412 (1906). Secretary Webster was addressing an incident of claimed anticipatory self-defense, the *Caroline* affair of 1837. Nevertheless, the quoted test reflects the customary law of self-defense generally both at the time of the *Caroline* incident and since that time. Also, it gives content to the principle of military necessity, identified in the preceding extracts by Adam Roberts (Reading 12) and Harry Almond (Reading 13) as central to legal judgments about warfare, in general, and environmental warfare, in particular.

On the other hand, as stated in W. Arkin, D. Durrant & M. Cherni, *On Impact: Modern Warfare and the Environment–A Case Study of the Gulf War* (1991), at 115, "[i]t is in the interpretation of military action, and specifically the concept of" military necessity "(the anticipated value of one's own action), that there is significant international disagreement as to proper conduct during war." Indeed, according to the same authors,

---

45. The Nuremberg Judgments were rendered primarily against Germany and Japan, and covered some environmental damage through reparations or demands for compensation. The fundamental principle of the law of war–the principle of military necessity–was ap-plied to render all destruction of property unlawful unless it was "imperatively demanded by the necessities of war." *Cf.*, The Hostage Case, United States v. List (Trial of War Criminals 1950) *reprinted in* LEON FRIEDMAN, THE LAW OF WAR 1303, 1318 (1972).

Military necessity has ... become the main justification for deviation from restrictions in customary law.... While a number of principles relate to protection of the environment during warfare, they are all subordinated to the principle of military necessity. Even in the Geneva Protocols **[e.g., Basic Document 7.31]**, the new basic rule on protecting the natural environment (Article 35) is later subordinated to military necessity. Article 55 states that "*Care* shall be taken in warfare to protect the natural environment" (emphasis added), accepting that environmental protection is not absolute. Despite acknowledgment of the environmental effects of warfare, Richard Falk wrote in 1984, "to turn to international law for relief provides only the most scant basis for hope at present.... What is militarily attractive remains permissible, or at least not explicitly prohibited, whereas that which is of no evident relevance to war making is diligently proscribed."[h]

Id. at 116, 123.

A similar, even if somewhat opposing, viewpoint is expressed in Guy B. Roberts, *The New Rules for Waging War: The Case Against Ratification of Additional Protocol I*, 26 VA. J. INT'L L. 109, 146-47 (1985):

Article 35(3) [of Protocol I] introduces a new principle in the laws of war. It prohibits the use of "methods or means of warfare which are intended, or *may be expected*, to cause widespread, long term and severe damage to the environment." ... By including the "may be expected" language of article 35(3), the drafters provided a legal ground for challenging the use of any weapon that may affect the environment.... [T]he "may be expected" language of articles 35(3) and 55 opens the door for war crimes prosecutions in every case where the environment suffers incidental damage as a result of military operations. The articles impose vague, unworkable, and impractical requirements on military commanders in an effort to prevent all collateral ecological damage, and should not be ratified.

15. MYRES S. MCDOUGAL & FLORENTINO FELICIANO, LAW AND MINIMUM WORLD ORDER—THE LEGAL REGULATION OF INTERNATIONAL COERCION 521-24 (1961).

Throughout the sets of specific rules of warfare that authoritative decision-makers seek to prescribe and apply to specific problems ..., the familiar policies of military necessity and minimum destruction of values may be seen to recur continuously as basic themes.... Thus, it is commonly stated in the learned literature that three basic principles underlie the more detailed prescriptions of combatant law: the principle of military necessity, the principle of humanity, and the principle of chivalry. The principle of chivalry would seem little more than a somewhat romantic inheritance from the Medieval Ages when combat between mailed knights was surrounded by symbolic and ritualistic formalities. In an age increasingly marked by mechanized and automated warfare, the scope of application of chivalry as a principle distinct from humanity may very probably be expected to diminish in corresponding measure. The customary formulations of the remaining two principles in complementary terms and at highest level of abstraction appear, of course, at

h.   Richard A. Falk, *supra* Reading 11.

first glance, as largely tautologous: the principle of military necessity is said to be "subject to the principles of humanity [and chivalry]," while the principle of humanity is assumed to preclude only such kind or degree of violence as is "not actually necessary". Here, however, as in most of the other domains of the law of war, and of the law of nations generally, complementary general principles serve the important function of spotlighting broad categories of competing considerations that must be taken into account by decision-makers aspiring to rationality. What at highest level of abstraction may appear to be tautologous opposites may, in contexts of specific application of policies, be indispensable preliminaries to, and anticipations of, inquiries for detailed factors of contexts and their appropriate relation to overriding community goals.

The principle of military necessity and the principle of humanity may be seen to express a genuine, inclusive interest of states and peoples. Each territorial community has a most direct and immediate interest in maintaining its security, that is, protecting the integrity of its fundamental bases of power and the continued functioning of its internal social processes from the obtrusion of unlawful violence. Each such community has consequently an interest in authority to exercise the force indispensable and appropriate for maintaining or re-establishing its security. Each territorial polity has at the same time an interest in reducing to minimal levels the destruction of values, both of itself and others, that attends such efforts. As we have earlier indicated, this interest has at least two interrelated, component elements. The first element is expressed in the demands, characteristic of a public order of human dignity, that the least possible coercion—not to mention violence—be applied to individual human beings, and that all authorized control over human beings be oriented toward strategies of persuasion with widest possible participation in decision, rather than toward strategies of coercion. The second equally pragmatic element is that of demand for economy in the outlay and expenditure of resources and other base values for safeguarding or restoring security. There is no ineluctable necessity for postulating the priority of one of these basic, complementary interests over the other. The point which does not bear emphasis is that the whole process of authoritative decision with respect to combat situations is a continuous effort to adjust and accommodate the specific requirements of both these interests in a series of concrete contexts. Historically, of course, the line of compromise has, more frequently than not, tended to be located closer to the polar terminus of military necessity than to that of humanity. Paradoxical as it may seem, the observation may not be inappropriate, however, that contemporary weapons whose destructiveness almost surpasses understanding may yet tend to push the line of compromise more toward the other terminus.

The content which has traditionally been written into the concept of military necessity is the policy of permitting the exercise of that violence necessary for the prompt realization of legitimate belligerent objectives. In terms of a theoretical image of the process of combat, one can of course conceive of the achievement of a clearly specified objective as requiring, under a given set of conditions, and at a given moment, the application of a particular (and no longer) period of time against a particular base of enemy power. In point of practical fact, however, no such perfection is achievable. The actual determinations of the lawfulness of particular exercises of violence,

by military commanders on the spot as by war crimes tribunals reviewing the decisions of commanders, go forward in contexts of variables which, even when they can be identified, are hardly susceptible of precise quantification and measurement.

16.   Christopher Greenwood, *State Responsibility and Civil Liability for Environmental Damage Caused by Military Operations, in* PROTECTION OF THE ENVIRONMENT DURING ARMED CONFLICT 397–403 (R. Grunawalt et al. eds., 1996).

A.   *State Responsibility and International Environmental Obligations*

The starting point for this inquiry is that where the agents of a State cause environmental damage by conduct which is contrary to a rule of international law binding upon that State, the State incurs international responsibility. It is a long established principle of international law that "every internationally wrongful act of a State entails the international responsibility of that State".[46] According to the International Law Commission,

There is an internationally wrongful act of a State when:

(a) conduct consisting of an act or omission is attributable to the State under international law; and

(b) that conduct constitutes a breach of an international obligation of the State.[47]

This principle applies to breaches by a State of its international obligations relating to the environment, just as much as it does to breaches of other international obligations. Indeed, the International Law Commission has categorized "a serious breach of an international obligation of essential importance for the safeguarding and preservation of the human environment" as conduct which may give rise to an international crime.[48] Whether the Commission's attempt to create a concept of State crimes separate from other breaches by States of their international obligations will prove acceptable, and whether it will actually make any difference to the substantive law (as opposed to such issues as the standing to bring a claim), is debatable. What matters for present purposes is the clear recognition that a State incurs responsibility under international law for the breach of its environmental obligations.

It is, however, widely recognized that as a means of ensuring protection of the environment, State responsibility is subject to severe limitations. While there have been cases in which a State has brought a claim for environmental damage caused to its own territory or interests, it is unclear which State, if any, has standing to maintain an international claim regarding damage to the global commons. The concept of an *actio popularis* has not yet gained sufficient acceptance in international law. Moreover, although this problem may be eased if the concept of causing serious pollution as an international crime comes to be accepted (since every State could then claim to be entitled

---

46. International Law Commission (I.L.C.), Draft Articles on State Responsibility **[Basic Document 1.10]**, Part I, art. 1 [hereinafter Draft Articles].

47. *Id.* art. 3, n.1.

48. *See* the arbitration award in the *Trail Smelter Case* **[Basic Document 8.4]**.

to enforce the obligations concerned), this effect has yet to be felt and may be outweighed by other problems inherent in the concept of State crimes. In addition, proof of causation is often particularly difficult in environmental cases. Finally, there is considerable argument about the standard of responsibility (strict, absolute or fault based) in many of the treaties on the environment. The result is that State responsibility, while not to be dismissed, is not regarded as the most important means of enforcing international environmental law. Instead, attention has tended to shift towards preventive measures, such as the requirement to conduct an environmental impact assessment, and supervisory action by international organizations.

It should also be mentioned that the International Law Commission has adopted a series of articles, distinct from those on State responsibility, which deal with the notion that a State may incur liability for the injurious consequences of lawful acts. Whereas State responsibility is based upon the thesis that a State incurs certain obligations because it has done something unlawful, liability under the new articles will not be dependent upon the act which gives rise to the injurious consequences being characterized as unlawful. The new concept is likely to be of particular significance in the environmental field but has proved controversial.

B. *State Responsibility and Obligations Under the Law of Armed Conflict*

The armed forces of a State are clearly one of the "organs" of the State and when members of the armed forces of the State act in their official capacity, their conduct is attributable to the State. If, therefore, that conduct is contrary to an international obligation of the State, then the responsibility of the State is engaged. It was never contested, for example, that France incurred international responsibility as a result of the actions of French special forces in destroying the vessel Rainbow Warrior in New Zealand in July 1985.[49]

The fact that the State is engaged in an armed conflict and that the obligation which is violated is one derived from the law of armed conflict, rather than the law of peace, does not in any way prevent the State from being held responsible. Although the law of armed conflict is unusual in international law in holding individuals criminally responsible for violations of its rules, "individual responsibility is additional to, and not exclusive of, the responsibility of the governments concerned."[50] The responsibility of the State for violations of the laws of armed conflict committed by its armed forces is expressly provided for in Article 3 of Hague Convention No. IV, 1907 **[Basic Document 7.25]**, and Article 91 of Additional Protocol I, 1977 **[Basic Document 7.31]**, which are discussed below.

49. *See*, Ruling Pertaining to the Differences between France and New Zealand Arising from the Rainbow Warrior Affair, 26 I.L.M. 1346 (1987), and 74 I.L.R. 256 (1987) [*see also*, Section A of Chapter 3 in the first edition of this coursebook].

50. UNITED KINGDOM, MANUAL OF MILITARY LAW, Part III, 173 (1958). *See also* U.S. DEPART-

MENT OF THE NAVY, ANNOTATED SUPPLEMENT TO THE COMMANDERS' HANDBOOK ON THE LAW OF NAVAL OPERATIONS, NWP 9 (Rev. A)/FMFM 1–10 (1989), Chapter 6, n. 19; GERMANY, HUMANITARIAN LAW IN ARMED CONFLICTS MANUAL, para. 12M (1992).

There are several rules of the law of armed conflict which expressly concern the environment and the violation of which will entail international responsibility on the part of the State concerned:

(1) the Environmental Modification Treaty, 1977 (ENMOD) 1977 [**Basic Document 7.30**], prohibits the use of environmental modification techniques having widespread, long-lasting or severe effects as a means of warfare;

(2) Articles 35(3) and 55 of Additional Protocol I [**Basic Document 7.31**], prohibit the use of methods and means of warfare which are intended or may be expected to cause widespread, long-term and severe damage to the environment;

(3) customary international law is widely considered to include a prohibition on unnecessary and wanton destruction of the environment and a requirement that a belligerent show due regard for the protection of the environment.[51] Some commentators also maintain that the proportionality principle applies in this context, so that a military operation is prohibited if it is probable that it will result in damage to the environment which is excessive in relation to the military gain which the operation is expected to produce.

In addition, a number of rules which are not specifically directed towards environmental protection have important repercussions for the environment. Chief among these are the following:

(4) the prohibition on wanton destruction of property, that is to say, destruction not demanded by the necessities of war;[52]

(5) the prohibition on the use of chemical and biological weapons, both of which are capable of devastating environmental effects;[53]

(6) the restrictions placed on the use of mines, booby-traps and incendiary weapons;[54]

(7) the prohibition of attacks on objects indispensable to the survival of the civilian population, such as foodstuffs and drinking water;[55] and

(8) the prohibition (except in certain narrowly defined circumstances) of attacks upon works and installations containing hazardous forces, such as nuclear electrical generating stations.

Conduct which is imputable to a State engaged in an international armed conflict and which is contrary to any of these rules will engage the international responsibility of that State, provided, of course, that rule is applicable

---

51. *See* DEPARTMENT OF THE NAVY, THE COMMANDER'S HANDBOOK ON THE LAW OF NAVAL OPERATIONS, NWP 1–14M (1995), para. 8.1.3. This paragraph was added in this edition of the HANDBOOK.

52. *See* Hague Convention No. IV, Respecting the Laws and Customs of War on Land [**Basic Document 7.25**], art. 23(g) of the Regulations annexed thereto.

53. Geneva Gas Protocol, 1925, 26 U.S.T. 571; T.I.A.S. 8061; 94 L.N.T.S. 65; and Convention on the Prohibition of the Development, Production and Stockpiling of Bacteriological (Biological) and Toxic Weapons, 1972, 26 U.S.T. 583; T.I.A.S. 8062, and the Convention on the Prohibition of the Development, Production, Stockpiling, and Use of Chemical Weapons and on their Destruction, 1993, *reprinted in* 32 I.L.M. 804 (1993).

54. Conventions on Prohibitions or Restrictions on the Use of Certain Conventional Weapons Which May be deemed to be Excessively Injurious or to have Indiscriminate Effects, with annexed Protocols, 1980, *reprinted in* 19 I.L.M. 1524 (1984) Protocols II & III, art. 56.

55. Protocol I Additional to the Geneva Convention Relating to the Protection of Victims of International Armed Conflict, with Annexes [**Basic Document 7.31**], art. 54.

to that State in the conflict in question. In addition, it is open to argument that some of the provisions of environmental agreements not specifically concerned with armed conflict remain applicable in armed conflict and thus impose further restraints, the disregard of which by the armed forces of a State may engage that State's international responsibility. A belligerent may incur international responsibility for damage to the environmental rights of another belligerent or a neutral State. The same difficulties exist here regarding standing to claim in respect of damage to global commons.

C. Special Features of State Responsibility in the Context of International Armed Conflict

In one respect, the concept of responsibility for violations of the law of armed conflict goes beyond the normal principles of State responsibility. Article 3 of Hague Convention IV [**Basic Document 7.25**] states:

> A belligerent party which violates the provisions of the said Regulations shall, if the case demands, be liable to pay compensation. It shall be responsible for all acts committed by members of its armed forces.

Similarly, Article 91 of Additional Protocol I [**Basic Document 7.31**] provides:

> A Party to the conflict which violates the provisions of the Conventions or of this Protocol shall, if the case demands, be liable to pay compensation. It shall be responsible for all acts committed by persons forming part of its armed forces.

In each case, the first sentence merely states the well established principle that a State is internationally responsible for the acts of its officials, members of its armed forces and other "organs" of the State which are imputable to it. The actions of an organ of the State are imputable to that State if the organ in question was acting in its capacity as an organ of the State but not otherwise.[56] This principle has generally been given a broad interpretation, so that arbitral tribunals have held a State responsible for acts which were *ultra vires* provided that the soldiers in question acted, at least apparently, as organs of the State. Thus, the United States–Mexican Mixed Claims Commission held in the *Youmans* claim that:

> Soldiers inflicting personal injuries or committing wanton destruction or looting always act in disobedience to some rules laid down by superior authority. There could be no liability whatever for such misdeeds if the view were taken that any acts committed by soldiers in contravention of instructions must always be considered as personal acts.[57]

Nevertheless, the prevailing view is that, under the general rules of State responsibility, a State is not internationally responsible for wholly unofficial, private acts which it was not negligent in failing to prevent.

The second sentence of Article 3 of Hague Convention IV and Article 91 of Additional Protocol I thus go beyond this general rule by providing that, in the context of armed conflict, a belligerent State is responsible for "all acts committed by persons forming part of its armed forces". The use of the word "all" suggests that responsibility under this provision extends to that catego-

---

56. Draft Articles, *supra* note 1, art. 5.   **57.** 4 Reps. Int'l. Arb. Awards 110, 116.

ry of wholly unofficial, unauthorized acts of members of the armed forces for which the State would not otherwise be internationally responsible. That interpretation is confirmed by the *travaux preparatoires* of the Hague Convention, the records of the Second Hague Peace Conference of 1907. . . .

It seems clear, therefore, both from the text and the drafting history, that the second sentence of Article 3 was intended to make a State responsible for all violations of the Hague Regulations committed by members of its armed forces, even where those violations were completely unauthorized private acts.

* * *

Article 91 of Additional Protocol I **[Basic Document 7.31]** is in the same terms as Article 3 of the Hague Convention **[Basic Document 7.25]** and was clearly intended to have the same broad scope. Where it may, perhaps, differ is that the draftsmen of Article 3 seem to have contemplated mainly direct claims by individuals, rather than State to State claims, for wrongs done by identifiable servicemen, rather than injuries caused by, for example, long range bombardment. These limitations were clearly not envisaged when Article 91 of Additional Protocol I was adopted. Both provisions were drafted with claims by neutral States, as well as by belligerents, in mind. While the basic principle that a State is responsible for violations of the law of armed conflict committed by members of its armed forces is undoubtedly part of customary law, and thus applicable to violation of all rules of the law of armed conflict irrespective of their source, it is open to debate whether the extended concept of responsibility for wholly private acts recognized in Article 3 of Hague Convention IV and Article 91 of Additional Protocol I applies to breaches of rules not contained in those two treaties.

It follows, therefore, that a State which is a party to an international armed conflict will incur international responsibility for damage to the environment caused by acts of members of its armed forces if those acts are in breach of one of the rules set out in the preceding section of this paper. If the rule is contained in the Hague Regulations or Additional Protocol I, responsibility will be engaged even if the servicemen in question were acting wholly outside the scope of their official duties and this was obvious to all concerned. If, therefore, fleeing soldiers from an army in which all discipline had collapsed set fire to oil installations in the course of looting and thus caused damage to the environment, this act would engage the responsibility of their State as a result of Article 3 of Hague Convention IV and, if applicable, Article 91 of Additional Protocol I, even if the State would not have been held responsible under the normal principles set out in the International Law Commission's draft.

Although there have been cases in which one belligerent has paid compensation to another (or to its nationals) for damage caused by violations of the laws of armed conflict—usually as a result of the treaties concluded at the end of the Second World War—effective reliance on the principles of State responsibility in this area have been rare since then. There have been a number of occasions on which a belligerent has paid compensation, usually without admission of liability, to a neutral State for damage caused by its armed forces. The United States, for example, received compensation from Israel for the attack on the USS *Liberty* in 1967 and from Iraq for the attack on the USS *Stark* in 1987. The United States also offered an *ex gratia* payment to the families of those killed when the USS *Vincente* shot down a civil airliner in 1988 at a time when United States forces were engaged in fighting with Iranian forces. On the whole, however, State responsibility has not proved a particularly effective means of enforcing the law of armed conflict.

17.   C. Szasz, *Remarks on the Gulf War: Environment as a Weapon*, 85 A.S.I.L. Proc. 215, 219–20 (1991).

We come now to the interesting question of who, if anyone, may be liable to take corrective action or to pay compensation in respect to [sic] the massive environmental harm that has evidently occurred due to the military actions in the [Persian] Gulf. In this connection it may be useful to recall that the International Law Commission has for years been considering two relevant subjects: "State Responsibility" and "International Liability for Injurious Consequences Arising out of Acts not Prohibited by International Law."[i] Though ... at least some of the actions damaging to the Gulf environment may indeed have been prohibited by international law, it may be useful to note that under the subject the ILC is currently considering a draft article which states that: "if the transboundary harm proves detrimental to the environment of the affected States," then the state of origin must bear the costs of reasonable restorative measures or pay compensation, including for harm to person and property in the affected state. Although the situations to which that rule would be addressed would differ substantially from those that occurred in the Gulf, because of the clearly wrongful nature of some of the acts and because it is not clear whether actions taken by Iraq within Kuwait are "transboundary," we can assume that the proposed ILC draft is a fortiori of the actual legal situation in the Gulf.

In its draft articles on "State Responsibility," the Commission has agreed that the breach of an international obligation entails responsibility, and that such breaches can be classified as either "crimes" or "delicts." In the former category, the ILC would include a "serious breach of an international obligation of essential importance for the safeguarding and preservation of the human environment, such as those prohibiting massive pollution of the atmosphere or of the seas."

In a sense, it is unnecessary to speculate further on whether Iraq is responsible for any environmental damage that it has caused, because this point is explicitly covered in ... Security Council Resolution [687] on the terms of the definitive ceasefire.[j] By accepting these terms, Iraq has therefore agreed that it "is liable under international law for any direct loss [or] damage, including environmental damage and the depletion of natural resources" that resulted from its invasion and occupation of Kuwait.

That massive deliberate offense against the environment—such as those that evidently occurred in the Gulf—constitute international crimes appears to be an idea whose time has come. I have referred to the ILC's draft articles on "State Responsibility" which would classify massive pollution of the atmosphere or the seas as an international crime. Under another long-pending subject—the Draft Code of Crimes Against the Peace and Security of

---

i. *See Attempts at Codification*, Chapter 5, section C, *supra*, at 347.

j. *See infra* Reading 18.

Mankind[k]—the Commission last year received a proposal of its Rapporteur to the effect that the concept of "crimes against humanity" should include "any serious and intentional harm to a vital human asset, such as the human environment."

18.   United Nations Security Council Resolution 687 (Concerning the Restoration of Peace and Security in Iraq and Kuwait), Adopted at the 2981st meeting, April 3, 1991, paras. 1, 16, 18, 19, 33, 34, U.N. Doc. S/RES/687 (1991), *reprinted in* **30 I.L.M. 847 (1991).** [Basic Document 7.32].

The Security Council,

Recalling its resolutions 660 (1990) of 2 August 1990, 661 (1990) of 6 August 1990, 662 (1990) of 9 August 1990, 664 (1990) of 18 August 1990, 665 (1990) of 25 August 1990, 666 (1990) of 13 September 1990, 667 (1990) of 16 September 1990, 669 (1990) of 24 September 1990, 670 (1990) of 25 September 1990, 674 (1990) of 29 October 1990, 677 (1990) of 28 November 1990, 678 (1990) of 29 November 1990 and 686 (1991) of 2 March 1991,

* * *

Conscious of the need to take the following measures acting under Chapter VII of the Charter,

1.   Affirms all thirteen resolutions noted above, except as expressly changed below to achieve the goals of this resolution, including a formal cease-fire;

* * *

16.   Reaffirms that Iraq, without prejudice to the debts and obligations of Iraq arising prior to 2 August 1990, which will be addressed through the normal mechanisms, is liable under international law for any direct loss, damage, including environmental damage and the depletion of natural resources, or injury to foreign Governments, nationals and corporations, as a result of Iraq's unlawful invasion and occupation of Kuwait;

* * *

18.   Decides also to create a fund to pay compensation for claims that fall within paragraph 16 above and to establish a Commission that will administer the fund;

19.   Directs the Secretary–General to develop and present to the Security Council for decision, no later than thirty days following the adoption of the present resolution, recommendations for the fund to meet the requirement for the payment of claims established in accordance with paragraph 18 above and for a programme to implement the decisions in paragraphs 16, 17 and 18 above, including: administration of the fund; mechanisms for determining the appropriate level of Iraq's contribution to the fund based on a percentage of the value of the exports of petroleum and petroleum products from Iraq not to exceed a figure to be suggested to the Council by the Secretary–General, taking into account the requirements of the people of Iraq, Iraq's payment capacity as assessed in conjunction with the international financial institu-

k.   *See infra* Reading 23.

tions taking into consideration external debt service, and the needs of the Iraqi economy; arrangements for ensuring that payments are made to the fund; the process by which funds will be allocated and claims paid; appropriate procedures for evaluating losses, listing claims and verifying their validity and resolving disputed claims in respect of Iraq's liability as specified in paragraph 16 above; and the composition of the Commission designated above;

* * *

33.   Declares that, upon official notification by Iraq to the Secretary–General and to the Security Council of its acceptance of the provisions above, a formal cease-fire is effective between Iraq and Kuwait and the Member States cooperating with Kuwait in accordance with resolution 678 (1990);

34.   Decides to remain seized of the matter and to take such further steps as may be required for the implementation of the present resolution and to secure peace and security in the area.

19. Hague Convention (No. IV) Respecting the Laws and Customs of War on Land, Oct. 18, 1907, arts. 2, 3 and Annexed Regulation 23(g), 36 Stat. 2277, T.S. No. 539, 1 Bevans 631 [Basic Document 7.25].

20. Geneva Convention Relative to the Protection of Civilian Persons in Time of War, Aug. 12, 1949, art. 146, 6 U.S.T. 3516, T.I.A.S. No. 3365, 75 U.N.T.S. 287 [Basic Document 7.26].

21. Legal Principles for Environmental Protection and Sustainable Development Adopted by the Experts Group on Environmental Law of the World Commission on Environment and Development, June 1986, Principle 21, in Environmental Protection and Sustainable Development (1987) [Basic Document 1.22].

22. Principles of International Law Recognized in the Charter of the Nuremberg Tribunal and in the Judgment of the Tribunal, Aug. 2, 1950, 2 Y. B. Int'l L. Comm'n 374 (1950) [Basic Document 7.27].

23. Draft Articles on the Draft Code of Crimes Against the Peace and Security of Mankind (as Revised by the Int'l L. Comm'n Through 1991), arts. 1, 14, 26, U.N. Doc. A/46/405 (1991), 30 I.L.M. 1584 (1991) [Basic Document 7.28].

24. Louis René Beres, *Toward Prosecution of Iraqi Crimes Under International Law: Jurisprudential Foundations and Jurisdictional Choices*, 22 Cal. W. Int'l L.J. 127, 127–34 (1991).

Between October 1943 and January 1944, the United States and Great Britain, bowing to rising pressure for post-war punishment of "Hitlerite Criminals," worked to establish a United Nations Commission for the Investigation of War Crimes (commonly known as the United Nations War Crimes Commission—UNWCC). Once established, the Commission, meeting in London in 1944, assembled lists of war criminals and planned for the creation of special war crimes tribunals. As is now well-known, the special trial of major Nazi leaders began in November 1945, a little more than three months after victorious allied powers authorized proceedings in their London Charter of August 8, 1945.

Today, shocked by evidence of Iraqi atrocities against civilians and combatants of diverse nationalities, a victorious coalition should ... begin preparations for what amounts to "another Nuremberg." ...

How should the coalition begin? ... As of late September 1991, there was considerable talk of a return of coalition military forces to Iraq. Although the rationale of such a return would be to ensure Iraqi compliance with authoritative cease-fire expectations ..., a reinserted multinational force (or even a U.S. military force under U.N. auspices) could be used to identify and apprehend alleged Iraqi criminals. From a jurisprudential perspective, of course, it would be entirely proper to reintroduce appropriate military forces for the sole purpose of such identification and apprehension (subject, of course, to the norms of *jus in bello*), but this is unlikely for both tactical and political reasons.

Ideally, apprehension of Saddam Hussein and his military leaders would be made possible via the established mechanisms of extradition or prosecution and the associated means of "indirect enforcement" (prosecution within authoritative municipal courts in the absence of a permanently-constituted international criminal court or ad hoc, Nuremberg-style tribunal), but these prospects are extremely remote. Other possibilities include *in absentia* trials or custody via abduction.

Regarding *in absentia* trials, the terms of the Charter of the International Military Tribunal [at Nuremberg], annexed to the London Agreement, are valid: "The Tribunal shall have the right to take proceedings against a person charged with crimes set out in Article 6 of this Charter [crimes against peace; war crimes and crimes against humanity] in his absence, if he has not been found or if the Tribunal, for any reason, finds it necessary, in the interests of justice, to conduct the hearing in his absence."

Regarding custody by *abduction* ... , there is almost always a presumption of sovereign immunity, a binding rule that exempts each state and its high officials from the judicial jurisdiction of another state. Although the rule of sovereign immunity is certainly not absolute in the post-Nuremberg world order, the right of one state to seize a high official from another state is exceedingly limited....

Exactly what kinds of Iraqi crimes are involved? Judging from persistent and well-documented reports of horrendous crimes, crimes so terrible in law that they mandate universal cooperation in apprehension and punishment (what the lawyers call *crimen contra omnes*, crimes against all), they concern (1) barbarous and inhuman assaults against the people of Kuwait and other nationals in Kuwait; (2) barbarous and inhuman treatment of coalition prisoners of war in Iraq and Kuwait; and (3) aggression and crimes of war against noncombatant populations in Israel and Saudi Arabia. All of these violations under international law, of course, are in addition to the original crimes against peace committed against Kuwait on August 2, 1990.

Washington and its allies must also decide on how broadly they wish to prosecute Iraqi crimes. In this respect, the special post World War II war crimes planning group had a somewhat easier task, focusing primarily on particular Nazi groups that were defined as inherently criminal (e.g., the SS and the Gestapo). Following the defeat of Saddam Hussein, however, it appears that most of the crimes against humanity committed by Iraq were unplanned and individually-conceived atrocities. This means that the coalition lists of suspected war criminals could become so large as to be altogether unusable. Alternatively, coalition prosecution could focus essentially or even entirely on Saddam Hussein and his leadership elite, a judicial strategy that would permit many or all rank-and-file Iraqi criminals to avoid punishment, but would at least stand some chance of far-reaching and practical success.

The United States slowly backed off from President Bush's intra-war plans for trials of Saddam Hussein and his military leadership. The principle reason for this diminished enthusiasm lies in geopolitical factors, especially the fear that the U.S.-led prosecution would not play well in the Arab world. In the U.S. Congress, certain individual members have argued for appropriate trials.

Finally, it should be noted that a coalition agency charged with creating "another Nuremberg" could adopt the solution favored by the United States, the Soviet Union, Great Britain, and France in 1945. Here, a specially-created tribunal would be established for the trial of major criminals (that is, Saddam Hussein and the surviving members of his Revolutionary Council) while the domestic courts of individual coalition countries would provide the venue for trials of "minor" criminals (that is, of ordinary soldiers and their civilian collaborators). As in the distinction employed to prosecute Nazi offenses, the separation of *major* and *minor* criminals concerns matters of rank or position, and would have nothing to do with the seriousness or horror of particular transgressions. Moreover, because the Iraqi crimes make their perpetrators "common enemies of mankind" under international law, *every* country now has the legal right to prosecute these crimes in its own courtrooms.

The crimes committed by Iraq are reminiscent of Nazi crimes of an earlier era, and warrant similar forms of trial and punishment. *Now* is the time for the U.S. and its partners to establish the necessary legal machinery.

Discussion Notes/Questions

1. We speak of damage to the environment as a result of intended and unintended acts of war. But what do we mean by "the environment"? Does it matter? Are mitigating solutions likely to depend on how we conceptualize it? Consider David Tolbert, *Defining the "Environment"*, in ENVIRONMENTAL PROTECTION AND THE LAW OF WARFARE (G. Plant ed., 1992), at 259–60:

> [T]ension in defining environmental damage stems from an underlying conceptual problem which arises from what the "environment" is and how we define it. If the "environment" is defined in terms of human relationships to the resources of nature, then the "environment" becomes a term that simply describes a type of economic resource and environmental damage is simply a calculation of resultant economic and/or social loss arising out of injury to that economic resource. Although there is undoubted economic dimension to the environment . . . , such a "human-centric" definition equates one consequence of environmental damage—damage to humans and their interests—as the sole or major determinant of environmental damage. [It is] submitted that for the "environment" to have any real meaning it must be defined in terms that do not principally rely on humans;* * * [And] one particularly good

example in the area of armed conflict which takes a "nature-centric" approach, the Environmental Modification Convention of 1977 (ENMOD) [**Basic Document 7.30**] which seeks to prohibit "environmental modification techniques" of the "natural processes—the dynamics, composition or structure of the earth, including its biota, lithosphere, hydrosphere and atmosphere, or of outer space". Thus this approach does not measure environmental degradation in terms of impact on human beings (although humans would clearly benefit from the enforcement of the treaty provisions), but in terms of the elements of the natural environment—water, air, space, seas and living matter, etc.

What are the consequences of taking a "human-centric" (i.e., homocentric) view of the environment? A "nature-centric" view? Should warfare that is intentionally destructive of the environment be seen as a "crime against humanity," as the Rapporteur to the International Law Commission in respect of its Draft Code of Crimes Against the Peace and Security of Mankind has proposed (see Reading 23, *supra*), or should it be viewed as a "war crime"? What difference might it make? Is it reasonable to conclude that a "human-centric" view of the environment might limit compensation for environmental damage to human losses resulting from the destruction, whereas a "nature-centric" outlook would extend compensation for damage to wildlife and the natural environment as such?

2. However "nature-centric" the ENMOD Convention [**Basic Document 7.30**] may be, it is not perfect. In *Some Considerations on the Review of the 1977 Environmental Modification Techniques (ENMOD) Convention*, 6 Ital. Y. B. Int'l L. 96, 98–103 (1985), Antonio Filippo Panzera notes the following criticisms:

a) according to the language of Art. 2 (which is supported also by the logical context and by the preparatory works), the Convention is concerned with environmental modifications produced by the deliberate use of special techniques intended for such purpose (which are prohibited) and not also (as would have been desirable) with environmental modifications produced "indirectly" or by the use of conventional weapons or weapons of mass destruction;

b) the Convention only partially prohibits techniques that are able to modify the environment for military—or at least hostile—purposes because it prohibits only techniques "having widespread, long-lasting or severe effects".... On the contrary, it appears to legitimize the use of techniques that are below this already high "threshold";

c) in the real life it is not always easy to distinguish between peaceful aims ... and hostile aims ... in the use of environmental modification techniques;

d) the Convention prohibits the use of environmental modification techniques but not research and stockpiling activities and, in general, any kind of preparatory activity;

e) for the purpose of stimulating broader participation in the Convention, Art 1, n. 1 prohibits only the hostile use of techniques of environmental modification that may cause "damage or injury *to any other State Party*", and not to third States as well;

f) the control mechanism in Art. 5 appears weak. Indeed, the Consultative Committee of Experts' role is restricted to the mere verification of facts, whereas any possible decision is entrusted to the [U.N.] Security Council, with the drawback of the possible Permanent Members' resort to the veto;

g) sanctions are not provided in the hypothesis of an established breach of the Convention's obligations.

Do you agree that these criticisms render the ENMOD Convention essentially useless? Why? Why not? What might you recommend to improve or strengthen it?

3.   Articles 35 and 55 of 1977 Geneva Protocol I [**Basic Document 7.31**], as we have seen, attempt to safeguard the natural environment against wartime activities. They provide important protections not previously found in the law. Significantly, however, such countries as France, the United Kingdom, and the United States, all key players in the 199091 Persian Gulf War, object to these provisions, refusing to consider them as binding principles of customary international law. As conveniently summarized in W. Arkin, D. Durrant & M. Cherni, *On Impact: Modern Warfare and the Environment: A Case Study of the Gulf War* 12324 (1991), a Greenpeace study:

The US (and most western military powers') rejection is rooted in the concept of military necessity. The US government's position is that Article 35 is not part of customary law. The objection centers on the language of Article 35 of Protocol I, which prohibits acts that would have "widespread, long term and severe damage," while not defining these effects in the text. During the most recent debate about the Protocols in 1987, Michael J. Matheson, Deputy Legal Adviser to the US State Department, reiterated that US objection:

We, however, consider that another principle in Article 35, which also appears later in the Protocol, namely, that the prohibition of methods or means of warfare intended or expected to cause widespread, long-term and severe damage to the environment, is too broad and ambiguous and is not part of customary law.

One opponent of the Protocols argued that Article 35 was objectionable, as it would open the door for war crimes prosecutions whenever the environment suffered serious environmental damage. However, an advocate of the Protocols, its US negotiator, Ambassador George Aldrich, argued that "collateral damage from conventional warfare such as that which occurred in France in World War I was not intended to be covered.... [L]ong term should be understood in terms of decades."

The US also does not support ... the new restrictions contained in the Protocols (Article 52) on attacking dangerous works and installations. The Joint Chiefs of Staff conducted a study of the military implications of Protocol I, concluding that it was "militarily unacceptable" because of new restrictions on objects of bombardment (as well as for other reasons). Abraham Sofaer, [former] State Department Legal Adviser, wrote that the new law "would protect objects that would be considered legitimate military objectives under customary international law." Sofaer argues that the Protocol would provide almost complete prohibition, and exempt such targets from the traditional considerations of proportionality:

It is clear ... that civilian losses are not to be balanced against the military value of the target. If severe losses would result, then the attack is forbidden, no matter how important the target. It also appears that Article 56 forbids any attack that raises the possibility of severe civilian losses.

As a result of the U.S. objections and those of France and the United Kingdom as well, Articles 35 and 55 appear to have had little international impact. Is this appropriate? Should the objections of a few nations be allowed to undermine the effectiveness of an otherwise widely endorsed agreement? How might such a world order situation be altered? What would you propose?

4. It is widely appreciated that a nuclear war would have devastating effect upon the natural environment. It would risk the end of human civilization as we know it in large part because of its probable climatic impacts (e.g., "nuclear winter"). Thus, in its July 1996 advisory opinion on the *Legality of the Threat or Use of Nuclear Weapons*, 1996 I.C.J. (general list No. 93), the International Court of Justice stated, at 15:

> The Court recognizes that the environment is under daily threat and that the use of nuclear weapons could constitute a catastrophe for the environment. The Court also recognizes that the environment is not an abstraction but represents the living space, the quality of life and the very health of human beings, including generations unborn. The existence of the general obligation of States to ensure that activities within their jurisdiction and control respect the environment of other States or of areas beyond national control is now part of the corpus of international law relating to the environment.

Nevertheless, the Court concluded, at 16, that "existing international law relating to the protection and safeguarding of the environment does not specifically prohibit the use of nuclear weapons," only that "it indicates important environmental factors that are properly to be taken into account in the context of the implementation of the principles and rules of law applicable in armed conflict"— e.g., the principles of necessity and proportionality. The Court reasoned: "the issue is not whether the treaties relating to the protection of the environment are or are not applicable during an armed conflict, but rather whether the obligations stemming from these treaties were intended to be obligations of total restraint during military conflict. ... The Court does not consider that the treaties in question could have intended to deprive a State of the exercise of its right of self-defence under international law because of its obligations to protect the environment." *Id.* The "treaties in question" to which the Court was referring included the 1976 ENMOD Convention **[Basic Document 7.30]** and the 1977 Additional Protocol I to the 1949 Geneva Conventions Relating to the Protection of Victims of Armed Conflict **[Basic Document 7.31]**.

Do you agree with this judgment? Disagree? Since when is a state's right of self-defense not limited by its environmental (and humanitarian) obligations? What might be a consequence of the Court's finding? Does it imply the need for some new treaty law? Does it make any difference? Is it possible to use nuclear weapons without violating the principles of necessity and proportionality? What, if anything, would you recommend to reverse the present commitment to nuclearism? In particular, how would you ensure national and international security without reliance on "the bomb"? For some thoughts along these lines, see ALTERNATIVE SECURITY: LIVING WITHOUT NUCLEAR DETERRENCE (Burns Weston ed., 1990). For additional discussion concerning the hazards of nuclearism, see Problem 7–3 ("The Atomic Steel Mill") in Chapter 7, *supra*.

5. The history of environmental warfare can be traced back over two thousand years. As early as 401 B.C., the Greeks employed honey poisoned with gray anotoxins to render Pompey's troops incompetent during the Spartan Wars. Troops were led into valleys where poisoned honey was located and then attacked after eating the honey, when in a weakened condition. During the Fourteenth Century, the Tartars hurled plague victims over the walls of Kaffa to spread the disease. And during the French and Indian wars, smallpox was deliberately spread

among American Indians via contaminated blankets. *See* R. Root-Bernstein, Biology: Infectious Terrorism 44 (1991).

In modern times, given our systems of water supply and air ventilation in many large buildings, it has become even easier to imagine biological and environmental warfare. Experiments document the ease with which agents such as *Giardia lamblia*, a diarrheal micro-organism, can be spread through public water systems. The release by the British of anthrax on a small, uninhabited island in the Pacific was so successful that the island remains uninhabitable due to contamination some forty years later. In short, technology now makes the release of toxins and genetically altered substances into the civilian environment easy and untraceable, capable of affecting humans, animals, agriculture, and the wider environment sometimes in irreversible ways. Release of chemicals via large "spillage" as in the case of the Persian Gulf War (and Khalifan) are now threatening to damage the environment and affect civilian populations for many years to come. Release of flood waters has also become a real concern, as it is not difficult to destroy a dam or other hydroelectric facility with modern weapons. For useful summary and detail, *see* Roof Bernstein, *supra.*

How do ENMOD [**Basic Document 7.30**] and Geneva Protocol I [**Basic Document 7.31**] address such environmental threats? Would the spreading of a disease in the course of a war violate the text of either agreement? If so, how? If not, how would you amend these agreements so that they might address such threats directly and explicitly? Would it be better simply to draft an entirely new convention?

6. In his introduction to *Environmental Protection and the Law of War* (G. Plant ed. 1992), Glen Plant identifies "four camps" representing a "spectrum of views" on the state of international environmental law relative to armed conflict. He summarizes, at 15–16:

> The holders of the spectrum of views on the state of the law applicable to deliberate and collateral damage to the environment in the context of international armed conflict can ... be roughly characterized into four hypothetical "Camps" as follows: *Camp 1*, those who consider the existing law relevant to environmental protection in wartime to be an amalgamation of principles established in the customary international law of war and a number of codifying provisions to be found in the Regulations attached to the Hague Conventions of 1899 (II) and 1907 (IV) [**Basic Document 7.25**] and in the Geneva Conventions of 1949 [**Basic Document 7.26**] and that this law reflects environmental concerns and is adequate to cover the worst environmental excesses of any foreseeable war; *Camp 2*, those who accept this but consider Protocol I to the 1949 Conventions [**Basic Document 7.31**] also to represent customary law, including among several relevant provisions two directly and expressly referring to environmental protection, Articles 33(5) and 55, and that this law, together with other relevant instruments such as the ENMOD [**Basic Document 7.30**] and the Inhuman Weapons Conventions (where they apply), is adequate to protect the environment in wartime, needing no further elaboration; *Camp 3*, those who consider the existing law of war, whatever it may be, to be inadequate or at least in need of restatement and who contemplate various means for improving the standards of, adherence to or implementation of that law, whether by using existing instruments and mechanisms or by developing new ones, such as a new Geneva-style Convention; this Camp generally inclines in favour of ensuring that developments in the international environmental law of peacetime are

fully reflected in the law of war, but considers that the matter should be tackled essentially within the framework of the law of war; and *Camp 4*, which considers the distinction between wartime and peacetime acts in this context to be so vague, irrelevant or misleading that, if any new development is to take place, it should be concerned with environmental destruction in all scenarios, whether wartime or peacetime.

In which "camp" or "camps" do you fall? Why?

7. As by now must be clear, strengthening and enforcing the ENMOD Convention [**Basic Document 7.30**] and Geneva Protocol I [**Basic Document 7.31**] in order to help safeguard the natural environment against the ravages of war is a matter of obvious priority. Perhaps not so obvious, however, is the possibility of assisting this process at the local level and not simply on the international plane. In August–September 1990, for example, the Eighth United Nations Congress on the Prevention of Crime and the Treatment of Offenders, meeting in Havana, Cuba, adopted a resolution on "The Role of Criminal Law in the Protection of Nature and the Environment," in which the UN Congress called upon states to enact and enforce national criminal laws to protect nature and the environment. Does such a call add force to the argument that such serious violations of international environmental values as environmental warfare should constitute international crimes? Why? Why not?

8. In *International Liability of States for Marine Pollution*, 21 Can. Y. B. Int'l L. 85, 88, Günther Handl writes that even if *prevention* of environmental harm is the best policy, state responsibility for such damage "would have to be emphasized as a key element." In other words, compensation for environmental damage often will be an important way to guarantee the international legal obligation not to do harm to "the environment of other States or of areas beyond the limits of national jurisdiction," per Principle 21 of the 1972 Stockholm Declaration of the United Nations Conference on the Human Environment [**Basic Document 1.12**]. However, as pointed out in Luan Low & David Hodgkinson, *Compensation for Wartime Environmental Damage: Challenges to International Law After the Gulf War*, 35 Va. J. Int'l L. 405 (1995), wartime environmental damage is typically not compensable under customary notions of *jus in bello*; and while compensable under Paragraph 16 of Security Council Resolution 687 [**Basic Document 7.32**] relative to the Persian Gulf War, that initiative, based on the *jus ad bellum*, may be said to have limited precedential value. Thus Low and Hodgkinson write, at 483: "The challenges for international law . . . are to provide obligations which directly protect the environment in wartime and to ensure that there is an adequate endorsement mechanism through the provision of liability and compensation. . . . Only when the legal system meets *both* challenges will international law offer full protection to the environment in wartime." What can you recommend that might fulfill this call to action?

9. In response to criticisms of existing international law of war as regards protection of the environment, many have called for a fifth Geneva Convention to improve the status of the environment in the law of war. Glen Plant calls for a new convention rather than continued reliance on the 1949 Geneva Conventions and their supplementary protocols. In so doing, he lists "the common ground on the law of war," as follows:

1.   The law of war has been concerned with environmental protection since ancient times at least in the sense of prohibiting wanton destruction of forests, orchards, fruit trees and vines and forbidding the poisoning of wells, springs and rivers.

2. Deliberate and wanton destruction of the environment in circumstances where no legitimate military objective is being served is contrary to international law.

3. The principle of proportionality between means and methods employed in an attack and the military objective sought to be attained by it, the prohibition against military operations not directed against legitimate military targets, the prohibition against the destruction of enemy property not imperatively demanded by the necessities of war and other well established principles of customary international law have the indirect effect of protecting the environment in many wartime situations.

4. The Martens Clause, formulated in its most modern version in Protocol I [**Basic Document 7.31**], reads as follows:

> In cases not covered by this Protocol or by other international agreements, civilians and combatants remain under the protection and authority of the principles of international law derived from established custom, from the principles of humanity and from the dictates of public conscience.

Thus the customary law of war, in reflecting the modern increase in concern for the environment as one of the dictates of public conscience in the sense understood in that Clause, now includes a requirement to avoid unjustifiable damage to the environment.

5. Violations of Article 23(g) of the Regulations attached to the Hague Convention of 1907 (IV) Respecting the Laws and Customs of War on Land [**Basic Document 7.25**], or of Article 53 of the 1949 Geneva Convention (IV) Relative to the Protection of Civilian Persons in Time of War [**Basic Document 7.26**], which prohibit destruction by an Occupying Power of enemy property not required by military necessity, give rise to civil liability. Wanton destruction is considered a grave breach, for which individual criminal responsibility can be attributed by virtue of Article 147 of the latter Convention.

6. States should ensure the wide dissemination and effective implementation of their existing obligations under the law of armed conflict as they may be relevant to the protection of the environment, as well as proper instruction of the military in their application. They should be adequately incorporated into military manuals and rules of engagement, in particular, through instructions to military commanders on the planning and preparation of military activities.

Glen Plant, *Introduction, in* ENVIRONMENTAL PROTECTION AND THE LAW OF WAR 17–18 (G. Plant ed. 1992). How, given this "common ground," might a better convention be conceived and drafted? Could it adequately address the problem of environmental protection in time of war? Would it need to prescribe a new category of crime—crimes against nature or crimes against the environment—to supplement the existing "crimes against the peace," "war crimes," and "crimes against humanity" categories of international crime?

9. *Bibliographical Note.* For further discussion concerning the principal themes addressed in this problem, consult the following specialized books/monographs and articles:

(a) *Specialized Books/Monographs.* W. Arkin, D. Durrant & M. Cherni, On Impact: Modern Warfare and the Environment–A Case Study of the Gulf War (1991); Armed Conflict and the New Law: Aspects of the 1977 Geneva Protocols and the 1981 Weapons Convention (M. Meyer ed. 1989); Arms Control and Disarmament Agency, Environmental Warfare: Questions and Answers (1976); S. Baxter, William III and the Defense of European Liberty 1650–1702 (1966); B. Bolt, Nuclear Explosions and Earthquakes (1976); P. Brickhill, Dam Busters (1951); S. Dycus, National Defense and the Environment (1996); Environmental Warfare: A Technical, Legal and Policy Appraisal (A. Westing ed. 1984); Environmental Hazards of War (A. Westing ed. 1990); Explosive Remnants of War: Mitigating the Environmental Effects (A. Westing ed. 1985); F. Kalshoven, Constraints on the Waging of War (1987); Nuclear Weapons and the Law (A. Miller & M. Feinreider eds. 1984); G. Plant ed., Environmental Protection and the Law of War: A "Fifth Geneva" Convention on the Protection of the Environment in Time of Armed Conflict (1992); Protection of the Environment During Armed Conflict, (R. Grunawalt, et al eds. 1996); B. Ramberg, Destruction of Nuclear Energy Facilities in War: The Problem and the Implications (1980); A. Westing, Ecological Consequences of the Second Indochina War (1976); A. Westing, Warfare in a Fragile World: Military Impact on the Human Environment (1980); Cultural Norms, War, and the Environment (A. Westing ed., 1988).

(b) *Specialized Articles/Book Chapters.* J. van Aartsen, *Consequences of the War on Agriculture in the Netherlands*, 37 Int'l Rev. Agriculture 5S–34S, 49S–70S, 108S–123S (1946); G. Aldrich, *Prospects for US Ratification of Additional Protocol I*, 85 Am. J. Int'l L. 1 (1991); D. Atlas, *Paradox of Hail Suppression*, 195 Science 139 (1977); F. Barnaby, *Environmental Warfare*, 32(5) Bull. Atomic Scientists 36 (1976); G. Boucher, A. Ryall & A. Jones, *Earthquakes Associated with Underground Nuclear Explosions*, 74 J. Geophysical Research 3808 (1969); A. Boyle, *State Responsibility for Breach of Obligations to Protect the Global Environment*, in Control Over Compliance with International Law 69 (W. Butler ed. 1991); C. Covey, S. Schneider & S. Thompson, *Global Atmospheric Effects of Massive Smoke Injections from a Nuclear War: Results from General Circulation Model Simulations*, 308 Nature 21 (1984); R. Davis, *Weather Warfare: Law and Policy*, 14 Ariz. L. Rev. 659 (1972); P. Ehrlich & H. Mooney, Extinction, Substitution, and Ecosystem Services, 33 BioScience 248 (1983); A. Ehrlich, *Nuclear Winter: A Forecast of the Climatic and Biological Effects of Nuclear War*, 40(4) Bull. Atomic Scientists 1S (1984); P. Ehrlich *et al.*, *Long-term Biological Consequences of Nuclear War*, 222 Science 1293 (1983); R. Falk, *Environmental Warfare and Ecocide*, 4 Bull. Peace Proposals 1 (1973); S. Fetter, & K. Tsipis, *Catastrophic Releases of Radioactivity*, 244(4) Scientific American 33 (1981); C. Greenwood, *State Responsibility and Civil Liability for Environmental Damage Caused by Military Operations*, in Protection of the Environment During Armed Conflict 397 (R. Grunawalt, et al eds., 1996); J. Goldblat, *Environmental Warfare Convention: How Meaningful Is It?*, 6 Ambio 216 (1977); L. Green, *The Environment and the Law of Conventional Warfare*, 29 Can. Y. B. Int'l L. 222 (1991); R. Kerr, Cloud Seeding: One Success in 35 Years, 217 Science 519 (1982); A. Leibler, *Deliberate Wartime Environmental Damage: New Challenges for International Law*, 23 Cal. W. Int'l L. J. 67, (1992); R. Manchee et al. *Bacillus Anthracis on Gruinard Island*, 294 Nature 254 (1981), 295 id. 362, 296 id. 598; ___, *Decontamination of Bacillus Anthracis on Gruinard Island*, 303 Nature 239 (1983); I. Mason, *Review of Three Long–Term Cloud–Seeding Experiments*, 109 Meteorological Magazine 335 (1980); J. Muntz, *Environmental Modification*, 19 H.I.L.J. 384 (1978); A. Roberts, *Environmental Issues in International Armed Conflict: The Experience of the 1991 Gulf War*, in Protection of the Environment During Armed Conflict 222 (R. Grunawalt, et al eds. 1996); B. Schafer, *The Relationship Between the International Law of Armed Conflict and Environmental Protection: The Need to Reevaluate What Types of Conduct Are Permissible During Hostilities*, 19 Cal. W. Int'l L. J. 287 (1989); R. Turco, O. Toon, T. Ackerman, J. Pollack & C. Sagan, *Nuclear Winter: Global Consequences of Multiple Nuclear Explosions*, 222 Science 1283 (1983); C. Sagan, *Nuclear War and Climatic Catastrophe: Some Policy Implications*, 62 For. Aff. 257 (1983–84); M. Schmitt, *Green War: An Assessment of the Environmental Law of International Armed Conflict*, 22 Yale J. Int'l L. 1 (1997); E. Weiss, *Weather as a Weapon*, in Air, Water, Fire: The Impact of the Military on World Environmental Order 51 (R. Russell ed. 1974); E. Weiss, *Weather Control: An Instrument of War?*, 17 Survival 64 (1975); A. Westing, *Geophysical and Environmental Weapons*, in Weapons of Mass Destruction and the Environment 49 (SIPRI eds., 1977); A. Westing, *Environmental Consequences of Nuclear Warfare*, 9 Environmental Conservation 269 (1982); C. Wunsch, *Environmental Modification Treaty*, 4 A.S.I.L.S. Int'l L. J. 113 (1980).

Part III

The Global Environment, International Law, and the Future

INTRODUCTION

The future is an integral part of the human condition, and may be thought of in both the short and the long term. Of course, precisely what is meant by either of these time spans is to large extent a subjective matter. For the hungry and otherwise deprived, for example, the future is substantially a day-to-day continuation of a relatively unchanging past and a seemingly unchangeable present. For the educated and otherwise fortunate, it can span generations, even centuries, and involve ideals and assumptions about possibility that transcend past and present constraints and inadequacies.

This latter conception of the future is a relatively new one in human experience. Also, it is largely a Western invention. Stemming primarily from the scientific and industrial revolutions (each relatively new developments in the historical sense), it contrasts sharply with the cyclical model of the future found primarily in Eastern and animist societies wherein the predestined sequences of birth, death, and rebirth move eternally toward the unknowable source of all origins. It embodies, in short, the idea of progress—both material, in terms of the enhancement of human well-being in the present or near future, and metaphysical, in terms of the perfectibility of human nature itself.

In this Part III, as befits our acculturation, we adopt this relatively recent and originally Western conception of the future and invite you to consider with us, and with this historical-cultural conception in mind, the strengths and weaknesses of international law and legal process as a vehicle for safeguarding the global environment in the future. Also, as befits our status of relative privilege, we ask you to do so with a time-horizon that is not constrained by the burdens of day-to-day survival.

We begin, in Chapter 12, with a relatively long-term view of the future, with a time horizon ranging from seventy-five to hundred years. Our focus here is on the way international environmental law is made and re-made to meet the challenges of a relatively predictable future. Predicting the future may be the business of futurists, but preparing for the more or less predictable future—i.e., the probable future—most certainly can and must be the business of lawyers. In Chapter 12, therefore, we introduce you to how, through international negotiation (the principle means of making international law at this stage in history), the international legal process makes normative adjustments to scientific probabilities—in particular, large-scale probabilities that demand to be taken into account if the global environment is to be preserved in whole or in part. We invite you, that is, to experience (and thereby hopefully to understand) the thrills and frustrations of negotiating, in a simulated multilateral negotiation exercise, the demands of global warming or climate change. Global warming, or climate change, is among the most grave and pressing problems facing our planet. It begs, therefore, to be studied and thoroughly comprehended in its own right. We take this point seriously, but we use this modern phenomenon to help you understand, as well, how nations negotiate the short-term future. As will be seen, this exploration is not for the faint-hearted.

Finally, fresh from multilateral negotiation, and located within a similar time span, you will be in a position to tackle our last chapter (Chapter 13). What will be the environmental problems of the future and how will international law develop in relation to them over this time span? How will or might it be strengthened? What role will or might international organizations play? How will or might the law and the specialized regimes that will likely have developed relate to one another? These sorts of questions will be familiar to anyone who has taken seriously our "suggested reflective assignment" in each Part II problem wherein we have repeatedly asked you to "[c]onsider (and recommend) alternative norms, institutions, and/or procedures that you believe might do better than existing world order arrangements to contend with situations of the kind posed by [the problem at hand]" and to do so "without insisting upon *immediate* feasibility." Still, we are not unmindful of the fact that there are many imponderables in the long-term environmental future of this planet. We have tried to capture as many of the important themes as space allows, and leave for you the ultimate question: Can we cope with the future? The judgment, in the end, is yours.

Chapter 12

GLOBAL WARMING: NEGOTIATING THE LONG–TERM FUTURE

STABILIZING GREENHOUSE GASES: NEGOTIATING A PROTOCOL[a]

SECTION 1. FACTS[b]

A. *Nature and Causes of the Phenomenon*

Enormous quantities of heat trapping or infrared trapping gases, known as greenhouse gases (GHGs), are emitted into the atmosphere today. In the right quantities GHGs help support life and ecosystems on earth by maintaining a relatively constant surface temperatures that average nearly 60°F. Where they are not present, as on Mars, the surface temperatures are very low and average only 39°F, and where GHGs are present in excess, as on Venus, surface temperatures are very high and average approximately +810° F.

The earth must radiate energy away in an amount equal to that absorbed from the sun if surface temperatures are to remain in balance. GHGs, at their natural level, maintain such a heat balance. They enable the earth to trap infrared radiation that warms surface temperatures while at the same time permitting excess heat to escape. If the GHGs are allowed to build, this energy balance will be upset, and trapped infrared radiation will cause a rise in surface temperature.[c] Unfortunately, each year human activities discharge six billion tons of carbon dioxide and significant quantities of other GHGs such as methane and nitrous oxides, that are upsetting the environmental balance hitherto maintained by atmospheric gases that blanket the earth.[d]

---

a. This exercise originated in Professor David A. Wirth's exercise on negotiating a short-term Protocol controlling greenhouse gases. He retains the copyright in that exercise, and the authors and publishers are grateful to him for permission to use the conception he developed. The authors of this course book have, modified and adapted his exercise in response to recent developments. Our debt to Professor Wirth is nonetheless deep.

b. Significant parts of the materials in the facts are reproduced from Lakshman D. Guruswamy & Brent R. Hendricks, International Environmental Law In a Nutshell, Ch 6 (1997).

c. Joseph C. Dragan & Stefan Airinei, Geoclimate and History at 44–52 (1989).

d. John Firor, The Changing Atmosphere: A Global Challenge 51 (1990).

Debate continues as to the extent and impact of global warming [*See* **Readings 2, 3, 4, 5 & 6** *infra*]. Scientists using mathematical models forecast an abnormal degree of global warming as a result of increased levels of CO_2 and other GHGs [*See infra,* **Box 2**]. Other scientists challenge this assessment claiming actual data, such as surface temperature measurement, does not support this conclusion, and argue that theories of global warming are predicated on unreliable mathematical models,[e] and unproven theories of cooling.

Despite the fact that the awesome complexity of atmospheric mechanisms cannot fully be replicated by mathematical models,[f] a large majority of the scientific community agree that global climate change will negatively impact earth's environment. Indeed, there is a strong general consensus among the international scientific community that some action should be taken now to limit or reduce atmospheric GHGs on a global basis, because corrective actions will be ineffective after climate change has gained momentum.[g]

Data relevant to the causes of climate change are available from the 1950s when the global monitoring of climate began. Since then, data has been collected in strategically located measuring stations that monitor many parameters of climate. In order to obtain information prior to the 1950s other techniques are used. For example, CO_2 present in the historical atmosphere is trapped in polar ice caps, and these ice layers are tested at various depths to determine concentrations of CO_2 present in the atmosphere when that ice layer was deposited. This data is then interpreted by scientists using computer models in an effort to predict the amount of GHGs worldwide, and correlate atmospheric concentrations with climate change.

We know for sure that Carbon Dioxide (CO_2) is the most abundant GHG. Other GHGs include methane (CH_4), nitrous oxide (N_2O), ozone (O_3) and halocarbons (human-made compounds that contain chlorine or bromine and carbon atoms).[h] Since the beginning of the industrial revolution, or about 1800, atmospheric CO_2 concentrations have increased about 25%. Atmospheric methane (CH_4) has more than doubled, but it may be stabilizing. Atmospheric nitrous oxide (N_2O) has increased about 12%. Ambient ozone, on the other hand, has actually been decreasing because atmospheric chlorine may be destroying it. Halocarbons are human-made, and because of reduction activities spurred by the Montreal Protocol, their levels seem to be stabilizing.

A growing scientific consensus holds that atmospheric CO_2 levels will increase between one hundred and two hundred percent by 2100 if no changes

e. Patrick J. Michaels & David E. Stooksbury, *The Failure of the Popular Vision of Global Warming,* 9 ARIZ. J. INT'L & COMP. L. 53–82 (1992)

f. INTERGOVERNMENTAL PANEL ON CLIMATE CHANGE, CLIMATE CHANGE 1995: THE SCIENCE OF CLIMATE CHANGE 14 at Box 1(1996); JOSEPH C. DRAGAN & STEFAN AIRINEI, GEOCLIMATE AND HISTORY 27 (1989).

g. INTERGOVERNMENTAL PANEL ON CLIMATE CHANGE, CLIMATE CHANGE 1995: CONTRIBUTIONS OF WORKING GROUPS I, II & III (1996); *see infra,* Reading 2.

h. Inventory of U.S. Greenhouse Gas Emissions and Sinks: 1990–1994, USEPA ES2–4 (1995); INTERGOVERNMENTAL PANEL ON CLIMATE CHANGE, CLIMATE CHANGE 1995: THE SCIENCE OF CLIMATE CHANGE 14–20 (1996).

are made to current policy and practice.[i] This could correspond to a mean global temperature increase from 1.5°C to 3.5°C, with a best estimate placing the increase near 2.5°C.[j] Over the past century, data reveals a 0.5°C increase in average global temperature, that has not yet made a discernible difference to the earth's environment. However, larger temperature increases such as those now predicted to occur over the next century may cause a different result.

Many naturally existing processes keep the CO_2 level in check by providing "sinks" that mitigate the effects of accumulated GHGs. The workhorse of these processes is common photosynthesis. Forest vegetation converts CO_2 to oxygen (O_2) in the presence of sunlight during photosynthesis. Another photosynthetic contributor is ocean phytoplankton. Scientific theory suggests that rising levels of CO_2 actually stimulate the production of phytoplankton to compensate for additional CO_2.[k] Moreover, a number of other factors such as aerosols, volcanic activity and variations of the Sun's energy output act as cooling or negative radiative forces.[l]

B. Impacts

In 1988, the Intergovernmental Panel of Climate Change (IPCC) was formed jointly by the World Meteorological Organization (WMO) and the United Nations Environment Programme (UNEP) to evaluate the scientific phenomenon of global warming and its effects on earth's community. Several hundred working scientists participated in three individual IPCC working groups named "Working Group I: Scientific Assessment", "Working Group II: Impacts, Adaptation and Mitigation" and "Working Group III: Socio-economic and Cross-cutting Issues" which assess, respectively, scientific information, response strategies and socio-economic impacts. The working groups reports were published in 1990, and updated in 1992, 1994 and 1996.

The IPCC concluded in its original report that global climate change might have its greatest impact in the polar regions, melting polar ice caps and causing a rise in sea-level of about 1 meter by 2100 and a rise in temperature of the surface ocean layer of between 0.2°C and 2.5°C.[m] They predicted that climate changes will affect agriculture, forestry, natural terrestrial ecosystems, hydrology, water resources, human settlements, oceans and coastal zones, seasonal snow cover, permafrost, and ice. Specific predictions were difficult on a regional scale since climate varies regionally. The IPCC supplements confirmed the original findings and provided additional supporting data and a refinement of specific predictions. According to the IPCC evaluations, the most pronounced impacts will be related to water resources. Rising global

---

i. "If carbon dioxide emissions were maintained at near current (1994) levels, they would lead to a nearly constant rate of increase in atmospheric concentrations for at least two centuries, about 500 ppmv (approaching twice the concentration of 280 ppmv) by the end of the 21st century." Intergovernmental Panel on Climate Change, Climate Change 1995: The Science of Climate Change 3 (1996).

j. Intergovernmental Panel on Climate Change, Climate Change 1995: The Science of Climate Change 23, 39–40 (1996).

k. Jane S. Shaw and Richard L. Stroup, *Getting Warmer? Planning for Global Warming*, Nat'l Rev., July 14, 1989 at 26.

l. Intergovernmental Panel on Climate Change, Climate Change 1995: The Science of Climate Change 14 (1996).

m. Intergovernmental Panel on Climate Change, Climate Change: The Intergovernmental Panel on Climate Change Impacts Assessment 1–1 (1990).

temperatures will change existing patterns of precipitation, which in turn will cause meteorological shifts affecting seasonal snow patterns. Additionally, melting polar ice caps are expected to cause a rise in sea level which will directly impact commercial marine industries like shipping and fishing. Sea level rises will also severely challenge coastal land use. Agriculture will follow precipitation and temperature, and entire species will either adapt to the new habitats, shift locations or face localized and potentially widespread extinction.

Human settlements will also change as world population and trading centers are typically located on coasts. Developing countries and areas with significant lowlands may be unable to survive the health impacts of changing water and food supplies. Finally, human migration may disrupt settlement patterns and cause social instability. In light of the fact, however, that global warming may lead to winners as well as losers, diplomatic progress has been inhibited by geographical differences in the impact of global warming effects, and the remote manifestation of actual changes to the ecosystem.

C. Legal Response

i. 1992 Framework Convention on Climate Change (FCCC)

The international law response to the threat of global warming was first expressed in the 1992 Framework Convention on Climate Change (FCCC) **[Basic Document 3.21]**. Though there was a substantial political base which desired long-term quantitative emission limits, eventually a "go-slow" approach prevailed. The short negotiating period, combined both with the enormous economic stakes and a substantial amount of scientific uncertainty, resulted in the adoption of only cautious controls in the final version of the treaty.

The FCCC, however, is not an empty framework treaty whose substantive details entirely await further elaboration; instead, it is a framework convention with a number of built-in requirements. Most significantly, developed countries must strive to reduce their overall emissions of greenhouse gases (GHGs) to 1990 levels by the year 2000. In addition, developed countries have a general commitment to make financial and technological transfers to developing countries. Furthermore all parties—both developed and developing countries—must develop inventories of greenhouse gases (GHGs), as well as national mitigation and adaptation programs. The FCCC, however, provides different timetables and requirements for both categories of parties with regard to inventories and other programs, and the Conference of the Parties (COP) has established different guidelines for the national reports communicating such programs to the COP.

In mandating different requirements for developed and developing countries, as well as making further delineations within those groups, the FCCC embraces the concept of "common but differentiated responsibility" (CBDR) (Preamble 6, 10). This principle recognizes that only international cooperation will help to resolve a problem of the magnitude of global warming, but that in responding to the problem different states have different social and economic conditions that affects their response capabilities. CBDR also incorporates the equitable notion that developed countries, which have the largest share of historical and current emissions of GHGs, should take the first painful actions to ameliorate the problem. As we shall see, however, the exact application of CBDR remains in controversy concerning a number of issues.

ii.   1997 Kyoto Protocol

A second step in the global response to climate change was taken in Kyoto in 1997 [**Basic Document 3.25**] and in Buenos Aires in 1998[n]. After intense negotiation at Kyoto, the developed countries agreed to reduce GHGs to 5% below their 1990 levels between 2008 and 2112 [*See infra*, **reading 1**]. The Kyoto Protocol which embodied this agreement also provided a basis for emissions trading, primarily between developed countries.[o] The Kyoto Protocol, however, has not been implemented. Despite the fact that the U.S. has signed the Kyoto Protocol, the U.S. Senate which must approve such a treaty remains adamant in its refusal to ratify the Kyoto Protocol.[p] Additionally, a number of the industrialized (Annex 1) countries have failed to carry out the emission reductions to which they had agreed. The faltering attempts made at the COPs in Buenos Aires in 1998 did little to remedy this problem. Consequently, the Kyoto Protocol's objectives of reducing greenhouse gases (GHGs), primarily carbon dioxide, to a level that is 5% below 1990 discharges by 2112, are receding into the distance and appear effectively unattainable.

Furthermore, an increasing number of scientists in the United States and Europe are casting doubt on the speed and impact of global warming as predicted by the IPCC. These scientists [*See, e.g.,* **Readings 5 & 6**] argue that the IPCC predictions, and the Kyoto targets, based on bad science, inflict crippling costs in a foolhardy and premature attempt to arrest the increase of carbon dioxide. Even if global warming were taking place because of a doubling of carbon dioxide, some developed countries contend that it is quite possible to cope efficiently and effectively with any problems arising by mitigation and adaptation, rather than by the painful and costly cutting down of emissions.

n. This was the fourth meeting of the Conference of the Parties (COP 4) to the 1992 Climate Change Convention.

o. The Kyoto Protocol allowed for three types of implementation based upon: 1) joint implementation between Annex 1 (developed) countries; 2) Clean development mechanisms (between developed and developing countries; and 3) new flexibility mechanisms such as the creation of a "bubble" for the European Union.

p. S. Res. 98, 105th Cong. (1997) was unanimous and,

Resolved, That it is the sense of the Senate that–

(1) the United States should not be a signatory to any protocol to, or other agreement regarding, the United Nations Framework Convention on Climate Change of 1992, at negotiations in December 1997, or thereafter, which would–

(A) mandate new commitments to limit or reduce greenhouse gas emissions for Annex I Parties, unless the protocol or other agreement also mandates new specific scheduled commitments to limit or reduce greenhouse gas emissions for Developing Country Parties within the same compliance period, or

(B) would result in serious harm to the economy of the United States; and

(C) any such protocol or other agreement which would require the advice and consent of the Senate to ratification should be accompanied by a detailed explanation of and legislation or regulatory actions that may be required to implement the protocol or other agreement and should also be accompanied by an analysis of the detailed financial costs and other impacts on the economy of the United States which would be incurred by the implementation of the protocol or other agreement.

The resolve that developing countries should also limit their GHGs in tandem with developed countries remains so firm that the Clinton Administration has decided not to submit the Kyoto Protocol for Senate approval.

But what is even more disturbing is that even if the Kyoto Protocol were fully and faithfully implemented, GHGs will double to their pre-industrial levels by 2100, and quadruple within another 50 years.[q] As to the increasing volume of carbon dioxide emissions some commentators from developed countries [*See* **Reading 4**] suggest that, developed countries could comfortably adapt or mitigate the consequences of a doubling of GHGs. They proceed to argue that GHG reductions, in the long term, would occur naturally with the advance of technology, following investment cycles based on demand. According to them, future carbon dioxide reductions should be left to the development of new reduced carbon technologies and better sources of energy driven by markets that demanded cleaner and cheaper energy.

Historically, contributions to atmospheric GHGs have been made by the industrialized countries, led in volume by the United States. Unfortunately, forecasts for the next century show significant increases in emissions from developing nations, and emissions from China and India will probably overtake those of the United States and the European Union by 2015. In light of the developing country position the Legislative branches of the United States have resolved that any responsibility for reducing carbon dioxide cannot be borne by the developed countries alone, and must be accepted by the developing countries. They point out that China, India and Brazil are already discharging more carbon dioxide than the E.U. and the U.S. put together.

The refusal of the developing countries to control their emissions as part of the global effort to stabilize concentrations of GHGs presents a major diplomatic challenge. Current efforts to include developing countries with emission reducing framework of the Kyoto Protocol have proven unsuccessful.[r] By any analysis, portentous implications arise from the present diplomatic deadlock with regard to the cooperation of developing countries, and the rising concentrations of GHGs. The negotiating exercise that follows seeks to examine some of these formidable issues and challenges you to build cooperation among members of the global community, who despite their differing economic and social priorities, confront a common threat to their security.

D. *Negotiating a New Protocol*

It is with the facts and arguments in mind that Amazonia, Annam, the Federation of Columbia, Friesland, Hanguo, Kuroshio, New Polynesia, Rajapur, Savoy, Volhynia, and Yoribo [**Schedule A**] have come together to further negotiate a Long–Range Protocol on Stabilizing Greenhouse Gases (LRP) in fulfillment of Art 2 of the 1992 United Nations Framework Convention on Climate Change.

Despite protracted negotiations over the past ten months, the State parties remain deadlocked on four issues. *First,* should the objective of the

q. Intergovernmental Panel on Climate Change, Climate Change 1995: The Science of Climate Change 25 (1996).

r. The issue of binding emission controls on developing countries did not even make it to the agenda at the fourth conference of the parties (COP4) at Buenos Aires in Nov. 1998. The efforts of the United States to include developing countries in the effort to stabilize GHGs were successfully thwarted by China and the "Group of 77". Env't Rep. (BNA) (June 8, 1998) While Argentina agreed to voluntary emissions limitations, it is an exception to the overwhelming opposition of developing countries to submit to any GHG limitations. William Stevens, *Argentina Takes a Lead in Setting Goals on Greenhouse Gases*, N.Y. Times, Nov. 12, 1998, at A7.

new Protocol be to stabilize greenhouse gases (GHGs) before they double their pre-industrialized levels, or should the Protocol attempt to stabilize GHGs at double the pre-industrialized levels with a view to averting their quadrupling? Second, what are the effects and impacts of a doubling of GHGs from pre-industrial levels, and are adaptation and mitigation the only practicable way of dealing with such impacts? *Third,* should developed (Annex 1)countries alone, as opposed to developing countries, be involved in the reduction of GHGs? *Fourth,* should a scheme of tradeable emission rights be established as part of a system of joint implementation, and, if so, what additional institutions and mechanisms are necessary for the successful administration of a system of tradable emission rights? The debate in respect of these issues has been intense.

On the first and second issues, a minority of industrialized countries, led by the Federation of Columbia, have argued that it is unnecessary to stabilize GHGs before they double from pre-industrialized levels. They contend that the conclusions of the IPCC, that the present levels of GHGs have lead to global warming, and that disastrous consequences would result if no immediate action were taken to arrest the increase of GHG emissions, are scientifically unsupportable. In any event they argue, even if doubling of GHG emissions did lead to a small temperature increase of 1 degree Centigrade, the consequences of such warming can more efficiently be dealt with by mitigation and adaptation rather than by cutting down GHG emissions. These nations are opposed by a large majority of countries who believe that the findings of the IPCC are valid and that immediate action should be taken to arrest the growth of GHGs as soon as possible. They strongly oppose postponing action until GHGs have doubled from pre-industrial levels.

On the third issue a number of developing countries, led by Rajapur and Hanguo, who rely on coal for their future industrial development, strenuously object to making any obligatory reductions in GHGs. They are adamant that global warming is the creation of the developed countries and that the duty to find solutions remains that of the developed countries alone. Developing countries were exempted from any effort to reduce GHGs in the Kyoto Protocol, which placed that responsibility on the developed countries alone. The developed countries should not be allowed to retract from that position.

As for tradeable emission rights, some countries, particularly the island nations, plead that the interdiction of a phenomenon that imperils their very existence demands strong commands and strict enforcement, and cannot be left to the vagaries of a market system. They advocate a drastic reduction of carbon dioxide and other GHG emissions. Others contend, in contrast, that a market system of tradable emission standards is the most efficient and effective way of regulating GHGs. They point out that the international legal system does not possess the enforcement and supervisory agencies that are a *sine qua non* for a command and control system. Since we have a weak legal system at best, they argue, there is little option but to rely on what the international legal order does possess: an established system of world trade.

These issues were heatedly debated in a number of COPs, and a consensus has emerged only with regard to a few matters. The COP has agreed by consensus that the long term accumulation of GHGs in the atmosphere would dangerously affect the climate system as contemplated by Art. 2 of the

Climate Change Treaty. They also agreed by consensus that they should attempt to stabilize carbon dioxide at 550 pp which is approximately double the pre-industrial levels of 280 pp, and prevent GHG accumulations from tripling and quadrupling. Even those developed countries who balked at the Kyoto timetables and reductions, have agreed that a quadrupling of GHGs may prove dangerous to the climate system of the world. However, these developed countries do not agree that action needs to be taken speedily, and it is anticipated that this will prove to be a difficult negotiating exercise.

In light of the fact that the Kyoto Protocol is still being implemented, and that controversy continues to surround the underlying science, it was decided that the Long–Range Protocol (LRP), while taking cognizance of the Kyoto Protocol, should follow an independent negotiating path. The LRP would be a new Protocol under the Climate Change treaty permitted to reassess the scientific evidence and draw up its own GHG reduction timetables and schedules.

The Secretariat established by the Conference for the LRP negotiation, upon the request of the Conference, has provided a Draft LRP, more fully described as the Draft of a Long–Range Protocol on Greenhouse Gas Emission Reductions [**Schedule B**] that could be used as a negotiating instrument. **Schedule A** describes the 11 negotiating parties.

SCHEDULE "A"

Amazonia is a tropical country covered by lush tropical forests. Unfortunately, it has received considerable unwelcome international attention for the destruction of its forests by colonists. Indeed, satellite photographs documenting forest burning and clearing for use in cultivation and as pasture land have demonstrated that Amazonia is probably the largest single contributor to biotic emissions of CO_2. Also, Amazonia is a newly industrialized country interested in substantially increasing its industrial production in the coming years.

Annam is an impoverished developing country with one of the last centrally-planned economies on the planet. Rice, whose cultivation is the principal source of Annam's methane emissions, is also that country's food staple.

The Federation of Columbia (FC) is a large, sparsely-populated, resource-rich industrialized democracy with a market economy. Indeed, the FC is one of the world's principal trading nations. It also is among the least efficient users of all forms of energy in the world. Recent statements by the Government of the Federation of Columbia have indicated a new willingness to accept more stringent targets for reducing greenhouse gases, though its resolve to break its great dependence on fossil fuels is not at all clear.

Friesland is a democracy that has had considerable success as a trading nation in recent years, thanks in large part to the efficiency of its industry and economy as a whole. Although its industrial emissions of CO_2 are not inconsiderable, they are among the lowest in the world per unit of industrial output.

Hanguo is a large developing country with, like Annam, a centrally planned economy. Hanguo's emissions of CO_2 are expected to increase dramatically in coming decades as Hanguo's huge coal reserves are tapped to fuel a hoped-for rapid industrialization.

Kuroshio is a small, very wealthy industrialized democracy with a market-oriented economy. With a small land mass and few natural resources, Kuroshio's staggering success is attributable to trade. Some of Kuroshio's territory is at risk from sea level rise.

New Polynesia is a tiny low-lying island nation that stands to suffer severely from sea level rise.

Rajapur, like Amazonia, is a heavily forested developing country that has been cutting down these forests as part of its development effort, and resents restrictions on its proclaimed right to develop its own natural resources. It is also a significant rice producer and opposes any restrictions on the right to feed its people. Its biotic emissions of CO_2 are high.

Savoy is an industrialized democracy with a market economy. A number of years ago, the Government of Savoy decided to proceed with nuclear power as its principal means of generating electricity. Accordingly, even with no international action Savoy's emissions of CO_2 are expected to remain stable or to decrease somewhat over the next several decades.

Volhynia, like the Federation of Columbia, is a large, sparsely-populated industrialized country rich in natural resources that has been a major geopolitical force. However, thanks to a bureaucratic command economy and a nonconvertible currency and in contrast to the FC, Volhynia has not been a major economic force in the world economy. It is now in the process of making the difficult transition to a free market economy. Volhynia's commitment to reducing GHGs has been tempered by the absence of a satisfactory source of fuel.

Yoribo, like Hanguo, is a less developed country whose primary objective is to develop economically. Its emissions of CO_2 in coming decades are expected to increase, although in Yoribo's case those increases are most likely to come from rapid population growth.

SCHEDULE "B"

DRAFT OF LONG–RANGE PROTOCOL ON GREENHOUSE GAS EMISSION REDUCTION

(Draft LRP)

THE PARTIES TO THIS PROTOCOL,

Noting the continued increase of greenhouse gases, and the specific increases in emissions of carbon dioxide, and the need to reduce and stabilize anthropogenic emissions in order to ensure that greenhouse gas concentrations do not present a dangerous anthropogenic interference with the climate system,

Recognizing the need to further increase technological and financial assistance to developing nations;

Further recognizing the need for using market based flexibility mechanisms for controlling global warming;

Have agreed as follows:

Article 1

Definitions

The definitions set forth in Article 1 of the 1992 Framework Convention on Climate Change, and the Kyoto Protocol, shall apply with respect to this Protocol.

Article 2

Obligations

1. Within three years of the coming into force of this Protocol, the COP acting upon the advice of the Secretariat, the Subsidiary Body for Scientific and Technological Advice, and the Scientific body for Implementation established under articles 9 & 10 of the Climate Change Convention, and such other bodies or persons as it may choose, shall formulate a global long-range strategic plan (GLRSP), and a series of five year global operational plans (GOP's).

2. The GLRSP will define the final global emission reduction and stabilization objectives (GERSOs) and targets for all GHGs, maintaining an adequate margin of safety, and having regard to the best available technology. The final objectives and targets will ensure that the total emission of GHGs will be stabilized at 550 pp by the year 2070.

3. The GOPs will embody incremental, progressive five yearly measures, targets and objectives, demonstrating and insuring that GERSOs are achieved and realized by the year 2070.

Article 3

Caps and Allowances

Within two years of the fixing of GERSOs, the COP, acting upon the advice of the Secretariat, the Subsidiary Body for Scientific and Technological Advice, and the Scientific body for Implementation established under articles 9 & 10 of the Climate Change Convention, and such other bodies or persons as it may choose, shall draw up baselines for each GHG within every State Party, and allocate to such parties their emission caps and allowances for each GHG.

Article 4

National Implementation Plans

1. All Parties taking into account their common but differentiated responsibilities and their specific national and regional development priorities:

(a) Shall within two years of the coming into force of this protocol, develop, formulate and submit to the COP, a national strategic implementation plan (SNIP), along with five year National Operational Plans (NOPs). These national co-relatives of the GLRSP and GOPs, will demonstrate and verify each Party's progress toward achieving the GERSOs.

(b) SNIPs and NOPs will enumerate specific measures and limitations that will enable each Party to meet the GERSOs in article 2, in conjunction with the caps and allowances in article 3.

(c) Developed (Annex 1) countries who fail to meet the reduction targets in their NOPs, shall spend between one half to one percent (0.5—1 %) of their GDP every year following such failure on energy conservation, alternative energy sources, new technology, and other necessary measures, until they achieve the targets set out in their NOPs. Developed (Annex 1) countries will annually deposit one twentieth of one percent (0.20%) of their GDP into a special fund called the global warming contingency fund (GWCF) beginning one calendar year after the coming into force of this Protocol. The monies so deposited will be invested by the fund managers in a manner that enables depositor countries to access these funds as and when they might require the money for the purposes of fulfilling their obligations under this Protocol.

(d) A majority of at least two thirds (2/3rds) of the COP, acting upon the advice of the Secretariat, the Subsidiary Body for Scientific and Technological Advice, and the Scientific body for Implementation established under articles 9 & 10 of the Climate Change Convention, shall approve, reject, or modify such NIPs and SNIPs, within six months of submission.

Article 5

Emissions Trading

1. Based on the emission caps and allowances in article 3, and in accordance with its provisions, each State Party shall provide the Secretariat with a yearly assessment of unused quotas in order that they be presented at the scheduled meetings of the Conference of the Parties. Annual assessments shall be filed no later than 31 December of each year.

2. At the end of each year a State Party that has not used its emission allowance is entitled to trade or offset its unused allocation with another State Party that is then entitled to emit carbon dioxide to the extent of the unused allowance. State Parties may enter into agreements that facilitate such exchanges, provided that:

(a) Any such project has the approval of the Parties involved;

(b) Any such project provides a reduction in emissions by sources, or an enhancement of removals by sinks, that is additional to any that would otherwise occur;

(c) It does not acquire any emission reduction units if it is not in compliance with its obligations under article 2;

(d) The acquisition of emission reduction units shall be supplemental to domestic actions for the purposes of meeting commitments under article 2.

4. The Conference of the Parties, serving as the meeting of the Parties to this Protocol may, at its first session or as soon as practicable thereafter, further elaborate guidelines for the implementation of this article, including verification and reporting.

5. Any Party may authorize legal entities to participate, under its responsibility, in actions leading to the generation, transfer or acquisition under this Article of emission reduction units.

6. The Secretariat shall develop a global warming index for all greenhouse gases (GHGs) and maintain a register of emission allocations, as part of an emissions trading or offsets system.

Article 6

Transfer of Technology

The nations identified in Annex 1 of the Convention on Climate Change may make technology transfers to developing nations that may take the form of pollution abatement equipment, technology or expertise. Such technology transfers may form part of the process of an emissions trading or offsets system.

Article 7

Entry Into Force

1. This Protocol shall enter into force for the signatory Parties on the ninetieth day after the date of deposit of the twenty-fifth instrument of ratification, acceptance, approval or accession.

2. For each State or regional economic integration organization that ratifies, accepts or approves the Protocol or accedes thereto after the deposit of the twenty-fifth instrument of ratification, acceptance, approval or accession of the Protocol, shall enter into force on the ninetieth day after the date of deposit by such State or regional economic integration organization of its instrument of ratification, acceptance, approval or accession.

Article 8

Implementation

1. The Secretariat shall monitor the compliance with provisions of this Protocol, and its officers shall have the right at any time to enter any country a State Party to this Protocol, to inspect any facility or secure any information necessary for the purpose of implementation.

2. Disputes about implementation shall be dealt with by the Conference of the Parties.

3. The Secretariat shall report annually to the Conference of the Parties on the compliance of each State Party.

SECTION 2. QUESTIONS PRESENTED

1. Will the doubling of GHGs from their pre-industrial level present a dangerous anthropogenic interference with the climate system as referred to in Art 2 of the Climate Change Convention?

2. At what level and within what time frame should GHGs be stabilized?

3. Should all countries, including developing countries, be parties to efforts at lowering or stabilizing GHGs?

4. Should a scheme of tradeable emission rights be established as part of a system of joint implementation, and, if so, what additional institutions and mechanisms are necessary for the successful administration of a system of tradeable emission rights?

SECTION 3. ASSIGNMENTS

The purpose of this exercise is to simulate a real international negotiation. This can be structured in a number of ways, and the precise approach will be in the hands of your instructor.

There are, however, a number of key procedural points to remember. International negotiations of this sort usually require unanimous consent; majority voting as occurs in domestic legislatures plays little or no part in international negotiations. A consensus must be reached. But in this negotiation it is necessary to look carefully at Article 15 of the 1992 United Nations Framework Convention on Climate Change [**Basic Document 3.21**] concerning amendments and compare it with Article 17 concerning the adoption of protocols. In this negotiation it is a protocol that is being negotiated.

Further, how the negotiations proceed is in the hands of the negotiating State representatives. There are no rules of procedure apart from those that can be inferred from the 1992 Framework Convention on Climate Change itself. The Secretariat (possibly your instructor) provides clerical services and circulates paper, but it cannot make decisions, although sometimes it can influence them. Members of the Secretariat usually are international civil servants, and, in this instance, they are members of the Secretariat established under Article 8 of the 1992 Framework Convention.

The most likely way to structure the negotiation is for class members to be assigned as members of a delegation from each of the countries participating in the negotiation. The negotiation could begin with a five-minute opening statement from each delegation as to the stance their country takes and the proposals it intends to make. Often the most productive negotiations will occur in informal groups outside the plenary negotiating meeting. Nevertheless, it will be necessary to have some discussions regarding the procedure to be adopted at plenary sessions. The negotiation will continue for as many days as your instructor determines. Usually at an international negotiation the negotiating parties will decide who is to chair the meeting or sessions and generally it is the head of one of the delegations present. It may be, however, that your instructor will prefer to act as the chair in this instance.

Supplementing the facts set out above, will be confidential negotiating instructions that each of you will receive from your respective foreign ministries. Between sessions, even before the first session, you may request clarifications or additions to your confidential instructions. The Chair (your instructor?) will act as the sole repository of confidential communications from all countries, and any clarifications or additional information offered by her or him will be deemed to be the official instructions of your country.

Finally, you are welcome—indeed, encouraged—to communicate with representatives of other delegations between sessions, and particularly in advance of the first session. For example, you may wish to circulate a written version of your opening statement either before or after you deliver it. The Secretariat (your instructor?) will make every effort to distribute documents to all delegations within twenty-four (24) hours of receipt, but only those documents that are intended for general distribution. Bilateral or other confidential communications should be undertaken directly with the other participating delegations. *However, whatever the distributional character of the document, be sure to mark it for distribution with your name, the date, and a heading "Proposal of the Delegation of X" or similar description identifying your role.*

A. Reading Assignment

Study the Readings presented in Section 4, *infra*, and the Appendices to the Draft LRP set forth in Section 5, *infra*.

B. Negotiating Assignment

Assume that you are a member of one of the delegations to the LRP negotiation (as designated by your instructor); then, relying upon the Readings and upon the confidential negotiating instructions for your country distributed by your instructor, negotiate a LRP scheduled to be signed at a Summit of Heads of State, already determined to take place no longer than two weeks after the date the SGHGC negotiating meeting commences.

C. Post–Negotiation Writing Assignment

Prepare a memorandum from your delegation to your Foreign Office justifying and explaining the final LRP negotiated between you and your associate negotiating diplomats.

D. Suggested Reflective Assignment

Consider (and recommend) alternative norms, institutions, and/or procedures that you believe might work better than existing world order arrangements to contend with situations of the kind posed by this problem. In so doing, but without insisting upon immediate feasibility, identify the particular transition steps that would be needed to make your alternatives a reality.

SECTION 4. READINGS

1. Laura B. Campbell and Chad W. Carpenter, *Analysis and Perspective: From Kyoto to Buenos Aires: Implementing the Kyoto Protocol on Climate Change*, 21 BNA-INT'L ENVT REP. 711–756 (July 22, 1998).

Introduction

On December 10, 1997, after long and arduous negotiations, the nations gathered in Kyoto, Japan, for the third Conference of the Parties to the United Nations Framework Convention on Climate Change ("COP–III" of the "FCCC") adopted the Kyoto Protocol, a historic international environmental agreement that creates specific, legally binding emission reduction targets for greenhouse gases ("GHGs").

* * *

Major Issues for Negotiation

Background on the Kyoto Protocol

Article 3 of the Kyoto Protocol requires countries listed in Annex I to the climate change convention (industrialized countries) to meet quantified emission limitation and reduction commitments by the period 2009–2012 with respect to six greenhouse gases: carbon dioxide, methane, nitrous oxide, hydrofluorocarbons (HFCs), perfluorocarbons (PFCs), and sulfur hexafluoride (SF_6). Under the Protocol, each of the gases will be converted into common units based on their 100–year Global Warming Potential (GWP), which represent their respective radiating forces.

The emission limitations imposed on Annex I countries will reduce overall global emissions for these countries by at least 5 percent below 1990 levels over the commitment period 2009–2012. The concept of a "commitment period" was chosen over a "commitment date" in order to add flexibility to the system and decrease the risk of yearly fluctuations in GHG emissions based on economic performance in a given year.

The baseline for the emissions target is also described in Article 3. For industrialized countries, the emissions target for carbon dioxide, methane, and nitrous oxide is based on emissions that took place in 1990, while 1995 emissions serve as the baseline for HFCs, PFCs, and sulfur hexafluoride. In contrast, countries with economies in transition such as Poland, Hungary, Romania, and Slovakia may use different base years from those noted above if the bases were established in their first national communications.

Under Article 6, countries can receive credit for afforestation, reforestation, and other activities that create so-called sinks to absorb greenhouse gases and result in a net reduction in emissions.

The protocol also recognizes "differentiation" in countries' abilities to reduce their greenhouse gas emissions by varying the percentage of emission reductions required among countries. For example, some of the key emission reduction commitments are: European Union—8 percent, United States–7 percent, Japan–6 percent, and Canada–6 percent. Australia is permitted to increase its emissions by 8 percent.

Utilizing cost-effective cooperative measures to achieve emission reductions was first mentioned in FCCC Article 3 (21:3901). In 1995, the first Conference of the Parties to the FCCC ("COP–1") decided to develop a pilot program on Activities Implemented Jointly ("AIJ") to test the possibilities of cooperative mechanisms for realizing emission reductions.

The Kyoto Protocol retained the idea of the cooperative measures but divided AIJ projects into two flexibility mechanisms: joint implementation (between Annex I parties) and the Clean Development Mechanism (between Annex I and developing countries). The protocol also included new flexibility mechanisms: aggregate targets as embodied in the creation of a "bubble" for the European Union and emissions trading.

Article 4 of the protocol provides for "joint implementation" among Annex I (industrialized) countries to meet their emission limitation commitments. The concept underlying the joint implementation scheme is that because greenhouse gases mix globally in the atmosphere, actions to reduce emissions taken anywhere generate equal global benefits. Therefore, if emission reductions can be achieved more economically in one country than another, the protocol will allow a country to "take actions" and/or "carry out projects" to reduce emissions in another country and receive credit against its own emission reduction obligations

* * *

Joint Implementation

Under Article 6, Annex I parties may work together to meet their emission targets and may transfer or acquire emission reduction units ("ERUs") resulting from projects and activities implemented in other Annex I countries. Although the term "joint implementation" is not actually included in Article 6, delegates in Bonn used the term for reference. Article 6 contains a provision to include projects that enhance carbon sinks-the natural ecosystems that sequester carbon-and grants parties the right to authorize participation of legal entities.

According to the protocol, Joint Implementation "JI" projects must be "supplemental" to any domestic activities to reduce emissions. However, "supplemental" is not defined, and parties disagree on its meaning in the context of JI. Another contentious issue involves the requirement that the emission reductions be "additional" to what would otherwise occur assuming business as usual. Some proposals define "additional" using a financial test that considers whether project funding would have been available in the absence of JI.

In Bonn, most Annex I countries supported JI and a liberal reading of the term "supplemental." In contrast, many members of the negotiating group consisting of the G–77 countries and China (basically, the developing countries) viewed JI as a way for developed nations to avoid cutting domestic emissions. Nevertheless, most countries agreed that flexibility mechanisms were necessary in order to ensure that the developed countries adopt ambitious targets.

Clean Development Mechanism

Under Article 12, the Clean Development Mechanism ("CDM") allows governments or private entities in industrialized countries to implement emission reduction projects in developing countries to meet their emission targets. The industrialized nations would receive credit for these projects in the form of "certified emission reductions" ("CERs").

Several inconsistencies exist in the construction of Article 12 in relation to the other flexibility mechanisms. CDM activities are not required to be "supplemental" to domestic actions, thereby allowing an Annex I country to forego domestic measures and meet its obligations through CDM credits. Also, Article 12 does not include a provision concerning carbon sinks. Several countries in Bonn, notably the United States and Canada, proposed that carbon sinks be included under the CDM as opposed to JI projects, which do not begin accruing credits until the beginning of the first commitment period in 2008, countries could begin accruing CER credits in 2000.

Few issues regarding the CDM were resolved in Bonn. Several approaches to organizing the CDM have been suggested. Countries or companies seeking to engage in multilateral projects could invest in a central independent fund, from which the organization managing the fund would choose projects for implementation. If the project produces emission reductions, each investing entity would receive credit for its proportional contribution.

Emission reductions from CDM projects must be "additional" to what would have otherwise occurred, meaning that the difficult issue of baseline emission levels needs to be resolved.

A system of certifying and verifying ERUs must also be developed to maintain credibility. Article 12 states that emission reductions must be "real, measurable, and long-term," and an "independent auditor" should conduct verification of the project activities.

One approach could be a "ton-year" accounting system that examines the residency life of carbon in the atmosphere and multiplies this by the amount of tons emitted. Assuming that the residency life of carbon in the atmosphere is 200 years, one ton emitted would equal 200 "ton-years". This amount could then be offset by a project that sequesters an equal amount of "ton-years" even if it does not exist for 200 years. A second suggested approach could be "real-time" accounting, which considers the residency life of carbon and the polluting activity it offsets.

Another problem to be resolved is "leakage" that occurs when a project does not decrease overall emissions of a country but simply shifts them to another locale. When projects displace economic activity, it will likely resurface elsewhere.

Additionally, the protocol states that "a share of the proceeds from certified project activities be used to cover administrative costs" and to assist developing countries in meeting the costs of "adaptation," and these terms must also be defined. Funds from certified project activities are most likely to be disbursed to developing countries to conduct self-assessments and produce strategic plans on how to adapt.

The United States strongly supports the use of the CDM mechanism and sees it as an economically efficient means of achieving its emissions target. The United States argues against imposing limits on the use of CDM projects to achieve national emission requirements. The European Union, however, would like to limit the use of credits from CDM projects, particularly projects to enhance sinks. Developing countries fear that the CDM will be used to avoid domestic emission reductions in industrialized countries, but most also recognize that the CDM could dramatically increase capital flows into their countries.

Emissions Trading

The provisions of Article 17 of the protocol on emissions trading allow an Annex I country with an excess of emission units, presumably from reducing domestic emissions below its commitment levels, to sell credits to another Annex I country that is unable or chooses not to meet its commitments by means of domestic emission reductions. Emissions trading is probably the most contentious of all the flexibility mechanisms provided for in the protocol, and principles, rules, and guidelines under which trading will be carried out need to be developed.

One concern about trading is that it will allow some developed countries to avoid domestic actions. This has fueled a dispute over a "cap" on the amount countries are allowed to trade. The debate centers on a phrase in Article 17 stating that trading should be "supplemental" to domestic actions to meet emission reduction requirements.

Another issue is how to establish a dependable verification system so that countries can trade without the fear of purchasing worthless credits that do not result in actual emission reductions. Developing such a system presents serious technical difficulties because of the inherent uncertainty in verifying GHG emissions.

Given the uncertainty in verification, the need to develop a liability system to deal with "bad trades" was also discussed. Under the U.S. sulfur dioxide trading system, the seller is liable if credits are oversold or worthless. Under an international carbon trading system, some have called for shared liability between buyer and seller. Proponents of shared liability argue that, in many cases, the buyer may be in a better position to judge the integrity of the carbon credit, but those opposed to the idea argue that the buyer is less able than the seller to ensure the integrity of the credit and therefore should not be liable for the seller's irresponsibility.

Developing country participation in a trading regime will likely require them to assume emission limitations. However, no decision was reached in Kyoto on commitments by developing countries. It has been proposed that developing countries should assume voluntary commitments to be set by the countries themselves. Critics argue that such voluntary commitments for developing countries would create an incentive for setting unrealistically high targets.

Some countries have called for a standardized system for setting voluntary targets, while others, particularly developing countries, argue that targets based on per-capita emission levels would create the most equitable and enduring system. On the other hand, the per-capita approach is also seen by many countries as politically unrealistic.

The United States will continue to champion unlimited emissions trading and favors a simple set of trading rules to minimize confusion. In Bonn, a group of nations consisting of the JUSCANZ countries (Japan, the United States, Canada, Australia, and New Zealand) and Iceland, Norway, and Russia jointly submitted a paper proposing rules for an emissions trading system. Under this proposal, the tradable unit would be an Assigned Amount Unit ("AAU"). AAUs would be denominated in "CO_2 equivalence" and would express one metric tone of CO_2 equivalent emissions.

Each country listed in Annex B of the Kyoto Protocol (industrialized countries) could issue serialized AAUs from its "assigned amounts." AAUs would be valid until used to offset emissions for the purposes of contributing to compliance.

Under the proposal, countries could trade directly and/or authorize legal entities to acquire and/or transfer AAUs. Each Annex B country would need to comply with Article 5 of the protocol concerning national emission estimation systems and Article 7 on emission inventories. The proposed system would also require countries to establish and maintain a national system for recording their "assigned amounts" and tracking AAUs that are held, transferred, or acquired; to report annually on trading activities; and to submit to a compliance assessment at the end of the commitment period.

The European Union (EU) supports emissions trading in principle but wants to ensure that an adequate international compliance regime is in place before trading begins. The EU has also introduced a proposal on international emissions trading that differs from the JUSCANZ proposal in how it addresses the following issues:

● The supplemental nature of trading related to domestic emission reduction measures;

● The need to ensure that trading is environmentally effective;

● Compliance mechanisms;

● Market transparency;

● Risk and liability rules;

● Reporting requirements; and

● Eligibility to trade.

Several G–77 countries remain skeptical about an emissions trading system and want to ensure that a verification and compliance system are in place before trading is allowed. These countries are concerned that trading will be used by developed countries to avoid domestic actions. They argue that countries such as Russia and Ukraine who have experienced an economic decline since 1990 will have a huge surplus of credits to trade and that buying these credits will not improve the environment. At the same time, this surplus of "hot air" available for trading could flood the market and create an inexpensive means for countries such as the United States to avoid domestic action.

Carbon Sinks: Land Use Change and Forestry

Carbon sinks are natural systems such as forests, wetlands, and oceans that absorb and sequester carbon. According to Article 3, the net change in GHG emissions from direct human-induced land use change since 1990 will be considered in determining GHG commitments. Many believe that means for measuring carbon sequestration of land use change and forestry activities are so scientifically uncertain that they jeopardize the credibility of the entire protocol. Many scientists, however, argue that existing technology can accurately measure carbon sequestration for aboveground carbon.

Under Article 3.4 of the protocol, additional land use change and forestry activities that result in carbon sequestration may be added to those activities already eligible to offset emissions. Currently, Article 3.3 of the protocol recognizes only afforestation, reforestation, and deforestation as eligible activities. Several countries were keenly interested in adding soil sequestration to the list of activities eligible to offset emissions. Several studies are now being conducted by research groups to improve the monitoring tools for carbon sequestration in soil. According to the protocol, if additional sinks are included they could be retroactively applied to the emission reduction targets for the first commitment period.

* * *

Group Commitments: Allocations Under the EU Bubble

Under Article 4.1, Annex I countries can meet their commitments jointly by creating a voluntary group, or "bubble," and countries within a bubble can trade with few restrictions. If the countries under the bubble meet its overall reduction commitment, then all its members are deemed to be in compliance. If the bubble does not reach its commitment, however, each of the countries covered under the bubble retains responsibility for meeting its individual emission reduction target.

The European Union and its member countries agreed to the Kyoto Protocol. Under the protocol, the EU is allowed to meet its overall target by trading emissions among its member countries. Meeting its EU-wide targets through trading, however, required the EU to allocate emissions among its members, a very difficult political process.

On June 18, 1998, after two days of bargaining, the EU countries agreed on the individual reductions that each must make to honor the EU-wide commitment to curb emissions by 8 percent. Each country must produce a plan, in coordination with the EU in Brussels, to implement its commitments. In meeting these commitments, it is likely that the main tools governments will employ are taxes and, to a lesser extent, a system under which companies and countries may trade emissions

Germany , the Netherlands, Denmark, and Austria-among the "greenest" EU countries-joined Belgium and Luxembourg in demanding a smaller share of the burden than they had agreed to last year. The United Kingdom, with its own longer-term target of a 20 percent cut, was the only state offering to increase its emission reductions. It agreed to raise its share to 12.5 percent from 12 percent. Germany agreed to reduce its emissions by 21 percent.

Group Commitments: Proposal for JUSCANZ Bubble

On June 29, 1998, the United States proposed a group approach for industrialized countries in the Pacific Rim to meet emission reduction targets, basically as an alternative to the EU's bubble and in light of the slow progress to date in defining the parameters of an international emissions trading scheme. So far the Japanese government has reserved comment on the U.S. proposal, but pressure on Japan to adopt the proposal is expected to increase as some other Pacific Rim nations support the idea.

Group member envisaged as participating in the U.S. strategy include Australia, New Zealand, and Russia, in addition to Japan and the United States. Japanese officials said the U.S. proposal calls on Pacific Rim nations to jointly attain their emission reduction targets mainly by using Russia's expected unused emissions quota in exchange for environmental technical assistance from Japan and the United States.

* * *

According to Article 25 of the protocol, at least 55 parties to the climate change convention must ratify or accede to the protocol for the agreement to enter into force. Furthermore, the Annex I parties that ratify the protocol must account for at least 55 percent of the total carbon dioxide emissions in 1990. Currently 42 countries have signed the Kyoto Protocol, representing 39 percent of the Annex I carbon dioxide emissions. The United States, accounting for 35 percent of 1990 Annex I emissions, has not yet signed or ratified the agreement. Although the protocol could enter into force without the United States, this scenario is very unlikely because it would require ratification by nearly all other Annex I parties.

The United States, however, is unlikely to ratify soon. In July 1997, a Senate bill was passed 95–0 calling on the president not to sign the Kyoto Protocol unless developing countries decide to take on commitments to reduce emissions and the president could ensure the protocol would not hurt the U.S. economy.

Congressional discomfort with President Clinton's support of the protocol prompted lawmakers to slash nearly $200 million earmarked for energy efficiency and research into renewable technologies, and Clinton's five-year, $6.3 billion climate initiative has been severely cut.

Spending legislation pending before the House would order the EPA and the White House Council on Environmental Quality not even to conduct education or information seminars on global warming or spend any money in "contemplation" of the Kyoto treaty being ratified.

Opposition to a global warming treaty is so strong in Congress that many lawmakers want to eliminate funding for even talking about climate change-whether in public forums or administration planning sessions. Senior administration officials are even more concerned that the bill could stifle any informed debate on global warming. Clinton has already ruled out sending the Kyoto treaty to the Senate this year for ratification, fearing rejection.

2. THE INTERGOVERNMENTAL PANEL ON CLIMATE CHANGE, CLIMATE CHANGE 1995: THE SCIENCE OF CLIMATE CHANGE 3–7, 14,–20, 23, 25–27, 31, 39–40, 312, 324 (1996).

Summary for Policymakers

- Considerable progress has been made in the understanding of climate change science since 1990 and new data and analyses have become available. Greenhouse gas concentrations have continued to increase

- Increases in greenhouse gas concentrations since pre-industrial times (i.e., since about 1750) have led to a positive radiative forcing of climate, tending to warm surface and to produce other changes of climate.

- The atmospheric concentrations of greenhouse gases, inter alia carbon dioxide (CO_2), methane (CH4), and nitrous oxide (N_2O) have grown significantly: by about 30%, 145% and 15% respectively (values for 1992). These trends can be attributed largely to human activities, mostly fossil fuel use, land-use change and agriculture.

* * *

- Many greenhouse gases remain in the atmosphere for a long time (for CO_2 and N_2O, many decades to centuries), hence they affect radiative forcing on long time-scales.

* * *

- Growth in the concentration of CFCs, but not HCFCs,[s] has slowed to about zero. The concentrations of both CFCs and HCFCs, and their consequent ozone depletion, are expected to decrease substantially by 2050 through implementation of the Montreal Protocol and its Adjustments and Amendments.

- At present some long-lived greenhouse gases (particularly HFCs (a CFC substitute)),[t] PFCs and SF_6[u] contribute little to radiative forcing but their projected growth could contribute several percent to radiative forcing during the 21st century.

* * *

- A range of carbon cycle models indicates that stabilization of atmospheric CO_2 concentrations at 450, 650 or 1000 ppmv could be achieved only if global anthropogenic CO_2 emissions drop to 1990 levels by respectively, approximately 40, 140 or 240 years from now, and drop substantially below 1990 levels subsequently.[v]

- Any eventual stabilized concentration is governed more by the accumulated Anthropogenic CO_2 emissions from now until the time of stabilisation, than by the way those emissions change over the period. This means that, for a given stabilized concentration value, higher emissions in early decades require lower emissions later on.

* * *

Climate has changed over the past century

- At any one location year-to-year variations in weather can be large, but analyses of meteorological and other data over large areas and over periods of decades or more have provided evidence for some important systematic changes.

- Global mean surface air temperature has increased by between about 0.3 and 0.6°C since the late 19th century; the additional data available since 1990 and the re-analyses since then have not significantly changed this range of estimated increase.

- Recent years have been among the warmest since 1860, i.e., in the period of instrumental record, despite the cooling effect of the 1991 Mt. Pinatubo volcanic eruption.

---

s. CFCs and HCFCs belong to a class of substances titled "halocarbons", because they contain Chlorine, Florine or Bromine, elements that are members of group VII on the periodic table.

t. HFCs are hydroflourocarbons, a CFC replacement in many industries. They do not contain Chlorine, so they do not deplete the ozone layer, but they are still potent greenhouse gases.

u. PFCs (Perfluorocarbons) and SF_6 (Sulfur Hexafluoride) are industrial gases that are very stable, and as a result have a long life in the atmosphere. The IPCC report states that they do not currently contribute greatly to global warming, but that they might become more important as their atmospheric concentrations increase because they are so stable.

v. *See infra*, Figure 12-3(a) & (b).

- Night-time temperatures over land have generally increased more than daytime temperatures.

- Regional changes are also evident. For example, the recent warming has been greatest over the mid-latitude continents in winter and spring. with a few areas of cooling, such as the North Atlantic ocean. Precipitation has increased over land in high latitudes of the Northern Hemisphere, especially during the cold season.

- Global sea level has risen by between 10 and 25 cm over the past 100 years and much of the rise may be related to the increase in global mean temperature.

- There are inadequate data to determine whether consistent global changes in climate variability or weather extremes have occurred over the 20th century. On regional scales there is clear evidence of changes in some extremes and climate variability indicators (e.g., fewer frosts in several widespread areas: an increase in the proportion of rainfall from extreme events over the contiguous states of the USA). Some of these changes have been toward greater variability: some have been toward lower variability.

- The 1990 to mid–1995 persistent warm-phase of the El Nino–Southern Oscillation (which causes droughts and floods in many areas) was unusual in the context of the last 120 years.

The balance of evidence suggests a discernible human influence on global climate

Any human-induced effect on climate will be superimposed on the background "noise" of natural climate variability, which results both from internal fluctuations and from external causes such as solar variability or volcanic eruptions. Detection and attribution studies attempt to distinguish between anthropogenic and natural influences. "Detection of change" is the process of demonstrating that an observed change in climate is highly unusual in a statistical sense, but does not provide a reason for the change. "Attribution" is the process of establishing cause and effect relations, including the testing of competing hypotheses. Since the 1990 IPCC Report, considerable progress has been made in attempts to distinguish between natural and anthropogenic influences on climate. This progress has been achieved by including effects of sulphate aerosols in addition to greenhouse gases, thus leading to more realistic estimates of human-induced radiative forcing. These have then been used in climate models to provide more complete simulations of the human-induced climate-change "signal". In addition, new simulations with coupled atmosphere-ocean models have provided important information about decade to century time-scale natural internal climate variability. A further major area of progress is the shift of focus from studies of global mean changes to comparisons of modeled and observed spatial and temporal patterns of climate change.

The most important results related to the issues of detection and attribution are:

- The limited available evidence from proxy climate indicators suggests that the 20th century global mean temperature is at least as warm as any other century since at least 1400 AD. Data prior to 1400 are too sparse to allow the reliable estimation of global mean temperature.

- Assessments of the statistical significance of the observed global mean surface air temperature trend over the last century have used a variety of new estimates of natural internal and externally forced variability. These are derived from instrumental data, palaeodata, simple and complex climate models, and statistical models fitted to observations. Most of these studies have detected a significant change and show that the observed warming trend is unlikely to be entirely natural in origin.

- More convincing recent evidence for the attribution of a human effect on climate is emerging from pattern-based studies, in which the modeled climate response to combined forcing by greenhouse gases and anthropogenic sulphate aerosols is compared with observed geographical, seasonal and vertical patterns of atmospheric temperature change. These studies show that such pattern correspondences increase with time, as one would expect as an anthropogenic signal increases in strength. Furthermore, the probability is very low that these correspondences could occur by chance as a result of natural internal variability only. The vertical patterns of change are also inconsistent with those expected for solar and volcanic forcing.

- Our ability to quantify the human influence on global climate is currently limited because the expected signal is still emerging from the noise of natural variability, and because there are uncertainties in key factors. These include the magnitude and patterns of long term natural variability and the time-evolving pattern of forcing by, and response to, changes in concentrations of greenhouse gases and aerosols, and land surface changes. Nevertheless. the balance of evidence suggests that there is a discernible human influence on global climate.

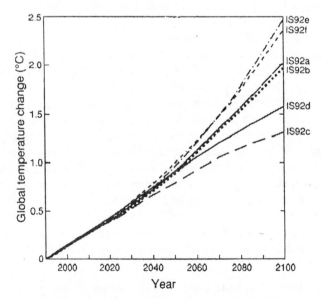

Figure 12-1 Projected global mean surface temperature changes from 1990 to 2100 for the full set of IS92 emission scenarios. A climate sensitivity of 2.5°C is assumed.

Climate is expected to continue to change in the future

The IPCC has developed a range of scenarios, IS92a-f [*See* Figure 12–1], of future greenhouse gas and aerosol precursor emissions based on assumptions concerning population and economic growth, land-use, technological changes, energy availability and fuel mix during the period 1990 to 2100. Through understanding of the global carbon cycle and of atmospheric chemistry, these emissions can be used to project atmospheric concentrations of greenhouse gases and aerosols and the perturbation of natural radiative forcing. Climate models can then be used to develop projections of future climate.

- The increasing realism of simulations of current and past climate by coupled atmosphere-ocean climate models has increased our confidence in their use for projection of future climate change. Important uncertainties remain, but these have been taken into account in the full range of projections of global mean temperature and sea level change.

- For the mid-range IPCC emission scenario, IS92a, assuming the "best estimate" value of climate sensitivity and including the effects of future increases in aerosol, models project an increase in global mean surface air temperature relative to 1990 of about 2°C by 2100. This estimate is approximately one third lower than the "best estimate" in 1990. This is due primarily to lower emission scenarios (particularly for CO_2 and the CFCs), the inclusion of the cooling effect of sulphate aerosols, and improvements in the treatment of the carbon cycle. Combining the lowest IPCC emission scenario (IS92c) with a "low" value of climate sensitivity and including the effects of future changes in aerosol concentrations leads to a projected increase of about 1.5°C by 2100. The corresponding projection for the highest IPCC scenario (IS92c) combined with a "high" value of climate sensitivity gives a warming of about 3.5°C. In all cases the average rate of warming would probably be greater than any seen in the last 10,000 years, but the actual annual to decadal changes would include considerable natural variability. Regional temperature changes could differ substantially from the global mean value. Because of the thermal inertia of the oceans, only 50 to 90% of the eventual equilibrium temperature change would have been realized by 2100 and temperature would continue to increase beyond 2100, even if concentrations of greenhouse gases were stabilized by that time.

- Average sea level is expected to rise as a result of thermal expansion of the oceans and melting of glaciers and ice-sheets. [See Figure 12–2] For the IS92a scenario, assuming the "best estimate" values of climate sensitivity and of ice melt sensitivity to warming, and including the effects of future changes in aerosol, models project an increase in sea level of about 5 cm from the present to 2100. This estimate is approximately 25% lower than the "best estimate" in 1990 due to the lower temperature projection, but also reflecting improvements in the climate and ice melt models. Combining the lowest emission scenario (IS92c) with the "low" climate and ice melt sensitivities and including aerosol effects gives a projected sea level rise of about 15 cm from the present to 2100. The corresponding projection for the highest emission scenario (IS92e) combined with "high" climate and ice-melt sensitivities gives a sea level rise of about 95 cm from the present to 2100. Sea level would continue to rise at a similar rate in future centuries beyond 2100, even if concentrations of greenhouse gases were stabilized by that time, and would continue to do so even beyond the time of stabilisation of global mean temperature. Regional sea level changes may differ from the global mean value owing to land movement and ocean current changes.

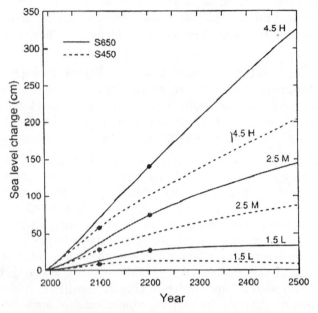

Figure 12-2 The global mean sea level response to the CO_2 concentration pathways leading to stabilisation at 450 (dashed curves) and 650 (solid curves) ppmv (see Figure 7a) for a climate sensitivity of 1.5, 2.5 and 4.5 °C. The changes shown are those arising from CO_2 increases alone. The date of concentration stabilisation is indicated by the dot. Calculations assume the "observed" history of forcing to 1990, including aerosol effects and then CO_2 concentration increases only beyond 1990.

* * *

- Warmer temperatures will lead to a more vigorous hydrological cycle; this translates into prospects for more severe droughts and/or floods in some places and less severe droughts and/or floods in other places. Several models indicate an increase in precipitation intensity, suggesting a possibility for more extreme rainfall events. Knowledge is currently insufficient to say whether there will be any changes in the occurrence or geographical distribution of severe storms, e.g., tropical cyclones.

- Sustained rapid climate change coud shift the competitive balance among species and even lead to forest dieback, altering the terrestrial uptake and release of carbon. The magnitude is uncertain, but could be between zero and 200 GtC over the next one to two centuries. depending on the rate of climate change.

There are still many uncertainties

Many factors currently limit our ability to project and detect future climate change. In particular, to reduce uncertainties further work is needed on the following priority topics:

- estimation of future emissions and biogeochemical cycling (including sources and sinks) of greenhouse gases, aerosols and aerosol precursors and projections of future concentrations and radiative properties;

- representation of climate processes in models, especially feedbacks associated with clouds, oceans, sea ice and vegetation, in order to improve projections of rates and regional patterns of climate change;

- systematic collection of long-term instrumental and proxy observations of climate system variables (e.g., solar output, atmospheric energy balance components, hydrological cycles, ocean characteristics and ecosystem changes) for the purposes of model testing, assessment of temporal and regional variability and for detection and attribution studies.

Future unexpected, large and rapid climate system changes (as have occurred in the past) are, by their nature, difficult to predict. This implies that future climate changes may also involve "surprises". In particular these arise from the nonlinear nature of the climate system. When rapidly forced, non-linear systems are especially subject to unexpected behavior. Progress can be made by investigating non-linear processes and sub-components of the climatic system. Examples of such non-linear behavior include rapid circulation changes in the North Atlantic and feedbacks associated with terrestrial ecosystem changes.

* * *

B.9 Emissions and concentrations of greenhouse gases and aerosols in the future

B.9.1 The IS92 emission scenarios

The projection of future anthropogenic climate change depends, among other things, on assumptions made about future emissions of greenhouse gases and aerosol precursors and the proportion of emissions remaining in the atmosphere. [See Table 12–1] Here we consider the IS92 emission scenarios (IS92a to f) which were first discussed in IPCC (1992). The IS92 emission scenarios extend to the year 2100 and include emissions of CO_2, CH_4, N_2O, the halocarbons (CF–Cs and their substitute HCFCs and HFCs), precursors of tropospheric ozone and sulphate aerosols and aerosols from biomass burning. A wide range of assumptions regarding future economic, demographic and policy factors are encompassed. In this report, the emissions of chlorine-and bromine-containing halocarbons listed in IS92 are assumed to be phased out under the Montreal Protocol and its Adjustments and Amendments and so a single revised future emission scenario for these gases is incorporated in all of the IS92 scenarios.

TABLE 12-1.

The common greenhouse gases, their origins, rates of buildup in the atmosphere, and their contributions to global warming in the 1980s.

Gas(1):	Principal Sources:	Current rate of annual increase and concentration:	Contribution to global warming (3);
CO_2	Fossil fuel burning (c.77%) Deforestation (c.23%)	0.5% (353 ppmv)	55%
CFCs & related gases (HFCs and HCFCs) (4)	Various industrial uses: incl. refrigerants foam blowing solvents	4% (280 pptv CFC-11) (484 pptv CFC-12	24%
CH_4	Rice paddies Enteric fermentation Gas leakage	0.9% (1.72 ppmv)	15%
N_2O	Biomass burning Fertilizer use Fossil fuel combustion	0.8% (310 ppbv)	6%

Sources and Notes: (1) Tropospheric ozone is not included in the table because, although its contribution is significant, it is very difficult to quantify. Ozone forms in the troposphere as result of chemical interactions between uncombusted hydrocarbons and nitrogen oxides produced by fossil fuel burning in the presence of sunlight.... (3) Note that these figures reflect understanding as of 1990. The 1992 IPCC Supplement concluded that ozone depletion by CFCs had been proceeding so fast that the radiative forcing contribution of CFCs is believed to have been approximately offset... This means that the proportional contributions of CO_2, HFCs, CH_4, and N_2O to global warming will all be higher than the figures given here. The 1992 IPCC Supplement did not give figures for how much higher. (4) Note that production of CFCs began only a few years before the Second World War. Now that these gases are known to deplete ozone, the chemical industry is preparing replacements: hydrochlorofluorocarbons (HCFCs) and hydrofluorocarbons (HFCs). Though HCFCs do not deplete ozone as badly as CFCs, both HCFCs and HFCs are potent greenhouse gases.

ppmv: parts per million volume; ppbv: parts per billion volume; pptv: parts per trillion volume.

Emissions of individual HFCs are based on the original IS92 scenarios, although they do not reflect current markets. CO2 emissions for the six scenarios are shown in Table 12-1.

The calculation of future concentrations of greenhouse gases, given certain emissions, entails modeling the processes that transform and remove the different gases from the atmosphere. For example, future concentrations of CO2 are calculated using models of the carbon cycle which model the exchanges of CO2 between the atmosphere and the oceans and terrestrial biosphere; atmospheric chemistry models are used to simulate the removal of chemically active gases such as methane.

All the IS92 emission scenarios, even IS92c, imply increases in greenhouse gas concentrations from 1990 to 2100 (e.g., CO2 increases range from 35 to 170%; CH_4 from 22 to 175%; and N_2O from 26 to 40%).

* * *

B.9.2 Stabilisation of greenhouse gas and aerosol concentrations

An important question to consider is: how might greenhouse gas concentrations be stabilized in the future. If global CO_2 emissions were maintained at near current 1994) levels, they would lead to a nearly constant rate of increase in atmospheric concentrations for at least two centuries. reaching about 500 ppmv (approaching twice the pre-industrial concentration of 280 ppmv) by the end of the 21st century.

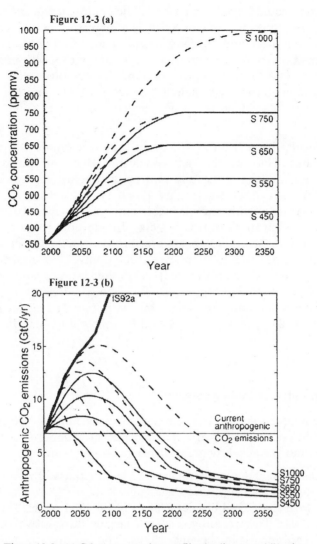

Figure 12-3. (a) CO_2 concentration profiles leading to stabilisation at 450, 550, 650 and 750 ppmv following the pathways defined in IPCC (1994) (solid curves) and for pathways that allow emissions to follow IS92a until at least 2000 (dashed curves). A single profile that stabilises at a CO_2 concentration of 1000 ppmv and follows IS92a emissions until at least 2000 has also been defined. (b) CO_2 emissions leading to stabilisation at concentrations of 450, 550, 650, 750 and 1000 ppmv following the profiles shown in (a). Current anthropogenic CO_2 emissions and those for IS92a are shown for comparison.

In IPCC (1994), carbon cycle models were used to calculate the emissions of CO_2: which would lead to stabilisation at a number of different concentration levels from 350 to 750 ppmv. The assumed concentration profiles leading to stabilisation are shown in Figure 12–3a (excluding 350 ppmv). Many different stabilisation levels, time-scales for achieving these levels, and routes to stabilisation could have been chosen. The choices made are not intended to have policy implications; the exercise is illustrative of the relationship between CO_2 emissions and concentrations. Those in Figure 12–3a assume a smooth transition from the current average rate of CO_2 concentration increase to stabilisation. To a first approximation, the stabilized concentration level depends more upon the accumulated amount of carbon emitted up to the time of stabilisation, than upon the exact concentration path followed *en route* to stabilisation.

New results have been produced to take account of the revised carbon budget for the 1980s , but the main conclusion, that stabilisation of concentration requires emissions eventually to drop well below current levels, remains unchanged from IPCC (1994) (Figure 12–3b). Because the new budget implies a reduced terrestrial sink, the allowable emissions to achieve stabilisation are up to or lower than those in IPCC (1994). In addition, these calculations have been extended to include alternative pathways towards stabilisation (Figure 12–3a) and a higher stabilisation level (1000 ppmv). The alternative pathways assume higher emissions in the early years, but require steeper reductions in emissions in later years (Figure 12–3b). The 1000 ppmv stabilisation case allows higher maximum emissions, but still requires a decline to current levels by about 240 years from now and further reductions thereafter (Figure 12–3b).

* * *

C.1 Has the climate warmed?

Global average surface air temperature, excluding Antarctica, is about 15°C. Year-to-year temperature changes can be computed with much more confidence than the absolute global average temperature.

The mean global surface temperature has increased by about 0.3° to 0.6°C since the late 19th century, and by about 0.2° to 0.3°C over the last 40 years, the period with most credible data (see Figure 12–4 which shows data up to the end of 1994). The warming occurred largely during two periods, between 1910 and 1940 and since the mid–1970s. The estimate of warming has not significantly changed since the IPCC (1990) and IPCC (1992). Warming is evident in both sea surface and land-based surface air temperatures. Urbanization in general and desertification could have contributed only a small part (a few hundredths of a degree) of the overall global warming, although urbanization influences may have been important in some regions. Indirect indicators, such as borehole temperatures and glacier shrinkage, provide independent support for the observed warming. Recent years have been among the warmest since 1860, i.e., in the period of instrumental record.

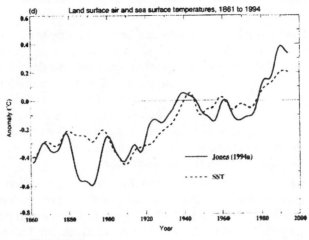

Figure 12-4

The warming has not been globally uniform. The recent warming has been greatest over one continent between 40°N and 70°N. A few areas, such as the North Atlantic Ocean north of 30°N, and some surrounding land areas, have cooled in recent decades.

* * *

Box 2: What Tools Are Used to Project Future Climate and How Are They Used?

Future climate is projected using climate models. The most highly developed climate models are atmospheric and oceanic general circulation models (GCMs). In many instances GCMs of the atmosphere and oceans, developed as separate models, are combined, to give a coupled GCM (termed here a coupled atmosphere-ocean model). These models also include representations of land-surface processes, sea ice related processes and any other complex processes involved in the climate system. GCMs are based upon physical laws that describe the atmospheric and oceanic dynamics and physics, and upon empirical relationships, and their depiction as mathematical equations. These equations are solved numerically with computers using a three-dimensional grid over the globe. For climate, typical resolutions are about 250 km in the horizontal and 1 km in the vertical in atmospheric GCMs, often with higher vertical resolution near the surface and lower resolution in the upper troposphere and stratosphere. Many physical processes, such as those related to clouds, take place on much smaller spatial scales and therefore cannot be properly resolved and modeled explicitly, but their average effects must be included in a simple way by taking advantage of physically based rela-

---

tionships with the larger scale variables (a technique known as parametrization).

Useful weather forecasts can be made using atmospheric GCMs for periods up to about ten days. Such forecasts simulate the evolution of weather systems and describe the associated weather. For simulation and projection of climate, on the other hand, it is the statistics of the system that are of interest rather than the day-to-day evolution of the weather. The statistics include measures of variability as well as mean conditions, and are taken over many weather systems and for several months or more.

When a model is employed for climate projection it is first run for many simulated decades without any changes in external forcing in the system. The quality of the simulation can then be assessed by comparing statistics of the mean climate, the annual cycle and the variability on different time-scales with observations of the current climate. The model is then run with changes in external forcing, for instance with changing greenhouse gas concentrations. The differences between the two climates provide an estimate of the consequent climate change due to changes in that forcing factor. This strategy is intended to simulate changes or perturbations to the system and partially overcomes some imperfections in the models.

Comprehensive coupled atmosphere-ocean models are very complex and take large computer resources to run. To explore all the possible scenarios and the effects of assumptions or approximations in parameters in the model more thoroughly, simpler models are also widely used and are constructed to give results similar to the GCMs when globally averaged. The simplifications may involve coarser resolution, and simplified dynamics and physical processes. An example is the upwelling diffusion-energy balance model. This represents the land and ocean areas in each hemisphere as individual "boxes", with vertical diffusion and upwelling to model heat transport within the ocean.

Early climate experiments, using atmospheric GCMs coupled to a simple representation of the ocean, were aimed at quantifying an equilibrium climate response to a doubling of the concentration of (equivalent) CO_2 in the atmosphere. Such a response portrays the final adjustment of the climate to the changed CO_2 concentration. The range of global warming results is typically between 1.5 and 4.5°C. The temporal evolution and the regional patterns of climate change may depend significantly on the time dependence of the change in forcing. It is important, therefore, to make future projections using plausible evolving scenarios of anthropogenic forcing and coupled atmosphere-ocean models so that the response of the climate to the forcing is properly

> simulated. These climate simulations are often called "transient experiments" (see Glossary) in contrast to an equilibrium response.
>
> The main uncertainties in model simulations arise from the difficulties in adequately representing clouds and their radiative properties. the coupling between the atmosphere and the ocean, and detailed processes at the land surface.

* * *

F.2 Projections of Climate Change

* * *

Using the IS92 emission scenarios, which include emissions of both greenhouse gasses and aerosol precursors projected global mean temperature changes relative to 1990 were calculated for the 21st century. Temperature projections assuming the "best estimate" value of climate sensitivity, 2.5° C, are shown for the full set of IS92 scenarios in Figure 12–1. For IS92a the temperature increase by 2100 is about 2° C. Taking account of the range in the estimate of climate sensitivity (1.5 to 4.5° C) and the full set of IS92 emission scenarios, the models project an increase in global mean temperature between 0.9 and 3.5° C. In all cases the average rate of warming would probably be greater than any seen in the last 10,000 years, but the actual annual to decadal changes would include considerable natural variability. Because of the thermal inertia of the oceans, global mean temperature would continue to increase beyond 2100 even if concentrations of greenhouse gasses were stabilized at that time. Only 50–90% of the eventual temperature changes are realized at the time of greenhouse gas stabilisation. All scenarios show substantial climate warming, even when the negative aerosol radiative forcing is accounted for. Although CO_2 is the most important greenhouse gas, the other greenhouse gasses contribute significantly (about 30%) to the projected global warming.

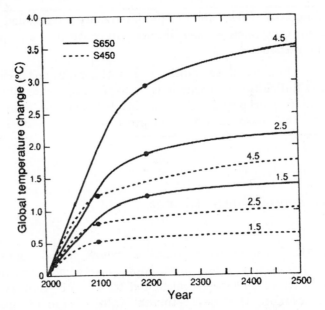

Figure 12-5 The global mean surface temperature response to the CO_2 concentration pathways leading to stabilisation at 450 (dashed curves) and 650 (solid curves) ppmv for a climate sensitivity of 1.5, 2.5 and 4.5 °C. The changes shown are those arising from CO_2 increases alone. The date of concentration stabilisation is indicated by the dot. Calculations assume the "observed" history of forcing to 1990, including aerosol effects and then CO_2 concentration increases only beyond 1990.

* * *

6.3.4 Longer Time-scale Projections

The IS92 emission scenarios give emissions only out to 2100. In almost all cases, projected values of global mean temperature are still rapidly rising at the end of the period. This raises the question of what might happen after 2100. As noted above, both the carbon cycle and the climate system have large inertia, so even if (for example) CO_2 emissions were to decline dramatically after 2100, temperature would continue to increase for some time. Figure 12–3a illustrates this. Here, anthropogenic emissions follow IS92a to 2100 and then are assumed to decline linearly to zero over 2100–2200 for CO_2, CH_4, N_2O, the halocarbons and the SO_2–derived aerosols. CO_2 concentrations in this scenario peak at around 850 ppmv in 2160, and decline to around 540 in 2500. Total radiative forcing also peaks around 2160, but temperatures continue to rise to 2200, declining only slowly thereafter.

While Figure 12–3a graphically illustrates the inertia of both the carbon and climate system, a more relevant set of long-term projections arises from the CO_2 concentration stabilisation profiles. [Figure 12-5] These illustrate, in an idealized way, possible future CO_2 concentration pathways and levels that might be achieved in response to Article 2 of the Framework Convention on

Climate Change, which call for eventual stabilisation of greenhouse gas concentrations at, as yet, unspecified levels.

3. T.M.L. Wigley, R. Richels & J.A. Edmonds, *Economic and Environmental Choices in the Stabilization of Atmospheric CO_2 Concentrations*, 379 NATURE 240 (1996).

The IPCC Working Group 1 (WGI) concentration profiles [(Figure 12–3)] ... show that stabilization requires an eventual and sustained reduction of emissions to substantially below current levels. Furthermore, some have interpreted the results for the IPCC pathways to imply that an immediate reduction in emissions (relative to the central IPCC "existing policies" or "business as usual" (BAU) emissions scenario (IS92a) is required to achieve any of the stabilization targets.

* * *

Viewing the stabilization issue as a carbon budget allocation problem helps explain why concentration pathways with higher near-term emissions have lower overall mitigation costs. Because cumulative emissions are approximately independent of the concentration pathway, for each stabilization level there is, roughly, a fixed allowable amount of CO_2 to be released. The basic choice is therefore how this budget is to be allocated over the time. From this perspective the reasons for drawing more heavily in under budget in the early years are: (1) Positive marginal productivity of capital. With the economy yielding a positive return on capital, the further in the future in economic burden (here, omissions reduction) lies, the smaller is this set of resources that must be set aside today to finance the burden. (2) Capital stock. Stock for energy production and use is typically long-lived (for example power plant, housing and transport). The current system is configured based upon a set of expectations about the future. Unanticipated changes will be costly. Time is therefore needed to re-optimize the capital stock. (3) Technical progress. There is evidence for past and potential future improvements in the efficiency of energy supply, transformation and end-use technologies. Thus, the availability of low carbon substitutes will probably improve and costs reduce over time. In addition, as the emissions budget will be somewhat larger (that is, greater cumulative emissions) for pathways with higher emissions earlier, dependence on higher cost, carbon-free alternatives is reduced.

* * *

The market (for example, agriculture, timber and fisheries) and non-market (for example, biodiversity, environmental quality and human health) implications of these results are unclear: do pathway-related differentials up to [sic]0.2° C in global-mean temperature and 4 cm in global-mean sea level change translate into significantly higher damages, and if so, are these large enough to offset the reduced cost of a more economical transition away from fossil fuels? The answer depends on the regional details associated with these changes, and the sensitivity is of impact categories to changes in important climate variables. Both aspects are highly uncertain. Nevertheless, it is clear that the choice of emissions path require state consideration of both costs and benefits.

4. Rob Coppock, *Implementing the Kyoto Protocol*, 14 ISSUES IN SCIENCE AND TECHNOLOGY 66-74 (1998).

The Kyoto Protocol to the United Nations Framework Convention on Climate Change is an agreement of historic proportions. Finally, the world is treating global warming seriously. The protocol could put us on a course that is less polluting, less damaging to agriculture and the international economy, and less threatening to human health. However, the protocol as written forces nations and industries into a crash program to slow global warming by dramatically reducing carbon dioxide emissions by 2010. The cost to enact the short-term plan will be unnecessarily excessive, and will actually make it more difficult to reach the fundamental emissions reductions required to stabilize the atmosphere for generations to come. The very same slowdown of global warming can be achieved more effectively and for far less cost, however, if a smarter implementation policy with a longer-term view is crafted. Emissions reductions would be phased in over more years, in parallel with the natural replacement of aging equipment, placing much less of a burden on industries and governments worldwide.

Thankfully, implementation of the protocol is far from a *fait accompli*. ... Before any more political momentum builds to ram the plan through, Congress and the world's governments should stop and consider a longer-term plan that can set the world on a more sensible and effective course.

Global warming guaranteed

Climate change is a long-term problem that can only be addressed adequately with a long-term outlook. The overall aim of the Framework Convention on Climate Change is to stabilize atmospheric concentrations of the so-called greenhouse gases at levels that will not be detrimental to human life or the environment. In implementing the framework convention, the Kyoto Protocol has been hailed because it establishes emissions-reduction targets for each industrialized country, a system for emissions trading among countries, projects between industrialized and developing countries, and a fund for developing country action. But what has been lost in the hoopla is that, even with the protocol's tough limits, the concentration of greenhouse gases in the atmosphere will have doubled by the end of the 21st century.

Ice core samples drilled in Greenland and Antarctica indicate that atmospheric concentrations of carbon dioxide were fairly constant at roughly 280 parts per million by volume (ppmv) before the beginning of the Industrial Revolution. They have risen to about 360 ppmv today. The protocol calls for industrialized nations to reduce their carbon dioxide emissions to 5 percent below 1990 levels between the years 2008 and 2012—I use the median date of 2010. But even then, the world will still be pumping substantial amounts of carbon dioxide into the atmosphere every year.

The key fact that is overlooked is that it takes hundreds of years for an injection of carbon dioxide into the atmosphere to dissipate. Although each atom of carbon in the atmosphere exchanges with the biosphere on an average of every four years, the atmosphere still exhibits the results of emissions from the early Industrial Revolution. Just as important, the concentration is cumulative. Even if all the world's nations cut annual emissions to 5 percent below 1990 levels by 2010, and held them there into the future, the atmospheric concentration of carbon dioxide would continue to rise. Furthermore, since developing country emissions are almost certain to exceed those from industrialized nations due to population growth and economic expansion, full implementation of the Kyoto protocol without additional measures would have little impact on the total accumulation of carbon dioxide in the atmosphere after a few decades. To keep atmospheric carbon dioxide at its current concentration is virtually impossible, even if the world's economies were drastically altered. The conclusion: Even with extreme short-term sacrifice, we are already committed to doubling the pre-industrial concentration. We will ultimately have to adjust to a warmer world.

The good news is that a doubling of carbon dioxide, though seemingly dramatic, is manageable, as we will see. It is not clear, however, how far beyond doubling we can go without triggering major environmental changes. But even if emissions rates were to increase somewhat over recent decades—a perhaps unavoidable outcome if populations and economies grow, increasing the emissions from power plants, vehicles, and heating and cooling buildings, the greatest contributors—it would take at least until 2150 to quadruple pre-industrial levels. And that would probably require returning to a coal-based energy system, another highly unlikely scenario, given industrial changes of the last 150 years. Doubling the atmospheric concentration of carbon dioxide is virtually guaranteed, while quadrupling it, or perhaps a bit more, seems to be the upper limit.

Given these boundaries, a realistic goal of international action would be to curb emissions to ensure that no more than a doubling of pre-industrial atmospheric concentrations occurs before the latter part of the 21st century. So far, the Kyoto agreement seems on target.

Is a doubling tolerable?

Before we consider how fast the world must act in order to hold concentrations to a doubling, let us consider if this level is tolerable.

Among the effects of pumping carbon dioxide into the atmosphere, two are particularly significant for climate change. First, it raises the average global temperature. This, in turn, changes the energy level in the atmosphere and oceans, which alters the earth's hydrologic cycle–the closed system of precipitation to earth and evaporation back to the skies.

There is direct, compelling evidence from measurements of bore holes in rock from many parts of the world that the 20th century has been substantially warmer than recent centuries. Not only has this century been the warmest of the last five, but the rate of temperature change is four times greater than that for the four previous centuries. These measurements show the present-day mean temperature to be a little more than 1.0°C warmer than five centuries ago. Of this change about half has occurred in this century alone.

There is also compelling evidence that the hydrologic cycle has increased in intensity this century, mostly due to rising global temperature. This could have more immediate and far-reaching environmental, economic, and social impacts than elevated temperature alone. For example, a more intense cycle causes storms to generate more precipitation, which could raise the moisture level of farmlands, affecting crops, and increase storm runoff that leads to floods or erosion of valuable property.

Nonetheless, several studies suggest that the economies of industrialized nations could easily adapt to the climatic consequences of a doubling of pre-industrial atmospheric carbon dioxide. That is because the rate of change will be slow. The trend this century has been about 0.05°C per decade. Investment cycles for most industrial sectors are rapid enough that suitable adjustments can be made along the way. Even agriculture ought to be able to cope. It takes about eight years to bring a new cereal hybrid into production, which would be needed to adjust to differences in soil moisture, and recent experience breeding disease-resistant rice suggests that genetic engineering can reduce this time. It also will not be long before agricultural implements are able to make "on-the-fly" soil-moisture measurement and precision delivery of fertil-izer to offset changes measured.

Rising warmth and moisture would also broaden the breeding grounds for insects, most notably mosquitoes, increasing their spread of diseases like malaria, dengue, and yellow fever. However, lifestyle and public health measures such as mosquito control, eradication programs, and piped water systems, which have wiped out these epidemics in the United States, will far outweigh the effects of future climate change.

Even the effort to counter a possible sea level rise of 30 [centimeters] by the end of the next century is not likely to be excessive. In urban and industrial locations, the cost of protective sea walls will be worth it. Elsewhere the coastline can be left to find its new level. The previously valuable property on the water's edge will be replaced by formerly inland property that becomes newly valuable because it is now next to water. Obviously there will be winners and losers, but then there always have been. Urban expansion will make winners and losers much more rapidly than climate change.

For industrialized countries, then, a doubling of carbon dioxide is not an economic problem. However, a doubling would definitely change particular ecosystems, and the most important question may be whether significant disruption will result. Plant and animal life in bodies of fresh water and in wetlands will face new conditions due to higher temperatures and altered precipitation, and may have difficulty producing sufficient organic sediment and root material to adjust. Other so-called "loosely managed ecosystems" have more capacity to adjust. Ecosystems in general will be forced to reconfig-ure into new communities more rapidly than they have since the end of the last ice age. But research indicates they should be capable of adjusting quickly enough to maintain the grand mineral and nutrient cycles upon which life on earth depends.

The story is different for developing countries, however. In areas already sorely stressed by environmental problems that cause considerable human suffering, climate change poses a direct threat to humanity. These nations may not have the money to alter farming so it can respond to changing soil moisture, for example, or to implement widespread control and eradication programs to battle the greater spread of disease by insects. Industrialized nations will have to help meet these new demands, just as with the problems of today. Many already are, moreover, and improvements in established programs should be able to offset the new challenges. Developing nations have so far to go, as is, that the added challenges imposed by global warming represent only a marginal increase. The additional suffering will be real, but pales in comparison to that brought about by much larger forces in these countries, such as war, oppression, and poverty.

If met with good planning, a doubling of the pre-industrial concentration of carbon dioxide poses a modicum of environmental problems, and little if any economic problems. The picture changes completely, however, if we ramp up to a quadrupling of the pre-industrial concentration. The consequences could be massive. Although we cannot say exactly how much temperature will have to rise before we confront serious thresholds, we can make some educated guesses. Various models indicate that crossing the 5°C threshold will change weather patterns and soil moisture enough that U.S. agriculture would have to shift to a completely different set of cultivars. Altered rainfall patterns could combine with dramatically reconfigured ecosystems to change the nutrient flows in soils across the entire Midwest, seriously threatening the productivity of the nation's bread basket. Studies in Texas show that bottom-land hardwood forests of the coastal plain might be unable to rebound from fires or storms, affecting the viability of both preserved and commercial forests there.

At some point, continued temperature rise will trigger an even greater global disaster, as well. Salinity and temperature differentials in the oceans are important in driving what is called the deep ocean conveyer, a huge flow that sinks in the North Atlantic, runs around the African cape, and empties into the Pacific Ocean. Up-welling currents from this conveyer carry nutrients to the major fishing areas of the world. There is evidence that sufficient warming could increase precipitation in the North Atlantic basin enough to change salinity and alter ocean temperatures to a degree that would slow or even stop the conveyer. At a minimum, ocean fishing worldwide would be affected. The consequences for weather would be drastic around the world, dwarfing anything that has been dished out by the El Niño Southern Oscillation, a periodic shift in ocean temperatures and flows in the South Pacific. Though nobody knows what the consequences of stopping the deep ocean conveyer would be, it is thought that Europe would cool dramatically as the warm Gulf Stream halts.

The world may be able to adjust to a doubling of the pre-industrial concentrations of atmospheric carbon dioxide. But continued increases will eventually reach a point that can only be called "scary."

Too much too soon

Since the world should be able to handle a doubling of carbon dioxide concentrations, but there is reason to worry when levels rise much beyond that, it seems the Kyoto Protocol's overall aim of reducing emissions is the right goal. But ironically, the protocol's provisions may make it harder to achieve the long-term emissions reductions that are needed to stabilize atmospheric concentrations of greenhouse gases.... Unfortunately, if the signatory nations attempt to fulfill the commitments they made to reduce emissions by 2010, they are likely to take actions that are too expensive and less effective than smarter alternatives.

To start, there is a serious question whether many nations can even hit the target. Only two of the industrialized countries that committed in 1992 to voluntarily reduce emissions to 1990 levels have done so—the UK, because it eliminated coal subsidies and switched to North Sea gas, and Germany, which shut down inefficient and uneconomical factories in the former East Germany. Both of these steps were one-time windfalls. Now, suddenly, the protocol expects all the other countries that have not been able to reduce emissions over the last seven years to reduce them to five percent or more below 1990 levels in the next twelve years.

Doing so will require concerted effort. In the United States, the Department of Energy's Energy Information Administration projects that carbon dioxide emissions will rise 30 percent by 2010 if no actions are taken, requiring a reduction in annual emissions of about 400 million tons to achieve 1990 levels. The Environmental Energy Technologies Division at the Lawrence Berkeley National Laboratory calculates that United States emissions could be reduced about half way to 1990 levels by adopting efficiency approaches that would cost about $50 per ton of avoided carbon emissions. If the burden for this reduction were equally spread across all sources of emissions, and costs were passed on to consumers (which they would be), this would correspond to an increase in the price of gasoline of 12 cents per gallon. An American Petroleum Institute study estimated that it would cost about $200 per ton to get all the way down to the 1990 level. Even if actual emissions reductions are less expensive than these estimates, the cost will be considerable. Yet the United States committed to a greater reduction in Kyoto—7 percent below 1990 emissions; achieving the additional reduction would cost even more.

For the rest of industry, meeting the Kyoto targets will force companies in virtually every sector to engage in massive retrofitting of equipment, to put in place technology that emits less and/or is more energy efficient, thereby reducing emissions. Retrofitting is almost always more expensive than waiting to install new equipment when old equipment has reached its natural end of life, but retrofitting is the only way to meet the short deadline. Electric utilities will have to tear out thousands of costly pieces of equipment long before their lifetimes have expired, which is normally 25 or 30 years, severely compromising their balance sheets—and our utility rates. Or they will have to add emissions control equipment to be used until current equipment is retired; when the new, less polluting equipment goes online the installed equipment will no longer be needed.

Equipment would have to be prematurely replaced in commercial and residential buildings as well, to improve the efficiency of commercial equipment, lighting, and heating and ventilation systems, and of residential heating, air conditioning, and lighting systems.

The United States' commitment to reduce emissions more than 30 percent below what they otherwise would be in 2010 will require massive changes that hold deep implications for industrial practices and consumer's habits. There is little evidence that our country, or any other industrialized country, is willing to make the huge investments required on the time-scale set by the Kyoto Protocol. The Clinton Administration's answer is that tax incentives, research subsidies, and trading will enable the United States to meet its target with only "modest" price hikes on the order of 4 to 6 cents per gallon of gasoline. But this assessment assumes we can cut our abatement costs in half, thanks to emissions trading with other industrial countries, and by another quarter from trading with developing countries. As we shall see, whether mechanisms will be put in place to realize these cost reductions efficiently is dubious at best. Robert Stavins, an economist and professor of public policy at Harvard's John F. Kennedy School of Government, thinks the Administration's claims are optimistic. "It is true that the impact can be relatively small——if this is done in the smartest possible way. But if we don't do it that way it will cost 10 times what the administration is saying."

There is a further problem with the strategy embodied in the Kyoto protocol. The investments required to meet the targets by 2010 are likely to use up funds that would have been used to replace aging equipment with new, more efficient, more expensive technology. If a utility or manufacturer is forced to spend precious capital on a retrofit, now, it won't have the money to install more efficient equipment later.

And there's the rub. Remember that curbing emissions to 5 percent below 1990 levels will not stabilize atmospheric concentrations of greenhouse gases. In particular, emissions of carbon ultimately will have to be essentially eliminated. The gain from rushing to meet the targets in 2010 is nowhere near worth the economic pain.

Better ways to reduce emissions

The question, then, is whether it is more effective to require a manufacturer or utility to spend money on retrofits to meet the short-term deadline, or to allow it to phase in more efficient equipment as old machinery becomes obsolete. Let's consider a few examples.

The pulp and paper industry is very energy intensive and creates volumes of pollutants, including chlorine and ozone used to make paper white. Under the Kyoto Protocol, paper manufacturers or the utilities that deliver power to them would have to undertake costly actions to reduce carbon dioxide emissions. Meanwhile, a new bleaching process is being developed that does not require either chlorine or ozone, and would reduce energy consumption by 50 percent. The process has yet to be perfected, and is unlikely to be widely deployed by 2010, but it might be in wide use by 2015. If manufacturers must spend large sums now, investment in the new process will be slowed, delaying its deployment, and thus delaying a natural reduction in energy use and thus carbon dioxide emissions. If the industry did not have to divert funds to short-term reductions, it might even be able to bring the new process online sooner, which would reduce not only carbon dioxide emissions, but chlorine and ozone emissions, and lower energy costs.

In the metal casting industry, there is new technology being developed that would increase the yield of the casting process from 55 percent to 65 percent. The higher yield equates to a reduction in the amount of raw material and electricity needed for processing. Both gains translate into less carbon dioxide emissions. Again, spending money to bring this process online benefits both global warming and the manufacturer's costs. The alternative— more short-term emissions control—raises costs for everyone.

Another good example comes from the commercial building sector. Studies show that replacing static insulation (put in walls and roofs to increase thermal resistance) with dynamic systems like computer-controlled windows and sensor-controlled ventilation systems could reduce a building's energy load for heating and cooling by 35 to 45 percent. Even if the technology becomes standard in new buildings, new buildings comprise only two to three percent of the existing building stock in any given year. Nearly 80 percent of the commercial buildings existing in 1997 will still be occupied in 2010. Retrofitting existing buildings with dynamic insulation systems would be extremely expensive; it is far more cost effective simply to wait for the natural turnover to improve the energy consumption—and therefore carbon emissions—than to force costly retrofits now.

Electric utilities will be among the hardest hit. They will have to add costly equipment that will be used for only a few years beyond 2010. It will then be obsolete, as more efficient generation equipment becomes available. Forcing the short-term expense will rob funds the utilities could use to buy more expensive, but more efficient, equipment when the current generators must be replaced. The expense will raise costs for all customers, and jeopardize the utility's ability to bring online more efficient equipment, which would lower costs for everyone in the long run. Such expenditures are doubly questionable when stabilizing atmospheric concentrations requires so much more in the long run. A much bigger kick would come from wider use of combined systems such as cogeneration, where waste heat from electricity generation is used to power industrial processes or heat buildings. Again, meeting short-term targets will eat up funds and slow options with ultimately bigger payoffs.

When these kinds of case studies are made in industry after industry, it becomes clear that rushing to meet the artificial Kyoto deadline of 2010 will raise short-term costs considerably, and siphon off money that could be used for smarter, long-term investments that will not only achieve the same carbon dioxide reductions, but also lower costs and the emission of other pollutants as well.

There is even less incentive for retrofits in the industrialized nations, because combustion (the principal source of energy) is expected to grow dramatically in developing countries as they become more populated and economically active. The aggregate emissions from developing countries will soon exceed those of the industrialized world. Given that, all the pain of implementing the Kyoto Protocol in industrialized nations will lead to only a pencil-thin-line deviation in the graph depicting carbon dioxide concentrations in the earth's atmosphere.

Failure to comply

There is another reason to favor a longer-term implementation of the Kyoto Protocol: There is serious doubt as to whether countries will make the short-term investments necessary to reach the 2010 deadline.

The proponents of the protocol argue that once proper incentives exist, all kinds of cheap and even profitable ways of reducing emissions will be found. One of the most highly touted is a provision in the agreement allowing countries to trade emissions rights so they can reach the limits they agreed to in the protocol. If a country reduces emissions below its limit, it can sell rights to a country that's over its threshold to apply the amount of the shortfall. For example, if one nation is 10 units below its limit, it can sell those units to a polluting country. If that country is 15 units above its limit, it would only have to reduce its emission by 5 units to meet its requirement. The proponents point to the resounding success of the United State's sulfur emissions trading scheme used by industry, which has reduced overall emissions to about 40 percent below target at much less cost than was anticipated.

However, emissions trading in the Kyoto scheme will be much more difficult to establish. First, there is a big flaw: The trading is to be between countries. But countries don't pollute; companies and households do. A nation wishing to create a shortfall will have to somehow get industry and homeowners to comply. And a country buying a credit will somehow have to collect the funds from all its polluting sectors. Each of these arrangements will be a practical nightmare.

There are other complications. The most efficient trading programs establish a free market in emissions permits, where private entities execute trades with minimal bureaucratic red tape. This kind of efficiency is unlikely when governments famous for bureaucracy are executing the trades. Also, each trader has to have a recognized emissions baseline so that proper shortfalls and excesses can be negotiated. However, setting baselines for different countries will be extremely difficult; how would emissions or credits from electricity generated in France but consumed in Germany be allocated? Finally, if the U.S. sulfur emissions trading scheme is any guide, there will have to be an overseer of the process that has the power to prevent governments from skewing arrangements to their benefit; establishing who or what will fill that role will be a true challenge. Preferences for organizing the trading system are likely to be in conflict, too; tradition in Europe and Japan favors greater governmental control, whereas the United States has had positive experience with private mechanisms. It is unclear how to address these issues in an international trading scheme.

The Kyoto Protocol also provides for industrialized countries to undertake joint projects with developing countries. An industrialized nation would receive a credit toward meeting its own target equal to the amount of emissions it helps reduce in a developing country. However, this "clean development mechanism" is viewed with suspicion by many in the developing world. They fear that rich industrialized countries will use their greater financial power to avoid emissions restrictions by purchasing emissions reductions from poorer countries and slowing their development in the process. The protocol provides no mechanism for addressing such concerns, nor does it specify how to determine meaningful baselines against which reductions can be measured.

Participation by developing countries is another weak plank in the protocol's short-term platform. The lack of early commitment by key developing countries not only aggravates concerns in the United States and other industrialized countries about international competitiveness, but raises the possibility of developing countries becoming "locked-in" to more fossil fuel intensive technologies. Just as available funds in industrialized countries are likely to be used for retrofits, precluding investments in longer-term alternatives, funds in developing countries might be invested in less efficient energy production technology that will subsequently be expensive to replace. The lack of commitments from developing countries in the Kyoto Protocol must be changed in the long run. It would be much better if they begin now to develop their power and industrial infrastructure with the most efficient new technologies emerging in the coming decades. Furthermore, the U.S. Senate, which ultimately must ratify the treaty, expressed its unwillingness in a 95–to–0 vote last year to support any treaty not including full participation of developing countries. The Clinton Administration has stated that it will not submit the treaty for ratification until major developing countries have committed.

From the scientific perspective, it is not necessary to involve all developing countries. The eight countries currently producing the largest carbon dioxide emissions are the United States, Russia, Japan, Germany, the United Kingdom, Canada ... and China and India. Adding a few rapidly industrializing countries, such as Brazil, Indonesia, Mexico, and South Korea, would encompass well over 60 percent of the world's current emissions and the bulk of its coal resources, the most carbon-intensive of fuels. Commitment by Europe, Japan, and the United States to reduce their domestic emissions with the possibility of joint implementation among this relatively small set of countries could effectively address the climate change problem.

The list of serious controversies that must be overcome in implementing the Kyoto Protocol is significant. They will make achieving a rational and effective plan in Buenos Aires a few short months from now extremely difficult.

Missing pieces

Indeed, the national negotiators at the Kyoto meeting apparently concluded that the only way to reach agreement there was to leave most of the difficult issues to be worked out later. Their scope is daunting. How they are worked out before and during the November Conference of the Parties will largely determine the protocol's value.

Several crucial features have thus far been left out. These include the rules and institutions that will govern the international trading of emissions credits among industrialized countries, and the joint implementation between industrialized and developing countries. Also missing are procedures for identifying whether a nation's actions satisfy the protocol's rules. The equally critical criteria used to judge compliance and any penalties for noncompliance are not specified, either.

The protocol states that the methods by which a country measures emissions, and calculates whether it is meeting emission targets, are to be based on the work of the Intergovernmental Panel on Climate Change—an international group of government scientists that has assessed and summarized the science base—and the Subsidiary Body for Scientific and Technical Advice, an entity of the Framework Convention on Climate Change. These must be worked out and approved by the Conference of the Parties. The protocol also specifies that expert review teams, selected from professionals nominated by signatory nations and appropriate intergovernmental organizations, will provide a thorough and comprehensive technical assessment of all aspects of the implementation by a signatory nation. Appropriate guidelines and methods are to be determined at the Buenos Aires meeting. Clearly, there is a lot to be decided at the Conference of the Parties. Yet even if all these issues can be successfully resolved, the protocol is still missing features that are crucial for successful climate control.

The first is an adequately long-term perspective. Most glaring is the absence of what might be called "futures trading" in emissions credits. There is a provision which allows a country that reduces its emissions below its commitment in one control period to "bank" that credit for application in a later period. But no credit is given for current actions that would reduce emissions in future periods. This actually creates a disincentive for investments in the massive infrastructure changes and new technologies needed to meet the long-term goal of atmospheric stabilization. For example, if the pulp and paper industry were to invest heavily in developing the new bleaching process between the years 2000 and 2012, but the process was not widely implemented until, say, 2015, it would receive no credit for that investment under the Kyoto Protocol—even though, in the long term, it would reduce emission by much more than any short-term investment could. A provision should be added to the protocol that allows the possibility of credits for investments made in one phase that will reap benefits in a later phase.

A second missing feature is an effective Secretariat. Not all issues of certification, verification, and compliance in national assessments, emissions trading, and joint implementation can simply be farmed out to external expert teams, as the protocol provides. The protocol establishes a central Secretariat, but it virtually ignores the Secretariat's role and functions. To implement the protocol, the Secretariat will require a high level of technical expertise and considerable manpower, especially if sanctions with teeth are envisioned. The German government has agreed to host the Secretariat, but for this body to effectively implement the protocol, it will need a much more significant stature. The Conference of the Parties should add language to the agreement clarifying the functions of the Secretariat, providing for a competent staff, and establishing a funding mechanism.

Expecting the Conference of the Parties to manage all these large tasks by November borders on the ridiculous. But even after all these questions are answered, there remains yet another step. The overall structure of the implementing scheme needs an appropriate degree of flexibility. The experience of the International Atomic Energy Agency, which also operates in an international arena marked by considerable scientific and technical complexity, is instructive here. Part of its success in handling technical issues that also touch domestic, social, and economic activities is its flexible implementation regime. The international legal order for nuclear energy is a mix of legally binding rules and agreements, advisory standards, and regulations. The mix constantly changes, with today's non-binding standards becoming tomorrow's binding commitments. Suitable flexibility will be equally helpful in the area of climate control. Yet it remains to be included in the protocol's provisions.

A better implementation plan

The likelihood of the Kyoto Protocol being worked out by November is slim. And that is perhaps good. A doubling of the concentration of carbon dioxide is virtually assured. So before the signatory nations spend considerable effort blazing a path to implementing the protocol, they would be much better off to slow down and consider whether a longer-term framework that achieves the same delay in doubling wouldn't make much more economic sense.

Do not misread my argument. I am not calling for a do-nothing-now policy. I am calling for a different, smarter implementation strategy to reach the end-goal of the climate convention. The nations of the world cannot simply wait until technology ages to replace it, because at that time what is needed is unlikely to be available. What the world must do is invest, now, in technology that is far more efficient with much lower emissions and that will be ready for widespread deployment as current equipment is retired.

Neither nations nor industries have limitless resources. Instead of spending excessive amounts of money for costly, short-lived retrofits to meet an arbitrary deadline of 2010, the protocol should encourage research and development investments that will ensure a more effective, less costly fix for the longer-term problem.

Rather than get buried in the myriad bureaucratic details now required of the November meeting, the Conference of the Parties should initiate a strategic assessment of energy-intensive industries, to see where the greatest gains can be made and where technology such as paper bleaching, metal casting, and cogeneration is already waiting in the wings. The signatory nations should develop the equivalent of a critical technologies list for the utility industry, heavy industry, transportation, housing, and so on. The U.S. government's experience in identifying critical technologies for defense, and in technology road-mapping that has proven useful for overcoming problems in the integrated circuit industry, could inform these efforts.

The Conference of the Parties should also focus on creating a system of phased-in emissions targets, rather than the shear wall of 5 percent below 1990 levels by 2010. For example, to lessen the consumption of fossil fuels, it would be much more tenable for the United States government to install a gradually increasing gasoline tax of, say, a few cents a year for 20 years, than to rapidly hike the price by 2010. And if manufacturers can plan on replacing technology over its full life span, they will be much more financially able to develop truly efficient new technology.

Finally, the Conference of the Parties should make provisions for a futures trading system in emissions credits, to inspire investment today that will benefit us all tomorrow.

Should Congress ratify the Kyoto Protocol? It depends on what happens in Buenos Aires. If the Conference of the Parties can achieve the kinds of strategic, long-term adjustments just mentioned, the protocol would be much more cost-effective. Congress should support this kind of plan and help provide the details. If, however, the Conference of the Parties simply pushes ahead on the short-term road it has already set, the world's nations may be better off scrapping the Kyoto Protocol and starting over.

5. Uncertainties in Climate Modeling: Solar Variability and Other Factors, Before the Senate Committee on Energy and Natural Resources (1996)(testimony of Sallie Baliunas, Senior Scientist, George C. Marshall Institute)<http://www.marshall.org/baliunas.html>.

The possible outcomes resulting from the predicted rapid and dramatic rise in global temperature deserve serious thought. What are the scientific facts in support of the claim that human-made global warming will be significant (i.e., larger than the natural fluctuations of climate) and even possibly catastrophic? How is it known that computer simulations of the climate, forecast 100 years into the future, are accurate?

One starts by testing the computer simulations against the record of temperature change of the last 100 years. In the last 100 years, the global average surface temperature of the earth has risen about 0.5 C. Also during that interval the concentration of anthropogenic greenhouse gases has increased in the atmosphere. The increase in concentration is roughly equivalent to a 50% buildup in carbon dioxide alone. That substantial buildup gives a way to test the computer simulations of climate change due to greenhouse gases from human actions. That is, by studying the temperature response to the 50% increase over the last 100 years the computer simulations can be tested against the actual response of the climate.

The computer simulations say that the global temperature should have risen in the last 100 years by roughly 0.5—1.5 C (aerosols, whose theoretical effect is included in that range, will be discussed below).While the magnitude of the rise, as post-predicted by the computer simulations, seems to agree with the observed temperature rise of 0.5 C, it is inconsistent with the timing of the warming.

The record of global temperature [figure 5] shows that most of the warming of the last 100 years occurred before 1940. But most of the anthropogenic greenhouse gases entered the atmosphere after 1940. Human-made greenhouse gases cannot cause a warming that took place before they existed in the atmosphere. Therefore, most of the 0.5 C rise must be natural. Only a small part of the 0.5 C rise—no more than a few tenths degree—could have been caused by human-made greenhouse gases. In other words, the 0.5—1.5 C warming predicted by the computer simulations exaggerates the greenhouse effect produced by the equivalent 50% buildup of carbon dioxide.

The solar influence

If the anthropogenic greenhouse gases did not cause most of the warming early in the century, then what did? One possibility is that the total energy output of the sun changes, thereby causing some warming and cooling. The evidence for this is in two parts: first, the sun has been observed by NASA satellites to vary in total energy output in step with the 11–year sunspot cycle of magnetic changes in the sun. Although the satellite records only began in the late 1970s, which is too short a time to obtain information on century-long climate variations, the association of brightness changes with surface magnetic changes allows us to obtain information on the sun's brightness changes going back several centuries, because records of the sun's magnetism are available over that long period.

The length of the sunspot cycle is a particularly interesting proxy for changes in the sun's brightness. Chart 2 compares the sunspot cycle length with surface temperatures going back to 1750. The correlation is nearly perfect.

The second part of the evidence for a solar influence on the climate is as follows. The sun's magnetic record can be converted to estimated brightness changes, using data from the sun and other sun-like stars, and input to a climate simulation.... If the sun has changed brightness in the way the magnetic records have indicated, then changes in sun explain more than half of the variance of the temperature record from 1880–1993. The results for the sun suggest that its brightness changes have had a significant impact on climate change. A brighter sun may be the explanation for a substantial part of, and possibly most of, the 0.5 C global warming observed in the last 100 years.

Aerosols

Pollutants such as sulfur dioxide complicate predictions of global climate change. Aerosols form a haze that absorbs or reflects sunlight causing a cooling that offsets some of the predicted greenhouse warming. Aerosols may also alter cloud properties.

Studies of the response of climate change to aerosols are based on computer simulations. The theoretical effect of aerosols has been to cool the climate forecasts, both for the present and the future, and bring the computer forecasts more in line with the recent global temperatures. (However, allowing for the theoretical cooling effect of aerosols cannot explain the observed warming prior to 1940.) The modeled effect of aerosols does not change the conclusion that the computer simulations of climate are greatly exaggerating the size of the greenhouse warming.

Regional results and the "fingerprint" studies

"Pattern" studies of anthropogenic greenhouse gases with the added effect of aerosols are considered in ensemble, region by region, and with height. They form the basis for the claim that the anthropogenic effect on climate has been detected. But checking the forecasts in specific regions shows instead that the simulations fail to agree with observations. For example, two regions where the aerosol effect should be verified are heavily-industrialized Europe and North America. There the aerosol effect worsens agreement of the computer simulations with the temperature observations.

Moreover, the combined greenhouse plus aerosol model can be tested with data from the region where the computer simulations predict the most warming, namely the troposphere over the southern oceans. That test shows no net rise in temperature from 1958 to the present.

Satellite temperature measurements

NOAA satellites have been measuring the temperature at a height of a few kilometers in the atmosphere essentially over the entire earth since 1979. These records have smaller systematic errors than the surface records, which, unlike the satellite records, come from a variety of instruments, techniques and measurement histories, and whose coverage is sparse over large areas like the southern ocean. The very precise satellite record shows no net warming over the last 17 years—contrary to the forecasts calculating the effect of the recent rapid increase in human-made greenhouse gases.

Temperature in the Arctic

Most computer simulations also post-predict a major, rapid warming in the Arctic, especially in the winter. The temperature record in the Arctic is thus a very sensitive test of the computer simulations. But over the last 50 years no net warming of the surface has been observed. The simulations also post-predict that the Arctic should have warmed by a degree or so in the last 17 years, the period during which satellites have made precise readings of the Arctic. Over the periods under study, the average temperature of the Arctic has not warmed. In the test of the Arctic records the computer forecasts exaggerate, by a very large amount, the warming that should have occurred.

Error budget and uncertainties in the computer simulations

Apart from the possible uncertainty of a significant solar variability effect in global climate change, there are other major uncertainties in the computer simulations. These uncertainties are demonstrated by the fact that simulations of the present-day climate differ from one another by 5°C in the tropics (and nearly 20°C in the polar regions).

* * *

Summary

No evidence can be found in the observations of the global temperature for a dangerous warming derived from human actions.

The computer simulations of climate, which estimate a warming of roughly 1°C over the last 100 years, have overestimated the warming that has actually occurred by a factor of three or more. The same computer simulations projecting for the next 100 years (the time frame cited for the equivalent of a doubling of carbon dioxide) must be corrected for these overestimates of past warming. When corrected, the forecasted warming for the next 100 years is a few tenths C. That warming, spread over a century, will be negligible compared to the natural fluctuations in climate.

Furthermore, delaying the onset of drastic emission reductions by as much as 25 years results in a penalty of only 0.2°C in added temperature by 2100, according to the current computer forecasts which are known to be exaggerating the warming. Investing in and waiting for better climate science would be appropriate, considering that the IPCC-forecasted warming has dropped by nearly a factor of two just in the last six years.

6.   Robert C. Balling Jr., *The Global Temperature Data*, 9 RE-SEARCH AND EXPLORATION 201-207 (1993).

By the end of the 1970s, climatologists monitoring global temperature records had seen decades of cooling. Aware of multiple glacial episodes over the past one million years they warned the public of the possibility of a return to colder climates in the immediate future. Yet, somehow, little more than a decade later, climatologists are once again in the spotlight, but this time the threat appears to come from the potentially dire consequences of global warming. At this time the spotlight is even brighter, and many more people seem to be listening. In this stage of environmental awareness, this latest doomsday scenario is an unparalleled hit! Surprisingly little was said in the public arena about global warming before the summer of 1988. However, during that summer, much of the United States experienced drought. The Southeast had one of the hottest summers on record; the Mississippi River nearly ran drive; Yellowstone Park burned to the ground; hurricane Gilbert slammed the Gulf states; and on and on. A few climatologists appeared in the public eye claiming that these events were consistent with the climate consequences of an accelerated greenhouse effect. We learned that the Earth was warming, and we discovered that many years in the 1980s were marked by record-breaking temperatures. The greenhouse effect became front page news. Suddenly new books on the subject were published, scientific documentaries were on television weekly, and op-ed pieces filled newspapers. The message was simple—human activities were increasing atmosphere greenhouse gas concentrations, these gases would act to warm the Earth, and climate catastrophe was certain. We were told to act now to avoid the apocalyptic, and if we did not, the calamities of 1988 would revisit again and again.

However, since 1988, an amazing amount of research has come along that cast serious doubts about the impending disaster. The temperature record has been scrutinized with vigor; a satellite-based global temperature record has been developed and analyzed; and the role of other gases has been examined more carefully. In the years following the summer of 1988, the estimated temperature rise for the middle of the next century has been reduced, and it is likely to be reduced even further. The greenhouse effect seems far less threatening today than a few years ago; even greenhouse benefits are now being discussed more freely in the scientific literature.

The common ground

For decades scientists have argued about the climate outcome of the doubling of the greenhouse gases and debate is likely to continue long into the future. Nested within that debate are some areas of little or no disagreement. No one disagrees that various greenhouse trace gases are increasing in atmosphere concentration due to human activities. CO_2, CH_4, N_2O, various CFC, and many other minor gases have been released by our activities, and their concentrations have increased exponentially. When the effects of these gases are expressed in CO_2 equivalents, we find the equivalent CO_2 has increased from near 310 ppm in 1890 to approximately 430 ppm in 1990. In the past 100 years, the levels of equivalent CO_2 have increased 40 percent.

The second point of virtually no debate is that the numerical climate models, well terrific scientific achievements, are still crude representations of the Earth-ocean-atmosphere system. The models are primitive with respect to ocean-atmosphere interactions, cloud processes, ice feedbacks, and biological mechanisms. Gross features of the climate system can be simulated by the models, but as of today, their predictions for climate change in the world of double CO_2 are nested in great uncertainty.

The third important point of limited debate is that Earth's atmosphere has warmed over the past 100 years. Meticulous assemblage of temperature records from the land-based stations and ship reports has led researchers to conclude that the planetary temperature has increased by approximately ½ degree centigrade over the past 100 years. So first glance, the greenhouse debate would seem completely one-sided—the trace gases are building up any atmosphere, the numerical climate models predict global warming, and planetary temperatures of the past century have been increasing. How can there be a debate when the evidence seems so overwhelming? There is a lot more to this story.

Global temperatures

As mentioned, researchers have reconstructed the planetary temperature from millions of observations taken around the world. A plot of annual temperatures for the past 100 years (1891 to 1991) reveals rather steady warming from 1891 to 1940, slight cooling from 1940 to the mid-1970s, and a sharp rise in global temperature in most recent decade. Based on these data, the nine warmest years since 1891 all occurred in the 1980s and early 1990s, and the total amount of warming was 0.46 degrees centigrade. In the eyes of many, this plot of global temperatures is "at least not inconsistent" with a catastrophic greenhouse effect.

However, a number of critical issues must be brought into the debate. The amount of warming over the record is 0.46 degrees centigrade. The amount of warming from 1891 to 1940 is 0.33 degrees centigrade. Seventy percent of the warming the past century occurred before the second world war. The timing of the warming is not consistent with the timing of the buildup of the greenhouse gases.

It is highly unlikely that all of the 0.46 degrees centigrade of warming can be ascribed to the greenhouse effect. For example, many researchers have concluded that as cities grow they tend to warm the local area. This urban heat-island effect contaminated temperature record by generating localized warming that influences the meteorological equipment. Best estimates are that "global warming" is inflated by between 2 and 20 percent by the urban heat Island contamination in the climate record

Urban warming is not the only signal in the temperature record that clearly is not related to the greenhouse gases. Throughout many semiarid and arid regions of the world, over grazing is altering surface vegetation cover. In the overgrazed areas, plant cover is removed or reduced, and more exposed soil is left behind. Meager precipitation levels strike the overgrazed areas, the water quickly runs off, and less moisture is available for evaporation or transpiration. Less of the incoming sunlight is used in the evapotranspiration processes, and more of the Suns energy warms the Earth and the air. This leads to warming and—in fact, the desertification warming signal could account for 2 to 10 percent of the observed warming of the past century.

In addition to the urban heat-island and desertification effects, climatologists fully recognize that any number of natural phenomena could be responsible for the observed pattern in global temperatures. For example, volcanic eruptions ejected enormous quantities of dust into the stratosphere, and this stratospheric dust can block incoming sunlight and cool the earth. Although none of the estimates of stratospheric dust loads is considered perfect, it is still recognized that 20 to 35 percent of the warming of the past century can be explained by variations in stratospheric dust.

Obviously, the total energy output of the Sun could play a major role in governing the planetary temperature. For many years, some scientists have argued strongly in favor of this mechanism as a primary control of planetary temperature, while others have rejected the idea that small variations in solar output can explain much of the trend of the past century. Recently, two researchers have found that the length of the solar sun spot cycle is related strongly to the fluctuations in temperature on Earth. Although the physical mechanism responsible for the linkage remains elusive, it is noteworthy that 75 percent of the observed global warming in this century can be statistically explained by variations in the length of the solar sun spot cycle.

Heat islands, over grazing, volcanic eruptions, and sun spot's obviously account for some of the warming, if not all of the warming, of the past century. In addition, climatologists fully recognize that the climate system displays a high level of natural variability that could also account for the observed warming. Great uncertainty is remaining in the accuracy and reliability of the instruments used to measure the temperatures of the planet, changes in the station distribution could also be biasing the record, and there is statistical uncertainty in the calculation of the actual trend in temperature over the past century. It is quite possible that none of the warming of the past century is related to the 40 percent increase in equivalent CO_2; oppositely, the natural forces could produce a cooling effect that is being masked by greenhouse response well above the observed 0.46 degrees C.

Uncertainty in the trend of planetary temperature has been compounded by recent satellite measurements of planetary temperature. Within the lower part of the atmosphere, molecular oxygen emits energy in the microwave portion of the electromagnetic spectrum; the amount of energy emitted is directly related to the atmosphere temperature. Polar-orbiting satellites sensing this energy estimate planetary temperature free from many problems inherent in the network of thermometers near the surface. The satellite based temperature record extends from 1979 to the present, and the satellite data show a slight warming of 0.03 degrees C in this period. The near surface air temperature data show warming of 0.20 degrees C for the same period. Due to the relatively short time span, the differences can not be considered statistically significant. Nonetheless, it is certainly noteworthy that the satellite-based temperature data show warming during a time when the equivalent CO_2 levels rose most rapidly.

Even before the geography of the expected and observed temperature trends is discussed, or the timing of the warming is examined, or changes in other variables are brought into the debate, it is clear that the apocalyptic view of the greenhouse effect gets little support from the global temperature record. And we can not forget that there's nothing sacred about a 100 year record. Over much longer time scales, we are fully aware that the Earth has experienced many warmings and many coolings that had nothing to do with human induced changes in greenhouse gases. In fact, the warming of the past century may be far more related to an unusual cool period in the 1880s and 1890s than to any unusual warming in the late 20th century.

The Role of Sulfates

What we are left with in the greenhouse debate is a suite of numerical models all predicting warming with the buildup of greenhouse gases, and a climate record that shows some underlying warming over the past century.

Most climatologists agree that the amount of warming, even if all of it is attributed to the increased concentration of greenhouse gases, is lower than expected given the output of numerical models. It is entirely possible that the models are correct in their predictions for 2 X CO_2 despite the apparent challenge imposed by the climate record.

Simulating climate change for a doubling of CO_2 is, in fact, an extreme hypothetical exercise. We recognize that human activities produce copious amounts of CO_2 and other greenhouse gases that may warm the planetary atmosphere. However, just as greenhouse gases are increasing exponentially . . . global SO_2 emissions are also increasing exponentially. Clean air legislation in the developed world has led to a recent decrease in SO_2 emissions in eastern North America and Western Europe, but the SO_2 emissions in the rest of the world continue to rise rapidly. In addition, natural sources of sulfur materials may be stimulated to emit more sulfur molecules into the atmosphere. Despite our best intentions, atmospheric SO_2 levels continue to increase along with greenhouse gases; the bulk of these SO_2 emissions occurs in the industrialized northern hemisphere.

Just as CO_2 has a net warming effect on the planet, the sulfate particles produced from SO_2 result in a net cooling effect by: reflection of incoming sunlight . . .; brightening clouds by acting as condensation nuclei; and, extending the life-span of existing clouds. To this point in time, the cooling effects of these particles may be equal in magnitude to the warming effects of the greenhouse gases–we may inadvertently have created something of a climate wash-out.

* * *

Conclusions

Understanding the causes of trends and variations in the global temperature record has been a matter of great interest in climatology for several decades. However, the recent attention associated with the greenhouse issue has heightened pressure on climate scientists to generate concrete answers to some difficult and complex questions. Never before has so much interest been generated in studying the global temperature records of the past century.

As we have seen, the best records available show nearly 0.5°C warming since the 1890s. However, to suggest that all of this warming has been caused by the increased concentration of greenhouse gases is foolish. Given the uncertainties in the temperature record, the timing of the observed warming, and the likelihood that many other factors contributed to the rise in temperature, we can hardly argue that the global observational record supports the more extreme, but highly popularized, 2 X CO_2 predictions from the numerical models. Unless some process has been forcing an otherwise natural cooling throughout the past 100 years, analysis of the global temperature record suggest that the numerical models are overestimating the global temperature sensitivity to the buildup of greenhouse gases.

Given the uncertainties in the numerical models of climate, and given their present shortcomings in accurately duplicating the observed temperature patterns over the past century, we should not hurry into corrective policies based on their predictions. Given the large amount of research currently under way, we can assume that our knowledge of greenhouse-related phenomena will increase enormously over the next decade. While others speak loudly of acting now, several scientists showed, using a numerical climate model, that implementing these policies in 10 years makes little difference as to future temperatures. They speak of a window of opportunity to get the science right and then to make policy decisions. We must be very careful not to base potentially expensive, unnecessary and useless policy decisions on the tremendous "hype," hysteria, and emotions that now surrounds the greenhouse issue.

Chapter Thirteen

THE FUTURE OF INTERNATIONAL ENVIRONMENTAL LAW

It is time now to take stock and to reflect upon the long-term future of international environmental law—where it is going, where it will end up over the long haul. Such reflection is necessarily speculative. Predicting the future, particularly the long-term future, is a notoriously inaccurate enterprise. The questions are hard. The variables are many.

By now you should have a good command of the structure of public international law as it applies to global environmental problems. You should be familiar, as well, with at least the major doctrines, principles, and rules involved. Still further, you should be familiar with the international institutions and organizations, both public and private, that are active in the field, and with the procedures or techniques by which governments and citizens go about protecting and attempting to enhance the natural environment. Intergovernmental negotiation is key, of course. You should appreciate that intergovernmental negotiation is central not only to the invention and development of new international environmental law norms, but also to their application or enforcement and even to their termination where called for.

All the international environmental law-making and law-applying to which you have been exposed, however, does not dispel the fact that the international legal system, at least as it relates to the natural environment, contains glaring weaknesses in many respects—the way it is made, the time it takes to make it, the monitoring of state behavior to see that it is observed, the enforcement of its norms when it is not. To these weaknesses must be added the perplexing nature of the global environmental *problématique* itself, dealt with in Chapter 4. How the science and ecology of the various elements of that *problématique* will unfold tomorrow and the day after is something about which there is substantial uncertainty; it contains many imponderables. And so we are presented with a complex matrix of considerations that makes ever more complicated the difficult task of defining not simply where we are but where we ought to be going.

Precisely how our world will evolve normatively, institutionally, and procedurally as it faces up to present and future environmental challenges is beyond the scope of this chapter. Prediction in this exact sense is not this chapter's mission. There are, however, two general predictions we are prepared to make based on present knowledge. They constitute, indeed, the mainsprings of the inspiration that led to the production of this coursebook in the first place.

First is the conclusion that the challenges to the environmental health and well-being of our planet are not only formidable, but likely to grow steadily worse. As the preceding problem chapters have demonstrated, the atmosphere, hydrosphere, lithosphere, and biosphere are all in peril from pollution and other forms of environmental degradation. The pressures of population and the drive for economic growth appear to be producing a situation that requires the imposition of limits. A stable and comfortable future for life on Earth appears, indeed, to depend on it. True, there is no universal agreement on either the scope of the problems or their gravity. But there does appear to be sufficient cause for alarm, raising serious issues of policy for national and international decision-makers, issues that are a long way from being resolved at a satisfactory pace or in a satisfactory manner.

The second conclusion derives from the first and revolves around the capacity of international law itself. Concerted, collective action by the world community is urgently needed on a wide range of fronts, we believe, but we question whether the international legal tools required to meet the challenge are sufficiently at hand. Unpalatable as it may be to many national governments, halting environmental degradation in all its many forms is going to require international regulation and control on a substantial and unprecedented scale. Quite apart from perfecting the regulatory mechanisms we have already at our disposal, there is a huge need to restrengthen old and invent new norms, institutions, and procedures to stop national and provincial governments and their societies, developed and developing alike, from pleasing themselves to the disregard of the global environment and humanity's collective interest in it. But is the world community and its essentially voluntarist legal system up to the task? An affirmative answer to this key question is by no means certain, as Andrew Hurrell and Benedict Kingsbury make painfully clear in *The International Politics of the Environment* 47 (1992):

> Can the existing international system, dominated by sovereign states but powerfully shaped also in relation to environment and development issues by multinational corporations, international institutions, and non-governmental scientific and political groups, respond adequately to the burgeoning environmental challenges? States have achieved the requisite degree of co-operation in relation to some of the less difficult issues, including marine pollution, Antarctica, the protection of the stratospheric ozone layer, and to a lesser extent acid raid and the transboundary movement of hazardous wastes. More complex and difficult problems have at least been accorded recognition on the international agenda, and new forums and institutional responses have begun to appear.

> It would be wrong to assume, however, that the universal rhetoric of ecological interdependence translates readily into effective international action. Even in established environmental regimes, implementation and enforcement lag far behind the achievements of standard-setting. The potentially vast magnitude of the climate change issue, and the fundamental scientific uncertainties about it, render economic and social analysis and political decision-making deeply problematic, and threaten to

exceed the present capacities of the system. The environmental issues whose roots lie in the absence of, or unsustainability of, development in the South and in eastern Europe are even wider in scope, and raise fundamental issues about the distribution of power, wealth, and resources, and about the values which should or will determine that distribution. Even where states are able to reach agreement on general principles in these areas, concrete measures and effective institutional structures may be much more elusive. . . .

Such, in any event, is the environmental challenge facing international law and organization today: how to develop the norms, institutions, and procedures—the organizing elements of any social order—that can ensure ecological balance (and dependent human happiness) for centuries to come.

This central challenge cannot be met, of course, without the help of all the instruments of public policy, most especially, perhaps, the economic instrument. In our search for innovative procedures to assist restrengthened and new norms and institutions, we ask, for example, whether systems of national accounting require revision to account for the use of resources in the production of wealth and whether the exchange of debt for future environmental protection is truly a useful mechanism. Of course, we are conscious that, as lawyers, we may be out of our depths when it comes to understanding and evaluating proposals that are not strictly legal in character. But because of the multi-disciplinary nature of the global environmental challenge, this is an exploration that as lawyers qua policy-planners and decision-makers we nevertheless must undertake. While we recognize that it is in the development of legal norms, institutions, and procedures that generally lawyers can be most effective—and this is where we have placed our emphasis in this final chapter—we also recognize that the legal profession itself must be reoriented and retooled if it is going to make a genuinely progressive environmental difference.

Thus, we may not leave you on an optimistic note. The future may seem more professionally intimidating than inviting, and the skills and labors required to solve the problems outlined in this coursebook certainly rival—possibly even exceed—those of Hercules. But with a combination of analytical creativity, cooperation, and determination we lawyers can be up to the task. Such, in any event, is the demand of the new international environmental order. International law and organization exist within the context of international economics and politics. The challenge is as much economic and political as it is legal. But getting the legal framework in fundamental good order is an essential pre-requisite for success.

In the following two introductory extracts, we invite you to begin thinking about how the international legal system might be put in good order to meet the global environmental challenge successfully. The first extract, by Professor Richard A. Falk, recommends that we see the challenge in macrohistorical perspective, contending that the world community is presently embarked upon a period of major world order transformation, filled with crisis but also with opportunity. The second, by Professor Sir Geoffrey Palmer, assumes this macrohistorical perspective and offers us a lawyer's preliminary glimpse into the kinds of normative, institutional, and procedural adjustments the world community must be prepared to make if in fact it is going to be successful in meeting the global environmental challenge.[a]

RICHARD FALK, REVITALIZING INTERNATIONAL LAW 3, 5–8 (1989).

A major reorganization of international life is taking place at the present time that will produce drastic modifications of the world-order system that has prevailed since the Peace of Westphalia.... [It] seems to be a reversal of the shift completed in the middle of the seventeenth century, by which time medieval Europe had given way to the modern state system. The seventeenth century completed a long process of historical movement from nonterritorial central guidance toward territorial decentralization, whereas the contemporary transition process seems headed back toward nonterritorial central guidance....

* * *

In this spirit of seeking to grasp world-order patterns, and more especially the characteristics of a transition period during which one pattern gives way to another, several main questions help clarify the roles of international law and international lawyers. What can we learn from this prior transition process that culminated in the birth of the state system? What roles were played by international law and lawyers? To what extent is this historical experience transferable to the present transition context? How can international law and international lawyers help assure the emergence of a new poststate system of world order that is relatively more peaceful and just? To what extent does the participation of international lawyers reflect specific national, ideological, cultural, socioeconomic concerns? Is it possible to formulate a position on the means and ends of transition that could serve as the basis for a transnational or global consensus? Could such a consensus provide the normative grounding for a political movement dedicated to global reform?

* * *

The main features of the position here can be set forth in summary form:

1. The state system is being superseded by a series of interlocking social, cultural, economic, political, technological, and ecological tendencies that are likely to eventuate in some form of negative utopia, i.e., in a very undesirable and dangerous structure of overall response (or nonresponse) to the problems posed by the deepening crisis in the state system.

2. Although this disquieting outcome seems probable as of now, it is not inevitable. Positive paths are also available. Premised on an affirmation of the wholeness of the planet and the solidarity of the human species, they could

---

a. The terms "normative" and "institutional" are well known to lawyers. So also is the term "procedural," which to jurists ordinarily signals "[a] set of established forms or methods for conducting the affairs of a business, legislative body, or court of law." THE AMERICAN HERITAGE DICTIONARY OF THE ENGLISH LANGUAGE 1444 (3rd ed. 1992). Here, however, we use the term "procedural" (or "procedure") in a broader sense, to refer to "[a] manner of proceeding; a way of performing or effecting something.... A series of steps taken to accomplish an end...." *Id.* We prefer this more inclusive definition because, while not excluding the particularistic meaning ordinarily given the term by jurists, it is, we believe, more appropriate to the nature of the global environmental *problématique* and to the demands of its challenge.

bring about a rearrangement of power, wealth, and authority more beneficial than anything the world has heretofore known.

3. Initially, the global reform movement needed to promote such a positive outcome has to take principal shape outside of and mainly in opposition to the centers of presently constituted political and economic power: in many societies it will have to be populist and antigovernmental in character and origin. Governments are not necessarily adversaries, and one objective of a popular movement is to encourage the emergence of political leaders more attuned to the need and opportunity for global reform.

4. The principal initial focus of a movement for positive global reform should involve education-for-action; that is, a demonstration that the felt needs and frustrations of people in a variety of concrete social circumstances around the world arise from the inability of states or the existing multinational actors to find short-range, middle-level, and long-range solutions to the distresses and dangers of our world.

5. The case for global reform should be premised on a basic assessment of structural trends and options. It need not rest altogether on the collision course that apocalyptic reformers are conveniently programming to take effect around the year 2000.[1] We should be somewhat suspicious about the recent show of millennial egoism, the idea that either we change by the year 2000 or everything is lost. There is a temptation to deliver an apocalyptic sermon to the wayward citizenry of Nineveh, but such a message would probably be shaped by the characteristic desire of mortals to witness the completion of their own reform projects within the compass of their probable lifetimes. My inclination is to adopt the perspective of that retired French general who wanted to plant in his garden some species of trees he had grown to love during his years as a colonial administrator in an Asian country. When told by his gardener that such trees would not blossom for seventy years, long after his death, the general is supposed to have said, "In that case, don't wait until after lunch to plant them."

The language and sensibility of law tend to be static. New modes of thought, new orientations are needed if law and lawyers are to adopt a dynamic, process-oriented perspective. Such an outlook is obviously essential to the whole idea of a transition process in the course of which the very framework of legal relations would undergo fundamental change. Can we develop an interpretation of that transition process [that] international lawyers can use to analyze the main developments of the international life that call for the application of legal techniques such as negotiation, adjudication, treaty making, and institution building? Without such an interpretation the characteristic problems of the day—whether they be the status of prisoners of war, claims to impose or disrupt an oil embargo, the status of military reprisals, or satellite surveillance—are fed back into an obsolete framework of interstate relations where the irrelevant cynicism of the Machiavellians jousts with the irrelevant moralism and legalism of outmanned idealists. We do not need judgments of approval nearly as much as we need a set of values that can inform a strategy of change. What was "realism" a generation ago when

1. *See, e.g.,* BARRY COMMONER, THE CLOSING   BOMB (1975).
CIRCLE (1971); PAUL EHRLICH, THE POPULATION

the state system was able to deal adequately with the main problems of the day becomes "crackpot realism" in the current world setting. Regardless of our normative outlook, we require a new framework to comprehend the dynamics of global transformation.

Discussion Notes/Questions

1. If national sovereignty is the great obstacle to progress, how can its consequences be ameliorated or avoided? Is it realistic to think that sovereignty will simply fade away in time as increasing numbers of international conventions are negotiated to deal with the global environmental problems?

2. If Professor Falk is right in his analysis of the need to reform public international law in general, what implications does it have for international environmental law? To what extent are the environmental issues separate and discrete from the general issues of public international law? To what extent are they the same?

3. Should a movement for global reform encompass all of international law or merely concentrate upon the environment? Are the legal techniques outlined by Professor Falk—negotiation, adjudication, treaty-making, and institution-building—just as applicable to international environmental law as they are to public international law generally?

4. Is it likely that the world can overcome the divisions of national identity, territorial sovereignty, ideological beliefs and cultural diversity to forge a common international approach? If so, how? If not, why not?

Geoffrey Palmer, *New Ways to Make International Environmental Law* 86 Am. J. Int'l L. 259, 260– 64 (1992).

The proposition that the world faces serious global environmental problems hardly needs demonstration or rehearsal. It was the reason that led to the establishment of the [1992] United Nations Conference on Environment and Development [UNCED] to begin with. Ozone depletion, climate change and biodiversity are the issues that have the most public prominence, but there are many others. They include the quality and supply of fresh water; protection of the oceans; deforestation, desertification, and drought; the management of biotechnology; the management of wastes, including toxic chemicals and other hazardous wastes; urban slums; and poor human health conditions. In recent times, the issues have been couched in security terms. Security of adequate food supplies is an obvious one, but the issues of energy can be dealt with from the same angle. As Peter Sand has recently put it,

> if global environmental security is taken to mean security against those risks that threaten our common survival, the focus of collective legal action may indeed be sharpened considerably. A tentative priority list of 'genuine survival risks would thus, as a minimum, have to include the following essential concerns:
>
> —climatic security
>
> —biological security
>
> —chemical security.[2]

A myriad of other issues concern the health of our planet and the capacity to sustain life upon it. The whole question was summed up by the World Commission on Environment and Development as one of sustainable development.[3] To produce the conditions necessary for sustainable development, a great deal more in the way of regulation and prohibition will be required at the international level than we have been prepared to tolerate up to now. In this respect, both developed and developing countries have an interest in resisting change—their freedom of action as nations is likely to be reduced and they know it—hence the lack of enthusiasm for new institutions and methods of international lawmaking.

In truth, the United Nations lacks any coherent institutional mechanism for dealing effectively with environmental issues. Strengthening its capacity and structure should be high on the list of priorities for the 1992 Conference on Environment and Development. The [UN] Charter itself **[Basic Document 1.3]** provides no environmental organ, an omission that would most certainly be rectified if it were being drafted today. In no respect is the Charter more a product of its times than in its disregard of the environment. Aside from a reference to "good neighbourliness," it contains nothing. At present, environmental responsibilities are divided among a number of the specialized agencies, including the Food and Agriculture Organization [FAO], the World Health Organization [WHO], the World Meteorological Organization [WMO], the International Maritime Organization [IMO], the UN Educational, Scientific and Cultural Organization [UNESCO] and the UN Development Programme [UNDP], with a coordinating and catalytic role assigned to the UN Environment Programme (UNEP). UNEP itself is a creature of a mere General Assembly resolution.[4] The Economic and Social Council [ECOSOC] has the task of coordinating all of these diffuse efforts and it is fair to say that the task has not been accomplished.

UNEP was established to act as a focal point for environmental action and coordination within the United Nations. It lacks any formal powers. Under its Executive Director, Dr. Mostafa Tolba, it points out environmental problems to nations and suggests solutions. In fact, it does much more than its limited powers suggest. It has become an agency that sets out to produce concrete results in terms of treaties negotiated. In my opinion, without UNEP, the system to prevent ozone depletion now in place would not have been developed.

UNEP can push states, probe their policies and plead with them; it cannot coerce them. UNEP lacks teeth. It has no executive authority. Partly for this reason, UNEP has made generous use of "soft law" instruments in the international consensus building that it engages in. All UNEP programs are financed by direct, voluntary contributions from member states. It has a Governing Council composed of representatives of fifty-eight member states.

---

2. Peter Sand, International Law on the Agenda of the United Nations Conference on Environment and Development 15 (on file, Victoria University of Wellington). The paper is based on a background report prepared for the Aspen Institute International Environmental Policy Meeting, July 1991.

3. WORLD COMMISSION ON ENVIRONMENT AND DEVELOPMENT, OUR COMMON FUTURE 320 (1987).

4. Institutional and Financial Arrangements for International Environmental Co-operation **[Basic Document 1.13]**.

UNEP has access to excellent scientific advice not filtered through nation-states. Given the nature of UNEP's constitution, its achievements are substantial, but it is not an adequate international organization for protecting the world's environment.

Various suggestions have been made to strengthen UNEP. The most important were the recommendations of the World Commission on Environment and Development in 1987. The commission recommended a major reorientation and refocusing of programs and budgets on sustainable development among all UN organizations. The commission saw UNEP as the principal source of environmental data, assessment and reporting and as an advocate of change and cooperation. It was to be the lead UN agency in restoring, protecting and improving the ecological basis for sustainable development. Its catalytic role was to be extended.

Recent attempts to improve the coordination of international environmental protection include the System–Wide Medium–Term Environment Programme, an effort to address all the activities in a single document and to provide a framework and strategy.[5] The Committee of International Development Institutions on the Environment, although not part of the UN system, offers some opportunities for integrating environmental issues into the plans of financial and developmental organizations.[6] Regional coordination mechanisms do exist and have been effective; but, by definition, these cannot take a global approach. In particular, one finds yawning gaps in the organizational framework for carrying out effective monitoring and assessment regarding such concerns as climate change, ozone layer depletion, water quality, living marine resources, sustainable development in some areas and biodiversity.

Many of these problems are widely recognized, but the logical inference from the facts seems politically unpalatable; the only way to cure the problem is to create a proper international environmental agency within the United Nations system that has real power and authority. At the same time, other environmental components within the UN system should be restructured and reorganized. That restructuring needs to be rigorous if resources are to be saved and priorities redirected. With determination the task could be achieved without spending more resources in total than are expended now. They should be regrouped and reorganized.

If we consider the new instruments that have developed in the international law for the environment in the last twenty years, we would be pardoned for thinking that the record is a good one. It is certainly substantial. The proliferation of international agreements has been enormous. There are more than a hundred multilateral instruments in force, many of which were negotiated since the Stockholm Declaration **[Basic Document 1.12]**. The UNEP register listed 152 as of May 1991.[7] In the years since the Stockholm Declaration, there have been some prodigious achievements in the negotiation of conventions dealing with global environmental problems. The United Nations Convention on the Law of the Sea **[Basic Document 4.20]** is an obvious example, although perhaps less successful than the Regional Seas

5. G.A. Res. 32/197, 32 U.N. GAOR Supp. (No. 45) at 121, U.N. Doc. A/32/45 (1977).

6. *See* CIDIE Secretariat, Action and Inter-action: The Role and Potential of CIDIE (1988).

7. Register of International Treaties and other Agreements on the Environment, U.N. Doc. UNEP/GC.16/Inf.4 (1991).

Programme, which was less ambitious.[8] The many famous victories include instruments on long-range transboundary air pollution,[9] notification and assistance regarding nuclear accidents,[10] endangered species,[11] and the movement and disposal of hazardous waste.[12] The Vienna Convention for the Protection of the Ozone Layer **[Basic Document 3.14]** and its progeny amount to perhaps the most substantial achievement of all.

Many of these instruments were stimulated by the activities of UNEP, which has launched various initiatives to develop new policies: action plans, a multitude of soft law instruments and framework conventions. UNEP's Montevideo plan set out a comprehensive program for the progressive development of international environmental law that . . . is in the course of being revised for the next ten years.[13]

While the number of instruments is impressive, and some of them will have slowed down degradation, it cannot be assumed that they have led to an improvement in the overall situation. A strong argument can be made that, during the time these instruments were being developed, the environmental situation in the world became worse and is deteriorating further. There is no effective legal framework to help halt the degradation. Furthermore, many international agreements do not necessarily mean many ratifications. Frequently, there appears to be a long lag in securing widespread ratification because of insufficient incentives for nations to sign up. Many other nations simply seem not to address the issues, not regarding them as of sufficient priority compared to domestic concerns. Nor is there any institutional mechanism to provide nations with incentives to comply when they have ratified. Moreover, ratification itself says nothing about whether the agreed standards are being observed. In many instances monitoring is difficult; in some instances it is simply not being done. Sometimes the instruments themselves provide for proper assessment; the Montreal Protocol **[Basic Document 3.18]** is the best example. But every time a new instrument is negotiated, fresh machinery has to be devised.

The making and negotiation of the instruments themselves has to start anew each time. No organization commands clear power to coordinate international environmental negotiations. Each negotiation proceeds differently. The ozone negotiations were conducted in a different way and serviced by a different organization from those on climate change. Such an approach carries the grave risk that on each occasion the wheel must be reinvented. Common elements are not necessarily treated the same way.

8. For details of the Regional Seas Programme, *see* PETER SAND, MARINE ENVIRONMENT LAW (1988). *See also* [the 1976] Barcelona Convention for the Protection of the Mediterranean Sea against Pollution **[Basic Document 4.15].**

9. Convention on Long–Range Transboundary Air Pollution, Nov. 13, 1979 **[Basic Document 3.8].**

10. Convention on Early Notification of a Nuclear Accident, Sept. 26, 1986 **[Basic Document 3.16];** Convention on Assistance in Case of a Nuclear Accident or Radiological Emergency, Sept. 26, 1986 **[Basic Document 3.17].**

11. Convention on International Trade in Endangered Species of Wild Fauna and Flora, Mar. 6, 1973 **[Basic Document 6.5].**

12. Convention on the Control of Transboundary Movements of Hazardous Wastes and Their Disposal, with Annexes, Mar. 22, 1989 **[Basic Document 5.6].**

13. UNEP, Montevideo Programme for the Development and Periodic Review of Environmental Law, ad hoc meeting of senior government officials expert in environmental law (Nov. 6, 1981); UNEP Governing Council Decision 10/21 (May 31, 1982).

There is no institutional machinery to evaluate gaps that may be found in the international framework of agreements or to develop means of assigning priorities among competing claims for attention. Nor is there any way of ensuring that environmental issues are effectively coordinated with and integrated into other activities that may be progressing at the international level. Scientific data and input, which are critical on the global issues, need to be assembled and tested before the political decisions are taken. Yet on each occasion the data are assembled in a different fashion. Institutional means need to be devised to channel scientific and technical expertise to the appropriate policy needs.

If an institutional home for the conduct of the negotiations themselves could be devised, it would cut the substantial costs of dealing with the global issues. Instead of having a new group of nations assemble to discuss each problem by holding a series of international meetings at different locations around the world in an effort to hammer out a consensus on the provisions of a multilateral convention, there could easily be a uniform method for bringing the nations together, conveying the relevant scientific information to them and conducting the negotiations. Such procedures offer the possibility of appreciably reducing the cost of all the present diplomatic activity, as well as increasing the coherence of the rules.

One of the biggest obstacles that must be overcome in international negotiations is the rule of unanimous consent. This rule impels each negotiating body to search for the lowest common denominator; it adds to the difficulty of negotiations because sometimes a single nation can resist the development of a common position and demand concessions as the price of securing unanimous consent. While it is doubtful that the rule of unanimous consent can be banished from international global negotiations, the introduction of new institutional mechanisms may provide ways around it, which would speed up the process and result in instruments of greater potency.

What is missing from the present institutional arrangements is the equivalent of a legislature; some structured and coherent mechanism for making the rules of international law. For such a institution to succeed, it must have access to high-quality streams of advice. An effective way of ensuring the availability of appropriate scientific information is essential. To maintain the authority of the rules that are made, international efforts must be devoted to effective monitoring, assessment and enforcement.

In sum, the methods and techniques now available to fashion new instruments of international law to cope with global environmental problems cannot meet that challenge. The emerging issues are so big and so all-embracing that current ways of doing things will not solve these problems. The institutional mechanisms within the United Nations system are not capable of handling the issues. The time has come for "something more innovative, for a conceptual leap forward in institutional terms."[14]

Discussion Notes/Questions

1. What normative, institutional, and procedural solutions would you suggest for dealing with the global environment? Of these, is it norms or institutions or procedures that are the most important?

14. General Debate Statement of New Zealand Government, U.N. Doc. A/44/PV.15, at 61, 76 (1989 Rt. Hon. Geoffrey Palmer).

2.   Is reasonable to expect the United Nations system to be at the forefront of addressing global environmental problems? Is it necessary and, if so, desirable or practicable to amend the U.N. Charter to provide responsibility for the environment? If so what changes would you suggest? If not, why not?

3.   Should the United Nations Environment Programme (UNEP) be expanded, restructured, and given overall responsibility within the United Nations system for environmental issues? How has the Commission for Sustainable Development changed the institutional landscape?

4.   Can the techniques of environmental diplomacy be altered to provide less cumbersome methods of negotiating international environmental conventions? If so, how? If not, why not?

5.   What are the limitations of an institutional approach? Is it realistic to think that a redistribution of the wealth will take place between nations? Can environmental progress be made without it?

6.   How does Palmer answer the above questions? What, if anything, is wrong with his diagnosis of the problem?

We turn now to a consideration of the principal normative, institutional, and procedural policy options known to be actually or potentially available in response to the global environmental challenge. We proceed from a self-consciously evaluative perspective. Consider carefully the questions following these readings.

A.   NORMATIVE OPTIONS

In an omitted portion of the above extract by Richard Falk, the author observes that "a new framework to comprehend the dynamics of global transformation" should help to mobilize a normative consensus that challenges the prevailing ethical currents of neo-Darwinian sentiment and policy. Richard Falk, *Revitalizing International Law* 8 (1989). Falk continues (on the same page):

> Presently, the process of transition is dominated by those who believe that the privilege of the few in the face of the misery of the many is either inevitable or actually beneficial, providing a necessary foundation for human excellence and accomplishment. The central feature of the normative challenge that I would propose as a counter rests upon an acceptance of human solidarity and all its implications, especially a shared responsibility to seek equity and dignity for every person on the planet without regard to matters of national identity, territorial boundary, or ideological affiliation.

The following extracts, specifically addressed to the global environmental challenge, manifestly accept this normative perspective.

**Alexandre Timoshenko, *Ecological Security: Global
Change Paradigm* 1 Colo. J. Int'l Envtl. L. &
Pol'y 127, 135–43 (Summer 1990).**

International policy based on the concept of ecological security requires long-term stability of interstate relations and unified behavior of states in the environmental sphere. International legal instruments serve to achieve these requirements by furthering the elaboration and adoption of legally binding principles and norms of state behavior. The practice of socialist countries illustrates the important role of these instruments. For example, a Declaration of Warsaw Treaty member states titled "The Arms Race Consequences for the Environment and Other Aspects of Ecological Security" states that "international ecological security demands adoption of obligatory principles and norms of state behavior."[15] It is possible that the future system of ecological security can be based on existing achievements of international environmental law. The process of norm-creating and codification in the field of international environmental law, however, should be considerably reinforced. It is thus necessary to formulate a set of fundamental principles containing basic obligations of states in the area of environmental protection.

Ecological security principles must reflect the basic features common to any security system. The most elaborate security system is military security—a system with a number of theoretical models. These models can be found in existing arms limitation treaties and in draft agreements. The creative use of a military security model is suggested because this model has reached a sophisticated level of development and because military security and ecological security have common aims—the protection of human civilization from the threat of self-destruction and the development of conditions for its survival.

With these preliminary notes in mind, the eleven ecological security principles are outlined with a discussion of their potential for resolving the global warming problem.

1. Right to a Favorable Environment. A workable theory of ecological security is not confined to state activity; it begins with the interests and participation of individuals. This is recognized in the principle of a right to a favorable environment. The right to a favorable environment is a combination of both environmental law and the rights inherent in the ecological security concept. Traces of this principle are found in the 1972 Stockholm Declaration **[Basic Document 1.12]**. This principle is the key element in the ecological security system. It should be considered an inalienable component of human rights and freedoms and be included in any future declaration of peoples' rights. To benefit from the right, however, individuals must recognize the corresponding obligation to observe requirements of the ecological imperative.

2. Equality. The principle of equality in ecological security is genetically linked with the fundamental international principle of sovereign equality that establishes equality of rights and obligations of states. Since all states have an equal right to ecological well-being, the principle of equal ecological security bars the achievement of ecological well-being by one state or group of states, to the detriment of the lawful rights and interests of other states. Clearly, unilateral efforts by states directed to bettering their national environment that do not have negative transboundary impacts do not infringe upon this principle. Existing practice shows, however, that unilateral efforts do not result in substantial improvement of the environment on a global scale.

The principle of ecological equality also prohibits the transfer of pollutants between states. Likewise, the building of ecologically harmful industries and the dumping of toxic wastes in other states cannot be tolerated under the ecological security regime nor can the rapacious exploitation of the natural

15. PRAVDA, July 17, 1988 (in Russian).

resources of other countries. An extraordinary example of this prohibition was experienced by the Mobro garbage barge that traveled for 162 days and 6000 miles looking for a place to dump its 3100 tons of garbage, believed to contain hazardous materials. It was rejected by three developing countries and several states in the United States before returning full circle to New York.[16]

* * *

3. Prohibition of Ecological Aggression. The principle of prohibition of ecological aggression is derived in substantial part from the 1977 Convention on the Prohibition of Military or Other Hostile Use of Environmental Modification Techniques **[Basic Document 7.30].** The principle is evidenced by the UN General Assembly resolution "On the Historic Responsibility of States for the Protection of Nature of the Earth for the Benefit of Present and Future Generations" **[Basic Document 1.19]** that declares illegal military activities that cause serious harm to the environment. Under Soviet [now Russian] legal doctrine the deliberate and hostile modification of the environment— ecocide—is unlawful and considered an international crime. The principle was endorsed when previous acts of ecocide in Vietnam and other Indochinese countries were condemned by world public opinion. Moreover, the International Law Commission in its Draft Articles on State Responsibility **[Basic Document 1.10],** Article 19, considers mass pollution of the biosphere to be an international crime.[b]

* * *

Despite this consensus on the need for the principle of prohibition of ecological aggression, the principle needs to be clarified and more fully developed. The definition of aggression adopted by the UN General Assembly in 1974 [13 I.L.M. 710 (1974)] must be amended. In particular, we must develop a better sense of what qualifies as ecological aggression and determine the juridical consequences for violating the principle.

4. Enforcement and Monitoring. Enforcement measures, such as monitoring state compliance with treaty provisions, are fundamental to ecological security. Only a developed system of national and international control procedures can guarantee state observance. Such control procedures include international requests that a state comply with the obligations after a violation has been observed, on-site inspections and investigations, consultations, creation of permanent international control institutions, and the participation of competent international organizations.

* * *

5. Information Exchange. The principle of enforcement is closely linked with the principle of regular exchange of information on ecological situations at national, regional, and international levels. Information exchange helps to ensure that ecological security is observed.

---

16. *The End Begins for Trash No One Wanted,* N.Y. Times, Sept. 2, 1987, at B1, col. 4 (late ed). When the trash was finally incinerated in New York officials discovered that the garbage contained no hazardous waste.

b. For pertinent commentary, see the extracts by Spinedi and Abi Saab in Chapter 5(D)(1) ("The Teachings of Publicists—Harmful Acts: Forms and Implications"), at p. 362-63, *supra.*

The implementation of this principle requires legally binding international arrangements on the frequency, quantity, mechanisms, and channels of information exchange. In addition, data must be compiled under a uniform method so that it can be easily interpreted by receiving states. Information on the latest scientific research and monitoring data, alternative techniques, and means of controlling pollutants must be exchanged so that all states can participate to their fullest capacity in controlling global warming.

6. *Scientific and Technological Cooperation.* Practical implementation of ecological security must include the principle of scientific and technological cooperation. The disparities in economic and technological development among countries are well established. A successful global ecological security regime must take advantage of the latest achievements in the fields of ecologically safe technologies, environmental control, monitoring, and low-waste and resource-saving technologies. Scientific and technical contributions from all members of the international community should be encouraged to ensure a concerted development of ecologically expedient technologies. Developments in science and technology must be widely accessible. Access, however, can come only after substantial changes are made in the system of international technical assistance. Developing countries are critical to the ecological security system primarily because they are the largest source of natural resources and other environmental values. Moreover, from the time of the Stockholm Conference developing countries have recognized that international environmental protection is inseparably linked with the interests of socioeconomic and scientific-technological development.

* * *

7. *Prevention of Transboundary Environmental Harm.* Foreseeing and preventing anthropogenic climatic changes are among the most important and urgent tasks put before the international community. The principle of prevention is evidence of the change in conceptual orientations. Prior to its development, international environmental regulation was primarily based on the "react-and-correct" model. Environmental degradation occurred first, then steps were taken to remedy the harm. The weakness of this model is that it does not allow for adequate evaluation, compensation, or restoration of environmental damage.

The principle of prevention of transboundary environmental harm follows the "foresee-and-prevent" model. Under this model steps are taken to prevent environmental deterioration before it ever occurs. The prevention principle has been suggested in a number of international documents. The Helsinki Final Act [14 I.L.M. 1292 (1975)] states that "damage to the environment is best avoided by preventive measures." The 1982 Nairobi Declaration has a special chapter dedicated to prevention of ecological harm. It provides that "prevention of damage to the environment is preferable to the burdensome and expensive repair of damage already done."[17] The modern conception of environmental protection both on a national and an international level should

---

17. Declarations on the World Environment, U.N. Doc. EP/GC.10/2 (1982). The Nairobi Declaration was adopted by 105 governments at the UNEP Governing Council Special Session, commemorating the tenth anniversary of the 1972 Stockholm Conference on the Human Environment.

thus focus on expedient preventive measures as opposed to post hoc alternatives.

The principle of prevention is an aggregate of several requirements of international environmental behavior, including use of environmental impact assessments (EIAs); notification of activities that can cause substantial transboundary environmental harm; dissemination and availability of relevant information on such activities; and international consultation on activities with actual or potential harmful transboundary consequences. EIAs are the most important element of the prevention principle. They are based on existing national practice and positive international law, and exemplify the "foresee" element of the "foresee-and-prevent" model. The governing bodies of the UNEP and the ECE [Economic Commission for Europe] have both commissioned special expert groups to elaborate on the elements of an international impact assessment mechanism. Senior advisors to the ECE governments on environmental and water problems have recommended the drafting of a European convention on this matter. A UNEP special expert group has also been researching uniform international procedures for EIA's. These procedures are aimed at the assessment of both short-and long-term ecological consequences. Impacts on all categories of natural objects both within and outside national jurisdictions should be assessed.

8.   Cooperation in Emergency Ecological Situations. Many experts agree that the number of industrial accidents resulting in serious ecological harm has grown. Natural catastrophes causing destruction of industrial and energy plants, which would result in considerable environmental damage, are an ever-present possibility. Not surprisingly, some scientists claim that the destructive potential of serious industrial catastrophes is comparable to that of military threats. The ecological security system must include the principle of cooperation in emergency ecological situations. The tragic experience at Chernobyl is an example of the need for a well-developed, legally binding mechanism of interstate cooperation in emergency ecological situations.[c] The consequences of Chernobyl could have been minimized had there existed relevant mechanisms of international cooperation such as early warning notification, exchange of information, and international assistance. Traces of the need for cooperation in emergency ecological situations can be found in provisions of the United Nations Convention on the Law of the Sea [**Basic Document 4.20**], space law,[18] and the latest conventions adopted under the aegis of the International Atomic Energy Agency (IAEA).[19]

Recent UNEP initiatives suggest ways to implement the principle of cooperation in ecological emergencies. After a number of chemical industry catastrophes with serious environmental harm received international attention, UNEP submitted a proposal to governments to draft and adopt two international conventions. The purpose of the conventions is to create a mechanism of international cooperation in case of serious chemical catastrophes. One convention would create an international legal mechanism of

c.   For pertinent discussion, see *supra* Problem 7–3 ("The Atomic Steel Mill") in Chapter 7.

18.   *See, e.g.,* Treaty on Principles Governing the Activities of States in the Exploration and Use of Outer Space, Including the Moon and Other Celestial Bodies [**Basic Document 3.3**].

19.   *See e.g.,* IAEA Convention on Assistance in the Case of a Nuclear Accident or Radiological Emergency [**Basic Document 3.17**].

urgent assistance from the world community; the other would impose an obligation to notify concerned countries of chemical catastrophes with transboundary consequences. The notice would include the type of chemical pollution, possible consequences, countermeasures already taken or planned, and the source of pollution.

* * *

9. *Peaceful Settlement of International Disputes.* Article 33 of the UN Charter **[Basic Document 1.3]** establishes the principle of peaceful settlement of international disputes. Today many disputes arise out of consequences suffered as a result of transboundary environmental damage caused by another state or states. Experts from UNEP consider these transboundary consequences to be a potential impetus for military retaliation. The ecological degradation resulting from these transboundary disputes is worsening and the number of disputes is expected to increase. Therefore, special dispute settlement instruments should be created and based on general provisions contained in the UN Charter. One possible measure to this end is the creation of a special permanent chamber of the International Court of Justice (ICJ) to deal with environmental matters.[d] Establishing an independent judicial body analogous to the judicial mechanism provided by the 1982 UN Convention on the Law of the Sea is another possibility.

10. *International Responsibility for Environmental Harm.* The principle of international responsibility for environmental harm was strongly recommended in Principle 22 of the 1972 Stockholm [Declaration] **[Basic Document 1.12]**: "States shall cooperate to develop further the international law regarding liability and compensation for the victims of pollution and other environmental damage caused by activities within the jurisdiction or control of such States to areas beyond their jurisdiction."

Despite this recognition of responsibility for environmental harm, cooperation of states in developing this area of international law has been minimal; it can therefore not be implemented without a detailed body of secondary norms. The International Law Commission in Article 19 of its Draft Articles on liability for damage arising from lawful acts **[Basic Document 1.9]** mentions international responsibility for environmental harm only once in the context of discussing international crimes. UNEP also addressed the issue of developing the institution of ecological responsibility in 1976 and 1977 but failed to work out a substantial recommendation. The Organization for Economic Co-operation and Development (OECD) has engaged in similar discussions on the notion of state obligation in the environmental field.

Treaty practice is an unlikely vehicle by which to establish an institution of ecological responsibility. The overwhelming majority of environmental treaties do not contain provisions regulating responsibility. In the rare treaties that do mention ecological responsibility, the relevant provisions contain only general language usually referring to future agreements on responsibility procedures. For example, Article 13 of the 1976 Barcelona Convention for the Protection of the Mediterranean Sea against Pollution **[Basic Document 4.15]** is titled "Liability and Compensation." Despite this title it mentions only a general obligation of the parties "to cooperate in formulation and

---

d. This measure has in fact been effected. *See supra* ch. 3, at note 183.

adoption of appropriate procedures for the determination of liability and compensation for damage resulting from the pollution of marine environment deriving from violations of the provisions of this Convention and applicable Protocols." Provisions of similar generality are found in the 1974 Helsinki Convention on the Protection of the Baltic Sea [**Basic Document 4.13**].

A precise and juridically explicit formulation of the principle of ecological responsibility is important for two reasons: (1) It would provide a stimulus for the elaboration of a relevant institution of international environmental law; and (2) it would reinforce the prevention mechanism by determining the illegality of substantial transboundary environmental harm and by providing appropriate sanctions. At a minimum, judicial standards should require the termination of harmful activity and compensation for damage.

11. Sustainable Development. Adherence to, and implementation of, the concept of sustainable development must also be included in the ecological security framework. Both sustainable development and ecological security have ecologically safe development as their nucleus. Sustainable development is an offshoot of the eco-developmental doctrine that calls for sound ecological, economical and social development. Eco-development is primarily concerned with fulfilling the basic human needs—food, water, and shelter—of populations in developing countries. The scope of sustainable development is broader as it seeks to meet the interests of all states. The concept requires states to conserve those ecosystems and ecological processes that are critical to the normal functioning of the biosphere. States must also conserve biological diversity and observe standards of optimal sustainability while using biological resources and living ecosystems.

A major premise of sustainable development is that prevention of environmental harm is economically more advantageous than is a post hoc attempt at corrective measures. Before sustainable development can be implemented, multiple programs and organizational structures must be supported by relevant legal instruments. . . .

Discussion Notes/Questions

1. Do we need a comprehensive single code of international environmental law? Is such an approach either practicable or desirable?

2. What criticisms can be made of the eleven ecological security principles isolated in the extract? Together do they add up to an integrated intellectual conception?

3. Are the principles of ecological security compatible with one another? To what extent do contradictions reside among them?

4. If those principles were all adopted and followed, would they be sufficient to protect the global environment? What gaps would exist?

5. Is the author's final assertion correct that no progress is possible without a sound legal basis?

————

William M. Lafferty, *The Politics of Sustainable Development: Global Norms for National Implementation* **5** ENVTL. POL. **185, 185–94 (1996).**

The notion of "sustainable development" has in recent years achieved a popularity approaching that of "democracy". Just as every country and ideology after the Second World War wished to profile itself as "democratic", we find the same trend today with respect to "sustainable development". The underlying idea of sustainability is, of course, much older than the 1987 report from the Brundtland Commission. It is, however, only since the publication of *Our Common Future* that sustainability, coupled to the notion of "development", has become a rhetorical talisman for our common present. Pity the politician, the party programme, the long-term plan or the international agreement that does *not* pay respect to the idea. The prospect of a non-sustainable society is on a par with that of a non-democratic society. It is simply not on.

Yet there is a tremendous diversity of definitions and interpretations. Competing understandings of "sustainable development" are surely as numerous as competing understandings of "democracy". The idea has evolved into an "essentially contested concept", an idea characterised by different types of "vagueness" over which we pursue endless semantic debates. For many, this points towards a relatively simple solution: avoidance. Unclear concepts lead to unclear communication, and unclear communication is the source of both nonsense and trouble. Any idea that attempts to attach relatively simple normative connotations to the complex notion of "development" as applied to widely diverse global settings and populations, deserves to be scrapped.

There is, of course, much to be said for this position, particularly from a scientific and analytic point of view. The matter can, however, be viewed in another light. As conceived here, the most significant potential of the concept lies in neither science nor academic analysis but in politics. The promulgation of the idea by politicians and bureaucrats is in inverse proportion to its rejection by critical social scientists. The more the politicians use it—the less the intellectuals like it. There is surely an interesting problematic here for political psychologists, but this is less important in the present context than the problem of implementation. Denying the usefulness of "sustainable development" as an analytic concept, or the attractiveness of it as a normative concept, does nothing to affect either its popularity or import as a political concept.

* * *

As I see it, there are a number of very good reasons for taking the politics of sustainable development seriously, regardless of how individual politicians and bureaucrats may use or abuse the idea. The structure of the argument is as follows:

(1) the concept of sustainable development, as originally expressed in *Our Common Future,* is both more coherent and potentially more radical than both its political adherents and critics seem to be aware of;

(2) the concept can be viewed as expressing essential normative standards for a global ethics of environment-and-development. As such, it fulfils two important criteria for ethical legitimacy—consensualism and realism;

(3) the more general normative standards of the concept have been translated into relatively specific and wide-ranging operational goals;

(4) there exist political fora, institutions and procedures for realising these goals;

(5) these political mechanisms are imperfect and incremental, but there is, at present, no more effective way to seek progress with respect to global environment-development problems.

* * *

Sustainable development is a normative concept used to prescribe and evaluate changes in living conditions. Such changes are to be guided by four principles:

(1) They aim to satisfy basic human needs and reasonable standards of welfare for all living beings (Development I);

(2) They aim to achieve more equitable standards of living both within and among global populations (Development II);

(3) They should be pursued with great caution as to their actual or potential disruption of biodiversity and the regenerative capacity of nature, both locally and globally (Sustainability I);

(4) They should be achieved without undermining the possibility for future generations to attain similar standards of living and similar or improved standards of equity (Sustainability II).

* * *

Sustainable Development as a Global Ethic

Given the prospect that the above definition expresses a reasonable summary of what *Our Common Future* intended, why and how can we understand the position as a global ethic? What force does it have as moral prescription, and why should we endorse it as a potentially effective norm-set for positive environment-and-development change?

There are, of course, numerous views as to the nature of ethics. Moral statements aim to convince us of good and bad behaviour, but they do so in different ways, with different arguments as to the legitimacy of their claims. For present purposes, we can be extremely simplistic by identifying two major modes for achieving ethical legitimacy and compliance: "realism" and "consensualism". The choice of these two orientations is conditioned by two vital premises as to how change should be accomplished. The first is that compliance should be achieved through rational argument directly related to the problematic, and the second is that any sanctions involved must derive from reasonable democratic procedures.

The realist mode argues for compliance on the basis of presumed ontological truth. What is right or wrong is derivable from a correct understanding of the phenomena relevant to the problematic. The oldest and most resilient form of this mode of ethics is the morality of natural law. Once we have understood the innate workings of the real world (as discoverable by science), we will then know how to act with respect to that world. Goodness attaches to the natural, badness to the unnatural. Both positivist and phenomenological approaches to the real world support ethics in this mode.

The consensual mode seeks moral validity through collective agreement. Theories of the real world are too indecisive and contingent to provide adequate ethical foundations. The debate as to correct epistemology leads to the deconstruction of scientific method as a decisive criterion for truth. Morality as a guide for action can only be secured through critical dialogue and consensual acknowledgment. The greater the degree of consensus as to right or wrong, the greater the force of moral prescription, and the greater the chances of moral compliance.

As outlined above, the concept of sustainable development can be shown to derive force from both of these modes of ethical legitimacy. With respect to the aspect of "physical sustainability", the norm-set is validated by the enormous weight of scientific evidence and argument as to the degenerative effects on the environment from human intervention. It is clearly no accident that several of the more decisive texts and many of the most prominent activists of the early environmental movement came from the natural sciences. Natural science arguments, supported by natural science data, have been at the core of demands for global environmental change from the start. They have provided these demands with a legitimacy and force that modern humanism lacked in its attempt to reverse the negative effects of industrialism. It is an interesting commentary on the foibles of ideological development and change, that modem environmentalism should anchor its moral appeal in positivist science at a point in history when the critical-scientific basis of Marxism was being definitively undermined. Where indeed would the argument for environmentalism-as-progress be if it were not for the natural scientists—a point which the Brundtland report makes explicit in its admonition for more direct links between the scientific community and NGOs.

In addition to its realist appeal, however, the demand for sustainable development, in both its physical and equity aspects, derives clear moral support from its widespread endorsement as a consensual norm. Regardless of which school of ethics one adheres to, there can be no doubt that if the goal is mobilisation for change within the realm of democratic procedures and institutions, the stronger the potential for consensus the better. And whereas philosophers of consensual ethics promote the correctness of their position in terms of abstract consensus, the concept of sustainable development has been the subject of very real and widespread agreement. We need only mention the Rio Declaration, *Agenda 21,* the Maastricht Treaty, and the numerous other conventions and action programmes within both the United Nations and the European Union, to illustrate the point. When, previously, has such a clearly prescriptive idea received such diverse and comprehensive voluntary support? Regardless of differences of interpretation, and making no presumptions as to sincerity of commitment, the world-wide acknowledgment of the principle of sustainable development gives credence to the claim of a global ethic. A foundation has been laid which ideological purists may reject, and cynical politicians exploit, but which normative pragmatists can and should work with.

Admittedly, the entire complex of values, declarations, conventions and institutions may reflect no more than rhetorical inflation and political expediency. The "consensus", it could be argued, is a consensus in word only. The understandings of the more than 170 governments assembled in Rio as to what sustainable development *actually* implies vary so much as to belie the image of a coordinated commitment. A political compromise does not constitute either a common goal or a consensual plan of action.

No one would want to deny the potential validity of such a perspective. Yet the import of the critique is neither new nor decisive. Democratic majorities are always subject to interpretation and second-guessing. In the present case, however, we are not dealing with a simple majority, but with global unanimity. Furthermore, we are not dealing with highly vague, rambling and usually neglected party-political platforms, but with specific documents which, in most cases, have been meticulously negotiated over many years. If we are to admit the open nature of the Rio documents because they reflect political compromise, we must also admit the relatively high degree of specificity and commitment which results from the long and intense preparatory process leading up to Rio.

Negotiations among the fundamental global interests represented in Rio led not only to problems of interpretation and the assessment of potential change, but to a broad scope of principles and action directives which *only* such a process of negotiation could produce. In contrast to the partisan bodies which normally author political platforms, the body that first composed and then signed off on the Rio Declaration, *Agenda 21* and two binding conventions (on climate change and biodiversity), constituted an Assembly of the Whole. In this fact alone lies a unique consensual mandate: unique in its breadth of representation; unique in its adherence to the principle of sustainable development; unique in the specificity of both its prescriptions and admonitions for change; and unique in the scope and purpose of its newly established mechanisms for implementation.

None of this is to say, of course, that the goal of sustainable development is unanimously understood, or that the changes advocated at Rio are sufficient to halt and reverse global environment-and-development degradation. What it does say is that the UNCED process has established new standards for global politics in this area, and that it has also put into place a network of fora and arenas for pursuing these standards within specific action frameworks. The process in no way guarantees progress toward a global sustainable society. But the prospect of resolving the trade off between global ecological balance and global welfare equity in a relatively peaceful and democratic fashion under any *other* normative regime, is surely less likely.

From Ethics to Implementation

What is contended, therefore, is that the politics of sustainable development are at once more normatively constrained and more instrumentally specific than any form of global politics thus far developed. Furthermore, it is maintained that there are clear possibilities of exploiting the normative position to exert political pressure on domestic regimes. Governmental leaders become bound up, and to a certain degree carried away by the momentum of international and regional environment-and-development processes. They either compete in capturing, or belatedly give their active support to, the moral cutting edge of the persuasion. The role of environmental journalists and

NGOs has been crucial in forcing this development, but the functional need for creating "new politics" at home has also been a factor.

What is important, however, is that when the leaders return home they leave behind a wealth of publicly recorded statements, documents, accords, procedures and institutions—records which clearly can be used to press for domestic political compliance. The politics of sustainable development are not only the politics of UNCED, UNEP, UNDP, CSD and the EU. They are also the *potential* politics of national and local change under the onus of supranational commitments. Gro Harlem Brundtland may, as a national politician and Prime Minister of Norway, regret her reference to the results of Rio as "promises made by world leaders". But her observation in the same context that the promises in question "can only be fulfilled in time to secure our future if governments are inspired and pressured by their citizens" stands as a rallying cry for political mobilisation and change.

It thus becomes increasingly important to objectify, analyse and make better known the parameters for sustainable-development politics. The emerging global game is of great significance in its own right, but there are also important implications for regional, national and local development. The slogan "Think globally, act locally" can only be given more widespread and concrete meaning if voters become better schooled in the intricacies of the environment-and-development relationship, and more aware of the moral and practical potential for local-global linkages.

During the past twenty years or so, the global arena for environment-and-development politics has emerged as a clearly identifiable political system. There are actors, roles, routines, settings, and an increasingly distinct political culture. Each major political milestone, from the Stockholm Conference in 1972 to the Rio Summit in 1992, has established new precedents for how future events and procedures should be structured. A pattern of relationships between governments, international administrative organisations, business groups, voluntary organisations and the media has emerged within a common historical framework.

Discussion Notes/Questions

1. Does sustainable development provide the normative solution? Are analogies with democracy valid?

2. Is sustainable development an analytical concept, an ethical concept, a political concept, or a combination of the three?

3. What is the relationship between normative options, and institutional and procedural solutions?

———

Edith Brown Weiss, *International Environmental Law: Contemporary Issues and the Emergence of a New World Order* 81 GEO. L. J. 675, 702–07 (1993).

Increasingly, notions of equity or fairness are the focus of pointed conflict in the negotiation and implementation of international environmental instruments. For equity to have meaning, it must be defined. The traditional notion of equity that has formed the basis of numerous environmental accords is one of national sovereign rights to exploit resources within a country's jurisdiction or control, combined with rights to shared or common resources (whether for natural resources or for pollution emissions) on a first-come, first-served basis. However, this traditional equity ethic has been deteriorating, and a new ethic is in the process of emerging. The search for a consensus on a new definition of equity is likely to be one of the major factors shaping international environmental accords in the future.

The controversy over the definition of equity lay at the heart of the U.N. Conference on Environment and Development debates. The Rio Declaration on Environment and Development **[Basic Document 1.29]**, a nonbinding legal instrument, explicitly reflects this concern with equity. Among other things, the Principles of the Declaration address obligations intended to "decrease the disparities in standards of living and better meet the needs of the majority of the people of the world";[20] provide for priority treatment to "the special situation and needs of developing countries, particularly the least developed and those most environmentally vulnerable";[21] and recognize that "[i]n view of the different contributions to global environmental degradation, States have common but differentiated responsibilities."[22] By contrast, twenty years earlier the U.N. Stockholm Declaration on the Human Environment **[Basic Document 1.12]** referred only to the need to consider "the systems of values prevailing in each country and the extent of the applicability of standards which are valid for the most advanced countries but which may be inappropriate and of unwarranted social cost for the developing countries,"[23] and, as was also expressed in the Rio Declaration, the need for financial and technical assistance.[24]

In international environmental law, the two issues that have given definition to equity are the allocation of natural resources and the responsibility and liability for pollution. Both have traditionally been based on rights acquired on a first-come, first-served basis, subject to increasing demands for equitable sharing of the burden of conserving natural resources and controlling pollution.

The right of countries to control the exploitation and use of natural resources within their own jurisdiction or control has been repeatedly reaffirmed in international legal instruments.[25] Traditionally states have also claimed the right to exploit resources outside national borders in commonly held areas on the basis of a first-come, first-served ethic in the absence of agreement to the contrary. This method of exploiting resources is reflected in the initial allocations of the geostationary orbit, the radio frequency spectrum, international waterways, fisheries, marine mammals, birds, and ocean miner-

---

20. Principle 5, Rio Declaration on Environment and Development **[Basic Document 1.29]**.

21. *Id.*, principle 6.

22. *Id.*, principle 7.

23. Declaration of the United Nations Conference on the Human Environment **[Basic Document 1.12]**, Principle 23.

24. *Id.*, principle 12. The Rio Declaration **[Basic Document 1.29]** deliberately does not use the term "technical assistance," which some countries view as unnecessarily narrow in scope and possibly condescending. Rather, the relevant article focuses on cooperation.... [*See*] Rio Declaration, Principle 9.

25. Principle 21, Stockholm Declaration **[Basic Document 1.12]**; Principle 2, Rio Declaration **[Basic Document 1.29]**. The Stockholm principle has been commonly regarded as reflecting customary international law, and hence being binding on all states.

al resources. Most international agreements have at least implicitly started from this ethical presumption. Countries have then voluntarily agreed to constraints on their operational behavior affecting these shared or common resources. The two notable international agreements that did not begin with this first-come, first-served presumption, but rather started from a notion of shared responsibility for the resources at issue, are the Convention on the Law of the Sea[26] and the Wellington Convention on Antarctic Mineral Resources **[Basic Document 2.7]**, both of which resulted in complicated allocation schemes that have never gone into effect. Increasingly, however, areas once considered to be *res nullius* or belonging to no one are treated as part of the "global commons."

The second primary focus of international environmental legal instruments has been on controlling pollution. Again, states have traditionally asserted the right to pollute at self-determined levels. International instruments have limited these rights. In practice this has meant that states that were able to industrialize first, or those that have vast territories, have been able to establish pollution levels quite independently of other countries.

In instances of transborder pollution, states have the responsibility under Principle 21 of the Stockholm Declaration to ensure that "activities within their jurisdiction or control do not cause damage to the environment of other States or of areas beyond the limits of national jurisdiction." But increasingly the effects of pollution are felt on a regional basis, which means that more detailed, regionally-focused control arrangements are needed. Countries have found it difficult to reach consensus on the base line year for establishing acceptable pollution levels. The problem is that countries that are beginning to industrialize and trying to reach parity with more industrialized countries do not want to be burdened with an early base line year; and those industrialized countries that have already started controlling pollution want to receive appropriate credit in the selection of the base line year. In the regional context of the U.N.-ECE, the concern is not only with equitably allocating acceptable levels of pollution for those countries that are still industrializing, but also with treating equitably those countries that have already reduced pollution levels significantly in advance of the target base year.

The equity issues that are most controversial in the international community concern responsibility for the prevention of harm to global resources and liability for their damage. The Rio Declaration addresses these issues in its reference to "common but differentiated responsibilities" arising from "the different contributions to global environmental degradation,"[27] and in its concern with liability issues and the polluter pays approach in internalizing environmental costs.[28]

The controversial issues in defining equity with regard to pollution control are multiple: whether to establish common or differentiated pollution control standards (as in the per capita chemicals consumption base line standard for developing countries in the Montreal Protocol[29]), what flexibility

---

26. Convention on the Law of the Sea **[Basic Document 4.20]**, Part XI ... (chapter on seabed minerals).

27. Principle 7, Rio Declaration **[Basic Document 1.29]**.

28. *Id.*, principles 13 & 16.

29. Montreal Protocol on Substances that Deplete the Ozone Layer **[Basic Document 3.18]**, Article 5.

there should be in the time frame for meeting standards (as in the ten year delay permitted for developing countries in meeting Montreal Protocol chemical phase-out requirements), the extent to which countries should be held responsible for activities that contributed to global environmental degradation in the past (for example, liability for effects of ozone depletion on inhabitants of the southern hemisphere), the extent to which a group of countries should be held responsible to particular countries who may suffer harm tomorrow from actions taken globally today (for example, the claims of island countries that industrialized countries establish a trust fund today to cover the costs of the rise of ocean levels due to global warming tomorrow), and the more general question of the responsibility of the present generation to future generations for the care and use of the planet.

In developing a new definition of equity for environmentally sustainable development, several factors and issues must be noted and addressed. First, the global environment knows no political boundaries, its components are spatially and temporally interdependent. This means that no one country or even group of countries has the capability to protect the environment over time by its own isolated efforts. Consequently, there is an incentive for all countries to reach consensus on an equitable and effective basis for allocating responsibility for maintaining the planet.

Second, developing countries have control over resources that are important to the industrialized world, just as the industrialized world has always had control over resources needed by the developing world. The debates during the Biological Diversity Convention **[Basic Document 6.11]** reflect this fact; the developing countries realized that the best reserves of biological diversity lie within their boundaries. In some ways this gave them bargaining power in the negotiations.

Third, developing countries are likely to suffer most from environmental degradation. This is both because poverty is a primary source of environmental degradation and because when rapid, human-induced global environmental change occurs, these countries have the least capacity to adapt.

Finally, future generations are, in my view, becoming a party to debates about equity. Sustainable development is inherently intergenerational, as are the agreements we negotiate. Yet future generations' interests have not been identified and adequately represented in the negotiations, the implementing measures, or in the compliance mechanisms of international environmental agreements. The present generation obviously has a built-in bias in favor of itself. Indeed the instruments that we have developed in the marketplace to consider environmental effects on future generations, namely externalities and discount rates, start from the perspective of the present generation. Thus, as we consider the future, it will be important to develop an international consensus on the definition and outlines of the concept of intergenerational equity.

Discussion Notes/Questions

1. How can the ideas of equity and fairness be given greater particularity in the international environmental area? Do they have a specialized meaning in that context?

2.   Can equity and fairness develop into potent norms of customary international law? How long will it take? How might it be prevented?

3.   Is Professor Weiss correct that a new definition of environmental equity is emerging? How might one argue against such a proposition?

4.   Is the North/South debate likely to be quelled in the foreseeable future? Will advanced nations voluntarily give up their privileged position? Why? Why not?

5.   What interest has the present generation in the welfare of future generations?

6.   We are much better off in material terms than our parents' generation. Is it not reasonable to expect that the same will be true for our children and grandchildren? Why? Why not?

7.   What criticism can be made of Professor Weiss's concept of intergenerational equity, if any? In this connection, review Lawrence Summers, *Summers on Sustainable Growth*, The Economist, May 30, 1992, at 65, *reproduced at* 280 in Chapter 4, *supra.*

8.   Do we have enough information to take intergenerational equity into account even if we want to?

B.   INSTITUTIONAL OPTIONS

"Government," Edmund Burke once wrote, "is a contrivance of human wisdom to provide for human wants."[f] In the last thirty to forty years, beginning perhaps with the publication of Rachael Carson's *Silent Spring* (1962), international ecological well-being has emerged as a conscious human want and the development of governing institutions capable of achieving it an increasingly urgent contrivance to challenge human wisdom. Some of these institutions must be developed at the national level, clearly. But as the world struggles more and more with environmental problems that demonstrate no inclination to remain confined within national frontiers, the need for international institutions has become manifest. The following readings, divided to highlight global intergovernmental institutions, regional regimes, and nongovernmental (i.e., citizen action) organizations, give some indication of the intellectual and operational progress made so far.

1.   GLOBAL INSTITUTIONS

Robert Keohane, et al., *The Effectiveness of International Environmental Institutions, in* INSTITUTIONS FOR THE EARTH: SOURCES OF EFFECTIVE INTERNATIONAL ENVIRONMENTAL PROTECTION 3, 19–24 (Robert Keohane, et al. eds., 1993).

[A]t the level of international society, effective management of environmental problems requires three fundamental conditions to be met. First, governmental concern must be sufficiently high to prompt states to devote scarce resources to solving the problem. Since concern is typically generated by political action within societies, it is unlikely to be sufficient without active networks of individuals and groups, linked to the political system, pointing out environmental hazards and demanding action on them.

---

f.   EDMUND BURKE, REFLECTIONS ON THE REVOLUTION IN FRANCE 88 (12th ed. 1793).

Second, transboundary and commons problems cannot be effectively resolved without a hospitable contractual environment. By this phrase we mean that states must be able to make credible commitments, to enact joint rules with reasonable ease, and to monitor each other's behavior at moderate cost so that strategies of reciprocity can be followed. In short, it must be feasible for governments to make and keep agreements that incorporate jointly enacted rules, without debilitating fear of free-riding or cheating by others.

Finally, states must possess the political and administrative capacity to make the domestic adjustments necessary for the implementation of international norms, principles, or rules. By political and administrative capacity we refer not only to the ability of governments to make and enforce laws and regulations, but also to the broader ability of actors in civil society to play an effective role in policy making and implementation. On the side of the state, the issue is broadly political as well as administrative, since the legitimacy of governments, and the degree to which they receive loyalty from their subjects and honest service from their own officials, are often open to question. Civil society, for its part, must be capable of generating discussion and criticism of governmental action and inaction, and of participating in finding and carrying out policies that respond to environmental problems. Developing countries and the governments of Eastern Europe have typically lacked adequate capacity on both the governmental and societal dimensions—governments have often been unable either to understand or to regulate the impact of their citizens and industrial enterprises on the natural environment; and groups within civil society that could have been the source of information and criticism either do not exist or have been repressed.

Any particular international environmental issue will emerge onto the international political agenda with given values of concern, the contractual environment, and capacity—what we label "the three Cs." Any effective action of international institutions with respect to the global environment is likely to follow a path that increases concern or capacity, or improves the contractual environment. Since we are interested in the impact of international institutions on environmental quality, we are able to focus our analysis by emphasizing how international institutions affect the values of the three Cs. If governmental concern, the quality of the contractual environment, or political and administrative capacity are low, action on environmental problems will suffer.

In fortuitous cases, concern, capacity, and the contractual environment are all favorable to effective management, and international institutions either are not needed or can succeed with minimal effort. This was probably the case in the 1911 Fur Seal Treaty [37 Stat. 1542, U.S.T.S. 564]. . . . In most other cases, however, conditions are not initially ripe for successful joint management. Institutional effectiveness, in such cases, can be assessed by judging the extent to which they perform functions that boost the three Cs.

Institutions can offer rewards or punishments contingent on state policy in order to increase governmental concern, and government preferences may change in response to the resulting shifts in material incentives. For example, international population institutions have sought to alter government policies by providing technical and financial assistance to national family planning programs, and the Montreal Protocol **[Basic Document 3.18]** contained provisions calling for trade sanctions against non-signatories. Institutions can also generate new information that alters states' perception of the consequences of their actions. Institutional responses to the acid rain problem caused a number of states to redefine their views concerning the atmospheric transport and ecological effects of sulfur dioxide. That perceptual shift helps account for much of the change in policies witnessed in Europe. Sometimes such a process of redefinition of interest occurs through the interaction of institutional activity and networks of scientists and experts known as epistemic communities.

Institutions can also heighten state concern by magnifying public pressure on recalcitrant states. Peter Haas and Marc Levy find, for example, that public exposure in high-level meetings concerning the North Sea and acid rain, respectively, engendered political responses within the United Kingdom that contributed directly to policy changes there[g].... Institutions can shape domestic politics by providing information that is useful to particular domestic factions, by helping bureaucracies fight turf battles, and by generating salient public commitments around which political actors can focus domestic debates. International institutions can interact with nongovernmental organizations (NGOs) and environmental movements to increase public concern, either through cooperative programs or as a result of public criticism of the international institutions and national policies by NGOs leading environmental movements. Robert Paarlberg ... finds evidence for these effects within developing countries, which helps explain changes in their behavior toward pesticide imports.[h] NGOs and environmental movements are often important sources of governmental concern about the natural environment.

In seeking to improve the contractual environment in order to enhance the ability to make and keep agreements, institutions have a variety of means at their disposal. They can reduce the costs of negotiating agreements by generating information about potential zones of agreement and providing a forum for bargaining. [It has been found] that international institutions had this effect in the case of stratospheric ozone depletion, making it possible to advance negotiations in response to rapidly changing—and increasingly frightening—scientific findings. The monitoring activities of international institutions can also be vital to the ability of states to make and keep agreements. Wherever states have reason to fear the consequences of being cheated, monitoring can help reassure them that such cheating will be detected in time to make appropriate adjustments. Monitoring makes state commitments more credible, thereby increasing the value of such commitments. In addition, international environmental institutions can create timetables for action, regular policy reviews, and other mechanisms that call for states to demonstrate repeatedly their commitment to solving the problem at hand. Such regular interactions may encourage a process of reciprocity by creating more opportunities for revealing intentions and responding to the actions of others.

g. Marc Levy, *European Acid Rain: The Power of Tote–Board Diplomacy,* in INSTITUTIONS FOR THE EARTH: SOURCES OF EFFECTIVE INTERNATIONAL ENVIRONMENTAL PROTECTION 75 (Peter Haas, et al. eds., 1993) [hereinafter INSTITUTIONS FOR THE EARTH]; Peter Haas, *Protecting the Baltic and North Seas,* in INSTITUTIONS FOR THE EARTH 133.

h. Robert Paarlberg, *Managing Pesticide Use in Developing Countries,* in INSTITUTIONS FOR THE EARTH 309.

Finally, in seeking to augment political and administrative capacity, institutions can foster the transfer of information, skills, and expertise necessary for effective domestic programs. This is the central goal for population institutions and the revised prior informed consent process governing pesticide trade. In addition to these direct information-dissemination and training activities, institutions can build coalitions with development banks and foreign aid agencies in order to funnel major quantities of aid toward projects that will help weak states increase their administrative capacity. Institutions can also help build capacity by providing a public commitment to a set of norms and principles, which domestic proponents of adjustment measures can use in attempting to overcome their opponents in funding and turf battles.

Lessons and Conclusions

[W]e find evidence for institutional effectiveness operating through all three roles—boosting concern, building capacity, and facilitating agreement. Often a single institution affects behavior in all three ways. It is important, therefore, for both analysts and practitioners not to presume that international environmental institutions only perform one family of tasks when they study past institutions and create new ones. The most effective institutions tailor their interventions to political situations they face.

In answering the puzzle of effectiveness, we show that state sovereignty is not incompatible with international progress in solving difficult problems. Institutions do not need enforcement powers to succeed, and it is unrealistic to hope that governments will grant them such powers. But at the same time that institutions must respect the legal integrity of the nation-state, we conclude that the most effective institutions penetrate the state politically to a high degree. Such penetration often makes use of political allies outside the formal institutional apparatus. Indeed, intergovernmental organizations can be expected to be more effective as catalysts for transnational networks of nongovernmental organizations and transgovernmental linkages among sympathetic governmental bureaucracies, than as independent actors. For instance, nongovernmental organizations, interacting with UNEP [the United Nations Environment Programme] and the FAO [Food and Agriculture Organization], have played a critical role (using the media) in putting issues of chemical pesticides on the international agenda, even in the absence of strong pressure to do so from powerful governments.

International institutions do not supersede or overshadow states. They lack resources to enforce their edicts. To be effective, they must create networks over, around, and within states that generate the means and the incentives for effective cooperation among those states. . . .

Discussion Notes/Questions

1.   Are the three roles of boosting concern, building capacity, and facilitating agreement discussed by Keohane, Haas, and Levy the most important issues?

2.   What is the role of legal norms under the institutional approach of Keohane, Haas and Levy?

3.   Do you accept the proposition that state sovereignty is compatible with environmental progress? Other authors have questioned that view.

4. Do you think the government of the United States would find congenial the views expressed by Keohane, Haas, and Levy? What about other governments?

Paul Szasz, *Restructuring the International Organizational Framework, in* ENVIRONMENTAL CHANGE AND INTERNATIONAL LAW: NEW CHALLENGES AND DIMENSIONS 340, 356–76 (Edith Brown Weiss ed., 1992).

In designing plans for establishing new international organizations or restructuring existing ones, account should be taken of the capacity of international organizations to learn—from their own experience and from that of others. . . .

Changes to Be Considered

1. *Assignment of New Responsibilities and Powers to Principal UN Organs*

Various suggestions have recently been made, that because of the importance of environmental concerns these ought to be assigned not merely to one of the numerous subsidiary organs of the United Nations but rather to one of the limited number of its principal organs, either one of those already in existence or to a specially created one. Some of those suggestions are merely aimed at giving greater visibility and weight to environmental issues and debates, while others would be designed to utilize the potentially binding force of the decisions of certain principal organs either to create new international environmental law or to enforce it. These various suggestions will now be examined in respect of each of the principal organs.

(a) The General Assembly

As already mentioned, the General Assembly, whose present workload is both heavy and weighted with items of historical but not necessarily current importance, has found it difficult to concentrate sufficiently on environmental issues and thus to give them the attention that many now believe they deserve. While the question of how the Assembly might shed or redistribute some of its existing load goes generally beyond the bounds of the present study, it should be pointed out that it has been recognized that the Fourth Committee, which deals with questions of decolonization and with the few remaining small non-self-governing territories, has for some time been due for retirement, with its remaining items perhaps assigned to the Special Political Committee. While it might be tempting to consign the Fourth Committee entirely to environmental concerns, to do so would disregard two important points: the fact that, interesting and important as these issues might be, they have not yet attained in the international community the prominence that would justify such an exclusive assignment of some two months debate in a plenary organ of the Assembly; furthermore, it is clear (e.g., from the name assigned to the 1992 Conference) that the General Assembly sees environment and development as inextricably linked. Consequently, a more acceptable proposal would appear to be to redistribute the current load of the Second Committee between that and the Fourth with one of them taking all environment or development related issues while all other economic and financial ones go to the other.

Although the General Assembly is already the most important international legislative body, in terms of the number and variety of the international law-making treaties it has adopted or caused to be adopted through conferences and other devices, not to speak of its numerous formal declarations that catalyze the creation of new customary and conventional law, the chances are minimal that it will soon or even in the foreseeable future be granted genuine legislative powers—i.e. authority to adopt legal rules that thereby become binding on states. Aside from the revolution in international legal thinking that the grant of such power to any global organ would entail, the Assembly notoriously suffers from a fatal flaw that would seem to disable it from such a role: its voting system. Although mistakenly sometimes characterized as "democratic," the assignment of the same voting power to a state of over a thousand million inhabitants as that enjoyed by a state with a population of some twenty thousand, disqualifies the Assembly from consideration as the sole approver of any generally binding norms. While it could of course be argued that the same Charter amendment that would be required to give legislative (rather than mere recommendatory) force to certain Assembly decisions could also change the voting rules for such decisions, it is only realistic to recognize that even if the majority of states might be willing, should they consider it absolutely necessary, to create new organs or organizations with expanded powers and an appropriate decision-making process to match, it is most unlikely that they will permit the voting rules of the General Assembly itself to be altered for such a purpose. What might, however, be considered is to have the Assembly act in tandem with some special environmental (or even broader) body (such as the new principal organ proposed under heading (e) below), so that an effective law-making decision would require adoption by both organs: by the Assembly representing classic sovereign equality and by a specially balanced organ whose decisions reflect in some realistic way genuine power and interest relationships; this would in effect be a bicameral (or possibly even a still more complex multicameral) world parliament, a device for which some precedents already exist in international constitutional law and indeed in the UN itself (e.g., the necessary collaboration of the Security Council and the General Assembly in taking decisions about UN membership, in electing the Secretary–General and, in a different way, the Judges of the World Court).[32]

For the same reason, i.e. its skewed voting system, as well as because of its size and consequent procedural awkwardness, the General Assembly cannot be seriously considered as an organ to which to assign enforcement powers relating to environmental rules or violations.

(b) The Security Council

The idea of assigning to the Security Council certain functions related to environmental management, particularly in dealing with emergency or otherwise serious situations, has at least two bases: The first ... is that critical environmental problems present, in effect, "security" issues, i.e. they are related to human survival in the same or a sufficiently similar sense as those war/peace questions over which the Council already has explicit competence;

---

32. Respectively UN Charter [**Basic Document 1.3**], articles 4–6 & 97, and article 10(1)-   (2) of the ICJ Statute [**Basic Document 1.4**].

the other is that the Council, uniquely among UN or indeed intergovernmental organs, disposes (at least in principle) over powers to compel states to comply with its decrees, or to suffer economic, diplomatic, or even military pressures and penalties that the Council can insist that other states impose on any offender.[33]

As to the first point, while the argument that environmental threats may indeed concern human security may be intellectually convincing, it should be noted that the language of the Charter [**Basic Document 1.3**], not to speak of the clear record of the original meaning, does not easily lend itself to such an interpretation—and that in an area where the classical rules of treaty interpretation require that in dealing with duties or burdens imposed on States Parties to a treaty a strict rather than a liberal construction be applied.

Secondly, in trying in effect to hitch a ride on the compulsory powers that are given to the Council by Chapter VII of the UN Charter, it should be noted that these powers were not designed for dealing with environmental rather than military concerns. In effect, it would be a case of using an inappropriate instrument to perform a potentially delicate operation—perhaps it can be pulled off successfully, but it certainly would not be either the surgeon's or the patient's choice. Nevertheless, there is one attractive feature to such proposals: if it should prove (as is not unlikely) that it is too controversial and therefore difficult to negotiate a treaty assigning true legislative powers to the United Nations or to a new international organization (which would require the concurrence of all significant states) or to amend the UN Charter in that sense (which would require only the concurrence of two-thirds of the membership, but these must include all five permanent members of the Security Council), it could be argued that the Council already has, albeit in yet undeveloped form, the necessary legislative powers under Article 25 and Chapter VII of the Charter.

The principal difficulty, however, is that neither the composition nor the voting system of the Security Council appear suitable for assigning environmental tasks to that organ. Even aside from the question whether that composition and that system are still appropriate even for the functions for which the Council was originally designed, it would seem absurd if at this time this completely different function (i.e. environmental protection) would be subjected to a system in which the five states who were the principal victors in the Second World War (but which do not include two of the most powerful economies, those of Germany and Japan) would have a veto power over environmental enforcement actions. It may indeed be sensible and even necessary that any such compulsory powers not be easily exercised and that therefore one or more states or groups of states should be able to prevent such exercise by a veto, but the states and the particular voting powers that one would assign them would presumably be quite different from those specified in Articles 23 and 27 of the Charter.

Consequently, to the extent that a Charter amendment would be required to give the Security Council responsibilities in respect of the enforcement of environmental rules or the prevention of environmental violations, it would

---

33. Articles 41 and 42 of the UN Charter   articles 25 and 48(1).
[**Basic Document 1.3**], read together with

seem more sensible, if it is desired to vest such powers in a UN organ, to create a new principal organ for that purpose. This is discussed under heading (e) below.

On these several grounds, there is no reason to try to involve the Security Council either in the process of environmental legislation or even in considering and debating such issues. Although it is true that the Council enjoys possibly the highest visibility among UN organs, it would seem likely that instead of enhancing environmental issues with its prestige it would find its own role diminished by dealing with matters for which it is clearly unsuited.

(c) Trusteeship Council

It has been suggested that with the achievement of independence of practically all trust territories, the Trusteeship Council is now or will soon be without any function, and consequently could assume the task of environmental watchdog for the UN System.

While perhaps superficially plausible, this proposal has really nothing to commend it. In the first place, there is no Law of Conservation of UN Principal Organs. If one or more organs lose their functions, they should be abolished or abandoned, whether or not any other tasks remain unassigned in the international constellation; on the other hand, if there are tasks that should be performed by new types of principal organs, these should be established as and when sufficient political agreement as to such a requirement can be achieved.

More importantly, the Trusteeship Council is even more unsuitable, from every point of view, than the Security Council to carry out any meaningful environmental tasks. Its Charter functions are irrelevant for that purpose and it has no powers, such as the Security Council has, that would be even potentially valuable in any other field; the powers it does have: to consider reports, to examine petitions, and to provide for periodic visits, are ones that the General Assembly could assign to a suitable subsidiary organ. Most importantly, its composition: all UN Members administering trust territories plus all other permanent members of the Security Council plus enough members elected by the General Assembly to balance the number of administering and non-administering states, is completely unsuitable and certainly unadaptable to the needs of an environmental organ.

Again, since a Charter amendment would be required to adapt the Trusteeship Council to assume any environmental functions, it would be better to consider the establishment of an entirely new organ.

(d) The Economic and Social Council

Although in a sense ECOSOC would appear predestined to be at least one of the principal UN organs to deal prominently with environmental questions, in fact that organ would, for various reasons, be a very weak reed to lean on for this purpose.

To dispose first of any potential role of this Council as an effective legislative or enforcement body, it should be pointed out that though only a third as large as the General Assembly, with 54 members it is still too large for a body to which a delicate task such as the diplomacy required for effective enforcement actions could be entrusted. Furthermore, even though its smaller size permits a slight mitigation of the one-nation-one-vote defect of the Assembly (in that a smaller proportion of small and weak states are elected to the Council compared to the larger and more significant ones), this is still not sufficient to reassure many crucial states that ECOSOC decisions normally reflect a realistic political base. This is especially so because, under Article 67(2) of the Charter, all Council decisions must be taken by a simple majority—i.e. the specification of any higher majorities is constitutionally precluded.

Turning now to the potentiality of the Council as an important forum for environmental debates, it must be pointed out that the Council has not, particularly in recent years, managed to play such a role either in respect of that subject or any other (such as human rights or development, its principal preoccupations). Why that should be so has been extensively examined, with suspicion concentrating on the fact that, because of two increases in its size to reflect the growth in the Organization's membership, the Council has become too large to be an effective intimate forum and too small to be fully representative. Voices have even been raised to suggest that ECOSOC be entirely abolished, with its tasks being taken over by the present plenary Second and Third Committees of the General Assembly, in which all significant Council debates are in any event rehashed; should ECOSOC disappear, these Committees might be authorized to meet between regular sessions of the Assembly, i.e. during the spring and summer. Given this general mood about the Council, it would not seem wise to plan to make it into a showcase for environmental concerns.

(e) A new principal organ

For the reasons sketched above, none of the four principal UN organs so far considered (i.e. all those having a representative character) would seem suitable to assume important responsibilities for either environmental legislation or enforcement—though the General Assembly itself might become one of the most important public environmental fora. If "governmental" responsibilities are to be exercised within the United Nations—and this itself is not entirely clear, in light of the alternatives discussed in particular under heading 4 below—it would then seem necessary to create one, or possibly two new organs for that purpose; moreover it would seem that because of the importance of the proposed tasks, and the need in any event to amend the Charter to endow the Organization itself with the required powers, such organ(s) should be created as principal one(s).

Faced with the prospect of having, in any event, to amend the Charter to create the proposed principal organ(s), it might in the first place be thought that all things are possible, both in terms of the powers of the new entity and in terms of its composition and decision-making rules. While technically this may be true, some constraints should be kept in mind so as not to appear to be utterly utopian: in the first place, the United Nations is an international and not a supranational organization, and consequently it would not seem appropriate, and especially not timely, to try to endow it with excessive powers over its members; secondly, the Organization is an intergovernmental one, so that the principal actors in any new organ should be governments acting through representatives, rather than other types of entities; lastly, account should be taken of the extensive experience of the international community with a large variety of decision-making devices to find one that would seem appropriate for the purposes designated here.

As to powers, one that should obviously be considered is a legislative or norm-making one.... [T]he principal weakness of the existing international legislative process is not in the formulating and adoption stages—though these too could be improved—but in the final one, that of bringing new legislation into force, against the suspicion or at least the inertia of the domestic authorities of most states. Indeed, the most important reason for contemplating the creation of a new principal organ within the United Nations is to overcome this handicap by endowing some properly constructed organ with authority to impose environmental rules on the entire UN membership and possibly even, by analogy to Article 2(6) of the Charter, on the few remaining non-members. Obviously, this proposed Charter power will have to be carefully circumscribed to make it at all acceptable to the world community, so that the burdens that may be so imposed not be capable of becoming excessively heavy or intrusive, or liable to distort international power or domestic social relations.

The other, and perhaps more plausibly acceptable, power that should be considered is that of enforcement of existing rules and responsibilities. As already mentioned in connection with the examination of a possibly expanded role of the Security Council (heading [b] above), it may be hoped that in due course the international community will mature enough to be able to assign serious enforcement functions in relation to environmental protection to an international organ, just as it did, in 1945, in principle assign such functions in relation to preserving international peace and security to the Security Council. By analogy to Article 39 of the Charter, the proposed organ might be empowered to determine the existence of any threat to the environment or any breach of an international environmental regime. By analogy to Article 40 it would first call on the state(s) to take certain provisional measures to avert the threat or the breach. Then, by analogy to Article 41, it might call on other states to take suitable economic, communication-related, or diplomatic measures *vis-à-vis* the offending entities. The articles relating to military measures (4247) would presumably not be directly relevant but some inspiration might be drawn from them for designing in advance certain sanctions that could be put into place readily as and when required.

Though these two potential functions are evidently not unrelated, they also present sufficient differences that it is not clear that they can and should be assigned to the same organ. In particular, any legislative organ must be large enough to be considered reasonably representative of the world community—even if it is provided (as suggested towards the end of heading [a] above) that any proposed legislation must also be approved by the General Assembly. On the other hand, an organ charged with enforcement should, by analogy with the Security Council, be small enough to be able to act effectively.

What is clear is that any organ to which either of the proposed formidable powers are entrusted would have to be carefully composed as is the Security Council. Evidently there would have to be a heavy role for the principal economic powers, though that might be achieved through devices other than assured permanent membership, i.e. by relying on certain indices (corresponding to those that determine membership in a number of international organs); naturally, there would also have to be appropriate representation of the less powerful states, using selection formulae similar to those that are already customary in the international community. As to the decision-making process, while consideration might be given to allowing certain members (and not necessarily only any "permanent" ones) to exercise a veto, it would seem better instead to require very high qualified majorities (e.g., 90 per cent) for certain types of decisions. Finally, consideration might also be given, in connection with these features, to some form of weighted voting, to reflect more sensibly—as in most of the international financial institutions—the influence in the real world of each member state.

Evidently, all the above-mentioned aspects will require extensive negotiations, which are not likely to be brought to fruition until the world community realizes the absolute importance of being able to rely on enforceable international regimes to save it from environmental catastrophes.

(f) The Secretariat and the Secretary–General

There can, of course, be no question of assigning any independent legislative or enforcement powers to the UN Secretary–General. However, he would, under Charter Article 98 and in accordance with well-established practices, have important responsibilities in assisting any competent representative organs in formulating proposed environmental norms and in actually carrying out or at least coordinating any enforcement measures decided on. By analogy to Charter Article 99 he might even be given the power to call to the attention of the competent organs the need to initiate norm-making or enforcement actions.

A question that may be asked, however, is how an Environment Secretariat might best be structured to offer the maximum effective support to the responsible representative organs. For this two models present themselves: that of a unit of the central secretariat (such as the Department for Disarmament Affairs or the Human Rights Centre) or that of a quasi-autonomous organ (such as the present UNEP, or UNDP or UNICEF) equipped with its own representative organ and led by an executive head who, though nominally selected by the Secretary–General and answerable to him, is confirmed by the General Assembly and is dependent on the support of his agency's special political organ, and also has considerable independence in dealing with his staff. The first model, which is more characteristic of policymaking units, evidently gives the Secretary–General a more important role and also a greater stake in the operation of the entity; the latter, which is used mostly for operational organs, gives greater scope for leadership by a dedicated executive head who has responsibilities for only a single programme—in this instance: environmental protection.

One further point to be considered in this connection is the bureaucratic level of the executive head of the secretariat unit. UN departments are normally headed by under-secretaries-general, as are most of the quasi-autonomous units. However, during the past two decades two still higher posts have been established, whose status is explicitly stated to be equal to that of the "executive head of a major specialized agency": one is the UNDP Administrator, the other the Director–General for Development and International Economic Cooperation, who presides over a cluster of departments and other units. The question is whether the secretariat units charged with environmental protection should, if part of the central secretariat, also be subordinated to the Director–General, into whose ambit they would naturally belong, or whether the environmental executive head, whether or not he leads a quasi-autonomous unit such as the UNDP Administrator, also be appointed at the level of those two officials; such an arrangement would of course enable him to speak on terms of greater authority with the heads of the independent agencies.

Some of the above-explored changes would be a natural consequence of establishing the new environmental organ(s) discussed under (e) above, but any or all of them could also be carried out if there should be no current enhancement of the political organs but merely an increase in the budgetary commitment and thus in the staff of the present UNEP in order to reflect the growth in its tasks and responsibilities.

(g) The International Court of Justice

The principal judicial organ of the United Nations is entirely capable, within the general powers it already has to settle disputes between consenting states and to respond to requests for advisory opinions from duly authorized organs of the UN system, to play a useful role in administering an international environmental regime.

Under Article 26(1) of its Statute, the Court has the power to form chambers "for dealing with particular categories of cases," and it has been pointed out that it could, under this power, create a chamber for dealing with environmental disputes;[i] Whether this would be at all useful would depend on whether there would be a sufficient flow of such cases that the existence of such a chamber (which could consist of any number of judges in excess of two) would on the one hand relieve the full Court of a burden that it could not conveniently carry out by itself, and on the other permit the judges assigned to the chamber to acquire sufficient expertise so that organ would commend itself to states as a particularly attractive forum to which to submit disputes of this type.

Actually, the second condition mentioned above is one unlikely to be realized: the Court, which is necessarily composed of senior international lawyers, is unlikely, either as a whole or through a dedicated chamber, to acquire a real expertise in the scientific and technical aspects of environmental disputes—though this objection might be met by appointing some expert assessors who could participate in the work of the chamber without a vote. Consequently, a different model commends itself: The international community could, either by treaties or by decisions of the General Assembly, establish one or more environmental courts to settle disputes under particular regimes (e.g., all those relating to the atmosphere, or all those relating to IMO-administered ocean-pollution treaties); naturally, in each case the states concerned would have to agree. These courts, staffed with technically expert judges, could then serve as the fora of first instance for these disputes, while any residual questions of international law (e.g., relating to treaty interpretation) could be referred to the ICJ either by the States Parties to the dispute or

i. This measure has in fact been effected.

by use of the advisory proceeding device activated by a suitable organ authorized to address requests to the ICJ (which might be the court of first instance itself, if it is one created as an organ of the United Nations).[j]

The ICJ could also become more readily available to the international environmental community by use of its advisory competence. First of all UNEP, or whatever organ succeeds it as the lead organ within the United Nations for environmental matters, might be authorized by the General Assembly to request advisory opinions of the Court within the scope of the organ's activities. Furthermore, various treaty organs associated with the UN system might be assisted in securing legal advice from the Court by authorizing a suitable UN organ, such as UNEP, to pass on their queries to the Court. Although the Court might well be reluctant to permit such a device to be used to settle disputes between states that could submit them directly to the Court's contentious jurisdiction, it would still be useful both for the settlement of disputes to which an international organization, such as a treaty organ, is a party, and to resolve genuine legal queries that arise in the course of formulating new or administering existing international environmental regimes.

2. Improving and Extending Subsidiary Organs

(a) Upgrading UNEP

If the proposals discussed under heading 1(e) above are carried out to establish one or more new principal UN organs to deal with environmental matters, then these would presumably replace the existing UNEP Governing Council. With respect to the Environment Secretariat, heading 1 (f) explored various possible enhancements and transformations, at least some of which might be undertaken even without any change in the political organs.

In any event, if the United Nations does assume, with or without a Charter amendment, greater responsibilities in respect of environmental protection, then a corresponding upgrading and transformation of UNEP will be called for. The principal feature of such enhancement should of course be the provision of greater financial resources, preferably reliably from assessed contributions, but perhaps reinforced with political arrangements for more generous voluntary ones. As to functions, those of the Programme itself (as distinguished from that of its organs: the Council, Environment Secretariat, and Fund) might be defined, though the lack of such specificity has not so far hampered its operations. For example, norm-making, and in particular the progressive development and codification of international environmental law, might be explicitly referred to[k] and perhaps spelled out in terms of specific procedures to be followed; however, while such specificity might to some extent strengthen the treaty-making activities of UNEP (which, as pointed out above, are already quite vigorous), it might also inhibit the fruitful inventiveness with which these activities have so far been pursued.

j. Under Charter Article 96(2), the U.N. General Assembly is empowered to authorize other U.N. organs or any specialized agency to request advisory opinions "on legal questions arising within the scope of their activities."

k. This is a power specifically assigned to the General Assembly by Charter Article 13(1)(a), and which the latter has often partially delegated to various organs, such as the International Law Commission (ILC).

One other way in which such an enhancement could come about would be through a steady increase in the number of treaty organs that UNEP arranges to service. Presumably each such treaty organ would have its own budget, the financing for which would be provided by those states that are parties to that treaty regime, or possibly in part by contributions from interested non-parties. The advantages and disadvantages of relying on such treaty regimes are discussed under heading 3 below.

Finally consideration might be given, and this is discussed under heading 4 below, to transforming UNEP into an independent international intergovernmental organization, preferably into a specialized agency.

(b) Organs for Coordination and Cooperation

The Administrative Committee on Co-ordination (ACC), with the assistance of [the interagency board of Designated Officials for Environmental Matters], apparently carries out its environment-related tasks as well as necessary and feasible, given the difficulty of coordinating a number of international entities that were deliberately created separate for diverse political reasons and that ultimately answer to different constituencies. Evidently, if other parts of the UN system are changed, e.g., if UNEP were to be superseded or supplemented by a new specialized agency, this would have to be reflected in ACC's membership and perhaps in its operations.

Whatever new intergovernmental organizations are created within or at the periphery of the UN system, they would presumably be encouraged to participate in the "common system of personnel administration" and to utilize the several organs established therefor, and also to participate in other joint administrative organs that assist governments in imposing certain common standards on operationally diverse international organizations.

3.   Treaty Organizations and Organs

For the most part modern multilateral treaties do not only establish rights and obligations for States Parties, but also create some sort of organs to help to develop and implement the consequent legal regime. This has been particularly true of environmental treaties which mostly function in rapidly developing fields in respect of which it is recognized that static legal obligations can in no way suffice, and which are complicated enough so that at least some of the parties, and perhaps all of them, require assistance and probably some stimulation in executing the undertakings adopted.

In some cases such a treaty creates what is merely a minimal, though complete, international organization consisting of at least one political representative organ (e.g., periodic meetings of States Parties), an expert organ to carry out further studies, to receive reports from the individual parties, and to make proposals to the meetings of parties, and a secretariat, perhaps consisting of only a few persons, to service the political and any expert organs. Such organizations typically rely for many purposes (e.g., premises, nonspecialized secretariat services, etc.) on larger, established international organizations, often the one under whose auspices the founding treaty was negotiated.

In other cases the international organization is not quite complete typically lacking any independent secretariat. When this is so, the treaty normally foresees that some other organization, again typically the sponsoring one, will provide the secretariat services on a temporary or permanent basis. When such arrangements are instituted some of the activities of the assisting organization become partially governed by the representative and other organs being serviced, so that these are then referred to as "treaty organs" of the servicing organization.

Evidently, both these types of arrangements are potentially very flexible, and this is one of their attractions to those formulating the treaties in question. Often enough the latter are actually fooled into believing that some absolute savings can be achieved by not providing for the establishment of a new secretariat, which are known to be expensive and with a Parkinsonian drive to self-enhancement. What is often forgotten is that the missing secretariat is merely established within the bowels of the sponsoring organization, with all the usual requirements for budgetary support and tendencies to grow.

An excessive proliferation of such mini and incomplete international organizations is, however, undesirable from a different point of view. Evidently, it is more difficult to coordinate and supervise the separate activities, decisions, and staffs of numerous small organizations than to do so in respect of one or two large ones with prominent executive heads who make periodic reports on all the activities of their organizations to well-attended periodic meetings of representative organs. One solution is to combine a number of such organizations and organs operating in related fields into a single one, in effect consisting of a sizeable secretariat simultaneously servicing many different representative and expert organs; this is the design of the World Intellectual Property Organization (WIPO), a UN specialized agency.

4. Specialized or Related Agencies of the UN

More and more, in arranging for the international governance of some field or activity, the emphasis has shifted from the static to the dynamic, in that the States Parties agree not so much to any specific obligations but rather establish a mechanism for studying the subject in question, for formulating guidelines and rules to be followed by states or other entities, for giving technical or material assistance in complying with such standards, for monitoring compliance, for advising what to do if lack of compliance is detected, and for taking any consequent action decided through an agreed procedure.

The normal instrument of choice to take the actions summarized above is an intergovernmental organization, established at an appropriate level, i.e. universal, regional, subregional, or defined by some other relevant criterion. As is well known, during the past decade some hundreds of such organizations have been created, including many at the worldwide level, to deal with subjects as diverse as labour conditions, public health, maritime affairs, or intellectual property. On the other hand, a few international organizations have a wider mandate, dealing with many different subjects. Whether or not a particular subject, such as environmental protection, should be dealt with in a specialized or in a general organization depends in part on whether the nature of the subject requires a sufficient assignment of material and human resources to justify an independent entity, on how closely that subject is related to others that should be dealt with in a more general context, and on whether political or other factors suggest that the subject requires attention close to the centre or may be assigned to the periphery of the relevant international system. As conditions change, the answer to these questions may also change: thus, in 1950, the International Refugee Organization (IRO), originally established at the conclusion of WWII as a UN specialized agency, was reduced to becoming a quasi-autonomous UN organ, the Office of the High Commissioner for Refugees (UNHCR); on the other hand, in 1975 it was decided that the United Nations Industrial Development Organization (UNIDO), which had originated as a Secretariat unit and had later become a quasi-autonomous UN organ, should be converted into a specialized agency with the same name.

Evidently, not all independent international organizations are UN specialized agencies, which are defined in UN Charter Article 57 as "established by international agreement and having wide international responsibilities . . . in economic, social, cultural, educational, health and related fields" that are brought into relationship with the United Nations by means of an agreement concluded pursuant to Charter Article 63(1). Thus, to qualify, an organization's tasks cannot be so narrow as to negate the characterization of "wide . . . responsibilities"; it cannot be merely regional, for then it might more appropriately become a specialized agency of one of the regional organizations (such as the Organization of American States—OAS); it has to have a sufficiently large membership so as to associate with the United Nations on a par with the other worldwide organizations whose activities it coordinates through ECOSOC and the ACC; and it has to agree to conclude a relationship agreement that implies a certain subordination to the central organizations and a willingness to cooperate with it and the other specialized agencies, in part through common administrative or coordinating organs. If for some reason any of these factors are absent or distorted, then the organization may still become one "related" to the United Nations (such as the IAEA), or merely tied to it by a cooperation agreement (such as the World Tourism Organization—WTO).

The question therefore is whether the field of environmental protection is one suitable for the establishment of an, or perhaps of even more than one, independent international organization, and whether such organization should then aspire to specialized agency status.

* * *

This having been said, it should once more be recalled that amendment of the UN Charter is not an easy or well-established route, unlike the frequent resort to the establishment of new organizations to meet particular urgent needs of the world community; as recalled above, there is even a precedent (that of UNIDO) for converting a quasi-autonomous UN organ, such as UNEP now is, into a specialized agency. Moreover, if the primary roles of the new organization are to carry out studies, assist in voluntary monitoring, provide technical assistance, raise consciousness about environmental matters, and to serve as a secretariat and general support for environmental treaty organs and organizations, then an independent organization, but preferably one within the UN system, might provide the best combination of flexibility and coordination.

Instead of or in addition to converting UNEP into an independent agency, it is also possible that one or more international organizations be established to deal with specific important environmental problems or areas, such as the implementation of a regime to deal with climate change or more generally with protecting the atmosphere. Whether such organizations would qualify as, and would wish to become, specialized agencies would depend on their membership and on their perceived role in the world community.

Discussion Notes/Questions

1. Is it realistic to expect the United Nations to be restructured?

2. Are there good arguments for restructuring the United Nations quite apart from international environmental considerations?

3. If you were to advise the Secretary–General of the United Nations, what changes in the United Nations system would you suggest be made to better cope with the international environmental challenge?

4. What obstacles to implementation do you see to the ideas advanced by Szasz?

5. Do any of the approaches discussed by Szasz appeal more than the others? Which? Why?

Geoffrey Palmer, *New Ways to Make International Environmental Law* 86 Am. J. Int'l L. 259, 279– 82 (1992).

There are basically four policy options in the institutional area. First, things could be left as they are. Second, UNEP could be strengthened and given formal responsibilities. Third, the secretariat approach of the Vienna Convention **[Basic Document 1.7]** could be embroidered upon and developed so that a series of secretariats operate for separate environmental issues. At present, that is the way things are heading. The fourth broad option is to create a new international institution.

To take the high road now will require considerable political commitment, but it is likely to ensure that there will be less trouble later on. International norms gain legitimacy from the process by which they are arrived at. An enduring institutional framework in which the processes are thorough and based on solid scientific data, and in which there is plenty of opportunity for refinement and debate, is likely to serve the world best in the long run.

What form should a new institution take? The most ambitious course is to create a new organ in the United Nations by amending the Charter **[Basic Document 1.3]**. It would be the best possible outcome of the 1992 Conference on Environment and Development. But the procedures for changing the Charter are by no means easy, and the permanent members of the Security Council have a veto. Although I favor creating a new UN organ, it is not the only option. An easier choice to achieve, and one that could provide a workable institutional framework, would be to create a new specialized UN agency.

Of course, it would be possible to expand and develop the United Nations Environment Programme, negotiate a charter for it, and charge it with some extra responsibilities. Or such bodies as the General Agreement on Tariffs and Trade **[Basic Document 7.1]** and the International Monetary Fund could serve as models for a new environmental organization. But, to my mind, the most useful model is the one that has been developed over many years by the International Labour Organisation.

One feature of the ILO's approach is the direct involvement of nongovernmental organizations in setting the standards. The ozone work demonstrated that environmental decisions have enormous impact on the business community. Widespread consultation with industry is necessary at the domestic level both to provide information about the problem and to work through the practical difficulties of compliance. In New Zealand the Ministry for the Environment was able to implement a tough policy without objections from industry as a result of such consultation.

In addition, many environmental organizations have more expertise on some global environmental issues than governments. Governments of smaller countries, in particular, often lack the background and manpower to develop the necessary expertise. The better course is to share information and hold consultations with environmental NGOs so that the approaches to be taken at international conferences can be worked out on the basis of the best available knowledge and judgment.

The International Labour Organisation is the most advanced supertreaty system in terms of providing legislative outcomes of any of the international agencies. Borrowing loosely from the ILO Constitution, a new International Environment Organization could be established with the following features.[34]

(1) A General Conference comprising all members, to be called together annually and more often if the Governing Council so decides. The conference shall consist of four representatives from each member; two shall be government delegates and the two others shall represent business and environmental organizations, respectively.

(2) A Governing Council of forty people—twenty representing governments, ten representing business organizations and ten representing environmental organizations.

(3) The ability of the conference to set international environmental regulations by a two-thirds majority of the votes cast by delegates present. The regulations would become binding without further action. There would also be provision for recommendations to be made to members.

(4) A Director–General and staff of the International Environment Office, to have explicit international responsibilities for educating people about the global environmental problems and what they can do to help.

(5) The office to have defined functions for gathering information and monitoring compliance, including verification of compliance with the regulations. There should be regular reviews of the environmental policies of member states and their compliance with the regulations.

(6) A thorough preparatory process, in which there are ample notice, thorough scientific and technical preparation, and consultation before regulations are made.

---

34. All the features summarized in the next piece of text can be found in the Constitution of the International Labour Organisation [Basic Document 1.2] and Standing Orders of the International Labour Conference (International Labour Office, Geneva, 1955).

(7) Formal provision for authoritative and widely representative scientific advice and papers to be available to the organization.

(8) Detailed requirements for nations to report annually on action taken to implement agreed regulations. The environment and business representatives would be required to report separately from governments.

(9) Provision for any member to be able to submit complaints regarding nonobservance in respect of any other member to the International Environment Office.

(10) Discretion of the council to refer such complaints to a commission of inquiry for a full report. The commission shall consist of three appropriate experts of recognized impartiality and be chaired by a lawyer. The commission is to make findings of fact and rule on the steps to be taken to deal with the complaint and the time by which the steps must be taken. Refusals by governments to accept these findings are to be referred to the full conference.

(11) Authority for the council to recommend measures to the conference to secure compliance when it is lacking.

A word needs to be said here about the last feature, on measures to secure compliance. For them to be effective, there must be some strong incentives to join the organization and stay in it. For many countries these will probably reside in technical assistance, information, advice, technology transfer and even financial assistance for dealing with environmental problems. From a practical point of view, the sanctions should include the withholding of benefits by the organization and of direct contacts with delinquent governments, and the mobilization of the politics of shame. Few nations like to be regarded as international pariahs and shame as a sanction ought not to be underestimated.

The great advantage of creating a new international organization of the type outlined is that it allows the technique of prolepsis to be used to arrive at rules that are binding, without the requirement of unanimity. It maximizes the prospects of observance of those rules by mandating explanation for their adoption and monitoring for compliance with them. It establishes a dispute settlement mechanism that is part of the institutional structure and not remote from it. What it does not do is overcome the need for consent by a nation to join the organization and remain a member. The incentives for that will have to be supplied by peer pressure and political means. But I do not regard it as unrealistic to think that we will reach the point where the norms are binding on every nation in the international community. It may happen quite quickly.

Many nations, particularly the most powerful and certainly the United States, are likely to be opposed to the creation of such an organization. There appears to be a broad consensus among governments that the creation of new institutions should be avoided when possible. In some quarters those sentiments derive from the ponderous nature of some UN structures and the impenetrable bureaucratic thickets surrounding them. Many nations reshape and reorganize their domestic agencies periodically. Such an effort ought to be made at the UN level. If the position is taken that the total outlay for bureaucratic resources must not exceed what it is now, great and beneficial restructuring could be achieved. It would involve cutting away existing overlaps in international agencies. Without a new institution, progress will be too slow and unsystematic. How much better it would be to have a coherent set of procedures and institutions for creating the norms. The ability to respond to the global challenges we face will be greatly reduced unless a new organization with clean lines of jurisdiction and new powers is created.

Discussion Notes/Questions

1. What flaws can you detect, if any, in the Palmer proposal?

2. Where does Palmer's proposal fit in relation to the Szasz analysis?

3. Would a proposal like Palmer's work? Is it practical or is it utopian?

U.N.G.A. Res. 47/191, Institutional Arrangements to Follow up the United Nations Conference on Environment and Development [Basic Document 1.31].

Editors' Note: The Commission on Sustainable Development

Much of the negotiation at the June 1992 United Nations Conference on Environment and Development (UNCED) in Rio de Janeiro, as well as preceding it, eschewed the creation of new international institutions. There was no real enthusiasm for restructuring the existing international institutions of the U.N. system either. There were too many vested interests.

But at a late stage, agreement was reached to establish a Commission on Sustainable Development to oversee and monitor the progress made by nations relative to their pledges in the Rio Declaration on Environment and Development **[Basic Document 1.29]** and Agenda 21. The details of the initiative were not settled at UNCED—these were left to the General Assembly debates in New York City in Fall 1992, where the structure of a new organization was agreed to and its terms of reference established.

The main purpose of the new Commission on Sustainable Development is to "monitor progress in the implementation of Agenda 21." [m] The Commission will review information provided by governments and review progress. The Commission itself "shall meet once a year for a period of two to three weeks." [n]

The resolution setting up the Commission goes to considerable pains to define its relationship with other U.N. and intergovernmental bodies. Despite these efforts it is obvious that serious problems of policy coordination, overlap, and duplication remain. The same resolution of the General Assembly recites that the Secretary General will establish a new Department for Policy Coordination and Sustainable Development. [o]

---

m. G.A. Res. 47/191 **[Basic Document 1.31]**, para. 3(a).

n. *Id.* para. 9.

o. *Id.* para. 32.

William M. Lafferty, *The Politics of Sustainable Development: Global Norms for National Implementation* 5 ENVTL. POL. 185, 194–96 (1996).

Of special interest for the politics of implementation at present, is the latest addition to the environment-and-development arena, the United Nations Commission on Sustainable Development (CSD). Established by the General Assembly in December of 1992 under the umbrella of the UN Economic and Social Council (ECOSOC), CSD has a small secretariat and an assembly of representatives from 53 governments. Its specific mandate is to follow up and implement the massive *Agenda 21*. More than any other document, *Agenda 21* is the successor to *Our Common Future*. Its categories are, to a large degree, those established by the Brundtland Commission. The document addresses (in 470 pages and 40 chapters) topics varying from radioactive waste and toxic chemicals to "Children and Youth in Sustainable Development". It was endorsed by virtually all national delegations to Rio as a "global partnership for sustainable development", with the signatories committing their respective governments to the development and implementation of national "plans of action". It is this process that CSD is designed to monitor and promote.

There are already numerous versions of the Agenda available (original, short, annotated, critical), and it has quickly superseded *Our Common Future* as the most quoted, misrepresented, widely discussed and little-read document of the UNCED process. Without going into detail, I would like to stress one feature of the document which is, I believe, underplayed—namely, that the prescriptions and coverage of the Agenda are as much devoted to the political, economic and financial aspects of sustainable development as they are to environmental degradation and conservation. This differentiation is clearly visible in the structure and content of the report itself, with 25 of the 40 chapters devoted to issues *other than* biogeospheric degradation. But it emerges even more clearly in the operative standards and procedures adopted by the CSD at its initial session in New York in May of 1993.

Box 13–1 lists the 13 general guidelines which the Commission has laid down for the secretariat's analytic reports and recommendations for national implementation. A quick run-down of the list shows that it is more concerned with issues of political and economic relevance than with issues related to the natural environment. Part of this has to do with the fact that CSD has limited resources and cannot be expected to monitor environmental phenomena which are already under observance by other international bodies. More specifically, however, the profile is attributable to what can be referred to as CSD's "compensatory role" *vis a vis* Rio. It was widely acknowledged in the aftermath of the Rio conference that two issues of key concern for Southern countries were not adequately covered by the concluding documents: the financing of sustainable development in the South, and the transfer of technologies necessary for more sustainable economic production. CSD was implicitly given responsibility for these tasks, and proceeded forthwith to establish high-profile "work-groups" on both issues.

These developments mean that CSD has been placed in the front line of sustainable-development implementation. Not only is the Commission to monitor and highlight national efforts with regard to the overall goals of *Agenda 21,* it must also bear the responsibility of carrying forward the crucial North—South issues of financial aid and the transfer of technology. The CSD must, in other words, keep UNCED "honest" with respect to both its public and hidden agendas. From the point of view of political analysis, it is not too strong a proposition, I believe, to maintain that the long-term implications of UNCED now rest with the CSD. The new body has been entrusted with a heavy responsibility for securing progress on the key issues of Rio. If it fails (and a discontinuation has already been aired in open session), the future of both *Agenda 21* and the Rio Declaration will be dim indeed.

Figure 1

UN COMMISSION FOR SUSTAINABLE DEVELOPMENT:
GENERAL GUIDELINES FOR MONITORING IMPLEMENTATION OF AGENDA 21

1.   Policies and measures at national level to meet *Agenda 21* objectives, including national sustainable-development strategies and major activities and projects undertaken;

2.   Institutional mechanisms to address sustainable-development issues, including the participation of NGOs and major groups in these mechanisms;

3.   Assessments of progress achieved to date, with statistical sheets and tables;

4.   Measures taken and progress achieved to reach sustainable production and consumption patterns and life-styles, to combat poverty, and limit demographic impact on the planet's life-supporting capacity;

5.   The impact of the environmental measures undertaken on the national economy, including the social impact of such measures;

6.   Experiences gained, for example, descriptions of successful policies and projects that can serve as models, and particularly strategies that improve both social conditions and environmental sustainability;

7.   Specific problems and constraints encountered, including those related to finance and technology and to the adverse impact of economic and trade policies and measures, particularly on developing countries;

8.   The adverse impact on sustainable development of trade-restrictive and distortive policies and measures, and progress in making trade and environment policies, mutually supportive in favour of sustainable-development;

9.   Assessments of capacity, or the availability of domestic human, technological, and financial resources;

10.   Assessments of needs and priorities for external assistance in finance, technology transfer, co-operation, and capacity building, and human-resources development;

11.   Implementation of Agenda *21* commitments related to finance (including the 0.7 per cent of GNP aid target) and to technology transfer, co-operations, and capacity building;

12.   Assessments of the effectiveness of activities and projects of international organisations, including international financial institutions and funding mechanisms;

> 13. Other environment-and-development issues, including those af-
> fecting youth, women, and other major groups.

Source: Agenda 21, ch. 33, *Means of Implementation: Financial Resources and Mechanisms*
[Basic Document 1.30].

Discussion Notes/Questions

1. What are the major challenges faced by the Commission on Sustainable
Development (CSD)? To what extent is it likely to achieve progress in addressing
the global environmental challenge?

2. Are the coordination provisions G.A. Res. 47/191 likely to work? Why?
Why not?

3. What is the best argument in favor of the CSD?

Editors' Note: The Global Environmental Facility

A relatively new international institution, the Global Environmental Facility
(GEF), promises to be of considerable importance in the future. It was set up in
late 1990—in response to a proposal by France—as a three-year experiment by the
World Bank, in cooperation with the United Nations Environment Programme
(UNEP) and the United Nations Development Programme (UNDP) to fund
projects on global warming, pollution of international waters, the destruction of
biological diversity and depletion of the ozone. At the 1992 Rio Conference
(UNCED), the role of the Facility was expanded by several means. First, there
were express references to the GEF in the conventions signed at Rio. For example,
the Framework Convention on Climate Change **[Basic Document 3.21]** designates the Facility to serve as its financial mechanism on an interim basis and, in
article 21, refers to the need to restructure the Facility and make its membership
universal, a reflection of the fact that the developing countries, in contrast to the
countries who provide the GEF's money, opposed its existing structure and
insisted that it be restructured. Chapter 33 of Agenda 21 (Means of Implementation: Financial Resources and Mechanisms) **[Basic Document 1.30]** sets out the
consensus reached at Rio regarding the GEF and should be read in conjunction
with this note.

At present, the GEF is an umbrella for three separate funds. The "core fund"
(as it is known), which is a global environment trust fund, is perhaps the most
important. There are also a number of co-financing arrangements that are
available on concessionary terms. The third fund, the "Montreal Protocol Fund,"
has been set up to help developing countries comply with the provisions of the
1987 Montreal Protocol on Substances that Deplete the Ozone Layer **[Basic
Document 3.18]**. These funds are administered somewhat differently, with the
responsibility tending to be split between UNEP, the UNDP, and the World Bank
itself. The Bank acts as administrator of the Facility and repository of the Trust
Fund. It also is responsible for investment projects.

The struggle at Rio and since regarding the role of the GEF simply underscores a continuing struggle between the developed and developing worlds that
pervades many international environmental issues. Their interests are different,
suspicion between them is considerable, and as a consequence there are many new
chapters to be played out before these issues of equity and finance are put to rest.

Discussion Notes/Questions

1. What is the fairest way of financing international environmental projects?

2. How should an international institution which gives out money for environmental projects be structured as between donors and donees? Is there any alternative to the prospect that those who pay will decide upon what the money is spent?

3. What do you think are the prospects for the GEF? For further commentary that will help you to answer this question, see Section 3 ("The Economic Instrument"), *infra*.

2. REGIONAL REGIMES

PETER SAND, LESSONS LEARNED IN GLOBAL ENVIRONMENTAL GOVERNANCE 9, 12–14 (1990).

Regionalization. Custom-built asymmetrical regimes are, of course, more easily achieved among regional groups of countries, where economic and other trade-offs can compensate for the asymmetries. Furthermore, if broadening the scope of an international regime means lowering its common denominator (with universal membership at the absolute bottom line), then the reverse should also be true: restricting membership should raise the standard, particularly where such restriction reflects an element of geographic or other affinity between members.

Does international experience in environmental governance bear out this observation? Certainly, the degree of institutional cooperation accomplished under regional agreements for marine environment protection—such as the 1974 Helsinki and Paris Conventions for the Baltic and the North Sea **[Basic Document 4.13]** and the NEP regional seas agreements starting with the 1976 *Barcelona Convention for the Protection of the Mediterranean Sea Against Pollution* **[Basic Document 4.15]**—has consistently been higher than under comparable global regimes, except possibly for ship-based pollution regulation by the International Maritime Organization (IMO).[35] At a time when the U.N. Law of the Sea Convention **[Basic Document 4.20]** (with its chapter XII on global protection and preservation of the marine environment) has still not entered into force, more than 50 states are already legally bound by conventions and protocols concluded under U.N. environment programs for the Mediterranean, the Caribbean, the West–Central African coast, the Red Sea, the Gulf, and the Southeast Pacific.[36] And while UNEP's own global guidelines on off-shore mining (1982) and on land-based marine pollution (1985)[37] generated little more than lip-service from governments, many countries did accept emission standards and specific regional commitments to prevent and abate marine pollution under the UNEP-sponsored Athens (1980) and Quito (1983) Protocols on pollution from land-based sources [19 I.L.M. 869 (1980) & UNEP Reg. p. 199] and under the Kuwait (1989) Protocol on pollution from exploration and exploitation of the continental shelf.[p]

But if regionalization can raise the level of standards, it can also introduce further asymmetries or reinforce existing ones. Far from offering a

---

35. *See, e.g.,* Douglas Johnston & Larry Enomoto, *Regional Approaches to the Protection and Conservation of the Marine Environment, in* THE ENVIRONMENTAL LAW OF THE SEA 285–385 (Douglas Johnston ed., 1981).

36. Text and membership lists in PETER SAND, MARINE ENVIRONMENT LAW IN THE UNITED NATIONS ENVIRONMENT PROGRAMME (1988).

37. *Id.* at 226, 235.

p. Citation unknown.

panacea for all transnational environmental problems, regional regulation may be manifestly unsuitable for some. For instance, when the *Organisation for Economic Cooperation and Development* (OECD) in 1984 initiated a regional draft convention for transboundary shipments of hazardous wastes, it was able to draw on a higher level of solidarity and consensus among its membership (limited to Western industrialized states) than would have been conceivable under a worldwide treaty. On the other hand, it soon became clear that the very prospect of tightened waste controls in the OECD region had an undesired spill-over effect, reorienting trade flows to countries outside the region that were unlikely to abide by OECD-imposed regulation. The OECD member states eventually had to abandon their project in favor of a less ambitious but globally applicable regime under UNEP auspices, the 1989 Basel Convention **[Basic Document 5.6]**. However, with the *Organization of African Unity* (OAU) now drafting a separate regional agreement on the topic,[38] the waste trade issue will continue to provide trial-and-error lessons in transnational regime-building.

Promoting Over–Achievement. To be sure, the Basel Convention does not prevent additional regional action. Article 11 actually reserves the right of any party to enter into other arrangements that are "not less environmentally sound" than the agreed-upon global standards. The European Community has already announced its intention to implement the convention by tighter requirements, as it previously did with such other treaties as the Council of Europe's 1968 Strasbourg *Agreement on the Restriction of the Use of Certain Detergents in Washing and Cleaning Products* [788 U.N.T.S. 181, E.T.S. 64]. (The Strasbourg Convention, which required detergents to be at least 80 percent "biodegradable," was upstaged by a 1973 EEC Detergents Directive requiring at least 90–percent biodegradability.)[39]

A number of environmental agreements expressly confirm the right of parties to take more stringent measures individually or collectively. Examples are the 1973 Endangered Species Convention **[Basic Document 6.5]**, the 1985 Ozone Layer Convention **[Basic Document 3.14]**, and its 1987 Montreal Protocol **[Basic Document 3.18]**. Under "framework" conventions, this right is frequently exercised in optional additional protocols concluded between some parties only.

* * *

In regional integration regimes, however, difficulties can arise. In the European Economic Community (EEC), for instance, there have been protracted quarrels over stricter national standards regarding fuel quality and engine emissions and over national subsidies for the purchase of "clean cars." Although article 130T of the EEC Treaty as revised by the 1986 *Single European Act* **[*see* Basic Document 1.6]** expressly authorizes more stringent national measures for environmental protection "compatible with this treaty," and article 100A(4) enables member states to derogate from agreed harmonization measures for environmental reasons, a country planning to do so must first notify the EEC Commission (which may object in case of non-

---

38. OAU Resolution CM/RES. 1225(L) of 21 July 1989.

39. Council Directive 73/404, The Approximation of the Laws of the Member States

Relating to Detergents, 1973 O.J. (L 347) 51, *as amended by* Directive 86/94.

compatibility) so as to avoid arbitrary restraints of trade. In the end, it is the trade regime that determines, if not the "bottom line," at least the margin of tolerable asymmetries in the EEC's environmental regime.

Discussion Notes/Questions

1.   Some environmental issues are inherently regional in nature, such as pollution of the Mediterranean Sea for example. Are they better dealt with regionally? Even where regional actions in themselves cannot provide a solution, is it possible that regional groupings of nations at international negotiations can make a big impact by pushing an agreed regional line? How many situations can you think of where a regional approach would be helpful? What criteria would you use?

2.   Recall Problem 10–1 ("Driftnet Fishing in the South Pacific") in Chapter 10, *supra*. There, a regional approach spread and became a universal international approach. Do you think that is likely to happen often?

3.   What are the dangers of a regional approach, as identified by Peter Sand?

4.   Is the EEC an example of a regional approach? *See* F. Abbott, *Regional Integration and the Environment: The Evolution of Legal Regimes*, 68 Chi.-Kent L. Rev. 173 (1992). Are there other areas of the world where such a regime is like to develop? If so, where and why? If not, why not?

3.   NONGOVERNMENTAL (CITIZEN ACTION) ORGANIZATIONS

Dan Tarlock, *The Role of Non–governmental Organizations in the Development of International Environmental Law* 68 Chi.-Kent L. Rev. 61, 69–75 (1993).

NGOs perform at least four related functions. They bring neglected as well as transcendent perspectives to bear in different fora, they monitor the environmental impacts of various activities, and they participate directly in resource allocation. In short, they increasingly perform roles traditionally assigned to state agencies.

A.   Infusion of Alternative Perspectives Into Narrow Mission Programs

The case for NGOs rests on the premise that non-governmental entities have a positive role to play in contributing new information and perspectives to policy formulation. This role is a major extension of their traditional role as information synthesizers. NGOs have deep roots in the international community; they reflect a long tradition of international scientific meetings and semi-official international organizations, but their role has evolved to one of claimed parity with established governmental institutions. The modern NGO as a direct political actor with non-state interests in the international affairs emerged at the 1972 United Nations Conference on the Environment in Sweden. NGOs did not have a substantial direct influence on the conference but they gained a legitimacy that they lacked before Stockholm.

The Stockholm Conference is generally counted as one of the most successful environmental conferences. It projected environmental concern into international politics where it remains an expanding priority. It also articulated a set of principles that remain the starting point for discussions of international law and treaty standards and it institutionalized this concern within the United Nations through the U.N. Environmental Program. Much of the success of the conference was the result of careful preparation and masterful diplomacy by conference secretary general Maurice Strong. However, the presence and participation by NGOs created a precedent that remains.

NGOs now seek political parity to counter the narrow self-interest politics of nation states. If politics is all interest groups, then all interest groups should have access to decision making processes. In the United States the opening of both administrative and judicial processes to interest group plaintiffs was justified because it furthered interest group liberalism. Environmental advocates in both Europe and the developing world have admired and emulated this model. As a Ugandan emigree teaching in the United States recently put it, "[e]ffective environmentalism is virtually impossible without basic democratic conditions."[40]

The international law argument for NGOs' status is also a major extension of the argument for citizen or public interest standing in the United States. United States law draws a sharp distinction between adjudication and political action which will not hold in the international context. In the United States, the case against the citizen suit is that it politicizes the judiciary. This is a false concern since courts are limited to cases and controversies under Article III. To cabin citizen standing, United States courts grant "injured" public interest plaintiffs standing only to enforce existing statutory mandates ignored by the agency. Citizen standing is justified by notions of pluralism that define legitimate decisions as those based on all legitimate view points. The idea of judicial participation in the establishment and enforcement of environmental priorities appeals to environmentalists in strong central administrative states as well, and this argument has become the basis for the integration of NGOs into the international community.

The analogy between domestic citizen standing and NGO participation in international law-making is apt, but concerns about the NGO role are more justified because there are no institutional constraints on NGO roles. This is a matter of considerable concern because in many international agencies the split between politics and technical expertise is a matter of great concern, and it is harder to maintain the line between the two. International organizations often provide an effective forum for developing countries to vent their frustrations, and NGOs can veer from articulating scientific positions that try to bring disparate interests together to articulating polarizing positions. NGO actions reflect the full range of contributions and have generally been hailed as positive. However, NGOs are not bound by the limitations of domestic law because their international legal status is different. At the present time NGOs participate at the discretion of the international organizations of the states. Some organizations have procedures to accredit NGOs.

NGO access is often more difficult, but once access is obtained, NGOs are free to use their influence to define agendas as they choose. Under the United States model, citizen suits are open to all who have standing and the law of standing does not screen directly for citizen competence. The idea of a case

40. Ibrahim J. Wani, *Poverty, Governance, the Role of Law, and International Environmentalism: A Critique of the Basel Convention on Hazardous Wastes*, 1 KAN. J. L. & PUB. POL'Y 37, 41 (1991).

limits what the NGOs can do in a law suit. No similar limitation exists at the international level. The limitations, such as they are, are solely on access to a process. International organizations have adopted Professor Jaffe's suggestion that courts screen citizen plaintiffs. This allows agencies to limit participation to those most likely to advance the work of the agency but this procedure is biased in favor of well-financed groups.

Putting fresh alternative approaches on the table has been the bread and butter activity of NGOs. Most governments still pursue short-term economic development with little serious consideration of alternatives such as sustainable development. For example, a group of Spanish NGOs issued a report which not only criticized the Madrid–Seville high-speed train, but offered a detailed blueprint for sustainable rural development. The report recommends that rural areas participate in the coastal and urban boom in Spain by being allowed to market their natural value and products to urban dwellers under carefully controlled conditions.[41]

One of the major success stories of NGOs has been the role that they have played in the transformation of the World Bank's mission, which is under continuing criticism for its support of projects with large adverse environmental and social consequences. NGOs lobbied the Bank directly as well as the United States Congress, and in the past few years Congress has enacted legislation requiring that U.S. agencies urge the Bank to adopt environmentally responsive lending policies.[42] Since 1986, the Bank has taken impressive steps to make sustainable development the operating standard for future loans. My colleague Bartram Brown has evaluated efforts to politicize the technical mission international organizations. He distinguishes between political activity which is unrelated to the mandate of the agency and impairs its ability to carry out its mission and that which enhances mandates. NGO pressure, aided by United States legislation, is an example of beneficial political pressure because "the Bank's ability to function and to fulfill its mandate has been enhanced by these reforms. It is true, of course, that the Bank's Charter never specifically mentions protecting the environment ... nonetheless this objective is very much consistent"[43] with its mandate to improve the world standard of living through useful projects.

B. The Articulation of Universal Perspectives

NGOs play a role which is both similar and more powerful than public interest plaintiffs in domestic law. In domestic law, public interest adds a perspective to that of the agency by presenting the court with an ignored statutory or constitutional value. This is a familiar role for NGOs and commentators have urged that international agencies allow widespread NGO participation. In the international arena, NGOs often play a more transcendent role. They offer a fundamentally different perspective from ones urged by nation states. One of the major criticisms of international environmental law making is that it is overly constrained by the state sovereignty which allows states to put state interest first in international negotiations. When

---

41. *Development Plans Being Pursued at Expense of Environment, Groups Claim*, 15 INT'L ENVTL. REP. (BNA) 18 (Jan. 15, 1992).

42. 22 U.S.C.S. § 2621–m (Law. Co-op. 1992).

43. *See* BARTRAM S. BROWN, THE UNITED STATES AND THE POLITICIZATION OF THE WORLD BANK: ISSUES OF INTERNATIONAL LAW AND POLICY 238 (1992).

agreement is reached, it reflects the lowest common denominator. NGOs, in contrast, are not bound by state interest but can articulate and advocate a global perspective. This can be a modest role such as the presentation of neutral scientific information to break a deadlock over the science of an issue or the articulation of the heretical idea that there should be no compromise on environmental issues.

The flip side of transcendence is, of course, ideological intransigence which can conflict with the underlying science as well as with legitimate non-environmental concerns. The positions taken by international wildlife organizations at the 1992 Kyoto Convention on International Trade in Endangered Species (CITES) **[Basic Document 6.5]** illustrate the problem of NGO inflexibility. Several southeast African nations wanted to relax the CITES ban on trade in elephant hides and tusks.[q] Relaxation was successfully opposed by many wildlife conservation NGOs, supported by thirty United States Senators, who saw the problem as a standard anti-species conservation move. However, the issue is more complicated. The nations, the United States Fish and Wildlife Service, and other NGOs saw the issue as a sustainable development problem and were willing to entertain the counter-environmentally intuitive proposal that limited trade in elephant products was not inconsistent with species conservation.[44] There is no requirement that politics produce rational or right decisions, but the ability of NGOs to block creative science-based solutions is troublesome.

C. Direct Participation in Enforcement

NGOs are playing an increasing role in the enforcement of international environmental standards. There is no basis for this role in international law but nonetheless NGOs have carved out a role. Under United States law and the laws of a few European countries, citizen organizations have a statutory enforcement role through the ability to bring citizen suits. There is no corresponding role in international law both because of the principle that only states have standing and the law of effective judicial and administrative enforcement mechanisms. Paradoxically, the non-role of the International Court of Justice and the limited enforcement powers of the United Nations Environmental Program have given NGOs the flexibility to play more diverse and creative roles.

NGO participation in the area of environmental norms is the easiest to justify, especially in developing countries which lack an effective regulatory infra-structure. NGOs are free to do what international law proscribes—to intervene in a nation's affairs which would fall under that nation's exclusive sovereignty under classic international law. NGOs are not bound by the non-intervention principles of international law. They are free to lobby international organizations as well as to use their influence to shape domestic political agendas. For example, recently a coalition of local and international environmental groups played a significant role in persuading the government of Honduras to reject a United States corporation's proposal to construct a

q. For pertinent commentary, see Problem 10–2 ("Poaching Elephants in Usambara") in Chapter 10, *supra.*

44. Steven Weisman, *Bluefin Tuna and African Elephants Win Some Help at a Global Meeting*, N.Y. Times, Mar. 11, 1992, at A8.

large pulp and paper mill because the project threatened to destroy a tropical forest.[45]

D. Direct Participation in Resource Allocation

NGOs have played their most creative role in pioneering incentives for developing nations to adopt environmental practices. Inter-generational equity requires that environmental protection be integrated with economic development. The north-south split is the most difficult unresolved environmental issue and the resolution of this issue increasingly drives global environmental issues. The issue has been framed as a classic redistribution issue: the north took resources from the south through colonialism and transformed them through technology and must now make restitution. The actors have been states and state-controlled multinational organizations such as the World Bank. Since World War Il, there has been limited technology transfer in the form of foreign assistance. After the OPEC oil embargo and consequent rise in the price of oil, money flowed into private and public banks and was recycled to developing countries in the form of loans. These loans are now a crushing debt burden for many countries and puts intense pressures on countries to continue to exploit rapidly their natural resources bases. This burden has also provided a small but growing window of opportunity for NGOs to change internal resource use priorities.

In 1984, Thomas Lovejoy proposed a new form of private debt relief: debt-for-nature swaps.[r] In brief, NGOs purchase from a bank a portion of the debt of developing countries faced with a write-off or write-down prospect. Developing country "paper" is plentiful and relatively cheap. The NGO must fund a debt instrument with hard currency that the developing country would like to retire as quickly as possible, often high interest, short term bonds. After the NGO purchases the instrument, it is converted into the local currency of the debtor country and the debt service is applied to purchase land threatened by development or to finance a conservation program. Debtor countries gain the benefit of servicing its debt with local rather than hard currency, subject to NGO control over the country's natural resources. Banks may deduct the original amount of the debt donated rather than the current fair market value of the debt. This strategy has been adopted by the United States government because it makes the best of a bad situation, helping developing nations with crushing debt burdens, and offers a modest way to support sustainable development projects.

In 1987, Conservation International purchased $650,000 of Bolivian debt for Citicorp at an 85% discount and cancelled the debt in return for Bolivia's promise to protect 3.7 million acres of rain forest surrounding the Beni Biosphere reserve. The World Wildlife Fund used the proceeds of its swap to fund an Ecuadorian NGO. A Mexican environmental group, Pronatura, negotiated a $3,000,000 swap with its government in 1991.

Debt-for-nature swaps are unlikely to be a major vehicle for developing country debt relief but they have considerable potential to save high priority

---

45. *Ecological Concerns Prompt Government to Reject Proposals from West*, 15 Int'l Envtl. Rep. (BNA) 192–93 (Apr. 8, 1992).

r. For pertinent commentary, see Catherine O'Neill & Cass Sunstein, *Economics and the Environment: Trading Debt and Technology for Nature*, infra; see also supra Problem 10–3 ("A Rain Forest and the Guahibo Are Threatened in Amazonia and Caribia").

natural areas such as rain forests. From a legal point of view the most interesting aspect of debt-for-nature swaps is the creative NGO circumvention of the basic principle of international law, proclaimed by the United Nations at the height of the Cold War, that each nation has the right to exploit its natural resources. Debt–for–Nature Swaps have been criticized as a new form of economic imperialism, but the device is preferable to traditional economic development which was dictated by the donor country and the World Bank. There are, however, many difficult issues to be faced in the future. For example, the traditional model of resource preservation, the protected enclave such as a national park, has limited application to the rain forests and other productive but environmentally sensitive areas of the developing world.

Steve Charnovitz, *Two Centuries of Participation: NGOs and International Governance* 18 MICH. J. INT'L L. 183, 274–86 (1997).

NGO ROLE: BENEFITS AND PROBLEMS

There are several potential benefits of NGO involvement. First, NGO networks can deliver technical expertise on particular topics needed by government officials. Second, NGOs can facilitate a negotiation by giving politicians access to competing ideas from outside normal bureaucratic channels. Third, NGOs can help government officials test controversial proposals by providing rapid feedback. Fourth, NGOs can help governments secure ratification or implementation of new treaties. Fifth, NGOs can vocalize the interests of persons not well represented in policymaking. Sixth, NGOs can help IGOs fulfill the role of being fiduciaries for future generations. The fact that some NGOs persist over decades shows that their programs have intergenerational authenticity. Seventh, NGO involvement may enhance the accountability of IGOs. Eighth, NGOs may enhance the accountability of governments by monitoring negotiating efforts. NGOs can also press compromises upon reluctant negotiators. Ninth, NGOs may strengthen international agreements by monitoring governmental compliance. Tenth, the consultation process may improve the behavior of NGOs by giving them a greater stake in policymaking.

Although there is universal agreement that NGO involvement in developing projects can be constructive, some government officials—for example, from China and India—resist expanding the NGO role in policymaking. Several problems are raised. First, the vast number of NGOs makes deeper participation impractical. Second, because many NGOs are from industrial countries, they amplify certain views—for example, on human rights or the environment—that may not be reflective of the views of developing countries. NGOs from developing countries may also be less well-financed than their industrial country counterparts and therefore less able to participate effectively. Third, and more fundamentally, some government officials argue that NGO involvement in international organizations is unnecessary because NGOs can seek influence through their own governments.

The first problem is one of numerosity. The NGO population increases daily. Numerosity could be tackled the same way we deal with it in national governance—by establishing elections for NGO representatives. But this raises difficult problems of how to weight votes, given that NGOs have different size memberships and that individuals may join more than one NGO. In the absence of formal selection procedures, one might look to informal ones. So far, NGOs have been able to work out among themselves how to allocate limited opportunities to attend meetings. For example, the European Environment Bureau coordinates the activities of over sixty NGOs with an interest in the European Union's environmental policymaking. For human rights, a liaison committee was set up to select NGO representatives during the Human Rights conference in 1993. Whether these informal practices will continue to work as NGOs multiply and become more diverse remains to be seen.

The second problem is one of imbalance among NGO participants. The earliest manifestation of this problem occurred in 1921 in the dispute concerning the Dutch worker delegate to the ILO. This was solved by alternating representatives. The growing number of NGOs in developing countries may help redress geographic imbalance.

Another facet of the balance issue is whether business groups should be able to participate. Some would draw the line between non-profit organizations, like the ICC, and profit-seeking enterprises, like ITT. Yet it seems inconsistent to exclude business entities while allowing the participation of NGOs that have business entities as members. Moreover, with the advent of database software and phone banks, it has become very easy to create organizations of like-minded individuals. ITT, for example, could create an international NGO of ITT employees and suppliers. Any system that tries to limit consultative status to certain kinds of NGOs is going to have a hard time justifying and policing its eligibility criteria.

The third problem is the easiest to address because it rests upon a faulty assumption. There is no requirement under international law that States have democratic governments. NGOs may be seeking input into an international organization precisely because a national government is not responsive. But even if national NGOs ought to keep their grievances at the national level, that says nothing about the grievances of *international* NGOs. It is illogical to tell an NGO like the ICC or the International Confederation of Free Trade Unions to channel its concerns through its own government. Such an instruction negates the purpose of the organization. As John Dewey pointed out in 1920, voluntary associations "do not coincide with political boundaries. Associations of mathematicians, chemists, astronomers; business corporations, labor organizations, [and] churches are trans-national because the interests they represent are worldwide."[s] The case for permitting participation by international NGOs is strong for one more reason. Many NGOs are likely to push for socially beneficial policies. It is no accident that NGOs organize internationally to promote collective goals like peace and the protection of the global commons. While national NGOs may advocate militarism or protectionism, such goals will rarely inspire true international coalitions.

Although participation by NGOs does not mesh well with a State-centric view of global governance, such participation is consistent with earlier conceptions of the law of nations that reached individuals. Many NGOs have

---

s. JOHN DEWEY, RECONSTRUCTION IN PHILOSOPHY
205 (1920).

international outlooks and favor multilateral agreements. If allowed to participate, NGOs will lodge complaints in order to promote compliance by States with their treaty obligations. Many NGOs will also try to help underdeveloped, small States that lack the influence implied by their sovereign equality to larger States. Moreover, it would seem unfair to accuse NGOs of undermining international law when so many NGOs served on the front lines of developing positive international law.

Although the State-centric view continues to pervade international law, this dogma is losing coherence. One challenge is the increasing number of States. Another is the heterogeneity of States. After all, how much commonality really exists between China and the Marshall Islands? Are they both "powers," to use the old term for participants in international conferences? The dichotomy between States and NGOs is also challenged as NGOs gain some characteristics of States, such as a permanent population (dedicated members) and a capacity to conduct international relations. Although the ILO is recognized as an exception to the State-centric view, international law has not yet fully caught up to the reality of NGO participation.

A sixty-two year old decision from an Italian Court may point the way to how international law should treat NGOs. In that dispute, which involved the Sovereign Order of Malta, the Court opined that it is impossible to deny to "international collective units a limited capacity of acting internationally within the ambit and actual exercise of their own functions, with the resulting international juridical personality and capacity which is its necessary and natural corollary."[t] The Court viewed the Order of Malta as having juridical personality because of the "universal character of its aims and ideals."[u]

* * *

TECHNIQUES OF NGO INVOLVEMENT

* * *

Part One of this article demonstrated a variety of ways that NGOs have participated in international organizations. It may be useful to catalog them briefly:

1. An individual from an NGO can be included on a government delegation to an international conference. The role of the individual is to advise a government; he is not free to conduct negotiations uninstructed by the government. An early example of this method was the mixed delegation sent by the United States to the First Pan American Conference. In 1994, the Cairo Population Conference urged governments to include NGOs on delegations to conferences where population and development are being discussed.

2. An individual from an NGO can be included on a national delegation to an international conference. The role of the individual is to represent the NGO; she is free to conduct negotiations uninstructed by her government. The principal example is the ILO.

---

t. *Nanni and Others v. Pace and the Sovereign Order of Malta, in* 8 ANNUAL DIGEST OF REPORTS OF PUBLIC INTERNATIONAL LAW CASES, 1935–1937, at 2, 5 (Hersh Lauterpacht ed., 1941).

u. *Id.* at 6.

3.   NGOs can send delegates to semi-public international conferences. An early example was the International Statistical Congress, which had representatives from governments and learned societies. A current example is the IUCN, whose membership includes seventy-five States, 105 government agencies, and 699 NGOs.

4.   An international organization can establish a formal advisory group that includes individuals from NGOs. These individuals are chosen for their expertise, not to represent the NGO. An early example was the Consultative Committee established by the League Council in 1927. A current example is the UN Advisory Board on Disarmament Matters.

5.   An international organization can give NGOs an opportunity to participate in ongoing policy development. An early example was the League's Organization for Communications and Transit. A current example are the conferences of the Convention on International Trade in Endangered Species in which NGOs have substantial input.

6.   An international organization can enlist NGOs in the implementation of programs. Some early examples were humanitarian operations coordinated by the International Relief Union. Some current examples are the assistance projects administered by the U.N. High Commissioner for Refugees.

7.   An international organization can give NGOs an opportunity to participate in an official conference to draft a treaty. An early example was the League's Conference on Customs Formalities in which the ICC participated and signed the Final Act. NGO participation in environmental treaty drafting today is less formal and often is part of a government delegation. The new ECOSOC resolution declares that NGO participation in U.N. conferences "does not entail a negotiating role."

8.   An international organization can give NGOs an opportunity to participate on a preparatory committee for an international conference. An early example was the participatory meetings for the U.N. Conference on Trade and Employment in 1946—47. A recent example was the preparatory meetings for the UNCED conference of 1992.

9.   An international organization can hold a special session to give NGOs an opportunity to make presentations. An early example was the League's conference on narcotics in 1924. A more recent example occurred in 1986, when NGOs were invited to address a Special Session of the General Assembly on Sub–Saharan Africa.

10.   An international organization can include NGOs as members. An early example was the International Bureau of Education. A current example is the International Commission for Scientific Exploration of the Mediterranean Sea whose membership includes twenty-two governments and eleven scientific committees.

While instances of most of these techniques can be found in contemporary practice, some of them seem underutilized, particularly numbers four, five, and nine. Even today, much NGO activity at IGO conferences is unofficial and informal. The participation is sometimes no deeper than what occurred at the Hague Peace Conferences. In a recent report, Rubens Ricupero, the Secretary-General of UNCTAD, states that "[b]y and large, multilateral institutions have so far failed to give these new actors [NGOs] adequate room to express themselves and to make their weight felt.'"

NGOs are here to stay. The challenge for policymakers therefore is to structure NGO involvement so as to optimize the benefits for international organizations. We need continuous experimentation with new methods to permit "interpenetration of extranational and extragovernmental forces."

The most intensive form of participation—full voting rights like those enjoyed by NGOs in the ILO—is unlikely to be replicated in the near future. As Michel Hansenne, the ILO's Director-General, pointed out, "[i]t is striking that all international institutions established since 1919 should have espoused the principle of the government being the sole representative of States.'" Visionary proposals for an NGO assembly in the U.N. do not seem politically feasible. But it might be feasible to establish more advisory committees similar to what the League had in a few areas and to what the OECD now has for trade unions and business groups.

One difficulty with establishing advisory committees is determining whose advice to seek. In environmental policy, individuals opposed to stronger regulation have found it useful to create new organizations with environmentally friendly names. There is no way to distinguish such top-down organizations from grassroots organizations. It would seem as legitimate for the public to organize anti-environmental-regulation groups as pro-environmental-regulation groups. The diminishing costs of communication with like-minded individuals—for instance, through the Internet—may change the way we think about "organizations" in the future.

A related issue is the involvement of unorganized individuals. It seems clear that many of the advantages from the participation of NGOs could also be obtained from individuals. There is no reason, other than practicality, for distinguishing between the Cousteau Society and Jacques Cousteau himself. The new ECOSOC guidelines do not address individual participation.

Another issue is to what extent governments should subsidize NGOs in order to fructify NGO participation. Some governments regularly do this. This had led to legal problems for some NGOs; for example, the Thai government is investigating some NGOs for accepting financial support from abroad without Thai government approval. The impact of such subsidies on the dynamics of NGO involvement needs further study.

Finally, NGOs sometimes ponder whether it is in their interest to enhance formal involvement in international organizations. Formal involvement provides an opportunity to influence decisionmaking, but also leads to a danger of co-optation. It seems likely that some NGOs will seek formal roles, while others will want to remain more independent so that they can feel freer to criticize.

Discussion Notes/Questions

1. Are NGOs likely to advance progress on environmental issues? What about NGOs that are opposed to further international environmental protections? Is the NGO influence a benign one whatever policy stance they take?

v. *Report of the Secretary–General of the United Nations Conference on Trade and Development to the Ninth Session of the Conference*, U.N. Doc. TD/366, at 74, 78 (1996).

w. INTERNATIONAL LABOUR ORGANIZATION, REPORT OF THE DIRECTOR-GENERAL: DEFENDING VALUES, PROMOTING CHANGE (I.L.C., 1994).

   2. Do NGOs represent the public interest or vested private interests?

   3. On what basis should NGOs have a greater say than individuals?

   4. Do the fundamental principles of democracy require NGO involvement?

C. PROCEDURAL OPTIONS[x]

A world community that aspires to ecological security for present and future generations can provide no security at all without truly effective procedures for ensuring that the old Adam of sovereignty and narrow vested interests will not defeat environmental goals and norms defined by the common inclusive interest. Some procedural options were noted in the immediately preceding section wherein we considered institutional options for meeting the global environmental challenge. But we did so only indirectly, as a consequence of the inevitable interplay of institutional and procedural elements in any governance system. Here, we do so directly, in quest of enforcement mechanisms and modalities that can give real teeth to an international environmental law that, so far, remains in doubt as an effective respondent to the global environmental challenge. In so doing, we focus on the potential dynamism of international environmental regimes, the utility of domestic law approaches, and the power of the economic instrument as a technique of guidance and persuasion.

1. INTERNATIONAL ENVIRONMENTAL REGIMES

Thomas Gehring, *International Environment Regimes: Dynamic Legal Systems* **1 Y. B. Int'l Envtl. L. 35, 47–54 (1990).**

Dynamic Legal Systems

A. The Legal Structure

International environmental regimes discussed in the present paper are based on formal multilateral conventions. Fundamental obligations are codified in formal protocols and/or annexes to these conventions. Usually, a regime's formal legal structure consists of a relatively stable framework convention with a high threshold for amendments, and protocols and/or annexes featuring a simplified amendment procedure. To ease the adaptation of this structure as necessary, a number of techniques are used. For example, provision is occasionally made for amendments of the formal legal structure to enter into force for countries that fail to give timely notice of their objection. Similarly, decisions to adjust control measures regarding substances controlled by the Montreal Protocol [**Basic Document 3.18**] become binding on all parties to the Protocol when approved by a two-thirds majority. These steps tend to speed up the process of adapting legal obligations to changing cognitive expectations considerably. Nevertheless, the regulation of important aspects of the normative structure of international regimes must occur outside this body of formal treaty law.

First, diplomatic conferences are, all too often, not in a position to deal with all relevant questions relating to an adopted instrument. Relatively minor, but nevertheless important, issues are frequently excluded from an

x. *See supra* note a.

agreed "package deal" on the understanding that negotiations thereon will immediately ensue. For example, upon the adoption of the Montreal Protocol, a resolution of the diplomatic conference requested that the Executive Director of UNEP convene a working group to prepare a report clarifying data reporting requirements. Based on this report, the First Meeting of the Parties to the Montreal Protocol adopted decisions on the confidentiality of data and on the clarification of definitions and terms. These "clarifications" are, in fact, interpretations of more general treaty obligations. They were adopted by consensus and thus have become part of the normative expectations built up within the regime.

Second, authoritative interpretations by the permanent conferences of international regimes may close unintended gaps left open in prior negotiations. At the request of the Soviet Union, the Montreal Protocol, under certain conditions, permits an increase of production beyond 1986 levels. At its first meeting, the conference "decided" by consensus that such a production increase may not be used for export to non-parties of the Protocol. The Executive Body for the Geneva Convention bridged a gap in the SO_2–Protocol in a similar fashion, i.e., by way of interpretation. Contracting parties undertake to reduce SO_2 emissions by at least 30% by 1993 at the latest. The Protocol, however, does not address the period after 1993. Therefore, the Executive Body "noted a common understanding among the Parties"[60] that an increase in such emissions after 1993 would be inconsistent with the Protocol.

Third, a permanent conference of parties might choose to circumvent, or even ignore, certain provisions of the relevant framework convention. At the Second Meeting of the Parties to the Montreal Protocol, states adopted a comprehensive "Amendment" to the Protocol. Formally, amendments to protocols enter into force after "at least two-thirds of the parties of the protocol concerned" have submitted their instruments of ratification, acceptance or approval. Yet, the 1990 Amendment requires only 20 such instruments to enter into force, i.e., of only one-third of the parties. While the intention not to delay the Amendment's entry into force may be understandable, the approach is not sanctioned by the language of the Convention. Thus, states may have tacitly amended the relevant provision of the Convention however ambiguous the formal legal foundation of this step may be.

Fourth, equally significant is the procedure by which States at the First Meeting of the Parties to the Montreal Protocol adopted the "Ozone Depleting Potential" (OPD) figure for one of the controlled halons. Since Annex A to the Protocol called for this figure "to be determined," discussion arose on the question of whether the figure had to be inserted by way of an amendment to the Annex or whether a mere interpretation sufficed. The latter approach was chosen for the sake of simplicity. Hence, the First Meeting of the Parties decided "to accept the value for the Ozone Depleting Potential (ODP) for halon 2402 as 6,0" and to request that the Secretariat inform the depository that the parties agreed to accept this figure by consensus and that, accordingly, the depository should insert this figure to replace the words "to be determined" in Annex A to the Montreal Protocol. Given the circumstances of

60. *See* Report of the Seventh Session of   22.
the Executive Body, ECE/EB.AIR/20, at para.

this particular issue, a mere interpretation did not suffice. Instead, the depository had to modify the text of the annex by inserting the agreed-upon figure. Yet this was done neither according to the ordinary amendment procedure as provided for in the Vienna Convention [on the Protection of the Ozone Layer **[Basic Document 3.14]**], nor any specific provision of the Protocol: its sole basis was the consensus among the parties to the Protocol.

Fifth, and even more surprising, is that by a simple decision the Second Meeting of the Parties to the Montreal Protocol established an Interim Multilateral Fund to support ozone-friendly technology in developing countries. Neither the framework convention nor the Protocol contains a specific legal basis for such a far-reaching step which places comparatively heavy financial obligations on member states. It is obvious that negotiators did not consider this issue at the time the Protocol was adopted in 1987. The decision, which entered into force immediately, involves a financial commitment of up to US$240 million for the first three-year period (1991–1993). The contracting parties agreed to contribute to the fund in accordance with the United Nations assessment scale. Contributions thus must be considered virtually "mandatory," even though language of this kind was avoided. Politically, an early establishment of the funding mechanism was desirable to induce developing countries to join the Protocol and accept its obligations. The fact remains, however, that establishment of a multimillion dollar fund simply by a decision of an intergovernmental body is an internationally unprecedented event.

All these decisions remain below the level of formal treaty law. On the one hand, interpretations of a given treaty adopted by the consensus of contracting states would appear to be unproblematic; on the other hand, circumvention of applicable provisions of the relevant framework convention and the establishment of a multi-million dollar multilateral fund by decisions of the conference of the parties might be viewed as presenting a more difficult issue. However, the effectiveness of all these decisions, indeed, of virtually all substantive decisions adopted so far within the two international environmental regimes discussed, rests on consensus among the parties. Regardless of any possible uncertainty about the legal basis and formal legal effects of these decisions, they have become part of the normative structures of the international regimes concerned; consensual decisions will not be challenged on formal grounds because negotiations bring participating states to the point at which they are able and willing to accept the decisions. Thus, formal soundness may be sacrificed in exchange for pragmatic and swift decision-making by consensus. In short, the normative structure of a regime reflects varying degrees of formal law, or, in other words, is only partially reflected in instruments that rise to the level of international treaty law proper.

B.   The Judicial Function

An essential component of any legal system, including sectoral legal systems, is the mechanism for dispute settlement. Disputes have both an individual and a group aspect. On the individual side, parties directly involved in a given conflict may be primarily concerned with settling their respective substantive claims without much regard for the normative implications for the regime as a whole. They will, at first, attempt to reach an acceptable settlement whether by negotiation, conciliation, third-party arbitration or court litigation. While the dispute settlement clause of the Vienna Convention on the Protection of the Ozone Layer, which also applies to the Montreal Protocol, offers almost all of these options, many countries favored compulsory dispute-settlement. There is, however, little prospect that states will ever use the third-party dispute settlement option because states are generally reluctant to submit disputes to impartial third-party institutions. Thus, for a number of reasons, negotiations remain the most important way to settle disputes in the contemporary international legal order.

There is another, more principled factor that discourages submission of disputes on the interpretation or application of norms that are part of the normative structure of dynamic international regimes to third-party adjudication: disputes submitted either to the International Court of Justice or to an arbitration commission have to be settled in accordance with recognized rules of international law. Yet, the body of normative expectations commonly accepted within the regime extends well beyond formally accepted international law. Hence, because the basis for judicial decision-making is separated, to a certain extent, from the body of normative expectations governing the particular issue-area, third-party adjudication could generate new problems.

In any event, every dispute about an individual actor's compliance with the norms of a legal system also has a collective aspect because the parties, as a group, will primarily be interested in protecting the stability of the legal regime. In particular, the group will seek to protect basic normative expectations against incidental or unintended modifications threatened by disputes among individual parties. Thus, when international environmental cooperation is located within a sectoral legal system, non-cooperation or non-compliance with normative expectations by an individual actor automatically rises to the level of a dispute between that offender and the other parties as a group.

This "group aspect" calls for a different procedure for dispute settlement. The relevant provision of the Montreal Protocol makes abundantly clear that its concern is not disputes between two (or a small number of) parties, but rather disputes pitting a single party against the other parties as a group. Thus, the parties are requested to "consider and approve procedures and institutional mechanisms for determining non-compliance with the provisions of this Protocol and for treatment of Parties found to be in non-compliance."[61]

According to the "non-compliance procedure," adopted on an interim basis at the Second Meeting of the Parties, a complaint has to be addressed by one or more parties to the Secretariat of the Protocol. After giving the alleged offender an opportunity to reply, the Secretariat will transfer the submission to a five-party Implementation Committee. This committee will then consider the complaint and report to the meeting of parties. In following this procedure, conflict between individual parties will be avoided from the beginning. The Secretariat, an institution jointly established by the parties, will formally submit the complaint and the conference of parties, acting in its capacity as the highest decision-making body of the regime, will eventually decide on possible action. Nevertheless, the procedure contains an element of compulsion, because it may be triggered without the consent of the offending party.

61. Montreal Protocol, article 8 **[Basic Document 3.18]**.

While disputes submitted to arbitration are to be settled in accordance with international law, submissions to the non-compliance procedure are to be considered "with a view to securing an amicable resolution of the matter on the basis of respect for the provisions of the Protocol."[62] No reference is made to provisions of international law outside the regime's normative structure. On the contrary, amicable resolution of the conflicts, and respect for the provisions of the Montreal Protocol, are the sole criteria for findings of the Implementation Committee. To be sure, this does not imply that the basic rules of international law will be widely disregarded. Rather, it liberates the Committee from the limits established by formal international law, provided that the two above-mentioned criteria are fulfilled. In short, the Committee will be able to ignore certain rules of international law whose application might not be considered desirable, and it may draw upon the body of normative expectations developed within the regime regardless of the formal legal status of any particular rule.

Upon the committee's submission of a report, the conference of parties' decision making relies on similar criteria and "may, take into consideration the circumstances of the case, decide upon and call for steps to bring about full compliance with the Protocol ..., and to further the Protocol's objectives."[63] Again enforcement of the law is not the task of the conference. Instead, the conference of the parties seeks to bring about compliance with the Protocol in light of the circumstances of the case. Instead of sanctions, assistance and support might be more appropriate depending upon the context. Moreover, the conference is not obliged to decide, and it may choose not to respond at all. In short, the conference remains master of the process and retains all the options as it is not restricted to the strict application of formal law.

In adopting the non-compliance procedure, the conference of parties has established an internal quasi-judicial mechanism. Disputes may be settled within the sectoral system, without reference to institutions outside the regime, through utilization of the regime's permanent communicative process and collective appraisal by an audience that has participated in the development of the body of norms governing the issue-area. It may be assumed that future disputes will be settled along the lines of this procedure.

Compared to the sophisticated apparatus of the ozone protection regime, the regime on long-range transboundary air pollution is far less elaborate. The Geneva Convention does not contain detailed provisions on dispute settlement. But let us assume a contracting party to the SO_2 Protocol does not meet its obligation to reduce emissions by 30% in 1993. In that case, third-party settlement of the conflict involving the application of international law proper is unlikely to occur. The offending country will not risk being found in violation of international law or being held liable for damages.

The group of parties making up the Executive Body will, however, have to address the issue in one way or another. A conflict between individual countries is, therefore, almost automatically converted into a situation in which the offender faces the entire community of parties. Similar to the dispute settlement process within the framework of the Montreal Protocol,

62. UNEP/OzL.Pro.2/3, Annex III, para. 6 of the non-compliance procedure.

63. UNEP/OzL.Pro.2/3, Annex III, para. 7 of the non-compliance procedure.

the Executive Body may not feel obliged to apply international law strictly. It might instead choose from a range of responses that fall short of the application of formal law. In short, any norm of the sectoral system, regardless of its formal legal status, might come into play. As is the case with the Montreal Protocol, the Executive Body will remain master of this dispute settlement process. Thus, despite the differences in the development of institutionalized procedures, non-compliance cases can be expected to be handled very similarly in both regimes: the communicative processes of international environmental regimes internalize the judicial function. The regimes provide for internal dispute settlement mechanisms that may or may not be formalized, but which, on all accounts, must be considered highly satisfactory.

The conference of parties is undoubtedly the most appropriate forum to decide disputes involving claims seeking to modify the normative structure of a sectoral legal system. Not only will the conference of parties seek to shape consensus on the conflict issue, but once consensus has emerged, it tends to modify or confirm authoritatively, as the case may be, the normative structure of the regime. Further, the conference of parties may be in a better position to settle disputes about the interpretation and application of law. While third-party institutions will have to base their decision upon formal legal principles, the parties as a group will decide by shaping consensus on the interpretation of norms in light of the factual circumstances. Such a consensus interpretation may imply a change in normative expectations. Even so, it will reinforce the stability of the sectoral legal system as a whole.

Discussion Notes/Questions

1.   Is it correct that an international regime can develop a policy dynamic of its own and progress due to its own impetus?

2.   Multilateral conventions providing for secretariats, regular meetings, monitoring and reports may have effects that make irrelevant the weaknesses of international law. How far can this idea be stretched?

3.   If international organizational systems can develop the dynamic outlined in the foregoing extract, are we home free? Why? Why not? Are there any international environmental problems that could not be dealt with that way? If so, which?

4.   What if important state actors elect to remain outside the regime?

5.   Are the insights of the Gehring extract compatible with the approach adopted by Keohane, Haas, and Levy *supra*. With which are you most sympathetic? Why?

———

Kal Raustiala & David G. Victor, *Conclusions, in* THE IMPLEMENTATION AND EFFECTIVENESS OF INTERNATIONAL ENVIRONMENTAL COMMITMENTS: THEORY AND PRACTICE 659, 676–89 (David C. Victor et al. eds., 1998).

Systems for Implementation Review (SIRs)

At the national level, in most well-functioning polities institutions are in place to monitor, assess, and enforce the implementation of laws. The international system lacks such extensive structures, but the need for these functions remains. Some states attempt to translate their international obligations into action but fail. Others attempt to "free ride." Still others have the will and capacity to implement environmental commitments but are reluctant to adopt costly measures without assurance that other societies are bearing similar costs. Often, effective international cooperation also requires the ability to assess and adjust commitments in light of new information. These situations can be addressed when procedures exist to collect and assess data on whether countries are meeting their commitments; to handle the implementation problems that are identified, such as by mobilizing technical assistance, political pressure, or sanctions; and to assess the adequacy of existing commitments and future options. The actors and institutions that perform these functions comprise what we term *systems for implementation review* (SIRs).

* * *

Trends in SIRs. SIRs are becoming more common and more elaborate. In at least one major subset of environmental accords—fauna and flora agreements—SIRs have steadily become more complex and appear to be making an increasing contribution to the effectiveness of agreements. Early agreements included no provisions for reporting and review; since the 1950s, nearly all agreements do. Today, the "standard" wildlife agreement includes regular reporting, regular reviews of implementation, regular reviews of the adequacy of commitments, and opportunities for non-state actors and experts to contribute information and participate in implementation review. With such a relatively high level of implementation review as the standard, it has been easier for some agreements to go even further: 4 of the 19 wildlife agreements concluded since 1970 even have provisions for on-site inspections.

In addition to John Lanchbery's study of a large sample of fauna and flora agreements (Chapter 2), the other case studies in the first part of the book also show that SIRs have become more extensive and intensive over time. As parties have become more intent on addressing the environmental problems at hand, they have responded both by making commitments more stringent *and* by enhancing SIRs. However, parties that have been wary of international commitments have also been wary of implementation review. The Montreal Protocol illustrates a tradeoff between the stringency of possible commitments and the extent of implementation review: developing countries opposed adoption of a rigorous review procedure but accepted commitments to sharply cut consumption of ozone-depleting substances. But in other cases, when parties have favored deeper cooperation, more stringent commitments and extensive implementation review have gone hand-in-hand.

In the Baltic Sea regime, donors have made financial and technical assistance conditional upon extensive implementation review; in the European air pollution regime, the 1994 Sulphur Protocol includes a noncompliance procedure to help ensure that its more stringent, costly emission controls are implemented fully.

Data Quality. Data are the backbone of SIRs. Without data on the environmental problem at hand and the extent of implementation activities it is impossible to review implementation, identify and handle implementation problems, and assess the adequacy of existing commitments. The main source of such data is the typical requirement in an international environmental agreement that each party report data on its own behavior. Previous studies have demonstrated that such national data reports are typically late and incomplete. We found that many international agreements now benefit from extensive efforts to improve reporting rates; financial assistance has helped many countries to report data and the end of the Cold War has reduced the political barriers to data reporting in transition countries.

However, all of our case studies demonstrate that a more intractable problem of data *quality* remains: national data often are not comparable, and their accuracy is often low or unknown. In the Baltic Sea regime, the quality of reported data was initially low and improved only through several rounds of active efforts to compare and apply data to the assessment of Baltic Sea quality and regulatory priorities. In the best-developed systems, the quantity and quality of data that are collected typically fall well short of what is needed for SIRs to reach their full potential. Even in the most extensively developed data collection system—that of the European air pollution regime . . .—it took nearly two decades of effort among countries with high administrative capacity to build up an integrated scheme for collecting data for use in models of the transport and chemistry of European air pollution. That experience shows that data collection can be useful for designing more effective international regulatory regimes, but if policymakers want such capacity, they must begin early. In that case, data collection efforts began even before the first round of substantive commitments was negotiated.

Addressing Implementation Failures and Noncompliance: Management versus Enforcement. Finally, the studies have considered many of the ways that the operation of SIRs has contributed to the effectiveness of international environmental accords. Of particular interest is what happens when an SIR uncovers an instance of inadequate implementation. Often such scrutiny of implementation failure has been triggered by formal noncompliance with international commitments, which underscores that while compliance is often a poor measure of whether an international agreement is effective, it is nonetheless important. Here, we briefly consider the two most important hypotheses: one, that failures to implement international environmental commitments are best "managed" in a nonconfrontational manner; the other, that coercive "enforcement" techniques are needed. The two schools of thought reflect different visions of how the international system works, the possibilities for governance with international law, and the policy tools that are available and should be used to handle implementation problems.

The "managerial" approach to compliance holds that states have a propensity to comply. Instances of noncompliance, for the managerialists, are seldom deliberate and usually result from problems of capacity, treaty ambiguity, and/or uncontrollable social or economic changes. Noncompliance is a problem to be solved, not an action to be punished. Solutions include greater transparency, nonadversarial forms of dispute resolution, and technical and economic assistance. Conversely, the "enforcement" school builds on traditional realist models of state behavior and argues that states in fact calculate the costs and benefits when they choose whether to comply. Hence the proper policy response to extensive noncompliance is to increase costs through enforcement measures. Proponents of enforcement strategies argue that when cooperation has historically been at its deepest, enforcement measures have

played important roles. Moreover, successful instances of intensive cooperation—such as the General Agreement on Trade and Tariffs—World Trade
Organization system and the European Union (EU)—contain enforcement
provisions that have grown stronger as the regime has grown deeper.

Our research provides a mixed message for this debate. The studies
suggest that most implementation problems are not willful violations. We find
little evidence of states strategically calculating whether to comply with
extant international obligations, in part because states that adopt the most
stringent international commitments—usually advanced industrialized countries—typically face domestic pressure to address environmental problems.
The only cases that illustrate such strategic behavior are those that concern
the USSR before transition, when the government suppressed facts and public
influence, thus limiting domestic pressure to address pollution, and when the
command system facilitated a unitary approach. Moreover, as the managerialists expect, the most serious failures to meet international commitments
identified in this study clearly stemmed from unanticipated factors. The
failure of Russia and a few other transition countries to eliminate ozone-
depleting substances reflects that these countries have limited ability to
control the firms within their borders. Similarly, the Norwegian central
government does not have direct control over municipalities, whose cooperation has been needed (but not forthcoming) to reduce nutrient pollution
flowing from wastewater treatment plants into the North Sea. However,
classifying these implementation problems as willful or accidental is difficult;
arguably, they merely reflect that governments have not given sufficient
priority to implementation and compliance.

Fundamental to this question of whether noncompliance is mostly an
unanticipated or a calculated phenomenon is the fact, noted earlier, that
compliance rates for binding commitments, which are the instruments most
extensively used in international environmental governance, are generally
very high. Few of the implementation problems identified in this study
actually constitute formal noncompliance. The practice of adopting binding
international commitments with which compliance is possible explains why
those few violations reflect miscalculation rather than mischief—states do
carefully calculate their interests when negotiating and joining international
agreements. High compliance may also explain why it is often difficult to
mobilize international responses to implementation problems—because few
such problems have actually yielded noncompliance few have triggered response mechanisms such as noncompliance procedures.

Regarding the instruments used, we find support for both managerial and
enforcement models. Most cases of actual or possible noncompliance are
"managed" through discussions and negotiations. Increasingly, resource
transfers ("carrots") have been part of the management approach. Managerialists claim that stronger responses to implementation problems, such as
sanctions and other "sticks," typically are not available in the international
system; they also argue that, even if they were, such techniques would not be
as effective as the management approach. Our studies only partially confirm
that expectation. The regimes examined in this volume that have been
marked by the most extensive cooperation, such as the Montreal Protocol,
have had at their disposal powerful incentives and disincentives—tools of
enforcement. When such tools have been used, they have worked, especially

when the sanction has been to withdraw assistance (i.e., to stop supplying "carrots"). Under the Montreal Protocol, funding for developing countries is withheld if those countries do not report their baseline data within one to two years of their first funded projects. Meeting that standard is relatively easy; nonetheless, all failures to report data have been met by a threat to cut funding, and almost immediately the needed data have been supplied by the delinquent governments. Similarly, the threat of denied GEF funding played a major role in the effective handling of the Russian and East European noncompliance cases. In practice, however, the operation of the Protocol's Non-Compliance Procedure generally has been nonconfrontational and has followed the management mode. "Sticks" have rarely been used and, perhaps, are rarely needed because the occasional use of strong measures may send a signal that deters other potential violators, although properly evaluating their deterrent role is difficult.

Other cases confirm that sticks can be essential for handling poor implementation. ENGOs enforced the implementation of whaling norms by mobilizing consumers against whaling countries, with some influence on whaling practices, especially in Iceland. In the Convention on International Trade in Endangered Species of Wild Fauna and Flora (CITES), multilateral sanctions have been applied. Trade in CITES specimens with Thailand and with Italy was temporarily banned after those parties repeatedly failed to implement domestic legislation and control trade as required by CITES. The United Arab Emirates was expelled from CITES, and thus excluded from trade in CITES specimens, because it persistently violated controls on trade in ivory. These cases also confirm that it has been much easier to trigger the mechanisms for applying such sticks when there has been a formal verdict of noncompliance.

The means for handling compliance problems at the international level shares some features with domestic regulatory enforcement. Studies on the implementation of domestic air pollution regulations in the USA, for example, show that compliance schedules are often negotiated between government agents and polluters; many penalties that are authorized by statute are actually never applied and few violations are strictly punished. That is, compliance with domestic regulatory law is also mostly managed, not strictly enforced. A critical difference between international and domestic regulation is that at the international level the range of international enforcement measures is typically much narrower. The ability of international institutions to apply large sticks or carrots to specific instances of noncompliance, as evident in the Montreal Protocol, is still unusual. As at the domestic level, the need for such measures may also be rare, but some instances do arise, and thus the ability to credibly threaten strong responses to violations makes other, softer management responses more effective. In contrast, at the international level the compressed range of available responses to implementation problems suggests that the ability to deter implementation failures may be small. Moreover, the management approach may be weakened because there are few stronger tools available when management fails. Indeed, the Russian case of noncompliance with the Montreal Protocol is one such instance where management efforts had repeatedly failed and were rejuvenated only because stronger measures were available and used.

The Choice of Legal Instruments

Although this book focuses on the implementation process, the case studies have allowed us to speculate about which types of legal instruments induce the most implementation activity and thus are likely to be the most effective. The choice of instruments is a central issue facing negotiators of international agreements; our analysis of the choices builds on several other studies that have explored which instruments are most effective under different conditions.

Conventional wisdom holds that the most effective international commitments are legally binding. Yet our cases point to many instances where nonbinding agreements have had greater influence on behavior, especially when parties have sought the benefits of international cooperation but have been uncertain of their ability to implement commitments. Four cases—regulation of NOx, protection of the Baltic and North Seas, and regulation of trade in hazardous chemicals and pesticides—show how the effectiveness of international cooperation rose with the adoption of nonbinding instruments. In none was the improvement a sole result of the choice of legal instrument: nonbinding instruments allowed but did not directly cause more effective cooperation.

Nonbinding commitments have aided cooperation and implementation in several crucial ways. States appear to have been more willing to adopt commitments that are both clear and ambitious when they have been codified in nonbinding form. Clear commitments have been more effective because they are more easily translated into specific actions, regulations, and other incentives for target groups. They are also more readily reviewed and evaluated by the international community. The ambitious nonbinding North Sea commitments to cut major pollutants 50—70% were highly specific and thus it has been easy to assess whether national performance has met the goals. The Baltic Sea JCP has produced highly detailed priorities for action, making transparent the principal causes of Baltic pollution and the cost of necessary policy responses. JCP priorities have not been followed fully, but they have helped to direct and coordinate funding, which would not have been possible if goals had been vague.

Ambitious commitments have spurred wider and more intensive efforts to change the behavior of target groups. When the legally binding Protocol to freeze emissions of NOx was signed in 1988, a small group of countries simultaneously adopted a more ambitious nonbinding Declaration to cut emissions by 30 percent. While it is difficult to ascribe a strong impact to either agreement, at least in the Netherlands and Norway the existence of more ambitious nonbinding commitments forced governments to explore the need for additional regulations that they otherwise would not have considered. Norway has since rejected the Declaration, but only after serious efforts to make additional cuts in NOx emissions. The flexibility of the Declaration allowed Norway to consider deeper cuts that it clearly was not contemplating under the binding NOx Protocol, without fear that it would be locked in if the additional cuts proved infeasible. The ambitious nonbinding Ministerial Declaration to cut the main Baltic Sea pollutants by 50 percent has required Finland and Sweden to implement additional measures, whereas earlier international commitments required little additional action.

Both these benefits—clarity and ambition—have been most evident when parties have been uncertain what they can implement. When uncertainty has been high, most governments have approached binding commitments with caution: they have signed only what they could implement, and thus binding commitments have typically required only modest, if any, change in behavior ex ante and have been accompanied by high compliance rates ex post. In contrast, governments have been less hesitant to adopt clear and ambitious commitments if they are nonbinding, even when implementation uncertainty creates risks of noncompliance. Indeed, compliance with nonbinding commitments has been low, but in many cases the influence of those commitments on behavior has been high. In short, contrary to popular wisdom, compliance and effectiveness are often inversely related.

Another attribute of nonbinding agreements that allows for more effective cooperation is flexibility in participation. In both the NOx and North Sea cases, a small "club" of countries used nonbinding instruments to move forward with deeper cooperation. In both cases, nonbinding agreements allowed the benefits of "minilateralism"—focused cooperation among a small number of motivated parties—when it was politically or symbolically difficult to exclude laggards from formal, "binding agreements." In the North Sea regime, ministerial-level conferences oriented around nonbinding declarations made it easy to exclude laggards Spain and Portugal. Neither state contributed significantly to North Sea pollution, but both had been formal participants (and slowed work) in the legally binding conventions. Without those two states, the only remaining laggard was the UK. Isolated, branded the "Dirty Man of Europe," faced with a growing domestic green movement, and under high-level pressure at the North Sea Ministerial Conferences, the UK switched positions and North Sea cooperation moved forward rapidly. Nonbinding instruments made it easier to isolate and pressure the UK and made it easier for the UK to adopt the stringent commitments once it had changed its position.

Our studies also demonstrate that nonbinding instruments can be effective in cases where the environmental problem at hand has been ambiguous but stakeholders nonetheless have wanted to start the process of international cooperation. In the case of regulating trade in hazardous chemicals and pesticides, when the nonbinding PLC system was adopted it was unclear which substances should be included in PLC and how PIC should work in practice. The nonbinding instrument created a voluntary scheme that could be adjusted easily and rapidly. None of the important rules was formalized; rather, the system evolved as the participants—industry, public interest groups, government officials, international organizations, experts—gained experience. In 1989, when PIC was adopted, advocates of tight trade regulations saw the adoption of a nonbinding system as a setback. They favored a binding alternative, but many exporting nations would not have consented to a binding PIC system in the late 1980s. (At this writing a binding treaty, modeled closely on the nonbinding system, is being negotiated.) In retrospect, the benefits of wide participation and "learning by doing" have been extremely important and probably would not have been nearly as abundant if PIC had been binding in its early stages. Once industry support was assured (which often occurs when nonbinding measures are backed by the credible threat of binding law), the nonbinding instrument yielded effective international environmental governance at the early learning stages of the regime. The presence of a system for implementation review provided information feedbacks and facilitated "learning by doing."

In sum, while prior studies have extolled nonbinding instruments because they enter into force immediately, without ratification, our cases point to other benefits that are more important. Such instruments have allowed parties to adopt clearer and more ambitious goals, especially when they are unsure of what they can implement. This central benefit of nonbinding instruments has also contributed to two other benefits. Parties that have wanted deeper cooperation have used nonbinding instruments to create a smaller club of like-minded enthusiasts. Moreover, the flexibility of nonbinding instruments has facilitated learning by doing, which has allowed more effective cooperation when it has been unclear how best to cooperate.

Taken together, these benefits suggest a new approach to international environmental governance that makes more extensive use of nonbinding instruments, especially at the early stages of cooperation. It is contrary to the current conventional wisdom, which leads diplomats and policy advocates to focus on negotiating binding commitments and to resort to nonbinding commitments only when binding efforts fail. Our evidence does not apply under all conditions: notably, if the goals, means, and ambitions of cooperation are clear then a binding instrument may be more appropriate (or, perhaps, the choice of instrument does not matter).

While advocates of binding measures fear that parties to nonbinding commitments will readily defect, the perils of defection have been reduced through transparency and extensive implementation review. The North Sea case provides an example and points to two important elements of the review process. First, effective reviews have looked at policies and plans, not only at simple indicators of compliance. Such reviews have made it possible to assess whether countries are on track to meet international commitments and whether existing commitments are adequate. In contrast, simple compliance reviews focus on ex post assessments. Second, in the North Sea case, reviews have been part of the Ministerial Conferences and thus have been backed by periodic high—level political attention. The presence of high-level government officials has made scrutiny of national performance more effective because such officials often have the power to change policies that are criticized in reviews and have the authority to forge agreements with their counterparts in other countries, including agreements that require extensive and costly implementation. Review procedures—SIRs—are likely to be critical for ensuring that noncompliance with ambitious nonbinding commitments, which is common, is not merely a sign of inaction.

Legally binding commitments nonetheless retain an important role as one of many international policy instruments. Indeed, the benefits of nonbinding instruments often have been most evident when applied in tandem with legally binding measures. The North Sea Ministerial Declarations and the NOx nonbinding Declaration were conceived as part of a broad complex of instruments that includes both nonbinding and binding commitments. Domestic efforts to pressure governments and target groups to implement international commitments may be more effective when they can refer to a binding instrument, even if its commitments are modest while more ambitious commitments are found only in nonbinding instruments. The existence of a core binding commitment may serve as a necessary rite of passage, helping to raise the profile and effectiveness of all efforts—binding and nonbinding, formal and informal. Binding commitments can also serve as a backstop if ambitious nonbinding commitments are abandoned, such as in the case of Norway's efforts to regulate NOx.

This new approach to international environmental governance, which places greater emphasis on nonbinding instruments and on regular and extensive implementation review, can and should become more common in handling the new generation of environmental problems. These problems are marked by the need for costly but uncertain changes in behavior as well as ambiguity as to the best means of achieving such changes. In that category today are problems such as climate change and loss of biological diversity, which may require fundamental changes in the ways that modern economies use and value natural resources. Fundamental changes are difficult to plan and implement according to exacting, binding targets.

Discussion Notes/Questions

1. How should Raustiala and Victor's conclusions be applied to climate change?

2. Is the withholding of financial assistance an appropriate "stick"?

3. What are the key factors for determining whether a binding or non-binding instrument will be most effective?

4. Why is data gathering so important?

2. DOMESTIC LAW STRATEGIES

David Wirth, *A Matchmaker's Challenge: Marrying International Law and American Environmental Law* 32 VA. J. INT'L L. 377, 392–99, 414–19 (1992).

III. DISCONTINUITIES BETWEEN THE INTERNATIONAL AND DOMESTIC LEGAL SYSTEM

The international legal system, like national law, is constantly changing. International responsibilities of the United States may be affected by orders and judgments of the International Court of Justice, decisions of international arbitral tribunals, binding international agreements, the evolution of customary standards and norms, and other multilateral instruments. Difficulties can nevertheless arise at the interface between international and national law. These interstices in the legal framework fall into at least two generic categories. First, developments on the international level may diverge from existing domestic legislative and regulatory schemes. Second, the implementation of international duties at the national level may encounter legal complications. This section examines case studies of each type of discontinuity.

A. *Executive Agreements Affecting Domestic Environmental Regimes*

The principle that an international agreement and a statute should be reconciled whenever possible finds its most frequent application where there is an apparent conflict between an earlier international agreement and a later statute. However, two recent cases—both of which interpret environmental statutory schemes—suggest that courts may construe the requirements of existing domestic law in light of a subsequent international agreement. This approach can on occasion disrupt existing legislative and regulatory structures in unpredictable and arguably unintended ways when, as in each of these cases, international obligations are contained in an executive agreement entered into based on the Executive Branch's unilateral interpretation of a statute and without Congressional approval or participation.

In *Japan Whaling Association v. American Cetacean Society*,[64] the Supreme Court construed the Packwood Amendment to the Magnuson Fishery Conservation and Management Act[65] and the Pelly Amendment to the Fishermen's Protective Act of 1967[66] in light of a subsequent executive agreement[67] with Japan. The existence of that agreement was decisive in the Court's rejection of arguments that a federal official had violated a statutory directive.

Shortly after World War II, more than forty nations entered into a multilateral agreement known as the International Convention for the Regulation of Whaling **[Basic Document 6.2]** that created the International Whaling Commission (IWC). The IWC has the power to set limits on the harvesting of various whale species. An "opt-out" procedure allows each nation party to the Whaling Convention unilaterally to reject these quotas, rendering them legally ineffective with respect to that country. Although the quotas are binding on member nations that do not opt out, the IWC nevertheless has no power to impose sanctions for violations.

The Pelly and Packwood Amendments attempt to reinforce the Whaling Convention on the domestic level by requiring the Secretary of Commerce to monitor the whaling activities of foreign nationals and to investigate potential violations of the Whaling Convention. Upon completion of this investigation, the Secretary must promptly decide whether to certify conduct by foreign nationals that "diminishes the effectiveness" of the Whaling Convention. After certification by the Secretary, the Packwood Amendment directs the Secretary of State to reduce the offending nation's fishing allocation within the United States' fishery conservation zone by at least fifty per cent.

In 1981, the IWC established a zero quota for harvests of sperm whales. During the next year, the Commission ordered a five-year moratorium on commercial whaling to begin in the 1985–86 season and to continue until 1990. Japan filed timely objections that effectively relieved it, as an international legal matter, from compliance with the sperm whale quotas for 1982 through 1984. Nonetheless, the potential sanction under the Pelly and Packwood Amendments by the United States threatened Japanese whaling for the 1984–85 season. After extensive negotiations, the United States and Japan concluded an executive agreement in which Japan agreed to catch no more than 400 sperm whales in each of the 1984 and 1985 seasons. Japan also agreed to cease commercial whaling by 1988, three years after the date specified by the IWC. In return, the United States agreed not to certify Japan under the Pelly and Packwood Amendments.

---

64. 478 U.S. 221 (1986).

65. 16 U.S.C. § 1821(e)(2).

66. 22 U.S.C. § 1978.

67. Agreement Concerning Commercial Sperm Whaling in the Western Division Stock of the North Pacific, Nov. 13, 1984, United States–Japan, T.I.A.S. No. 11,070.

Suit was brought by several environmental organizations to compel the Secretary of Commerce to certify Japan. The Supreme Court, reversing both the District Court and the Court of Appeals, decided that the Secretary had no mandatory duty to certify in response to IWC quota violations. Although the bulk of the opinion deals with the construction of the Pelly and Packwood Amendments, it is clear that the chosen interpretation was strongly influenced by the existence of the agreement with Japan as an acceptable, if alternative, means of achieving the statutory goal.

The international agreement at issue in this case was an executive agreement, entered into on behalf of the United States by the President without consent or input from the Congress. Neither of the applicable legislative enactments authorized the negotiation of the agreement, nor was the particular agreement with Japan endorsed by the Congress either before or after its conclusion. Although the question remains the subject of considerable debate, some authority suggests that such an agreement must be consistent with existing legislation. The Court avoided this problem by interpreting the conflict out of existence, but simultaneously contorted the statutory framework.

Greenpeace USA v. Stone[68] is among the most recent cases addressing environmental effects outside the United States under the National Environmental Policy Act of 1969 (NEPA).[69] The court in that case made clear that its conclusion that NEPA did not apply was strongly influenced by an agreement that the court found had been made between President Bush and Chancellor Kohl of Germany.

This case concerned a plan of the United States Army and the Department of Defense, together with the German Army, to remove obsolete chemical weapons from a storage site in Clausen, Germany. The weapons were to be transported by rail and ship to Johnston Atoll, a United States Territory in the Pacific Ocean, pursuant to a Congressional mandate directing the destruction of the entire United States chemical weapons inventory by 1997. Environmental Impact Statements (EISs) required by NEPA had been prepared for the federal actions on Johnston Atoll. Plaintiffs challenged the Government's failure to prepare a comprehensive EIS covering all aspects of the transportation and disposal of the European stockpile, including transit through Germany and transport over the ocean.

Relying on the political question doctrine, the court denied plaintiffs' motion for a temporary restraining order enjoining the removal of the stockpile from Germany. In both that decision and an opinion denying plaintiffs' further motion for a preliminary injunction, the District Court gave substantial weight to foreign policy concerns. In particular, the court emphasized the significance of what it characterized as an agreement between President Bush, through Secretary of State Baker, and Chancellor Kohl, according to which the United States pledged to remove the stockpile by December 1990. The court explicitly articulated the crucial importance of this purported agreement to its reasoning.

68. 748 F.Supp. 749 (D.Haw.1990), *appeal dismissed as moot*, 924 F.2d 175 (9th Cir. 1991).

69. 42 U.S.C. §§ 4321–4370.

Like the agreement in *Japan Whaling*, the Bush–Kohl arrangement in the *Greenpeace* case was concluded without Congressional participation. Indeed, by comparison with the instrument in *Japan Whaling*, this "agreement" was never reduced to a single written instrument and was closer to a unilateral statement of purpose. If so, that undertaking would not even rise to the level of an international agreement in the legal sense.

NEPA is the "basic national charter for protection of the environment."[70] A cornerstone of NEPA law is the necessity to provide opportunities for public input, including notice of a proposed action, an opportunity to comment on a draft EIS, and the necessity for Executive Branch agencies preparing EISs to respond to public comments. As a general matter, these requirements apply as well to international agreements. Accordingly, if the Bush–Kohl arrangement is an international agreement, as the court seemed to accept in its opinion, that agreement might well have been subject to NEPA and its implementing regulations, including provisions for full disclosure and public participation. The court did not discuss whether NEPA applied to the creation of the Bush–Kohl arrangement instead of its implementation, thereby excluding the statute's application at both stages. If, on the other hand, that arrangement did not rise to the level of an international agreement, the implications are even more profound. Then the court's opinion strongly suggests that the routine, day-to-day conduct of foreign relations by the Executive Branch—often undertaken in secrecy without notice to, input from, or scrutiny by the Congress or the public—may frustrate or attenuate otherwise dispositive statutory directives.

* * *

IV. STRENGTHENING THE NEXUS BETWEEN INTERNATIONAL AND DOMESTIC LAW

This uneasy interface between international and national law has potentially far-reaching, but as yet largely unappreciated, implications.... At least two initiatives would tend to minimize [the] divergences between the international and national legal systems while preserving the integrity of the international obligations of the United States.

* * *

A. *Congressional Participation in International Agreements Not Expressly Contemplated by Statute*

The *Japan Whaling* and *Greenpeace* cases demonstrate the disruptive effect international agreements can have on domestic legislative regimes. Existing statutory and regulatory schemes can mesh smoothly with treaties and executive agreements authorized by the Congress through legislative participation in defining the terms of those international instruments. Moreover, Congressionally-sanctioned international agreements have the imprimatur of the legislative branch as the law of the land. By contrast, executive agreements not expressly contemplated by statute, even if not strictly inconsistent with existing law, can nonetheless modify or even frustrate the operation of existing legislation and regulation without the participation of the legislative branch.

---

70. 40 C.F.R. 1500.1 (Council on Environmental Quality implementing regulations).

That an "agreement can be given effect without the enactment of subsequent legislation by the Congress," as set out in State Department policy, is not by itself necessarily sufficient evidence of consistency with Congressional intent as expressed in an existing legislative scheme. Nor does that test provide adequate legal justification as a matter of course in the absence of express prior statutory authorization for the choice of an executive agreement instead of either an article II, section 2 treaty or a Congressional–Executive mechanism requiring the participation of the legislature. The mere existence of statutory authority in a particular area does not consequently imply that an executive agreement that has domestic legal effect and that purports to rely on that authority is consistent with the underlying Congressional purpose. Further, reliance on an executive agreement not expressly contemplated by statute could be questionable when implementation is intended to be accomplished by new regulations or rulemakings pursuant to existing statutes. In such a case, the international agreement could compromise the regulatory process, thereby undermining important principles of administrative law like those in the APA. Finally, even when both statutory and regulatory authorities are in place, the choice of an executive agreement would be inappropriate because of its tendency through international processes to constrain future legislative and administrative choices.

However, as State Department policy also recognizes, resolution of the historically delicate question of "choice of instrument" is quite sensitive to context. In such situations, silence, indifference, or acquiescence by the Congress can carry legal significance. To overcome potentially difficult questions concerning the necessary threshold level of Congressional interest and thorny interbranch disputes that can arise on a case-by-case basis, Congress ought to consider enacting legislation that would articulate the requisite legislative concern for each executive agreement not previously authorized by statute that falls within the enumerated powers of the Congress and that is intended to have domestic legal effect. Legislative participation in formulating and giving domestic legal effect to international agreements within realms of statutory concern will almost by definition tend to assure greater consistency with overall statutory purposes. For instance, the legislation might require the Executive Branch to transmit interim drafts of this sub category of executive agreements to relevant Congressional committees and establish a process for regularized consultation with those committees. The Congress could also enact legislation with instructions to the judiciary that executive agreements on matters within the enumerated powers of Congress must be explicitly authorized by statute to have effect as domestic law. Alternatively, the Executive could itself decide to alter its practice in this with respect to this sub-category of executive agreements.

For this same sub-category of agreements, there should also be an explicit instruction to the courts to decide questions of statutory interpretation notwithstanding the political question doctrine and foreign affairs implications. Further, the legislation should address the current overly broad discretion of the courts, short of a conclusion of nonjusticiability through application of the political question doctrine, haphazardly to take broad account of foreign relations concerns in judicial decisions with few apparent standards. Instead, Congress ought to substitute principles governing the judicial calculus to clarify the legal force of an Executive Branch action taken in an international context, within the enumerated powers of Congress, intended to have domestic legal effect, and not expressly authorized or participated in by the Congress.

B. Regularized Public Participation on the National and International Levels

Perhaps the most obvious divergences between international and national law involve considerations of process. For example, if the Uruguay Round proposals on harmonization of sanitary and phytosanitary standards are adopted, GATT dispute settlement mechanisms will become a forum in which United States regulations on pesticide residues could be challenged as a matter of international law. However, unlike domestic legislative, administrative, and judicial processes, those mechanisms are secret and inaccessible to the public. In the Mexican Tuna case the Executive Branch—in secret and with no formal opportunity for Congressional or public input—was responsible for vigorously defending a policy it reluctantly adopted only after flouting three statutory directives and resisting a court order. Such "cognitive dissonance" may be an endemic artifact of our domestic constitutional structure of separation of powers, in which the President both carries out the law and serves as the "sole organ of the nation in its external relations." The posture of the Mexican Tuna case and the Uruguay Round, which would give foreign governments the authority to challenge United States pesticide residue limitations, nevertheless throws the closed nature of GATT dispute settlement into sharp relief and pointedly demonstrates the failure of that procedure to insure even a modicum of accountability to the public.[y]

As more environmental threats that are governed by or overlap with domestic regulatory structures are addressed in the international arena, there is a commensurately increasing need for improved processes for public participation on the international level. To ameliorate the effects of resulting discontinuities, multilateral fora like GATT might adopt rules of procedure that regularize and greatly expand public access to, and public accountability of, their law-making, law-enforcing, and adjudicatory processes. Without question, improved access and public participation at the international level is the most desirable way to reconcile these disparities, while simultaneously furthering the larger public policy goals of improving the legitimacy and accountability of the international legal system. However, much can also be done at the purely national level in the absence of progress on the international level or until multilaterally agreed-upon measures are implemented.

First, the APA's foreign affairs exception should be reevaluated. The underlying justification for that provision is no longer warranted, if it ever was. The foreign affairs exception is a crude and unsophisticated mechanism governing a sphere of the law that has become increasingly nuanced and complex. Environment, like foreign trade, clearly falls within the enumerated powers of the Congress. The national legislature has reacted to both issues with complex webs of statutory and regulatory directives. For that reason, both areas are fundamentally different from traditional security and foreign affairs concerns like the conduct of war and the recognition of foreign

y. For pertinent commentary, see *supra* Problem 11–1 ("The Environment and GATT Collide in Albion").

governments entrusted by the Constitution to the President. Likewise, international undertakings on both environmental and foreign trade matters governed by statute are well within the reach of Congressional law-making authority. Accordingly, the unusual deference to the Executive Branch contained in the APA exception merely because of the international context for decision-making is not warranted.

Second, Congress should replace the sweeping APA exemption with comprehensive new legislation that articulates how basic principles of American public law will be applied in a foreign affairs context. At a minimum, this legislation should establish standards for distinguishing between those domains such as war and recognition of foreign governments—that are appropriate for an exemption like that currently in the APA and those—like environment—that are not. For the latter category, outcome-neutral procedures analogous to notice-and-comment rulemaking and judicial review under the APA should be established, with processes tailored to meet the needs of governmental decision-making in national, bilateral, and multilateral contexts. For instance, the legislation might require publication of interim drafts of international agreements in the Federal Register, with a subsequent opportunity for formal public comment to United States negotiators, unless the President provides compelling reasons, such as overriding national security concerns, to justify a waiver.

Discussion Notes/Questions

1. What lessons can be learned from Professor Wirth's analysis of the whaling developments?

2. What is the importance of public input in international negotiations?

3. Is it better for international environmental law to be made in negotiations by nation states free from the influences of legislatures and domestic public opinion? Why? Why not?

4. How does the domestic law of judicial review in the United States affect internationally negotiated outcomes?

5. In 1996, the American Society of International Law's (ASIL) Interest Group in International Environmental Law undertook a comparative study of the application of international environmental law by domestic courts. A recent article by Daniel Bodansky and Jutta Brunnee, *The Role of National Courts in the Field of International Environmental Law* 7 RECIEL 11 (1998), is based on the ASIL study. The authors note that cases involving international environmental law have been too sporadic for national courts to play a significant deterrence role, but courts have contributed to dispute-resolution and implementation in individual cases. The authors note that existing case law suggests various options for strategic litigation. However, they caution that the role which national courts can reasonably and legitimately play in implementing international environmental law must be more carefully examined.

Lakshman Guruswamy, *Global Warming: Integrating United States and International Law* 32 ARIZ. L. REV. 221, 253–63 (1990).

A. THE NEED FOR INTEGRATION

Issues of science and science policy concern only one aspect of global warming. We must also address the problem within a more overtly political framework. In the past, global insecurity was posed by military threats and armed aggression. The threat to security as Lester Brown pointed out with percipience and insight, "may now arise less from the relationship of nation to nation and more from the relationship of man to nature."[71] In light of such a peril the demand to redefine national security to include environmental dangers is difficult to resist. The security problem global warming presents cannot be solved between two superpowers or even by the efforts of the major industrialized countries. Safeguarding the world requires a truly global effort. This effort must include the domain of international law.

Both the United States and the international community face a common foe, and need to arrive at measures that can succeed against it. Recognition that United States policy is addressing a common global problem makes it evident, at both national and international levels, that the fashioning of common policies between the United States and the international community of states presents an eminently sensible and rational way of meeting the challenge. To the extent that it is a common problem, we must search for common answers acceptable to all countries and capable of incorporation into both international and national legal systems. If, therefore, the United States can pioneer strategies, policies and laws that could be adapted by the rest of the international community, it would in fact be providing solutions at the levels of both national and international law. Consequently, United States environmental laws dealing with global warming that integrate national, comparative and international approaches, will constitute a rational and compelling legal response to a global peril.

Hitherto environmental problems usually were experienced, detected and interdicted within local or national boundaries. National legal systems possessed the jurisdictional power and the capacity to solve them. Unfortunately, global warming cannot be solved in this way. It arises because the atmospheric commons, shared by all nations, has been polluted by the very nations that depend on it. Unilateral national legislation adopted by the United States prohibiting such pollution, will not solve the problem when other nations continue to pollute. The United States is only one (though perhaps the most important) among 160 nation states. The problem insists on common and concerted action at both global and national levels.

But this is no occasion to invoke, far less celebrate, existing international law. That law possesses neither the jurisdiction and institutions, nor substantive law and remedies, to deal with the problem. Alas, international law as well as national laws permit the pollution of the global commons. Even in a shrinking, interdependent role, international law is premised upon national sovereignty, and nation states insist upon the sovereignty, supremacy and independence to determine their own course of action. Consequently, when we confront problems that have outstripped and outgrown the existing capacity of both national and international legal systems, we also confront a glaring lacuna in the law.

The legal gap referred to can only be overcome by a new generation of United States environmental laws that seek to integrate international and national policy and law. Integration is an elastic term encompassing a spectrum of meanings ranging from implementation to unification. For our

---

71. Lester Brown, Human Needs and the Security of Nations 6 (1978).

purposes integration is synonymous with compositeness rather than unity. It ensures that United States law will cohere with international law to form an identifiable whole. Integration generates United States and international lawmaking but does not call for the unification or uniformity of such laws. . . .

* * *

C. AN ENTREPRENEUR FOR INTERNATIONAL LAW

United States leadership is the necessary catalyst in the formation of effective international law controlling global warming. International law is still at an early, even primitive, stage of development, and has not matured into a legal system, as that term is ordinarily understood. It is unnecessary to explore the well recognized distinctions between developed national legal systems and the undeveloped state of international law except to point out that international law does not possess a binding law-making agency or international legislature, it has no law interpreting body or court with universal compulsory jurisdiction, and no law enforcing or policing agencies. In short, there are no international institutions, comparable to those within the United States, that can create new laws dealing with global warming.

It is sadly true that answers to global problems emerge with excruciating tardiness out of a primitive system of international law. Timely answers cannot be extracted from the Byzantine mix of policies meshed within the international social, scientific, and political milieu embraced by these problems. In comparison to domestic law, international law making is generally very slow and unproductive. It will remain so despite what appears to be an emerging scientific consensus on the gravity of these problems, and the expectation that legal measures and controls must be fashioned because they are the only rational way of averting evident danger.

Unfortunately, legal action is based on political realities and not scientific rationality. Harvey Brooks points out that past attempts to use international scientific networks to influence national political decisions have had limited success largely because of a lack of political sensitivity.[72] Proposed measures have to be measured by the pulse of the political process and cannot only be taken on the basis of more scientific information or expertise. Law making is difficult enough in the United States. Those difficulties are multiplied in the international context. The complications of crossing from cognition to solution are compounded by the fact that the international "legal system" is so much weaker than a national legal system. The international community may agree on what the environmental problems are, and even on what ought to be done about them, but international political and legal processes hardly lend themselves to the expeditious translation of "ought" to "is."

In this situation of cumbersome and sometimes irrational international lawmaking the United States can make a critical contribution to the emerging tapestry of environmental law and policy. The process of working towards the creation of national law will equip and enable the United States to press for the acceptance of a global convention. The intervention of the United States as a superpower and an economic giant in favor of a treaty on global warming

---

72. Harvey Brooks, *The Role of International Research Institutions, in* SCIENCE FOR PUB- LIC POLICY 151–52 (Harvey Brooks & Chester Cooper eds., 1987).

will be critical if not decisive. Because the United States is, arguably, still the most important environmental player on the global scene and its internal actions will make a critical contribution to the speedier evolution and creation of new international law.

The recent response to ozone depletion, which is analogous to global warming, is instructive of the way in which the first question concerning the likelihood or certainty of risk evoked similar answers from United States and international lawmakers. Scientists found mounting evidence that chlorine containing substances, more specially fully halogenated chlorofluorocarbons (CFC's), when released into the atmosphere, slowly migrate into the stratosphere and are broken down by solar radiation. The chlorine atoms so produced catalyze a series of reactions that ultimately destroy ozone. Authorities estimated that such a destruction of ozone would admit greater solar UV–B radiation that would lead to increased basal skin cancers and squamous-cell cancers.

Under the auspices of the United Nations Environment Program (UNEP), a global framework convention for the protection of the ozone layer—the "Vienna Convention for the Protection of the Ozone Layer" **[Basic Document 3.14]**—was signed in 1985. It was an umbrella convention containing broad obligations lacking specificity. More specific and binding rules were to be elaborated in the form of protocols and technical annexes. The lack of agreement on more concrete measures was partly attributable to the absence of scientific proof of CFC damage. Shortly after the Vienna Convention concluded, scientists discovered a hole in the ozone layer over Antarctica, and found that there had been a dramatic forty percent decrease of springtime ozone between 1977 and 1984. They realized that the scientific conclusions on which the Vienna Convention relied had seriously underestimated the extent of ozone depletion. The new scientific findings led to a burst of activity, led by the United States, that culminated in the Montreal Protocol **[Basic Document 3.18]**. It might be pointed out that the ozone hole did not conclusively prove the culpability of CFC's. Be this as it may a scientific consensus emerged, which the United States argued, warranted international action. Such action was in fact taken. The ozone story illustrates the importance of an entrepreneur capable of employing scientific findings to advance international lawmaking.

Furthermore, United States law could be adopted or could generate similar laws in other countries. The foreign impact of United States environmental law and policy has been formidable. The National Environmental Policy Act (NEPA) revealed how environmental impact could be ascertained and become part of the broader policy-making framework. The EPA demonstrated that a centralized pollution inspectorate could become a reality, while citizen suits offered an antidote against administrative apathy. Freedom of information opened the doors to environmental participation. Even the much maligned, rigorous, combative character of environmental laws dealing with air and water pollution, are now seen as the wave of the future. International law is a consensual law that arises only if nations agree to its creation. The nations which emulate United States laws will be among the lawmakers of international law, and it would be perfectly natural for them to agree to international law that mirrors their own preferences.

Discussion Notes/Questions

1. Is Professor Guruswamy's approach compatible with that of Professor Wirth, *supra*? Why? Why not?

2. Can international and domestic environmental law be successfully integrated as Guruswamy suggests? What obstacles are there to such an approach?

3. Can some of the primitive characteristics of international law be eliminated by linking it to domestic law on environmental issues? If so, how? If not, why not?

4. How do the complexities of science as they affect international environmental issues fit into the international/domestic law interface in Guruswamy's view?

5. Does the United States, as the world's only superpower, have a heavier responsibility to integrate its legal approaches than other countries?

6. If the United States has a leadership role, how is it to discharge that obligation?

3. THE ECONOMIC INSTRUMENT

HILLARY FRENCH, AFTER THE EARTH SUMMIT: THE FUTURE
OF ENVIRONMENTAL GOVERNANCE 38–45 (1992).

In national governments, the finance and commerce ministries often hold sway over environmental protection ministries in interagency struggles. At the international level as well, power rests with the institutions charged with managing the world economy. Strengthening global environmental governance will thus depend in large measure on substantially reforming today's leading international economic institutions—the World Bank, the International Monetary Fund, and the General Agreement on Tariffs and Trade **[Basic Document 7.1]**.

These organizations have achieved considerable successes in the task granted them by governments when they were created after World War II—stabilizing the world monetary system and preventing a return to the protectionism of the thirties that contributed to the global depression. But the environment was not recognized to be inextricably linked with the economy at that time, as it is beginning to be now. The globalization of the world economy, combined with the power of the World Bank, IMF, and GATT to affect policies, means that a growing amount of *de facto* environmental governance is now taking place through the "back door"—via these organizations.

The World Bank exerts considerable influence in the countries to which it makes loans, through the projects it chooses to finance and the conditions it places on how the money is spent. All too often this influence has been negative, with the bank underwriting ecological debacles, such as large hydroelectric dams that have forced over a million people to relocate, and regional development programs that have stripped tropical rainforests. In recent years, its record has improved somewhat.[z] In 1987, under pressure from environmental groups and the U.S. government, Bank president Barber

z. *See supra* "Editors' Note: The Global Environmental Facility," at Section B.1.

Conable announced several measures aimed at making sustainable development a greater priority throughout the bank's massive annual lending program ($23 billion in 1991). He created a central environment department and environmental units in each regional bureau, and announced that environmental impact assessments would be required for all projects. The amount of money devoted to freestanding environmental loans also began to increase. In 1991, such loans amounted to $1.6 billion, up from some $400 million in all previous years combined.[73]

Despite this progress, the bank has a long way to go before it can claim to have taken the sustainable development message to heart. The new environment department is committed to change, but it has so far had limited success in making its influence felt throughout the immense organization of nearly 6,000 employees in 53 offices around the world. By and large, the bank's ranks continue to be filled with economists who view environmental protection as an amenity rather than a fundamental precondition for sustainable development. Though the World Bank claims to be working to better integrate environmental concerns throughout its lending program, critics say that in many cases the environmental component of projects is so small as to border on irrelevance. And the bank continues to invest primarily in large, capital intensive projects that are relatively cheap to administer, rather than in the smaller-scale, grassroots efforts that are often needed. It also slows its own movement toward more enlightened lending practices by shrouding its operations in secrecy. The World Bank views itself as accountable to governments alone. As a result, local people and non-governmental groups cannot gain access to most of its documents, let alone participate in a meaningful way in the planning or implementation process even though these documents may determine the fates of their communities.

While the ecological impacts of the World Bank and regional development banks have received considerable attention in recent years, the IMF's environmental role has been largely overlooked. The fund was originally created to provide short-term balance of payments support for needy countries in order to help stabilize the world economic system. During the eighties, it played a central role in efforts to resolve the international debt crisis. In fiscal year 1991, the fund loaned out $20 billion. In return for access to IMF financing, the fund requires recipient countries to adopt "structural adjustment programs" that include a range of policy measures intended to set the recipient's economic house in order so that it will be creditworthy. Common policy prescriptions include steep cuts in government expenditures, reductions in subsidies, devaluation of currencies, and reduction of trade barriers.

The products of often difficult negotiations between IMF officials and recipient governments, these programs have been roundly criticized in recent years. Many development experts and Third World governments charge that the reduced subsidies and slashed governmental expenditures generally prescribed in structural adjustment programs are a bitter medicine which usually hurts the poor disproportionately. In some cases, it is even questionable whether the programs are helpful to the country's economic health in the long run.

73. WORLD BANK, THE WORLD BANK AND THE
ENVIRONMENT: A PROGRESS REPORT (1991).

But the environment, too, can be a victim of IMF structural adjustment programs. The emphasis on boosting exports to earn foreign exchange can lead to the destruction of natural resources such as forests, wetlands, and mangroves, and to excessive development of ecologically damaging industries such as mining. Requirements that countries drastically reduce governmental expenditures can cause the elimination or postponement of crucial governmental activities, such as wildlife management or enforcement of environmental laws. Finally, to the extent that structural adjustment programs hurt the poor, they will often also hurt the environment, given the tendency for poverty and environmental degradation to go hand in hand. For instance, unemployed laborers might increasingly make their way into the tropical rainforest to engage in slash-and-burn agriculture.

If environmental reform were treated as an important element of structural adjustment, these programs could be a powerful tool to encourage environmentally beneficial programs—while still achieving their original objectives of economic stabilization. Already, some policies promoted by structural adjustment programs are having positive environmental results. For instance, cutting subsidies to ecologically damaging industries, such as mining and energy development, helps to achieve both economic and environmental goals. A recent loan agreement with Haiti pointed out that government-imposed trade barriers on agricultural products were having the unintended effect of aggravating soil erosion by encouraging grain production on marginal lands. Removing the barriers, as the loan agreement recommended, would be an environmental gain. But at the moment, any environmental benefits are merely incidental by-products of the IMF's policy prescriptions rather than integral goals. Only when the fund's managers recognize that environmental health and economic prosperity are inextricably linked will this change.

Unfortunately, the IMF is resisting even the most elementary environmental reforms. The U.S. Congress passed a bill in 1989 directing the U.S. treasury department to use its influence at the fund to promote such reforms, including the creation of an environmental department, procedures for more consultation with the public, and the weighing of environmental considerations in policy framework papers prepared jointly by the recipient country, the fund, and the World Bank. So far, however, the IMF has done little more than assign three economists to do environmental research. In February 1991, the fund's Executive Directors explicitly rejected the idea of creating an environment department. Environmental groups are lobbying Congress to turn down a proposed capital increase for the fund unless it begins to make environmental protection more of a priority.

The international community is also beginning to pay attention, finally, to the effect of world trade agreements and institutions on the environment. Commercial interests, environmentalists, and government authorities alike have worried that new environmental policies might be on a collision course with free trade obligations. The question of how best to reconcile these goals has been debated for several years within the European Community, and emerged as a major issue in negotiations over a North American Free Trade Agreement in 1991. In addition, environmentalists have grown concerned that the current round of trade negotiations within GATT could lead to the erosion of hard-won environmental gains.

Their concern reached a crisis point with a September, 1991 ruling by a GATT dispute resolution panel suggesting that the use of trade sanctions for environmental purposes is at odds with GATT rules.[aa] The panel upheld a Mexican charge that a U.S. embargo on Mexican tuna violated GATT rules. The embargo had been imposed in accordance with a U.S. law that forbids the import of tuna from countries employing fishing practices that have been restricted at home because they fatally ensnare large numbers of dolphins along with the tuna. Consideration of the ruling by the full GATT General Council has been indefinitely deferred by joint agreement of the United States and Mexico. Yet the ruling itself was a clear signal that, unless GATT is amended, countries may encounter legal difficulties in using trade sanctions to promote environmental goals.

There are many other ways in which free trade and environmental goals can conflict. Product standards can have the effect of discriminating against foreign-made products—such as cars not meeting domestic automobile fuel efficiency standards, or beverages sold in non-returnable bottles—whether or not this was their intent. Other important conservation strategies also can constrain trade. For example, some countries have banned the export of unprocessed logs, which hastens deforestation while creating few jobs. Japan, the leading importer of tropical logs from Southeast Asia, has charged that these bans violate GATT rules.[74]

Import taxes on products made in countries with lax environmental standards have also been attacked as trade barriers. The usual motivation for these taxes is to ensure that domestic producers are not put at a competitive disadvantage by having to meet strict environmental standards. But these levies also help prevent the export of hazardous industries to countries where regulation is lax. Such countries are in essence subsidizing domestic industries at the environment's expense, a practice that is coming to be known as "ecological dumping." But trade agreements have yet to recognize this concept. Instead, they tend to regard environmentally-motivated import tariffs as unfair trade barriers.

The most logical solution to the trade and environment dilemma is to negotiate strict international environmental standards that require companies in every country to play by the same rules. This "level playing field" would insure both free trade and environmental protection in an increasingly global economy. But there are practical difficulties in negotiating a common policy. Forging a consensus among countries that have varied commitments to environmental protection and are at different stages of economic development is difficult. Some analysts fear that any achievable international standard would be a least common denominator that would eviscerate the environmental laws of more progressive countries.

Short of this, it might be possible to amend the GATT and other trade agreements to explicitly recognize that nations have the right to set their own domestic environmental laws, to clarify that trade sanctions have a legitimate

aa. For pertinent commentary, *see supra* Problem 11–1 ("The Environment and GATT Collide in Albion").

74. CHARLES ARDEN-CLARKE, THE GENERAL AGREEMENT ON TARIFFS AND TRADE, ENVIRONMENTAL PROTECTION AND SUSTAINABLE DEVELOPMENT (1991); FRANCOIS NECTOUX & YOICHI KURODA, TIMBER FROM THE SOUTH SEAS: AN ANALYSIS OF JAPAN'S TROPICAL TIMBER TRADE AND ITS ENVIRONMENTAL IMPACT (1989).

role to play in environmental policymaking, and to permit import levies that discourage "ecological dumping". Since the tuna ruling, international environmental groups and the chairman of the U.S. Senate's International Trade Subcommittee, Max Baucus, have called for the negotiation of such an environmental code. Though this would satisfy most environmentalists, it would do little to address the concerns of those who worry that environmental policies are impeding free trade. Developing countries are particularly wary of barriers to their products that could be erected on pseudo-environmental grounds.

* * *

The GATT itself is taking some halting steps toward grappling with the problem. A moribund working group on the relationship between trade and the environment, first established in the early seventies, has recently reconvened to discuss these difficult questions. But environmental groups fear the emphasis is mistakenly being placed on eliminating environmental policies that impede free trade, rather than vice-versa. Many developing countries, on the other hand, are strongly opposed to even discussing the connection between trade and the environment, given their worries that the industrialized world is using ecological concerns as an excuse to erect more barriers to their products.

One troublesome aspect of the growing power of institutions such as the World Bank, the IMF, and trade agreements to affect environmental policy is the fact that the world's more powerful countries exert a disproportionate influence in these bodies. To developing countries, it often appears that the rich countries are hypocritically imposing environmental conditions on them while being unwilling to take actions themselves to solve problems such as global warming. One way to right this imbalance is to consider alternative schemes for distributing voting power in these bodies, as has been proposed for the Washington, D.C.-based Global Environment Facility [GEF].[bb] Opening these notoriously secretive international institutions to more extensive public participation would also help ease their inequitable distribution of power. Rather than rich countries manipulating the poor ones, world public opinion would be shaping governments.

Discussion Notes/Questions

1. How much effort needs to be given to the development of economic institutions in responding to the global environmental challenge?

2. Is there really a conflict between GATT and the environment, or does there just appear to be?

———

Robert Repetto, *Balance Sheet—Incorporating Natural Resources in National Income Accounts* 34 ENV'T. 13–17, 44 (1992).

Whatever their shortcomings, the national income accounting systems used by governments to assess macroeconomic performance are undoubtedly

bb. *See supra* "Editors' Note: The Global Environmental Facility" at Section B.1.

one of the 20th century's most significant social inventions. Their political and economic impacts can scarcely be overestimated. However inappropriately, they serve to divide the world into "developed" and "developing" countries. In the developed countries, whenever the quarterly gross domestic product (GDP) figures emerge, policymakers stir. Should the latest figure be lower, even marginally, than those of the preceding three months, a recession is declared, the strategies and competence of the federal administration are impugned, and public political debate ensues. In the developing countries, the rate of growth of GDP is the principal measure of economic progress and transformation.

National income accounts have become so much a part of society that it is hard to remember that they have been in use for only 50 years: They were first published in the United States in 1942. It is no coincidence that, during the last half century, governments have taken responsibility for the growth and stability of their economies and have invested enormous amounts of talent and energy in understanding how economies can be better managed.

The aim of national income accounting is to provide an information framework suitable for analyzing the performance of a country's economic system. The current System of National Accounts promoted by the United Nations is a historical artifact, heavily influenced by the theories of the British economist John Maynard Keynes in the 1930s. The system reflects the economic preoccupations of that time: the business cycle and persistent unemployment in industrial economies. Because raw material prices were at an all-time low in the 1930s, Keynesian economists paid little attention to the possibility of natural resource scarcities. Consequently, even today, the contribution that natural resources make to production and economic welfare is hardly acknowledged in national income accounts. Capital formation is assigned a central role in economic growth theories, but natural resources are not treated like other tangible assets in the System of National Accounts.

The result is a dangerous asymmetry in the way people measure and, hence, the way they think about the value of natural resources. Manmade assets, such as buildings and equipment, are valued as productive capital and are written off against the value of production as they depreciate. Natural resource assets are not so valued: A country could exhaust its mineral resources, cut down its forests, erode its soils, pollute its aquifers, and hunt its wildlife and fisheries to extinction without affecting its measured national income. It is a bitter irony that the low-income countries most dependent on natural resources for employment, revenues, and foreign exchange earnings are instructed to use a system for national accounting and macroeconomic analysis that almost completely ignores their principal assets.

SHORTCOMINGS OF THE SYSTEM

The System of National Accounts (SNA) published by the United Nations Statistical Office provides a standard, internationally accepted framework for setting up national income accounts. SNA includes stock accounts that identify assets and liabilities at particular points in time and flow accounts that keep track of transactions during intervals of time. Flow accounts include all transactions of final goods that determine the level of national income, or GDP, including capital formation and depreciation, purchases of goods and services, payments to wage and profit earners, and import payments and export revenues for goods and services. Flows and stocks are linked, in that flows are equal to differences between stocks and stocks are equal to accumulated past flows. With a few specific exceptions, only goods and services exchanged in the market economy are included in national income accounts. This is so because market prices offer a ready way to establish value.

National income accounts have become the basis for almost all macroeconomic analysis, planning, and evaluation. SNA is supposed to be an integrated, comprehensive, and consistent accounting framework; unfortunately, however, it is not. SNA gives inconsistent treatment to the consumption of capital goods and natural resources. The value of capital goods, such as buildings and equipment, declines with use because of physical wear and obsolescence. This gradual decrease in the future production potential of capital stocks is directly integrated into national flow accounts by a depreciation allowance that amortizes the asset's value over its useful lifetime. (Depreciation is the decline in the present value of a future income flow because of an asset's decay or obsolescence.) Depreciation of tangible, reproducible capital is subtracted from GDP in calculations of net domestic product. This subtraction reflects the fact that a nation must invest enough in new capital goods to offset the depreciation of existing assets if the future income-producing ability of the entire capital stock is to be preserved.

The United Nations recommends that countries create balance sheet accounts that include some natural resources, such as tree plantations, and nonrenewable resources, such as agricultural land and subsoil minerals, along with financial assets and stocks of capital goods. Rather than integrate changes in natural resource stocks directly into national flow accounts, however, the United Nations recommends that stock accounts of natural resources flow through separate "satellite" or "reconciliation" accounts.[cc]

Logically, if a country's national balance sheets indicate at two points in time that a natural resource, such as the forest, has been depleted, the flow accounts for the intervening years should show a capital consumption or depreciation allowance. If the forests have expanded, the accounts should show a corresponding amount of capital formation. This change would reflect perhaps the most basic identity[dd] in all of accounting—namely, that the difference in stocks between two points of time equals the net flow in the intervening period. SNA violates this basic accounting identity.

Reconciliation accounts, or accounts that reconcile apparent differences or discrepancies in other accounts, are, however, a poor substitute solution. They provide a means of recording changes in the value of net assets between successive measurement dates without having to show any effect on the income of the intervening period. Recording these changes in reconciliation accounts is likely to minimize their consideration in national policy analysis.

Ironically, SNA does classify as gross capital formation those expenses incurred in "improving" land for pastures, developing or extending timber-

cc. UN DEPARTMENT OF ECONOMIC AND SOCIAL AFFAIRS, PROVISIONAL INTERNATIONAL GUIDELINES ON THE NATIONAL AND SECTORAL BALANCE-SHEET AND RECONCILIATION ACCOUNTS OF THE SYSTEM OF NATIONAL ACCOUNTS STATISTICAL PAPERS, SERIES M, no. 60 (1977).

dd. Identity is a term used in economics to mean a relationship that is, by definition, true and is described in mathematical terms.

producing areas, or creating infrastructure for the fishing industry. SNA records such actions as contributing to recorded income and investment even though they sometimes destroy the income-producing potential of natural resources through deforestation, soil erosion, and over-fishing. This loss of capital—as natural resources are used beyond their capacity to recover—is not recorded in national income and investment accounts. The national accounts thereby create the illusion of income development when, in fact, national wealth is being destroyed. Thus, economic disaster masquerades as progress.

Several misunderstandings underlie this anomalous treatment of natural resources. First, it is a misconception that natural resources are so abundant that they have no marginal value. Whether or not they enter the marketplace directly, natural resources make important contributions to long-term economic productivity and so, strictly speaking, are economic assets. Another misunderstanding underlies the contention that natural resources are free gifts of nature, so that there are no investment costs to be written off. The value of an asset is not its investment cost but, rather, the capitalized present value of its income potential. Many companies valued by the stock market to be worth many billions of dollars have as their principal assets the brilliant ideas and inventions of their founders. The Polaroid camera, the Apple computer, and the Lotus spreadsheet are good examples. These inspired inventions are worth vastly more than any measurable cost their inventors incurred in developing them and, as the products of genius, could also be regarded as free gifts of nature.

The UN Statistical Office justifies its treatment of natural resources on the grounds that natural resources are nonmarketed goods and that their economic values cannot be readily established. This notion also is wrong. Indeed, the United Nations itself provides guidelines for valuing natural resource assets in the stock accounts that could be applied just as well to the flow accounts: The assets' market values are to be used if available; if not, the discounted present value of the stream of rents or net revenues from the asset is to be used instead.

THE SCOPE OF NATURAL RESOURCE ACCOUNTING

A growing number of experts have recognized the need to correct SNA's environmental blind spots. Several member nations of the Organization for Economic Cooperation and Development, including Canada, France, the Netherlands, Japan, Norway and the United States, have proposed or established systems of environmental accounts. Although natural resources take priority in the Norwegian and French systems, the U.S. and Japanese systems have focused on pollution and environmental quality. Canada and the Netherlands have combined elements of both approaches.

Norway and France have established extensive resource-accounting systems to supplement their national income accounts. The Norwegian system includes accounts for such material resources as fossil fuels and other minerals, such biotic resources as forests and fisheries, and such environmental resources as land, water, and air. The accounts are compiled in physical units of measurement, such as cubic meters or tons, and are not integrated with the national income accounts. However, resource accounts, especially those for petroleum and gas, have been expressed in monetary terms for use in macroeconomic planning.

The French natural patrimony accounts are intended as a comprehensive statistical framework to provide authorities with the data they need to monitor changes in "that subsystem of the terrestrial ecosphere that can be quantitatively altered by human activity."[ee] Like their Norwegian counterparts, these accounts cover nonrenewable resources, the physical environment, and living organisms. Because material and energy flows to and from economic activities form only a subset of these accounts, they are conceptually much broader than the national income accounts.

Compiling such environmental statistics may well encourage decision makers to consider the impacts of specific policies on national stocks of natural resources. Physical accounting by itself has considerable shortcomings, however. For instance, it does not lend itself to useful aggregation: Aggregating wood from various tree species into a single number of cubic meters obscures wide differences in the economic value of different species. Aggregating mineral reserves into a single number of tons obscures vast differences—caused by grade and recovery costs—in the value of deposits. Yet, maintaining separate physical accounts for particular species or deposits yields a mountain of statistics that is not easily summarized or used. A further problem with physical accounting is that such accounts do not enable economic planners to understand the impact of economic policies on natural resources or, thereby, to integrate resource decisions, which presumably is the main point of the exercise. There is, however, no conflict between accounting in physical and economic units because physical accounts are necessary prerequisites to economic accounts. If measurement of economic depreciation is extended to cover natural resources, physical accounts are inevitable byproducts.

The limits to monetary valuation of natural resources are set mainly by the remoteness of the resource in question from the market economy. Some resources, such as minerals, enter the marketplace directly. Others, such as groundwater, contribute to market production and can readily be assigned a monetary value even though they are rarely bought or sold. Still others, such as noncommercial wild species, are quite remote from the marketplace in that they do not contribute directly to production and can be assigned a monetary value only through quite roundabout methods involving many questionable assumptions. Although research into the economic value of resources that are remote from the market is to be encouraged, common sense suggests that highly speculative values should not be included in official accounts.

In industrial countries, where pollution and congestion are mounting while economies are becoming less dependent on agriculture, mining, and other forms of primary production, economists have proposed systems of environmental accounting that go well beyond the scope of natural resource accounting. One approach considers how GDP might be modified by the costs and benefits associated with pollution and its abatement.[ff] Other economists

ee. P. Corniere, *Natural Resource Accounts in France: An Example—Inland Water,* in OECD, INFORMATION AND NATURAL RESOURCES (1986).

ff. Orris Herfindahl & Allen Kneese, *Measuring Social and Economic Change: Benefits and Costs of Environmental Pollution,* in THE MEASUREMENT OF ECONOMIC AND SOCIAL PERFOR-

have proposed general systems to account for the impacts of economic activities on the environment broadly defined to include all land, water, and atmospheric resources.[gg]

To see, for example, how industrial countries are affected by the bizarre anomalies in the current SNA, consider how SNA treats toxic wastes. If toxic substances leak from a dump and pollute soils and aquifers, measured income does not fall despite the possibly severe impairment of vital natural resources. If the government spends millions of dollars to clean up the mess, however, measured income rises (other things being equal) because such government expenditures are considered to be purchases of final goods and services. If industry itself undertakes the cleanup, even under a court order, income does not rise because the same expenditures are considered to be intermediate production costs when they are made by enterprises. If the site is not cleaned up and nearby residents suffer increased medical expenses, measured income again rises because household medical expenses are also defined as final consumption expenditures in the national income accounts.

Clearly, environmental factors should be accounted for more completely. One aspect of environmental accounting—natural resource accounting—attempts to inject some environmental realities into national income accounting, but it excludes transitory environmental externalities, such as air pollution. There are good reasons to focus rather narrowly on accounting for renewable natural resources: The principal natural resources, such as land, timber, and minerals, are already listed under SNA as economic assets, although they are not treated like other tangible capital, and their physical and economic values can be readily established. Demonstrating the enormous costs of natural resource degradation to a national economy is an important first step in establishing the need for revamping national policy. It also helps people recognize the need for further developing environmental accounting methodologies.

Developing countries whose economies are dependent on natural resources are becoming particularly interested in developing an accounting framework that accounts for these assets more adequately. Work is already under way in the Philippines, China, India, Brazil, Chile, Colombia, El Salvador, and other developing countries.

* * *

Introducing such an accounting system will require that key international economic institutions—such as the World Bank, the other multilateral development banks, the International Monetary Fund, and the Organization for Economic Cooperation and Development—begin to compile, use, and publish revised estimates of net national product and national income. All such institutions should ready themselves to provide technical assistance to the growing number of national statistical offices that wish to adopt these changes and make such estimates for themselves.

MANCE: STUDIES IN INCOME AND WEALTH (Milton Moss ed., 1973); Karl–Goran Maler, *National Accounts and Environmental Resources*, 1 ENVTL. & RES. ECON. 1 (1991).

gg. For a survey of approaches taken, see Robert Eisner, *Extended Accounts for National Income and Product*, 26 J. ECON. LIT. 1611 (1988).

Finally, the United Nations should announce that the distortions in the treatment of natural resources will be removed in the ongoing revisions to SNA. This would be a timely and feasible way to ensure that the process begun at the UN Conference on Environment and Development in Rio de Janeiro in June goes forward with all deliberate speed in coming years. No other single action would go further to raise consciousness about the link between economic growth and the wise use of natural resources.

Discussion Notes/Questions

1. Is it beneficial to have environmental concerns recognized by a system that clearly is not designed to deal with them?

2. Would global politics be changed if National Systems of Accounts reflected the "wealth" of the South more accurately?

3. Has Repetto overestimated the educational function of such changes?

4. Under a revised System of Accounts, how might those resources that are remote from the marketplace be recognized? What about environmental features that have no marketplace value? Does the System of Accounts require assessment and critique at a more fundamental level?

THEODORE PANAYOTOU, GREEN MARKETS: THE ECONOMICS
OF SUSTAINABLE DEVELOPMENT 105–16 (1993).

Achieving Sustainable Development through Policy Reform

Virtually every developing country faces some degree of deforestation, watershed destruction, soil erosion, insecure land use, excessive pesticide application, and inefficient water use.

Issues of more localized interest include shifting cultivation in Southeast Asia, overgrazing in Africa and the Near East, water-logging in South Asia (Pakistan) and the Near East (especially Egypt), cattle ranching subsidies in Latin America (Brazil), and desertification in the arid lands of India, the Middle East, and Africa. Governments around the world are increasingly recognizing that this environmental degradation poses growing threats to the sustainability of the growth process. In response to these concerns, governments have changed existing policies and introduced new policies and programs. Increasingly, policy successes, though still far fewer than policy failures, are easier to find.

A policy success is a government intervention, or the elimination of one, that improves the allocation of resources and reduces the degradation of the environment. Policy successes can be classified into three groups: First is the reduction and eventual elimination of policies (taxes, subsidies, quotas, and public projects) that distort well-functioning markets or exacerbate market failures. The radical change in Indonesian policy toward pesticides in recent years is a case in point. Following economic analysis that showed negative returns from insecticides and agroecological research that confirmed the link between insecticide use and the surge of brown planthopper that threatened 70 percent of Java's rice crop, a 1986 presidential decree banned fifty-seven registered brands of broad-spectrum insecticides, twenty of which were heavily subsidized by the government. The same decree established integrated pest management as the national pest control strategy for rice. Likewise, Brazil recently reduced or eliminated most of the credit subsidies and tax breaks for the conversion of natural forests in the Amazon to privately lucrative but socially unprofitable ranches.

The second form of policy success is the correction or mitigation of market failures through interventions that improve the functioning of the market or result in outcomes superior to those of the free market. For instance, Singapore uses marginal cost pricing to control urban congestion, while China has introduced water pricing to deal with water shortages.

A third kind of policy success is the internalization of environmental, social, and other side effects of public projects and sectoral and macroeconomic policies. Examples include the Dumoga-Bone irrigation project and national park in Indonesia, which uses water pricing to improve irrigation efficiency and to fund the management of a watershed area that has been declared a national park, and the inclusion of environmental provisions in several structural adjustment programs.

Other cases of policy success exist as well. Recently there has been a shift toward reducing subsidies in the Philippines, Pakistan, Tunisia, and Morocco. In many cases, the pressure comes more from a need to reduce the burden on the budget rather than the burden on the environment, although the latter is increasingly a factor as pesticide and fertilizer subsidies are considered in macroeconomic and trade policy reform discussions and negotiations for structural adjustment loans (SALs). Iona Sebastian and Adelaida Alicbusan report that the Philippines, Nepal, Morocco, and Tunisia have agreed to reduce their fertilizer subsidies as part of SAL packages.[hh]

With regard to land ownership. Tunisia, Morocco, Nepal, and Thailand have recently accelerated their land titling programs to improve security of ownership, while Papua New Guinea recognizes and protects customary communal tenure over land and forest resources. Kenya has seen a resurgence of self-help groups that effectively manage community resources.

Needed Policy Reforms

Policy reform is simply the restructuring of government interventions from areas of policy failure to areas of policy success. The absolute level of government intervention may not change and may in fact decrease depending on the magnitude of market distortions to be eliminated relative to market failures to be corrected or mitigated.

This analysis of environmental degradation reveals the root causes of natural resource depletion and environmental degradation: policy distortions and market failures, and the corollary failure of underinvesting in human resource development and employment alternatives. These root causes also point toward the type of policy overhaul necessary to improve resource management and make the development process more sustainable. A comprehensive policy reform should have five components:

hh. Iona Sebastian & Adelaida Alicbusan, World Bank, Sustainable Development: Issues in Adjustment Lending Policies (Environmental Division Paper No. 1989–6, (1989).

1. It should eliminate or at least reduce policy distortions that favor environmentally unsound practices at the same time as they discriminate against the poor, reduce economic efficiency, and waste budgetary resources.

2. It should correct or at least mitigate market failures such as externalities, insecurity of ownership, and absent or imperfect markets that result in overexploitation of resources, through a system of institutions, incentives, regulation, and fiscal measures.

3. It should include investment in human resource development and rural industry to provide alternative employment to disadvantaged groups such as shifting cultivators, landless farmers, and underemployed workers, to lessen the pressure on natural resources and their use as a last resort activity.

4. It should apply broad social cost-benefit analysis to all public projects by: (a) casting them in the overall sectoral and macroeconomic policy context; (b) taking into account all benefits and costs, whether near or distant, whether economic, social, or environmental, and whether quantitative or qualitative; and (c) avoiding projects that lead to irreversible changes in the environment or foreclosure of options.

5. It should build analytical capability and institutional capacity for analyzing, formulating, and implementing policies and projects that have environmental dimensions.

This is a tall order and requires considerable political will, but movement in this direction is both necessary and feasible. It is necessary because the current situation is clearly untenable: not only are the current trends of resource depletion and environmental degradation unsustainable, but if they are continued they will undermine otherwise successful development strategies. Policy reform is feasible because the proposed policy reform would promote several national objectives with minimal trade-offs and budgetary costs: increased economic efficiency and growth, resource conservation and environmental protection, reductions in income inequalities, and, in some cases, savings in or additional sources of government revenues. The substantial policy reforms that have occurred in other areas such as taxation, the exchange rate, and general macroeconomic policy suggest that the political will for change does exist among policy makers.

The first priority is to eliminate, reduce, or cushion policies that have significant environmental costs or perverse incentives that encourage resource depletion and environmental degradation beyond the level that is even privately optimal. Unless these perverse incentives are removed, project investments aimed at improved use and conservation of natural resources are unlikely to succeed, and when they do, their impact will be unsustainable, lasting only as long as the project. Reforming policies that are detrimental to both the economy and the environment is also the easiest place to start because no difficult development-environment trade-offs or budget outlays are involved. If anything, eliminating policy distortions usually reduces budget outlays, in many cases reduces government expenditures, and may even generate additional budget revenues. The distributional implications are also positive since many of these distortions are sources of not only inefficiency and resource depletion, but also inequity. Finally, eliminating policy distortions can be done by adjusting prices, taxes, and subsidies, which is easier than introducing new instruments or developing new institutions to deal with market failures. Therefore, eliminating policy distortions is the place to start, but it is only a start, because without correction or at least mitigation of market failures, a country cannot achieve efficient use and conservation of resources.

The overall objective of policy reform is to reestablish the link between resource scarcity and resource prices that has been severed by a constellation of subsidies, perverse incentives, and unmitigated market and institutional failures such as insecure land tenure, open-access fisheries and forests, and unaccounted environmental externalities. Reestablishing the link between resource scarcity and resource prices is critical to improving resource management and sustainable development. Population growth, economic growth, and improvement in the quality of life are all increasing the demand for a dwindling supply of natural resources and environmental amenities. This demand, if not reflected in higher resource prices or if cushioned through subsidies, will result in accelerated resource depletion and environmental degradation, culminating in unsustainable development. If, on the other hand, the growing resource scarcity is reflected in increasing resource prices, it will stimulate efforts to reduce the growth of demand through resource conservation, improved efficiency, and substitution and to expand supply through recycling, exploration, imports, and development of substitutes. It will also encourage structural change in the use of natural resources, which will go from being sources of raw materials and dumpsites for waste disposal to being sources of environmental amenities and improved quality of life, consistent with growing incomes and expanding material wealth. These very responses to growing resource prices would result in both economic growth and environmental conservation through more efficient resource use, increased substitution of lower-cost, more abundant sources of supply, increased investment in human capital, and technological development.

Discussion Notes/Questions

1.   Would Panayotou's economic solution suffice? Or, does it need to be completed by other approaches?

2.   Panayotou notes that the solution requires considerable political will. Does that exist? If not, why not?

3.   Do you agree that the root causes of natural resource depletion and environmental degradation are policy distortions and market failures? How does this analysis relate to the perspectives set out in Chapter 4?

Catherine O'Neill & Cass Sunstein, *Economics and the Environment: Trading Debt and Technology for Nature* 17 COLUM. J. ENVTL. L. 93, 107–10 (1992).

1.   HISTORY

The idea that debt might be exchanged for nature was originally proposed in 1984 by Dr. Thomas E. Lovejoy, then Vice–President for Science at the World Wildlife Fund ("WWF"). Lovejoy noted that programs calling for the management of natural resources were often eliminated by countries that needed to reduce spending. Such countries thereafter relied on foreign donors to obtain the funds necessary to support national parks. According to Lovejoy, it would be a simple and direct solution for developed countries to take advantage of the debt crisis to deal with environmental problems that threatened developing and industrialized nations alike. The solution was to create transactions by which public or private actors in developed countries would agree to retire some of the debt of a developing nation in return for an agreement to protect natural resources.[ii]

The idea was implemented for the first time in 1987. Lender banks, especially frustrated that debts had appeared to become uncollectible, sought new means for alleviating this liability. A number of conservation organizations offered to acquire foreign debt from the banks and then retire the debt in return for conservation. The first swap occurred in July 1987, as Conservation International ("CI"), a private organization, purchased $650,000 of Bolivia's commercial debt through Citicorp Investment Bank for $100,000. In exchange the President of Bolivia agreed to set aside over four million acres of tropical forest for national protection and to create a $250,000 fund for managing the area.[jj]

Many debt-for-nature trades have followed. In December 1987, Ecuador and the United States branch of WWF ("WWF–US") completed an exchange involving the purchase of $1 million of Ecuadoran debt at thirty-five cents on the dollar; this exchange was the first of a $10 million debt-for-nature program approved by the government of Ecuador. The second exchange under the Ecuadoran program, involving the remaining $9 million, took place in April 1989. The Nature Conservancy ("TNC") and the Missouri Botanical Gardens joined WWF–US as purchasers of the debt at twelve cents on the dollar.[kk]

Costa Rica participated in its first of five exchanges in February 1988. A recent swap, in March 1990, brought the total face value of Costa Rican debt exchanged to $79,253,631. The purchasers of the debt involved in the various Costa Rican exchanges included WWF–US, TNC, Holland, Sweden, and the National Parks Foundation of Costa Rica, with WWF assistance.[ll]

WWF–US has completed two swaps in the Philippines, the most recent of which occurred in August 1990, exchanging an aggregate of $1,290,000, at rates of 51 and 48.75 cents on the dollar respectively.[mm] WWF–US' two exchanges in Madagascar involved a total of $3,030,475; in Zambia, WWF–International purchased debt with a face value of $2,270,000; and in Poland, WWF–US purchased $50,000 of debt.[nn] TNC and the Puerto Rican Conservation Trust, in March 1990, bought debt of the Dominican Republic having a face value of $582,000.[oo]

---

ii. *See* Thomas Lovejoy III, *Aid Debtor Nations' Ecology*, N.Y. TIMES, Oct. 4, 1984, at A31.

jj. *See* World Wildlife Fund, The Bolivian Case (undated and unpublished document, available from WWF, Washington, D.C.).

kk. *See* World Wildlife Fund, Officially Sanctioned and Funded Debt–For–Nature

Swaps to Date: December 1990 (unpublished table, available from WWF, Washington, D.C).

ll. *Id.*

mm. *Id.*

nn. *Id.*

oo. *Id.*

2. MECHANICS

The mechanics of debt-for-nature swaps follow a basic pattern. An interested group, usually an international nongovernmental organization ("NGO"), purchases, on the secondary market, developing country debt held by an international lender. The price is discounted from the face value of the debt. The purchasing group then trades its right to repayment of the debt for a commitment on the part of the developing nation to protect, in some fashion, the environmentally vulnerable lands within its territory. This trade may involve exchanging the debt instrument directly for legislative protection by the debtor country government. Alternatively, it may involve transferring the debt to a debtor country conservation organization, which will then turn it over to its government in exchange for local currency or local currency bonds to be used to finance a conservation program managed by the local group.

* * *

3. ENVIRONMENTAL COMMITMENTS

The environmental commitments undertaken in the various swaps accommodate a broad array of ecological and policy goals of the various developing countries. These commitments range from the preservation of specific areas, to the creation of programs for education and training, to the establishment of funds for environmental uses whose details are left to later determination. In the Bolivian arrangement, for example, the government elevated to the highest legal protective status the existing 334,200–acre Beni Biosphere Reserve. It also created, with the same level of legal protection, an adjoining 877,205–acre reserve, as well as an additional 2,870,561–acre buffer zone—the Chimane Forest Reserve—to be developed in a sustainable manner. Finally, Bolivia designated the local currency equivalent of $250,000 for the establishment of an operational fund for the management of the Biosphere Reserve. . . .

Discussion Notes/Questions

1. What are the weaknesses of a trading-debt-for-nature approach, if any? Are there some environmental problems that are not susceptible to this approach? Do debt-for-nature swaps offer any solution to the problem of depleting resources?

2. What incentives do debt-for-nature swaps offer to halt destructive environmental practices?

3. Can you think of other unusual or innovate solutions (such as debt-for-nature swaps) to address the global environmental challenge?

———

Daniel M. Putterman, *Model Material Transfer Agreements for Equitable Biodiversity Prospecting* 7 COLO. J. INT'L ENVTL. L. & POL'Y 149, 149–52 (1995).

Genetic resources have been traded across the world for centuries, though rarely to the advantage of biodiversity-rich source nations. Today, genetic resources are used primarily as the source of new, economically valuable chemical compounds, genes, or germplasm by industries in such sectors as pharmaceuticals, agrochemicals, consumer products, enzymes, biotechnology, and seeds. The combined world market for pharmaceuticals alone exceeds $210 billion annually. A thriving trade in genetic resources continues today, though mainly through a network of brokers and other middlemen. Unfortunately, it is still rare that source countries realize reasonable benefits from this trade.

While Article 15 of the United Nations Convention on Biological Diversity (Biological Diversity Convention) recognizes sovereign rights of national governments over genetic resources, there has been a call for a recognition of "local" sovereignty over these resources at the level of rural communities. Although most national legal systems have yet to address this sovereignty issue ..., there is now widespread recognition of the potential to profit from the equitable and sustainable development of genetic resources.

To date, only a handful of attempts to incorporate genetic resources trading into national economies—and to link this trade to community development or biodiversity conservation—are noteworthy. Usually, such attempts at equitable "biodiversity prospecting" (or "bioprospecting") center around the creation of collaborative research agreements between source country institutions and Northern, or industrialized country, corporations. Treating genetic resources as their new "comparative advantage" in the world marketplace, business-savvy researchers, conservationists, and policy makers in some source nations have successfully attracted Northern capital in exchange for access to these resources. Although it is advantageous to trade genetic resources for cash and market share (royalty rights), many have recognized the critical need to acquire new technology to add value to these resources and have successfully negotiated cooperative research and development agreements (CRADAs) incorporating such technology transfers.

II.   MATERIAL TRANSFER AGREEMENTS:
A CONVENIENT EXPEDIENT

The purpose of this paper is to illustrate that material transfer agreements (MTAs) can be used as convenient tools with which the citizens of developing countries can facilitate equitable collaborative research and development with genetic resources. MTAs are special types of contracts routinely used by the biotechnology industry and academic researchers in Northern countries to facilitate the sharing of biological research material for mutual gain. MTAs define the rights and obligations of all parties, including third parties, involved in a transfer of biological material. MTAs can be relatively concise documents, yet sufficiently flexible to be useful in a large number of research and development scenarios. It is these characteristics of MTAs that make them particularly useful to citizens of developing countries wishing to encourage research and development with genetic resources.

* * *

The purpose of these agreements is to enable basic or applied research and development with genetic resources while defining source country and local community rights to the material. Distinctions are made between tangible property, intellectual property, and traditional knowledge. Regarding the first category, genetic resources are treated as tangible property, much like oil, natural gas, minerals, or timber. These resources, which have a market value, can be traded for monetary gain or for such nonmonetary benefits as technology or research services. The MTAs incorporate an option to allow rural communities to trade genetic resources found on community land as communal property.

The second category, intellectual property, refers to knowledge or inventions created by researchers in the conventional sense of formal research and development. Conventional intellectual property may be eligible for legal protection under Northern intellectual property law, such as patents, plant variety protection, or trade secrets.

The third category, traditional knowledge, is defined by these MTAs as a type of intellectual property not formally recognized by Northern intellectual property law. Nevertheless, the MTAs incorporate mechanisms allowing rural communities to claim ownership of their traditional knowledge. This is accomplished through optional clauses which treat traditional knowledge as trade secrets, a legal tactic not unlike that used by collaborating industries in Northern countries which seek to share unpatentable biological material for mutual gain. Trade secret protection for traditional knowledge presupposes that such knowledge is not already widely known, perhaps confined only to a particular rural community or better still, to certain individuals within the community.

Discussion Notes/Questions

1. Will MTAs promote environmental protection? Why? Why not?

2. Are MTAs a legal or an economic mechanism?

3. Do MTAs satisfy the equity concerns embraced by the sustainable development concept?

CONCLUSION

We have reached a stage in the evolution of international society at which thinking about the future of world order has become widespread, and not just on the part of utopian advocates of world government. Corporate and financial leaders, as well as more reflective diplomats and scholars, have come to believe that some form of global integration and governance is inevitable, and they have come to believe this in relation to the global environmental challenge especially. The uncertainty that exists—and there is a great deal of uncertainty—is in the particulars and, perhaps most of all, in whether the world community can muster the political will and other resources that are needed to fashion the particulars in a timely—and humane—manner. It is from this perspective that the next three concluding readings should be considered. The first was written *before* the United Nations Conference on Environment and Development (UNCED) in Rio de Janeiro in June 1992, but in anticipation thereof. The last two were written after.

GERALD PORTER & JANET WELSH BROWN, GLOBAL ENVIRONMENTAL
POLITICS 143, 144–59 (1991).

A new agenda of global environmental problems will demand international attention in the final years of this century and into the next.... Three broad alternative strategies have been suggested by governments and analysts for creating and strengthening the needed global environmental regimes over the next decade:

- A continuation of the political process that has brought incremental changes in global diplomacy during the last two decades

- An effort to achieve a new level of North–South partnership on both economic progress and environmental and resource conservation to revitalize environmental cooperation

- An attempt to create new institutions of global environmental governance that would reduce the power of individual states to block or weaken environmental agreements and ensure that they are adequately enforced

THE INCREMENTAL CHANGE APPROACH

The first possible approach to environmental regimes is based on continued incremental changes. It would eschew any radical changes in either policy framework or institutional structure at the global level. Incrementalism denies the need to take into account the interrelatedness of all global issues and forces, dealing with issues on a case-by-case. It assumes that reasonable progress can be made on global environmental challenges within the parameters of existing global political institutions, diplomatic practice, and socioeconomic realities.

Although a number of industrialized and developing states have called for a much bolder approach to managing environmental problems, the incremental change strategy would continue the approach that has characterized the negotiation of international environmental agreements over the past decade or more. It must be distinguished from an approach involving no changes, which is no longer possible given increasing threats to the environment and rising popular interest in international action on environmental issues. Over the past two decades, multilateral environmental negotiations have become more sophisticated as diplomatic innovations have minimized some of the pitfalls in traditional multilateral environmental treaties.

* * *

Incremental change as an approach does not preclude imaginative ways of building flexibility and adaptability into environmental agreements. Agreements negotiated on the basis of an incremental strategy would leave room for more aggressive measures in the future. Whereas traditional multilateral diplomacy tends to set commitments that are not easily adjusted to changing reality, environmental agreements such as CITES **[Basic Document 6.5]**, the London Dumping Convention **[Basic Document 4.11]**, and the 1987 Montreal Protocol **[Basic Document 3.18]**—all products of such incremental change diplomacy—have included provisions for regular consultations of the parties to make new decisions in response to new scientific evidence or shifts in political attitudes.... [But an] incremental change approach, as the name implies, would settle for modest progress toward effective regimes, on the assumption that further increments of progress will follow later....

This approach depends on future strengthening of initially weak regimes. But reasonable projection of greenhouse-gas emissions, tropical deforestation, diversity loss, or toxic chemical pollution over the next two decades ... would suggest that an incremental change approach is unlikely to build the momentum necessary to reverse these serious trends before environmental degradation gets much worse.

THE GLOBAL PARTNERSHIP APPROACH

A second approach to global environmental regimes, reflecting major shifts in the policies of key industrialized and developing states, is a concerted effort by industrialized and developing countries to collaborate widely on sustainable development....

Instead of trying to separate issues of debt, trade, financial flows, and technology transfer from global environmental negotiations, a global partnership strategy would make cooperation on such North–South economic issues a central feature of environmental diplomacy. It would start from the assumptions that the environment and natural resources can only be conserved under conditions of sustainable global development and that the present world economic system makes sustainable development impossible. It also recognizes the political reality that developing countries will [increasingly] demand some linkage between global environmental agreements desired by most industrialized states and demands regarding North–South economic relations. The ... strategy thus represents a holistic, as opposed to an incremental approach to the formation of environmental regimes.... [It] would not be a single all-encompassing agreement, negotiated at a single conference.... [It] would require a series of new arrangements covering a range of issues, all of which would probably take many years, even given a conscious decision by key actors to pursue it.

* * *

[However, a] global partnership approach to regime creation would require a level of political will to address global environmental problems that does not appear to exist now. There is still strong resistance in the United States, Japan, and Germany to the kinds of resource transfers envisioned in this approach, and removal of protectionist barriers is still blocked by special interests throughout North America, Western Europe, and Japan. There are significant barriers to such a partnership in many developing countries as well. The willingness to raise the price of petroleum, which is necessary to achieve energy-efficiency gains in the developing countries, is limited by the fears of weak states that their political survival may depend on continuing to provide subsidized energy to urban dwellers.

Hopes for a North–South partnership approach depend on a recognition of mutual dependence and self-interest among countries, both North and South. The highly industrialized countries must accept the fact that they cannot solve global environmental problems without the cooperation of the developing countries. The developing nations must recognize that they cannot pursue a sustainable development strategy without the cooperation of the partnership of the highly industrialized countries of the North. Very important also to achieving successful partnership is the development of more precise indicators for measuring progress toward agreed-on goals. Some of these indicators—for greenhouse-gas emissions, forest loss, health, and education—are already in use, but others measuring biological diversity, marine pollution, and equity are still being developed.

* * *

Critics claim the costs of this approach will be too high; proponents counter that the costs of not taking it will be fatal. Better estimates of the costs of alternative strategies are clearly needed, but even some establishment institutions like the Asian Development Bank are now suggesting that switching to sustainable development strategies is not prohibitively expensive and that initially funds can be found by taking funds from less sustainable development efforts.

THE GLOBAL GOVERNANCE APPROACH

The third approach to environmental regimes—global environmental governance—has been increasingly advocated in recent years by unofficial observers and, more significantly, government officials. The approach is founded on the widespread perception that existing national and international institutions and international law are inadequate to the environmental challenges facing the globe in the coming decades. . . .

The global environmental governance approach suggests that only far-reaching institutional restructuring at the global level can stem the tide of environmental disruption and natural resource depletion. . . . The most ambitious proposal for institutional restructuring is the call for a global environmental legislative body with the power to impose environmental regulations on nation-states. The idea surfaced at an international conference at The Hague in March 1989 sponsored by the French, Dutch, and Norwegian prime ministers. . . . The final declaration, adopted by twenty-four heads of state, called for a U.N. authority that could take effective action "even if . . . unanimous agreement has not been achieved."[pp]

This pathbreaking document . . . anticipates a truly supranational institution capable of overriding national sovereignty on matters of global environmental concern. The acceptance of such an institution by most of the industrialized states suggests a significant trend toward global governance of the environment. The opposition of the United States, the Soviet Union, Britain, China, and Japan, who are more reluctant to yield their sovereignty over an issue area as vital as the environment, remains a major obstacle. . . . Another potential problem is the sensitivity of most developing states to intrusions by the industrialized world on their sovereignty. The question that many developing countries may ask themselves is whether they could count on the developing country majority to kill global legislation that would not be in their interests.

* * *

   pp. Declaration of the Hague, Mar. 11, 1989 **[Basic Document 1.24]**.

The main argument against an institution of global governance in the past, apart from the assertion that humanity does not face any real global ecological crisis, has been that its scope raises the transaction costs of a regime. It is argued by some scholars that establishing a centralized system of worldwide enforcement of environmental agreements would require large-scale monitoring and policing capabilities as well as the power to enforce economic sanctions. But the costs of monitoring and enforcement may depend less on the structure of the authority than it does on how difficult the problem is to monitor, how strong the incentives are for compliance, and how committed the international community is to ensuring compliance. A wide range of costs is possible under either decentralized or centralized authority structures. Neither satellite monitoring of deforestation nor trade sanctions against violators of a convention, for example, would be notably more expensive if carried out under the auspices of a global authority than if done through multilateral coordination.

Another argument against a global environmental authority is that most compliance with international regimes has little to do with fear of sanctions, suggesting that no overarching institution is needed.

Although that observation is undoubtedly true, it sidesteps the more important question. The regimes already formed have consisted of those acceptable to the parties participating. In the future, mankind may need to carry out international environmental regulation that is not acceptable to all significant states. Under the present system that cooperation could be blocked by one or a few intransigent states. A global environmental authority, on the other hand, would have the power to enforce regulations on states that would otherwise not adhere to the regime. It is hoped that political change in all countries with significant responsibility for global environmental issues will make such a global environmental authority unnecessary, but there is as yet no guarantee that the change will have uniform results.

Less ambitious proposals for global institutional reform involve the creation of a counterpart to the U.N. Security Council to deal with environmental threats.... The purpose of [these] proposals is to create a body that could negotiate quickly and effectively on global environmental threats and take emergency action. Although some situations do require emergency measures ..., what is needed is long-term cooperation across a broad array of issues. An Environmental Security Council, therefore, would probably add little to the ability of the world system to create effective environmental regimes.

Another component of the global governance approach would be the development of international legal concepts that further reduce the zone of absolute sovereignty of individual states in issues affecting the global environment. The idea of the "common heritage of mankind," which was included in the 1982 UNCLOS Treaty **[Basic Document 4.20]**, marks the first major step away from the old legal order based on the assumption that sovereign states could do whatever they pleased outside the jurisdiction of other states. But [so far] the idea has no binding force because the Law of the Sea Treaty is not operative. Similarly, the concept of responsibility to future generations or

intergenerational equity has [so far] no legal status because future generations are not [yet] recognized as subjects under existing international law.

* * *

One of the objectives of the global governance approach would be to make
the "common heritage of mankind" and "intergenerational equity" legal
principles applicable to all global environmental issues that touch on threats
to the global commons or natural resources affecting the interests of future
generations. Such a revolutionary development in international law would
presumably go hand in hand with the transformation of the international
system by the creation of a global environmental authority.

The global governance approach, which seemed hopelessly idealistic only
a few years ago, has suddenly been given legitimacy by the support it has
received from most industrialized states. In the states that remain opposed,
however, one should not underestimate the strength of nationalistic resistance to giving up sovereignty over environmental policy. The creation of a
global environmental authority may be seen as appropriate to a later stage of
evolution in global environmental politics. As political efforts on behalf of
such an authority would be in competition with the more immediate objective
of pressing for a global bargain, there is a danger of putting the institutional
cart before the political horse.

CONCLUSION

The stakes in global environmental politics are bound to increase further
in the coming decade[s] as environmental issues such as global climate
change, continuing rapid urban growth, tropical deforestation, international
battles over water, and land-based sources of ocean pollution are affected by
economic development strategies and production techniques in both developed
and developing countries. The choice of broad approaches to forging new
environmental regimes and strengthening existing ones involves judgments
about what is politically feasible as well as diplomatically and environmentally
effective.

The incremental approach may produce some progress on all fronts, but
some of the political obstacles to effective regimes on the major issues now
confronting the international community would not be confronted directly or
promptly under this strategy. A global partnership, on the other hand, would,
if achieved, allow a qualitative leap forward in environmental cooperation but
may be politically impossible because of the lack of vision and political
leadership among key industrialized countries to come to grips with North—
South structural issues. And the global governance approach, which has much
to recommend it, may have even less support among major industrialized
states unless there is a dramatic new impetus for addressing North—South
economic inequalities in the coming decades. The incremental approach,
requiring no dramatic political change, is obviously the one most likely to be
pursued.

Global security politics will clearly affect the prospects for strong international environmental regimes.... The evolution of the global economy will
also play a part in shaping global environmental regimes.

Even more fundamental in determining the fate of global environmental politics in the coming decades, however, is the trend in popular consciousness and the level of activism regarding environmental threats.... [T]he rise of strong domestic political constituencies for international cooperation on the environment in several states has already made a crucial difference.... If there is one force that could sweep away the formidable obstacles to strong new global environmental regimes, it is the support of voters and grassroots activism throughout the highly industrialized world.

* * *

Something going beyond traditional power politics is clearly at work in global environmental politics.... Most people able to look beyond the daily needs of physical survival appear to understand that irreversible damage to the earth's natural systems and resources, some of which would profoundly affect the lives not only of future generations but most of the people alive today, is at stake. The issue, therefore, is not whether nation-states will move toward progressively more effective cooperation on global environmental threats, but whether they will do so rapidly enough.

Edith Brown Weiss, *International Environmental Law: Contemporary Issues and the Emergence of A New World Order* 81 Geo. L. J. 675, 707–10 (1993).

In June 1992, 178 countries met in Rio de Janeiro, Brazil, for the United Nations Conference on Environment and Development, which was the twentieth anniversary of the United Nations Stockholm Conference on the Human Environment. The Rio Conference was an occasion to consider how far we had come in the last twenty years, and how far we need to go in the next twenty. As we look ahead to the future, it is clear that new directions in the environmental world order are emerging. These trends can be categorized both in immediate, and somewhat narrow terms, and in long-range, broader terms.

A.   The Immediate Trends

In the next two decades, the joining of environmental protection and economic development will grow. The burgeoning new field of environment and trade reflects this linkage. While trade law has operated under the relatively unified and broad framework of the General Agreement on Tariffs and Trade[89] for more than forty years, fledgling international environmental law still consists only of many separate and disparate legal instruments. It is not surprising then that most environment and trade issues are discussed almost exclusively within the GATT context. The environment and trade issues move in two directions: environmental protection practices affect trade, and trading practices affect environmental conservation. Thus, it will be important to move to a *modus vivendi* in which environmental and trade concerns are accorded comparable legitimacy, and both are viewed as important elements of sustainable development.

More generally, in the quest for environmentally sustainable development, the focus will likely move to considering environmental concerns at the

---

89. General Agreement on Tariffs and Trade, [**Basic Document 7.1**].

front end of the industrializing process, so as to prevent pollution, minimize environmental degradation, and use resources more efficiently. This should mean an increasing concern with making the whole system of production environmentally sound. If so, international environmental law will reflect this emphasis by focusing on standards and procedures for preventing pollution and minimizing environmental degradation, rather than on liability for damage, and on providing incentives to companies to use environmentally sound processes.

Second, the formulation of nonbinding legal instruments, or "soft law," is likely to increase more rapidly than the negotiation of formal international conventions. This is because when the instrument is nonbinding, agreement is normally easier to achieve, the transaction costs are less, the opportunity for detailed strategies to be set forth are greater, and the ability to respond to rapid changes in our scientific understanding of environment and development issues are more vast.

Third, the growing adoption of new approaches, duties, and procedures in international environmental accords is likely to continue. These include the precautionary principle or approach and the duties to consult with affected states, to prepare an environmental impact assessment before undertaking certain projects, to provide emergency assistance for environmental accidents or disasters, to monitor activities, and to make relevant information available.

Finally, UNCED and the 1992 Rio Declaration[90] may be viewed as legitimizing the importance of public participation in environmental decision-making and of public access to relevant information. The international institutional system in which environmental legal instruments are imbedded is likely to continue to become more diverse and to include increasingly larger numbers of nongovernmental organizations of various kinds. While four decades ago we could speak of an international system focused almost exclusively on nation-states and their subunits, today the system includes national governments (and local governments), intergovernmental organizations, and nongovernmental organizations as essential components constantly interacting. NGOs are likely to continue to expand their influence in the negotiation, implementation, and compliance process of international environmental legal agreements. The information revolution should greatly facilitate this increased role of NGOs in international environmental decisionmaking.

B. THE BROADER PERSPECTIVE

The concept of national interest, which has long been used to address foreign policy decisions, is not a very useful construct for analyzing global environmental problems in the long-term. National interest can be defined as national preferences, or the preferences of a country's decisionmakers. On the global scale these interests are often considered in terms of a zero-sum gain. The implicit assumption is that one country's national interest is necessarily opposed to another's. But when addressing global environmental issues the interest is a common one: the overall maintenance of the world's environmental systems. This becomes apparent as we look into the future because no

---

90. Rio Declaration on Environment and Development, June 13, 1992, 31 I.L.M. 874 **[Basic Document 1.29]**, Principle 10.

community today can by itself conserve the planet for even its own descendants.

The physical setting in which all peoples are locked together in a common global environment for the foreseeable future means that it is increasingly futile to posit national interests that over the long term can be opposed to another country's national interest in the environment. The rapid advances in international cooperation, as demonstrated in international environmental law, suggest countries are implicitly beginning to recognize this need to coordinate long-term interests.

The international environmental agreements negotiated during the last two decades reflect a commonality of interests. In many international legal instruments, states have agreed to constrain "operational sovereignty," while continuing to retain formal national sovereignty. The conventions on ozone depletion, transboundary shipments of hazardous waste, air pollutants such as nitrogen oxides and volatile organic chemicals, and the Antarctic environment illustrate this constraint. In other agreements, states have arguably strengthened their operational sovereignty by focusing on national plans and actions and dissemination of these documents to other parties to the agreements. The recant Framework Convention on Climate Change **[Basic Document 3.21]** and the Convention on Biological Diversity **[Basic Document 6.11]** reflect this approach. Nonetheless in these instances, states have set up an international process for monitoring the health of the environment and for providing other benefits to parties. In the climate change convention, the international procedures are sophisticated and far-reaching, and they could lead to substantial international consideration and evaluation of national measures to mitigate climate change. Thus, the international environmental agreements examined in this article point in the same direction—a recognition of the benefits of international cooperation and an increased willingness to agree to obligations directed to protecting the environment.

While countries may share a commonality of interests in maintaining the robustness and integrity of our planet, there are deep differences among them over the equitable allocation of burdens and benefits in doing so. These were vividly displayed at the Rio Conference meeting and are reflected in more recent agreements. Moreover, states do not agree on priorities—whether to satisfy immediate needs to alleviate poverty and local environmental degradation or longer-term needs to protect the robustness and integrity of the biosphere. The clashes extend to communities and groups at the local and transnational levels. These clashes could intensify in the next two decades, as countries (and communities) try to reach consensus on what is equitable in the context of environmentally sustainable development. Unless resolved, they could lead to inefficient and ineffective outcomes that are inadequate to the task of conserving our global environment and ensuring sustainable development for future generations.

Editors' Note

The foregoing analysis of what went on at Rio in 1992 is relatively optimistic. While not quarrelling with the prognosis of possible future trends, however, it is possible to read the results of the United Nations Conference on Environment and Development (UNCED) another way, particularly against the pre-Rio backdrop laid out by Porter and Brown, *supra*. It cannot be suggested with any credibility that matters would have been better were UNCED never to have taken place. Clearly it raised consciousness, knowledge, and concern around the world—it had a substantial educational effect. And there were some solid achievements; the paradigm of sustainable development was embraced officially by all the nations attending. But whether that paradigm (considered in Chapter 4, *supra*) can deliver better environmental outcomes must remain a moot point given the intellectual contradictions residing within it. Agenda 21 **[Basic Document 1.30]** was adopted and will provide some benchmarks against which to measure future developments in a number of critical areas. Furthermore, there were some important conventions that came out of Rio: the Framework Convention on Climate and Change **[Basic Document 3.21]** and the Convention on Biodiversity **[Basic Document 6.11]**.

It remains the conviction of the authors of this coursebook, however, that more should have been achieved at Rio and that it is prudent to be skeptical about its achievements. A great deal had been promised for Rio, and so it is perhaps not surprising that it did not rise to meet those expectations. The Secretary–General of UNCED, Maurice Strong, claimed that the Conference would "define the state of political will to save our planet."[qq] Many of the speeches by world leaders at the Conference engaged in similar rhetorical flourishes. But the actions did not match the lofty rhetoric. In theory the need for international environmental governance was supported by many countries, but when it came to implementation the results were decidedly weak.

The failure at Rio was a failure of commitment and vision, a failure of political leadership; the progress made there was simply insufficient to deal with the environmental problems that face the world. The biggest diplomatic meeting in the history of the world did not summon the collective political resolve necessary to deal with the global environmental challenge. Rio may have started trends that will end up changing peoples' attitudes, and that is in no way to be discounted. But, in the end, action is necessary. Twenty years after the United Nations Conference on the Human Environment in Stockholm, which produced the Stockholm Declaration of the United Nations Conference on the Human Environment **[Basic Document 1.12]**, the condition of our planetary environment is worse than it was then, and we seem no closer to getting a grip on the problems involved.

And so, regrettably, we end upon a somewhat pessimistic note. Only the future can tell whether we are right or wrong.

But we are not without hope. Nor should you be. For the first time in more than half a century, a serious revived interest in normative, institutional, and procedural change has emerged on the global plane. The profound and profoundly exhilarating world events of the last several years attest to this development. The eruption of inter-ethnic horror in the Balkans and elsewhere most certainly gives one pause, but it still is hard not to be awed by the ending of the Cold War and the accompanying disengagement of East–West military forces, the democratization of Eastern Europe, the persistent even if slowed integration of Western Europe, the credible possibility of some all-European unity down the road, the beginning of the end of the heretofore intractable Israeli–Palestinian crisis, and, not least, the rollback of apartheid in Namibia and South Africa. Separately and

qq. Statement by Maurice F. Strong, Secretary–General, United Nations Conference on Environment and Development at the Opening of the United Nations Conference on Environment and Development, June 3, 1992 (transcript available from UNCED).

together, these events lead one to appreciate that "reality" is never fixed and that the magnitude of the struggle for an ecologically responsible world order is not so overwhelming as to be beyond human capacity.

Of course, the struggle for an ecologically responsible world order is going to require numberless diverse acts of heroism—that is, in the stirring words of novelist Russell Banks, quoted at the outset of this text, "constant heroism, systematic heroism, heroism as governing principle." But therein lies the basis of our hope. We believe there is heroism in all of us. We need but reach into ourselves and act upon it. In the end, it is a matter of courage and belief.

Discussion Notes/Questions

1.   Are you optimistic or pessimistic about the general outlook for the global environment? On what do you base your views?

2.   Of all the options available for making future progress, which is the most important in terms of priorities? How should priorities be determined in an area such as global environmental protection? Politics, it is often said, is the language of priorities. How would you determine the priorities?

3.   How important is the law in the wider scheme of the global environmental issues?

4.   Will you sleep comfortably at night having completed this course?

5.   Who, ultimately, is responsible for the future?

6.   *Bibliographical Note.* For further discussion concerning the principle themes addressed in this chapter, consult the following specialized materials:

(a) Specialized Books/Monographs. L. Caldwell, International Environmental Policy: Emergence and Dimensions (2 ed. 1990); P. Elkins, A New World Order: Grassroots Movements for Global Change (1992); P. Holdgate, From Care to Action: Making a Sustainable World (1996); J. Laurenti & F. Lyman, One Earth, Many Nations: The International System and Problems of the Global Environment (1990); D. Lumsdaine, Moral Vision in International Politics: The Foreign Aid Regime, 1949–1989 (1993); D. Reed, The Global Environmental Facility: Sharing Responsibility for the Biosphere (1991); Preserving the Global Environment: The Challenge of Shared Leadership (J. Tuchman Mathews ed., 1991); B. Urhquart & E. Childers, A World in Need of Leadership: Tomorrow's United Nations (1990).

(b) Specialized Articles/Book Chapters. F. Abbott, *Regional Integration and the Environment: The Evolution of Legal Regimes,* 68 Chi. Kent L. Rev. 173 (1992); T. Bigg, *Institutions for Global Environmental Change—The UN Commission on Sustainable Development: a Non–Governmental Perspective* 5 Global Envtl. Change 251 (1995); C. Brown, *Facilitating joint implementation under the Framework Convention on Climate Change: Toward a greenhouse gas emission reduction protocol* 14 Envtl. & Plan. L. J.356 (1997); A.N. Craik, *Recalcitrant Reality and Chosen Ideals: The Public Function of Dispute Settlement in International Environmental Law* 10 Geo. Int'l. Envtl. L. Rev. 551 (1998); P. Doran, *The U.N. Commission on Sustainable Development* 5 Envtl. Pol. 100 (1996); C.P. Graffy, *Water, Water, Everywhere, Nor Any Drop to Drink: The Urgency of Transnational Solutions to International Riparian Disputes* 10 Geo. Int'l. Envtl. L. Rev. 399 (1998); L. Guruswamy, *Global Warming: Integrating United States and International Law,* 32 Ariz. L. Rev. 221 (1990); D. Hunter, *Toward Global Citizenship in International Environmental Law,* 28 Willamette L. R. 547 (1992); J. Juergensmeyer & J. Nicholas, *Debt for Nature Swaps: A Modest but Meaningful Response*

to Two International Crises, 5 Fla. Int'l L. J. 193 (1990); L. A. Kimball, *International Law and Institutions: The Oceans and Beyond,* 20 Ocean Development & Int'l L. (1989); A.R. Lucas, *The North American Agreement on Environmental Cooperation: International Environmental Jurisdiction over the Energy Sector,* 16 Energy Nat. Resources L. 84 (1998); D. Magraw, *Legal Treatment of Developing Countries: Differential, Contextual, and Absolute Norms,* 1 Colo. J. Envtl. L. & Pol'y 69 (1990); P.J. Nelson, *Deliberation, Leverage or Coercion? The World, NGOs and Global Environmental Politics* 34 J. Peace Res. 467 (1997); *Restoring Participatory Democracy: Why the United States Should Listen to Citizen Voices While Engaging in International Environmental Lawmaking* 12 Emory Int'l. L. Rev. 1215 (1998); S. Rubin & S. Fish, *Biodiversity Prospecting: Using Innovative Contractual Provisions to Foster Ethnobotanical Knowledge, Technology, and Conservation* 5 Colo. J. Int'l. Envtl. L. & Pol'y 23 (1994); P. Thacher, *Alternative Legal and Institutional Approaches to Global Change,* 1 Colo. J. Int'l Envtl. L. & Pol'y 101 (1990); A. van Buitenen, *The United Nations Commission on Sustainable Development: Securing the Outcomes of UNCED?* 7 Leiden J. Int'l. L. 89 (1994); K. von Moltke, *International Commissions and Implementation of International Environmental Law,* in International Environmental Diplomacy 87 (J. Carroll ed., 1988); D. Wirth, *Legitimacy, Accountability, and Partnership: A Model for Advocacy on Third World Environmental Issues,* 100 Yale L. J. 2645 (1991); O. Young, *The Politics of International Regime Formation: Managing Natural Resources and the Environment* 43 Int'l Org. 349 (1989); C. Zheng–Kang, *Equity, Special Considerations, and the Third World,* 1 Colo. J. Envtl. L. & Pol'y 57 (1990).

Index

BIODIVERSITY—Cont'd
Debtor-nature, see Debt-for-Nature Exchanges
Definition, 334
Deforestation, see Deforestation
Ehrenfeld, 837
Exclusive territorial sovereignty, 885–888
Findley, R., 888–890
General Agreements on Tariffs and Trade (GATT) and, 929–930
Guruswamy, L., 981–982
Indigenous rights, see Indigenous Rights
National Academy of the Sciences, loss of biodiversity, 837
Obligation to protect, 981–982
Rio Declaration, 890
Species extinction and, 258
Stewardship sovereignty, 887–888
Sustainable development,
　Benefits of, 888
　Compensatory payments, 889–890
　Costs of, 888–889
　Economic analysis of, 888–890
　Exclusive territorial sovereignty and, 885–888
　Need for, 886–887
　Stewardship sovereignty and, 887–888
Sustainable use, 982–983
Tarlock, A., 885–888
World Resources Institute, 255–258, 789

BIOSPHERE
See also, Biodiversity; Endangered Species; Deforestation
Definition, 334
Geophysics, 255

BOLIVIA
Debtor-nature exchange, 862, 1199, 1242, 1243

BOTSWANA
Elephants, 843, 844, 845, 847, 851, 856, 863

BRAZIL
Antarctic Treaty, consultative party, 395

BRUNDTLAND COMMISSION
Generally, 319–323, 325, 530–531, 979
Sustainable development, 319–323, 325

BULGARIA
Antarctic Treaty, non-consultative party, 395

CANADA
Acid rain, effects, 474–476
Arctic Council member, 11
Canadian forests, effects, 474–476
Ecofeminism, example of, 315
Forests, effects of acidic deposition and ozone, 474–476
Ozone, impact in United States and Canada, 474–476

CARBON DIOXIDE
See Greenhouse Gases; Ozone Layer

CARBON MONOXIDE
See Greenhouse Gases; Ozone Layer

CFCS
See Greenhouse Gases; Ozone Layer

CHERNOBYL ACCIDENT
See also, Nuclear Accidents
Effects, 542, 543, 550–551, 552, 567–568
International Atomic Energy Agency (IAEA) and, 542–543
　Alteration of priorities alter Chernobyl accident, 548
Layard, A., 546–549
Liability, evolution of, 549–557
McClatchey, D., 549–557
Post Accident Review Meeting, report to, 543
Reform after, 546–549, 568–569
State responsibility, see State Responsibility and International Liability

CHILE
Antarctica,
　Claimant state, 385
　Jurisdictional claims, 385, 386
Antarctic treaty,
　Consultative party, 395
　Participant, 395

CHINA
Antarctic Treaty, consultative party, 395
Human rights, 1030–1039
Kristof, N., 996–1000
Nuclear submarines, 3
One-child family policy, 1030–1039
Population control, 996–1000, 1001–1002, 1004, 1030–1039, 1040
　Gender ratio, 999–1000
Statist and rule-oriented definition of international law adopted by, 18
United Nations, resolutions and declarations of, 163

CHLOROFLUOROCARBONS (CFCS)
See Greenhouse Gases; Ozone Layer

COMMISSION FOR ENVIRONMENTAL CO-OPERATION
See also, North American Agreement for Environmental Cooperation
Bolinger, C., 969–974

COMMON HERITAGE PRINCIPLE
Antarctica, 447–449, 454–455, 989
Biodiversity, 986
Common heritage of mankind, 418–419, 445, 447–449, 450, 454, 986
Commons regime, 444–450
Elephants, common heritage arguments, 866

CONCEPTUAL PRAGMATISM
Antipathy for by New Stream Scholarship, 40
Attempt to mediate between naturalism and positivism, 40–41
Criticism of New Stream Scholarship (also known as Critical Jurisprudence and Critical Legal Studies), 48
Schools of,
　Idealism,
　　Alvarez, A., 41
　　Bedjaoui, M., 41, 48
　Policy-approach,
　　Higgins, R., 48
　　Lasswell, H., 41, 48